1988

GENERAL HISTORY OF AFRICA · III

Africa from the Seventh to the Eleventh Century

6192PRE1 3.11.87 K00 L04

Unesco General History of Africa

Volume I	Methodology and African Prehistory (Editor J. Ki-Zerbo)
Volume II	Ancient Civilizations of Africa (Editor G. Mokhtar)
Volume III	Africa from the Seventh to Eleventh Century (Editor M. El Fasi) (Assistant Editor I. Hrbek)
Volume IV	Africa from the Twelfth to Sixteenth Century (Editor D. T. Niane)
Volume V	Africa from the Sixteenth to Eighteenth Century (Editor B. A. Ogot)
Volume VI	The Nineteenth Century until 1880 (Editor J. F. A. Ajayi)
Volume VII	Africa under Foreign Domination, 1880–1935 (Editor A. A. Boahen)
Volume VIII	Africa since 1935 (Editor A. A. Mazrui) (Assistant Editor C. Wondji)

UNESCO International Scientific Committee for the Drafting of a General History of Africa

GENERAL HISTORY OF AFRICA · III

Africa from the Seventh to the Eleventh Century

EDITOR M. EL FASI

ASSISTANT EDITOR I. HRBEK

HEINEMANN · CALIFORNIA · UNESCO

First published 1988 by the
United Nations Educational, Scientific
and Cultural Organization,
7 Place de Fontenoy, 75700 Paris

and

Heinemann Educational Books Ltd
22 Bedford Square, London WC1B 3HH
P.M.B. 5205, Ibadan P.O. Box 54314, Nairobi
PO Box 10103, Village Post Office, Gaborone
EDINBURGH MELBOURNE AUCKLAND
SINGAPORE KUALA LUMPUR NEW DELHI
KINGSTON

First published 1988
in the United States of America by the
University of California Press
2120 Berkeley Way, Berkeley
California 94720, United States of America

Heinemann Educational Books ISBN 0 435 94809 1

Unesco ISBN 92-3-101 709-8
University of California Press ISBN 0-520-03914-9

Filmset in 11 pt Monophoto Ehrhardt by
Eta Services (Typesetters) Ltd., Beccles, Suffolk
Printed in Great Britain by
Butler & Tanner Ltd, Frome and London

Contents

* *Note*: The official designation of Côte d'Ivoire is *Côte d'Ivoire* in all languages but with respect to the English practice, Ivory Coast will be found in this book.

Note on chronology

It has been agreed to adopt the following method for writing dates. With regard to prehistory, dates may be written in two different ways.

One way is by reference to the present era, that is, dates BP (before present),the reference year being +1950; all dates are negative in relation to +1950.

The other way is by reference to the beginning of the Christian era. Dates are represented in relation to the Christian era by a simple + or − sign before the date. When referring to centuries, the terms BC and AD are replaced by 'before the Christian era' and 'of the Christian era'.

Some examples are as follows:

(i) 2300 BP = −350
(ii) 2900 BC = −2900
AD 1800 = +1800
(iii) 5th century BC = 5th century before the Christian era
3rd century AD = 3rd century of the Christian era

List of figures

The publishers would like to thank the following for supplying maps and/or drawings for this volume: Professor B. W. Andah, Professor J. Anquandah, Professor A. Bathily, Professor T. Bianquis, Professor J. Devisse, Mme B. Domenichini-Ramiaramanana, Professor C. Ehret, Professor I. Hrbek, Professor T. N. Huffman, Professor S. Jakobielski, Professor S. Lwanga-Lunyiigo, Professor F. de Medeiros, Professor D. W. Phillipson, Professor Thurstan Shaw, Professor P. Vérin.

List of plates

Acknowledgements for plates

Brett, Dr M., 9.1, 11.1
Centre national de la recherche scientifique, Paris, 28.2
Devisse, J., 7.3, 14.1, 14.5, 28.9, 28.10
El Fasi, HE Mr Mohammed, 10.1
Fehervari, Dr G., 7.6
Freer Gallery, Washington, 7.4 (a), 7.4 (b)
Gado, B., 28.3
Hachette (Albert Shoucair), 7.5
Holl, A., 15.1, 15.2, 15.3
IMRS, Nouakchott, 5.1, 14.2, 14.3, 14.6, 14.7, 14.9, 28.4
Jansen, G., 28.8 (b), 28.8 (c)
Maret, P. de, 23.1, 23.2
Meillassoux, C., 27.1
Ministry of Culture and Tourism, Algeria, 13.3 (a)
Ministry of Culture of Ethiopia, 19.1, 19.2, 19.3
Ministry of Culture, Morocco, front cover photograph, 10.2
Musée royal de l'Afrique centrale 28.1 (a)–(g)
Musée d'Histoire naturelle, Paris 25.1
Nantet, Bernard, 3.1, 13.3 (b), 14.4, 14.8, 28.6, 28.11
National Commission for Museums and Monuments, Lagos, 16.1 (a)–(h)
National Institute of Archaeology and Art, Tunis, 10.4 (a), 10.4 (b), 10.5
Office de la topographie et de la cartographie, Tunis, 12.1
Research Centre for Mediterranean Archaeology, Polish Academy of Sciences, Warsaw, 8.1, 8.2, 8.3, 8.4, 8.5
Réunion des musées nationaux, Louvre, 2.1, 2.2
Shaw, Thurstan 17.4 (a)–(f), 28.7 (a), 28.7 (b)
Stelling, F., 28.8 (a)
Terrasse, H., 13.1
Topkapi Saray Museum (Reha Günay), 26.1
UNESCO 7.1 (A. Khalil), 13.2 (a)–(b) (Dominique Roger)
Unwin, Sheila 21.1
Van Grunderbeek, M. C., Roche, E., Doutrelpont H., 6.2 (b)–(d)
Van Grunderbeek, M. C., Roche, E., Doutrelpont, H., Craddock, P., 6.2 (a)
Van Noten, F., 6.1
Werner Forman Archives, 2.3, 10.6, 11.2
Willett, Frank, 17.1, 17.2, 17.3, 28.5

Preface

AMADOU-MAHTAR M'BOW
Former Director-General of Unesco

For a long time, all kinds of myths and prejudices concealed the true history of Africa from the world at large. African societies were looked upon as societies that could have no history. In spite of important work done by such pioneers as Leo Frobenius, Maurice Delafosse and Arturo Labriola, as early as the first decades of this century, a great many non-African experts could not rid themselves of certain preconceptions and argued that the lack of written sources and documents made it impossible to engage in any scientific study of such societies.

Although the *Iliad* and *Odyssey* were rightly regarded as essential sources for the history of ancient Greece, African oral tradition, the collective memory of peoples which holds the thread of many events marking their lives, was rejected as worthless. In writing the history of a large part of Africa, the only sources used were from outside the continent, and the final product gave a picture not so much of the paths actually taken by the African peoples as of those that the authors thought they must have taken. Since the European Middle Ages were often used as a yardstick, modes of production, social relations and political institutions were visualized only by reference to the European past.

In fact, there was a refusal to see Africans as the creators of original cultures which flowered and survived over the centuries in patterns of their own making and which historians are unable to grasp unless they forgo their prejudices and rethink their approach.

Furthermore, the continent of Africa was hardly ever looked upon as a historical entity. On the contrary, emphasis was laid on everything likely to lend credence to the idea that a split had existed, from time immemorial, between a 'white Africa ' and a 'black Africa', each unaware of the other's existence. The Sahara was often presented as an impenetrable space preventing any intermingling of ethnic groups and peoples or any exchange of goods, beliefs, customs and ideas between the societies that had grown up on either side of the desert. Hermetic frontiers were drawn between the civilizations of Ancient Egypt and Nubia and those of the peoples south of the Sahara.

It is true that the history of Africa north of the Sahara has been more closely linked with that of the Mediterranean basin than has the history of sub-Saharan Africa, but it is now widely recognized that the various civilizations of the African continent, for all their differing languages and cultures, represent, to a greater or lesser degree, the historical offshoots of a set of peoples and societies united by bonds centuries old.

Another phenomenon which did great disservice to the objective study of the African past was the appearance, with the slave trade and colonization, of racial stereotypes which bred contempt and lack of understanding and became so deep-rooted that they distorted even the basic concepts of historiography. From the time when the notions of 'white' and 'black' were used as generic labels by the colonialists, who were regarded as superior, the colonized Africans had to struggle against both economic and psychological enslavement. Africans were identifiable by the colour of their skin, they had become a kind of merchandise, they were earmarked for hard labour and eventually, in the minds of those dominating them, they came to symbolize an imaginary and allegedly inferior *Negro* race. This pattern of spurious identification relegated the history of the African peoples in many minds to the rank of ethno-history, in which appreciation of the historical and cultural facts was bound to be warped.

The situation has changed significantly since the end of the Second World War and in particular since the African countries became independent and began to take an active part in the life of the international community and in the mutual exchanges that are its *raison d'être*. An increasing number of historians has endeavoured to tackle the study of Africa with a more rigorous, objective and open-minded outlook by using – with all due precautions – actual African sources. In exercising their right to take the historical initiative, Africans themselves have felt a deep-seated need to re-establish the historical authenticity of their societies on solid foundations.

In this context, the importance of the eight-volume *General History of Africa*, which Unesco is publishing, speaks for itself.

The experts from many countries working on this project began by laying down the theoretical and methodological basis for the *History*. They have been at pains to call in question the over-simplifications arising from a linear and restrictive conception of world history and to re-establish the true facts wherever necessary and possible. They have endeavoured to highlight the historical data that give a clearer picture of the evolution of the different peoples of Africa in their specific socio-cultural setting.

To tackle this huge task, made all the more complex and difficult by the vast range of sources and the fact that documents were widely scattered, Unesco has had to proceed by stages. The first stage, from 1965 to 1969, was devoted to gathering documentation and planning the work. Operational assignments were conducted in the field and included campaigns to collect oral traditions, the creation of regional documentation centres for oral traditions, the collection of unpublished manuscripts in Arabic and

Ajami (African languages written in Arabic script), the compilation of archival inventories and the preparation of a *Guide to the Sources of the History of Africa*, culled from the archives and libraries of the countries of Europe and later published in eleven volumes. In addition, meetings were organized to enable experts from Africa and other continents to discuss questions of methodology and lay down the broad lines for the project after careful examination of the available sources.

The second stage, which lasted from 1969 to 1971, was devoted to shaping the *History* and linking its different parts. The purpose of the international meetings of experts held in Paris in 1969 and Addis Ababa in 1970 was to study and define the problems involved in drafting and publishing the *History*; presentation in eight volumes, the principal edition in English, French and Arabic, translation into African languages such as Kiswahili, Hausa, Fulani, Yoruba or Lingala, prospective versions in German, Russian, Portuguese, Spanish and Chinese, as well as abridged editions designed for a wide African and international public.[1]

The third stage has involved actual drafting and publication. This began with the appointment of the 39-member International Scientific Committee, two-thirds African and one-third non-African, which assumes intellectual responsibility for the *History*.

The method used is interdisciplinary and is based on a multi-faceted approach and a wide variety of sources. The first among these is archaeology, which holds many of the keys to the history of African cultures and civilizations. Thanks to archaeology, it is now acknowledged that Africa was very probably the cradle of mankind and the scene – in the neolithic period – of one of the first technological revolutions in history. Archaeology has also shown that Egypt was the setting for one of the most brilliant ancient civilizations of the world. But another very important source is oral tradition, which, after being long despised, has now emerged as an invaluable instrument for discovering the history of Africa, making it possible to follow the movements of its different peoples in both space and time, to understand the African vision of the world from the inside and to grasp the original features of the values on which the cultures and institutions of the continent are based.

We are indebted to the International Scientific Committee in charge of this *General History of Africa*, and to its Rapporteur and the editors and authors of the various volumes and chapters, for having shed a new light on the African past in its authentic and all-encompassing form and for having avoided any dogmatism in the study of essential issues. Among these issues we might cite: the slave trade, that 'endlessly bleeding wound', which was responsible for one of the cruellest mass deportations in the history of man-

1. Volume I has been published in Arabic, Spanish, Portuguese, Chinese and Italian; Volume II in Arabic, Spanish, Portuguese, Chinese and Korean; Volumes IV and VII in Spanish.

kind, which sapped the African continent of its life-blood while contributing significantly to the economic and commercial expansion of Europe; colonization, with all the effects it had on population, economics, psychology and culture; relations between Africa south of the Sahara and the Arab world; and, finally, the process of decolonization and nation-building which mobilized the intelligence and passion of people still alive and sometimes still active today. All these issues have been broached with a concern for honesty and rigour which is not the least of the *History*'s merits. By taking stock of our knowledge of Africa, putting forward a variety of viewpoints on African cultures and offering a new reading of history, the *History* has the signal advantage of showing up the light and shade and of openly portraying the differences of opinion that may exist between scholars.

By demonstrating the inadequacy of the methodological approaches which have long been used in research on Africa, this *History* calls for a new and careful study of the twofold problem areas of historiography and cultural identity, which are united by links of reciprocity. Like any historical work of value, the *History* paves the way for a great deal of further research on a variety of topics.

It is for this reason that the International Scientific Committee, in close collaboration with Unesco, decided to embark on additional studies in an attempt to go deeper into a number of issues which will permit a clearer understanding of certain aspects of the African past. The findings being published in the series 'Unesco Studies and Documents – General History of Africa'[2] will prove a useful supplement to the *History*, as will the works planned on aspects of national or subregional history.

The *General History* sheds light both on the historical unity of Africa and also its relations with the other continents, particularly the Americas and the Caribbean. For a long time, the creative manifestations of the descendants of Africans in the Americas were lumped together by some historians as a heterogeneous collection of *Africanisms*. Needless to say, this is not the attitude of the authors of the *History*, in which the resistance of the slaves shipped to America, the constant and massive participation of the descendants of Africans in the struggles for the initial independence of America and in national liberation movements, are rightly perceived for what they were: vigorous assertions of identity, which helped forge the universal concept of mankind. Although the phenomenon may vary in

2. The following eight volumes have already been published in this series: *The peopling of ancient Egypt and the deciphering of Meroitic script; The African slave trade from the fifteenth to the nineteenth century; Historical relations across the Indian Ocean; The historiography of Southern Africa; The decolonization of Africa; Southern Africa and the Horn of Africa; African ethnonyms and toponyms; Historical and socio-cultural relations between black Africa and the Arab world from 1935 to the present; The methodology of contemporary African History; Africa and the Second World War; The Educational Process on Historiography in Africa; Libya Antiqua.*

different places, it is now quite clear that ways of feeling, thinking, dreaming and acting in certain nations of the western hemisphere have been marked by their African heritage. The cultural inheritance of Africa is visible everywhere, from the southern United States to northern Brazil, across the Caribbean and on the Pacific seaboard. In certain places it even underpins the cultural identity of some of the most important elements of the population.

The *History* also clearly brings out Africa's relations with southern Asia across the Indian Ocean and the African contributions to other civilizations through mutual exchanges.

I am convinced that the efforts of the peoples of Africa to conquer or strengthen their independence, secure their development and assert their cultural characteristics, must be rooted in historical awareness renewed, keenly felt and taken up by each succeeding generation.

My own background, the experience I gained as a teacher and as chairman, from the early days of independence, of the first commission set up to reform history and geography curricula in some of the countries of West and Central Africa, taught me how necessary it was for the education of young people and for the information of the public at large to have a history book produced by scholars with inside knowledge of the problems and hopes of Africa and with the ability to apprehend the continent in its entirety.

For all these reasons, Unesco's goal will be to ensure that this *General History of Africa* is widely disseminated in a large number of languages and is used as a basis for producing children's books, school textbooks and radio and television programmes. Young people, whether schoolchildren or students, and adults in Africa and elsewhere will thus be able to form a truer picture of the African continent's past and the factors that explain it, as well as a fairer understanding of its cultural heritage and its contribution to the general progress of mankind. The *History* should thus contribute to improved international cooperation and stronger solidarity among peoples in their aspirations to justice, progress and peace. This is, at least, my most cherished hope.

It remains for me to express my deep gratitude to the members of the International Scientific Committee, the Rapporteur, the different volume editors, the authors and all those who have collaborated in this tremendous undertaking. The work they have accomplished and the contribution they have made plainly go to show how people from different backgrounds but all imbued with the same spirit of goodwill and enthusiasm in the service of universal truth can, within the international framework provided by Unesco, bring to fruition a project of considerable scientific and cultural import. My thanks also go to the organizations and governments whose generosity has made it possible for Unesco to publish this *History* in different languages and thus ensure that it will have the worldwide impact it deserves and thereby serve the international community as a whole.

Description of the Project

B. A. OGOT

Former President, International Scientific Committee for the Drafting of a General History of Africa

The General Conference of Unesco at its 16th Session instructed the Director-General to undertake the drafting of a *General History of Africa*. The enormous task of implementing the project was entrusted to an International Scientific Committee which was established by the Executive Board in 1970. This Committee, under the Statutes adopted by the Executive Board of Unesco in 1971, is composed of thirty-nine members (two-thirds of whom are African and one-third non-African) serving in their personal capacity and appointed by the Director-General of Unesco for the duration of the Committee's mandate.

The first task of the Committee was to define the principal characteristics of the work. These were defined at the first session of the Committee as follows:

(a) Although aiming at the highest possible scientific level, the history does not seek to be exhaustive and is a work of synthesis avoiding dogmatism. In many respects, it is a statement of problems showing the present state of knowledge and the main trends in research, and it does not hesitate to show divergencies of views where these exist. In this way, it prepares the ground for future work.
(b) Africa is considered in this work as a totality. The aim is to show the historical relationships between the various parts of the continent, too frequently subdivided in works published to date. Africa's historical connections with the other continents receive due attention, these connections being analysed in terms of mutual exchanges and multilateral influences, bringing out, in its appropriate light, Africa's contribution to the history of mankind.
(c) *The General History of Africa* is, in particular, a history of ideas and civilizations, societies and institutions. It is based on a wide variety of sources, including oral tradition and art forms.
(d) The *History* is viewed essentially from the inside. Although a scholarly work, it is also, in large measure, a faithful reflection of the way in which African authors view their own civilization. While prepared in an inter-

national framework and drawing to the full on the present stock of scientific knowledge, it should also be a vitally important element in the recognition of the African heritage and should bring out the factors making for unity in the continent. This effort to view things from within is the novel feature of the project and should, in addition to its scientific quality, give it great topical significance. By showing the true face of Africa, the *History* could, in an era absorbed in economic and technical struggles, offer a particular conception of human values.

The Committee has decided to present the work covering over three million years of African history in eight volumes, each containing about eight hundred pages of text with illustrations, photographs, maps and line drawings.

A chief editor, assisted if necessary by one or two co-editors, is responsible for the preparation of each volume. The editors are elected by the Committee either from among its members or from outside by a two-thirds majority. They are responsible for preparing the volumes in accordance with the decisions and plans adopted by the Committee. On scientific matters, they are accountable to the Committee or, between two sessions of the Committee, to its Bureau for the contents of the volumes, the final version of the texts, the illustrations and, in general, for all scientific and technical aspects of the *History*. The Bureau ultimately approves the final manuscript. When it considers the manuscript ready for publication, it transmits it to the Director-General of Unesco. Thus the Committee, or the Bureau between committee sessions, remains fully in charge of the project.

Each volume consists of some thirty chapters. Each chapter is the work of a principal author assisted, if necessary, by one or two collaborators. The authors are selected by the Committee on the basis of their *curricula vitae*. Preference is given to African authors, provided they have requisite qualifications. Special effort is also made to ensure, as far as possible, that all regions of the continent, as well as other regions having historical or cultural ties with Africa, are equitably represented among the authors.

When the editor of a volume has approved texts of chapters, they are then sent to all members of the Committee for criticism. In addition, the text of the volume editor is submitted for examination to a Reading Committee, set up within the International Scientific Committee on the basis of the members' fields of competence. The Reading Committee analyses the chapters from the standpoint of both substance and form. The Bureau then gives final approval to the manuscripts.

Such a seemingly long and involved procedure has proved necessary, since it provides the best possible guarantee of the scientific objectivity of the *General History of Africa*. There have, in fact, been instances when the Bureau has rejected manuscripts or insisted on major revisions or even reassigned the drafting of a chapter to another author. Occasionally, specialists in a particular period of history or in a particular question are consulted to put the finishing touches to a volume.

The work will be published first in a hard-cover edition in English, French and Arabic, and later in paperback editions in the same languages. An abridged version in English and French will serve as a basis for translation into African languages. The Committee has chosen Kiswahili and Hausa as the first African languages into which the work will be translated.

Also, every effort will be made to ensure publication of the *General History of Africa* in other languages of wide international currency such as Chinese, Portuguese, Russian, German, Italian, Spanish, Japanese, etc.

It is thus evident that this is a gigantic task which constitutes an immense challenge to African historians and to the scholarly community at large, as well as to Unesco under whose auspices the work is being done. For the writing of a continental history of Africa, covering the last three million years, using the highest canons of scholarship and involving, as it must do, scholars drawn from diverse countries, cultures, ideologies and historical traditions, is surely a complex undertaking. It constitutes a continental, international and interdisciplinary project of great proportions.

In conclusion, I would like to underline the significance of this work for Africa and for the world. At a time when the peoples of Africa are striving towards unity and greater cooperation in shaping their individual destinies, a proper understanding of Africa's past, with an awareness of common ties among Africans and between Africa and other continents, should not only be a major contribution towards mutual understanding among the people of the earth, but also a source of knowledge of a cultural heritage that belongs to all mankind.

1

Africa in the context of world history

I. HRBEK

If an extraterrestrial visitor had looked at the Old World at the beginning of the seventh century of the Christian era and had then revisited it after five centuries – by 1100 – he might well have come to the conclusion that the world was on the way to becoming Muslim.

At the time of his first visit, the community around the Prophet Muḥammad, who preached the new religious system, Islam, in the small town of Mecca, lost in the boundless wastes of the Arabian desert, did not count even a hundred people fighting for survival against the growing hostility of their compatriots. Five centuries later the adherents of this faith were to be found on a territory stretching from the banks of the Ebro, the Senegal and the Niger in the west, to the Syr-Darya and the Indus in the east, and from the Volga deep in the heart of the Eurasian continent to the East African coast.

In the central parts of this territory the Muslims formed the majority of the population whereas in some fringe areas they were rulers or traders, expanding further and further the Islamic frontiers. Although at this time the Islamic world had already lost its former political unity, being divided into many mutually independent states, and had even lost some of its territories (in northern Spain, in Sicily and just at the end of the period also a small territory in Palestine and Lebanon), it still represented a fairly homogeneous culture and civilization whose creativity was far from being exhausted.

In the meantime Islam had ceased to be an exclusively Arab religion; the new faith showed the capacity to win over and assimilate ethnic elements of the most diverse origins, fusing them into a single cultural and religious community. Islam, born in the sun-scorched peninsula of Arabia, was later able to acclimatize itself in various regions of the world and among such diverse peoples as the Persian, Egyptian and Spanish peasants, the Berber, Somali and Turkish nomads, the Afghan and Kurdish mountain-tribes, the Indian pariahs, the Soninke traders and Kānemi rulers. Many of these peoples became in their turn fiery champions of Islam taking the torch from the Arabs and expanding the faith in new directions.

No wonder that such a magnificent achievement would have impressed our hypothetical extraterrestrial visitor, as it has many historians who have not hesitated to call the period from the seventh to the eleventh century – and even beyond – 'the Islamic age'. This label does not imply that the Muslim peoples dominated the whole world or that they exercised a decisive political, religious or cultural influence outside their own sphere. We have to understand it in relation to other cultural zones and in the sense that the Islamic world was during that period the most dynamic and the most progressive in several fields of human activity. It would, of course, be misleading to neglect the changes going on in other zones or to underestimate the achievements of other peoples in Africa, Asia and Europe at the same time, since there already existed germs of later evolution that did not remain without impact on the destinies of the world.

The rise of Islamic civilization

The Arab conquest was in many ways similar to but also in many ways different from all other conquests known to the world. First, although inspired by a religious teaching, the Arabs did not expect the conquered people, in principle, to enter their religious community; the conquered people were allowed to maintain their old religious allegiances. But after a few generations the majority of the urban population adopted Islam and even those who did not do so tended to use Arabic as a common medium of culture. The Arab empire had been conquered by a pastoralist military force but this force was led by urban merchants who were already acquainted with the culture of the occupied lands. The empire created by the Arabs, in contrast to those founded by other pastoralists, stayed in one piece and endured. In contrast also to, let us say, the Mongols, the Arabs did not adopt the local languages and religious systems but instead imposed their own language and allegiance on the various peoples they had conquered.

The Arab conquests in the seventh and eighth centuries produced two momentous and enduring effects. The more immediate and dramatic was the creation of a new world state in the Mediterranean Basin and the Near East. The second effect, less rapid and tumultuous but no less important, was the development of a new world culture within this state.

The Arab world state was launched as an imperial system with a rapidity seldom matched in history. Within a century of their appearance on the world scene, the Arabs held sway from the Pyrenees on the border of France to the Pamirs in Central Asia. Spain, North Africa, Egypt, the former Byzantine territories south of the Taurus Mountains and the Persian empire in the east were welded together into an imperial realm that rivalled that of Rome at its peak.

For a little over a century the Arab conquerors were able to hold their subject lands together. After the mid-eighth century, various regions began to break away and non-Arab Muslims began to assert their right to share in the rule of state and society. In the west, Spain, North Africa and later Egypt gradually achieved independence and went their own ways. In the east, various dynasties of Persian and Turkish (but culturally Persianized) origin emerged until they became masters of the eastern parts of the Caliphate. By the end of the eleventh century the original Arab empire had long since ceased to exist. It was transformed into a bewildering array of petty states, regional powers and contending dynasties, few of them of Arab origin.

Thus the Arab empire of the first conquerors was transformed into the Muslim world of the Middle Ages. It was a world and not an empire, a political realm consisting of individual and often mutually hostile states, yet aware of common identity that distinguished it from the other world regions. It was Muslim, not solely Arab, based upon a common religion rather than on ethnic bonds.

The second enduring result of the original Arab conquest was the creation, within this Muslim setting, of a new world culture. The Arab conquerors used both their new faith, Islam, and their military prowess to establish an empire but the culture they brought from their desert home was rather unsophisticated and simple. Compared with the rich Classical, Hellenistic or Persian heritage, found in the conquered countries, the Arabs' cultural contribution was rather limited although in many ways significant. Apart from the religion, they contributed their language as the main vehicle of administration, literature and science and also their poetry and aesthetic values.

The distinctive and rich civilization that characterized the Muslim world at its height came into being through the amalgam of varied traditions of all the people who adopted Islam or lived under its sway. It inherited not only the material and intellectual achievements of the Near Eastern and Mediterranean world but also appropriated and absorbed many elements of Indian and Chinese origin and transmitted them further.

It would be erroneous to see the Muslim civilization merely as a simple conglomerate of bits and pieces of borrowed cultural goods. At first, of course, many traits were appropriated directly without any reshaping but gradually they were combined, enlarged and developed into new patterns that served both as resource and stimulus to creative Muslim sciences, artistic expression and technological innovations. In this way emerged the Muslim civilization with its own distinctive pattern corresponding to the new universalistic spirit and new social order.

Geographic and economic factors

The flowering of this civilization was made possible by a set of favourable, dialectically interlocked factors. The Muslim empire was erected in the region of the most ancient world civilization. The conquering Arabs found there an age-long tradition of urban life and urban economy; very quickly they seized this opportunity and besides settling in ancient towns they founded many new ones. It was this urban character of the Muslim world and civilization that most profoundly marked its difference from the Christian West in the early Middle Ages. The existence of many populous cities in the Muslim empire was of considerable importance for the economy of the empire as a whole and especially for its commercial relations with other parts of the Old World. It was in the Muslim core lands that the most important centres of economic and cultural life were to be found, Western Europe offering at that time a quite different picture of scattered rural communities with only a minimum of commercial and intellectual activity. Thus the major trends of social and economic development in the Muslim world were exactly contrary to those that characterized the history of Europe at the same period.

The incorporation of so many countries in the Muslim empire created conditions for the expansion of trade activities on a scale that had been impossible to achieve when the region was politically fragmented. From the late seventh century to the end of the twelfth century the Muslim empire functioned like a free-trade area. The commodities produced in one part of the world became available in other parts so that a uniformity of consumer goods existed among a large, diverse population inhabiting a wide territory. The Muslim world, lying midway between East and West, served also to disseminate technological innovations among the peoples of outlying areas. The increased commercial activity between various parts of the Muslim world and beyond its frontiers stimulated local production of commodities for markets in other places. It also stimulated advances in applied and theoretical techniques, for example in navigation and the allied fields of shipbuilding, astronomy and geography as well as in commercial and banking practices.

The economic boom that had started in the eighth century and continued for some centuries was also to a great extent brought about by the flow of precious metals to the central lands of the Near East. Gold dinars were minted for the first time at the end of the seventh century by the Umayyads and circulated mainly in the former Byzantine provinces whereas the eastern parts had remained for a long time traditionally the silver area. The increase of gold supply in the ninth century led to a change in the monetary system of the Muslim empire: the countries where from time immemorial only silver coins had circulated, went over to bimetallism and all mints in the eastern parts of the Caliphate began to strike gold dinars. In the western part of the Muslim world the situation was different; for a long time the Maghrib and Muslim Spain remained in the orbit of silver currency, mainly for want of easily accessible gold mines. This began to change only in the tenth century with increased gold imports from the Western Sudan of West Africa, to reach its highpoint with the Almoravid dinar, a coinage that became internationally recognized.[1] The issue of great quantities of excellent gold and silver coins had many consequences for economic life in the Muslim countries. Production was stimulated as people increased consumption of various goods but at the same time there was a steep rise in prices.

As a region the Muslim empire was favoured also by its central position in the heart of the Old World. By their domination of the isthmus area between the two great maritime domains of the Mediterranean and the Indian Ocean the Muslims gained a decisive advantage in long-distance trade. The sheer extent of the Muslim world from the shores of the Atlantic to the Chinese borders created a unique situation; it was the only one of the great cultural areas to be in direct contact with each of the others – with Byzantium, with Western Europe, with India and China. This geographical position also allowed it to enter into contact with the great frontier areas and new peoples – in the Eurasian fluvial plains, in Central Asia, across the Sahara in the Sudanic Sahel, in South-east Asia. These were the regions where Islam expanded after the first wave of the conquests following mainly the major long-distance trade routes, either the great continental route – the route of steppes, deserts and oases going from Central Asia to West Africa – or the maritime one leading to the countries around the Indian Ocean and to East Asia.

This central position predestined the Muslim world to the role of intermediary – or channel – between all the other regions of the Old World. Together with commercial commodities transported by land and sea routes went many new ideas and concepts, and innovations in technology and sciences. Some of them were accepted only by the Muslim peoples but many more were transmitted further to neighbouring areas. The actual routes or dates of cultural or material borrowings are in most cases obscure but there is no doubt that they were transmitted. The case of paper serves as an early example of an important product that was sent all the way from China to Europe via Muslim lands. Originally a Chinese invention, it was introduced to the Muslim empire by Chinese prisoners-of-war who were brought to Samarkand in 751. These Chinese papermakers taught the Muslims the technology of its production and Samarkand became the first place outside China to have a paper industry. From there the industry spread to Baghdad, then to Arabia, Syria and Egypt and lastly to Morocco (in the ninth century) and to Muslim Spain (in the first half of the tenth century). There the town of Játiva (Arabic, Shaṭiba) became the main centre of the industry whence the technology was introduced in the twelfth century to Catalonia, the first European country to produce paper. It is not necessary to stress the far-reaching consequences of the spread of one of the greatest inventions for culture and civilization in general.

In a similar way the Indian invention of positional notation in mathem-

1. Cf. C. Cahen, 1981.

atics, the so-called Arabic numerals, was early (already in the eighth century) adopted by the Muslims (who called them Indian numerals) and at some time between the end of the ninth century and the middle of the tenth century the Western world came to know this system. The adoption of positional notation by the Muslims made possible the evolution of algebra, a branch of mathematics which until that time had not been the object of any serious, systematic study; the algebraic mathematics then became the foundation without which the modern branches of mathematics and natural sciences would have been impossible.

The Islamic world and Africa

Let us now turn to Africa and African peoples in the context of the Muslim world and its civilization. At first we shall consider those parts of the continent that became an integral part of the Muslim empire as a result of the first wave of conquests, i.e. Egypt and North Africa, then we will turn our attention to the regions that felt in various ways the impact of Islam or Muslim peoples without being politically integrated within any of the great Muslim states of the time.

The history of Islamic Egypt between the seventh century and the end of the eleventh century offers a fascinating picture of the evolution of an important but rather peripheral province of the Caliphate to become the core land of a new powerful Fāṭimid empire; from a mere granary to become the most important entrepôt for trade between the Mediterranean and the Indian Ocean; from the situation of a rather poor relative in the field of Muslim intellectual activities to become one of the main centres of Arab cultural life. In relation to other parts of Africa, Egypt played manifold roles; it was the starting point both of the Arab conquests in the Maghrib in the seventh century as well as of the Hilālī invasion in the eleventh century. The first led to the Islamization of North Africa, the second to its Arabization. It was from Egypt that Arab Beduins began their advance to the south and made their way gradually into Nubia thereby paving the way for the eventual downfall of its Christian kingdoms and the Arabization of the Nilotic Sudan. Although Egypt lost its Christian character during this period and the majority of the population was converted to Islam, the Alexandrian patriarchate still retained its control over the Monophysite churches in Nubia and Ethiopia and at times became the tool of Egyptian politics in these countries.

It must not be forgotten, too, that Egypt was the final destination of many black African slaves imported from Nubia (in accordance with the famous *baḳt* treaty), Ethiopia, and the Western and Central Sudan. Amongst this unfortunate human merchandise was one slave – Kāfūr – who emerged eventually as the virtual ruler of the country. Others, in their thousands, served as members of the armed forces who wielded considerable influence in domestic politics. The vast majority, however, were employed variously in humble and menial positions.

Although the prominent role of Egypt as the champion of Islam against the European Crusaders and the Mongol invaders came only later (in the twelfth and thirteenth centuries), it was made possible by the political and economic consolidation of the previous centuries.

In the Maghrib the conquering Arabs encountered staunch resistance from the Berbers and it was not until the end of the seventh century that the main regions were subdued. The majority of the Berbers then adopted Islam and although they resented the political domination of the Arabs, the Islamic faith gained vigorous new adherents among them who helped to expand it across the Strait of Gibraltar as well as across the Sahara. The Berber warriors formed the bulk of the Muslim army that conquered Spain for the Umayyads, of the Aghlabid troops that took Sicily away from the Byzantines, and of the Fāṭimid contingents in their victorious campaigns in Egypt and Syria.

North Africa occupied an essential strategic place in the Muslim world both politically and economically. It was from the Maghrib that the conquest of Spain and Sicily started with all its consequences for the history of the western Mediterranean and Europe. It constituted the important connecting link that permitted contact between civilizations and through which various influences flowed in both directions. Muslim domination reintroduced the Maghrib into the orbit of an extensive world-wide economy in which it played a very important role; during this period it underwent new demographic growth including major urbanization, and new economic and commercial prosperity.

From the religious point of view the role of the Berbers was twofold. First, their democratic and egalitarian traditions led them very early on to adhere to the teachings of those Islamic sects that preached these tendencies. Even though Berber Khāridjism was crushed after having flourished for several centuries and continued to exist in only a few communities, the spirit of reform and populism remained part and parcel of Islam in the Maghrib. It revealed itself in the great movements of the Almoravids and Almohads as well as in the proliferation of the *ṣūfī* brotherhoods.

The second important role of the Berbers – seen both in Islamic and African perspective – was to introduce Islam to trans-Saharan Africa. The caravans of the Berber traders that crossed the great desert to the more fertile regions of the Sahel and the Sudan carried not only material products but also new religious and cultural ideas that had found a response at first among the commercial class and later at the courts of African rulers.[2] A second wave of Islamization of the Sudanic belt came about in the eleventh century with the rise of the Almoravids, a genuinely Berber religious movement. The imprint of Berber Islam with its reforming spirit never

2. For further information on the spread of Islam, see Chapter 3 below.

died out in the Sudan and it came to the fore most markedly in the nineteenth-century *djihāds*.

It was the opening up of the Sahara and the Sudanic zone that gave North Africa it specific significance for the economy of the Muslim world. When Sudanese gold started to flow in steadily increasing quantities to the Mediterranean coast it brought about an economic boom permitting many dynasties in the Muslim west to go over from silver to gold currency. The exploitation of the Saharan salt mines became more intensive in response to the growing demand for this indispensable mineral in sub-Saharan Africa. According to a recent authority the trade with sub-Saharan Africa was through many centuries probably the most profitable branch of the Muslim foreign trade.[3]

The Sudanic zone of West Africa was one of the African regions that were not conquered by the Arabs or other Muslim peoples and thus never formed a constituent part of the Caliphate; nevertheless it felt an ever-increasing impact from the Muslim world through commercial and cultural contacts and became to a certain degree integrated into its economic structure. A similar situation obtained, with some important deviations, on the East African coast.

Since Classical times this coast had been visited for commercial purposes by merchants from southern Arabia and Persia. After the rise of Islam and the foundation of the Islamic empire there emerged on the Indian Ocean a vast commercial network controlled by Muslims, mostly Arabs and Persians; it had stretched from the Persian/Arabic Gulf[4] and (later) the Red Sea to India, Malaya, Indonesia and southern China and included the East African coast, the Comoros and also parts of Madagascar. The prosperity of the coastal towns belonging to this network depended to a large degree on the general economic situation of the whole Indian Ocean area, particularly that of the Muslim countries. And since this economy was steadily expanding in the period under discussion, especially after the Fāṭimids had started to develop their commercial relations with the Indian Ocean, East African coastal settlements with their exports of gold, iron, hides and other commodities played a still more important role in the whole network. Not only the material welfare of the coastal cities benefited from this process but indirectly so did Islam as a religion and culture, contributing thus to the flowering of the Swahili culture in the next centuries.

There is no doubt that the rapid expansion of Islamic power did considerable damage to the economic life of Ethiopia by cutting it off from access to the Red Sea and by monopolizing the trade in adjacent regions. The repercussions of this were also felt in the political sphere; the country was politically fragmented and for more than two centuries the central authority of the state was weakened. Another result of the Muslim

3. E. Ashtor, 1976, pp. 100–2.
4. The official name is 'Persian Gulf'.

supremacy in the coastal regions was the shifting of the centre of the Ethiopian state southwards and a more energetic expansion in this direction. These southern regions in their turn became the core from which the revival of the Christian Ethiopian state started in the ninth century. From the tenth century on there began a new period of Islamic penetration of the Ethiopian interior by Muslim merchants from the Dahlak Islands and Zaylāʿ and also the foundation of the first Muslim states in the southern parts of present-day Ethiopia. Thus by a combination of various factors the essential conditions were created for the long struggle between Islam and Christianity in the next centuries for the domination of the Ethiopian region.

If one tries to sum up the role that the rise of the Islamic empire played in regard to Africa during these five centuries, the conclusion will be as follows:

(1) The Mediterranean façade of the continent, from the Isthmus of Suez to the Strait of Gibraltar, and the adjacent Atlantic coast had been incorporated as an integral part of the Islamic world. It had ceased forever to be part of the Christian world and even served as the starting point for further Muslim expansion in Spain and Sicily on the one hand and in the Sahara and the Sudanic zone of West Africa on the other.

(2) In north-eastern Africa it had brought about the weakening of the Christian states of Nubia and Ethiopia, though neither of them was conquered. Whereas Nubia had come more and more under the economic and political control of Muslim Egypt and nomadic Arabs had begun to penetrate it so that it eventually lost its Christian character, Ethiopia had survived as an independent political and cultural unit although it had to accommodate its external relations to the growing Muslim influences surrounding it.

(3) The Sahara and large parts of the Sudan had now been linked through the trade network to an Islamic economic sphere in which their main exports – gold and slaves – played an increasingly important role. The religion and culture of Islam had penetrated along the trade routes, becoming gradually incorporated into the African ways of life.

(4) In East Africa the role of international trade controlled by the Muslims was similar with the important exception that the Muslim merchants had restricted their activities to coastal settlements and Islamic influence did not penetrate into the interior. But the growing demand, in Muslim countries and India, for Zimbabwe gold even seems to have led to some changes in the Zambezi region. Some parts of Madagascar and the Comoro Islands were also made a part of the great Indian Ocean commercial network.

Thus in the first five centuries of the Islamic era large parts of the African continent had come directly or indirectly under the impact of the new

Islamic empire. In some regions this had helped break down former isolation from the outside world, and the external contacts offered the possibility of cultural exchange and borrowing. The adoption of Islam by the ruling classes of some of the West African states and East African coastal towns forged the links of these states and regions with the Muslim world. In West Africa where states had existed before the coming of Islam, their further expansion into large empires seems to have been fundamentally a reaction to the development of trade with North Africa.[5]

The contacts of the Muslim world with tropical Africa were important, too, in another way: the accounts of Arab geographers and historians are an indispensable and unique corpus of information about these regions.[6] Without these we would know much less or hardly anything at all about the politics, economics and cultures of many African peoples during a crucial period of their history. This aspect, too, should not be forgotten in the general assessment of the interaction between the Muslim world and Africa.

Africa and medieval Europe in the age of transition

At the time when Muḥammad started to preach the new faith in faraway Arabia, the western peninsula of the huge Euro-Asiatic continental mass, known as Europe, was divided into three areas that differed profoundly in their stages of general development: the Byzantine empire, the former Roman provinces of Western Europe now under the domination of various Germanic peoples, and lastly the part to the east of the Rhine and north of the Danube inhabited by Germanic and Slavonic peoples, many of them still on the move to their more permanent homes.

The Byzantine empire

Only the Byzantine empire could claim to continue Graeco-Roman tradition and to have a developed state organization with an efficient administration, a prospering money economy and a high degree of cultural activities in many fields. After surviving the upheavals of the first great migrations of peoples the empire was able in the sixth century – under Justinian – to reconquer and re-establish its domination in most of the central and western Mediterranean and to make it again a Byzantine lake. From its Asiatic provinces and Egypt, the part of the empire least touched by migrations, the Byzantines attempted to re-open the trade routes to the East both on land (the Great Silk Route to China) and on sea (through the Red Sea to India). These attempts were, however, frustrated by the other great power in the area, the Sassanid Persian empire, which ruled all the

5. J. D. Fage, 1964, p. 32.
6. Cf. Unesco, *General History of Africa*, Vol. I, ch. 5 for an evaluation of these sources.

Irano-Semitic core area save the Syrian end of the Fertile Crescent. The struggle between these empires continued from the mid-sixth century until the first third of the seventh century with supremacy alternating between the Byzantines and Persians, although the latter eventually gained the upper hand.

This heavy struggle had exhausted both sides financially and militarily to such a degree that they showed themselves shortly afterwards unable to withstand the onslaught of the new dynamic force of Muslim Arabs. This onslaught spelt the disappearance of the Sassanid empire forever, whereas Byzantium lost some of its most valuable provinces; Syria and Egypt, during the first wave of the Arab conquest, and all North Africa by the end of the seventh century.

Throughout the ninth and tenth centuries the fighting between the Arabs and the Byzantines degenerated into frontier clashes in Asia Minor and northern Syria without much changing the balance of power, even if the empire was able to reconquer parts of Syria and Mesopotamia during the time of political disintegration of the eastern Caliphate.

The Arabs – exhausted as a political force – were then replaced by the Saldjuk Turks who resumed the Muslim advance in Asia Minor, definitively taking its major part by the end of the eleventh century. This new Muslim offensive constituted one of the main causes of the Crusades.

In relation to Africa the Byzantine empire ceased to play any significant role in the course of the seventh century. Egypt was lost very quickly and sporadic attempts to reconquer it from the sea were not successful; some coastal regions of North Africa remained in Byzantine hands until the end of the same century, the delay in ousting them being caused by civil wars among the Arabs who for some decades stopped their offensive. The Orthodox state Church of the Byzantines had never been strong in the African provinces because the Egyptians adhered tenaciously to their Monophysite creed, and the North African urban population to the Roman Church. Whatever influence the Orthodox Church had had in previous centuries, it lost for ever through the Muslim conquest. Although Nubia had never formed a part of the Byzantine empire, Byzantine cultural and religious influence remained comparatively strong there even after the Arab conquest of Egypt, especially in Makuria, the central of the three Christian Nubian states, which adopted – in contrast to the others – the Orthodox (Melkite) creed. The administration was modelled on Byzantine bureaucracy, the higher classes dressed in Byzantine manner and spoke Greek. But gradually the links with Byzantine culture and religion were weakened and at the end of the seventh century the king of Makuria introduced Monophysitism into his state which was now united with the northern Nobadia.[7] This change led to a strengthening of the ties with Coptic

7. On the question of Orthodox and Monophysite religion in Nubia cf. Unesco, *General History of Africa*, Vol. II, ch. 12; Vol. III, ch. 8.

Egypt and partly with Syria and Palestine, too, where Nubian Christians found more inspiration in contacts with their Monophysite coreligionists.

During its struggle against Persia, Byzantium was interested in an alliance with Christian, although Monophysite, Ethiopia. The Arab expansion cut off Byzantium from the Red Sea and the trade with India, thus making the alliance impossible as well as impracticable. As Monophysite Christianity became more and more the symbol of the Ethiopian state and nation, hostile both to Islam and to any other form of Christianity, it developed its own original identity without any reference to Byzantine models, either in theology or in artistic and literary expression.

Western Europe

When we turn our attention to the western provinces of the former Roman empire, i.e. the part we call usually Western Europe, we encounter here, on the eve of the period under discussion, a situation totally different from that of Byzantium. All the territory to the west of the Rhine and to the south of the Alps including parts of the British Isles, had become, between the fourth and the seventh centuries, the theatre of the great migration of Germanic peoples.

These migrations left Western Europe to a high degree devastated; urban life declined and social life became highly localized in small agglomerations of population. Western Europe ceased to be an urban civilization, and became a civilization of small agricultural settlements which maintained only vestiges of mutual relationship.

The general disorganization of life changed Europe between the fifth and tenth centuries into a congeries of small disconnected territories. Its societies lived practically in the forests and plains where people fought desperately to survive until the next harvest; to have enough to eat every day was the prerogative of a few great and powerful men. These societies could have hardly adopted the ways of classical urban civilization.

During these troubled times trade, local as well as long-distance, could hardly progress; a tendency to autarkic economy on all levels led to the progressive disappearance of market exchange and the money economy. As cash became rarer, payment for necessary goods and services was made in agricultural products; the land and its tenure were now the chief source – besides war – of wealth and power. The peasants working on these lands entered, voluntarily or under duress, into various kinds of contractual relationship with their landlords giving a greater or larger part of their products in exchange for security and defence against foreign or domestic enemies. In this way there slowly emerged the feudal system which characterized the historical process in Europe for many centuries to come.

During the seventh century, at a time when the Byzantine empire had to fight against invaders from south and north, Western Europe, not yet threatened by external foes, was able to reorganize itself into some more-or-less stable territorial units. In the west the Visigoths dominated the entire Iberian peninsula, in Gaul and adjacent lands the Frankish Merovingians established their domination and in England the Anglo-Saxons founded their kingdoms. Italy was at the end of the century divided among the Byzantines in the south and the newly arrived Germanic Longobards in the north. In the course of the next centuries the Catholic creed was adopted by all Germanic peoples in Western Europe. Thus, by the seventh century Western Europe, divided ethnically, politically and economically, acquired an element of religious and cultural unity.

The Arabo-Berber conquest of Visigothic Spain at the beginning of the eighth century amputated a considerable part of the Latin West. The Franks were able to stop further Muslim penetration into Gaul but Arab incursions and raids on coastal places in southern France and in Italy continued for more than two centuries, contributing to general insecurity in the Mediterranean. Nevertheless at the end of the same century the first and for a long time the only successful attempt to give political unity to Western Europe was made; it was the work of the Carolingians. Charlemagne's predecessors unified the Frankish territories between the Pyrenees and the Rhine and repulsed the attacks of other Germanic peoples from the east. Charlemagne (768–814) himself incorporated the majority of eastern Germans into his state and established a frontier against the Slavs on the Elbe. The northern half of Italy as well as some territories in northern Spain also fell under Frankish domination and it is no wonder that Charlemagne – as the most powerful monarch in the Latin West – was crowned Emperor in 800. But many parts of Western Europe remained outside his empire: the British Isles, the larger part of Spain under Muslim rule, and southern Italy still in Byzantine and Longobardian hands.

With Charlemagne is connected the famous thesis of the Belgian historian Henri Pirenne that has led to vigorous debates concerning the relationship between the emergence of the Muslim empire and the fate of Western Europe.[8] The Pirenne thesis claims, in a generalized way, that it was not the invasions of the 'barbarian Germanic tribes' in the fifth century that ended Rome's control of trade in the Mediterranean Basin but rather the creation of the Muslim empire. The wresting of North Africa and the eastern provinces from Byzantium by the Arabs created a final break between East and West. This forced Western Europe to turn inward upon itself and its own resources, substituting for the maritime economy of the Merovingians the landlocked and continental Carolingian economy, so that Western Europe became poor and barbarian. 'Without Muḥammad, no Charlemagne' runs the Pirenne formula; in this view the founder of the Western empire appears rather as a symbol of renunciation than of a

8. H. Pirenne, 1937; A. F. Havighurst, 1958.

renewed greatness and thus marks a change of direction in the destinies of the Latin West. Stagnation was overcome only after the tenth century with the emergence of a new European urbanism which, in the final analysis, enabled the rise of modern society.

Although this thesis has been finally rejected by the majority of historians, its main merit was to have drawn attention to important problems of change in medieval economies and to the rise of European feudalism. It also made historians aware of the impact of the Arabs and their domination of North Africa on developments in Europe, a long-neglected theme.

Whether there was a total closure of the Mediterranean and an interruption of long-distance trade as a result of the Arab conquests, or only a diminution in its volume – those were the moot points in the discussion – seems to be less relevant in view of the chief weak point of the Pirenne thesis, namely that this interruption should have had such far-reaching consequences. The long-distance trade, however lucrative or voluminous, did not play the decisive role in the social and economic life of Western Europe attributed to it by Pirenne. Consequently its interruption could not have caused such profound changes in the economic structure. The autarkic latifundium, which seriously menaced even the existence of towns in the empire, had existed long before the Germanic and Arab conquests.

The lasting Arab and Islamic impact on Europe did not result from the military confrontation or the interruption of trade contacts across the Mediterranean but rather from the long years of Muslim rule in Spain and Sicily. Through the innovations brought to these regions, new crops, agricultural processes and technology, and – mainly in sciences and philosophy – new concepts were introduced into a Europe that was less developed in these matters than the Islamic world. Although the European Renaissance began later – from the thirteenth century onwards – the foundations from which it arose were laid in the period of the greatest flowering of Islamic civilization, between the eighth and twelfth centuries.

Eastern and Northern Europe

In the rest of Europe – beyond the ancient Roman frontiers on the Rhine and the Danube – the westward migrations of Germanic tribes opened the way for Slavonic expansion which took two general directions: southwards across the Danube to the Balkans and westwards into the territory of present-day Poland, Czechoslovakia, Hungary and the German Democratic Republic. In the Balkans the ancestors of Yugoslavs and Bulgars, after crossing the Danube in the sixth century, attacked Byzantine European provinces and gradually settled there, changing totally the political and ethnic pattern.

With regard to the Muslim world the Slavonic peoples were to play for some centuries a similar role to that of black Africans; they were imported

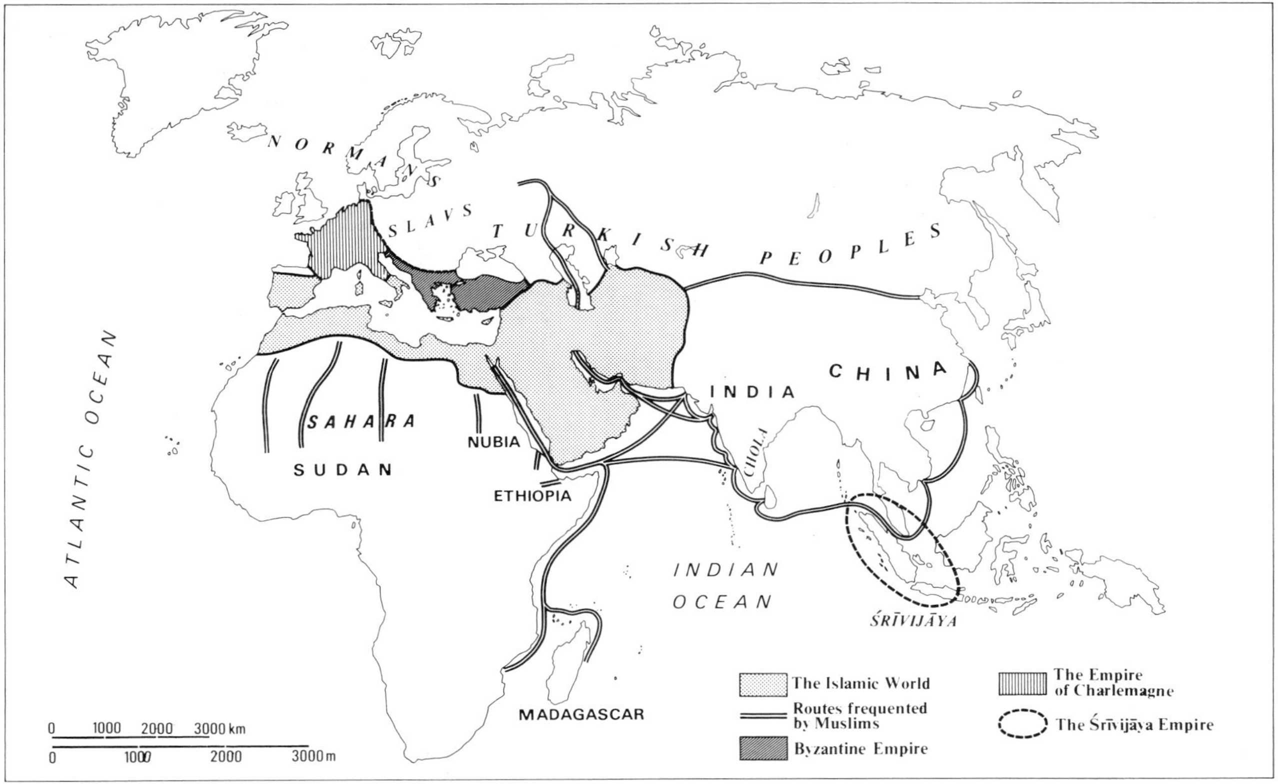

FIG. 1.1 *The Old World.* c. 230/845

thither as slaves.[9] As victims of incessant wars and raids waged against them mostly by their German neighbours, or of their own internecine wars, they were not only retained as a labour force in Europe but were also exported abroad to the Muslim countries. Those captured in central Europe went through the Frankish state to Muslim Spain, whereas those from the Balkans were mostly sold by the Venetians to North Africa. Called by the Arabs 'al-Ṣaḳāliba' (sing., al-Ṣaḳlabī) they were employed mainly as soldiers, in state administration and, when castrated, in harems.[10] Whereas in Muslim Spain the term 'al-Ṣaḳāliba' soon expanded to designate all European slaves of whatever nationality, in the Maghrib and in Fāṭimid Egypt it retained its original meaning. And it was here that the Slavs of Balkan origin did play an important role, participating as soldiers and administrators in the consolidation as well as expansion of the Fāṭimid power.[11] The most famous among them was Djawhar, the conqueror of Egypt, founder of Cairo and of the al-Azhar University. Although the Slavs were soon absorbed, ethnically and culturally, by the Muslim Arab society in the Maghrib and Egypt, they nevertheless did contribute to the shaping of the destiny of these parts of North Africa in the course of the tenth and eleventh centuries.

With the adoption of Christianity the majority of Slavonic peoples entered into the community of European 'civilized' nations and ceased to be sold as slaves abroad. At the end of the eleventh century the states of Bohemia, Poland, Croatia, Serbia and Bulgaria already existed, whereas in the east the state of Kiev accomplished the unification of the majority of eastern Slavonic peoples.

Between the eighth and tenth centuries another group of peoples from beyond the horizon of Mediterranean nations emerged on the European scene, the Viking (or Norman) invaders, conquerors and merchant-adventurers who from their Scandinavian homes attacked coastal regions, and along rivers even some parts of the interior, from their technologically advanced ships. These attacks and raids were repeated over many years and caused heavy devastation and general insecurity in many regions such as the British Isles and France; but some Normans (called by the Arabs 'al-Mādjūs') reached as far south as Muslim Spain and even Morocco. In Eastern Europe the Vikings (known here as Varyags) combined raids with

9. It is significant that in all West European languages the word for 'slave' (Sklave, esclave, esclavo, escravo, etc.) is derived from the ethnonym 'Slav', the name various Slavonic peoples used for themselves. This points to the fact that during the formative period of European national languages, which coincides precisely with the period under discussion, the Slavonic prisoners of war must have formed the main bulk of the slave population in Western Europe.

10. The castration, being forbidden by the Muslim law, was performed already in Europe with the town of Verdun as the most important place so that Reinhard Dozy called it a 'eunuch factory'.

11. Cf. Chapter 12 below.

commerce, establishing their factories along the Russian river system. Descending the Volga they reached the Caspian Sea and made contact with the countries of the Caliphate; sometimes they plundered the coastal regions of Transcaucasia, sometimes they travelled as merchants as far as Baghdad, trading in furs, swords and slaves.

Until the eleventh century the Normans, with the exception of the above-mentioned raid on the Moroccan coast in 858 or 859 which remained an ephemeral episode, did not enter into any direct contact with Africa. A group of Normans settled permanently in northern France (Normandy) founding there a strong state. Apart from conquering England in 1066, these same Normans also carved out for themselves a state in southern Italy. From here they undertook the conquest of Muslim Sicily making it their base for further expansion directed partly to North Africa. For one century the Normans of Sicily became an important factor in the political history of Muslim North Africa.

The Muslim raids from the south and Norman incursions from the north deeply influenced Western Europe. It became almost impossible to offer a centralized and organized resistance to these sudden attacks on so many places. Thus the local defence was organized by local lords; in consequence they became more and more independent of their nominal rulers, kings and emperors, and in many cases became even more powerful and wealthy than these. This process of gradual dissolution of centralized authority had already begun in the mid-ninth century and strengthened the already existing tendency to feudal fragmentation.

A relative security returned to Europe by the eleventh century; the dangerous invasions and migrations with their accompanying upheavals came to an end and in large parts of the continent a more-or-less permanent ethnic pattern emerged. From now on changes in political frontiers or the emergence and disappearance of states were due mainly to dynastic policies and aspirations, not to migrations of whole peoples.

It would not be inappropriate to call the period between the seventh and eleventh centuries in Europe the age of transition or transformation, in the sense that during these centuries there emerged a new Europe which differed profoundly from the Europe of Classical times.

New nations living in Antiquity beyond the horizon of the Greeks and Romans and therefore not considered belonging to Europe, became accepted into the European community by their adoption of Christianity and its cultural values and by their adherence to the common political system. The continent was politically and even more so economically fragmented into innumerable small units but already in the eleventh century there was a vague but growing awareness of religious and cultural solidarity especially vis-à-vis the Muslim world. But this awareness was not strong enough to stop the quarrels between the Orthodox and Catholic Churches or to avert the great schisms of the mid-eleventh century.

The eleventh century also marks the end of the transitional period in the economy; serfdom was from now on the dominant mode of production in medieval Europe in which ties of vassalage were also dominant, forming thus the socio-political structure properly called feudal. In some parts of Western and Northern Europe, after a long stagnation, agriculture went through a process of innovation with the introduction of the heavy plough, open fields, triennal rotation, all of which improved methods of producing food. There also emerged new technologies in industrial production such as the application of water power in cloth-making or to activate hammers and bellows in producing more and better iron and iron implements. Transport was made easier on land by the invention of the whippletree for long wagons and the better harnessing of horses; much improvement was also made in ship construction.

No less important was the rise of European towns after so many centuries of decadence. Most spectacular was the revival of Italian towns, especially the ports of Venice, Amalfi, Pisa and Genoa. Before the tenth century their merchants had already started to develop trade with the Byzantine empire as well as with Muslim countries of North Africa and the Near East, exporting timber, metals and slaves, and importing luxury goods such as silk fabrics and spices but also flax, cotton, olive oil and soap. In the eleventh century the Italian merchant republics already dominated the Mediterranean trade; the most active among them, Venice, was given free-trade privileges in all Byzantine ports by the Byzantine emperor and nearly monopolized maritime transport so that Byzantium became a commercial colony of the Venetians.

In the eleventh century Western Europe, until then involved in the struggle for survival in the face of many invasions, gained enough forces to abandon the defensive and prepare to take the offensive.

The offensive started in Sicily; between 1060 and 1091 the Normans conquered the entire island from its Arab rulers and founded a strong state from which they attacked the North African coast and its towns. In 1085 Toledo, one of the most important Muslim cities in Spain, fell into the hands of the Christians. Although the Christian offensive was then halted by the interventions of Berber Almoravids and Almohads for more than a century, this date nevertheless marks the real beginning of the *reconquista*, the Spanish Muslims being driven permanently onto the defensive.

By the end of the century the First Crusade – the earliest serious overseas enterprise and one in which various European peoples were represented – had also achieved its first success with the conquest of Jerusalem and some other towns in the Levant. For nearly two hundred years the Europeans, called Franks by their Muslim enemies, animated at the beginning by a sincere religious zeal and later by the more mundane interests of feudal lords and Italian merchants, tried to incorporate the eastern Mediterranean into their sphere of influence. But the Muslim counter-offensives, in spite of further Crusades, gradually eroded the Latin states in the Levant and succeeded at the end of the thirteenth century in expelling the last Crusaders from Palestine. In the meantime the Byzantine empire, regarded by the Westerners with envy and hostility, became the main victim of the Crusades, emerging at the end much weaker than before. The real victors of this two centuries' long struggle were the Muslims and then the Italian republics which became great mercantile powers.

In the preceding pages we have amply shown the various implications which the Muslim presence on the southern shores of the Mediterranean in North Africa had on Western Europe. Although we do not subscribe fully to Pirenne's thesis, it nevertheless remains a historical fact that with the Arab conquest of North Africa the Mediterranean Basin ceased to be a part of a single large cultural area as it has been in the preceding millennium and became divided between the European (or Christian) and the Arabo-Berber (or Muslim) zones, each with its own culture and going separate ways.

From the Western European point of view, Africa became identified with the Muslim world as it was from this region that the main incursions and invasions, but also various influences and ideas, were coming. When more intensive commercial contacts between the northern and southern shores of the Mediterranean developed later, Africa, which the Europeans then came to know, was still Muslim Africa. It is thus not surprising that Africa was identified with the arch-enemy of Christianity, and its inhabitants, irrespective of their colour, were regarded and treated accordingly.[12] The lack in Europe of any direct contacts with Africa beyond the Muslim sphere must have inevitably led to the emergence of a very distorted image of the continent and particularly of its black inhabitants. Some recent studies, mainly those by J. Devisse and F. de Medeiros[13] have clearly shown how both this ignorance, and the presumed identification of black Africans with Muslims, fashioned the European image of black Africans as the impersonation of sin, evil and inferiority. It was in those early medieval times that European negative attitudes, prejudices and hostility to peoples of black skin emerged, to be later strengthened by the slave trade and slavery.

Africa, Asia and the Indian Ocean

Since the general aspects of the Indian Ocean factor in African history, particularly those of a geographical and oceanographical nature, are discussed in Volume II of the *General History*,[14] we shall here examine only such developments that were significant in the period between the seventh and eleventh centuries.

12. The term 'Moors' (and other derivates of Lat. Mauri) signified for a long time both the Muslims and the blacks; only later the distinction was being made between 'white Moors' and 'black Moors' (Blackamoors); cf. J. Devisse, 1979a, pp. 53–4 and notes on p. 220.

13. ibid., pp. 47ff., and *passim*; F. de Medeiros, 1973.

14. Cf. Unesco, *General History of Africa*, Vol. II, ch. 22.

In the course of the last two decades a few specialized colloquiums and some collective studies have been dedicated to the problem of relations between different parts of the Indian Ocean region;[15] a common feature of them was to call attention to extant problems and to indicate orientations for future research rather than offering definitive answers to a great number of as yet unsolved questions of paramount interest for the history of Africa and the adjacent islands.

The period under discussion is especially beset by these unsolved problems. The main difficulty arises from the fact that owing to some peculiar coincidences – in contrast to the preceding and subsequent periods – our knowledge about the history of the Indian Ocean and the relations between the countries bordering it, is based on rather slender evidence.

It consists up to now of a few, mostly second-hand accounts written by Muslim authors after the tenth century, of some scattered archaeological findings of goods of Asian provenance on the East African coast and on the islands, and of some parallels in the material culture. The situation is not helped by the insufficiency of historical material originating in South India and South-east Asia whose history at this period is far less well known than that of the Islamic countries to the west of India. Another difficulty concerns the dating; in Africa we do find some plants of unquestionably Asian origin, and some African languages – particularly Kiswahili – contain many Indian loan-words, but to pinpoint the precise time of their introduction is problematic. As for other problems and questions that are waiting to be tackled, it suffices to look at the long list catalogued in the report of the Unesco meeting on historical relations across the Indian Ocean[16] to see the enormous research that needs to be done before a clearer picture of the mutual contacts in this region emerges.

Muslim commerce

The important place that the Islamic empire held in inter-continental relations was demonstrated earlier on in this chapter and we do not propose here to recount all the factors that played a role in establishing its predominance in the fields of economics, trade, navigation etc.

In contrast to the Mediterranean Sea, the Indian Ocean has been in general an ocean of peace. The trade relations between its peoples, going back to early times, though not always advantageous in the same way to all participants, were only rarely disturbed by wars. Permanent trade tendencies seem to have been stronger than transitional political ones, the push towards economic exchanges stronger than political antagonism. In the early medieval Mediterranean, Muslim and Christian powers were involved in a continuous struggle and although commercial contacts never

15. Cf. mainly D. S. Richards (ed.), 1970; M. Mollat, 1971; Colloque de Saint-Denis, 1972; H. N. Chittick and R. I. Rotberg (eds), 1975; Unesco, 1980.

16. Unesco, 1980.

totally ceased, the state of war was not generally favourable to trade. By contrast, the expansion of Islam in the Indian Ocean had not negatively influenced Arabo-Persian trade activities since the merchants were anxious not to disturb established commercial relations through forceful conversion.

This does not mean, however, that the Indian Ocean trade has been an idyllic one. In addition to the slave trade, which was often accompanied by warlike deeds and the use of force, there existed throughout the period large-scale piracy. But it should be pointed out that it never reached the extent known from the Mediterranean where it was inflamed and even justified by religious differences.

There were some other negative factors that interfered with the otherwise continuous prosperity of the Muslim enterprise. In the second half of the ninth century two incidents seriously disrupted the Indian Ocean trade. The first was the great Zandj revolt in the region of lower Iraq and the Persian Gulf in the years 252/866–270/883.[17] Some of the most important ports – Baṣra, Ubulla, Abadan – were devastated and Baghdad was cut off from access to the sea. The merchants of these ports who survived the massacres fled into the interior or to other ports, and many ships were lost. For more than fifteen years the maritime trade in this region stagnated from want of merchant capital, goods and ships.

The second blow to the Muslim trade occurred almost simultaneously, in 265/878, when the forces of the Chinese rebel Huang Ch'ao sacked Canton and massacred a huge number of foreign traders, mostly from Muslim countries. The lives of some merchants were apparently spared, for according to the narrator of this disastrous incident, the rebels oppressed Arab shipmasters, imposed illegal burdens on the merchants and appropriated their wealth.[18]

Two calamities of this order could not, of course, occur without leaving traces on Muslim merchant seafaring. The ports at the terminal of the Persian Gulf went through a period of decline and in the East the Muslim merchants preferred to stop at Kalah (on the west coast of the Malayan peninsula) at that time a part of the Śrīvijāya empire of Sumatra (cf. pp. 27–9 below) and to meet there with their Chinese counterparts.

In spite of the calamities of the ninth century, and the monopolistic tendencies of the Śrīvijāya rulers, the Muslim trade gradually recovered and slowly started to regain its former importance. Not even some disasters of the tenth century, such as the sack of Baṣra by the Ḳarmatians from eastern Arabia in 308/920, the burning of the whole Omani fleet in 330/942 by the ruler of Baṣra besieged by this fleet, or the earthquake that destroyed Sīrāf in 366/977, were able to stop the movements of Muslim ships on the sea-lanes of the Indian Ocean.

17. Cf. Chapter 26 below.
18. G. F. Hourani, 1951, pp. 77–9.

The eleventh century witnessed a major shift in the Muslim trade caused by the decline of the Abbasid Caliphate in the Middle East and the simultaneous rise of the Fāṭimids on North African soil. The age-old rivalry between the route terminating in the Persian Gulf, and the route leading through the Red Sea, was then resolved to the advantage of the latter after many centuries in which it played a minor role in Indian Ocean commerce.

So far we have spoken about the role of the Muslim Arabs and Persians in Indian Ocean interrelations. What about the others; Africans, Indians, Indonesians and Chinese? To what degree did these peoples participate in these relations? Did their cultural and material interchange occur through direct or only through indirect contacts?

All this is connected with another problem: do we not overestimate or exaggerate the part played by Muslims in the Indian Ocean merely on the grounds that the evidence and documentation for their activities is at present the most abundant? Only a careful study of all available evidence could bring a definitive answer; already the discovery of some new facts and aspects of the question permits a better assessment of the role played in Indian Ocean relations by non-Muslims. Nevertheless the overall picture of Muslim predominance in this area seems to be unaffected by the recognition of other peoples' roles.

This is only natural: the dominant position of Muslim trade did not emerge 'ex nihilo', it reflected the dynamics of the whole socio-economic structure of the Muslim world in these centuries as well as its favourable geographical situation on the crossroads of continents. As mentioned earlier, none of the cultural areas of the Old World was able at this time to sustain continuous contacts with all the others; the Islamic area was the only one to develop a truly intercontinental trade network. And the period between the seventh and eleventh centuries was just the time when this intercontinental trade evolved to reach its maturity, even if its greatest expansion was to be achieved only later.

Chinese commerce

Now to the participation of other nations; we will deal firstly with the Chinese, mainly for the reason that there are already some exhaustive studies on their enterprise in the Indian Ocean and contacts with Africa.[19] Chinese contacts in ancient and medieval times with the other main areas of the Old World – India, western Asia and the lands around the Mediterranean – were established almost entirely through the export trade in which the most important commodity was silk and, later, chinaware.

Although China already possessed the necessary technical knowledge

19. Cf. J. J. L. Duyvendak, 1949; T. Filesi, 1962, 1970.

and means for long-distance sea voyages on the Indian Ocean under the T'ang dynasty (618–906), she did not employ her own ships for trade beyond the Malayan peninsula. The reasons for Chinese absence from the Indian Ocean were of a cultural and institutional order.[20] In the centuries immediately preceding the rise of Islam, Ceylon (now Sri Lanka) was the main entrepôt for sea trade between China and western Asia. Ships from Champa or Indonesian states used to sail as far west as Ceylon; from here westwards the trade was in the hands of Persians and Axumites.

The Chinese came to know the Indian Ocean through Indian, Persian and later Arab intermediaries. They presumably were not aware of the existence of another continent at the other side of the ocean. The fragmentary accounts in Chinese literary sources about Africans and Africa seem to be drawn from Muslim accounts. In consequence they came to think of the Africans as subjects of Muslim rulers and of their countries as forming part of the Arab empire.[21] African commodities wanted and welcomed by China were easily obtainable through foreign merchants who came in their own ships to Chinese ports.

Among the African goods that reached China the most important were ivory, ambergris, frankincense and myrrh as well as Zandj slaves.[22] In the well-known account of Ibn Lākīs about the attack on Ḳanbalū (Pemba) in the year 334/945–6 by the Wāḳ-Wāḳ people, the Chinese are also said to demand tortoiseshell and panther skins.[23]

For some time the opinion was held that the history of East Africa has been written in Chinese porcelain.[24] Indeed, in East African coastal cities an enormous quantity of Chinese porcelain has been found, so that this ware must have formed an important part of Chinese exports to Africa. Sherds which closely correspond to finds on the East African coast have also been found in Somalia and South Arabia; all this indicates that the whole area of the western Indian Ocean may be considered as forming one single area from the point of view of imports of this type.[25] But the bulk of the Chinese porcelain belongs to a period later than the eleventh century. A similar situation obtains for Chinese coins found on the coast. The evidence thus points to the conclusion that whereas African commodities formed a constant part of Chinese imports from early times, the arrival of Chinese goods in significant quantities could be placed only in the period after the eleventh century. As mentioned above, the exchange between China and Africa was not direct, but passed through the Muslim trade network in the Indian Ocean.

20. Wang Gungwu, 1980.
21. ibid.
22. Cf. Chapter 26 below.
23. Buzurg ibn Shahriyār, 1883–6; cf. also Chapter 25 below.
24. Sir Mortimer Wheeler, quoted by G. S. P. Freeman-Grenville, 1962a, p. 35.
25. ibid.

Indian commerce

The entire problem of India's role in the Indian Ocean, particularly in the first millennium of the Christian era, is still open. It concerns mainly the participation of Indians in international trade, and the Indian influence on various parts of this region. The task of solving this complex problem is not made easier by the almost total lack of evidence of Indian provenance in the period under discussion.

One of the first observations that springs to mind is the great difference between the Indian impact on the eastern and western parts of the Indian Ocean area; throughout the whole of South-east Asia the Indian cultural influence is more than evident both in material and spiritual spheres, notwithstanding the fact that in some parts it was overlaid later by Islam. On the opposite side of the Indian Ocean there is nothing comparable to Borobudur, the Old Javanese Ramayana epics, Balinese Hinduism, the Sanskrit loan-words in dozens of languages and so on. It seems as if the Indians had established a north-south line across the Indian Ocean, deliberately deciding to turn their eyes only eastwards and to avert them from the west. This must have occurred sometime in the middle of the first millennium; in the first centuries of the Christian era there is enough evidence of Indian ships plying between India and the western parts of the ocean and of Indian influence in Ethiopia and even Nubia, but as has been rightly remarked by D. K. Keswani,[26] this glorious period of Indian maritime activities did not last very long. But even so, the Indian cultural impact in this part of Africa is weaker than that in South-east Asia and not comparable with it. Later, at the time of the flourishing of the East African coastal cities, the Indians started to participate in steadily growing numbers in the trade between Africa and India but it was then too late for Indian culture to exercise any deeper influence on the already Islamized coastal society.

In the period between the seventh and the eleventh centuries, relations between Africa and India seem to have been at their lowest ebb.[27] Contact nevertheless existed, and was mostly connected with the exchange of goods. One of the most important African commodities exported to India has always been ivory. The ivory trade flourished already in Antiquity and there is hardly any Arabic source that does not mention it when describing the East African coast. Al-Mas'ūdī (d. 345/956) wrote that ivory from East Africa was destined for export to India and China and adds that its main entrepôt was Oman. This confirms the already expressed suggestion that there was no direct connection between Africa and India at this time.[28] As

26. Cf. D. K. Keswani, 1980, p. 42.

27. There is evidence about the activities of Indian pirates operating from Socotra during this time, but pirates do not usually fulfil the role of cultural apostles. Al-Muḳaddasī, 1877, p. 14; al-Mas'ūdī, 1861–77, Vol. 3, pp. 36–7; cf. G. F. Hourani, 1951, p. 80.

28. Cf. G. S. P. Freeman-Grenville, 1962a, pp. 201–2, who discusses the commercial and nautical reasons for the lack of direct communications.

for other export goods no evidence is available from these centuries but we have to bear in mind that al-Idrīsī's (d. 549/1154) well-known report of African iron exports to India relates in all probability to earlier times and therefore to our period. This African product played an important role in the development of one branch of Indian industry, the production of steel blades. It seems that this is one of the rare occurrences of African export goods that did not belong in the category of primary commodities; it must be stressed here that Africa did not export iron ore (in any case too bulky a cargo for the capacity of contemporary vessels) but already a processed product, probably pig-iron.[29]

Although in later periods many people of African origin imported as slaves came to prominence in India, nothing similar occurred in our period. Some African slaves were certainly exported to India via Arabia or Persia but so far no corresponding documents or other evidence has come to light. Nor do we have sufficient indications about population movements in the opposite direction, of Indians towards Africa. In many oral traditions from the coast and adjacent islands there are many references to people called Debuli (Wadebuli) who are believed to have arrived at the coast even before the Shirazi and thus before the twelfth century. Some ancient buildings are connected with them. Their name is considered to be derived from the great port of al-Daybul (Dabhol) in the mouth of the Indus River.[30] The date of their arrival at the coast is highly controversial, some traditions placing it before the conversion of the coastal towns to Islam, others connecting it with the introduction of firearms, and thus rather late. Only one person with the *nisba* al-Dabuli is recorded, a man whom the Portuguese installed as sultan of Kilwa in 1502.

All this does not exclude the possibility that some people of Indian origin had settled – most likely as traders – on the coast in earlier times. But in any case their number would not have been great since otherwise more concrete traces, in written sources or in material culture, would have been preserved. Kiswahili contains, indeed, many loan-words of Indian origin but until now it has been impossible to determine the epoch in which they were introduced. However, owing to the well-documented increase of Indian expatriates in later centuries, these loan-words seem to have been borrowed comparatively recently, certainly not in the period under discussion.

Contacts with Indonesia

Whereas the contacts between Africa on one hand, and China and India on the other, have been, as indicated, indirect rather than direct, there existed on the other side of the Indian Ocean one region that left indubitable traces

29. Al-Idrīsī, 1970, Vol. 1, Iḳlīm I/8, pp. 67–8.
30. Cf. J. M. Gray, 1954, pp. 25–30; G. S. P. Freeman-Grenville, 1962a, pp. 202–3.

in at least some parts of Africa. The Indonesian contribution to the peopling of Madagascar has been long recognized. At present one of the main tasks of Malagasy history is to elucidate the process of mingling of elements of Indonesian and African origin in the Malagasy culture. As these and cognate problems of Malagasy history are discussed in other chapters of this work,[31] we shall deal here only with those topics that have a direct bearing on the African continent.

It seems now that the impact of the Indonesians on the African mainland has been exaggerated. There is virtually no evidence for direct Indonesian penetration of East Africa similar to what obtains in Madagascar. Until now no archaeological, linguistic or somatic data have been discovered to demonstrate a prolonged presence of Indonesians. The theory of H. Deschamps[32] that before settling in Madagascar the proto-Malagasy made a stay on the coast of Africa where they mixed or married with Africans, lacks any supporting evidence. Raymond Kent has expanded this hypothesis, assuming a movement from Indonesia into East Africa before the arrival of the Bantu-speaking groups; later the Indonesians and Bantu met and mixed in the interior and from this mingling the Afro-Malagasy population resulted. The expansion of the Bantu to the coastal areas forced this population to migrate to Madagascar.[33]

These theories were developed on the ground that the Indonesians were believed to be unable to accomplish a non-stop migration across the Indian Ocean. As a corollary to this some further stopping places like the Nicobars, Sri Lanka, India, the Laccadives and Maldives are mentioned so that the Indonesian migration is seen as a series of relatively short springs from island to island with some stops in India and East Africa. Such a reconstruction is in itself not impossible or improbable but similar stops must have been of rather short duration as the Indonesians have left no discernible vestiges of their presence in these places.

Much has been made, chiefly by G. P. Murdock, of the so-called 'Malaysian botanical complex' comprising such plants as rice, bananas, taro (cocoyam), yams, breadfruit tree and others that came to form the staple food of many Africans. Murdock and others believed that this complex had been brought to Madagascar during the first millennium before the Christian era by migrants from Indonesia who travelled right along the coast of southern Asia before reaching the East African coast. Leaving aside the complex problem of the origin of these plants, it should be pointed out that the diffusion of cultivated plants does not depend on physical migrations of the peoples who first started to cultivate them or had earlier adopted them, as is more than clearly demonstrated by the diffusion of some American crops through western and central Africa after the sixteenth century. This, of course, does not exclude the possibility that some

31. Cf. Chapter 25 below and Unesco, *General History of Africa*, Vol. II, ch. 28.
32. H. Deschamps, 1960.
33. R. K. Kent, 1970.

of the South-east Asian plants were introduced later to the African mainland from Madagascar.

There is, however, no doubt that the Indonesians were capable and accomplished navigators and that they undertook many voyages in all directions from their island homes. Apart from being perhaps the first to open maritime commerce with China, they were particularly active on the sea routes towards India. In Sumatra and Java there emerged in the second half of the first millennium great maritime powers such as the empire of Śrīvijāya in Sumatra (seventh to thirteenth centuries) and the state of the Śailendra dynasty (eighth century) in Java which later also came to power in Śrīvijāya.[34]

We are here concerned merely with those aspects of their history that relate to the general situation in the Indian Ocean region on the one hand, and to their possible contacts with Africa on the other. The Śrīvijāya state, with its first centre in south-eastern Sumatra, emerged as a maritime power in the second half of the seventh century. During the following centuries its territorial as well as commercial expansion continued and when in the tenth century the first accounts of Arabic/Persian geographers started to appear, the Śrīvijāya ruler became for them the 'Maharaja' par excellence, being the most powerful and important sovereign of the whole region, the 'King of the isles of the eastern seas'. The Śrīvijāya rulers imposed their control on the main export ports in the region, thus securing a vast monopoly on the spice trade. The control of the Malacca Strait gave them an enormous advantage since all maritime traffic had to flow through it and to call at its ports. The relations with the Cholas in South India on the one hand, and with China on the other, were continuous and friendly until the first quarter of the eleventh century.

After the almost total destruction of the Muslim merchant colony in China in 265/878 (cf. p. 21 above) and the ensuing decline of direct Muslim–Chinese trade, the Śrīvijāya's rulers seized the opportunity to insert themselves into this lucrative enterprise; the eastbound Muslim ships met with the southbound Chinese ships at Kalah in the Malacca Strait, a port under the suzerainty of the Śrīvijāya empire. At the same time the ships of Śrīvijāya participated in the Indian Ocean trade; the close contacts with South India are documented by inscriptions in Buddhist monasteries and schools of Negapatam. As for the voyages to the western Indian Ocean we dispose of a few but extremely important Arabic texts. The first is the well-known account about the attack of the Wāḳ-Wāḳ people on Ḳanbalū (Pemba) in 334/945–6.[35]

The mention of the whole year's journey necessary to accomplish the

34. Cf. D. G. Hall, 1964, pp. 53ff.

35. Cf. Buzurg ibn Shahriyār, 1883–6, pp. 174–5; a full translation of this account is to be found in Unesco, *General History of Africa*, Vol. II, pp. 706–7, where the second sentence should read: '... they arrived in about a thousand of ships and fought vigorously against them (inhabitants of Ḳanbalū) but were not able to defeat them.'

voyage from their homes to East Africa already led the narrator to the conclusion that the islands of Wāḳ-Wāḳ are situated opposite China. G. Ferrand has shown that under the term Wāḳ-Wāḳ the Muslim authors understood two regions or people, one somewhere in the south-western part of the Indian Ocean, including Madagascar and the African coast to the south of Sufāla, the other in South-east Asia, in present-day Indonesia.[36] Various fables and 'mirabilia' were narrated about them and successive authors added a lot of contradictory details so that the picture is highly confused. But it seems that until the present nobody paid attention to the curious coincidence that the Wāḳ-Wāḳ appear in Arabic geographical literature always in connection with those areas where people of Indonesian/Malayan origin lived together with or were neighbours of or mixed with the Negroids. This seems to be confirmed by al-Bīrūnī[37] who says that the peoples of the Wāḳ-Wāḳ island are dark-skinned although in their neighbourhood live others of lighter skin and resembling the Turks (the Muslim stereotype for the Mongoloids). Al-Bīrūnī had in mind here parts of South-east Asia and his Wāḳ-Wāḳ is either New Guinea (Irian) where a locality called Fakfak is still to be found, or some of the Moluccas Islands partly inhabited by Melanesians, or both. Many Muslim authors were not always capable or they did not care to ascertain the precise ethnicity of the people called Wāḳ-Wāḳ. So each single reference has to be analysed in its own context before reaching the probable concrete meaning of the term.

In this case some details of Ibn Lākīs' narrative point unmistakably to South-east Asia as the home of these Wāḳ-Wāḳ people. And since we know that at this period the Śrīvijāya empire was the major maritime power in the eastern Indian Ocean, it is not too far-fetched to see in this long-distance expedition an attempt to expand the area of Śrīvijāya's trade network in order to reach directly the sources of African commodities, thus evading the Muslim monopoly. It was perhaps not the first voyage of this kind, and it is possible that these expeditions began at the time when Muslim commercial activities were severely restricted by the Zandj revolt as well as by the expulsion of foreign merchants from Chinese ports in the second half of the ninth century. How far these expeditions – and al-Idrīsī confirms that Indonesian ships continued to visit African shores and Madagascar in later centuries, too – were related to the new waves of Indonesian migrations to Madagascar between the tenth and twelfth centuries, remains an as yet unsolved problem. On the other hand it is not excluded that these late migrations were in some way connected with the invasions or raids of the South Indian Cholas on Śrīvijāya in the first half of the eleventh century that considerably weakened the state and could have led

36. G. Ferrand, 1929. For the most up-to-date discussion on this problem, see G. R. Tibbets, 1979, pp. 166–77.

37. Al-Bīrūnī, 1887, p. 164; for English translation, see 1888, Vol. 1, pp. 210–11.

to flights and movements of population. The difficulty of coming to more certain conclusions is due to lack of adequate sources for Śrīvijāya history.

Conclusion

In comparison with the preceding period the extent and character of mutual contacts between the African continent and other parts of the Indian Ocean region underwent some quantitative and qualitative changes.

First we can observe a steadily increasing presence of Middle Eastern peoples in all parts of the area and particularly on the East African coast. There the Arabs and Persians were able to develop further their commercial activities whose foundations had already been laid in the first centuries of the Christian era. This new expansion was connected with the rise of the Caliphate as a unifying political, cultural and economic great power. With this background it was possible for the Muslims to monopolize the East African trade and achieve a dominating position in the external relations of this region. While these contacts undoubtedly contributed to the flourishing of some coastal cities as centres of international trade and led to the rise of an African entrepreneurial class, it should not be forgotten that at the same time great numbers of African slaves were exported outside the continent to contribute to the economies of various Asiatic countries, mostly in the Middle East.

Secondly there was a marked decline of direct contacts with India. Before the seventh century Ethiopian ships traded with some Indian ports and these relations are well attested by hoards of Indian (Kushan) coins found in Ethiopia as well as by many traces of Indian influence in Ethiopian material and intellectual culture. Between the seventh and eleventh centuries nothing comparable is to be observed; it was due mainly to the passing of the traffic between India and Ethiopia into the hands of Muslims who imposed their own cultural layers on these relations.

Thirdly, nothwithstanding the Muslim preponderance in the Indian Ocean the Indonesians were still able to maintain contacts with Madagascar and even with some parts of the African coast. Their impact on the mainland, however, must have been negligible; assertions of some scholars about the decisive contribution of Indonesia to African culture are to be considered as hypotheses without sufficient evidence. The situation in the case of Madagascar is, of course, quite different as the Indonesian connection is more than evident.

We shall now investigate the role played by peoples of African origin in the Indian Ocean context. In assessing it we should bear in mind that during this period only a tiny part of the African continent, i.e. the narrow coastal strip, was in contact with the outside world. The number of Africans with any opportunity to exercise any influence or to be exposed to it, must have been rather restricted. There was thus a substantial difference from the situation obtained in West Africa where cross-cultural contacts occurred on a wider and deeper front. But even so, their role has been in no way negligible, on the contrary, it was the Africans who contributed substantially to profound changes in the destinies of a great empire. The Zandj revolt, an authentic social rising, had far-reaching consequences in many fields – political, social, economic. The uprising shattered the unity of the Muslim empire as great provinces broke away from the Caliphate, and it paved the way for the downfall of the old Abbasid regime. The political crisis ushered in by the Zandj revolt had deepened the cleavage between the social classes, and the well-to-do classes, being afraid for their privileges, began to put their confidence in the professional armies of Turkish and other mercenaries as the only force capable of keeping order; this heralded the new era in the history of the Muslim Middle East. The revolt also taught a lesson to the Muslim ruling classes; never again do we find in the Muslim East any large-scale enterprise based on concentration of slave labour and it seems that the exploitation of slaves in agriculture and irrigation was abandoned. This in turn led in the next century to the rise of feudalism as the prevailing mode of production in eastern Muslim countries, the slave exploitation giving way to the feudal one. Whether there was as a consequence a decrease in the number of imported African slaves is, in the absence of any statistics, an open question. Another consequence of the Zandj revolt seems to have been a hardening of racial feelings in those times; the black Africans came to be held in contempt, in spite of the teachings of Islam, and there emerged in Muslim literature many previously unknown themes expressing a negative attitude towards blacks.

Other aspects of African history during this period were partly due to the interaction of various Indian Ocean regions. Among them we should mention the growth of the participation of towns on the East African coast in the international maritime trade. Even if the shipping was controlled by foreign merchants, the producers and exporters were African coastal peoples. Although the full flowering of Swahili political, economic and cultural life occurred in the next centuries, it was in our period that its foundations were laid.

2 The coming of Islam and the expansion of the Muslim empire

M. EL FASI and I. HRBEK

In Chapter 1 an attempt was made to look at the main events in the Old World in their relations to African history in the period between the first/seventh and fifth/eleventh centuries. This survey indicated that one of the most dynamic forces at work during this period was Islamic society in all its manifestations in the spheres of religion, politics, economics and culture.

The purpose of this chapter is to describe the coming of Islam, its political expansion and doctrinal evolution, as the background needed for a better understanding of historical and ideological issues that will be dealt with or touched upon in this as well as in the remaining volumes of the *General History of Africa*.

Preliminary remarks

From the Islamic point of view it is not correct to say that the Prophet Muḥammad is the founder of Islam or that he was preaching a new faith. Islam is not the name of some unique faith presented for the first time by Muḥammad, as he was the last of the prophets each reiterating the faith of his predecessor. This is based on the following Islamic doctrine: God having, since He created men, sent prophets to guide them and to show them the best path to follow on earth and prepare for their eternal bliss, decided at last that mankind had reached such a degree of perfection that it was fit to receive His last revelation and to understand and appreciate the laws that should govern its behaviour in every field. His choice for the role of this last prophet fell on an Arab from the town of Mecca called Muḥammad ibn ʿAbd Allāh, belonging to the tribe of Ḳuraysh.

Muḥammad's predecessors in the prophetic missions were – apart from some lesser figures – Abraham, Moses and Jesus Christ, who all preached belief in one unique God on the ground of scriptures that were sent and revealed to them from Heaven. Those who believed in those prophets and scriptures, Jews and Christians, are called *ahl al-Kitāb* (people of the Book) and as possessors of a part of the revealed truth, have the right to special consideration from Muslims. It was God's purpose from the start to let all mankind believe solely in Him as the highest being. Thus the successive messages contained two main tenets: monotheism and universality. The first people to be given this message were the Jews but in the course of their history they deviated from the original message by usurping the monotheistic belief for themselves and denying it to others. To rectify this deviation from His original purpose God sent Jesus, who indeed restored the universality of monotheism. But the Christians, like the Jews, deviated, this time by proclaiming Jesus son of God and thus abandoning the monotheistic creed. And it was Muḥammad who was entrusted with the mission of bringing the whole of humanity back to genuine universal monotheism, Islam. Muḥammad is thus not the founder of Islam, a religion that already existed,[1] but the last in the chain of the prophets, being the 'Seal of the prophets' (*kh̲ātimu l-anbiyā'*). Islam thus venerates all preceding prophets as messengers of God's will. According to the Islamic doctrine, Jesus was a mere mortal, although it was God's will to make his birth a miracle like the creation of the first man, Adam, ancestor of the human race. It does not follow that he had the least particle of divinity. His mother, the Virgin, our lady Miryam – *mawlātunā Miryam* as the Muslims call her – enjoys the greatest respect in the Islamic world. Jesus was not killed by the Jews but God recalled him to His presence. He did not need to redeem the sin of Adam since God forgave Adam before compelling him to leave paradise and live on earth.

Muḥammad himself insisted that he was only a man and made a clear distinction between his humanity and his role as Prophet: 'I am a mortal like you. In matters revealed to me by God, you must obey my instructions. But you know more about your own worldly affairs than I do. So my advice in these matters is not binding.'[2] But since it was inconceivable that Muḥammad as the Messenger of God would act contrary to Divine will, belief in his guidance in worldly matters became firmly established in the Islamic faith. We will return to the role of Prophetic tradition (*sunna*) later.

The life of Muḥammad

It would obviously take too long to recount the Prophet's life here in detail. Since there exists a vast literature in several languages dealing with it, we will point out only the main events.

The Arabian peninsula on the eve of the seventh century of the Christian era was inhabited by a great number of politically independent tribes who together formed a linguistic and cultural community. The majority of

1. C. Qoran, 28:53 where the people of the Book say: 'Verily before it [i.e. the Qoran] we were Muslims'.

2. It is therefore erroneous to call the Muslims Muḥammadans or Islam Muḥammadanism. These words were introduced into European languages on the model of Buddhism and Christianity, religions in which the founders are worshipped as divine beings.

them were nomads (Beduins) but in South Arabia as well as in numerous oases sedentary populations practised agriculture. Along the ancient trade route leading from the shores of the Indian Ocean to the Mediterranean existed a few towns whose inhabitants were engaged in commerce but still retained the customs and moral code of the nomads. Mecca was the main commercial and religious centre of Arabia. The religion of the pre-Islamic Arabs was largely animistic and gods or spirits believed to inhabit blocks of stone, rocks, trees or wells were worshipped. Some of the gods were of astral origin (the Sun, the planet Venus). There was also a notion of a supreme being called Allāh but he was not the object of worship; more important seems to have been the worship of Al-Lāt, 'the goddess'. The idols of some of these gods were set up in an ancient sanctuary in Mecca known as the Kaʿba. In general the Arabs in these times – both nomadic and sedentary – cared little for religious matters, religion being for them only a part of the customs of their forefathers.

In Arabia there were also large settlements of people of Jewish faith; many of them were converted Arabs who lived mainly in oases and had a similar 'tribal' organization to the Arabs, who practised traditional religion. Christianity had found its way into Arabia very early; its main centres were in South Arabia (Nadjrān) and on the fringes of the desert in Mesopotamia and Transjordan. Individual Christians were scattered in all towns while in the desert lived solitary monks.

But it was first to the pagan Arabs that Muḥammad was sent with the Divine message. Born in Mecca after his father's death and early orphaned, he had spent his life as a trader until he was 40. He was known for his probity and justice in all his dealings; in no other way was he distinguished from the others. In about the year 610 of the Christian era he received the first revelation of God. Dictated to him by the angel Gabriel this ordered him to preach Islam to his fellow men. These first revelations centred on the unity of God and the last day and exhorted men not to neglect religion in favour of worldly business. They also contained a statement of the principles of equality of all men without regard to their social position or wealth.

When Muḥammad started his preaching and assembled around himself a small community of believers, the Meccan oligarchy of wealthy merchants and bankers soon became aware of the revolutionary content of the message and considered it a threat to their privileges. There was also the danger that Mecca as the centre of Arabic traditional religion with its sanctuary of the Kaʿba would lose its importance through the new religion. The annual pilgrimage visited by thousands of the Arabs from the whole peninsula, was a source of considerable profit for the Meccan merchants. And although Muḥammad at the beginning did not aspire to any political leadership in Mecca, his moral and intellectual qualities strengthened by his Prophetic mission and communication with God made him in the eyes of the oligarchy a dangerous rival. So the history of Muḥammad and his community until the year 622 is a story of persecution and even attempts

ان الله وملائكته يصلون على النبي يا ايها الذين امنوا صلوا عليه وسلموا تسليما

on the Prophet's life. Under these circumstances the Prophet ordered several of the new converts including one of his daughters and her husband to emigrate to Christian Ethiopia where they were friendlily received by the Negus.[3] The idea of leaving a country where injustice, oppression and persecution are prevalent, and taking refuge somewhere else where the Muslims can gather their forces before returning to renew their quest for life according to Islamic principles, is a key idea in Islam, repeated often in the subsequent history of many Islamic revivalist movements.

When the persecutions reached their peak, Muḥammad and his followers moved to the oasis town of Yat͟hrib, subsequently called Madīnat al-Nabī (the City of the Prophet), shortly to be known as Medina. This happened in the year 622 of the Christian era and that date is the first year of the Muslim calendar. The transfer from Mecca to Medina is called *hid͟jra*; the usual translation 'the flight' is incorrect as the true meaning of the Arabic word is 'severing previous tribal ties and entering into new ones'.

Muḥammad was invited to Medina by its inhabitants who came to be known as *Anṣār* (the Helpers); the Meccan emigrants were called *Muhād͟jirūn* (those who undertook the *hid͟jra*, or Emigrants) and these two groups form together the *Aṣḥāb* – the Companions – (of the Prophet). In the next years until his death in 11/632 the Prophet strengthened and governed the Muslim community (Arabic, *umma*), beat off the attacks of his Meccan enemies and gained supremacy by means of diplomacy and war over a wide confederacy of the Arab 'tribes'. When he was sufficiently strong he returned to Mecca as the victor and religious and political leader whose authority was supreme. At the time when God recalled him from this life, Muḥammad was virtually lord of most of Arabia and already prepared to expand Islam outside the peninsula.

The Qoranic teachings

Both in Mecca and Medina the Prophet received a continuous flow of revelations in the form of verses (*āya*, pl., *āyāt*) arranged in chapters (*sūra*, pl., *sūrāt*). The 114 *sūra*s of unequal length form together the Qoran.

The Qoran is not a 'holy book' written by Muḥammad. The word means

3. Cf. Chapter 19 below.

PLATE 2.1 *Representation of Medina: this plaque shows, in elevation, the Mosque of Medina built on the site of the house of Muḥammad, whose tomb is situated in the prayer room. After accomplishing the pilgrimage to Mecca, many Muslims come to Medina to honour the memory of the Prophet. These plaques, which decorated the walls of the mosques from the seventeenth century onwards, were probably donated by pilgrims.*

إن أول بيت وضع للناس للذي ببكة مباركا وهدى للعالمين فيه
آيات بينات مقام ابراهيم ومن دخله كان آمنا ولله على الناس حج
البيت من استطاع اليه سبيلا ومن كفر فان الله غني عن العالمين
باب ابراهيم
مقام حنفي
مقام ابراهيم
قبة عباس

recitation and what Muḥammad did was to recite the word of God spoken to him by the angel Gabriel. 'The Qoran is purely divine, while at the same time being intimately related to the inmost personality of the Prophet Muḥammad. The Divine Word flowed through the Prophet's heart.'[4] It is not, as generally believed, the Bible of Muslims; the position of the Qoran in Islam is quite different because for Muslims the Qoran is what Christ himself is for the Christians: the Word of God. The nearest parallel in Islam to the Christian New Testament as the record of Jesus's deeds and sayings is the *ḥadīth*. It would be therefore highly blasphemous to attempt to apply textual criticism to the Qoran as was done with the Bible, whereas criticism of the *ḥadīth* is permissible and has since early times been exercised by Muslim scholars.

The teachings of the Qoran are comprehensive and destined to give man guidance in his relations with God as well as with other members of human society. The Qoranic precepts and principles form the basis of the Islamic faith.

The first principle is the absolute monotheism expressed in perhaps the shortest and simplest credo of any religion in the world: 'There is no god but God and Muḥammad is the Prophet of God.' To pronounce this short sentence (*shahāda*) is all that a convert to Islam needs to do to become a Muslim. The belief in Muḥammad's prophetic nature is an integral part of this credo because without his prophetic mission the perfection of Islam would not exist.

The *shahāda* thus forms the first of what are called the 'Five Pillars of Islam' (*arkān al-islām*). The second is the duty of every Muslim to perform ritual prayer (*ṣalāt*) five times a day. The prayers fix the minds of the believers on God throughout the whole day. It is recommended that prayers should be performed in common with others standing and sitting in ordered rows; all believers pronounce them facing the direction of Mecca. An indispensable part of the prayer is the prescribed ablution before its performance. Thus the prayers have also a practical hygienic value and instil in men the values of collective discipline.

The third pillar is the fast (*ṣaum*) which consists of forgoing all material pleasures (eating, drinking, sexual relations etc.) from dawn (not from

4. R. Fazlur, 1966, pp. 33ff.

PLATE 2.2 *Representation of Mecca: this plaque, which was made in Iznik, shows in elevation, the plan of the Great Mosque of Mecca with its seven minarets. In the middle of the courtyard one can see the Ka'ba – said to have been built by Abraham – in an angle of which is embedded the Black Stone that every Muslim should, if possible, come to worship at least once in his lifetime. Each small building – and each door – is designated by its name in Naskhi script. Above the plan a Qoranic inscription, also cursive (Sūra 3: 90–2), recalls the duty of pilgrimage.*

sunrise as is often believed) to sunset during Ramaḍān, the tenth month of the lunar year. Hence the expression 'to observe Ramaḍān', meaning to observe the Muslim fast. The sick, persons travelling during Ramaḍān, women in labour, workers engaged in arduous tasks and warriors in campaign are exempt from the fast provided that they fast for an equivalent number of days at another time of the year. Fasting is an act of renunciation, of self-denial and as such enhances the spiritual life. It also teaches the rich to undergo the pangs of hunger and so to sympathize with the poor who suffer these privations during the whole year.

The fourth pillar is a highly important obligation to society. It is the compulsory alms known as *zakāt* which consists in giving to the poor and to certain categories of needy persons a part of the goods that have remained in one's possession for the whole year. This portion varies from 2.5 per cent to 10 per cent. The *zakāt* not only emphasized the importance of charity but was also necessary in the early days of Islam to sustain the community which was composed largely of poor emigrants without any means. The *zakāt* was collected by the Islamic community (*umma*) and then divided among the categories indicated by the Qoran. It corresponded to the modern social welfare of the state.

The fifth pillar is the annual pilgrimage to Mecca (*ḥadjdj*). This institution reflects Islam's continuous concern that men should get to know one another and meet as often as possible. It is in the *ḥadjdj* that the universal message of Islam is most visible and evident as the Muslims from every corner of the world assemble in the month of *Dhu l-ḥidjdja* at Mecca to perform various ceremonies whose purpose is to commemorate Abraham's sacrifice at this place. The pilgrimage is obligatory for every Muslim but he is compelled to carry out this duty only if he has the means to do it, if there is no danger on the journey, or if his health is good. He must also be able to leave his family with sufficient means during his absence. For all these reasons the number of people able to carry out this duty is small in relation to the total number of Muslims. But even so, the *ḥadjdj* is the largest multinational gathering of human beings on the face of the earth today. Those who perform it are given in these few days a visible proof that they are members of a vast worldwide brotherhood of Islam without distinction of race or language. It fills the pilgrim with a deep awareness of Islamic values and makes him a venerated person after his return as one who was present at the place where the Prophet Muḥammad lived and where God revealed the Qoran.

Another set of Muslim beliefs is contained in Sūra 4, verse 135: 'Believe in God and in His Prophet and in the Book which He has sent down to His Prophet and the books which He sent down formerly. He who disbelieves in God and His angels, His books and His apostles and the Last Day, has strayed away [from the truth].'

The Day of Judgment is one of the cornerstones of the Islamic faith; the whole history of mankind will find its end by the resurrection and the Day

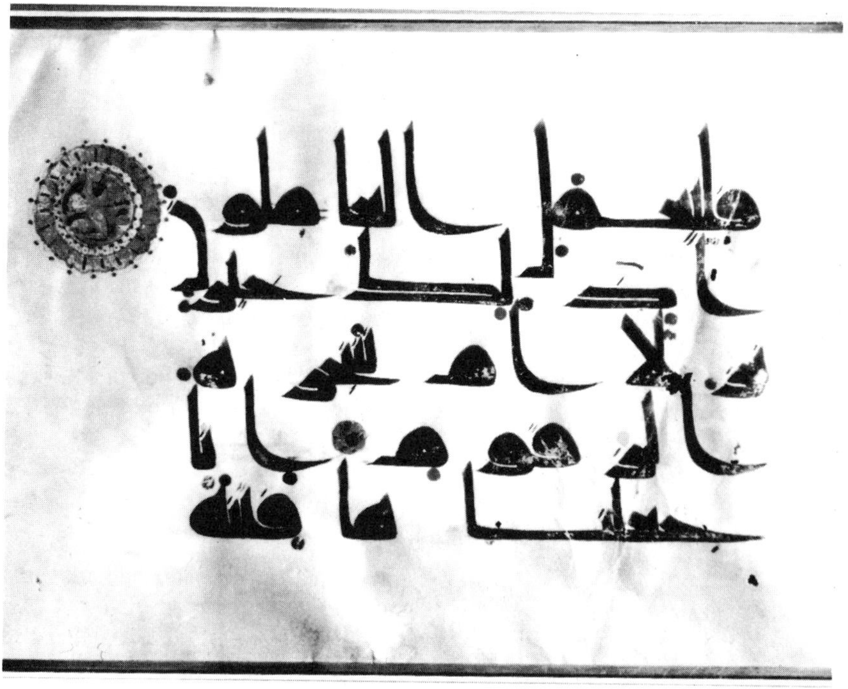

PLATE 2.3 *Qoran leaf in Kufic script, ninth century, Abbasia (Iraq)*

of Judgment. The dead await this hour in their tombs whereas the Prophets and martyrs go directly to paradise. All people will appear at the Last Judgment before God to be judged according to their deeds and then sent either to paradise (*djanna*, lit. garden) or to hell.

The Qoran also contains a number of prohibitions and recommendations for the worldly life. It forbids the eating of pork and some other animals and the drinking of wine and other alcoholic drinks. In Sūra 17, verses 23–40 we find guidance for everyday behaviour: ostentatious waste, pride and haughtiness are condemned and the Faithful are ordered to give just weight and measure.

Although slavery is considered to be a recognized institution, slaves must be kindly treated, allowed to marry and encouraged to buy their liberty. Masters are recommended to free slaves who are believers.[5]

Islam proclaims the equality of men and women. The Prophet proclaimed that 'Women are fully men's sisters before the law.' Customs wholly alien to the orthodox doctrine have masked this fine aspect of Islam. But in law Muslim women have enjoyed a legal status that women in other

5. For a discussion of the Islamic attitude to slavery, cf. Chapter 26 below.

religious systems might until recently have envied them. Muslim women have always had the right to go to law without referring to their husbands and to administer their property independently of them. A woman is not required to bring her husband a dowry, it is the latter who is compelled to pay the bride a certain sum and to give her certain gifts, all of which becomes the wife's personal property.

The Qoran allows a man four legal wives; it thus constituted progress compared with pre-Islamic times when polygamy was unrestricted. Islam, moreover, subjected polygamy to such conditions that it could be regarded as having taken a step towards the abolition or at least a diminution of this social phenomenon. This is clearly to be seen from these Qoranic verses: 'Marry of the women who seem good to you, two or three or four; but if you fear that you cannot do justice [to so many] then marry one only or any female war-captive you may possess' (4:3) and 'You will not be able to deal equally between your wives, even if you wish it' (4:129).[6]

S̱harīʿa and fiḳh

Islam is not only a religion, it is a complete way of life, catering for all the fields of human existence. Islam provides guidance for all walks of life; individual and social, material and moral, economic and political, legal and cultural, national and international.[7]

The *s̱harīʿa* is the detailed code of conduct comprising the precepts governing modes and ways of worship and standards of morals and life. It consists of laws that allow and prescribe and that judge between right and wrong. Though each Prophet had the same *dīn* (religious faith), he brought with him a different *s̱harīʿa* that would suit the conditions of his time and his people. Muḥammad as the last Prophet brought with him the final code which was to apply to all mankind for all time to come. The previous *s̱harīʿa* were thus abrogated in view of the comprehensive *s̱harīʿa* of Muḥammad.

The sources of the Islamic *s̱harīʿa* are the Qoran and the *ḥadīt̲h̲*, i.e. the words and deeds of the Prophet Muḥammad preserved and handed down by his Companions. Thousands of *ḥadīt̲h̲*s were sifted and collected by scholars in collections of traditions, the most famous of them being those of al-Buk̲h̲ārī (d. 256/870) and Abū Muslim (d. 261/875). The content of the Prophetic tradition is called *sunna*, i.e. the conduct and behaviour of Muḥammad.

The science that codifies and explains the prescripts of *s̱harīʿa* is called *fiḳh* and the scholars who are concerned with it are the *faḳīh*s (Arabic pl.,

6. The famous Egyptian thinker Muḥammad ʿAbduh (d. 1323/1905) considered on the strength of the interpretation of these verses that the Qoran imposed virtually monogamy. Cf. R. Levy, 1957, p. 101.

7. K. Aḥmad, 1976, p. 37.

fuḳahā') or doctors of law; *fiḳh* being the Islamic science par excellence, the *faḳīh*s are considered as scholars (*'ulamā'*, sing., *'ālim*).

After the great conquest of many countries with different social and economic conditions inherited from ancient times, a number of problems were encountered by the Muslim community. Others arose from the establishment of a state widely different from and more complex than the original community in Medina. Since the Qoran seldom deals with particular cases and sets out only general principles governing the lives of Muslims, it soon became apparent that the answers to some problems confronting the Muslim community were to be found neither in the Holy Book nor in the *ḥadīth*s of the Prophet. So two additional sources were added to the Islamic law. First, the reasoning by analogy (*ḳiyās*) that consists of comparing the case for which a solution is sought with another similar case already settled on the strength of the Qoran or a particular *ḥadīth*. Secondly, the answer to a problem might be also resolved by the consensus of eminent doctors of law (*idjmā'*).

Between the second/eighth and third/ninth centuries eminent scholars in various intellectual centres of the Muslim world, particularly in Medina and Baghdad, codified the whole of the Islamic law into a coherent system. Their individual approaches to this enormous task differed and so emerged four legal schools (*madhhab*, pl. *madhāhib*) named after their founders who bear also the honorific title of *Imām*.

These four *madhāhib* are the Hanafi, Māliki, Shāfi'i and Hanbali schools. All of them are completely orthodox (Sunnite) and differ mainly on points of detail; it is not proper to call these schools sects. The founders of these schools codified the law on the basis of the principles set out above and added others. While unanimously agreed on the text of the Qoran and on the *ḥadīth*s regarded by all Muslim scholars as the most authentic, each *Imām* by personal preference (known as *idjtihād*) gave priority to one or other of the other sources of the law.

Although there were various shifts in the course of history, each of these schools is now adhered to in specific geographical areas: the Hanafite school is dominant in those regions that came under the sway of the Turkish dynasties, i.e. Turkey, Syria, Iraq, Central Asia and northern India/Pakistan; the Shāfi'ite *madhhab* is to be found mostly along the shores of the Indian Ocean, from southern Arabia and East Africa to Indonesia; Mālikism very soon implanted itself in North Africa, Muslim Spain and in the western and central Sudan. The last school, the Hanbali, which was formerly widely adhered to in Syria and Iraq, is now virtually confined to Saudi Arabia.

The differences between the various *madhāhib* are not fundamental, they mostly concern details of ritual and minor points of law. One of the central features of Islamic law is the assessing of all human acts and relationships in terms of the following concepts: obligatory (*wādjib*), recommended (*mandūb*), indifferent (*mubāh*), reprehensible or disapproved (*makrūh*) and forbidden (*maẓhūr*). The whole of Islamic law is permeated by religious and ethical considerations such as the prohibition of interest on loans or unjustified enrichment in general, the prohibition of gambling and other forms of speculation, the concern for equality of two contracting parties and the concern for a just average, together with abhorrence of extremes.

Another feature that distinguishes *fiḳh* from other legal systems is that it was created and developed by private jurists. It did not grow out of an existing legal system: it created itself. The state did not play the part of legislator, it did not decree the laws and there were for a long time no official codes of laws issued by state organs. Instead the laws were incorporated in scholarly handbooks that had the force of law and served as references in actual juridical decisions.

Islamic religious structure, true to its egalitarian principles and conscience, had never produced any form of external organization or any kind of hierarchy. There is no priesthood and no church. Everybody is his own priest and there is no intermediary between the believer and God. Although it recognized *idjmāʿ*, the consensus of doctors of law as a valid source of doctrine, there was neither council nor curia to promulgate its decisions.

The consensus was reached informally, either by tacit assent on the part of those qualified to express their opinion or sometimes by prolonged debate in writing before an agreement was reached by the majority. Thus the elaboration of Islamic doctrine in all fields developed, pushed forward by a number of eminent and brilliant thinkers who followed the famous saying of the Prophet: 'Seek science from the cradle to the grave.'

It happened, however, that the '*ulamā*' in their quest for establishing Islamic precepts for every minute detail of worship and everyday life were too much absorbed by the formal side of the Divine law leaving not enough place for individual devotion. Thus a reaction against the intellectualism and formalism emerged in the form of Islamic mysticism, sufism.[8] There was already a strong note of asceticism and mysticism among the early Muslims and many famous mystics before the twelfth century contributed positively to the intensification of the Islamic faith. On the other hand some adherents of sufism were prone to neglect religious obligations of the *sharīʿa*, considering themselves absolved from the universal obligations of the Muslim. In the eleventh century the great theologian al-Ghazālī (d. 505/1111) achieved the incorporation of sufism into orthodoxy by stressing both the necessity of a personal approach to God and the duty to follow the prescripts of the *sharīʿa* as being inseparable parts of Muslim religious life. Soon afterwards the *ṣūfī*s began to organize themselves in mystical associations or brotherhoods (Arabic, *ṭuruk*, sing. *ṭarīḳa*) around different spiritual leaders known as *shaykh*s. The oldest of these *ṭarīḳa*s is

8. From Arabic *ṣūf*, wool, to denote the practice of wearing a woollen robe. In Arabic Sufism is called *taṣawwuf*.

the *Ḳādiriyya*, founded in Baghdad by ʿAbd al-Ḳādir al-Djīlānī (d. 561/1166) which soon expanded into various Muslim countries. With time the number of the *ṭarīḳa*s increased so that nearly every Muslim belonged to this or that *ṭarīḳa* and participated in the mystical exercises called *dhikr* (invocation or litany).

From these respectable and recognized brotherhoods must be separated the cult of saints who are called *marabouts* in the Maghrib; many of these *marabouts* exploited naive Muslims by pretending to perform miracles, by preparing various amulets and talismans, and by claiming to have a direct access to God thus being able to intercede for others. This is highly un-Islamic as every Muslim is his own priest and only God may be venerated and directly approached. Islam makes man completely independent of all beings except God. From the point of view of genuine Islam the cult of 'saints' is the result of a parasitical excrescence.

The Islamic sects

The origin of the main divisions into sects is political; it became a matter of doctrinal divisions only later.

The chief problem around which the opinions of early Muslims revolved was that of the succession of Muḥammad, not as a Prophet – as he was the last of the Prophets – but as the head of the Islamic community. During his lifetime the Prophet indicated on several occasions that the valid system for governing the community was *shurā* or consultation, today known as democracy. After his death his immediate successors were elected and began to be designated as caliphs. The first four caliphs, called by Muslims *al-khulafāʾ al-rashidūn* (the rightly guided caliphs) were Abū Bakr, ʿUmar, ʿUthmān and ʿAlī; all of whom belonged to the Ḳuraysh tribe and were related to Muḥammad by marriage. ʿAlī, moreover, was the Prophet's cousin. When the third Caliph, ʿUthmān, was murdered by a group of Muslims who had revolted because they were offended by some of his policies, ʿAlī ibn Abī Ṭālib was elected Caliph in Medina, then the capital. His appointment, however, was not accepted by some companions, particularly Muʿāwiya, Governor of Syria. The result was civil strife between the followers of ʿAlī and those of Muʿāwiya. The Caliph ʿAlī agreed to the setting up of an arbitration commission consisting of two members, one representing him and the other Muʿāwiya. But many of ʿAlī's followers rejected that solution and expressed their disapproval by seceding from him; hence their name Khāridjites (from Arabic, *kharadja* – to go out). They regarded the arbitration – which did not end favourably for ʿAlī – as an act of treason against God, the sole arbiter. During the first/seventh and second/eighth centuries, and in some places even later, the Khāridjites revolted again and again against the caliphs and the central government of the Umayyads and then the Abbasids, mostly in Iraq, Arabia, Iran and adjacent countries. The Khāridjites very early split into many sects that differed both in theory and practice. But there were some common features. They insisted on the importance of acts, not only faith, and asserted that anyone guilty of grave sin was an unbeliever and an apostate and should therefore be killed. One of their main doctrines concerned the *Imāmate*, that is the leadership of the Muslim community. In contrast to other Muslims who considered that the *Imāmate* (or Caliphate) is the prerogative of certain lineages (either the Ḳurayshites in general or specifically the family of ʿAlī), the Khāridjites insisted that anyone, even a black slave, could be elected as the head of the Muslim community if he possessed the necessary qualifications of piety, integrity and religious knowledge. These democratic tendencies, verging sometimes on anarchy, attracted many people who were dissatisfied with the government for one reason or another. In general the Khāridjites, although democratic, pious and preaching a purified Islam, repulsed many by their intolerance towards other Muslims and thus constituted only minorities in the eastern lands of the Caliphate. In the Maghrib some of the Khāridjite sects, the Ibāḍites, the Nukkārites and the Ṣufrites found a fertile soil for their doctrines among many Berbers dissatisfied with the oppressive Umayyad regime.[9]

Those Muslims who stayed with ʿAlī were those who were persuaded that the Caliphate (they preferred to call this institution *Imāmate*) should go to the family of the Prophet, represented by ʿAlī and his descendants from his marriage with Fāṭima, the daughter of Prophet Muḥammad. They were called *Shīʿatu ʿAlī*, i.e. the party of ʿAlī, whence their name Shīʿites in European languages. Whereas the Khāridjites differed from orthodox Islam on political and ethical issues only, the Shīʿites went further and added many new doctrines of purely religious content. The Shīʿites rejected the principle of the consensus of the community, and substituted for it the doctrine that there was in every age an infallible *Imām* to whom alone God entrusted the guidance of mankind. The first *Imām* was ʿAlī, and all succeeding ones were his direct descendants. The *Imām*s are considered to be divinely appointed rulers and teachers of the faithful, and to possess superhuman qualities which were transmitted to them from the first man, Adam, through Muḥammad. For these reasons they are the only ones to have the right to lead the Muslim community; the Shīʿites believe that even after the last *Imām* has 'disappeared' from the world, he continues his guidance as the 'hidden *Imām*'. He will reappear one day to restore peace and justice to the world as the *Mahdī* (the divinely guided one).

Shīʿism very soon split into a large number of sects between which the main difference arose from the question of who should be the 'hidden *Imām*'. The most important in the course of history became the group called the Twelvers (*Ithnāʿ asharīyya*) which recognizes the twelfth descendant of ʿAlī, Muḥammad al-Mahdī, who disappeared in 266/880. The stronghold of the Twelvers today is Iran where this brand of Shīʿism

9. See Chapters 3, 9–12 below.

has been the state religion since the eleventh/sixteenth century. Significant groups are found also in Iraq, Syria, Lebanon and India. During the Abbasid Caliphate the adherents of Twelver Shīʿism were more numerous, mainly in the big cities.

Those Shīʿites who recognized the seventh *Imām*, Ismāʿīl, separated themselves from the main body and became known as Ismāʿīliyya or the Seveners (*Sabʿiyyūna*). Apart from beliefs held in common with other S͟hīʿites, the Ismāʿīliyya developed a set of special doctrines based mostly on Neo-Platonism, such as the theory of emanation of the world intellect that manifests itself in Prophets and *Imāms*. In their exegesis of the Qoran they looked for hidden meanings accessible only to initiates. The Ismāʿīliyya functioned for a long time as a secret society; it came into the open with the coming of the Fāṭimids who were the most successful among all the S͟hīʿite branches and founded an empire that stretched from the Atlantic to Syria and Ḥid͟jāz.[10] Late offshoots of the Ismāʿīliyya were the Druzes in Lebanon and Syria and then the 'Assassins' (al-Has͟hīs͟hiyyūn), a terroristic sect, who were active in the period between the sixth/twelfth and eighth/fourteenth centuries in the Middle East with centres in Iran and Lebanon.

From the struggle among the Muslims orthodoxy at last emerged victorious in the shape of Sunnism, comprising adherents of the *sunna*, i.e. the way of the Prophet. Sunnites comprise today more than 90 per cent of the world's Muslim population. The doctrinal differences between the Sunnite and S͟hīʿite Islam are these: the sources of Sunnite laws are the Qoran, the *ḥadīt͟h* of the Prophet, the consensus of the community and analogy, whereas the four bases of Shīʿite law are the Qoran, the *ḥadīt͟h* of the Prophet and of the *Imāms*, the consensus of the *Imāms*, and reason. Although the S͟hīʿites perform the pilgrimage to Mecca, they prefer to visit the tombs of ʿAlī and his son Ḥusayn in the towns of Nad͟jaf and Kerbelā in Iraq.

Not all descendants of ʿAlī and Fāṭima – those who have the right to the honorific title *s͟harīf* – were *eo ipso* adherents of Shīʿite doctrines. The majority of *S͟harīfs* were and are Sunnites. In many parts of the Muslim world where the *s͟harīfs* came to power as sultans or emirs, as in Morocco (the Idrīsids and the two S͟harīfian dynasties of Saʿdis and Alawis) or the Hashimites in Ḥid͟jāz, Iraq and Jordan, they followed the path of orthodoxy and never claimed any of the supra-human qualities ascribed to the *Imāms* by S͟hīʿites.

Nevertheless one concept of S͟hīʿite origin, the belief in the coming of the *Mahdī*, penetrated into Sunnite Islam. It was not an official teaching as in S͟hīʿism but on the level of popular religion in which the *Mahdī* is seen as a Messiah who will return to the earth, slay the anti-Christ and fill the world with justice as it was before filled with injustice and tyranny.

10. Cf. Chapter 12 below.

Through the centuries *Mahdīs* appeared in various Muslim countries from time to time, the most famous examples being those of the Sudanese *Mahdī* Muḥammad ibn ʿAbdallāh and the Somali, Muḥammad ibn ʿAbdille.

Islamic attitudes towards non-Muslims

Islam makes a sharp distinction between those non-Muslims who belong to a religious system with revealed Books, that is the *ahl al-Kitāb* ('People of the Book') and those non-Muslims considered to be polytheists, idolaters or adherents of traditional religions. In conformity with the doctrine of the successive revelations and of the Prophetic chain, the Jews and the Christians as possessors of the Holy Books are not forced to adopt Islam. This tolerance was applied also to the Zoroastrians as well as to the adherents of some ancient Near Eastern religious systems known as the Sabeans and later even to the Hindus (notwithstanding their multitude of gods) and the Buddhists.

As regards the second group, since the Prophet Muḥammad was sent to preach Islam particularly to those who as yet have not received any revealed guidance, he and his successors were obliged to combat traditional religion and to convert the 'infidels'. These were given the choice of either becoming Muslims or fighting; in the case of defeat their lot was captivity and slavery.

There are many erroneous conceptions about the *dj̲ihād*. This word is usually, but erroneously, translated as 'holy war' but nothing of this sort is encompassed in the term which means 'effort to the utmost of one's capacity'. The true meaning of the word is best illustrated by the saying of the Prophet on returning from an expedition against an Arab *ḳabīla* that adhered to traditional religion: 'We have returned from a lesser *dj̲ihād* to accomplish the greater *dj̲ihād*', that is, to struggle for inner perfection.

As far as the *dj̲ihād* as warlike activity is concerned, there was in the early days a tendency to make it the sixth 'Pillar' of Islam, mainly among the K̲h̲āridj̲ites, but this was not generally accepted. The legal schools (with the exception of the Hanbalites) considered *dj̲ihād* an obligation if certain conditions were fulfilled, among them that the unbelievers should begin hostilities and that there should be a reasonable hope of success. In special situations *dj̲ihād* becomes an individual duty incumbent even on slaves, women and minors; this happens when the enemy attacks Muslim territory and whoever abstains from this duty is a sinner and a hypocrite.

The wars of expansion of the Islamic state after the death of the Prophet were not directed to the religious conversion of the conquered peoples since the majority of these adhered to religions with revealed scriptures, being Christians, Zoroastrians and Jews. These peoples were obliged to pay the poll tax (*dj̲izya*) and then became protected (*d̲h̲immī*) without being forced to abandon their religions. The conversion to Islam of individuals or even of groups was a very minor part of the aim of the *dj̲ihād*; the essential aim was the expansion of the Islamic state as the sphere within which the *sharī'a* was paramount. This came to be expressed in the distinction between *Dār al-islām* and *Dār al-ḥarb*, the sphere of Islam and the sphere of war. The term *Dār al-islām*, or the Islamic *oekoumene*, does not imply that all its inhabitants must be Muslims but rather that it is the part of the world where Islamic social and political order reigns supreme and Islamic public worship is observed. The *Dār al-ḥarb* is the opposite of the *Dār al-islām*, the rest of the world that is as yet not under Islamic sway; theoretically it will one day disappear and integrate into the Islamic *oekoumene* as expressed in the Qoranic words (9:33): 'He it is who sent his Messenger with guidance and the religion of truth to make it prevail over all religions despite the pagans.'

Nevertheless, from the third/ninth century onwards, when the universal Caliphate broke up into smaller states, a relation of mutual tolerance was established between the Muslim world and the *Dār al-ḥarb*; its conquest was postponed from the historic to the messianic time. Political and commercial relations with European, Asiatic and African states were governed by the recognition of some of them as belonging to an intermediate category. *Dār al-ṣulḥ*, the sphere of truce. This provided the main legal basis for peaceful contacts and communications with non-Muslim states. Another measure to facilitate these contacts was the introduction of the safe-conduct, called *aman*, which the head of a Muslim state could give to the subjects of any non-Muslim state (they were then called *musta'minūn*) and this made possible not only diplomatic exchanges but also the residence of European and other merchants in Muslim countries.

Islamic expansion, the rise and fall of the Caliphate

Some aspects of the rise of the Islamic world and its impact on various parts of Africa were already touched upon in the preceding chapter. Here we propose to present a brief outline of the political history of the Caliphate from the death of the Prophet Muḥammad to the end of the fifth/eleventh century. As the history of the African parts of the Islamic world are fully covered in a number of chapters in this Volume, we will focus our attention more on the developments in its more eastern provinces. This is necessary not only owing to the obvious importance of the Islamic world as the leading cultural area of the period but more so because the repercussions of the historical changes in Persia, Arabia and adjacent countries were of immediate importance in the Indian Ocean region and thus in parts of East Africa, too.

Under the first four caliphs (*al-khulafā' al-rashīdūn*, 'the rightly guided caliphs'), Abū Bakr, 'Umar, 'Uthmān and 'Alī,[11] Muslim Arabs started

11. Abū Bakr, 11/632–13/634 'Umar, 13/634–23/644 'Uthmān, 23/644–35/656 'Alī, 35/656–40/661.

their expansion outside the Arabian peninsula. The nomadic Arab *ḳabīlas*, united now by the bond of a common faith and forbidden by it to continue their internecine fighting, led by a pleiad of brilliant generals of Meccan origin, won in a few years a series of victories over the armies of the two great powers, the Byzantine empire and Sassanid Persia. The campaign against the Byzantines in Syria took only two years before the emperor and his troops evacuated these provinces forever in 15/636. The conquest of Persia lasted longer and after initial setbacks the Arabs went from victory to victory. The battle of Ḳādisiyya and the occupation of the capital, Ktesiphon, in 16/637 opened all the fertile lowlands of Iraq west of the Tigris to the Arabs. From their newly founded military bases of Baṣra and Kūfa the Muslim armies penetrated the Iranian highlands in pursuit of the retreating Persian armies. The last great battle at Nihāwend (21/642) sealed the fate of the Sassanid empire. The Muslims then occupied other parts of Iran and pushed their advance to the east so that by 29/650 they stood on the borders of India, in northern Iraq, in Armenia and on the Amu-Darja (Oxus).

After the conquest of Syria the Arab armies turned towards Egypt which offered an even easier field of conquest. Between 18/639 and 21/642 the whole of Lower Egypt with its capital, Alexandria, fell to the invading forces and Byzantium thus lost another rich province. It served later as the starting point for a further Arab advance into North Africa.[12]

One of the principal reasons for the lightning successes of the Muslims was the financial and military exhaustion of both empires after their long series of wars. In addition, the Byzantines were hated by their Semitic and Coptic subjects because of their oppressive taxation and their persecution of the 'heretical' Monophysite churches. The situation in the Sassanid empire was somewhat similar; the most fertile provinces of Iraq were inhabited by the Christian Aramaic-speaking peoples who stood in opposition to the Zoroastrian ruling classes. Just before the Arab onslaught dynastic strife had torn apart the empire, weakening its political and military structure. In general in most of the conquered countries the local inhabitants offered no resistance to the invading Arabs as they had little or nothing to lose by the change of masters; in some cases the Muslims were even welcomed.

The civil war after the death of ʿUthmān between ʿAlī and Muʿāwiya, which ended with the death of the former and the coming of the Umayyad dynasty to power in 41/661, as well as the need for the dynasty to consolidate its power, stopped the external expansion of the Arab state for some years. But already in the reign of Muʿāwiya the frontiers were expanded in North Africa under ʿUḳba ibn Nāfiʿ, and in the east, where the entire province of Khurāsān (north-eastern Iran and Afghanistan) was conquered and the River Oxus crossed (between 43/663 and 54/674). Twice at this time

12. Cf. Chapters 7, 8 and 9 below.

the Arab armies penetrated to the walls of the Byzantine capital but in both cases were unable to conquer it. A third and most serious attempt was made much later, in 98/716–17, when the Arabs unsuccessfully attacked Constantinople from sea and land. It was left to the Ottoman Turks to add this bastion of Eastern Christianity to the Islamic world in the ninth/fifteenth century.

A second wave of conquests on all fronts was launched under the Caliphs ʿAbd al-Malik (65/685–86/705) and al-Walīd I (86/705–96/715); in the West the whole Maghrib was subjugated and Spain invaded, in the north-east Central Asia (Transoxania) was conquered and at the same time the Arab armies pushed as far as the Indus River, adding the new province of Sind to the Caliphate. Campaigns in Transcaucasia achieved the incorporation of Georgia and Armenia into the orbit of the Arab empire. Further advance in the West was stopped by the Franks, while the attempts to the north of the Caucasus were frustrated by the Turkish Khazars, so that for a long time the Pyrenees and the Caucasus marked the limits of the empire.[13]

Thus a hundred years after the Prophet's death the Arab state already comprised an enormous territory that became the core of the Islamic world. At this time the Arabs were its undisputed masters and formed the exclusive ruling class. The Umayyad policy was to perpetuate this situation in which all non-Muslims had to pay taxes, whilst Muslim Arabs were exempt and even had pensions paid out to them from these revenues. The Arab ruling class did not look favourably therefore on mass conversions in the conquered lands and the new Muslims, each of whom had to attach himself to an Arab *ḳabīla* as a client (*mawlā*, plural *mawālī*), still had to pay the taxes as before. On the other hand the conquered peoples, be they Persians, Copts or Arameans (in Syria and Iraq) were employed in growing numbers in an increasingly complex state administration. The Arabs, with their unsophisticated background of nomadic life, were unable to cope with the enormous administrative problems arising from the continuing expansion. Thus they willingly adopted the Byzantine and Sassanid administrative systems already existing in the provinces and left their running in the hands of the converted natives. The contradictions arising from the fact that a minority usurped all the political power together with the economic privileges, while the majority, although already Muslim, was denied access to them, were the main causes of the crisis that ended with the fall of the Umayyads and the coming of a new dynasty, the Abbasids. The victory of the latter was made possible by the support of all the dissatisfied elements, mostly non-Arab Muslims, who claimed their full share in a community founded on the principle of equality among all believers. The Abbasid revolution put paid to the 'Arab kingdom' – as the Umayyad period is

13. The Arab troops defeated by Charles Martel at Poitiers in 114/732 seem to have been merely a raiding party, not an army of occupation. Whether the campaigns against the Khazars aimed at the total conquest of the South Russian steppes is open to question.

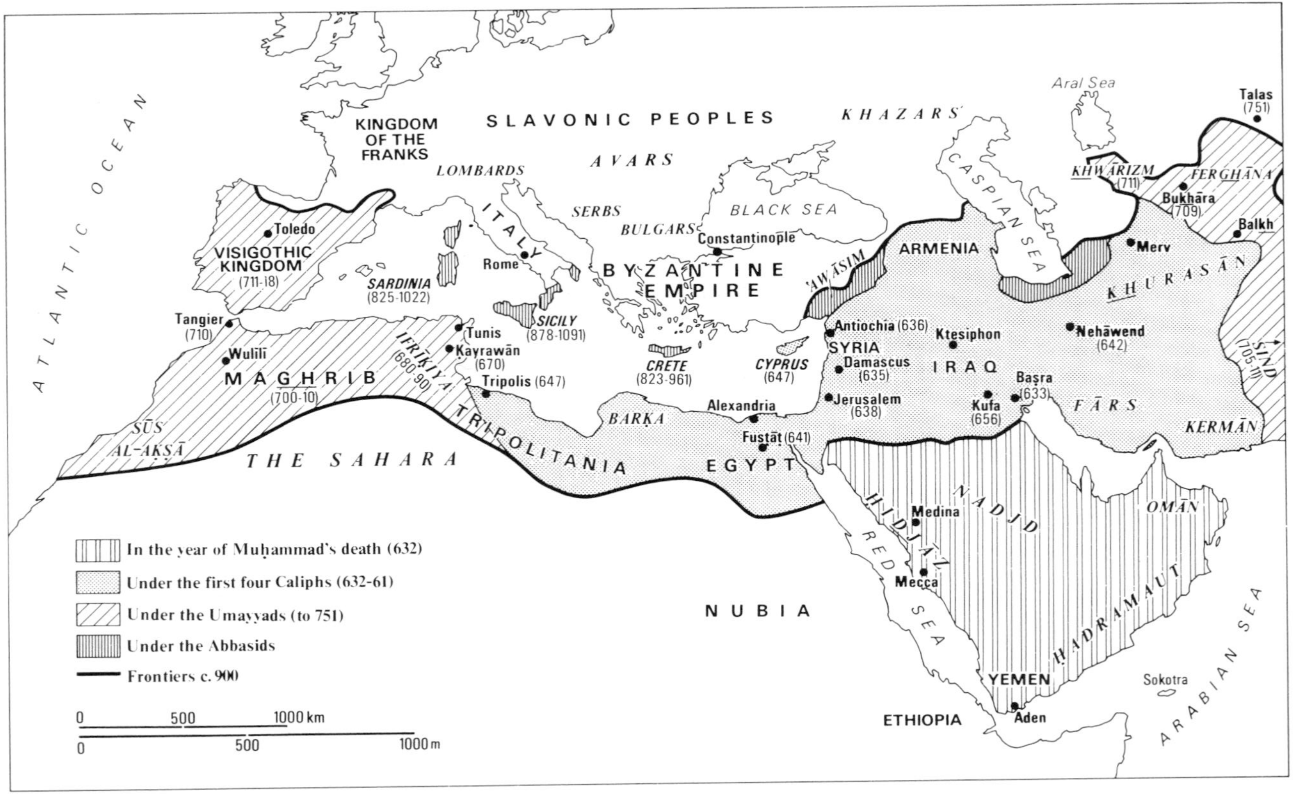

FIG. 2.1 *The expansion of the Islamic state*

sometimes called – and inaugurated the Islamic empire where distinctions followed religious, not national lines. The Arabs lost the privileged status conferred on them as the first bearers of Islam but Arabic continued to be the language of the state, literature and science employed widely by peoples of non-Arab origin.

Under the Umayyads the centre of the empire was Syria with its capital at Damascus; although the eastern provinces were in no way neglected, most attention was naturally turned to the Mediterranean world, Egypt, North Africa and Spain.

The transfer of the capital from Syria to Iraq where the Abbasids founded Baghdad (in 144/762) was not only a geographical shift of the centre of gravity of the empire, it was also a symbolic act opening a new era. In place of the Umayyad emphasis on Arabism, their successors laid stress on Islam as the basis of their regime and the promotion of orthodox Islam became one of the chief tasks of the caliphal administration.

During the first century of Abbasid rule the territory of the Caliphate continued to expand but on a less grandiose scale than before: the Caspian provinces were annexed and in 212/827–8 the dependent dynasty of the Aghlabids began to conquer Sicily. On the other hand the Abbasid realm had been from the start much smaller than that of the Umayyads since Muslim Spain never belonged to it. A totally independent dynasty had already been founded in Spain by a scion of the house of Umayya in 138/756 and this lasted for two-and-a-half centuries. In the course of the first fifty years of their rule the Abbasids lost control of all the African provinces west of Egypt either to the Khāridjites or the Idrīsids; in 184/800 the governor of Ifrīḳiya, al-Aghlab, became virtually independent and founded his own dynasty.[14]

The causes of the gradual disintegration of great empires in former times are well known: the impossibility with the available means of communication to control effectively from one centre an enormous realm composed of countries with heterogeneous populations on various cultural and economic levels, and, as corollary to this, the tendency of provincial governors to break away from the central government. In the case of the Abbasid Caliphate these general causes were intensified by the presence of dissident movements of heterodox sects, often combined with social upheavals.

Until the second half of the third/ninth century, however, a succession of remarkably efficient caliphs was able to maintain effective rule and control. But after the Zandj revolt[15] the inevitable process of disintegration gained momentum as an array of short-lived local dynasties emerged in Iran and Central Asia as well as in Arabia and Syria. During the fourth/tenth century even the core of the Abbasid realm, Iraq, fell under the sway of the Shīʿite dynasty of the Buwayhids, who made the Abbasid caliphs

14. Cf. Chapter 10 below.
15. Cf. Chapters 1 above and 26 below.

their puppets. In the west the Fāṭimids founded a rival caliphate and began to put into effect their grandiose plans of domination over the whole Islamic world. They did not succeed entirely but detached Egypt, Syria and Arabia from the Abbasid territory. And since in 317/929 the Spanish Umayyad ʿAbd al-Raḥmān III took the caliphal title of the 'Prince of the believers' (*amīr al-muʾminīn*) there were for a while three caliphs in Islam. Although in the mid-fifth/eleventh century the Turkish Saldjuks, who adhered to Sunnite Islam, liberated the Abbasids from the yoke of the Buwayhids, they were in no way prepared to restore the political power of the caliphs of this dynasty.

The Central Asiatic Turks had been a dominating factor in Muslim Near Eastern countries since the third/ninth century; the armies of the Muslim states were composed mostly of the Turkish cavalry and Turkish generals (*amīr*s) soon assumed the role of kingmakers. The novelty of the Saldjuk invasion was that a whole Turkish people was now on the move to conquer most of western Asia for themselves. This move inaugurated the era of Turkish pre-eminence in the political and military history of large parts of the Islamic world. Taking the torch from the Arabs the Turks expanded Islam in various directions. Already the predecessors of the Saldjuks, the Ghaznavids of Afghanistan, had launched the military conquest of India to the east of the Indus River; in their steps followed other dynasties so that the mightiest of them, the Great Mughals, who came to power in the tenth/sixteenth century, could claim that the greater part of India belonged to *Dār al-islām*.

The Saldjuks themselves added to the Islamic world many new territories in eastern and central Asia Minor, the great bastion of the Byzantine Christian empire which had for so long stood in the way of Muslim advance. In the following centuries the rest of it fell under the sway of other Turkish dynasties; the crowning of the new Turkish Muslim offensive came about with the conquest of Constantinople in 857/1453 by the Ottoman sultan Meḥmed II Fātiḥ.

In the eighth/fourteenth century the whole Islamic world with the exception of the Maghrib and Muslim Spain came under the rule of the Turkish or the Turkicized Mongol dynasties who gave a new vigour to Islam. The great historian Ibn Khaldūn considered the almost universal supremacy of the Turks in Islam as a proof of God's concern for the welfare of the Muslims. At a period when the Muslim world went through a crisis and became weak and defenceless, God in His wisdom had brought new rulers from among the Turks to revive the dying breath of Islam and restore the unity of the Muslims.[16]

In terms of the development of Islamic religious thought the Abbasid period represents a formative period for various branches of religious sciences, particularly of jurisprudence (*fiḳh*) and of speculative theology

16. Ibn Khaldūn, 1867, Vol. 5, p. 371.

(*kalam*). These branches evolved not in a straightforward way but they took their shape as a result of fierce debates within the Muslim community itself and of controversies with outside opponents, mostly Christians and Manicheans (called *zindīḳs*).

A fundamental place in the birth and development of Muslim thought as a whole is held by the *Muʿtazila*. This is a name given to an early school of Muslim religious thinkers who, influenced by Greek philosophy, wished to place at the service of Islam the resources of reason and thereby take these weapons from their opponents and turn them against them. In European literature the Muʿtazilites are sometimes called 'freethinkers' or 'liberals' but those labels are erroneous. The *Muʿtazila* was not a sect and among its adherents were numbered Sunnites and Shīʿites alike; they tried to present the dogmas of Islam as acceptable not only to faith but also to reason and also to give a systematic presentation of religious beliefs. Among the themes dealt with by the Muʿtazilites the principal ones concerned the nature of God, the nature of the Qoran and man's relation to God. They insisted on the unity and oneness of God, even rejecting the real attributes of God and all forms of anthropomorphism. As far as concerns the Qoran, they held the opinion that it was not eternal but created in time. The last great theme derived from the Islamic tenet about the Divine justice. The *Muʿtazila* found it difficult to reconcile the doctrine of predestination with the goodness of God; it was abhorrent to them to think that man would be punished for deeds which God had commanded him to perform. God is always obliged to command good and since He does not desire evil, He does not ordain it; it is man who creates evil. For some time in the first half of the third/ninth century the Muʿtazilite doctrine achieved the status of the Abbasid state religion; the Muʿtazilites were highly intolerant of the view of others and insisted with force on having theirs widely accepted. But after a brief reign as the dominant school they were in their turn persecuted and suppressed. However, in spite of the rejection of its main doctrines the *Muʿtazila* was of crucial importance for the development of Sunnite orthodox theology. By forcing the orthodoxy to rethink some fundamental issues of the faith it was indirectly responsible for the definitive formulation of the beliefs of 'those who are faithful to the tradition of the Prophet' (*ahl al-sunna*) as represented by the teachings of the prominent figures of the Islamic theology like al-Ashʿarī (d. 324/935) and al-Bāḳillānī (d. 403/1013).

These Sunnite theologians lived and worked at a time when the prospects of Sunni Islam and of the Abbasid Caliphate were at their lowest ebb. The schismatic Fāṭimids reigned over a half of the Islamic world and threatened the rest ideologically and politically. The Shīʿā was flourishing even within the Abbasid domain where the Buwayhids made the caliphs into puppets. Petty Shīʿite dynasties governed in parts of Arabia, in Syria and northern Iran.

The coming of the Saldjuks did more than restore the territorial unity of Islam; it was accompanied by a great religious revival of Sunni orthodoxy.

It is interesting to note that this revival of orthodoxy and the reaction against heterodoxies started almost simultaneously in the East (the Saldjuks) and the West (the Almoravids); in both cases the bearers of the orthodoxy were recently converted nomadic peoples from the fringes of the Islamic world. The religious zeal and military prowess of the Turks and Berbers also found expression in the renewal of the struggle on the frontiers with the Christians, in Anatolia as well as in Spain.

Conclusion

The end of the fifth/eleventh century was thus marked in the Islamic world by significant changes on many levels. In political terms it heralded the definitive preponderance of the Turks in the East and of the Berbers in the West. The Fāṭimids, whose power reached its zenith just in the middle of the century, had by its end lost their Maghriban provinces (to the Zīrīds and the Hilālī Arabs) as well as Syria with Palestine but retained their hold on Egypt and the Red Sea regions. The Saldjuk offensive against the Byzantines in Asia Minor evoked reaction in Western Europe which took the form of the First Crusade. Although the territorial gains of the Franks, as the Crusaders were called in Muslim countries, were not excessively large, the implantation of the Christians in the Holy Land and on the Mediterranean shores of Asia introduced a new political factor into the Near Eastern scene. It took nearly a century before Jerusalem was taken back by the Muslim armies, and another before the last remnants of the Christian states were wiped out.

In Muslim Spain the occupation of Toledo in 478/1085 and the Christian offensive against the Muslim *mulūk al-ṭawā'if* that followed threatened for the first time the existence of Islam on the Iberian peninsula. The danger was for a while stopped by the intervention of the Berber Almoravids. In the central Mediterranean the Muslims lost Sicily forever.

No less important were the changes in economy and trade. With the arrival of the Saldjuks the institution of *iḳṭā'* – a kind of system of military fief-holdings – became characteristic of the economic life and socio-political structures in large parts of the Muslim world. In spite of various interpretations of this institution it is clear that on it was built a production system typologically corresponding to European feudalism. Although in Egypt and the Maghrib this system developed fully only later, it became universal and typical until the twelfth/nineteenth century.

The period of the fourth/tenth and fifth/eleventh centuries also saw a gradual shift of the terminal of the Indian Ocean trade from the Arab/Persian Gulf to the Red Sea and thus to the Fāṭimid orbit. Egypt profited most from this change and became for a long time to come the main centre of the transit trade between the Mediterranean and the Indian Ocean. At the same time the Italian merchant republics monopolized the European side of the transit trade and soon also the maritime control of the eastern Mediterranean from where Muslim shipping almost disappeared.

We have already mentioned the triumph of orthodox Sunnite Islam in the fifth/eleventh century. Although the Shīʿā lost much both territorially and religiously, it continued to exist in many parts of the Islamic world; none the less with the gradual decline of the Fāṭimids the Shīʿite religion was deprived of its powerful exponents and it had to wait some centuries until the Safawid dynasty in Persia raised it once again to the level of a state religion.

Two measures contributed substantially to the victory of Sunnite Islam at this time: the first was the establishment of *madrasas*, higher religious institutions for the education of the *ʿulamāʾ*. Although a few schools of the *madrasa* type existed in the East already before the Saldjuks, it is generally accepted that under this dynasty on the initiative of the famous vizier Niẓām al-Mulk (d. 485/1092) the *madrasas* became universal religious teaching institutions, being quickly established in nearly all Muslim countries. The *madrasa* was founded as a counterweight to similar institutions in Fāṭimid Egypt and to provide a more effective defence against the organized spread of Ismāʿīli propaganda; the *madrasa* was rightly called 'the bulwark of the orthodoxy'. The second contributory factor was the recognition and incorporation of sufism into the fold of official Islam and the emergence of ṣūfī brotherhoods; *ʿulamāʾ* became their members and were thus able to steer both the leaders and members towards orthodoxy and away from heterodoxy. Orthodox sufism as practised by the recognized *tarīḳas*, also stressed moral perfection, preached personal effort (the greater *djihād*) as an indispensable basis of Muslim social values and insisted on charitable acts and self-negation.

3

Stages in the development of Islam and its dissemination in Africa

M. EL FASI and I. HRBEK

General introduction

Islam – together with Buddhism and Christianity – belongs in the category of missionary religions, i.e. those in which the spreading of the truth and the conversion of 'unbelievers' were considered a duty by the founder of the religion and then by the whole community. Muslims employ for the proselytizing activity the Arabic word *daʿwa*, whose literal meaning is 'call, appeal, invitation', in this case to the truth of the Islamic faith.

The duty to invite non-Muslims to accept Islam is contained in many Qoranic Sūras such as: 'Call unto the way of thy Lord with wisdom and fair exhortation; and reason with them in the kindest manner' (16:126) or 'Say to those who have received the Scripture and those who are ignorant: do you accept Islam? Then, if they accept Islam, they are rightly guided, but if they turn away, then thy duty is only to convey the message' (3:19). Similar exhortations are found in many other Sūras.

During Muḥammad's life Islam became the religion of the Arabs; it fell to his immediate successors, the first caliphs, to carry the new religion beyond the borders of the Arabian peninsula. There the Muslims encountered a different situation; whereas the majority of the Arabs had been adherents of traditional religion before their conversion (Arabic *mus̲h̲rikūn*, polytheists) the surrounding countries were inhabited by Christians, Jews and Zoroastrians, who were, according to the Islamic view *ahl al-Kitāb*, people of the Book, that is those who made use of revealed Scriptures and were thus adherents of a revealed, even if imperfect, monotheistic religious system. The attitude to these peoples did not entail any obligation on the part of the Muslims either to convert or to exterminate them, since ideologically Islam discourages compulsory conversion. The appeal it hopes to exercise consists in the existence and the availability of the ultimate truth made visible through the life of the Muslim community in which it is embodied. There was surely during the great Arab conquest no attempt to convert the *ahl al-Kitāb* by force.

Although generations of scholars have already clearly demonstrated that the image of the Muslim Arab warrior with sword in one hand and the

Qoran in the other belongs to the realm of mythology, this image still persists in popular writings on Islam and is generally believed in non-Muslim countries. This misinterpretation has arisen from the assumption that wars waged for the extension of Muslim domination over lands of non-Muslims were aimed also at their conversion.[1] Islamic political theory, in fact, requires control of the body politic for the Muslims, but it does not require bringing every subject of the Muslim state into the fold. The conquests during the first century of the *hidjra* were made not for conversion's sake but actually for the extension of the Islamic sphere of domination (*Dār al-Islām*). The Muslims were more interested in the incorporation of non-Muslims into the Islamic state, which in their eyes represented the ultimate realization of a divinely ordained plan for mankind, than in their immediate conversion.[2] Conversion was desirable from the religious point of view, but not necessarily from a governmental point of view.

The *ahl al-Kitāb* were given substantial autonomy in all ecclesiastical matters on the condition that they paid *djizya*, the poll tax. The Muslims were exempted from this tax and Muslim Arab warriors and their families were paid pensions from the central state treasury (*dīwān*) and also enjoyed a privileged social position. The obvious advantages of belonging to the faith of the victors were not lost on conquered peoples and many of them went over to Islam.

Under the Umayyads conversions became so numerous that the tax revenue in many provinces had fallen alarmingly low; the answer was an official policy which discouraged further conversions by ordering that the new converts should continue to pay land tax and poll tax as before. Only during the reign of the pious Caliph 'Umar II (99/717–101/720) who is said to have pronounced the famous sentence 'God had sent Muḥammad to call men to a knowledge of the truth and not to be a collector of taxes',[3] was this policy stopped for a short time, but later the general practice reverted to one of discrimination against newly converted Muslims. It was not until Abbasid times that the neophytes were integrated as full members into the Islamic community and that the Arabs lost their privileged position as the ruling class.

Not until the second and third centuries after the *hidjra* did the bulk of the Near Eastern people profess Islam; between the military conquest of the region and the conversion of its people a long period intervened. The motives which led to conversion were manifold – some were attracted by the simple and straightforward teachings of Islam, others wanted to escape tribute and taxes, and still others sought to identify themselves with the ruling class and participate fully in the emerging Islamic culture.

It remains true, nevertheless, that the Arab conquest resulted – not immediately but in the long run – in the Islamization of the majority of the

1. T. W. Arnold, 1913, p. 5.
2. I. Goldziher, 1925, p. 27.
3. Ibn Sa'd, 1904–40, Vol. 5, p. 283.

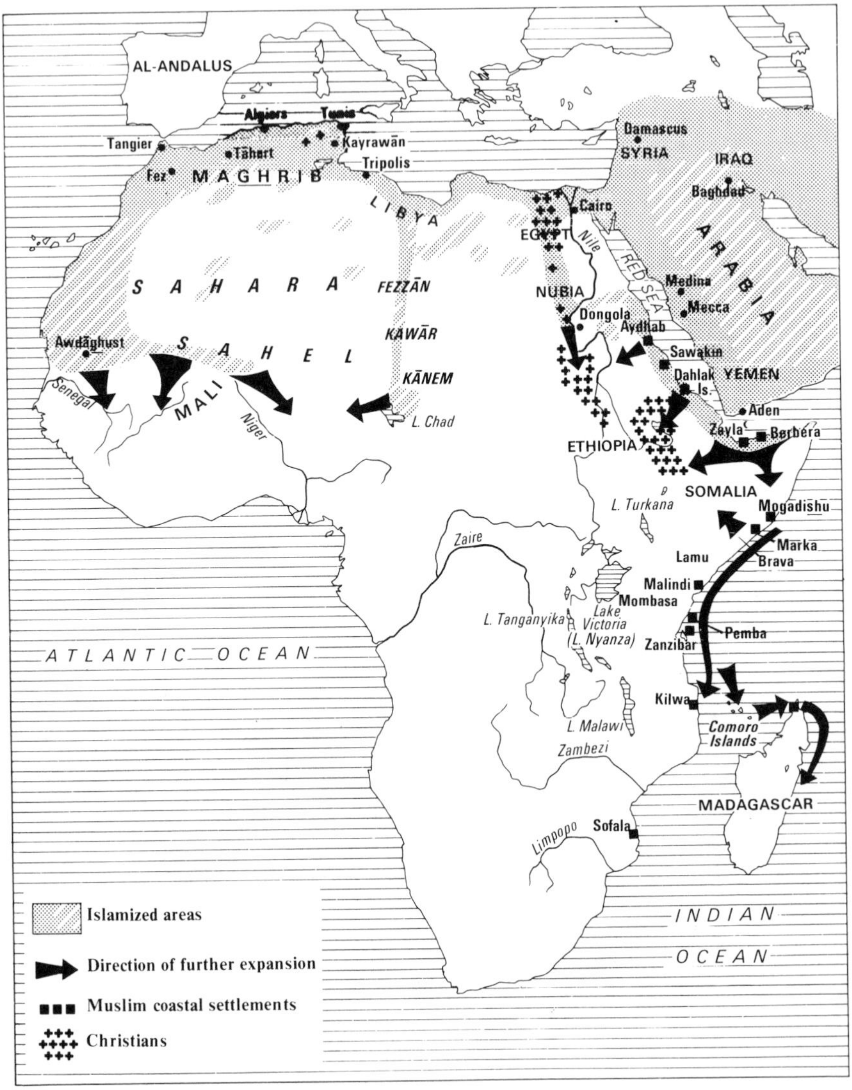

FIG. 3.1 *The Islamized areas of Africa by* c. *1100*

Near Eastern and North African populations. The rule of Muslim Arabs created political, religious, social and cultural conditions that favoured conversions to the religion of the politically dominant group without there being any need to employ force.

Part I: The Islamization of North Africa

M. EL FASI

Egypt

Egypt – then a Byzantine province – was the first African country to be invaded by the Arabs. Its conquest did not take long as the Byzantine garrisons were not numerous and the local Copts did not offer any resistance; on the contrary they welcomed the Arabs as deliverers from the Byzantine yoke.[4] They had suffered not only from a heavy tax burden and other forms of exploitation but also from religious persecution to which they were subjected as Monophysites by the official orthodox Byzantine church. This oppression had increased just before the Arab conquest through attempts to forbid the Coptic form of worship and through relentless persecution of Coptic clergy.

It may be suggested that this struggle between the two Christian churches in Egypt facilitated to some degree early conversions of Egyptians to Islam. The interminable theological controversies of the most abstruse and metaphysical character must have been unintelligible to the great mass of Christians who were doubtless also wearied and perplexed by the futility of them. Many of the Copts turned therefore to a faith that offered them a simple and clear truth about one God and his Prophet. This helps to explain the rapid spread of Islam in the early days of the Arab occupation.[5] Although in later periods the Copts were from time to time persecuted by some intolerant rulers and many of them were thus driven to abandon their faith, such cases were the exception rather than the rule. Paradoxically, it was under the Fāṭimids and Ayyubids – both dynasties considered to be champions of Islam – that the non-Muslim subjects enjoyed a freedom of religion rarely seen in earlier or later periods; this tolerance, by bringing Muslims and Christians together, led to the gradual disappearance of the Coptic language from everyday use and its replacement by Arabic. In the sixth/twelfth century only the more educated clergy knew the language and it even became necessary to translate liturgical books into Arabic to make

4. Cf. Chapter 7 below.

5. Even before the conquest was complete, thousands of Copts went over to Islam and later every year witnessed mass conversions. Jean de Nikiou, 1883, p. 560; Severus ibn al-Muḳaffaʿ, 1904, pp. 172–3.

PLATE 3.1 *Detail of a minbar (in carved cedar) from the Mosque of Ḳayrawān*

them comprehensible to the majority of the lesser clergy and the mass of Christians. The Copts filled many posts in the state apparatus, farmed the taxes and held in their hands financial and administrative responsibilities; in this they were not alone, as numerous other Christians (Armenians) and Jews were similarly employed.[6]

The Islamization and Arabization of Egypt was also furthered by the steady influx of Arab Beduins from the Arabian peninsula and the Fertile Crescent who settled down as peasants, mixed with the native Copts and thus increased the number of Arab-speakers and Muslims. Another factor leading to conversions was the increasing corruption and degeneracy of the Coptic clergy from the fifth/eleventh century onwards which resulted in the neglect of the spiritual and moral needs of the people. In the seventh/thirteenth century whole dioceses became Muslim since there were no priests, owing to a long quarrel between contending candidates to the Patriarchate of Alexandria, during which no new priests were ordained.[7]

The Islamization of Egypt was thus a rather complicated process in which many factors – sincere religious adherence, fiscal and social advantages, persecutions, the decay of the Coptic Church, and an influx of Muslims from abroad – played their role. The combined result was that Egypt in the Mamluk period was already a country with a Muslim majority and Coptic and Jewish minorities.

The Maghrib

The religious situation in North Africa to the west of Egypt was at the time of Muslim advance more complex than the one found in Egypt. The Romanized population in the towns and on the coastal plains had for a long time adhered to Christianity, whereas the Berbers in the interior remained largely adherents of traditional religion although some of the mountain inhabitants had adopted Judaism. Already under Roman and Byzantine rule the Christianized Berbers had been given to sectarianism: the Donatists and Circumcellions – sects that professed egalitarianism and a simple creed – revolted many times against Church authorities and refused to pay taxes, thus expressing the characteristic Berber love of independence and an aversion to state authorities.[8]

The dramatic story of the Arab conquest and of the fierce Berber resistance is fully discussed elsewhere in this Volume and does not need to be

6. Cf. G. Wiet, 1932, p. 199; C. Cahen, 1983, p. 87 et seq.
7. The decay is fully described by J. M. Wansleben, 1677 and by E. Renaudot, 1713.
8. Cf. on the situation in the Roman and Byzantine periods, Unesco, *General History of Africa*, Vol. II, ch. 19.

repeated here;[9] our task in this chapter is to describe the Islamization of the Maghrib.

The information we possess about the spread of Islam in this region is rather meagre; moreover the beginnings of Islamization are coloured in later Arabic sources by the ʿUḳba legend that transformed this gallant warrior into a peaceful missionary. It nevertheless remains true that through the foundation of Ḳayrawān in the year 50/670 ʿUḳba ibn Nāfiʿ created not only a military base but also an important centre for the radiation and propagation of Islam.

Although Ifrīḳiya (present-day Tunisia) had already become an integral part of the Caliphate in the course of the first century after the *hidjra* and the Arab domination here was more stable than in the rest of the Maghrib, the process of Islamization even here went rather slowly. In many regions, mainly in the Sāḥil, in the southern parts and in the zone of Mzāb, Romanized and Christian Africans continued to represent the majority of the population during the first two centuries after the conquest. In more remote parts, but also in some towns like Carthage and Tunis, small Christian enclaves were still found in later centuries: in Mzāb in the fifth/eleventh century, in Ḳafṣa in the sixth/twelfth century and in some Nafzāwa villages in the eighth/fourteenth century.[10] In the town of Tozeur the ancient Christian population persisted until the twelfth/eighteenth century.[11] In the fifth/eleventh century there were forty-seven bishoprics in the Maghrib; and in the city of Tunis a small community of native Christians, quite distinct from foreign Christian merchants, formed the bodyguard of the Ḥafṣid sultans in the ninth/fifteenth century.[12] But the very fact that these Christian remnants evoked the curiosity of observers in later centuries indicates that already by the fifth/eleventh century they lived among a majority of Muslims. Some papal documents from this century, lamenting the lack of clergy, also bear witness to the decay of Christianity in North Africa at this time.[13] This long survival of the native Christians is a strong argument against the supposition of forced conversion; as elsewhere it was general social conditions that led to a gradual change of religion. The conversion was doubtlessly aided by the active missionary activities of Muslim clergy and pious men from Ḳayrawān and other Islamic centres. And as in other parts of the Islamic world the spread of Islam was more rapid among the townspeople than in the countryside.

Although we are not able – for lack of sufficient evidence – to answer precisely why and how various Berber groups (and there were many dozens of them) adopted the religion of Islam, we can at least discern some general trends characterizing this process in its successive stages.

9. See Chapter 9 below.
10. T. Lewicki, 1951–2, pp. 424ff. See also A. Mahjoubi, 1966.
11. H. R. Idris, 1962, Vol. 2, p. 761.
12. Leo Africanus, 1956, Vol. 2, p. 67.
13. T. W. Arnold, 1913, pp. 126–7.

In the first stage many Berber groups, after offering a fierce resistance to the Arab armies, were subdued and converted. Conversions under these circumstances were largely formal and were probably restricted to chiefs and clan elders, who by this act recognized the sovereignty of their new masters. As soon as the Arab armies withdrew or were expelled – and this happened many times during the first/seventh century – the Berbers reverted to their traditional beliefs, considering themselves to be free of any political or religious allegiance. This led Ibn Khaldūn to his famous remark that the Berbers apostasized as many as a dozen times during the first seventy years of their contact with Islam.[14] When in 84/703 the last great Berber revolt under al-Kāhina was on the point of being crushed, this intrepid woman sent her sons to the Muslim camp with instructions that they were to embrace Islam and make common cause with the Arabs. Whether this act was prompted by the realization that further resistance was useless or by the wish to retain the chieftainship of the Djarāwa Berbers in her lineage, or both, is difficult to decide.

When the Arabs finally learned that it was beyond their capabilities to subjugate the Berbers by force,[15] they changed their policies: the famous governor Mūsā ibn Nuṣayr started to select young men of noble origin from among the prisoners, liberate them on the condition that they embraced Islam and then appoint them to high commands in the army.[16] This policy soon bore fruit as many Berber warriors encouraged by the example of their chiefs joined the Arab armies. The Arabs were aided in their effort to convert the Berbers by the successful invasion of Spain which almost immediately brought to their side large numbers of Berbers eager to participate in conquest and receive their share of booty. The Muslim army in Spain was composed mostly of recently converted Berbers and its first commander, Ṭāriḳ, was also a Berber. Thus shortly after the crushing of the last great resistance against the Arabs and Islam, thousands of Berbers joined both the armies and the faith of their enemy of yesterday. These conversions, however, only touched a minority of the population since large parts of present-day Algeria and Morocco remained beyond any effective Arab control and it took a long time before Islam penetrated into mountain areas.

Nevertheless, it can be said that during the first three or four decades of the eighth century Islam made considerable progress among the urban, rural and partly even the nomadic population in the plains and coastal strips. And it was precisely at this time that the characteristic Berber attitude towards the Arabs and Islam began to manifest itself: the Berbers were ready to accept Islam as a religion, or even the Arabic culture, and did so massively, but at the same time they resented being politically domi-

14. Ibn Khaldūn, 1925–56, Vol. 1, p. 21.

15. An Arab governor, Ḥassān ibn al-Nuʿmān exclaimed: 'To subjugate Africa is impossible!'

16. Al-Maḳḳarī, 1840–3, Vol. 1, p. 65.

nated by a foreign bureaucracy, representing a faraway sovereign, which discriminated against new converts, exacting from them heavy taxes as if they were unbelievers. To this was added the injustice suffered by Berber warriors in Spain where they were allocated less-fertile lands, although they had played at least as much part in the conquest as the Arabs.

Thus the stage was set for the next phase when the Berbers' struggle against foreign domination found its expression on an ideological level within the Islamic context. As a protest against the oppression of the orthodox Arabs they started to adhere to the doctrines of Khāridjism, the oldest Islamic politico-religious sect.

The Khāridjite political and religious teaching was democratic, puritan and fundamentalist, and in all these respects its adherents were radically opposed to the orthodox and absolutist Caliphate. From their egalitarian principles arose their doctrine concerning the choice of the *Imām* (the head of the Muslim community): he should be elected and not hereditary, and every pious believer, irreproachable in his morals and faith, whether Arab or non-Arab, a slave or a free man, could hope to attain the office of *Imām*.[17]

After leading several revolts against the Umayyads, the Khāridjites of the eastern provinces of the Caliphate – soon divided into a number of mutually hostile branches – were savagely repressed. Some survivors emigrated to North Africa to escape persecution and to preach their doctrine. There it fell on fertile ground among the Berbers, many of whom enthusiastically adopted it as the ideology of their struggle against Arab domination. The principle of equality of all believers corresponded both to their social structure and ideals as well as to the aspirations of those opposed to the heavy taxation and harsh treatment meted out by the Arab bureaucracy. No less attractive was the teaching that since all Muslims are equal, luxurious living and ostentation by some is sinful and that true believers should live soberly and modestly, practising charity and strict honesty in their personal or commercial dealings. This puritanical element must have exercised profound influence on the frugal Berber peasants and semi-nomads, scandalized by the luxury and immorality of the Arab ruling classes. Nowhere in the whole Islamic world did Khāridjism gain so many adherents as among the Berbers. As Reinhard Dozy aptly put it: 'Islamic Calvinism finally found in North Africa its Scotland'.[18]

In its two main forms – Ibāḍism and Ṣufrism – the Khāridjite doctrine spread chiefly among the Berber population in the area of steppes stretching from Tripolitania in the east through southern Ifrīḳiya to southern Morocco in the west, and particularly influenced the Berbers of the great

17. This doctrine was in opposition both to the Shī'ites who insisted that the Imāmate could be held only by members of the Prophet's family through his daughter Fāṭima and her husband 'Alī, and to the Sunnite view that only the members of the Ḳuraysh tribe from Mecca are qualified for this office.

18. R. Dozy, 1874, Vol. 1, p. 150; see also A. Bernard, 1932, p. 89.

Zanāta family.[19] In the middle of the second/eighth century the Khāridjites created two theocracies: the imāmate of Tāhert which commanded the allegiance of all Ibāḍites from Tripolitania to southern Algeria, and the smaller Ṣufrite principality in Sidjilmāsa. These states remained outside the control of the central Abbasid government or of the semi-independent Aghlabid governors of Ifrīḳiya until destroyed in the course of the fourth/tenth century by the Fāṭimids.[20]

It is obvious that the adoption of the Khāridjite doctrine by so many Berbers had its roots in the social and national opposition to the domination of Arab ruling classes. The Berber Khāridjism was in no case an anti-Islamic movement, on the contrary it was an expression of Berber acceptance of Islam as a religion. And through the incessant activities of numerous Ibāḍite *shaykh*s and scholars a large part of the Berbers became better acquainted with Islamic doctrine and duties, and were genuinely and not merely nominally converted.

Similarly the Berber resistance was not aimed against Muslim Arabs as such, but only against their ruling class. Berbers vigorously opposed any forceful or arbitrary imposition of foreign rule or rulers, but were ready to accept by free choice non-Berber Muslims as their chiefs. This happened in the case of the Persian Ibn Rustum in Tāhert, the Alid Idrīs in Morocco and the Fāṭimid ʿUbaydullah among the Kutāma Berbers. In all these cases these men were accepted not only as leaders of the anti-government opposition, but also for their specific Islamic appeal. This fact indicates yet again that the Berbers in question were already acquainted with Islam and sought to give an Islamic character to their opposition, whether Khāridjite (Ibn Rustum), orthodox Sunnite (Idrīs) or Shīʿite (ʿUbaydullāh).

There were also some attempts to found an exclusive Berber religion as a counterpart to Islam, the most famous and durable being that of the Barghawāṭa, a fraction of the Maṣmūda, who lived on the Atlantic plain of Morocco between Sale and Sāfī. Their chief, Ṣāliḥ ibn Ṭarīf, proclaimed himself a prophet in 127/744–5, composed a Qoran in the Berber language and issued a code of ritual and religious laws based mostly on local customs. Although all this put the Barghawāṭa religion outside the Islamic fold, its Islamic inspiration is clearly apparent and it represents one of the most original attempts to 'Berberize' the religion brought to the Maghrib from the East.

This heresy encountered much success among the Moroccan Berbers. Ṣāliḥ proclaimed himself ruler of a state independent of the Caliphate and his successors continued to dominate a large part of the Atlantic littoral until the fifth/eleventh century. They successfully defended their religion and state against all outside attacks, being finally subdued by the Almoravids, whose founder, ʿAbdallāh ibn Yāsīn, died fighting these heretics.

19. T. Lewicki, 1957, and also Chapter 13 below.
20. Cf. Chapter 12 below.

In other parts of northern Morocco, among the Awrāba, Miknāsa, Ghomāra and others, Islam had already made some progress in the course of the second/eighth century, but it seems that the real breakthrough and a more profound implantation occurred here during the rule of the Idrīsid dynasty.[21] The Berbers enthusiastically welcomed the founder, a scion of the Alid family, as faith in the special *baraka* (blessing power) hereditary in the line of Prophet's descendants had already begun to take root among the masses of believers, both in the East and the West. Invited to lead the anti-Abbasid movement, Idrīs seized the opportunity and after being proclaimed Caliph (in 172/788) launched an offensive to bring under the sway of Islam those Berbers who had not as yet been converted. This policy was continued by his son, Idrīs II, so that in the course of the next century northern Morocco was to a large extent Islamized, with the exception of the heretical Barghawāṭa. It should be pointed out that contrary to the opinion of some scholars,[22] the Idrīsids could not be counted as a Shī'ite dynasty as they never preached the Shī'ite form of Islam. The Islamization of the Berbers in the Idrīsid domain was aided also by the steady immigration of Arabs from Andalusia and Ifrīḳiya into the newly founded city of Fez which played a role in the western Maghrib comparable to that of Ḳayrawān in the eastern parts.

The Islamization of the whole Maghrib was substantially complete by the fourth/tenth century; only in some regions and towns did small Christian and Jewish communities still exist and a few Berber groups in remote mountain areas clung to their ancient beliefs while the 'heretic' Barghawāṭa were still unsubdued. But in the meantime the political and social conditions underwent many changes that deeply influenced the whole religious situation.

In these changes the role of the Fāṭimids was paramount, even if highly paradoxical. By sweeping away the Khāridjite states of Tāhert and Sidjilmāsa and by suppressing several Khāridjite revolts, the Fāṭimids dealt a mortal blow to Berber Khāridjism. But they were, however, unable to attract the Berber masses to their form of Islam, Shī'ism. Rather, the Berbers now turned to Sunnite Islam and especially to the Mālikite *madhhab* (religious-legal school). The surviving Khāridjites either retired to remote regions (Mzāb, Djabal Nafūsa, etc.) or gradually abandoned their doctrines and went over to Mālikism which was already firmly rooted at Ḳayrawān in Ifrīḳiya and in parts of Morocco. Khāridjism ceased to be the specific Berber form of Islam because at this time it lost its *raison d'être* as the expression of Berber opposition to foreign rule. There was no foreign domination in the Maghrib after the Fāṭimids transferred the centre of their empire to Egypt and left the Maghrib under the governorship of the Berber Zīrīds who in due time proclaimed their independence

21. On the beginnings of this dynasty see Chapter 10 below.
22. For example P. K. Hitti, 1956, pp. 450–1.

and swore allegiance to the Sunnite Caliph in Baghdad. Shortly afterwards the western part of the Maghrib came under the domination of the Berber Almoravids who exterminated the last vestiges of Khāridjism, Shīʿism and the Barghawāṭa heresy in this area, and established definitively the domination of the Mālikite school of Sunnite Islam.

Part II: The spread of Islam in Africa to the south of the Sahara I. HRBEK

Since the Islamization of the northern part of Africa came about as a result of the Arab conquest, it is often thought that the spread of this religion into tropical Africa followed a similar pattern, that is, that the local peoples were first subdued by the Arabs (or Berbers) and then forced to adopt Islam. The Almoravid conquest of Ghana is usually quoted as the most outstanding case of this kind of Islamization but recent research has demonstrated that such an interpretation of Ghana's conversion is not substantiated by available evidence (see below). External conquest by Muslim invaders played a negligible role except in the Eastern Sudan where extensive Arab settlement was of crucial importance for the dissemination of Islam. Even here, however, the conversion of autochthones followed much later. The conquest of African societies by local Islamized states was a significant factor in the Chad region or in southern Ethiopia, although there, paradoxically, the final extension of the Christian Amhara empire in the nineteenth century had a far more profound and permanent effect on the promotion of Islam than the military actions of previous centuries.[23] But in various parts of Africa to the south of the Sahara the normal course of the spread of Islam has been quite different as will be seen presently.

The Sahara

The Berbers of the western Sahara could have got into contact with Islam either through the Arab warriors who had penetrated their country from al-Sūs al-Aḳṣā or through the Muslim merchants whose caravans from Sidjilmāsa or from other towns of al-Sūs al-Aḳṣā had appeared on the western Saharan trade routes just after the Arab conquest of the Maghrib. These contacts certainly led to the conversion of some individual Berbers who served as guides and escorts for the caravans. In a few commercial and political centres along the routes where the Muslim traders had established themselves permanently, the influence of Muslim culture on the local population must have been more strong and profound.

The oldest information about the contacts between the Arabs and the

23. I. M. Lewis, 1974, pp. 108–9.

Saharan Berbers is an account of the expedition of ʿUḳba ibn Nāfiʿ to southern Morocco. In 63/682 he attacked the Massūfa Berbers to the south of al-Sūs al-Aḳṣā and after making some of them prisoners, he retired.[24] It seems that that expedition had reached as far as Wādī Darʿa (Oued Dra). Although much embellished by the later ʿUḳba legend, this expedition seems to have been only a kind of reconnaissance similar to that undertaken by the same Arab general in 47/666–7 to the south of Tripoli towards Fezzān and Kawār;[25] it is highly improbable that such short forays would have led to the Islamization of the local people.

Not much different were the campaigns of Mūsā ibn Nuṣayr, the Umayyad governor of Ifrīḳiya who between 87/705–6 and 90/708–9 had conquered, pacified and allegedly converted most of the Moroccan Berbers. He, too, entered al-Sūs al-Aḳṣā and even arrived at Sidjilmāsa and as far as to the town of Darʿa on the frontiers of the Massūfa territory.[26] But the same sources maintain that the definitive conquest of al-Sūs al-Aḳṣā and the conversion of its inhabitants occurred only as late as the 730s as a consequence of the expedition of Ḥabīb ibn Abī ʿUbayda.[27] The Arab army came back with many prisoners and a quantity of gold. Amongst the prisoners was a considerable number of the Massūfa; this indicates that these Berbers refused to accept Islam.

Further Arab military expeditions to the western Sahara stopped after the great Berber revolts in the 740s which had led to the decadence of Arab domination and a general anarchy in the Maghrib.

The first of the Saharan Berbers whose conversion is attested seem to have been the Lamtūna since Ibn Khaldūn wrote that they had accepted Islam shortly after the Arab conquest of Spain, in the second decade of the second/eighth century. On the other hand, al-Zuhrī (sixth/twelfth century) speaks of the conversion of the Lamtūna, Massūfa and Djuddāla during the reign of the Umayyad Caliph Hi*sh*ām ibn ʿAbd al-Malik (106/724–125/743).[28] Their Islam, however, must have been only a thin veneer for many centuries to come; the whole history of the beginning of the Almoravid movement offers eloquent evidence about the superficial Islamization among these three Berber peoples.

The Western and Central Sudan

Islam had been carried across the desert to the Western Sudan even before

24. Ibn Khaldūn, 1925–56, Vol. 1, p. 212; J. M. Cuoq, 1975, p. 330; N. Levtzion and J. F. P. Hopkins (eds), 1981, p. 326.

25. Ibn ʿAbd al-Ḥakam, 1947, pp. 63–5; J. M. Cuoq, 1975, pp. 45–6; N. Levtzion and J. F. P. Hopkins (eds), 1981, p. 12.

26. Al-Balādhurī, 1866, p. 230.

27. Al-Balādhurī, 1866, pp. 231–2; Ibn ʿAbd al-Ḥakam, 1947, pp. 122–3; Ibn ʿIdhārī, 1948–53, Vol. 1, p. 51; J. M. Cuoq, 1975, p. 46.

28. Al-Zuhrī, 1968, pp. 126, 181; J. M. Cuoq, 1975, p. 121; T. Lewicki, 1970.

the Maghrib and the Sahara themselves were fully converted. According to al-Zuhrī the rulers of the commercial town of Tādmekka, the Berbers of Banū Tānmak, were Islamized seven years after the people of Ghana, being forced to do this by newly converted Ghana.[29] It is, of course, quite possible that in this case the 'conversion' had meant the enforcement of orthodox Almoravid Islam among a people that already professed the Khāridjite faith. Tādmekka had been visited by Ibāḍī traders from North Africa since the third/ninth century and had become a centre of their missionary activities among the Sudanese peoples. The famous leader of the anti-Fāṭimid Khāridjite revolt in the fourth/tenth century, Abū Yazīd, was probably born in Tādmekka.[30]

This brings us to consider the role of the Khāridjites, especially the Ibāḍī sect, in the spread of Islam in the Sudan. Recent work by T. Lewicki on the Ibāḍites in North Africa, in the Sahara and in the Sudan has thrown much new light on the activities, commercial as well as missionary, of these puritanical Muslims. It is quite clear today that Ibāḍī traders penetrated the Sudan much earlier than orthodox Sunnites and it is likely that some of the first converts among the Sudanese were won for Islam solely by the proselytizing efforts of the Ibāḍites. The majority of the classical Arabic sources did not mention these activities, as their authors, being orthodox Muslims, were biased against the heretics;[31] only sporadically or in an indirect way do we learn from them about the Ibāḍite presence in the Sudan.[32] On the other hand, the writings of Ibāḍī authors from North Africa are full of information about the Ibāḍī trade network in the Sahara and the Sudan from the second/eighth century on. There is evidence of settlements of Ibāḍī merchants who came from Tāhert, Wargla, southern Tunisia and Djabal Nafūsa, in various Sudanese towns such as Ghana, Gao, Awdāghust, Tādmekka, Ghayārū, Zāfunu and Kūgha. The Khāridjites of the Ṣufri sect were ruling Sidjilmāsa, one of the most important northern termini of the caravan trade until the fourth/tenth century; the Ibāḍite dynasty of the Banū Khaṭṭāb in Zawīla (in the Fezzān) dominated the northern end of the important trade route from Libya to the Lake Chad Basin. The picture that emerges from recent research shows us the great extent of these trade relations. Although reports about the missionary activities of these merchants are not numerous, it can be surmised that their centuries-long presence in the most important Sudanese centres exercised a religious influence on the local inhabitants. The first converts

29. Al-Zuhrī, 1968, pp. 181–2; T. Lewicki, 1981, p. 443.

30. Ibn Ḥammād, 1927, pp. 18, 33–4; cf. Chapter 12 below.

31. Among many victims of the Almoravid conquest of the town of Awdāghust, al-Bakrī, 1913, p. 24 (J. M. Cuoq, 1975, pp. 91–2), regrets only the death of a Ḳayrawānī Arab, i.e. Sunni Muslim, and passes without comment the massacre of the Zanāta Berbers, in majority Ibāḍites.

32. Ibn Baṭṭūṭa, 1969, p. 395, mentions a group of white Ibāḍīs in Zaghari. Although the Ta'rīkh al-Sūdān, 1900, p. 61, describes Sonni 'Alī of Songhay as a Khāridjite, it seems that this term has here the general meaning of a heretic. Cf. T. Hodgkin, 1975, p. 118, n. 3.

would have been, of course, their Sudanese partners in trade. On the other hand, no traces of the religious tenets of the Ibāḍite faith remain alive in the Sudanese belt. It seems that only in the religious architecture can we detect more profound Ibāḍite influence: the minaret forms extant in many parts of the Sudan came originally from southern Tunisia, whereas the rectangular minbars are copies of those from Mzāb, the main Ibāḍite centre from the fourth/tenth century onwards.[33]

The early Ibāḍite influences in the southern Sahara and the Western Sudan were eradicated under the impact of the Almoravids who preached orthodox Islam and ensured that the Sudanese Muslims would thenceforth adhere to Mālikism. At the same time, in the fifth/eleventh century, the invasion of North Africa and the northern fringes of the Sahara by the nomadic Banū Hilāl contributed further to the decline of Ibāḍī communities and the definitive loss of their commercial preponderance in the caravan trade.

There are two curious episodes that could be interpreted as echoes of the former Ibāḍi influence in the sub-Saharan region. The Hausa legend of Daura contains the story of an Abuyazidu (or Bayadjidda), 'son of the King of Baghdad' and the legendary ancestor of the Hausa ruling dynasties. This Abuyazidu legend seems to be somewhat connected with the famous leader of the anti-Fāṭimid Khāridjite uprising, Abū Yazīd, who was killed in 335/947. Although it is historically impossible to identify these two as one person, it is nevertheless admissible to see in this legend a distant echo of an Ibāḍī tradition in the Sudan, the more so as we know that the historical Abū Yazīd was born of a Sudanese mother in Tādmekka (or Gao).[34]

Al-Dardjīnī (seventh/thirteenth century), an Ibāḍite author from the Maghrib, narrates an anecdote about his great-grandfather who about 575/1179–80 travelled to the Sudan and there converted the king of Mali (situated inland of Ghana) to Islam. This anecdote reminds one of the well-known story of al-Bakrī about the conversion to Islam of a king of Mallel; this must have happened before the work of al-Bakrī had been written (before 460/1068). The chronological discrepancy indicates that what we have here is a pious deceit by al-Dardjīnī who has ascribed to his ancestor the success of an anonymous missionary.[35] But this does not diminish the value of this anecdote as evidence for early missionary activities of the Ibāḍites and the awareness of this in later centuries.

How effective or profound this first wave of Islamization was is difficult to assess. Taking into account the situation of Islam in more recent times, it can be surmised that in a general way this early Islam contained many elements of various pre-Islamic faiths known in the Maghrib since the end

33. Cf. J. Schacht, 1954.

34. H. R. Palmer, 1928, Vol. 3, pp. 132ff.; W. K. R. Hallam, 1966, and the criticism of A. Smith, 1970.

35. Cf. J. Schacht, 1954, pp. 21–5; T. Lewicki, 1969, pp. 72–3; J. M. Cuoq, 1975, pp. 195–6; N. Levtzion and J. F. P. Hopkins (eds), 1981, pp. 368–9.

of the Roman epoch (Judaism, Christianity) as well as survivals from the Berber and African religions. No wonder that the intransigent orthodox (mainly Mālikite) reformers of the type of Ibn Yāsīn were horrified by the survivals of traditional religion and the 'mixed' nature of this early Islam in the Sahara and the Sudan. It took many centuries before the genuine Islam preached by a long chain of reformers and revivalists achieved some success.

To the Ibāḍites belongs the undeniable merit of having been the first to introduce Islam to the Sudanese peoples; even if their success cannot be quantitatively measured – and it seems that it was not very great – they laid the foundation on which later propagators of Islam were able to build a firmer structure.

The association of Islam and commerce in sub-Saharan Africa is a well-known fact. The groups most commercially active in later centuries, the Dyula, the Hausa and the Dyakhanke, were among the first to be converted when their respective countries came into contact with Muslims. The explanation of this phenomenon is to be found in social and economic factors. Islam as a religion born in the commercial society of Mecca and preached by a Prophet who himself had been for a long time a merchant, provides a set of ethical and practical precepts closely related to business activities. This moral code helped to sanction and control commercial relationships and offered a unifying ideology among the members of different ethnic groups thus helping to guarantee security and credit, two of the chief requirements of long-distance trade. As it was well put by A. G. Hopkins: 'Islam helped maintain the identity of members of a network or firm who were scattered over a wide area, and often in foreign countries; it enabled traders to recognise, and hence to deal readily with each other; and it provided moral and ritual sanctions to enforce a code of conduct which made trust and credit possible.'[36]

Muslims in these early days tended to form small communities dispersed along the main trade routes all over the Sahel and Sudan. In some capital cities like Ghana or Gao the merchants and Muslims – in fact, these categories were in most cases identical – lived in separate quarters, sometimes enjoying a certain political and judicial autonomy. This pattern was repeated until quite recent times not only in the trading centres but also in many villages where Muslims preferred to live separately from the pagan majority under the jurisdiction of their own *s͟hayk͟h*s or *ḳāḍī*s.

In their quarters they established mosques and soon acquired a distinctive character through some of their habits and customs associated with the practice of Islam such as the five daily prayers, the mode of dressing and the total abstention from alcohol by some pious Muslims.

Thus Islam appeared first not as a moving frontier of mass conversion in a continuous area but rather as a series of urban enclaves at the centres of

36. A. G. Hopkins, 1973, p. 64.

trade and political power while the peasants were only little touched by Islam.[37] These settlements along the trade routes and in the major centres constituted the nursery for the eventual propagation of Islam.

Of course, not every Muslim trader could have had enough time or inclination to do missionary work among the local people. But in the wake of the traders and with the growth of Muslim communities in many parts of the Sudan came Muslim clerics for whom religious activities were generally more important than commercial ones. At first they performed a variety of clerical functions for established Muslim communities to which they later added healing, divining and the manufacture and sale of charms and amulets. It was in this way that they won respect and prestige among non-Muslims whose religious tenets were not exclusive and who often sought the aid of these clerics in attempts to manipulate the world of the supernatural. The side of their activities that touched on magic and superstition constituted the major appeal of Islam in non-Muslim eyes in the Sudan countries. Interpretations of dreams, healing by faith, divining the future, belief in the power of prayer, especially of prayers for rain, were of great relevance.[38]

Since its appearance in West Africa Islam has always had to contend with non-Islamic customs and practices. For most converts, the acceptance of the new religion has never meant a complete abandonment of all non-Islamic practices associated with the African Traditional Religion. In fact, many initially accepted Islam because early Muslim leaders were liberal in their interpretation of what constituted the profession of Islam and were therefore very tolerant of some non-Islamic practices.

The second social group – after the merchants – to be converted to Islam were the rulers and courtiers. Whereas the adoption of Islam by the Sudanese traders through their contacts with North African counterparts went on gradually and unobtrusively for many years, thus failing to arouse the curiosity of the Muslim authors of our written sources, the conversion of a ruler had always attracted their attention, being an event duly recorded as a victory for Islam. We are therefore much better informed about the Islamization of the royal families and courts; moreover the given dates permit us to put this process into a relatively sure chronological framework.

It is generally admitted that the first ruler in the Western Sudan to become Muslim was Wār Dyābī of Takrūr on the lower Senegal. He had adopted Islam even before the rise of the Almoravids in the 420s/1030s. According to al-Bakrī he undertook to spread the new religion into the neighbouring country of Silla;[39] and in 448/1056 his son Labī joined

37. P. D. Curtin, 1975, p. 48.

38. H. J. Fisher, 1977, p. 316. But some clerics were less than zealous about spreading Islam to the unconverted, preferring to claim the monopoly of esoteric powers for their own group; cf. Y. Person, 1968–75, Vol. 1, p. 133.

39. Al-Bakrī, 1913, p. 172; J. M. Cuoq, 1975, p. 96; N. Levtzion and J. F. P. Hopkins (eds), 1981, p. 77.

Yaḥyā ibn ʿUmar in fighting the rebellious Djuddāla. Although the Fulbe-speaking people on the lower Senegal are today called Tukulor (but they themselves do not use the name), a distortion of Takrūr, it is not quite sure whether they already inhabited this country in the fifth/eleventh century. It seems more probable that the ancient Takrūr was peopled by the Soninke.[40] In later centuries the name of Takrūr tended to designate, in North Africa and in Egypt, all the Muslim countries of the Western and Central Sudan. Whether this usage goes back to the fact that Takrūr was the first West African Muslim country or to the fact that by the eighth/fourteenth century the people of Takrūr, at that time already Fulbe-speaking, had begun to produce the class of Muslim clerics (the Torodbe) who played such an important role in the Islamization of the whole Western Sudan, remains unsolved.[41]

An even earlier, pre-Almoravid, conversion of a local ruler occurred in Gao (Kāw-Kāw), where in about 400/1009–10 the fifteenth Dyā (Zā) ruler Kosoy adopted Islam.[42] Al-Bakrī does not mention the circumstances of this conversion but reports that when a new ruler was installed at Gao he was given a sword, a shield and a copy of the Qoran said to have been sent from a caliph as his insignia of office. He adds that the king professed Islam, never giving supreme power to anyone other than a Muslim.[43]

But the court ceremonial at Gao described by al-Bakrī was clearly non-Muslim. This pattern of Islam as the official royal religion with the mass of the populace non-Muslim and with a largely traditional court ceremonial remained a general fashion in many Sudanese states and is an indication of the very delicate balance which always existed between Islam and the indigenous religious structure.

To this same period also belongs the already mentioned conversion of the king of Mallal, one of the earlier chiefdoms of the Malinke. The ruler is reported by al-Bakrī to have been gained for Islam by a Muslim resident whose prayers brought a long-awaited rain to the country. Although the royal family and court became sincere Muslims, the rest of the people continued in their traditional religion.[44] This king proclaimed his allegiance to the new religion openly, being called 'al-Muslimānī'; but already his colleague, the ruler of Alūkan, had to conceal his Islam before his subjects.

The first establishment of Islam in the Central Sudan occurred in the fifth/eleventh century with the conversion of the *mai*s of Kānem.[45] In the *maḥram* (grant of privilege) of Ḥummay Djilmi (*c*. 472/1080–490/1097) we read that:

40. Wār Dyābē is a Soninke proper name; cf. C. Monteil, 1929, p. 8. The immigration of the Fulbe-speakers into the country on the lower Senegal began only later.

41. Cf. U. al-Naqar, 1969.

42. Ta'rīkh al-Sūdān, 1900, p. 5.

43. Al-Bakrī, 1913, p. 183; J. M. Cuoq, 1975, pp. 108–9.

44. Cf. note 35.

45. Cf. D. Lange, 1978.

> 'the first country in the Sudan which Islam entered was the land of Bornu. It came through Muḥammad ibn Mānī who had lived in Bornu for five years in the time of King Bulu . . ., fourteen years in the time of King Umme (Ḥummay). Then he summoned Bornu to Islam by the grace of King Umme ... *Mai* Umme and Muḥammad ibn Mānī spread abroad Islam to last till the day of judgment'.[46]

It is interesting that already under the reigns of some of Ḥummay's predecessors (from the beginning of the fifth/eleventh century) there lived at the court Muslim clerics who even instructed the rulers in Islamic precepts and read parts of the Qoran with them; nevertheless none of *mai*s publicly professed Islam. It is for this reason that al-Bakrī, writing a generation before Ḥummay, considers Kānem to be still a kingdom of 'idolatrous Negroes' although exposed to Muslim influences, illustrated by the interesting story of the presence there of some Umayyad refugees who 'still preserve their Arab mode of dress and customs'.[47] The son and successor of Ḥummay, Dūnama (490/1097–545/1150) undertook two pilgrimages to Mecca, being drowned on the second occasion.[48]

The fifth/eleventh century seems to represent the period of the first real breakthrough for Islam in the Western and Central Sudan: from the lower Senegal to the shores of Lake Chad Islam was accepted by various rulers and chiefs, thus gaining an official recognition in the framework of African societies. The same century also brought about the conversion of the most famous and at the time most powerful of the Sudanese states, that of Ghana.

It used to be thought that this conversion was brought about as a result of the Almoravid conquest of Ghana in 469/1076. Recent research by scholars such as D. Conrad, H. J. Fisher, L. O. Sanneh and M. Hiskett,[49] has, however, cast serious doubts on this view and it is becoming increasingly accepted that no such conquest ever took place and that the two powers in fact maintained friendly relations throughout. As a recent authority has concluded, 'it seems more likely that the Soninke of Ghana were on good terms with the desert Almoravids, that they became their allies not their enemies, and were peacefully persuaded by them to adopt Sunni Islam as the offical religion in the Ghana empire.'[50] From Arabic sources, principally al-Bakrī, we know about a large Muslim community in the capital in the pre-Almoravid period, consisting not only of merchants but also of courtiers and ministers. The rulers of Ghana had thus already been exposed to Islamic influences for a long time; it is also likely that Islam came to Ghana first in its K͟hāridjite form. The conversion mentioned by

46. H. R. Palmer, 1928, Vol. 3, p. 3; reprinted also in H. R. Palmer, 1936, p. 14ff.
47. Al-Bakrī, 1913, p. 11; J. M. Cuoq, 1975, p. 82; cf Chapter 15 below.
48. Diwan of the Sultans of Bornu; H. R. Palmer, 1936, pp. 85–6.
49. D. Conrad and H. J. Fisher, 1982, 1983; L. O. Sanneh, 1976; M. Hiskett, 1984.
50. M. Hiskett, 1984, p. 23.

al-Zuhrī – that the people of Ghana were converted by the Lamtūna in 469/1076[51] – could therefore mean merely an imposition of the orthodox Mālikite Islam on a previously Ibāḍite community as was earlier done in Awdāghust. The most important achievement of the Almoravid intervention was doubtless the conversion of the king and his court.[52]

Also rejected by revisionist scholars is the view that the conquest and enforced Islamization of Ghana led to a massive population movement of the Soninke who opposed Islam and preferred to leave their ancestral homes rather than abandon their traditional religious beliefs.[53] Since no such conquest or enforced Islamization took place the migration which did occur could not be attributed to these factors.

It would be, of course, mistaken not to acknowledge the profound impact of the Almoravids and the changes that their intervention brought to the Sudan. But these changes were of a quite different order to those supposed by the adherents of the migration theory. The Soninke really started to disperse but it was a continuation of a process that had begun much earlier. The Islamized Soninke merchants – the Wangara of the Arabic sources – gradually established their commercial network in the Sahel and to the south of it, towards the fringes of the tropical forest. Far from being averse to Islam they in fact substantially helped to spread this religion to non-Muslim parts of the Sudan where neither Arabs nor Berbers ever penetrated. The Soninke who moved from Dya (Dia) on the Niger to a new centre at Dyakhaba on the Bafing became known as Dyakhanke. They adopted the Malinke language and developed a closely knit community in which clerical and commercial activities went hand in hand.[54] Other traders of Soninke origin, but often linguistically Malinkized, developed other trade networks: the Dyula mostly to the southern parts, the Marka in the Niger Bend and the Yarse in the Voltaic states. Most of their history and their role in spreading Islam belong to later centuries but it was in the period immediately following the Almoravid intervention in Ghana that this process gained its initial momentum.

There is no doubt that after the Almoravid intermezzo Islamic activities south of the Sahara became more intensive. The Islamization of the *Mai* Ḥummay of Kānem is sometimes ascribed to Almoravid influence but this is unlikely. There were, as we have seen, other Sudanese rulers who became Muslims before the rise of the Almoravids. It would seem that in the fifth/eleventh century the dynamics of previous development in many Sudanese states had reached a stage in which the adoption of Islam offered a certain set of advantages to the ruling classes and to a widening group of

51. Al-Zuhrī, 1968, p. 180ff; J. M. Cuoq, 1975, p. 119.

52. M. Hiskett, 1984, p. 26.

53. This concept stood at the roots of the theory that the ancestors of the Akan peoples of the modern republic of Ghana (Akan being allegedly a corruption of Ghana) came from ancient Ghana after its conquest by the Almoravids.

54. On the Dyakhanke cf. L. O. Sanneh, 1979; P. D. Curtin, 1971.

local traders. These advantages became even more apparent in the following centuries, in the period of the rise of the great Sudanese empires, Mali and Songhay.

Reasons of state that led to a degree of Islamization in the formerly non-Muslim empires were both internal and external. The external ones were connected with trade since the function of these empires from the economic point of view was the control and exploitation of the Sudan's trade with North Africa. The ruling class had a real interest in presenting an Islamized front – by the organization of its courts and by performing the pilgrimage – in order to establish and improve good relations with its North African clients and partners.[55] In the internal sphere one of the great problems of the imperial rulers was how to secure the allegiance of other subjected pagan clans and peoples which possessed totally different ancestor and land cults from those of the ruling dynasty. A universal religion such as Islam seemed to offer a suitable solution; an effort was made to implant it at least among the heads of other lineages and clans and to establish a new common religious bond. The increasing extent of the empires made the effective administration of the realm more complicated; in this respect the help of Muslim scribes and other literate persons was indispensable for correspondence and control of state affairs. The influence of Muslim clerics at the courts must have been great, thus preparing the ground for the ultimate conversion of the ruler and his family.

This does not mean that the kings were necessarily very devout or deep Muslims. They also had to reckon with the local customs and traditional beliefs of the majority of their non-Muslim subjects who looked upon the rulers as incarnations of or intermediaries of supranatural powers. None of the rulers had the political power to enforce Islam or Islamic law without compromising the loyalty of the non-Muslims. This helps to explain the numerous pagan rites and ceremonies at the courts of Muslim kings like the *mansas* of Mali and of the *askiyas* of Songhay, men who had performed the pilgrimage and were commonly considered to be devout Muslims.

In the Mali empire the Islamization of its rulers occurred at the end of the seventh/thirteenth century under the descendants of Sundiata. Although Ibn Baṭṭūṭa and Ibn Khaldūn maintain that this founding hero was converted to Islam,[56] the Malinke oral tradition vehemently insists on his character as a 'pagan' magician and denies any conversion. But already Sundiata's son and successor Mansa Uli performed the pilgrimage during the reign of the Mamluk sultan, Baybars (658/1260–676/1277). Under his rule Mali expanded over the Sahel and took control of the trading towns of Walāta, Timbuktu and Gao, thus coming into a more direct contact with Islamized peoples than in the centuries before.[57] From his reign onwards

55. C. Coquery-Vidrovitch, 1969, especially p. 73.

56. Ibn Baṭṭūṭa, 1969, Vol. 4, p. 420; Ibn Khaldūn, 1925–56, Vol. 2, p. 110; J. M. Cuoq, 1975, pp. 310, 344.

57. Cf. J. L. Triaud, 1968, p. 1329ff.

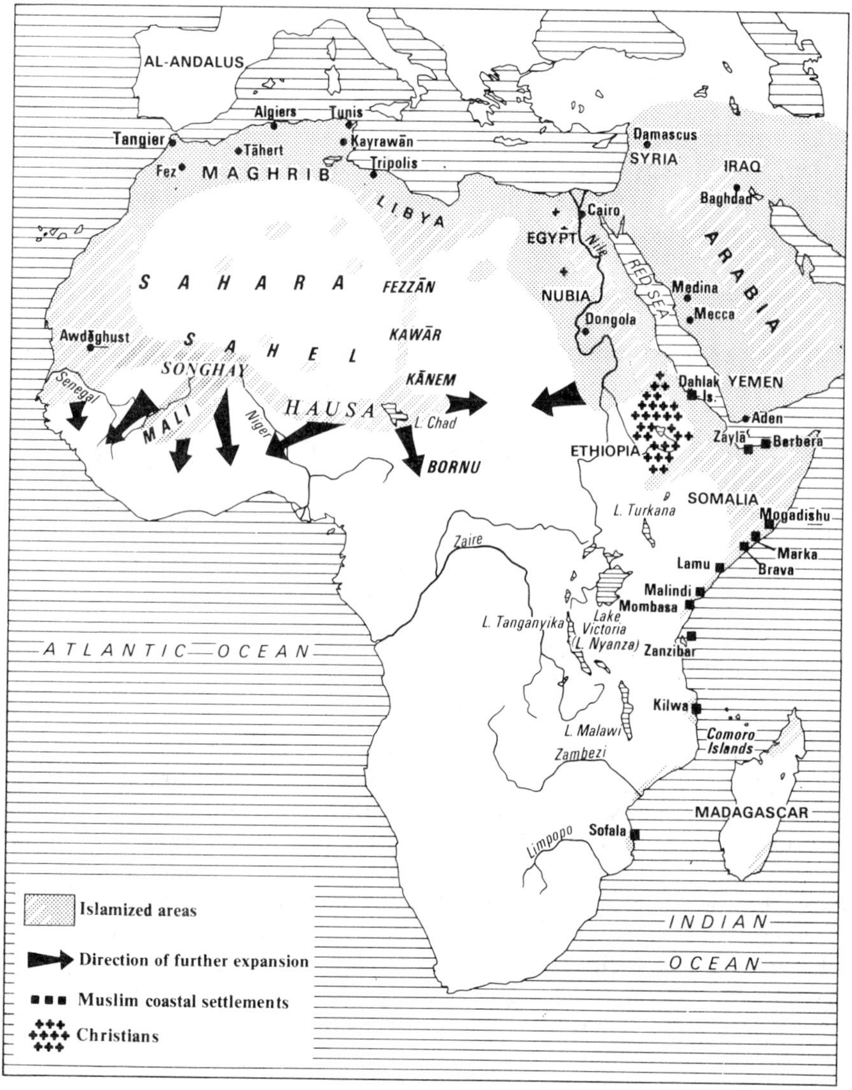

FIG. 3.2 *The Islamized areas of Africa by* c. *1500*

the royal pilgrimage became a permanent tradition among the *mansas*. The Islamic outlook of the empire took shape in the eighth/fourteenth century under Mansa Mūsā (*c*. 712/1312–738/1337) and his brother Mansa Sulaymān (*c*. 738/1341–761/1360) who encouraged the building of mosques and the development of Islamic learning. Ibn Baṭṭūṭa, an eye-witness, praised the zeal of the Malian Muslims in memorizing the Qoran and in attendance at the public prayers. The general feeling one has in reading his account is that Mali in the mid-eighth/fourteenth century was a country in which Islam had already taken root and whose inhabitants followed the main Islamic precepts. He does not mention any pagan religious practices and apart from the nakedness of women he did not observe anything prohibited by Islamic law.[58]

The general security reigning during the heyday of the Mali empire was favourable to the expansion of trade in the Western Sudan. Muslim traders operated various trade networks across the entire empire and even ventured beyond its frontiers. More and more Malinke were converted as well as some people from other ethnic groups like the Fulbe in the Senegal Valley and in Masina. An important development was the emergence and growth of a local clerical class that was concentrated in the main political and commercial towns, in Niani and Gao, but particularly in Jenne and Timbuktu. There is sufficient evidence to show that at least until the ninth/sixteenth century the majority of Muslim scholars in Timbuktu were of Sudanese origin; many of them studied in Fez and excelled in Islamic science and piety to such a degree as to arouse the admiration of foreign visitors.[59] All the main offices in Timbuktu (*ḳāḍīs*, *imāms* and *khaṭībs*) were held by black Muslims who had come from the interior of the Mali empire. A similar situation obtained in Jenne and also in Dyagha (Dya) whose inhabitants Ibn Baṭṭūṭa praised as 'Muslims of old and distinguished by their piety and their quest for knowledge.'[60] The establishment of a class of learned Muslim scholars and clerics of Sudanese origin was an important event in the history of Islam in Africa south of the Sahara. It meant that from then on Islam was propagated and spread by autochthons armed with the knowledge of local languages, customs and beliefs; this knowledge facilitated their missionary work and assured them a greater success than that obtained by their North African coreligionists in earlier times. In the eyes of the Africans Islam ceased to be the religion of white expatriates and, because it was now carried by Africans themselves, it became an African religion.

The influence of this new class of African clerics was felt as far as the Central Sudan. Until the eighth/fourteenth century the region between Lake Chad and the middle reaches of the Niger had formed something of a

58. Ibn Baṭṭūṭa, 1969, pp. 423–4; he encountered similar nakedness in the Maldive Islands without doubting the genuineness of the Islamic faith of their inhabitants.

59. Cf. Ta'rīkh al-Sūdān, 1900, pp. 78–84.

60. Ibn Baṭṭūṭa, 1969, Vol. 4, p. 395.

backwater in the spread of Islam, Hausaland in particular having been barely touched by missionary activities. Then, under the reign of *Sarki* Yaji of Kano 'the Wangarawa came from Melle bringing the Muslim religion'.[61] According to Palmer's chronology, Yaji ruled from 750/1349 to 787/1385; but the recently discovered eleventh/seventeenth-century *Chronicle of the Wangarawa* explicitly states that these missionaries arrived in Kano during the reign of Muḥammad Rumfa (867/1463–904/1499) having left their original home in the year 835/1431–2.[62] The chronological difficulties in early Hausa history being well known, it is not surprising that scholars disagree as to the date of the first introduction of Islam into Hausaland. Notwithstanding the arguments forwarded by the editor of the *Chronicle of the Wangarawa* it seems more likely that the entry of these Muslims had occurred during the eighth/fourteenth century under Yaji and not under Rumfa a century later. Yaji is presented in the *Kano Chronicle* as a strict Muslim requiring his subjects to pray; and many *sarakuna* between him and Rumfa, apart from bearing Muslim names, are depicted as Muslims.[63] Under the immediate predecessor of Rumfa, Muslim Fulbe (Fulani) came from Melle 'bringing with them books on Divinity and Etymology' whereas formerly the Hausa Muslims had only had books on the Law and the Traditions.[64]

It is, of course, possible that Hausaland received several waves of Wangara Muslims at different times and that their earlier representatives had succeeded in spreading Islam mainly among the traders whereas the group recorded in the chronicles preached the new religion to the ruling classes.[65]

It was in the second half of the ninth/fifteenth century that a strong Islamic tradition began to be established. Three major rulers, perhaps contemporaries, Muḥammad Rabbo in Zaria, Muḥammad Korau in Katsina and Muḥammad Rumfa in Kano altered the character of Hausa development by introducing or confirming Islam. Apart from the fact that he was the first Muslim *sarki* of Zaria, nothing is known about Muḥammad Rabbo. The next ruler of Katsina, Ibrāhīm Sūra, is remembered as a severe master who imprisoned those who refused to pray, whereas his son ʿAlī was called *murābiṭ* (man of the *ribāṭ*). Many of these rulers came under the influence of the great Muslim reformer Muḥammad al-Mā<u>gh</u>ilī who at Rumfa's request wrote the *Obligations of Princes* as a guide for the conduct of Muslim rulers.[66] There are also accounts of the arrival of *<u>sh</u>ārīf*s (descendants of the Prophet) in Kano at that time; their presence led to the

61. *Kano Chronicle*, in H. R. Palmer, 1928, Vol. 3, p. 104.
62. M. A. Al-Hajj, 1968, p. 7ff.
63. The main weakness of the *Wangarawa Chronicle* lies in the fact that it confuses the arrival of the Wangarawa with that of the reformer al-Mā<u>gh</u>ilī which happened at the end of the ninth/fifteenth century.
64. *Kano Chronicle*, in H. R. Palmer, 1928, Vol. 3, p. 111.
65. Cf. S. A. Balogun, 1980, pp. 213–14.
66. On al-Mā<u>gh</u>ilī see A. A. Batrān, 1973.

strengthening of the faith and the elimination of some pagan survivals. Islam was at that time still permeated by many local customs and practices and some rulers asked guidance for correct conduct not only from al-Māghilī but also from the famous Egyptian scholar al-Suyūṭī.[67]

Even after these attempts to foster its strength Islam was by no means generally accepted. It became the religion of small communities of traders and professional clerics; the court circles were influenced superficially, whereas the masses of people continued in their traditional beliefs. But gradually Islamic concepts and attitudes became more pervasive creating a situation of 'mixed' Islam. Important for further spread of Islam in those parts of the Sudan was the ready acceptance of it by the Hausa traders who became – after the Dyula – the second most active Muslim commercial class. With the opening of trade routes to the kola-producing countries in the hinterland of the Gold Coast (present-day Ghana) – where they met with an eastward movement of the Dyula – they carried Islam to the forest fringes.

By the tenth/sixteenth century the position of Islam had been further improved by the policies of *Askiya* Muḥammad of Songhay as well as by the exodus of the *mai*s from Kānem to Borno and the long rule of Idrīs Alaōma. It is supposed that the intervention of that ruler in Mandara in favour of one of his protégés paved the way for the introduction of Islam into that country and it may be that at that time the Tubu adopted the religion. The newly founded Bagirmi became a Muslim state in the same century and some time later, through inspiration drawn from Bagirmi, ʿAbd al-Karīm was able to weld Wadai into a state that was at least nominally Muslim.

At the other end of the Sudanese belt, in Senegambia, that period also witnessed an Islamic offensive. At the beginning of the tenth/sixteenth century the great majority of the Gambian populations were already considered to be Muslim.[68] In the second half of the century the spread of Islam was even more manifest in connection with the progress of the Tukulor in Futa Toro. Nearly everywhere on the coast Muslim clerics (called by the Portuguese *bixirim*) circulated, propagating the faith of Islam, prohibiting the consumption of pork and distributing amulets. Three *ribāṭ*s on the bank of the Gambia specialized in the formation of clerics who were then sent to proselytize in all neighbouring countries.[69]

There were also, of course, some setbacks in the progress of Islam. The Mosi (Mossi) people in the Niger Bend had resisted the spread of Islam for a long time in spite of their having already come into contact with it in the eighth/fourteenth century when they had attacked and sacked Timbuktu

67. In his letter to Ibrāhīm Sūra al-Suyūṭī wrote: 'I have been informed that among the people of Gobir are those who sacrifice a male or female slave if they are ill claiming that this will be their ransom from death.' Cf. T. Hodgkin, 1975, p. 119.

68. D. Pacheco Pereira, 1956, pp. 69–73.

69. M. F. de B. Santarem, 1842, p. 29.

and even Walāta.[70] In the closing years of the next century *Askiya* Muḥammad launched a *djihād* against them because of their rejection of his summons to adopt Islam. But not even the defeat of his army could persuade the Mosi ruler to abandon his traditional religion and the majority of his subjects followed his example. The Mosi kingdoms started to be penetrated by Muslim merchants (Yarse) only after the eleventh/seventeenth century and it was as late as the thirteenth/nineteenth century that some Mosi were converted.

Another island of traditional religion was formed by the Bambara in the territory of the ancient Mali empire. And even the Islamic culture of Mali regressed after the decline of the empire; having lost their external possessions and being separated from the Saharan trade the Malinke lived in small *kafu* (chiefdoms) without any central administration and without urban life. Islam, being abandoned by the political class, was represented by the commercial group (Dyula) or by the clerics (*moriba*) only.[71]

But in general, by the tenth/sixteenth century Islam was established all along the Sudanese belt from the Atlantic to Lake Chad and beyond. The ruling classes of all the great states and of the majority of the smaller ones were at least nominally Muslim. In all the towns and in many villages there lived communities of African Muslims of various ethnic origins, sometimes Muslims only in name, but often men of piety and learning with a wide outlook and in contact with the wider world to the north of the Sahara. Although the majority of the peasants were only lightly touched by this universal religion, Islam had become, after so many centuries of its presence, a familiar phenomenon, a part of the cultural scene in West Africa.

Nubia and the Nilotic Sudan

The Islamization of Nubia and the Nilotic Sudan has been – and indeed still is – a continuing process. Although Nubia had been in contact with Islam since the time of Arab conquest of Egypt in the early first/seventh century, Islam's spread there was blocked by the existence of the Christian Nubian states and the attachment of the Nubians to their Christian faith. The Muslims from Egypt tried in 31/651–2 to conquer Nubia and even penetrated as far as Dongola but the fierce resistance of the Nubians forced them to seek a truce. The ensuing treaty, commonly called the *baḳt*,[72] was a non-aggression pact which allowed the Nubian state of al-Maḳurra to retain its independent status. It conferred on the subjects of each side the right to travel and trade freely in the other's territory and stipulated also

70. It is, however, not sure, in the light of recent research, whether these Mosi were identical with those of the Volta Basin, cf. Unesco, *General History of Africa*, Vol. IV, ch. 19.

71. Y. Person, 1981, pp. 614, 641.

72. On the *baḳt* cf. Chapter 8 below.

that the lives of Muslims in Nubia were to be safeguarded.[73] The treaty remained in force for six hundred years, an exceptionally long term indeed for an international agreement to last. It shows also that the Muslims had abandoned the idea of occupying Nubia; they were more interested in putting an end to Nubian raids and keeping the country as a sphere of influence. Although there were occasionally attempts to convert the rulers (for example at the beginning of the period of Fāṭimid rule in Egypt), the general policy of the Muslim Egyptian governments was to leave the Christian kingdom undisturbed.

The friendly relationship between Egyptian rulers and Nubian monarchs opened the doors for the penetration of Muslim traders. In the capital of al-Maḳurra there existed, from early times, settlements of Arab merchants who inhabited – in accordance with the pattern established in the whole Sudanic belt – separate quarters of the town. Although it does not seem that these merchants actively propagated the Islamic religion, they nevertheless brought the first elements of the new faith into this hitherto wholly Christian region.

The Islamization (and the Arabization, too) of Nubia was the work of quite different agents. Already in the second/eighth century some Arab nomadic groups had started to move from Upper Egypt towards Nubia, choosing mainly the region between the Nile Valley and the Red Sea littoral. In the fourth/tenth century they were already established in the extreme north of Nubia and at the same time some of the Nubians to the north of the Second Cataract had been converted to Islam.

Another gateway for the penetration of Islam, although of less importance than the Nile corridor, was the Red Sea littoral. There the Arab merchants had already started to settle in coastal towns like ʿAydhāb, Bāḍīʿ and Sawākin in the second/eighth century. The hinterland was inhabited by the turbulent nomadic Bēdja whose repeated incursions harassed Upper Egypt for a long time. The Muslim governments tried to pacify them by treaties similar to that concluded with the Nubians but as the Bēdja were without any centralized political organization, these treaties covered only a part of their groups. Nevertheless the Bēdja chiefs allowed the settlements of Muslim merchants on their territories, thus opening this region to the influence of Islam.

This influence was strengthened by the immigration of some Arab nomadic groups into the Bēdja country where their members intermarried with the Bēdja ruling families; their children became chiefs of some of the Bēdja groups. This process was repeated over a long period of time and Muslims thus gained prominence. A similar process of intermarriage went on in Nubia, too, and led to the establishment of powerful Muslim lineages. The Islamization of the Bēdja was also stimulated between the

73. Here we deal only with those parts of the treaty which have a direct bearing on the spread of Islam.

fourth/tenth and seventh/thirteenth centuries by the development of trade routes across the Bēdja country from the Nile Valley to Red Sea ports. The northernmost Bēdja groups, the Hadāriba and ʿAbabda, gradually became Arabized, even adopting fictitious Arab genealogies, but their ancient beliefs were only thinly disguised by Islam. Other groups did not feel the influence of the Muslim Arabs so strongly but even they in the long run accepted Islam, or at least some of its precepts. It can be said that by the eighth/fourteenth century the majority of Bēdja were formally Islamized; that is to say they considered themselves Muslims and were recognized as such by their coreligionists but with many of their traditional beliefs and practices still alive.

In the meantime northern Nubia witnessed an uninterrupted flow of Arab immigrants; until the end of the sixth/twelfth century, as long as the kingdom of al-Maḳurra still remained independent, this flow took rather a form of gradual infiltration of small Beduin groups. With the Mamluk interventions in the internal strife of the royal family, the Nubian kings became vassals or puppet rulers. In 715/1315 the Mamluks chose as Nubian king a prince who was already converted to Islam; this event heralded the beginning of the decline of Nubian Christianity. The passing of power into the hands of a Muslim turned Nubia from a *Dār al-ḥarb* to a *Dār al-Islām*; the payment of *d̲j̲izya* (poll tax) to the Muslim rulers of Egypt ceased.[74] The Islamization of the rulers also brought an end to the *baḳt*.

The disintegration of the northern Nubian kingdom, to which the earlier penetration of Arab tribesmen had substantially contributed, facilitated the great Arab breakthrough to the rich pasture lands beyond the Nubian desert. Although these Arab Beduins were nominally Muslim, there is no reason to suppose that their Islam was any less superficial than that of other nomads. They can hardly be considered as fanatical proselytizers for their faith. On the other hand the end of the Christian dynasty and thus the end of Christianity as a state religion must have greatly facilitated the acceptance of Islam by the sedentary population along the Nile Valley. Additional factors contributing to the decline of Nubian Christianity included the growing isolation from the outside world, and also the deterioration of the status of Christians in Egypt from where most of the higher clergy came. Christianity was not wiped out at once but it lingered on over a long period and rather died out by internal weakness. Its place was taken gradually by Islam. In the more southerly state of ʿAlwa it remained alive until the beginning of the tenth/sixteenth century when it was overthrown by the joint action of Arab 'tribesmen' and the Fund̲j̲.

At this time the Arab nomads had already penetrated into the D̲j̲azīra (Gezira), between the Blue and White Niles, as well as into the Buṭāna, between the Atbara River and the Blue Nile. There they settled in the

74. Ibn K̲h̲aldūn, 1956–9, Vol. 5, pp. 922–3.

metropolitan area of ʿAlwa and in Sennār and progressed to the south as far as the island of Aba on the White Nile. In a similar way the Arabs penetrated into Kordofān and southern Dārfūr.

In the wake of the nomadic Arabs came Muslim clerics and holy men. They arrived from or had studied in the older lands of Islam and they were the first to bring to this country some knowledge of the Holy Law (*sharīʿa*). The earliest of these pious missionaries was a Yemeni, Ghulām Allāh ibn ʿAyd, who came in the second half of the eighth/fourteenth century to the Dongola region; he found the Muslims in a state of ignorance due to lack of teachers.[75] In the following centuries the missionaries of *ṣūfī* orders began to settle in the Sudan and to contribute to the preaching of Islam. They succeeded in converting the Fundj, a dark-skinned people, whose immediate provenance was the upper Blue Nile. Under the rule of Fundj kings Islam was encouraged and many scholars and pious men migrated to their kingdom. By the tenth/sixteenth century the southern frontier of Islam was stabilized along the line of the 13°N parallel of latitude. The process of Islamization was accompanied by a process of Arabization that left its mark on a large part of the country.[76]

The Horn of Africa

The penetration of Islam into Ethiopia followed two major trade routes leading into the interior from the Dahlak Islands and Zaylāʿ. The Dahlak Islands had become Muslim at the beginning of the second/eighth century and at the same time other coastal places on the Red Sea shores began to be settled by Muslims, mostly of Arab or other non-African origin. From these centres Islam was propagated among the local, predominantly nomadic peoples along the coast, but the impact of Islamization was not strong until after the fourth/tenth century.

Although the great number of Arabic inscriptions found on the Dahlak Islands indicate the wealth and importance of the Muslim community which developed later into an effective sultanate,[77] the islands do not seem to have played a great role in the spread of Islam into the interior regions of Ethiopia. The main obstacle was the solid establishment of the Christian Church in northern Ethiopia among the Tigré-speaking and Amharic-speaking peoples. The rulers undoubtedly welcomed Muslim merchants from the coastal settlements – Dahlak being for a long time the only commercial outlet for the Ethiopian kingdom – but they forbade them to propagate their faith. Nevertheless in the third/ninth century Muslim communities had already emerged in the main centres and along the major trade routes. Trade in Ethiopia, and particularly the long-distance caravan

75. Y. F. Hasan, 1966, pp. 154–5.
76. On the spread of Islam in the Nilotic Sudan, cf. J. S. Trimingham, 1949.
77. On these inscriptions see B. Malmusi, 1895; G. Oman, 1974a, 1974b.

trade had been monopolized since these early times by Muslims as the Christian society had always looked down on commercial activities and crafts.[78] Traces of early Muslim communities have been found in the fully Christian province of Tigré;[79] the merchants presumably had freedom of movement and were allowed to settle with their families and servants in the Christian kingdom.[80]

While the Dahlak Islands were certainly the gateway for the founders of Muslim communities in northern Ethiopia, those in the south, in the Shoa province, must have received their inspiration from Zaylāʿ, an important port in the Gulf of Aden. In this respect Zaylāʿ has been of greater importance than Dahlak and it was in these southern parts of the Ethiopian region that Islam was destined to play a most prominent role.

The situation in the hinterland of Zaylāʿ was quite different from that prevailing in the north: it was a frontier region for both Christians and Muslims who started a struggle there to win for their respective faiths the souls of the large indigenous population with traditional religious beliefs. Side by side with this religious competition went the struggle for political and economic domination which was to continue for many centuries to come.

During the second/eighth and third/ninth centuries Islam became firmly established in the coastal areas of the Gulf of Aden; during the next centuries its political and religious significance in the whole region and especially in the interior increased. The conditions that allowed the growth of Islamic influence were partly internal, the decline of the Christian kingdom, and partly external, the rise of Fāṭimid power in the Red Sea followed by a revival of trade. More and more Muslim traders penetrated the southern interior, founding small communities and political units. This created favourable conditions for the arrival of Muslim clerics who began to convert the local people to Islam.

The early Muslim trading cities and principalities on the shores of the Gulf of Aden began to expand along the Harar plateau at the end of the fourth/tenth century. By the beginning of the next century the expansion of Islam had led to the founding of Muslim sultanates among the Semitic-speaking and Cushitic-speaking peoples of the region. A local Arabic chronicle maintains that the first prince of the sultanate of Shoa had already begun to rule at the end of the third/ninth century, but it is more likely that the foundation of this state came about only at the beginning of the sixth/twelfth century.[81] The ruling lineage claimed an origin from the well-known Ma<u>kh</u>zūmī family of Mecca. There were also other non-Ma<u>kh</u>zūmī principalities of Arab origin in this region.

78. Cf. M. Abir, 1970, p. 123.

79. M. Schneider, 1967.

80. Cf. al-Masʿūdī, 1861–77, Vol. 3, p. 34 on the Muslim families in 'Haba<u>sh</u>a' as tributaries to the local peoples.

81. E. Cerulli, 1941, pp. 5–14; cf. Chapter 20 below.

One of the more important Muslim kingdoms was that of Ifāt, whose rulers also claimed descent from the family of the Prophet Muḥammad through Abū Ṭālib; in 684/1285 its greatest Sultan, ʿUmar Walasma, annexed the sultanate of Shoa to the Ifāt state.

Arabic and Ethiopian sources indicate the existence of at least three Muslim kingdoms apart from Ifāt: Dawāro (to the west of the Harar region), Sharka in Arusi, and Bālī, south of Dawāro. In later times we find mention of some other states like Hadyā, Ārababnī and Darah. Hadyā in particular became famous after the seventh/thirteenth century as a centre of the slave trade.[82] Ifāt remained for a long time the leading Muslim state thanks to its strategic position on the important trade route leading from Zaylāʿ to the provinces of Amhara and Lasta as well as to other Muslim principalities.

Although from the seventh/thirteenth century on the Solomonid emperors gradually annexed the Muslim states and principalities in the south, the caravan trade on the plateau remained to a large extent in the hands of Muslims.

How far and deep the Islamization of the local people, apart from the merchants and courtiers, went in these early centuries, is difficult to assess. The chronicle of the Shoa sultanate reports major conversions in the interior only by the beginning of the sixth/twelfth century, especially on the eastern foothills of the Shoan plateau. In the Harar area Arab inscriptions dated to the seventh/thirteenth century bear witness to the existence of well-developed Muslim communities, thus confirming the importance of Harar as a diffusion centre of Islam in this area.[83] During the Christian offensive to the south Islam undoubtedly suffered losses in influence and numbers; it nevertheless continued to be professed by many ethnic groups not immediately touched by the offensive, like the Afar and Somali. When in the tenth/sixteenth century Aḥmad Grañ started his *djihād* against Christian Ethiopia, he was able to recruit into his army Afar and Somali from the plains as well as the various Semitic-speaking and Cushitic-speaking peoples from the plateau, who had long been under Islamic influence. Even if this attempt to found a Muslim Ethiopian empire in the end failed, the eastern and southern fringes of Ethiopia remained firmly in the Islamic orbit.[84]

While the early spread of Islam in Ethiopia can be traced with the help of written documents, the beginnings of Islamization of the Somali are more obscure. We certainly have some records of Arab geographers about coastal towns like Zaylāʿ, Berberā, Mogadishu, Brava and Marka, and even some dated inscriptions from these places, but as far as concerns developments in the interior where the great mass of the Somali were living, only some general traits can be deduced from historical traditions. There is no

82. Al-ʿUmarī, 1927, pp. 20ff.
83. R. P. Azaïs and R. Chambord, 1931, Vol. 1, pp. 125–9.
84. On the Islamization of Ethiopia cf. J. S. Trimingham, 1952.

doubt that the Somali groups living along the coast of the Gulf of Aden came very early into contact with Muslims. Arab and Persian merchants seem to have been the first settlers in coastal towns where they intermarried with local women and eventually merged with local Somali inhabitants. They brought with them Islam as a religion, and influenced the Somali living in these settlements and in the immediate hinterland, who gradually became Muslim, too. But it took some centuries before the impact of these Muslims achieved more permanent success. Somali traditions record that Shaykh Darod Ismāʿīl arrived from Arabia, settled among the Dir, the oldest Somali stock, married a Dir woman and later became the ancestor of a huge clan family called after him, Darod. This cannot be dated with certainty but it is generally accepted that this event occurred in the fourth/tenth or fifth/eleventh century. There is a similar tradition about the arrival, some two centuries later, of another Arab, Shaykh Isḥāḳ, the putative founder of the Isaq Somali, who settled to the west of the Darod.[85] Although many traits of these patriarchs are legendary, it appears that the traditions reflect a period of intensive Islamization among the northern Somali, as well as the growth and expansion of the Darod and Isaq clans at about this time. The creation of big clan families unified by the bond of Islam released the internal dynamic forces and prompted a general movement of these groups into the interior of the Horn in a generally southward direction. It can be surmised with some certainty that during these migratory movements, the already Islamized clan families exercised a proselytizing influence on the hitherto untouched Somali-speaking groups. How long it took is impossible to ascertain.

The Somali living along the Indian Ocean coast became acquainted with Islam from the coastal towns of Mogadishu, Brava and Marka in a similar way to their counterparts in the north. Already in the first half of the fourth/tenth century Arab and other Muslim merchants had established themselves in considerable numbers in these towns. These first settlers were later followed by many successive waves of immigrants from Arabia, Persia and even India. An eventual merging with the local inhabitants gave rise to a mixed Somali-Arab culture and society. It was not uniform throughout the coastal towns but its most important common feature was its Muslim character. These coastal towns, being primarily trading posts, must have been in regular contact with the Somali of the hinterland. Whether they contributed to the spread of Islam in the same degree as did the profoundly Islamized northern groups, remains unknown.

A special feature of Somali Islam is that it was not accompanied by Arabization. Although the Somali are proud of their traditions, which proclaim their descent from noble Arab lineages, and their language contains a large number of Arabic loan-words, they never lost their own ethnic identity, in contrast to what happened in North Africa or in the Nilotic Sudan.

85. E. Cerulli, 1957–64, Vol. 1, pp. 60–1.

This can be explained by the fact that the Arabs never migrated massively to the Horn of Africa but came rather as individuals, merchants or clerics, who were soon absorbed in Somali society.[86]

The East African coast and the Islands

The coming of Muslim Arabs and Persians to the East African coast and the Comoro Islands and Madagascar and their settlement there is discussed in detail in other chapters of this Volume.[87] Here we will be concerned only with the spread of Islam; in this respect the region offers – in the period under review – a picture widely different from the parts of tropical Africa already discussed. Whilst in the Sudan belt or among the Somali Islam gradually penetrated entire peoples and influenced more or less the lives of African ethnic groups, no corresponding impact was felt among the Bantu-speakers and other peoples of East Africa. True, Islam flourished here, but only as a religion of immigrants from overseas living in closed-class communities in coastal or insular settlements. Although archaeology as well as Arabic sources provide ample evidence for the Islamic character of many coastal towns stretching from Lamu to Mozambique, at the same time they confirm that Islam did not penetrate into the interior and that neither the Bantu-speakers nor any other ethnic groups were touched by this religion until the thirteenth/nineteenth century. Islam attained success only among those coastal peoples who came into immediate contact with the Arab and/or Persian expatriates in the towns. There are reports that even villages in the vicinity of Muslim settlements were inhabited by 'unbelievers' (*kāfir*s), victims of slave raids.[88]

The society of coastal cities was doubtless Islamic but not Arabic. The immigrants, never very numerous, intermarried with African women and became integrated with the local inhabitants. Their descendants of mixed blood soon abandoned Arabic for Kiswahili which gradually evolved as the lingua franca for all Muslim communities along the coast. But for a long time to come the Islamized element in East Africa was a tiny minority, which looked towards the ocean rather than to Africa itself.

An exception to this general rule was the penetration of Muslim, mostly Swahili merchants, into the hinterland of present-day Mozambique and into Zimbabwe. Chinese and Persian ceramics dated to the seventh/thirteenth and eighth/fourteenth centuries found in Zimbabwe are indications of commercial relations with the coastal settlements, particularly with Kilwa and its southern outposts like Sofala. Later, from the ninth/fifteenth

86. Many originally Arab families were gradually Somalized; the Mukrī clan, from which the chief *ḳāḍī* of Mogadishu has been always nominated, changed its name into a Somali one, Rer Faḳīh. Cf. J. S. Trimingham, 1952, p. 215.

87. Cf. Chapters 21 and 25 below.

88. Cf. Ibn Baṭṭūṭa, 1969, Vol. 2, p. 193.

century on, at the time of the decline of the Kilwa-Sofala gold monopoly, the traders based on Angoche and Mozambique entered into brisk trade contacts with the rising Mutapa empire. The Portuguese sources from the tenth/sixteenth century abound with accounts of the presence of thousands of 'Moorish' merchants active in the Mutapa empire whose competition was bitterly resented by the Portuguese. The importance of Muslim traders in the empire is shown also by the fact that the second wife of the *mwene mutapa* was minister for Muslim affairs. The majority of these traders were black Africans, either Swahili immigrants from the older coastal centres to the north, or local people who had adopted the international trading culture of Muslim urban societies.

The penetration of coastal Muslims into the interior of south-eastern Africa did not leave any discernible Islamic heritage among the peoples of the region. To all intents and purposes Islam failed to be accepted as a religion by the Africans in the interior in spite of their centuries-long contacts with Muslims. The traditional maxim that the spread of Islam followed the activities of Muslim traders seems not to be applicable to this area for reasons still to be investigated.

The coastal Muslims showed a more proselytizing spirit in the Comoro Islands. The 'Shirazi', to whom the Kilwa Chronicle ascribes the Islamization of Kilwa, are said also to have settled on Anjouan, and the local traditions on the islands confirm this in a general way. The chronology of these events is rather uncertain but it is likely that the first Muslims came around the seventh/thirteenth century; as everywhere they mixed with the local Malagasy and Africans on the islands and gave rise to a people known as Antalaotra ('people of the sea') whose language is a dialect of Kiswahili enriched by many Malagasy loan-words. According to recent studies the final Islamization of the Comoro Islands occurred in the ninth/fifteenth century.[89]

In spite of the considerable progress achieved during the last few decades in the study of Islam on Madagascar, there still remain more unanswered than answered questions. There is no doubt that Islamized peoples, be they of Arab or more likely of Kiswahili origin, were installing themselves from the fourth/tenth century onwards on the north-western coast and on nearby small offshore islands, as witnessed by archaeology, oral traditions and early Portuguese accounts. The culture of the first settlers offers many analogies with that of the East African coast between Lamu and Kilwa. On the north-eastern coast there flourished between the fifth/eleventh and eighth/fourteenth centuries a variant of the ancient Swahili culture of the north-west. The Islamized inhabitants of these settlements traded with East Africa, the Persian Gulf, South Arabia and East India exporting, in particular, vessels made from chlorite schists. From the north-east the Islamized peoples spread along the whole east coast as far as

89. Cf. C. Robineau, 1967.

Fort-Dauphin. The ebb and flow of the Muslim immigrants seems to have followed in a general way the expansion of the Indian Ocean trade network, particularly of its East African component.

The traditions of some Malagasy groups claim an Arab origin for their ancestors, not only in the north but especially in the south-east. Among these groups the most important are the Zafiraminia, the Onjatsy and the Antemoro. The 'Arab' immigrants were gradually assimilated to the local Malagasy population and all that remained of their Islamic civilization was the Arabic script – the *sorabe* – vague memories of the Qoran and some socio-religious practices (mostly in the field of geomancy and magic). The scribes (*katibo*) and soothsayers (*ombiasy*), specialists in the writing and interpreting of the *sorabe* were held in veneration – the veneration of the written word is a typically Islamic feature – but there are traces neither of any Islamic institutions nor of mosques. We could thus hardly speak of these groups as Muslims.

On the other hand, the Muslims in the north, being in continuous contact with the outside Islamic world, and strengthened by waves of new immigrants, retained their religion and even spread it to some of their Malagasy neighbours. The profoundly Islamic character of the settlements is confirmed by early Portuguese visitors in the tenth/sixteenth century, who spoke of many mosques and of *shaykh*s and *ḳāḍī*s as representatives of political and religious authority. As in the Comoro Islands, the inhabitants of these city-states were known as Antalaotra, an expression still used today to denote a category of Islamized inhabitants of Madagascar.

In conclusion it should be stressed that in Madagascar Islam did not play the same role as in other parts of tropical Africa where in the course of time it became the religion of entire ethnic groups and profoundly influenced African societies. It never superimposed its own culture over the Malagasy one; on the contrary, in more remote parts of the island a reverse process, i.e. the absorption of Islamized people by the local cultural milieu, can be observed.[90]

Conclusion

Between the first/seventh and tenth/sixteenth centuries Islam was established through large parts of Africa. Its dissemination had not been a uniform and linear process in all areas since in each part of Africa different methods, ways and agents were employed. We can roughly discern the following patterns of Islamization:

(1) The Arab conquest of Egypt and North Africa. Although it was

90. The problems of Islam and its influence on Madagascar are discussed in P. Vérin (ed.), 1967; and in Chapter 25 below. See also Unesco, *General History of Africa*, Vol. IV, ch. 24.

not accompanied by any enforced conversion of the Coptic and Berber autochthons, it nevertheless created social and economic conditions which in due course led to the acceptance of Islam by the majority of local peoples.

(2) The commercial activities of Muslims, firstly the long-distance or overseas trade, later the regional one, functioned as a stimulus to Islamization in much of tropical Africa. The first agents were merchants of Arab (in the east predominantly from Arabia itself), Persian (in the same region) and Berber (in the west) origin. From the fifth/eleventh century on, the proselytizing was continued through the activities of Muslim Africans: Soninke, Malinke, Fulani, Kānembu, Hausa, etc.

(3) The clerics or holy men were the first to introduce Islam among the Somali, whereas in other regions they contributed to the deepening of faith among already formally Islamized peoples (West Africa and eastern Sudan) and to spreading it further in the wake of merchants.

(4) In the Nilotic Sudan Islamization followed the penetration of Arab nomads, whereas in Somaliland the migrations of some clan families to the south were a contributory factor to the spread of the new faith to other groups.

In North Africa, in Nubia and in Ethiopia the incoming Muslims encountered a rival monotheistic faith, Christianity. The resistance of local Christians to Islamization varied according to local political and social conditions. In the Maghrib where the Christians represented only a minority (mostly of mixed or foreign origin), Islamization has been more complete and Christianity died out by the fifth/eleventh century. In Egypt the process took a longer time being accelerated only under the Fāṭimids; Islamization has never been complete, as about 10 per cent of Egyptians still belong to the Coptic Church.

In Christian Nubia, by contrast, the impact of Islam until the end of the seventh/thirteenth century was minimal but during the next two centuries Christianity gradually vanished, being superseded by Islam. Only in the Ethiopian highlands were the Christians able to resist. Neither the peaceful penetration of Muslim merchants nor the military campaigns of Muslim states to the south of the plateau shattered the fidelity of Ethiopians to the faith of their fathers. Although Christianity in Ethiopia emerged from this centuries-long struggle victorious, it remained an isolated outpost amidst a Muslim sea.

4

Islam as a social system in Africa since the seventh century

Z. DRAMANI-ISSIFOU

Islam as a religion, and thus as a constituent part of spiritual and social culture, is one of the fundamental aspects of modern African civilizations, to such an extent that many inhabitants of the continent often regard Islam and Africa as being a single entity. Indeed, Africa and the religion of Islam are old acquaintances. Even before the *hidjra* certain companions and converts, on the orders of the Prophet, had found refuge in Ethiopia at the court of the ruler of Axum. This little community of refugees, which included relatives of Muḥammad and some of the first Meccan converts to Islam, was very generously received by the sovereign. Hardly eight years after the death of the Prophet, Islam was gaining a firm foothold in Egypt; the conquest of the north of the African continent was to be completed during the following century.

Islam was carried by a people – the Arabs – who had in pre-Islamic times been the repository of varied forms of cultural life which arose in the desert and in the towns and which the Byzantines, the Persians, the Christians and the Jews had endeavoured to influence. The message of Islam was expressed in a language in which God had 'sent down His word'; quite apart from questions of linguistic pride,[1] it was invested with the certainty of having brought about a unified Arab culture. Islam could therefore be the bearer of a cultural hegemony which was a source of conflicts with other cultures rooted in other types of societies. The pre-Islamic cultures and societies dominated by Islam in the Near East were worthy of note, in particular, by reason of their written heritage. There is no need to dwell on the subject here. The case of African cultures and societies is more difficult to deal with. As in many other cases, the oral transmission of their knowledge, the implicit nature of their rich and ancient cultural life, means that factual evidence concerning them is often derived from external sources; in this instance, the evidence comes from Arab historiography which is

1. In order to form an adequate idea of the consequences of this sublimation of the Arabic language it is necessary to remember the immense effort made in the third/ninth century to translate into Arabic everything in pre-Islamic cultures that was of any significance. This is not without points of similarity with what had been accomplished by Latin-speaking Christians three or four centuries earlier.

marred by prejudice and by ideological assumptions which must be identified and clarified. If this is not done, there is once again the risk that the history of Africa will seem to be a history without any inherent originality and will appear, for long periods of time, as an 'object-history', the history of a land that was conquered, exploited and civilized. Indeed, since, unlike the inhabitants of the Near East and the Ethiopians, they did not possess a Book which is the pledge of a Divine revelation, the black Africans and their religion were, from the outset, categorized among the peoples without a respectable religion, incapable of acquiring the status of peoples 'protected' by Islam and therefore as hardly likely to possess respectable languages and cultures.[2]

Islam, African peoples and their cultures

Islam proclaims a profound unity which does not theoretically preclude cultural diversity. It strongly affirms the unity of the human race and recognizes all men as having an identical nature, created by God. They all belong to the 'race' of Adam to whom God has granted, in pre-eternity, the 'primordial pact'. At this level of theoretical generality the profound unity of Islam could not raise any problems for Africans. It did, on the other hand, raise very serious problems for the Egyptian Christians, the Ethiopians and in general for Christian and Jewish monotheists. The Sūra entitled 'The Table'[3] establishes a historical continuity after Abraham, through Moses, Jesus and Muḥammad, three Messengers of a single God. The human beings who received the message of the first two Prophets failed to remain faithful to it; the rigour imposed by the third Prophet concerning the observance of divine commands is explained both by man's tendency to infidelity and by the fact that the revelation through Muḥammad is, historically, the last.

Underneath this unity which, except for Christians and Jews, is easy to grasp and to accept, there appears a second level of contact with Islam: the observances that denote that one belongs to the Muslim community and thus, also, the possible prohibition on engaging in forms of religious life other than those required by the Qoran. The obligations are well known: they are contained in the 'five pillars' of Islam: the *shahāda* or profession of faith which is expressed in the affirmation 'there is no divinity but God, and Muḥammad is the Prophet of God'; the *ṣalāt* or set of ritual prayers,

2. This question is important in that it was one of the most hotly debated problems at the Arab-African Symposium held in Dakar from 9 to 14 April 1984 by the African Cultural Institute (ACI) and the Arab Educational, Scientific and Cultural Organization (ALECSO) on the subject of the 'relations between African languages and the Arabic language'. The general conclusions of the Symposium were that no African language suffered any adverse effect at all as a result of its contacts with the Arabic language. This view of the matter is one with which we do not at all agree.

3. Sūra 5.

five times a day; the fast of *Ramaḍān*, one month per year; the *zakāt* or legal almsgiving which provides for the support of the poor and of orphans; and, lastly, the *ḥādjdj*, or Pilgrimage to Mecca, once in a believer's lifetime, if this is materially possible. Unity in the faith and in religious practice, the fraternal solidarity among believers who are all 'brothers', hospitality and justice which flow from this sense of community: these, similarly, pose no serious theoretical problems. The social ideal of the Muslim faithful is seen as being adapted to the forces of human nature by practising mutual assistance, hospitality, generosity, the honouring of commitments towards members of the Community (*umma*), first, but towards other communities, too, and the tempering of desire. Beyond that, this ideal offers through *djihād* (the holy war)[4] and the sacrifice of one's life, the opportunity to transcend oneself. This is the expression of the profound unity which characterizes Islam and which gives it its uniqueness. This spirit of community is clearly compatible with deep-seated African traditions of social organization. Muslim texts coincide with underlying African assumptions: in the *ḥadīth* of Gabriel, al-Bukhārī wrote that Islam is also 'giving food [to the hungry] and giving the greeting of peace [*salām*] to those whom one knows and to those whom one does not know'[5] or again: 'None of you becomes a true believer if he does not desire for his [Muslim] brother what he desires for himself'.[6] However, this unity coexists with a truly personal moral responsibility; no one can be charged with the fault of another; everyone must be responsible for his own actions. Thus, the sense of community, the feeling that one is part of a whole, is united, as though by a dialectical process, with a concern for one's own destiny and for one's own obligations. The believer is aware of being in a personal relationship with God who will require him to give an account of himself.

It must at the outset be noted that the act of embracing Islam is an individual one; if it is to be a responsible act it must be freely chosen: moral and physical coercion are prohibited by the Qoran. But it is also an irreversible act: it is a *social* conversion which denotes the act of joining a community of a new type and severing links with other types of socio-cultural community. This is a fundamental point at issue for the relations between the Muslim world and the societies and cultures of Africa. *Historical* situations are certainly varied, both in time and space. An African of a different religion could not be forced to embrace Islam; however, his religious status – without a Scripture – made him entirely dependent on Islam and with no protection *vis-à-vis* the Muslim community.

We have thus moved towards a third and much more dramatic level of contacts: that of the law. It was almost three centuries before legal rules were established in the Muslim world in accordance with the Qoran and the teachings of the Prophet – the *Sunna*. These rules involved a compila-

4. *Djihād* means literally: 'effort to achieve a certain aim'; cf. Chapter 2 above.
5. Al-Bukhārī, 1978, Vol. 2, p. 37.
6. Al-Nawāwī, 1951, pp. 21, 33, 36, 42, 43.

tion of 'all the [Prophet's] sayings, deeds, ways of eating, drinking, dressing, accomplishing his religious duties and of treating both believers and unbelievers'.[7] The law – *sharī'a* – gathers together the Qoranic prescriptions[8] supplemented by the prohibitions and clarifications contained in the jurisprudence – *fiḳh*. The law has been interpreted by four schools of jurisprudence in varying ways and in a spirit which differed in its degree of literalness and rigour. One interesting feature of the debate on the relationship between Islam and African societies is that the legal schools of jurisprudence with which the Africans had to deal were not the same in the west of the continent as they were in the east. The west, from the Maghrib to West Africa, bore the deep and almost exclusive imprint of Mālikism. The Māliki school, which was more formalistic than certain other juridical schools, particularly after its triumphs in the fifth/eleventh century, was brought in conjunction with Sunnism to a high degree of intransigence by the jurists (*fuḳahā'*). These played a highly important role, in particular from the fifth/eleventh to the tenth/sixteenth century. To the east, Shāfi'ism, which was strongly established in Egypt and was more liberal, was generally predominant in the Horn of Africa and on the East African coast. Numerous subtle distinctions can probably be accounted for by this fact.

Lastly, it must be added that the fifth/eleventh century witnessed a movement in two directions which are contradictory only in appearance. On the one hand, the increasing rigour of Sunnism, from the time when the Turks became dominant in Baghdad, which was ultimately triumphant and which tended to impose uniformity, through the law, on the authority of the state and on education, and a single Muslim rite; on the other hand, the reappearance of mystic currents of thought – sufism – which had long been opposed and which sought to express religious feeling through asceticism and rejection of the world. The Maghrib was the first to extend a warm welcome to these mystics.[9] In the seventh/twelfth century ṣūfī brotherhoods began to appear, the first of which was that of the Ḳādirīyya, associated with Baghdad; in Morocco, the Shadhiliyya brotherhood was popularized by al-Djazūlī in the ninth/fifteenth century and played both a political and a religious role. Both these fifth/eleventh-century trends had profound repercussions on the relations between Islam and African societies. The first, which was dominated by Mālikism, made the Muslim community more intransigent in its dealings with African cultural traditions.

7. R. Blachère, 1966, p. 92.

8. The juridical conditions governing the life of the Muslim individual in his community are defined in the Mu'āwalāt of the Qoran. These consist mainly of Sūras 2, 4 and 5 and of some 500 verses.

9. According to H. Massé, 1966, p. 175: 'Perhaps in no other Muslim country was the cult of saints taken to greater extremes; it can be said without hesitation that it constitutes the sole religion of rural people, particularly women accompanied by the rites of animism and nature worship'.

The other spread with great success the cult of holy men – the bearers of the blessing (*baraka*) that was equal to that which the *ḥādjdjīs* derive from the Pilgrimage. These took on the role of healers and divines and thus Islamized certain very ancient aspects of the daily life of the Africans. In the eyes of simple people who are always ready to believe in miracles, the saints and *marabouts* seemed more accessible than the majestic and distant God of Islam. More important still, the cult of local saints sometimes negated the obligation of the Pilgrimage to Mecca and sometimes incorporated an earlier cult. In this way there developed first in the Maghrib and then, particularly after the eleventh/seventeenth century in West Africa, the character of the *marabout*,[10] a dominant social figure of western Islam.

Thus the development of Islamic law, its sponsorship of specialists supported by the state, and the rise of mysticism, concern the life of African societies much more intimately than faith or mere observance. In these doctrinal matters the meeting was not to be as easy as earlier meetings had been. The danger here was one of confusion between the norms of the social life of the Near East and the faith of Islam.

There was a risk that a fourth dimension would play a part: that of cultural emulation of the Arab model, thus implying renunciation of African cultural traditions and total endorsement of the values of the Arab world whether they were regarded as desirable and superior or whether they were imposed. In this context there was a possibility of confusion between Arabization and Islamization.

This is something that can be gauged even before one embarks on an analysis of the process whereby Islam became established as a social system in Africa; it was a meeting between peoples, cultures and societies of different traditions, a meeting the results of which depended on the extent to which each side was able to distinguish between what was merely cultural and what was of general religious significance, and this was ultimately a question of the permeability of African societies and cultures, which were in no sense passive, to the new influences that came from the east.[11] This also means that any approach to Islam as a social system implies a study of

10. The word does not have the same sense in the Maghrib and in black Africa. In the former it applies both to the saintly founder of the brotherhood and his tomb; in sub-Saharan Africa it denotes any person more or less versed in knowledge of the Qoran and other sacred texts and who uses such knowledge to act as an intermediary between the believer and God, while at the same time drawing on the traditional lore of divination and on the practice of talismans. He is regarded by the public as a scholar, in the religious sense of the term, as a magician and as a healer.

11. Many assumptions and propositions have taken this theme as their foundation. The question whether a black Islam existed has been examined. To do so is perhaps to overlook the monolithic nature of the religion in question and to dwell more on the sociological aspects of its place in the world than on the metaphysical and theological aspect of the matter. The very clear approach which is that adopted in this Volume – the social system – seems, at the present state of knowledge, to accord better with the conclusions that can be drawn today.

the phenomena of Islamization and conquest, the meeting of peoples. The fact of geographical co-existence made it inevitable that there would be dialogue between Muslims of diverse origins and between Muslims and non-Muslims through the delineation of Islamic space within which the following problem is posed: is there, or is there not, unity in the monolithic meaning of the term or is there unity in diversity?

A period of easy co-existence: the fifth/eleventh century

The tenacious struggle of the Berbers against certain forms of Islamization[12] has all too often been cited as evidence to support the claim that in black Africa the conquest was violent. In fact, the Arabs often halted in their progress southwards when they encountered resistance which was too difficult to overcome in historical and political contexts that were unknown, little known or difficult to control: hence their very limited incursions towards Nubia, towards the Fezzān and Kawār, towards the Sūs and the western Sahara.[13] In these regions, the leaders of the empire applied the same policy as they did north of the Pyrenees or in central Asia: being aware of the risks inherent in massive military defeats, they confined themselves to incursionary expeditions entrusted to small groups. In spite of the triumphal tone in which some of these incursions were later celebrated, they did not have far-reaching effects and their results were in most cases compromises which provided a safe means of supplying the Muslims with slaves[14] but which ensured that the populations of the south enjoyed peace. The Islamization of the north of the continent in Egypt and in the Maghrib, took, in the long term, forms which are considered in other chapters of this Volume.[15]

In fact, the penetration of Islam into black Africa had very complex and essentially non-violent aspects during this initial period as is shown by many recent studies:[16] the Berbers of the desert, or those of them who embraced Islam, the Ibāḍite or Ṣufrite merchants, and the representatives of Fāṭimid interests played roles that were different but were not marked by significant violence. Opinions vary even on the methods employed by the Almoravids in their dealings with the black peoples at the end of this

12. See Chapter 3 above.
13. See Chapter 3 above.
14. About 500 slaves a year delivered to Aswān by the King of Nubia; 360 – a symbolic figure – delivered by the Fezzān and by Kawār (Ibnʿ Abd al-Ḥakam, 1948, p. 63); in other words a total of some 1300 to 1500 slaves a year.
15. See Chapters 3 above, Chapters 7 and 9 below.
16. See Chapter 3 above and T. Lewicki, 1981; D. C. Conrad and H. J. Fisher, 1982, 1983. These authors have tried to show that the Almoravid episode was not as violent as has hitherto been claimed. Cf. Z. Dramani-Issifou, 1983b; 'The historical relations between the Arabic language and African languages', report to the Arab-African symposium in Dakar (cf. note 2 of the present chapter). In that report see principally notes (11) and (26). See also A. R. Ba, 1984.

first period. There has no doubt been too great a tendency to rely on historical writings that were of wholly Arab or Arab-Berber origin and were strongly influenced by the victory of the believers over the unbelievers, even if they were 'people of the Book' and the glorification of certain heroes, the most popular of whom and the most widely celebrated in mythology was ʿUḳba ibn Nāfiʿ.

This situation has given rise to a muted and subtle debate in which there are differing ideological assumptions. The debate involves two opposing tendencies in historical explanation, or rather interpretation, of the conversion of Mediterranean Africa to Islam. In general, Eastern and Middle Eastern historians, whether Arabs or otherwise, those from the regions of Africa which have come under the cultural influence of the Middle East (Egypt, the Sudan, Libya and Tunisia) and those of the rest of the Maghrib who are in addition specialists in Islamic studies, have difficulty in accepting – or unequivocally reject – the thesis of the Arab conquest as a preliminary to the conversion of populations. In support of their point of view they argue that Islam does not allow conversions by force. The other specialists in African history, almost all of them, like the former, specialists in Muslim matters and the expansion of Islam, are divided between those who support their analyses by referring to the phenomenon of the conquest and those who accept the conquest as a fact but view it in its correct historical proportions as a long-term phenomenon. The latter include Westerners, sub-Saharan Africans and, to a very limited extent, historians of the Maghrib (particularly Morocco) specializing in Berber studies. Is this no more than an academic dispute? We do not think so and we believe that this debate is important for the understanding of the entire range of human and cultural factors which brought the Arabs into contact with the peoples of Africa. In short, we think that the encounter between these peoples was initially more a political and economic matter than a religious one.

In fact, in the early centuries, the Muslim world had preoccupations which were very different north of the Sahara on the one hand, and south of the Sahara and in East Africa on the other.

In the first case the strategic considerations were of immense importance both as a springboard for further expansion towards Spain, the Mediterranean islands and Italy and for the defence of a bastion against any return of the warring Christians who remained a constant threat.

Seen from this twofold standpoint, Egypt occupied a position of worldwide importance of which the Byzantines were well aware. It was vital to keep Egypt within the House of Islam – *Dār al-Islām* – and its inhabitants had to be induced, by the most varied means, not to break the agreement obtained from them at the time when the Arab troops established themselves. Here the highly structured organization of the Islamic community predominated; Christians and Jews were obliged to take their part in it as *d͟himmī*.

In a few centuries, the Berbers occupied vast areas from the Atlantic to the Nile; they travelled through them and controlled them by means of the camel. They led highly varied forms of life ranging from the completely sedentary to the fully nomadic.[17] To the north of the African continent they were also obliged to conform to the warlike and therefore political demands of the *Dār al-Islām*; although efforts were made by the orthodoxy to eliminate the dangerous – and persistent – traces of religious syncretism, the Berbers were allowed to retain for a long time a degree of originality within Islam and a certain linguistic autonomy. Moreover, for a long time a tolerant view was taken of their respect for traditions which did not affect the essential features of Muslim life. A striking example concerning Ibn Tūmart is given by Ibn Khaldūn:

> He took pleasure in frequenting the mosques and, in his youth, he was given the nickname of Asafu, that is to say, Brightness, because of the large number of candles that he was in the habit of lighting.[18]

Ibn Tūmart was thus showing a traditional Berber fondness for lights to which Saint Augustine had also referred.[19] Other and more far-reaching examples of the survival of these practices may be cited. In certain tribes of the Awrās, of Kabylia, of the Nile and the Atlas, the Berbers preserved their language and their customs, the sources of their originality. For instance, customary law and non-Qoranic judicial organization are characteristic features of Berber law as exemplified by the collective oath as a means of proof, as are the regulations and scale of penalties known by the name of *lḳānūn* (*ḳānūn*), and justice administered by judge-arbiters or village assemblies. Such customs did not come into conflict with Qoranic law, but they may have constituted an element of resistance to the standardizing progress of Mālikīte Sunnism in the Almoravid period;[20] in any case, we find these features reflected in the organization of the Almohad empire. In return for this relative liberty,[21] the Berbers of the north allowed themselves to be integrated, and granted their military assistance even though the latter was sometimes the subject of bargaining between rival princes, in particular in the fourth/tenth and fifth/eleventh centuries. After the major confrontations of the second/eighth century, the territorial and political integration of the Berbers of the north was more or less an accomplished fact; it was vital for the Muslim world.[22]

17. See Chapter 9 below.
18. Ibn Khaldūn, 1925–56, Vol. 2, p. 163.
19. For denunciation of funeral feasts in the cemetery with candles, see J.-P. Migne (ed.), Vol. 33, p. 91.
20. The Mālikite school considers *al-ʿamal*, the customary usages, as one of the juristic principles. The appeal to a custom is possible if it does not contradict Islam; it was thus thanks to the Mālikism that Berber customs were recognized in North Africa.
21. See Chapter 3 above, Chapter 9 below.
22. See Chapter 3 above, Chapter 9 below.

South of the Atlas and on the East African coast there was no imminent danger that required comparable policies. The mass of the nomadic Berbers to the west joined Islam fairly quickly. Arabic sources remain vague on this point. Even Ibn Khaldūn contradicts himself: he says, on the one hand that the Lamtūna 'embraced Islam some time after the conquest of Spain by the Arabs'[23] and on the other, that they were converted 'in the third century of the *hidjra*'.[24] As T. Lewicki shows, it appears from the present stage of research that the Islamization of the Berbers in contact with the black populations began during the years 117/735–122/740. This was a beginning, for during the same decade the Massūfa Berbers resisted Islam.[25] Thus, there was no haste and no pressure to achieve integration: as late as the eighth/fourteenth century, Ibn Baṭṭūṭa noted that, in more than one respect, the social traditions of the desert Berbers which he, as a Muslim, found deeply shocking, remained intact: Muslim law was not strictly respected, still less so the rules of marriage and the Arab principles of decency.[26]

The Muslims, therefore, had strong reasons for showing prudence when they entered regions of the continent inhabited by peoples with a strong cultural and social identity – even if more than one author found this coherent identity surprising – and where, contrary to what was for a long time thought and written, there existed ancient states that were as powerful as those in North Africa or in Western Europe at the same date. The world of the Soninke, to the west, that of the Zaghāwa or the Kānembu in the centre, that of the Bantu-speakers to the east, surprised the Muslims who were not slow in making major ethnographical descriptions of them. They did not seek to convert them and still less to make them abandon their religious, cultural and social practices, before the sixth/twelfth century. For a long time they were content to coexist as merchants, a situation which was of benefit to them and in which they enjoyed for the most part cordial relations with the black princes and merchants. This policy, moreover, was not without benefit even from the religious point of view. We are now gaining a better knowledge of the ways in which the conversion took place, probably in the tenth century, of the princes and merchants in the Senegal Valley.[27] We are also well aware of the case of Gao. The historian Ibn al-Ṣaghīr wrote in 290/902–3 a chronicle on the Rustumid *imāms* of Tāhert. He mentions that between 159/776 and 166/783 there were commercial relations between Tāhert and Gao, the ruler of which claimed to be a Muslim.[28]

At Kānem, the rulers converted to Islam, probably during the fifth/

23. Ibn Khaldūn, 1925–56, Vol. 2, p. 65.
24. ibid., p. 67.
25. See Chapter 3 above, Chapter 11 below.
26. J.-L. Moreau, 1982, p. 99.
27. See Chapter 3 above, Chapter 13 below.
28. J. M. Cuoq, 1975, pp. 55–6; Chapter 3 above; T. Lewicki, 1962, p. 515; Z. Dramani-Issifou, 1982, pp. 162–4.

eleventh century, even before the change of dynasty which brought Hummay (478/1085–490/1097) to power;[29] the latter may have been responsible merely for the introduction of Sunnism, in which case the event was contemporary with what was being done further west by the Almoravids. It is likely that trade in the region of Lake Chad played an important role in Islam's progress southwards. To some extent, conversion was a means of protecting oneself against being sold into slavery, a flourishing trade on the route between Lake Chad and the Mediterranean according to al-Ya'ḳūbī,[30] as early as the third/ninth century. This is a form of social change for African societies, somewhat unexpected for Islam but undoubtedly important.[31] It did not probably play the same role at that time in East Africa as there was a decline in the sale of Zandj slaves after the revolt which bears their name and which ravaged Iraq in the third/ninth century.[32] Equally reliable information is not at present available on this period concerning the East African coast and Madagascar as for West and Southern Africa, apart from interesting descriptions such as that of al-Mas'ūdī.

Thus, without wars, without violent proselytism, Islam advanced on African soil prior to the sixth/twelfth century.[33] These advances had no decisive bearing on *Dār al-Islām*; they were not irreversible; they took far greater account of princes and merchants than of cultivators. At least it can be said that, before the great efforts to extend *Dār al-Islām* which developed from the fifth/eleventh century onwards, certain major achievements had been made. Coexistence had had more striking results than may appear even if it was accompanied by major compromises.

Often what took place was no more than a formal conversion of the prince: the anecdote relating to the conversion of a chief of Mallal, which is cited several times by Arab authors, eloquently bears out this point;[34] later we shall refer to the somewhat surprising fact that the Mansa of Mali, when in Cairo during the Pilgrimage, showed a very superficial knowledge

29. D. Lange, 1977, p. 99.

30. J. M. Cuoq, 1975, pp. 48–9.

31. For the region of Chad, this fact is of great historic interest judging by the persistent references in the source literature, until the modern age, of the sale of slaves from the regions of central Africa.

32. See Chapter 1 above, Chapter 26 below.

33. The range of problems posed in general terms by the relations between the populations of Mediterranean Africa, the Sahara and Sudanic Africa (chronology, nature of these relations, formation of states, etc.) have been raised and discussed with the help of appropriate hypotheses by a considerable number of researchers. Among the most recent, the following may be mentioned: T. Lewicki, 1976; J. Ki-Zerbo, 1978; J. Devisse, 1982; Z. Dramani-Issifou, 1982. There are certainly many others whom we have not mentioned, but we draw the reader's attention in particular to the constructive scientific quality of the studies by two young Senegalese researchers on Takrūr and its associated problems. These are Y. Fall, 1982, pp. 199–216 and A. R. Ba (1984) in his thesis on Takrūr.

34. J. M. Cuoq, 1975, pp. 102 and 195–6. See also Chapter 3 above.

of the Muslim rules of life.[35] If this is true of the princes who were soon to be criticized by pious jurists for their 'false Islam', what is to be said of the 'converted' merchants who were loyal associates for short-term commercial purposes but were probably rather superficial Muslims. As for the rural world, there was no question of influencing its beliefs and practices: that would have meant disrupting an entire society and its modes of production. It remains possible, moreover, like a king of the Kongo in relation to Christianity at the end of the fifteenth century, that the rulers who converted to Islam saw a very definite advantage in doing so: they were thereby enabled to shed the numerous obligations inherent in the exercise of power in Africa, with its organized counterbalances that controlled its execution, and not to share the advantages of the new faith with their dependants. Up to a certain point Islam was able, as long as there were no strong religious counterbalances south of the Sahara, to exalt the ancient powers and even the authority of kingship: the question is one that warrants serious study.

Other types of compromise, even more important, emerge from Arab sources. It is an often repeated commonplace to refer to the disappearance of gold when the producers were converted to Islam. This possibility was equally disastrous for the north (as the client) and for the rulers who were the middlemen. Thus the gold producers were not converted, and they were very numerous.[36] In the eighth/fourteenth century thought was given to endowing this exceptional situation with an appearance of legality: al-ʿUmarī explains that the Mansa of Mali tolerated in his empire 'the existence' of populations still practising traditional religions which he exempted from the ṭax that was imposed on unbelievers but which he employed in gold-mining.[37] The situation appears to have remained much the same until quite recent times. The fundamental reason really is that gold prospecting and production were accompanied by a number of magical operations and were bound up with a system of beliefs of which we can still discern traces.[38]

The same applied to iron which provides perhaps an even clearer example than gold. In many areas, accounts describing power relations indicate the close association between royal authority and the master smelters and smiths. The figure of the 'blacksmith' is also associated with magic, with the dangerous power of the ironmasters. With the passage of time, this 'type' becomes more and more antithetical to that of the *marabout*; in 1960 the Soviet scholar D. Olderogge drew attention to this opposition and developed a parallel line of reasoning to the above.[39]

The *marabout* – or, more simply, the bearer of Muslim law – was to

35. Al-ʿUmarī in J. M. Cuoq, 1975, pp. 273 *et seq.*
36. See Chapter 14 below.
37. Al-ʿUmarī in J. M. Cuoq, 1975, pp. 280–1.
38. J. Devisse, 1974.
39. D. Olderogge, 1960, pp. 17–18.

eliminate the influence of the iron-worker: as A. R. Ba showed in his thesis, 'Le Takrūr des Xe–XIe siècles', Islamization as it was becoming established, even if it remained urban and gregarious, seems to have been accompanied by a break in the earlier alliance between royal power and the iron-workers. The latter were first debarred from all political influence and were feared on account of their magical and economic power and gradually formed an isolated group hemmed about by prohibitions but still feared. They were not excluded from economic life, since their role was essential. Gradually there arose around them the notion of caste: in the twelfth/eighteenth century, their religious and social isolation was considerable: the contempt in which they were held provides an indication of the fear inspired by their magic and their longstanding reputation as men of power. This example probably indicates what a long and slow process was the introduction of the Muslim social system, and how cautious it was when it first came into contact with such deep-rooted habits; it may also provide a different insight into the account of the confrontations between the Sumaoro, surrounded by 'bad pagan blacksmiths' and Sundiata who was also an ironmaster but no longer gave in to pressures from adherents of traditional religions. Hence the importance of the theoretical battle that was joined concerning the personal commitment of the Sundiata to Islam.

The groups of Muslim merchants established south of the desert ultimately agreed to live there in minority communities that were partly Islamized by the Africans but in no way dominant; they accepted, from the autochthonous rulers a treatment comparable to that accorded to Christian or Jewish minorities in Islamic lands but were probably excused the payment of taxes. This explains the success of the Muslim quarters, close to the royal cities and in many cases with their own mosques, which did not however exert any pressure on the population as a whole.

The Ibāḍites[40] clearly played a major role during this period. Their easy relationship with the *Sūdān* (Negroes) may be noted with some surprise, particularly as they behaved with such acrimony towards other Muslims. This is probably one indication of the excellent relations which, for centuries, the Saharan Berbers maintained with the black populations.

Ibāḍite sources that have recently emerged from the obscurity in which religious orthodoxy kept them for centuries[41] give a good account of the situation. They provide examples of genuine mutual religious tolerance and of a large measure of understanding – which would probably have been intolerable from the point of view of the Mālikite Sunnis – towards African cultures impregnated with traditional religion designated as 'pagan' and their social practices.

After the brilliance of the Fāṭimid fourth/tenth century, so important for Africa, things changed everywhere with the triumph in the fifth/eleventh

40. The founder of this sect was 'Abdallāh ibn Abāḍ, but as the spelling Ibāḍ (and Ibāḍites) is traditionally adopted, we continue to use it.

41. T. Lewicki, various works (see bibliography), and see Chapter 11 below.

century of Sunni orthodoxy and the emergence of religious phenomena that were far less ready to display tolerance, such as the Almoravid movement, at least in its African aspects. Even in East Africa, the sixth/twelfth century saw a hardening of Muslim attitudes towards African cultures and societies. This was the beginning of a second period in which the efforts of Islam were increasingly directed towards the standardization of patterns of life in the lands under its control.

Social and cultural tensions related to the success of Islam after the middle of the fifth/eleventh century

The causes of tension

If the *ḥadīth* which states that 'the angels do not enter a house where there is a dog' were to be taken literally, there would have been no future for contact between Islam and the peoples of Africa since, in African societies, dogs are a permanent feature of domestic life. It is also to be noted that Islam resolutely opposed the excessive manifestations of the keeping of dogs, in particular cynophagy.

Everything depended in the last analysis in the social sphere on the permeability of African societies to any changes proposed or imposed by Islam since there were no obstacles in principle to the adoption of Islam's belief in a single God.

The black African societies which were penetrated by Islam were rural; they had functional links with the land and with all features of their immediate environment (mineral, vegetable, air and water). In these agrarian cultures, based on the oral tradition, it may be possible to see analogies with certain socio-cultural aspects of the pre-Islamic Arab World. That does not mean that the social structures of the Islamic world resembled those of Africa. In African societies the nuclear family – man, wife, children – was unknown as an autonomous unit; the extended family consisting of the descendants of a common ancestor bound together by ties of kinship and land, was the basic component, united by a high degree of economic solidarity. The history of the flourishing of these basic social groups, up to the limits of segmentation, the history of the various ways in which they associated together in larger groups, recognizing a common ancestor – more or less fictive – or working a common stretch of terrain, need not be retold here. The important thing is that these communities, whatever their size, considered that their bonds – even if they were fictive – were religious and were shared by the totality of their ancestors, the living and children as yet unborn, in an unbroken chain of generations, having a sacred bond with the soil, with the bush, and with the waters, which provided food and were objects of worship. These socio-religious structures could not be dissociated without destroying the entire balance of their life;

they had a sense of oneness, thanks to a long historical awareness of a common past and the slow pace of the changes to which they were subject. Beside them, other more complex societies existed: those in which favourable geo-economic conditions had made it possible to amass reserves that justified the existence of social categories specializing in distinct tasks. Some categories were socio-economic in nature and ensured an increasing division of labour. Others were socio-religious: they maintained, through the activity of magicians, diviners, healers and intercessors between the visible and the invisible, a social cohesion that would otherwise have been threatened by the division of labour; still others represented a more highly developed political organization than in the purely agrarian societies. In all cases, however, the African man retained his vision of the world as a vast confrontation of forces that were to be exorcised or exploited. As Joseph Ki-Zerbo rightly puts it: 'in this ocean of dynamic and conflicting currents [man] made himself into a fish in order to swim'.[42] Within two different frameworks, one more urban and the other always rural, African societies have taken widely divergent forms depending on whether the people were savanna-dwellers or forest-dwellers, sedentary or nomadic, cultivators or stock-raisers, hunter-gatherers or members of an urban community. Very often, however, the unity of the religious perception of social relationships prevailed over differences in material detail; very often, the role of the mother and the woman in the transmission of property remained considerable. The forms of life remained very remote from that of the clan and of the patrilineal family of the Arabs with which Islamic law is in almost perfect harmony.

It was, of course, in this field that tensions and conflicts arose, particularly when, above all in West Africa, pressure was exerted by Muslim jurists who would have liked to induce the Africans to commit themselves more fully to a 'model of society' which such jurists assumed to be Islamic even though it was perhaps primarily Near Eastern. However, the forms taken by these tensions varied widely from one region to another and at different times, depending also on relationships of strength of every kind, primarily numerical, between Muslims and non-Muslims, and between Muslims from the east and the north and African Muslims. Thus, when we endeavour to appraise the way in which Islam transformed or failed to transform the societies of black Africa, we are dealing with a rich and complex history.

When the scene of events was a town, it was probably permissible in the fourth/tenth century, as it is today in Rwanda,[43] to abandon any reference to ancient rural alliances and to change one's name and merge into a new Islamic community which satisfied all one's needs, and to establish in that community, when the time came, a new family on new ideological founda-

42. J. Ki-Zerbo, 1978, p. 177.
43. J. Kagabo, 1982.

tions. The change of name permits an elegant and simple transfer, from the social point of view, from the original community to the Muslim community.[44] In Sahelian Africa, this transfer seems to have been easy but, rightly, it does not denote a total break: a Muslim name, strongly Africanized – Muḥammad sometimes becomes Mamadu, ʿAlī becomes Aliyu[45] – is added to the existing African names: these are only Islamized in the long term and in accordance with very precise codes. The process is one of slow fusion whether in the case of kings, merchants or rural dwellers, even later than the sixth/twelfth century. The same was not the case in other regions of the continent where onomastic breaks were massive and dramatic.[46] The Muslims themselves were, of course, divided as to the attitude to be adopted towards the African socio-cultural traditions. The jurists from the north, armed with their learning and proud of the society they represented, tended to see in the 'non-conformist' actions of black societies the proof that they belonged to a world that was alien to Islam and must be opposed; the black Muslims who were born in these societies and who wished to live in them, sometimes as small and tolerated minorities, were much more inclined to regard the practices of African religions as not constituting a real obstacle to the acceptance of Islam; their tolerance might be very extensive and their coreligionists from the north readily accused them of permissiveness, of collusion or even of treason to Islam. It was, however, the latter rather than the former who, as we shall see, ensured the most lasting successes of Islam from the sixth/twelfth to the tenth/sixteenth century.

Juridical intransigence, indeed, was a cause of extreme tension over the question of altering the matrilineal rules of succession in favour of the patrilineal practices imposed by the Qoran. No comprehensive study has yet been made showing the successive stages of this conflict which undoubtedly arose as early as the fifth/eleventh century and whose most celebrated instance was the consultation of al-Māghilī to which we shall refer later: the author stated that those who rejected Muslim legislation and applied a matrilineal line of inheritance were not Muslims.[47] Pressure on this matter was clearly exerted first of all on those who held power: genealogies reveal hesitation between the two forms of succession.[48]

It was probably in connection with the concept of the ownership of goods that the incompatibility between one society and the other proved the strongest. When al-Bakrī spoke of the 'bizarre decisions' of ʿAbdallāh ibn Yāsīn,[49] he displayed the distaste of an individual and individualistic

44. In Somalia this change was total.

45. Ben Achour, 1985. This is not restricted to black Africans only. In Berber languages Muḥammad becomes Ḥammū, Moḥa, Mūḥ; Fāṭima becomes Ṭamū, Ṭima, etc.

46. These examples are strictly comparable in the case of the conversion to Christianity, for example after 1930 in Rwanda-Burundi.

47. J. M. Cuoq, 1975, p. 424.

48. J. M. Cuoq, 1975, p. 344, for example.

49. Al-Bakrī, 1913, pp. 319 *et seq.*; cf. Chapter 13 below.

owner towards 'socializing' forms, equality and the redistribution of property which the Almoravid cleric wished to impose. All the more reason, then, that the African community of land, work and harvests was barely comprehensible to Muslims accustomed to individual family and urban wealth. Once more, the consultation of al-Māghilī raises, in different terms, the problem of the ownership of goods and his reply was, once again, a radical one.[50]

The apparently milder protests against 'African immorality' were equally ineffectual: the excessive laxity in the behaviour of women, their failure to wear the veil,[51] nudity among adolescents; Arab writers could do no more than record[52] or denounce[53] the 'scandals' which offended their sight.

At all these levels underlying their respective and hardly compatible forms of organization, the differences between Arab-Muslim societies and African societies, whether they were Muslim or otherwise, remained unreconciled between the sixth/twelfth and the tenth/sixteenth centuries. They no doubt tended to see these opposing forms of social life as indicating an incompatibility between Islam and African religion.

The role played by African rulers

Whether friends of Islam or Muslims, from the fourth/tenth century in the Takrūr, or from the sixth/twelfth century in Mali, for example, African rulers in general accepted fairly readily a division of space and labour which ensured that the administrators they required would be available to them in the towns which had been wholly or partly Islamized, while the rural world constituted an inexhaustible source of compliant agricultural manpower whose conversion was not a matter of urgency. Islamic practice seems to have adjusted to this situation: after all, it recognized a privileged territory – *Dār al-Islām* – side-by-side with the territory inhabited by the infidels and the pagans – *Dār al-Kufr*, *Dār al-ḥarb*. Being content with the conversion of the princes who, in the long term, were the guarantors of the conversion of the masses, Islam probably adopted a 'pastoral' attitude which was also to be found in Christian Europe at the same periods.[54]

African rulers, even if they were Muslims, cannot by any stretch of the

50. J. M. Cuoq, 1975, pp. 410 *et seq.*

51. Veil wearing is not a religious obligation in Islam and the veiling of women as understood in some Muslim countries, is not orthodox.

52. Ibn Baṭṭūṭa in J. M. Cuoq, 1975, p. 311.

53. Al-Māghilī in J. M. Cuoq, 1975, p. 431.

54. Although historical comparisons must not be taken to unreasonable extremes, it is none the less interesting to note that the methods used by both Christianity and Islam to penetrate and establish themselves in 'pagan' societies often display important analogies: the violence of Christianity, however, was incomparably greater, for example against the Slavs and the Scandinavians.

imagination be said to have been active proselytizers. However, there was no lack of attempts to achieve political and social integration on the Islamic model, both on their part and on that of their Muslim advisers from sub-Saharan Africa. They are sometimes even accused of cultural imitation. One thinks, for example, of Mansa Kankū Mūsā returning from the east with the architect al-Sāḥilī, or Askiya Muḥammad I or the dynast of Kano, Muḥammad Rumfa, both of whom called on the services of the pious cleric of Tlemcen, al-Mā<u>gh</u>ilī, or on those of the Egyptian al-Suyūṭī, or of the emperor Mansa Sulaymān of Mali (742/1341–761/1360), a friend of the Marinid Sultan Abū'Inān, who attracted Mālikite scholars and clerics to his court. Many authors tend to endorse the severe judgement pronounced by al-Idrīsī: 'men of learning and distinction are almost unknown among them, and their kings only acquire what they know about government and justice from the instruction of learned visitors from further north'.[55] This opinion probably overlooks two essential things; the first is that this judgement does not allow for circumstances and it reinforces the pernicious notion that nothing of importance came from Africa itself, but always from outside. Furthermore, and this is still more serious, to think like al-Idrīsī is to forget that African societies, long before their contact with Islam, invented forms of political organization of which we are today gaining a better knowledge but of which both Muslims and Christians knew nothing for centuries. The ways in which power was exercised, which formed an integral part of the African religious sense, could not be abandoned without the consent of society as a whole and without total submission to Islam: we have already referred to the anecdote which is told differently by al-Bakrī and by al-Dar<u>dj</u>īnī,[56] concerning the conversion of a king of Mallal in the fifth/eleventh century. He adopted Islam in highly dramatic circumstances after a drought in order to obtain from the God of the Muslims the rain that was necessary for the survival of his people: in so doing, he was acting in accordance with an African model of power. The price of the conversion was a heavy one: the destruction of all the instruments of the ancestral religion, the hounding of sorcerers, the devastation of age-old traditions. The response of the people was unexpected: 'we are your servants, do not change our religion!'. We are thus entitled to wonder whether the black rulers did not take from Muslim society, with its belief in a single God, what was convenient and effective for the administration of their empire and whether these attempts at 'modernization' did not constitute a series of attempts to establish a balance between the 'weight' of pre-Islamic African traditions and the 'requirements of the new religion'.

Using a few specific examples, we can examine the real scope of the royal policy of integration with Islam.

The eighth/fourteenth century is often regarded in the historiography of

55. B. Lewis, 1982, p. 61.
56. J. M. Cuoq, 1975, pp. 102 and 195–6.

Africa south of the Sahara as being the age which saw the high point of the empire of Mali, characterized by remarkable economic development, political influence on an international scale involving diplomatic relations with Morocco and Egypt, and, above all, by the decisive establishment of Islam. It was thus a triumph of the Muslim religion which is powerfully underlined by Jean-Luc Moreau when he writes: 'With the empire of Mali, Islam embarked on yet another phase in the Western Sudan: it was, at least in part, the initiator of a new society'.[57] Joseph Ki-Zerbo represents Mansa Mūsā as 'a fervent Muslim [who] gave new impetus to the expansion of Islam'.[58]

Although there is no doubt of the Islamic piety of Mansa Mūsā, the pilgrim king, and without denying that, mainly in the towns, Islam was to some extent established, we think that these two authors who are, moreover, not the only ones, have been misled both by the relatively large mass of documents on Mali in the eighth/fourteenth century[59] and by the triumphant euphoria of the Arab and Sudano-Berber sources of the eleventh/seventeenth century. Moreover, Ki-Zerbo himself acknowledges that: '...the peasant masses (who formed the overwhelming majority of the populations of Mali) retained their animistic faith and this was tolerated by the Mansa in exchange for their obedience and their taxes'.[60] Furthermore, we cannot see how Mansa Mūsā would have managed to give fresh impetus to the 'expansion of Islam' as, in common with all the other rulers of Mali, he did not launch a holy war (*djihād*).

Let us look one and a half centuries ahead: the end of the ninth/fifteenth century and the tenth/sixteenth century provide other examples of the desire expressed by certain Muslim clerics to bring about a profound transformation of African habits, and of the indecisive response of rulers to such pressure.

Askiya Muḥammad, who seized power by means of a *coup d'état*, made considerable efforts to achieve political and social integration in line with the ethic of the Qoran. In order to legitimize his *coup d'état* he resorted to every means afforded by the Muslim religion. With the support of the 'Muslim party' of the scholars of Timbuktu, he made the Pilgrimage to Mecca at the end of the ninth/fifteenth century. The title of caliph (*khalīfa*) invested him with spiritual authority in the Sudan. In the interior, he sought the advice almost exclusively of Muslim scholars. Faced with the difficulty of resolving the social problems raised by part of the inheritance he had received from Sonni ʿAlī the Great, he requested four consultations from three outstanding jurists: ʿAbdullāh al-Ansammānī of Takedda, al-Suyūṭī, and al-Māghilī. The latter appears to have taken the greatest trouble. At the request of the *askiya* he wrote a kind of handbook of the

57. J.-L. Moreau, 1982, p. 103.
58. J. Ki-Zerbo, 1978, p. 136.
59. Ibn Baṭṭūṭa, al-ʿUmarī, Ibn Khaldūn, etc.
60. J. Ki-Zerbo, 1978, p. 136.

perfect Muslim prince, the *Answers to the Questions of the Emir al-Ḥādjdj ʿAbdullāh ibn Abū Bakr*.[61] At the request of another black ruler, al-Mā<u>gh</u>ilī wrote a book in the same style: *The Obligations of Princes* (Risālat al-Mulūk), intended for the king of Kano, Muḥammad Rumfa (870/1465–905/1499).

Askiya Muḥammad, wishing to conform to the model of what was required of a caliph, adopted the oriental insignia of power: a seal, a sword, a Qoran; he declared Friday to be the day of the weekly audience, he undertook holy wars – though without success – against the 'infidels'. He was no more successful however, than the emperors of Mali who had preceded him in distancing himself from the African traditions which enjoined him to retain the ancestral attributes inherited from the time of the Shi: a drum, sacred fire, precise regulations concerning dress, hairstyle, regalia, the catching of the ruler's spittle, the existence in the higher administration of the *Hori farima*, in other words the high priest of the worship of ancestors and genies.

Ultimately, he did not put into practice the unbending advice given by al-Mā<u>gh</u>ilī against the 'false Muslims' by whom, according to the jurist, the *askiya* was surrounded. The teachings of al-Mā<u>gh</u>ilī remained dormant in West Africa until ʿU<u>th</u>mān Dan Fodio turned them into a doctrine and a weapon to use against the princes who were then of no further use to the expansion of Islam.

In Bornu, the successor to the state of Kānem, the rulers (*mai*) who were true living gods, nevertheless filled their courts with learned Muslim *imāms*. These tried in the reign of ʿAlī ibn Dūnama (877/1472–910/1504) to bring the morals of the notables into line with Qoranic prescriptions. The 'sultan' acquiesced but the notables refused to comply. Similarly, the justice administered by the *ḳāḍi* was confined to the towns and did not replace the law of African groups. Parts of Hausaland, which were converted to Islam in the eighth/fourteenth century by Fulani and Wangara missionaries, rulers and zealots, experienced the same difficulties in inducing rural, or even urban, populations to adopt the Muslim religion. In Katsina, after the visit of al-Mā<u>gh</u>ilī to try and purify the lukewarm Islam of the Hausa, 'sacred woods of the animists were razed to the ground and in their place mosques were built'. The Near Eastern form of life was dominant in Muslim society: the harem and the veil for women, the employment of eunuchs, a fiscal system based on the Qoran and so forth. But these changes did not last. Ultimately, the apparent inaction of the kings was probably an indication of their awareness that social pressures would lead to the rejection of Islam.

It was outside their control, 'at the grass-roots', that the most substantial advances of Islam were ultimately achieved during these centuries. African

61. Z. Dramani-Issifou, 1982, pp. 34–40. Text of al-Mā<u>gh</u>ilī in J. M. Cuoq, 1975, pp. 398–432.

merchants, Wangara and later Dyula and Muslim missionaries of all types carried the message of the Prophet out to the countryside and to the towns as far as the forest fringe. This slow expansion did not, for sound reasons, overturn the habits of societies within which small groups of Muslims were coming into existence. Such societies continued, for example, to produce the cultural wares in keeping with their traditions: the remarkable discovery in recent years of an art of statuary in terracotta in the middle of 'Muslim' Mali bears witness to this.[62]

The results

In the present state of research, the results are very difficult to assess and their apparent contradictions are disconcerting.

There is no doubt that the art of writing and techniques of weighing[63] were introduced by Islam south of the Sahara as early as the fourth/tenth century. To what extent did these two innovations upset earlier habits? What were the earlier habits as regards conservation of traces of the past, counting and mathematical knowledge?

It may justifiably be said that literature in the Arabic language south of the Sahara seems to have paid no regard to African cultures and their languages. In order to be sure of this it would be necessary to ascertain and evaluate the contents of libraries which are now being studied in Mauritania, Mali, Burkina Faso, Niger, Chad and the Sudan. It would also be necessary to make a scientific study of the development of certain African languages in contact with Arabic. It is probably correct to say that those who were literate 'in Arabic' ignored ancient African cultures both because they were 'pagan' and, more simply, because they were unaware of their existence; in that regard they showed themselves to be as unperceptive as the majority of Christian missionaries some centuries later. It would probably be unjust to regard such ignorance as denoting preconceived contempt for African societies and cultures.

It may be said that these scholars north of the Sahara who were, in most cases, unacquainted with the region up to the ninth/fifteenth century (although the same is probably not true in East Africa), brought with them their own preoccupations. After the seventh/thirteenth century these seem no longer to have had the brilliance of the great age of Arab-Muslim culture; even though Morocco in the seventh/thirteenth century, for example, seems to have had several great thinkers; it may be that many branches of knowledge withered at that time in the Muslim world, even though some continued to flourish. It may be that authors of the past were copied too much and that legal formalism prevailed over living thought. Here again,

62. On the subject of this art: B. de Grunne, 1980. See also (*La*) *rime et la raison*, 1984 and Unesco, *General History of Africa*, Vol. IV, illustrations nos. 6, 11, 12 and 14.

63. J. Devisse, D. Robert-Chaleix *et al.*, 1983, pp. 407–19.

in order to reach valid conclusions, it will be necessary to wait until thousands of manuscripts, so far not studied even if they have been catalogued, have been analysed; we shall need, for example, to be aware of the treasures of the Ḳarawiyyīn Library of Fez and the Bibliothèque Royale at Rabat where so many manuscripts from Timbuktu and works on Africa are housed.

At present it seems that it was normal, at the outset, for educated Malinke, Fulani, Soninke, Berbers or Negro-Berbers, such men as Mourimagha Kankoi of Jenne, Baghayogho, Kāti, ibn Dansal al-Fūlānī, Aḥmed Bābā, ibn al-Mukhtār Gombele of Timbuktu, and so forth, who were committed to the letter and spirit of Islam, to think in Arabic, write in Arabic and produce commentaries on books belonging to the Islamic tradition. This Islamo-centrism no doubt made the universities of Timbuktu seem less brilliant than black Africans today would wish, as they can discern in those universities, as far as our present knowledge goes, hardly a trace of their cultural past.[64] This being so, there is only one comment to be made: the Muslim scholars belonged to a fairly closed world and were still a minority group facing a mass of adherents of African traditional religion, whom they thought themselves duty bound to convert and perhaps to guide towards other styles of life; thus they were not predisposed to become enlightened historians of the African past or even sympathetic observers of the life of autochthonous societies which they considered to be 'pagan'.

It is probably in this area that research is least advanced and where the researcher has the greatest difficulty in maintaining objectivity.

Islamization–Arabization

It was probably in Kānem and in East Africa that the last transformation of African society first took place: the 'Arabization' of their origins and their past; West Africa was not slow in taking the same path.

When, in the seventh/thirteenth century, the genealogists of the Kānembu dynasty tried to reconstitute the noble lineage of the reigning princes, they did not demur to make one vitally important innovation, namely to seek those origins in the East and even in biblical traditions.[65] This was the inception of an idea that was to prove enormously successful and to bring about a profound change in the cultural relationship between African societies and the Muslim world. Any prince of any standing had to come from the East; the only noble origins were those of the East and no past was to be so spoken of except if it were related to the Prophet, his family or his companions. A start was made (not, by any means, for the last time) on the rewriting of African history and the 'new history' was to strike

64. Z. Dramami-Issifou, 1982, pp. 196–203.
65. D. Lange, 1977.

a blow at the obsolescence and the absurdity of the cosmic or animal origins with which African societies sometimes endowed themselves.

Genealogical literature was to flourish after the eighth/fourteenth century in East Africa where it became one of the weapons in the ideological conflict between opposing Muslim tendencies and between reigning houses as late as the thirteenth/nineteenth century.[66] A great deal of work remains to be done to clarify this literature. In West Africa, the transformation of the stories concerning the origin of the 'Mandingo' was spectacular;[67] that of the origins of the founders of the Wagadu was equally so. Gradually, every Islamized group of any importance discovered an ancestor from Arabia. This considerably strengthened a theory of biblical origin according to which African populations came from the Middle East, with all the diffusionist consequences that this theory implied. Another aspect was the propensity for discovering 'white' origins – in this case Arabic and Persian – for everything of any value in Africa even if that meant totally devaluing the most anciently attested African cultures. Thus began the eclipse of African history which was later to be considerably exacerbated by the Europeans.

No dominant family or group ultimately escaped this logic of 'Arabization'.[68] In the thirteenth/nineteenth century, the Yarse of Burkina Faso in their turn claimed Arab origins at a time when their commercial supremacy, which dated from two centuries earlier, and the privileged position which had earned them a real historical compromise with the Mosi of Ouagadougou seemed to them to be in jeopardy.[69] Even the remote Betsileo of central Madagascar, who had no Muslim tradition, were fascinated by the 'civilizing model' of Islam and sought out Arab origins for their princes; they were not, incidentally, the only ones to have done so in Madagascar.[70]

In the last analysis, there is nothing surprising in the fact that Islam inspired such confidence and infatuation. The phenomenon is one which ought to be studied dispassionately since it is so important and, for several centuries, was so characteristic of an 'oriental' temptation for Islamized African societies.

This 'genealogical snobbery' provided a guarantee of the age and quality of the Islamic practices of those who traced their origins to Arab ancestors; it also guaranteed the 'historic rights' of aristocracies that were becoming established. It finally took on so much importance, particularly in the region between Lake Chad and the Nile, that it became the normal process of the Arabization-Islamization of many groups. The Maba are a good case in point. Islam had been gaining ground in Kānem when the Bulala arrived

66. M. Rozenstroch, 1984.
67. A. Condé, 1974.
68. D. Hamani, 1985.
69. K. Assimi, 1984.
70. E. Flacourt, 1913.

and helped to extend its influence eastwards through contact with other peoples including the Maba. The latter, until the ninth/fifteenth to tenth/sixteenth century, had not been exposed to any Islamic influence. The actual or mythical arrival among them of an Arab claiming to be of Abbasid origin, called Djāmē at the end of the tenth/sixteenth century, changed the course of events. Djāmē chose a wife belonging to a Maba clan and his entry into the Maba group made things simpler. As the new religion progressively gained more ground, certain Maba clans laid claim to an Arab-Muslim origin. The contact that had existed between the Arabs and the indigenous populations just prior to the penetration of Islam had no religious or cultural implications. Such contacts were based mainly on the black slave trade, and on the trade in gold and ivory. The Arab *ḳabīla*s referred to the Maba as 'ambāy' (primitives) whereas the indigenous peoples dignified their guests by the name of 'aramgo' (savages, barbarians, anarchists). Until that time they had not been brought together by language or by religious outlook. Before long the Arabs married into the great Maba families; they became semi-sedentary and more or less adopted the Islamic traditions of the Maba. The influences were in both directions. The Maba learned the language of the Arabs and thus considered that they had no difficulty in understanding the Qoran. Religion commanded the observance of Islamic rites and also the language of the Qoran. As the teaching of Islam spread, the Maba 'sought not only to imitate the Arab model offered by Islam but also to identify themselves with the Arabs. In each clan, the chief who was installed and maintained by power sought out an origin in the Arab-Muslim world: the line was traced back in most cases to the family of the Prophet or, more modestly, to one of his four direct companions'. Moreover, writes Issa Khayar, 'to adopt the religion of the Arabs, the customs of the Arabs, the language of the Arabs, to ally themselves with the other Arab or Muslim peoples, was the irresistible trend of the entire Maba society'.[71]

Islamization, together with Arabization, had very important repercussions on the whole of Maba society. The Maba unconsciously tried to rewrite their history by fabricating fictitious genealogies accompanied by a complete change of names.

Such more or less collective changes of name explain the difficulty encountered by present-day historians in studying the sequence of past events. From the point of view with which we are concerned, the example of the Maba is remarkable in many ways. In their case, as in that of the Waddaians in general, their own system of cultural values underlies and cohabits with the Islamic ethic. But Islam, because of the cultural dynamism conferred on it by a written and oral system of teaching, tended to overshadow and to overthrow these traditional socio-cultural values, which became latent.

71. I. H. Khayar, 1976, pp. 43–4.

The last link in the chain of transformations brought about by Islam in the life of African societies is probably the most significant of all. It leads to a total 'deculturation' of the societies in which it gains a complete hold, creates a 'black Arabism' which seems like a historical contradiction and which culturally impoverishes the Muslim community. Many African societies did not react like the Maba. They assessed the damage implied by the alternatives offered or imposed. On occasion their reaction was even to reject Islam. Ultimately those most concerned by this problem were those who, having been kept aside from the transformations brought about by Islam, suffered from them because of the contempt for their beliefs and an ideology that viewed them as no more than an inexhaustible source of slaves of which the main beneficiaries were the proponents of Islam and the black states engaged in the slave trade. In many cases, therefore, mistrust arose and induced a certain number of African societies to open rejection and confrontation.

The interrupted dialogue: the late tenth/sixteenth – early eleventh/seventeenth centuries

The end of the tenth/sixteenth century and the beginning of the eleventh/seventeenth century mark an important stage in West African history. This period has with some justification been described as a turning point. We would prefer to regard it as an interlude which comes at the end of a long and extremely rich period which saw the emergence and development of the principal black sub-Saharan states and the confrontation of two world views, that of the traditional religions of the African continent and that of Islam. It was also the starting point of another, admittedly shorter, period of serious disturbances and uncertainty during which the Muslim religion apparently paused in its expansion or even, in many regions, retreated. The main impression given is that the majority of the African peoples which had had contacts with Islam returned to their origins. This interlude is seen to have been historically necessary when one analyses the role of Islam as a motivating force in African socio-economic relationships, a role which appeared to offer a greater threat where Islam was less firmly established: sedentary agrarian societies were dominated by African oligarchies when it advanced; under cover of Islam, entire regions of the continent became reserves of slaves.

It was in the Songhay empire, under the leadership of Sonni ʿAlī (868/1464–897/1492) that this anti-Muslim reaction took its most vigorous form; it was directed not against persons but rather against the influence of the ideology they professed which was regarded as incompatible with traditional African values. A number of circumstances favoured the conduct of what really ought to be termed a counter-offensive.

During the last quarter of the eighth/fourteenth century and during the early years of the following century there was a weakening, followed by the almost total disappearance of the central authority of Mali which had been a source of political cohesion between the various peoples of which the empire was composed. Spurred on by the exactions of certain rulers of Mali, satellite states, regions, country areas and urban centres found it easier, the more remote they were from the capital, to cast off the central authority. The rich, cosmopolitan urban populations, well organized and structured by Islam, began to act as autonomous or even independent merchant republics. This was the case with Jenne, Walāta and Timbuktu, for example. In the new Songhay empire, which, by conquest, had inherited the eastern provinces of Mali, the relations between Sonni ʿAlī and these towns, particularly Timbuktu, rapidly deteriorated into serious conflict. Economic and strategic reasons were among the causes of the conflict but the determining factor seems to have been the reason of state rooted in the primacy of the imperial authority. Sonni ʿAlī, the emperor magician, raised in the ethos of the all-powerful African monarch – who was, after all, known as Dāli, in other words the All Highest – could not bear to see his supernatural power, which was recognized by the great mass of his subjects who adhered to African traditional religions, challenged by the Muslim scholars of Timbuktu, who were, moreover, foreigners.[72] The Berbers, the Negro-Berber half castes and the Fulani formed, indeed, the overwhelming majority of the population of that town. The city was therefore severely harassed in the person of its scholars much to the discomfiture of the learned authors of the *Tārīkh*s.[73] The reign of Sonni Alī was marked by the bringing into line of Timbuktu, by the supremacy of Gao,[74] and in a sense by the backlash of African traditional religion against Islam. The *coup d'état* of 898/1493 organized by Askiya Muḥammad and the desire to make the 'Islamic option' irreversible can be explained only in this context.

Apart from two interludes – the reigns of the *askiya*s Muḥammad I (898/1493–934/1528) and Dāwūd (956/1549–990/1582) – during which a relative revival of interest in Islam was manifested by those two rulers, the end of the tenth/sixteenth century was marked by the Moroccan conquest. The collapse of the political framework and the disorganization of the social fabric led to a definitive decline of the Songhay cities. Resistance to the occupying Moroccan force over the course of some ten years brought about a southwards movement of populations, mainly into Dendi. These populations organized themselves as little independent states with socio-religious structures drawn from the ancestral traditions and kept nothing of Islam except their names.

A pamphlet by Aḥmad Bābā (963/1556–1038/1628), generally known by the name of *Miʿrādj al-Suhūd*, written between 1001/1593 and 1025/1616,

72. A. Konaré-Ba, 1977.

73. Ta'rīkh al-Sūdān, 1900, pp. 105, 107, 110 and 115; Ta'rīkh al-Fattāsh, 1913–14, pp. 80, 84 and 94.

74. Z. Dramani-Issifou, 1983a.

provides an insight into the extent of the social upheavals caused by the Moroccan conquest and by the intensification of slavery at the turn of the eleventh/seventeenth century. Having been called on by the merchants of Tūwāt to give his opinion (*fatwā*, *fatāwā*) on the subjugation and sale into slavery of certain populations of the Songhay empire, Aḥmad Bābā took the opportunity to describe the social and religious scene in the greater part of the Nigerian Sudan in the early eleventh/seventeenth century. In this description, which aspires to be in conformity with Islamic ethics, the author, wishing to defend populations which had been the victims of lawless capture, shows that the economic activities of the time relied mainly on the trans-Saharan black slave trade. He drew attention to the extent and variations of the Islamization of the peoples of the region, and the retreat of the Muslim religion emerges clearly.

Still more significant than this retreat is the social and religious disarray in the political vacuum created by the disappearance of the Songhay state and the disorders of the Moroccan occupation, the emergence of an 'animistic' kingdom ostensibly professing allegiance to African values. This was the Banmana (Bambara) kingdom of Segu during the eleventh/seventeenth century. This was caused both by the destruction of the 'imperial Muslim power' and also by the decline in the urban fabric of the empire and the open rejection of Islam which had taken place in rural environments since the seventh/thirteenth century, in spite of the *mansa*s of Mali and the *askiya*s of Songhay.

Islamic contact with Africa proved one of the most fruitful human ventures in world history. Islam offered what might be termed 'a choice of society'. Its implications were variously conceived at different times and in different places in the black continent. The stakes were high: neither more nor less than a change in outlook, in ways of conceiving and representing the world, in behaviour. It was a matter of exchanging one's own culture for that of another, in short of becoming someone other. In spite of the resistance that was shown between the first/seventh and the start of the eleventh/seventeenth centuries, Mediterranean Africa accepted the Muslim option. It was Islamized and started to become Arabized.

In the rest of Africa, Islam did not find the propitious historical circumstances which explain its success in the east and north of the continent and in Spain. Although it was neither a conqueror nor totally in control of power, which it had to leave in the hands of princes who were still imbued with African traditions – even though they sometimes made themselves 'foreigners' to the peoples whom they ruled by their own conversion and often, thanks to the profits earned by such rulers from the sale of slaves – Islam obtained substantial religious results south of the desert and in East Africa. By the tenth/sixteenth century Islam had still not found an overall solution which would enable it to integrate black societies and their cultures without problems in the House of Islam. The subsequent interlude was not any more conducive to the discovery of such a solution.

Lastly, on more than one point, social integration was to occur in the course of revolutionary events in the twelfth/eighteenth and early thirteenth/nineteenth centuries: those events alone, in certain regions, were to make Islam into a comprehensive expression of the social and cultural life of the people.

5

The peoples of the Sudan: population movements

F. DE MEDEIROS

The problem and the sources

At the present stage of African historiography, study of the movements that culminated in the establishment of the peoples of the Sudanic zone of West Africa is an indispensable but extremely complex task.

The context in which the question arises is clouded by debates that give prominence to presuppositions concerning the cultural supremacy of certain groups from the north and east. This is a problem of major concern which must be constantly borne in mind in the course of our examination in so far as it has a bearing on the methods and the main lines of emphasis of African history; it calls for strenuous critical thinking and a commensurate effort of empathy.

In most books and monographs on African history, population movements occupy a prominent place; they are usually introduced before any other topic is developed, with the widespread notion of 'migrations'. The vast area occupied by the Sudan was conducive to movement, contacts and exchanges; in the absence of solid geographic and chronological points of reference, there is a strong temptation to invoke outside influences. Similarly, use is often made of oral tradition which goes back to the beginnings of the peoples of the Sudan in an attempt to establish a connection between their cultures and the culture of prestigious ancestors. Finally, the very theme of 'migrations' lends itself to new interpretations that utilize, among other procedures, comparative investigations, seeking to rediscover in the facts and realities of African history patterns and structures originating in more ancient cultures that are taken as models.

The Hamitic hypothesis, which served to explain the evolution of African cultures in ancient times, has been widely used as a palpable interpretative framework.[1] According to this theory, the 'Hamites' were an African people distinct from the other blacks of sub-Saharan Africa from the standpoint of race (Caucasian) and linguistic family. The northern branch

1. R. Cornevin, 1960, pp. 70–1 tries to account for the two terms 'Chamite' and 'Hamite', but he endorses the former; cf. C. G. Seligman, 1930, 1935.

of the 'Hamites' would, therefore, include the inhabitants of the Sahara, the Berbers, the Tubu and the Fulani. The 'Hamitic' hypothesis draws a clear distinction between the pastoral 'Hamites' and the agricultural blacks, considering them as two separate and well-defined categories.

Because of their 'natural' kinship with the peoples who founded the Mesopotamian and Egyptian civilizations of the Middle East, the Hamites are regarded as having been responsible for all the progress and innovations made by and in Africa. That being so, the occupation of pastoral cattle-breeder is credited with cultural superiority. These white nomads would, it is said, have transmitted the elements of 'civilization' to the sedentary blacks.[2]

Authors like M. Delafosse, H. R. Palmer and Y. Urvoy in particular, who have provided much of our knowledge about the peoples of the Sudan, deliberately adopted this diffusionist standpoint;[3] Urvoy is even convinced that 'the whites brought the seed of a superior type of organization' to Africa.[4] Contemporary African historiography is becoming sensitive to the ideological presuppositions inherent in such assumptions which are being subjected to methodical criticism.[5] But it must be admitted that much arbitrary data of this type is still fashionable in textbooks and other works. For although these theories and their influence are now being challenged in earnest, it is far harder to replace them with fresh contributions based on the results of research (which has itself become more rigorous).

Another set of problems stems from the fact that we do not have the material for an exhaustive treatment of this subject. The period in question – the first/seventh century to the fifth/eleventh century – usually comes under the heading of the 'dark ages'.[6] And yet despite the recent expansion of African historical studies, the information we have for the early periods is still incomplete.

It is true that the Arab conquest of North Africa ushered in a period of contacts calculated to yield more reliable information than the previous centuries. But the limitations of the written sources originating from the Arab geographers are now becoming more and more apparent.[7] Conceived from the standpoint of their own cultural environment, they are fragmentary, and reflect considerable gaps as regards the specific question of the peoples of the Sudan. Their authors were mostly easterners such as al-Ya'ḳūbī, who never went beyond the Nile delta. Some of them had to take account of the interests and expansionist designs of the masters who had sent them to collect information, as with Ibn Ḥawḳal (who worked for the Fāṭimids). Al-Bakrī is undoubtedly the author whose contribution has

2. C. G. Seligman, 1930, p. 96.
3. M. Delafosse, 1912; H. R. Palmer, 1936; Y. Urvoy, 1936, 1949.
4. Y. Urvoy, 1949, pp. 21–2.
5. W. MacGaffey, 1966; E. R. Sanders, 1969.
6. See the titles of the works of E. F. Gautier, 1937 and R. Mauny, 1971.
7. Cf. Unesco, *General History of Africa*, Vol. I, ch. 5.

proved to be the most important; but he did not know the countries he described from Spain, and the facts in his account come mainly from the works of earlier authors (largely thanks to the official archives of the Caliphate of Cordova) and from the stories of travellers he questioned.[8] In all likelihood, none of these writers visited the Sudan before Ibn Baṭṭūṭā (eighth/fourteenth century).

But the subject can be approached from a new angle. The collections of Arab sources of J. M. Cuoq and of N. Levtzion and J. F. P. Hopkins are invaluable works of reference alongside the individual studies, especially when research in the field is making progress.[9] A positive attitude towards oral tradition is found throughout Africa. The Wagadu legends, accounts by chroniclers and traditionists from Mali and 'Mandingo' land, and Songhay, Zarma, Hausa, Fulani (Peul) and Mosi (Mossi) traditions, together with the archaeological work being carried out from Mauritania to Chad, make it possible to view the subject in a more critical light and to widen the field of information.

The area in question is enormous. The Land of the Blacks – *Bilād al-Sūdān* – now denoted by the name Sudan comprises not only the Senegal, Niger and Chad basins but also ports of the savanna and forestlands further south. Here documentary material is even scantier, and research is in its infancy. Work is in progress at Kong (Ivory Coast), Begho (Ghana) and Poura (Burkina Faso); but apart from Taruga and Ife in Nigeria these sites cannot compare with what has been achieved at Tis̲h̲īt, Tegdaoust or Kumbi Saleh or in Dogon country. This wealth of investigations in the Sahel in fact provides valuable material for a reassessment of the Sudan's relationship with its Saharan fringes, which can hardly be ignored. This in turn makes it possible to see under what conditions the peoples of the Sudan occupied their environment, and how they fitted into it and acquired their cultural resources.

The northern border

We have long been accustomed to looking at the sub-Saharan area through what may be called 'the spectacles of Islam', that is, seeing its history exclusively through the eyes of the Muslim society settled in North Africa, which is our main source of written literature. The Muslim period and the new situation it introduced in the Maghrib unquestionably represents a major stage in our knowledge of the sub-Saharan area. The study of the peoples of the Sudan starts here, for Muslim Arab culture and society brought with it impressions that affected its relationship with the Sudan. This is useful historical material and Arabic sources are viewed with favour, coupled with the prestige of the written word so prized by the

8. Cf. Chapter 14 below.
9. J. M. Cuoq, 1975; N. Levtzion and J. F. P. Hopkins (eds), 1981.

'People of the Book'. But if we step back a little from this very widespread attitude we find that knowledge of the Sudan and its peoples is largely influenced and determined by the concerns of the Eastern and Maghribi Muslim world.

The tendency to look at the 'Land of the Blacks' from a North African viewpoint goes back a very long way. It originated in antiquity, when the 'known world' around the Mediterranean basin was the geographical centre of the world. This structure did not change fundamentally during the Islamic period. Moreover this predominance of the north to the neglect of sub-Saharan Africa, at least until the ninth/fifteenth century, is reflected in many contemporary works which were certainly not written by supporters of diffusionism. The result is an imbalance between a plethora of writing about ancient and medieval trans-Saharan traffic on the one hand and very incomplete knowledge of the black peoples during the same period on the other. But this fact is itself a sufficient reason to look at the northern approaches to the Sudan, which connect through the Sahara with Berber country.

The Berbers played an important role in West Africa from the point of view of population movements. Since prehistoric times they were constantly active in the Sahara, as far as its southern edges. Their ancestors from the Fezzān, the Garamantes, are said to have been active intermediaries between Provincia Africa and the Land of the Blacks during the Roman period.[10]

The Berbers, who had never really formed part of the zone controlled by successive hegemonies in North Africa, from the Carthaginians to Byzantium, found their mobility in the direction of the desert enhanced by the increase in the number of camels. Whether it had previously resulted in the establishment of sedentary kingdoms and principalities far to the north or in the formation of major nomadic confederations adjacent to the desert and in the Sahara itself, the Berbers' independent attitude brought about prolonged opposition to the new Arab power; this expressed itself in various resistance movements, but especially in the favourable welcome given to the Khāridjite heresy.[11]

Indeed, it was the principalities and centres controlled by the Khāridjites which had the initiative in trade with the Sudan from the late second/eighth century. Djabal Nafūsa, Wargla, Tāhert and Sidjilmāsa were in one way or the other engaged in such activities.[12]

To the west the Berbers formed a great confederation, which al-Fazārī (second/eighth century) called the state of Anbiya; it probably consisted of the Massūfa, the Lamtūna and the Djuddāla.[13] Al-Ya'ḳūbī classified them among the Ṣanhādja, who played an important role throughout the western

10. Cf. R. C. C. Law, 1967a, 1967b.
11. See Chapter 3 above, Chapter 10 below.
12. See Chapter 11 below.
13. Cf. J. M. Cuoq, 1975, p. 42.

Sahara. This huge grouping must have been in contact to the south with the area controlled by Ghana. Another group of Berbers, the Hawwāra, originally from Tripolitania, marched with the Land of the Blacks. To avoid being conquered they went west, and while crossing the Maghrib took part in the various uprisings against the Arabs. In the second/eighth century they embraced Khāridjism. After Abū Yazīd's last Khāridjite revolt,[14] in which they took part, they dispersed westwards and eastwards, while some of them fled south. During this period their presence was reported in the Fezzān.

The Hawwāra were also in the Hoggar. The link between the ethnonym Hawwāra and the toponym Hoggar is an indication of this. Ibn Khaldūn, the historian of the Berbers, states that a fragment of the latter crossed the sands and settled next to the veil-wearing Lamṭa, who lived near the town of Kāw-Kāw (Gao) in the Land of the Blacks.[15]

The Ṣanhādja played an active role in the trans-Saharan traffic which took the western route: moreover, this explains the coming into being, in what had already been an occupied post in ancient times (and was henceforth to be known as Awdāghust), of a trading centre that soon came to be dominated by the Lamtūna and was inhabited in the third/ninth and fourth/tenth centuries by Berbers belonging to the region, blacks and traders from the north. A road linked Awdāghust to Sidjilmāsa the great caravan port of the Tafilālet in southern Morocco.

To the east the Ibāḍite Berbers played a similar role in the traffic leading to the outlets of Ifrīḳiya and Tripolitania. They took part in the trade in black slaves brought from the land of the Zaghāwa, in Kānem. The Berber capital, Zawīla, was the hub of this trade, acting as a warehouse for slaves waiting to be sent north.

Writing about this trade, al-Ya'ḳūbī was not greatly upset by the fact that Ibāḍite Muslims were trading in black pagans; he merely showed slight surprise on learning that 'the kings of the blacks thus sell blacks for no reason, and without the motive of war'.[16] The slave trade thus seems to have been not a sporadic occupation for those engaged in this traffic but a steady economic activity dependent on the needs of the Maghribi and Mediterranean market, i.e. on the laws of supply and demand. Thus these Ibāḍite Berbers (who were religious dissidents because they adopted Khāridjite doctrines) were in economic terms well integrated into the Muslim world. Their special position in relation to the Sudan made them the driving force of a large Arab-Berber grouping which extended as far as the southern Sahara.

Among the Saharan Berber groups, the Tuareg – the name by which they would later become known to us – occupied a special position. Their

14. See Chapter 12 below.

15. Ibn Khaldūn, 1925–56 Vol. 1, pp. 275–6; J. M. Cuoq, 1975, pp. 330–1.

16. Al-Ya'ḳūbī, 1962, p. 9; J. M. Cuoq, 1975, pp. 42, 48; see also Chapters 11 and 15 below.

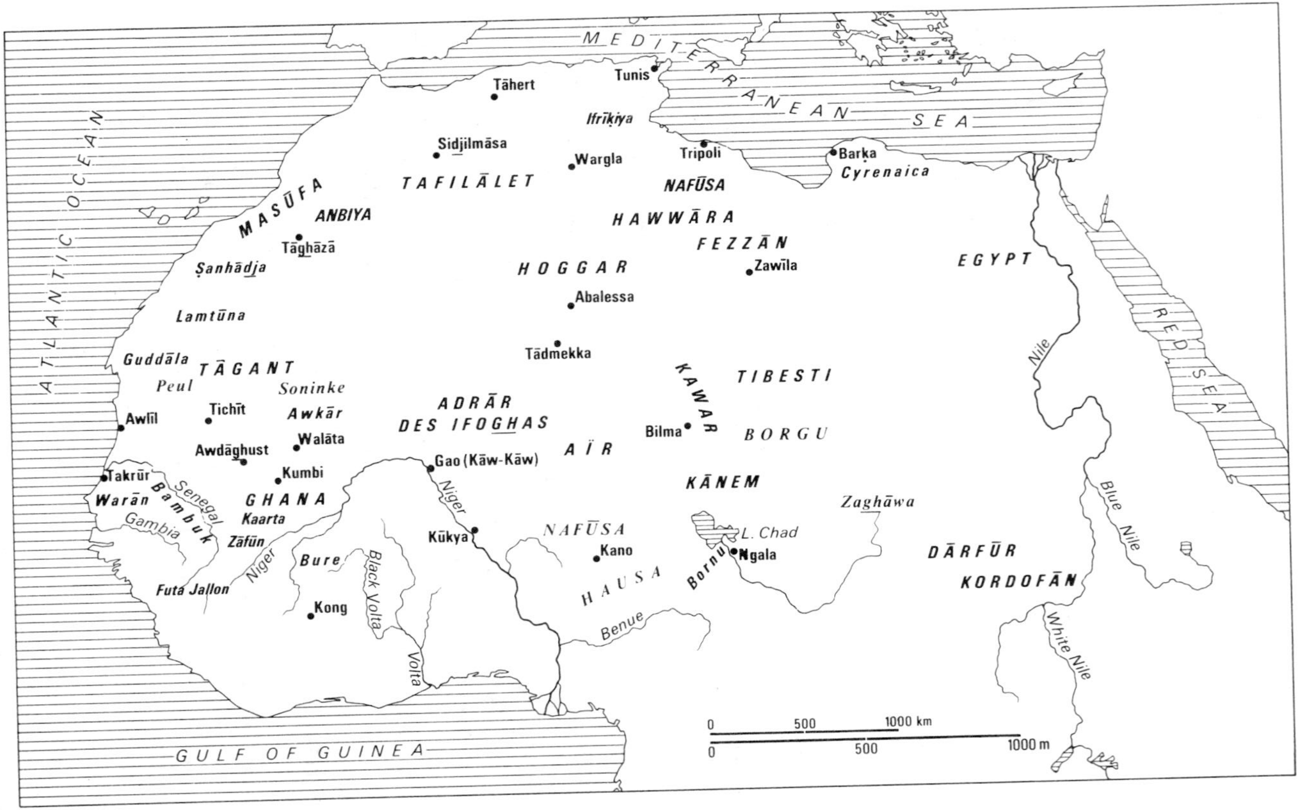

FIG. 5.1 *West Africa in the eleventh century*

area was relatively near the Land of the Blacks. They formed a number of confederations and occupied a territory extending from the Ghadamēs area in the northern Sahara to the Niger and beyond, their main settlements being in the massifs of Hoggar, Aïr and the Adrār des Ifoghas. They managed despite adherence to the Muslim religion to preserve fundamental aspects of their culture, such as their language, *tamashegh*, their script, *tifinagh*, and their social structure, with warrior, religious teacher, tributary, slave and craftsman classes. In their accounts of their origins they claim an ancestry which also indicates an undoubted cultural identity. According to their oral traditions the Tuareg are descended from Tin Hinan, a woman from the Tafilālet. This queen, the ancestress of the Kel Rela nobles, is said to have arrived in the Hoggar on a white she-camel accompanied by her servant Takamat, ancestress of the Dag Rali. Excavations carried out in 1929 and 1933 in a funeral monument at Abalessa, west of the Hoggar, seem to confirm these traditions. They brought to light a large quantity of objects dating from the fourth century of the Christian era, which also suggests the existence of an old route between southern Morocco and the Hoggar at a time when camels were in use.[17]

In anthropological terms the Tuareg in fact represent a halfway house between the Sahara and the Sudan. They fall into two groups: those who live in the Tassili-n-Ajjer and the Hoggar in the north and the southern branch, the Awellimid and the Kel Wi of Aïr who have intermarried with the black Hausa peoples. In the circumstances the black peoples must have exerted some cultural influence on the Tuareg. H. T. Norris notes that the Tuareg practise a type of divination called *tachchelt* ('the viper'), in which the reptile is questioned according to certain forms of words.[18] The snake also appears in many other circumstances, its meaning being ambiguous: it has a protective function, but it appears in dreams as a harbinger of ill fortune. On the strength of comparison with a similar legend reported by al-Bakrī and attributed to the Zāfḳāwa people of the Sudan, the author suggests cultural contacts between the Tuareg and Ghana.[19]

There are black peoples in the Sahara in the eastern and central desert and particularly in the west. The latter, the Harātīn, usually form part of the population of the oases of southern Morocco and Mauritania. The question of their origin is still debatable: they have been called black Berbers.[20] New approaches to the ancient peopling of the Sahara throw a different light on the issue. This problem can therefore only be dealt with as part of an overall study of the role of the Saharan environment in the development of the peoples of West Africa. There are plausible indications

17. M. Reygasse, 1940; 1950, pp. 88–108; M. Gast, 1972; see also Unesco, *General History of Africa*, Vol. II, ch. 20.

18. H. T. Norris, 1972, pp. 8–9.

19. Al-Bakrī, 1911, p. 173; 1913, p. 330.

20. Cf. G. Camps, 1969, pp. 11–17, 1970, pp. 35–45; H. von Fleischhacker, 1969, pp. 12–53.

that they are living specimens of black peoples whose southward movement goes back a very long way.

Integrative tendencies among African peoples in the melting pot of the Sudan

If we look at the question of the peoples of the Sudan from the standpoint of the fringe components, i.e. on the basis only of the impressions and interests of Mediterranean societies from the Maghrib eastwards, we are in danger of distorting the picture of the specifically West African environment and its peoples. The results of such an analysis are bound to be incomplete. It is true that our information is still fragmentary despite the progress made, and that many questions remain unanswered. We shall try first to demarcate the area within which African societies organized and structured themselves during the period concerned. Here we must use the results of work based on the latest research techniques, such as palaeoecology, palynology and archaeology. By combining their contributions with more easily available data from oral tradition and the Arabic sources, we may possibly arrive at some sound hypotheses. The work done in Mauritania on Saharan prehistory and later periods will serve as an example. In this respect the Adrār, Tāgant and Awkār areas stand out. The research projects carried out there by H. J. Hugot and P. Munson[21] can be regarded as a sample of what is needed in order to make headway with the question of population movements in other sectors of sub-Saharan Africa. They are directly concerned with the western sector of the 'Land of the Blacks', and hold out promising prospects for the understanding of groups as representative as the Fulani and the Soninke.[22] The study of relevant population movements in this area takes us back to the neolithic period in the Sahara, and particularly to the major geoclimatic event of the desiccation and desertification of this area. The process, which entered its active phase in about the fourth millennium before the Christian era, brought about considerable social and historical changes which affected the whole of the continent. It is now established that the population map of the neolithic Sahara was perceptibly different from the situation following the climatic change, and there are plausible indications of a sedentary majority black population. The first millennium of the Christian era may have been characterized by the continued existence of black peasant communities as well as entrenched cores among Libyco-Berber and then Berber nomads. Pressure from these latter set off a gradual southward movement, i.e. towards the habitat which the black peoples have largely retained. We must

21. P. Munson, 1968, 1970, 1971, 1980; H. J. Hugot *et al.*, 1973; H. J. Hugot, 1979.
22. See, on the geographical conditions of this region, C. Toupet, 1977.

now consider whether these hypotheses allow us to understand the very moot questions of the origins of Fulani and Soninke in the Sahel.

The Fulani inhabit a very large area of the West African savanna, and their presence in several regions between Senegal and Cameroon lends importance to the question of their provenance and the various stages of their journeyings.[23] Their way of life makes them sometimes seem marginal in relation to other groups, which tends to make the latter think that the Fulani are essentially unstable and always 'migrating'. This largely explains why diffusionist speculation has found in the Fulani fertile ground on which to deploy a variety of 'Hamitic' theories. The cradle of the Fulani has been sought in all sorts of areas, both inside and outside Africa: their ancestors were perhaps the Tziganes, perhaps the Pelasgians or, according to Delafosse, Judaeo-Syrians. Some people have thought they came from India, because of the supposed affinity of Fulfulde and Sereer with the Dravidian languages; others found anthropological and sociological similarities between the Fulani of the Adamawa and the ancient Iranians; some hold that they are descended from the Berber Arabs; while others again hold that they are Nubian, Ethiopian or at any rate East African in origin, and link them with the Nuba of Kordofān.[24]

Most of these theories are supported with various linguistic and anthropological arguments. None of them is really convincing. They all share the 'Hamitic' presupposition that the formation of the great states of the Sudan is primarily due to outside factors contributed by pastoral peoples such as the Fulani. These ideas are not supported by current studies, all of which tend to agree that the Fulani phenomenon belongs within the West African context and forms an integral part of its human geography, its historical development and its culture. There is no possibility of solving the problem of their origin and movements except in this context. From the linguistic point of view, improved knowledge of their vernaculars reveals that Fulfulde has an undoubtedly African substratum showing similarities to Wolof and Serer, though pre-Berber components have been grafted on to this core. As regards their provenance, the evidence points to southern Mauritania, where the Fulani were to be found at the beginning of the Christian era. Striking resemblances and influences of Fulfulde have been found in the toponyms of the Brakna and Tāgant areas of Mauritania. This set of hypotheses suggests that the Fulani are descended from the cattle rearers for which there is evidence in Mauritania datable to the third and second millennia before the Christian era. In the period that concerns us they moved at the same time as the black peoples towards the Senegal Valley, and played a part in the formation of some states, such as Takrūr. The Fulani presence in West Africa is especially evident in Futa Toro in the fifth/eleventh century, although they are not explicitly mentioned in

23. There is a great deal of literature on the Fulani; cf. C. Seydou, 1977.

24. The various hypotheses have been described by L. Tauxier, 1937 and D. J. Stenning, 1959.

the Arabic sources before al-Maḳrīzī and the *Kano Chronicle* (eighth/fourteenth to ninth/fifteenth century).

Something should be said at this point about the ethnonyms Fulani (Peul)[25] and Tukulor (Toucouleur): the Fulani (Peul) call themselves Pullo (in the singular) and Fulbe (in the plural). All those who speak their language – Pular or Fulfulde – are called Hal-pularen. The latter is also the term used by the inhabitants of Futa Toro whom European sources refer to as the Tukulor (Toucouleur). Ethnographers and other scholars of the colonial period who came in contact with the Fulbe in Senegal began calling the herdsmen the Fulbe (Fulani, Peul) proper while for the sedentary people speaking the same language they suggested the name Tukulor (Toucouleur), regarding them as a different ethnic group. Although the two groups have different customs, the differences are due to socio-economic factors and have nothing to do with ethnic, linguistic or cultural considerations. It is an irony of fate that in the region which was the point of departure of the migrations of the Fulbe towards the east, that is, the Senegal Valley (Futa Toro), the Fulbe should be called by a name that is alien to them.[26]

If speculations and hypotheses about the origin and prehistoric migrations of the Fulani are set aside, it is almost unanimously recognized today that in historical times the Fulani came from the Senegalese Futa and that the Senegalese group, the neighbour of their close relatives, the Sereer and the Wolof, should be regarded as the nucleus from which other groups whose language was Pular or Fulfulde spread out and emigrated towards the east and the south.

Between the fifth/eleventh century and the ninth/fifteenth century the Fulani moved towards Masina, passing through Diombogo and Kaarta. It should be noted that the Fulani settled by a process of gradual contacts. Thus small groups and families from Ferlo and Futa Toro settled in Futa Jallon. There was thus a slow integration as the result of interchange with the peoples who were already there when the Fulani arrived.[27] The Fulani's movements were nothing whatever like invasions; and hence they are not consonant with the usual scenario of the 'Hamitic theories' about the transformation of the archaic structures of the black peoples by 'white Hamites'. The question of the origin and movements of the Fulani is crucial to the history of the peoples of West Africa, for it affects all groups in the Western and Central Sudan. But other aspects of the Fulani's relations

25. The term Fulani is prevalent in English Africanist literature and the term Peul in French. This is largely because the French first encountered these people in a context (Senegal) where they retained their own name for themselves, whereas the English met them in northern Nigeria where those in political power had adopted the Hausa name, Fulani.

26. The Fulbe are called Fula by the Mandingo, Fulani (sing., Ba-Filanci) by the Hausa, Fellata by the Kanuri and the Arabs of the Sudan, and Fulani by the Arabs.

27. T. Diallo, 1972.

with these groups, especially the Wolof, the Sereer, the Soninke and the 'Mandingo', and also with the ancient kingdom of Ghana, need to be further investigated.

The foundation of Ghana, like the origin of the Fulani, has been interpreted in diffusionist terms, based on what was said by the authors of the *ta'rīkhs*; Delafosse attributes to Ghana Syro-Palestinian founders who came to the Soninke of Awkār from Cyrenaica, stopping on the way in Aïr and the Sudanic zone of Niger. These foreigners were supposedly the ancestors of the Fulani as well, and were said to have set up the powerful state of Ghana in the third century of the Christian era. Towards the end of the second/eighth century Soninke blacks with Kaya Maghan Cissé as their first king (*tunka*) supposedly drove the whites back towards Tāgant, Gorgol and the Futa.[28]

Paradoxically, the legends of the kingdom of Wagadu seem to lend colour to this. The versions reported by C. Monteil give Dina, the founder of Kumbi, capital of Wagadu, a Jewish origin (Job) in the case of the first version and an Iranian one (Salmān the Persian, companion of the Prophet) in the case of the second.[29] But the agreement suggested is more apparent than real, since an analysis of the Wagadu stories shows that they claim no basis in history. The point of these stories lies elsewhere, particularly in the religious and social spheres. In that sense they do not tie in with the circumstantial details contained in the theory of a Syro-Palestinian origin for the founders of Ghana.

It is now seems established that the neolithic population of the Sahara was quite dominated by blacks, traces of whom can be found as far as the Adrār. Following the change to a drier climate, the white population (the Libyco-Berbers) moved southwards, but came up against organized black peasants like those of Dhār Tishīt ancestors of the Soninke of Ghana. The defensive sites of Dhār Tishīt show that the blacks were indeed organized to resist the pressure of the Libyco-Berber nomads. Given these factors it seems likely that the foundations of an organized state like the Ghana of the Arabic sources date back to the first millennium before the Christian era and it is not impossible that the Chebka phase between −1000 and −900 is a credible hypothesis, as suggested by A. Bathily on an interpretation of Munson's work.[30]

Hypotheses about the very old establishment of Ghana by a black population, and its initial habitat in the neolithic Sahara in an area further north than later phases of Ghana, are not purely arbitrary, especially since the persistence of 'residual' elements right from the Arab period to our own time greatly adds to their plausibility. This at any rate is the conclusion to be drawn from the role attributed by the Arab geographers to the Gangara-

28. M. Delafosse, 1912, Vol. 2, pp. 198ff.
29. C. Monteil, 1953, pp. 370–3, 386, 389.
30. A. Bathily, 1975, especially pp. 29–33.

Wangara and the Bafūr, and especially from the existence to this day of Harātīn blacks scattered across the Sahara.

Even a study of Arab texts and the oral traditions shows that the blacks in historical times inhabited an area much further north than they do today. They controlled the Tāgant, Awkār, Hōdh (Ḥawḍ), Tīris and Adrār areas. Analysis of these texts and traditions makes it possible to situate the Soninke in Tāgant and Hōdh and the ancestors of the Serer and Fulani in other parts of present-day Mauritania. The last two groups had earlier lived together in southern Mauritania and afterwards in Futa Toro.[31] Whereas the Fulani remained in the Senegal Valley, the Serer moved further south towards the territory they now occupy in Sine and Salum.

Undue emphasis has often been placed on divisions between the Berber nomads and the sedentary black peoples and fierce, unrelenting and merciless struggles between them. While there is no denying the fact that these two groups clashed with each other, it should not be forgotten that the necessities of economic and political life led them to live and co-operate very closely together. That is why it is no longer valid to interpret the relations between the whites and blacks of the Sahel solely in terms of racial and religious confrontation.[32]

It is not enough to attribute the dispersion of the Soninke solely to the pressure exerted by the Berbers and especially the Almoravids; there were many factors, the foremost being the climatic factor. Their original habitat – Wagadu of Soninke legend – was situated in a region of unstable climate but well placed from the commercial standpoint. The Wagadu legend tells us that the people of Wagadu fled south after a drought that was to last seven years. This climatic disaster, which is reminiscent of the drought of the 1970s, seems to have been the primary reason for the dispersion of the Soninke. Their migrations took them over large parts of the Western Sudan, from Gambia as far as Songhay, but one very large group remained behind in their initial habitat in Awkār and Hōdh, where they established their first state, ancient Ghana. It is not yet possible to establish even a rough chronology of these events, but there is absolutely no doubt that the migrations of the Soninke extended over several centuries.

The emergence of the Sudanese hegemonies

During the first millennium of the Christian era, a succession of organized societies appeared in the central and eastern Sudan and developed into veritable states. Some like Kānem or Ghana became very powerful. Others in the process of formation like those of the Hausa, the Songhay and the Takrūr were less extensive. When the Muslims arrived in the Sudan during the first centuries of Islam, they found themselves in the presence of

31. See T. Diallo, 1972.
32. J. Devisse, 1970; S. K. McIntosh and R. McIntosh, 1981.

these groups and had to come to terms with them. While there are still gaps in our knowledge as to the stages in the formation of these states, we can trace them in broad outline by focusing on the groups that formed Ghana and Kānem.

Amongst the oldest homogeneous groups of the Sudan, the Kanuri people occupy a special place. Their origin dates back to the period after the desiccation of the Sahara. The black farming peoples withdrew around the residual depression of Lake Chad, distributing themselves on both sides of an area with a harsh climate, the triangle delineated by the line Borku–Azben–Chad. Whilst the so-called Chadic language peoples such as the Hausa settled to the west of this area, the Teda-Daza language groups, in particular the Kanuri, the Kānembu and Zaghāwa, occupied the east. Local traditions attribute the foundation of the Kānem state to an Arab hero, Sayf Ibn Dhi Yazan, who took control of a group of nomads, the Magumi, settled to the north-east of Lake Chad.[33]

In the Western Sudan the empire of Ghana was built up on a very broad ethnic base: the great Mande-speaking family extended from the southern forest land to the Sahel adjoining the Sahara. The kingdom of Ghana was located in the northern part, peopled by Soninke who were in contact with the white nomads of the Sahara. Oral traditions collected at Timbuktu some thousand years after the founding of Ghana relate that the first ruling dynasty of that country was white.

The frequency with which the oral traditions orginating in Sudanese societies themselves attribute their origin to white ancestors might seem surprising. That raises the question of the origin of state structures in the Sudan. However, the late date of these accounts and the situation of the black societies that produced them provide some answer to the question: those accounts simply project into the past facts that were contemporary with those societies. The oral traditions concerning white ancestors appear, in fact, in a context where the northern Berber groups play a dominant role.

The attitude of Arab authors towards this specific question provides some valuable information here: generally speaking there is a widespread tendency in the Muslim world to link the ruling classes of a group or dynasty to the Prophet or his entourage and thereby give legal sanction to their power.[34] However, Arab authors before the middle of the sixth/twelfth century make no mention of the white origin of the dynasties that ruled the Sudanese states, whether they speak of Ghana, Takrūr or Songhay. Al-Bakrī, who provides most information on the fifth/eleventh century, dispels all doubt on this question: Ghana was ruled by a black pagan king.[35] It was not until al-Idrīsī (sixth/twelfth century) that the theme of

33. See Chapter 15 below.
34. See Chapter 4 above.
35. J. M. Cuoq, 1975, pp. 99–100.

white origins was developed;[36] this theme accordingly falls into the context of the growing expansion of Islam in the Sudan. Al-Idrīsī, moreover, was the first to chronicle the events following the Almoravid conquest which was spearheaded by the Ṣanhādja Berbers of the western Sahara. Critical scrutiny both of the accounts transmitted by oral tradition and the texts of Arab writers before al-Bakrī clarify the reasons why the theme of white origins took on such importance; at the same time, the effort made to suppress it reveals the importance of the opposite thesis.

The states of the Sudan were specific creations of the black peoples. They were in contact with the Berbers of the southern edge of the Sahara, and maintained complex relations with these neighbours of white origin. Certainly the black farmers initially withdrew under the pressure of the nomadic herdsmen and settled in the less rigorous areas of the Sahel, but they later organized themselves so as to be in a better position to resist such pressure. The Sudanese found within themselves the political and social resources necessary to face up to the threats coming from the desert. But a permanent state of antagonism existed, for the powerful empire of Ghana was, from 380/990 on, in a position to dominate Awdāghust economically, thanks to the activities of the Zanāta who had come from North Africa, and so establish political hegemony. One century later, under pressure from the Almoravids, this same Ghana lost its indisputable primacy among the Sudanese states. Nevertheless, the state of tension that existed between the Berbers and the black peoples did not result in the Berbers taking over the Sudanese states, for the latter had built up a solid organization.

The basis of the prosperity of the Sudanese states

The coming into being and development of the states of the Sudan in the period under review were based on the use of certain instruments and techniques which made it possible for those who possessed them to impose their rule on the small groups of farmers and herdsmen of the Sahel. Two factors seem to have played a decisive role in this regard: the possession of iron and the use of horses and camels.

Some studies (for the moment, still fragmentary) about metals in Black Africa have pointed out the connection between iron and the formation of the large Sudanese states. Apart from the importance iron has for hunting and farming, it is a factor of military strength conferring its possessor with technical superiority over others. As far as the Sudan is concerned, the role of the army was decisive in the formation of states like those of Kānem or Ghana. Increasing interest is being shown in oral tradition having to do with the trade in iron and with blacksmiths who form a category of persons holding power in a variety of ways. This can throw light on the role of iron

36. J. M. Cuoq, 1975, p. 133.

in ancient times; but the question of the initial acquisition of techniques and their spread is much more complex and has been little studied.

Two hypotheses exist. According to the first, iron from the Middle East reached the Sudan through the Nile Valley via Meroe, an important and flourishing metallurgical centre.[37] From there it spread southwards and westwards into the savanna. According to the second hypothesis, the iron came from North Africa, and was brought by the Phoenicians and the Carthaginians (fifth century before the Christian era) to the Sudan. The weapons depicted on rock paintings discovered in the Sahara have been referred to in support of that theory. But objects found at Nok, in a region south of the Jos plateau in northern Nigeria, are evidence that iron metallurgy existed in ancient times in Black Africa. In the third century before the Christian era, iron was already widely used. These new facts point to the need to reassess previous theories and suggest several possible routes by which iron entered Africa, without excluding the possibility that some centres of iron-working grew up locally.

As has often been suggested, there is a close connection between iron and use of the horse because both are linked to the formation of the large states of the Sudan. It is known that there were horses in the Sahara during the second half of the second millennium and the first centuries of the last millennium before the Christian era. However, they followed population movements, the Barbary horse also being found in the Maghrib and the Dongola in the south-east. The Barbary (or Mongol) horse was used in West Africa in Hōdh and the Sahel as far as Jerma. But from the outset of the Christian era, the horse was replaced by the camel, an animal more resistant to the rigours of the desert, for trans-Saharan communications. The latter played a considerable role in the establishment of Sudanese dominion from Takrūr as far as Kānem. The camel was bred throughout the Sahel and was used for transporting salt and the rounding-up of slaves, to say nothing of its military importance.[38]

Features of an original civilization

In the present state of our knowledge about the peoples of the Sudan, much work is being done on trade between these peoples and their partners to the north – Berbers and Maghribis – to the detriment of the domestic trade within the black communities themselves. This is even more true of the relationships between the great Sahel states and the countries of the savanna and the forest.[39] Here the documentary material available is scanty, and current information is not helping to put the balance right.

37. On this question, see Unesco, *General History of Africa*, Vol. II, chs 11 and 21.

38. On the introduction of the different animals, and their importance, see H. J. Hugot, 1979.

39. See Chapter 14 below.

Nevertheless, we can analyse the position of the black states in the balance of power thus created by contact between the Berber and Maghribi peoples and the blacks of the Sudan through their trans-Saharan relations. The prevailing impression is that this was a massive piece of exploitation of the countries of sub-Saharan Africa by better equipped northern states, which had a greater variety of more highly developed instruments and techniques borrowed from a Mediterranean world swarming with up-to-date inventions of all kinds.

An old and relatively steady phenomenon like slavery, at least for certain areas, would suffice to demonstrate this. Much of the trade network seems to have been set up by the Maghribi and Saharan Berber masters responsible for establishing the main routes. They turn up both at the northern outlets and on the routes, which were studded with staging-posts. There were bitter struggles for the control of the routes, and the powers of the moment tried to ensure satisfactory safety conditions for the orderly conduct of an often very lucrative traffic. The question that then arises is how the states of the Sudan behaved in this situation, bearing in mind the many circumstances that favoured the people of the north and the consequent imbalance in their favour. The activities of the black states can be observed at three levels: the growth of their power, real control of the sector under their authority and their adoption of a policy suited to the interests of their people.

Al-Bakrī's descriptions of the kings of Ghana and Kāw-Kāw (Gao) give a series of details which show how the monarchy in both kingdoms was aggrandized to prompt the veneration of the people. The king of Ghana was distinguished by ritual apparel: only he and the heir apparent could wear sewn clothes, and he also wore a gilded cap and a turban, necklaces and bracelets. The king held audience to dispense justice in the setting of an impressive ceremonial, with strict etiquette described in minute detail by al-Bakrī. The latter mentions a practice of extreme importance because of its religious implications: the king's subjects prostrated themselves at his approach and threw earth on to their heads.[40] But this custom (hardly consistent with Islam) was spared to Muslims, who merely clapped their hands. Lastly, the grandiose ceremonies marking the king's funeral are described: the custom of burying servants with the sovereign, the sacrifices and libations offered to him, the sacred woods that sheltered the tombs of the kings and their inviolable character; all this helped to make the monarchy a sacred institution worthy of reverence.

As regards the king of Kāw-Kāw (Gao), al-Bakrī relates that his meal was accompanied by a special ritual: women dancing to the sound of drums, all business in town suspended during the king's meal, and public announcement of the end of the royal meal by shouts and yells.[41]

40. J. M. Cuoq, 1975, pp. 99–100.
41. J. M. Cuoq, 1975, p. 108.

Royalty of a sacred kind seems to have been a specific feature of the culture of the great black states of the Sudan, at least during the Islamic period. Attempts have been made to use the features of this type of monarchy as support for a diffusionist interpretation. But in the context of a medieval Sudan confronted with a relatively homogenous Muslim world this institution stands out as something indigenous: thus it is significant that the Arab geographers do not, for instance, describe the situation of an Islamized, integrated ruler like the ruler of Takrūr. Such an institution can also be regarded as an effective instrument in the hands of these societies for governing their states, especially in the case of kingdoms exerting hegemony over a very wide area, like Gao and Ghana.

While the kings of the Sudan had authority and power within their states, which they governed firmly by means of a suitable institution, mastery of external relations was not completely beyond them. Ghana's relations with the Berbers who reigned at Awdāghust from its foundation by the Lamtūna in the third/ninth century can be so interpreted. The rulers of Ghana extended their frontiers in all directions from the late second/eighth century onwards. The existence of a Berber trading centre at the extreme southern edge of the desert could be conducive to trade with the north, and from this point of view the town of Awdāghust had a *raison d'être*. All the same, the role of these traders had to be within limits compatible with Ghana's sovereignty. It was enough for them to be brokers and intermediaries in a traffic whose real southern terminus must have been Ghana. Escalation of their claims and the strengthening of Lamtūna power at Awdāghust could represent a threat to the state of Ghana, which reached the height of its power in the fourth/tenth and fifth/eleventh centuries. This is the explanation of the installation of a Soninke governor to control thenceforth the power of the Lamtūna. Soninke management seems to have fulfilled its purpose very efficiently, for the blacks were to keep control of the situation at Awdāghust until the Almoravids, chafing at their alliance with Ghana, destroyed it in 446/1055.[42]

Control of the political situation was inseparable from a real Soninke stranglehold over the entire economic sector in the area under their jurisdiction. One of the necessary conditions for this power was information about the sources of their prosperity. The rulers of Ghana exerted strict and effective control in this important domain, especially as regards the provenance of gold and how it was acquired. It is not impossible that this went back a very long way. A story such as that of the 'silent trade' in gold, very widespread even beyond Africa, may have served, *inter alia*, as a 'red herring'.[43]

The ruler of Ghana, in his efforts to control the springs of commercial transactions south of the Sahara, pursued an intelligent policy: he levied a

42. Cf. al-Bakrī in J. M. Cuoq, 1975, pp. 91–2. See Chapter 13 below.
43. On the 'silent trade', see P. F. de Moraes Farias, 1974.

PLATE 5.1 *The Mosque of Tegdaoust/Awdāghust, after excavation and conservation work on the walls. The ḳibla wall faces south-southwest.*

tax when goods were brought into or taken out of his territory. Traders had to pay twice on salt: one dinar on bringing it in and two dinars on taking it out. Ghana was thus the hub for the distribution of salt, a vital product in sub-Saharan Africa. According to al-Bakrī, the ruler of Ghana kept for himself all nuggets extracted, to avoid a slump in the price of gold.[44] Since he had a good understanding of the economic mechanisms of which Ghana was the hub, he meant to keep the monopoly of a product as vital as gold. Thus the black world organized its trading economy to withstand the power of the salt producers, salt being exchanged for gold.

This being so, it is hardly likely that trade and the whole system of economic exchanges it entailed was introduced to Ghana's blacks by the Libyco-Berbers, as has sometimes been suggested. The latter are supposed to have contributed not only the idea but also the techniques of this trade (including the slave trade), and to have brought about the birth of the state of Ghana. The control exercised by the Sudan's rulers over their own commercial sector rules such a hypothesis out of court. The case of the Sēfuwa of Kānem is instructive in this connection. Having taken over from the Zaghāwa rulers (Duguwa dynasty) when Kānem was Islamized, they realized that the religious development of the country could threaten their

44. J. M. Cuoq, 1975, p. 101.

economy, which was based primarily on the slave trade. The point was that it was forbidden to enslave a free Muslim. As D. Lange has demonstrated in his article on the progress of Islam and political changes in Kānem from the fifth/eleventh century to the sixth/twelfth century the Sēfuwa continued a type of politico-economic domination reminiscent of the practices of their non-Muslim predecessors during the Zag͟hāwa period.[45]

The kings of the Sudan showed great political skill in their relations with the Muslim world and the culture of all their northern partners with whom they had dealings. They used the abilities of the Muslims who frequented their states to their own advantage. According to al-Bakrī, the king of Ghana chose his interpreters, his treasurer and his ministers from among the Muslims.[46] Thus in entrusting some sectors of his administration to educated Muslims he expected some measure of efficiency from it. In return he tried to create favourable conditions for the practice of their religion. Ghana, like Gao, had a town next to the king's town in which the Muslims lived, with twelve mosques all with their *imāms*, muezzins and lectors. Lawyers and scholars also lived in this town. Lastly, Muslims were not obliged to comply with customs incompatible with their religious convictions.

As regards the ruler of Gao, he was normally supposed to be a Muslim. Moreover the attributes of royal authority handed over to him at his investiture comprised, besides the seal, the sword, and the Qoran 'supposedly', according to al-Bakrī, 'the gifts sent by the Emir of believers'.[47] But the fact that both sovereigns governed peoples who freely practised traditional religions raises the problem of the Sudan's relations with the Muslim world in this initial period of Islamization.[48]

On the whole their persistent attempts to control their environment in a responsible way can be regarded as a characteristic of the states of the Sahelian Sudan (corresponding to the known part of the Land of the Blacks). In this way we can see the emergence of a specific culture, deeply rooted in the world of traditional religion. The latter has often unobtrusively but effectively challenged much of the data which arrived with the pretensions and prestige of an apparently better-equipped society.

Conclusion

The study of population movements entails first and foremost a rigorously critical reappraisal of widespread notions about the 'migrations' of the black peoples over very long distances. The movements of the peoples of

45. D. Lange, 1978, p. 513; cf. Chapter 15 below.
46. J. M. Cuoq, 1975, p. 99.
47. ibid., p. 109.
48. On these issues, see Chapters 3 and 4 above, Chapter 28 below.

the Sudan before the fifth/eleventh century bore no resemblance to anarchic movements over enormous areas.

The first settlement dates from the end of the neolithic period when the erstwhile flourishing Sahara had become barren and forbidding after a 'slow agony'. The blacks who constituted the predominant population of the Sahara had to withdraw southwards into the Sahel to look for favourable agricultural conditions. They abandoned their lands to groups of specialized nomadic herdsmen who were able to adapt themselves to the new conditions while continuing to attempt to impose their rule on the peoples of the Sahel region, subjecting them to frequent pressure. The latter found there other groups of blacks with whom they aligned themselves in order to face the threats coming from the north. This gave impetus to the gradual development of socio-political units of varying size that extended from Kānem in the east to Takrūr in the west during the period preceding the arrival of Islam in the Sudan.

When the Muslims arrived in the Sudanese Sahara, they found themselves in the presence of a series of states, some of them fully established, others still in the process of formation. The powerful Soninke kingdom of Ghana dominated the extended Mande group in the region between the Senegal and Niger rivers while the nucleus of what would become the Songhay kingdom took shape in the eastern part of the Inland Niger Delta. That kingdom controlled the river traffic as well as the route linking the Niger to North Africa via Adrār des Ifoghas and the Hoggar. On the other side of Lake Chad, the Sao were in the process of consolidating their position and they acquired the instruments of their future policy of conquest. The use of horses and camels would aid them in their systematic expansion northwards where they would take their place among the Kanuri who were beginning to emerge as a group.

The arrival of Islam in the second/eighth century introduced a new factor which, in the century that followed, would stimulate increased economic and cultural exchanges. But it was above all the religious factor that was destined to play an important role in the political and social development of the region from the Maghrib to the Sudan.

The period from the second/eighth century to the fifth/eleventh century was decisive for the peoples of the Sudan. Because of the sound organization and powerfully centralized structure of their monarchies, they were able to realize the importance of trade with Mediterranean and Saharan Africa. However, their constant concern was to retain control over the transactions to prevent the Saharan intermediaries from gaining a stranglehold on trade and the sources of their prosperity. However, perceiving the cultural and economic advantages to be gained from the presence of their northern partners, they adopted a sufficiently tolerant attitude towards their outlook and religious demands and even went so far as to become converted to Islam while remaining rooted in their own religious traditions. In so doing, the Sudanese leaders, and above all those of Ghana, were able to withstand the competition of their neighbours, the Ṣanhādja, who were part of the Almoravid movement in the fifth/eleventh century. That prevented their complete decline despite the Almoravid onslaught and a temporary eclipse. In that way, the black states succeeded in safeguarding their personality and thus ensured the foundations of a lasting civilization whose subsequent development found expression in Mali, the Songhay empire and in the city-states of the Hausa.

Note of the Rapporteur of the International Scientific Committee

Research on iron metallurgy in Africa in ancient times is now making rapid strides and is no longer in the dark. The period of the great theoretical debates about the spread of this craft has come to an end. Excavations and confirmed datings have now proved that iron was being produced through the process of reduction in a furnace in several parts of the continent at least five centuries before the Christian era. Sites from that period have so far been located not only in Nigeria but also in the Aïr region of the Niger, present-day Mali, and in Cameroon, Tanzania, Rwanda and Burundi. Of course, this list is very provisional. Almost every year, new research findings change the overall picture, challenging postulates regarding the general or limited spread of that craft. Iron was also produced in the bend of the Senegal, the bend of the Limpopo and in Ghana from the first centuries of the Christian era. Many African and Malagasy researchers are now at work on this problem from Mauritania to Madagascar. The technological importance to be attached to this ancient African production of iron by the direct process has been shown at various meetings, such as the ones which took place in 1983 at the University of Compiègne, at the Collège de France in Paris (proceedings published) and at the University of Paris I (proceedings in the course of publication).[49] Research is also going on at the same time into the history of metallurgy. The essential work of revising the descriptive vocabulary of these technologies, too much of which was left vague and imprecise in the past, has also been begun.

49. The proceedings of the Compiègne meeting have been published, but neither entirely nor satisfactorily; those of the Collège de France meeting were published under the title: 'Métallurgies africaines', 1983. Mémoires de la Société des Africanistes, nº 9, published by Nicole Echard; as for those of the University of Paris I meeting, they are still in the course of publication.

6

The Bantu-speaking peoples and their expansion

S. LWANGA-LUNYIIGO and
J. VANSINA

Almost all the peoples occupying the southern third of the African continent, from the Cameroon–Nigeria sea coast in the west to the Somalia–Kenya coastline in the east and southwards as far as Port Elizabeth, speak a closely related group of languages known as the Bantu languages.

The Bantu family of languages

The Bantu family consists of over four hundred languages all deriving from the same ancestral language known as 'proto-Bantu'. This is a fact that has been established beyond doubt on the basis of lexical, phonetic, morphological (grammatical) and syntactic resemblances which cannot be accounted for by mere chance or by borrowings. A common parentage must be assumed. Take, for instance, the word meaning 'people' in the following languages:

Duala: *bato*	Bushong: *baat*
Fang: *bot*	Luba: *bantu*
Tio: *baaru*	Rwanda: *abantu*
Kongo: *bantu*	Shona: *vanhu*
Mongo: *banto*	Herero: *abandu*

All these words follow the same pattern. It can be seen that they all derive from the form made up of the root **-ntu* and the prefix **ba-*, denoting the plural. In addition, the differences between languages are regular, as may be gathered from other comparisons. For instance, a *-t-* in the second position of the root invariably becomes *-r-* in Tio. This rules out the possibility of fortuitous similarities and borrowings. A proto-Bantu glossary has been drawn up for over five hundred roots,[1] all following regular phonetic patterns.

But vocabulary is only one aspect of language. Analogies, even in points of detail, are also to be found in the morphological (grammatical) system of the Bantu languages. In the above example, the prefix governs the gram-

1. M. Guthrie, 1967–71, collected the available data. Compare A. E. Meeussen, 1969.

matical agreements (concordances) and belongs itself to a specific class of prefixes. The corresponding singular prefix is **mu-* which, combined with the root, forms the word meaning 'person'. The system of agreements, the formation of adjectives, all kinds of pronouns, the breakdown of the verb into prefix, marker, infix, stem, extension and ending and the way these elements function, the invariants, the deverbative formation of nouns are all as alike in the Bantu languages as is the grammatical structure of the Romance languages deriving from Latin. A common grammar of Bantu has in fact been produced.[2] What has been said of the morphology applies equally to the syntax and phonological system. All the evidence, therefore, bears out the fact that more than four hundred languages spread over one-third of the great landmass of Africa have their origins in a single ancestral language. The historical implications of such a vast phenomenon are evident.

Origins and subdivisions of the Bantu languages

The phenomenon of Bantu relationships was certainly one that did not pass unnoticed. As early as the beginning of the sixteenth century, the first Portuguese navigators were surprised by the linguistic bonds linking the inhabitants of the kingdom of the Congo and those of the continent's eastern seaboard. Since Wilhem Bleek[3] first identified the speakers of Bantu as a group in 1862, dubbing the family 'Bantu' because of the structure of the words meaning 'people', anthropologists, linguists, historians and others have been intrigued by the Bantu question and have tried to account for the origins and movements of the Bantu-speaking peoples. In 1886, H. H. Johnston outlined a theory for the identification of the birthplace of the proto-language and for retracing the history of its geographical expansion. His study, published between 1919 and 1922, was the first serious attempt to locate the origins of the Bantu and plot the stages of their dispersal. Using linguistic evidence, he located the ancestors of the Bantu in the Baḥr al-Ghazāl, 'not far from the Baḥr al-Jebel, to the east of Kordofān in the north, or in the Benue and Chad basins in the west'. According to him, the first movement of the Bantu was eastwards towards Mount Elgon and from there to the northern shores of Lake Victoria, mainland Tanzania and the Zairian forest, with the first large-scale incursion into central and southern Africa beginning around −300.[4]

In 1889, Carl Meinhof provided formal (phonetic) proof of the unity of the Bantu languages. Ever since then, linguists – often known as 'Bantuists' – have been adding to our knowledge of the Bantu linguistic

2. C. Meinhof, 1906. A new comparative grammar is being prepared in the Leiden and Tervuren centres.
3. W. H. I. Bleek, 1862–9.
4. H. H. Johnston, 1919–22.

family.[5] Two major theories have been put forward by linguists to account for the origins of the Bantu-speaking peoples. Joseph Greenberg thought that they must have originated in the area of greatest Bantu language divergence and, following this theory, he traced their origins to the middle Benue region of Nigeria, to the north-west of the vast territory where the Bantu languages are firmly rooted.[6]

As this conclusion was not accepted by the influential Bantuist Malcolm Guthrie, it was subsequently subjected to close investigation but is now accepted as accurate by all linguists. In Guthrie's view, the most likely location for the birthplace of 'proto-Bantu' was in the area of greatest Bantu language convergence, that is to say around the watershed of the Congo and Zambezi rivers, with a nucleus in the Shaba province of Zaire.[7] These conflicting hypotheses advanced by eminent linguists have been used by many specialists as the basis for their own theories on the origins and expansion of the Bantu.

Suggesting that the hypotheses of Greenberg and Guthrie were complementary, the distinguished historian Roland Oliver put forward a brilliant theory which divided the expansion of the Bantu from their original homeland in West Africa to southern Africa into four phases. These phases were as follows: (1) very rapid migration along the Congo (Zaire) waterways of small groups speaking 'pre-Bantu' languages, from the woodlands of central Cameroon and Ubangi to the woodlands south of the Zairian equatorial forest; (2) the gradual consolidation and settlement of the migrant peoples and their expansion through the southern woodland belt extending from coast to coast and embracing the central African region between the mouth of the Congo (Zaire) River in Zaire on the western coast and the Rovuma River in Tanzania on the eastern coast; (3) rapid Bantu penetration into the more humid region north and south of the area of their former lateral expansion and; (4) occupation of the remainder of present Bantu Africa, a process which began during the first millennium before the Christian era and only came to an end towards the middle of the second millennium of the Christian era.[8]

Since 1973, three groups of linguists working independently have proved that Guthrie was wrong. All three adopt a similar approach (based on studies of vocabulary) but they do not use the same data. In fact, one of the studies takes Guthrie's own data as its starting-point.

That the Bantu languages originated in the west has therefore been established. Ideally, one would have to discover the subgroups belonging to the family in order to retrace the routes by which these languages dis-

5. C. Meinhof, 1899. For a historical synopsis and bibliography, see J. Vansina, 1979–80.

6. J. H. Greenberg, 1972.

7. M. Guthrie, 1962.

8. R. Oliver, 1966; some years ago Oliver totally abandoned this theory. See R. Oliver, 1979.

persed and developed. In the comparative approach to historical linguistics, the primary task is to construct a genealogical tree in which the ancestor of the family is the direct antecedent of the ancestors of subgroups which are themselves the forerunners of the ancestors of language subgroups, etc. In order to do this, massive comparisons must be made both of basic vocabulary (lexicostatistics) and grammatical phenomena. So far, nobody has proposed a genealogical subdivision of the Bantu group of languages based on evidence solid enough to be acceptable. The reason is what is known among linguists as 'phenomena of convergence', that is to say massive borrowings among Bantu languages from the time of their common ancestor up to the present day. Among the similarities it is very hard to say what is a borrowing and what dates back to the ancestor of a common subgroup. This circumstance is itself of cardinal importance to historians, since it proves that various Bantu-speaking groups have remained constantly in close contact with their neighbours and have never been really isolated from one another.

The studies currently in progress are using computers and are constructing models of genetic divergence on the basis of comparative elements of basic vocabulary or – in very recent projects – grammatical elements.[9] It is now generally agreed among linguists that there were two major blocs of Bantu languages, the western bloc located principally in the equatorial forest regions and the eastern bloc extending from Uganda to the Cape.

Furthermore, the languages belonging to the eastern group are more closely related to each other than those of the western group. This implies that the expansion of the eastern group began at a later stage and occurred more rapidly than that of the western group, assuming that the rate of change and the amount of convergence were the same in each case, which is not necessarily true. At the other end of the time-scale, it is generally agreed that a number of small genetic groupings have their roots in the relatively recent linguistic past, for instance a Kongo genetic group and a genetic language group from the region of the Great Lakes. Recent studies have made it possible to track down these minimal groupings with increasing accuracy.

Experts did not wait for the results of these studies before subdividing the Bantu languages. As early as 1948, Guthrie began to apply what he called a practical system of classification, grouping blocs of geographically contiguous languages in zones 'of resemblance',[10] based on comparisons of

9. Y. Bastin, A. Coupez, B. de Halleux, 1981. Comparisons between the two types of data enable conclusions to be drawn with virtual certainty in the event of congruence. The western Bantu bloc differs quite sharply from the eastern bloc and within the former, a north-western group is clearly distinguishable from the central forest group. The computer programme is expanded as new data are gathered.

10. M. Guthrie, 1948.

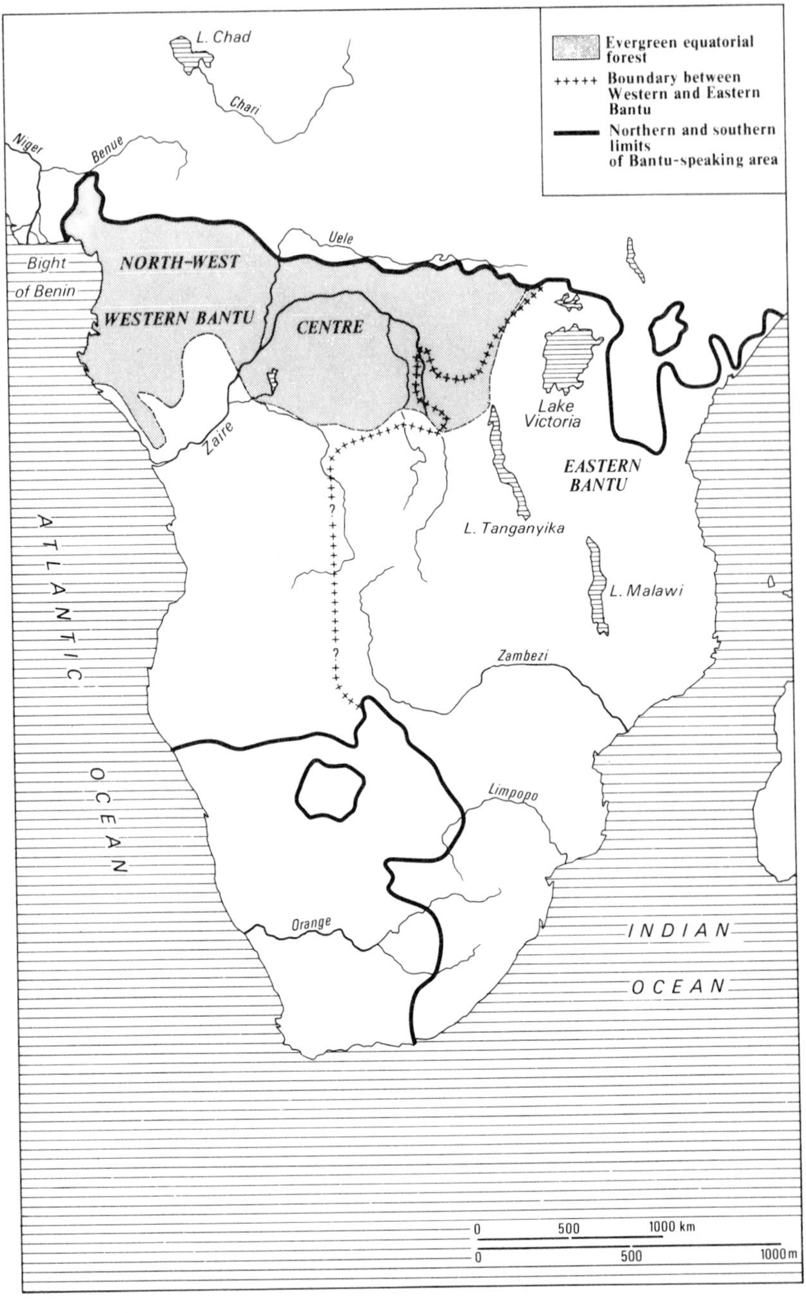

FIG. 6.1 *Bantu expansion*

existing data. These categories were only provisional and intended for practical purposes, but they proved so useful that they are still frequently employed today. Each zone is assigned a letter between A and T, followed by a figure for each smaller grouping and a second figure standing for the language itself. Thus, A70 refers to the so-called 'Pahouin' group of languages and A74 denotes the Fang language.

At first glance, this classification system appears to have no historical value, a fact that is borne out by increasingly elaborate attempts to devise a reliable system of historical classification. Even the subgroups designated by figures cannot always be compared. In addition, a practical system of classification cannot be used for the purposes of historical argument. For instance, the fact that the Banga of Gabon and the Bubi of Malabo Island both belong to the A30 group cannot be taken to indicate that the Bubi languages have their origins on the coast occupied by the Banga or that the Banga came originally from the island. In other words, the categories do not have the value of historical proof.

Broadly speaking, however, some zones clearly correspond more closely to genetic facts than others. Among those that have proved invalid, mention may be made of zone B (Gabon/Congo), Guthrie's former zone D, which has long since been reclassified under D and J, and, on somewhat less convincing evidence, zones F and D. Although the drawbacks of applying a system having no historical validity are enormous, linguists are none the less reluctant to use a system of notation or terminology based on genetic data until the subdivisions of the Bantu family have been established beyond doubt.

It promises to be a time-consuming task, first because the data currently available, even in respect of basic vocabulary, cover only about half of all Bantu languages, whereas in order to draw authoritative conclusions, the least that is required is correct linguistic notation, a more extensive vocabulary and an outline of the grammatical structure of each language. If these conditions were fulfilled, one could proceed with confidence. Thus the basic requirements for really definitive work are a comprehensive set of dictionaries and grammars. There are very few available at present. The bulk of the linguistic heritage of the Bantu-speaking peoples has not yet been recorded. A further difficulty lies in the fact that for much of their history the Bantu languages developed by a process of differentiation of one language, or a small number of languages, from the whole nucleus of languages, so that blocs of languages cannot be compared with one another as, for instance, in the case of the Indo-European languages. It will be necessary in the long run to obtain detailed knowledge of almost every Bantu language – especially in the west – in order to place it in its proper historical perspective.[11] There is no short cut.

11. The procedure is best described in B. Heine, 1973; B. Heine, H. Hoff, R. Vossen, 1977.

Linguistics and history

It is an undeniable fact that linguistic data have historical implications. The phenomenon of a single family of languages spread over such a wide area must have some significance beyond what meets the eye. But what exactly is it? All authors have assumed that the languages in question spread as a result of the migration of their speakers. There is also a tendency to juxtapose or even confuse language, culture and race. Many hope to rediscover a Bantu society, a Bantu culture or a Bantu philosophy still surviving, despite the geographical expansion from an original nucleus to the confines of the African continent and the lapse of thousands of years while the expansion was continuing. But just how valid are these assumptions?

The equation between language, culture and race does not, in any case, hold water. This is a fact that can easily be demonstrated. The Bira language, for instance, is spoken by farming and trapping communities in the forest of north-eastern Zaire and by pygmy hunters living in close contact with them or with other neighbouring crop-growers. The same language is therefore spoken by two different ethnic groups. The same language is also used by the Bira farmers of the savanna whose way of life differs sharply from that of the forest Bira.[12] So here we have one language which cannot even be associated with a single culture. On the contrary, each culture and each way of life is also found among people speaking different languages and living in communities adjacent to those of the groups mentioned above. The forest Bira have the same way of life as the Walese who speak a Central Sudanic language. The pygmies have the same lifestyle as neighbouring pygmy hunters who speak Sudanic languages, and the stock-breeders live like other stock-breeders speaking Central Sudanic, Bantu or even Nilotic languages. Hence, there is not any strict correspondence between language and culture.

It may, of course, be pointed out that the above cases are easily explained. The pygmies adopted the language of the farmers with whom they were associated. The latter, in the forest, adopted the culture of the peoples of the savanna when they emigrated to the savanna, unless the group first lived in the savanna and then adapted itself to the forest. But that is immaterial. The main thing is that originally there was only one community speaking that language and hence the correspondence between culture, language and race was valid. Many other cases could be mentioned, of course, in which culture, language and race overlap. One may go still further and point out that the original Bira-speaking community was undoubtedly not the only one in the race to which it belonged, nor even the only one with a specific way of life, form of society or expressive culture, but must certainly have shared them with speakers of other languages.

12. M. A. Bryan, 1959, pp. 89–90.

Although in the beginning there was a Bantu community, speaking the proto-Bantu language, belonging to a specific 'race' and with a characteristic way of life, the matter is still not entirely clear because data indicate that while the community's main occupation was fishing, some of its subgroups probably lived by farming instead. In addition, languages are our only source of information concerning the proto-Bantu culture. It is quite possible that situations such as that of the Bira existed at that time. Indeed, they must have existed subsequently, since autochthonous communities gave up their own languages and began to speak a Bantu language.

The other assumption, concerning the spread of the family of languages by migration, is not as watertight as it seems. The Romance languages, for example, did not spread through massive migration of the inhabitants of Latium. A whole range of socio-linguistic mechanisms exists which can lead to changes in the geographical location of languages, one of the most important being a change of language. A people may learn a foreign language, become perfectly bilingual and then abandon its own language for the foreign one. This is what happened in the case of the Sekyani of Gabon who are now all bilingual in Mpongwe and are beginning to lose their original language. The same is true of the inhabitants of the western Cape and southern Namibia, who lost the Khoi and San languages and now speak only Afrikaans. These changes are brought about by socio-cultural power relationships. The Roman empire accounted for the spread of the Romance languages, and the Chinese empire, with its steady stream of emigration from the north, accounted for the Sinization of southern China. Demographic processes also play a role. The Norman conquerors of England lost the use of the French language, having been assimilated by their more numerous subjects, and the same thing had happened previously in Normandy itself where they adopted the French language. Commercial or cultural predominance may also influence developments. The Sekyani adopted Mpongwe because it was the language of trade. The cultural predominance of France in Europe accounts for the spread of French in Belgium in the eighteenth century. In conclusion, it may be noted that quite frequently commercial, socio-political and even religious links may engender new common languages, derived from a language invested with prestige, for instance the Koines, the Creoles and the Sabirs. Judging by the massive scale of convergence phenomena among the Bantu languages, this type of situation must have arisen more than once. In the comparatively recent past, mention may be made of Lingala, Swahili or Monokituba as trading languages belonging to the Creole category.

To obtain a more accurate explanation for the expansion of the Bantu languages, historians must proceed by analogy and bear constantly in mind the whole range of socio-linguistic mechanisms involved. They cannot automatically ascribe everything to migration. In any case, given the probable population density prior to our own era, it is misguided to speak in terms of massive population movements. Local demographic superiority or social, economic, cultural or political advantages are far more likely to shed light on the phenomenon. In addition, the history of the spread of the Bantu languages is so long and the area affected so vast that it must be assumed that at one time or another the majority if not all of the factors known to us by analogy could have played a role.

In reality, the linguistic data are of direct use in only one respect, namely the reconstruction of the proto-Bantu community on the basis of what its vocabulary reveals; and the vocabulary, of course, corresponds to a whole period and not to a point in time, for the proto-Bantu language itself evolved, broke up into different dialects and became more sharply differentiated from other related languages. The Bantu vocabulary utilizable today[13] refers to the Bantu group narrowly defined, the 'Common Bantu' closest to us in time. While the evidence available makes it easy to reconstruct the vocabulary in terms of form, the same is not always true of meaning, since meaning also changes over time and may now vary considerably from language to language. For instance, the root **kùmù* means 'healer' or even 'diviner' in the east and 'chief' in the west and in one western bloc of languages (the A70s) it means 'one who is rich'. Of course, the meanings can be linked and we may envisage the proto-Bantu chief as being rich, a healer and a diviner. But the result may prove somewhat artificial. In this case, we have to opt for the meaning 'leader', which is correct but rather vague.

It may, however, be deduced from the old vocabulary that the community which spoke the ancestral Bantu language cultivated the yam, certain other roots and even cereals. The goat was the only domestic animal known. The community hunted (especially the wart hog) but their speciality was fishing. As we have seen, the language may very well have been common to two communities leading comparatively different lives. Kinship was a major principle in internal organization and the community had its specialists, leaders and religious experts. The notions of ancestry and belief in sorcery were well established. One can even form some idea of the attitude of groups of wife-givers to wife-receivers. But there is still a great deal of ground to be covered in the study of vocabulary, and if all goes well a far more lengthy description of this aspect of the question may be expected.

The vocabulary, correlated with archaeological data and a knowledge of the geographical origins of the community, enables us to provide a date for the beginning of the Bantu expansion. We are dealing with a Neolithic community that engaged in agricultural activities (cereal cultivation for instance) but was not familiar with metal-based technology. These clues enable us to narrow down proto-Bantu to the period between −1000 (or even earlier) and −400.[14]

13. M. Guthrie, 1967–71, Vol. 2; A. E. Meeussen, 1969.

14. T. Shaw, 1978, pp. 60–8, 78–80; P. de Maret and F. Nsuka, 1977, examine the question of metallurgy.

The expansion itself was an enormously long process, since even in the nineteenth century it was still not entirely completed in East Africa.[15] The first Arab travellers nevertheless brought back Bantu words from Africa's east coast. By about the eighth century, therefore, Bantu-speaking communities were already settled on the shores of the Indian Ocean. It follows that the Bantu expansion covered not only a third of the continent but a time-span of two to three thousand years. Under the circumstances, it is by no means surprising that we are left with only very general and often sharply divergent evidence of how it came to pass!

Linguistics and archaeology

The line followed by scholars is clear and is reflected in the way the beginnings of Bantu expansion were established. The vocabulary must be combed for information that can be confirmed by finds in archaeological sites. Again, but it is less conclusive, archaeological evidence of large-scale migrations can be compared with what is known about the spread of the Bantu languages.

In theory, this should provide the answer. However, when one considers that Indo-European specialists still hold widely divergent theories in their own field, in which all the languages are well described and excavations have been far more numerous than in Africa, it becomes clear that the task of reconstituting the processes is neither an easy nor a rapid one. Some of the more obvious difficulties may be mentioned. An early Iron Age site may date from after the first movement of expansion of the Bantu languages, but that does not imply that, later on, only the Bantu-speaking peoples of that third of Africa knew how to smelt iron. One cannot automatically attribute all Iron Age sites to communities speaking Bantu. There is evidence in East Africa of the very rapid spread of a type of pottery dating from the early Iron Age, and as the sites are all in the area of expansion of the eastern Bantu languages, this coincidence (and coincidence it is) has been taken as proof that these were the archaeological traces of the Bantu expansion.[16] In the first place, however, very few finds have been made at excavations in other parts of Bantu-speaking Africa. Secondly, it is just as plausible to suggest that this rapid spread of iron was the work of ironsmiths and potters who perhaps represented only a tiny minority of the population in which they settled.

We must constantly bear in mind the fact that archaeology cannot prove what language was spoken by the people who made or used the pottery, cultivated the cereals or fashioned the objects in metal, stone or bone discovered in the sites. Linguistic and archaeological data may, on the other

15. A case in point are the Mbugwe in Tanzania.
16. In particular, D. W. Phillipson, 1977, pp. 102–230 and especially pp. 210–30.

hand, be compared, and the more remarkable the correlation seems to be, the greater its value as evidence.

This is not the place for a review of the sites of the early Iron Age, since the subject was dealt with in several chapters of the preceding volume. Suffice it to note that the earliest sites of Bantu-speaking peoples are undoubtedly associated with tools classified as Neolithic and that the Iron Age sites in southern, central and eastern Africa *may conceivably* be associated with the traces left by speakers of Bantu languages.[17]

The Bantu expansion

Two theories have been put forward to explain the Bantu expansion from their original homelands. One is that the abandonment of a precarious hunting and food-gathering economy in favour of an agricultural economy led to a population explosion, which in turn led to migrations of people seeking space in which to live. Writing in the early 1960s, the archaeologist Merrick Posnansky suggested that the migrations of the Bantu peoples from West Africa to central Africa involved agricultural communities and that the movement gathered momentum after the agricultural techniques (banana and yam cultivation) introduced by the Indonesians between −400 and +200 spread to the forest peoples of central Africa.[18] Another theory, based on the notion of conquest, establishes a link between the expansion of the Bantu and the beginnings of the Iron Age. The working of iron, it is claimed, facilitated agricultural production by making tools more effective and enabled the Bantu to dominate the peoples in the areas where they settled. The main exponent of this theory, C. C. Wrigley, claims they 'were a dominant minority, specialized to hunting with the spear, constantly attracting new adherents ... by their fabulous prestige as suppliers of meat, constantly throwing off new bands of migratory adventurers, until the whole southern sub-continent was iron-using and Bantu-speaking'.[19] Judging by the pattern of migrations in the second part of the present millennium, other, probably more serious reasons can be adduced to explain the incessant movements of the Bantu during the first millennium of the Christian era in sub-equatorial Africa. Famine, the search for more favourable living conditions in the form of better farming and grazing land, epidemics, wars and a sheer spirit of adventure could also have motivated the early Bantu movements, but these factors have hitherto received only scant attention.

Turning to the population explosion and conquest theories, it should be noted that the introduction of agriculture was a gradual process and did not immediately displace the earlier hunting and food-gathering economy in sub-equatorial Africa. Indeed, these two types of economy supplemented

17. Cf. Unesco, *General History of Africa*, Vol. II, chs 25 and 27.
18. M. Posnansky, 1964.
19. C. C. Wrigley, 1960, p. 201.

one another, as they still do in some parts of Africa up to the present day. The beginning of agriculture should not therefore be seen as a dramatic turning-point. It was an evolutionary process which could not immediately have caused a demographic revolution leading to mass emigration of the Bantu in search of more living space. The working of iron only gradually revolutionized agriculture because only small quantities of the metal were initially produced in Bantu Africa. Iron technology did not by any means revolutionize agriculture during the early Iron Age. Up to the beginning of the present century, most forest and bush clearing was done by fire, and the digging stick survived into the twentieth century in Africa. How much more true then of the early Iron Age! Iron technology undoubtedly improved the arsenals of the Bantu of that period, the iron-tipped spear and arrow being the most notable additions, but for a long time after their invention they were probably not regarded as more effective than stone or bone-tipped arrows, wooden spears and clubs, and did not make their possessors more aggressive.

The expansion of the Bantu did not assume the dimensions of an exodus from one area to another. It was most probably a movement of small numbers of people from one village to the next and sometimes back again, a process that was repeated over and over again until successive generations reached all parts of sub-equatorial Africa, perhaps over the space of a thousand or more years. It should not be imagined that the Bantu migrations took the form of a linear progression, unidirectional, in a perpetual forward movement. On the contrary, over thousands of years, movements must have occurred in all directions.

All things considered, what can we say today regarding the Bantu expansion? Proto-Bantu was spoken close to an ecological dividing-line, hence in a comparatively rich environment in so far as the inhabitants were capable of exploiting it. Migration of surplus population, at least on a small scale, probably occurred here. In addition, there were movements of whole villages when, every ten years or so, they moved in order to be closer to newly cleared fields. Their penetration of the forest was most likely a gradual process. The distribution of the north-western languages, sharply divergent from those of the centre of the equatorial forest,[20] shows that they spread out in three main directions, first along the sea-coast towards the south, and across the sea towards Malabo Island. During this first movement, they may even have reached the Gabon estuary. The second movement took the form of a thrust along the edge of the forest towards the east, at least as far as the Sangha River. The third involved penetration of the forest from various points along its edge, either because of the normal advance of agriculture or perhaps again through the activities of fishermen on the Sangha.

The first achievement of the Bantu was mastery of the Zaire forest en-

20. There is a clear dividing-line in both lexical and grammatical classification.

vironment. The process of infiltration occurred in two phases: (1) from north to south, with the Bantu merely following the rivers and the narrow strips of alluvial land, and (2) through the progressive destruction of the primary forest by the Bantu agricultural populations advancing on a broad front.

Very little is known about the early agricultural and metallurgical history of the western proto-Bantu region. It has, however, been suggested that equatorial Zaire was an independent centre of agricultural development, a development due to the great importance attached to yams and palm oil.[21] On Malabo Island, agricultural development based on palm-oil production began in the sixth century and agriculture in the wider equatorial region probably began at much the same time. In the Stanley Pool/Kasai region of Zaire traces of a 'neolithic' culture have been found in the form of heavy stone picks, stone discs, polished stone axes, adzes and pottery. It is believed that the Bantu cultivated yams and oil palms but there is no direct evidence, since these activities leave little trace of their existence for the archaeologist.

There are two major early Iron Age traditions in Zaire, the Kasai/Stanley Pool tradition and the Shaba/eastern Kivu tradition. In the western proto-Bantu region (that of the Kasai/Stanley Pool tradition), no stratified sites have so far been investigated, although large quantities of 'dimple-based' pottery dating from the early Iron Age have been found on the surface. Unfortunately, it has not been possible to obtain isometric dates in this region, but it is reasonable to assume that the working of iron did not occur much earlier there than in the Shaba/eastern Kivu zone where carbon-14 dates in the fourth century were obtained for Shaba and in the first millennium of the Christian era for Kivu. While the stratified sites of Shaba give a clear date for the start of the Iron Age, those of Kivu do not, since comparable sites in Rwanda and Buhaya (Tanzania) have been assigned a much earlier date, around 300 to 500 years before the Christian era.

The agricultural innovations in the western proto-Bantu region started from within and although they encouraged population movements, it is fair to assume that such movements occurred for the most part within the region. The equatorial environment does not facilitate such movements and up to the end of the first millennium of the Christian era the western Bantu were probably the more stable of the two major Bantu groups. Although the evidence is scanty in this region, the Bantu were definitely using iron in the first millennium of the Christian era, but they are unlikely to have developed its use to the point where an improvement in plantation agriculture generated a population explosion leading to expansion, or where warfare was revolutionized to the extent of encouraging the western Bantu to embark on military campaigns outside their own region.

21. J. D. Clark, 1970, pp. 187–210.

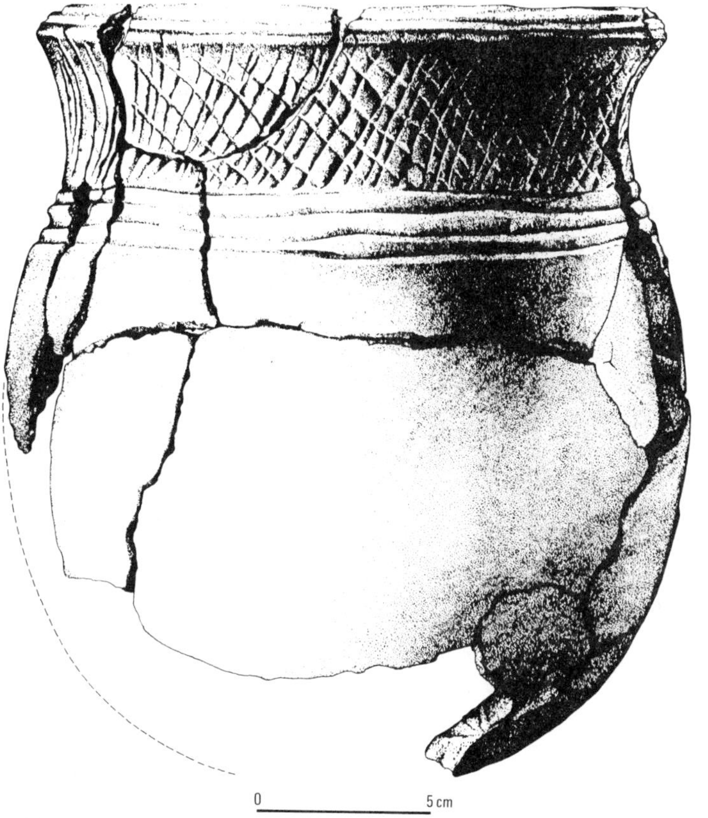

FIG. 6.2 *Almost complete specimen of early Iron Age pottery (Urewe) found above the hole designated as the grave of Mutara I Semugeshi, at Rurembo, Rutare, Rwanda (after F. Van Noten, 1972)*

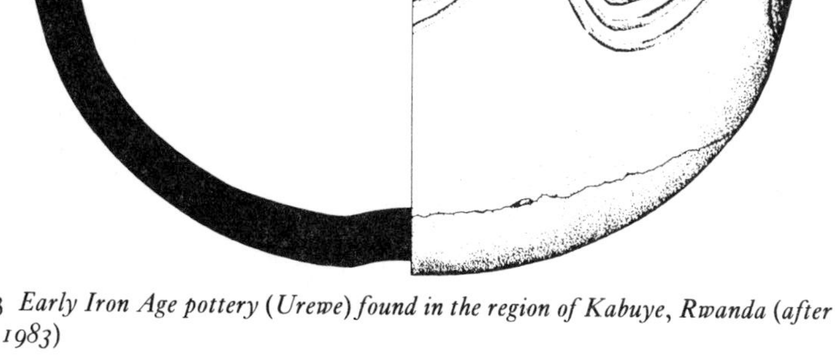

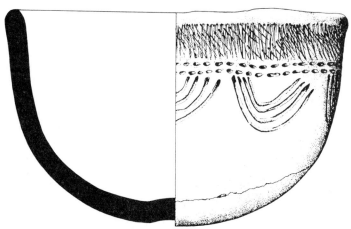

FIG. 6.3 *Early Iron Age pottery (Urewe) found in the region of Kabuye, Rwanda (after F. Van Noten, 1983)*

PLATE 6.1 *Banana plantation at Rutare (Rwanda)*

Nevertheless, given the overall distribution of the Bantu language groups, there must have been a much stronger thrust eastwards, along the edge of the forests, carrying the predecessors of the eastern Bantu languages as far as the Great Lakes. This theory is neither borne out nor invalidated by other data. No eastern Bantu languages are found in these regions although some languages spoken in the Sudan and in the eastern part of the Central African Republic might very well belong to that group. The only thing that is probable is the existence of the eastern group of languages. Furthermore, during this first stage, the expansion took place of the ancestors of other languages spoken by the western Bantu, especially the ancestor of the language bloc of the central forest towards the lands beyond Ubangi and Zaire. Assuming that a direct advance was precluded by the existence of a huge swamp, the second largest in the world, either the northern route, to the north of Dongo, or the southern route, to the south of the mouth of the Sangha, must have been taken. The geographic distribution of the languages belonging to this bloc indicates that the southern route was chosen, and the ancestral language may have been spoken between the Alima River and the forest, on the right bank of the Zaire/Congo. Subsequently, these languages were carried to all parts of the forest by fishermen advancing along the rivers that spread fanwise throughout the region, and by nomads wandering from village to village.

This region between the Alima and the forest contained a mixture of forest and savanna, similar to the area in which the proto-Bantu community has been located. But the languages advanced into sharply different environments, a development which could hardly have occurred without some interruption or at least deceleration in the movement of expansion. Gradually, for instance, some groups must have adapted to life in savannas where there was a lack of water, as is the case in the Bateke plateaux. In the east, on the other hand, there was an excess of water and some communities adjusted to swamp life, either then or much later. But the bulk of the languages were spoken by people who preferred life in the forest, either as farmers or fishermen. Some languages, however, were spoken in lower Kasai, in an environment with extremely rich aquatic resources but where the forest was reduced to narrow fringes along the watercourses, yet another variation of the savanna and forest environment. Finally, some other languages developed during this second stage in the south and south-west along the edge of the forest, which in that region extends in a north–south direction, and subsequently in lower Zaire in a fresh mosaic of forest and savanna.

No trace of autochthonous languages remains in this part of the western Bantu-language zone. How can we account for the assimilation of these autochthonous languages? The fact that the Bantu-speaking peoples lived in villages gave them an undeniable advantage over the less-settled hunters and food-gatherers. The village became the centre of the surrounding territory and the influence of its language grew accordingly as the territory was reorganized. The villages stimulated trade (in agricultural products!) and perhaps marital interchange, and there were probably also visitors who simply wished to satisfy their curiosity and for whom the village was a metropolis. In a forest environment, this is quite a plausible scenario and fits in well with the theory of rapid propagation of languages by fishermen along the major rivers and the sea-coast. These people were highly mobile, though, paradoxically, they also tended to build fairly large villages which could, in particularly favourable locations, become fairly permanent. They must have influenced the lives of the farming people all around them, either directly or through the trading of fish, pottery and sea-salt for the products of hunting or food-gathering. A look at the map enables us to say with certainty that the fishing communities were responsible for the high degree of linguistic homogeneity in the central basin because of their intensive contacts with the farmers. These contacts checked tendencies to linguistic divergence and favoured convergence, especially with regard to grammar.

It is not known when the western Bantu languages spread beyond the southern limits of the forest or even whether it was before or after metallurgy had become widespread in that area. In addition, recent data provide no conclusive evidence of the subsequent expansion of these languages to the south of lower Kasai and lower Zaire.

Many later linguistic movements occurred in that area. In the north, es-

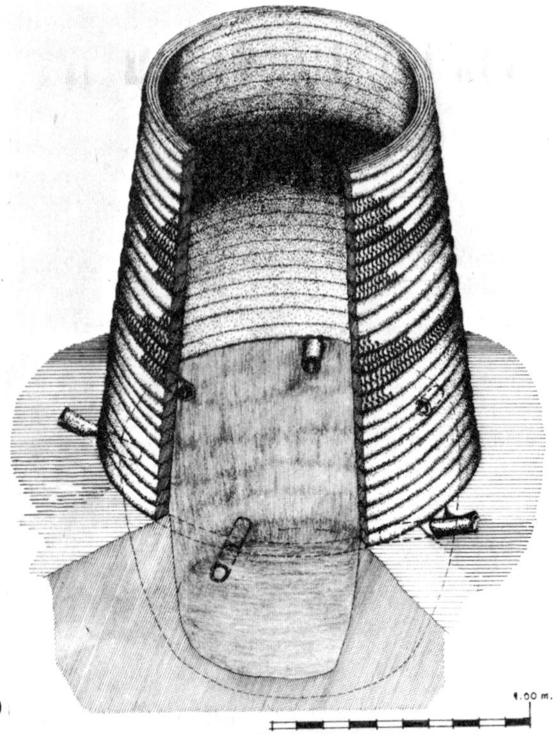

(a)

(b)

PLATE 6.2(a) (*left*) *A reconstruction of an Early Iron Age furnace in Rwanda: Nyaruhengeri I*
PLATE 6.2(b) (*left*) *Excavation of an Early Iron Age furnace: Kabuye XXXV*
PLATE 6.2(c) *Excavation of an Early Iron Age furnace: Nyaruhengeri I*
PLATE 6.2(d) *Excavation of an Early Iron Age furnace: Gisagara VI*

(c)

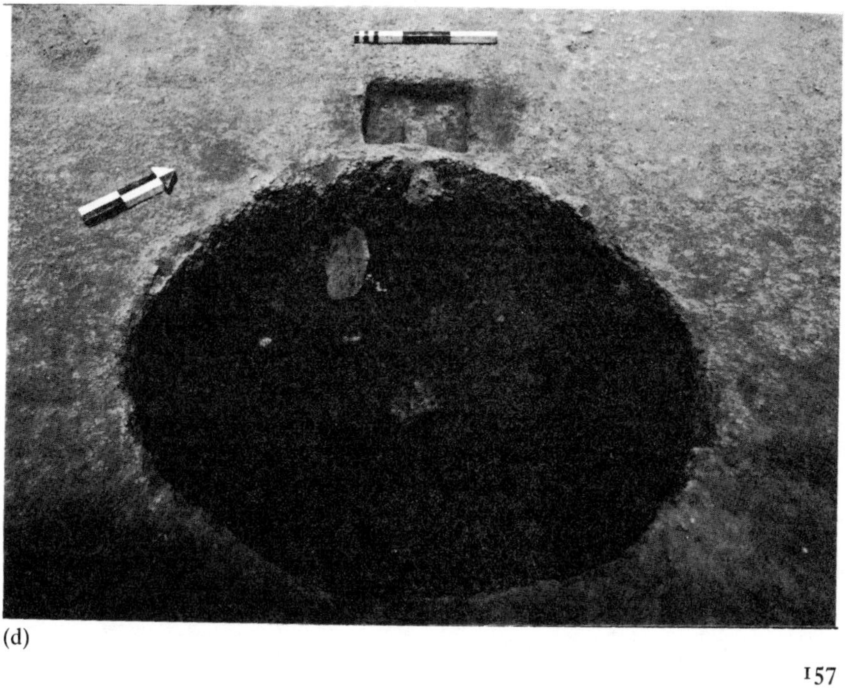

(d)

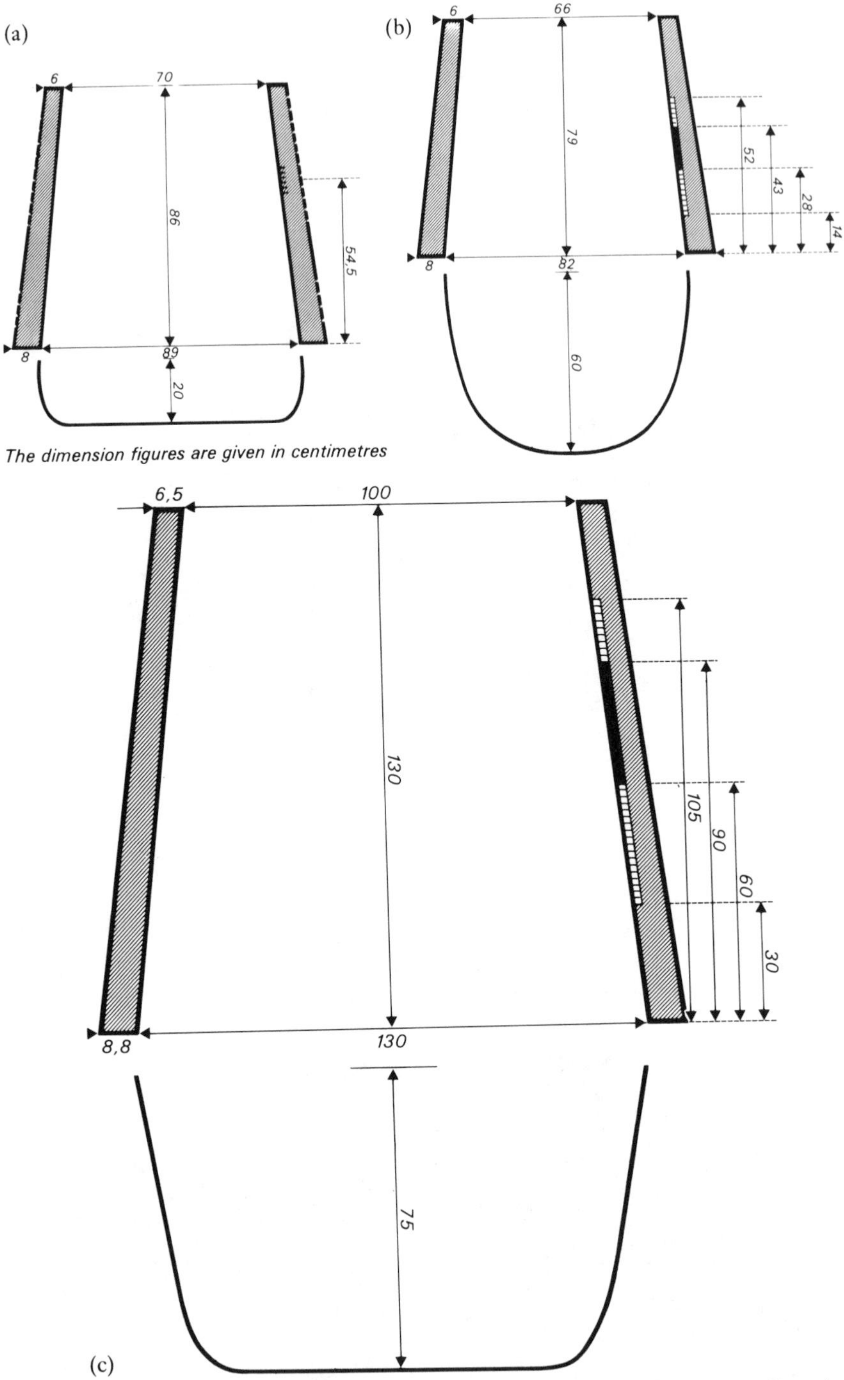

FIG. 6.4 (a)–(c) *Profiles of reconstituted Early Iron Age furnaces in the Butare area, Rwanda*
(*a*) *Gisaga vi* (+255) (*b*) *Kabuye xxxv* (+32) (*c*) *Nyaruhengeri I* (+380)

pecially between Ubangi and Zaire, from Bangui to the Uele River, movements in different directions were discernible. In some cases, Bantu languages displaced other linguistic groups (for instance the Mba-Mondunga group from Lisala to Kisangani); in others, they were overshadowed by the Central Sudanic languages, especially in Ituri where a large bloc of Bantu languages was, in addition, strongly influenced by the grammatical structure of those languages. In some cases exchanges between languages also occurred.

The linguist Christopher Ehret developed a theory to the effect that the Sudanic languages spread as far as southern Africa but were assimilated by the subsequent expansion of the Bantu. In his view, the eastern proto-Bantu around the western shores of Lake Tanganyika evolved in three successive series of communities between −600 and −400, namely the Lega-Guha, who occupied eastern Zaire to the west of the western Rift Valley system, the Lacustrine Bantu, who occupied the present territories of Rwanda, Burundi, western and southern Uganda (and probably parts of the interlacustrine belt of Tanzania), and the Tuli, who occupied a very extensive area in eastern, central and southern Africa. These Tuli were later to split into two groups, the Pela and the Pembele, the former including all speakers of Bantu dialects in Kenya and parts of Tanzania and the latter the Bantu-speaking peoples of most of Malawi, Mozambique, eastern Zambia and the whole of south-eastern Africa. By the end of the first millennium before the Christian era, these Pela and Pembele communities had emerged as different entities from their eastern proto-Bantu ancestors to the west of Lake Tanganyika and spread very rapidly during the first two or three centuries of the first millennium of the Christian era to eastern and southern Africa. The present Bantu-speaking peoples of these regions are their descendants.[22]

No linguist has followed up Ehret's theory, doubtless because the evidence on which it is based is still too slender. Even though some of the available archaeological data bear out certain aspects of Ehret's theory, it should be noted that so far, no archaeological research on the early Iron Age has been conducted in the region to the west of Lake Tanganyika which, in his view, is the area from which the eastern proto-Bantu split up into different groups. It must be admitted, however, that we still do not understand how the Bantu languages came to predominate in eastern Africa. It was a completely new environment, the indigenous populations were technically more advanced than the Bantu-speaking groups and some of them doubtless spoke Central Sudanic languages, at least in the north-western part of the region.

Linguistics shed less light on the expansion of the eastern Bantu languages than on what preceded it. Archaeology tells us that metallurgy was already quite advanced in that area by the last centuries before the

22. C. Ehret, 1973.

Christian era and that it spread from the Great Lakes to Transvaal and Natal in the first few centuries of the Christian era.[23] One is naturally tempted to visualize a corresponding linguistic movement extending from the Great Lakes to Cape Province and to conclude that it was technical superiority that enabled the Bantu languages to gain supremacy throughout the region. Towards the south, indeed, the advantage of technical superiority would also have included agriculture and animal husbandry. But at this point caution is indicated. Many languages in East Africa itself are so closely related that there is as yet no clear-cut system of subclassification, except for the languages to the south of the Limpopo and the Shona languages to the south of the Zambezi. Besides, we must bear in mind that eastern Bantu languages are also spoken further to the west, in south-eastern Zaire and in Zambia. And there is still some doubt regarding the position of the various languages from the south of lower Zaire as far as Namibia. These languages were, to say the least, strongly influenced by the eastern Bantu languages, and the regions where they are spoken, in the rare cases in which they have been explored archaeologically, do not correspond to the typical distribution of cultures in the early Iron Age.

It is still possible, therefore, to share Professor Ehret's view that these languages originated to the west of Lake Tanganyika and subsequently spread northwards and southwards. It is equally defensible to place their origins in the far north or in any one of a number of areas along the upper Kasai or the upper Zambezi. Nothing has yet been established beyond doubt.

Within that area, traces of non-Bantu languages are discernible in the southernmost Bantu languages which have borrowed some of their vocabulary and phonology from the Khoi and San languages. In East Africa, the geographical distribution of languages shows that their progress there was highly eventful. Bantu and other languages are closely intertwined, and even in the recent past non-Bantu languages have encroached on Bantu languages and vice versa. The Bantu expansion did not proceed without reverses. On the contrary, it is more than likely that reverses occurred and that the setbacks lasted for centuries, affecting large portions of the Bantu-speaking region. If this is so, however, it should be possible to find the traces of these other languages, as in the case of the Central Sudanic influences in eastern Zaire.

Our study comes to an end around the year +1100, when the Bantu had settled in most of sub-equatorial Africa (an area which they still occupy) and, most importantly, when their cultures had begun to assume well-defined regional characteristics. At the present stage of research, it is not possible to make a definite statement about the origins of the Bantu or why they expanded throughout the length and breadth of sub-equatorial Africa.

23. N. J. Van Der Merwe, 1980, pp. 478–85, especially p. 480; M. Hall and J. C. Vogel, 1980, for the latest developments; P. Schmidt, 1981, p. 36.

Of course, as linguistic research becomes more intensive and is extended to more and more Bantu languages, many new facts will come to light, since so many languages are still little known. The foregoing survey will certainly be expanded.

In conclusion, the need to separate linguistic data from archaeological data should again be emphasized. This is necessary in order to avoid the danger of confusing the probative value of different disciplines and, more important still, to avoid the intellectual danger of creating a myth – a powerful one but none the less unfounded. There is a temptation on hearing the word Bantu to associate it with an ethnic or national reality, whereas it is only a linguistic label. It does not denote a people or a society or a culture. Bleek's choice of a label was somewhat too apt and we must now defend ourselves against the consequences. For just as the 'Hamitic' myth grew out of the confusion of language, culture and race, so also a Bantu myth would be sure to develop from a similar confusion.

Editor's note

As this chapter is the work of two experts with different scientific training and divergent opinions, it consists, up to a point, of a combination of ideas. Surprisingly enough, the two authors agreed on the most important questions, thus bearing witness to the fact that years of fruitful discussion have resulted in genuine progress in the study of the Bantu question. On one point only was there serious disagreement, namely the theory put forward by one of the co-authors – S. Lwanga-Lunyiigo – whose view differs from that of most specialists in the field. We have therefore reproduced below what the author himself said in his original contribution.

Basing my conclusion on archaeological evidence, I suggested recently that the speakers of Bantu languages occupied from very early times a broad swath of territory running from the Great Lakes region of East Africa to the shores of the Atlantic in Zaire and that the supposed movement of Bantu-speakers from West Africa to central, eastern and southern Africa did not take place.[24]

The evidence indicates that peoples of Negroid physical type occupied sub-Saharan Africa from the Middle Stone Age and that it was from this Negroid stock that the speakers of Bantu languages emerged. It is possible that Bantu languages developed through the interaction of various early Negro communities, borrowing from one another and in this way helping to develop new 'Bantu' languages from the various Negro language amalgams. This does not, of course, rule out the genetic factor which points to a single origin of the speakers of related languages, but it should be pointed

24. S. Lwanga-Lunyiigo, 1976.

out that the genetic factor which linguists have advanced to explain the origin or origins of the Bantu-speakers is by no means exclusive.

Archaeological evidence indicates several areas of early Negro settlement in sub-Saharan Africa, areas of Negro communities which may have interacted with one another to form entirely new languages. In West Africa the earliest evidence of Negro existence comes from Iwo Eleru in western Nigeria where a 'proto-Negro' skull excavated there was dated to the early tenth millennium before the Christian era (−9250). Elsewhere in West Africa a Negroid skull was excavated at Asselar in Mali and was dated to the early seventh millennium (−6046). Other early Negroid remains excavated at Rop in northern Nigeria and Kintampo in northern Ghana were dated, respectively, to the second millennium (−1990 ± 120) and the fourth millennium before the Christian era. In East Africa the Negro clearly begins to emerge during the terminal Pleistocene/early Holocene period. At Ishango in eastern Zaire 'an indigenous Negro population emerges in Africa from the older palaeolithic stock'[25] between −9000 and −6500. The Kanga Negroid skeletal material in Kenya is dated to the third millennium before the Christian era. Southern African Negroes began to emerge during the middle Pleistocene.[26] These Negroes are represented by Broken Hill Man in Zimbabwe, by the Tuinplaats and Border Cave skeletons and by the late Stone Age skeletal material in the Cape Province of the Republic of South Africa.[27] The Oakhurst, Matjes Rock shelter, Bambandyanalo and Leopard's Kopje Negroid material further indicates that Negroes were already in existence in much of southern Africa in late Pleistocene/early Holocene times.[28] So the population from which the Bantu emerged was widespread in sub-Saharan Africa from the middle Stone Age onwards.

Whether the Bantu originated in West Africa, the Baḥr al-G͟hazāl region of the Republic of the Sudan, around the Congo–Zambezi river watershed or the interlacustrine region of East Africa, one factor seems to be well established. Whatever were the origins of the speakers of Bantu languages, they moved from their original homelands and eventually displaced and incorporated Khoisan and probably Sudanic stocks in vast regions of sub-equatorial Africa, an exercise they had largely accomplished by the end of the early Iron Age and the beginning of the second millennium of the Christian era.

25. J. de Heinzelin, 1962.
26. D. R. Brothwell, 1963.
27. ibid.
28. B. Wai-Ogosu, 1974.

7

Egypt from the Arab conquest until the end of the Fāṭimid state (1171)

T. BIANQUIS

Introduction

The Arabs had already conquered vast territories in Syria and Mesopotamia when they entered Egypt, attracted by the legendary opulence of its countryside, and its large industrious population. Through this territory, Islam, organized and triumphant, came in touch with Africa. Right up to the present, Egypt has retained this vital role of mediator between the Arab East and the black world.

Since the fall of the Ptolemies, a dynasty alien by origin and by language, Egypt had had no centre of authority on its own soil. A colony for exploitation by the Romans, then by the Byzantines, it produced a considerable proportion of the cereals fed to the populace in the imperial capitals. Its prosperity was vital to the security of the princes.

During the first two centuries of Islam there were few changes. However, the central authority, in Medina, in Damascus, finally in Iraq, varied its instructions according to whether its chief object was to convert the Copts to Islam or, on the contrary, to obtain a high yield from the gold and grain taxes demanded of them.

From the third/ninth century onwards, an inclination to resist the demands of the Caliphate was diplayed by those who were invested with authority in Egypt. Thus began a new history, that of the slow rise to autonomous, then independent, finally imperial authority. This transfer of political power from Baghdad, first to Fusṭāṭ, then to Cairo, followed a shift in the trade routes of the Gulf and Mesopotamia towards the eastern Mediterranean, the Nile Valley and the Red Sea. Nubia and the innermost recesses of Africa, unknown until then, came to play an active part, thanks to Egypt, in the economic exchanges of the Mediterranean world.

Egypt in subjection

The conquest

Byzantine Egypt was subjected to the authority of an Augustal duke resident in Alexandria. The country was divided into five duchies, each comprising two eparchies made up of a number of pagarchies. This strict territorial hierarchy, reflecting a society of highly organized dominant groups and dominated groups, was designed to facilitate the levying of taxes in cash and kind, the collection of the *annona*,[1] or wheat levy, and the financing of its transport to Constantinople, to which 2.5 million hectolitres of grain had to be brought each year before 10 October.

Territorial forces recruited in Copt families specializing in armed service maintained order in the countryside. They were necessary to strengthen the authority of those entrusted with tax collection; they were of scant military value and lacked mobility. The cities had to be surrounded by ramparts to ensure effective protection from nomad raiders.

The solicitude of the Byzantine state was directed to the population of Alexandria, Greek-speaking, Melchite Christians, whose culture and way of life approached those of the inhabitants of Constatinople. Responsibility in the provinces was taken over by high-ranking officials, also Greek, and Hellenized families with big landholdings.

The Copt peasantry had preserved the linguistic inheritance of Pharaonic Egypt. It rejected the Chalcedonian doctrine of the Melchites and held to Monophysitism. Each of the two churches had its Patriarch. The Copt religion expressed itself in a strong inclination towards monastic life, a trend strengthened by the large number of peasants fleeing to evade the pressure of excessive taxation. Rural activity and, more especially, a hermit's life in the desert on the fringe of the cultivated areas, were recognized values, whereas the towns, and above all Alexandria, represented disorder, debauchery and heresy.

The Persians conquered Egypt without difficulty in 619 and they remained there some ten years, persecuting the Greeks and members of the Melchite Church, but adopting a relatively benevolent attitude to the Copts. After their departure, the theologians of the Byzantine state tried to obtain general recognition for a doctrine acceptable to both churches: in this they failed and the persecutions started up again. The Arab conquest came at a time when the Egyptian population keenly resented the distant authority of Constantinople and its local representation in Alexandria. That population could not identify with the Byzantine state on either the political, religious or linguistic plane.

The Arab general, ʿAmr b. al-ʿĀṣ, entered Egypt at the head of a modest army in D͟hu l-ḥid͟jd͟ja 18/December 639. The conquest of Syria, which had just been completed, ensured that he would not have to face any offensive by land on the part of the Byzantines. ʿAmr occupied al-Arīs͟h, al-Farāma, and, advancing in a south-westerly direction along the eastern

1. *Annona*: wheat sent by certain provinces, including Egypt and North Africa, to Rome, when that city was the capital of the Empire, and later to Constantinople, so that the Emperors could distribute it to the population.

branch of the Delta, he reached Bilbays, then Heliopolis, east of the point where the Nile branches to form the Delta. Babylon (Bābalyūn), the strongest fortified town after Alexandria, lay just to the south, also on the right bank, facing the island of Rōda (Rawḍa).

The Byzantine defence was led by the Chalcedonian Patriarch Cyrus, and the commander-in-chief Theodore. 'Amr, who had received reinforcements, carried out expeditions in the Fayyūm and in the Delta while laying seige to Babylon, which fell in Djumāda l-āk̲h̲ir 20/April 641. In Radjab 20/June 641 began the siege of Alexandria, centre of Byzantium's maritime power in the southern Mediterranean. This gigantic fortified town, sheltering a population of six hundred thousand, finally capitulated and the Arabs occupied it in S̲h̲awwāl 21/September 642. The party dissensions that divided the Greeks, and their hatred of the Copts on religious grounds facilitated the task of the invaders. The Byzantine elite had been unable to arouse a spirit of resistance in the commonalty and the help given by the mother-city, Constantinople, had been inadequate.

Breaking with the tradition instituted by the Lagids of establishing the centre of political authority in the port of Alexandria, 'Amr chose Babylon, just between the Delta and Middle Egypt, as capital of the province. He settled the Arab ḳabīlas to the north of the fortress. A mosque, centre of religious and political assembly, set the seal on the unity of the new city, which was referred to as Fusṭāṭ, or Fusṭāṭ-Miṣr. The texts do not enable us to form an idea of this first town – doubtless a camp gradually replaced by houses, first of sun-dried clay bricks, then of burnt bricks and stone. Non-Arabs settled in the Ḥamrā's alongside the ḳabīlas.

From that time right up to the Fāṭimid period Alexandria was a town of secondary importance kept under close supervision by the provincial authority. For there was a risk of a Byzantine landing in its port, which would have made possible the establishment of a bridgehead in a milieu favourable to Byzantium. Indeed, in 25/645–6, the imperial navy briefly reoccupied the town, and its reconquest by the Muslims, led by 'Amr, who was called back for the purpose, was no easy matter.

It is difficult to describe the fiscal regime imposed on Egypt by the Arabs at the time of the conquest, for early works such as that of al-Balād̲h̲urī, report contradictory traditions. Egypt was either a land conquered by a bloodless capitulation – ṣulḥān[2] – or one wrested from its inhabitants by armed force – ʿanwatān.[3] In the former case the land remained in the hands of those who cultivated it; to keep it they were obliged to pay a tax in kind, sometimes called k̲h̲arād̲j̲,[4] in addition to the poll tax, sometimes

---

2. Ṣulḥ(ān): refers to the capture of a town by the Muslims by capitulation.

3. ʿAnwat(ān): refers to the taking of a city by the Muslim army by assault after refusal to capitulate.

4. K̲h̲arād̲j̲: land tax, sometimes paid in kind, levied on agricultural lands not abandoned at the time of the Islamic conquest; by extension, land taxes generally.

called *djizya*,[5] due in return for having their lives spared without being converted to Islam. In the latter case the land went to the Muslim community, which was free to employ conquered peasants whose lives had been spared as workmen or as tenant farmers.

The confusion may be due to the concern of the chroniclers of traditions to allude by a single legal formula to successive episodes far apart in time and in space. The Byzantine army was able to take up arms again, whereas the Copts, owing to the capitulation of the local territorial forces, had managed to keep their land. Elsewhere, the Muslim authorities sought some reason for refusing Arabs of the *ḳabīla*s parcels of land which cultivated by Copts produced a more regular yield.

The ambiguities of the situation following the conquest seem to have been turned to account. The existence of the treaty of capitulation seems to have stood in the way of the land claims of the Arab chiefs; Copts reluctant to meet the demands made on them seem to have been reminded that the land conquered by armed force could be taken away from them. The poll-tax paid by Christians and Jews varies according to the texts, ranging from one to four dinars per annum for every male over the age of 14. As for tax in kind, based on the area of the land worked, it consisted of provisions of grain, oil, vinegar, sometimes clothing or animals. By means of the Nile/Red Sea route, the victuals could be sent to Arabia; similarly, a large part of the gold collected was sent to the Caliph. Initially, the authorities fixed a total figure for the tax revenue demanded of each administrative division, leaving it to the tax collectors and the Church to distribute the load among individuals and among farms. This two-level fiscal system explains the difference between the facts described in the Greek papyri of Arab times and the theoretical systems worked out *a posteriori* by Arab historians. Caliph ʿUthmān, conscious of the danger represented by a provincial governor, with an army at his disposal, and in command of the gold that financed the Caliphate and the wheat that was consumed by its capital, suggested that ʿAmr place fiscal administration in the hands of the Governor of Upper Egypt, ʿAbd Allāh b. Saʿd, while retaining political and military reponsibility. ʿAmr refused to 'hold the horns of the cow while someone else milked it', a retort which situates him in the line of the Roman and Byzantine prefects. ʿAbd Allāh was appointed sole governor of Egypt in 23/644.

In 31/652 ʿAbd Allāh launched an expedition against Nubia, in present-day Sudan, and got as far as Dongola, upstream from the Third Cataract. The Christian population, close to the Monophysitic Church of Egypt, put up a fierce resistance. The invaders, discouraged by the precision of the archers, who pierced the eyes of the Arab horsemen, and by the poverty of

5. *Djizya*: poll-tax that had to be paid to the Islamic state by non-Muslims, in particular Christians and Jews, whose permanent presence in Islamic territory was tolerated. In return they were exempted from military obligations, had the right to practise their religion with discretion and were entitled to the protection of the Muslim ruler.

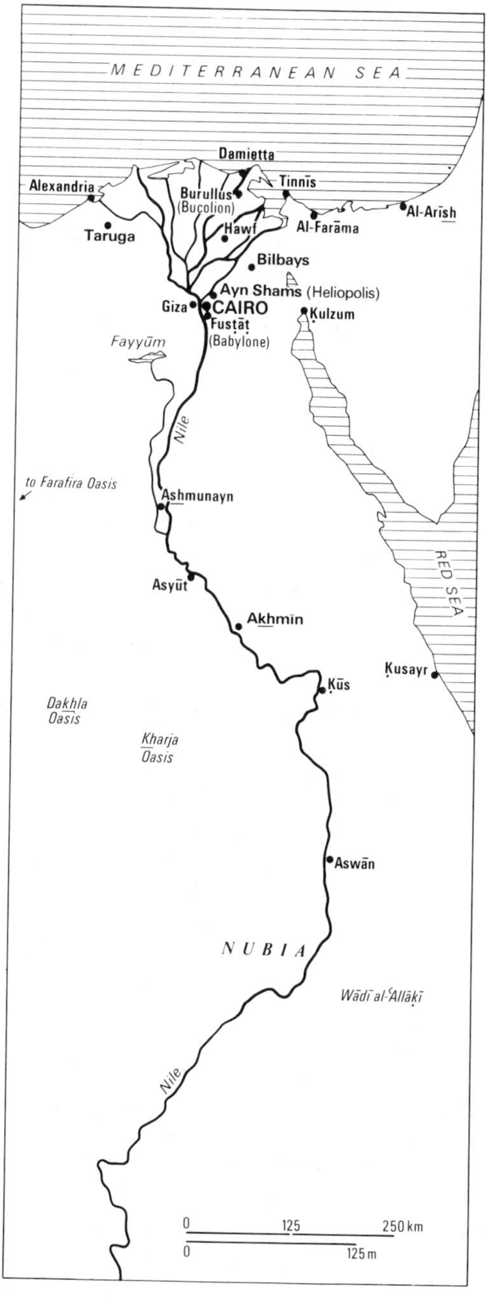

MEDITERRANEAN SEA
Damietta
Alexandria
Burullus
(Bucolion)
Tinnis
Al-Arish
Taruga
Hawf
Al-Farama
Bilbays
Ayn Shams (Heliopolis)
Giza
CAIRO
Kulzum
Fustat
(Babylone)
Fayyum
Nile
to Farafira Oasis
Ashmunayn
RED SEA
Asyut
Akhmin
Kusayr
Kus
Dakhla
Oasis
Kharja
Oasis
Aswan
NUBIA
Wadi al-ʿAllaki
Nile
0 125 250 km
0 125 m

FIG. 7.1 *Arab Egypt (after G. Duby, 1978)*

the country, preferred to negotiate. The *baḳt*,[6] signed with the Nubians provided that the latter would deliver slaves and would receive victuals and fabrics. Regarded by Muslim jurists as a trade treaty – and not as a political instrument – negotiated on equal terms with a handful of barbarians, this *baḳt*, amended on several occasions, was still in force at the end of the Fāṭimid period. Incidents sometimes broke out – raids by Nubian pillagers in Upper Egypt, struggles for the gold or emerald mines – but the country upstream of Aswān remained independent.

Islam easily took possession of immense territories in which political and social stratification was based on cultural oppositions; but when it came up against relatively homogeneous populations it failed. Its abandonment of Nubia made southern Egypt a 'land's end' for the time being and was to defer the Islamization of Nilotic Africa to the Mamluk period.

The Umayyads in Damascus

The installation of the Caliphate in Damascus in 41/661 represented a northward shift of the centre of the Islamic world. The maritime war between Arabs and Byzantines, which began with the Victory of the Masts won by the Egyptian seamen in 35/655, dealt a heavy blow to trade in the Mediterranean. From then onwards the Red Sea was abandoned in favour of the Gulf and land routes which, in Egypt, ran east–west, and no longer north–south.

The crisis that was to bring Mu'āwiya to the Caliphate began in 35/656 with the assassination of the Caliph 'Uthmān in Medina. The first crisis in the Islamic community during its period of growth led to its division into groups opposing each other on the relationship between religious law and political authority or on succession to the supreme magistracy. This early break in Arab-Islamic unity enabled new converts of all origins to fit easily into a disjointed structure and spared this religion the temptation of disputes over priority, of racialism and of an exclusive attitude. The various populations, on entering Islam, could bring with them elements of an earlier culture to which they were attached. The Copts, whose Christianity was simple, faithful and sensitive, had rejected the speculative theology of the Byzantines. They brought into an untroubled Sunnism their obsessive desire to keep in touch with the loved ones who had passed on. The Ḳarāfa cemeteries testify to the uncertain boundaries between the here and the hereafter to the same extent as the necropolises of the Old Kingdom.

The revolt which led to the assassination of the Caliph 'Uthmān, leader

6. *Baḳt*: from the Latin *pactum*, an almost unique instance of a bilateral treaty concluded by the Arabs with a people that refused Islam. The Nubians delivered slaves to the Muslims and received wheat, perhaps wine, and fabrics. Concluded under 'Uthmān in 651–2, the treaty was renewed and amended several times, remaining in effect until 1276, at which time Nubia was reduced and made subject to Mamluk Egypt by the armies of Baybars.

of the Umayyad party, started among the Arab troops in Egypt, and yet this province was associated, through the action of its Governor, ʿAmr, with the defeat of the claims of the Caliph ʿAlī both at Siffīn and at Adhruh. When ʿAmr died, ʿUtba, brother of Muʿāwiya, replaced him as governor of Egypt (44/664–5). Shīʿism therefore never had many followers in Egypt, despite the posthumous affection always shown for the descendants of the Prophet.

When the Arabs first came to Egypt they took over the Byzantine state set-up. The Greek language, the subordinate tax officials, the administrative divisions, the coins, were kept; the system went on functioning for the benefit of the new rulers of the country instead of Constantinople. The Monophysite Church retained its role of intermediary between the state and the villages and between the state and the individual. When the presence of the Arabs persisted, this respect for the past was no longer appropriate. The first step was to replace the Christian symbols, with which the Byzantine state stamped its coins and the papyrus used in its offices, by texts from the Qoran. In 87/706 Arabic had to be used for the drawing up of official instruments throughout the Caliphate. Bilingual, Arabic/Greek, papyri appeared in Egypt soon after the conquest and this practice was not to be abandoned until about 102/720. Greek texts dating right up to the end of the eighth century are to be found. In the first quarter of the second/eighth century Egypt went over completely to Arabic. Coptic survived in the countryside for two centuries, and longer in the Monophysite (Jacobite) Copt liturgy. By the fourth/tenth century, Egyptian historians, whether Chalcedonian or Monophysite, were writing their chronicles in Arabic. Unlike the Persians and the Turks, who adopted Islam but retained, or returned to, their national language and thus enjoyed cultural autonomy, the Egyptians became merged in the Arab-speaking world stretching from the Atlantic to Mesopotamia. Born in the Middle Ages, its bounds not reproducing those of any previously existing empire or any natural unity, the Arab-speaking world has survived up till the present, integrating Egyptian civilization for the first time into a wider framework than the Nile Valley. This Arab-speaking world is independent from any constraint from Islam, for many non-Muslims speak Arabic, whereas not many speak Turkish or Persian.

Under the Umayyad Caliphate, few Arabs lived in the Egyptian countryside and the presence of the Muslim soldiers, often Yemenite, among the Egyptians in the towns raised no problem. Mutual acculturation quickly took place and both parties acceded together to an urban way of life, previously reserved for the Hellenized classes. The number of persons not participating in agricultural production increased: soldiers drawing pensions in accordance with the *dīwān*, administrators, artisans working for the governor, military chiefs and fiscal administrators. However, the urban way of life entailed increased expenditure and from the 80s/700s onwards conquests slowed down and the treasury could no longer rely on the spoils of war. Fiscal pressure became more burdensome and levies were made to the detriment of the countryside.

Resistance to the new fiscal demands was passive at first, as in the Byzantine period. The peasants deserted the villages where they were registered, disappearing or becoming monks in order to evade the poll tax. When 'Abd al-'Azīz b. Marwān extended the poll tax to cover monks (65/685–85/704), the Copts found a solution in conversion to Islam. The Muslim authorities had to choose between encouraging conversions, which entailed a decrease in fiscal revenue, or amending the law with a view to not exempting new Muslims, so as to prevent conversions for selfish reasons. Ḳurra b. Sharīk, political and financial governor from 90/709 to 95/714, refused to abolish the poll tax for converted Copts and proceeded against fugitives, levying in addition special taxes to finance the naval war against Byzantium. He increased production by placing fallow land under cultivation and planting sugar cane. His successor was ordered by the Caliph Sulaymān b. 'Abd al-Malik to 'milk the cows dry and to shed blood until it was spent'. Caliph 'Umar b. 'Abd al-'Azīz (99/717–101/720) introduced a legal solution to the problem of conversions, which, as a fervent Muslim, he wanted to increase: he separated the person of the new Muslim, who was exempted from poll tax, from his land, which kept its previous status, and he continued to oblige whoever cultivated it to pay the *kharādj*, even converts.

As the taxes levied on the Egyptian countryside became more and more burdensome and the traditional means of evading them were then prohibited, in 107/725 the first Copt revolt broke out. The Muslim authorities settled the Ḍelta with Ḳaysite Arab *ḳabīla*s: some ten thousand men, accompanied by their families, arrived in three successive waves. In this way the control of the countryside was facilitated, while the Yemenite population, predominant at the time of the conquest, was counterbalanced. Again, in an attempt to achieve balance, this time directed against the influence of the Monophysite (Jacobite) Church, in 107/725 the Melchites were given their churches back. A Chalcedonian Patriarch was appointed with the agreement of Byzantium, although the Byzantine navy had effected a raid on Tinnīs in 101/720 and was to effect another in 118/736. Simultaneous recourse to military action and negotiation and a concern to balance the pressure of different social groups are both features of medieval Arab policy.

The great revolts at the beginning of the Abbasid Caliphate

In 132/750 the Umayyads were overthrown and their last Caliph was killed in Egypt in August. The wars between Ḳays and Yemenites had diverted their attention from the Khorasān, where discontent was developing among the non-Arab Muslim combatants. The seat of the Caliphate was transferred to Mesopotamia, beyond the historical bounds of the Hellenistic and Roman world, far indeed from Egypt. Damascus was eclipsed as an autonomous centre of authority. Mecca and Medina were abandoned by the Ḳurays͟hite aristocracy, that of the *s͟harīf*s in particular, sure of being well received by the Abbasid caliphs. The regional function of Fusṭāṭ, relay of a distant authority in Mesopotamia separated from the Mediterranean by vast steppes, was enhanced and broadened.

From 150/767 to 254/868, revolts continued almost without interruption in Egypt. Those of the Copts were stirred up by the replacement of the local Christian officials by Muslims, particularly in the small towns in the Delta. This was a further reason for the discontent of the Copts, who felt like aliens in their own country. As a result, between 150/767 and 155/772 the Delta Christians tried to drive out the Muslim officials by force. In 217/832, in the region of the Bucolics, in the north of the Delta, a rustic Christian population rose in rebellion: it was not easily put down. For the last time Christians had taken up arms alone against the Muslim authority in Egypt; in all the subsequent revolts they combined with Muslims in movements led by the latter.

From the third/ninth century onwards, the Arabs of the *ḳabīla*s and the soldiers were at the root of the main disturbances. The initial enthusiasm waned. Military engagements took place in Islamic territory, often against poor peasants: they could no longer be financed by the spoils of war. The soldiers had to be paid in peacetime and additional expenses had to be defrayed when they were in action. Their loyalty depended on the regularity of their pay. In the event of a revolt, local armies, too closely assimilated, were unreliable: troops were brought at great expense from Mesopotamia. In 193/809 a mutiny broke out in Fusṭāṭ and the following year the governor had a residence built outside the town on the hill where the citadel of Cairo was later to be erected.

The Arabs of the *ḳabīla*s, settled on the edges of the Delta, had retained a semi-nomadic pastoral way of life: they would have liked to use for pasture the fields cultivated by the Copts and they refused to pay the *k͟harādj* for the lands that they occupied. Other Arabs, on the contrary, had turned peasant, adopting the way of life and the customs of the Copts, from whom they were difficult to distinguish, since the latter were assimilating to the Arabs and Islam. All alike were up in arms against the tax collector.

Participation of Arabs from the *ḳabīla*s in the revolts is reported from 169/785 onwards, and the Ḥawf, the eastern Delta, was in a state of rebellion right up until 194/810. From 198/814 to 217/832 there was total anarchy in Egypt, the authority of Fusṭāṭ no longer being recognized except upstream, in Middle and Upper Egypt. Refugees from Cordova in Spain had constituted a state in Alexandria and held the western Delta. The eastern Delta, from Tinnīs to Bilbays and al-Farāma, formed another unit. Without entering into details, one might mention that the despatch of four thousand Turkish soldiers and the presence in Egypt of the Caliph al-

Ma'mūn were required to restore order in 217/832. From the following year onwards, the Arabs were excluded from the *dīwāns*: freed from military obligations, they were no longer entitled to the state pension.

For the descendants of the Arabs of the conquest three destinies were taking shape. The members of the aristocratic or merchant families of Arabia, those of the *ḳabīla*s settled around the old towns or in towns established in Iraq or in Egypt, had become urbanized. As officials, jurists and merchants, they benefited from the economic development of the cities, centres of prosperity that sprang from the extent of the market and their field of action, prosperity financed by the taxes levied in the countryside.

Other groups, as we have seen, assimilated with the indigenous rural populations and shared the burden of this taxation. Finally, many Arabs remained Beduins, whether semi-nomads settled on the fringe of the cultivated lands, as in Egypt, or real nomads wandering over the steppes. Thrown out of the armies, they became marginalized once more, while still being dependent on the laws of the market, which determined the prices of the grain they consumed. They displayed resentment and contempt in the face of the urban luxury from which they were barred. They were receptive to the claims of the Hasanid or Ḳarmatian rebels. The pillaging of caravans, and of holy places of weakly defended towns enabled them to regain possession of property amassed as the result of wars waged by their ancestors in former times. So the Arab conquest led to a situation in which, two centuries later, descendants of the victors were to be found both among those privileged by the regime and among the exploited and the rejected.

Egypt autonomous

The Tulunid dynasty

Under the reign of Caliph al-Muʿtaṣim (218/833–227/842) Turkish slaves were introduced into the Mesopotamian troops in such great numbers that they gained control of the army and exerted an influence on civil, fiscal and provincial administration. The Palatine troops had reduced to a figurehead a Caliph whom they set up or brought down as they wished. The administration of provinces or groups of provinces was entrusted to members of the Caliph's family or to Turkish chiefs, who continued to reside in Baghdad or Samarra, in their turn delegating the actual government of the province to a relation. For instance, Aḥmad b.Ṭūlūn, who arrived in Egypt in 254/868, appanaged by Bākbāk, had been given the *ṣalāt* (political and military authority over the province) but not the *kharādj* (financial and fiscal authority), which was retained by Ibn al-Mudabbir.

Thirty-three years of age, Ibn Ṭūlūn, like his Turkish comrades, was possessed of excellent military references, having served seven years at Tarsus against the Byzantines. However, he stood out from them by reason of his religious and literary culture. Throughout his lifetime he placed his intelligence in the service of an ambition beyond measure and seldom resorted to brute force. By 258/872, as a result of intrigues conducted in Samarra, Ibn al-Mudabbir was transferred to Syria.

Ibn Ṭūlūn had first to intervene in Upper Egypt, where three revolts broke out in 255/869 and 256/870. The Wādī al-ʿAllāḳī gold mines, south-east of Aswān, and the slaves of Nubia were tempting spoils. In 221/836 the treaty with Nubia had been renewed and the king's sons were received in Fusṭāṭ and Baghdad. The Bēdja nomads settled between the Nile Valley and the Red Sea had similarly concluded a treaty and one of them lived at Aswān. Under these circumstances the towns of the Ṣaʿīd went over to Islam and new trade links were established with the Red Sea and Arabia or with the Maghrib by the trails leading from the oases. In 259/873 the most dangerous of the rebels, Ibn al-Ṣūfī, defeated, took refuge in Arabia. Shortly afterwards al-ʿUmarī, who controlled the Wādī al-ʿAllāḳī mines, was killed. The security of the links with the south was ensured.

Ibn Ṭūlūn had considerable funds at his disposal and he turned them to account by constituting an army enabling him to intervene outside Egypt. He sent it to Tripolitania to put down a revolt, and in 256/870, when the tribute he sent to Iraq was seized in Syria, he was about to enter the country. However, the Caliph's entourage preferred to settle the affair without his help for his ambition was beginning to cause apprehension. Ibn Ṭūlūn had at his disposal the wheat of Egypt, the gold and the slaves of Nubia; the Caliphate needed the tribute he sent to Iraq in order to pay the troops, whereas he had nothing to expect from that institution. Two courses were tempting to the powerful governor of Egypt: to make himself independent of the Caliph like the princes of North Africa and keep the tribute for the financing of his army, or, conversely, to intervene in Iraq's domestic affairs. In 256/870 a new Caliph, al-Muʿtamid, had been installed and had entrusted his brother al-Muwaffaḳ with the eastern part of the empire. Ibn Ṭūlūn secured from the Caliph the responsibility for levying the *kharādj* in Syria and in Cilicia and, in exchange, he sent the tribute from Egypt to the Caliph direct for his personal needs. Al-Muwaffaḳ, who was faced with two dangerous revolts – those of the Saffārids in Persia and the Zandj black slaves in the south of Iraq – considered the amounts he received from Egypt insufficient. Out of a fiscal revenue of 4.3 million dinars, Ibn Ṭūlūn apparently sent 2.2 million a year to the Caliph, and in 876 an additional 1.2 million to al-Muwaffaḳ. At the same time, it is true, he was building an aqueduct and a hospital, and a new town north-east of Fusṭāṭ with barracks for his soldiers, a palace and a large mosque in the Samarra style. According to Ibn Taghrībirdī, these edifices were built with the gold – 1.5 million or 2.5 million dinars in weight – taken from a Pharaonic tomb discovered near Fusṭāṭ. Was this a legend to justify his refusal to give more assistance to al-Muwaffaḳ, engaged in a difficult war for the safety of the Caliph? At all events al-Muwaffaḳ sent an army to drive Ibn

Ṭūlūn out of Egypt, but the soldiers, not having been paid, disbanded at Raḳḳa.

In 264/878 Ibn Ṭūlūn invaded Syria without encountering any resistance except at Antioch. Ill-received at Tarsus in Cilicia, he had just installed a governor when he had to return to Egypt, his son al-ʿAbbās having revolted. The young prince was brought back to Fusṭāṭ as a prisoner in Ramaḍān 268/February 882 and Ibn Ṭūlūn, in undisputed command of Egypt and Syria, secretly invited the Caliph to come and reside in Fusṭāṭ. However, the Caliph, after an attempt at flight, was brought back to his capital and compelled to sign an instrument removing Ibn Ṭūlūn from office. The latter, in Dhu l-ḳa'da 269/May 883, assembled in Damascus *ḳāḍī*s, jurisconsults and *sharīf*s representing the Muslim people of Egypt, Syria and Cilicia and obtained a vote from them legalizing *djihād* against al-Muwaffaḳ, pressures imposed on the Caliph by him invalidating any instrument emanating from the Caliphate. The only ones to refuse to vote in favour were three Egyptians, including the *ḳāḍī* of Fusṭāṭ. Less than a year later, in Ramaḍān 270/March 884, Ibn Ṭūlūn fell ill and died in Fusṭāṭ.

He was succeeded by his son Khumārawayh, who managed to combine Tarsus and Djazīra (Upper Mesopotamia) with his principality, and in 273/886 the Caliphate acknowledged the sovereignty of the Tulunid dynasty over Egypt and Syria for a period of thirty years. In 279/892 the Caliph al-Mu'taḍid married Khumārawayh's daughter, Ḳaṭr al-Nadā, who brought him a million dinars, the wedding festivities were the most sumptuous in Arab history. In 282/896 Khumārawayh was assassinated in Damascus, leaving the treasury empty. The reign of his son Djaysh, then of his son Hārūn, completely ruined the dynasty which was incapable of defending Syria against the Ḳarmatians. This sect of Ismāʿīlite Alid origin, which arose in Mesopotamia in the second/eighth century, had exploited the bitterness of the Arabs of the *ḳabīla*s sent back to the desert when the Caliphate's armies had become Turkish or black. The Beduins invaded Syria from 289/902 onwards and easily overcame the Tulunid army of Damascus, commanded by Ṭughdj. Drawing the inference from this defeat, an Abbasid general, Muḥammad b. Sulaymān, entered Syria and crushed the Ḳarmatians in 290/903 then marched on Fusṭāṭ, which he entered on 20 Rabi'I 292/10 January 905. Hārūn b. Khumārawayh had just been killed.

Al-Kindī's account of the Tulunids provides evidence of an evolving social state. After the death of Ibn Ṭūlūn political authority was fragile; it was threatened by the prince's peers, his relations or his generals, who knew the military basis of his legitimacy. Once a prince was replaced by force, this group granted his successor the *bay*ʿa and had the mosque authorities recognize the innocence of the new prince with regard to any violence used to seize power from or take the life of his predecessor. Any act strengthening a *de facto* political authority capable of functioning was morally and

PLATE 7.1 *The Mosque of the Ibn Ṭūlūn in Cairo: partial view of the courtyard, the minaret and the pavilion of ablution*

PLATE 7.2 *Fāṭimid Mosque: eleventh-century decoration of the façade*

PLATE 7.3 *Tomb from the Fāṭimid era at Fusṭāṭ*

legally commendable. This easy consensus ill concealed the real disinterest of the religious authorities in the legal bases of a provincial authority so long as the *khuṭba*[7] was pronounced on behalf of the Caliph. The split between civil society and military comradeship began to appear. A sudden change of *ḳāḍī* or *imām* disturbed the marketplace more than a change of prince. Fusṭāṭ and Damascus, provincial towns of artisans and merchants, haggling and narrow-minded, distrusted the Tulunid princes, whose morals and culture were marked by a Persian indulgence. This nascent middle class identified itself with the mosque, *ahl al-masdjid*,[8] and regarded the securing of judicial responsibility as a promotion. It kept a close watch on the lower classes, *aṣfal al-nās*, sons of peasants or of soldiers, maladjusted to city life, and denounced them to the authorities if need be.

Another inadequacy of the dynasty was due to its army, incapable of coping with the extent of the territories to be protected and of encountering the armies of Cilicia, hardened by constant warfare. The Tulunid army was heterogeneous, comprising Turks, Daylamites, blacks, Greeks and Berbers. The latter stemmed from peoples settled in the Delta; the eastern Delta had supplied Arabs from semi-nomad *ḳabīla*s who constituted a formidable guard.

These weaknesses must not blind us to the irresistible progress of the Egyptian economy. The fury with which the Abbasid army pillaged Fusṭāṭ

7. *Khuṭba*: an oration delivered by the khaṭīb from the *minbar* of the great mosque at Friday mid-day prayers, in the course of which God's protection was invoked on behalf of the Caliph recognized in the city, and also on behalf of the ruler from whom the governor had received his delegated authority, where such was the case.

8. *Ahl al-masdjid*: mosque-goers, those who attended daily, generally merchants, tradesmen and jurists.

and destroyed all the Tulunid buildings with the exception of the great mosque proves that it was aware of that progress and of the threat it represented to Iraq's preponderance.

Fragile Abbasid restoration: anarchy

From the fall of the Tulunids in 292/905 to the installation of Muḥammad b. Ṭughdj as governor in 323/935 Egypt underwent a series of disorders which it would be idle to recount. Governors, whose functions were confined to military and political affairs, succeeded one another, while the al-Mādharā'ī family sat firmly at the head of the fiscal administration, even opposing certain nominations to the office of governor. The army, irregularly paid, took to pillaging. To escape this, the inhabitants of Fusṭāṭ got the mosque authorities to ask for the troops to be transferred to Giza, a logical request since that town was threatened by the Berbers. Settled on the left bank of the Nile, in the Delta, in the Fayyūm, they acted on behalf of the Ismā'īlite dynasty of the Fāṭimids established in Ifrīḳiya. Berber contingents had been merged with the Egyptian army together with the other troops recruited during the Tulunid period; only the Arabs from the *ḳabīla*s had been discharged. This mosaic of ethnic groups gave rise to disciplinary problems; the violent clashes between 'westerners' and 'easterners' were a prelude to the great encounters of the Fāṭimid period.

Two institutions characteristic of the second Arab Middle Ages, the *iḳṭā'*[9] and the *waḳf*[10] developed in Egypt at the end of the Tulunid period and during the disorders that ensued. The pay in cash and the allowances in kind due to the soldiers were the responsibility of the provinces in which the army was engaged. Now, whereas the disorders demanded the presence of the army, the financial services were the first to be affected, while on the other hand it was no easy matter to transport over a great distance the funds required by a large army. In order to decentralize the financial operation, the officer in command was given a mandate to collect taxes from a rural district and was wholly or partly responsible for maintaining the men whom he commanded, or in some cases owned. The *iḳṭā'* bound the officer in command to the territory he was helping to defend, while relieving the provincial administration of the burden.

9. *Iḳṭā'*: delegation of authority to levy taxes granted by the ruler to a military or civilian officer in a fiscal district as a reward for services rendered to the state. The concession was revocable.

10. *Waḳf*: an inalienable legal and religious donation made by the owner of a piece of real property to bestow the revenue from it on a religious institution or an institution of public or social interest and/or on the owner's descendants. The instrument of donation, drawn up in a recognized form and backed by a religious or charitable intention, provided for a trustee for the *waḳf* and the beneficiaries. If all else failed, the *ḳādī* could be asked to enforce compliance with the legitimate intentions of the founder. The desired effect of declaring private property a *waḳf* was to avoid the possibility of confiscation by the ruler or the dispossession of orphans during their minority.

Civil *iḳṭā*ʿs were no doubt constituted for the benefit of financial administrators, such as the Mādharā'ī, to guarantee their advances to the treasury. Their office undoubtedly enabled them to build up an immense fortune (they had one million dinars confiscated) in landed property and real estate: a fortune rapidly acquired, which was envied by those in power. The Mādharā'ī resorted to setting their property up in *waḳf*s to ensure that only their descendants would have the use of it.

As a result of these two institutions the towns weighed more heavily on the countryside, increasing the taxation of the agricultural yield, leaving the peasant at best the bare minimum for the subsistence of his family. It was impossible to put anything by. Then again, the existing situation was frozen and the field of action of the central or regional authorities was limited. At the same time the peasants ceased to have recourse to violence, at least in the form of large-scale revolts. This was due to the more widespread supervision of the countryside as a result of the *iḳṭā*ʿ and the absolute military superiority of the professional soldier over the armed civilian owing to the new techniques of fighting with sword or lance.

The Ikhshidids and Kāfūr

In Shaʿban 323/July 935, Muḥammad b. Ṭughdj, appointed governor of Egypt with responsibility for both the *salāṭ* and the *kharādj*, arrived in Fusṭāṭ. This twofold responsibility, which ran counter to the practice followed since the fall of the Tulunids, was obtained thanks to the support of al-Faḍl b. Djaʿfar Ibn al-Furāt, tax-inspector for Egypt and Syria. Ibn al-Furāt, who had been the vizier of the great Abbasid *amīr* of Baghdad, Ibn Rā'iḳ, to whom he was related by a matrimonial alliance, concluded a matrimonial alliance with Ibn Ṭughdj as well. He had begun to bring down the financial power of the al-Mādharā'ī family when he died in 326/938. His son, Djaʿfar b. al-Faḍl was vizier at the end of the Kāfūrid period and, much later, under the Caliph al-ʿAzīz. Alliances between a family of Iraqi civil financiers and tax-farmers and a Turkish or Persian governor or military chief were current during this period. With other financiers, the Banū al-Furāt brought from Baghdad to Fusṭāṭ a cultural environment favourable to Shīʿism, indirectly facilitating Fāṭimid propaganda.

Grandson of a Turkish soldier in the Samarra guard, son of a former governor of Damascus, Ibn Ṭughdj had exercised numerous commands. Appointed to Fusṭāṭ with the mission of protecting the western flank of the Caliphate against an imminent attack by the Fāṭimids, he was granted the right to constitute an autonomous principality. In 327/939, he was given, on request, the title of al-Ikhshīd, the Servant, a title traditionally borne by the princes of the Ferghāna. In the year of his appointment to Egypt, 323/935, he was forced to confront the Berbers, who had occupied the Island of Rōḍa (Rawḍa) opposite Fusṭāṭ and set fire to the arsenal on the island. After going off towards Ifrīḳiya, they came back in 324/936 with a Fāṭimid army to attack Egypt, but they were defeated. The wealth of Ifrīḳiya, the gold it received through the Sahara and its relations with Andalusia and Sicily had attracted considerable traffic coming from the Red Sea, and so trails parallel with the Mediterranean coast and linking North Africa with the Delta, the oases and Upper Egypt had increased in number. Their military control was difficult.

Going back to the Tulunid tradition, Ibn Ṭughdj regarded Syria as an integral part of his principality. He had to dispute that province with the military chiefs driven out of Mesopotamia, who saw in it a compensation. Ibn Rā'iḳ, turned out of Baghdad by his lieutenant Badjkam, attempted to conquer Syria in 326/938. After uncertain engagements, Ibn Rā'iḳ and Ibn Ṭughdj concluded a matrimonial alliance and divided the province between them, the south to the Ikhshīd, the north and Damascus to the former great *amīr* of Baghdad. In 330/942 the Hamdānid ruler of Mawsil, Nāṣir al-Dawla, had Ibn Rā'iḳ killed and in 332/944 he sent his brother ʿAlī, the future Sayf al-Dawla, to occupy Aleppo. At the same time the Caliph al-Muttaḳi, threatened in Baghdad by the Turkish *amīr* Tūzūn, took refuge in Raḳḳa, where Ibn Ṭughdj, like Ibn Ṭūlūn before him, went and invited the Caliph to take up residence in Fusṭāṭ. The Caliph returned to Baghdad where, in 334/945, the Persian *amīr* Muʿizz al-Dawla set up an Alid authority, the Buyid dynasty, for a century. Also in 334/945 Ibn Ṭughdj died after having agreed to make peace with the Hamdānid ruler of Aleppo. Unudjūr ibn al-Ikhshīd took up the struggle and in 336/947 divided Syria up with the Hamdānid ruler, whose right to the *djund*s[11] of Ḳinnasrīn-Aleppo and of Homs was recognized. The Ikhshidid ruler retained, along with Egypt, the *djund*s of Ramla-Palestine, of Tiberias-Jordan and of Damascus. The boundaries thus drawn were to remain in force for a century and a half, except during brief periods.

Ibn Ṭughdj had placed at the head of his army a black eunuch, Kāfūr, a remarkable personality, who combined indisputable military, administrative and diplomatic abilities with a deep Sunnite faith. Brought to Ḳūs as a slave when he was still a child, he identified more than any of his predecessors with the people of Fusṭāṭ, with whom he liked to mingle. After the death of Ibn Ṭughdj, Kāfūr directed the Ikhshidid state under the principate of Ibn Ṭughdj's two sons, Unudjūr (334/946–349/961) and ʿAlī (349/961–355/966). From 355/966 until his death in 357/968 Kāfūr exercised power in his own right in Egypt and southern Syria with the title of *al-Ustādh*, and his authority was recognized by the Abbasid Caliph.

The Kāfūrid period was marked by growing insecurity in Egypt and Syria. In addition to the Fāṭimid threats in the west there was the new aggressiveness of the Nubians in the south, who attacked the oases in 339/950 and Aswān in 345/956. The Beduins of Arabia and Syria fell upon caravans of pilgrims. In the opinion of some historians the Fāṭimids, too

11. *Djund*: territorial district corresponding to a military recruiting unit.

busy repressing revolts in North Africa, were following a policy of harrying Egypt through their allies, particularly the Ḳarmatians and the Nubians. On the other hand, these incidents can be connected with the frequency of food shortages in Egypt at the time owing to inadequate floods. The Beduins, like the Nubians, bought cereals and when the rise of prices in Egypt made the terms of exchange too unfavourable for them they resorted to armed force in order to eat cheaply.

Kāfūr therefore strengthened the army, introducing black slaves bought on the markets of Upper Egypt. These Kāfūriyya were never completely integrated into the Ikhshīdiyya – white *ghulāms*, Turks or Daylamites – and the two formed separate hostile groups. Kāfūr had pushed out those of his former comrades in arms whose presence might have been prejudicial to him and he had bought the loyalty of the others by granting them large *iḳṭā*ʿs. After his death the senior officers were unable to find a successor from among themselves and they allowed themselves to be manoeuvred by Ibn al-Furāt. The original system introduced by Kāfūr did not survive him. If there had been a man of his character among the military chiefs assembled in Fusṭāṭ in the spring of 358/969 a régime anticipating that of the Mamluks might have come into being on the banks of the Nile three centuries earlier than it did.

Imperial Egypt

The first three Fāṭimid *imāms* of Egypt

At the beginning of the summer of 358/969 the Fāṭimid general Djawhar gained a victory on both banks of the Nile downstream from Fusṭāṭ giving him access to that town and forcing the Ikhshidid and Kāfūrid chiefs to flee to Syria. The inability of the latter to unite and organize the defence of the country against the Berbers accounted for a defeat which their undeniable superiority in the technique of warfare ought to have spared them. The Fāṭimid victory had been prepared by propagandists with considerable funds at their disposal, who exerted their psychological influence on a public opinion disconcerted by the political vacuum that followed the death of Kāfūr and paralysed by the effects of a very serious famine. The Alid sympathies of the Iraqi notabilities of Fusṭāṭ had facilitated matters. Recourse to arms had brought to a successful issue a long process of destabilization of the state in Egypt. An understanding of political and ideological warfare enabled al-Muʿizz and his successors to achieve excellent results with mediocre armies.

Djawhar had just conquered Egypt for his master, the Fāṭimid *imām* al-Muʿizz, who had remained in Ifrīḳiya. Before inviting the latter to join him, Djawhar had two further tasks to carry out: creating a capital worthy of receiving a caliph and ensuring the security of the country. He founded Cairo (al-Ḳāhira), to the north of Fusṭāṭ, built a palace there for the *imām*, a mosque palatine, known today by the name al-Azhar, and barracks for the different army corps. He lost no time, for by 360/971 the first buildings were completed and Djawhar sent a message to his master announcing that he was awaited in his new capital.

Ensuring the security of Egypt was a more difficult matter. A few words on the Fāṭimid doctrine are required to situate it in the ideological struggles of the period. Al-Muʿizz claimed to be the descendant of al-Ḥusayn, the son of Fāṭima, daughter of the Prophet Muḥammad, and of ʿAlī, the Prophet's spiritual successor. This genealogical principle had been the pretext for the Alid revolts against the Umayyads, persecutors of the Family, then against the Abbasids, who were accused of having misappropriated the Family's inheritance. Alongside the Imamite Shīʿism, which recognized twelve descendants of ʿAlī there was the Ismāʿīli Shīʿism, which recognized only seven, and which embodied the most radical religious and social claims of the movement. Ḳarmatism, which stemmed from Ismāʿīlism, had taken up arms against the Abbasid theocracy at the end of the third/ninth century. Calling into question the religious rites and the social and family ethic, it was a response to the secret aspirations of those who had not become assimilated in the new urban centres. It could not win over the middle classes, with the exception of a few outstanding minds. The only way it could survive military defeat was to become institutionalized on the parcel of territory it controlled and to place its military force at the service of foreign ambitions.

The origin of the Fāṭimid movement was identical, but it had separated from the Ḳarmatians at the beginning of the fourth/tenth century, when the latter extended their influence to Syria. ʿUbayd Allāh al-Mahdī, the Fāṭimid *imām*, had left Salamiyya for Ifrīḳiya, where he established a caliphate. Relying on the devoted courage of a few Berber groups, his successors gained possession of the greater part of North Africa and Sicily. They made preparations for the conquest of Egypt, the last stage before that of Baghdad. The Islam they preached could scarcely shock Egypt: a few minor differences in ritual, equal rights to inheritance for women, but a rather harsh moral attitude towards them, were not enough to put off the Sunnites of Fusṭāṭ, who were, moreover, attracted by devotion to the Family. Djawhar, in his letter of *amān* to the people of Fusṭāṭ, had promised to re-establish pilgrimage, to resume *djihād*, to maintain the mosques and to pay those who served them. He did not have to face any religious opposition and he kept the same *ḳāḍī*, who continued to judge in the mosque of ʿAmr. It is true that alongside the public doctrine, close to Twelver Imamism, a secret doctrine was reserved for initiates.

The Ḳarmatians, who had openly condemned the rites, and pilgrimage in particular, did not resign themselves to the proximity of the Fāṭimids. The pretext for war was the invasion of Syria by a Berber army sent by Djawhar in the months following the fall of Fusṭāṭ. The former Ikhshidid domain – Ramla, Tiberias and Damascus – was conquered by the Kutāmite general Dja'far b. Falāh. Taking advantage of the weakened resistance of the Hamdānids as a result of the deaths of Sayf al-Dawla and of Nāṣir al-Dawla, Dja'far dispatched an army against Antioch, which the Byzantines had just occupied. However, Dja'far had to recall his army for he was attacked in Damascus by the Ḳarmatians, acting on behalf of the Abbasid caliph of Baghdad and coming to regain control of Syria. Since the death of Kāfūr they had brought this province into their orbit. Dja'far b. Falāh was killed in 360/971 and Syria was evacuated by the Fāṭimids. Djawhar repelled with diffculty the Ḳarmatians besieging Cairo.

In Ramaḍān 362/June 973 the *imām* al-Mu'izz took possession of his new capital and his palace. In the spring of 363/974, the Ḳarmatians attacked Cairo again, but, driven off by the *amīr* 'Abd Allāh, son of al-Mu'izz, they fell back on Syria, which they also had to abandon. Security was re-established in the east; in the north, commercial shipping in the Mediterranean was able to develop as a result of an agreement with Byzantium; in the south, the *baḳt* with the Christian sovereign of Nubia was renewed. In fact the real vocation of the Fāṭimid empire was trade. The influence of al-Mu'izz's adviser, Ya'ḳūb ibn Killis, was decisive in this respect. This Iraqi Jew, a merchant in Syria, a convert to Islam under Kāfūr, informer of al-Mu'izz at the time of the conquest of Egypt, and vizier during the greater part of the reign of al-'Azīz, son of al-Mu'izz, had elected to become erudite in Ismā'īlism. He applied an intelligent foreign policy. Preferring to support protectorates in Syria rather than to engage in costly military operations, he concerned himself mainly with the smooth functioning of economic relations. He owned agricultural concerns in that province, which enabled him to import wheat into Egypt in years of short supply, or even to export to Byzantium. This very profitable grain trade is still not well known by historians, whereas the activity of the Jewish merchants in Fusṭāṭ has been studied thanks to the documents of the Geniza of Old Cairo. It was a long-distance trade of high-priced or very high-priced merchandise linking southern Europe and North Africa to the Indian Ocean and the Horn of Africa. The Ismā'īlite merchants, too, were active in Yemen and in India, as also in Syria. They established communities professing their beliefs in the towns at which they stopped.

Once the Ḳarmatians were defeated and famine was a thing of the past in Egypt, pilgrimages could be resumed in 363/974 and the invocation on behalf of the Fāṭimid sovereign was pronounced in Mecca and Medina, then provisioned in wheat from the Nile. Pilgrims from all over the Islamic world took part in the glorification of the Cairo dynasty.

Under the reign of al-'Azīz (365/975–386/996) Egypt experienced calm and prosperity. Its influence spread over the southern Mediterranean, North Africa, the Arabian peninsula and central and southern Syria. In the latter province a very cautious policy was followed until the death, in 381/991, of Ibn Killis, particularly towards Tripoli, which constituted the coastal frontier with Hamdānids and the Byzantines and which made it possible to evacuate part of the Syrian wheat. From 382/992 to his death in 386/996, al-ʿAzīz launched more venturesome actions. Relying on an army that had been thoroughly reformed from 369/980 with the introduction of Turkish armoured horsemen and improvements in siege engineering, he attacked the Hamdānid ruler of Aleppo and his powerful Byzantine protector. At the same time he installed a Fāṭimid governor in Damascus and drove the Beduins out of Palestine. Al-ʿAzīz saw his generals triumph, but in the months preceding his death he tried in vain to assemble a powerful army to go and attack the Byzantines in person.

Al-ʿAzīz bequeathed a situation less brilliant than it appeared to be to his son al-Ḥākim, who reigned from 386/996 to 411/1021. The population of Fusṭāṭ and Cairo, the dual capital of the richest empire of the period, had increased tremendously. Berber, Turkish and black soldiers, Iraqi and Syrian merchants, artisans, mosque and other officials had flocked to these towns where gold was said to flow freely. The entry of tribute from the provinces and the taxes levied on traffic crossing Egypt caused the precious metal to accumulate. However, the main source of fiscal revenue, in metal and in kind, was, to their detriment, the Egyptian countryside or the artisans of the provincial towns. Tax-farmers and fiscal officials took a large part of what they collected for themselves. Often Jews or Christians, they had aroused in the Sunnites of Fusṭāṭ a tendency to reject minority groups, an attitude which was already to be observed in the time of Ibn Killis. The Cairo courtiers, the officials, the military chiefs and the big merchants possessed means of payment such that when shortages threatened, demand far exceeded the supply, aggravating price increases. Shortages then spread to the surrounding markets, stirring up the Beduins and the inhabitants of the provinces.

The rapid promotion of Turks in the army and the financial profit they derived thereby provoked the envy of the Berber tribes, which seized power on the death of Al-ʿAzīz, taking advantage of the youth of al-Ḥākim. The persecuted eastern soldiers allied with the Slav eunuchs (*al-saḳāliba*) and the Christian and Iraqi officials to eliminate the Berbers.

Al-Ḥākim was the last Arab sovereign in history to have exercised absolute power over a vast empire. He had no vizier, but a chief of *dīwān*, who also acted as an intermediary between the *imām* and his subjects. He very soon ceased to appoint an army chief, instead designating a general for the duration of operations. He had many dishonest *ḳādī*s executed, but when he came upon one of integrity, he respected his independence, with rare exceptions. In his youth al-Ḥākim had observed the parasitic behaviour of the courtiers of al-ʿAzīz. Later on, without the protection of his tutor, Bardjawān, he would have been killed by the Kutāmites. All his life he entertained hatred and contempt for the palace entourage. He liked to frequent Fusṭāṭ, its *sūḳ*s and its humble quarters, and, unlike his father and his grandfather, he was in direct contact with the Sunnite artisans and the merchants. He became aware of the burden imposed on the real country by the luxury and quickly made fortunes of the court and the barrier raised by the civil and military dignitaries between the sovereign and his subjects. He tried to remove this intermediary body by executing all those whom he suspected of dishonesty or personal ambition. He failed in this undertaking for it did not meet with the approval of the Sunnites of Fusṭāṭ. Suffering from the tensions imposed by absolute power, he tried to find a solution. However it was too much for him: his reason was clouded by fits of buffoonery and sanguinary, desperate madness.

His religious policy was inconsistent. He tried to win acceptance for the Fāṭimid ritual in Fusṭāṭ, then, in order to attract the Sunnites, he pressed Christians and Jews into converting to Islam and erected mosques over their places of worship. In 399/1009 he even had the Holy Sepulchre in Jerusalem pulled down. Around the same time, from 396/1006 to 404/1013, he adopted a tolerant attitude to the Sunnite ritual and appointed Sunnite teachers to the *dār al-ʿilm* which he founded.[12] Then he reverted to the prohibition of the Sunnite rite and in 408/1017 he let some Persians preach his divinity. This was a failure: the propagandists who had been unable to find refuge were massacred and in the following year al-Ḥākim saw the northern quarters of Fusṭāṭ sacked by the black soldiers. Feeling vaguely that he had failed in his attempt to found a direct monarchy on a consensus of the Sunnite urban middle classes, without having offices and the army acting as intermediaries, he lost interest in Fusṭāṭ, took to walking alone on the Mukattam and authorized Jews and Christians who so desired to abjure the Islam he had imposed on them ten years earlier. His murder, disguised as a disappearance, was instigated by his immediate entourage who feared further purges. Some of the adepts of his divinity founded the sect of the Druses in Syria.

The Arab 'tribes' had caused many disturbances during al-Ḥākim's reign. Abū Rakwa, an Umayyad, stirred up the Zanāta Berbers and the Banū Ḳurra Arabs to revolt in Tripolitania. Having defeated several Fāṭimid armies, he threatened Fusṭāṭ in 396/1006. The civilian population then showed its loyalty to al-Ḥākim: acts of treason were reported at the court and in Berber forces. Abū Rakwa was captured thanks to the support of the Nubians and executed near Cairo. The Fāṭimid army had shown signs of ineffectiveness and it had cost the treasury one million dinars to put it into action. So when, in 402/1011, the Ṭayy chief of Palestine, Ibn al-Dj̲arrāḥ, installed the Hasanid ruler of Mecca as Caliph in Ramla, al-Ḥākim bought over certain individuals close to Ibn al-Dj̲arrāḥ and obtained the anti-caliph's return to Mecca without having recourse to the army. Similarly, the conquest of the town and province of Aleppo in 407/1016 was the result of skilful diplomatic manoeuvres.

12. *Dār al-ʿilm*: house of learning, an institution for religious instruction and the propagation of doctrine, endowed with a public library, founded by the Fāṭimid *imām* al-Ḥākim. In certain respects it foreshadowed the Sunnite *madrasas* founded by the Seld̲jukids as centres for the dissemination of the dominant religious ideology.

The great crisis of the fifth/eleventh century

Under the reign of al-Ẓāhir (411/1021–427/1036), and under that of his son, al-Mustanṣir (427/1036–487/1094), the policy followed was no longer determined by the will of the *imām*, but by the complex interaction of pressure groups. Right up until 454/1062 the situation of the empire steadily deteriorated under the effects of the weaknesses mentioned earlier. The army was made up of a variety of ethnic groups, often mutually hostile, of different status; Berber or Arab allies, *ghulāms*, black slaves and mercenaries. In peacetime it consumed the greater part of the public revenue. When it went into action the troops had also to be equipped with mounts and weapons and to receive additional pay. Being a soldier meant being assured of a state pension more than exercising the profession of arms. Edicts reiterated the injunction to strike off the state pension registers descendants of soldiers who no longer served the state, but they tended to be laxly applied in practice. As each ethnic group was administered by a special *dīwān* and the funds at the disposal of the treasury did not increase in line with the number of persons entitled to pensions – the extended family of the *imām*, *sharīfs*, civil servants, troops – conflicts of interests constantly arose. Poorly paid, the soldiers pillaged the countryside and the suburbs. The army was no longer a factor in keeping order but was itself the basic cause of insecurity.

The towns were overcrowded: the cemeteries of the Ḳarafa were peopled by populations driven from the countryside by Beduin incursions; and the elite left the outlying districts to seek security in the centre of Fusṭāṭ or Cairo. The merchants awaited the great Muslim feasts with anxiety, for the crowds took to pillaging the closed *sūḳs*. Food shortages became more acute and more frequent. The city-dwellers grabbed the peasants' plough-oxen and also the land subject to inundation, where the notables of the regime raised huge herds, for the affluence of the towns increased the consumption of meat. Whenever a poor flood was anticipated, speculation pushed up the price of wheat. Al-Djardjarā'ī, vizier from 418/1027 to 437/1045, managed to put a stop to the price rises by imposing a single market for grain and encouraging price-cutting competition among the bakers, but all the high officials, including the *imām*, built up stocks and speculated.

A general destabilization of the population on the fringe of the desert also became apparent: the three great *ḳabīlas* of Syria – Ṭayy, Kalb and Kilāb – made an alliance in 415/1024 and emissaries contacted the tribes in the Delta and Tripolitania. A solidarity due to their circumstances overcame former mutual hostility; they wanted to obtain access to the cultivated lands for their herds and incidentally to pillage the towns. A climatic change – drier winters – may account for this. Up until 433/1041 the Fāṭimid general al-Dizbirī, though poorly supported by Cairo, held the tribes in check in Syria. In Upper Egypt advantage was taken of the treason of the Zīrīd Ibn Bādīs to send to Tripolitania and to Ifrīḳiya the Banū Hilāl and the Banū Sulaym who were ravaging the Ṣaʿīd (442/1050).

In 451/1059 the Fāṭimids won their last great diplomatic victory: a Turkish general, Al-Basāsīrī, sent the Abbasid Caliph al-Ḳāʾim into captivity and had the invocation pronounced in the mosques of Baghdad in favour of al-Mustanṣir. However, a few months later Tughril Bek, chief of the Seldjukids, the new Sunnite masters of the east, retook Baghdad and re-established al-Ḳāʾim. The situation was reversed in 462/1070, when the Fāṭimid general Nāṣir al-Dawla, in rebellion in Alexandria, recognized the Abbasid Caliphate and, in 464/1072, confining al-Mustanṣir in Cairo, called to the Seldjukids for aid. The Fāṭimid state might have come to an end on that occasion.

A great famine, which began in 454/1062 and was very serious from 457/1065 onwards, had starved to death a large part of the population of Egypt. Al-Mustanṣir sold the treasures of the dynasty and only survived by begging. The whole edifice, undermined by the parasites whom he had sheltered, was collapsing. In 466/1073 the *imām* called the Armenian Badr al-Djamālī, Governor of Palestine, to his assistance. This rough warrior came to Cairo in Djumāda 466/January 1074 and executed the chief officers, dispersed the dissident armies and reconstituted around his Armenian troops a small and effective army. He received the title of vizier with full powers. He then went and put down the blacks who were ravaging Upper Egypt, returning in 468/1076 to defend Cairo which had been attacked by the Turk Atsiz, an ally of the Seldjukids. In 469/1077, he drove the Lawāta Berbers out of the Delta, selling 20 000 women of that tribe on the market. In the meantime he had passed through Syria where he was unable to retake Damascus but managed to consolidate Fāṭimid rule over the ports of Palestine. He had the towns of Syria protected by stone walls and it was at Badr's command that the three monumental gates of Fāṭimid Cairo which still exist were built.

In order to enable the peasants to resume cultivation of their devastated fields he remitted three years' taxation. He reformed the administrative districts and restructured the state and the army, thus extending by a century the life of the Fāṭimid regime. The texts of al-Ḳalkashandī and other authors describing the functioning of Fāṭimid institutions refer to the state born of Badr's reform, which was very different from the first Fāṭimid state.

The sixth/twelfth century: death throes of the Fāṭimid regime

Following the 454/1062–468/1076 crisis, the Fāṭimid empire was dead. The invocation on behalf of al-Mustanṣir was no longer pronounced either in Ifrīḳiya, or in Mecca, or in Aleppo, or in Damascus. Egypt, reorganized around the Nile Valley, was recovering from its wounds. Alexandria was regaining its prosperity through trade with Italy, while Ḳūs, the prefecture of Upper Egypt, was distributing black slaves from Nubia and spices from

PLATE 7.4 *Egyptian (Fāṭimid) lustre-painted ceramics*
7.4(a) (left) Tenth-century vase; 7.4 (b) (right) eleventh-century bowl

India. In 487/1094 Badr died, and al-Mustanṣir's death followed. Badr's son, al-Afḍal, proclaimed al-Mustanṣir's young son, al-Ḥasan, as Caliph and immured his elder brother Nizār. The master of the Ismāʿīli *daʿwa* in Seldjukid territory, Ḥasan b. al-Ṣabbāḥ, recognized Nizār as *imām*; his movement, that of the *assassins*, which, like the Druse movement, developed solely outside Egypt, put an end to the traditional Fāṭimid *daʿwa*.[13]

Al-Mustanṣir had reigned for almost three-quarters of a century. In the period, not much longer, that elapsed before the dynasty died out, six caliphs succeeded one another. Not one exercised power in reality; not one chose his successor. Authority was in the hands of the military viziers: some of them conquered power at the point of the sword, some inherited it. Some of them were remarkable – as, for instance, Ṭalā'iʿ b. Ruzzīk – others were nothing but upstart brigands. In an Egypt in which the teaching of the Fāṭimid doctrine had apparently disappeared, they flaunted various religious convictions. Al-Afḍal Kutayfāt, who was Badr's grandson, established Twelver Imamism and installed four *ḳādīs* of four rites. Ridwān was a Sunnite and opened a Shāfiʿite *madrasa* in Alexandria. The people appeared to be indifferent to the coloration of Islam that held power; attachment to the dynasty was motivated only by pride in an Islamic power the centre of which was on Egyptian soil. Only the presence of a non-Muslim vizier, Bahrām, bearing the title of 'Sword of Islam' was not well received.

13. *Daʿwa*: designates both some particular Shīʿite doctrine, frequently Ismāʿīli or Fāṭimid, spread by clandestine or semi-clandestine missionaries, and the various resources made available to the latter for propaganda purposes.

Then, three years after Badr's death, the Franks entered Muslim territory, overthrew the Seldjukids and, in 492/1099, took Jerusalem. They defeated the Fāṭimids at Askalon. There things rested for many years, apart from a few skirmishes. There was no active complicity between Franks and Fāṭimids, but rather a certain nonchalance on the part of the latter, which is readily understandable. In the fourth/tenth century the Fāṭimid state's resources had been derived from the levying of tribute in metallic currency and from the grain trade. It had had to control extensive territories and hold the Syrian Bekā'a and Ḥawrān. In the sixth/twelfth century the price of grain had dropped after the demographic disasters of the fifth/eleventh century and also no doubt owing to the extension of lands under cultivation following another climatic change in Syria. Gold, which was rarer in Syria, circulated mainly between India and the West. So the Fāṭimids had only to hold the Nile Valley and the trading posts on the Palestine seaboard, frequented, like Alexandria, by Italian merchants. The army was grouped in the south of Palestine and in Egypt, ready to encounter the Seldjukids, who wanted to restore Sunnism in Cairo. For the Fāṭimids, the presence of the Crusaders in Syria – raising a barrier between the Seldjukids and Egypt and diverting traffic from the Red Sea to the Nile Valley – had its uses. Now, until 549/1154, when Nūr al-Dīn was installed in Damascus, there had been no sign of any Muslim solidarity for the purpose of driving the Franks out of Syria. Egypt, which suffered merely moral injury as a result of their presence, felt no more concerned than the other Muslim states.

Nūr-al-Dīn, relying on a powerful army, undertook the reconquest of Syria. The fragile Fāṭimid state, with its army divided into rival ethnic groups, had to choose between a policy of support for the counter-Crusade – a policy that exposed it to attack by the Franks–and an appeal to the latter against Nūr al-Dīn, who wanted to take over the Seldjukids' plan to restore Sunnism. The parties disputing power in Cairo chose in turn one or the other of these two alternatives, sometimes both at once, hoping to keep the situation in hand. They hastened the decadence of the state.

In 548/1153 the Crusaders abandoned their neutrality with regard to Palestine and seized Askalon. The installation of Nūr al-Dīn in central Syria prompted them to seek compensation in Egypt. The first concern of the Fāṭimid viziers, who were often former governors of Ḳūs, was the protection of the great southern Red Sea route to Alexandria via Upper Egypt. They would have been ready to pay Nūr al-Dīn large amounts in gold dinars for relieving them of the necessity of defending the eastern frontier. However, Ṭalā'i' b. Ruzzīk launched two expeditions in Frankish Palestine. He was victorious but obtained no lasting result, for Nūr al-Dīn had remained inactive. In 556/1161 the Franks launched an offensive against Egypt. They were to launch four more, some in response to appeals from the Cairo viziers, in the period up to 564/1169. It was only in 558/1163 that they came up against troops sent by Nūr al-Dīn and commanded by

Shirkūh and the latter's nephew, Ṣalāh al-Dīn. As a result of broken promises, sudden changes of alliance and betrayal on the part of the vizier Ibn Sallār and the Caliph al-ʿĀḍīd, these military actions came to nought. So in 564/1169 Shirkūh took the Fāṭimid vizier's office for himself. He died shortly afterwards and was replaced by Ṣalāh al-Dīn.

The last Fāṭimid vizier was therefore a Sunnite Kurd general, vassal of the Prince of Damascus, the Sunnite Turk Nūr al-Dīn, whose name was mentioned in the invocation, following that of the *imām*, al-ʿĀḍīd. This was an intolerable situation for the *imām*, who instructed Djawhar, a eunuch, to assassinate Ṣalāh al-Dīn. When the latter heard of it he had Djawhar executed. The black guard of Cairo mutinied. A very hard struggle ensued and al-ʿĀḍīd had to disavow the black soldiers who laid down their lives for him. The guard was massacred. Ṣalāḥ al-Dīn, to whom the Fāṭimid Caliphate's fiction was of use, refused to put a stop to it despite the reprimands of Nūr al-Dīn. However, in 566/1171 a Persian publicly pronounced the *khuṭba* on behalf of the Abbasid Caliph and so the Fāṭimid Imāmate of Egypt came to an end without there being any need for removing al-ʿĀḍīd. At that point the latter obligingly died a natural death. A regime that had lived for two centuries finally left the political scene without any display of emotion on the part of the population of Cairo.

Islamic monuments in Egypt built before 566/1171

Most of the beautiful monuments of Arab architecture that can be seen by visitors to Cairo date from the Ayyubid and Mamluk periods. In old Cairo and in the province of Egypt, apart from a few exceptions at Luxor, Ḳūs and Alexandria, the remnants of medieval architecture dating to the periods before the Crusades are in general Christian. However, the first five centuries of the Arab presence in Egypt have left some buildings to posterity. These are few in number, and have often been substantially rebuilt or altered. They are impressive, however, because of their scale, their style and the spiritual power that they have possessed since their first construction or have acquired in the course of history.

Four major mosques were founded by or on behalf of four prestigious rulers of Egypt. The great mosque of Fusṭāṭ was built close by the Nile by the governor, ʿAmr ibn al-ʿĀṣ in 20–1/641–2. Extended, altered and modernized on several occasions, it retains no visible traces of its original form. It is to be hoped that the Egyptian antiquities department, which conducted important investigations of the mosque site between 1970 and 1975 that threw light on the chronology of successive extensions, will publish the reports and photographs to which we can turn for further information.

In 265/879, Aḥmad ibn Ṭūlūn established the great mosque that bears his name on the high ground of al-Kaṭāʾiʿ to the north-east of Fusṭāṭ (Plate 7.1). Since it was never completely adopted by the population, it is much better-conserved and much less transformed than many other buildings of this period. In the heart of an animated and bustling city, it maintains a vast preserve of silence and devotion in an architectural framework that is austerely beautiful, severe and rigorous. The British historian, K. A. C. Cresswell has analysed this vast architectural ensemble; around an almost square courtyard with sides of 92 m open off four elegant and lofty porticoes. These incorporate five rows of pillars on the *ḳibla* side and two rows on the other three sides. Miṣr-Fusṭāṭ's vocation as one of the temporal and spiritual capitals of the Islamic world was affirmed for the first time with the foundation by a pious Turkish warrior of this admirable monument constructed in burnt brick, and profoundly impregnated with Asiatic influences.

When Djawhar founded Cairo in 359/970 for his master, al-Mu'izz, he established a great mosque in the heart of the capital, to the north of al-Kaṭā'i'. To this day it is known worldwide as al-Azhar. The animation that it manifests contrasts with the silence and solitude that entrances the visitor to the Ibn Ṭūlūn mosque. Cairo was founded by Africans; the acculturation of Africa to Islam was the achievement of the teaching provided by al-Azhar. The success of this institution as the privileged source for the diffusion of Muslim knowledge to both Arab and non-Arab peoples is sufficient indication that the building must have been extended on several occasions; indeed only the courtyard shows evidence of the original Fāṭimid plan. The whole history of Egypt and of its role beyond its frontiers is evident in this ensemble of buildings. The foundation of Cairo was indeed the beginning of a great adventure.

In 400/1010 al-Ḥākim established a great mosque on the northern outskirts of the city of Cairo. The sites of the four mosques we have described are evidence of the regular translation of the centre of gravity of the successive capitals of Egypt towards the north-north-east over the first three and a half centuries of the Islamic era. The true centre had, however, essentially been fixed by Djawhar, and al-Ḥākim was aware of this fact. His mosque never knew the success enjoyed by al-Azhar and, henceforth, it was above all either the city of Cairo or the area between it and Fusṭāṭ that received the principal buildings constructed for the use of the living by the Ayyubid and Mamluk princes. Long abandoned, the al-Ḥākim mosque was later restored for the use of the Ismā'īlites.

The grand vizier Badr al-Djamāli, an Armenian by origin, introduced building in stone to Cairo, where bricks had previously been used. He had the city walls of the capital reconstructed, and had monumental gateways erected. Three of these may still be admired: Bāb Zuwayla, to the south of the great axis of the Fāṭimid town; Bāb al-Futūḥ, to the north of this same axis; and Bāb al-Naṣr (Plate 7.5), to the north-east. The architectural conception behind these was skilful, seeking at the same time a majestic appearance and military effectiveness. Their realization was perfect thanks to careful stereotomy. Indeed, the heritage of the Byzantine stonemasons

PLATE 7.5 *Bāb al-Naṣr: one of the gates in the wall of the Fāṭimid city*

who had built many churches in Syria and Asia Minor in the sixth century had been preserved intact by the Armenians in their remote mountains. In the sixth/twelfth century, it was diffused once again across the whole of the Frankish and Muslim east.

Four smaller mosques date from the second Fāṭimid period. On the Moḳattam hill, the al-Djuyūshī mosque-martyry, founded in 478/1085, seems to watch over the destiny of the dead and the living of the great city;

PLATE 7.6 *Al-Djuyūshī Mosque: general view from the east*

its style, unusual in Egypt, once again evokes there the churches of Armenia (Plate 7.6). In 519/1125 the small al-Akmar mosque was built on the principal artery of Cairo, between the al-Ḥākim and al-Azhar mosque. Its façade in carved stone and its ornate main entrance announce a stylistic revolution in religious buildings. The dummy mausoleum dedicated to Sayyida Ruḳayya, built around 527/1133 in the cemeteries to the south-east of the Ibn Ṭūlūn mosque, attests to the desire of the Fāṭimid rulers to attract to Cairo all the pilgrims devoted to the Holy Family of Islam. It was with the same political and religious intention that in 555/1160 the vizier Ṣāliḥ Ṭalā'i' had the mosque that bears his name built to the south of the Bāb Zuwayla. Its beautiful façade, which takes up and develops certain elements of the al-Akmar mosque, modifying them to take account of the tastes of the day, is evidence of the rapid progress of religious architecture in the sixth/twelfth century and foreshadows the full blossoming of the art under the Ayyubids and Mamluks.

Conclusion

In 566/1171, more than five centuries after the conquest of Egypt by the Arabs, this land was the richest in the East. The ceramics, the glassware, the fabrics and the objects of metal and wood that came out of its workshops attained unparallelled perfection. Agriculture retained the characteristics it had acquired over several millennia, while integrating new crops that had come from Asia. Architecture, both religious and military, had produced powerful monuments; the following centuries were to be even more fruitful. A literature in Arabic was steadily developing and gradually losing its provincial character. The Iraqis and Syrians residing in the capital played an important role, but the quality of the historical works and of the descriptions of the features of the land of Egypt gave this literature its originality. Here again though, the richest works were to be written later.

Yet acculturation to Islam had been neither quick nor complete. A large proportion of the people, peasants of Upper Egypt or artisans of the provincial towns, had remained Christian. As for the Sunnites of Fusṭāṭ, they displayed indifference to the struggles for power that set against each other military chiefs – often risen from slavery – who were at the head of troops consisting of an admixture of different ethnic groups. An Egyptian personality, about which only a few texts tell us anything, was evolving slowly, in contrast with the rapid development of Fusṭāṭ and Cairo. Yet, in the following centuries the Islam of Africa was guided by the scholars and the *ṣūfīs* of Egypt.

It is time that historians brought together the elements that might make it possible to trace the rise of this deep river, so that the history of Egypt might not remain only that of its successive masters.

8

Christian Nubia at the height of its civilization

S. JAKOBIELSKI

Early relations with Muslim Egypt

The emergence of a powerful Christian kingdom to the south of the First Cataract on the Nile[1] created favourable development prospects for the Nubian population. Two factors made it possible for the kingdom to attain economic prosperity. The first was the uniting of the northern kingdom of Nobadia (Arabic, Nūba), having its capital at Faras, with the central kingdom of Makuria (Arabic, Muḳurra), with its capital at Old Dongola (Arabic, Dūnḳūla al-ʿAdjūz), and in conjunction with this, the creation of a strong central government. The second factor was the propitious settlement of relations with neighbouring Egypt by the signing of a treaty known as the *baḳt* following the Arab invasion of Dongola led by ʿAbdallāh ibn Abī Ṣarḥ in 651. Both of these facts in the history of Nubia are known mainly from reports by Arab historians and travellers, and have hitherto been only partly verified by archaeological investigations. So let us deal with these factors in detail.[2]

It appears that at the time of the Arab invasion, northern and central Nubia were united under King Qalidurut of Dongola. Thus ʿAbdallāh ibn Abī Ṣarḥ signed only one treaty – that in Dongola – paying no attention to Nobadia with whom the settlement of a correct relationship might seem to have been more important, since that country directly adjoined Egypt. The *baḳt* was a special form of treaty, having no precedence in the Muslim world. It was really a truce or pact of non-aggression. The complete text of this agreement has been preserved in the Khiṭaṭ of al-Maḳrīzī.[3] The text

1. For the earlier periods of Christian Nubia's history see Unesco, *General History of Africa*, Vol. II, ch. 12.

2. For main elaborations on the period discussed see J. W. Crowfoot, 1927; U. Monneret de Villard, 1938; P. L. Shinnie, 1954; 1971; 1978a; B. G. Trigger, 1965; O. Meinardus, 1967; I. Hofmann, 1967; Y. F. Hasan, 1973; G. Vantini, 1975; 1981a; W. Y. Adams, 1977, pp. 433–507; A. Osman, 1982a.

3. Cf. P. Forand, 1971, pp. 114–15; Y. F. Hasan, 1973, pp. 22–4; G. Vantini, 1975, pp. 640–2.

contains definitions of the following matters: the Arabs should not attack Nubia, under the terms of the agreement; and citizens of both countries should enjoy the right of free passage through the country in question as travellers but not as settlers, and under such conditions the authorities would be responsible for the safety of the other country's citizens. It also contained a clause providing for the extradiction of fugitives from one country to the other. The Nubians were to be responsible for the upkeep of the mosque built in Old Dongola to cater for visiting Muslims. Nubia also had imposed on her an annual tribute of 360 slaves, to be supplied to the Governor of Aswān. Another source (ʿAlī Khalīfa Ḥumayd b. Hishām al-Buḥayrī)[4] recalls that in exchange for those slaves, the Arabs should supply 1300 *ardeb* of wheat, 1300 *kanīr*[5] of wine and certain defined quantities of linen and cloth etc. Thus this treaty had some qualities of a trade agreement. In principle the truce was upheld throughout the next five centuries of Christian civilization in Nubia, and in its initial phase was crucial for maintaining peace and possibilities for national development at a time when Arab armies occupied large areas of North Africa and Spain and were threatening Byzantium.

With regard to the date when the two Nubian kingdoms were united, a hypothesis should still be mentioned[6] that ascribes unification to the activities of King Merkurios, who was crowned in the year 697, which date can be established thanks to foundation inscriptions of Bishop Paulos concerning the cathedral in Faras, dated to 707, and referring to the eleventh year of the reign of that king.[7] It appears that after the unification of his kingdom King Merkurios directed his attention principally towards the question of religious unity throughout Nubia, and at the beginning of the second/eighth century concerned himself with the subordination of the Nubian Church to the Monophysite partriarchate in Alexandria.

Both the unification of the land and later of the religion, i.e. the creation of a common plane embracing – under the auspices of the Monophysite Church from Egypt – the united kingdom of Nubia, the southern kingdom of Alodia (about which we know very little from this period), and including Ethiopia, undoubtedly created favourable conditions for the development of Nubia. The lack of any real threat from the Arabs and the possibility of carrying on trade with Egypt and maintaining contacts with Byzantium or at least with Jerusalem which was the goal of pilgrimages, led to the development of a distinctive Nubian culture in the subsequent period. This

4. G. Vantini, 1975, pp. 642–3; W. Y. Adams, 1977, p. 452.
5. For its suggested capacity cf. L. Török, 1978, p. 301, n. 3.
6. See Unesco, *General History of Africa*, Vol. II, ch. 12, pp. 333–4. On the date of the unification cf., for example, L. P. Kirwan, 1935, p. 61; U. Monneret de Villard, 1938, p. 80; K. Michałowski, 1965a, p. 16; S. Jakobielski, 1972, pp. 35–6; W. Y. Adams, 1977, pp. 453–4; G. Vantini, 1981a, pp. 71–2; Cf. also L. P. Kirwan, 1982.
7. S. Jakobielski, 1972, pp. 36–46; J. Kubińska, 1974, pp. 14–19.

could be seen in the growth and maturity of a literate civilization with its architecture and cultural traditions connected as much with the Coptic tradition as with the Byzantine, the latter being particularly influential as a source for models of state administration and court organization as well as in building construction and the arts and crafts.

Thus the end of the eighth century saw Nubia moving into its period of prosperity, which lasted up to the beginning of the second half of the twelfth century and was also conditioned by a favourable economic situation. One of the factors essential for this was the relatively high level of the waters of the Nile, which gave Nubian agriculture a chance to develop.[8]

Our knowledge of political events in this period is largely drawn from Arab sources and chiefly concerns the united kingdom of Nubia. Her borders stretched from al-Ḳasr in the north (a few kilometres to the south of Aswān) south to the area between the Fifth and Sixth Cataracts (al-Abwāb), where it encountered the northern border of Alodia (Arabic, ʿAlwa) with its capital at Soba, in the vicinity of modern-day Khartoum.

We know next to nothing of Alodia. An account by Ibn Sālim al-Aswānī, quoted by al-Maḳrīzī,[9] informs us that Soba possessed magnificent buildings and gardens as well as churches overflowing with gold. It is also reported that the king of ʿAlwa was mightier than the ruler of Makuria, had a formidable army and ruled over a land that was far more fertile. Recent excavations done in Soba by the Expedition of the British Institute for Eastern Africa have come close to verifying this view about the city's munificence.[10] A complex of churches and episcopal buildings of red brick have recently come to light. But this is still a very small part of the entire picture.

There are not even direct data about the unification of Alodia with Makuria, though in the mid-tenth century both courts were united by blood relationships. Ibn Ḥawḳal reported on this when he journeyed through Alodia about 945–50 and quotes the kings Stephanos, son of Georgios (II, King of Nubia) and his predecessor Eusebios.[11] In the mid-eighth century, King Kyriakos was described by the Coptic biographer Deacon Ioannes as being the ruler of the whole kingdom of Nubia, 'right as far as the southern end of the earth ...'[12] It seems, however, that judging by later reports, Alodia may have only temporarily been included within the united kingdom of Nubia, being for almost the entire period of Christianity in Nubia a separate state entity.

8. P. L. Shinnie, 1978a, p. 569; B. G. Trigger, 1970, p. 352.

9. G. Vantini, 1975, p. 613; cf. also A. J. Arkell, 1961, pp. 194–5; P. L. Shinnie, 1961, pp. 11–12.

10. Preliminary reports on these excavations, continued by the British Expedition since 1981, will appear in *Azania*. For previous works cf. P. L. Shinnie, 1961.

11. G. Vantini, 1981a, pp. 117–18. The name of King Stephanos is attested also in a graffito from Meroe: U. Monneret de Villard, 1938, p. 157.

12. G. Vantini, 1981a, pp. 75–7.

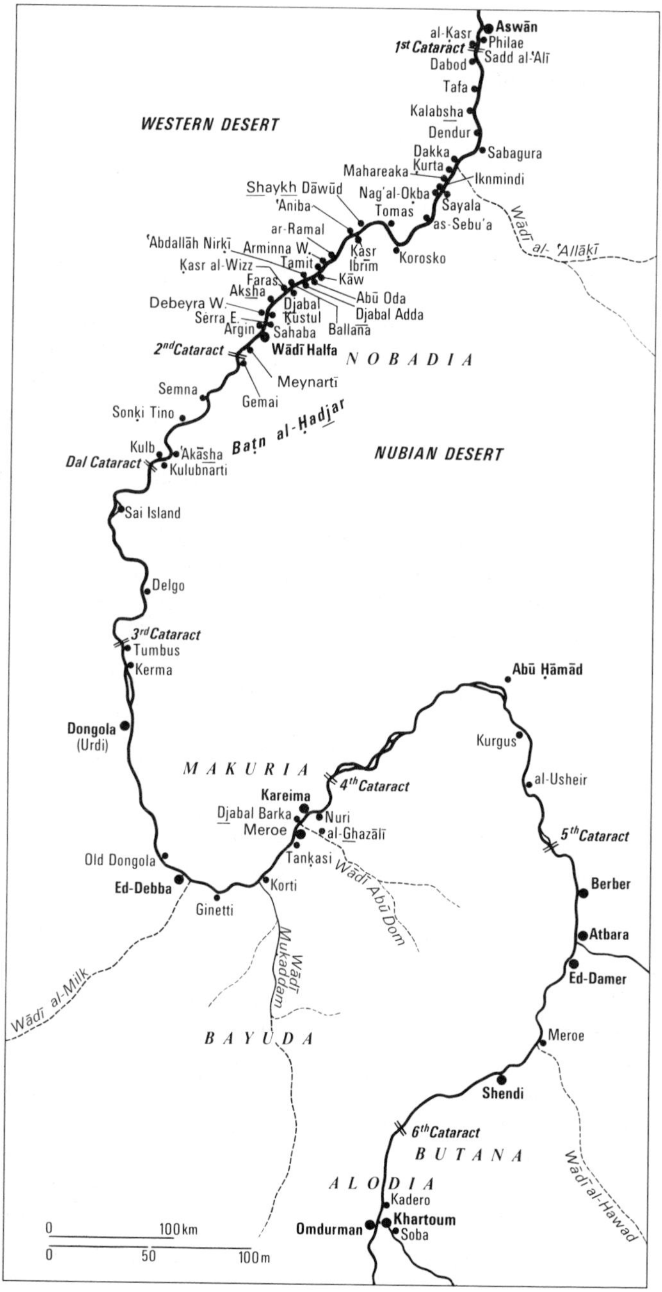

FIG. 8.1 *Christian Nubia*

East and west of the Nile

The eastern border of the kingdom of Nubia adjoined lands occupied by the Bēdja tribes. From the eighth to the tenth century, they were an important factor in shaping political relations in this part of the world. They had always constituted something of a threat to southern Egypt, which had been in danger from raids on the part of the earlier Blemmyes, a nomadic Bēdja people from the Eastern Desert.

By the beginning of the third/ninth century, most of the Bēdja peoples living in the Red Sea Hills area were still 'pagans', though some had nominally accepted the Christian faith, while still others – particularly in the north – seem to have been under the strong influence of Islam. In the year 831, as a result of continual border disputes, the Caliph, al-Mu'taṣim sent a punitive expedition against the Bēdja. After suffering defeat, their leader Ḳānūn ibn 'Abd al-'Azīz was forced to recognize the suzerainty of the Caliph. At that point a kind of treaty was negotiated and although it contained some clauses identical to those of the *baḳt* its meaning was altogether different. The Bēdja were to be subject to an annual tribute, with no guarantee on the part of the Arabs. The latter received the right to settle on Bēdja lands, whose ruler now found himself in the position of a vassal.[13]

The treaty did not put an end to hostilities, but rather created a situation conducive to further conflict. The lands occupied by these nomadic *ḳabīla*s abounded in gold mines (particularly in the Wādī al-'Allāḳī area) and Arab penetration into these lands grew in strength. Open war broke out again in the mid-ninth century, when the erstwhile leader of the Bēdja, 'Alī Bābā had to submit in the face of overwhelming Arab forces under the leadership of Muḥammad al-Ḳummī. According to certain Arab sources, the tribute by now amounted to approximately 2400 gm of gold annually.[14]

It was natural that the Bēdja should seek the protection of the Nubians since they were under constant threat. There are conflicting Arab reports on this matter, but there seems no doubt that Nubian forces were in some way involved in the above-mentioned battles. Ibn Ḥawḳal even reported that 'Alī Bābā and the Nubian King Yurḳī (Georgios) were both taken prisoner and brought before the Caliph al-Mutawakkil in Baghdad.[15] We shall return to the matter of the sojourn of King Georgios in Baghdad below. In any case, even during the period of its greatest prosperity, the kingdom of Nubia witnessed constant hostilities along the Red Sea, beyond Nubia's eastern borders.

Relations with those *ḳabīla*s living to the west of the Nile Valley followed a different trend. Though we have little information on this matter,

13. W. Y. Adams, 1977, pp. 553–4; Y. F. Hasan, 1973, pp. 38–41; G. Vantini, 1981a, pp. 92–3.

14. According to aṭ-Ṭabarī (d. 930), see G. Vantini, 1975, p. 99; 1981a, p. 95.

15. G. Vantini, 1975, p. 158, according to writings of Ibn Ḥawḳal (d. 988).

it seems from reports by Ibn Ḥawḳal that in a land many days' journey from the valley over the sandy desert, there lived some pastoralists called the Djibāliyyūn (Highlanders) and the Aḥadiyyūn, whom we may place in southern (Nuba Mountains) and northern Kordofān. The latter folk were supposed to have practised Christianity.[16] It has already been proved that there existed obvious linguistic links between certain groups in the Nuba Mountains (Dair, Dilling) and Dārfūr (Birgid, Midob, Tundjur) and those speaking the Nubian dialects in the Nile Valley,[17] which is evidence of contacts or migration. Contacts between the Nubian kingdom and that part of the Sudan have been partially confirmed archaeologically, for example in the finding of Christian pottery of the Nubian Classic Period at 'Ayn Faraḥ (northern Dārfūr) and of a slightly later type at Koro Toro in Chad.[18] According to Ibn Ḥawḳal, both of the above-mentioned peoples bore allegiance to the king of Makuria or the king of Alodia.[19]

It cannot be ruled out that Kordofān and Dārfūr were actually the source of the slaves which Nubia was obliged to supply to Egypt in accordance with the terms of the *baḳt*. We do not know to what extent slave-dealing was a state enterprise rather than an economic mainstay,[20] nor do we know to what extent these western areas of the present-day Sudan republic were colonized by the Nubians.

Dongola, Faras and other towns

Old Dongola, situated on the eastern bank of the Nile, halfway between the Third and Fourth Cataracts was the capital of the united kingdom of Nubia. The development of this town may be traced from the findings of excavations carried out there since 1964 by the Polish expedition. The early eleventh-century town of Dongola was described by Abū Ṣāliḥ in the following way: 'Here is the throne of the King. It is a large city on the banks of the blessed Nile, and contains many churches and large houses and wide streets. The King's house is lofty with several domes built of red-brick and resembles the buildings in Iraq . . .'[21] The results of excavations seem to confirm this account to the letter.[22] At the present time the town

16. G. Vantini, 1981a, pp. 140–1.

17. E. Zyhlarz, 1928b; R. Stevenson, 1956, p. 112; R. Thelwall, 1978, pp. 268–70; 1982. On the languages of the Sudan in general: J. H. Greenberg, 1963b, and R. Stevenson, 1971.

18. P. L. Shinnie, 1978a, p. 572 and R. Mauny, 1978, p. 327, note 2. On Nubian pottery at Tié (Chad) cf. A. D. Bivar and P. L. Shinnie, 1970, p. 301.

19. G. Vantini, 1975, pp. 165–6.

20. W. Y. Adams, 1977, p. 505.

21. K. Michałowski, 1966a, p. 290; Abu Ṣāliḥ, 1969, pp. 149–50; G. Vantini, 1975, p. 326.

22. For results of the excavations cf. K. Michałowski, 1966a; S. Jakobielski and A. Ostrasz, 1967–8; S. Jakobielski and L. Krzyżaniak, 1967–8; S. Jakobielski, 1970, 1975, 1978, 1982a, 1982c; P. M. Gartkiewicz, 1973, 1975; W. Godlewski, 1982a. Current reports on the excavations appear in *Études et Travaux* (Warsaw) beginning with Vol. 8 (1973); final publications will appear in the series *Travaux du Centre d'Archéologie Méditerranéenne de l'Académie Polonaise des Sciences* (Warsaw).

consists of a complex of ruins extending over an area of 35 ha, in which the remains of the earlier buildings are concealed under the structures of the Muslim period (ninth/thirteenth to fifteenth/nineteenth centuries). The central part of the town which is located on a rocky outcrop was once surrounded by massive walls. To the north extends the Christian city including the complex of churches discovered by the Polish archaeologists (which makes it possible to completely revalue the theories hitherto held about sacral architecture in Nubia, as will be described below). Further northwards extend a second/eighth- to third/ninth-century housing complex. The houses discovered here differ in their hitherto unencountered spatial layout as well as their functional programme (water supply installation, bathroom with heating system) and interiors decorated with murals.

The turn of the eighth century is taken as the date of the monumental two-storeyed royal building, situated on a rocky spur to the east of the centre of the town. Standing almost 11 m tall, this building contained the king's Throne Hall on its representative storey, decorated once with murals (Fig. 8.2), (for that reason it had been mistaken for a church). In 1317 it was converted by Sayf al-Dīn ʿAbdallāh into a mosque, which was used for religious purposes until the year 1969. The building itself had been destroyed and rebuilt many times and its external appearance has changed over the ages (Plate 8.1); it is however the only Christian Throne Hall surviving intact in all the areas which had once been under the cultural influences of Byzantium, and may have been modelled on the one which used to be in the Great Palace in Constantinople and is known only from descriptions.[23]

The other important sites in what was formerly Makuria have not yet been investigated. During this period an important centre was quite possibly the Island of Sai,[24] the seat of one of the bishoprics.

We have, however, more precise data from the northern part of the realm (the former Nobadia, also known in the sources as the province of Maris) obtained during the great Unesco campaign to save the monuments of Nubia from being flooded by the waters of the Nubian Lake in the 1961–6 period.[25]

Faras, also investigated at that time by the Polish team[26] with its

23. W. Godlewski, 1981; 1982a.

24. J. Vercoutter, 1970; U. Monneret de Villard, 1938, pp. 162–6; P. M. Gartkiewicz, 1982a, pp. 81–3.

25. For a bibliographical summary of the Unesco campaign see L.-A. Christophe, 1977; for recent discoveries and a new bibliography on sites excavated during the Nubian campaign, see J. Leclant, 1958–74; 1975–83; see also W. Y. Adams, 1966; 1977, pp. 81–90; F. Hinkel, 1978; for a catalogue of all archaeological sites in the territory of the Sudan see F. Hinkel, 1977– .

26. See Unesco, *General History of Africa*, Vol. II, ch. 12 and K. Michałowski, 1962, 1965c, 1967, 1974; (there is at pp. 312–14 a full bibliography concerning the site); S. Jakobielski, 1972; K. Michałowski 1979; G. Vantini, 1970a; M. Martens-Czarnecka, 1982a; P. M. Gartkiewicz, 1983.

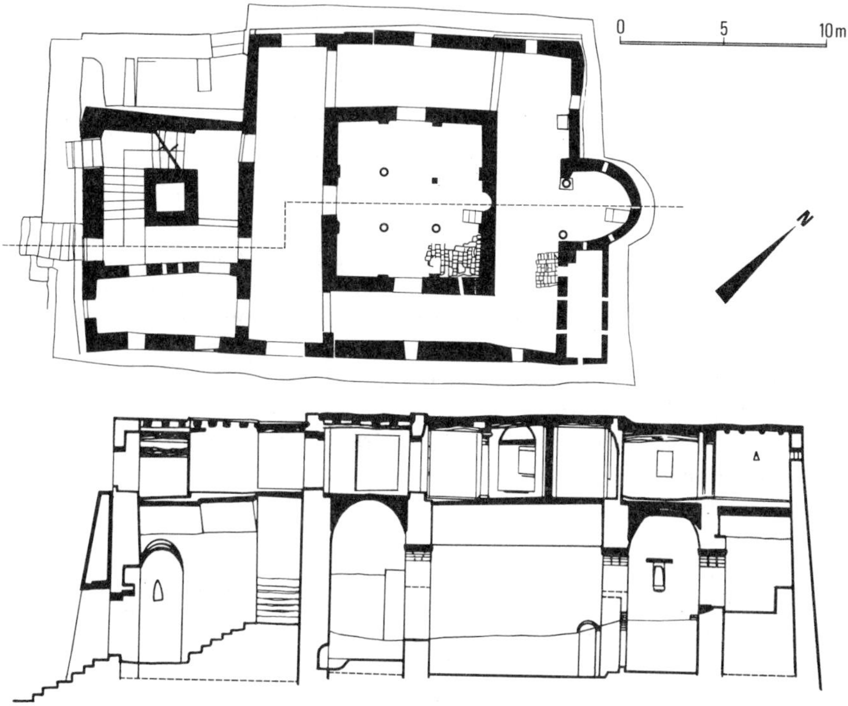

FIG. 8.2 *The mosque building in Old Dongola in its present state. Top: plan of the upper storey with the king's throne hall, converted to a mosque in 1317. Bottom: the east–west section of the building* (*elaborated by St Medeksza*)

PLATE 8.1 *The royal building in Old Dongola, converted to a mosque in 1317*

splendid cathedral, churches, palaces and monasteries, placed in the central point of the town and surrounded by the older walls, retained its role as the religious centre. This was now reinforced by the raising of Faras to the status of Metropolitan Bishopric with the assumption of the episcopate by a Nubian, Kyros (866–902) whose splendid portrait decorates the walls of the Faras Cathedral (Plate 8.2). The Metropolitan Bishop resided in Faras until the end of the tenth century, the last to bear that title being Petros I (974–99).

Faras probably also remained a centre of administration, the seat of the eparch, the royal administrator of the northern part of the kingdom, whose duties included not only control over the province, but also responsibility for contacts between the kingdom and Egypt. He was also the chief treasurer.[27] The Nubian administration, both royal and local in Nobadia, maintained various court functionaries. Their Greek titles, known from the Byzantine period in Egypt and North Africa, were adopted in Nubia, but their functions were not necessarily the same. Such titles[28] as *domestikos*, *protodomestikos*, *meizon*, *protomeizoteros*, *nauarchos*, *primikerios* and others can be found alongside many others, attested exclusively in the Old Nubian language.[29]

According to some scholars, the residence of the eparch was now transferred to the stronghold of Ḳasr Ibrīm;[30] the only archaeological site that has survived above the waters of the Nubian Lake, because it is located on a high rock. It is being investigated systematically by expeditions of the Egypt Exploration Society.[31] Apart from the cathedral, and the remains of its urban architecture, Ḳasr Ibrīm has provided us with a wealth of material discoveries and several hundred fragments of manuscript finds, among them ecclesiastical and literary writings, letters and documents.

Also of great importance was the vast town of Gebel Adda,[32] about a dozen kilometres to the north of Faras on the eastern bank of the Nile. These towns were quite possibly inhabited by several thousand residents, while other smaller centres such as Ḳurta, Kalābsha, Sabagura, Ikhmindī or Shaykh Dāwūd had usually been fortified in the previous period and

27. L. Török, 1978, pp. 298–9, 303–4. For the eparch's duties see especially, W. Y. Adams, 1977, pp. 464–7; J. M. Plumley and W. Y. Adams, 1974, p. 238.

28. U. Monneret de Villard, 1938, pp. 189–92; L. Török, 1978, pp. 305–7.

29. J. M. Plumley 1978, p. 233; A. Osman, 1982b, pp. 191–7.

30. Cf. J. M. Plumley, 1975a, p. 106; another opinion is expressed by W. Y. Adams, 1982, p. 29. There is no doubt, however, that Ḳasr Ibrīm was the eparch's residence in the Late Christian period.

31. Excavators' reports have been appearing regularly in the *Journal of Egyptian Archaeology* beginning with vol. 50 (1964); cf. also: J. M. Plumley, 1970, 1971a, 1975a, 1975b, 1978, 1982b, 1982c, 1983; W. Y. Adams, 1982; R. Anderson, 1981; P. M. Gartkiewicz, 1982b.

32. N. B. Millet, 1964, 1967; W. Y. Adams, 1977, pp. 494, 511, 535–6.

PLATE 8.2 *Portrait of Kyros, the Bishop of Faras (866–902): a mural from Faras Cathedral*

contained several hundred people each.[33] Still smaller centres – better known from excavations – such as Tamit, Arminna (Ermenne), Meynartī, Debeyra West (Fig. 8.3), or ʿAbdallāh Nirkī[34] have provided important information about daily life in Nubia in the Classic Christian Period. There are also typical monastic centres here like Ḳasr al-Wizz (Fig. 8.4), ar-Ramal in northern Nubia or al-Ghazālī in Makuria, in the desert not far from today's Merāwe.[35]

Economic and social conditions

Despite the wealth of archaeological remains, we know very little about the features of the Nubian civilization of the period under discussion that were most vital for the population. Settlements investigated, such as Debeyra West or Arminna, present a picture of a prosperous and at the same time surprisingly free and egalitarian society, where differences in social status were not necessarily reflected in material culture.[36] Small-scale farming continued to provide the basis of subsistence. Unlike in Egypt, farmers produced several crops a year. The chief crops cultivated were barley and millet. Dates were probably also of considerable economic importance. The area of land under cultivation was now clearly expanded, especially on the islands of the Second Cataract and in Baṭn al-Ḥadjar.[37] The farmers had been keeping cattle, sheep, donkeys and chickens while now their livestock also included pigs.

Most of the land was in small holdings, but in practice Nubians were tenant farmers, since according to law all land was owned by the king.[38] Taxation in Nubia was based on land tax (and possibly other taxes) and the clergy most probably served as tax-collectors.[39] Presumably Nubian monasteries were also endowed with landed estates for their support.

The villages and small towns were largely self-sufficient and Nubian craftsmen perhaps supplied most of the articles in daily use. Among the articles produced in great quantities during this period, the most remarkable were finely decorated pottery, superior to and not copies of contem-

33. W. Y. Adams, 1977, pp. 488, 494–5; P. M. Gartkiewicz, 1982a, p. 59; for a bibliography of the individual sites see L.-A. Christophe, 1977.

34. S. Donadoni (ed.), 1967; B. G. Trigger, 1967; K. R. Weeks, 1967; W. Y. Adams, 1964, 1965a; P. L. Shinnie, 1975; P. L. Shinnie and M. Shinnie, 1978; P. van Moorsel, 1970a; P. van Moorsel, J. Jaquet and H. D. Schneider, 1975; L. Castiglione, G. Hajnóczi, L. Kákosy and L. Török, 1974–5.

35. G. Scanlon, 1970, 1972; U. Monneret de Villard, 1935–57, Vol. I, pp. 132–42; P. L. Shinnie and H. N. Chittick, 1961; cf. also W. Y. Adams, 1977, pp. 478–9; S. Jakobielski, 1981, pp. 42–3.

36. W. Y. Adams, 1977, p. 501.

37. B. G. Trigger, 1970, p. 355.

38. L. Török, 1978, pp. 296–9.

39. W. Y. Adams, 1977, p. 503.

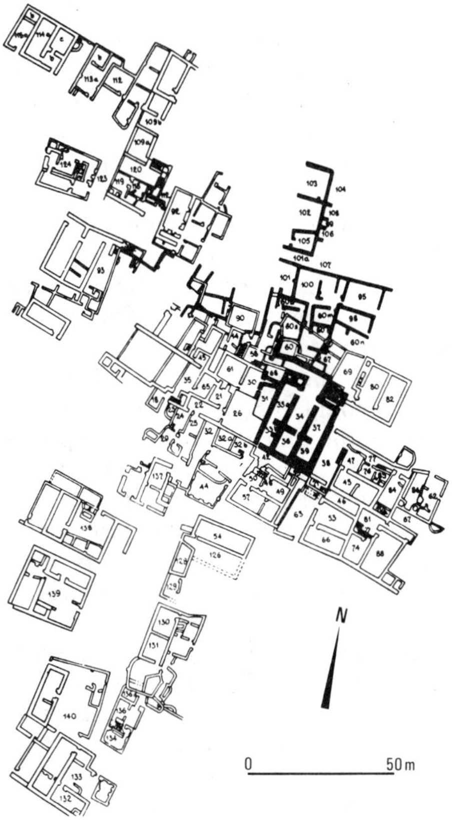

FIG. 8.3 *Plan of the Christian site of Debeyra West (24-R-8). Black areas indicate early buildings (after P. Shinnie, 1975)*

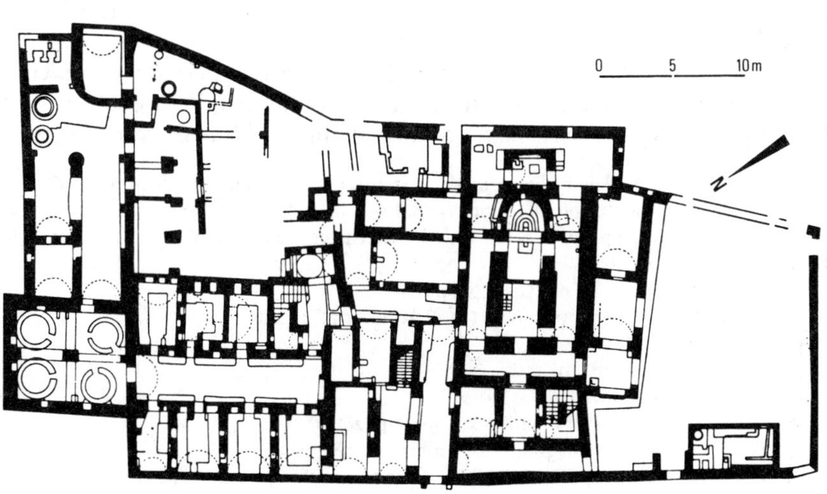

FIG. 8.4 *Plan of Ḳasr al-Wizz, a Nubian monastic complex (after P. M. Gartkiewicz, 1982a)*

porary Egyptian wares. The end of the eighth century saw the development of a new style in ceramics, known as Classic Christian.[40] This introduced a wealth of new forms (all kinds of vases, bowls and jars), decorated with bright colours and elaborate floral patterns and zoomorphic motifs. Here one may perceive Byzantine or even Persian influence.[41] Others consider that some of the wreaths and interlocking geometric figures in their decoration were copied from motifs used in contemporary Coptic manuscript decoration.[42] The Classic Christian artistic canon shows much more resemblance to that of Meroitic times than it does to anything in the intervening five centuries.[43] The sublime development of local production may have resulted from external causes. At some time during the second/eighth and early third/ninth centuries there was a marked decrease in the amount of Egyptian pottery imported to Nubia, especially of amphorae (and the wine they contained) produced in the Coptic monasteries of Upper Egypt. The accession to the throne of the Abbasid dynasty in Baghdad resulted in an increase in the persecution of the Copts and in restrictions which were placed on Egyptian monasteries.[44]

One of the greatest known Nubian potteries was the factory at Faras.[45] There must have been in Old Dongola itself or its vicinity some major production centre, which somewhat modified the style of decoration. Examples of similar pottery have also been encountered in the monastery at al-Ghazālī,[46] to the south of the Fourth Cataract.

Many of the local centres were producing crockery such as storage jars and cooking-pots or *ḳadūs*, a special vessel used on the *sāḳiya* (or water-wheel). The Classic Christian pottery produced during the third/ninth and fourth/tenth centuries was sufficient to satisfy completely the domestic needs of the country. It was only in the eleventh century that imported ceramics from Egypt (the so-called Aswān ware) began to appear alongside local products, as did glazed Arabic pottery which had never been copied in Nubia.[47]

Another important industry of the Classic Christian period was weaving. The main products were made from wool or camel-hair[48] by contrast with weaving in Egypt, where flax was predominant. Nubian woollen robes

40. Professor W. Y. Adams has provided extensive elaboration of Nubian pottery types. See W. Y. Adams, 1962b, 1967–8, 1970, 1978. For Classic Christian wares (a summary) see W. Y. Adams, 1977, pp. 495–9; Cf. also F. C. Lister, 1967; M. Rodziewicz, 1972; K. Kołodziejczyk, 1982.

41. P. L. Shinnie, 1978a, p. 570; 1965, p. 268.

42. K. Weitzmann, 1970, p. 338; W. Y. Adams, 1977, p. 496.

43. W. Y. Adams, 1977, p. 496.

44. P. L. Shinnie, 1978a, p. 570.

45. W. Y. Adams, 1962a.

46. P. L. Shinnie and H. N. Chittick, 1961, pp. 28–69.

47. W. Y. Adams, 1977, p. 499; P. L. Shinnie, 1978a, p. 570.

48. I. Bergman, 1975, pp. 10–12; P. L. Shinnie, 1978b, p. 259; J. M. Plumley, W. Y. Adams and E. Crowfoot, 1977, p. 46–7.

were mostly decorated with alternating stripes in bright colours or occasionally in a chequered design. Such robes have many analogies among those depicted in Nubian mural painting, such as at Faras and other sites. Judging from the finds, one of the greatest weaving centres was undoubtedly Ḳasr Ibrīm.

Nubian craftsmen also manufactured iron implements (hoes, knives, etc.) as well as leather products and all kinds of matting, basketry and artistic plaited goods made from palm-fibre (sandals, mats and *ṭabaḳ* plates), the tradition for producing which has been maintained until the present date.

Apart from these local products the material culture of the period discussed indicates the use of many articles of foreign origin. In addition to items mentioned in the *baḳt* treaty (wheat, barley, wine, but also linen, cloth and ready-made garments), the archaeological evidence demonstrates that Nubia imported from Egypt all sorts of glass vessels. However, the great diversity of forms and decorative technique – marvering, cut decoration, appliqués, painting – found on the vessels discovered, indicates that these were not of one origin. Among the liturgical vessels found in the cathedral of Faras was a beautiful chalice of dark-purple glass (Plate 8.3).[49]

Trade in Nubia was largely carried out through the system of barter. There was no monetary system, with the exception of the northern parts of Nubia where Egyptian coins were used in trading with the Arabs. Thus in foreign trade Nubia was compelled to pay with money but internal financial dealings were forbidden as is shown by the strict border (in reality a customs frontier) established in Upper Maḳs (ʿAkāsha) in the Baṭn al-Ḥadjar area, which separated the foreign trade zone from the heart of the country,[50] where foreign trade was under the strict control of the king. Nubia's exports consisted mainly of slaves but the traditional products, such as gold, ivory and skins must have played no mean role in foreign trade. The Dongola region must have also been in contact through Kordofān and Dārfūr with merchants operating trade routes in the countries of the Central and Western Sudan of West Africa.

Political history from the third/ninth century on

The best sources of information on the political events of this period are the writings of Arab authors: al-Yaʿḳūbī, al-Ṭabarī, ibn Ḥawḳal and Ibn Sālim al-Aswānī (the last two travelled in Nubia in person). There are also Christian sources: the writings of Severus, the Bishop of Ashmuneyn and those of Abū Ṣāliḥ the Armenian (both drew from Coptic documents) and

49. Now in the Sudan National Museum. Cf. K. Michałowski, 1964a, p. 196. On glass in Christian Nubia, see W. Y. Adams, 1977, pp. 499–500.

50. L. Török, 1978, p. 296; P. L. Shinnie, 1978b, pp. 260–2; on the trade see also R. Mauny, 1978, p. 335.

PLATE 8.3 *Glass chalice found in Faras Cathedral*

Michael the Syrian, who utilized the Chronicle of Dionisius, the Patriarch of Antioch.[51]

In the third decade of the third/ninth century Nubia took advantage of the unstable situation in Egypt caused by warfare over the succession to

51. All these sources are quoted in translation in G. Vantini, 1975. On the events in this period cf. U. Monneret de Villard, 1938, pp. 103–15.

Caliph Hārūn al-Rashīd and stopped paying the *baḳt*. As soon as Ibrāhīm (al-Muʿtaṣim) took over the Caliphate in 833, his actions to restore order included a letter sent to Zacharia, the King of Dongola requesting not only a resumption of annual tribute but also the repayment of all arrears. The Nubian king, who was unable to meet the demand, decided that his son Georgios, the one who subsequently – perhaps in 856[52] – became king of Nubia, should go to Baghdad to negotiate with the Caliph and at the same time to get an opinion of the military strength of the Abbasids.[53] Georgios was crowned as successor to the Nubian throne before he left for Baghdad in the summer of 835, accompanied by bishops and members of his court. His journey to meet the Caliph was an unprecedented event and a great political success for the Christian Nubian kingdom and was to make it widely known in the Near East. The embassy concluded a bilateral treaty revising the terms of the *baḳt* which was now declared payable once every three years. The arrears were cancelled. Georgios received abundant gifts from al-Muʿtaṣim and returned to Dongola sometime in 837, accompanied this time by the Alexandrian Patriarch Joseph for part of the journey home.

The story is known from many sources and there are also many confusions in the versions. Some sources say that the treaty was signed in Cairo sometime before 833, and it is not impossible that Georgios travelled to Baghdad twice, the other time under less happy circumstances – as a prisoner – together with the Bēdja king, ʿAlī Bābā in 852, but the source of this information is ambiguous.[54]

From the time of the long reign of Georgios I we have a detailed description of events that occurred in the seventh decade of the ninth century. This concerns the expedition into the heart of Nubia of the Arab gold prospector and theologian Abū ʿAbd al-Raḥmān al-ʿUmarī who, with his private army, succeeded in taking over for a time some of the gold mines near Abū Ḥāmād. King Georgios sent his troops under the command of his nephew Niuty to fight the invader. After several armed encounters with the forces of al-ʿUmarī, Niuty concluded an agreement with him. Then Georgios, treating Niuty as a traitor, sent first his eldest son and, later, Zacharia, the younger one, against Niuty. Zacharia made an alliance with al-ʿUmarī and then used some men of his to kill Niuty by a trick. Then Zacharia turned against al-ʿUmarī and forced him to withdraw northwards. There, in the Bēdja country al-ʿUmarī again got involved in fighting and local conflicts and was eventually treacherously killed by agents of Ibn Ṭūlūn.

The expedition of al-ʿUmarī was not an expression of official Egyptian policy towards Nubia, but it does clearly substantiate the fact that the Arabs were endeavouring to penetrate far into Nubia with the purpose no

52. S. Jakobielski, 1972, pp. 92–6. The date has been questioned by G. Vantini, 1981a, p. 112 where the year 839 is suggested.

53. Cf. G. Vantini, 1975, p. 317.

54. G. Vantini, 1970b; W. Y. Adams, 1977, p. 455; P. L. Shinnie, 1978a, pp. 578–9.

doubt – as in the conflict with the Bēdja – of ensuring the flow of gold from the south into Egypt. Al-Maḳrīzī gave a detailed account of al-ʿUmarī's adventure, probably culled from earlier writings, and informs us about the Nubian kings and their dynastic customs.

Georgios I, whose longevity is attested by several sources, reigned in Nubia until 915. The date of his death can be deduced from an inscribed lintel bearing a Coptic dedication of the Church on the South Slope of the Kom in Faras, erected in 930 by Iesou, the Eparch in the fifteenth[55] year of the reign of King Zacharia (III), Georgios's successor. As a matter of fact, Zacharia's claim to the Nubian throne did not arise from the fact that he was the son of Georgios but because he was at the same time the son of the king's sister's daughter, i.e. the sister of Niuty, who was the lawfully first in line to the throne. After the death of Niuty, Zacharia became the sole heir. Dynastic succession in Nubia depended exclusively on the endogamous principles of the matrilateral line, but because parallel-cousin marriage was commonly practised,[56] it often happened that a son succeeded his father on the Nubian throne.

The above-mentioned Coptic inscription also refers to Mariam, the mother of the king, attesting also to one of the significant court titles 'Queen Mother', otherwise known later as *nonnen* in Old Nubian texts.[57] Another Queen Mother, Martha, is represented under the protection of the Virgin Mary on one of the Faras murals[58] dated to the beginning of the fifth/eleventh century. This designation not only shows the importance of the maternal line in the system of succession to the throne but it equally reflects, perhaps, an ancient tradition in Meroitic Nubia which accords a considerable role to the king's mother.[59]

The fourth/tenth century in Nubia seems to have been a period of prosperity in the country, as was the second half of the previous century. This prosperity was apparently only disturbed by the great flood of the Nile, which led in some regions of Nobadia to the resettlement of the population. However, the Nubian state with its firm economic foundations succeeded in overcoming the difficulties. Historical events appear to indicate that the kingdom was a powerful one, and not only in the military sense.

In 956 Nubia was again at daggers drawn with Egypt. This time how-

55. In the publications of this text (S. Jakobielski, 1966b, pp. 107–9; 1972, pp. 110–13) an error was made in reading 'tenth' year instead of the correct 'fifteenth'. This led to establishing erroneously the date of death of Georgios I as 920 (the one commonly quoted) in place of the correct one: 915. Cf. S. Jakobielski, 1982b, p. 132, note 27.

56. A. Kronenberg and W. Kronenberg, 1965, pp. 256–60; cf. also S. Jakobielski, 1972, p. 113.

57. A. Osman, 1982b, p. 193.

58. The mural is now in the Sudan National Museum, Khartoum. Cf. K. Michałowski, 1964a, p. 203, Pl. XLIIb; 1967, pp. 154–7; Pl. 77–9; 1974, p. 48; J. Leclant and J. Leroy, 1968, Pl. LI; M. Martens, 1972, *passim*; B. Rostkowska, 1972, pp. 198–200.

59. S. Donadoni, 1969; B. Rostkowska, 1982b.

ever, it was not the Arabs who were the aggressors, but the Nubians, who raided and plundered Aswān. An Egyptian punitive expedition very soon after got as far as Ḳasr Ibrīm, but this was a short-lived success.[60] In 962 the Nubians occupied a large part of Upper Egypt as far as Akhmim. This incursion no doubt resulted from the prevailing situation in Egypt during the time of the last Sultans of Fusṭāṭ, the Ikhshidids (936–68) and could have been intended to bring about the victory of the Fāṭimids in this country, with whom Nubia later retained good relations.

The Nubian occupation of Egypt did not cease with the coming into power of the Fāṭimid Caliphate in 969. Perhaps the frontiers of the occupied area were only redefined so that Edfu still remained within the frontiers of Nubia. This city was an important centre of Nubian culture until the middle of the fifth/eleventh century.[61] This was also the time when the famous monastery of St Simeon near Aswān was rebuilt by the Nubians.[62]

Most of our information for this period is based on the writings of Ibn Sālim al-Aswānī, who *c.* 969 was entrusted with a mission to the Nubian ruler Georgios II. The king accorded the Arab embassy a warm reception. However, as Nubia was then a powerful state, the king was in a position to refuse payment of tribute as stipulated by the *baḳt* and conversion to Islam.[63]

Religious developments

Intensive persecutions of the Copts again occurred in Egypt at the end of the tenth century, during the Caliphate of al-Ḥāḳim (996–1021). At first, Nubia did not intervene on behalf of the Egyptian Coptic Church, perhaps because of its political friendship with the Fāṭimids, or for some other reasons, but the Nubians did eventually open their frontiers to refugees from Egypt and a vast number immigrated into Nubia.

In the fourth/tenth century, the Church in Nubia played a significant role in the affairs of the country; this is confirmed by the fact that when the Arab embassy came to Dongola in the time of Georgios II, the ruler called a council composed of bishops[64] to decide on the reply to be given to the Arabs. The king was later to act as an intermediary in purely ecclesiastical affairs as when he interceded on the request of the Ethiopian authorities

60. For a detailed consideration of these events see J. M. Plumley, 1983, p. 161; G. Vantini, 1981a, p. 116.

61. U. Monneret de Villard, 1938, pp. 124–5.

62. U. Monneret de Villard, 1927, pp. 24–36.

63. These are preserved only in quotations in the writings of al-Maḳrīzī and Ibn al-Salām al-Manūfī. Other sources are the writings of al-Mas'ūdī, Ibn al-Faḳīh and al-Ya'ḳūbī, cf. G. Vantini, 1975.

64. O. Meinardus, 1967, p. 150.

with the Patriarch Philotheos (979–1003) concerning the nomination of an appropriate metropolitan for Ethiopia.[65] This fact gives us proof of the concurrence between the interests of Church and State at that time. It also indicates the Church's affinities with Monophysitism and the cordial relationship existing between Nubia and Ethiopia.

From among seven of the Nubian bishoprics known from Arab sources, five of them – Ḳurta, Ḳasr Ibrīm, Faras, Sai and Dongola – have been confirmed by archaeological discoveries. The most complete data concerning the history of a bishopric has been established in the case of Faras where, thanks to the List of Bishops inscribed on one of the cathedral walls, tombstones and graffiti, it has been possible to establish[66] an unbroken chronological sequence of the dignitaries of the Church in this diocese from the time of its founding in the first/seventh century up to 1175. As was already mentioned, five of the bishops of the third/ninth and fourth/tenth centuries bore the title of Metropolitan of Pachoras (i.e. Faras). Thanks to portraits of bishops[67] preserved there in seventeen paintings, we know exactly what the Nubian bishops' vestments looked like over the different historical periods. Graffiti in Faras, Sonḳi Tino and Tamit may constitute a source of information about the ranks in the Church hierarchy.

The Monophysite character of the Nubian Church is attested by the numerous data concerning Faras and the other dioceses as regards the fourth/tenth century. However, the evidence from Faras suggests on the other hand that there was some variation in allegiance at the close of the fourth/tenth and the beginning of the fifth/eleventh century. In the years 997–9 we find two bishops simultaneously on the episcopal throne of Pachoras: Petros I (974–99) and Ioannes III (997–1005). A reasonable explanation could be that Ioannes represents a confession different to that of the Monophysite Petros, the Metropolitan of Faras, that is the Greek (or Melkite) faith. The situation is far from clear and the hypothesis put forward on the basis of the Faras evidence[68] has caused vivid discussion among scholars and some doubts.[69] Some historical facts are, however, worth mentioning here in support of the opinion that there was a Melkite take-over in the diocese. The episcopate of Ioannes comes just after the death of al-ʿAzīz who openly favoured the Melkites in Egypt, his wife (or concubine) being of that confession. One of her brothers, Jeremias, was appointed by al-ʿAzīz as the Patriarch of Jerusalem, the other, Arsenius,

65. U. Monneret de Villard, 1938, p. 125; A. J. Arkell, 1961, p. 190; G. Vantini, 1981a, pp. 123–4.

66. S. Jakobielski, 1966a; 1972, pp. 190–5; G. Vantini, 1981b.

67. K. Michałowski, 1974, p. 46; M. Martens-Czarnecka, 1982a, *passim*; S. Jakobielski, 1982b.

68. K. Michałowski, 1967, pp. 91–3; 1970, p. 14; S. Jakobielski, 1972, pp. 140–7; J. Kubińska, 1974, pp. 69–86.

69. P. van Moorsel, 1970b, pp. 281–90; T. Säve-Söderbergh, 1970, pp. 238–9; M. Krause, 1970, pp. 71–86; 1978; K. Michałowski, 1979, pp. 34–5.

became Melkite Patriarch of Egypt.[70] It seems likely that the Melkites profited considerably from the leniency of the Caliph, and their efforts to reclaim some of the episcopal sees could have been at times successful. Two successors of Ioannes on the episcopal throne in Faras – Marianos (1005–36) and Merkurios (1037–56) – were called in inscriptions 'his sons'. This expression can be understood to mean that they shared the same confession. Marianos, known from his magnificent portrait in Faras Cathedral (now in the National Museum in Warsaw) (Plate 8.4), died in Ḳasr Ibrīm, where his tombstone was found. From the text of this stele[71] one can deduce that he came to Faras having already been for two years bishop in another diocese. The text also says that he was 'envoy of Babylon' (i.e. Old Cairo), which is in perfect accord with his light complexion as represented on the Faras mural.

Not much is known about the nature of the liturgy in Nubia. Greek remained probably the most important language in the Church, being at the same time a sort of lingua franca in the whole Christian world of those times.[72] Alongside Greek, the Coptic language was also extensively used in Church writings, for official inscriptions and on tombstones. It was, however, perhaps mostly used by numerous Coptic communities inside Nubia. From the mid-tenth century on Nubia showed a considerable increase of texts written in the indigenous language known as Old Nubian (called otherwise Medieval Nubian), a language that is ancestral to the modern Mahas dialect of riverain Nubian and belongs to the Eastern Sudanic language group. Old Nubian is written in the Coptic alphabet (itself an adaptation of the Greek one) with the addition of four signs for specific Nubian sounds.

The earliest dated text attested in Old Nubian is a graffito left in 795 in the church of al-Sebūʿa by one Petro, a priest from Faras.[73] The textual material in Old Nubian is largely religious in character and the corpus of Old Nubian writings comprises canonical texts (Gospel fragments), codexes containing lives and sayings of the saints (among them the Miracle of St Menas)[74] and the Homily of Pseudo-Chrisostom,[75] prayer books, a litany to the Cross, and the extraordinarily rich collection of legal documents and letters found recently in Ḳasr Ibrīm[76] as well as quite a lot of Nubian or mixed Greco-Nubian graffiti. All this material is of the greatest

70. G. Vantini, 1970a, pp. 83, 98, 223; 1981a, pp. 145–7; W. H. C. Frend, 1972b, pp. 297–308; P. L. Shinnie, 1978a, p. 571.

71. J. M. Plumley, 1971b.

72. On languages in Christian Nubia in general see P. L. Shinnie, 1974; S. Jakobielski, 1972, pp. 12–16; W. H. C. Frend, 1972a; W. Y. Adams, 1977, pp. 484–6; T. Hägg, 1982.

73. F. L. Griffith, 1913, p. 61; E. Zyhlarz, 1928a, pp. 163–70.

74. E. A. W. Budge, 1909; F. L. Griffith, 1913, pp. 6–24. On Old Nubian literature in general see C. D. G. Müller, 1975, 1978. For main publications of other texts see F. L. Griffith, 1928; B. M. Metzger, 1968; J. Barns, 1974; G. M. Browne, 1982b.

75. G. M. Browne, 1983.

76. Cf. J. M. Plumley, 1975a, 1978; R. Anderson, 1981.

PLATE 8.4 *Portrait of Marianos, the Bishop of Faras (1005–36): a mural from Faras Cathedral*

importance not only from historical and religious points of view but also for linguistics, because both lexicography and Old Nubian grammar are far from being sufficiently elaborated[77] and the newly found texts remain largely unpublished.

For the greater part of the fifth/eleventh century not much historical information is available. The history records King Raphael reigning around 1002. Arab chronicles mention the revolt of Abū Raḳwa against the Fāṭimids in about 1006, when having met with defeat in his own country he fled to Nubia. Because of this, Nubia was again involved in the affairs of her northern neighbour. In general, however, during the 200-year long period of Fāṭimid rule in Egypt (969–1169) the two countries were at peace and Nubia maintained the best of relations during the reign of Caliph al-Mustanṣir (1036–94). The Nubians were now even being recruited to the Fāṭimid army and in the period of his rule, their number increased to 50 000. This information comes from the writings of Nāṣir-i Khusraw, who visited Egypt and Nubia in 1050.[78]

The information about the Nubian Church derived from the History of the Monophysite Patriarchs[79] mainly concerns the period of activities of the sixty-sixth Patriarch, Christodulos (1047–71). The first ten years of his patriarchate in Alexandria is the time which brought a renewal of the persecution against the Copts, which this time entailed the closing of their churches by the decree of Vizier al-Yazūrī, 1051–9. Christodulos, who was imprisoned for a time, sent two Egyptian bishops as envoys to the king of Nubia, requesting assistance and intervention. Through them the king sent funds to pay a ransom in order to free the Patriarch. A dozen or so years later he nominated a new metropolitan for Nubia (Dongola) – Victor. Christodulos's contacts with Nubian kings could have brought about the reinforcement of the Monophysite Church which, as the example of Faras has illustrated, was for some time in danger. The Patriarch was by this time on better terms with the vizier of Egypt, Badr al-Djamālī, who during the next mission from the patriarchate to the Nubian king, with Merkurios bishop of Wāsim as envoy, sent with him his own envoy Sayf al-Dawla to obtain the extradition from Nubia of the traitor Kanz al-Dawla, and was successful in doing so. Badr al-Djamālī shortly afterwards (1080) received the former Nubian ruler Salomon in Cairo. This king had abdicated in favour of his sister's son Georgios (III) so that he could devote his life to monasticism. We hear also about Nubian King Basilios reigning in 1089.

With the fall from power of the Fāṭimids (1170) the relations between Nubia and Egypt rapidly deteriorated. At about the same time, Nubia's Golden Age came to an end. Armed encounters with the troops of Ayyubid

77. F. L. Griffith, 1913; E. Zyhlarz, 1928a, 1932; B. H. Stricker, 1940; F. Hintze, 1971–7; G. M. Browne, 1979–81, 1982a.

78. Y. F. Hasan, 1973, p. 46; G. Vantini, 1981a, p. 129.

79. The source is Severus (Sawirus Abu' l-Bashar ibn al Mukaffa'), see G. Vantini, 1975, pp. 189, 209–18.

Sultan Ṣalāḥ al-Din (Saladin) opened the next period (called Late Christian) in Nubian history.

Arts and architecture

Architecture

The tenth and eleventh centuries in Nubia were an extremely favourable period for the development of arts and architecture. Research into sacral architecture is undoubtedly the key problem for the understanding of Nubian architecture in general.[80] Church-building was the most important aspect of architecture for the whole Christian world at this period and in it the art of building and architectural conceptions are most fully reflected. The material which we possess is apparently very rich. There are over 120 churches known in Nobadia and about 40 in Makuria.[81] Such an unequal distribution of the known churches in Nubia (and nearly all the northern ones have been excavated) has led to an acceptance of the opinion[82] that Nubian sacral architecture is derived only from the 'basilican' type of church, a type which in fact prevailed in the north. It was only when the Polish Expedition discovered the Old Church in Dongola and superimposed on its plan that of the Church of Granite Columns and also the Cruciform Church[83] that it became apparent that we have to deal here with two equally important tendencies in sacral architecture – the central design and the elongated basilican pattern – both exerting an influence on individual church edifices. The main trends in architecture are manifested, first of all, in the great structures created in cultural and administrative centres in which bishoprics were also located, like Old Dongola, Faras or Ḳasr Ibrīm. Parallel to this creativity there runs the development of provincial architecture that is modelled to a certain extent on the latter but has at its disposal limited possibilities as to the execution and material. This last line of development is responsible for the creating of the so-called 'typical Nubian plan' of church encountered mainly in northern Nubia in the Classic Christian and Late Periods. In this type most of the local, internal features are manifested. Such a church is normally a rectangular building, oriented east–west, divided by piers or columns into a nave and two aisles. A considerable part of the nave, in the east closed by an apse with semi-circular tribune, contains the presbytery (called the *haykal*) with

80. G. S. Mileham, 1910; S. Clarke, 1912; U. Monneret de Villard, 1935–57, Vol. 3; W. Y. Adams, 1965b; P. M. Gartkiewicz, 1975, 1980, 1982a, 1983; S. Jakobielski, 1981.

81. The 'inventory' of all known churches in Nubia was published by W. Y. Adams, 1965b; general conclusions are also found in W. Y. Adams, 1977, pp. 473–8.

82. W. Y. Adams, 1965b.

83. P. M. Gartkiewicz, 1975. An architectural monograph on those churches by P. M. Gartkiewicz (Dongola II) will appear in *CAMAP*, vol. 27 in 1984. Cf. also S. Jakobielski, 1982c and note 22 above.

an altar in the centre. On either side of the apse there are two rooms, the northern one served as a vestry and the southern as a baptistry.[84] They are connected by a narrow passage behind the apse. In the western part of the church two rooms are built at the corners. The southern one, as a rule, contains a staircase, the purpose of the northern one remains obscure. The entrances to the church lead from the south and from the north straight to the aisles. In the central part of the nave an ambo is placed at the north side.

In the entire sacral architecture certain periods and lines of development influenced also from outside Nubia, are to be identified[85] as follows:

First Period

Phase 1: the initial foreign influence on Nubia's religious architecture. Churches were based on an elongated uniaxial three-aisled plan. They were generally built of mud-brick and covered with wooden ceilings supported by mud-brick piers.

Phase 2: development of building activity. Erection of the great cathedrals of ashlar stone or burnt-brick. The plan remains the same, three- or five-aisled, roofs supported by columns. Alongside this activity, the tradition of building in mud-brick was still continued in smaller edifices. Barrel vaulting was being introduced. The most typical Nubian church building, already described, was developed during this phase.

Second Period

The evolution of types of churches combined with Armenian and Byzantine architectural influences completely transformed the conception of spatial form in buildings. During this period two tendencies were developed: whilst the traditional style maintained itself in the provinces, a new and official mode of building characterized by a central plan made its appearance in the capital. Burnt brick was widely used. In this period the Church of Granite Columns in Dongola was built, which comprised a composition of the cruciform design incorporated into a basilican interior. Nubian architecture reached the climax of its creative possibilities. One of the examples of the original conceptions of Nubian architects that profited from the architectural achievements of the wider Christian world is the Mausoleum (Cruciform Church) in Old Dongola, based on the plan of a Greek cross. Undoubtedly Dongola became in this period the main centre of architectural activities in Nubia (Fig. 8.5).

Third Period

In this period one cannot distinguish the main stream of continuation in the line of development. The building activities were dispersed into several

84. The problem of Nubian baptistries is discussed at length in W. Godlewski, 1978, 1979.

85. According to P. M. Gartkiewicz, 1980; 1982a, pp. 73–105.

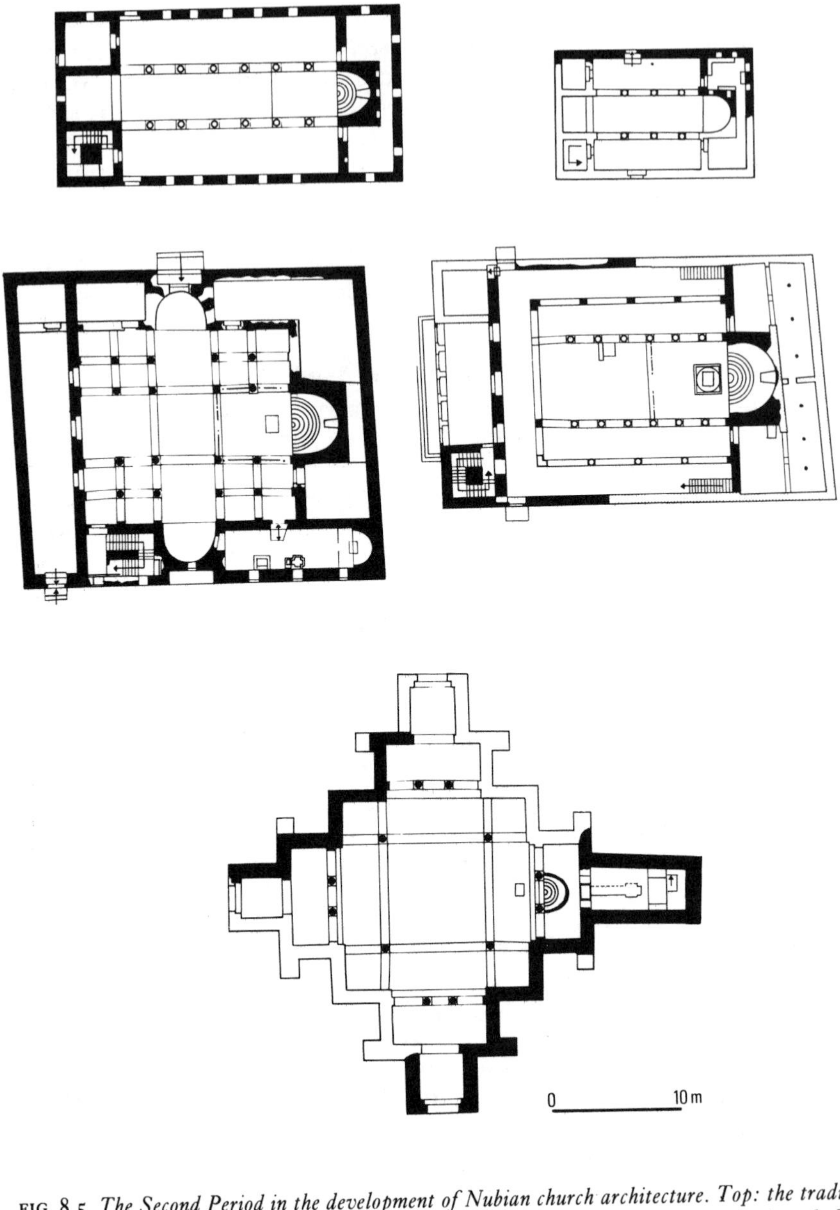

FIG. 8.5 *The Second Period in the development of Nubian church architecture. Top: the traditional (conservative) provincial building activity (B2); monastery church in Ghazāli and the church on the south slope of the Kom in Faras. Middle: the progressive line, main trend, first phase (A3); example of the spatial arrangement and central (Church of the Granite Columns in Old Dongola) or longitudinal plan (the Great Cathedral, Ḳasr Ibrīm). Bottom: Example of the main trend, second phase (A4), the Mausoleum in Old Dongola, a cruciform church (after P. M. Gartkiewicz, 1982a)*

centres absorbing diversified influences mainly of Byzantine origin. The common general feature was at that time the introduction of the domed covering towards the end of the tenth century. This conception was connected with the new approach to the form of a church in which the vertical axis was to play the most important role. Both the elongated (basilican) and the central-plan churches were now being transformed by the addition of domes in the central part and the replacement of columns with brick piers. Mud-brick is now commonly used again. Beside the rebuilding of the older churches, new ones were now being erected, the form of which resulted from various simplifications and local mutations of Nubian solutions (Fig. 8.6).

Church art

At the end of the eighth century, the standard decoration of the interior of sacral buildings became figurative mural painting, replacing the earlier architectural decoration (lintels, door-jambs and capitals decorated in relief). Examination of the set of paintings from Faras,[86] depicting – apart from the many representations of Christ and the Virgin Mary – saints and archangels, scenes from the Old and New Testaments and also portraits of local dignitaries presented under the protection of holy figures, have made it possible to get a coherent picture of the development of mural painting in Nubia which was different in its means of expression from this branch of art in the neighbouring countries.

Material from Faras has made it possible to distinguish and place in chronological order the various stylistic groups of painting some of which are mentioned in Volume II of the *General History of Africa*. Of these the violet style was predominant at the end of the second/eighth century, followed by the late violet and intermediate styles of the early third/ninth century and the white style of the second half of the third/ninth century, an example of which is the portrait of the first Metropolitan, Bishop Kyros (Plate 8.2). Murals of this early period inspired a new generation of local Nubian artists who in the fourth/tenth century created their own school of painting, the most characteristic features of which were the decorative forms where the foreign elements, transformed in a peculiar way, formed a kind of ornamentation that was unique to Nubia,[87] and a selection of colours that was characteristic for each period. Thus at the beginning of the fourth/tenth century, after a re-plastering of the Faras Cathedral interior had taken place, a new style which has been called yellow-red was de-

86. Cf. Unesco, *General History of Africa*, Vol. II, ch. 12, pp. 336–7; K. Michałowski, 1964b, 1966b, 1967, 1970, 1974; K. Weitzmann, 1970; G. Vantini, 1970a; M. Martens, 1972, 1973; M. Rassart, 1972; G. Vantini, 1981b; S. Jakobielski, 1982d; N. Pomerantseva, 1982.

87. M. Martens-Czarnecka, 1982a, 1982b, 1982c.

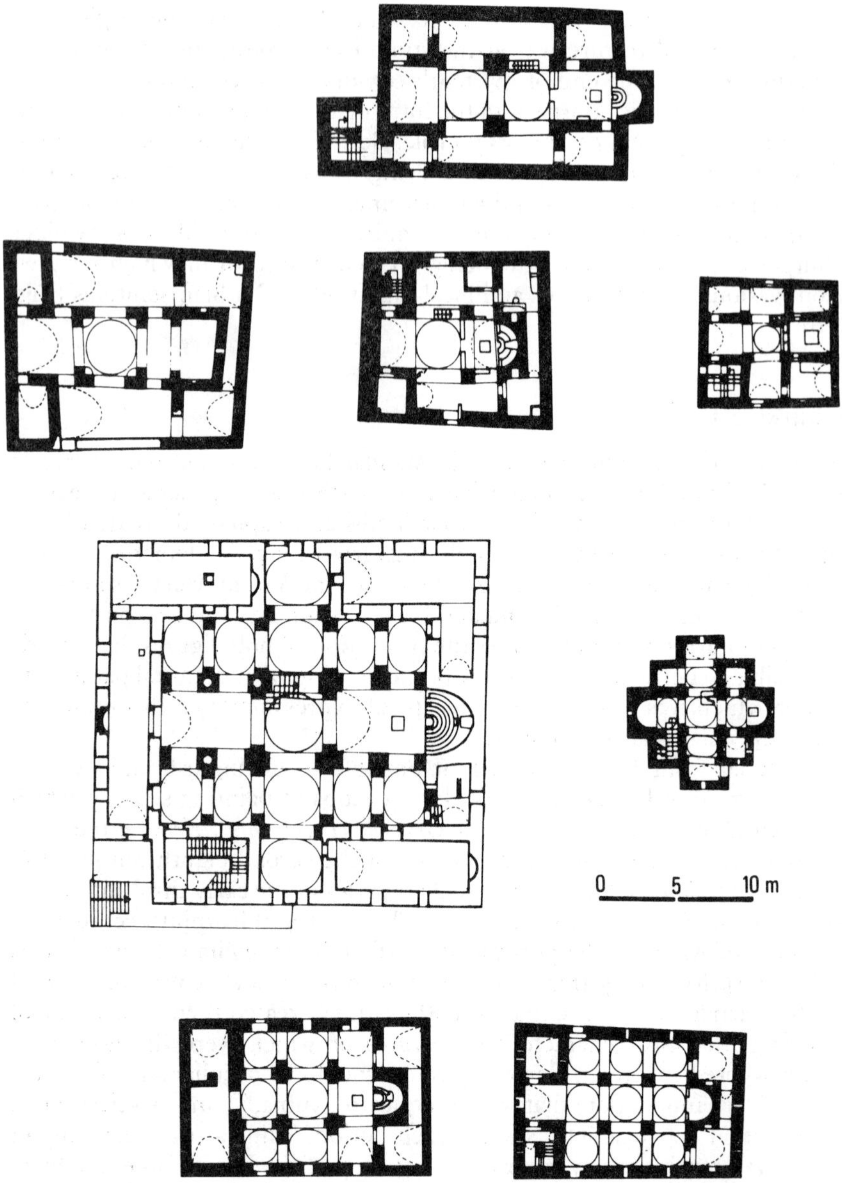

FIG. 8.6 *The Third Period in the development of Nubian church architecture. Examples of churches developed along diversified trends. Top: C1—influenced by domed basilica type (the Basilica at Tamit). Second row: C2—influenced by the double-shell composition (church at Nag' el Oḳba) or cross-in-square pattern (church at Sonḳi Tino). Third row: C3—influenced by domed-cross pattern (Faras Cathedral rebuilt by the end of the tenth century, and Church of Angels at Tamit). Bottom: C4—influenced by multi-axial hall composition (St Raphael Church at Kāw) (after P. M. Gartkiewicz, 1982a)*

veloped. It was then that the realistic trend of the white style was being abandoned in favour of far-reaching idealization and schematization of facial features. Embroidery and decoration of the robes of the figures represented now became apparent. As an example of this style, the portrait of King Georgios I may be used, added at the beginning of the fourth/tenth century to the composition of the Holy Virgin and Apostles in the apse of Faras Cathedral. After the great rebuilding of the Cathedral, which had occurred by the end of the fourth/tenth century the multicoloured I style was being created. This is one of the most widespread styles in northern Nubia, attested in several churches, for example in ʿAbdallāh Nirḳī, Sonḳi Tino and Tamit.[88] It is characterized by brilliant colours and lavishly ornate details in the treatment of robes, books, crowns and other items represented. Among forty-eight paintings of this style an outstanding example of this new art is the portrait of Bishop Marianos (Plate 8.4), painted in the opening years of the eleventh century. The great composition of the Nativity, now in the Sudan National Museum, Khartoum (Plate 8.5), comes from the same time; it is the largest mural in Nubia. We have here evidence that the Nubian artist had mastered the art of painting scenes with many figures on several planes one above the other. There is no strip composition here, which is so characteristic of the art of Egypt but a pattern of several groups (the Magi, shepherds, archangels, flying angels) closely interconnected as regards subject and form.[89]

One of the characteristically novel themes in Nubian painting is the representation of local nobles under the holy protection of Christ, the Virgin or the Archangel Michael. A stylistic canon applies here in which the authentic shade of secular personages' complexion is retained, unlike representations of Saints and Christ who were always shown as having white faces.[90]

The multicoloured style was continued until the end of the Christian Period in Nubia; its further developments are called Multicoloured II (second half of the fifth/eleventh century), Multicoloured III (sixth/twelfth century), and Late Style (seventh/thirteenth–ninth/fifteenth centuries).

The chronological order established for the Faras paintings has been confirmed by the discovery of other murals decorating Nubian buildings – to such a degree that they may serve as a basis for dating.[91] In this regard, investigations into Nubian painting have preceded work of this sort carried out on Coptic painting in Egypt, which hitherto has not been completely catalogued or classified.

88. P. van Moorsel, J. Jacquet and H. Schneider, 1975, pp. 54–131; S. Donadoni and S. Curto, 1968; S. Donadoni, 1970; S. Donadoni and G. Vantini, 1967–8; S. Donadoni (ed.), 1967, pp. 1–60.

89. K. Michałowski, 1974, p. 39. Cf. also, K. Michałowski, 1967, pp. 143–8, Pl. 63–9.

90. Cf. S. Jakobielski, 1982d, pp. 164–5; B. Rostkowska, 1982a, p. 295.

91. Cf. especially M. Martens-Czarnecka, 1982c.

PLATE 8.5 *View of the north transept of Faras Cathedral with the great mural of the Nativity in multicoloured I style, painted* c. *1000*

In general in the Nubian painting of the Classic Christian period one can see the predominant influence of Byzantine art (seen even in the profusion of ornamentation), which did not wholly replace Coptic elements prevailing in the earlier periods.[92] The main expression of this art exhibits purely local features typical only of Nubian painting.

Here one could draw attention to the iconographic value[93] of this branch of art in Nubia, which indicates a profound knowledge of the earliest traditions of Christian thought and the text of the Holy Scriptures. Nubia in its Golden Period remained, after all, an important limb in the Christian *oikoumene*,[94] and through its contacts (visible at least in local art and architecture) not only with Copts in Egypt and most probably with Ethiopia, but with the entire sphere of Byzantine culture, from Armenia to Syria and Palestine, drew inspiration from all these sources, creating in the process her own separate cultural personality.

92. On influences in Faras murals, cf. J. Leclant and J. Leroy, 1968; K. Weitzmann, 1970; P. Du Bourguet, 1970, pp. 307–8; M. Rassart, 1972, pp. 274–5; 1978; B. Rostkowska, 1981; M. Martens-Czarnecka, 1982d, pp. 111–16.

93. Among a great number of articles on this topic, cf. T. Gołgowski, 1968, 1969; P. van Moorsel, 1966, 1970b, 1972, 1975; E. Dinkler, 1975; T. Dobrzeniecki, 1973–5, 1974, 1980; L. Török, 1975; J. Kubińska, 1976; W. H. C. Frend, 1979; A. Łukaszewicz, 1978, 1982; E. Lucchesi-Palli, 1982; W. Godlewski, 1982b; cf. also note 86 above. For the state of elaboration of iconographical problems cf., especially K. Michałowski, 1974, pp. 42–63 (bibliography pp. 312–13); 1979, pp. 33–38; B. Rostkowska, 1982a, pp. 295–9.

94. *Oikoumene* (from *oikouménê* in Greek, meaning inhabited territory). Used by ancient geographers to designate that part of the Earth that was inhabited, as opposed to the Earth as a whole.

9

The conquest of North Africa and Berber resistance

H. MONÈS

In Volume II of the *General History of Africa* the reader may obtain an initial glimpse of the Berbers, their origins, their ethnic structure and some of their characteristics.[1] However, as this is the first chapter to deal with the Maghrib (Islamic North Africa exclusive of Egypt), it may be useful at this point to acquaint the reader with the Berbers as the Arabs found them at the time of the Arab conquest of the Maghrib, from 21/642 onward.

Some modern writers regard the term Maghrib as an anachronism since it now applies to only one part of the land in question. Some six hundred years ago Ibn Khaldūn (732/1332–808/1406) was of the same opinion; according to him, the term *al-Maghrib* was not so much a proper name as a geographical definition. He added, however, that by his time it has become the proper name for the particular territory concerned.[2]

E. F. Gautier began his work *Le passé de l'Afrique du Nord – les siècles obscurs* with a chapter strikingly entitled 'A country without a name'.[3] Presumably this is meant humorously, since *al-Maghrib* ('the west' of the land of Islam) was in fact, both historically and geographically, a clear and precise name for a clearly defined part of the world: that part of northern Africa (exclusive of Egypt) lying to the north of the great African desert, the Sahara.

Until recently North Africa (or the Maghrib) was considered, except for a few pockets of arable soil, to be an infertile land of rock and sand where, as in Arabia, the very poverty of the land made its inhabitants a proud, free, hardy people. In fact the Maghrib is far from poor. The coastal belt possesses ample resources of water and vegetation. The northern slopes of the Atlas Mountains afford excellent wooded pastureland and produce fine olive trees. In the north the coast and the mountain-sides enjoy all the mildness of a Mediterranean climate, referred to by Ibn Khaldūn as *mizādj al-tulūl*. The High Atlas plateau is covered with woodland and forest, and along the Atlantic coast lies a wide band of fertile soil.

1. Cf. Unesco, *General History of Africa*, Vol. II, chs 17, 18 and 19.
2. Ibn Khaldūn, 1956–9, Vol. 4, p. 193.
3. E. F. Gautier, 1937, p. 7.

The Atlas Mountains, with their abundant forests, arable lands and pastures, are both hospitable and beautiful. They were the cradle of one of the sturdiest and most enduring peoples on earth: the Berbers. Ibn Khaldūn is unstinting in his praise of the beauty and magnificence of 'the land of the Berbers' (*mawāṭin al-Barbar*), in which he includes Libya and a good part of the Sahara.

Having given this brief description of the geographical environment, we should say a word or two about the Arab and modern source texts dealing with the Arab conquest of North Africa. A number of old Arabic texts are still extant, written by such reputable historians as al-Balādhurī, Ibn 'Abd al-Ḥakam, Ibn al-Athīr, Ibn 'Idhārī, al-Mālikī, al-Dabbāgh, Ibn Khaldūn, Abū'l-'Arab Tamīm and al-Nuwayrī; these are a rich mine of largely trustworthy information.[4] Even so, they contain occasional inconsistencies, erroneous dates and contradictions, attributable to the gap of over two centuries between the conquest itself and the earliest of these historians' works. Most of the writers mentioned may be regarded simply as chroniclers and annalists without much critical sense; the sole exception is Ibn Khaldūn, a true historian who has left us not only much sound factual material but also a reasoned interpretation of the history of the Berbers. However, all these historians were Arabs, and their point of view was that of conquerors; the point of view of the Berber resistance remains unknown, even though some traces of their tradition have been preserved in the Arab chronicles.

Until very recently, North African studies were monopolized by French and Spanish scholars (and Italian scholars in the case of Libya), whose works covered the whole history of the Maghrib from antiquity to independence. While we must recognize the admirable work done by these historians in publishing, translating and interpreting the Arabic source texts, and their great contribution to the clarification of a variety of historical problems, it must nevertheless be remembered that the majority of their works date from the colonial era, and that their particular interpretations tended, to a large extent, to serve the objectives of colonial policies, as for example the integration of Algeria into metropolitan France. Today, thanks to the serious efforts of Arab scholars and others over the past twenty years, a new generation of historians has transcended the French scholars' judgements on virtually all the great historical problems of Islamic North Africa.[5]

The American researcher Edmund Burke III expresses the prevailing opinion on this development among historians in the following terms:

> The historical study of North Africa has until quite recently been an

4. See Bibliography.

5. Cf. A. M. Al-Abbādī and M. I. al-Kattānī, 1964; H. H. 'Abd al-Wahhāb, 1965–72; J. M. Abun-Nasr, 1971; H. Djait, 1973; H. al-Djanhānī, 1968; A. Laroui, 1970, 1977; H. Monès, 1947; M. Talbī, 1971; S. Zaghlūl, 1965; M. Brett, 1972; M. Churakov, 1960 and 1962; J. Wansbrough, 1968.

> almost exclusively French preserve. The few English-speaking historians who ventured to deal with the Maghreb did so at their peril, always vulnerable to criticism for not having sufficiently mastered the enormous French literature ... To a large extent this situation was an artifact of a colonial division of labour. The dictum that 'scholarship follows the flag' received empirical confirmation in the mutual myopia of national traditions of scholarship about the Islamic world.[6]

Nevertheless, the French historians' immense labours are worthy of the utmost respect and the greatest esteem, even though we may often disagree with the textual interpretations of such respected scholars as Henri Fournel, C. Diehl, E. Mercier, E. F. Gautier, H. Basset, William and George Marçais, R. Brunschwig, E. Lévi-Provençal, and C.-A. Julien, to name but a few.[7]

The Berbers on the eve of the Arab conquest

At the beginning of their conquest of North Africa, the Arabs discovered that the Berbers were organized, as they were themselves, in *ḳabīla*s. These *ḳabīla*s were divided into two categories: the Butr and the Barānis.

Oddly enough, the names of these two groups make their appearance only at the time of the Arab conquest, never before. Ibn ʿAbd al-Ḥakam, the earliest chronicler of the conquest, speaks matter-of-factly of the Barānis and Butr, but Stéphane Gsell, in his extremely detailed chronicle of the ancient history of North Africa, makes no mention of either of these names, nor indeed does Charles Diehl in his voluminous history of Byzantine Africa.[8]

The two terms Butr and Barānis sound Arabic: the Barānis are those who wear the *burnus*, a garment already known to the Arabs before their arrival in Africa, since ʿUmar ibn al-Khaṭṭāb, the second Caliph, is said to have worn one; and the Butr, according to Arab writers, were the descendants of a man named Mādghīs al-Abtar. *Abtar*, which is the singular form of Butr, means a man without offspring, or a man missing a hand or leg, or without headgear. Since the Butr can hardly have been descended from a man without offspring, we are left with only one explanation: Mādghīs, the ancestor of the Butr, was given the name of *abtar* because he wore no hood.

We cannot, in any case, accept any of these linguistic explanations. We can only recognize the fact that, on the basis of the testimony of Arab and Berber genealogists, Ibn Khaldūn, the historian of the Berbers, wrote that the Berbers had been divided into two blocs since time immemorial, and

6. E. Burke III, 1975, p. 306.

7. See Bibliography.

8. S. Gsell, 1913–28; C. Diehl, 1896. It is possible that this classification was applied to the Berber-speaking world by the Arab writers who created the vocabulary, on the basis of the familiar realities of life in the Middle East, where the Arabs were themselves divided into two great groups.

that their mutual hostility and incessant quarrelling had been the dominant factor throughout their history both before and after the advent of Islam.

According to E. F. Gautier, this classification corresponded to two different ways of life, the Barānis being sedentary mountain-dwellers and the sons of Mādghīs the Butr, being nomads of the plains. This is a hypothesis that many researchers have found attractive, but it is too speculative to be accepted without careful scientific scrutiny.[9] Even so, a classification into two great groups probably does reflect the feelings of the Berber population of the Maghrib themselves as regards their respective ancestries. It would seem that Berber and Arab genealogists constructed this division *a posteriori*, but in so doing took into account the facts of historical experience.

According to Ibn Khaldūn, at the time of the Arab conquest the main Butr confederations of *ḳabīla*s were those of the Zanāta, the Maṭghara and the Nafzāwa. The Zanāta seem to have enjoyed supremacy over the others, as they are said to have given their name to all the nomadic Butr groups. Zanāta was the grandson of a man named Māzīgh. It seems that the Barānis were also descended from Māzīgh. The word *māzīgh* means 'free man'.[10]

As regards the Barānis, and again according to Ibn Khaldūn, their most important confederations of *ḳabīla*s at the time of the conquest were the Awrāba, the Hawwāra and the Ṣanhādja.[11]

However, as soon as we move on to study the Arab conquest and the history of North Africa under Islamic domination, we find new *ḳabīla*s and tribal groupings emerging that prove to have been more important than those mentioned above. It should also be noted, however, that the genealogical tables given by Ibn Khaldūn were drawn up at a later period, certainly no earlier than the fourth/tenth or fifth/eleventh century, for political or dynastic purposes.

The tables themselves are full of contradictions, and vary according to the source consulted. The geographical distribution of the *ḳabīla*s poses another problem; one *ḳabīla* or confederation of *ḳabīla*s may, for example, have branches and offshoots in different parts of the Maghrib, especially after the invasion of the Banū Hilāl in the fifth/eleventh century.[12]

This is why, to avoid inaccuracy, we shall be well advised to restrict ourselves to a broad outline of the Berbers' tribal divisions at the time of the Arab conquest and afterwards, up to the sixth/twelfth century.

At the time of the Arab conquest, the Barānis were divided into a

9. E. F. Gautier, 1937, pp. 227–39; but cf. R. Brunschwig, 1974 and H. R. Idris, 1962, Vol. 1, pp. 4–6.

10. Some younger Maghribi scholars, fascinated by this name and its meaning, would like to replace the name 'Berber' by 'Imāzīghen' (plural of Amāzīgh). They consider 'Berber' a perjorative term, which in fact it is not; Berber is a proper noun which has lost all connotations of the term 'Barbaroi'.

11. Ibn Khaldūn, 1956–9, Vol. 4, pp. 282–96.

12. Cf. Chapter 12 below.

number of large groups such as the Ṣanhādja, Kutāma, Talkāta, Awrāba and Maṣmūda or Masāmida. The Zanāta (or Zanatians) inhabited Cyrenaica and Tripolitania, extending southward as far as the Djabal Nafūsa and the oases of Fezzān, the predominant confederations of *ḳabīla*s being those of the Hawwāra, Luwāta, Nafūsa and Zaghāwa.

These groups also ruled the eastern part of what is now Algeria, an area known during the Arab period as the al-Mzāb region. They occupied the pasturelands on the northern slopes of the Central Atlas Mountains as far as the Mulūya River. This was the homeland of that great group of *ḳabīla*s known as the Miknāsa, who extended southward as far as the fertile region of the Tafilālet oases.

The Kutāma and the Ṣanhādja inhabited the central Maghrib, including the Awrās massif and the Ḳabā'il country (Grande Kabylie), living in the regions around Tāhert and Tlemcen. This was the common homeland of a number of great groups: the Kutāma, who contributed to the establishment of the Fāṭimid Caliphate; the Talkāta, founders of the two Zīrīd emirates; the Awrāba, who played a major role in the foundation of the Idrīsid emirate in northern Morocco and other, smaller *ḳabīla*s. Ibn Khaldūn calls these Ṣanhādja of central Morocco 'the first generation of Ṣanhādja (*al-ṭabaḳa al-ūlā min Ṣanhādja*)'. There were other small enclaves of Ṣanhādja in the western Maghrib, the largest being that of the Haskūra who lived in the High Atlas, in Masmūda country; the Ṣanhādja later joined forces with the Masmūda, merging with them to create the Almohad empire.

A further group of Ṣanhādja inhabited an area stretching from the desert land south of Wādī Dar'a (Oued Dra) to the strip of the Sahara that lies along the Atlantic coast as far as the Senegal River. Their most important groups were the Lamtūna, Massūfa, Djuddāla, Gazūla (Djazūla), Banū Wārith, Lamṭa and Ṭarḳa. These last were in fact the famous Tuareg (al-Ṭawāriḳ), who have remained the lords of the great Sahara right down to our own day. All these groups were camel-breeding nomads.[13]

Ibn Khaldūn calls this Ṣanhādja group 'the second generation of Ṣanhādja (*al-ṭabaḳa al-thāniya min Ṣanhādja*)'.

Some genealogists entirely exclude the Kutāma from the Ṣanhādja and from the Berbers as a whole, holding them to be of Arab descent and giving them a South Arabian Himyarite ancestry.

But the most important Barānis group was that of the Masmūda or Masāmida. They controlled practically the whole of the western Maghrib with the exception of a few small enclaves of Ṣanhādja and Zanāta. The most important branches of this group were the Ghumāra (in the Tangier region and throughout the Rīf), and the Barghawāṭa who ruled the Sebū valley along with the Awrāba. The Masāmida inhabited the mountainous regions of the High Atlas and Anti-Atlas ranges and the fertile plain of Sūs, which stretches between the two Atlas ranges to the south of the Sirwa massif. These were the founders of the Almohad religious movement and

13. Cf. chapter 13 below.

empire, which subsequently united the Maghrib and Spain.[14] Among the larger *ḳabīla*s included in the group were the Hintāta, Haylāna (or Aylāna), Urīka, Hazardja, Masfīwa, Dughāgha, Hargha, Ahl-Tin mallal, Ṣawda, Ganfīsa, Banū Wawazgit, Fatwāka and Mastāna.

The above, of course, is only a very brief survey of the Berbers and their groups at the time of the Arabs' arrival in North Africa. Some resisted the Arabs, while others rallied to them and were converted to Islam during the long period of conquest.

Virtually all the Berbers followed their ancient cults of worshipping the forces of nature. The Arabs called them *mādjūs*, i.e. 'fire-worshippers', but in the context of the early history of Islam this term usually means simply 'pagans'.

Christianity had not become widely spread among the Berbers: only the inhabitants of the coastal belt, the people called *al-Afāriḳa* by the Arabs, were Christian. The Afāriḳa were a marginal people, a mixture of Berbers and Romanized Carthaginians, Romans, and Greeks. In comparison with the powerful Berber groups further inland they constituted only a small minority.[15] Among the Berbers properly so called, the spread of Christianity was slight: only in Zeugetania and Byzacena had it become established in the interior. Moreover, the Christians of Byzantine Africa were divided by schisms; for these Berbers, Christianity had long been a source of unity against Roman domination, and they had ardently embraced such heresies as Arianism and Donatism which stood in opposition to the doctrine of the Church of Rome. A similar situation developed later in opposition to Byzantine religious policies.

Judaism too had made many converts, and although it never played the role some writers have attributed to it, nevertheless it had spread throughout North Africa. The majority of native-born North African Jews are descended from those converted prior to the advent of Islam.[16]

The first stage of the conquest: the conquest of Cyrenaica and Tripolitania

In the year 20/641, the Treaty of Alexandria was concluded between ʿAmr ibn al-ʿĀṣ and the Patriarch Cyrus, the last Byzantine governor of Egypt, ratifying the conquest of his territory by the Arabs. Shortly thereafter, on 16 Shawwāl, 21/17 September 642, the last Byzantine garrison evacuated Alexandria.

But ʿAmr ibn al-ʿĀṣ, the conqueror of Egypt, thought it necessary to annex Cyrenaica as well; since the last reorganization of the Empire by the Emperor Maurice (582–602), Cyrenaica had in fact belonged to the province of Egypt, as had Tripolitania. ʿAmr marched on Cyrenaica at the be-

14. Cf. Unesco, *General History of Africa*, Vol. IV, ch. 2.
15. On the Afāriḳa, cf. T. Lewicki, 1951–2.
16. Cf. H. Simon, 1946 and H. Z. Hirschberg, 1963, 1974.

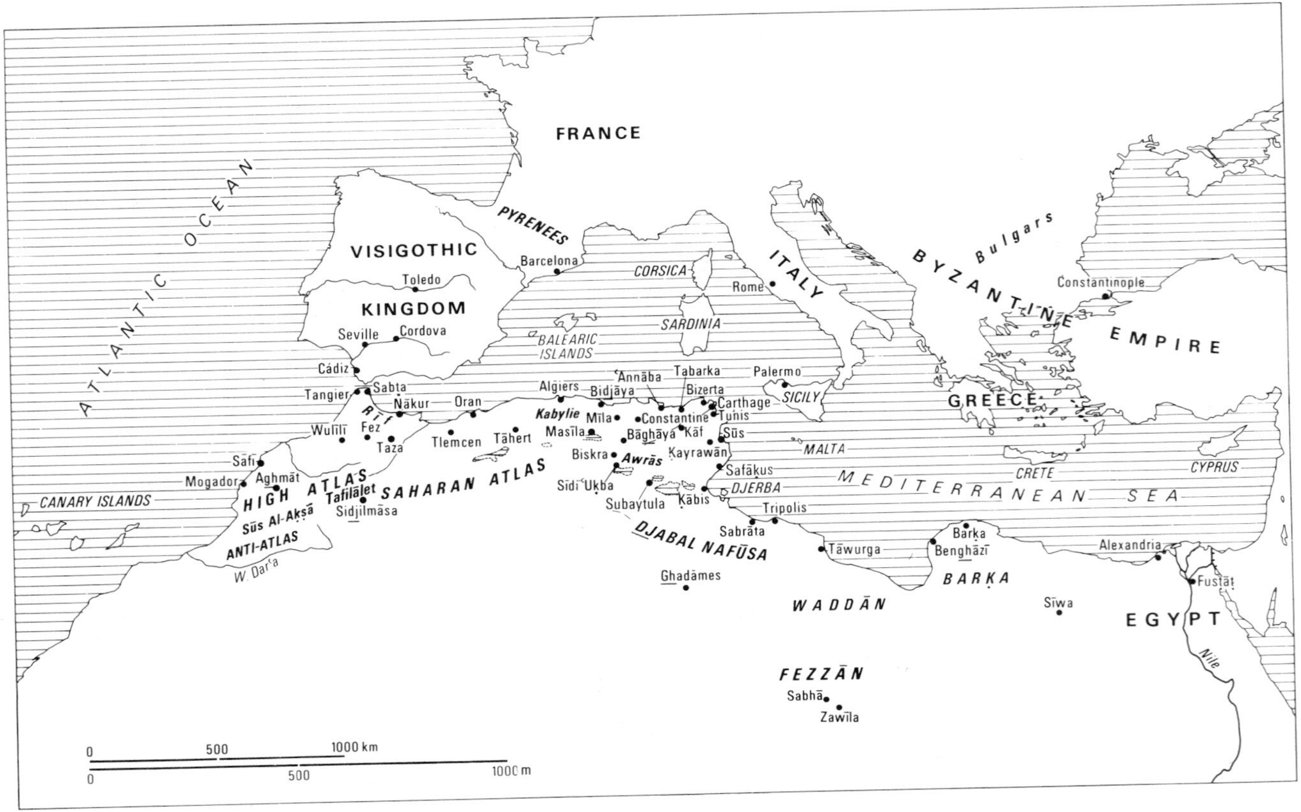

FIG. 9.1 *The Arab conquest of the Maghrib*

ginning of 22/643, and seized it almost without meeting any resistance. He found neither Greeks nor *Rūm* (Byzantines) to oppose him, only Berbers of the Luwāta and Hawwāra groups. These eventually surrendered and agreed to pay an annual tribute of 13 000 dinars, which thenceforth constituted part of the tribute payable by Egypt.[17]

In the Arabic source documents, Cyrenaica is sometimes referred to by the name Antābulus (i.e. Pentapolis, the Five Towns). It is also termed Ḳūrinā, a slight deformation of the Greek name Cyrene. All previous names for the region were soon to disappear in favour of the new name the Arabs bestowed on it: Barḳa, after a small town in the region (the contemporary al-Mardj).

At the same time, ʿAmr sent his lieutenant Nāfiʿ ibn ʿAbd al-Ḳays to occupy Zawīla, a small oasis between Cyrenaica and Fezzān that still exists today, a short distance south of Sabha. Zawīla is quite a long way from Barḳa, but seems in those days to have been the most important watering-place on the route to Fezzān. This detail shows how, right from the start, the Arabs deemed it necessary to conquer the hinterland as well as the coastal plain. Nāfiʿ ibn ʿAbd al-Ḳays left a garrison at Zawīla and rejoined ʿAmr at Barḳa. In Radjab 22/April or May 643, both returned to Egypt.

A year later, ʿAmr ibn al-ʿĀṣ and his lieutenants returned to accomplish one more step in the conquest of North Africa. Their objective was Tripoli, which at the time was an integral part of Byzantine Egypt, as was Barḳa. It was essential to annex the port of Tripoli, with its high walls and its flourishing trade; Greek ships dropped anchor there to buy the region's products, olives or olive oil, and wool, for the region was renowned for the quality of its sheep. ʿAmr captured Tripoli after a brief siege. To complete the work of conquest, he launched attacks by two columns: one, commanded by Buṣr ibn Abī Arṭāt, attacked Sabra or Sabrāta, the last great city of western Tripolitania, while the other, under the command of ʿAbd Allāh ibn al-Zubayr, took Waddān, the largest oasis in the hinterland of Tripoli. The occupation of Waddān effectively meant the annexation of the whole mountain region of Nafūsa. In those days the Djabal Nafūsa was covered with rich vegetation, olive groves and pastureland. It was also the bastion of the Nafūsa confederation.

ʿAmr ibn al-ʿĀṣ had thus put the finishing touch to his conquest of Egypt. The western frontiers of his province were secured. Beyond those frontiers lay the Byzantine province of Byzacena, corresponding approximately to modern Tunisia.

The first incursions into Ifrīḳiya

In the year 27/647, ʿAbd Allāh ibn Saʿd, the new governor of Egypt, launched an attack on Byzacena. At that time, the governor of Byzantine Africa was the Exarch Gregory (Djurghīr to the Arabs), who a few years

17. Ibn ʿAbd al-Ḥakam, 1922, pp. 170 *et seq.*

earlier had proclaimed himself independent and cut the province off from the rest of the empire. His army included many mercenaries and Berbers. The Arab and Byzantine armies met not far from Suffetula, which the Arabs call Subaytula (Sbeitla). The battle ended in a decisive victory: the Exarch Gregory was killed, his daughter captured along with many members of his household, and Subaytula occupied. Many Byzantines took refuge in Carthage, Sūs (Hadrumetum) and other ports, and many left Africa, never to return.

After his victory, ʿAbd Allāh b. Saʿd, who had quarrelled with his officers, returned to Egypt, but Arab columns carried out raids in all directions across the country, taking thousands of prisoners, especially at Thysdrus, a Roman fortress or theatre (known today as al-Djamm). Finding themselves utterly at his mercy, the African population appealed to ʿAbd Allāh ibn Saʿd and begged him to accept a substantial ransom as the price of his departure. The offer seemed acceptable to him; he agreed, took the ransom and left the country. The campaign ended in 28/649.

The second stage of the conquest

The campaigns of ʿAmr ibn al-ʿĀṣ and ʿĀbd Allāh ibn Saʿd may be regarded as the preliminary or preparatory stages of the conquest of the Maghrib. By now the Arabs had some knowledge of the country and its inhabitants. Some of those who had taken part in these campaigns had acquired useful experience. Since the expedition of ʿAmr ibn al-ʿĀṣ there had been a permanent garrison occupying Barḳa; another, smaller one was now established at Waddān. But all the Muslims' projects for conquest were paralysed for a period of nearly twelve years as a result of the civil war which raged among the Arabs between the middle of ʿUthmān's Caliphate (24/644–36/656) and the accession of Muʿāwiya ibn Abī Sufyān to the Caliphate in 41/661.

As soon as peace was restored within the Arab empire, the new Caliph, Muʿāwiya, founder of the Umayyad dynasty, decreed that conquest should be pressed forward on all fronts. In 43/663, Muʿāwiya appointed his supporter ʿUḳba ibn ʿAmīr al-Djuhanī to the post of Governor of Egypt, and appointed Muʿāwiya ibn Hudaydj al-Sākunī commander-in-chief of the Arab army which was to resume the conquest of the Maghrib.

During this period, circumstances worked to the Arabs' advantage in Africa. Profiting from the Arabs' long absence, the Byzantines had tried to re-establish their own authority there. The Emperor Constans II (641–68) sent out a new exarch, the Patrician Nicephorus, with orders to extract from the province an amount in tax revenue equal to the ransom they had paid to the Arabs. The people refused, as they were quite unable to produce such a sum. Tension built up and led, inevitably, to armed confrontation. It was at this point that the army of Muʿāwiya ibn Hudaydj appeared on the horizon, in 45/665. Mu ʿāwiya defeated Nicephorus easily, forcing him to take refuge within the walls of Hadrumetum (Sūs), and then launched an attack on him with a column of cavalry under the command of ʿAbd Allāh ibn al-Zubayr. The Arab horsemen captured Sūs and forced Nicephorus to take to the sea. In quick succession the Muslims then took Djalūla (Cululis), Bizerta, and the island of Djerba. In 46/666 they even ventured for the first time to undertake an incursion against the coast of Sicily.

In 50/670, the Caliph Mu'āwiya dismissed Ibn Hudaydj and appointed 'Uḳba ibn Nāfi' as commander-in-chief of the Arab forces in North Africa. This appointment was to prove decisive for the conquest. Setting out from Waddān, 'Uḳba undertook a long expedition, going by way of Fezzān and the south of Kawār. Wherever he went he took care to establish the authority of Islam firmly, building mosques and leaving garrisons and missionaries; then he moved north again as far as Ghadāmes. Here he was joined by 10 000 horsemen sent by Mu'āwiya to help him in his new mission. He began by attacking the last Byzantine strongholds standing between Gabès (Ḳābis) and the place where he had decided to establish what was to be both a military base and the political centre (*miṣr*) of his province. Without delay he set about the task of founding his capital, which he called Ḳayrawān, meaning 'camp' or 'arsenal'.

The building of the town began. Legend has it that 'Uḳba performed a number of miracles at this point; the heavens are said to have shown him the exact direction of the *ḳibla*, and in addition all snakes and other harmful creatures are said to have left the area at his command. This is part of the legend of Sīdī 'Uḳba, the first Muslim saint of Africa. With the founding of Ḳayrawān, one of the oldest and most venerable cities of Islam, the first Islamic province of North Africa was born. It was given the name of Africa (Ifrīḳiya). At the time, it covered more or less the same area as present-day Tunisia.

Having thus established a base from which to operate and having endowed the new province with a capital, 'Uḳba began to prepare his campaign; then came the unpleasant shock of learning that he had been relieved of his command (56/675). His successor, Dīnār ibn Abū al-Muhādjir, who held the post from 56/675 to 63/682, proved to be one of the most brilliant men ever to direct the Arab conquest of the Maghrib. On his arrival in Africa, he realized that the situation had shifted slightly to the disadvantage of the Arabs. Already the Byzantine Emperor Constantine IV (Pogonatus) had emerged victorious from the first major Arab attack and the siege of Constantinople which they had undertaken during the reign of the first Umayyad Caliph, Mu'āwiya. Constantine decided to take advantage of this victory to recover part of his lost territory. He retook Cyprus and some of the Aegean islands, and dispatched emissaries to re-establish contact with such Byzantines as remained in Carthage and other parts of the former province. After accomplishing this mission, the envoys won over to the Byzantine cause the most powerful contemporary Berber leader, Kusayla, chief of the Awrāba and of the Ṣanhādja confederation which ruled the whole of the central Maghrib.[18]

18. Ibn al-Athīr, citing Muḥammad ibn Yūsuf al-Warrāk as his authority, gives this name as Kasīla.

PLATE 9.1 *Part of the Byzantine fortifications of the city of Tebessa: Arch of Caracalla, originally in the centre of the Roman city, converted by the Byzantines into the north gate of a much smaller, walled town eventually conquered by the Arabs.*

Upon being informed of the situation in Ifrīḳiya, Abū al-Muhādjir, in accordance with the custom of the Arab leaders of his day, decided to meet the enemy as soon as possible. He therefore marched immediately to the territory of the Awrāba, in the Tlemcen region. Once there, he tried to make contact with the enemy before engaging battle. He met with Kusayla and succeeded in winning his confidence: he explained Islam to the Berber chief, assuring him that if he accepted the faith and rallied to its cause he and all his clan would become full members of the Muslim community.

Kusayla was convinced; he and all his tribesmen embraced the Islamic faith. The year was 59/678, a memorable date in the history of the Islamization of the Maghrib. The following year, in 60/679, Abū al-Muhādjir, with the help of his powerful ally, sent an army under the command of his lieutenant Sharīk ibn Sumayz al-Muradī to conquer the peninsula known today as Iḳlībiyya or Djazirat Bashū, but which for centuries bore his name: Djazirat Sharīk. Having taken the peninsula, Abū al-Muhādjir attacked Carthage, capturing Mila, a key stronghold of the Byzantines situated a short distance north of Cirta (modern Constantine).

Shortly after this success, Abū al-Muhādjir was relieved of his command and ʿUḳba was reappointed governor of Ifrīḳiya and commander-in-chief of the Arab army of the West, as a result of the death of Muʿāwiya and the accession of his son Yazīd in 61/680. This second appointment of ʿUḳba ibn Nāfiʿ at the head of the conquering Arab army of the West was unquestionably the most important event in the Arab conquest of North Africa. He restored the town of Ḳayrawān, repaired its mosque and declared his intention of opening up the whole of the Maghrib to Islam. Leaving a garrison of 6000 men in the capital, he marched off with 15 000 horsemen and several thousand of Kusayla's Berbers.

But instead of choosing the easy route along the coastal plain, he ventured into the Awrās Mountains, intending to attack the Berbers in the heart of their territory. First of all he launched an attack on Bāghāya, which had once been the centre of the Donatist schism under the Byzantines; indeed, there were still many of these Christian schismatics in the region, entrenched in their mountain fastness to escape the Byzantines. At ʿUḳba's approach they united with neighbouring Berbers in an attempt to halt the invaders. But to no avail: they were defeated, and the survivors fled for refuge to the mountains. ʿUḳba left them there in peace, for fear of losing valuable time. Thousands of Berbers and Christians (the Arab texts speak of Rūm) withdrew hastily westwards. Leaving Bāghāya behind him, ʿUḳba took Masīla by storm, and crossed the gorges of the Awrās, emerging close to Tiāret (Tāhert). There he was surprised to find thousands of Berbers – Luwāta, Hawwāra, Zugwagha, Matmāta, Zanāta and Miknāsa – waiting for him, together with a sizeable contingent of Rūm. ʿUḳba and his troops swooped down on them and scattered them in a fierce battle.

This victory gave ʿUḳba a reputation for invincibility. Impressed both by his victory and by his personality, thousands of Berbers converted to Islam and joined his army *en masse*. Leaving the Tiāret region he invaded the area around Tlemcen, the home of Kusayla and his Awrāba 'tribesmen'. Abū al-Muhādjir advised ʿUḳba not to attack these people, since they were already Muslims and their chief, Kusayla, was his own friend and ally. But ʿUḳba disregarded this excellent and sincerely offered advice and, with his host of fighters, swept into the heart of the Awrāba country. Kusayla was infuriated, but controlled his rage, deciding to take his revenge at an opportune time.

ʿUḳba then crossed the Mulūya River, went over the strategic Taza pass and marched on Tingis (Tandja, Tangier), where Julian, the governor of the town, contacted him,[19] advising him to move southward and conquer the Berber territories. ʿUḳba advanced swiftly toward the mountain strongholds of the Masāmida, the princes of the peaks, who fled in terror, withdrawing as far as Wādī Darʿa; ʿUḳba pursued them and inflicted a crushing defeat on them there. Moving north-eastward from Wādī Darʿa, he crossed the Tafilālet region and then cut across westwards towards Aghmāt-Urīka, where he built a mosque. He had another mosque built in Naffīs, a village on the stream of the same name.

From there, ʿUḳba marched south-westwards and reached the Atlantic coast at Sāfī, north of Mogador, near the village of Ighiran-Yattūf (Cap

19. It has now been established that Julian is not a personal name but a title, *comes julianus*, 'count of Julia Traducta', which was the Roman name for Tarifa. He was undoubtedly a Visigoth. It is for this reason that we find another *Julian* at the time of the conquest of Spain. Cf. J. Vallvé, 1967.

Guir). There, according to the legend, he rode on horseback into the sea, saying he had reached the end of the world fighting for God, and that if he could proceed no further it was because there was no more land to be brought into the fold of Islam.

But the return march was a tragic one. The men were exhausted, and after so long an expedition they were impatient to see their families again; 'Uḳba allowed those who wished to hurry on ahead, and in the end he was left with only 5000 men. This was the moment Kusayla had been waiting for to take his revenge. As they were passing through the Tlemcen region, his homeland, he abandoned 'Uḳba's camp and hastened into the very midst of the Atlas Mountains, where he contacted the Christians who had taken refuge there, and made an agreement with them to await 'Uḳba on a plain near Tahūdha, to the south of Biskra. 'Uḳba found himself surrounded by some 50 000 men. He displayed a degree of valour worthy of his reputation: dismounting together with Abū al-Muhādjir and the rest of his companions he hurled himself upon the enemy and met a hero's death. Almost all his men were killed (Dhu l-Ḥidjdja 63/August 683).

The tragic news alarmed the whole of the Maghrib. In Ḳayrawān, the Muslims were panic-stricken; the garrison left in haste and hurried eastwards. Kusayla marched on Ḳayrawān and seized it. He did not abjure the Islamic faith but simply proclaimed himself governor, treating the Arabs of the town with forbearance. Thus 'Uḳba's tale ends in catastrophe, but Ifrīḳiya was not lost to Islam. For the first time in history it was governed by a man of pure Berber stock: Kusayla, chief of the Awrāba.

'Uḳba's campaign was not a fruitless adventure. Despite its tragic end it was the most important and decisive expedition the Muslims had undertaken in the Maghrib. This man had been feared by the Berbers, but his courageous end made him a saint and martyr (*mudjāhid*). Sīdī 'Uḳba's tomb became the most venerated holy place in all North Africa.

The beginnings of Berber resistance

'Uḳba's campaign had one very important side effect: the Berbers came to realize that the Arab attack was directed against them, not merely against the Byzantines. It was now clear that the aim of the Arabs was to absorb the Berbers and the Berber territory into their empire and their religious community. Although the general Berber population had no objection to adopting Islam, their chiefs were unwilling to let themselves be absorbed into the empire of a foreign power. Kusayla's victory is the first demonstration of this feeling: he had been happy enough to be a friend and ally to the Arab governor Abū al-Muhādjir, but he refused to become subject to a remote caliph. On the other hand, the Umayyads were not prepared to grant sovereignty over the new province to a local chieftain, even if the latter was a Muslim. The Caliph 'Abd al-Malik ibn Marwān (66/685–

86/705) was for the time being not in a position to send reinforcements into Africa, but he never even considered the possibility of negotiating with Kusayla.

Not until 69/688 did a new army commanded by Zuhayr ibn Ḳays undertake the reconquest of the lost province. Kusayla, who had built up a Berber kingdom covering the Awrās, the area south of Constantine and the greater part of Ifrīḳiya (68/687–71/690) felt insecure in Ḳayrawān when he learned that the new Arab army was on its way. He decided to await the enemy at Mamma, a small village inhabited by the Hawwāra that lay between Ḳayrawān and Lāribus.

The battle of Mamma was decisive. The Arabs, now past masters in the arts of war, defeated the Berbers (71/690). Kusayla was killed, and his men suffered heavy losses. The Arabs pursued the fleeing survivors far into the Maghrib, as far as the Mulūya River in some instances. The Awrāba, at that time one of the most powerful Berber clans, were utterly crushed. Abandoning the area around Tlemcen they settled to the north of Sebū, around the town of Wulīlī (Volubilis). A large number of strongholds fell to Zuhayr, among them Sicca Vaneria (Shikkahāriya, the modern al-Kāf).

After his victory, Zuhayr stayed only a year in Ifrīḳiya before deciding to depart. As he was on his way to Egypt, however, a Byzantine fleet, seizing the opportunity afforded by the Arabs' war against Kusayla, landed at Barḳa and occupied it. Zuhayr was not far away when he heard of this; he marched on Barḳa with his vanguard, followed by the rest of the army, but was killed in the battle with the Byzantines.

The news of this Byzantine victory worried the Caliph ʿAbd al-Malik considerably, but it was four years before he was able to send into Ifrīḳiya the fresh contingents that were needed; he had too many urgent problems to resolve elsewhere. The new governor appointed by the Caliph was Ḥassān ibn al-Nuʿmān, who raised a large army and appropriated Egypt's tax revenues in their entirety to cover the costs of his new expedition; he wanted to complete the conquest of the Maghrib once and for all.

Ḥassān's first objective was to defeat the Byzantines and so prevent any alliance between them and the Berbers. After reaching Ḳayrawān, he marched on Carthage and destroyed its port in order to make it unusable for Byzantine ships. Then he sent out columns in all directions with instructions to expel the last remnants of the Rūm. Most of these fled for refuge to the islands of the Mediterranean. There was violent fighting around Istafūra (or Satfūra) and on the peninsula where Hippo Diarhytus (Bizerta), Hippo Regius (Bône, ʿAnnāba), and Tabarka stood; all of these were Byzantine colonies and fortresses, and all fell to the Arabs.

Having accomplished this much, Ḥassān considered his military tasks completed, and set about organizing the territory. But hardly had he returned to Ḳayrawān when alarming and unexpected news reached him: a Berber woman whom the Arabs called *al-Kāhina*, 'the priestess' or 'the prophetess', chief of the Djarāwa in the Awrās mountains, had assembled all the Zanāta of the region and announced that she would throw the Arabs out of Ifrīḳiya. Al-Kāhina – for it is under this Arab name that she has gone down in history – was, without a doubt, a fearsome woman, half queen, half sorceress, with dark skin, a mass of hair and huge eyes; according to the Arab chroniclers, when she was angry or possessed by her demons her eyes would turn red and her hair would stand on end. She is one of those curious figures around whom legends grow up.[20]

As the chief of a large Zanāta group, she had been very much disturbed by the unexpected victory of Kusayla, the Ṣanhādja chieftain who had imposed his rule over the region bordering on her own. Now that the Arab newcomers had defeated the Ṣanhādja and threatened to extend their domination to the whole of the Maghrib, her fears increased, and she determined to defy the Arabs.

News of the rising came as a surprise to Ḥassān, but he immediately went on the offensive against his new enemy. Al-Kāhina expected the Arabs to try to seize Bāghāya, which would have served as a good base from which to attack her in the Awrās; and so she occupied the town without delay, thus cutting off the route into the interior. Ḥassān advanced as far as Miskiāna, a small village on the stream of the same name, not far from the camp of the sorceress-queen. In 77/696 he launched his attack. The Djarāwa threw themselves on the Arabs so fiercely that the latter were driven back, leaving behind hundreds of dead and some eighty prisoners. So numerous were the Arab casualties that the earliest of our chroniclers, Ibn ʿAbd al-Ḥakam, calls the Wādī Miskiāna 'the wādī of the disaster'. Ḥassān beat a retreat to Barḳa. Al-Kāhina, satisfied with her victory, withdrew into the mountains instead of marching on Ḳayrāwan.

Thinking that the Arabs were interested only in plunder, she adopted a 'scorched earth' policy and had all the standing crops destroyed between the Awrās and Ifrīḳiya. This action turned the sedentary tribes against her, and it was not long before they sent emissaries to Ḥassān asking him to come to their assistance. The following year, in 78/697, the situation further deteriorated; the Byzantine emperor Leontius (695–8) sent out a fleet which sacked Carthage and killed many of the Muslims there.

Reinforcements did not reach Ḥassān until 80/699. The caliph ʿAbd al-Malik, tired of the interminable struggle for Africa, had decided to strike a decisive blow. The army with which Ḥassān marched against *al-Kāhina* was the largest ever seen in the region, the Arab troops being reinforced by thousands of Berbers, most of them Butr.

The final battle between Ḥassān and al-Kāhina took place in 82/701. The queen was killed and her followers routed. The Berbers of the Awrās immediately asked for amnesty, which they were granted on condition that they supply men to fight in the Arab armies. Twelve thousand men were sent to Ḥassān, who placed them under the command of the defeated

20. Cf. M. Talbi, 1971.

queen's two sons. All these fighting men, including the two young princes, adopted the Islamic faith.

Ḥassān thus had reason to feel that Berber resistance had been broken, and returned to Ḳayrawān. The next step was to make sure that the Byzantines would never be able to return, and to that end Ḥassān gave orders for the total destruction of Carthage. The work was done in 83/702; the tale of this city, so glorious in its day, was at an end.

But Ifrīḳiya had to have a large port, and Ḥassān now chose the site of an old Phoenician port, Tarses (Tars͟hīs͟h), lying south-west of Carthage on a shallow bay. Here he ordered that a new port should be built, and the Caliph sent him from Egypt a thousand skilled Coptic draughtsmen to help draw up the plans. A canal was dug and a shipyard or 'arsenal' (*dār al-ṣinā'a*) was built. Thus was born the port city of Tunis, in 83/702. Thirty years later, 'Ubayd Allāh ibn al-Ḥabḥāb (116/734–123/741); governor of the entire Arab Maghrib, transformed it into a truly great city. He had the shipyard enlarged and new docks constructed, and he encouraged migration into the city to populate it. He made Tunis the centre for all the great military camps in the region where Arab troops were stationed, and transformed its mosque into a cathedral mosque (*masd͟jid d͟jāmi'*). This was the famous Zaytūna mosque, one of the most important sanctuaries in the Islamic world.

Meanwhile, Ḥassān had begun to set up an administrative system for the new province of Africa. In this province he included the Tripolitania (Ṭarābulus) region, from Misrāta in the east to Tāwarg͟ha in the west, Ifrīḳiya proper, from Gabès to 'Annāba, and the Mzāb region from 'Annāba to the upper reaches of the Chélif River, south of Algiers. Thenceforth this whole area was regarded as the province of Africa. West of the Chélif stretched the Central Maghrib, and beyond that the Western Maghrib; these, in theory, were part of the Islamic empire, and there were already Muslim communities established there, but in fact no more is heard of the two Maghribs from the time of 'Uḳba's death until their real annexation to the Caliphate, which was to be the work of Mūsā ibn Nuṣayr and his sons.

For the time being, Ḥassān organized his province of Ifrīḳiya along the lines of the administrative system in force throughout the Islamic empire. In that empire, the previous administrative divisions of each province were invariably retained; at the head of each province the Muslims appointed a governor (*'āmil*), who himself chose a vice-governor (*wālī*) for each district; as a rule, taxes were levied at a rate of approximately 10 per cent on personal income. In Ifrīḳiya, where there were almost no Jews or Christians on whom to levy capitation tax (*d͟jizya*), this particular source of revenue, so important everywhere else–as in Egypt, for example–was presumably almost non-existent.

Ifrīḳiya was similar to Arabia in that both had societies organized in *ḳabīla*s. In Arabia, the government imposed a tax of about 2 per cent of each tribe's collective wealth in the form of camels and sheep. This was the *ṣadaḳa*, and the tax-collector was known as the *muṣaddiḳ*. The tax-collectors were sent out once or twice a year to the *ḳabīlas*. Ḥassān applied the same principle to the mountain and desert regions of his province. However, the government had to appoint a judge (*ḳāḍī*) for each tribal group and to send missionaries or teachers to instruct the population in the principles of Islam and to preside over prayers, and consequently hardly any revenue was raised from the *ḳabīlas*, as these various state functionaries were paid out of *ṣadaḳāt* contributions.

Ḥassān, at any rate, endowed his province of Africa with a sound administrative infrastructure. It is not surprising, considering the sheer size of its area, as outlined above, that this province should have become the keystone of the entire Arab edifice in North Africa. Ḳayrawān, thanks to its mosque – now entirely renovated through Ḥassān's efforts – became one of the most important centres of Islamic learning and culture.

Despite the absence of any Arab authority over the two Maghribs, Islam was making steady progress there, thanks to the many preachers who were to be found throughout the region, even in such remote areas as the region around Sūs, in the extreme south of Morocco. We are assured by reliable documents that at that time the Berbers were building mosques everywhere and endowing these cathedral mosques with pulpits (*manābir*) for public prayers. Where mosques had not been built with the *ḳibla* oriented exactly towards Mecca, the necessary corrections were being made. The pulpit of the Aghmāt Hilānā mosque south of Marrakesh, for example, is said to have been in use since 85/704.[21]

The conquest of the western Maghrib

Ḥassān ibn al-Nu'mān did not remain in office long enough to complete his work. In 85/704 he was replaced by Mūsā bin Nuṣayr, an astonishingly ambitious man of 60 with extravagant tastes who was a protégé of the governor of Egypt, 'Abd al-'Azīz ibn Marwān. He came to Ifrīḳiya bursting with energy despite his age and with an incredible thirst for adventure, conquest and glory. He began his campaign as soon as he reached Ḳayrawān. He wanted to subdue the central and western Maghrib, and reckoned that he could extract a fabulous booty from it. Unfortunately for him, the Maghrib held nothing comparable to the hoards of gold and precious stones that had been seized in Iran and Iraq when they were conquered. Here there was nothing but men, their families and their flocks.

As the objective for this first campaign, Mūsā chose a *djebel* south of Tabarka-Djabal Zaghwān (Zengitanus). This was the territory of some

21. E. Lévi-Provençal, 1956, p. 223. The *ḳibla* is the direction which Muslims must face while praying, the direction in which the Ka'ba lies. In a mosque it is also the niche that indicates this direction, a recess in the wall oriented towards the Ka'ba in Mecca.

subgroups of the Hawwāra and Djarāwa who had not yet made their submission. He launched a fierce attack and took a great many prisoners. This hard blow struck fear into the hearts of Berbers from one end of the Central Atlas to the other. As they began to flee towards the western Maghrib, Mūsā pursued them. After capturing a number of villages and compelling the submission of various *ḳabīla*s in the Rīf, where Kusayla's daughters had sought refuge, Mūsā occupied Tangier (Tandja) and offered protection to Ceuta (Sabta) and its governor, Julian. From there, Mūsā sent out flying columns headed by his four sons and other officers to sweep the western Maghrib in all directions. They caught up with the proud Maṣmūda on the Wādī Dar'a and defeated them in battle.

Most of the Berbers of the western Maghrib surrendered and converted to Islam. Mūsā created three new provinces: the central Maghrib with Tlemcen (Tilimsān) as its capital, the far western Maghrib (al-Maghrib al-Aḳṣā), with Tangier as its capital, and al-Sūs al-aḳṣā.

For each province he appointed a governor, who was based in the provincial capital with a strong garrison, made up of both Arabs and Berbers. In order to ensure the obedience of the conquered people, he took large numbers of fighting men as hostages (*rahā'in*) and incorporated them in his Muslim army. At Tangier, Mūsā appointed his son Marwān governor and allotted to him 17 000 soldiers of the Maṣmūda; subsequently he replaced Marwān with Ṭāriḳ ibn Ziyād.

Mūsā ibn Nuṣayr had thus completed the conquest of the whole Maghrib. It was a magnificent achievement, but he had employed cruel methods for which the Muslims were to pay dearly in due course. In 91/710 Mūsā returned to Ḳayrawān. The following year he was recalled and given the greatest task of his life: the conquest of the Iberian peninsula (al-Andalus).

The conquest of the Iberian peninsula (al-Andalus)

No study of the conquest of North Africa by the Muslims can reasonably ignore the salient role played by the Berbers in the conquest of the Iberian peninsula, or their contribution to the history of Islamic Spain and hence to Muslim hegemony in the Mediterranean.

The history and civilization of Islamic Spain constitute a monumental edifice, the foundations of which were laid by Arabs and Berbers together. The first Muslim military leader to undertake (in 91/710) a reconnaissance operation in southern Iberia to explore the possibilities for conquest was Tarīf, son of Zar'a ibn Abī Mudrik. Tarīf was one of the young generation of Islamized Berbers imbued with the military thinking of Ḥassān ibn al-Nu'mān and Mūsā ibn Nuṣayr. He successfully carried out the expedition, and a small port in southern Spain, Tarifa, is named after him. The Muslim general who first decided on the conquest of Spain was also a Berber: Ṭāriḳ ibn Ziyād ibn 'Abd Allāh ibn Walghū. His grandfather 'Abd Allāh had been a member of the Warfadjūma *ḳabīla* a branch of the Nafza;

he had been converted to Islam at ʿUḳba's instance and had served under the latter.

As we have seen, Mūsā had appointed Ṭāriḳ ibn Ziyād governor of the province of Tandja, or al-Maghrib al-Aḳṣā, 'the far western Maghrib', which covered what is today the southern part of the kingdom of Morocco. He commanded an army of 17 000 men, mainly Ṣanhādja.

With this expeditionary force and some additional Arab troops, Ṭāriḳ crossed the straits and disembarked near a rocky promontory which from that day to this has borne his name: Djabal Ṭāriḳ ('Ṭāriḳ's mountain'), or, as we now pronounce it, Gibraltar. In Shawwāl 92/August 711, he won his great victory over the Visigoth army, in which the last Visigoth king, Roderick, or Rodrigo (Rūdrīk in Arabic),[22] was killed in the battle. Wasting no time, Ṭāriḳ pushed on with his indefatigable Berber cavalry to Toledo (Ṭulayṭula in Arabic). After a forced march of over 500 km he seized the Gothic capital, thus taking full advantage of his initial success. Within a month, by Dhu l-Ḥidjdja 92/September 711, Ṭāriḳ, the first of the great Berber generals of western Islam, had already put an end to Visigothic rule in the peninsula and ushered in the era of Islamic Spain.

Mūsā ibn Nuṣayr joined Ṭāriḳ at once and finished the work of conquest with an army of 18 000 men, mainly Arabs. The two commanders met at Talavera, and Ṭāriḳ and his Berbers were given the task of conquering the north-west of Spain. This they set out to do, and within three months, in 93/712, they had swept the entire territory north of the Ebro as far as the Pyrenees and annexed the inaccessible Basque country. There they left a small detachment of men under Munūsa, a Berber lieutenant who was later to play a decisive role in the Muslim campaigns in southern France. Before the period of his command in Spain was over, Ṭāriḳ, with his Berber troops, conquered the whole of the region later to be called Old Castile, occupying Amaya, Astorga and finally León.

In the aftermath of these brilliant successes in Spain, Berbers by the thousand flooded into the Iberian peninsula. So great was their haste to come that some crossed the straits on tree-trunks. As soon as they arrived they took part in the conquest of the rest of the peninsula and in the Muslim campaign in the south of France. The battle of Poitiers, which put an end to the Muslims' successes in Gaul, took place in the autumn of 114/732. Thousands of Berbers stayed on in the south of France during the next forty years.[23] Many others settled in Spain (al-Andalus, the Arabic name of Islamic Spain), marrying either Arab or Ibero-Roman wives and becoming Muslim Andalusians. There were Berber colonies scattered throughout the peninsula. Their offspring were known as *muwalladūn*, i.e.

22. The site of the battle has never been determined with certainty. The most plausible suggestions have been the banks of the Guadelete or the Laguna de la Janda, or Jerèz de la Frontera. But I. Olagüe, 1974, ch. 2, has shown that the battle may have taken place near the Guadarranque River, not far from Gibraltar.

23. Cf. J. Reinaud, 1836; J. Lacam, 1965; and G. de Rey, 1972.

Andalusians with Arab or Berber fathers and Iberian mothers, and these made up 70 per cent of the population of Islamic Spain. These Andalusians of Berber origin, who were found in all social classes, have left us an endless list of famous names: generals, ministers, theologians, inventors, poets and artists.

The Berbers after the Arab conquest

Once the long-drawn-out conquest of North Africa by the Arabs (642–711) was over, we find a completely new country whose people were undergoing a total transformation in their social, and even ethnic, structures, their way of life, their way of thought and even their conception of the world. Their political, spiritual and cultural relations with the Christian world were severed for nearly ten centuries. From the Atlantic coast to Cyrenaica, the population now looked towards the Arab Muslim East. Little by little, as they became progressively Islamized and Arabized, they felt increasingly that they belonged to that world; such was the strength and depth of this tendency that some of the more important social groupings began to boast of remote pre-Islamic Arab forebears. Later on, professional genealogists worked out family trees that included Arab ancestors, and these were accepted by all Berbers as undisputed fact.

It is surprising to realize how irresistibly the Berbers were attracted to Islam. In the course of the conquest, they adopted the Islamic faith *en masse*, but at first this acceptance barely constituted more than lip-service. They continued to adhere to Islam because its clear and simple doctrine attracted them. Throughout the period of the conquest, Arab immigrants settled in all parts of North Africa. They came as peaceful newcomers, and were made welcome everywhere. Large Arab settlements were established in many areas in Cyrenaica and the provinces of Ifrīḳiya. They persisted for many years, especially in the two provincial divisions of Ifrīkiya and Mzāb. A considerable proportion of these colonists belonged to the great Arab confederation of Tamīm. Later, during the Aghlabid period (184/800–296/909), these Arab colonies fell into decadence and were gradually absorbed into the local population.

There were also small groups of Arabs, sometimes even single families or individuals, who settled among Berber tribes where they were regarded as teachers; they acted as *imāms* or religious leaders. This spiritual leadership often developed into political leadership as well, the Arab *imām* becoming the political head of the tribe. This development involved some Berberization of the Arab colonists in turn. One characteristic example is that of the Arab family of the Banū Ṣāliḥ ibn Manṣūr al-Yamanī. In 91/710, the Caliph ʿAbd al-Malik offered them as a gift the region of Nakūr, near what is today Alhucemas in northern Morocco. The family settled there, they intermingled with the local population, and the Berber came to recognize them as emirs. Similarly, the Banū Sulaymān ibn ʿAbd Allāh ibn al-Ḥasan, a family of descendants of the Prophet, established themselves in the Tlemcen area where they created a number of Arab-Berber emirates with the collaboration of the local Berbers, while their cousins the Idrīsids of Fez actively worked to promote the Islamization of the western Maghrib from 172/789 onward.

Very often these Arab colonists belonged to one or another of the dissident Islamic sects known as K͟hāridjites (*K͟hawāridj*) that opposed the Umayyad regime. These preached egalitarian doctrines that found ready acceptance among the Berbers.

The great conquests through which the Arabs had expanded beyond their peninsula had been carried out under the banner and in the name of the new Islamic religion. In this initial period, the terms 'Arab' and 'Muslim' meant the same thing. This tendency to regard ethnic group and religion as identical, instead of fading away as the peoples of the conquered territories were converted, was maintained and even strengthened with the advent of the Umayyad dynasty. The Umayyad empire was effectively an Arab kingdom headed by the Ḳurays͟hite aristocracy of Mecca, who had once been the Prophet's adversaries and had converted only at the last minute. This aristocracy ruled the Islamic state primarily for their own advantage, disregarding the democratic principles characteristic of Islamic doctrine. The new non-Arab converts continued to be treated as second-class citizens and did not enjoy the same rights as Arabs, especially with respect to the taxes to which they were subjected. Aiming to preserve their privileges and their revenues, the Umayyad caliphs apart from the pious ʿUmar ibn ʿAbd al-ʿAzīz (99/717–101/720) were never willing to grant the newly converted their rights as members of the Islamic community (*umma*) or to regard them as equal to the Arabs. It was this policy that produced such a profound crisis under the Umayyad regime, leading to the fall of the dynasty in the mid-second/eighth century. As has often happened historically, ethnic and social tensions found expression in dissident religious movements. In the case of the Berbers, all the necessary conditions were present. The last Umayyad governors introduced a harsh policy that soon provoked a hostile reaction: the Berbers were regarded as a vanquished people, to be governed by force, even though almost all of them had already converted to Islam, had fought for Islam, and therefore considered themselves an integral part of the Islamic empire, on an equal footing with the Arabs. The Berbers complained that they had been poorly rewarded for their services (as was most visibly the case in Spain, where they had been given the less fertile regions as fiefs). So the Maghrib turned away from the Sunnite orthodoxy which represented official Umayyad policy; instead it adopted K͟hāridjite doctrines. The K͟hāridjites succeeded in founding communities of their sect in all regions, including such mountainous areas as the D̲j̲abal Nafūsa, south of Tripoli. These centres of dissidence were established as much by the Berbers themselves as by the Arabs. Both together attacked the Umayyad administration. The general uprising against the Umayyads that began in the western Maghrib in 123/741 under the administration of the governor ʿUbayd Allāh ibn al-Ḥabḥāb was not, as has generally been asserted, a rising of Berbers against the Arabs to drive the latter out of the Maghrib altogether, but rather an Islamic revolt against the Umayyad administration. We shall describe this uprising in detail elsewhere in this volume.[24]

24. Cf. Chapter 3 above, Chapter 10 below.

10 The independence of the Maghrib

M. TALBI

The revolt and independence of the Maghrib

The Maghrib under the Umayyads

After the battle of Poitiers (114/732), the centripetal force that had irresistibly drawn a growing number of provinces, both to the East and to the West, into the orbit of Damascus, was spent. Eight years later, in 122/740, the contrary process began; the centrifugal reaction which was to lead to the foundation of several independent states. Between 78/697 and 122/740 there had been eight successive governors at Ḳayrawān, the regional capital from which all the western Muslim territories were administered, from Lebda, east of Tripoli, to Narbonne, beyond the Pyrenees. Direct government by Damascus of this vast area through Ḳayrawān lasted for only a little more than forty years. A period of time such as this may seem of little consequence when compared to the duration of Roman, Vandal and Byzantine domination. The results, however, were considerably more significant and more durable. Why is this so? Most probably because the native population, while rejecting foreign domination, gave its genuine support to the values that had been introduced by Islam. As we shall see, their commitment to these values was all the more profound because they contributed in a decisive way to setting in motion and stimulating the forces behind the struggle for freedom.

Rising anger

To understand the difficult beginnings of the new Maghrib, with its independence arising out of conquest, a clear distinction must be made between the presence of the Qoran and its historical interpretation. Interpretation almost always leads to misinterpretation. The result, in the event, was that the ideal of fraternity, which was supposed to govern relations between Muslims without any distinction as to race, colour or place, was very poorly applied in practice. There was, admittedly, no racism based on doctrine or principle, and no actual segregation, either. Be that as it may, the Arabs were often inclined to consider the Berbers as little more than 'the scum of the earth',[1] and spread humiliating *ḥadīth*s[2] about them that were no less harmful and repugnant for being unquestionably apocryphal. In all fairness, however, it must be said, so as not to convey the wrong impression, that some of the most generous Arabs attempted to ennoble them by devising for them some distant Arab, especially Yemenī,[3] ancestry. The aim was, in some measure, to use genealogical fiction, which exerted considerable influence at the time, to win over the Berbers, assimilate them and make brothers of them.[4] This reflected the hesitations and the ambiguous aspects which the Arabs' behaviour already showed towards the Berbers.

This hesistant approach was to be found in politics. Ḥassān b. al-Nuʿmān, taking up the policies of Abū al-Muhādjir Dīnār, friend and ally to Kusayla, integrated the Berbers into his army and involved them in the *fay*ʿ (sharing of land). His successor, Mūsā b. Nuṣayr (79/698–95/714), while reconciling considerable sections of the Berber population to himself and surrounding himself with numerous and faithful clients from their midst, including Ṭāriḳ, the celebrated conqueror of Spain, took up the vigorous style of ʿUḳba and waged his pacification campaigns in a forthright manner. Caliph Sulaymān b. ʿAbd al-Malik (96/715–99/717) replaced him by Muḥammad b. Yazīd, to whom he gave, among other things, rigorous instructions on fiscal equity. This trend was further accentuated by the very pious figure of ʿUmar b. ʿAbd al-ʿAzīz (99/717–101/720) whose governor, a *mawlā*[5] and also an ascetic, poured all his zeal into spreading Islam and giving it the best possible image. The reign of ʿUmar was unfortunately too brief. When he died, a new governor, Yazīd b. Abī Muslim, trained in Iraq at the austere school of al-Ḥadjdjādj, was dispatched to Ḳayrawān. So as to maintain the volume of taxes, which had been dwindling as a result of the numerous conversions to Islam, he decreed, contrary to the letter and spirit of the Qoran, that those who were newly converted to Islam should continue to pay the *djizya* (poll tax)[6] and went so far as to humiliate his Berber guards by having their hands branded. The guards subsequently assassinated him (102/720–1). This was the first sign of rising anger on the part of the local population and Ibn Khaldūn rightly sees in this the earliest manifestation of the Khārīdjite spirit in the Maghrib.[7]

From then on the situation grew steadily worse. It would be impossible to relate everything in detail here, so we shall therefore quote a text in full that provides a striking summary of the Berbers' grievances. The following may well actually reproduce the contents of the memorandum left as a last

1. Ibn Khaldūn, 1867, Vol. 6.
2. Ibn Khaldūn, 1867, Vol. 6, pp. 177, 181–9. On *hadīth* see Chapter 2 above.
3. Yāḳūt, 1866–73, Vol. 1, p. 369.
4. Ibn Khaldūn, 1867, Vol. 6, p. 187.
5. *Mawlā* (pl. *mawālī*): non-Arab Muslim, attached as client to an Arab tribe.
6. *Djizya*: poll-tax, paid by the non-Muslims (Christians, Jews, etc.).
7. Ibn Khaldūn, 1867, Vol. 6, pp. 220–1.

resort with Hishām b. ʿAbd al-Malik (105/724–125/743) by the delegation led by Maysara who, after his final fruitless attempt, was to launch the revolt that marked the beginning of the independence of the Maghrib:

> Maysara set off for the Orient at the head of a delegation of some ten persons in order to have a meeting with Hishām. They requested an audience and encountered many difficulties. They then went to find al-Abrash and asked him to bring the following to the notice of the Prince of Believers:
>
> Our Emir goes campaigning with us and his Arab troops. When he captures any booty, he excludes us from the share-out and says to us: 'They are more entitled to it than you'. We said to ourselves: 'All right! Our combat in God's cause is all the more pure as a result because we get nothing out of it. If we are entitled to it, we give up our entitlement willingly for their profit; and if we are not entitled, in any event we did not want any booty'. They continued: When we attack a city, our Emir also says to us: 'Forward!' and he keeps his Arab troops in the rear. We said to our people: 'Again, all right! Forward! Your share in the battle for God's cause is all the greater and you are of those men who bear the burden for their brothers. Thus have we saved them, paying with our own lives, and we have sacrificed ourselves in their stead'.
>
> Then it was the turn of our flocks. They set about disembowelling the pregnant ewes in search of the foetuses' white fleeces for the Prince of Believers. They disembowelled a thousand ewes for one single fleece. We said to ourselves: 'How simple it all is for the Prince of Believers! But we put up with everything; we let them do whatever they wanted'.
>
> They then pushed our humiliation to the point of abducting any of our daughters who was comely. We then observed that we could find nothing in God's Book or in Tradition to justify that. And we are Muslims.
>
> Now we wish to know – did the Prince of Believers desire all this, yes or no?[8]

Khāridjism, a revolutionary doctrine

Maysara, known as the Despised One (*al-haḳīr*), was a former Berber water-carrier who had become converted to Ṣufrite Khāridjism. Under the Umayyads, Khāridjism had been the strongest revolutionary force. It had arisen from the *fitna*,[9] or the major crisis that had shaken the Muslim community after the assassination of ʿUthmān (35/656), and had been forged

8. al-Ṭabarī, 1962–7, Vol. 6, pp. 254–5.
9. *Fitna*: rebellion or civil war among Muslims.

first of all into a political theology. This theology had as a common basis, to be found in all forms of Khāridjism, the principle of an elected *imām*, the highest leader of the community, without distinction as to race, colour or country, power thereby being invested in the best man, 'even if he were an Abyssinian slave with a slit nose'.[10]

There were four movements in Khāridjism that can be listed in descending order of revolutionary extremism: the Azāriḳa, the Nadjadāt, the Ṣufrites and the Ibāḍites. The first and most violent of these, the Azāriḳa, was exterminated in the Orient by the very forceful al-Ḥadjdjādj around 81/700, and the Nadjadāt had practically disappeared from the political scene a few years earlier, around 74/693, before the Maghrib was completely conquered. Subsequently, only the Ṣufrites and the Ibāḍites remained. It can be said with some degree of certitude that their propagandists headed westwards around 95/714. It was as if they had shared out their respective areas of influence; the Ṣufrites to the west of Ḳayrawān and the Ibāḍites to the east of it.

What were they bringing to the Maghrib? A revolutionary strategy that had been conceived and put into practice in the East, together with a doctrine adapted to that strategy. The strategy combined *ḳu'ūd*,[11] clandestine subversive action under the cover of *taḳiyya*[12] or tactical dissimulation, with *khurūdj*,[13] open insurrection launched at the appropriate time. The doctrine stressed the absolute equality that reigns among all Muslims, and the illegal nature of the ruling authority of the Umayyads who had come to power through violence. It condemned the unjust nature of this authority, which had repeatedly violated the letter and the spirit of the Qoran, particularly in fiscal matters. All the main ideological themes were supported by *ḥadīths* (sayings of the Prophet) that can be found in the Ibāḍite *Musnad*[14] of Ibn Abī'l-Rabī' and elsewhere. There are, however, no traces of Ṣufrite writings, but it seems quite reasonable to believe that the two currents – between which there was no hostility – were in agreement on fundamental issues. Revolt against Umayyad tyranny, therefore, was preached not merely as a right but also as an imperative religious duty.

It should also be pointed out that Khāridjism exercised an appeal on account of its austere and rigorous nature. It is quite obvious that there was perfect complementarity between the doctrine, on the one hand, and the psychological, socio-economic or physical environment, on the other. The actual geographical setting was also of some significance. As R. Dozy once wrote, in a few lines that have retained all their vigour despite the passing

10. Al-Rabī' b. Ḥabīb, *Musnad*, No. 819; A. J. Wensinck, *et al.*, 1933–69, s.v.

11. *Ku'ūd*: literally 'sitting', subversive actions aimed at weakening the established order.

12. *Taḳiyya*: dissimulation of true belief in order to escape persecution.

13. *Khurūdj*: going out of clandestinity to open revolt.

14. *Musnad*: collection of *ḥadīths* arranged according to the names of transmitters, not according to subject matter.

of some hundred years: in the Maghrib, 'Muslim Calvinism had at long last found its Scotland'.[15] However, apart from this almost biological complementarity, the root of the success of Khāridjism is to be found in the fact that the Berbers were caught in the midst of a storm. They felt frustrated, humiliated and oppressed and their grievances had not aroused any interest in Damascus. The storm was now ready to burst; a tide of bitterness had welled up in their hearts. The Ṣufrite and Ibāḍite movements were going to unleash this.

Victories and setbacks

Maysara thus led the revolt under the banner of Ṣufrism (122/740) and was granted the title of caliph,[16] in accordance with the doctrine whereby supreme authority is invested in the most praiseworthy of men, without distinction as to race or social status. Nevertheless, the reign of the first Berber caliph was to be very short. Having retreated to Tangier in the face of the enemy, he was relieved of his command and executed. It was his successor, Khālid b. Ḥumayd al-Zanātī who won the resounding victory of the Battle of the Nobles (123/741), which was a humiliating slaughter of the flower of the Arab aristocracy. Towards the end of the same year, this victory was followed by another, equally brilliant and just as complete, on the banks of the Sebū. Among those who died was Kulthūm b. ʿIyāḍ who had been dispatched hurriedly from the East with a sizeable army to save the situation. Everything seemed to suggest that a Berber state was about to be born in the Maghrib, united in the spirit of Ṣufrism.

This was not to be. As triumph came nearer, the seeds of discord were sown among the ranks of the victors. The following year, at the walls of the besieged city of Ḳayrawān, there were two rival armies. The first, which had established its camp at al-Asnām, was led by ʿAbd al-Wāḥid al-Hawwārī, while the second, which had chosen to encamp at al-Ḳarn, was led by ʿUkāsha. They were defeated one after the other, most unexpectedly, by Hanẓala b. Ṣafwān (early 125/743). Rejoicing took place as far away as the East where al-Layth, the Egyptian rival to Mālik, founder of Mālikism, compared this victory to that of Badr.

The new political map and external relations

The Ṣufrite kingdoms

The map of the Maghrib was completely changed after the turmoil.

15. R. Dozy, 1932, Vol. 1, p. 149.

16. Ibn ʿAbd al-Ḥakam, 1947, pp. 124–5; Ibn ʿIdhārī, 1848–51, Vol. 1, p. 53; Ibn Khaldūn, 1867, Vol. 6, p. 221.

Ḳayrawān, admittedly, had stood firm, but all the western and central Maghrib now lay beyond the reach of the authority of the East.

The Khāridjite democratic spirit, with its excessive concern for self-rule, allied to tribal sectarianism, had led to a multitude of states rising from the ruins of centralized Arab authority. The smaller of these states, with their fluctuating boundaries and uncertain life-span, are scarcely known to us. Only the largest kingdoms, which played a leading part in events, have left their mark on history.

The first of these to have been set up was Tāmasnā, on the Atlantic coast of Morocco, between Salé and Azemmour, and was better known under the disparaging term of the kingdom of the Barghawāṭa. It was founded by Ṭarīf, of the Zanāta, who had taken part in the Ṣufrite attack on Ḳayrawān. It was here that Berber nationalism was carried to the extreme. Ṣufrite Khāridjism had, in fact, facilitated political freedom, but the spiritual domination of Islam, that is to say submission to ideas imported from abroad, remained. The fourth king of the Banū Ṭarīf dynasty, Yūnus b. Ilyās (227/842–271/884) decided to endow his people with a national religion, based on Islam, so as to emancipate them more fully. He declared his grandfather, Ṣāliḥ b. Ṭarīf, to have been a prophet and attributed to him a Qoran in the Berber language and a whole range of prescribed rites and dietary restrictions even more demanding than those of Islam, and thus considered superior. This, in short, amounted to a kind of cultural emancipation aimed at putting the finishing touches to the political emancipation that had already been achieved. This process, *mutatis mutandis*, is not unlike certain contemporary phenomena of decolonization. The Banū Ṭarīf succeeded in preserving their independence and their originality for centuries and this is further illustrated in the way their Sunnite Muslim enemies could not refrain from praising their courage and their moral conduct.

While the kingdom of Tāmasnā was being formed, the kingdom of Tlemcen (124/742–173/789), was founded in the central Maghrib by Abū Ḳurra, whose father's name – Dūnnās[17] (=Donnus) – testifies to his Christian origin. Abū Ḳurra had also taken part in the abortive assault on Ḳayrawān. According to Ibn Khaldūn[18] he was raised to the dignity of caliph. His Zanāta kingdom did not, however, outlive him for long. On 15 Radjab 173/8 December 789, Tlemcen, without the slightest resistance, fell under the rule of the Idrīsids.

The third Ṣufrite kingdom, that of the Banū Wasūl, better known as the Banū Midrār, was founded at Sidjilmāsa (140/757–366/976), on what may have been an ancient site, by the Miknāsa Berbers. The kingdom, encompassing the oasis of the Tafilālet and stretching as far as the Darʿa, enjoyed a peaceful existence until 296/909 when the Fāṭimids came to power. The

17. Ibn Ḥazm, 1962, p. 51.
18. Ibn Khaldūn, 1867, Vol. 6, p. 267.

future Fāṭimid caliph, ʿUbayd Allāh al-Mahdī, entered Sidjilmāsa disguised as a merchant, where, after some hesitations, he was eventually imprisoned. At the end of 296/September 909, Abū ʿAbd Allāh al-Dāʿī took the town by storm and freed him. Al-Yasāʿ b. Midrār was executed and replaced by a Fāṭimid governor who did not manage to stay in power for more than two months. The Banū Wasūl regained power over the town and were able to govern it despite all obstacles, discarding Ṣufrism for Ibāḍism and finally for Sunnism, until they were ousted, once and for all, by the Zanāta Banū Khazrūn, backed by the Umayyads of Spain. Sidjilmāsa was, first and foremost, a major Saharan trading centre, a resting place on the gold route and a focal point for trade between the countries to the south of the Sahara, the Maghrib and the East.[19] Sidjilmāsa, which no longer exists today, has left behind it the memory of a great trading centre whose prosperity and fine dwellings (*ḳsārs*) were praised by geographers. Preliminary excavations conducted on the site were regrettably abandoned.[20]

The Ibāḍite kingdoms

The sphere of influence of Ibāḍism was initially limited to Tripoli. It was an uncomfortable position. It was vital that Tripoli, the key point on the lines of communication between east and west, should be properly defended so as to maintain the link between Ḳayrawān and the seat of the Caliphate. Thus no publicly recognized Ibāḍite kingdom was ever able to maintain its authority there for any length of time. As described above, insurrection came first from the west; it was Ṣufrite in ideology and led by the Zanāta. The Ibāḍites, who were more moderate and, by necessity, more cautious, began by simply adopting a wait-and-see attitude. They had first organized themselves, in accordance with their theology which admitted the *ḳuʿūd* and *kitmān*,[21] in preparation for when the right moment came.

This happened in 127/745. Damascus was in the grip of anarchy and Ḳayrawān had fallen into the hands of ʿAbd al-Raḥmān b. Ḥabīb, whom we shall return to later. This man made the mistake of having the Ibāḍite leader of the province of Tripoli, ʿAbd Allāh b. Masʿūd al-Tudjībī executed. The execution was the signal for *khurūdj* (open insurrection). The two Ibāḍite leaders, ʿAbd al-Djabbār b. Ḳays al-Murādī and al-Ḥārith b. Talīd al-Ḥaḍramī, both Arabs, scored victory after victory and finally took

19. Cf. Chapter 11 below.

20. These excavations were started at the request of Mohammed El-Fasi, Minister of Education at the time, but were subsequently abandoned by his successors, although showing signs of promise. Mr El-Fasi has drawn our attention to the fact that they led to the discovery of 'water-ducts with pipes that were enamelled internally', which would indicate 'an advanced level of civilization'.

21. *Kitmān*: clandestinity.

over the whole of the province of Tripoli. Unfortunately for them, like their Ṣufrite brethren, they too fell under the curse of dissension. They were subsequently discovered dead, each run through with the sword of the other. A Berber, Ismāʿīl b. Ziyād al-Nafūsī, became leader and besieged Gabès. This was to no avail, however, as ʿAbd al-Raḥmān b. Ḥabīb managed to defeat him in 131/748–9 and regained Tripoli, where he massacred the Ibāḍites on a large scale so as to rid the province of heresy.

All this was in vain, however, as Ibāḍism survived, and merely reverted to clandestinity, or *ḳuʿūd*, with the appropriate structures of *kitmān*, or secrecy, and *taḳiyya*, or tactical dissimulation, which ensured that it could survive until the time came for a new resurgence (*zuhūr*). Ibāḍism was to come violently to the fore again on two occasions. It seized power in Tripoli in 137/754, thanks to the state of anarchy which prevailed after the assassination of ʿAbd al-Raḥmān b. Ḥabīb. From Tripoli, Abū'l-K͟haṭṭāb went on towards Ḳayrawān, which had meanwhile been occupied and cruelly treated by the Ṣufrite Warfad͟jūma from southern Tunisia. He entered the city in Ṣafar 141/June–July 758 and appointed as governor ʿAbd al-Raḥmān b. Rustum, the future founder of Tiāret. At long last, K͟hārid͟jite banners fluttered in the wind throughout the Maghrib. Was this the end of its link with the East? In fact, this was not to be. In Rabīʿ I 144/June–July 761, Ibn al-As͟hʿat͟h came to raise yet again the black standard of the Abbasids at Ḳayrawān. Nevertheless, ten years later, the insurrection broke out once more with exceptional violence. Most of the K͟hārid͟jite leaders took part, including Abū Ḳurra and Ibn Rustum, without succeeding, however, in maintaining their alliance. In actual fact, only Abū Ḥātim, the Ibāḍite, who had come from Tripoli, put a stranglehold on the capital of Ifrīḳiya and reduced the inhabitants to eating their cats and dogs. At the beginning of 155/772, the starving city fell once more into the hands of the Ibāḍites, but for only a few months. On 19 D͟jumādā' II 155/27 May 772, Yazīd b. Ḥātim al-Muhallabī put an end, once and for all, to the attempts of the Ibāḍites to seize power in the eastern Maghrib.

Tiāret (Tāhert) was the only Ibāḍite state to have been successfully established for some length of time (144/761–297/910). It was founded by the Persian, ʿAbd al-Raḥmān b. Rustum who had managed to escape from Ḳayrawān when it was besieged by Ibn al-As͟hʿat͟h. Around 160/778, he was raised to the status of *imām* and his influence soon made itself felt in the Orient, whence the Ibāḍite congregation sent him substantial funds which contributed to consolidating the new state. The dynasty he founded, despite schisms of a serious nature, was never really challenged. The Rustumid state stretched from the central Maghrib as far as the D͟jabal Nafūsa, rather in the manner of a discontinuous and rather fluid plasma which engulfed the Ibāḍite faithful. This state, with its ill-defined boundaries, never possessed any complex structure and, beyond the limits of the city of Tiāret itself, the *imām*'s authority was much more of a spiritual than of a temporal nature. Despite conflicting doctrines, the Rustumids established strong ties of friendship with the Umayyads of Spain and displayed with regard to their neighbours to the east and to the west a position of neutrality which was discretion itself. Only *imām* ʿAbd al-Wahhāb (168/784–208/823) intervened against the Aghlabids by fruitlessly lending his support to the endeavours of his followers from the Djabal Nafūsa to seize Tripoli (196/811–12). Subsequently, in 283/896, Tiāret stood by when Ibrāhīm II, in a battle at Mānū, crushed the Nafūsa who had been the spearhead of the kingdom and the faithful followers of the *imām*.

The decline of Khāridjism and the founding of the Idrīsid kingdom

Khāridjism did not enter the Maghrib alone. At virtually the same time, the *iʿtizāl*[22] of the Wāṣilite tendency also won over a number of followers, and the Ibāḍites were obliged to call upon their wisest scholars to compete against them in the public contests of eloquence which created a sensation and were long remembered. A *muʿtazilite* princedom, governed by a Berber, Ibrāhīm b. Muḥammad al-Muʿtazilī, had even been successfully established at Ayzaradj to the west of Tiāret. Was it the only one of its kind?

Shīʿite proselytism, aimed initially at the East, neglected the Maghrib to begin with. From the middle of the second/eighth century, however, it began to constitute a serious rival there to Khāridjism, which suffered serious setbacks. The reason for this change can be found in the abortive rebellion led by Muḥammad al-Nafs al-Zakiyya at Mecca in 145/762 and in the bloody repression that ensued. Many ʿAlids either elected or were forced to seek refuge elsewhere. Some settled in the Maghrib where they indulged in vigorous religious and political proselytism, greatly assisted by the aura of their descent from the Prophet himself. Abū Sufyān and al-Hulwānī came to settle in the western confines of Ifrīḳiya in 145/762, where they began to lay the first foundations for the eventual advent of the Fāṭimids. One of the brothers of al-Nafs al-Zakiyya is said to have been sent to the Maghrib on a mission of reconnaissance and proselytism. Thus Khāridjism, with its democratic spirit, was beginning to give way to a diametrically opposed doctrine, theocratic Shīʿism, which taught that supreme authority must be exercised for the welfare of all by the *imām* by divine right, descended from the Prophet's line through ʿAlī and Fāṭima.

This doctrinal change was at the root of the success of the Idrīsids. Banished from the East after the abortive revolt at Fakh (169/786), Idrīs I, one of the brothers of al-Nafs al-Zakiyya, after a detour via Tangier 'where

22. *Iʿtizāl*: a trend of Muslim theology, of which the teaching is called *muʿtazila*; cf. Chapter 2 above.

he did not find what he was looking for',[23] eventually came to Wulīlī (Volubilis), an old centre of Christian civilization, where he was welcomed on 1 Rabīʿ I 172/9 August 788 by the leader of the Awrāba Berbers, the Muʿtazilite ʿAbd al-Ḥāmid. Six months later, he took the oath of investiture, the *bayʿa*. He immediately embarked on a vast campgaign of expansion and Islamization. Tlemcen soon opened its gates to him. His actions caused such concern to the Abbasid caliph that the latter had him assassinated (179/795) by a doctor, al-Shammākh al-Yamānī, sent specially from Baghdad and assisted in his task by Ibrāhīm b. al-Aghlab who was governor of the Mzāb at the time. Nothing was solved by the assassination. Idrīs I left behind him his Berber *djāriya* (slave), Kanza, who was pregnant. The child was named after his father and government was exercised for him until he could take the oath of investiture or *bayʿa*. Baghdad, however, remained on its guard. An ʿAlid, even if he was partly of Berber stock, could constitute a threat, even in a remote area on the fringe of the civilized world. The Caliphate therefore attempted, through Ḳayrawān, by means of intrigue and bribery, to crush any subversion in its embryonic stage. Rāshid, the faithful client of Idrīs I and one of the best allies of Idrīs II in childhood, lost his life in the cause. Was it to avoid the disadvantages of too lengthy a period of regency that it was decided to proceed with the investiture of Idrīs II as quickly as possible? This in fact took place as early as 187/803, but it is not known under which title; it was possibly that of *imām*, in accordance with Zaydite doctrine. This, however, did not put an end to conspiracies. In 192/808, Idrīs II gave orders for the execution of Isḥāk b. Muḥammad b. ʿAbd al-Ḥamīd – the leader of the Awrāba who had been at the root of his father's success – for having had dealings with the Aghlabid enemy. Was this a genuine accusation or rather indicative of a desire for emancipation? Was it perhaps to escape from the domination of his Berber protectors that the young king established his quarters the following year on the left bank of the Wādī Fās and surrounded himself with Arabs? With time, however, hostilities between Aghlabites and Idrīsids gradually died away. Each of the movements became too absorbed in its internal problems. It also became clear that the Idrīsids did not constitute a danger for their neighbours, and still less so for the Caliphate. Their original Shīʿite beliefs were soon discarded for Sunnism. Thus, to all intents and purposes, the Maghrib came to be divided into three spheres of influence: the Aghlabids in the east, the Khāridjites in the central region, and the Idrīsids in the west.

Idrīs II pursued the policies introduced by Idrīs I. From Volubilis, and later from Fez and beyond, overall policy consisted of Islamization and Arabization and of extending the borders of the kingdom within the limits of the spheres of influence stated above. Idrīs II ensured that his authority was recognized by the Maṣmūda of the High Atlas, retained Tlemcen

23. Ibn Abī Zarʿ, 1936, Vol. 1, p. 7.

within his orbit, seized Nefīs in the south, but failed in the west where he met with resistance from the Barghawāṭa who were occupying the Tāmasnā plateau along the Atlantic coast.

When he died (in Djumādā II 213/September 828), he was the ruler of a large and prosperous kingdom which he divided between seven of his ten sons. This division of the kingdom turned out to be quite disastrous, but it was not initially as complete as had been thought. Muḥammad (213/828–221/836), the eldest son of Idrīs II, was granted Fez and thereby received the right of overlordship. Theoretically, the kingdom remained united. His brothers, comfortably endowed, were supposed to be his vassals and remain under his authority. In actual fact, the arrangement worked badly. The achievements of Idrīs I and Idrīs II in the form of political unification and expansion were followed by the gradual disintegration of the kingdom. Subsequently, with the death of Yaḥyā II (245/859), who was notorious for his loose living, the senior branch of the family lost its regal authority. This fell into the hands of the younger branch, the Banū ʿUmar of Rīf. From then on, the crisis took a turn for the worse and was little more than a monotonous series of internal quarrels, disturbances and bloody fights which terminated only when the dynasty came to an end in 375/985. Having vanished from Morocco, it reappeared in 407/1016 in Cordoba in the person of a short-lived caliph, ʿAlī b. Ḥammūd, a descendant of the Banū ʿUmar.

The far from brilliant and yet inevitable end of the Idrīsid dynasty should not conceal the very important part it played in the destiny of Morocco. From the political standpoint, the Idrīsids were responsible for the emergence of a Moroccan national consciousness that can be traced right through to the present day. It was the Idrīsids who actually constituted Morocco and gave the country its first capital, Fez. In the extreme west of the Maghrib, Fez was to play the part that had been conferred on Ḳayrawān in Ifrīḳiya and on Cordoba in Spain. Thanks to Lévi-Provençal, we now know that Fez was founded first of all by Idrīs I who, in 172/789, built the city on the right bank of the Wādī Fās, populated by Berbers, and subsequently by Idrīs II who, in 193/809, erected a new and better planned one on the left bank opposite the first city.[24] Initially each of the two cities had its own fortified wall, and it was not until the advent of the Almoravids that they were unified. As it benefited from an extremely favourable position on the major east–west axis along the Taza valley, and possessed ample supplies of water, wood, stone for building and clay for pottery, Fez developed rapidly and was the pride of the Idrīsids. As the spiritual centre of the new state, it was and has remained ever since, an intellectual centre of the first order.

At the outset, the kingdom of the Idrīsids, established as it was in a Berber environment, was no more Arab than the kingdom of the Rustu-

24. E. Lévi-Provençal, 1938.

PLATE 10.1 *A general view of Fez with, in the foreground, the outer city wall, which was rebuilt several times by successive dynasties*

PLATE 10.2 *The minaret of the Ḳarāwiyyīn Mosque in Fez*

mids had been Persian. Nevertheless, by accepting refugees from Ḳayrawān and Cordoba, Fez rapidly became an irresistible centre of Arabization. As early as 189/805, the city welcomed five hundred horsemen, composed of Ḳays, Azd, Mudlidj, Banū Yaḥṣūb and Ṣadaf, who had come from Ifrīḳiya and Spain. It was from these men that Idrīs II, when he built his new residence, formed his first Arab court. In 202/817–18, Fez opened its gates to the crowds of survivors from the revolt of Cordoba and, in 210/825–6, to new immigrants from Ifrīḳiya. Finally, the still famous mosque and university of al-Ḳarawiyyīn was founded by a woman from Ḳayrawān in 245/859. This was to play a decisive role in the religious and cultural history of Morocco. Thus Fez became a capital that was Arab, both politically and intellectually, within a Berber environment. Fez constituted a point of departure for the progress of Arabization and Islamization, not so much through war as through a process of osmosis and influence. Although the Idrīsids were originally Zaydite Shīʿites, they do not appear to have made any particular effort to impose their doctrine. In fact, they seem to have encouraged the spread of the teachings of Mālik, the great scholar at Medina, perhaps because he had never made any mystery about his sympathy for the ʿAlids, especially during the revolt led by al-Nafs al-Zakiyya, the brother of Idrīs I. Thus Mālikism became the dominant school in Morocco during the reign of the Idrīsids.

It should be noted that the success of the Idrīsids had a contagious effect. Other descendants of ʿAlī came to win away the central Maghrib from Khāridjism with some successs. Al-Yaʿḳūbī, who toured the region between 263/876 and 276/889 listed no fewer than nine ʿAlid emirates.[25] The boundaries between these various states were naturally neither rigid nor closed. Despite political conflict and vituperation, people and goods moved quite freely throughout the region, and consequently so did ideas.

The first attempt at independence in Ifrīḳiya

After the Battle of the Nobles (122/740), local Arabs began to realize how cut off they had become from their fellow Arabs in the East. Already humiliated and shocked by their defeat, they then had to suffer, on the part of the 'Easterners' who had been dispatched to their aid, the disdain that had usually been reserved for the Berbers. On the banks of the Chelif, the Ifrīḳiyan army, commanded by Ḥabīb b. AlīʿUbayda b. ʿUḳba b. Nāfiʿ, a grandson of the conqueror of the Maghrib, almost turned its weapons, before the very eyes of the Berbers, on the 'foreign' reinforcements sent from the East under the command of Kulthūm b.ʿIyāḍ and his cousin, Baldj, such was the offensive nature of the taunting sarcasm these had inflicted on them. In answer to this, ʿAbd al-Raḥmān b. Ḥabīb proposed a duel between his father and Baldj. An open fight was narrowly avoided.

25. Al-Yaʿḳūbī, 1870–94.

PLATE 10.3 *The Ḳubba Barādiyyīn in Marrakesh: decorative detail beneath the dome*

This incident, however, together with many other corroborating factors, illustrates a phenomenon vital if one is to understand the subsequent development of the situation, namely the growth of a genuine local national consciousness in the minds of the Arabs of the Maghrib, particularly among those of the second or third generation who, having been born in the country, had never seen the East. It is this phenomenon that will provide a basis for understanding a whole series of events that would otherwise remain unintelligible.

It is thus easier to understand how ʿAbd al-Raḥmān b. Ḥabīb, who had embodied Ifrīḳiyan dignity in the face of Baldj's disdain, succeeded in expelling from Ḳayrawān Hanẓala b. Safwān (covered in glory from his victory over the Berbers, but nevertheless a 'foreigner') and in founding the first independent state in the eastern Maghrib (127/744–137/754). Acting undoubtedly in collusion with the leaders of the Ifrīḳiyan army, he had only to land at Tunis from Spain where he had prepared his plot, in order to be raised to power. With independence, the Ifrīḳiyan army immediately recovered from its recent humiliation and defeat and regained its former mettle. We are told that under the command of ʿAbd al-Raḥmān b. Ḥabīb, the army 'would never again admit to defeat'[26] and inspired terror

26. Ibn ʿIdhārī, 1848–51, Vol. 1, p. 61.

wherever it went. In 135/752–3, it successfully attacked Sicily, Sardinia and Tlemcen.

ʿAbd al-Raḥmān b. Ḥabīb was at the head of a state with an Arab leadership and living under a Sunnite doctrine; a doctrine that was anxious to preserve the spiritual unity of the Muslim community (*umma*). In view of this, he was bound to seek a *modus vivendi* with the Caliphate, i.e. with Damascus first, whose end was near, and then with Baghdad. He took without demur the oath of allegiance (*bayʿa*) to the Abbasid Caliph. This meant that he officially recognized the new regime hoping, in return, for the sake of his own power, for *de jure* recognition that would confirm and strengthen the independence which existed in fact. Al-Ṣaffāḥ (132/750–136/754) gave the impression of having implicitly accepted such a development in relations between Baghdad and Ḳayrawān. However, his successor, Abū Dja'far al-Manṣūr (136/754–158/775) clearly expressed his desire to return to the situation as it was before, especially with regard to fiscal regulations and the traditional supply of slaves. ʿAbd al-Raḥmān b. Ḥabīb knew only too well how disastrous the consequences of such demands would be. He gave the Caliph a blunt answer: 'Today, Ifrīḳiya has become entirely Muslim. We no longer have the right either to make slaves or to bring pressure to bear on the population. Above all, make no demands on me for money'.[27] This was the breaking point, followed shortly afterwards by the assassination of ʿAbd al-Raḥmān b. Ḥabīb and by the failure of the first attempt at independence which he represented. This independence collapsed into anarchy, which Ibāḍite Khāridjism attempted to use to its advantage but to little lasting avail.

The Aghlabids

Abū Djaʿfar al-Manṣūr succeeded in bringing Ifrīḳiya back into the fold for another forty years or so (144/761–184/800). Over that span of time, the country only experienced law and order when the first two Muhallabids (155/772–174/791), after the second abortive attempt of Ibāḍism to establish itself at Ḳayrawān, managed to assert themselves through their personal stature and experience. Their efforts constituted a timorous attempt at establishing a dynasty. This did not, in fact, meet with success and, from 178/794 onwards, the bitterness of the struggle between the rival factions of the *djund* (Arab army) to seize power by force reached such intensity that Ifrīḳiya became completely ungovernable. The region was now just a source of unending concern to the Caliphate, and weighed heavily on the treasury. Besides, Baghdad was increasingly in a position in which it could not afford to intervene militarily. Heeding the wise counsel of Harthama b. Aʿyān, Hārūn al-Rashīd decided accordingly to grant Ifrīḳiya the in-

27. Ibn al-Athīr, 1885–6, Vol. 5, p. 314.

dependence that it would undoubtedly have taken by force. This decision was all the more easily arrived at through the opportune presence of a valid representative, Ibrāhīm ibn al-Aghlab, the founder of the Aghlabid kingdom (184/800–296/909).

Ibrāhīm b. al-Aghlab was not an unknown figure. His father had governed Ifrīḳiya (148/765–150/767) and had died there. He himself was appointed vice-governor of the Mzāb (179/795) by Harthama b. A'yān, who was governor of Ifrīḳiya at the time (179/795–181/797), and immediately gave proof of his allegiance to the Abbasids by contributing effectively to the struggle against the Idrīsids. In 181/797, he was raised to the rank of governor and soon had yet another opportunity to display his loyalty and discipline. In the contest for power launched by the insurrection of Tammām, vice-governor of Tunis, he chose to play the part of a champion of legality. He defeated the rebel and re-established the legal governor, the colourless Muḥammad b. Muḳātil al-ʿAkkī. Had he been totally disinterested in acting in such a way? Was his action the result of a shrewd calculation? Whatever his motives, the fact remains that he was insistently urged and invited to take al-ʿAkkī's place. He only gave in to these solicitations on his own terms, namely that he would accede to the status of emir provided that he could not be unseated and that the title would be hereditary. He offered in exchange to give up the subsidy of 100 000 dinars made over to Ifrīḳiya from the *kharādj* of Egypt and to contribute, for his part, an annual due of 40 000 dinars to the treasury of Baghdad. Al-Rashīd accepted the proposal, which in fact was quite advantageous to both parties. Ifrīḳiya could not indeed remain the exception to the rule and be left out of the movement for independence launched in 122/740 by the revolt of Maysara. However, the independence of Ifrīḳiya was achieved through negotiations, without any schism or break with Baghdad.

The first three rulers of the new dynasty devoted their efforts to consolidating their regime. Naturally, they were not able to avoid rebellions within their army. The most serious of these insurrections, which nearly toppled the Aghlabid throne, was fomented by Manṣūr al-Ṭunbudhī (209/824–213/828). Its ultimate failure marked the beginning of a period of peace and maturity during which Ifrīḳiya enjoyed a period of legendary prosperity. Abū Ibrāhīm Aḥmad (242/856–249/863) left behind him the memory of an ideal prince, entirely devoted to the interests of his subjects. He had many *ribāṭ*s[28] built for the defence of the coast and, to ensure an adequate water supply for Ḳayrawān, he equipped the city with cisterns which arouse admiration even today. The golden age, followed soon after by the decline, occurred under the reign of Ibrāhīm II (261/875–289/902) which began very auspiciously. His subjects enjoyed a system of equitable justice and wise government. However, the king unfortunately suffered from melancholia and his mind gradually became unbalanced. He made

28. *Ribāṭ*: cf., for the various meanings of the term, Chapter 13 below.

PLATES 10.4a–b *The ribāṭ of Sūs. Excavations revealed that it was built on pre-Islamic foundations*

PLATE 10.4(a) (*above*) *View of the surrounding wall, single entrance gate and minaret tower*

PLATE 10.4(b) (*below*) *Inner courtyard showing the two-storey structure: the small dome crowns the monumental entrance*

more and more exactions and committed more and more political errors, providing Shīʿite proselytism with excellent advantages.

Shīʿite proselytism, with Abū ʿAbd Allāh al-Dāʿī as spokesman preaching among the Kutāma Berbers of Kabylia, proclaimed the advent of the *Mahdī*, or Saviour, who would establish a paradise of justice on earth where the Divine Sun, rising in the west, would shine at last with equal intensity on all. Proselytism of this kind met with success, and the Aghlabid regime, possessing vast material resources but deprived of popular support, was accordingly overwhelmed by the hordes sweeping down from the impoverished mountain areas and taking possession of the fertile valleys. The decisive blow fell in the region of El-Kēf, at al-Urbus (22 Djumādā II 296/18 March 909). Ziyādat Allāh III, carrying off the riches hoarded by his ancestors, fled at night by torchlight from the opulent princely city of Raḳḳāda which had been founded by his grandfather. On the following day, the city was looted and plundered.

The independence movement whose ebb and flow we have just studied was not limited to the Maghrib. Spain, for instance, underwent very similar developments but was hardly influenced by Khāridjism. Here, the struggle took place primarily between the two major Arab tribal groups, who were traditional enemies, the Ḳays and the Kalb. Yūsuf b. ʿAbd al-Raḥmān al-Fihrī, a cousin of ʿAbd al-Raḥmān b. Ḥabīb, seemed at first to be gaining the upper hand (129/747–138/756). His plans were finally thwarted by a leading figure, the Umayyad, ʿAbd al-Raḥmān b. Muʿāwiya b. Hishām b. ʿAbd al-Malik, whose mother, Rāh, was a Berber captive from the Nafza tribe. He escaped to the Maghrib from where, after a veritable odyssey, he was able to re-enter Spain and found an independent emirate. In 316/929, the eighth sovereign of the dynasty, ʿAbd al-Raḥmān III, transformed the emirate into a caliphate, thereby following the example set by the Fāṭimids. This was the golden age of Muslim Spain.

External relations

The Maghrib of the Middle Ages, with its extension into the Iberian peninsula, had interests which lay in two directions; northwards, to the Christian world, a land of trade and *djihād* and southwards, to Africa south of the Sahara, the source of gold. With the advent of the Arabs, the Maghrib entered into a particularly active phase of its history characterized by territorial and economic expansion, a process that was both violent and peaceful.

The tide of expansion beyond the Pyrenees was halted once and for all in 114/732. The emirs of Cordoba were subsequently forced into a defensive *djihād* aimed at containing Christian pressure on their northern border. The final loss of Barcelona as early as 185/801 illustrates the very modest success of the *djihād*. The final thrust from the Maghrib towards Europe was launched in the third and fourth centuries from Ḳayrawān. Ziyādat

Allāh I (201/817–223/838), to relieve some of the pressure on Ifrīḳiya which was enduring constant rebellions within the *djund*, seized the opportunity offered to him by Euphemius, the patrician of Sicily, for intervening in the island, despite opposition from most of the *faḳīhs*, who wished to abide by the treaties binding the two kingdoms. The attack was led by Asad b. al-Furāt, a *ḳādī* who was in favour of the campaign. The conquest, in which Ḳayrawān was opposed by Byzantium, soon became a difficult and laborious task. Begun in 212/827, it did not end until some fifty years later with the capture of Syracuse (264/878). In the meantime, the Aghlabids settled in Calabria, in southern Italy, from where they harassed several southern towns. The foray most sorely felt by all Christendom was that against Rome, which was attacked from the sea on 23 August 846. After three months of devastation, during which even the Holy Places were not spared, the tragedy came to an end when, on the journey home, the army perished in a storm. The alarm that gripped all of southern Italy was increased still further when Ibrāhīm II, assuming personal responsibility for directing operations, landed on Italian soil in Radjab 289/June 902, fired by the foolish design of reaching Mecca via Rome and Byzantium. The venture came to a close some months later when the emir, suffering from dysentery, expired beneath the walls of Cosenza (17 Dhu l-Ḳaʿda 289/23 October 902). From then on, the retreat began. It should be noted that these events enabled a small Muslim emirate, founded by mercenaries who were initially in the pay of the Italian princes, to hold its ground in Bari from 847 until 871.[29]

These violent clashes, which are but the accidents of history, should not conceal from us the existence of peaceful, fruitful relations which were maintained even during the hostilities. Fifty years of conflict, marked by some twenty naval expeditions launched between 84/703 and 135/752, mainly against Sicily and Sardinia, were followed by fifty years of total peace in the western Mediterranean (752–807) during which truces were concluded and ambassadors exchanged. The best known of these missions was the one which set off from Baghdad via Ḳayrawān to Carolingian Gaul in the spring of 801. Contrary to what H. Pirenne thought, there was no break between the Empire of Muḥammad and that of Charlemagne.[30] Trade was maintained and even included materials of strategic value, such as copper, iron or weapons – which Ifrīḳiya supplied to Sicily – despite the ban imposed by the Church on the one hand, and the protests of the *faḳīhs* on the other. At the height of the war in Sicily, Naples, Amalfi, Gaeta, Venice and Genoa, among other ports, maintained their trade with the Maghrib and did not hesitate to conclude alliances with it. One particular event is of special significance. In 266/880, just off the Lipari Islands, an Aghlabid fleet suffered a severe defeat. It was reported that the quantity of

29. Cf. G. Musca, 1964.

30. On the Pirenne thesis see Chapter 1 above.

oil seized was such that it brought about an unprecedented drop in the price of this commodity in Byzantium. It was quite obviously a trading fleet on its way to Italy which was caught up unexpectedly in the battle. This goes to show that the trade routes established since Antiquity were still in use and had weathered upheavals of all kinds. There are many other indications pointing in the same direction. One, in particular, deserves to be stressed here, namely that the papal bulls of John VIII were written on Muslim papyrus.

Relations with Africa south of the Sahara were devoid of violence during the period under consideration. Africa, admittedly, supplied slaves, but this was not, within the context of the period, necessarily a violent activity, nor for that matter a specifically African concern. Naples, for instance, sold white slaves or *ṣaḳāliba*[31] to the Maghrib, and the part played by Verdun in the trading of eunuchs is well known. In this instance, it would be useful to remind ourselves of the fact that the term 'slave' is derived from the medieval Latin *sclavus*, which came from slavus (=Slav). The Slavs, traded under the name of Ṣaḳāliba, had constituted an abundant source of servile labour in the Middle Ages. In Ḳayrawān or in Cordoba, the Africans purchased in the regions south of the Sahara served primarily in the army. They thereby contributed very efficiently to Ifrīḳiyan expansion in Sicily and southern Italy, and inside Muslim Spain they consolidated the authority of the Aghlabid and Umayyad emirs.

Trade with sub-Saharan Africa went back to early Antiquity and was conducted mainly along two routes, one along the Atlantic coast, and the other ending at Zawīla in the south of Libya. The volume of trade was, however, modest. As the Maghrib entered the Arab Muslim world, trade, from the eighth century onwards, developed on an unprecedented scale. The main trade route at that time linked Awdāghust (Tegdaoust?) to Sidjilmāsa which was a veritable fountainhead for the distribution of gold from *Bilād al-Sūdān*. We know the surprise and admiration felt by Ibn Ḥawḳal,[32] the geographer and merchant, when he visited Awdāghust in 340/951 and saw a cheque for 42 000 dinars made out to a merchant of the city by a colleague from Sidjilmāsa. The cheque, symbolizing the volume of trade between these two centres, also demonstrates that the banking system, which has been studied so painstakingly by Goitein with regard to the East, through the documents of the Geniza,[33] also underpinned the trading activities of the western territories of Islam. Sidjilmāsa was like the hub of a wheel from which the routes, like spokes, led off to Fez, Tangier and Cordoba; to Tlemcen and Tiāret; and towards Ḳayrawān and the East. These trade routes continued towards Europe across Sicily and Italy,

31. Mr Mohammed El-Fasi informs me that 'even today, houses in Fez still have a room on the first floor called *Ṣaḳlabiyya*, because it was reserved in former times for the white slaves (Ṣaḳāliba).

32. Ibn Ḥawḳal, 1938, pp. 96–7; N. Levtzion, 1968a; J. M. Cuoq, 1975, p. 71.

33. S. D. Goitein, 1967.

across the Iberian peninsula, or more directly via what Charles Courtois called the 'island route' which went past Sardinia and Corsica and ended up in Provence.[34]

Within this framework of multiple movements of people and goods, the wealthy merchant was also on occasion an ambassador or an influential political figure. This is precisely what happened to 'Muḥammad b. 'Arafa, a fine, distinguished and generous man who was sent to bear a precious gift to the King of the Sudan by Aflaḥ b. 'Abd al-Wahhāb' (208/823–258/871), *imām* of Tiāret.[35] Muḥammad b. 'Arafa, who was immensely wealthy, subsequently held the highest positions in the Rustumid capital. The embassy with which he was entrusted was the earliest one that we know, from diplomatic records, to have taken place between the Maghrib and sub-Saharan Africa.

Society and culture

Density and variety of population

The Maghrib of the Middle Ages was never as populous as it was in the third/ninth century, a fact which accounts in some way for its expansion overseas. Furthermore, the prevailing trend at the time, quite unlike that of later periods, was towards the sedentarization of the nomads who populated the central Maghrib and the areas bordering on the Sahara, and towards urbanization. The four major political and cultural capitals of the region – Ḳayrawān. Tiāret, Sidjilmāsa and Fez – were the fruit of an Arab Muslim culture. Ḳayrawān in the third/ninth century certainly had several hundred thousand inhabitants, and Ibn Ḥawḳal believed that Sidjilmāsa was equally populous and prosperous.[36] The concentration of the population in towns was not the same throughout this part of the world. The eastern Maghrib, Sicily and Spain, for instance, were the most urbanized areas. It is not possible, here, to mention all the major towns. Let it be noted, however, as a guide, that Cordoba is estimated to have had a population of a million in the fourth/tenth century.[37]

The distinguishing feature of society was its very varied composition. The population of the Maghrib had as its basis the Berbers, mentioned in the previous chapter, who were themselves very diverse. Spain was populated mainly with Iberians and Goths. Various foreign elements were merged with these two basic substrata, especially at the outer limits of the region. Until the mid-fifth/eleventh century, the Arabs were few in number. In Ifrīḳiya for instance, there were several tens of thousands, pos-

34. C. Courtois, 1957.
35. Ibn al-Saghīr, 1975, p. 340; J. M. Cuoq, 1975, p. 56.
36. Ibn Ḥawḳal, 1938, p. 96.
37. E. Lévi-Provençal, 1950–3, Vol. 3, p. 172.

sibly a hundred thousand or a hundred-and-fifty thousand at the most. The Arabs were even less numerous in Spain and there were practically none in the Maghrib, where traces of their presence can only be found in Tiāret, Sidjilmāsa and Fez. The Berbers, mostly from northern Morocco, had for their part spread into the Iberian peninsula where they outnumbered the Arabs. In addition to these, there were two other ethnic components whose numbers and specific role are even harder to evaluate. On the one hand, there were the Europeans – peoples of Latin, Germanic or even Slavonic origin – considered globally to be Ṣaḳāliba, or slaves; on the other hand, there were the blacks, inextricably associated with the life of wealthy or comfortably-off families or who served in the personal guard of the emirs, as has already been stated.

The social strata

Medieval society in the western territories of Islam was composed, as in recent Antiquity, of three categories of men: slaves, former slaves, generally called *mawālī*, and freemen by birth.

The slaves were very numerous in major urban areas, but virtually unknown in areas with a predominantly nomadic population and strong 'tribal' structures. If we estimate them to have formed one-fifth of the population of the major cities of Ifrīḳiya and Spain, one has the impression, reading the documents we have at our disposal, that this is well below the real figure. As in other social strata, there were those that were fortunate and those that were less so. The slaves were to be found in the harems – as white or black favourites and eunuchs – as in every sector of economic life and at all levels, ranging from the wealthy steward managing his master's fortune, to the hard-working peasant or the wretched servant who was the hewer of wood and drawer of water. Generally speaking, however, the status of the slave was unenviable, despite the safeguards provided by the *fiḳh* or law, and the exceptional success of certain slaves. Their economic role was, however, immense as they were the machine tools of the time. One has the clear impression that, in the eastern part of the Maghrib and in Spain, a very considrable proportion of domestic, craft and rural workers were slaves or semi-slaves, especially on the large estates that sometimes encompassed several villages. However, the status of the slave, no matter how unpleasant it might have been, never lasted indefinitely. There was always a way out. It is a well-known fact that the Qoran lays considerable emphasis on the merits of enfranchisement. Accordingly, the ranks of slaves, through the combined effect of enfranchisement and the purchase of liberty, were constantly thinned out as slaves aspired to move up to another and equally numerous social category, that of the *mawālī*. Social mobility, which really did exist, worked in favour of freedom.

The *mawālī*, though legally free through enfranchisement, continued to live in their former master's entourage, thereby constituting his clientele. A motley collection of humble folk also belonged to the *mawālī*. Non-Arabs, they deliberately put themselves under the protection of an influential person, an Arab, and adopted his *nisba* or 'tribal' ancestry and consequently became a member of his *gens*. Both patrons and clients found advantage in the organic ties of the *walā*.[38] The client benefited from his master's protection, while the patron acquired prestige and power according to the size of his clientele.

The freemen in general were divided into two classes: the aristocratic minority, influential and usually wealthy, the *khāṣṣa*; and the majority of plebeians, the *ʿāmma*. The *khāṣṣa* was the ruling class, with somewhat ill-defined boundaries. It consisted of the elite by birth or by military tradition, the intellectual elite, and, in general, all persons of any wealth. The affluence of some members of the *khāṣṣa* – such as the Ibn Ḥumayd, a family of Aghlabid viziers who had grown immensely rich through the ivory trade – occasionally reached fabulous proportions. The *ʿāmma*, on the other hand, was composed of a variety of peasants, small farmers, craftsmen, shopkeepers and a mass of labourers who hired out their services in the fields and in the towns. At the lowest levels of the *ʿāmma*, the most wretched lived in almost complete destitution. None the less, hope of gaining admittance to the *khāṣṣa* was not denied to the members of the *ʿāmma*. No rigid legal structure acted as an obstacle to this.

Religious and racial osmosis

On top of the ethnic and social barriers between men were others of a religious nature which did not necessarily follow the same paths. At the time of the conquest of the Maghrib, traditional religion, Judaism and Christianity existed side by side. Islam attracted a following from all social classes and by the ninth century had become without any doubt the religion of the majority. While virtually nothing remained of traditional religion, Judaism and Christianity retained a considerable following among the native populations. These followers were the traditional *dhimmī*s, or protégés of Islam, who, in addition to religious freedom, enjoyed a separate fiscal and legal status. In Spain, they had a *comes* as their leader, sometimes referred to also as *defensor* or *protector*. Apart from occasional short periods of agitation, many anecdotes point quite clearly to the fact that *dhimmī*s and Muslims led the same kind of life and usually lived on good terms with each other. There is no indication of the existence of a ghetto or of any religious riots. What is more, the degree of harmony was such that in some instances, certain Christians, particularly in the lower classes, gave genuine veneration to the celebrated Muslim ascetics in their community. Harmony of this kind went one stage further within the confines of family life. *Djāriya*s, or slave-wives to Muslims, who had retained their Christian or Jewish convictions,

38. *Walā*: relationship between the master and the dependent person or freed slave.

were, in fact, quite common. The children born of such mixed marriages usually took up their father's religion. Sometimes, however, a strange compromise was reached, as in the case of certain social groups in Sicily where the daughters adhered to the religon of their mother.

Similarly, colour prejudice was quite unknown in the western territories of Islam during the Middle Ages. The Arabs undoubtedly believed themselves to be superior, as we have already stressed, but they mingled willingly with other races. Black *d̲j̲āriya*s were appreciated no less than others, and mulattoes, free from any complex whatsoever, moved freely at any level in the social hierarchy. Religious and racial diversity was thus an inherent part of the basic structure of the family unit. Hence, as inter-religious and inter-racial marriages became more frequent, family lineage, despite the leading role conferred on the father by Arab tradition, became more obscure. It is a fact of life that blue blood gradually thins and loses its colour. In short, Hispano-Maghribian society, amazingly tolerant as it was during a medieval period reputed to have been one of fanaticism, and particularly composite and heterogeneous at its two extremes, was a network of cells which were both very specific and also intimately inter-related through a system of multiple and intricate ties.

Language, arts and sciences

Several languages were spoken in the western territories of Islam during the period under consideration. First and foremost were the Berber dialects, all very different from each other, and very widespread throughout the Maghrib especially in the rural and mountainous areas where Arabic could not easily penetrate. These dialects, however, never followed the armies to the northern coast of the Mediterranean. Indeed, no trace whatsoever of Berber dialects has been found in Spain and Sicily where the local tongues had to compete exclusively with Arabic. In Spain, a Hispano-Romance language, derived from Latin, did develop and came to be widely used both in the countryside and in the cities. Similarly, traces have been found of an Ifrīḳiyan-Romance language which must have been particularly widely used among Christian city-dwellers.[39] All these were essentially oral languages. The only cultural or written language was Arabic, which was used not only by the Muslims, but also by the *d̲h̲immī*s who, judging by the example of the Jew, Maimonides,[40] were able to use it in some instances for expressing particularly vigorous ideas.

There were a considerable number of cultural centres. Every provincial capital, and all the major towns had their poets, their *adīb*s (men of letters) and their theologians or *faḳīh*s. There were times when the most famous theologians were sought out – as when Tiāret was threatened by the *iʿtizāl*

39. T. Lewicki, 1951–2.
40. Maimonides (d. 1204), a native of Cordoba, a famous physician and philosopher.

– even in the fastnesses of the mountains of Nafūsa. However, the only detailed information we have at our disposal today concerns the three centres that were unquestionably the most outstanding, viz. Ḳayrawān, Cordoba and Fez. In these centres, as throughout the western territories of Islam, literature drew most of its inspiration from the East. Throughout the breadth of Islam, it was the same poets and the same *adībs* who awakened admiration, and the same literary paths that were pursued. The *riḥla* or journey, combining the virtues of study with those of a pilgrimage, maintained close and uninterrupted communication between the capitals of the West and those of the East. The peoples of the Maghrib, in particular, entertained for their masters in the East admiration that verged on superstition. People and ideas moved from one country to another at a speed that is all the more surprising as communications were slow, arduous and even dangerous. The best illustration of the presence of Eastern culture in the heart of the Muslim West is perhaps the *'Iḳd al-Farīd*, the anthology compiled by the *adīb* from Cordoba, Ibn 'Abd Rabbihi (246/860–328/939).[41] It is composed essentially of extracts from Eastern authors, so much so that al-Ṣāḥib b. 'Abbād, the celebrated Buyid vizier and man of letters of the second half of the fourth/tenth century, is said to have exclaimed on looking at it: 'These are our own goods being sent back to us!'

Nevertheless, Ḳayrawān, Cordoba and the other big towns had poets and men of letters who, although they did not attain the renown of the great Oriental poets, would not have been out of place in the *'Iḳd*. In Cordoba, for example, there were the eulogist, Ibrāhīm b. Sulaymān, who sang the praises of 'Abd al-Raḥmān II (207/822–238/852), Faradj b. Sallām, lexicographer, poet and doctor of medicine who, while on a journey in Iraq, befriended al-Djāḥiẓ (d. 255/868) whose works, especially the *Bayān*, he introduced into Spain; and 'Uthmān b. Muthannā (179/795–273/866) who brought back from the Orient the *Dīwān* by the illustrious Abū Tammām who had been his master in poetry. In Ifrīḳiya too, no less than in other parts of the Muslim world, there was among the educated classes a taste for verse, and everyone was something of a poet. There were even some princes who were quite proficient at writing verse, such as Muḥammad b. Ziyādat Allāh II (d. 283/896) who compiled two anthologies, both of which have unfortunately been lost: *Kitāb Raḥāt al-Ḳalb* and *Kitāb al-Zahr*. Mention should also be made of *Lakīt al-Mardjān*, *Risālat al-Wāḥida* and *Ḳuṭb al-Adab*, all lost, by Abū' l-Yusr al-Kātib (d. 298/910–11) who had directed the chancellery for the Aghlabids and the Fāṭimids. The capital of the Aghlabids also had its philosophers who were sufficiently eminent to have been classified separately by al-Zubaydī in his *Ṭabaḳāt al-Naḥwiyyīn* (The Classes of Grammarians). It would seem, however, that philosophy, which was already beginning to achieve some

41. Ibn 'Abd Rabbihi (1876).

recognition in the Orient with al-Kindī (d. *c.* 256/870), was not, and never was to be, accepted in Ifrīḳiya. The city that Sīdī 'Uḳba dedicated to the defence of Islam could not come to terms with freedom of thought that was as suspicious as this. This discipline was as yet only in its infancy, even in Spain where it was subsequently explored by masters of world renown, especially Ibn Masarra (d. 319/931).[42]

Throughout the Muslim world of the Middle Ages, people not only enjoyed occasional indulgence in verse writing and philosophical discussion, but also enjoyed drinking (some intoxicating drinks, such as *nabīdh*, were considered lawful by certain schools of *fiḳh*), singing and dancing, especially at the court and in aristocratic or bourgeois circles. A whole set of rules of etiquette, which is reflected in literature, was instituted to govern polite conduct in such circumstances. Ifrīḳiya and Spain in particular, were no exceptions to the rule. The *djāriya*s, trained in the singing and dancing schools of Medina and Baghdad, were much sought after and their price sometimes involved stupendous sums. Famous composers were similarly sought after. One of these, Ziryāb (173/789–238/852) built up a private fortune and exerted considerable influence. Ziryāb was black and was a *mawlā* of the Abbasids. As such, he was admitted to the famous singing and dancing school directed by Isḥāḳ al-Mawsilī (150/757–235/850). By the skill he acquired and by the gifts he displayed, he soon provoked his master's feelings of jealousy and had to go into exile. After spending some time in Ḳayrawān he went to Cordoba at the invitation of al-Haḳam I (180/796–206/822) who sent Manṣūr, a Jewish singer at court, to meet him. Al-Haḳam died in the meantime and Ziryāb was welcomed by his successor, 'Abd al-Raḥmān II (206/822–238/852) with princely courtesy. Ziryāb brought profound changes to the customs of the court and the ruling class in society. He brought with him refinement and the courtly spirit. He taught the men and women of the court how to behave at table, how to wear make-up, how to groom their hair and adapt their mode of dress to the time of day or to circumstances. Ziryāb's music, aided by certain instrumental improvements of his own invention, soon replaced all the old melodies and has lived on through the centuries until today. The *mālūf*, which is still in fashion in the Maghrib today and Spanish *flamenco* are remotely descended from the revolution brought about in music by Ziryāb.[43]

At this time, science had barely gone beyond the stage of infancy in Spain. In Ḳayrawān however, the school of medicine, with such masters as Isḥāḳ b. 'Imrān and Ziyād b. Kalfūn (d. 308/920–1) already enjoyed a certain renown. The third/ninth century should be remembered especially, apart from achievements in military and court architecture, for two of the finest monuments of Islam, the mosque of Ḳayrawān, which was built

42. Cf. M. Asín Palacios, 1914.
43. On Ziryāb see E. Lévi-Provençal, 1950–3, Vol. 2, pp. 136 ff.

PLATE 10.5 *The great lake of Raḳḳāda, near Ḳayrawān. Massive embankments served as a breakwater against waves whipped up by the wind*

chiefly by the Aghlabids, and the mosque of Cordoba which, although founded by ʿAbd al-Raḥmān I in 169/785, did not reach completion until two centuries later under the rule of the mighty 'Master of the Palace', Ibn Abī Āmir (377/988). It should also be noted that the celebrated university and mosque of al-Ḳarawiyyīn, in Fez, was founded in 245/859 by a woman from Ḳayrawān.

Religious thought

Throughout the Middle Ages, cultural matters remained essentially in the hands of ecclesiastics, that is to say, *faḳīhs*, in the Muslim world. In the third/ninth century no school of thought had yet gained the upper hand, so there existed relative freedom of thought and the violence of passionately held beliefs. Strangely enough, the capital city where freedom of thought was most inhibited was Cordoba. There was greater tolerance, as Ibn al-Ṣaghīr has proved, at Tiāret, though it was dominated by the Ibāḍites, reputed for their intransigence. As for Ḳayrawān, it is an accepted fact that from the mid-third/ninth century onwards, the Great Mosque was open to the various circles of Ibāḍites, Ṣufrites and Muʿtazilites, who dared to plead and openly teach their 'unorthodox' or 'heretical' opinions before the

PLATE 10.6 *Door and blind arches of the west façade of the mosque at Cordoba*

very eyes and ears of the Sunnites. This tolerance, however, whether broad or limited, was not, of course, indifference. Not by any means. The debates were lively, vociferous and sometimes led to violent disputes followed by blows. This was the case, for example, of Asad (d. 213/828), the undisputed champion of Sunnism in his day, who, with kicks, made Ibn al-Farrā', the leader of the Mu'tazilite school, retract there and then a statement that dared to contradict him, before his own congregation, on the question of the vision of God in eternity.[44]

The third/ninth century was an era with a passion for law and theology, a vast enterprise for constructing and organizing the present and the future. Assertions, denials, refutations and counter-refutations followed each other in succession, either verbal or written, but invariably vehement and indignant. On the one hand, the Mu'tazilites in power in Ḳayrawān delved into the arsenal of dialectics, while on the other, the Sunnites, who constituted a majority within the population and often played the part of the opposition, drew their inspiration from tradition. The Ancients and the Moderns were already at loggerheads! We shall be publishing in the near future a collection of polemical works which conjure up the atmosphere that prevailed in Ḳayrawān at the time.

What was the subject of conversation? *Irdjā'*, or faith and redemption. Was faith merely a matter of conviction or was it the formulation of beliefs and their translation into deeds? Practical problems of politics and ethics stood out against the backcloth of this abstract and metaphysical debate. The question of free will and predestination or *ḳadar* was also an obvious subject for discussion. As the central, formative problem of the *i'tizāl*, *ḳadar* has been at the root of much controversy in all religions and philosophies without anyone ever having really succeeded in squaring the circle. We know today that this problem fired the enthusiasm of the Ifrīḳiya people and that the debates held beneath the walls of the *ribāṭ* at Sūsa led to considerable commotion. There was lively enthusiasm for a host of other questions: the attributes of the Deity; the vision of God in the afterlife; the essence of the Qoran; etc. Theology, therefore, was at the very heart of all discussions and pervaded all aspects of public life. The third/ninth century can therefore be said to have been a period of intense intellectual activity.

Subsequently, from the mid-third/ninth century onwards – when Saḥnūn (160/777–240/854) expelled the 'myrmidons of heresy' from the Great Mosque of Ḳayrawān – when orthodoxy was beginning at last to gain the upper hand, the wrangling went on unabated. Disputes emerged and developed within Sunnism and similar feuds were occurring in the ranks of the Ibāḍites or Ṣufrites.

Against this background of passion, polemics and strife, the presence of a few illustrious *faḳīh*s stood out clearly. In Spain, there were 'Īṣā b. Dīnār (d. 212/827), 'Abd al-Malik b. Ḥabīb (d. 238/852), and, above all, Yaḥyā b.

44. M. Talbi, 1966, p. 220.

Yaḥyā al-Laythī (152/769–234/849), the Berber *mawlā*. In Ḳayrawān, there were Asad b. al-Furāt (142/759–213/828) and his rival, Saḥnūn b. Sa'īd al-Tanūkhī. All, except Asad, who was claimed especially by the Hanafites, were instrumental in the triumph of Mālikism in the western territories of Islam. Saḥnūn played a particularly decisive role in these developments, and his *Mudawwana*, a monumental legal compendium, put into writing and led to the ultimate pre-eminence of the teachings of Mālik. Saḥnūn was to become venerated as a master and had a remarkable number of disciples. We are told that there were some seven hundred 'genuine luminaries in every town'. These luminaries spread the word not only in Ifrīḳiya but also in Spain. Spaniards indeed flocked to Saḥnūn's lessons in great numbers. They were spoken of in Ḳayrawān in the third/ninth century as the Scots and Germans were to be spoken of later in Paris. 'Iyāḍ, in his *Madārik*, quotes the names of fifty-seven Spanish *faḳīh*s who had carried back to their homeland the teachings of the master of Ḳayrawān and had made known throughout their country his principal work, the *Mudawwana*.[45]

The period which we have just considered, all too briefly, was a decisive one in the history of the Maghrib. It was then that this part of Africa acquired its independence, succeeded in tracing its borders, which have remained virtually unchanged to the present day, and fashioned the principal features of its cultural and spiritual identity.

45. M. Talbi, 1962.

11 The role of the Sahara and Saharians in relationships between north and south

T. LEWICKI

In this chapter we shall be discussing the history of the Sahara and the role played by that desert in the relations between North Africa and the Sudan between the second/eighth and sixth/twelfth centuries. The sole sources of information on which we can draw to retrace the past of the Sahara during that period, apart from archaeology and tradition, are written sources of Arab origin. The information they provide about the Sahara dates only from the second/eighth century and was initially very sparse. It was not until the fourth/tenth century that it became more plentiful, coming to a peak in the fifth/eleventh and sixth/twelfth centuries in the two great geographical works of al-Bakrī and al-Idrīsī, which abound in details concerning the Sahara and the Sudan.[1]

Ecology and population

Owing to the fact that the transition from non-desert to desert areas is generally a gradual process, the boundaries of the Sahara are fairly vague. If, however, various geographical factors are taken into account, and especially the climate, the boundaries of the Sahara can be defined as follows: in the east the natural boundary of the Sahara (including the Libyan Desert) is the Nile, and in the west the Atlantic Ocean. In the north the Sahara extends as far as the Libyan Plateau, the Syrte Desert, Djabal Nafūsa, Shoṭṭ Djarīd, Shoṭṭ Meghīr, the Saharan Atlas and Wādī Dar'a, thus taking in the trade centres in the north of the Sahara, such as Fezzān, Ghadāmes, Wādī Rīgh, Wargla and Sidjilmāsa, which grew rich through trading with the Lands of the Black (*Bilād al-Sūdān*). As for the southern boundary of the Sahara, it passes roughly through the mouth of the Senegal River, the top of the loop of the Niger River and through the Chad basin (taking in Ennedi), joining up again with the Nile at around 16°N latitude. The dryness of the air and the lack of water, which are basic

1. For this reason, we have slightly overstepped the chronological limits laid down for this volume.

features of the Saharan climate, cause the grazing lands of the Sahara to be very scattered and the palm groves and garden centres there to be rather insignificant, with the exception of the northern Sahara. Partly as a result of these factors, this desert was very thinly populated in the early Middle Ages, as it is today, and vast stretches of the Sahara, as for instance Madjābat al-Kubrā in the western Sahara and the Libyan Desert, were with few exceptions, completely uninhabited. Despite these facts, however, the Sahara was not only a barrier but also a link between the countries of northern Africa and the Sudan, playing an extremely important role in relations, particularly trade relations, between north and south. The rare and difficult caravan routes that crossed this desert were frequented, during the Muslim period, by traders from the Maghrib, Ifrīḳiya, Egypt and the various trade centres of the northern Sahara. In this trade between the northern countries and the Sudan the main role was in fact played by North African and Egyptian merchants, alongside Ibāḍite Berber traders from Bilād al-Djarīd and Sidjilmāsa.

From the second/eighth to the sixth/twelfth centuries the population of the Sahara was extremely mixed. The western and central Sahara was inhabited by peoples of Berber stock sometimes mixed with black African blood. As for the eastern Sahara, including the Libyan Desert, its northern part was also inhabited by people of Berber stock, while its southern part was peopled by negroid people belonging to the various Tubu groups, such as the Zaghāwa, the Teda and the Daza. These peoples reached as far north as the Kufra and Taizerbo oases, that is to around the 26°N line of latitude. It is to be noted that certain features of Tubu anthropology and culture suggest a considerable degree of Libyco-Berber interbreeding. It is also to be noted that, during the period under consideration in this chapter, there was no lack of Arabs in the Sahara, including city-dwellers and nomadic herdsmen.

The Berber population of the Sahara, which played an extremely important role in the establishment of relations between North Africa and Egypt, on the one hand, and the Sudan on the other, belonged to two main Berber branches, namely the Ṣanhādja and Zanāta branches. The Ṣanhādja were mainly nomadic, raising camels, sheep and goats. As for the Zanāta and the other Berber groups related to this branch, such as the Mazāta and the Lawāta, they were partly nomadic and partly sedentary peoples. The impressive oases of Sūf, Wādī Rīgh, Wargla, Tidikelt and Tuwāt in the Algerian Sahara were founded by fractions of these groups, probably after the period of Roman domination. These people were experienced well-sinkers who bored underground water catchment and supply conduits, known as *kanāt* in classical Arabic and *foggāra* in the Arabic dialect of southern Algeria. They also sank artesian wells there. These two practices have a very long history in North Africa and the method of sinking artesian wells was described in the eighth/fourteenth century by the Arab historian Ibn Khaldūn who makes mention of such wells in the villages of Tuwāt,

Gurāra, Wargla and Rīgh.[2] It appears that the Zanāta, whom the Arab invaders encountered in Tripolitania, learnt the art of boring *foggāras* and artesian wells from the ancient Libyco-Berber peoples of the eastern Sahara. As for the artesian wells in the Egyptian oases, they are mentioned, among others, by Olympiodor, a Greek writer of the fifth century of the Christian era. It is further to be noted that Herodotus (fifth century before the Christian era) mentions the abundance and fertility of the palm trees growing in Augīla (Awdjīla) and in Fezzān where the Garamantes lived.

During the period with which we are concerned here, only the Tubu of the southern half of the eastern Sahara still observed their traditional religion. All the other Saharans, except perhaps a number of Judaized Zanāta in the northern Sahara, gradually became converted to Islam. The Islamization of the Berbers inhabiting the Sahara began as early as the first half of the second/eighth century. According to Ibn Khaldūn, the Ṣanhādja group of Lamtūna who led a nomadic existence in the western Sahara did not embrace Islam until some time after the conquest of Spain by the Arabs, in other words, in the early half of the second/eighth century.[3] Ibn Khaldūn's words are corroborated by a passage in the geographical treatise of al-Zuhrī (*c.* 546/1150), according to which al-Murābiṭūn (the Almoravids), that is to say the Lamtūna of the western Sahara, were converted to Islam during the reign of Caliph Hishām ibn ʿAbd al-Malik (105/724–125/743), at the same time as the inhabitants of the oasis of Wargla.[4]

It is very likely that the Ṣanhādja and the Zanāta of the Sahara, like the Berbers of North Africa, originally adopted the orthodox form of the Islamic faith. But later, when the North African Berbers rejected Sunnism, owing to the political and fiscal oppression of the Umayyad caliphs, and, around the middle of the second/eighth century, joined (particularly the groups descended from the Zanāta) two Khāridjite sects opposed to the Sunna, namely the Ṣufrite sect (of radical tendencies) and the Ibāḍite sect (more moderate). The Saharan Zanāta, or at least some of them, also adhered to these two sects. The Saharans descended from the Ṣanhādja who were vaguely Muslim in the second/eighth century, did not become orthodox until the middle of the fifth/eleventh century, as a result of Almoravid propaganda. As for the Berbers descended from the Zanāta who lived in the villages of the Tripolitanian Sahara, Sūf, Wādī Rīgh and Wargla, they very early on embraced Ibaḍīsm, a faith that had been adopted by their brethren in the eastern and central areas of the Berber region, who founded there several imāmates or states. These started with a small imāmate founded in 125/743 by members of the Hawwāra, Nafūsa and Zanāta peoples in the north-western part of Tripolitania, and finished with the Rustumid *imāmate of T*āhert, whose first head, ʿAbd ar-Rahmān ibn Rustum, was elected *imām* in 162/776–7. This imāmate survived until

2. Ibn Khaldūn, 1925–56, Vol. 3, p. 286.
3. ibid., Vol. 2, p. 65; N. Levtzion and J. F. P. Hopkins (eds), 1981, p. 327.
4. Al-Zuhrī, 1968, p. 181; N. Levtzion and J. F. P. Hopkins (eds), 1981, p. 99.

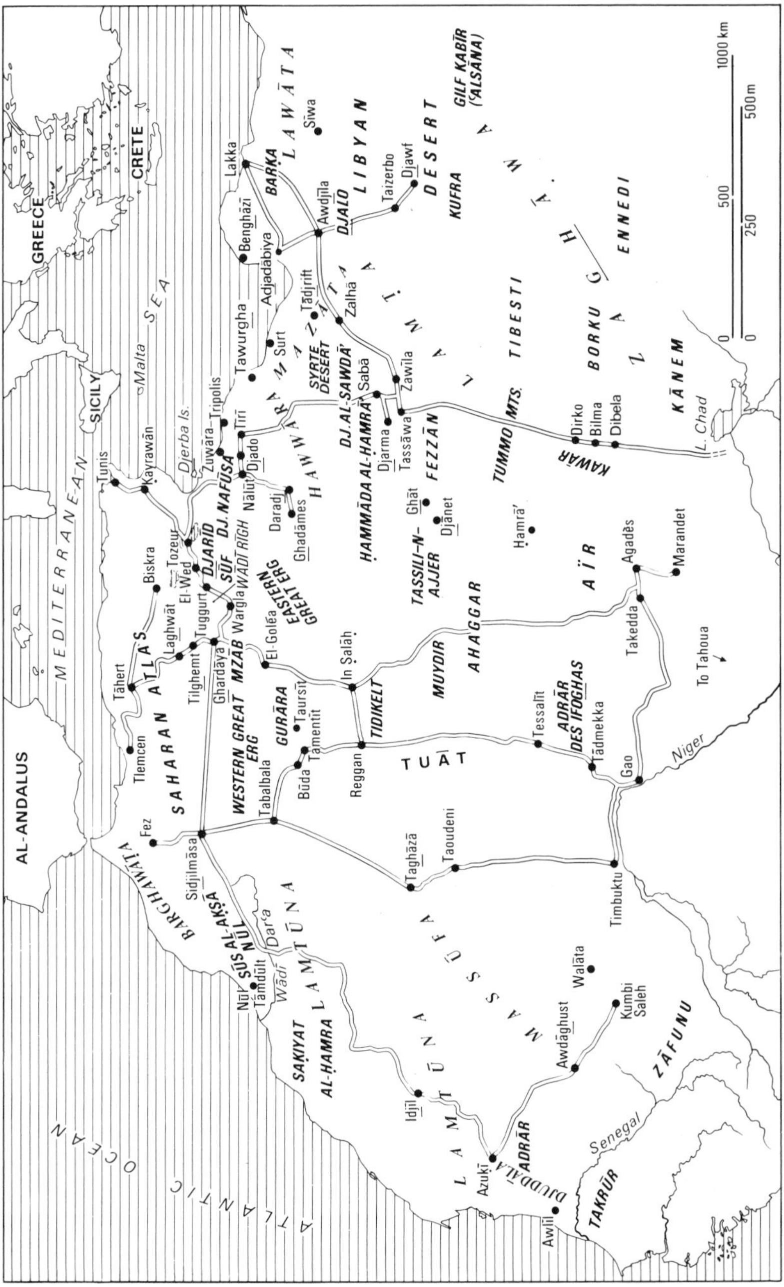

FIG. 11.1 *The Sahara*

297/909, when it fell before the army of Abū ʿAbd Allāh al-Shiʿī, who founded the powerful Fāṭimid empire on the ruins of that state and of other Muslim states of North Africa.[5]

All the Ibāḍite Berbers of North Africa recognized the supremacy of the Tāhert imāmate which took in, in the south, the oases of Wādī Rīgh and Wargla. It was to Sadrāta, a town located in the oasis of Wargla, that the last Rustumid *imām* of Tāhert fled after Tāhert had been conquered by the Fāṭimid army; for a time the thought was entertained there of restoring the Ibāḍite imāmate.

The Miknāsa, who adopted the Ṣufrite beliefs, settled in Tafilālet in the south-east of present-day Morocco, where they founded a small Ṣufrite state, the capital of which became the city of Sidjilmāsa, founded in 140/757–8. This city, which was governed by the dynasty of the Banū Midrār and was located on the edge of the desert, soon became a major centre for trade with the Sudan and was ruled by the Ṣufrite chiefs until the middle of the fourth/tenth century. Despite differences of dogma, relations between the Ibāḍite dynasty of Tāhert and the Ṣufrite princes of Sidjilmāsa were very friendly. Indeed Arab sources reveal a marriage alliance between these two dynasties in the late second/eighth century and in the early third/ninth century. No doubt the increasing role played by the city of Sidjilmāsa in trans-Saharan trade was the cause of this rapprochement.

Lastly, some groups of the Zanāta, living in the south-western part of present-day Algeria and in the Saharan villages, joined the movement of Muʿtazila, or Wāṣiliyya, which was opposed to orthodox Islam just like the Khāridjites.[6] It may be assumed that the area occupied by the Muʿtazilite Zanāta included, on one side, the high plateaux south of Tiāret and, on the other, the Mzāb region whose inhabitants were Wāṣilites before being converted to the Ibāḍite faith.

The city of Sidjilmāsa in Tafilālet, capital of the Ṣufrite state of the Midrārites, was one of the termini of a caravan route linking North Africa to the ancient kingdom of Ghana, the 'land of gold' of the medieval Arab geographers. Through it passed a trade route to the city of Tāhert (present-day Tiāret), the capital of the Ibāḍite imāmate of the Rustumids. At the time of the reign of the first *imām*, between 160/776–7 and 168/784–5, this became an important political and economic centre. This notable market city attracted not only a large number of North African traders, both Ibāḍite and non-Ibāḍite, but also enterprising Arab merchants from Ḳayrawān, Baṣra and Kūfa. This is revealed to us by Ibn al-Saghīr, an historian of Tāhert, who wrote around the beginning of the fourth/tenth century.[7] A route linking Tāhert to the western Sudan led through Sidjilmāsa to Ghana. Another route linked Tāhert to the city of Gao; it was already in

5. Cf. Chapter 3 above, Chapter 12 below.
6. Cf. Chapter 10 above.
7. N. Levtzion and J. F. P. Hopkins (eds), 1981, p. 24.

use before the death of the Rustumid *imām*, ʿAbd al-Wahhāb in 208/823.[8] This latter route appears to have passed through the oases of Wādī Rīgh and Wargla which were also involved in Tāhert's Sudanese trade. The Saharan Ibāḍites continued to engage in trade with the Sudan even after the fall of the Rustumid state in 297/909.

Alongside the Ibāḍite merchants of Wādī Rīgh and Wargla, the Ibāḍites of Ghadāmes and Zawīla (in Fezzān) also organized distant expeditions to various Sudanese regions, together with the Ibāḍite merchants of Bilād al-Djarīd in southern Tunisia and traders from Djabal Nafūsa. The Berber traders who engaged in these relations generally belonged to the various groups of the Zanāta. As for the Saharans of Ṣanhādja stock, they often served as guides for the caravans equipped by North African traders from Sidjilmāsa, Tāhert, Tlemcen, Ḳayrawān or Tripoli, and also escorted these caravans under the protection of the Ṣanhādja chiefs of Awdāghust, Tādmekka and other places.

Following this rapid review of the ethnic, religious and economic situation of the Saharan peoples, we shall consider the history of the particular regions of the Sahara during the period covered in this volume.

The Libyan Desert

Four oases in the Libyan Desert, namely, Khārja, Dākhla, Farāfra (known by the medieval Arab geographers as Farfārun) and Baḥriyya (Bahnāsat al-Wāh) formed, at the time of the Arab conquest of Egypt, a small Muslim state governed by the Al-ʿAbdūn dynasty, of Lawāta Berber origin. This state was first mentioned in the latter half of the second/eighth century by the geographer and astronomer al-Fazārī. He called it ʿAmal Wāh or the 'Land of the Oases'.[9] Later, around the middle of the fourth/tenth century, al-Masʿūdī gave a brief description of the Land of the Oases based on an account dating from 330/941–2. A Berber prince called ʿAbd al-Malik ibn Marwān ruled there with several thousand horsemen under his command. In addition to the Lawāta Berbers, there was in the Land of the Oases a large Christian population of Coptic origin and there were also Arab nomads belonging to the Banū Hilāl tribe. The princes of this state lived in two districts of Dākhla, one of which was called al-Kalamūn and the other al-Ḳaṣr. Several routes linked the Land of the Oases to the various Egyptian cities on one side and the oasis of Santarīya (Sīwa) on the other. The oases contained a large number of date palms and other fruit trees and also alum mines.[10]

A route said to be ten days' walking distance long linked the oasis of

8. ibid., p. 25.

9. Al-Masʿūdī, 1861–77, Vol. 4, p. 39; N. Levtzion and J. F. P. Hopkins (eds), 1981, p. 32.

10. Al-Masʿūdī, 1861–77, Vol. 3, pp. 50–2.

Bahnāsat al-Wāh (Baḥriyya) to the oasis of Santarīya or Sīwa (formerly Ammonium) which, in the fourth/tenth–sixth/twelfth centuries, was the meeting-point of all the western routes. The most important of these routes linked Santarīya to Egypt on one side and the Maghrib and Kawār on the other. Al-Idrīsī speaks of a route linking Santarīya to the port of Lakka (east of Tobruk) and adds that Santarīya abounded in palms and fruit trees. Santarīya appears to have long remained independent of Egypt. It was not until the seventh/thirteenth century that it was annexed to the province of Alexandria.[11]

In the most remote part of the Land of the Oases there was a very prosperous region, known as Wāh Ṣebrū ('the oasis of Ṣebrū'), to which access was very difficult and where, in the eleventh century, 'no one ever came except for a few travellers who had lost their way in the desert'.[12] The anonymous author of the geographical treatise entitled *Kitāb al-Istibṣār*, composed in 587/1191, adds that that region, which he calls *Wāh Ḍbr* (which is but a corruption of Ṣebrū), abounded in date palms, cereals and all kinds of fruit, as well as in gold mines.[13] In my view the mention of gold mines is no more than an allusion to the gold trade with the Western Sudan, whence gold used to be transported to Egypt. Far more precise is the information supplied by al-Idrīsī, who speaks of the ruins of a once flourishing and populated city, known as S̲h̲ebrū or S̲h̲ebrō, where there were said to be only few palm trees and where the Arabs went on excursions. To the north-east of this city was a lake on whose banks people known as the Kawār (Tubu?) nomads camped. To the north of this region were the oasis of Santarīya (Sīwa) and the city of Zāla (Zella).[14]

A look at the map of the Libyan Desert reveals that the only large oasis in that desert whose position corresponds exactly to the information provided by the early Arab geographers concerning Ṣebrū (Ḍbr, S̲h̲ebrū) (apparently this name derives from the Copt word for village, *tchobro*) is the Kufra group. There is an abundance of water there; it flows through marshes and lakes watering the luxuriant plantations. Dates, figs and lemons are grown there, together with cereals. The present-day inhabitants belong to the Zāwiya people, Arabized Berbers who came down from the north around the middle of the eleventh/eighteenth century. The conquerors found there a non-Muslim people (Kufra; *kufarā'* = 'infidels') belonging to the Tubu who had founded a small state there. After the conquest of Kufra by the Zāwiya, the local Tubu withdrew to the Tibesti mountain range or else were annihilated by the newcomers. Only a few hundred individuals of Tubu origin remain today in the Kufra oasis and they are completely Islamized and subject to the Arabs. As for the lake mentioned by

11. Al-Idrīsī, 1866, pp. 41–2; N. Levtzion and J. F. P. Hopkins (eds), 1981, p. 126.
12. Al-Bakrī, 1911, text pp. 15–17; 1913, translation, pp. 38–40.
13. *Kitāb al-Istibṣār*, 1852, pp. 33–6.
14. Al-Idrīsī, 1866, p. 41; N. Levtzion and J. F. P. Hopkins (eds), 1981, p. 125.

al-Idrīsī, situated at the foot of an inaccessible mountain in Shebrū, it lies at the foot of Djabal Buzeima (Bzēma) in the oasis of that name.[15]

The ancient caravan route that linked Egypt to Ghana before the fourth/tenth century, alluded to by Ibn Ḥawḳal in the latter half of the fourth/tenth century, probably passed through the Kufra oasis. This route was used earlier, in the time of Aḥmad ibn Ṭūlūn (254/868–270/884), and would appear, after reaching Kufra, to have then headed off in the direction of Wādī al-Namūs and Wādī al-Kabīr, passed through Fezzān, and from there to have gone on to Kawār, Gao and, lastly, Ghana.[16] It is likely that this is the route of which Ibn al-Faḳīh speaks (fl. 290/903) in a section of his treatise, probably derived from an earlier source:

> The route from Ghana to Egypt leads through the land of a people known as the Kāw-Kāw [Gao], then through that of a people known as the Maranda, then through that of a people known as the Murrawāt, and from there to the Egyptian oases in Malsāna.[17]

Maranda is Marandet, an important waterhole south of Agadès. As for Malsāna, this place is probably to be identified with the mountain of ʿAlsānī or al-Idrīsī's ʿAlsānā, identical, in all probability, to the plateau of Gilf Kabīr, located to the west of Dākhla.

Ten days' walking distance, across a sandy plain where water was scarce, lay between Santarīya (or Sīwa) and the Awdjīla group of oases (referred to by the ancient authors as Augila), famous for its date trees. This group included, besides the oasis of Awdjīla proper, the city and the oasis of Djālū (Djalo). The capital of this region, was, according to al-Bakrī, the city of Arzākīya which contained several mosques and bazaars. The whole region was covered with villages, date trees and fruit trees. Dates from Awdjīla were exported to the city of Adjadābīya (Adjedabia). The population of Awdjīla was no doubt of Berber stock and was probably composed of groups of the Lawāta, like the population of Santarīya and Barḳa. The descendants of the early inhabitants, Berbers by their ethnic group and by their language, now go by the name of the Awdjīlī. Al-Idrīsī emphasizes that the capital of Awdjīla, although small, was densely populated and that its inhabitants engaged in active trade. For Awdjīla was at the crossroads of several trade routes and was an important centre on a route to the Sudan. Through this oasis one gained access to 'the greater part of the Land of the Blacks, for instance, to Kawār and Kāw-Kāw [Gao]'.[18] We know nothing about the history of Awdjīla during the first centuries of Islam. It is not impossible that it remained independent. Later, in the third/ninth–sixth/twelfth centuries, it already formed part of the Arab provinces of Barḳa.

To the west of the oasis of Awdjīla and the province of Barḳa stretched

15. See T. Lewicki, 1939, 1965c. Regarding the Tubu migrations, cf. J. Chapelle, 1957.
16. Ibn Ḥawḳal, 1938, p. 61; N. Levtzion and J. F. P. Hopkins (eds), 1981, p. 45.
17. Ibn al-Faḳīh, 1885, p. 68; N. Levtzion and J. F. P. Hopkins (eds), 1981, p. 27.
18. Al-Idrīsī, 1866, p. 132; N. Levtzion and J. F. P. Hopkins (eds), 1981, p. 129.

the province of Surt or Sirt which took in all the eastern part of Tripolitania. This is a Saharan region where the desert known by the name of the Syrte Desert extends as far as Syrtis Major. This province owed its name to that of Surt, a large city possessing a mosque and a few bazaars surrounded by date trees. Its inhabitants, traders, spoke 'a kind of dialect which was neither Arabic, nor Persian, nor Berber nor Copt'.[19] It may conceivably have been ancient Punic.

The province of Surt included two districts during this period, the first of which, Surt proper, corresponded to the coastal area, while the second, Waddān (so called after a city belonging to the modern oasis of Djofra), corresponded to the inland region. The first of these districts is known by the name of *arḍ Surt* ('land of Surt'), while Waddān was still regarded between the third/ninth and sixth/twelfth centuries as a district (*ʿamal*) and indeed as a separate country (*arḍ*). These two regions of the province of Surt were peopled by the Mazāta Berber group whose neighbours were the Lawāta of Barḳa and the Hawwāra who had settled in central Tripolitania. The western boundary of the teritory of the Mazāta ran close to Tawargha (present-day Tawurgha), while in the south the area they inhabited extended beyond Djabal al-Sawdā (Djabal Sōda), whose population was at war with the Mazāta in the third/ninth century. The latter formerly represented the majority of the inhabitants of Waddān, where, however, there were also two Arab groups. The desert city of Tādjrift was peopled by a mixture of Mazāta and Arabs. During that period the oasis of Zalhā (or Zella) also formed part of Mazāta territory, as emerges from a passage in the work of al-Bakrī.[20]

The Mazāta of eastern Tripolitania came under the sway of Ibāḍism at an early date, the district of Surt being one of the provinces of the short-lived Ibāḍite state founded in Tripolitania by the Imām Abūl-Khaṭṭāb ʿAbd Allāh ibn al-Samḥ al-Maʿāfirī (131/757–8–135/761). The Ibāḍite faith remained alive for a long time in Tripolitania, and the Mazāta continued to profess it until around the end of the third/ninth century. In 26/646–7 the city of Waddān was conquered by an Arab officer named Buṣr ibn ʿAbi Arṭāṭ who demanded from its inhabitants a heavy tribute of three hundred and sixty slaves. When, later on, the people of Waddān refused to pay this tribute, ʿUḳba ibn Nāfiʿ of illustrious name conducted a further expedition against that territory in 46/666–7, and, after punishing the king, again secured payment of the tribute.[21] The city of Waddān was linked by a route to the city of Maghmadās (the Macemades Selorum of ancient authors), situated on the Mediterranean coast, and to the city of Djarma (formerly Garama). This was no doubt the route used to import the slaves who made up the tribute paid to the Arabs by the people of Waddān. The slaves were black prisoners from the regions of Kawār, Tibesti and Kānem.

19. Al-Bakrī, 1911, p. 11.
20. ibid., p. 11–12.
21. Ibn ʿAbd al-Ḥakam *apud* N. Levtzion and J. F. P. Hopkins (eds), 1981, pp. 12–13.

These prisoners were probably transported by the same route as that used, according to Herodotus, by the ancient Garamantes to give chase to the Ethiopian troglodytes.[22] Throughout the period Waddān engaged in trade with the Land of the Blacks; the route between Wāddan and the Land of the Blacks passed through the city of Zawīla in Fezzān.

Another route linking Wāddan to Awdjīla passed through the city of Zalhā (Zella), where dates were extremely plentiful. It was also a stopping place on the route leading from northern Tripolitania to Fezzān and the Land of the Blacks. According to al-Bakrī (Muḥammed Ibn al-Warrāḳ), this area was inhabited by the Mazāta;[23] however, al-Idrīsī, who knew it by the name of Zāla, states that its inhabitants belonged to the Hawwāra, adding that they were traders.[24]

The Arab sources do not make much mention of Ḥammāda al-Ḥamrā' and the surrounding mountains, with the exception of al-Bakrī who gives a description of the route that led from the trading city of Djādū (Djado or Giado), capital of the eastern part of Djabal Nafūsa, to the city of Zawīla, the important caravanserai situated on the route leading to the region of Kawār and the other Lands of the Blacks.[25] However, a three-day desert crossing on foot was necessary before reaching Tīrī or Tīra, a locality situated on the side of a mountain and containing a large number of date palms.[26]

On the western borders of Ḥammāda al-Ḥamrā', between the plateaux and the Eastern Great Erg, lies the Saharan oasis and city of Ghadāmes. This place, which in remote antiquity was already the most important stopping place in the desert (known as Cydamus or Kidamē by the ancient authors), owed its importance to its geographical position. It was the gateway through which merchants passed on their way from Tripolitania to the Land of the Blacks. The route that linked the trading city of Sharūs in Djabal Nafūsa to the Takrūr region passed through Ghadāmes. Still today, in the vicinity of Sharūs, a trail can be seen that leads to Ghadāmes, which goes by the name of *trīḳ al-Sūdān* ('the Sudan trail'). This no doubt is the route spoken of by Yāḳūt (after a sixth/twelfth-century source) which led to the region known as Zāfunu (Diafuunuu) in upper Senegal.[27]

22. Cf. Unesco, *General History of Africa*, Vol. II, ch. 20.

23. Al-Bakrī, 1911, p. 12; 1913.

24. Al-Idrīsī, 1866, pp. 41–2; N. Levtzion and J. F. P. Hopkins (eds), 1981, p. 129.

25. Al-Bakrī, 1911, p. 10; 1913, pp. 26–7; N. Levtzion and J. F. P. Hopkins (eds), 1981, pp. 63–4.

26. The word *tira* means 'writing' in Berber. However, if a dot is added to the third Arabic letter of this word, another Berber word can be obtained, namely, *Tīzī*, which means 'slope'. This is perhaps Mizda (Musti Vicus of old), a stopping place situated on the shortest route leading from the city of Tripoli and from Djabal Nafūsa to Fezzān. According to the Ibāḍite chronicles, the *manzil* ('stopping place') of Tīrī already existed in the third/ninth century; at that time it was peopled by Ibāḍites.

27. N. Levtzion and J. F. P. Hopkins (eds), 1981, pp. 170–2. Concerning Zāfunu, cf. T. Lewicki, 1971a.

Al-Bakrī has described a route that started from Tripoli, passed through Djabal Nafūsa and Ghadāmes, and ended in Tādmekka in the western Sudan.[28] It is likely that, after Ghadāmes, this route passed through the territory of the Askār Berbers (present-day Tassili-n-Ajjer) which was eighteen days' walking distance from Ghadāmes according to al-Idrīsī.[29]

The inhabitants of Ghadāmes had since ancient times been engaged in a limited form of agriculture (they grew mainly dates there) and also in trans-Saharan trade. Medieval Arab sources make mention of this city at a very early date. The Arab historian Ibn ʿAbd al-Ḥakam speaks of the capture of Ghadāmes by the Arab general ʿUḳba ibn Nāfiʿ in the year 46/667.[30] The population of the city consisted of several Berber groups, one of which, the Tināwuta, had already been mentioned in the second/eighth century. Moreover, the Berber language is still spoken in Ghadāmes.

The inhabitants of Ghadāmes, converted to Christianity in the first/seventh century, appear at a very early date to have adopted Ibāḍite beliefs, apparently at the same time as their neighbours in the north, the Nafūsa who inhabited present-day Djabal Nafūsa and with whom they had close relations. At the beginning of the third/ninth century the people of Ghadāmes took up the dissident doctrines of the Ibāḍite sects of Khalafīya and Nukkār, and only through the military intervention of the Nafūsa was pure Ibāḍism-Wahbism re-established there. At the time the population of Ghadāmes was governed by the Ibāḍite *mashāyikh* (*shaykhs*).[31]

At a short distance to the east of Ghadāmes lies the oasis and city of Daradj (referred to in the Ibāḍite chronicles as Dardj or Adradj) which was an important Ibāḍite Berber centre. It is not inconceivable that Dardj derives its name from the Tanāta branch of the Banū Idradj (Tdrj being an erroneous form of the word), mentioned by Ibn Ḥawḳal along with the Waradjma, the Banū Būlīt and other Zanāta groups of southern Tunisia.[32] It is further to be noted that a route passing through Sināwan and Dardj linked Ghadāmes to the city of Nālūt (or Lālūt), situated in the western part of Djabal Nafūsa.

Between Fezzān and Lake Chad

In the southern part of Tripolitania lies the vast desert region of Fezzān, a

28. Al-Bakrī, 1911, p. 182; N. Levtzion and J. F. P. Hopkins (eds), 1981, p. 86.

29. N. Levtzion and J. F. P. Hopkins (eds), 1981, p. 121; J. M. Cuoq, 1975, p. 153. The Āzḳār are the nomadic Berbers of Fezzān or Adjdjer Tuaregs. Al-Idrīsī, 1866, p. 36.

30. Ibn ʿAbd al-Ḥakam, cf. N. Levtzion and J. F. P. Hopkins (eds), 1981, p. 12.

31. In the seventh/fourteenth century the inhabitants of Ghadāmes still professed the Ibāḍite faith. Now they are all fervent Sunnites.

32. Ibn Ḥawḳal, 1964, p. 104; T. Lewicki, 1959.

group of oases situated between Hammāda al-Ḥamrā' in the north, Tassili-n-Ajjer in the west, the Tibesti foothills in the south and the Libyan Desert in the east.

As for the ancient civilization of the Garamantes, it did not cease to exist until after the Arab conquest of the Maghrib, and there are now reasons for thinking (on the basis of the carbon-14 dating of certain excavated materials) that this civilization was not destroyed until between the second/eighth and fourth/tenth centuries by the Arab conquerors. One is led to believe that the main cause of the fall of the civilization of the Garamantes was the expedition led by the victorious Arab general Ibn al-Ash'ath who, in 145/762–3, conquered the kingdom of Zawīla in eastern Fezzān and massacred the inhabitants of the capital. It should be pointed out, moreover, that the kingdom of Zawīla survived this shock and existed around the end of the third/ninth century as an independent state.

The kingdom of Zawīla took in only part of present-day eastern Fezzān. It was founded either in the late first/seventh century or in the early second/eighth century.[33] As for all the rest of Fezzān, it formed, between the second/seventh and the sixth/twelfth centuries, a separate kingdom, an outgrowth of the kingdom of the Garamantes, which is referred to by the medieval Arab authors by the name of Fezzān.[34]

This state is mentioned in Arab sources as early as the year 46/666–7. Thus the historical work of Ibn 'Abd al-Ḥakam tells us that 'Uḳba ibn Nāfi', after conquering the city of Waddān, set off for the city of Djarma (Djerma), capital of Greater Fezzān, whose king surrendered and whose inhabitants were converted to Islam. 'Uḳba ibn Nāfi' then made his way to the other 'castles' of Fezzān, going right up to the ones furthest north.[35]

Starting from the late second/eighth century the inhabitants of Fezzān became Ibāḍites and, from the outset, they recognized the supremacy of the Rustumid *imāms* of Tāhert. For some time, however, they were followers of the Ibāḍite heretic Khalaf ibn as-Samḥ. At the time of al-Ya'ḳūbī (at the end of the third/ninth century) Fezzān formed a vast state governed by an independent chief (*ra'is*).

Al-Ya'ḳūbī also mentions the capital of Fezzān, which was a large city.[36] He was no doubt referring to Djarma which flourished for several hundred years more, up to the sixth/twelfth century. At that time there was also in Fezzān, in addition to Djarma, another large city, namely, Tassāwa (Tessaoua), which the 'Blacks' (Fezzānis?), according to al-Idrīsī, called

33. The city of Zawīla is known to have not yet come into existence at the time of 'Uḳba ibn Nāfi''s expedition into Tripolitania in 46/666–7.

34. This kingdom was at war with the Mazāta of eastern Tripolitania. This war seems also to have contributed, together with the expedition led by Ibn al-Ash'ath against the city of Zawīla, to the fall of the ancient civilization of the Garamantes.

35. Ibn 'Abd al-Ḥakam *apud* N. Levtzion and J. F. P. Hopkins (eds), 1981, pp. 12–13.

36. Al-Ya'ḳūbī, 1962, p. 9.

'Little Djarma'.[37] The Arab sources also contain mention of other cities in Fezzān. Among these, al-Bakrī draws attention to a city by the name of Tāmarmā, situated on the route leading to Djādū in Djabal Nafūsa. This city is completely unknown to us and its name should, so we think, be corrected to read 'Tāmzawā', in other words present-day Tamzaua (Tamséua). The Ibādite authors knew it by the name of Tāmzāwat. Al-Bakrī also mentions the large city of Sabhā, which is to be identified with the present capital of Fezzān, designated as Sabhah on our maps. Sabhā possessed a cathedral mosque and several bazaars. The Ibāḍite chronicles refer to this city by the name of Shabāha.[38]

The population of medieval Fezzān was made up of various ethnic groups forming a people known as the Fezzān.[39] Ibn Ḥawḳal mentions in the fourth/tenth century a Berber people known as the Adjār Fezzān whom he numbers among the Zanāta 'tribes'.[40] There appears to be a link between the first part of this name and the name of the present-day area of Agar or Aggar in Fezzān, a short distance away from Tassāwa. In addition to the Fezzān (also Fazzāna), there were also other groups in this region. Al-Bakrī mentions the Banū Kaldīn (or Kildīn) who inhabited the city of Tāmarmā (Tāmzawā), together with the Fazzāna.[41] The Kaldīn were probably the same as the Kadīn (Kildīn) who, according to Ibn Khaldūn, were related to the Hawwāra.[42]

The inhabitants of Djarma (and apparently of all the other 'castles' of Fezzān) who, as early as the year 569, were Christians, were converted to Islam following the Arab invasion of 46/666–7. They subsequently took part in the Ibāḍite movement in Tripolitania (in 126/743–4) and suffered losses, like the Ibāḍites of Waddān and those of Zawīla, following the expedition led by the Abbasid general Ibn al-Ash'ath in 145/762–3. At the time of the Rustumid *imām* 'Abd al-Wahhāb ibn 'Abd al-Raḥmān (d. 208/823) the Fezzani were already Ibāḍites. Thus it is that the Ibādite chronicles mention several outstanding figures from Fezzān who lived at that time.[43]

The Ibāḍites of Fezzān appear, in the early third/ninth century, to have thrown in their lot with the Ibāḍite dissident Khalaf ibn as-Samḥ who, having revolted against the Rustumid *imāms* of Tāhert, succeeded in bringing almost all of Tripolitania under his sway, with the exception of Djabal Nafūsa, whose inhabitants, who professed the Ibāḍite-Wahbite religion, remained faithful to the Rustumids.[44] However, during the first

37. Al-Idrīsī; cf. N. Levtzion and J. F. P. Hopkins (eds), 1981, p. 120.
38. Al-Bakrī, 1911, p. 11.
39. Al-Ya'ḳūbī, 1962.
40. Ibn Ḥawḳal, 1964, p. 104.
41. Al-Bakrī, 1911, p. 10.
42. Ibn Khaldūn, 1925–56, Vol. 1, p. 177.
43. T. Lewicki, 1957, p. 341.
44. ibid., p. 342.

half of the third/ninth century, Fezzān was again regarded as a region with an Ibāḍite-Wahbite population.

The second state that existed in Fezzān between the second/eighth and sixth/twelfth centuries, the kingdom of Zawīla, owes its name to the city of Zawīla (present-day Zawīlah), which was its capital. It is not mentioned at the time of the expedition led by ʿUḳba ibn Nāfiʿ into the interior of Tripolitania and to Kawār in 46/666–7, but appears in the sources for the first time a century later, at the time of the wars between the Sunnite Arabs and the Ibāḍite Berbers. After the victory achieved, in 144/761–2, by Ibn al-Ashʿath over Abu ʾl-Khaṭṭāb, the Ibāḍite *imām* of Ifrīḳiya, the Arab army captured the city of Zawīla, whose Ibāḍite Berber inhabitants were put to the sword and whose chief, ʿAbd Allāh ibn Hiyān al-Ibāḍī, was killed. Despite these occurrences, Zawīla long remained a major Ibāḍite centre. Al-Yaʿḳūbī notes the presence there, in the latter half of the third/ninth century, of an Ibāḍite people who practised date growing and traded with the countries of the Sudan.[45]

Around the beginning of the fourth/tenth century it appears that the city of Zawīla was abandoned, probably after the war waged by its inhabitants on the Mazāta of eastern Tripolitania. Al-Idrīsī's mention of the foundation of Zawīla in 306/918 (by which is to be understood, rather, the rebuilding of that city) is no doubt to be interpreted with reference to that war. According to al-Idrīsī, Zawīla was founded to serve as a residence for ʿAbd Allāh ibn al-Khaṭṭāb al-Hawwārī and his family.[46] According to Ibn Ḥawḳal (*c.* 988), the dynasty of Banūl-Khaṭṭāb was descended not from the Hawwāra but, rather, from the Mazāta.[47]

The chief resources of Fezzān (I am thinking of the Djarma and Zawīla regions) were crops, particularly palm tree and cereal crops. Most of the information concerning these crops is derived from al-Bakrī, who speaks of a large number of date palms in Tāmarmā (Tāmzawā), Sabāb and Zawīla and describes the growing of cereals and the use of camels in irrigation. He also mentions the fact that the plant which yielded indigo dye was grown in Sabāb.[48] Al-Idrīsī also speaks highly of the date palms of Zawīla and mentions the growing of palm trees, millet and barley in Tassāwa.[49] As for irrigation, J. Despois assumes that the technique of *foggāra*s (underground catchment conduits) became widespread in Fezzān at the end of the Roman period.[50] The Arab authors provide some information about crop irrigation. Thus, according to al-Bakrī, the crop-growing area in Zawīla was irrigated by means of wells operated by camels, which are still used in

45. Al-Yaʿḳūbī, 1962, p. 9; cf. N. Levtzion and J. F. P. Hopkins (eds), 1981, p. 22.
46. Al-Idrīsī, 1866, pp. 37–8; cf. N. Levtzion and J. F. P. Hopkins (eds), 1981, p. 122.
47. Ibn Ḥawḳal, 1964, p. 104.
48. Al-Bakrī; cf. N. Levtzion and J. F. P. Hopkins (eds), 1981, p. 64.
49. Al-Idrīsī, 1866, pp. 35–6.
50. J. Despois, 1965.

Fezzān, and al-Idrīsī says that palm trees, millet and barley were irrigated (in Djarma and Tassāwa) by means of a machine known as an *indjāfa*, which the inhabitants of the Maghrib knew by the name of *khaṭṭāra*.[51]

Alongside crop-growing, Fezzān's main activity was trans-Saharan trade, for this region is, after the Nile, historically the most important channel of communication with the countries south of the Sahara. The Garamantes had already brought to the Tripolitanian ports of Leptis Magna (Lebda), Oea (Tripoli) and Sabratha (Zuwāra) products from their countries and from the interior of Africa, such as dates, ivory and precious stones known as garamantiques. From the dawn of the Muslim era the Fezzani also engaged in the trade in black slaves. Trade was carried on along a very ancient route, which was already known to the Garamantes in the fifth century before the Christian era and which linked Tripoli and the other cities on the coast of Tripolitania to Kawār and Kānem in central Africa. It led through the city of Zawīla and Djabal Nafūsa, whose main city, Djādū, still contained bazaars and a large Jewish population in the fourth/tenth and fifth/eleventh centuries. Trans-Saharan trade was the reason for the settlement in Zawīla, alongside the Ibāḍite Berbers, of people of highly varied stock, originating from Khurāsān, Baṣra and Kūfa. The Zawīla traders mainly exported black slaves captured from the Sudanese peoples of Mīrī, Murrū, Zaghāwa and others, most of whom belonged to the Teda-Daza group.[52]

In the fifth/eleventh century al-Bakrī describes three routes that linked the city of Zawīla to Tripolitania proper and to Egypt. The first went to the city of Djādū and then to Tripoli. The second linked Zawīla to the city of Adjadābīya at the eastern edge of Tripolitania. The third route linked Zawīlā to Fusṭāṭ, the capital of Egypt. Al-Bakrī also alludes to a caravan route which went from the city of Zawīla to the region of Kānem, forty days' walking distance from that city.[53]

To the south of the Tummo Mountains, which constituted the southern boundary of Fezzān, there is a chain of oases which facilitate communication with Kānem. This is the finest caravan route of the Sahara, despite the dunes that lie between Bilma and Dibella (Dibela). This route has been used since very remote times. The best-known oases forming part of this chain are those of Kawār (referred to as Kawār by the medieval Arab geographers and as Kaouar today). They had been known for centuries as a result of the trans-Saharan trade that was carried on along these routes. In 46/666–7, when ʿUḳba ibn Nāfiʿ took possession of all the *ḳṣūr*s (castles) of Fezzān, moving from the north to the south, the inhabitants informed him that beyond this region lay the *ḳṣūr*s of Kawār, the chief one of which

51. Al-Bakrī, 1911, p. 11; al-Idrīsī, 1866, p. 35. The machines in question are *shadūfs*, which are still used in the Fezzān and which are known as *keṭṭāra*.

52. Al-Yaʿḳūbī, 1962, p. 9; cf. N. Levtzion and J. F. P. Hopkins (eds), 1981, p. 22.

53. Al-Bakrī, 1911, p. 11; cf. N. Levtzion and J. F. P. Hopkins (eds), 1981, pp. 63–4.

(*ḳaṣaba* or *gaṣba*), referred to as Khāwār by al-Bakrī was a very large fortress.[54]

A brief description of Kawār is given by Ibn ʿAbd al-Ḥakam and also by al-Yaʿḳūbī, but it was left to al-Idrīsī to give us more detailed information. Among these 'cities', al-Idrīsī mentions al-Ḳaṣaba ('the chief city'), which is the same as Ibn ʿAbd al-Ḥakam's Khāwār, which was a rather insignificant place at the time of that geographer. Ḳaṣr Umm ʿIṣā, placed by al-Idrīsī at two days' walking distance south of al-Ḳaṣaba, should, in my view, be identified with the village of Aschenumma described by Nachtigal, which is now a place of no importance.[55]

At a distance of forty Arab miles, that is 80 km, from Ḳaṣr Umm ʿIṣā, al-Idrīsī places the city of Ankalās, which was the largest city in Kawār and the most important as regards trade, and at the same time the place of residence of the local chief.[56] Ankalās might be identified with the village of Dirki where, at the time of Nachtigal's stay in Kawār, the sovereign of that region resided. This village (also called Dirko by the Teda) was, according to Nachtigal, the oldest and the largest in Kawār.

The last place in Kawār to be mentioned by al-Idrīsī (who lists the inhabited areas in this region, going from north to south) is the small city of Tamalma (or Talamla), situated in the southern part of that region. Following J. Marquart we may identify Talamla with the modern city of Bilma (or rather Bilmāʿ).[57]

According to al-Yaʿḳūbī, the region of Kawār at about the end of the third/ninth century contained a mixed population, made up of Muslims of every origin, the majority of whom were Berbers.[58] These were Ibāḍite Berber traders from Fezzān, Djabal Nafūsa and Waddān. Alongside the Berbers (and no doubt also the Arab traders), the region of Kawār contained an autochthonous population belonging to the Tubu (Teda-Daza) group, referred to by the Arab geographer Ibn Saʿīd (before 685/1286), who calls the inhabitants of Kawār 'the Blacks' and who says that they adopted the customs of the whites.[59] Already in the third/ninth century this population was Muslim and probably Ibāḍite.

The resources of the inhabitants of Kawār who, according to Arab

54. Ibn ʿAbd al-Ḥakam *apud* N. Levtzion and J. F. P. Hopkins (eds), 1981, pp. 12–13; Al-Bakrī, 1913, p. 12. Khāwār appears to have been identical to Gissebi (Guesebi) in northern Kawār, a few kilometres to the south-west of present-day Aney. The name 'Gissebi' (Guesebi) seems to be but a corruption of the Arab term *ḳaṣba* or *gaṣba*.

55. G. Nachtigal, 1879–89, Vol. 1, p. 511. The name given to this castle (*ḳaṣr* in Arabic), i.e. Umm ʿIṣā (Umm Aysa in Arabic dialect) is but a metathesis of that of Aschenumma (Asche-n-ummạ for, ʿAysa-n-umm). R. Mauny, 1961, p. 141, identifies this place with present-day Bilma.

56. Al-Idrīsī, 1866, p. 39; cf. N. Levtzion and J. F. P. Hopkins (eds), 1981, pp. 123 *et seq.* According to R. Mauny, 1961, this is modern Kalala.

57. J. Marquart, 1913, p. 80.

58. Al-Yaʿḳūbī *apud* N. Levtzion and J. F. P. Hopkins (eds), 1981, p. 22.

59. Ibn Saʿīd *apud* N. Levtzion and J. F. P. Hopkins (eds), 1981, pp. 192–3.

sources, were rather well-to-do, derived from crops (dates), the mining of alum, and trade, particularly the slave trade. Camels were also bred there for the use of the local traders and the fish that abounded in the large lake in the vicinity of Abzar were caught and salted. However, the main source of wealth of the inhabitants of Kawār was the mines, which contained a variety of alum known by the name of *kawārī* whose exceptional purity is praised by al-Idrīsī.[60] According to this author, these mines were located to the south of Kawār, in Ankalās and Abzar, as far westward as the western Berber region, and also in the Wargla oasis. R. Mauny, curious as to the nature of these famous alum mines in Kawār, located in areas where today there are only saltworks, takes the view that al-Idrīsī was thinking of sodium sulphate which, broadly speaking, is an alum and which today is no more than the by-product of salt extraction in Kawār. In Bilma the proportion of sulphate contained in salt may be as much as 79 per cent. Thus, continues Mauny, 'when alum was of considerable commercial value (in the Middle Ages it was used to fix dyes on materials) there was no reason not to collect separately the salt containing the largest proportion of sulphate and to sell this product under the name of alum'.[61]

Apart from alum, the main source of wealth of the inhabitants of Kawār was the slave trade. Large numbers of black slaves were brought from Kawār to the markets of Djarma, Zawīla and Waddān, whence they were exported to the Maghrib and Ifrīḳiya, as well as to Egypt. Apparently this trade already existed in antiquity and was practised by the Garamantes.

The ancient and medieval history of Kawār is not known to us. It seems that in the ninth century this region was independent. Subsequently, the sultanate of Kawār was brought under the dominion of the kingdom of Zaghāwa or Kānem, which we shall be discussing later. At all events, such was the situation of that region in Yāḳūṭ's time (1220).[62]

Alongside the Tubu Kawarians and the Ibāḍite Berbers who, together with Arab traders, inhabited the villages of Kawār, there were also Lamṭa Berbers in that region of the Sahara, most of whom led a nomadic existence in the western Sahara, especially to the south of Sūs. According to al-Ya'ḳūbī,[63] these Lamṭa of the central Sahara inhabited the area between Kawār and Zawīla extending towards Awdjīla. It appears that later they helped to form the Tubu or Teda-Daza or that they withdrew to Aïr where they joined the local Tuareg.

The peoples of the Tubu or Teda-Daza-Zaghāwa, who have since very early times occupied the oases of Kufra in the Libyan Desert, as well as the region of Kawār, also constituted the population of the southern fringe of Fezzān, the Djādo plateau and the Tibesti mountain range. They also inhabited and still continue to inhabit Borku (as well as Bodélé and Baḥr

60. Al-Idrīsī, 1866, p. 39; cf. N. Levtzion and J. F. P. Hopkins (eds), 1981, p. 123.
61. R. Mauny, 1961, pp. 141, 334–6, 452.
62. Yāḳūṭ, 1866–73, Vol. 3, p. 142.
63. Al-Ya'ḳūbī, 1962, p. 9.

al-Ghazāl), which is a vast and very low-lying desert basin between Tibesti and Chad, as well as the plateaux of Ennedi and the areas to the north of Wadaī and to the north-west of Dārfūr. The Tubu group which still today continues to live in the last-mentioned areas goes by the name of the Zaghāwa. This name seems to have been at the time we are discussing the term used by the Arab geographers to designate virtually all the branches of the Tubu with the exception of the Goran and the nomadic inhabitants of Kawār and the Kufra oasis, described by al-Idrīsī as the 'nomads of Kawār'.[64]

It should also be added that the Arab author Wahb ibn Munabbih who wrote before 110/728 refers, alongside the Zaghāwa, to the Sudanese people of Kurān (or Korān) whose name is also to be pronounced 'Gorān'. This name is still preserved today and is given by the Arabs to the Daza, a branch of the Tubu living to the north and north-east of Lake Chad.[65]

As for the name 'Zaghāwa', mentioned by Wahb ibn Munabbih (apparently as that of the northern branch of the Tubu, i.e. the Teda) among the names of the peoples descended from the Biblical Ham, alongside the Korān, the Nubians, the Abyssinians, the Berbers and the Zandj of east Africa, it is not unknown to the other medieval Arab authors. It is cited as one of the Sudanese toponyms in the work of the astronomer Muḥammad ibn Mūsā al-Khuwārizmī (d. 220/835 or 232/846).[66] Al-Ya'ḳūbī mentions the people of Zaghāwa among the slaves that were exported from Zawīla[67] and in his historical works speaks of this people in more detail: the Zaghāwa settled in a place known as Kānim or Kānem where they lived in reed huts. There they founded a kingdom.[68]

It appears that Kānem had maintained relations with the Ibāḍites of Djabal Nafūsa since very early times. For we know that Abū 'Ubayda 'Abd al-Ḥamīd al-Djināwunī, who governed Djabal Nafūsa as the representative of the Rustumid *imāms* of Tāhert and who lived in the early half of the third/ninth century, besides knowing the Berber language and Arabic, was also familiar with that of the Kānem (*lugha kānimiya*).[69] The Arab geographer al-Muhallabī (d. 380/990) tells us that the Zaghāwa were a Sudanese people living to the south of the Maghrib. There they founded a vast state that bordered on Nubia; ten days' walking distance separated these two kingdoms.[70]

64. Al-Idrīsī, 1866, pp. 12–15; cf. N. Levtzion and J. F. P. Hopkins (eds), 1981, p. 125.
65. Ibn Ḳutayba, 1850, pp. 12–13; cf. N. Levtzion and J. F. P. Hopkins (eds), 1981, p. 15; J. Chapelle, 1957.
66. Al-Khuwārizmī, 1926, p. 6; cf. N. Levtzion and J. F. P. Hopkins (eds), 1981, p. 7.
67. Al-Ya'ḳūbī, 1892, p. 345; 1962, p. 9.
68. Al-Ya'ḳūbī, 1883, p. 219; cf. N. Levtzion and J. F. P. Hopkins (eds), 1981, p. 21.
69. Cf. T. Lewicki, 1955, pp. 92–3 and 96.
70. Yāḳūt, 1866–73, Vol. 2, p. 932. According to another part of the description of the Zaghāwa, al-Muhallabī said that between the Zaghāwa and the city of Dongola in Nubia there were twenty stages; al-Muhallabī *apud* Yāḳūt, Vol. 1, p. 277.

In the north, the kingdom of the Zaghāwa or Kānem extended as far as Bilma and al-Ḳaṣaba in Kawār. The land of the Zaghāwa (the reference here is to Kānem) was not a desert area and its inhabitants subsisted on their crops, chiefly millet and legumes. They also possessed herds of sheep, cattle, camels and horses. At the time when al-Muhallabī was writing, the Zaghāwa of Kānem were still infidels; they venerated their king whom they worshipped in the place of God. They went about naked, merely covering their loins with the skins of animals, with the exception of the king who wore woollen trousers and a silk garment from Sūs (Morocco).[71]

Ibn Ḥawḳal seems to identify the land of the Zaghāwa with Kānem. He mentions the existence of a route that linked the land of the Zaghāwa (Kānem) with Fezzān, that is, apparently Djarma, the capital of that region; two months' walking distance lay between Fezzān and Zaghāwa, which seems to me to be an exaggeration.[72]

Kānem was not unknown to al-Bakrī, according to whom this region lay on the other side of the desert of Zawīla, forty days' walking distance from that city. The inhabitants of that region were at the time 'idolaters'.[73]

Al-Idrīsī, to whom we are indebted for a highly detailed description of the Sahara and the Sudan, devoted several passages in his work to the Zaghāwa and the Kānem (he distinguishes between the two ethnic groups). Kānem was a kingdom whose sovereign inhabited the city of Mānān. The soldiers of the king of Kānem wore no clothes, as at the time of al-Muhallabī one hundred and fifty years previously. In addition to Mānān, al-Idrīsī mentions another city in Kānem, Andjīmī (present-day Ndjimī). Six days' walking distance from Andjīmī lay the city, or rather the centre, of the Zaghāwa, around which lived several branches of this people, who were camel-breeders. Al-Idrīsī tells us nothing about the political situation of this Tubu group which, at that time, was probably independent of the king of Kānem. Speaking of the Zaghāwa, he stresses that the territory of the Zaghāwa borders on Fezzān, thereby including the region of Kawār in the territories inhabited by the Zaghāwa.[74] In another chapter, al-Idrīsī speaks of two centres of the Zaghāwa, to wit, Saghāwa (which is probably identical to Sakawa, the name given to the Zaghāwa in the southern part of present-day Wadaī) and Shāma (perhaps present-day Tin-Shaman, north of Agadès). The resources of these Zaghāwa branches derived from stock-raising (they subsisted on the milk, butter and meat of their herds) and

71. Cf. N. Levtzion and J. F. P. Hopkins (eds), 1981, pp. 171, 173.

72. Ibn Ḥawḳal, 1938, p. 92; cf. N. Levtzion and J. F. P. Hopkins (eds), 1981, p. 46.

73. Al-Bakrī, 1911, p. 11; 1913, p. 29; cf. N. Levtzion and J. F. P. Hopkins (eds), 1981, p. 64. Al-Bakrī apparently gleaned this information from a source prior to the fifth/eleventh century, perhaps from a geographical work by Ibn al-Warrāk (d. 362/973), since the fifth/eleventh century may be considered to have witnessed the beginnings of Islamization in that region, the population of which finally embraced Islam after 500/1107.

74. Al-Idrīsī, 1866, pp. 33 *et seq.*; cf. N. Levtzion and J. F. P. Hopkins (eds), 1981, pp. 114 *et seq.*

sorghum-growing. Among the Zaghāwa in Shāma and Saghāwa there also lived a group of Berber origin known as the Sadrāta. These were nomads whose way of life was in all aspects like that of the Zaghāwa. They were thus in the process of becoming assimilated with the Teda-Daza-Zaghāwa.[75]

The northern Sahara

The northern Sahara embraces all the region situated between the Atlas in the north and the Ahaggar (Hoggar) in the south, to the west and south-west of Ghadāmes. It is a territory where, amidst the calcareous *hammāda*s and sand dunes of the Western Great Erg and the Eastern Great Erg (the *blēd al-atesh*, or 'land of thirst'), there are wells and magnificent oases (the *blēd al-bīyār*, or 'land of wells'). At the edge of the crop-growing land (mainly palm groves) in these oases are fortified villages (known as *ḳṣūrs* in literary Arabic). They were established, as were the palm groves and the *foggāras* that irrigate them (particularly in Tuwāt), by various Ibāḍite, Muʿtazilite and even Jewish groups of the great Berber branch of the Zanāta.

These oases can be divided into three groups:

(1) The eastern oases, irrigated by artesian wells, concentrated around the foot of the Atlas.
(2) The western oases which are irrigated by *foggāra*s, forming a strip some 1200 km long which runs between the Saharan Atlas of Figuīg on one side and Tidikelt on the other.
(3) Half-way between these two groups lies a third important group of oases – the Mzāb.

The most easterly of these three groups of oases is that of Sūf, surrounded on all sides by the sand, on the route that leads from Djarīd to Tuggurt and Wargla. Right from the beginning of the period of Arab domination in North Africa, if not even before, this oasis was of some importance, being one of the stages on the trade route linking southern Tunisia, inhabited between the second/eighth and sixth/twelfth centuries by the Ibāḍite Berbers, to the Ibāḍite Berber centres of Wādī Rīgh and Wargla and also to the Sudan. We do not know the period in which the palm groves and villages of Sūf were established. The first mention of this oasis is to be found in the ancient Ibāḍite chronicles, where it is referred to as Sūf or Asūf. In the latter half of the fourth/tenth century Sūf was inhabited by Ibāḍite Berbers who maintained close relations with Djārīd, and especially with the city of Tozeur. The inhabitants of Sūf belonged to the various branches descended from the Zanāta or related to that Berber family (like the Lawāta). It is further to be noted that to the north of Sūf,

75. Al-Idrīsī, 1866; cf. N. Levtzion and J. F. P. Hopkins (eds), 1981, pp. 119–20.

PLATE 11.1 *Tenth-century mosque in the city of Tozeur, Djarīd*

towards the district of Nefzāwa, the Banū Mūlīt, who also formed part of the Zanāta, lived as nomads in the fifth/eleventh century.[76]

A hundred or so kilometres west of the oasis of Sūf are to be found the many large oases of Wādī Rīgh, situated in a gully 20 km wide. In the period under consideration, Wādī Rīgh, which is known to us from Arab sources (and especially the Ibāḍite chronicles) by the name of (Wādī) Rīgh or Arīgh, was dotted with several cities and fortified villages (*ḳuṣūr*). Later, at the time of Ibn Khaldūn), (eighth/fourteenth century), there were some three hundred of these. We know the names of several of these places, such as Adjlū al-Gharbiyya (western Adjlū), Adjlū al-Sharkiyya (eastern Adjlū), Tīdjīt, Ḳaṣr Banī Nūba, Tighūrt (present-day Tuggurt) and Waghlāna. In addition to these five cities, the Ibāḍite sources mention several of lesser importance which are difficult to identify, except perhaps for Tīn Tamerna, probably identical to Tamerna, Tīn Islīmān (Sīdī Slīmān), to the north of Tuggurt, and the oasis of Aḳūḳ (Gūg).

Rīgh or Arīgh derives its name from the Rīgha Berbers, a group of the Maghrāwa belonging to the great Zanāta family. However, in addition to the Rīgha, there were other Zanāta groups, such as the Banū Wartīzalen,

76. We are not acquainted with the history of Sūf. We do know, however, that Sārāt al-Lawātīya, an Ibāḍite woman of some repute who lived during the latter half of the fifth/eleventh century, came from this oasis. It was at the time of this woman that an Ibāḍite caravan returning from Tādmekka (in Adrār des Ifoghas, to the north of Gao) passed through Sūf, probably on its way to Tozeur.

Banū Wīlīl, Banū Zalghīn, Banū Itūfa, Maghrāwa, Banū Yandjāsen and Banū Lant. Among other Berbers who inhabited Wādī Rīgh or led a nomadic existence in the vicinity of those oases, mention should also be made of the Banū Warmāz (Warzemār) and the three peoples who lived as Bedouins, the Banū Warsifān, the Banū Ghomāra (or Ghomra) and the Banū Sindjāsen. It is not impossible that the latter were identical to the Banū Sindjās, a branch of the Maghrāwa who, according to Ibn Khaldūn, still inhabited Wādi Rīgh in the eighth/fourteenth century.

Very little is known about the history of Wādī Rīgh before the sixth/twelfth century. The autochthonous population attribute the origin of their wells to Dhu 'l-Karnayn (the man with two horns), or in other words Alexander the Great. However, no mention was ever made of the oases of Wādī Rīgh by the ancient writers and they were no doubt established after the period of Roman domination in North Africa. The first reference to this region in the written sources has to do with the great Berber nomad chief Yabīb ibn Zalghīn who lived at the time of the Rustumid *imām* Aflaḥ ibn 'Abd al-Wahhāb (208/823–257/871).

In the latter half of the fourth/tenth century the population of Wādī Rīgh was mainly composed of various groups of Ibāḍite Maghrāwa. In 471/1078–9 a civil war began which caused the downfall of this group of oases. A further war took place in Wādī Rīgh in 502/1108–9. It is also to be noted that, in the fourth/tenth and fifth/eleventh centuries, the oases of Wādī Rīgh played an important role in the lives of the North African Ibāḍites.

The most important of all the eastern oases of the northern Sahara is that of Wargla, known to the medieval Arab geographers as Wārdjlān or Wārḳlān. We know nothing about the origins of Wargla, having no information regarding this oasis prior to the Arab conquest. However, it is not impossible that, at the time of the later Byzantine empire, there already existed in that place a village which was a stage on the caravan route linking Numidia to the Hoggar and probably also to the Niger Bend. It was by means of this route that trade was carried on between Numidia and the central Sahara. This trade must have been fairly modest in antiquity. The name 'Wargla' can be found in that of the Moorish 'tribe' of the Urceliani, referred to by Corippus in the sixth century.[77] It was perhaps people belonging to the Urceliani who built dwellings in Wargla at a time prior to the Muslim invasion. As well as these primitive dwellings, there were also in the oasis of Wargla several real towns which were already there at the time of the arrival of the first Arabs in the Maghrib, i.e. around the middle of the first/seventh century. V. Largeau[78] refers to eleven towns or villages which existed at that time in the oasis of Wargla, the ruins of which are still visible.

77. Corippus, 1970, p. 128; T. Lewicki, 1976, p. 10.
78. V. Largeau, 1879, *passim*.

Wargla is mentioned in the Arab sources for the first time (as Wārḳlān) during the period of the Umayyad Caliph Hishām ibn ʿAbd al-Malik (105/724–125/742). According to al-Zuhrī (mid sixth/twelfth century), it was during this period that the inhabitants of Wargla were converted to Islam.[79]

It appears that the inhabitants of the oasis of Wargla very soon, like nearly all the other Berbers, adopted the Khāridjite doctrines in protest against the oppressive rule of the orthodox government. They became Ibāḍites, adhering to the most moderate branch of that sect and they soon entered into close relationship with the Ibāḍite *imāms* of Tāhert.[80]

As for the city of Sadrāta or Sedrāta, it seems to have been the capital of the oasis of Wargla between the fourth/tenth and sixth/twelfth centuries. The name of this city derives from that of the Sadrāta Berbers, another group of which inhabited the Mzāb, in the vicinity of Biskra. The ruins of Sadrāta are 14 km south of the city of Wargla. In these ruins the vestiges of a mosque have been found and of the tomb of the *imām* Yaʿḳūb ibn Aflaḥ, the last Rustumid *imām*, who fled to Wargla following the capture of Tāhert by the Fāṭimid army in 296/908.[81] In 322/934 Sadrāta was besieged by the Fāṭimid army and its inhabitants abandoned the city and took refuge in Karīma (present-day Gara Krīma, south of Wargla).

Later, at the time of al-Bakrī (fifth/eleventh century), there were seven 'castles' in the oasis of Wargla, the largest of which was known as Aghren en-Ikammen in Berber, a name which is completely unknown to the Ibāḍite authors. Alongside these cities and 'castles', the written sources mention several Berber towns or villages located in the oasis of Wargla, such as Fadjūha, Ḳaṣr Bakr (or Tīn Bakr, Ḳaṣr Banī Bakr), Aghlām, Tīn Imṣīwen, Tīn Bā Māṭūs, Tamāwāṭ and Ifrān.

Thanks to the written sources, and especially the Ibāḍite chronicles, we also have some information about the composition of the population of the oasis of Wargla between the second/eighth and sixth/twelfth centuries. We saw earlier that the name of the oasis derives from that of the 'tribe' of the Urceliani or Wārdjlān, a branch of the Zanāta which founded it, according to Ibn Khaldūn. It has already been stated that among the early inhabitants of Wargla there was also a group of the Sadrāta, which belonged to a branch of the Lawāta. Among other Berbers who inhabited the oasis of Wargla, mention should also be made of the Banū Yādjrīn (or Yāgrīn), known as the Yāḳrīn (or Yagrīn) by Ibn Ḥawḳal, the Tināwata, known from Ghadāmes, the Banū Warzemār, a group of which led a nomadic existence in the vicinity of Wādī Rīgh, and the great *ḳabīla* of the Banū Wartīzalen who also inhabited Wādī Rīgh earlier.[82] In addition to the

79. Al-Zuhrī, 1968, pp. 181, 340.
80. Cf. T. Lewicki, 1976, pp. 9–11.
81. Cf. M. van Berchem, 1952, 1954.
82. Ibn Ḥawḳal, 1964, pp. 103–4.

Wahbite or Nukkārite Ibāḍite Berbers, there was in Wargla no lack of orthodox Mālikite Muslims whom the Ibāḍites sometimes called the Ashʿarites. It is also to be noted that Yāḳūt, in his brief description of Wargla, mentions, alongside the Berbers, the presence of an ethnic group known as the Madjdjāna.[83] These were African Christians of Roman origin who emigrated to Wargla after the fall of Tāhert, following the last Rustumid *imām*, whose faithful servants they were.[84] It appears that the Berber inhabitants of Rīgh and Wargla had already largely interbred with the blacks before the sixth/twelfth century.[85]

All the towns and cities of the oasis of Wargla formed part of the district known in the fifth/eleventh century as *iḳlīm Wārdjlān* ('district of Wardjlān'). At the beginning of the fourth/tenth century in the oasis of Wargla there was a *rāʾis* ('chief') who lived in Tāghyārt. Al-Wisyānī mentions a *rāʾis* of Tāghyārt named Ismāʿīl ibn Kāsin, flanked in Wargla by the *wulāt Wārdjlān* ('governors of Wārdjlān'), who were no doubt subordinate to this *rāʾis*. In the early half of the fifth/eleventh century there were in Wargla twenty-three *mutawallī*, probably town administrators, whose powers, however, we know nothing about.[86] In addition to the *rāʾis* and governors, the Ibāḍite sources mention the existence in Wargla of notables (who probably consisted primarily of the leading merchants), known as *aʿyān* and *akābir*. Such was the situation at the beginning of the tenth century. It is further to be noted that, in the oasis of Wargla, a certain role was also played by councils in which were represented the inhabitants of all the villages in that oasis. These councils met once in the village of Tamāwāt.

After the fall of the Rustumid imāmate, whose sovereignty was recognized by the inhabitants of Wargla, this oasis became completely independent despite the efforts of the Fāṭimids who, in the first half of the fourth/tenth century, attempted to conquer it, no doubt because of its economic importance. Later Wargla was for some time ruled by the dynasty of the Banū Ḥammād. Thus it was that the Ḥammādite sultan al-Nāṣir ibn ʿAlannās (454/1062–482/1089) was represented by a governor in that oasis.

The commercial role of Wargla was considerable owing to the fact that this city was the starting-point of the route followed by all the North African and Egyptian merchants who travelled to the Western Sudan. Let us now consider Wargla's relations with the major trade centres of North Africa and the markets of the Western and Central Sudan.

83. Yāḳūt, 1866–73, Vol. 4, p. 920.
84. Cf. T. Lewicki, 1976, pp. 79–90.
85. The ethnic situation in Wargla and Wādī Rīgh must have been similar at that time to what it was at the beginning of the tenth/sixteenth century, as described by Joannes Leo Africanus, who says in his *Description of Africa* that 'the men are for the most part Negro ... because these people have many black female slaves with whom they sleep, with the result that they have black children'. Cf. Leo Africanus, 1956, pp. 437 *et seq.*
86. T. Lewicki, 1976, pp. 10–11.

As early as the mid-third/ninth century a direct route, which passed through Laghwāt, linked Wargla to Tāhert, while another trade route existed between Wargla and the city of Sidjilmāsa, which constituted the most important northern terminus of the caravan routes between northern Africa and the Western Sudan and the destination of the gold and slaves from Ghana and the land of Wanḳāra. Originally Wargla was merely one of the stopping places on the great route between the Sudan and Egypt; this route passed through Tripolitania and Djarīd on its way first to Wargla and then to Sidjilmāsa. However, the merchants of Wargla soon began to take an active part in the trade between Sidjilmāsa and the gold-bearing lands of the Western Sudan. There is frequent mention by the Arab geographers of merchants from Wargla in that city, who had apparently come via the Sidjilmāsa route, although it is not impossible that these merchants travelled to Ghana and Wankāra by the route leading from Tādmekka and Kāw-Kāw (Gao).[87]

Another route linked the Mzāb (present-day Zībān) to the city of Wargla and the Land of the Blacks. It is known to us thanks to al-Idrīsī, who adds that this was the route used to export dates from the Mzāb to the Sudan.[88]

The next trade route was the Wargla–Tlemcen route which is known to us from al-Bakrī, who also mentions a route linking the capital of the Ḥammādite state Ḳalʿa Abī Ṭawīl (Ḳalʿa Banū Ḥammād. the ruins of which now lie 30 km away from Bordj Areridj) to the city of Wargla.[89]

The most ancient and, at the same time, the most direct route linking Wargla, and thereby the whole of the Maghrib, to the Sudan was that leading from Wargla to Tādmekka in Adrār des Ifoghas (the present-day ruins of Es-Sūk, at a distance of 45 km from the village of Kidal), and from there to the city of Gao. According to al-Bakrī, this route began in Tādmekka and went to Ḳayrawān, passing through Wargla and Ḳaṣṭīliya (Tozeur).[90] We know from the Ibāḍite sources that trade between Wargla and Tādmekka was carried on as early as the latter half of the fourth/tenth century and that one of the items traded was clothing, which was exchanged for gold.[91]

In addition to the Wargla–Tādmekka–Gao route there was another major trans-Saharan route that linked the city of Wargla to the markets of

87. The earliest mention of the direct route linking Egypt to Sidjilmāsa is to be found in the Ibāḍite chronicle of Abū Zakarīyāʾ al-Wardjlāni (sixth/twelfth century) and concerns an occurrence dating from the fourth/tenth century. This route passed through Tozeur and Wargla and led directly to Sidjilmāsa. Cf. T. Lewicki, 1960.

88. Al-Idrīsī, 1866, p. 4; N. Levtzion and J. F. P. Hopkins (eds), 1981, p. 108.

89. Al-Bakrī, 1911, p. 182; 1913, p. 340; N. Levtzion and J. F. P. Hopkins (eds), 1981, p. 86.

90. N. Levtzion and J. F. P. Hopkins (eds), 1981, pp. 84–71; cf. T. Lewicki, 1976, pp. 32–41.

91. N. Levtzion and J. F. P. Hopkins (eds), 1981, pp. 89, 91. It was apparently the same route that was taken by Kaydad, the father of Abū Yazīd Makhlad to travel to Tādmekka and Gao. The latter was born in Tādmekka *c.* 272/885. Cf. Chap. 12 below.

PLATE 11.2 *One of the oases of the Mzāb*

the Western Sudan. I am referring here to the Wargla–Ghana route. This route was far more important than the Wargla–Tādmekka one as the city of Ghana was a major storage place for the gold brought from the gold-bearing regions of Bambuk and Buré. The Wargla–Ghana route passed through the city of Sidjilmāsa, in the land of Tafilālet, which was a major Saharan emporium, the true gateway to the Sudan. The sovereigns of Sidjilmāsa (who belonged to the Miknāsa, related to the Zanāta) professed the beliefs of the Ṣufrite sect, closely related to those of the Ibāḍites, and were on respectful terms with the Rustumid *imāms* of Tāhert. It appears that the Wargla–Sidjilmāsa route passed through El-Goléa. As for the second part of the Wargla–Ghana route, after leaving Sidjilmāsa, it went on to the city of Tāmdūlt in Sūs al-Aḳṣā (Tāmdūlt is present-day Wāḳa in south-western Morocco). We know of this route thanks to al-Bakrī who also gives us the names of the following two stages, namely Īzil, which is Kēdiat d'Idjīl, and the city of Awdāghust, an important market in the southern part of present-day Mauritania, where today lie the ruins of Tegdaoust.[92] According to al-Zuhrī, the route from Sidjilmāsa to Ghana also passed

92. Al-Bakrī, 1911, pp. 155 *et seq.*; 1913, pp. 295 *et seq.*; N. Levtzion and J. F. P. Hopkins (eds), 1981, pp. 66–9. For an examination of the information provided by al-Bakrī, cf. V. Monteil, 1968. See below.

through the city of Azuḳī (Azugī) in the Mauritania Adrār.[93] There was also another route from Wargla to Ghana which passed through Tād-mekka. The most direct route between Wargla and Tāhert passed through the region of the Mzāb, through Tilghment and Laghwāt, i.e. through the middle group of oases of the northern Sahara, situated between Wādī Rīgh and Wargla on one side, and Tuwāt-Gurāra on the other.

According to Ibn Khaldūn, the name of the Mzāb derives from that of a Zanāta group that founded the villages in this region. However, the Banū Mzāb and the region itself were known to the Ibāḍites as early as the third/ninth century by the Arabized name of Mus'ab. The Ibāḍite chronicles mention the Banū Mus'ab or Djabal Mus'ab, which corresponds to the present-day Mzāb. The Banū Mus'ab originally professed the Mu'tazilite doctrine, but later (in the fifth/eleventh century) they were converted to the Ibāḍite faith.

Among the towns founded in the northern Sahara by the Zanāta, mention should be made of the fortress of Tālghement (present-day Tilghement or Tilrhemt) and the city of Laghouat (Laghwāt), already known in the fourth/tenth century by the name of al-Aghwāt, which was under the domination of the Zanāta chief, al-Khayr ibn Muḥammad ibn Khazar al-Zānātī.

Another important city in this region was the *ḳṣar*, El-Goléa, now known as Taurīrt al-Mānia, which, in all likelihood, connected Wargla to the Sidjilmāsa route. It also appears that the route leading from Wargla to Tādmekka branched off at El-Goléa. El-Goléa is mentioned by al-Bakrī by the name of al-Ḳal'a ('the Fortress'). It was a highly populated city 'which contained a mosque and the remains of a few ancient monuments'.[94] El Goléa lies to the east of the Western Great Erg on a cone-shaped mountain which, according to local tradition, was formerly surrounded by vast cereal fields and a large number of palm trees irrigated by twenty-four *foggāra*s.

The western group of oases in the northern Sahara is formed by Gurāra, Tuwāt and Tidikelt, which possess a clearly marked geographical unity. Of these three, Gurāra is the most populated and has the most water and palm trees. Tuwāt forms a 'streets of palm trees' more than 200 km long between Būda and Taurīrt; it is less heavily populated than Gurāra and the number of palm trees contained by this group of oases is only slightly higher than the number of date palms in Gurāra. Lastly, the number of palm trees in Tidikelt is only half that of Gurāra. The oases of the western group are irrigated by means of underground water catchment and supply conduits, known as *foggāra*s.

The history of Gurāra, Tuwāt and Tidikelt up to the eighth/fourteenth century is practically unknown. It is generally assumed that all these oases were established only recently, in the sixth century of the Christian era in

93. Al-Zuhrī, 1968, pp. 190 *et seq.*; N. Levtzion and J. F. P. Hopkins (eds), 1981, pp. 95–8.

94. Al-Bakrī, 1911, p. 77; 1913, pp. 156–7.

the case of Gurāra and as late as the eleventh/seventeenth century in the case of some of the oases of Tidikelt. In Tamentīt, in Tuwāt, a stone idol with a ram's head has been found, which gives grounds for thinking that this place was inhabited before the Islamic period by a Libyco-Berber people, probably originating from eastern Libya where they adopted, perhaps in Sīwa, the cult of Ammon with the ram's horns. These newcomers also learned from the eastern Libyans the art of boring *foggāra*s.

As for the Judaization of the Saharan Berbers, this probably began in the second century of the Christian era and was the consequence of the dispersal of the Jews of Cyrenaica who, after the repression ordered by the Roman emperor Trajan, fled to Mauritania and the Sahara. Later there was a further Jewish immigration to Gurāra and Tuwāt. According to local tradition, a synagogue was built in Tamentīt in the year 517 of the Christian era, and another in 725.[95]

The Zanāta groups made a further thrust towards Gurāra and Tuāt in the mid-fifth/eleventh century. This second move was occasioned by the invasion of the Banū Hilāl and also by the invasion of the Almoravids in Morocco, following which some of the Berbers, Zanāta and others, either Muslim or converted to Judaism, escaped to the Sahara.

The central Sahara

In the centre of the Sahara and south of El-Goléa and Wargla lies a highland region known as Ahaggar or the Hoggar, which extends north-east into Tassili-n-Ajjer and westwards into Muydir. Two other massifs form a continuation of Ahaggar southwards, namely Aïr and Adrār des Ifoghas. These Saharan regions were peopled in the second/eighth–sixth/twelfth centuries by various Berber groups descended from the branch known as the Ṣanhādja, who were the ancestors of the present-day Tuareg. During this period no large city or palm grove existed in Ahaggar or Tassili-n-Ajjer.

In Adrār des Ifoghas and Aïr, on the contrary, there were, as we are told by medieval Arab sources, true cities, the inhabitants of which engaged in trade but where there was a complete lack of palm trees and gardens (*aghren*), as was the case in Tādmekka in Adrār des Ifoghas, or where such vegetation was rather insignificant.

Tassili-n-Ajjer derives its name from the Adjdjer or Azger Berbers, the earliest description of whom is given to us by al-Idrīsī.[96] According to that author, who calls the Adjdjer by the name of the Āzḳār (for Āzgār), these people were camel-drivers whose political centre, which may have been in

95. Regarding Judaization, cf. H. Z. Hirschenberg, 1974, Vol. 1; the commercial role of the Jews is discussed by M. Abitbol, 1981.

96. Al-Idrīsī, 1866, pp. 36 *et seq.*; N. Levtzion and J. F. P. Hopkins (eds), 1981, pp. 121–2.

the region of present-day Ghāt or Djānet, was eighteen days' walking distance from Ghadāmes and twelve from the city of Tassāwa in Fezzān. It appears that the latter route is identical to the ancient route of the 'Garamantean chariots' which, in the first millennium before the Christian era, linked Fezzān to Gao, passing through the region of Ajjer, Ahaggar and Adrār des Ifoghas. The existence of this ancient route is proved by the discoveries of Abalessa and by several ancient coins found in the vicinity.

As for the Azḳār–Ghadāmes route (the starting-point of which was probably somewhere near Ghāt or Djānet), it must be the same as the northern part of the Tādmekka–Ghadāmes route described in the fifth/eleventh century by al-Bakrī. However, the exact whereabouts of the stages on this route are unknown to us.

We know very little about the history of Ahaggar between the second/eighth and the sixth/twelfth centuries. Local tradition has it that, before Islamic times, there lived in Ahaggar an idolatrous Tuareg-speaking people by the name of the Isebeten (or Isabeten, sing. Asabat) who practised a pre-Tuareg form of agriculture (fig trees, vines and palm groves) and possessed irrigation channels. The present-day *ḳabīla* of the Dag-Ghāli claims to be descended from these Isebeten and to be the true owners of the land. Later Ahaggar was invaded by the Lamṭa and then by the Hawwāra who gave it its name (through the change of the Berber phoneme *ww* into *gg*, attested by Ibn Khaldūn). According to that author, a group of the Hawwāra crossed the sands and settled alongside the 'veil-wearing' Lamṭa who lived near the city of Kāw-Kāw (Gao) in the 'Land of the Blacks'.[97] Ibn Baṭṭūṭa, who crossed the Ahaggar region, tells us that its inhabitants wore a veil over their faces.[98] It seems that the arrival of the Ahaggar-Hawwāra in the territory where they now live must have been connected with the defeat inflicted upon the Hawwāra of Awrās by the Fāṭimid prince al-Mu'izz in 342/953 and to the routing of these rebels, some of whom fled 'as far as the Land of the Blacks', apparently in the direction of present-day Ahaggar.

The Arab sources mention several regions (or places) in Aïr that were already known in the third/ninth century. Al-Ya'ḳūbī mentions there – among the kingdoms under the sway of the Sudanese state of Kāw-Kāw (above the loop of the Niger) – kingdoms that were probably located in Aïr. These were the kingdoms of Maranda, al-Hazban (in the manuscript al-Harbar) and Tikarkarīn (in the manuscript Tidkarīr).[99]

The first of these kingdoms, which is also known to us from the *Kitāb al-Buldān* of Ibn al-Faḳīh al-Hamadānī (written about 290/903) and, later, from the geographical works of Ibn Ḥawḳal and al-Idrīsī, derives its name

97. N. Levtzion and J. F. P. Hopkins (eds), 1981, p. 327.

98. Ibn Baṭṭūṭa, 1969, Vol. 4, pp. 444 *et seq.*; N. Levtzion and J. F. P. Hopkins (eds), 1981, p. 304.

99. Al-Ya'ḳūbī, 1883, p. 219; N. Levtzion and J. F. P. Hopkins (eds), 1981, p. 21.

from the small town and water-hole (present-day Marandet) situated to the south of Agadès. The remains of an ancient village can still be seen there that have, according to R. Mauny, provided us with vestigial evidence of an ancient copper foundry.[100] According to Ibn al-Faḳīh, the people known as the Maranda lived to the north of Kāw-Kāw and their 'land' (or rather their capital) was a stopping place on the major trans-Saharan route leading from Gao to the oases of Egypt.[101] In the latter half of the fourth/tenth century Ibn Ḥawḳal mentions Maranda as a stage on the route leading from Ghana to Adjadābīya in Cyrenaica. It lay one month's walking distance away from the city of Kāw-Kāw (Gao), constituting the following stage (after Gao) on this route which then passed through the city of Zawīla in Fezzān.[102] According to al-Idrīsī, Maranda was a highly populated city, 'a refuge and a place of rest for those who come and go in the course of their travels and expeditions'. However, according to the same author, 'travellers seldom pass by there'.[103]

As for al-Hazban (al-Hazbin), we are indebted for the correct form of the word to J. Marquart who identifies it as Azben or Azbin.[104] This, according to H. Barth, was the early name of Aïr, used by the black or mixed-race population of that region, still in use at the time of that traveller, i.e. around the middle of the nineteenth century.[105]

The third kingdom cited by al-Ya'ḳūbī goes by the name of Tikarkarīn; this is the Berber feminine plural of Takarkart, a name which reappears on our maps as Tacarcart. This cliff is situated halfway between the city of Tahua and that of Agadès, in a region where there is no lack of evidence of an ancient civilization. In the eighth/fourteenth century Ibn Baṭṭūṭa speaks of a Berber sultan by the name of at-Takarkarī who had a dispute with the sultan of Takedda (present-day Azelik) in the south-western part of Aïr. In another part of Ibn Baṭṭūṭa's work the sultan in question bears the name of al-Karkarī, without the Berber prefix *Ta*.[106]

Alongside Azbin which, as we just saw, is the early name for Aïr, a few Arab sources also contain a reference to this last name. It appears in the writings of al-Bakrī in the form of Hayr or Hīr.[107] The modern Arabic form of this name is Ahīr and, in Tamashek, Aïr.

The massif of Adrār des Ifoghas was not unknown either to the early Arab geographers, mainly on account of the city of Tādmekka (today the ruins of Es-Sūḳ, 45 km north of the present-day village of Kidal), which

100. R. Mauny, 1961, p. 138.
101. Ibn al-Faḳīh, 1885, p. 68; N. Levtzion and J. F. P. Hopkins (eds), 1981, p. 27.
102. Ibn Ḥawḳal, 1938, p. 92; N. Levtzion and J. F. P. Hopkins (eds), 1981, p. 46.
103. Al-Idrīsī, 1866, p. 41; N. Levtzion and J. F. P. Hopkins (eds), 1981, p. 125.
104. J. Marquart, 1913, pp. lxxviii and cix–cxvi.
105. H. Barth, 1857–8, Vol. 1, p. 382.
106. Ibn Baṭṭūṭa, 1969, Vol. 4, p. 442; N. Levtzion and J. F. P. Hopkins (eds), 1981, p. 303.
107. Al-Bakrī, 1911, p. 183; N. Levtzion and J. F. P. Hopkins (eds), 1981, p. 87.

was its political centre. Tādmekka was also an important stage on the caravan route leading from Gao to G͟hadāmes and the city of Tripoli. Nine days' walking distance lay between Gao and Tādmekka and forty between Tādmekka and G͟hadāmes, by way of the region of Sag͟hmāra and four deserts, described by al-Bakrī.[108]

The Sag͟hmāra were Berbers who lived in a region extending to the north, or rather the north-east, of Tādmekka, to a point six days' walking distance (i.e. about 120 km as the crow flies) from the ruins of Es-Sūk. They also inhabited the area under the dominion of Tādmekka, which lay south of this city, opposite the city of Gao. H. Lhote identifies this group with the Tuareg Isekkamaren (sing. Asekkamar), some of whom still nomadize today in Adrār des Ifog͟has.[109]

Tādmekka already existed in the third/ninth century and was an important trade centre, visited mainly by Ibāḍite Berber merchants from Wargla, Djarīd and Djabal Nafūsa who frequented this city to obtain the gold that was brought in large quantities from the gold-bearing areas near Ghana. It also served as a storage place for merchandise from the Mag͟hrib, especially clothing, which was brought in by the Wargla route. Tādmekka was better constructed than Ghana and Gao but had no crops.[110]

In the fourth/tenth century Tādmekka formed a state governed by the kings belonging to the Banū Tānmak (a branch of the Ṣanhādja). According to Yāḳūt, the name of this state was Tādmāk and its capital was called Zakrān, which should be amended to Akrām (or Agrām). However, the inhabitants of that city did not belong to the Berber branch of the Ṣanhādja but to the Zanāta. While the Zanāta inhabitants of the capital were, from the third/ninth century onwards, Ibāḍite Muslims, the Ṣanhādja of Tādmāk did not become Muslims until 503/1109–10.[111]

Another ancient city, Tasalīt, is an old site where ancient mines have been discovered and where there was copper and an ore slightly reminiscent of turquoise, formerly used to make the famous 'pearls of Gao'. In my view, this was the city known as Tasalā or Tasalī, mentioned by al-Zuhrī. According to that geographer, the city of Tasalā or Tasalī was nine days' walking distance from Tādmekka, which suggests that it corresponded to present-day Tasalīt, which lies 180 km north of Es-Sūk as the crow flies. The people of Tasalā/Tasalī, like those of Tādmekka, were at war with the inhabitants of Ghana; they converted to Islam in 503/1109.[112]

Six days' walking distance from Tādmekka, according to al-Bakrī, lay a region known as Tūtak or Tawtak which possessed underground salt

108. Al-Bakrī, 1911, pp. 181–2; 1913, pp. 339–43; N. Levtzion and J. F. P. Hopkins (eds), 1981, pp. 85–6.

109. H. Lhote, 1955, pp. 126 *et seq.*

110. N. Levtzion and J. F. P. Hopkins (eds), 1981, pp. 86–7.

111. Yāḳūt, 1866–73, Vol. 2, p. 938; cf. T. Lewicki, 1981, pp. 439–43.

112. Al-Zuhrī, 1968, pp. 181–2; N. Levtzion and J. F. P. Hopkins (eds), 1981, pp. 98–9.

mines.[113] The province of Tūtak derives its name from a branch of the Ṣanhādja known to us from Ibn Ḥawḳal's list of Berber *ḳabīlas*.[114] We are unable to ascertain the exact whereabouts of this region. It is not impossible that its name, as well as that of the tribe of the Tūtak, is connected with that of the Taïtok, a noble Tuareg group now living in Ahnet, a region to the north of Adrār des Ifoghas and to the north-west of Tamanraset.

The western Sahara

The ethnic and political situation of this part of the Sahara, which extends westwards from Adrār des Ifoghas and southwards from Morocco as far as the Atlantic Ocean, is known to us, for the period from the first/eighth to the sixth/twelfth centuries, from Arab sources.

The earliest information concerns the expedition led by the general 'Uḳba ibn Nāfi' in southern Morocco. In 62/682 this commander entered the province of as-Sūs al-Aḳṣā and even crossed its southern borders into the Sahara, where 'he attacked the Massūfa and, having taken many of them prisoner, retraced his steps'.[115]

The purpose of the expedition led by 'Uḳba ibn Nāfi' was not in our opinion the permanent Arab conquest and Islamization of southern Morocco and the western Sahara, although a medieval Arab historian speaks of the conversion to Islam, under the pressure of this general, of the south Moroccan Berbers of the Djazūla group. It appears, however, that its purpose was rather to reconnoitre the gold-bearing regions of the Western Sudan, and in this it was similar to that undertaken by the same 'Uḳba ibn Nāfi' in 47/666–7 in order to survey the trade route leading from the coast of Tripolitania through Fezzān and Kawār to Lake Chad.

Twenty-five years after 'Uḳba ibn Nāfi', the new Arab governor of Ifrīḳiya, Mūsā ibn Nuṣayr, conquered, pacified and converted to Islam the major part of the territories of present-day Morocco. Between 87/705–6 and 90/708–9 Mūsā ibn Nuṣayr penetrated as far as the region of as-Sūs al-Aḳṣā whose inhabitants adopted the Islamic faith and received as their governor Marwān, the son of Mūsā ibn Nuṣayr.

But it was not until during the administration of the governor of Ifrīḳiya, 'Ubayd Allāh ibn al-Ḥabḥāb (116/734–122/740), that this province was finally conquered and converted to Islam, as a result of the expedition led by the Arab general Ḥabīb ibn Abī 'Ubayda. This expedition was directed not only against southern Morocco but also against the Western Sudan.

113. Al-Bakrī, 1911, p. 183; 1913, p. 344; N. Levtzion and J. F. P. Hopkins (eds), 1981, p. 87.

114. Ibn Ḥawḳal, 1938, p. 106; N. Levtzion and J. F. P. Hopkins (eds), 1981, p. 50; cf. T. Lewicki, 1959.

115. Ibn Khaldūn, 1925–56.

Ḥābīb ibn Abī ʿUbayda returned victorious from this expedition, bringing back a large number of prisoners and a considerable quantity of gold.[116]

It appears that his son Ismāʿīl continued the expeditions against the Berbers leading a nomadic existence in the western Sahara. No doubt these are the expeditions referred to by the eminent Muslim sectary Abul Khaṭṭāb al-Azdī (or al-Asadī) who died in 145/762 or 147/764. In one of his accounts, transmitted by Ibn al-Faḳīh, he cites the following words of the Arab commander al-Mushtarī ibn al-Aswad: 'I organized twenty war expeditions against the land of Anbiya, starting from as-Sūs al-Aḳṣā. I saw the Nile [i.e. the Senegal River]; between that river and a salt sea [i.e. the Atlantic Ocean] stood a sandy hill at the foot of which the river had its source'.[117]

This account also contains the first reference to the name Anbiya (the pronunciation of which is uncertain) to designate the territories lying between as-Sūs al-Aḳṣā and the Senegal River. The name appears later in the work of al-Fazārī (*c.*172/788), transmitted in part by al-Masʿūdī (d. 345/956) to designate the territories situated between Sidjilmāsa and the kingdom of Ghana, or in other words roughly the whole of the western Sahara.[118] According to another passage in Ibn al-Faḳīh's work, this region extends over a distance representing seventy nights' travel through plains and deserts.[119] At the end of the third/ninth century al-Yaʿḳūbī speaks of the Anbiya as a Berber people of the Ṣanhādja (Zenaga) group, whose country extended from Sidjilmāsa to the city and Berber Kingdom of Ghast (referred to by other authors as Awdāghust) on the south-eastern fringe of the territories with which we are concerned here.[120] The implication is that this mysterious name contains a veiled reference to the most ancient federation of Berbers in the western Sahara. According to Ibn Khaldūn, this federation was composed of the Massūfa, the Lamtūna and the Djuddāla; he gives the date of its fall as 306/919.[121] It was against this very federation that the Arab expeditions organized by the governor ʿUbayd Allāh ibn al-Ḥābḥāb were directed.

It appears, however, that these expeditions lasted only a short time and that fairly soon an agreement was reached between the Muslims of North Africa and the chiefs of the Anbiya federation, which subsequently made it possible to pacify the territories of the western Sahara. This gave rise to favourable conditions for trans-Saharan trade in these territories and for the propagation of the Muslim religion, brought about mainly by the

116. Cf. regarding these expeditions, T. Lewicki, 1970.

117. Ibn al-Faḳīh, 1885, p. 64; N. Levtzion and J. F. P. Hopkins (eds), 1981, p. 27.

118. Al-Masʿūdī, 1861–77, Vol. 4, pp. 37 *et seq.*; N. Levtzion and J. F. P. Hopkins (eds), 1981, p. 32.

119. Ibn al-Faḳīh, 1885, p. 81; N. Levtzion and J. F. P. Hopkins (eds), 1981, p. 28.

120. Al-Yaʿḳūbī, 1892, p. 360; N. Levtzion and J. F. P. Hopkins (eds), 1981, p. 22.

121. N. Levtzion and J. F. P. Hopkins (eds), 1981, p. 328. Concerning the origin of the name 'Anbiya' cf. H. T. Norris, 1972, p. 72.

North African merchants who were at the same time missionaries preaching the Faith of the Prophet. It is in our view to this brief period that the following words of Ibn Khaldūn refer: 'When Ifrīqiya and the Maghrib were conquered [by the Arabs] merchants penetrated the western part of the land of the Sūdān and found among them no king greater than the king of Ghāna'.[122]

These relations between the Muslim Maghrib and the Western Sudan led to a degree of rapprochement between the North African merchants and the Berber nomads of the western Sahara; the first conversions to Islam of the Berbers in this region were one of its consequences.

The first Ṣanhādjā chief to reign in the western Sahara was Tīlūtān ibn Tīklān (or Itlūtān ibn Talākākīn) who belonged to the 'tribe' of the Lamtūna. According to Ibn Abī Zar', he reigned over all the desert and more than twenty Sudanese kings paid him tribute. His territory extended over an area 'three months long and three months wide'. He could mobilize 100,000 thoroughbred camels. His reign was long and he died at the age of eighty, in 222/837. His grandson al-Athīr ibn Bātin succeeded him and reigned until his death in 287/900. The last king of the state of the Ṣanhādja was the son of al-Athīr, Tamīm, who ruled over these tribes until 306/918. He was slain by the Ṣanhādja notables who rose up against him. As a result, a breach occurred between the Ṣanhādja tribes, and it was not until 120 years later that they reunited under the command of the emir Abū 'Abd Allāh Muḥammad ibn Tīfāt (Tīfawt), known by the name of Tārsina, one of the chiefs of the Lamtūna (460/1035). His reign lasted only three years. It was followed by that of his brother-in-law, Yaḥyā, al-Djuddālī, who became the chief of the federation of the Ṣanhādja. It was through him that the Ṣanhādja 'tribes', who had hitherto been only superficially Muslim, were converted to Sunnism by the missionary 'Abd Allāh ibn Yāsīn al-Djazūlī, whom the emir Yaḥyā ibn Ibrahīm brought back with him when he returned from his journey to North Africa.[123]

According to a tradition recounted by Ibn Khaldūn, supreme authority among the Ṣanhādja lay with the Lamtūna, who already formed a large kingdom at the time of the Umayyad emir 'Abd ar-Raḥmān (139/756–172/788). Ibn Khaldūn then lists the sovereigns of the Ṣanhādja state up to Awrāken ibn Ūrtantak.[124]

Another source cited by Ibn Khaldūn mentions the most famous of the Ṣanhādja kings, who reigned 'throughout the Sahara' during the fourth/tenth century. He was Tīnazwa ibn Wanshīk ibn Bīzār, also known as Barūyān ibn Washīk ibn Izār. It appears that this prince was the same as

122. N. Levtzion and J. F. P. Hopkins (eds), 1981, p. 332.

123. Ibn Abī Zar', 1843–66, p. 76. Concerning Ibn Yāsīn and the beginning of the Almoravids, cf. Chapter 13 below.

124. Ibn Khaldūn, 1926–56, Vol. 1, p. 236.

the one known to al-Bakrī by the name of Tīn Yarūtān ibn Wīsnū ibn Nazār, who reigned between 350/961 and 360/974.[125] Ibn Ḥawḳal mentions King Tanbarūtān ibn Isfishār, whom he calls the 'prince of all the Ṣanhādja' and who may also have been the same person.[126]

After crossing the land of Anbiya, one reached according to al-Ya'ḳūbī the region known as Ghasṭ, a pagan kingdom whose king made forays into the Land of the Blacks.[127] Some of the inhabitants of this region lived in permanent settlements. It consisted of the Berber city and kingdom better known to the ancient Arab authors by the name of Awdāghust, which was an important trade centre, ten days' march from the city of Ghana. Our source for this information is the Arab geographer and traveller Ibn Ḥawḳal who passed through Awdāghust in 340/951–2 and who adds that two months' march lay between Awdāghust and the city of Sidjilmāsa.[128] According to al-Muhallabī (writing around the end of the fourth/tenth century), Awdāghust was the name of a vast region and also of its capital, situated more than forty days' march from Sidjilmāsa across sand and desert. According to another passage from the same source, Awdāghust contained fine markets, and travellers flocked in from all sides; the inhabitants were Muslims. The chief of the region was a man belonging to the Ṣanhādja group.[129]

According to al-Bakrī, in the years from 350/961 to 360/971 the state of Awdāghust was ruled by a king known as Tīn Yarūtān from the tribe of the Ṣanhādja whose empire extended over two months' march. It thus appears that for a while the kingdom of Awdāghust belonged to the federation of the Ṣanhādja groups.

More than twenty black kings recognized the king of Awdāghust as their sovereign. Later, the Berber king of Awdāghust recognized (up to 446/1054) the supremacy of the black king of Ghana (unlike the Lamtūna, Massūfa and Djuddāla who were independent of Ghana). Awdāghust at that time was a densely populated big city whose large and wealthy population was composed of Arabs and Berbers (including members of the Nafūsa, Lawāta, Zanāta, Nafzāwa and also the Berkadjāna groups). In the Awdāghust market 'thronging with people at all times of the day' purchases were made with gold dust.[130]

Awdāghust stood in a sandy plain at the foot of a mountain bare of vegetation; it was surrounded by gardens and date palms. It apparently corresponds to Tegdaoust, the ruins of which lie to the south-west of Tichitt

125. ibid.; al-Bakrī, 1911, p. 159.

126. Ibn Ḥawḳal, 1964, p. 98; 1938, p. 100.

127. Al-Ya'ḳūbī, 1892, p. 360; 1937, pp. 226–7; 1962, p. 31.

128. Ibn Ḥawḳal, 1964, pp. 90–100; N. Levtzion, 1968a, is of the opinion that Ibn Ḥawḳal never got as far as Awdāghust.

129. Cf. D. Robert, S. Robert and J. Devisse (eds), 1970, pp. 19–20.

130. Al-Bakrī, 1911, pp. 50–3.

(some 200 km away) and west-north-west of Kumbi Saleh (or old Ghana) at a distance of some 400 km.[131]

In the first half of the fifth/eleventh century the Berber, apparently Muslim, kingdom of Awdāghust was subject to the pagan Sudanese kingdom of Ghana. It was on these grounds that Awdāghust was attacked and conquered by the Lamtūna, Massūfa and Djuddāla of the former Ṣanhādja federation, transformed around the mid-fifth/eleventh century into an Almoravid state.

Most of the inhabitants of the western Sahara between the first/seventh and fifth/eleventh centuries were Berbers of the Ṣanhādja branch (Lamtūna, Massūfa and Djuddāla). The Lamtūna and Djuddāla lived in the far south of the Islamic region, in the neighbourhood of the blacks, and once formed part of the great Ṣanhādja state of Anbiya. According to al-Idrīsī, the region of Tāzukkāght (present-day Sakiyyat al-Ḥamrā) belonged to the Lamtūna.[132] The territories of the Lamtūna also took in, to the north, the region of Nūl in southern Morocco.[133] Further south, their territories extended to Īzal (or Ayzal), which corresponds to present-day Kēdia d'Idjīl. Even further south we know of a region known as Lamtūna which lies to the north-west of the region of Tāgant in south-east Mauritania. Around the year 446/1054 the Lamtūna also occupied the Mauritania Adrār (Adrār Tmār), subsequently known as Djabal Lamtūna. This was a region covered with date plantations, established by a people who had settled in the area long before, the Bafūr, as they are referred to by local tradition and by certain Portuguese authors.

The chief city of Djabal Lamtūna was Azuḳī which grew up between the fifth/eleventh and sixth/twelfth centuries around the Almoravid fortress of the same name. It was an important stopping place on the route leading from Sidjilmāsa to the Western Sudan. The blacks knew this city by the name of Kūkadam (al-Idrīsī) or Kākadam.[134] It corresponds to present-day Azougui, a small settlement possessing ancient Almoravid and pre-Almoravid ruins in northern Mauritania, not far from the modern town of Atār.[135]

The Banū Massūfa lived in the desert in the region traversed by the route linking the city of Sidjilmāsa to the city of Ghana. They possessed no

131. Regarding the Tegdaoust excavations, cf. D. Robert, 1970; D. Robert, S. Robert, J. Devisse (eds), 1970; C. Vanacker, 1979.

132. The name 'Tāzukkāght' (for Tazuggaght) is the feminine form of the Berber word *azeggagh*, 'route'. The name 'Sakiyyat al-Ḥamrā'' means 'the red trench'. This region was already known to Ibn Khaldūn and its centre, al-Ḥamrā', appears on Abraham Cresques' map (fourteenth century) under the name of Alamara.

133. Nūl, or rather Nūl Lamṭa, still exists today in the plain of Wādī Nūn around Goulimine in south-west Morocco, between the Anti-Atlas and Wādī Dar'a. Cf. V. Monteil, 1968, pp. 97–8.

134. Al-Idrīsī, 1866, pp. 59–60; Yāḳūt, 1866–73, Vol. 4, p. 229.

135. R. Mauny, 1955a.

city except for that of Wādī Dar'a or Tīyūmetīn, five days' distance from Sidjilmāsa.[136]

Around the middle of the sixth/twelfth century the Massūfa went as far south as the city of Azukī. In the south-east lay the saltworks of Taghāzā which came into their possession; through this area passed the caravan route leading to Iwālāten (or Walāta), an important trade centre on the southern edge of the western Sahara under the dominion, in the eighth/fourteenth century, of the kings of Mali.

To the south-west of the territory occupied by the Banū Lamtūna, from the fifth/eleventh century onwards, lived the Ṣanhādja group of the Banū Djuddāla, probably descendants of the ancient Getulians. According to al-Bakrī, they dwelt directly to the north of lower Senegal near the sea, from which they were separated by no other group. The Djuddāla thus inhabited present-day south-western Mauritania and also the area surrounding al-Djabal al-Lammā' (Cap Blanc).[137]

As regards the inhabitants of the kingdom of Awdāghust, most of them were nomads and were Ṣanhādja (Zenaga) in the strict sense. Its capital was, as we saw earlier, inhabited by natives of Ifrīkiya and members of the Barkadjāna, Nafūsa, Lawāta, Zanāta and, above all, Nafzāwa peoples; there were also a small number of people from all the major Muslim cities. These were Ibāḍite traders from the various groups that had settled in Djabal Nafūsa, Bilād al-Djarīd, and in the oases of Sūf, Wargla and Wādī Rīgh. Ibāḍite sources in fact contain occasional mention of the travels of Ibāḍite traders from these regions to Awdāghust.

It emerges from archaeological excavations, and from the traditions collected by French scholars, that, in certain areas of the western Sahara, alongside the nomad population, there were also groups of agriculturalists whose descendants have survived to the present day. We possess some Portuguese manuscripts, dating from the ninth/fifteenth to the tenth/sixteenth centuries, from which it is possible to discover the nationality of these agriculturalists. According to these sources, they belonged to two different groups. The white agriculturalists were known as the Baffor or Abofur (in local traditions Bafūr) and the black agriculturalists as the Barbar (Barbara, Barābir, Barbaros), related to the Soninke.

The most ancient of these groups left in the Mauritanian Adrār a considerable number of ruined villages and archaeological sites.[138] These ancient sites are attributed by local traditions to a mysterious people known as the Baffor, Abofur or Bafour, who inhabited the Mauritanian Adrār just

136. According to V. Monteil, 1968, p. 90, this city was in the region of present-day Tagounit, 20 km to the north of the bend in the Dar'a river.

137. C. E. de Foucauld, 1940, mentions a 'tribe' of Tuareg marabouts in Aïr and Azawagh known as the Ighdālen. It appears that these are the descendants of the Djuddāla of the early Middle Ages.

138. See R. Mauny, 1955a.

before the arrival of the Lamtūna.[139] According to some traditions, the Bafour were whites (which the author considers to be the most likely) belonging to the Berber group of the Zanāta.[140] According to Mauritanian tradition, the non-Muslim autochthonous inhabitants of Adrār Tmār were agriculturalists and were responsible for the planting of the first palm trees in Adrār. The Bafour might, we think, be identified with the Libyan (Moorish) tribe of the Bavares, active in the western part of North Africa in the third and fourth centuries of the Christian era. They subsequently emigrated to present-day Mauritania, and left their culture and their name to the inhabitants of Adrār Tmār which, in the early sixteenth century, was still known as the 'mountain of Baffor', as recorded in one part of the account given by Valentim Fernandes.[141]

According to Arab sources of the sixth/twelfth century (*Kitāb al-Istibṣār* and al-Zuhrī), the blacks known as the Barbar or Barbara (Arabic plural: Barābir) formed the population of the Sudanese land of Zāfunu, corresponding to present-day Diafunu. They counted among the Djanāwa, that is to say the blacks, and also, according to al-Zuhrī, lived in the centre of the desert (probably the deserts and steppes of south-east Mauritania) and in areas in the vicinity of Ghana and Tādmekka (north of Gao), the inhabitants of which invaded their lands in order to take slaves. They had their kings and wore animal skins, as was normal for a people partly composed of nomads. The Barbara believed themselves to be the noblest of the Sudanese peoples and claimed that the sovereigns of Ghana came from their 'tribe'.[142]

The Barbara would thus appear to be a group of the Soninke. Might not al-Barābir (Barbara, Barbar) be identified with a black people known as al-Barbar who, so local tradition has it, formerly inhabited the city of Tichitt in south-eastern Mauritania? Some observers identify this legendary people with a people of black-skinned agriculturalists referred to as the Barbaros in the ancient Portuguese chronicles and appearing in the fifteenth and sixteenth centuries of the Christian era in the Mauritania Adrār, alongside the 'Azenègues' or Berber Zenaga (Ṣanhādja).

The foregoing is an account of the history and historical geography of the Sahara from the first/seventh to the sixth/twelfth centuries. We have done no more here than relate the basic facts, referring the reader to the Arab sources and special monographs dealing with this period.

139. Cf. A. J. Lucas, 1931; C. Modat, 1919.

140. These traditions are corroborated by an interesting passage in the *Kitāb al-bāyan al-mughrib* of Ibn 'Idhārī al-Marrākushī (early fourteenth century) who, speaking of the campaigns of Ibn Yāsīn, founder of the Almoravid state, relates the following: 'Near to where the Lamtūna lived there was a mountainous region inhabited by non-Muslim Berber tribes. 'Abd Allāh ibn Yāsīn invited them to adopt the faith. They refused. Yaḥyā ibn 'Umar ordered that they be attacked: the Lamtūna raided them and took prisoners whom they shared among themselves'.

141. P. de Cenival and T. Monod, 1938, p. 154; T. Lewicki, 1978.

142. *Kitāb al-Istibṣār*, 1852; al-Zuhrī, 1968, p. 181.

12 The emergence of the Fāṭimids

I. HRBEK

The establishment of the Fāṭimid dynasty: the role of the Kutāma

At the end of the third/ninth century a large part of the Muslim West (the Maghrib and Spain) was already outside the effective control of the Abbasid Caliphate of Baghdad: the Umayyads were established firmly in al-Andalus, the Idrīsid dynasty held sway over some cities and Berber groups in the Muslim Far West (al-Maghrib al-Akṣā), and on the fringes between the sown and the desert several Khāridjite states stretching from Djabal Nafūsa to Sidjilmāsa led their independent lives. Only the Aghlabids in Ifrīḳiya still paid allegiance to Baghdad but after one hundred years of virtual independence their links with the Abbasids were merely formal.[1]

In religious terms – and it should not be forgotten that in Islam the political and religious spheres are closely interwoven – the Maghrib was divided between the orthodoxy of Sunna with Ḳayrawān as one of the strongholds of the Mālikite legal school, and the heterodoxy of various Khāridjite sects (Ibāḍites, Ṣufrites, Nakkārites, etc.). Although the Idrīsids belonged to ʿAlī's family and their establishment was preceded by Shīʿite propaganda, it seems that the doctrinal tenets of the Shīʿa, as elaborated in the East, were not much propagated and even less followed in their realm.

All this was changed with the coming to North Africa of a vigorous and extremely active form of the Shīʿa, the Ismāʿīliyya, at the end of the third/ninth century. An essential part of Shīʿite creed is the dogma that the leadership (*imāmat*) of the Muslim community belongs rightly to the descendants of Muḥammad through his daughter Fāṭima and her husband ʿAlī, the fourth caliph. Unlike the Sunnite caliph the Shīʿite *imām* had inherited from Muḥammad not only his temporal sovereignty but also the prerogative of interpreting the Islamic law (*sharīʿa*), the *imāms* being infallible and impeccable. ʿAlī, the first *imām*, was succeeded by his son al-Ḥasan and then by his other son al-Ḥusayn in whose line the *imāmat* then continued. Another part of the *imāmat* doctrine is the belief that the last of

1. Cf. Chapter 10 above.

the visible *imāms* did not die but went into hiding from which he will in due time emerge as the *Mahdī* ('the divinely guided one') to restore true Islam, conquer the whole world and to 'fill the earth with justice and equity as it is now filled with oppression and tyranny'. On the question, however, of who should be the last visible and who the first hidden *imām* (and thus the *Mahdī*) the Shī'ites split into many groups. A majority consider the hidden *imām* to be the twelfth one, Muḥammad, who disappeared in 264/878 without leaving offspring. His adherents are known as the Twelvers (*Ithnā-'ashariyya*) and form today the main body of the Shī'ites.

Another group, although agreeing with the Twelvers as to the succession down to the sixth *imām*, Dja'far al-Ṣādiḳ, diverged at this point, professing the *imāmate* of Dja'far's eldest son Ismā'īl (d. 144/760) in preference to his brother Mūṣā who was recognized by the majority of the sect. Ismā'īl (and later his son Muḥammad) thus became in their eyes the seventh and hidden *imām*; the sect took the name of Ismā'īliyya and its adherents are also known as the Seveners (*Sab'iyya*).

The history of this sect and the early development of its specific doctrines through which it differs from the other Shī'ites are rather obscure. As is often the case with dissident sects, the Ismā'īli movement split into several branches; one of the main points of divergence concerned the nature of the *imāms*. On one side were those who retained the original doctrine and their devotion to the hidden *imām* Muḥammad ibn Ismā'īl, maintaining also the belief that 'Alī and Muḥammad ibn Ismā'īl were prophets, and that the latter, on his reappearence as the *Mahdī* would bring a new *sharī'a*. The other wing, the one from which the Fāṭimids emerged, accepted the doctrine according to which there were visible *imāms* at the head of the Muslim community. The official Fāṭimid version claims that the line of the Fāṭimid caliphs was preceded by the series of 'hidden *imāms*' descended from Muḥammad ibn Ismā'īl. But during the early days of their rule in North Africa their doctrine had a peculiar feature: the second ruler of the dynasty, al-Kā'im bi-Amr Allāh had a special status and was considered as the *Mahdī* who would usher in the messianic era. Only when his death dispelled the hopes set on him, did the figure of the *imām* as a temporal and spiritual leader assume a central position in Ismā'īli thought and that of the *Mahdī* was pushed into the background.

The Ismā'īlites organized some of the most subtle and effective political and religious propaganda. Their leaders began to send missionaries (*dā'ī*, plur., *du'āt*) from their places of retreat, one of the most important being in Salamiyya in Syria, to preach their doctrines, mainly the early return of the hidden *imām* as the expected *Mahdī*. They gained numerous adherents in various provinces of the Islamic world, in southern Iraq, in Bahrayn, in Persia and also, in the Yemen. Ismā'īlism appealed to various social strata discontented with the established order, promising a new era of vague social justice and reform that would come with emergence of the *Mahdī*. In each region the missionaries skilfully exploited particular grievances of the

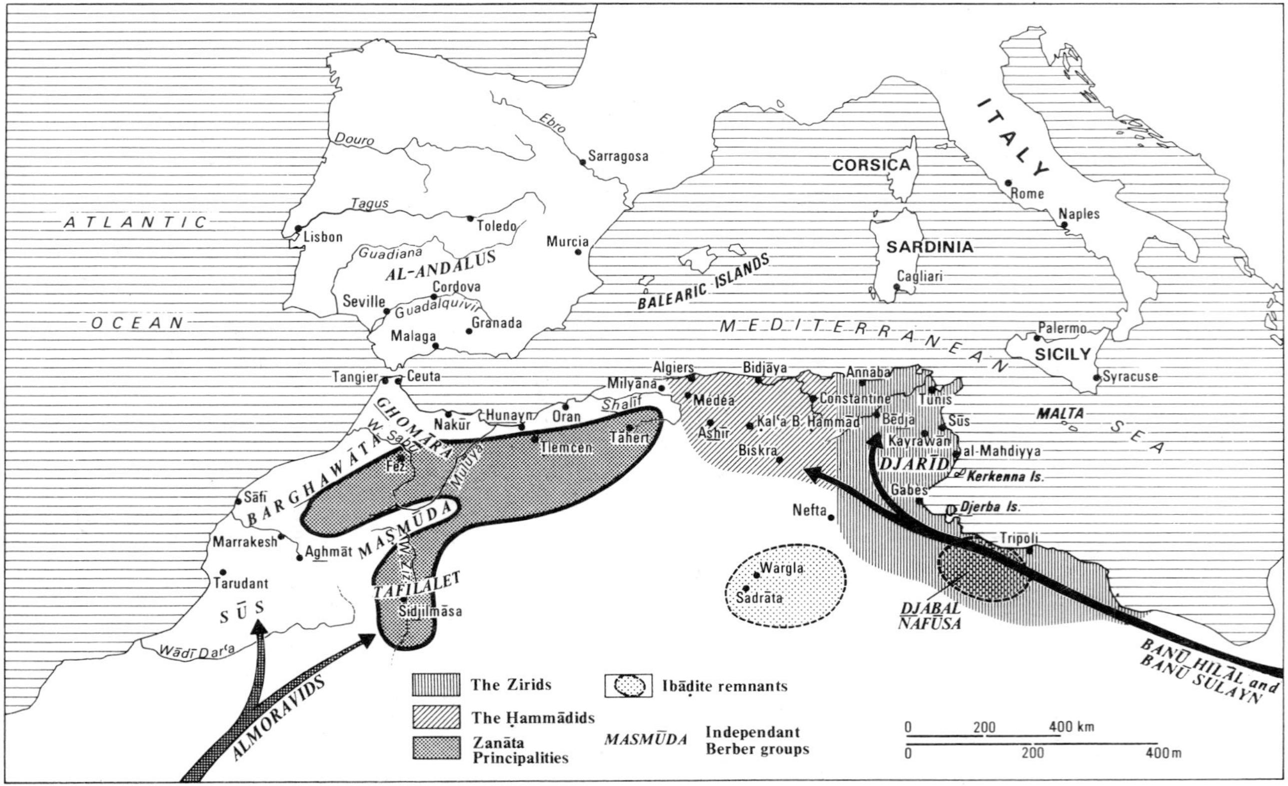

FIG. 12.1 *The Maghrib in the first half of the fifth/eleventh century*

population; in some parts they succeeded in founding small states but nowhere did their propaganda achieve such a success as in North Africa, at first among the Kutāma Berbers. Only the Fāṭimids among all the Ismāʿīli Shīʿa branches were able to found and maintain an empire that lasted for more than two centuries and that came within reach of attaining the universal goal of the doctrine.[2]

The Kutāma branch of the Berbers inhabited the region of Little Kabylia between Djidjelli, Satīf and Constantine on the easternmost fringe of what was formerly Roman Mauritania. Although the Aghlabids considered themselves officially masters of that area, they only rarely tried to execute their rights there so that the Kutāma were virtually independent. Ibn Khaldūn points out that 'they were never subjugated by the Aghlabids'.[3] In spite of minimal interference from the Aghlabids the Kutāma were animated by a profound aversion towards the Arab conquerors and rulers of Ifrīḳiya; they demonstrated it by often granting refuge to numerous deserters from the Aghlabid *djund*.

The truce between the Aghlabids and the Rustumids of Tāhert at the end of the third/ninth century enabled the former to start a fresh attempt to subjugate the Kutāma. Their armies began to occupy some fortified places on the approaches to the Kutāma independent zone. With the loss of hope for Rustumid help the influence of Kharidjism among the Kutāma, never very strong, declined and the way was opened for Ismāʿīlite propaganda. The Shīʿite creed was not entirely unknown in the Maghrib as during the third/ninth century two missionaries, Abū Sufyān and al-Hulwānī had led a successful although short propaganda campaign in those regions.[4]

More durable, and in the last analysis of decisive importance, were the activities of another propagandist (*dāʿi*), Abū ʿAbd Allāh al-Shiʿī, a native of Yemen, who was sent among the Kutāma towards the close of the century. Acquainting himself with some Kutāma *shaykhs* during their pilgrimage to Mecca he accompanied them to their native land in 280/893.

It is not entirely clear what special appeal for the Kutāma was represented by the Ismāʿīlite Shīʿism preached by Abū ʿAbd Allāh. It is difficult to discern any clear social character in the Fāṭimid branch of Ismāʿīlism. In the Maghrib they exploited the general discontent of the local population and to some degree the Kutāma expansionism but even those Berbers have never assimilated their doctrines. Once in power in the Maghrib and later in Egypt the Fāṭimids did not implement – and never intended to – any social transformation; their theoretical writings do not even mention similar preoccupations. It was in the other branch of Ismāʿīliyya, the Karma-

2. Literature about the Ismāʿīliyya is rather abundant; the most important and recent studies are those by B. Lewis, 1940; W. Ivanow, 1952; A. S. Tritton, 1958; W. Madelung, 1961; S. M. Stern. 1961.

3. Ibn Khaldūn, 1925–56, Vol. 2, p. 31.

4. F. Dachraoui, 1964.

tians in Bahrayn and eastern Arabia, that the primitive social ideas of the movement stressing social justice and egalitarian ideals were incarnated. Nothing distinguished the Fāṭimid regime, in social terms, from all other Islamic regimes.[5]

Whatever the reasons, the majority of the Kutāma was soon won over by Abū ʿAbd Allāh's propaganda to the cause of the descendants of ʿAlī and Fāṭima represented then by the *imām* ʿUbayd Allāh. In a few years the various Kutāma clans were unified into one strong army held together by *ʿaṣabiyya* (ethnic solidarity) combined with loyalty to the Fāṭimid *imām* as the expected *Mahdī* who would deliver the world from the hands of oppressors, be they the Aghlabids or their distant Abbasid masters in Baghdad.

The decisive struggle against the Aghlabids started in 290/903 when the Kutāma troops descended from their mountains into the plains of Ifrīḳiya. The Aghlabid armies were easily defeated and in a few years the greater part of Ifrīḳiya was in the hands of Abū ʿAbd Allāh; the sympathy of the people to his cause was increased by his fiscal policy since he proclaimed illegal all the non-canonical taxes and restituted to the inhabitants of the conquered towns the booty taken from them by the Kutāma. By contrast, Ziyādat Allāh III, the last Aghlabid emir, had increased the fiscal burden in order to finance his army; a step highly unpopular among the masses. After a prolonged campaign, Ḳayrawān, the capital of Ifrīḳiya, was conquered by Abū ʿAbd Allāh. Realizing that this was the final defeat, Ziyādat Allāh left his residence in Raḳḳāda and fled to Egypt. The Aghlabid period in North African history came to an end.

After the first successes of his followers in Ifrīḳiya, *imām* ʿUbayd Allāh, who until then had lived in Salamiyya in Syria, decided to move into the Maghrib. Instead of joining Abū ʿAbd Allāh in Ifrīḳiya, he went to Sidjilmāsa, the capital of the Khāridjite Midrārid state in southern Morocco. That is a curious episode and no conclusive answer as yet has been found to explain it. What was the purpose of his going to the Far West and among the worst enemies of the Shīʿa when there was already a large area under the control of his followers? Was his aim to establish in Sidjilmāsa a second centre and lay hands on the flow of gold coming there from the Sudan?[6] Whatever his original purpose, some time after his arrival he was put under house arrest and later into prison by al-Yasāʿ ibn Midrār.

In 296/909 Abū ʿAbd Allāh led the Kutāma army to Sidjilmāsa to free his master; in the course of that expedition and with the help of the local inhabitants he had overthrown the Rustumids in Tāhert. Sidjilmāsa capitulated without any fighting and ʿUbayd Allāh was set free.[7] In the next year he triumphally entered Raḳḳāda where he was proclaimed

5. C. Cahen, 1961, pp. 13–15.
6. J. Devisse. 1970.
7. Some Sunni historians maintain that ʿUbayd Allāh was killed in prison and that Abū ʿAbd Allāh found there only his servant whom he had presented to his followers as the true *Mahdī*. Cf. Ibn Khallikān, 1843–71, Vol. 3, s.v. ʿUbayd Allāh.

'Prince of the faithful' (a caliphal title) and 'Mahdī'; according to the Ismā'īlite doctrine that meant the end of the epoch of tyranny and the beginning of a new 'golden' era.

The origin of 'Ubayd Allāh and thus of the Fāṭimids is still wrapped in obscurity. Muslim historians are divided into two camps on the question of the legitimacy of their claims. The enemies of the Fāṭimids denied their descent from 'Alī and Fāṭima and declared them to be impostors; it is noteworthy that no dispute as to the genuineness of their descent had arisen until the year 402/1011 when the Abbasid Caliph in Baghdad issued a manifesto signed by several Sunnite and Shī'ite notables, among them many *sharīfs*, declaring the falsity of the Fāṭimid claims.[8] In later times we find among the supporters of their legitimacy even some notable Sunnite historians such as Ibn al-Athīr, Ibn Khaldūn and al-Maḳrīzī. This is rather a complex problem and even modern scholarship has not found a satisfactory solution.[9] But most important was the firm belief of their immediate followers in North Africa in their 'Alid descent.

'Ubayd Allāh al-Mahdī, who reigned from 297/909 to 322/934, established himself first in Raḳḳāda but shortly afterwards began to build a new capital – al-Mahdiyya – on the eastern coast, where he transferred his seat in 308/920. Later, after Abū Yazīd's revolt, the Caliph al-Manṣūr (334/946–341/953) founded a new capital to the east of Ḳayrawān, Ṣabra-Manṣūriyya, finished in 337/949. There his successors resided until 362/973 when al-Mu'izz, the last of the North African Fāṭimids, left it definitively for Egypt.

The foundation of a Shī'ite state in North Africa sealed the break-up of the Muslim world into three mutually hostile empires: the Abbasid Caliphate in Baghdad, the Fāṭimid Caliphate in North Africa and the Umayyad Emirate in Spain; shortly afterwards, in 318/929, the Umayyad emir of Cordoba 'Abd al-Raḥmān III confronted with the spectacle of two caliphs – a heretical one in Tunisia and an orthodox one far away in Baghdad – proclaimed his own Caliphate. Thereafter there were for some time three caliphs in Islam. The collapse of the Umayyad Caliphate in 422/1031 reduced the number again to two and the extinction of the Fāṭimids in 567/1171 brought it to one, that of the Abbasids in Baghdad.

The struggle for hegemony in North Africa

While the overthrow of the Aghlabid dynasty and the occupation of Ifrīḳiya proper were accomplished in a relatively short time, further Fāṭimid conquests in the Maghrib proved to be more difficult and time-

8. Text of the manifesto is presented by many historians, cf. P. H. Mamour, 1934, p. 201 ff.

9. Apart from the studies quoted in note 2 above, see also ibid., W. Ivanow, 1942, 1952; al-Hamdani, 1958 and M. Canard, 1965.

PLATE 12.1 *Aerial view of the peninsula of Mahdiyya (in the 1970s)*

consuming. This was partly because of the insecure internal situation of their realm, partly because of the narrow basis of their military strength.

The new doctrine of Ismā'īli Shī'ism could not fail to bring trouble to a region already split between Mālikite Sunnism and Khāridjism in its Ibāḍite and Ṣufrite forms. All these groups accepted the rule of the Fāṭimids only grudgingly and often manifested their opposition, which was either sternly suppressed or extinguished by bribery. The mainstay of Sunnite opposition was Ḳayrawān, the famous centre of Mālikite orthodoxy, whose great influence among the townspeople and rural population continued undiminished. Although these Sunnite groups never openly revolted, their passive resistance and the possibility of their joining forces with the more radical Khāridjites contributed to the difficulties of the dynasty. The caliphs openly expressed their contempt for and even hatred of the local inhabitants and we can surmise that these feelings were reciprocal.[10]

From the very beginning the Fāṭimids regarded North Africa merely as a springboard for further conquests towards the East in order to supplant the Abbasids and to fulfil their universalistic dreams. These grandiose projects forced them to keep up powerful and expensive armed forces both on land and sea. Although the *dā'ī* Abū 'Abd Allāh initially gained consider-

10. Cf. many instances of this attitude in M. Canard (ed.), 1958.

able sympathy by suppressing many unlawful taxes, this policy was soon changed and the Fāṭimid state re-introduced a number of non-canonical taxes, both direct and indirect, tolls and various other contributions. In the chronicles we find an echo of the general discontent provoked by the fiscal regime of the rulers 'for whom all the pretexts to fleece the people were good.'[11]

Military establishment was at the beginning rather precarious as the sole supporters of the dynasty were the Kutāma and some other branches or clans of the Ṣanhādja. These tribal contingents, moreover, could be held under discipline only by the promise of plunder and booty; if not satisfied, they were inclined to revolt. That inclination was demonstrated already two years after ʿUbayd Allāh's accession to the throne when he had Abū ʿAbd Allāh and his brother assassinated for reasons that are not quite clear to us.[12]

In response the Kutāma rose in revolt and proclaimed a new *Mahdī*, a child; the revolt was soon suppressed with much bloodshed. Although it is generally believed that the Kutāma formed the mainstay of the Fāṭimid power structure – and there is no doubt that they helped the dynasty in its conquest of the Maghrib and Egypt and played there a role that should not be underestimated – there are many instances of their revolts, disloyalty and disturbances. In such a situation it was only natural for the founder of the dynasty to look elsewhere for more trustworthy recruits for his army. He found them in various Slavonic people from the Balkan peninsula: the *Ṣaḳāliba* (sing., *Ṣaḳlabī*) as they were called by the Arabs, had already served as guards under the last Aghlabids but it was under ʿUbayd Allāh and his immediate successors that the *Ṣaḳāliba* troops became the second – and more stable – pillar of the Fāṭimid military and even administrative system.[13] The *Ṣaḳāliba*, mostly of South Slavonic (Dalmatian, Serbian, Bulgarian, etc.) origin came to Ifrīḳiya through various channels, either as slaves imported and sold by the Venetians or as captives from Arab raids on the coasts of the Adriatic Sea. In the Fāṭimid empire they played a role similar to that of the Turkish slave-soldiers in the more eastern parts of the Islamic world, and served not only as the elite troops but also as administrators, governors and courtiers, being known for their military prowess as well as for their loyalty. Some of them attained the highest posts, like Djawhar, the future conqueror of Egypt and founder of Cairo and the al-Azhar Mosque and university. Under al-Muʿizz two of the *Ṣaḳāliba*, Ḳayṣar and Muẓaffar, were nominated governors of the western and eastern provinces respectively in North Africa and there were many others in the immediate entourage of the caliphs.

11. Ibn ʿIdhārī, 1948–53, Vol. 1, pp. 186 ff.

12. The conflict between the *Mahdī* and his *dāʿī* arose either because the latter had doubts of him really being the *Mahdī*, or because his master was afraid of Abū ʿAbd Allāh's great power and gifts of persuasion.

13. On the role of *Ṣaḳāliba* in the Fāṭimid empire, cf. I. Hrbek, 1953.

It was the help of these two bodies of troops – the Kutāma and the *Ṣaḳāliba* – that turned the small Fāṭimid realm in Ifrīḳiya into an Empire stretching from the Atlantic to Syria, and into one of the Mediterranean big powers in the fourth/tenth and fifth/eleventh centuries. The black Africans on the other hand did not play the same role as later during the Egyptian phase. They did, however, serve as troops in the army, being called Zawīlī after the great slave market in Fezzān. This points to the Chad region as their country of origin.[14]

Although the Fāṭimids are considered to be the first dynasty to establish the political unity of the whole of North Africa (Ifrīḳiya and the Maghrib), a close look indicates how tenuous their authority was westwards of Ifrīḳiya proper. It would be tedious to attempt to enumerate or describe all the campaigns undertaken in the Maghrib during the reigns of ʿUbayd Allāh, al-Ḳāʾim, al-Manṣūr (334/946–341/953) and al-Muʿizz (341/953–365/975). Many regions or towns subdued by the Fāṭimid armies were to be repeatedly reconquered as the local people, chiefs or emirs always took the first opportunity to liberate themselves from foreign domination. So Tāhert was first seized in 295/908, to be reconquered in 299/911 and in 322/934, Fez was taken for the first time in 308/920 and retaken in 322/930, 423/935–6 and 347/958. The same is true of Sidjilmāsa where the Fāṭimid governors rotated with Midrārid emirs. Even Awrās, a region close to Ifrīḳiya, was only pacified in 342/953.

Some regions in North Africa never came under the authority of the Fāṭimids. After Tāhert had been taken, the last Rustumid *imām* fled with his people to Wargla where the Ibāḍites, although not attempting the foundation of a new *imāmat*, remained independent and even spread to the Mzāb. The Djabal Nafūsa, an ancient stronghold of the Ibāḍites, was never conquered and throughout the fourth/tenth century was the centre of a small independent state.

During the fourth/tenth century the whole belt along the northern fringes of the Sahara remained in the hands of the Zanāta who controlled the terminals of the caravan trade going to the Lake Chad region and to Gao. The Fāṭimid caliphs were never able to bring that part of the Maghrib under their domination; it was in the westernmost terminal, Sidjilmāsa, that they attempted to tap the influx of Sudanese gold so much needed for their grandiose conquest plans. It seems that the control of the western gold route, not the colonization of the whole Maghrib was the chief aim of their North African policy.[15]

The Fāṭimid attempts to implement that policy were continuously thwarted both by local centrifugal forces and by external foes joined together in common opposition against the Shīʿite dynasty. The traditional rivalry between the Ṣanhādja and the Zanāta Berbers, conditioned by their

14. Ibn Ḥammād, 1927, pp. 34–5.
15. J. Devisse, 1970, p. 144.

different ways of life, commercial interests and religious allegiance, was soon integrated into a more grandiose duel fought in the fourth/tenth century by the great powers of Western Islam – the Umayyads of Spain and the Fāṭimids of Ifrīḳiya. Having no common frontiers those two empires nevertheless carried on a deadly struggle for hegemony through their Berber allies who acted as intermediaries; whereas generally (there were some exceptions) the Zanāta and particularly the most formidable amongst them, the Maghrāwa, represented the interests and claims of the caliphs of Cordoba, the Ṣanhādja groups, especially the Banū Zīrī, stood firmly on the Fāṭimid side.[16] For one and a half centuries, both antagonistic alliances knew alternately successes and setbacks but as long as the Fāṭimid base of power remained in Ifrīḳiya (until the eighth decade of the fourth/tenth century), the Ṣanhādja–Fāṭimid alliance got the upper hand. During that period their armies at least twice reached the western Maghrib: in 322/934 a Fāṭimid army led by Mayṣūr al-Ṣaḳlabī reconquered Fez and re-established the Idrīsids in their domains under a Fāṭimid protectorate. On a greater scale was the campaign of Djawhar in 347–8/958–9; with a huge Kutāma and Ṣanhādja army under Zīrī ibn Manād, he subdued large parts of Morocco as far as the Atlantic Ocean, with the exception of Tangier and Ceuta which remained in Umayyad hands. Not even that great success established a durable Fāṭimid control over those distant regions for some eight years later Djawhar had to undertake a second expedition into the same area to bring it again under the sway of his masters. Shortly afterwards, with the main Fāṭimid forces concentrated on the attack of Egypt, the western Maghrib slipped away into the Umayyad orbit and was for ever lost to the Fāṭimids and their Zīrīd vassals.

In the background of the Fāṭimid–Umayyad and Ṣanhādja–Zanāta struggle loomed from the start the vision of the Sudanese gold and of control over the terminals of the caravan routes. Scholars are only beginning to appreciate the implications of that factor for North and West African history, particularly for the interpretation of Fāṭimid history.[17]

The growing discontent of large strata of population with the fiscal and religious oppression of the Fāṭimids has already been mentioned. Until the last years of al-Ḳā'im's reign the external manifestations of discontent did not attain any dangerous form and some occasional local revolts or riots were easily suppressed. Then, in 332/943–4 there suddenly broke out a terrible revolt, or rather a genuine revolution, that came near to destroying the whole Fāṭimid state. Its leader was Abū Yazīd Makhlad ibn Kaydād, commonly called Abū l-Ḥimār (the man on the donkey) born either at Tādmekka or at Gao (Kāw-Kāw) in the Sudan as a son of a Zanāti mer-

16. On the rivalry between the Ṣanhādja and Zanāta cf. H. Terrasse, 1949–50, Vol. 1; L. Golvin, 1957; H. R. Idris, 1962 and E. Lévi-Provençal, 1950–3, Vol. 2.

17. The pioneer work on this problem was done by J. Devisse, 1970; see also C. Cahen, 1981.

chant from Bilād al-Djarīd and his black slave girl.[18] Since his early youth Abū Yazīd had excelled as a scholar and teacher of Ibāḍite dogmatics and soon became one of the leading figures of the Nukkārite branch, the most radical Ibāḍite wing. When ʿUbayd Allāh al-Mahdī established the Shīʿite domination, Abū Yazīd dedicated all his powers of oratory, missionary zeal and growing influence to mobilizing people for the destruction of the ungodly dynasty. From Djarīd, where his agitation aroused the suspicion of the authorities, he fled to the central Maghrib. Both among the Berbers of the Awrās Mountains and the peasant masses of the plains he preached a holy war against the Fāṭimids, propounding the establishment of a democratic state led by a council of pious *shaykh*s and run according to the Khāridjite doctrine. He gained some support from the Spanish Umayyads and entered into a rather uneasy alliance with the orthodox Mālikite bourgeoisie in Ḳayrawān. His army of fanatical adherents swept over the plains of Ifrīḳiya six months after the beginning of the open revolt, conquered Ḳayrawān (in 333/944) and defeated the Fāṭimid troops in several fierce battles. Thereafter, for ten months, Abū Yazīd laid siege to al-Mahdiyya, the last stronghold of Fāṭimid rule, defended by the Caliph al-Ḳāʾim with his Kutāma and *Ṣaḳāliba* troops. The Shīʿite domination in North Africa was on the brink of collapse.[19]

A prolonged siege by an unprofessional army always saps its strength and morale and soon Abū Yazīd's contingents of tribal levies started to disperse and go home. Not even the death of al-Ḳāʾim in 334/946 improved the deteriorating situation of the revolt.

The new Caliph, al-Manṣūr, soon undertook energetic steps to quell the uprising; with fresh forces, mainly from Sicily, he reconquered Ḳayrawān and during a six months' campaign he decisively defeated the Khāridjite army. Abū Yazīd continued to defend himself with his last adherents for one year in the Hodna Mountains; in 336/947 he succumbed to injuries inflicted on him in one of the skirmishes with the Fāṭimid troops. For another year the fighting was prolonged by his son Faḍl but after the death of the latter the waves of revolt gradually ebbed away.

Abū Yazīd's revolt was the greatest ever undertaken against the Fāṭimids and it nearly succeeded in overthrowing their regime. A new revolt of the Wahbite Ibāḍites in 358/968–9 led by Abū Khazar in Bilād al-Djarīd, the Mzāb and Tripolitania, whose main contingents came from the Mazāta Berbers, did not seriously endanger it, being suppressed after a short time.[20] Al-Manṣūr's victory over Abū Yazīd heralded the beginning of a gradual decline of Khāridjite fortunes in North Africa. After the invasion by the Banū Hilāl in the fifth/eleventh century the decline was even accelerated; the most rigorous Ibāḍites withdrew to a few remote regions

18. Ibn Ḥammād, 1927, p. 33 on Tādmekka; Ibn Khaldūn, 1925–56, Vol. 3, p. 201 on Gao.
19. On the revolt see R. Le Tourneau, 1953.
20. Ibn Khaldūn, 1925–56, Vol. 2, p. 548.

whereas the majority of them were gradually converted to orthodox Sunni Islam.

Imperial policy: Sicily, the Mediterranean and Egypt

The Fāṭimids inherited an interest in the island of Sicily from their predecessors, the Aghlabids. The Aghlabids took more than seventy years 212/827–289/902 to make themselves complete masters of Sicily and for the next two hundred years the island formed a province of the Islamic world.[21] The Fāṭimid beginnings on the island were not auspicious as two successive governors sent after 297/909 by ʿUbayd Allāh were driven out by the local inhabitants who in 300/912 elected a governor of their own, Aḥmad ibn Ḳurhub. He declared for the Abbasid Caliph and twice sent his fleets against Ifrīḳiya. In the second attempt he suffered, nevertheless, a defeat. After four years of independent rule Ibn Ḳurhub was abandoned by his troops and delivered to the Fāṭimids who had him put to death in 304/916. Only then did Sicily revert to the Fāṭimid domain but in the next three decades the island was the scene of many disturbances that almost amounted to civil war. The various elements of the Muslim population, the Arabs (both from Spain and from North Africa) and the Berbers, lived in constant friction complicated by the feuds arising from the old rivalry between the South Arabian Yemenites (including Kalbites) and the North Arabs. Only after 336/948 when the caliph sent al-Ḥasan ibn ʿAlī al-Kalbī (d. 354/965) as governor, did the situation improve with the re-establishment of order. Under him and his successors, the Kalbite dynasty, Muslim Sicily became a prosperous province which at the same time gained more and more autonomy.

The Muslims in Sicily built a better structure upon what were solid Byzantine foundations. They lightened somewhat the heavy burden of Byzantine taxation and they split many latifundia into small estates intensively cultivated by tenants and peasant proprietors. They also enriched Sicilian agriculture with new techniques and plant varieties. Muslim writers stress the wealth of metals and other minerals, one of which, sal-ammoniac (ammonium chloride), was a valuable export. It was in this period that the cultivation of citrus fruits, sugar-cane, palms and mulberries began. Cotton cultivation also continued for a long time, disappearing only in the eighth/fourteenth century. Still more significant was the progress of market gardening: onions, spinach, melons and other vegetables were transmitted through Sicily to Western Europe.

Equally important was the bilateral staple trade with Ifrīḳiya which sent oil in exchange for Sicilian grain and timber; this last commodity, whose shortage was notorious in other Islamic countries, enabled the Aghlabids and after them the Fāṭimids to build strong navies and emerge as major

21. On the history of Muslim Sicily see the classic work of M. Amari, 1933–9.

maritime powers in the central Mediterranean. And Sicily was also the main source of seasoned sailors for manning the Fāṭimid (and later the Zīrīd) fleets.

Control over Sicily gave the Fāṭimids a strategic preponderance in the Mediterranean, and Palermo became an important naval base. In order to replenish their war-chest destined for their costly plans of conquest, the Fāṭimid caliphs counted on the gains from raids against the shores of Christian Europe and Muslim Spain, organized either by privateers or by the state itself. Already under ʿUbayd Allāh, Malta, Sardinia, Corsica, the Balearic and other islands felt the power of the fleet which he had inherited from the Aghlabids. The Fāṭimid fleet was especially active between 309/922 and 316/929 when nearly every year it raided both shores of the Adriatic Sea, the Tyrrhenian coast and southern Italy (chiefly Taranto and Otranto). The expedition of 323/934–5 was also very successful; the fleet harried the southern coast of France, took Genoa and coasted along Calabria carrying off slaves and other booty. Abū Yazīd's revolt seems to have curtailed these naval activities and it was not until the reign of al-Muʿizz that the raids again reached a greater scale. In 344/955–6 the Fāṭimid fleet raided the coast of Umayyad Spain and a year later Djawhar won a great success against the Byzantine navy and disembarked troops in southern Italy. But his fleet was scattered by a storm on the return voyage and suffered some losses. The maritime preponderance of the Fāṭimids in the Mediterranean was so great that some centuries later Ibn Khaldūn nostalgically noted that 'the Christians were unable to let float on the sea even a board'.[22]

The occupation of Sicily naturally brought the Fāṭimids into a conflict with the Byzantines, the former masters of the island. Owing to the rising seapower of the Fāṭimids and due to the changing political situation in the Mediterranean, the Byzantines were soon driven into a defensive position and sought to conclude a truce. Already under ʿUbayd Allāh the Byzantine emperor had concluded a treaty by which he undertook to pay an annual tribute of 22 000 gold pieces. The Caliph, from his side, wanted to strengthen his position vis-à-vis the Byzantines by attempting to conclude an alliance with the Bulgars: a Bulgarian embassy visited the court at al-Mahdiyya but on their return voyage, in the company of Fāṭimid ambassadors, the ship was captured by the Byzantines and the projected alliance fell through. When the Byzantine emperor had freed the Fāṭimid envoys the Caliph reduced the above-mentioned tribute to a half in recognition of this magnanimity.

During a revolt of the Byzantine population of Girgenti in Sicily in the time of al-Ḳāʾim, the emperor attempted to support the rebels but without much success. Under al-Muʿizz during the hostilities with the Spanish Umayyads, who obtained some help from the Byzantines, the emperor

22. Ibn Khaldūn, 1925–56, Vol. 2, p. 202.

proposed to the Caliph that he would withdraw his troops if al-Muʿizz was willing to grant him a long-term truce. Al-Muʿizz refused and only after his fleet achieved some success and reverses was he prepared to accept Byzantine ambassadors and conclude a five-year truce (in 346/957–8).[23] Some years later the Byzantines refused to continue the payment of the tribute and renewed hostilities in Sicily; their army, however, suffered a disastrous defeat at the Battle of Rametta and their fleet was beaten in the naval Battle of the Straits in 354/965. The negotiations that followed resulted in a peace treaty in 356/967, since al-Muʿizz wanted to have his flank secure during the Egyptian campaign.

The imperial idea was inherent in Ismāʿīli ideology, of which the Fāṭimids were the most prominent champions; among all the Ismāʿīli Shīʿa branches only they came within reach of attaining the ecumenical goal of their doctrine. They considered their North African kingdom as merely a preparatory stage, a necessary power base on the road to the creation of a universal Ismāʿīli empire ruled by the Prophet's descendants in accordance with the esoteric doctrine of the Ismāʿīliyya. Only domination over the heartland of Islam – the region from Egypt to Iran inclusively – could bring this project of universal empire nearer to realization, not the rule over peripheral Ifrīḳiya and the Maghrib. Nevertheless, the caliphs were realistic enough to see that for the time being this region must form their economic and strategic basis. And it was, indeed, the resources of North Africa – both human and material – that enabled the dynasty to launch the victorious march to the East.

Soon after establishing his rule in Ifrīḳiya, ʿUbayd Allāh al-Madhī considered – rather prematurely – that the time for the conquest of Egypt had arrived. Under the command of his son al-Ḳāʾim he launched two expeditions, in 301–2/913–15 and 307–9/919–21. After some initial successes that brought the Fāṭimid army beyond Alexandria and as far as the gates of al-Fusṭāṭ and, on another occasion, to Fayyūm, these campaigns ended in heavy defeats. In the second expedition the whole Fāṭimid fleet was destroyed. The only tangible result was the permanent occupation of Barḳa (Cyrenaica) which created an important glacis for future conquests. A third expedition to Egypt in 325/925, undertaken by al-Ḳāʾim after his accession to the throne, proved again to be unsuccessful. The repeated failures were due mainly to the insufficient resources of the dynasty in the early stage. It was nearly half a century before the economic, military and political situation of the Fāṭimid state improved to such a degree as to make a new attempt to conquer Egypt successful. In the meantime Ifrīḳiya with its direct dependencies (Sicily, parts of Algeria and Libya) went through a period of unprecedented efflorescence due partly to its role as one of the main Mediterranean trade entrepôts, partly to the control over the gold imported from the Western Sudan. The Fāṭimid army and navy were

23. Cf. S. M. Stern, 1950.

forged into efficient tools by experiences gained in many campaigns in the Maghrib and in the central Mediterranean, where several generals and admirals showed qualities of leadership. And last but not least the Fāṭimids were able to establish a very efficient centralized administration which assured smooth functioning of supply services for their armed forces.

These achievements as well as the success of Fāṭimid armies in the Maghrib allowed the fourth Caliph, al-Muʿizz, to prepare and launch the final attack on Egypt. The carefully planned conquest, which was also facilitated by skilful political propaganda was achieved without much difficulty by Djawhar, who entered al-Fusṭāṭ on 12 Shaʿbān 358/1 July 969. Shortly after the conquest of al-Fusṭāṭ, Djawhar started to build a new capital, Cairo – in Arabic, al-Ḳāhira[24] – and in the next year laid the foundations of the al-Azhar mosque. Four years after the conquest, in 362/973, al-Muʿizz moved from Ifrīḳiya to Cairo making Egypt the centre of an empire that survived its original founders and lasted for more than five centuries.[25] This shift of the Fāṭimid centre to the East had profound and manifold consequences for the history of North Africa.

The return to Berber hegemony[26]

In the heavy fighting against Abū Yazīd's revolt, the Talkata, a branch of the Ṣanhādja, led by Zīrī ibn Manād, had proved their loyalty to the Fāṭimid cause. In recognition of this the Caliph had given Zīrī, after the defeat of Abū Yazīd, the command over all the Ṣanhādja and their territory.[27] During the remaining Fāṭimid period in the Maghrib, Zīrī and his son Buluḳḳīn led many victorious campaigns against the Zanāta and the Maghrāwa in the central and western Maghrib either independently or in alliance with Fāṭimid generals. Later, in the time of al-Muʿizz, the Zīrīds were entrusted with the governorship of the central Maghrib (Ashīr, Tiāret, Baghāya, Msīla, Mzāb) and of the towns they had founded (Algiers, Milyāna, Médea).

It was thus only natural that the Caliph, before leaving definitively for Egypt in 359/972, should nominate Buluḳḳīn ibn Zīrī[28] as his lieutenant over all the western part of the empire. Although at first glance this event does not seem to be revolutionary, in reality it inaugurated a new epoch in North African history. Until the coming of the Zīrīds all the main dynasties had been of Eastern origin; the Idrīsids, the Rustumids, the Aghlabids,

24. So called, because on the day of its foundation the planet Mars (al-Ḳāhir, lit., the subduer) was in the ascendant.

25. For the history of the Fāṭimids in Egypt see Chapter 9 above and Unesco, *General History of Africa*, Vol. IV, ch. 15.

26. The most detailed and recent study of the post-Fāṭimid epoch is H. R. Idris, 1962; cf. also L. Golvin, 1957.

27. Ibn Khaldūn, 1925–56, Vol. 2, pp. 539–40.

28. Zīrī ibn Manād was killed in 360/971 in a battle against the Maghrāwa.

the Fāṭimids. The Zīrīds were the first reigning house of Berber origin; moreover, they opened the period of Maghriban history which was to see political power in the region held exclusively by Berber dynasties (the Almoravids, the Almohads, the Zayyanids, the Marinids, the Ḥafṣids).

Another change, although of lesser importance, was the rise of the Ṣanhādja. The Fāṭimid army sent to conquer the East consisted mostly of the Kutāma and from that time on Kutāmis were found all over Egypt, Palestine and Syria as commanders, as insurgents or as private citizens. The exodus of the Kutāma warriors opened the way for the Ṣanhādja Berbers to establish and consolidate their hegemony over the eastern part of the Maghrib.

Under the first three Zīrīds – Bulukkīn (361/972–373/984), al-Manṣūr (373/984–386/996 and Bādīs (386/996–406/1016 – the relations with the Fāṭimids remained in general correct. The tribute to Cairo was paid regularly and the emirs occasionally sent precious gifts to the caliphs who, nevertheless, surrounded the emirs with representatives whose role was to control them. At the same time the Zīrīds tried to acquire more real independence without renouncing the *de jure* suzerainty of the Fāṭimids. These, of course, were aware of this trend but for various reasons did not wish it to come to an open rupture and therefore employed at times more devious means to recall their vassals to obedience. When al-Manṣūr deposed a powerful Fāṭimid representative in Ifrīḳiya and proclaimed himself to be more than a simple administrator who could be exchanged by a stroke of pen, no open reaction followed from Cairo. But a *dāʿī* was sent to the Kutāma instructing them to rise against al-Manṣūr (in 375/986). After some years of fighting the revolt was suppressed with exceptional cruelty and the *dāʿī* executed. The Kutāma as a political and military factor in the region were definitively finished and the Zīrīd authority strengthened. Although Bādīs showed more subservience towards Cairo and was duly rewarded with the province of Barḳa, he did not receive any help from his suzerain when his uncle Ḥammād proclaimed himself independent. It seems that the Fāṭimids, more and more absorbed by their Eastern politics, were gradually losing interest in the western parts of the empire; whether this had been caused by the economic decline of Ifrīḳiya or by the inability of the Fāṭimids to intervene there militarily, or both, is difficult to decide. When, in the middle of the fifth/eleventh century, the final rupture at last occurred, the Fāṭimids retaliated not by direct intervention but in a devious way; by sending hordes of nomadic Arabs against their former vassals.

The first two Zīrīds, Bulukkīn and al-Manṣūr, continued a vigorous offensive against the Zanāta and their Umayyad protectors in the west. Under Bulukkīn the Zanāta were expelled from the central Maghrib and the emir reconquered nearly all Moroccan territory with the exception of Umayyad Ceuta. As soon as his army retreated, the Zanāta between Tanger and the Mulūya River started again to name the caliph of Cordoba in their *khuṭbas*. At the beginning of his reign al-Manṣūr made an unsuccessful attempt to re-establish his influence in Fez and Sidjilmāsa (385/985); occupied by the Kutāma revolt and realizing that a total occupation of the western Maghrib with its turbulent population was beyond his capabilities, he renounced the offensive and turned his attention more to the consolidation of the central province, Ifrīḳiya.

The reign of Bādīs witnessed some profound changes which left their marks on the political map of the Maghrib. The first was the vigorous offensive of the Zanāta (principally the Maghrāwa) who attacked the central Maghrib in 389/998–9 and reached as far as Tripoli. At the same time the Zanāta groups living in Zīrīd territory revolted and were even joined by some members of the Zīrīd family. The situation was saved by the military prowess of Ḥammād ibn Bulukkīn, an uncle of Bādīs, who by vigorous campaigns pacified the central Maghrib and repulsed the Zanāta, driving them to Morocco. Bādīs was forced to give his uncle large fiefs in the central Mahgrib, where in 398/1007–8 Ḥammād founded his own capital, the fortress Ḳalʿa of the Banū Ḥammād, one of the most imposing architectural monuments in North Africa. Its strategic position was even better than that of Ashīr, the original seat of the Zīrīds, as it dominated important trade routes and a large region. In a short time Ḥammād proclaimed his independence (in 405/1015) severing relations with the Fāṭimids and transferring his allegiance to the Abbasids. Thus the Ṣanhādja dynasty split into two; the Zīrīds, who retained Ifrīḳiya proper, and the Ḥammādids, who ruled over the central Maghrib. Although Bādīs, and after his death, his successor al-Muʿizz (406/1016–454/1062) in the end defeated Ḥammād, they were forced to recognize the independence of the latter; an uneasy peace followed between the two branches.

Ḥammād's change of allegiance led to a revival of Sunnite activities. The majority of the population in Ifrīḳiya and the central Maghrib had always stood in opposition to the Ismāʿīli Shīʿa, the official religion of the Fāṭimids and the Zīrīds, but this opposition was rather passive. In the last year of Bādīs' reign, however, the first massacres of the Shīʿites occurred in Bēdja and Tunis, followed later by large-scale anti Shīʿite pogroms in Ḳayrawān and elsewhere in Ifrīḳiya, when thousands of Shīʿites were killed and their houses plundered. This movement, which expressed the feelings of both urban and rural masses, showed clearly to al-Muʿizz, just at the beginning of his long reign, the dangers of a sectarian government imposed upon a generally orthodox Sunni population. It does not mean that the religious question played the most important part in the rupture between the Zīrīds and Fāṭimids that occurred in the middle of the fifth/eleventh century but it was certainly a contributory factor in the decision of al-Muʿizz to throw off his allegiance to the Fāṭimids in Cairo and to return to the orthodoxy. That the changing of allegiances between the Abbasids and Fāṭimids was motivated primarily by other than religious reasons is demonstrated by the policies of the Ḥammādids; already the founder of the dynasty.

Ḥammād reverted to the Fāṭimid allegiance in the later years of his reign, whereas his son, al-Ḳā'id (419/1028–446/1054) changed twice in the course of five or six years, paying allegiance first to the Abbasids and then to the Fāṭimids.

The unity of the Maghrib, sought but never permanently achieved by the Fāṭimids, did not survive their withdrawal to the East. The fissiparous tendencies of the Berbers and their opposition to political centralization proved stronger than the feeble attempts of the Zīrīds to continue the unifying policies of their suzerains. In the first half of the fifth/eleventh century the political map of the Maghrib offered the following picture: (1) To the east, in Ifrīḳiya, the Zīrīd realm constituted the most advanced and relatively stable state. (2) To the west of the Zīrīd emirate the Ḥammādids had established their independent state which permanently fought with the Zanāta and occasionally with the Zīrīds. (3) After the withdrawal of the Fāṭimids and the fall of the Umayyad Caliphate in Spain, various groups of the Zanāta seized the opportunity to found a number of independent statelets, in Tlemcen, in Sidjilmāsa, in Fez and elsewhere. They never formed any centralized political organization but rather a linguistic and ethnic group united only by their hostility to the Ṣanhādja. (4) On the Atlantic coast the heretical Barghawāṭa were able to preserve their independence against the attacks of the Zīrīds and later those of the Zanāta. (5) The Ghomāra held a similar position in northern Morocco, strengthening their independence even more after the decline of the Umayyads. (6) The numerous Masmūda groups in southern Morocco in the Anti-Atlas and in the Sūs continued their independent existence of small communities without any higher organization (see Fig. 12.1).

In general the situation of the Berbers resembled that obtaining before the Arab conquest; the Arab element was represented only in towns and its strength diminished gradually from east to west. Parallel with it went also the political structure: in Ifrīḳiya the state system was the most developed, but in the western parts of the Maghrib the societies did not as yet reach the level of state formation.

The religious situation underwent profound changes in the post-Fāṭimid period: by the mid-fifth/eleventh century the whole Maghrib presents itself as an orthodox Sunnite region with no traces of Shī'ism and with only a few minor enclaves of Khāridjism. This change may be explained as a direct consequence of the return of political supremacy to the Berbers. Under these conditions Khāridjism had lost its *raison d'être* as an ideology of Berber resistance to the Arab conquerors and dynasties professing the Sunnite form of Islam. It belongs also to the ironies of history that the Fāṭimids, one of the most successful and powerful Shī'ite dynasties, had – by inflicting heavy defeats and losses on North African Khāridjism – opened the way for the definitive victory of Sunnite Mālikism in the eastern and central Maghrib. After Abū Yazīd's defeat Khāridjism ceased its existence as a political power in North Africa.

Surviving only in small peripheral communities, it practised defensive rather than offensive politics. But the victory over Khāridjism did not help the Shī'ite cause, it served merely to give more chance to Sunnite renaissance.

The Banū Hilāl and Banū Sulaym invasion

When the Zīrīd al-Mu'izz ibn Bādīs had at last, in 439/1047, broken with his Fāṭimid suzerain al-Mustanṣir and recognized the Abbasid Caliph of Baghdad, thus abandoning the Shī'ite creed for the Sunnite one, the revenge of the Fāṭimids took a peculiar form. Owing to the impossibility of sending an army against the recalcitrant vassal, the visier al-Yazūrī advised his master to punish the Ṣanhādja by handing over Ifrīḳiya to the horde of nomadic Arabs of the Banū Hilāl and Banū Sulaym, who lived at that time in Upper Egypt.

It was apparently not too difficult to persuade the chiefs of both *ḳabīla*s to undertake the westward migration as it promised them rich booty and better pastures than those in Upper Egypt. Since the nomadic Arabs were notorious for being a turbulent and undisciplined element, it must have been quite clear from the start that they would neither bring North Africa back under Fāṭimid sway nor constitute an orderly vassal state there. It was, on the part of the Fāṭimids, not an attempt to regain the lost provinces but an act of pure revenge against the Zīrīds as well as a way of getting rid of the unwelcome and turbulent nomads.

The Arabs started to migrate in 442/1050–1 and in the first stage ravaged the province of Barḳa; the Banū Hilāl then moved farther to the west leaving Barḳa to the Banū Sulaym, who remained there for some decades before moving again. When the vanguard of the Banū Hilāl appeared in southern Tunisia, al-Mu'izz, unaware of al-Yazūrī's scheme, did not immediately recognize what a scourge was nearing his domain. On the contrary, he tried to enlist the invaders into his service as potential allies and even married one of his daughters to one of the great Hilāli chiefs. On his invitation the majority of the Banū Hilāl left Barḳa and soon their hordes had overrun the southern parts of the Zīrīd emirate. The ever increasing pillaging of villages and towns destroyed al-Mu'izz's hopes of making the nomads the mainstay of his armed forces. He tried to stop their incursions but in several battles among which that of Ḥaydarān in the region of Gabès (in 443/1051–2) became the most famous,[29] his army – composed largely of black contingents – was utterly routed in spite of its numerical superiority. The countryside, the important villages and even some towns fell into the hands of nomadic chiefs and anarchy and insecurity spread further and further. Although al-Mu'izz married three of his daughters to Arab emirs this did not check the continued devastation and

29. Cf. M. Brett, 1975.

was no more effective than his return to Fāṭimid obedience in 446/1054–5. Finally, in 449/1057 the Zīrīd was forced to abandon Ḳayrawān and take refuge in al-Mahdiyya which became the new capital of his now very reduced state. Immediately afterwards Ḳayrawān was sacked by the Banū Hilāl, a disaster from which it never recovered.

When the Arabs invaded the central Maghrib, the Ḥammādids of Ḳal'a were gradually drawn into the complicated interplay of rivalries between the *ḳabīla*s and tried to acquire some advantages from the troubles of the Zīrīd cousins. Using one section of the Banū Hilāl as auxiliaries, they attacked Ifrīḳiya, thus causing further devastation. In 457/1065 the Ḥammādid al-Nāṣir, at the head of a large coalition of Berbers and Banū Hilāl (Ṣanhādja, Zanāta and the Hilāli sections of Athbadj and 'Adī) fought against other Arab sections (Riyāḥ, Zughba and Banū Sulaym), suffered a heavy defeat at Sabība. Although the immediate consequences were less abrupt than those following the defeat of the Zīrīds at Ḥaydarān, the grip of the Banū Hilāl became gradually so strong that al-Nāṣir had to abandon his capital, the Ḳal'a, for Bidjāya (Bougie) which was founded shortly before, and to leave the southern parts of his domain to the nomads. Bidjāya became the new capital of the Ḥammādid dynasty, to fall – as did al-Mahdiyya – into the hands of the Almohads half a century later. In the meantime the nomadic Arabs, who came with their families and herds, occupied large parts of Ifrīḳiya and central Maghrib, founding numerous independent principalities which led incessant wars among themselves, against the remnants of Zīrīd and Ḥammādid states as well as against other small states that emerged from the ruins, thus increasing the general anarchy and decline of economic life. The grip of the Banū Hilāl on the country remained unchallenged until in the middle of the sixth-twelfth century the arrival of the Almohads restored order.

Such is, in brief, the account of the Hilālian migration as narrated in Arabic contemporary or later sources. Among these Ibn Khaldūn has been the first to stress the destructive role of the Beduins, comparing them with a 'cloud of hungry locusts'.[30] Modern historians have in general followed Ibn Khaldūn's view and have even stressed the negative aspects of the Arab nomads' arrival by calling it 'the Hilālian catastrophe' and pointing out the various adverse consequences that this event has had for North African history.

In recent years an attempt to revise the hypothesis of the Hilālian catastrophe and some of the related issues has been undertaken. It is now maintained, for example, that the Arab nomads were not so numerous, that their invasion was not so destructive and that already before their arrival there had appeared signs of decline in the economies and societies of North Africa.[31] Moreover, the emigration of the Arabs from Egypt is now con-

30. Ibn Khaldūn, 1925–56, Vol. 2, p. 35.

31. Cf. the polemics by C. Poncet, 1954, 1967, on one side, and H. R. Idris, 1968a, 1968b, and C. Cahen, 1968 on the other hand.

sidered to have been caused mainly by the economic situation (a catastrophic dearth and hunger under al-Mustanṣir's reign) and not by political considerations.[32] The debate has contributed to the clarification of many points and has to some degree rectified the one-sided view of the Hilālians as the chief and sole culprits of the decline.

Nevertheless it should be stressed that the arrival of a large body – whatever their precise numbers – of nomadic Arabs was a turning point in North African history from many points of view. Although the process of Arabization was already well advanced, at least in Ifrīḳiya, large parts of the countryside remained inhabited and cultivated by a Berber-speaking population. Whereas the Arabs of the first conquest of the second/eighth century had been absorbed in the Berber population, the Banū Hilāl and Banū Sulaym started a reverse process, not as a deliberate policy but as a consequence of the necessary modus vivendi between the sedentaries and nomads. Some Zanāta groups – particularly the Banū Marīn – were forced to retreat westwards to make space for the Arabs. Although the Arabs penetrated neither the littoral regions nor the mountain massifs which became the refuge of the sedentary Berbers, the plains of the eastern half of the Maghrib fell gradually under their influence. Most of the present-day rural dialects of Arabic in North Africa go back to the nomadic vernacular brought by the Banū Hilāl and Banū Sulaym. In terms of Islamization, by contrast, their contribution was minimal or even nil since the Islam of the nomads was rather superficial and the entire population of the areas invaded by them had already been Muslim for centuries.

As for the harm done by their arrival, it is generally agreed to have been extensive, even if the term 'catastrophe' seems to be rather an exaggeration. There is no doubt that the presence of thousands of nomads with their herds must have had major consequences for the economic life of the country and that the area of pastures must have increased to the detriment of cultivated fields. The former equilibrium between the nomadic and sedentary elements in North Africa was thus – for some centuries to come – disturbed, with the result that many parts of the fertile land were abandoned by agriculturalists and left to the Beduins.

The anarchy, a natural consequence of the collapse of the Zīrīd and later Ḥammādid states, might have been not so general as described by Ibn Khaldūn, since many Arab chiefs, starting to found their own statelets, established some order, but it must be borne in mind that general security suffered from the presence of too many independent and unruly Arab groups.

Although the harm suffered by Ḳayrawān and by other towns through the Arab conquest was serious, more fatal proved to be the impact on external relations, which became dependent on the changing moods of roaming nomads. The decline of towns in the interior was comparatively rapid

32. Cf. the recent study by R. Daghfūs, 1981.

and while Ḳayrawān was destined to lose much of its former importance, the Ḳal'a of Banī Ḥammād ceased gradually to exist. The anarchy also spilt back towards Egypt where the Lawāta from Cyrenaica ravaged the west and north and overran the Delta.

The principal casualties of the unrest exacerbated by the nomads were the Zīrīd and Ḥammādid emirates which eventually survived only in the coastal strips around al-Mahdiyya and Bidjāya (Bougie). The progress of the Arab nomads in the interior did contribute to the orientation of the Ṣanhādja Berbers towards the sea and it even accentuated the dichotomy between the inland regions and the littoral. On the ruins of the Zīrīd and Ḥammādid states piracy prospered. Bidjāya, better situated than al-Mahdiyya (which lacked timber for ship-building) became an important maritime centre and entered into a brisk trade with other parts of Mediterranean, mainly with the Italian towns. The Ḥammādids were able, at the beginning of the sixth/twelfth century, to conquer and dominate the Djerba Island.

The economy of North Africa as it existed formerly had been seriously undermined. Even if we now prefer to speak of an Hilāli infiltration rather than of an invasion, the results were the same. The pre-eminently sedentary and agricultural economy of the eastern Maghrib gradually gave way to an economy with a preponderance of nomadic and pastoralist elements, a real revolution about which al-Bakrī and al-Idrīsī have left sufficient evidence. These profound changes in the eastern part, moreover, took place at the same time that the western regions of the Maghrib were coming under the impact of another group of nomads, the Almoravids. Both events inaugurated a new chapter in the history of the Maghrib.

13 The Almoravids

I. HRBEK and J. DEVISSE

At much the same time as the Banū Hilāl and the Banū Sulaym began to penetrate North Africa from the east[1] there started at the opposite end of the Maghrib a movement of the desert Berbers who in a short time were to invade the western and central part of the region. Both these simultaneous movements, the Almoravids from the west and the Hilāli from the east, were expressions of nomadic dynamism and both led to a temporary control by the nomads over sedentary societies and established state organizations. It seems that it was precisely the case of the Almoravids and the Hilāli that inspired the great Maghribi historian Ibn Khaldūn with the idea of the military preponderance of nomads over sedentaries, which forms one of the cornerstones of his socio-historical theory.

The political, economic and religious background of the Almoravid movement

The generally accepted account of the beginnings of the Almoravid movement relates how Yaḥyā ibn Ibrāhīm, one of the leaders of the Djuddāla Berbers from the Western Sahara, who was on his way back from the pilgrimage to Mecca, asked Abū ʿImrān al-Fāsī (d. 430/1039), a famous Mālikite jurist of Ḳayrawān,[2] to send somebody with him to instruct his people in the genuine Islamic religion as they were rather ignorant of it. Since Abū ʿImrān could not find anybody in Ḳayrawān willing to go and live among the savage Ṣanhādja in the desert, he advised Yaḥyā to visit one of his former students, Waggāg ibn Zallū al-Lamṭī in Malkūs near Sidjilmāsa, and obtain help from him. Waggāg then recommended as the most

1. Cf. Chapter 12 above.

2. On Abū ʿImrān, see H. R. Idris, 1955, p. 54; the visit of Yaḥyā ibn Ibrāhīm must therefore be dated before Abū ʿImrān's death. The dates 444/1052–3 given by Ibn ʿIdhārī, 1948–51, Vol. 3, p. 242, or 440/1048–9 in *Al-Ḥulal al-Mawshīyya*, 1936, p. 9; J. M. Cuoq, 1975, p. 365; N. Levtzion and J. F. P. Hopkins (eds), 1981, p. 311, are thus erroneous.

promising missionary his pupil ʿAbdallāh ibn Yāsīn al-Djazūlī, whose mother was originally from the Sahara.[3]

Another tradition preserved by al-Ḳāḍī ʿIyāḍ (d. 544/1149) and Ibn al-Athīr (d. 630/1233) mentions neither Yaḥyā ibn Ibrāhīm nor Abū ʿImrān al-Fāsī but has another Djuddāla pilgrim, Djawhar ibn Sakkam, on his way back from Mecca, directly asking Waggāg for somebody to teach his people Islam and its religious duties. Waggāg had formerly built a house in the Sūs for the purpose of study and piety called *dār al-murābiṭīn*. It was among the members of this *dār* that Waggāg chose ʿAbdallāh ibn Yāsīn, 'a man of learning and piety'.[4]

Despite these discrepancies in the sources the following facts remain incontestable:

(1) The superficial state of Islam among the Ṣanhādja in the Western Sahara.
(2) The wish of some Djuddāla leaders to improve this situation.
(3) The influence of the pilgrimage on the awareness of these men of the low standard of Islam among their compatriots.
(4) The connection of the Almoravid movement with the militant Mālikism represented by the link between Abūʿ Imrān, Waggāg and ʿAbdallāh ibn Yāsīn.

All these points indicate that the religious factor played a decisive role in the rise of the Almoravid movement; but since every religious movement is born in a concrete social setting and reflects its stresses and contradictions, it is necessary to analyse all the circumstances in order to establish, as far as possible, its true motives and causes.[5]

In the first half of the fifth/eleventh century the region of Morocco and the area south of it as far as the Senegal River were inhabited by the Berbers who were splintered into many hostile and warring factions. Morocco itself had been for the preceding century the object of the struggle between the two western great powers, the Spanish Umayyads and the Fāṭimids. These dynasties had intervened there directly only on rare occasions leaving the actual fighting to their Berber allies; in general (there were some exceptions) the Umayyads were represented by the Zanāta group, whereas the Fāṭimids, especially after the transfer of their

3. Al-Bakrī, 1913, p. 165; V. Monteil, 1968, pp. 59–60; J. M. Cuoq, 1975, p. 87; N. Levtzion and J. F. P. Hopkins (eds), 1981, p. 71.

4. Cf. H. T. Norris, 1971, pp. 255–6; J. M. Cuoq, 1975, pp. 125–6; N. Levtzion and J. F. P. Hopkins (eds), 1981, pp. 101–3.

5. Some modern scholars tended to minimize the religious aspects of the movement, reducing it to a mere conflict of material interest between the nomads and sedentaries or between various Berber groups, cf. A. Bel, 1903, p. vii; H. Terrasse, 1949–50, Vol. 1, pp. 217 ff; Vilá, 1956, p. 57; cf. the opposite views of P. F. de Moraes Farias, 1967, p. 798, and H. T. Norris, 1971, pp. 267–8. This chapter tries to take into account all aspects of the movement and to interpret them in a dialectical way as interdependent causes.

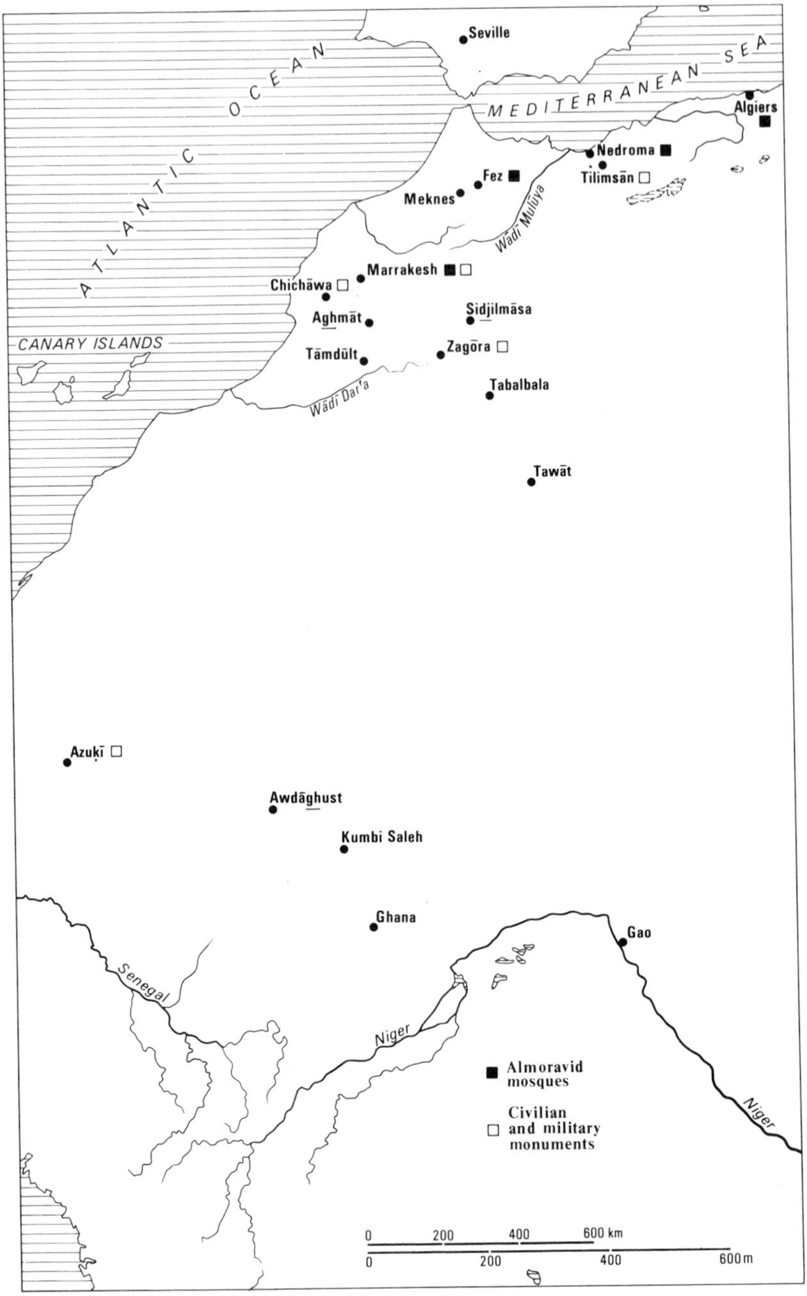

FIG. 13.1 *The Almoravid empire: towns and monuments*

capital from Ifrīḳiya to Egypt, reserved this task for the Ṣanhādja Zīrīds as their lieutenants.[6] One of the principal aims of this struggle was control over the trade routes to the Western Sudan and/or over the gold trade. The disintegration of the Umayyad caliphate in Spain did not diminish the fierceness of the struggle since various Zanāta principalities in Morocco continued it on their own account, fighting not only against the Zīrīds but often also among themselves. The Banū Ifran were established at Salé and Tadla while the Maghrāwa who had already proclaimed their independence from the Umayyads in 390/1000, gradually extended their domination from Fez to Sidjilmāsa, Aghmāt, Tāmdūlt and those parts of Wādī Dar'a until then under the control of the Saharan Ṣanhādja. The continuous fighting and general anarchy made life and normal economic activities under the Zanāta regime unbearable.[7] It seems that Berber particularism reached just at that time its extreme point; it was felt by some responsible chiefs and leaders that a radical change was needed. Under prevailing conditions only an Islamic movement could provide a unifying factor among the Berbers.

A similar situation existed to the south of Morocco among the 'veiled' (*mulaththamūn*) Saharan Ṣanhādja. These nomadic Ṣanhādja (distinct from the sedentary Ṣanhādja of Ifrīḳiya) were composed of three main branches: the Massūfa in the north and east (in Wādī Dar'a, Ḥawḍ, Taghāza), the Lamtūna in the centre and south (in Adrār and Tāgant), and the Djuddāla (or Guddāla) to the west in the Atlantic Sahara.[8] Until the beginning of the fourth/tenth century the Berbers of the Western Sahara were known as the Anbīya[9] and it still remains uncertain whether that was a designation of a loose confederacy of the three main branches[10] or another name for one of them.

That there were some attempts during the fourth/tenth century to unify the Ṣanhādja – perhaps in order to obtain a better control of the trade routes or to make conquests in the Sudan – is attested by Ibn Ḥawḳal and al-Bakrī, who refer to a certain Tīn-Barūtān (or Tīn-Yarūtān) as 'the king

6. Cf. Chapter 12 above.

7. Ibn Abī Zar', 1843–6, Vol. 1, pp. 71–2 describes in detail the deterioration of the political and economic conditions during the second quarter of the fifth/eleventh century. Ibn 'Idhārī, 1948–51, Vol. 4, p. 10 (N. Levtzion and J. F. P. Hopkins (eds), 1981, pp. 219 ff), narrates that Ibn Yāsīn on his return from al-Andalus through Morocco observed with amazement the splintering of the country into numerous hostile *ḳabīlās*. The Berbers acted in the same way, if not worse, as the *Mulūk al-ṭawā'if* in al-Andalus. A Masmūda man answered his question as to whether these people did not believe in God and Muḥammad with the words: 'Yes, but no one among us tolerates that somebody from another tribe is above him.'

8. Ibn Khaldūn, 1925–56, Vol. 2, p. 64; J. M. Cuoq, 1975, p. 332; N. Levtzion and J. F. P. Hopkins (eds), 1981, p. 327 enumerate seven Ṣanhādja groups: the Djuddāla, Lamtūna, Massūfa, Watzīla, Tārgā, Zaghāwa and Lamṭa but seem to consider only the three first as of the 'race of the Ṣanhādja', the others being 'their brothers'.

9. No satisfactory explanation of this name had as yet been offered.

10. This is the opinion of J. Marquardt, 1913, p. 325.

of all the Ṣanhādja' or as 'the ruler of Awdāghust' between 340/951 and 350/961.[11] Although none of the authors mentions the branch to which Tīn-Barūtān belonged, it is likely that he was a Lamtūna.[12] The nature and scope of this confederacy is nowhere explained and we are not informed whether all three main branches of the Ṣanhādja were part of it.

According to Ibn Abī Zar', a comparatively late author (he wrote *c.* 726/1326), there followed in the Western Sahara a lengthy period of disunity, confusion and anarchy among the Ṣanhādja, who could not agree on a single ruler until the time of *amīr* Abū 'Abdallāh Muḥammad, known as Tārashna al-Lamtūnī, whom they made their leader.[13] Now a Tārasna (or Tārashna) al-Lamtūnī is mentioned by al-Bakrī as the Lamtūna chief who was killed somewhere in the Sudan fighting the blacks,[14] presumably shortly before the rise of the Almoravids. After his death he was succeeded as ruler of the Ṣanhādja by his son-in-law, Yaḥyā ibn Ibrāhīm al-Djuddālī, the man who introduced 'Abdallāh ibn Yāsīn among the Ṣanhādja.[15]

This account, although not above suspicion of being a later attempt to streamline the pre-Almoravid history of the Ṣanhādja,[16] reflects in general the anarchic conditions in the area to the south of Morocco, where short periods of unity among the Ṣanhādja branches were followed by disunity, rivalry and fierce fighting. No confederation was able to retain supremacy in the desert and its leadership changed frequently.[17]

This state of affairs among the Ṣanhādja groups was not without effects on their economic prosperity. Although nomadic pastoralism formed the way of life for the majority of the desert Ṣanhādja, participation in the caravan trade between the Maghrib and the Sudan that went across their territory, represented a welcome addition to their income. Their chiefs derived many advantages from the control of the routes as well as of the trade centres by levying dues, fees and presents for their protection or services.

Until the third quarter of the fourth/tenth century the Ṣanhādja confederacy under the strong leadership of Tīn-Barūtān controlled the very important salt mines at Awlīl and held the monopoly of the salt trade going through Awdāghust to Ghana. Although according to archaeological evidence the town of Awdāghust had as yet not reached its zenith, it was

11. Ibn Ḥawḳal, 1938, pp. 100–1; J. M. Cuoq, 1975, pp. 73–4; al-Bakrī, 1913, p. 159; V. Monteil, 1968, p. 53 (this latter author gives faulty dates of 961 and 971).

12. The close relations with *Bilād al-Sūdān* as well as his being called 'the ruler of Awdāghust' indicate that he was based in the southern parts of the desert, as were the Lamtūna.

13. Ibn Abī Zar', 1843–6, Vol. 1, p. 76; J. M. Cuoq, 1975, p. 231 quoted also in Ibn Khaldūn, 1925–56, Vol. 1, p. 236; J. M. Cuoq, 1975, p. 333.

14. Al-Bakrī, 1913, p. 164; V. Monteil, 1968, p. 59; J. M. Cuoq, 1975, p. 86.

15. Ibn Abī Zar', 1843–6, Vol. 1, p. 76 indicates that 120 years elapsed between Tīn Barūtān and Tārashna, but this is too long a time period. Al-Bakrī gives no dates.

16. Cf. N. Levtzion, 1978, pp. 653–5; 1979, p. 90.

17. The Moorish tradition speaks of about sixteen such confederations in the Western Sahara during the last three centuries; F. de La Chapelle, 1930, p. 48.

nevertheless an important commercial centre, dominated by the Ṣanhādja chief and inhabited by a Ṣanhādja majority.[18] But after 360/970 the trade of Awdāghust began to be dominated by the Zanāta and Arab traders of Ifrīḳiya. How this change came about is not entirely clear but until the Almoravid conquest of Awdāghust in 446/1054 the Ṣanhādja were nearly totally excluded from the lucrative trade. Another serious blow to Ṣanhādja prosperity had been the opening of a new salt mine at Tantintal (Taghāzā) which started to supply Ghana and other parts of the Sudan with that precious commodity thus breaking the Awlīl monopoly.

The weakening of the Ṣanhādja at the end of the fourth/tenth and the beginning of the fifth/eleventh century had allowed the Maghrāwa Berbers of Sidjilmāsa to gain control and occupy extensive pastures in the Dar'a, at Aghmāt and at Tāmdūlt which were vital for the nomadic economy of the northern Ṣanhādja groups.[19]

Thus in the first half of the fifth/eleventh century the Ṣanhādja of the Western Sahara lost much of their former preponderance both in the north and in the south where their hereditary enemies, the Zanāta Berbers, took over not only the termini of the trans-Saharan routes (Sidjilmāsa and Awdāghust) but also their best pastures.

Turning now to the religious conditions prevailing in the westernmost part of the Islamic world just before the rise of the Almoravids, we find not only a variety of heterodox sects but also varying degrees of Islamization going from a very superficial knowledge of the main tenets of this religion among the desert and mountain Berber groups to highly developed Islamic institutions in some towns and regions.

Among the heterodox sects the most interesting was that of the Barghawāṭa, a Berber group living on the Atlantic plains of Morocco between Salé and Sāfī. Their religion was already founded in the second/eighth century by a 'prophet' called Ṣāliḥ, who produced a Qoran in the Berber language and developed a set of doctrines in which old Berber beliefs were mixed with Islamic elements. Although the Idrīsids, Umayyads and Fāṭimids attempted occasionally to uproot this heterodoxy, they had never defeated the Barghawāṭa; the *djihād* against them was a permanent obligation for the inhabitants of the *ribāṭ* (fortified monastery) built at Salé against their incursions into the 'land of Islam' (*Bilād al-islām*).[20]

In the southern parts of Morocco, in the Sūs region, in the Atlas Mountains as well as in the Dar'a valley had lived groups of Shī'ites of various denominations. But the most important non-orthodox sect among the Berbers were the Khāridjites, especially the 'Ibāḍites.[21] Although after the advent of the Fāṭimids and the unsuccessful revolt of Abū Yazīd in Ifrīḳiya the political role of the Khāridjites in the Mediterranean Maghrib had

18. Cf. J. Devisse, 1970, pp. 121–2.
19. Ibn Khaldūn, 1925–56, Vol. 1, p. 257.
20. Cf. R. Le Tourneau, 1958 and Chapter 3 above.
21. Cf. Chapters 10, 11 and 12 above.

diminished, they still retained strong positions and influence in the Sahara and the Sudan, especially as traders and missionaries.[22] For some reason the ʿIbāḍite doctrine particularly attracted the Zanāta branch of the Berbers whereas the Ṣanhādja were more inclined to adopt Shīʿite Islam and later Sunnite Islam in its Mālikite form.

All the early Arabic sources about the rise of the Almoravid movement are unanimous about the superficial Islamization of the Saharan people and stress their religious ignorance and negligence. There were, of course, some persons among the chiefs and leaders with a more profound knowledge of Islam, people who performed the pilgrimage to Mecca and even some *faḳīh*s who tried to improve the religious situation of their compatriots. Some small centres of militant Mālikism existed in southern Morocco, like the *dār al-murābiṭīn* of Waggāg ibn Zallū, but it seems that until the emergence of ʿAbdallāh ibn Yāsīn their efforts did not bring any appreciable improvement.

The role played by the Pilgrimage to Mecca and of travel through the more advanced Muslim countries in enlarging the religious and cultural horizon of pious visitors from the Islamic periphery is well known. The pilgrims became aware of the deep contrast between the superficial Islam of their own people and the Islam as practised in the central parts of the Islamic *oekoumene*.[23] Throughout history a number of reformers or revivalists in the Maghrib, in the Sahara and in the Sudanese belt have been stimulated by the experience of Pilgrimage.

The first half of the fifth/eleventh century witnessed a revival of orthodox Sunni Islam in the Muslim world from the Maghrib in the west to Iran in the east. It emerged partly as a vigorous reaction against the attempts of Shīʿite dynasties like the Fāṭimids and Buwayhids under whose domination a large part of Muslim countries lived, to impose their specific creed on the hitherto Sunnite population.[24] Outstanding in the ideological struggle against the Shīʿa and other heterodoxies were the Mālikite *faḳīh*s of North Africa especially those from the ancient Mālikite stronghold at Ḳayrawān.[25] The Mālikite *faḳīh*s encouraged the Zīrīds to leave the Fāṭimid orbit and to recognize the Abbasids as supreme heads of the Islamic community; the same *faḳīh*s instigated anti-Shīʿite pogroms in Ifrīḳiya, their aim being to eradicate from this region any heresy or any other *madhhab* (school of Islamic jurisprudence) than their own.[26] One of the leading figures of Ḳayrawān and the most active and militant Mālikite was precisely that Abū ʿImrān al-Fāsī whom the Djuddāla chief Yaḥyā ibn Ibrāhīm met in Ḳayrawān in 430/1038–9.

22. Cf. Chapters 3 and 11 above.
23. Cf. Chapter 8, note 94 above.
24. See Chapter 2 above.
25. On Mālikism in Ifrīḳiya, see H. R. Idris, 1955 and 1972; H. Monès, 1972.
26. 'The year 440/1048 marks the definitive victory of Mālikism in the Muslim West'. E. Lévi-Provençal, 1948, p. 251.

The beginnings of Ibn Yāsīn's reforming activities

Not much is known about 'Abdallāh b. Yāsīn's life before he was sent to the desert Ṣanhādja. He came from the Djazūla, a Berber group in southern Morocco, his mother being originally from the village of Tamāmānāwt on the fringe of the desert bordering with Ghana.[27] Some later sources indicate that he had studied for seven years in Muslim Spain[28] but al-Bakrī, who was a near contemporary, expresses grave doubts about the extent of Ibn Yāsīn's knowledge of the Qoran and Islamic law.[29] Even his position in Waggāg's *Dār al-murābiṭīn* is not quite clear; he seems to have remained obedient to Waggāg as the head of the school and spiritual leader until the latter's death, an indication of a rather subordinate standing. On the other hand Waggāg's choice of him as missionary to the Ṣanhādja must have been based on recognition of the quality of his religious knowledge and strength of character.[30]

The history of Ibn Yāsīn's reforming activities among the Ṣanhādja is known only in a general way; the chronology is uncertain and confused and there are at least two long periods (the first between 430/1039 and 440/1048 and the second between 446/1054 and 450/1058) on which we are without any concrete information. We can discern in Ibn Yāsīn's activity in the desert two phases: in the first he tried to improve or reform the faith among the Djuddāla and succeeded in grouping around himself a number of followers. This phase lasted from *c.* 430/1039 to 445/1053 and ended with a violent clash between the reformer and the Djuddāla leaders, with the result that Ibn Yāsīn was expelled. In the second phase, which lasted until his death in 451/1059, the Lamtūna became the mainstay of the Almoravid movement.

At first, under the protection of Yaḥyā ibn Ibrāhīm, all went comparatively well; in the words of Ḳāḍī 'Iyāḍ:

> he made [Ibrāhīm] and his people understand his code of living and his idealism . . . he demanded and imposed a severe and strict observance, in changing unlawful practice and in the severe chastening [of those] who did not accept the path of true guidance. He continued to enjoy hospitality amongst those *ḳabīla*s, until he became dominant among them, and they proclaimed the true faith there.[31]

From that long period only two events are recorded: an attack against the Lamtūna, who were defeated in their mountains (Adrār) and the founda-

27. Al-Bakrī, 1913, p. 165.
28. Ibn 'Idhārī, 1967, Vol. 4, pp. 9–10; *al-Ḥulal al-Mawshiyya*, 1936, p. 10.
29. Al-Bakrī, 1913, pp. 169–70. But if should not be forgotten that this author, a sophisticated Andalusian scholar, was biased against the rude Saharan Berbers.
30. Ḳāḍī 'Iyāḍ, *apud* H. T. Norris, 1971, p. 256: "Abdullāh b. Yāsīn was acknowledged to be a man of learning and piety.'
31. Cf. H. T. Norris, 1971, p. 256. Other sources speak in similar terms.

tion of the town of Arat-n-anna where in accordance with Ibn Yāsīn's egalitarian ideas all houses were to have the same height.[32]

After more than ten years of residence among the Djuddāla Ibn Yāsīn clashed with the *faḳīh* Djawhar ibn Sakkum and two Djuddāla nobles, 'Ayār and In-Takkū. The cause of this split appears to have been a combination of religious differences and a struggle for power after the death of Yaḥyā ibn Ibrāhīm al-Djuddālī.[33]

Ibn Yāsīn's strict demands concerning discipline and the observation of all religious duties as well as his puritanic and egalitarian ideas probably did not find the resonance he expected; being rather a harsh master he displayed a disregard for the social values and taboos common to Ṣanhādja society. In the succession struggle after Yaḥyā's death he apparently took the side of an unsuccessful pretender[34] and was forced to leave his abode at Arat-n-anna.[35] This whole episode shows that Ibn Yāsīn's means of power were rather limited and did not allow him to enforce his will.

During and after the crisis Ibn Yāsīn had the full support of his master Waggāg who although disapproving of his pupil's extremism and excessive bloodshed, backed him and wrote a strong reprimand to all who showed disobedience. He sent Ibn Yāsīn again to the Ṣanhādja, this time to the Lamtūna, led by Yaḥyā ibn 'Umar. It was among the Lamtūna that Ibn Yāsīn found the necessary political support for the implementation of his aims. This was the turning point in the history of the Almoravid movement and the main reason for the dominance of the Lamtūna. All this happened before 447/1055 and it seems that at that time there existed serious tensions between the Djuddāla and Lamtūna, caused probably by diverging policy as to the future orientation of the movement.[36]

Ibn Yāsīn's retreat and then his return for a second mission can be considered a sort of *hidjra* and we can observe in many of his acts a re-enactment of early Islamic usages. One of the aspects of this revivalism was the reform of traditional Berber military tactics in order to re-enact the original ways of waging the *djihād*.[37]

32. Al-Bakrī, 1913, p. 165. Although Arat-n-anna is commonly identified with the present-day Aratane, a well between Tichīt and Walāta in eastern Mauritania, there are archaeological objections to this supposition. Cf. D. Jacques-Meunier, 1961. Aratane is a widely distributed toponym, cf. H. T. Norris, 1971, p. 258.

33. It is not certain what happened to this man who brought Ibn Yāsīn to the Saharan Ṣanhādja. According to some historians he had already died before the Djuddāla expelled Ibn Yāsīn, while according to the others his death took place before the 'island retreat', cf. below.

34. A. M. al-'Abbādī, 1960, p. 149; H. T. Norris, 1971, pp. 260–2.

35. Al-Bakrī, 1913, p. 165. 'They [the Djuddāla] refused to listen to his advice, took away from him the treasure administration, demolished his house and pillaged its furniture and all effects it contained.'

36. J. Devisse, 1970, p. 115, n. 10.

37. Cf. on this aspect the penetrating analysis of P. de Moraes Farias, 1967, pp. 811–17 and some remarks by H. T. Norris, 1971, p. 266, n. 45.

The transformation of a reform movement into a *djihād*

The dominance of the Lamtūna in the movement has been the reason that they are very often identified as the Almoravids par excellence. Before we continue the history of the movement we should discuss the problem of the origin of the name Almoravids (Arabic, *al-Murābiṭun*).

Until recently it was held that it is derived from *ribāṭ* (*al-Murābiṭun* = the people of the *ribāṭ* or *rābiṭa*) – a word whose accepted sense is 'fortified frontier or coastal post' or 'a fortified centre for religious and ascetic practice and/or the propagation of the faith'. This interpretation is based only on the account of a comparatively late Arabic author Ibn Abī Zarʿ (d. after 726/1326) according to whom Ibn Yāsīn withdrew after the disagreement with the Djuddāla to an island where with seven companions he had built a *rābiṭa*; later he indoctrinated many other disciples in this place and called them *al-Murābiṭūn* because of their adhesion to this *rābiṭa*.[38] Ibn Khaldūn (d. 808/1406) also speaks about Ibn Yāsīn's retreat to an island but does not make any reference to a *ribāṭ* in the sense of a fortress or hermitage.[39] None of the more ancient sources refer to the existence of such a building and P. de Moraes Farias rightly remarks that 'one wonders why the account given by Ibn Abī Zarʿ has been accepted without challenge by most historians'.[40]

The recent scholarship represented by A. M. al-ʿAbbādī, A. Huici Miranda, P. de Moraes Farias, H. T. Norris, A. Noth, N. Levtzion and F. Meier,[41] has definitely abandoned the idea of *al-Murābiṭūn* meaning 'people of the *ribāṭ*'. The name seems to be derived from the Qurʾānic meaning of the root *r–b–ṭ* which is very close to that of waging *djihād* in a correct way, although the term also contains the idea of pious acts, dedication to the cause of Islam. *Ribāṭ* could also delineate the whole corpus of Islamic teaching (*daʿwat al-ḥakk*, 'summons to the truth') laid down for the Ṣanhādja by Ibn Yāsīn.[42] It is not impossible that the name *al-Murābiṭūn* is in some way connected with Waggāg's *dār al-murābiṭīn* where Ibn Yāsīn lived before his mission.

The final proof that there was not a *ribāṭ* (a fortified outpost) on an island has been brought by the archaeological expedition of the Institut fondamental de l'Afrique noire on the island of Tidra near the Mauritanian

38. Ibn Abī Zarʿ, 1843–6, Vol. 1, p. 79; cf. the criticism of this source by A. Huici Miranda, 1959a, pp. 155ff.; 1960, pp. 513ff.

39. Ibn Khaldūn, 1925–56, Vol. 1, p. 238; the text shows that the members of the community lived amidst the natural surroundings of a thicket without building anything like a *ribāṭ* or *rābiṭa*.

40. P. de Moraes Farias, 1967, p. 805.

41. Cf. Bibliography.

42. Originally *rabaṭa* means to bind, to tie up; *ribāṭ* – ribbon, band, ligature; *rābiṭa* – bond, tie, link, later also confederation, league, union etc. The semantic development to fortified outpost and all cognate meanings is discussed in P. de Moraes Farias, 1967, pp. 813 ff, and in greater detail by F. Meier, 1981, pp. 80 ff.

coast in 1966. No vestiges of any *ribāṭ* could be found on this island. Any building of the kind mentioned by Ibn Abī Zarʿ is a physical impossibility there owing to the lack of clay and stones.[43] On the other hand the reports on the retreat of Ibn Yāsīn and his early followers to an island in the sea seems not improbable in the light of the comparison of Ibn Abī Zarʿ's account to the results obtained by the field work on Tidra. Therefore the report of Ibn Khaldūn about the life of the first Almoravids in a thicket cannot be entirely excluded.

Ibn Yāsīn's retreat – a conscious imitation of Prophet Muḥammad's *hidjra* – is difficult to date exactly; it occurred probably before 444/1052–3 since within a year after this the followers of Ibn Yāsīn had attacked the town of Sidjilmāsa. When Ibn Yāsīn emerged from his retreat and found in the Lamtūna his most devoted followers, especially among their chiefly family, represented by Yaḥyā ibn ʿUmar and his brother Abū Bakr, the movement entered a decisive phase. From a reform movement it became a militant one whose members were ready to spread his teaching among other Ṣanhādja and even beyond either by persuasion or by *djihād*. Although Ibn Yāsīn wanted from the start to give his movement a supra-tribal character, the *al-Murābiṭūn* were and remained members of some concrete Berber groups. The leadership was in the hands of the Lamtūna under their chief Yaḥyā ibn ʿUmar, to whom Ibn Yāsīn delegated the military command as *amīr* and the other founding branches, the Massūfa and Djuddāla (at least at the beginning) followed this general command. The members of the different tribes were more or less left under the leadership of their traditional chiefs and remained tribal warriors as before but now under the banner of Islam.

There emerged a pattern of dual leadership since Ibn Yāsīn attended not only to the religious and judicial affairs of the community but also administered the public treasury and held the supreme authority, even over Yaḥyā ibn ʿUmar.[44] He even took part personally in campaigns.

The unification of the Ṣanhādja was not an easy task; the Djuddāla who were defeated by the Lamtūna after Ibn Yāsīn's return to the desert and coerced to rejoin the movement, remained hostile and seceded at the earliest opportunity. When the main Almoravid army fought in southern Morocco, the Djuddāla revolted and Yaḥyā ibn ʿUmar was sent against them but apparently without any success as he was besieged by the Djuddāla at Azuḳī (Azugī) in the Adrār.[45] The first *amīr* of the Almoravids was killed (in 448/1056) in the battle at Tabfārīllā where his army, although reinforced by the troops of Labī ibn Wār-Dyābī, the chief of Takrūr, was

43. Cf. H. J. Hugot, 1966, pp. 555 ff and 1019 ff; P. de Moraes Farias, 1967, pp. 821–43; a recapitulation by A. Gaudio, 1978, pp. 52–5.

44. Al-Bakrī, 1913, pp. 166–7. Ibn Yāsīn ordered the flogging of Yaḥyā who submitted to it even before he knew the reason for it.

45. Azuḳī is situated about 15 km from Aṭār, which, according to al-Bakrī, had been built by Yaḥyā's brother Yannū ibn ʿUmar. On this site, see B. Saison, 1981 (Plate 13.1).

defeated.[46] No other attempts were made by the Almoravids against the Djuddāla but relations remained strained. On the other hand members of this branch participated later in the Almoravid campaigns in the Maghrib and the Djuddāla were counted among the true Almoravids. More obscure were the relations with the Massūfa: according to Ibn Khaldūn there occurred a conflict between them and the Lamtūna but it seems that it was quickly settled and in subsequent exploits the Massūfa and Lamtūna formed a firm alliance. As for other Berbers, the Lamṭa were subdued at an early stage and rallied themselves to the Almoravid cause, as did even some Zanāta and Masmūda.

Despite all the internal dissensions and secessionist tendencies the new politico-religious system and common interests brought unity to the Ṣanhādja Berbers. Those of them who lived along the trade routes were interested in regaining control over these and over the trade. The associated *ḳabīla*s in the north, the Lamṭa and the Djazūla,[47] as well as some of the Lamtūna wanted to regain the rich pastures between the Atlas Mountains and the Sahara. The common enemy in both cases were the Zanāta. Although not all the Zanāta professed the Khāridjite faith, many of them did and their heresy added another reason for the Mālikite Almoravids to attack them. To a certain degree the Almoravid conquest was a vengeance of the desert Ṣanhādja on the Zanāta, who in the preceding period had gained an upper hand in the western Maghrib. Of no small importance for their initial successes were the nearly anarchic conditons prevailing in Morocco under the Maghrāwa dynasties as many people greeted the conquering Almoravids as liberators from the Maghrāwa oppression.[48] Within five years, between 446/1054 and 451/1059 the Almoravids had broken the Zanāta supremacy in north-western Africa. The first campaigns were directed against the Zanāta domains in the Dar'a valley and then against Sidjilmāsa whose inhabitants complained to Ibn Yāsīn about the tyranny of the Maghrāwa ruler, Mas'ūd b. Wānūdīn. After the failure of peaceful settlement the Almoravids conquered the town, killed Mas'ūd and installed there their own governor. Having thus seized the northern terminus of the caravan trade the Almoravid army immediately returned to the south against Awdāghust. After its conquest they pitilessly massacred its Zanāta inhabitants. Thus the second terminus of the trans-Saharan route fell under their authority and with it also the control of the western trade.[49]

46. Al-Bakrī, 1913, pp. 167–8. On Takrūr, see now A. R. Ba, 1984.

47. Among the spiritual leaders of the movement Waggāg belonged to the Lamṭa, Ibn Yāsīn to the Djazūla.

48. The Mālikites of North Africa played, since the Fāṭimid period, a role of champions of oppressed people; the Almoravids, at least during the initial stage, remained true to this tradition and gained much sympathy by their abolition of all illegal (non-canonical) taxes.

49. Cf. J. Devisse, 1970, pp. 152 ff on the conquest and its impact on the whole economic situation in the Maghrib, the Sahara and the Sudan.

In the meantime the population of Sidjilmāsa, apparently discontented with the harsh regime introduced by the puritanical Almoravids, revolted and massacred the small garrison. A new campaign was necessary to re-establish the situation. During the absence of the main Almoravid army there occurred the already mentioned secession of the Djuddāla in the south and also the death of Yaḥyā ibn ʿUmar. The northern wing commanded now by Abū Bakr, who became the new *amīr* after the death of his brother Yaḥyā, reconquered Sidjilmāsa and the pastures of the Darʿa.

In the few next years Ibn Yāsīn proved to be not only a religious reformer and a hard warrior but also an accomplished politician. By a fine diplomacy he had achieved the peaceful submission of the Maṣmūda Berbers of the Atlas Mountains and, in a similar way, after prolonged negotiations, the important town of Aghmāt with the whole Sūs region fell under his control (in 450/1058). To cement the new alliance, Abū Bakr married Zaynab, a daughter of the chief of Aghmāt and this step assured the Almoravids bloodless occupation of vast regions in southern Morocco. It goes without saying that all the various heresies and heterodoxies flourishing in this part of Morocco were extirpated and the Mālikite school in its Almoravid form was introduced everywhere.

But in the struggle against the most formidable foe of the orthodoxy, the Barghawāṭa, the Almoravids suffered their first serious setback; in 451/1059 they were defeated and Ibn Yāsīn was killed in obscure circumstances in the battle near Kurīfalat.[50] His successor at the head of the Almoravid community was Abū Bakr ibn ʿUmar.

Although the founder's death led to a temporary crisis (it is reported that at that point the Massūfa revolted), it speaks for the solidity of Ibn Yāsīn's achievement that the whole movement did not crumble but did find, after a short time, a new and even greater vigour that enabled it to continue victoriously both the spread of the new doctrine and the conquests.

With the passing away of Ibn Yāsīn the religious community transformed itself into a kingdom. As the spiritual leadership began to lose its former importance,[51] the office of *amīr* achieved the primacy and the holder of it had founded a dynasty. At the same time a hierarchy developed: the first in the realm were the Lamtūna, the branch of the rulers, so that the Almoravids were often designated as *al-Lamtūniyyūn al-murābiṭūn* or more simply *Lamtūna*. The title *al-murābiṭ* was restricted to the members of the three founding branches whereas the members of other *ḳabīla*s such as the Djazūla, Lamṭa, Maṣmūda and others who served in the army

50. Al-Bakrī, 1913, p. 168. The place is situated about 40 km south of Rabat.

51. Ibn Yāsīn was succeeded as religious commander by Sulaymān b. ʿAddū, another companion of Waggāg b. Zallū. There were then some other jurists like Imām al-Ḥaḍramī, the *ḳāḍī* of Azuḳī, or Limtād al-Lamtūnī, but none of them achieved the influence and status of the movement's founder. Cf. H. T. Norris, 1971, pp. 267–8.

PLATE 13.1 *Marrakesh: excavations in the first Almoravid palace*

were not considered *al-murābiṭūn* but were called 'followers' (*al-hasham*). The restriction of the name to the founding branches indicates the rise of an aristocracy.

The 'veiled ones' (*al-mulaththamūn*) is another name given to the Almoravids; it is derived from the traditional custom of the desert Ṣanhādja of wearing a mouth veil. In Muslim Spain the veil was considered a privilege of the true Almoravids and its wearing was forbidden to all but the Ṣanhādja[52] It was something like a uniform or distinctive dress of the ruling class.

The history of the first ten years of Abū Bakr's rule (until 462/1069) is obscure and no details are known about Almoravid activities.[53] A long time was perhaps needed for consolidation of the new leadership and to overcome crises natural in a recently formed confederation of groups with strong traditions of independence.

With the foundation of Marrakesh as the new capital to the north of the

52. Cf. E. Lévi-Provençal, 1934, pp. 200–18. On the origin and purpose of the veil among desert Berbers a number of studies exist, cf. R. Corso, 1949; J. Nicolaisen, 1963; J. H. Keenan, 1977; H. T. Norris, 1972, pp. 19–41; F. Meier, 1981, pp. 143–63.

53. That even the contemporaries did not know much about the events is confirmed by al-Bakrī's statement (1913, p. 170) that 'at present [i.e., in 1067–8] . . . their power is dispersed and incoherent and their dwelling-place is the Sahara.'

Atlas Mountains in 463/1070 a new chapter in Almoravid history began.[54] This date is significant, too, in the sense that at that time the split of the Almoravid movement into two wings had occurred, the southern led by Abū Bakr and the northern with Abū Bakr's cousin Yūsuf ibn Tāshfīn at its head.[55] This split came about gradually and unintentionally; even before the construction of Marrakesh was finished Abū Bakr was recalled to the desert where serious conflicts between the Lamtūna and the Massūfa threatened the unity of the movement. Yūsuf ibn Tāshfīn became his deputy in the north with the task of continuing the campaign against the Zanāta.[56] After settling the dispute in the Sahara, Abū Bakr returned to the north to assume again the leadership of the whole movement. But in the meantime Yūsuf ibn Tāshfīn had consolidated his position, having strengthened his army by buying black slaves from the Sudan and Christian captives from Spain so as not to be solely dependent on the Ṣanhādja warriors. Naturally enough he was not prepared to yield his powerful position to his cousin although he still acknowledged him as his superior. For various reasons Abū Bakr did not want to press his claim[57] and gracefully handed over the authority to Yūsuf. According to the revised chronology this happened in 465/1072; Abū Bakr then returned definitively to the Sahara and never returned to the north. Nevertheless, he was recognized as the head of the whole Almoravid empire until his death in 480/1087. The gold Almoravid dinars were struck up to this date in the name of Abū Bakr ibn ʿUmar and even Yūsuf ibn Tāshfīn continued to pay him nominal allegiance.[58]

54. As many Arabic sources indicated that Marrakesh was founded in 454/1062, this date was long accepted without comment. E. Lévi-Provençal, 1957; A. Huici Miranda, 1959b and G. Deverdun, 1959–66 have critically examined all the literary and archaeological evidence and established the new date.

55. The relationship of the first Almoravid *amīrs* is shown in the following simplified genealogy:

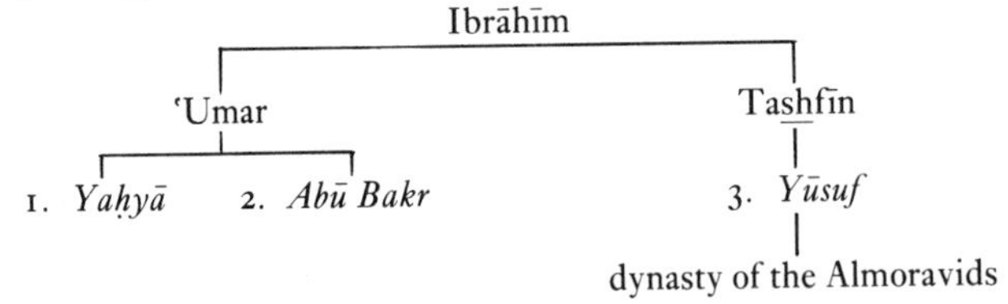

56. At the same time Abū Bakr divorced Zaynab who next married Yūsuf ibn Tāshfīn bringing him a large fortune.

57. He himself proclaimed that he could not live out of the desert, cf. *Al-Ḥulal al-Mawshiyya*, 1936, p. 15. Although this attachment to the nomadic way of life certainly played a role in Abū Bakr's decision, it should not be forgotten that his armed forces were much weaker than those of his cousin.

58. Ibn Tāshfīn's name appeared on the coins only after 480/1087, when he became in name as well as in practice the sole ruler of the Almoravids.

The conquests in the north

In the years between 468/1075 and 476/1083 the Almoravid army led by Yūsuf ibn Tāshfīn had gradually conquered Morocco and the western regions of Algeria. Fez had fallen to them in 468/1075 followed by other towns on the Atlantic plain. Seven years later Tlemcen and Oran were conquered and in 476/1083 the Almoravid army secured control of the Gibraltar Strait by the conquest of Ceuta. This had brought Muslim Spain into the horizon of the desert warriors.

There the once flourishing Umayyad caliphate had crumbled in the first decades of the fifth/eleventh century. From its ruins emerged a conglomeration of petty states that spent themselves in fratricidal quarrels and were unable to resist the vigorous attempts of the northern Christian states to subdue them. No less than twenty such petty states had arisen in various provinces or towns under emirs and kinglets known collectively as *mulūk al-ṭawā'if* ('party kings', Spanish, *reyes de taifas*).

The Christian offensive culminated in the conquest of Toledo (Arabic, Ṭulayṭula) in 478/1085 and it soon became apparent that the Christians were aiming at the total absorption of the *mulūk al-ṭawā'if* and not only on imposing vassalage and tribute on them. Muslim jurists had become alarmed by this state of affairs which threatened to uproot Islam and its civilization in al-Andalus. As the Muslim kinglets were totally unable to offer any serious resistance to the advance of the Christians, only the invitation of help from abroad remained as an alternative. Under the circumstances the sole power that would be able to accomplish this task were the Almoravids who were now in full vigour and renowned as a religious body dedicated to *djihād*. At the invitation of the Abbadid ruler of Seville, al-Muʿtamid, the Almoravid army under Yūsuf ibn Tāshfīn crossed the Strait of Gibraltar in 479/1086.[59] After an unopposed march through southern Spain the Almoravid army inflicted a spectacular defeat on the Castilian army under King Alfonso VI at al-Zallāḳa (Sagrajas) near Badajoz.[60] A wave of enthusiasm spread over al-Andalus and Yūsuf returned to Morocco in accordance with his previous promise. A year later the death of Abū Bakr made him nominal as well as de facto sovereign of the empire.

But the grave problems of Muslim Spain were far from being definitively settled. Shortly after Ibn Tāshfīn's retreat new discord among the petty rulers permitted the Christians to resume their attacks. The Almoravids were called again to intervene and in 481/1088 they scored another victory in the battle of Aledo. In spite of this the *mulūk al-ṭāwāʿif* showed an open hostility to their deliverers whom they feared no less than their Christian foes, and Ibn Tāshfīn left al-Andalus for the second time.

59. Letter of invitation in al-Maḳḳarī, 1855–61, Vol. 2, p. 674. To his critics who foresaw the danger of the Almoravid take-over in al-Andalus, al-Muʿtamid replied that he would rather be a camel-driver in Africa than a swineherd in Castille.

60. Cf. on this battle E. Lévi-Provençal, E. Garcia Gomez and J. Oliver Asín, 1950.

PLATE 13.2(a) *Almoravid decoration: detail of a bronze door (Fez)*

PLATE 13.2(b) *Almoravid decoration: a bronze door-knocker* (*Fez*)

His patience was now exhausted and in 483/1090 he came back, but this time as conqueror rather than ally. Armed with *fatwās* (legal opinions), signed by numerous Moroccan and Andalusian *fuḳahā'*,[61] he led the campaign against the *mulūk al-ṭawā'if*, who were accused of various anti-Islamic sins such as collaboration with the Christians, corruption and illegal taxation. In a systematic campaign the Almoravid army conquered or occupied all the main towns and by 487/1094 the whole of Muslim Spain was annnexed, with the exception of Toledo which remained in Christian hands, and Saragossa where the dynasty of Banū Hūd was allowed to subsist and to form a buffer state. All the old Muslim rulers were deposed[62] and the unity of Muslim Spain – now under the rule of the Almoravids – was re-established.[63]

In the east the Almoravid conquests only reached the town of Algiers and its immediate region. Why they stopped there without accomplishing the unification of the whole Maghrib by penetrating farther eastwards into Ifrīḳiya remains obscure. They certainly did not come up against the Hilāli Arabs who at that time were roaming in the more southerly regions of Ifrīḳiya and eastern Algeria. Although the Ḥammādid state of central Algeria offered some resistance to the Almoravid advance and there was even some fighting around Tlemcen in which the Ḥammādids were victorious, it seems that the Almoravids were rather reluctant to attack vigorously a people belonging to the same branch of the Ṣanhādja. But the most likely reason seems to be the worsening situation in Muslim Spain which absorbed more and more of the attention of Yūsuf ibn Tāshfīn; since his limited manpower was not sufficient for fighting on two fronts he had decided to concentrate on the campaign against the Christians, conscious of the Almoravid fame as fighters for Islam.

What had originally been no more than a local reform movement among the desert Berbers had become an empire extending from the Ebro to the Senegal; its sweep of nearly thirty degrees of latitude covered a great diversity of landscapes, zones of economic activity, and cultural traditions, from the most fertile plains of Spain and Morocco to the deserts of Mauritania.

The new situation south of the Sahara

Unfortunately much less is known about the situation in the southern part

61. Even the great Iraqi scholar al-Ghazālī (d. 505/1111) supported Ibn Tāshfīn's war against the Andalusian kinglets. This did not save his books from being later burned by the Almoravid *fuḳahā*.

62. Al-Mu'tamid of Seville was sent to Morocco where he lived in chains and in utter destitution until his death in Aghmāt in 488/1095; he lamented his fate in elegies that belong to masterpieces of Arabic poetry.

63. Valencia, where Rodrigo Diaz de Vivar, known as Cid and hero of the great Spanish epic, established an idependent principality, fell into the Almoravid hands only in 495/1102.

of the Almoravid empire than about that in the north. The big difficulty is the scarcity of source material: the written sources come from Arabic historical literature written far away from the scene of events in space and sometimes in time and the oral ones have undergone many changes, which (although they are beginning to be subjected to critical study) still make them difficult to use. The former come from Muslims in the north, the latter from black Africans in the Sahel, who although they may already have been Muslims did not necessarily adopt the same viewpoints as the men from the north of the continent.

We do not know with any certainty the situation that existed in the Senegal Valley. It now seems beyond doubt that the key points where settlements and markets developed were not on the coast but a good way inland. We now know from excavations that Sintiu-Bara[64] was an important site as early as the fifth to sixth centuries of the Christian era,[65] that Ogo was a big settlement, and that iron was smelted there in the ninth century.[66] Both al-Bakrī and al-Idrīsī mention the name Silla in various forms, and there are several places with this name in the Kaedi area. A recent article[67] suggests that the site of one of them, Sillā Rindaw, goes back to the period we are dealing with: the traces of iron-working found there – not yet accurately dated but probably ancient – certainly show the importance of the investigations that need to be carried out in this area.[68] All the prospecting and research carried out in the last few years on both the Mauritanian and the Senegalese side of the river suggests that valuable information will be gained from archaeological research in the coming decades.[69]

Though the texts are unclear and difficult to interpret, we gather from al-Bakrī and al-Idrīsī that Sillā and Takrūr, neither of them yet adequately pinpointed, jointly dominated the middle Senegal River in economic terms

64. The spelling of the name of this site is something of a problem. G. Thilmans and A. Ravisé (1980) spell it Sintiou, in accordance with French phonetics; Y. Fall (1982) and most Senegalese authors now spell it Sincu.

65. G. Thilmans and A. Ravisé (1980).

66. See B. Chavane, 1985.

67. Y. Fall, 1982.

68. D. Robert-Chaleix and M. Sognane, 1983.

69. B. Tandia, 1982–3, among many other studies. The main results of prospecting in Mauritania in June 1982 from Selibaby to Boghé are as follows. A large number of fluted pots were found comparable to the Sintiu-Bara ones regarded as dating from the fifth to sixth centuries: such pots have been found on the Senegalese side at Cascas, Sintiu-Bara Matam, Ogo and Bakel, and on the Mauritanian side in twenty places exactly opposite the above-mentioned sites. This could be a cultural indicator of great importance. A large quantity of rope-twisting discs were found (see R. Mauny, 1955b; G. Thilmans, 1979, p. 29) at thirty-seven sites on the Mauritanian side (and in many cases on the Senegalese side). Thousands of bases of iron-smelting furnaces were found (see D. Robert-Chaleix and M. Sognane, 1983).

in the fifth/eleventh and sixth/twelth centuries.[70] Thus all the evidence combines to show conclusively that this middle region of the river was busy – particularly in the realm of fishing – and powerful, between the sixth and twelfth centuries. Only faint echoes of this come through in the written sources and oral traditions and much more work will be needed to obtain results, though they will certainly prove to be spectacular.

A little further south, it is thanks to T. Lewicki that we have a somewhat better knowledge of a kingdom that long remained in the shadows, namely Diafunu (Zāfun-u). We learn that this kingdom became Muslim in the fifth/eleventh century, and that it was situated roughly around the confluence of the Kolombiné and the Senegal.[71]

Azuḳī, which according to preliminary investigations[72] was active between the end of the fourth/tenth century and the middle of the sixth/twelfth century, was probably a very important staging-post in this 'Senegalese system'.[73]

All this information, mostly obtained within the last fifteen years, still does not enable us to reconstruct the exact history of this area, which was so important for its contacts with the Almoravids. Abdurahmane Ba's recent thesis[74] puts forward attractive hypotheses about the very early existence of dynasties allied to the iron producers, who with their allies warred with black pre-Almoravid Islamizing forces from Takrūr (and probably also from Diafunu). Sillā was not yet Muslim in the eleventh century.

The political life of this area is beginning to emerge from the shadows, at least in terms of hypotheses. It is still hard to be sure whether Sillā, Takrūr or Diafunu exercised most control over the traffic in gold, which is known to have come from more southerly areas, the most northerly being between Falamé and Bafing. It will be seen below[75] that the establishment of the Almoravids in the south of what is now Mauritania had an undeniable effect on the geography of the gold trade and on the competition between rival towns on the Senegal.

The question is whether the Almoravids found Muslim princes on the Senegal with whom the Berbers had been in contact since the beginning of Islamization in this area, or whether they started and accelerated the conversion of the towns on the middle Senegal. The answer to this question is

70. A. R. Ba, 1984.

71. T. Lewicki, 1971a; Lewicki gives the Arabic transliteration as Zāfun(u).

72. B. Saison, 1981.

73. The spelling of the name of this place by Arab authors poses major problems. The various manuscript readings and possible vowel patterns yield a number of different spellings.

74. A. R. Ba, 1984.

75. See Chapter 14 below on the subject of the routes described by al-Idrīsī, which gave considerable importance to the Senegal Valley as against the routes taken in the previous two centuries.

very interesting. The most recent studies[76] tend to suggest that Islamization predated the Almoravid period, and may have brought about the downfall of an earlier Takrūr dynasty which was too closely bound up with the 'pagan' iron-smelters and magicians. Much work remains to be done on these questions, but research is moving quickly. In any event, it is now clear that Islam played a very important role in the Senegal Valley[77] in the fourth/tenth and fifth/eleventh centuries, and that the understanding between the Almoravids and the black Muslim rulers probably played a great part in the success of the veiled warriors from the north; in the Senegal Valley they found fighting men, slaves and gold.[78]

Further east the situation was certainly less favourable for the Almoravids. The Inland Niger Delta was of course a trading area and was urbanized before the advent of Islam.[79] The bulk of the gold produced, as far away as the forest lands, was probably brought together in this area, and the black gold merchants who collected it were in touch with Ghana to the north, and probably sometimes also with Gao, by the fourth/tenth century at the latest. The princes who governed these two towns regulated the sale of gold to the north. The ruler of Ghana was not a Muslim at the time of the Almoravid expansion, though he maintained excellent relations with the Muslims. Many of the latter, as research at Kumbi Saleh has shown,[80] lived in this market town, where the ruler of Ghana was glad to welcome them and where they could pray in a monumental mosque, certainly from the fourth/tenth century on.[81] The whole Ghana – Inland Niger Delta system, organized long before the Almoravids and certainly hostile to the Ṣanhādja,[82] was accustomed to trading with the Ifrīḳiyan merchants. There was thus likely to have been a clash between the Almoravids and the

76. See A. Ba, 1984. See also the doctoral thesis presented in Dakar by Mr Oumar Kane in December 1986 which indicates – by reference to Soninke traditions – that some Soninke (or *Jula*) merchants introduced Islam south of the Senegal River, possibly as early as the ninth century, but at the latest by the tenth century. Eleven maraboutic Soninke families of the Futa Toro maintain that their origins may be traced back to this period. Mr Kane points out that the verbs *julde* (to pray) and *julaade* (to trade) are derived from the word *Jula*. Even if those Soninke merchants were no more than guides for Muslim tradesmen from the north, they were nevertheless responsible for introducing Islam to Africa some time well before the Almoravid period. In a different way, this point is also clearly made by al-Bakrī.

77. There is a well-known reference in al-Bakrī (J. M. Cuoq, 1975, p. 90) to the fact that Lâbi (?), son of Wār Dyābi, chief of Takrūr, was with Abū Bakr in 1056. This certainly seems to suggest that Takrūr had at that time been Muslim for at least two generations.

78. See below Chapter 14, in particular on the idea of rival systems based on the towns on the Senegal and Ghana at this time.

79. S. K. McIntosh and R. J. McIntosh, 1980; J. Devisse, 1982.

80. S. Berthier, 1983. See also *Annales de l'Institut Mauritanien de Recherches Scientifiques*, 2nd year.

81. This is the view nowadays suggested by carbon-14 datings for the earliest periods of the organization of the town and its mosque.

82. See J. Devisse, 1970.

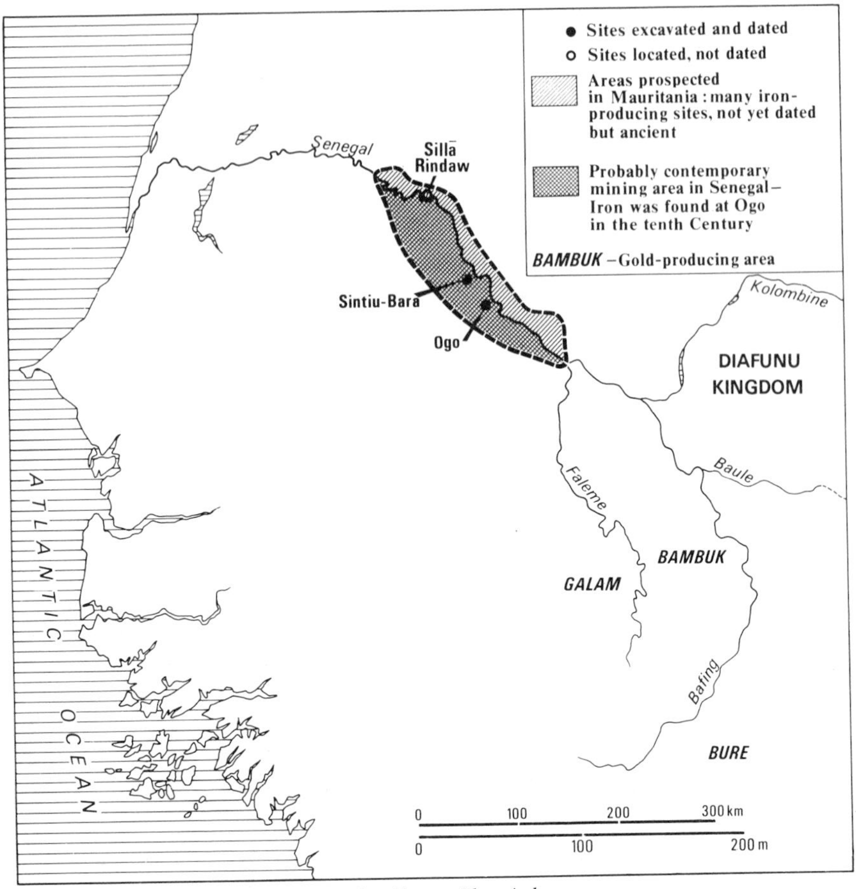

FIG. 13.2 *Localities on the Senegal in the Almoravid period*

Ghana system; and this is all the more probable because the latter, merely by virtue of the facts of geography (which it made the most of) had a sort of side-door to gold through the towns on the Senegal. At present, however, it is very difficult to judge what form this confrontation could have taken.

In order to answer this question we should first need to gauge exactly the forms and degree of Islamization attained in the Sahel when the Almoravid movement developed. All research nowadays combines to suggest that the first rational, concerted major effort at conversion (*djihād*) was the work of Saharans – the Almoravids – and dates from the fifth/eleventh century.[83] In the preceding two or three centuries the progress of Islam was probably

83. Ibn Sammak (1381) in J. M. Cuoq, 1975, p. 364.

more sporadic, and linked to the presence of the merchants from the north and urbanization.[84]

We are probably entitled to think that an initial phase of Islamization, sometimes very 'individual', and in the case of the Fāṭimids[85] perhaps 'statal' and hence very ideological, had an occasional effect on the termini of the Saharan trade without greatly affecting the rural areas and without making much effort at education or religious training. The first communities at Awdāghust, in Ghana, and perhaps at Tādmekka, Gao and no doubt some other towns on the Senegal or the Inland Niger Delta belong to this period; the famous anecdote about the conversion of the King of Mallal should perhaps also be assigned to this time.

The Almoravids took their role as reformers and teachers of Sunnism very seriously. They did not start from scratch,[86] but they gave the Muslim community of West Africa a geographical dimension, probably for the first time: after them it had more distinct boundaries than before. The upheaval south of the Sahara brought about by the Almoravid conquest was certainly considerable; and moreover it was combined with the general counter-offensive of Sunnism that marked the fifth/eleventh century, after the Shī'ite triumphs of the preceding century. It is against this background that it should be possible to assess relations with Ghana.

Ghana officially went over to Islam at the end of the fifth/eleventh century, having been conquered or converted to Māliki Sunnism; it may also have helped to bring about Tādmekka's transition to Sunnism.[87] Archaeological evidence is still vague. Admittedly traces of probable destruction have been found deep down, nearly 5 m below the present surface; admittedly the dimensions of the mosque changed after the end of the fifth/eleventh century; and admittedly the great market town on the spot called Kumbi Saleh developed most conspicuously in the seventh/thirteenth and eighth/fourteenth centuries.[88] These clues go some way to suggest destruction by the Almoravids, who had no more reason to spare their Zanāta enemies here than at Awdāghust.[89] But conclusive proof is still lacking: and in any case, as with Awdāghust, any raid that there may have been would not have led to the disappearance of the market town; quite the con-

84. See Chapter 3 above.

85. Refers to the case of Awdāghust, now under investigation. See also Chapter 12 above.

86. See Chapter 3 above.

87. J. M. Cuoq, 1975, p. 120 (al-Zuhrī's text): 'In the vicinity of Ghana, fifteen days' journey away, there are two towns: the first is Silla, the second Tādmekka. These two towns are nine days apart. The people of these two towns became Muslim after those of Ghana, seven years later, after wars between them and many rebellions. The people of Ghana sought help from the Murābitūn in order to defeat them'. T. Lewicki, 1979, p. 166 quotes this text, and introduces another transliteration of the first place name, namely N-s-la. See also D. C. Conrad and H. J. Fisher, 1982, 1983.

88. S. Berthier, 1983.

89. J. Devisse, 1970.

trary. Archaeology still has some basic questions to answer: for the moment they do not seem to interest many people.

The question is, if there was a clash, what happened to the royal capital?[90] Did it withdraw further south, or did it also adopt Islam? What were the subsequent relations with the neighbouring Soso to the south, whose eighth/fourteenth-century and ninth/fifteenth-century texts tell us that they defeated an enfeebled Ghana?[91] Thus at present the whole fate of the 'Ghanaian system' linked with the Inland Delta[92] mainly escapes us and this is a great pity.

R. M. A. Bedaux has no hesitation in regarding the warlike movements that possibly then affected the Sahel as the cause of the occupation or re-occupation of important sites in the Inland Niger Delta,[93] and also of the settlement of the Tellem in the old Tolloy sites on the Bandiagara cliff.[94] Some authors even think that the upheaval gradually reached the Chad area.[95]

The princes of Gao were Muslims as far back as the fourth/tenth century.[96] Traces of relations with Almoravid Spain, likewise difficult to interpret, appear at the end of the fifth/eleventh century. Royal funerary steles[97] have been found in the Gao-Sane necropolis to the north of Gao. The two earliest of these steles may have been carved from Spanish marble;[98] they relate to monarchs who were undoubtedly Muslim and probably Sunnite. At present little more is known about them.[99]

We do not even know the precise outcome of Abū Bakr's efforts to con-

90. See the arguments against the presupposed conquest of Ghana by the Almoravids in D. C. Conrad and H. J. Fisher, 1982.

91. J. M. Cuoq, 1975, p. 343 (Ibn Khaldūn, p. 388) (al-Maḳrīzī): the translations need to be carefully revised. The texts, being difficult, are open to readings very different from those of the author.

92. See Chapter 14 below.

93. R. M. A. Bedaux, T. S. Constandse-Westermann, L. Hacquebord, A. G. Lange and J. D. Van der Waals, 1978.

94. R. M. A. Bedaux and R. Bolland, 1980.

95. H. T. Norris, 1972. This interpretation is not accepted by all research workers. On this point also much work remains to be done.

96. Al-Muhallabī (d. 990) in J. M. Cuoq, 1975, p. 77: 'The king of the country proclaimed himself Muslim in the presence of his subjects, and many of them proclaimed themselves Muslim likewise'. On the role Tāhert may have played in this field, see T. Lewicki, 1962.

97. J. M. Cuoq, 1975, p. 111 *et seq.*

98. J. Sauvaget, 1949. See also M. M. Viré, 1958, pp. 368–76.

99. Mr Paulo de Moraes Farias, of Birmingham University, who has already made signal contributions to the history of the Almoravids, is working with Malian, Mauritanian and French research workers on a comprehensive study of the inscribed steles of the Sahel area. We should thanks to him know much more about them in a few years' time. See also J. O. Hunwick, 1980.

vert the Sahel. The date and place of his death vary considerably according to the sources.[100] The oral sources in Mauritania are also vague.[101]

Obviously the last word has yet to be said, and the history of the Almoravids[102] still has big surprises in store, even as regards religion: for the first time a coherent Sunnite realm presented a comprehensive front and a border for *Dār al-islām* as against a black world with different religious systems. In the face of these societies that Islam regarded as 'pagan', tolerance and indifference were no longer appropriate. This novelty was pregnant with important developments for the succeeding centuries.

The organization of a space stretching from the Ebro to the Senegal: the failure of the Almoravids

The economies of the northern part of the Almoravid bloc were already highly organized before the Ṣanhādja conquest. From now on they benefited from the flow of gold from West Africa. For too long people have written that the Almoravid conquests devastated the western seaboard of Africa. The progress of research in recent years has shown that on the contrary the Sahel areas were at that time very highly integrated with the northern economies. The setting up or strengthening of new staging-posts on the connecting routes between Senegal and Morocco shows that the tracks carried considerable traffic.[103] Some historians sometimes take the view that the Almoravid bloc was amicably shared, in the full meaning of the word, between Abū Bakr and Yūsuf ibn Tāshfīn. This view is disproved, first, by the fact that coinage continued to be struck in Abū Bakr's name at the Sidjilmāsa mint until his death, and secondly by the discovery in Mauritania of dinars struck in Andalusia in the sixth/twelfth century;[104] the flow in this vast empire was from north to south. Moreover it could not have been otherwise, given the great need for southern gold in the north.[105] The long Atlantic seaboard linking countries with complementary

100. The first (undated) reference to Abū Bakr's death is in a late seventh/thirteenth century text (J. M. Cuoq, 1975, p. 176). In the seventh/thirteenth century Ibn al-Athīr (Cuoq, p. 194) placed it in 462/1069–70. In the eighth/fourteenth century authors hesitated between 469/1076–7 and 480/1087–8. Similar uncertainty exists about the date of death of ʿAbd Allāh ibn Yāsīn, viz. between 450/1058 and 452/1060.

101. A. Ould el-Bah, 1982.

102. Two important theses are awaited from French historians, V. Lagardère and A. Nègre, who have already published interesting preliminary studies.

103. See Chapter 14 below. Azuḳī, in what is now Mauritania, Tabalbala, in eastern Morocco, and Zagōra and Tāmdūlt, in southern Morocco, are among the relatively important towns probably built by the Almoravids. On Azuḳī see B. Saison, 1981; on Tabalbala see F. D. Champault, 1969; on Zagōra see J. Meunié and C. Allain, 1956. On Tāmdūlt see B. Rosenberger, 1970b.

104. G. S. Colin, A. O. Babacar, N. Ghali, and J. Devisse, 1983.

105. See Chapter 14 below: in particular, Fig. 14.6 of the Almoravid mints.

PLATE 13.3(a) *Almoravid coins and stamping tools found in Algeria*

PLATE 13.3(b) *Almoravid gold coins*

economies must, therefore, be regarded from an economic point of view as a whole. Hence the demand for products 'from the south' in all probability increased until the middle of the sixth/twelfth century. The maintenance of this economic unity did not of course prevent the existence of two administrations, one in Marrakesh and the other in the Sahel; two armies, one in the south, faithful to camels, and the other entirely on horseback from the end of the fifth/eleventh century.[106] and perhaps two different political climates.[107] But economic unity is firmly attested by the sources. Southern Morocco benefited greatly from this boom. Al-Idrīsī eloquently describes this increase in wealth in the case of Aghmāt-Warīka, quite close to the Tīnmāl area, birthplace of the Almohad movement. 'The people of Aghmāt,' he says:

> are Hawwāra, Arabs who have become Berbers by close contact. They are rich merchants, and live well. They go into the countries of the blacks with caravans of camels carrying quintals and quintals of goods: copper, brass, blankets, woollen garments, turbans, cloaks, glass beads, mother of pearl, precious stones, spices of all kinds, perfumes and wrought ironwork ... Under the rule of the Mulaththamūn [Almoravids] no one was richer or more well-to-do than the people of Aghmāt. They put markers at the doors of their houses to show the extent of their wealth.

Aghmāt was not alone in benefiting from the economic boom. The whole of the mountainous part of Morocco supplied increased quantities of copper, iron and silver for export: and in the sixth/twelfth century there were real battles for control of the mines between the supporters of the Almohads and those of the Almoravids.[108] Excavations in the Chichāwa area[109] west of Marrakesh have revealed the lavishness of living conditions in the Almoravid period: the stucco work[110] and painted decorations[111] are worthy of comparison with others found in the north and south.

Naturally economic prosperity, which obviously only reached certain urban circles and people close to those in high places, made for the development of sometimes ostentatious luxury, which the Almohads were to condemn forcefully. Many sumptuously decorated mosques date from this

106. Details taken from V. Lagardère, 1983.

107. See above, p. 350.

108. There is an excellent and very accurate translation of al-Idrīsī's text in M. Hadj Sadok, 1983, pp. 73–4.

109. B. Rosenberger, 1970; P. Berthier, 1962, pp. 75–7.

110. P. Berthier, 1962, for comparison with others in Spain from the same period. See C. Ewert, 1971 (reviewed by B. Rosenberger in *HT*, **12**, 1972, pp. 219–21).

111. The geometrical decorations in red on a white background at Chichāwa are obviously related to the ones of the same period found at Marrakesh. We may well wonder whether they are not also related to the decorations at Walāta, in Mauritania.

time (see Fig. 13.1) but so do fine secular monuments, some of which, such as the fountain at Marrakesh, have survived to this day. No town has yielded more important remains than Marrakesh, the Almoravids' most original piece of town planning. Al-Idrīsī gives us an interesting picture of the town at the time when it was built. '[It] is on level ground, and adjoining it there is but one small hill called Idjalliz, from which the stone was taken for the building of the palace of the "Emir of the Muslims", 'Alī ibn Yūsuf ibn Tāshfīn, known as Dār al-Ḥadjar [the stone house]. There is no stone at all there apart from this hill: so the town has been built of clay, baked brick and rammed earth'.[112] Archaeology has made it possible to find this palace, a 'marvel of architecture' in this area for the period in question;[113] and it has also made it possible to reconstruct part of the plan of the Almoravid mosque and completely extricate a superbly decorated fountain given to the inhabitants for their ablutions.[114] The northernmost tip of the Almoravids' lavish decoration was in Spain, on the Ebro, in the Aljaferia at Saragossa: nothing now remains of it but parts of arches.

According to G. Wiet and E. Lévi-Provençal,[115] Marrakesh also became a brilliant literary centre. Here court poets from Spain continued careers begun under the *reyes de taifas*[116] but ruined by the Almoravid conquest of al-Andalus and the initial severity that accompanied it. This initial severity, which aroused, for example, al-Bakrī's profound reservations about the Almoravids, died down in time both in actions and in behaviour. The Islamic culture of the day had been, for the first time on such a scale, transplanted to Morocco. With it came luxury and a taste for a sumptuous life style: the Almoravids were to be reproached for this by their enemies. But the legal severity of the *fuḳahā'*, the allies of the ruling house, which often contrasted with the permissiveness of the glittering life in Marrakesh, had not disappeared. It imposed a sometimes paranoid Māliki Sunnism, a fact of great importance for the history of Western Islam, including Islam in Africa but one which by its excesses also aroused many hostile reactions.[117]

V. Lagardère's work has brought out quite recently the depth of animosity aroused in Spain and Morocco, and perhaps even further afield, by the hostile policy imposed on the ruling house by the Mālikite *fuḳahā'*. The latter attacked in particular the works of al-Ghazālī, which had then been

112. M. Hadj-Sadok, 1983, p. 75.

113. J. Meunié and H. Terrasse, 1952, pp. 11–19 and 20–1: painted decorations like those at Chichāwa.

114. H. Terrasse, J. Meunié and G. Deverdun, 1957.

115. G. Wiet, 1966, pp. 230–1; E. Lévi-Provençal, 1948, particularly pp. 239–318.

116. After the famous book by H. Pérès (1953) the reader may consult S. Khalis, 1966.

117. V. Lagardère (1981) has convincingly shown that the Almoravids, though briefly tempted by exposure to Shāfi'ism and Sufism, reverted under 'Alī b. Yūsuf b. Tāshfīn to uncompromising Mālikite severity.

introduced into the West and whose mystical tone perplexed the *fuḳahā'* who supported the Almoravids. A letter dated November 1143 from the Almoravid monarch Abū Marwān ʿAbd al-Malik b. ʿAbd al-Azīz to a future *ḳāḍī* of Valencia clearly shows the feelings and anxieties of the ruling power at that time: 'When you come across a heretical book or the fomenter of some heresy, be wary of them, and especially of the works of Abū Ḥāmid al-Ghazālī. Track them down, so that their memory may be totally destroyed, by an unceasing auto-da-fé [sic]; carry out searches and require oaths of those you suspect of hiding some'. The atmosphere in the last decades of Almoravid power was poisoned by the repressive measures of the Mālikite jurists, who had the support of the princes; this repression lent colour to the reproaches addressed to the ruling dynasty, in particular by the infant Almohad movement. According to V. Lagardère, even the legitimacy of the ruling house seemed to be called into question by the interpretation of a very popular text by Al-Ghazālī:

> The period before Islam was nothing but error and blindness. Then, thanks to the Prophethood, it was the turn of Truth and the right path. The Prophethood was followed by the Caliphate, and the Caliphate by the monarchy; the latter then turned to tyranny, pride and vanity. Now since we find that there is a divine tendency to bring things back to their point of departure, it follows that truth and the Prophethood will inevitably be brought back to life by holiness . . .

This was saying fairly clearly that the ruling power, tyrannical, proud and vain as it was, had, despite the formal support of the Mālikite jurists, neither dynastic justification nor underlying religious worth.[118] The 'legitimist'–vis-à-vis the Abbasids–opposition, which was unitaristic and close to Ibn Tūmart's Ghazalian aspirations, stands out much more clearly in this context.[119]

In a succession of articles, V. Lagardère is studying the weakness of the Almoravid administration.[120] This was almost non-existent at local level: power was exercised through relatives and clients. In more than one case the misdeeds condemned in the rulers of al-Andalus in the early years of rectitude soon reappeared, particularly in the realm of taxation. The rigidity flaunted in the legal field and in inquisitorial procedures[121] cannot conceal a certain doctrinal ambivalence, and revolts were not infrequent.

118. The texts quoted are taken from V. Lagardère, 1983.

119. V. Lagardère, 1981, p. 53, emphasizes that Ibn Tūmart was a disciple of Abū Mūsā ʿIsā b. Sulayman ar-Rafrāghī, who came from the province of Tādilā and had been nurtured on contemplative oriental teachings; even if the Almohads did not invoke his texts, the similarity is interesting.

120. V. Lagardère, 1978, 1979, 1983. Further studies are on the way.

121. The sentence passed on the works of al-Ghazālī, which were destroyed by fire on the orders of the Almoravids, casts a disagreeable shadow over their ruler (V. Lagardère, 1983).

The one that was to sweep away the dynasty developed in the Atlas, and the Almoravid government could do nothing but contain it as long as possible. The weapon Yūsuf ibn Tāshfīn had used against the *reyes de taifas* at the end of the fifth/eleventh century was to be turned against the Almoravids, who were accused in their turn of oppression, injustice, corruption, debauchery and lack of rigour in religion. The undeniable wealth of the Almoravid state apparatus was to fail to withstand the onslaught of the Almohads, fiery as it was and well organized in their mountain bases.

History has for far too long been very hard on the Almoravids, who have been charged with every possible mistake and suspected of intervening like 'barbarians' in a Spain in which compromises between Muslims and Christians were arrived at on the basis of capitulations. They upset too many established interests for their irruption to be easily forgiven; and they introduced too many new faces, including some blacks, to escape arousing mistrust and hostility. It will be very interesting in the years to come to observe the process (already begun) of rehabilitation of this dynasty and the quest for a better, more balanced appraisal of its historical role. It is already fascinating to try to gauge what impression the Almoravids have left on collective memories. The experiment already carried out in this field by a young Mauritanian research worker shows how valuable such investigations would be if they were performed systematically.[122]

122. See A. Ould el-Bah, 1982.

14 Trade and trade routes in West Africa

J. DEVISSE

Over the past twenty years research has considerably changed the information base available for the study of this subject. There have been many archaeological discoveries, especially south of the Sahara, and numismatics has taken a great leap forward as a result of laboratory research on the Islamic coinages, particularly for our period. Progress has also come from a critical re-reading of the written sources and the application of the methods of economic history to these remote periods. Nearly all recent work has cast great doubt on findings that were taken for granted two decades ago; and has also radically changed the spirit of research itself and opened up new and far-reaching avenues of enquiry.

From the outset two precautions must be taken. The first is one of method: the mere reporting of archaeological discoveries is not sufficient to link up the various sets of indications that are revealed. Micro-analysis and small-scale certainty must henceforth give way to the requirements of economic history, with its statistical or at any rate serial methods, its anxiety for an overall view and its keenness to work on a broad canvas.

The second preliminary precaution, failing which much of the reasoning to follow would remain obscure, is an elementary one of vocabulary. It is generally accepted that a local trade economy based on the barter of consumer goods or locally made products existed very early on, and certainly for our period, both in Africa and elsewhere. It does not directly affect the subject of this chapter. A long-distance trade economy involving merchants rested on the existence of a demand for certain rare and costly products (such as salt, kola, gold, wheat, fabrics and copper) which had to come from 'elsewhere'. These and many other commodities formed the basis of a trade that only became trans-Saharan when demand in the north irreplaceably complemented that in the south. This should never be forgotten. New needs for new products could be created among distant trading partners on the basis of existing routes; dangerous very long-distance trade could only be established if it reflected imperious needs.

Above all, however, our study of the development of the trans-Saharan gold trade will be meaningless unless we remember two key ideas, the demand for and the supply of coinage.[1] Demand for trading tokens arises when there is a desire for a medium that temporarily preserves the freedom of choice of the party who has just sold a product by means of a token which is not necessarily the product supplied by the buyer. Archaeology and written sources have demonstrated sufficiently clearly the existence of such tokens (for example little copper crosses, iron objects and fabrics) throughout Africa in the period under consideration for there to be no need to re-open the discussion. Africa was familiar with the need for tokens as currency. It also knew the value of gold, and how to build up gold reserves as tangible nest-eggs for hard times.

Thus trans-Saharan trade was not a timeless phenomenon. In the form of an annual crossing by camel caravans in search of gold in the south, it arose and developed in ways that we need to recognize and study. It also underwent major changes, which we need to follow as best we may.

The Sahara, a gulf that has widened since the Neolithic period

Possible ways of crossing the desert

From the point of view of trans-Saharan links the period between the seventh and eleventh centuries of the Christian era was of crucial importance. This was when the lines of regular links, along routes which changed over the years, grew up between the Mediterranean economies, with, in particular, their demand for gold, and those of the southern Saharan Sahel and the savannas which in turn linked it to the forest region, which used salt but produced little of it. But the origins of these crossings has for long been a moot point.

The cultural unity of the Sahara of the hunters and its southern fringes has quite recently been authoritatively established for very early periods[2] but this applies to the Nile area, the central Sahara from the Hoggar to Tibesti, and the Saharan Atlas. It leaves entirely out of the discussion what are now south-western Algeria and Mauritania and Mali.[3] For the latter areas Hugot has clearly shown that before the third millennium before the Christian era, when the intensified spread of the desert wrecked earlier efforts, there was no active Neolithic life in the Sahara. The large quantity

1. On the idea of the need for and supply of coinage see C. Cipolla, 1961; G. P. Hennequin, 1972, 1974. 'Demand' may be appraised by means of various descriptive sources, coin finds, and gold and silver remains unearthed by archaeologists. 'Supply' is directly related to the various kinds of evidence of coinage struck. It is studied nowadays by a revival of traditional numismatics and by an entirely new approach to numismatics based on statistical series. The results of investigation have for some years now been radically affected by laboratory work.

2. J. Leclant and P. Huard, 1980, especially the conclusions, pp. 517–28.

3. ibid., map p. 80.

of potsherds found are evidence of this.[4] The Sahara became difficult to cross as the isohyets moved further and further apart to north and south.

Looking at the present-day isohyet map (Fig. 14.1), we see the wide area of totally inadequate or very poor grazing which over nearly a thousand kilometres separates the areas of better grasslands to north and south. This situation is probably not fundamentally very different, by and large, from that of 1500 or 1600 years ago,[5] although countless local deteriorations have aggravated the situation in places[6] and very recent crises have again revived the question of further desertification in the southern Sahel region of the Sahara.

Except at a few rare points where the northern and southern 50 mm isohyets are close together, crossing the Sahara necessitates either finding reliable wells and oases or else travelling with mounts that are economical water users[7] and carrying much of the water needed for human survival.[8] This crossing is dangerous, and is certainly not attempted without good reason.

This observation, on which all researchers are nowadays in agreement, makes the old discussions about major Saharan crossings in more remote periods[9] somewhat academic. Even if it is one day established that they took place, the inexorable drawing apart of the two edges of the desert[10] would have made it difficult or impossible for travellers to cross in one continuous journey by the end of what is usually called Antiquity.[11] An important role in cross-desert links was to be played by peoples, probably Berber-speakers, who settled in the Sahara in circumstances and at dates

4. H. J. Hugot, 1979, especially, pp. 213 *et seq.*; J. -P. Roset, 1983; *Revue de géographie et de géomorphologie dynamique*, special issue, 1976; R. Kuper (ed.), 1978; *Colloque de Nouakchott*, 1976; C. Toupet, 1977; H. J. Hugot, 1979, pp. 673 *et seq.*

5. The literature on the climatic evolution of the Sahara has today reached a high degree of consensus. See for example on the human consequences: R. Kuper (ed.), 1978; H. J. Hugot, 1979; J. Leclant and P. Huard, 1980; and on changes in living conditions the gripping pages in T. Monod, 1958, about the Madjābat al-Kubrā. See also: S. E. Nicholson, 1979, pp. 31–50; the abstract of S. E. Nicholson, 1976, an important thesis. Generally speaking, the progress of research on the history of environmental evolution in West Africa may be followed in the *Bulletin de l'ASEQUA* (Dakar).

6. J. Devisse, D. Robert-Chaleix *et al.*, 1983, contains a detailed study on the historical evolution of the water table at Awdāghust and the probable causes of this collapse.

7. On the camel and its place in history see R. Mauny, 1961, pp. 287 *et seq.*; C. de Lespinay, 1981.

8. T. Monod, 1973a, p. 31, shows that the Sahara is the most inhospitable of all deserts, 60 per cent of its area being arid and 15 per cent of that completely devoid of vegetation.

9. For instance O. du Puygaudeau, 1966, pp. 37 *eq seq.*

10. On the consequences of this drawing-apart in the south see the very stimulating studies by S. Daveau and C. Toupet, 1963; C. Toupet, 1977. These have illustrations for the period under consideration.

11. The most recent work comes down against regular trans-Saharan trade relations after the end of the Neolithic period; see Unesco, *General History of Africa*, Vol. II, ch. 20; J. Desanges, 1976, pp. 213, 374; G. Camps, 1980, p. 65 *et seq.*

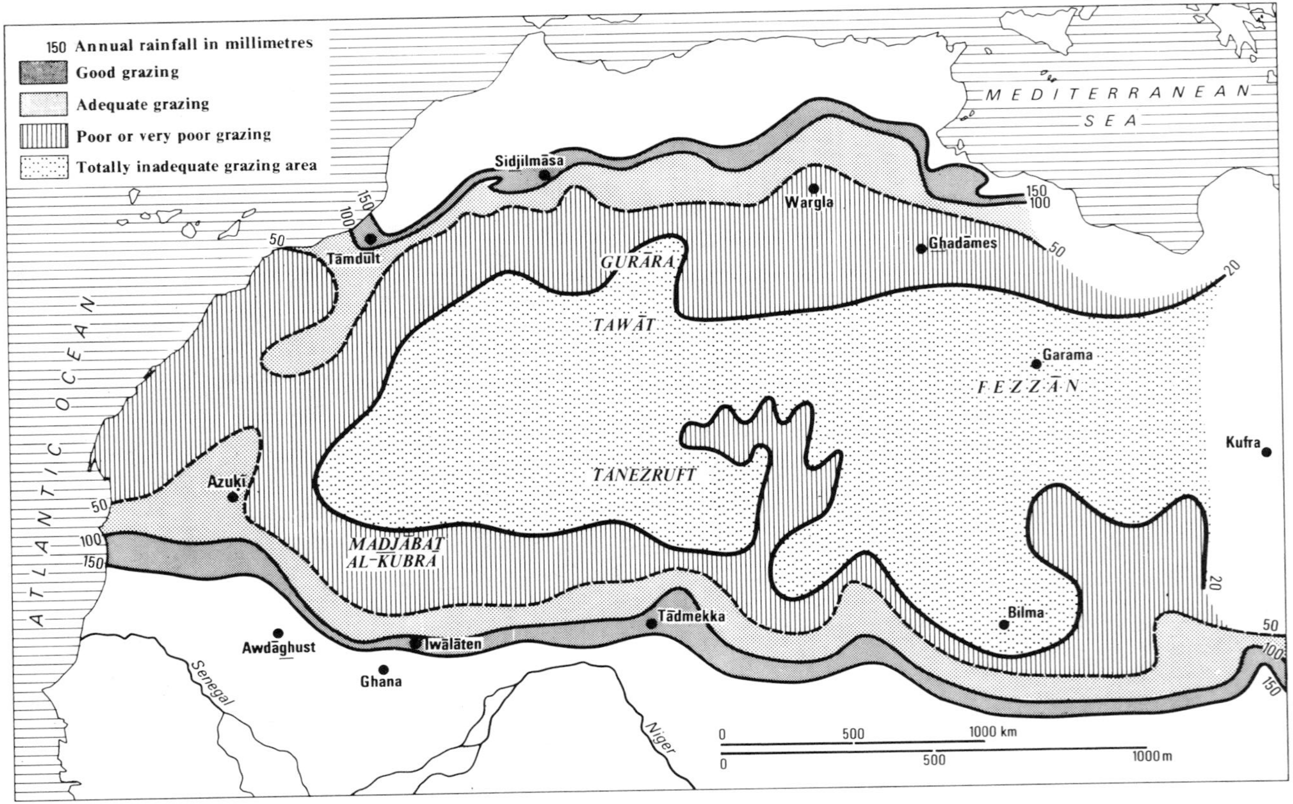

FIG. 14.1 *The desert area to be crossed: map showing present-day isohyets (after Hugot, 1979; Godinho, 1956)*

about which we know little, but between the fourth and seventh centuries of the Christian era.[12] Little is known about the economic role of these Saharan groups before the eighth century. This is no reason to deny that partial links existed, through them, between North Africa and points quite deep in the desert,[13] or even with the south of the desert and the Sahel area.

The 'Berber' confederations of the fifth and sixth centuries[14] were the first to be in a position to attempt the crossing, thanks to the rapid spread of the camel for some centuries.[15] The point is that this was the only animal that could have made possible the long expeditions of between one and two thousand kilometres between the two edges of the Sahara. Neither chariots (no longer widely believed to have been used for commercial purposes),[16] horses (then recently introduced into the Sahara),[17] donkeys (old and frugal habitués of these parts) nor the slow-moving draught oxen attested by rock art[18] met the needs of difficult, heavy, long-distance trade. The characteristic feature of caravans, at least from the tenth century onwards, was to be the number of beasts of burden carrying impressive loads to be exchanged for the main product sought to the south of the Sahara, gold.

An important consideration was the choice of a route that limited risks. The pains taken by Arab authors of the tenth, eleventh and twelfth centuries to describe the minutiae of trans-Saharan trade routes shows clearly that any improvization was likely to be disastrous. There were special transit areas, suggested by the physical conditions and later to be consecrated by custom. There is sometimes mention of a coastal route (al-Bakrī refers to it in the eleventh century without regarding it as of real importance[19]); recent research has brought out its difficulties and hence its dangers: between latitudes 26°N and 24°N, the completely inhospitable coast is devoid of any trace of human existence, even for the Neolithic period.[20]

Further east, in what is now Mauritania, travel was favoured by the fact

12. See H. T. Norris, 1972; T. Lewicki, 1978; G. Camps, 1980; and Chapter 11 above.

13. See Unesco, *General History of Africa*, Vol. II, pp. 514–15.

14. Unesco, *General History of Africa*, vol. II, p. 508 and G. Camps, 1980. The possible presence of Berber-speaking Jews in these areas has also been discussed.

15. Recent accounts (C. de Lespinay, 1981; H. J. Hugot, 1979, p. 145) point out that no trace of dromedary bones has been found in properly dated Neolithic sites in the Sahara, and that their representation in painting and carving came later.

16. G. Camps, 1980, p. 65; H. J. Hugot, 1979, pp. 566 *et seq.*

17. H. J. Hugot, 1979, pp. 111 *et seq.*

18. H. J. Hugot, 1979, p. 675, pp. 574–5; Hugot believes in the historical importance of ox-carts; but they seem to be unsuitable for real trans-Saharan trade, although (as H. J. Hugot, 1979, shows clearly on p. 573) they may have played a role in the transport over short distances of materials such as timber, clay and reeds, particularly in the southern savannas of the Sahel.

19. J. M. Cuoq, 1975, p. 95.

20. N. Petitmaire, 1978, p. 327; complemented by J.-C. Rosso and N. Petitmaire, 1978.

that the northern and southern 50 mm isohyets come closer together: this was to be the site of Azukī. Still further east were the Saura valley, Gurāra and Tawāt in the north, and these soon attracted the attention of caravan travellers.[21] The exceptional importance of this route was to make it one of the transit points most frequented by caravans from the tenth century onwards. Still further east, it was necessary to go to Wargla, in the Mzāb, and to slip southwards to Adrār des Ifoghas and the valley of Tilemsi[22] to find a route as easy as the foregoing. But Wargla does not appear in history until the eighth century:[23] perhaps it was then a staging-post on the route from Tāhert to Gao.[24] Near it grew up Isedraten (Sadrāta), the town of refuge for the Ibāḍites driven out of Tāhert by the Fāṭimid victory at the beginning of the tenth century. Isedraten did not survive for long in a hostile environment.[25] But the Mzāb, where towns developed in the eleventh century,[26] and Wargla, which was prosperous from the tenth, were a focus for the development of trans-Saharan relations comparable to Tawāt.

In the last quarter of the eighth century people at Tāhert reckoned that 'the routes leading to the Sudan are open to business and trade'.[27] The first move towards links with the *Bilād al-Sūdān* can thus be dated from the second half of the eighth century; but these links were not firmly established or attested until the tenth century. While the Berber-speakers were the first to experiment with trans-Saharan routes, to open them to regular trade needed economic incentives and human determination of which Tāhert had only glimpsed the first stirrings. 'Natural conditions' were not enough to create routes; for that economic needs were required.

Further east the existence of early links becomes more apparent as we get nearer to the Nile. But the work so far published does not allow the drawing of a very definite route. The role of the Garamantes remains a subject of controversy.[28] It is now thought that trade took place between the Fezzān and the Lake Chad area, and also that Kawār supplied salt to the south.[29] But we cannot yet sketch out a pattern for any trade there may have been with the peoples living south of Lake Chad.[30] A route from

21. See J. L. Echallier, 1970, who dates the earliest settlements in Tawāt and Gurāra to the tenth century.

22. J.-P. Blanck, 1968, shows that the valley of the Tilemsi was probably still dry 5500 years before the Christian era, and certainly was 10 000 years ago.

23. T. Lewicki, 1976.

24. ibid., p. 12.

25. The town was abandoned during the eleventh century.

26. H. Didillon, J.-M. Didillon, C. Donnadieu and P. Donnadieu, 1977, p. 32; A. Ravereau, 1981.

27. T. Lewicki, 1962.

28. See R. C. C. Law, 1967b; J. Desanges, 1962, 1976; G. Camps, 1980.

29. D. Lange, 1978, pp. 497–9.

30. J.-P. Lebeuf, A. M. D. Lebeuf, F. Treinen-Claustre and J. Courtin, 1980; J.-P. Lebeuf, 1981. In the latter summary work the author envisages the southward movement from north of Lake Chad in the ninth century of hunters using spears.

Chad to Tripolitania may perhaps have served for the export of slaves from a date impossible to specify; this is the inference from reading al-Yaʿḳūbī, who described the situation in the middle of the ninth century.[31]

As we get nearer the Nile the networks are much longer-standing on the river and on a route parallel to it on the west along the chain of oases. There were also east–west links between these oases and the river[32] and caravan links with the Red Sea from at least the Hellenistic era.[33] Nothing changed from the early days of Pharaonic Egypt until the period under consideration, with the probable exception of one parameter: relations with Nubia. These had been frozen by a pact (*baḳt*) between the Muslim masters of Egypt and the Makurra dynasty: concluded for the benefit of both parties.[34] This provided for the annual delivery of several hundred black slaves to the north, and was implemented fairly correctly until the time of the Mamluks. The Nubian buffer probably blocked direct access by the Muslims of Egypt via Dārfūr to the Chad Basin. This remained the case until the fourteenth century, a fact of great economic significance. This never stopped the Muslim masters of Egypt getting at the gold reserves of Wādī al-ʿAllāḳī and Nubia but it complicated their links with the *Bilād al-Sūdān*. The only way open lay along an old route, the first section of which was well known to Antiquity, from the Nile to the oasis of Sīwa. In the fifth and sixth centuries shrewd monks set up on this route a trade in relics of St Menas, whose monastery is on the outskirts of Alexandria.[35] Various studies suggest that, further on, the route went through the oasis of Kufra.[36] It then probably crossed Kawār from east to west, passing through al-Ḳaṣāba (Gezabi),[37] and reached Marandet (Maranda) and Gao.

Al-Yaʿḳūbī speaks of this route, vaguely but in the present tense, in the ninth century.[38] A century later Ibn Ḥawḳal regarded it as abandoned because it was too dangerous.[39] Ibn Ḥawḳal's descriptions mark a significant departure. If we draw an overall plan (Fig. 14.2) of the routes he described, we find that he considered the 'Egyptian' route to be in decline, but also that he 'disregarded' links between the areas where the Ibāḍites

31. J. M. Cuoq, 1975, p. 49. See D. Lange and S. Berthoud, 1977, pp. 34–5, whose hypotheses seem entirely reasonable.

32. On the system of routes see Unesco, *General History of Africa*, Vol. II, ch. 20.

33. On the development of these links with the Red Sea in the Fāṭimid period see J.-C. Garcin, 1976, pp. 71 *et seq.*

34. On the *baḳt* see L. Török, 1978. For the Fāṭimid period, see I. B. Beshir, 1975. See also Chapter 8 above.

35. J. Devisse, 1979a, pp. 38 *et seq.*

36. T. Lewicki, 1965c.

37. D. Lange and S. Berthoud, 1977, p. 33. On this route see Chapter 11 above.

38. J. M. Cuoq, 1975, p. 49.

39. Ibn Ḥawḳal, 1964, pp. 58, 153.

lived and the Sudan[40] and devoted his attention only to the 'Fāṭimid' route from Sidjilmāsa to Ghana. Moreover, he says explicitly that this was the busiest route 'in his day'.[41] Once this route passes to the south of Ghana, the information on it given by Ibn Ḥawḳal is glaringly inaccurate, with fanciful localizations and completely vague distances. Moreover, on the map he appended to his own text Ibn Ḥawḳal was careful not to mark the names he quoted (Sāma, Kūgha, Ghiyārū and Kuzam), which were repeated by his successors: he contented himself with saying that this area comprised 'districts in the domain of the Blacks'.[42]

This should be a warning to us: everything to do with the description of the routes is political and stems from choices made by the writer. This is particularly flagrant in the case of the old Egyptian route, of which an Iranian source, the *Ḥudūd al-'Alām*, said in 982–3 that it took eighty days to traverse, with only one place where there was water and fodder and that the Egyptian merchants used it to take 'salt, glass and lead' to the *Bilād al-Sūdān*.[43]

Ibn Ḥawḳal's neglect of the Egyptian route was probably not the result merely of ideological and political factors, but probably reflected radical economic changes between the ninth and the tenth centuries. Neither al-Bakrī nor al-Idrīsī, the two great chroniclers of trans-Saharan routes, were to mention the Egypt route again: something had certainly happened between the ninth and tenth centuries that led to its abandonment.

In fact the key events were to take place in the ninth, tenth and eleventh centuries between Tripolitania, Chad and the Atlantic; the other area, around the Nile, had quite a different destiny reserved for it.

Life in the Sahel zone as revealed by recent archaeological research[44]

Recent research on iron and copper[45] in West Africa is alone enough to cast doubt on most of the received ideas about pre-Christian periods. In the period before the great commercial crossings of the Sahara these two essential commodities were marketable at long range south of the desert without intervention from the north.[46] If we look at the map of the

40. ibid., p. 68: he calls the Ibāḍites and Nukkārites 'impious hypocrites' and 'schismatics'.

41. ibid., p. 58.

42. ibid., p. 61.

43. J. M. Cuoq, 1975, p. 69.

44. See J. Devisse, 1982, who gives the recent bibliography and a map of the sites, and S. K. McIntosh and R. J. McIntosh, 1981.

45. In addition to S. Bernus and P. Gouletquer, 1974, 1976; see D. Calvocoressi and N. David, 1979, and D. Grebenart, 1983.

46. See in particular R. J. McIntosh and S. K. McIntosh, 1981; S. K. McIntosh and R. J. McIntosh, 1980b. I adopt most of their conclusions.

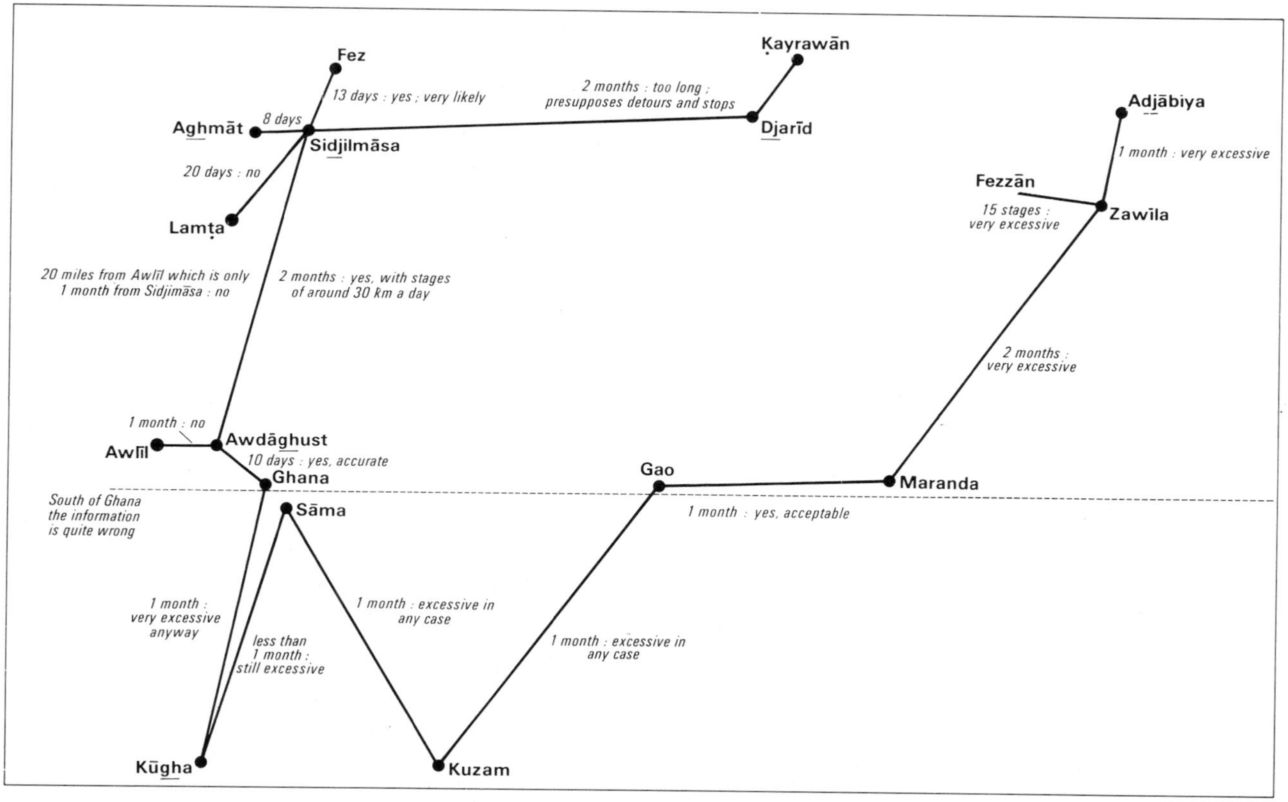
Fez
13 days : yes ; very likely
Kayrawān
2 months : too long ;
presupposes detours and stops
Adjābiya
Aghmāt
8 days
Sidjilmāsa
Djarīd
1 month : very excessive
20 days : no
Fezzān
Lamṭa
15 stages :
very excessive
Zawīla
20 miles from Awlīl which is only
1 month from Sidjimāsa : no
2 months : yes, with stages
of around 30 km a day
2 months :
very excessive
1 month : no
Awlīl
Awdāghust
10 days : yes, accurate
Ghana
Gao
Maranda
South of Ghana
the information
is quite wrong
Sāma
1 month : yes, acceptable
1 month :
very excessive
anyway
1 month : excessive in
any case
less than
1 month :
still excessive
1 month : excessive in
any case
Kūgha
Kuzam

FIG. 14.2 *Trade routes described by Ibn Hawkal*

sites[47] recently reported on by archaeologists, which are dated, we learn some surprising things about the importance of the Middle Niger Valley and the Senegal area in these recent discoveries.

Before the fifth century, sites in the Bandiagara-Tolloy area (fifth to second century before the Christian era), the Jenne-Jeno area (Phase I from −200 to +50 and Phase II from +50 to +400) and the Begho area have produced evidence of the intensity of activity in these three areas.

For the fifth, sixth and seventh centuries of the Christian era, without taking note of influences from across the Sahara, excavations have shown that there was activity both in the Senegal Valley[48] and in the southern half of that country. It was also present, remarkably, from Niani to Tondidaru, along the valleys of the Niger as far as the outskirts of present-day Niamey. Marandet, Ife and sites in Ivory Coast also show great activity. Community life, with metal-working, division of labour, and trade, was organized in the Sahel before any signs of the appearance of a powerful Saharan trade. We can now say, without fear of being proved wrong by future research, that all the infrastructure of settlement and economic life in the valleys of the Senegal and Niger, and no doubt further south, was in existence during these 'obscure centuries'.[49]

Going on to the eighth and ninth centuries, we see that apart from development (which incidentally still continued in the tenth and eleventh centuries) the only novelty was the emergence of the market towns of the north (Tegdaoust and Kumbi Saleh). The tenth and eleventh centuries were characterized by the same tendencies, with the rise of Azuḳī and then Walāta and the further growth of activity in the Senegal and Niger areas.

Detailed examination of the site findings strengthens the conviction that important Sahelian cultures are being resurrected by research; cultures with which the traders from the north were to come into contact. For the periods before the seventh century, Tondidaru,[50] Jenne-Jeno[51] and Bandiagara[52] have yielded a rich harvest. The comments of S. K.

47. See R. J. McIntosh and S. K. McIntosh, 1981; J. Devisse, 1982.

48. Very recent research, still unpublished, on the Mauritanian bank of the Senegal River yields a surprising crop of new facts. Forthcoming publications of the Institut Mauritanien de la Recherche Scientifique are worth following closely.

49. Of course this leap backwards in our knowledge is not proof that between the fifth and seventh centuries we are at the *beginning* of organized life, trade and cultural development in Sahelian Africa. Recent discoveries relating to iron and copper would alone suffice as a warning against any such new error of judgment. These discoveries cast doubt on the indications given by J. Anquandah, 1976, in his description of the economic development of the Sahel.

50. J. F. Saliège, Y. Person, I. Barry and P. Fontes, 1980. Very exact corrected carbon-14 datings: 1330 BP–40, 1245 BP–40, i.e. between +620 and +655.

51. S. K. McIntosh and R. J. McIntosh, 1980b. According to these authors there was town life on the site from the second century of the Christian era; they estimate the area of the town as 40 ha in about 900–1000.

52. R. M. A. Bedaux, 1972.

McIntosh and R. J. McIntosh are particularly important as regards the trade in copper and iron in the Inland Niger Delta.[53] For the various regions of Senegal the information is less detailed[54] but even the size of the areas prospected has given rise to some debatable but not negligible estimates of the density of settlement between the river and the Gambia during the first millennium.[55] The site of Sintiu-Bara, not yet completely published, has yielded bronze equipment of great interest.[56] The discovery at sites on the river of many discs used in ropemaking for this period is still too recent to be interpreted with certainty; it also implies quite a high degree of technological development.[57] For the eighth and ninth centuries and perhaps even for an earlier date Tegdaoust has yielded abundant consistent traces of copper-alloy metallurgy, one of the raw materials for which probably came from Akdjudjt.[58] The earliest archaeological evidence of the use of *cire perdue* moulds has been found there for the same early periods:[59] this local metallurgy, apparently continuous with that studied by N. Lambert,[60] certainly played an inter-regional economic role very early on.

Lastly, bringing together the still meagre data about adaptation to the environment, stockbreeding, agriculture and food, we find that even for this period before the eighth to ninth centuries archaeological research has given some important recent results. At Jenne-Jeno fish and two kinds of bovids were eaten from the earliest period; and rice (*Oryza glaberrima*) was perhaps also eaten,[61] being attested after +400 and before +900 (Phase III) alongside a variety of millet.[62] But life expectancy seems to have still been short, to judge by the age of the skeletons found: six probably did not live beyond twenty-five years, one beyond thirty years, three between thirty and thirty-five years and one between forty-five and fifty-five years.[63] At Tegdaoust beef was plentiful from the earliest times (eighth century or earlier); fowls – guinea fowl – and domestic animals or livestock

53. In particular there were some rare imports of copper in Periods II and III (50–400 and 400–900) which obviously could not have come from the trans-Saharan trade; S. K. McIntosh and R. J. McIntosh, p. 76. On pp. 444–5 the authors use the same argument with regard to iron, which was not produced locally and was probably traded with iron-producing areas upstream.

54. See G. Thilmans, C. Descamps and B. Khayat, 1980.

55. V. Martin and C. Becker, 1974b. See *Atlas National du Sénégal*, 1977, sheet 8, p. 51 for prehistoric sites in Senegambia.

56. A. Ravisé and G. Thilmans, 1978; G. Thilmans and A. Ravisé, 1980.

57. G. Thilmans, 1979 records discoveries on forty-two sites, ten of which have yielded more than ten examples. A ropemaking disc has apparently also been found at Tegdaoust, see D. Robert, 1980.

58. See C. Vanacker, 1979, pp. 136 *et seq.*; J. Devisse, D. Robert-Chaleix *et al.* 1983; J. Polet, forthcoming; D. Robert-Chailex, forthcoming; B. Saison, forthcoming.

59. D. Robert-Chaleix, forthcoming.

60. See N. Lambert, 1971.

61. S. K. McIntosh and R. J. McIntosh, 1980b, p. 188.

62. ibid., p. 190.

63. ibid., pp. 177 *et seq.*

made up an important part of the diet.[64] At Niani sorghum is attested in the eighth–ninth centuries, lentils probably in the ninth–tenth centuries.[65]

Thus nowadays everything points to the fact that the societies with which the men from the north were to come into contact via the Sahara were cohesive and well organized, had towns and were capable of trading, sometimes over a long distance. Moreover, from the latter point of view it is noteworthy that salt-trading networks probably existed from this period.[66] Here we must remember the testimony of the *Ḥudūd al-ʿAlām*, quoted above, and also that of al-Muhallabī, which shows that in the tenth century the main wealth of the princes of Gao lay in their salt reserves.[67]

The situation north of the Sahara

It will suffice for our purpose to pick out those features of the situation north of the Sahara that may be important for economic history[68] and the history of trans-Saharan links.

In what is now Morocco, five areas concern us. One, in the Atlantic plains and much of the Rif, was inhabited by peoples that were long to remain independent. The most representative, the Barg͟hawāṭa, resisted all domination, at least until the Almoravid period: nevertheless they played a certain role, as yet not well understood, through their trading links with Muslim Spain in particular; they seem to have had no links with the Sahel. The Idrīsids who were divided into many ruling branches, dominated not only the north, around Fez, their capital and their creation, and Meknes, but also the Middle Atlas. To judge by the work so far published, they had no links with black Africa.[69] In the north a string of ports, from Ceuta to Honayn, provided a continual link through coasting trade with neighbouring Spain: these ports were always fairly directly dependent on the economy of Andalusia.[70] The Sūs, between the Atlas and the Anti-Atlas, from very early on enjoyed the reputation with Arab authors of a land of

64. J. Devisse, D. Robert-Chaleix *et al.*, 1983.

65. W. Filipowiak, 1979, pp. 107, 113.

66. J. Devisse, 1970: between the Atlantic coast and the Niger: Tāgant in Mauritania and Awdāg͟hust were important staging-posts; similar trade probably took place between Kawār and Chad (D. Lange and S. Berthoud, 1977), between Aïr and the neighbouring areas, and so on. This is also the view of S. K. McIntosh and R. J. McIntosh, 1980b, p. 446, who believe, without studying the record further, that the salt trade was very lively south of the Sahara from the fifth century onwards.

67. J. M. Cuoq, 1975, p. 78.

68. On trade links between regions in the north of the continent, see C. Vanacker, 1973.

69. D. Eustache, 1970–1. According to the catalogue painstakingly compiled by this author, there is no trace of the minting of gold by the Idrīsids; the argument is strong, but not conclusive as regards links with the south.

70. If Ibn Ḥawḳal is to be believed, in the tenth century Spanish influence extended as far as Sebū on the Atlantic coast; see Ibn Ḥawḳal, 1964, p. 77.

plenty.[71] It is here that Tāmdūlt[72] emerged as an early terminus for the southward routes. Others multiplied on both sides of the Atlas and in the Dar'a Valley until the tenth century. Lastly, on the Sahara side of the Middle Atlas, Sidjilmāsa (about whose foundation al-Bakrī reports several contradictory versions) began, certainly by the second half of the eighth century, to act as a caravan port for links with the south.[73]

The south, as all the authors tell us, was the realm of the great cameleers, lords of the desert, who knew neither bread nor agriculture and lived in close symbiosis with their camels. They included the Banū Masūfa, mentioned by Ibn Ḥawḳal as early as the tenth century; they had an excellent knowledge of the routes, went veiled, and crossed the desert in winter.[74] A little earlier Ibn al-Faḳīh mentioned the Lamṭa, who already made famous shields 'which they temper for a whole year in sour milk. Swords bounce off these shields'.[75] These are thought to be the 'adargues' of which R. Mauny has written at length.[76] T. Lewicki has recently discussed the Islamization of these groups;[77] a good deal of discovery no doubt remains to be done on this difficult topic.

Once the Berbers had been pacified, and especially in the Aghlabid period, Ifrīḳiya took on greater importance. Of most interest to us here, in the context of trans-Saharan links, is the existence of a dinar coinage which deserves attention.[78] For this purpose we have a survey by A. S. Ehrenkreutz[79] covering Aghlabid dinars, all of an excellent degree of fineness (on average 98.99 per cent pure).[80] Chronological classification shows that the coinage with the lowest degree of fineness dates from the beginning of the ninth century, and that after 817 the degree of fineness was very high; the coins which were 100 per cent gold were struck between 841 and 863.[81] Hence the Aghlabids obtained gold for their coinage. It remains an open question whether a large part of this gold came from the conquest of Sicily[82] or whether it was brought from the *Bilād al-Sūdān* in the ninth

71. Ibn Ḥawḳal, 1964, p. 89.

72. B. Rosenberger, 1970b, p. 106 the town existed in the tenth century; al-Ya'ḳūbī mentions it.

73. Al-Ya'ḳūbī (see J. M. Cuoq, 1975, p. 48) said that this town in the country of the Blacks could be reached in about fifty days. For Ibn Ḥawḳal, 1964, p. 97, as early as the tenth century, Sidjilmāsa's trade with the south was 'uninterrupted'.

74. Ibn Ḥawḳal, 1964, p. 100.

75. J. M. Cuoq, 1975, p. 54; the text dates from 903.

76. R. Mauny, 1961.

77. T. Lewicki, 1970.

78. This is dealt with too superficially in J. Devisse, 1970, p. 140.

79. A. S. Ehrenkreutz, 1963.

80. ibid., p. 251: only one contains only 83 per cent of gold; of the others six contain between 95 and 97 per cent, twenty-two contain 99 per cent, and three contain 100 per cent of gold.

81. ibid., p. 252.

82. This hypothesis is advanced by M. Talbi, 1966, p. 250–1.

century.[83] Historians are still debating this question.[84] For one thing, we do not have for the Aghlabid period results of the kind emerging from the important laboratory research carried out by R. Messier for the dinars of the following periods.[85] For another the documentation is meagre and difficult to interpret. In his very many studies of the Ibāḍiṭes,[86] T. Lewicki has stressed that they were a political and ideological barrier to the southwards penetration of the Aghlabids; he has never said or shown, however, that even though they monopolized traffic on the Saharan routes they did not sell gold to the governors of Ḳayrawān. Al-Bakrī, in the ninth century, attributes the digging of wells on the Tāmdūlt–Awdāghust road to ʿAbd al-Raḥmān b. Abī ʿUbayda al-Fihrī. The latter seized control of the government of Ifrīḳiya in 749;[87] he was assassinated in 755. A recently published source states that in 752–3 he sacked Tlemcen and subjugated the whole of the Maghrib.[88] An expedition to the lands of gold a good deal earlier – around 734 – supposedly at the behest of the governor of Ifrīḳiya[89] is attributed to the same man. Even if the raid is historical, and even if it led to the digging of the wells (the southernmost of which was on the 23rd parallel of latitude *at the most*), this is far from saying that a route was organized to Awdāghust (on the 17th parallel) and the land of gold.[90] It seems odd that an Ifrīḳiyan should have wanted to have such a western route explored rather than the more obviously accessible one through the Mzāb. It is not now possible to know in detail what economic links there may have been between Ifrīḳiya and West Africa in the eighth and ninth centuries, or even whether the Aghlabids had a consistent policy on this matter. At the very most it may be more or less assumed that the Ibāḍites, rulers of the area extending from southern Tripolitania – Djabal Nafūsa – to what is now western Algeria, themselves tried at that time to organize a regular trans-Saharan link. The presence of gold in Ifrīḳiya suggests this; and the certainty that links existed between Tāhert and Gao gives this hy-

83. ibid., p. 458 points out the high proportion of blacks in the Emir's guard; it is true that they could have come from the Chad area via the slave export route referred to above. Be that as it may, the fact that blacks came to Ifrīḳiya is indirectly confirmed by a recent study of the temporalities of Monreale Abbey after the Norman conquest in the eleventh century: blacks from Ifrīḳiya formed part of the abbey's Muslim labour force; see H. Bercher, A. Courteaux and J. Mouton, 1979.

84. H. Djaït, M. Talbi, F. Dachraoui, A. Bouib and M. A. M'Rabet (n.d.), p. 57 think that links with black Africa are still in the realm of hypothesis. M. Talbi, 1966, p. 173, considers that the high level of activity in Ifrīḳiya in the tenth and eleventh centuries referred to in letters from Jewish merchants studied by S. D. Goitein suggests that the same level of activity already existed in the ninth century. This postulates the importation of African gold.

85. See p. 386 below.

86. The bibliography is mainly in J. Devisse, 1970, p. 124.

87. See E. Lévi-Provençal, 1960.

88. H. R. Idris, 1971, p. 124.

89. Ibn ʿAbd al-Ḥakam, 1922, p. 217.

90. See S. Daveau, 1970, pp. 33–5.

pothesis still greater credibility. Thus Tāhert became one of the main keys to the first regular trans-Saharan links known to us. These links were with Gao, not with Ghana, and it would be reasonable to wonder whether the traders of Tāhert did not try to supply Gao with the salt that its princes stockpiled and resold. Lastly, we must remember that the *imām* of Tāhert entered into a matrimonial alliance with the Midrārites of Sidjilmāsa in the hope of securing a share in the growing trade of the western route.

Thus for the eighth and ninth centuries, until or unless better documentation becomes available to research workers, in particular by excavating at Sidjilmāsa and Tāhert, we are for the present reduced to hypotheses about the establishment of what were to be the great northern termini of the trans-Saharan trade (Tamdūlt, Sidjilmaša, Tāhert, Wargla and the towns of the Djarīd) and the early organization of the trans-Saharan caravans.

Hence again, as in the case of the Egypt route, it must be pointed out at once that all the parameters of the problem change with the descriptions of Ibn Ḥawḳal, who refers to a situation in the middle of the tenth century, and also with that of al-Bakrī, who through his many borrowings from the tenth-century author al-Warrāḳ also sometimes speaks of the situation in that century. Everything leads us to assume that the crucial events that led to a regular trans-Saharan trade took place in this century, or during the period from 850 to 950.

What trade, in search of what goods?

Seen from the eighth century, the preceding 2000 years had increased the geographical difficulties of communication between the two areas just considered: but, as a counter to this, an invaluable means of crossing the desert, the camel, had been available in this area for some centuries.

But an essential link was missing: what was there to be obtained on the other side of the desert? For the south, the answer is probably very little! The needs of a very different diet from that of the Mediterranean, both in products consumed and in their balance, were certainly better met by the adjacent south than from the trans-Saharan north. Salt, while not plentiful, was no doubt in relatively good supply thanks to the number of production techniques and of collection and manufacturing points. We must probably not let ourselves be misled by the Arabic sources after Ibn Ḥawḳal; these give the impression that Sahelian Africa was completely without salt and at the mercy of the merchants from the north to supply this product.

In fact, while not denying the huge disparity between the price of salt imported from the north[91] and that current on the Mediterranean, there are some nuances to be made. Ibn Ḥawḳal, al-Bakrī and al-Idrīsī all report that Awlīl continued to produce and export salt. According to Ibn Ḥawḳal

91. J. Devisse, 1970, pp. 111 *et seq.*, with the nuances introduced here.

it was the main mine south of the Sahara.[92] Al-Bakrī described life in the salt-producing area, where turtles were eaten[93] on a part of the coast that also supplied ambergris.[94] Al-Idrīsī shows that the mine still played an important regional role and that its output, carried by boat on 'the Nile', reached the whole of the *Bilād al-Sūdān*.[95] Everything in the accounts of Ibn Ḥawḳal and subsequent authors goes to show that the traders from the north, initially *customers* of Awlīl, and obliged, on leaving this mine, to go through Awdāghust (remarkably situated at a good water-supply point between the coast and the Niger Valley), gradually discovered a way of shortening such a route by using reserves of salt placed on the north–south route in the middle of the Sahara. They thus found a way to put increased pressure on the salt market in the south, and through the examples of Ghana and Awdāghust intensified the impression of an unsatisfied demand; whereas in fact increasing pressure was put on the sale of a product whose extraction and transportation were a monopoly. But the history of the production and consumption of salt in the savanna and the forest has still to be written, and this output probably escaped the pressure from the north. The south did not need more copper (contrary to the opinion held twenty years ago) or iron, which was already produced in a scattered but adequate way. What demand there was thus came more from the north than from the south.

As regards West Africa and our period, the demand for slaves has probably been greatly exaggerated. Claude Cahen has pointed out that the value of long-distance trade, according to Arabic sources of the ninth and tenth centuries,[96] could be very clearly assessed in terms of real profit margins, taking account of the seriousness of the risks run. He also pointed out that the slave trade does not in general seem to have been a source of big profits.[97] But the importation of slaves, says Cahen, was indispensable, for 'the general economic boom . . . demanded and allowed the employment of a growing labour force, which was most easily obtained through the slave trade.'[98] The traffic in slaves thus represented a definite flow, but probably not the main economic driving force; and hence it does not explain trans-Saharan trade. The annual demand was probably limited[99] and better

92. Ibn Ḥawḳal, 1964, p. 91; he seems in fact to know no other.

93. R. Mauny, 1961, p. 260.

94. ibid., p. 155.

95. ibid., p. 407.

96. C. Cahen, 1977, p. 339. Sources studied: *Tabassur al-Tidjāra* (Iraq, ninth century) and *Maḥāsin al-Tidjāra*, by the Fāṭimid subject Abū l-Faḍl and ad-Dimashqī.

97. ibid., p. 341: very high prices were the exception; in general selling prices were between 30 and 60 dinars.

98. ibid.

99. The example of the *baḳt* between Nubia and Egypt gives food for thought: five hundred slaves at the most were handed over at Aswān each year in exchange for goods which the Nubian court needed.

organized in the north-east quadrant of the continent than in the north-west.

According to the evidence, the north was not in need of food: the distance, and the disparity in staple foods, suggest that people did not cross the Sahara for millet, kola (which only appeared in the north after the thirteenth century) or pepper which the Arab merchants were to fetch from Asia; African 'peppers' being marketed on a small scale only much later. Similarly there is nothing to suggest that people came south for indigo-dyed fabrics: besides, there is no evidence that they were produced on a large scale before the eleventh century.[100]

We are thus irresistibly thrown back on the product of which all the Arab authors speak and to which all the historians have paid attention: gold. An enormous amount–both good and bad–has been written on this subject. Our concern here is not archaeological or ethnological but above all economic: namely to determine when, under what conditions and for what purposes the demand for gold in the north led to the organization of regular trade with the Sahel.

The Muslim world, a major consumer of gold, especially after the reforms at the end of the seventh century, behaved in relation to its fringes as an enormous zone of demand. In this period gold was much more likely to have come from Asia, Nubia or from the recycling of Pharaonic treasures than from West Africa or from what is now Zimbabwe.[101] The Muslim west, except (as we have seen) for Ifrīḳiya under the Aghlabids, did not mint gold before the tenth century.[102] But, from then on, it became a major consumer of gold for coinage. It is also from then on (and this is of course no coincidence) that information about African gold production – coming, moreover, from Western authors for the first time – became (at least relatively) less mythological and more geographically accurate.

A lengthy digression is in order at this point. All the Muslim theorists of coinage drew a fundamental distinction between crude, unrefined gold and silver and these metals once they were struck into coins. At Mecca, just before the *hidjra*, crude gold was called *tibr* and minted gold *'ayn*.[103] In a

100. All the foregoing is very likely as regards the links between North Africa and the *Bilād al-Sūdān*. A distinction should probably already be made for Tripolitania: the fact that Ibn Ḥawḳal speaks of the production and export of woollen fabrics at Adjadābiya (Ibn Ḥawḳal, 1964, p. 63) raises the question of the possible rôle of Kawār alum, in terms similar to those appositely used by D. Lange and S. Berthoud, 1977.

101. There is a vast and tedious bibliography on these questions. Among recent work it is worth consulting: C. Cahen, 1979, 1980. It should be pointed out here that R. Summers, 1969 considers that the mining of southern gold started in the sixth century, that it was already developed by the eighth century, and that it supported a large annual export trade from the tenth century on. Nobody has so far built up from these data an overall economic study of the marketing of southern gold, like the one that many of us have carried out for West African gold.

102. Most recently; C. Cahen, 1979.

103. G. P. Hennequin, 1972, pp. 7–8, note 5.

fairly recent article[104] R. Brunschwig draws the same distinction between *tibr* or *sābika* (ingot) and dinars. This simple fact dictates caution about translating the word *tibr* as 'gold dust'. The summary of the occurrence of *tibr* and *dhahab* in the sources translated by Cuoq seems worthy of comment.[105]

For the earliest authors, al-Fazārī and Ibn al-Faḳīh,[106] *dhahab* denotes gold, including that 'which grows like carrots'.[107] In view of the great importance generally attached to al-Bakrī's text on this point, we asked a young Tunisian research worker, an Arabist and a very good linguist, for as exact a translation as possible.[108] Here it is:

> If a lump[109] of gold is found in any of the mines of his country, the king picks out the best,[110] but he leaves the scraps of crude gold for the people.[111] Otherwise pure gold[112] in the hands of the people would become too plentiful, so that its value would drop. The lump weighs anything from one *ūḳiya* to one *ratl*. It is reported that he has one at home like an enormous pebble.[113]

This translation brings a new solution to the interpretation of the pair *tibr–dhahab*. In all the books he consulted Ghali found the meaning of *tibr* as given above: native gold, not minted, not worked, perhaps as specks or dust; in every case, gold in the rough state as opposed to worked gold (*dhahab*).[114] Conversely *dhahab* in every case implies a refining process, designed to obtain the purest metal, whether gold or silver.[115] Thus the

104. R. Brunschwig, 1967.

105. J. M. Cuoq, 1975.

106. ibid., pp. 42, 54.

107. Later, in the fourteenth century, al-'Umarī says that the roots of the *nadjīl* are *tibr* (J. M. Cuoq, p. 273), even though a little further on he speaks of the extraction of *dhahab* (J. M. Cuoq, p. 280).

108. This was Mr Nouredine Ghali, who is studying for a doctorate in history.

109. The Arabic word *nadra* suggests rarity: Ghali stresses that it refers to a lump of pure gold mixed with the ore.

110. The Arabic word *astaṣfā* suggests the idea of 'creaming off' or 'taking the best'.

111. Arabic, *al-tibra daḳīka*. For *tibra*, see *al-Mundjid fi'l-lughat wa'l-adab wa'l-ulūm* (Beirut, 1975), p. 58c which gives: 'gold not minted or worked, in its matrix'.

112. In this case the Arabic word used is *al-dhahab*, which is thus clearly distinguished from the preceding term.

113. Elsewhere this passage is translated as follows: V. Monteil, 1968, p. 73: 'If native gold is found in any mine in the kingdom, the king appropriates it: he leaves only the gold dust for his subjects ...' J. M. Cuoq, 1975, p. 101: 'If gold nuggets are found in the mines of the country, the king keeps them for himself; the gold dust he then leaves for his subjects ...'

114. R. Blachère, M. Chouémi and C. Denizeau, 1967– , Vol. 2, p. 984 give a quotation probably taken from Ibn 'Abd al-Ḥakam: 'he exchanged with Zurâra native gold [*tibr*] for fine gold [*dhahab*]'.

115. Mr Ghali provided me with a quotation – without indication of author – from *al-Mundjid fi'l-lughat wa'l-adab wa'l-ulūm* pp. 239c, 240a: 'he found the *dhahab* in his ore; he was amazed, as though he were going mad'.

distinction between unworked gold and the 'core of pure metal' cleared of its matrix seems to us quite adequate for an understanding of al-Bakrī's text. A little further on in his text, al-Bakrī writes that the Naghmārata trade in *tibr*.[116] There is only one possible explanation for this contradiction: namely that *tibr*, left for private individuals, may have been marketed by specialist merchants, the Naghmārata (ancestors of the Wangara?), operating outside the sovereign's control. But then what is to be made of al-Bakrī's own explanation[117] to the effect that the sovereign regulated the circulation of gold by keeping the nuggets, so that the metal did not depreciate through overabundance? Are we to suppose that inconsistency in economic matters was normal in Ghana? We do not believe it. The traditional distinction between nuggets and dust does not hold water. The real distinction is a different one: 'pure' gold, which by definition the ruler set aside for himself and which was intended for coinage, was *dhahab*. How else could an eleventh-century Andalusian, brought up in Arab culture, express himself? *Tibr* was 'native' gold, also of very high quality, marketed outside the channels controlled by the ruler.

A century later, al-Idrīsī, who was extremely well informed (contrary to what has often been written about him), provided fresh details.[118] According to his account, merchants from the north took gold (*tibr*) from Takrūr[119] and the Wangara supplied gold (*tibr*) which was then minted at Wargla.[120] His text leaves no doubt: the Wangara could not operate without being controlled by the sovereign of Ghana.

It seems to us that to draw a diametrical opposition between 'nuggets' as the translation of *dhahab* and 'gold dust' as the translation of *tibr* has greatly impoverished the discussion; the distinction between untreated gold and minted gold leaves it more open. The debate can no doubt only be definitely resolved by card-indexing and systematically translating all the usages of both words. Meanwhile, we should like to suggest that other hypotheses might help to solve this problem.

Lastly, the word *dhahab* is little used in the Arabic sources about West Africa. Though found in the eighth and tenth centuries, it hardly occurs at all after al-Bakrī except in two fourteenth-century sources.[121] By contrast the continuity in the use of the word *tibr* is remarkable.[122] Ibn Khal-

116. J. M. Cuoq, p. 102.

117. ibid., p. 101.

118. See T. Lewicki, 1966, a well-documented study.

119. J. M. Cuoq, p. 129.

120. ibid., p. 164.

121. Al-ʿUmarī (J. M. Cuoq, 1975, pp. 264, 265) is in the last resort not much clearer than al-Bakrī: the sultan, he says, has under him the country of the refuge of gold (*tibr*), but if he conquered one of the towns of gold (*dhahab*) (p. 265), production would stop. The distinction becomes clear if we accept that *dhahab* really refers to 'the government's gold'.

122. Al-Masʿūdī (J. M. Cuoq, 1975, p. 62); Ibn Ḥawḳal (J. M. Cuoq, p. 75); al-Bakrī (J. M. Cuoq, p. 84, p. 101, p. 102); al-Idrīsī (J. M. Cuoq, pp. 129–64); Abū Ḥāmid al-Gharnāṭī (J. M. Cuoq, p. 169) and so on, until the end of the fifteenth century.

dūn[123] and then Ibn Ḥadjar al-ʿAskalānī[124] perhaps provide a partial answer, especially the latter who states that *tibr* meant untreated gold.

From now on we for our part have no hesitation in replacing the pair 'dust–nugget' with the pair 'untreated gold–refined or worked gold', which is a much more important distinction for economic history.

If we go a step further we may be able to understand why in the context of the *Bilād al-Sūdān* the word *dhahab* was gradually given up in favour of *tibr*. *Tibr* has in the long term probably denoted West African gold, in whatever form it was received (specks, dust, nuggets or ingots) and regardless of its socio-economic origins, as a specific quality of gold pure enough even without refining to be used directly for coinage. It did not need 'purification' because it contained few impurities and was unalloyed. In fact laboratory research[125] has shown that this gold contains silver and a small percentage of copper.[126] Indeed, R. A. K. Messier aims to use this small percentage of copper to identify, among the dinars he has studied, those which were struck from West African gold.[127] The laboratory analyses we are now carrying out on gold from Falémé and certain Almoravid dinars[128] confirm Messier's findings and add slightly to their precision: we find percentages of silver comparable to those he has published, but also small but characteristic traces of platinum which he does not mention.[129]

This semantic problem with a bearing on economics is obviously complicated; one day it will have to be definitively cleared up.

If (as we think) *tibr* indeed denotes (at least from the eleventh century onwards) the quality of West African gold that could be used without refining or alloying for minting coinage, this would explain both why al-Bakrī says this gold is the best in the world and also people's keenness to obtain it. A recent survey in the archives of Genoa confirms that after the fourteenth century the Genoese also tended to use *tibr* to denote a quality of gold.[130]

The Arab sources attest that gold existed in wrought form in West Africa; but apparently those in power south of the Sahara, whether Muslim

123. J. M. Cuoq, pp. 347 *et seq.*

124. ibid., p. 394.

125. R. A. K. Messier, 1974.

126. During the excavations at Tegdaoust we found in a ninth-century stratum a fragment of crucible enclosing a little lump of gold. This lump was encased in copper oxide.

127. R. A. K. Messier, 1974, p. 37: there is less than 1.5 per cent of copper in this gold, which for the author rules out the possibility that it was added through alloying.

128. These studies will be published shortly by the Institut Mauritanien de la Recherche Scientifique.

129. I am indebted for this information to Mr S. Robert, Research Attaché at the Institut Mauritanien de la Recherche Scientifique.

130. J. A. Cancellieri, 1982. The author writes (p. 14) that neither the older term *paliola* nor, after 1400, *tibar* specifically denote gold dust; on p. 16 he concludes that this is *unrefined* 21-carat gold, and on p. 20 says of *tibr* that it is crude gold, that has not had its fineness improved.

or not, never, even after 1050, turned this gold into coins. To this day no trace of a die or mint has been found south of the desert. The fact leads us to ask some essential questions in the field of economic history. Given the way this gold was produced from thousands of widely separated shafts, would the direct use of gold for coinage have been feasible in the south? Would not this gold, even struck into coins weighing 4 gm, have had far too much purchasing power for the type of local trade (as was also the case at the same period for the transactions of Mediterranean societies)?[131]

According to Muslim jurists, however, the use of wrought gold or ingots was legal for all types of transactions in both the south and the north. The Muslim theorists laid it down that there should be no difference in exchange between dinars from different mints – except for obviously debased coinage – or between dinars and gold ingots.[132] Wrought gold, if of good quality, was of course covered by this system of exchange control.

In the north, especially from the tenth century onwards, the minting of coinage by the authorities became the rule.[133] This was the result partly of growing aspirations to territorial hegemony by the Western Muslim powers, and the progress of their administration, and partly of the general economic situation of the West as a whole. Trade appeared in response to the annual currency requirement at the behest of the gold-minting dynasties in North Africa and then in Spain (the Aghlabid governors of Ifrīḳiya in the ninth century; the Fāṭimids of Ifrīḳiya in the tenth century; the Umayyads of Spain in the tenth century; the Fāṭimids of Egypt after 970; the Zīrīds of Ifrīḳiya, and then the Almoravids. But of course it was especially when the Fāṭimids, the Umayyads and then the Almoravids undertook coinage on a scale unprecedented in the Muslim West that the vitality of the trans-Saharan trade became apparent.

Who were the intermediaries between the scattered production of *tibr* in the south and its increasingly well-organized consumers in the north? The Arabic sources present things as a matter of course: Ghana took on the task. But we are told nothing about the historical steps that led to this; nothing about any middlemen – merchants are probably not mentioned until the tenth century – between the miners and other merchants.

Attempts have recently been made to assess the annual minting capacity

131. See P. Grierson, 1961, p. 709.

132. G. P. Hennequin, 1972, p. 9, note 4: 'precious metals have almost always preserved their 'paramonetary' rôle as universally acceptable goods, in competition with minted coinage'. Hennequin goes on to write (p. 10) that: 'the minting of the metal makes it a monetary token, by giving it a sort of added value. This added value always exists, *at least in qualitative terms*'.

133. ibid., p. 9, does not hesitate to write: 'What brings money into being, in the sense in which we understand it, is action by the authorities', and in note 2 on p. 9: 'the fact that any monetary token is accepted without restriction for payments to the authorities is enough to guarantee its acceptance in private transactions, even if it does not necessarily lead to the immediate elimination of competing instruments and hence to a monopoly by the favoured token'.

in Umayyad Spain. Such estimates should of course be treated with caution. The fact remains that in 1009–10, a year of heavy minting,[134] 40 000 dinars were struck, using about 160 kg of gold. Such a figure bears little relation to the derisory number of specimens now preserved in museum collections.[135] The same author believes that the annual minting in Tulunid Egypt between 879–80 and 904–5 was not more than 100 000 dinars,[136] or about 400 kg of gold. The annual minting requirement in the north cannot be accurately estimated on the basis of these two orders of magnitude. It may be supposed to have fluctuated around one tonne at the most, even allowing for rivalry and competition (which by eliminating rivals, always operated to the advantage of a single beneficiary, the Aghlabids, the Fāṭimids, then the Umayyads, then the Zanāta and then the Almoravids; the case of the Zīrīds is far harder to analyse).

In any event, and even allowing for the needs of jewellery, the building-up of savings and annual losses of coinage, it is difficult to imagine that the tonnage imported annually could have been much over two tonnes, three at the most. These figures, perhaps make those put forward by Mauny in 1961[137] seem a little high. Having set the average gold needs of the north from the tenth century onwards at three tonnes a year (an arbitrary figure, and certainly too high), we see that this is not an impossible task: it represents thirty to forty camel-loads. The obvious proliferation of travellers, and information from the Arabic sources, leave the impression that these figures are much too modest and that the caravans contained more camels, at least on the outward journey, and grew in number every day. Here we see the full difficulty of quantitative history for these early periods.[138] In any case, we now have the serious problem of the obvious physical imbalance between the weight of the material to be brought across the desert from the north (and hence the number of camels on the outward journey) and the much smaller weight on the return journey. What became of the redundant camels? Were they eaten, or sold in the Sahel, in which case their numbers must have rapidly increased? Another piece of research still to be carried out.

Whether we adopt our suggested 'floor' figure of about three tonnes or R. Mauny's figures, these weights (derisory in present-day economic

134. A. S. Ehrenkreutz, 1977, p. 270.

135. There are innumerable reasons why coins disappear; see P. Grierson, 1975.

136. See J. Devisse, 1970.

137. Estimated annual exportable production at: Buré: 4 tonnes; Galam: 500 kg; Poura Lobi: 200 kg; Gold Coast and Ivory Coast: 4 tonnes; Kpelle, Sierra Leone: 300 kg (R. Mauny, 1961, pp. 310–22). It is true that these estimates rested on present-day production figures. A recent study by Mr Kiethega takes the view that production in the Poura area of Burkina Faso between the sixteenth and the nineteenth century probably never exceeded 50 kg a year on average (J. B. Kiethega, 1983).

138. Be it noted also that even if we keep a figure close to R. Mauny's, i.e. about 6–7 tonnes a year, this would still give only a small number of mounts going back to the north.

terms) require comment. The fact that they are so low explains not only the bitter rivalry for control of the routes and the extent to which their surveillance or the plundering of the caravans was necessary or profitable, but also the extent to which each of the northern termini for the circulation of this gold needed regular annual journeys by the Saharan caravans to maintain the credibility of its coinage (given that the Muslim West had no other major source of gold). Similarly we can now see why, when Mansa Kankū Mūsā much later brought about a ton of gold to Cairo, the gold price was upset. It would be childish to suppose that a flood of gold came out of West Africa every year.

We can also make very rough estimates of the work represented by this annual exportable output, plus perhaps the same amount of gold again consumed locally, if we remember that one shaft yielded between 2.5 gm and 5 gm of gold. Between 240 000 and 480 000 shafts thus had to be dug each year, which represents a considerable mobilization of labour. Even if we add on the output from gold-washing, the fact remains that this activity, which after all was seasonal, must have mobilized hundreds of thousands of people in West Africa each year once the demand was strong and regular.

When did the regular annual caravan trade supplying gold for the Muslim mints begin?

We can rule out the first half of the eighth century, which saw disturbances in the north, hesitant attempts to cross the desert, and raids that may have been spectacular but were quite ineffectual. On the other hand the possibility of regular trade arises seriously for the second half of the eighth century and the ninth century, when Sidjilmāsa was founded or developed, Tāhert was booming and Ibāḍite trade was developing. We cannot yet really answer the question, but it seems to us that this period could well have been that of the still hazardous and timid trading suggested by the texts of al-Yaʿḳūbī or even Ibn Ḥawḳal. It may be worth mentioning here what the latter wrote, probably of a considerably more recent period, when he reported what a witness had told him: 'I have heard', he said, 'Tanbarūtān ibn Isfishār, who was then the prince of all the Ṣanhādja, say that he had been governing this people for twenty years and every year was visited by groups he did not know ...' The excavations at Tegdaoust, almost certainly the site of the ancient Awdāghust, have yielded valuable information on the very period, eighth to ninth centuries, about which so little is still known.[139] Copper metallurgy has already been reported above: there are abundant remains: crucibles, *cire perdue* moulds, slag and small ingots. This does not imply trans-Saharan links, but it does imply trade[140]

139. On the chronology of the site see J. Devisse, D. Robert-Chaleix *et al.*, 1983, and J. Polet, forthcoming; D. Robert-Chaleix, forthcoming; B. Saison, forthcoming.

140. The plethora of shells imported from the Atlantic coast (D. Robert, 1980, p. 209 and B. Saison, 1979) imply regular links with the coast. The possible use of copper from Akdjudjt has been mentioned above.

PLATE 14.1 *An example of locally made pottery moulded in imitation of thrown pottery imported from the Maghrib (probable date: tenth–twelfth centuries)*

and the sale of products. Gold was certainly produced:[141] it necessarily came from the south. The presence of spindle whorls[142] implies spinning and probably cotton, though we cannot say more for the moment, these objects being rare for this period. A type of local pottery with white-painted decoration,[143] very characteristic of the eighth to ninth centuries, also raises interesting problems: it is somewhat reminiscent of similar ware from the Christian period in Nubia (Plate 14.1).[144]

The objects imported from the north are of still greater interest: there are not yet many of them, but they are evidence of desert crossings. Precious and semi-precious stones (to be discussed more fully further on) and glazed pottery have already been found. Very careful examination as to

141. D. Robert, 1980, p. 209, fragments of a crucible with particles of gold; B. Saison, 1979, p. 688; pan of a small scale for weighing gold? J. Devisse (unpublished report): fragment of crucible containing gold coated with copper.

142. D. Robert, 1980, p. 209; B. Saison, 1979; J. Devisse, D. Robert-Chaleix *et al.*, 1983. In his thesis on the Saharan Neolithic (1979), H. Hugot says that spindle whorls were present in the Sahara during the Neolithic period.

143. See B. Saison, 1979, e.g. pp. 548–9. It occurs in excavation reports, and was still being made in the tenth century. These pottery types are unlike those found at Jenne-Jeno (S. K. McIntosh and R. J. McIntosh, 1980b, p. 453) or at Kūgha (quoted by ibid.).

144. See S. Wenig (1978), Vol. 1, p. 132, plates 98, 99; p. 133, plate 100; Vol. 2, p. 321, plate 285; p. 322, plate 288.

provenance has not yet yielded absolutely positive conclusions, except in one case: some postsherds from the lower levels of the site come from Ifrīḳiya.[145] Glassware, we also now know, crossed the Sahara.[146]

Not finally identified as to provenance but definitely from the north, these precious 'goods' found at Tegdaoust are the result of a purchase, or more probably a barter transaction. The date of the levels at which they were found is undoubtedly earlier than 900. They are no doubt the first definite evidence of the existence of trans-Saharan links in the eighth and ninth centuries.

All the trends of the argument having been brought together, it is now time to show how matters probably developed between 900 and 1100 or thereabouts.

The development of trans-Saharan trade from 900 to 1100

The growth of currency needs: the Fāṭimids in Ifrīḳiya; Umayyad competition; the Almoravids

At the end of the seventh century, the Umayyad sovereigns in the east wished to give to the community whose caliphs they were a coinage both appropriate to the new religion and also economically strong. The Muslim world had for two centuries lived on the theoretical idea of an ideological unity of the coinage, struck in the name of the only acknowledged Caliph ruling in Damascus and then in Baghdad. Thus for a Muslim (as witnesses a sixteenth-century text by al-Maḳrīzī) the coinage, obviously an economic fact of life, was also the mark of a certain image of authority.[147]

In the Muslim world, as in the Roman tradition, the minting of coins was a regal prerogative[148] which the rulers enforced more or less strictly. This monopoly of minting coinage[149] had nothing to do with the legal cur-

145. B. Saison, 1979, p. 688; J. Devisse, D. Robert-Chaleix *et al.*, 1983; C. Vanacker, 1979.

146. J. Polet, 1980, p. 92; C. Vanacker, 1979.

147. Muslim authors, especially from the tenth century onwards, constructed theories of the use of coinage. According to R. Brunschwig (1967, p. 114), who has made a close study of this question, one of the earliest, Ibn Miskawayh, writing in about 980, showed that communal life and the division of labour gave rise to the need for objects of reward, which were then used to pay for other work and objects and were accepted without question. It was essential for these objects to be fairly rare: gold was chosen for its permanence and ease of melting. Later, according to Brunschwig, 1967, Ibn Khaldūn stated that the function of coinage was to preserve wealth, and that it should circulate as a standard of value and not be kept as personal property. The Qoran points in the same direction when it says (Sūra 9:34): 'Those who treasure up gold and silver and do not expend them in the way of Allah will meet painful punishments'.

148. Some historians (G. P. Hennequin, 1972, p. 9) tend to consider that coinage only exists as the result of action by the authorities.

149. On these points, see P. Grierson, 1975, pp. 130 *et seq.*

rency of the coins minted,[150] the tokens accepted in transactions still being a matter for agreement between the parties. It was obviously more convenient to use coins that inspired confidence by virtue of the integrity of their minting. The latter, a regal prerogative and purveyor of tokens for fiscal relationships between the ruler and his subjects, could thus also be accepted in an ideal case as a good referee for economic transactions. In such a case the coinage proclaimed the glory and integrity of him who ordered it and proclaimed on the faces of the coins the glory of God, his Prophet and the ruling dynasty.

A map (Fig. 14.3) of the gold mints just before the Fāṭimids seized power tells us much. There was one at Ḳayrawān in the hands of the Aghlabids and one at Miṣr-Fusṭāṭ controlled by the Ikhshīdids. Most of the gold was minted either by Syria/Palestine under the control of the Ikhshīdids or in the realms of the Abbasids. Neither Spain nor the north of the continent of Africa struck much gold during this period. Indeed, the Umayyads of Spain[151] and the Idrīsids in what is now Morocco used local resources to strike silver dirhams.[152] For the coinage of silver, another mint took on some importance (Fig. 14.4), namely Sidjilmāsa, the growth in whose economic rôle we have also seen: this mint certainly received southern gold, but did not mint it. The Fāṭimids' gold policy radically altered this state of affairs;[153] the tenth century saw the opening of gold mints in parts of the Muslim world where there had not been any, under the strict supervision of the two rival dynasties, the Fāṭimids of Ifrīḳiya and the Umayyads of Spain (Fig. 14.5).[154] Rivals to the Abbasids in the East and proclaiming the decadence of that caliphate and their own intention of reunifying the Muslim world which the Abbasids had allowed to fall into decline,[155] the Fāṭimids owed it to themselves ideologically to mint

150. There is much discussion among historians as to whether minting gave the metal used an actual added value or merely a psychological one (because of the confidence the coins inspired). In any case, every government whether in the West, Byzantium or the Muslim world sought to enforce its right to mint the metal of its choice. In this sense there was rivalry or even conflict between governments which had little direct connection with the real value of their coinage. See G. P. Hennequin, 1972, p. 10.

151. On the conditions, rules and forms of minting, see the very detailed study in P. Grierson, 1975.

152. M. Barcelo, 1979, p. 313. There was no minting of gold in Spain between 127/744–5 and 316/928, i.e. for 189 years. The minting of dinars was resumed in 928 (see J. Devisse, 1970, p. 148). An even more significant fact is that the few coins struck in Spain between 93/711–12 and 127/744–5 were struck on the Ifrīḳiyan model; hence they gave al-Andalus no political or economic independence.

153. See Fig. 14. 4. Sources: D. Eustache, 1970–1; B. Rosenberger, 1970a. Datings have been obtained for the Moroccan silver mines: *BASEQUA*, 1978, No. 52–4, p. 19. Djebal AWAM: one dating, +1020 ±90 = between 840 and 1020. Zgunder in Tizi Ntest: +1250 ±90 = between 610 and 790.

154. J. Devisse, 1970, 1979b. See Fig. 14.5. See also C. Vanacker, 1973, map No. 7.

155. See E. Lévi-Provençal, 1950–3, Vols 2 and 3; J. Devisse, 1970.

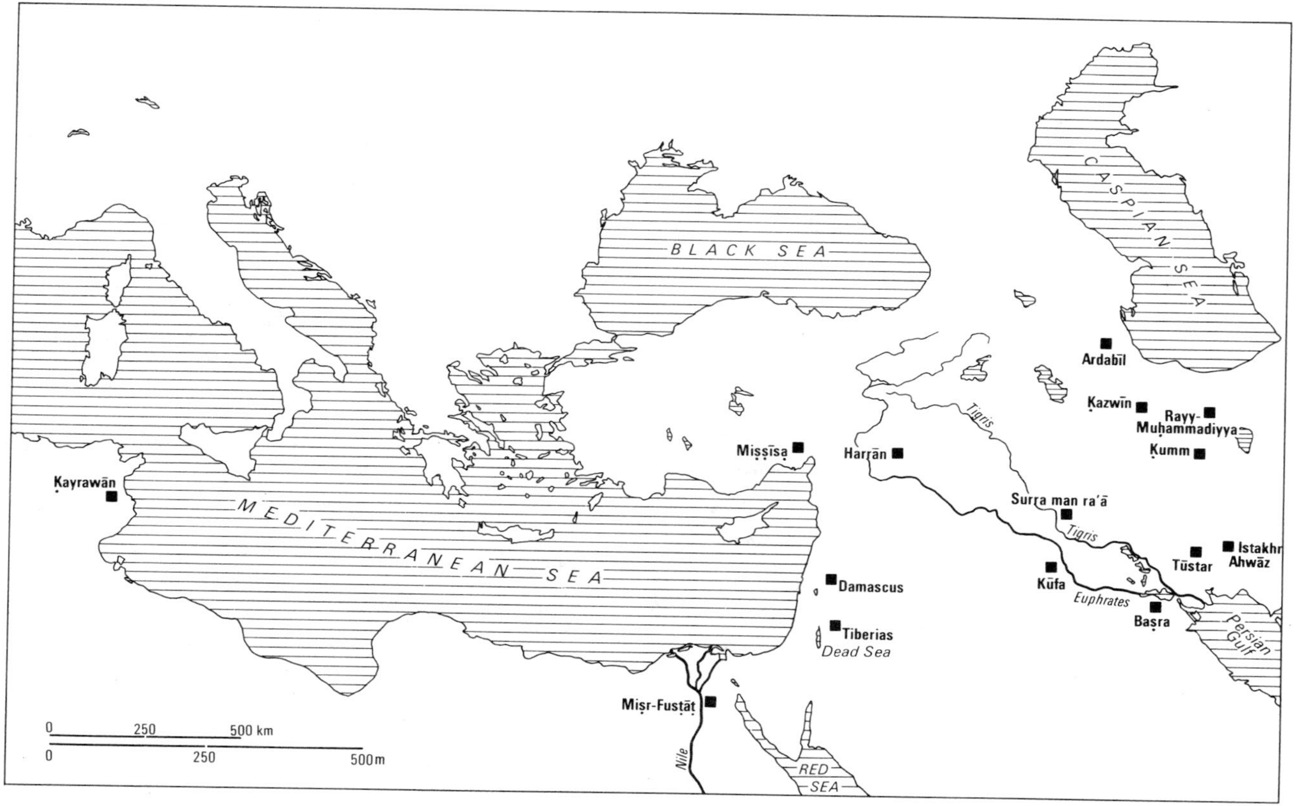

FIG. 14.3 *Gold mints on the eve of the Fāṭimid conquest*

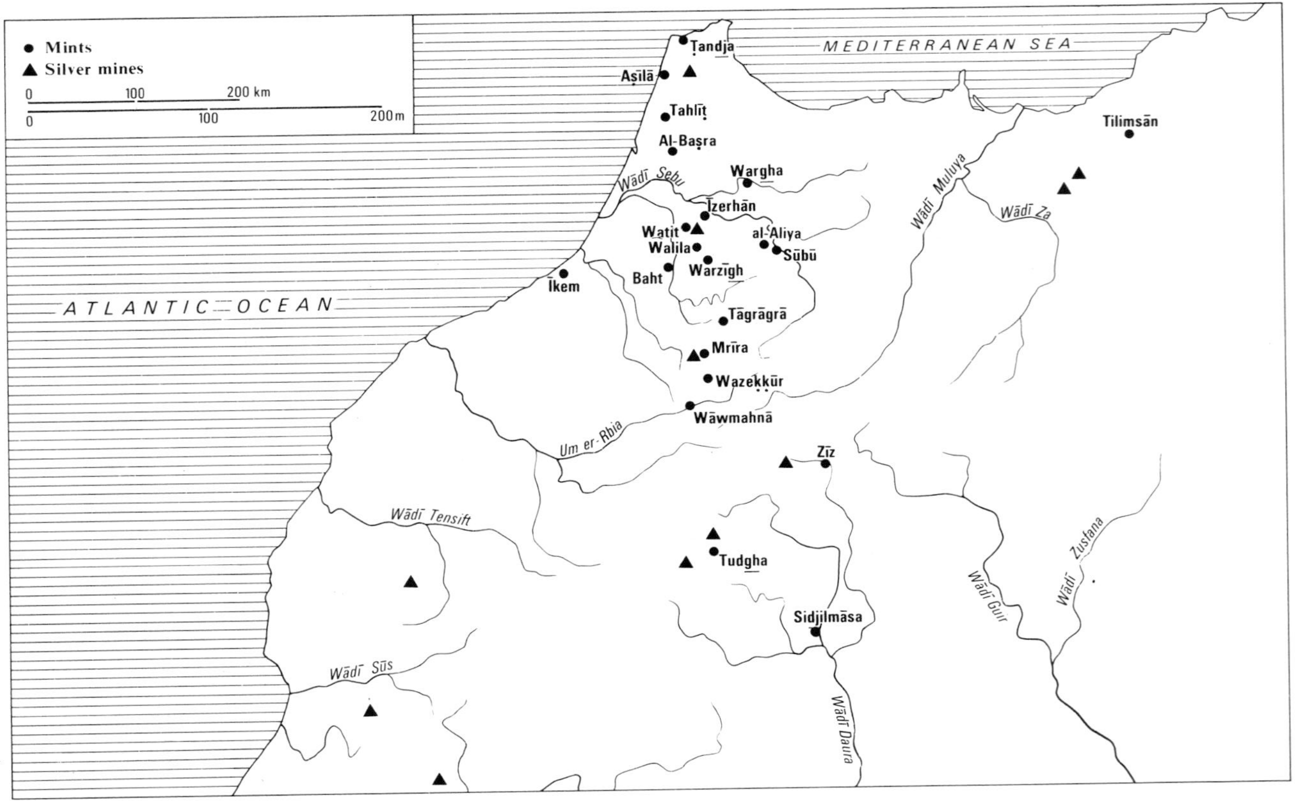

FIG. 14.4 *Minting of dirhams in the Western Maghrib during the Idrīsid period*

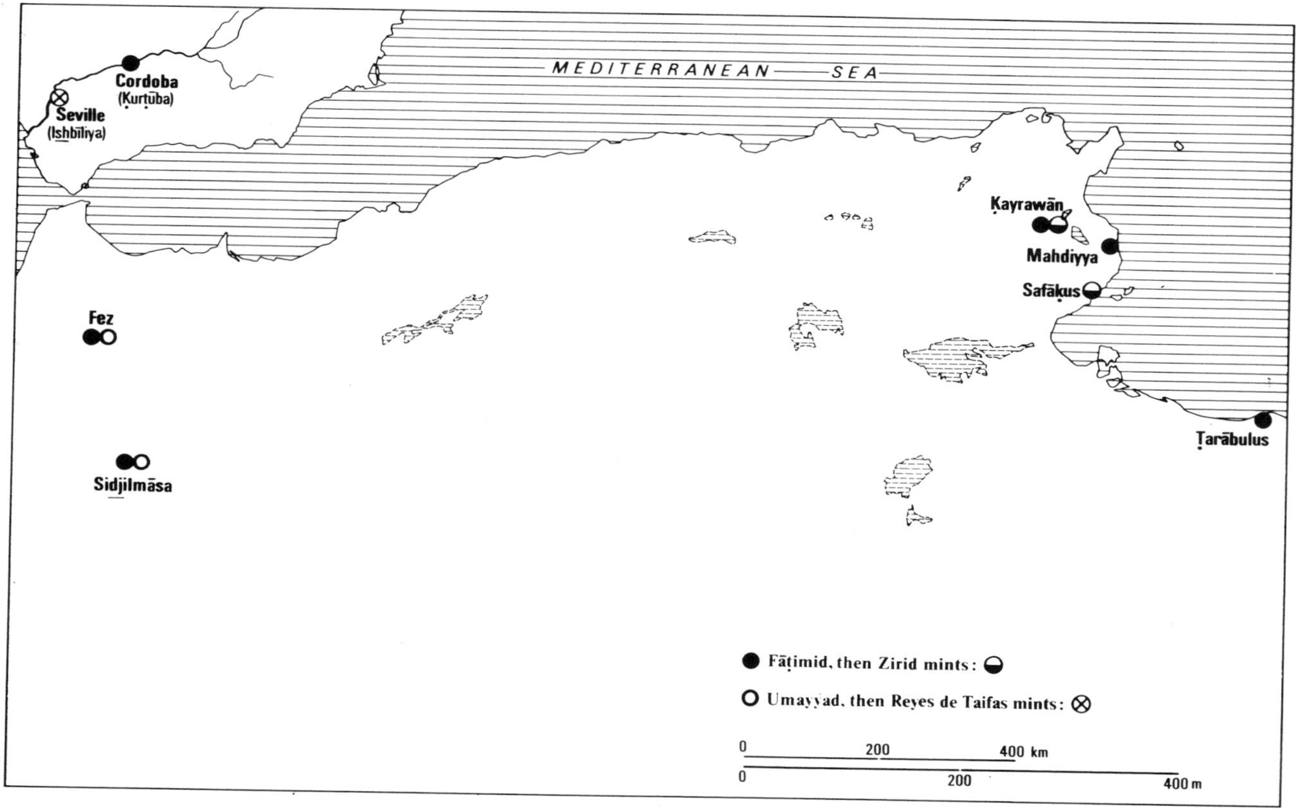

FIG. 14.5 *Minting of gold in the West Muslim world after 910*

gold. They were the first in Islam to be so bold as to strike caliphal gold coins in competition with the hitherto acknowledged authority: and their coins were intended to demonstrate the power and glory of the new authority.[156] This was no easy task. Though the Abbasid coinage was much weakened and its standard of fineness had become rather poor, the coinage of those who governed Egypt in the name of the Abbasids remained of a high standard of fineness.[157] If a Fāṭimid gold coinage was to be imposed it would therefore need to inspire confidence at least equal to that of the Egyptians.[158] The Fāṭimids' need for gold was obviously motivated by three factors, ideology, political realism and economic realism.[159] Their coinage is thus unprecedentedly important for the history of African economic relations. It started an ideological war of currency in the Muslim West that was not to end with them.[160]

Study of the Fāṭimid coinage shows that once the caliphs had overcome the grave difficulties of the mid-tenth century, they were at pains to mint coins with a high standard of fineness, and thus to build up both a reserve of precious metal and an international capital of credibility. This was an overall policy which merits closer study than it has so far received.[161] After 953 and in particular after 975, dinars struck in the name of the Fāṭimids, whether at Sidjilmāsa or Mahdiyya were in demand by traders as far away as the East because of their exceptional quality.[162]

Today, when so many data point in the same direction, we should not be surprised that the Fāṭimids sought to provide a plentiful supply of gold coinage, given a demand which they had themselves largely helped to

156. M. Canard, 1942–7.

157. On these points, recently the subject of very serious studies, see C. Cahen, 1965; A. S. Ehrenkreutz, 1963 (value of Aghlabid dinars, p. 250; value of Ikhshīdid dinars, p. 257–8; and an important overall comparison of the standards of fineness of Eastern and Western coins, p. 264); A. S. Ehrenkreutz, 1959, had already shown (pp. 139 *et seq.*) the relative weakness of the Abbasid coinage: after the middle of the ninth century the standard of fineness sometimes dropped to 76 per cent, and few coins between 95 per cent and 99 per cent purity exist. On the other hand the Ikhshīdid dinars examined (p. 153) are excellent: two contain 96 per cent gold; four, 97 per cent; twelve, 98 per cent; and ten, 99 per cent.

158. It must not be forgotten that until 969 Egypt was the Fāṭimids' continual political and strategic target.

159. As an importer of Sicilian grain (M. Brett, 1969, p. 348) and of costly Eastern produce from Egypt, Ifrīḳiya, despite its exports, had a deficit on its balance of trade which necessitated the export of coinage (see S. D. Goitein, 1973).

160. See A. Launois, 1964, for the period up to the Almoravids inclusive, then K. Ben Romdhane, 1978, for the Almohad period.

161. A. S. Ehrenkreutz, 1963, shows the value of the dinars struck, especially after 953 (pp. 256–7). The table this author gives for dinars struck in Egypt after 969 is also very illuminating: many coins contain between 97 and 100 per cent gold (p. 259). Comparison with the Aghlabid coinage (p. 257) reveals concern to do at least as well as their predecessors. See also J. Devisse, 1970. A few pages have been devoted to coinage by F. Dachraoui, 1981.

162. S. D. Goitein, 1967, p. 234; 1973, p. 30. See also J. Devisse, 1970, p. 144.

create and which was probably not primarily economic.[163] Nor should we be surprised at the pains taken by the Fāṭimids to organize the annual trans-Saharan gold trade on a quite unprecedented basis. I was already convinced that this was so in 1970[164] and the results of research at Tegdaoust have more than confirmed my conclusions at that time. Glass weights, all Fāṭimid (Plate 14.2) have been found, some of them in a stratigraphic position such that they have helped to date the site.[165] Their arrival coincides with the peak in the town's importing activity and its most spectacular urban development. It is no surprise for us today to read what al-Muhallabī wrote in the last quarter of the tenth century, that is to say at a time when Fāṭimid supremacy was not yet manifestly challenged: the people of Awdāghust became Muslims in the time of the Mahdī ʿUbayd Allāh.[166] We have no hesitation in saying today that though the Fāṭimids always had difficulty in making their way via Wargla and Tādmekka, the Ibāḍite route to black Africa, they made the Sidjilmāsa–Ghana route the main avenue to black African gold for at least two centuries and the supply line for their gold coinage and the building up of their war treasure.[167] Moreover, as long as they stayed in Ifrīḳiya, after the defeat of Abū Yazīd, they struck coins that inspired confidence in merchants.[168]

But the bitter struggle waged by the third caliphate from Cordoba against Fāṭimid hegemony, the successes achieved by the Cordoban agents after the Fāṭimids' departure for Egypt, the diversion of gold to Spain or at least to the western Maghrib and the transfer of the Sidjilmāsa mint to the Umayyads show that by the last decade of the tenth century at the latest, without any change in the annual demand for gold, the beneficiaries of this influx were no longer the Fāṭimids. Here again we must be on the look-out for information from excavations[169] or laboratory research. The

163. It is as important to take account of the Fāṭimids' 'gold diplomacy' as to consider the natural flow of the economy. This 'gold diplomacy' was directly ostentatious like the Egyptian 'journey' of 969 or channelled through their agents and customers. It was intended to proclaim of the glory of the dynasty, to which the Fāṭimids were so sensitive that they had their accredited propagandists. But their monetary policy in turn probably greatly intensified economic activity in Ifrīḳiya in the second half of the tenth century and at the beginning of the eleventh. See above, S. D. Goitein, 1967, 1973; M. Brett, 1969.

164. J. Devisse, 1970, p. 141 *et seq.*

165. On these glass tokens, see chapter by Launois and Devisse, in J. Devisse, D. Robert-Chaleix *et al.*, 1983. There is much controversy about these glass weights, not those of our period but those that were made by the Fāṭimids of Egypt: see P. Balog, 1981 and M. L. Bates, 1981.

166. J. M. Cuoq, 1975, p. 76.

167. Because of them the road from Sidjilmāsa or Tamdūlt by various routes to the land of the blacks became far the best described by Ibn Ḥawḳal and al-Bakrī. We shall revert to this point later.

168. S. D. Goitein, 1967, pp. 237 *et seq.*, gives very specific examples of this success.

169. Be it noted here that less than one-fifth of the uniformly built-up area (12 ha) has been excavated, and certainly less than two-thirds of the very historically significant complex of ruins around Noudacke.

PLATE 14.2 *Tegdaoust/Awdāghust: Fāṭimid glass weight, tenth century*

last Fāṭimid weights so far found at Tegdaoust date at the latest to a little later than 1000; they may be earlier. R. Messier reports that the Fāṭimid dinars struck in Ifrīḳiya certainly seem to him to contain 'Sudanese gold', but that the same is no longer true of Fāṭimid dinars struck in Egypt.[170] The author puts the date of the change at 1047, at the time of the break between the Zīrīds and the Fāṭimids. In his opinion 47 per cent of the dinars struck before then contained western gold, against only 24 per cent for the following period.[171] We believe that the findings would probably be still more significant, even for the Zīrīds, if the chronological bar were put at about 1000. The point is that everything suggests that supplies of western gold to Ifrīḳiya stopped after 990, and that this radical change in

170. R. A. Messier, 1974, pp. 38–9; in Egypt they contain more copper than they should if it were 'Sudanese gold'.

171. ibid., 1974, p. 39.

the gold routes had consequences for Ifrīḳiya indications of which reverberate through all S. D. Goitein's publications.[172]

The last ten years of the tenth century saw a radical change in western Muslim gold coinage, with the boom in Spanish coinage[173] and the beginning of an unprecedented awakening to international trade of the parts of West Africa closest to the Atlantic.

When, having taken over the title of Caliphate, Umayyad Spain also decided to mint gold, after 929, the coinage was none too good: it only really became of good quality after 987–8. In 988–9 dinars struck at Sidjilmāsa for the Umayyads appeared.[174] But the minting remained predominantly concentrated in the Cordoban mints, under the eye of the authorities.

To appreciate the 'world' importance of these phenomena, a brief detour into Christian Europe is called for. Although not very many gold coins from the Muslim world have so far been found in the West, research now enables us to have a somewhat clearer idea of the West's relationship to the gold coinage of Islam. C. Cahen has shown the importance throughout the West of the engraved coin without an effigy to which the Westerners gave the name of *mancus* (from the Arabic root *naḳasha*, passive participle *manḳūsh*, 'engraved').[175]

It used to be thought that Christian Spain interested itself in dinars fairly late, in the eleventh and twelfth centuries,[176] but even then it was noted that Galicia wanted to have gold coins as early as the beginning of the ninth century, and the Asturians in the last quarter of that century. The Christians' aim was to lay hands on coins that would enable them to buy luxury goods from the Muslim south, the only possible supplier. P. Bonnassié's very fine recent work[177] takes us a good deal further. Gold coins from the south were known in Catalonia in 972: after 996 the references increase in number, and between 1010 and 1020 there was a veritable flood of gold. Between 1011 and 1020 53 per cent of property transactions were settled in gold coinage, as against 1 per cent between 971 and 980.[178] The references to *mancus* recorded by Bonnassié divide up as follows: 981–90: 78; 991–1000: 1071; 1001–10: 1220; 1011–20: 3153. The author notes that

172. S. D. Goitein, 1962, p. 570: much gold and silver was exported to Egypt; letters from Jewish merchants living in Tunisia speak of the decline of trade between 1030 and 1040, whereas letters at the beginning of the century were still speaking of prosperity. About 1040 a letter says that 'the whole of the West is henceforth worthless'; S. D. Goitein, 1966, pp. 308–28. On these points we cannot agree with M. Brett who continues to ascribe to the Hilālian invasion a 'catastrophic' importance for the economic life of Tunisia (M. Brett, 1969, p. 348). R. Messier also is against this view: 1974, p. 35.

173. J. Devisse, 1970, pp. 146 *et seq.*

174. ibid., p. 148.

175. C. Cahen, 1965, pp. 417–19; 1980.

176. J. Gautier-Dalché, 1962.

177. P. Bonnassié, 1975, pp. 372 *et seq.*

178. ibid., p. 373.

the abruptness of the phenomenon surprised people at the time.[179] Bonnassié concludes that real gold coins were in circulation in Christian Catalonia in the final period of the Umayyads;[180] and he, too, thinks that a lot of gold came from West Africa to provide for this coinage. In 1018, thanks to this influx of gold, the Catalans were in a position to strike their first gold coins since the ninth century. After 1020 the decline was rapid.[181]

We only need to compare these results with those we put forward in 1970 to see a very clear chronological agreement. This leads the economic historian to two important conclusions. The first is that small though the quantities of gold imported were, it was immediately absorbed as coinage, and that this coinage circulated very quickly.[182] There are reasons therefore for thinking that part of the African gold could, at least by the twelfth century, have passed into Western gold coins. The second conclusion is that the need for gold was so great that the 'frontiers' were then disturbingly permeable. All this throws even more light on the reasons for the bitter competition between western Muslim countries to obtain African gold.

The Umayyad episode was even shorter than the Fāṭimid, but it obviously kept up the pressure of heavy demand on African gold production and on the trans-Saharan traffic. The *reyes de taifas* also struck a little gold, inefficiently and with difficulty. But the real relief came later with the Almoravids. We of course only need to deal here with the Almoravid coinage and economy to show that this last phase of our period was probably the most brilliant and the most important for the history of trans-Saharan links, though in many respects still the least known.

A look at a map of the places where the Almoravids struck gold (Fig. 14.6) at once shows major innovations. The eastern half of the Maghrib was quite without mints, and Tlemcen itself was only a marginal mint. On the other hand the territory of what is now Morocco, except for the Atlantic plains south of the Sebu, was well supplied. The termini of the trans-Saharan trade (Sidjilmāsa, Aghmāt and Nūl Lamṭa) struck gold, so did Fez and Marrakesh, the capitals, and Salā, a strategic town (Fig. 14.6). There were seven mints in the western Maghrib and fourteen in Spain,[183] we are a long way from the concentration and supervision of the earlier periods,

179. ibid., p. 374. He gives a great wealth of detail. There are references to gold *mancuses*: in 1010 a Spanish counterweight (*pensum*) was obtained to weigh them (p. 376). The successive coinages of the masters of Cordoba can be identified (p. 378) and their respective values distinguished.

180. ibid., pp. 378 *et seq.*

181. ibid., p. 388.

182. P. Bonnassié, 1975, shows how the Catalans acquired this gold, and does not rule out the possibility that some of it went back to the south to pay for their purchases.

183. R. Messier, 1980: out of 1503 dinars studied, 663 came from Maghribī mints, 214 from Sidjilmāsa, 173 from Aghmāt, 118 from Fez, 78 from Nūl, 67 from Marrakesh and 13 from Tlemcen; 840 came from the Spanish mints. These figures of course refer to specimens so far discovered and preserved, not to the total of examples struck in the period.

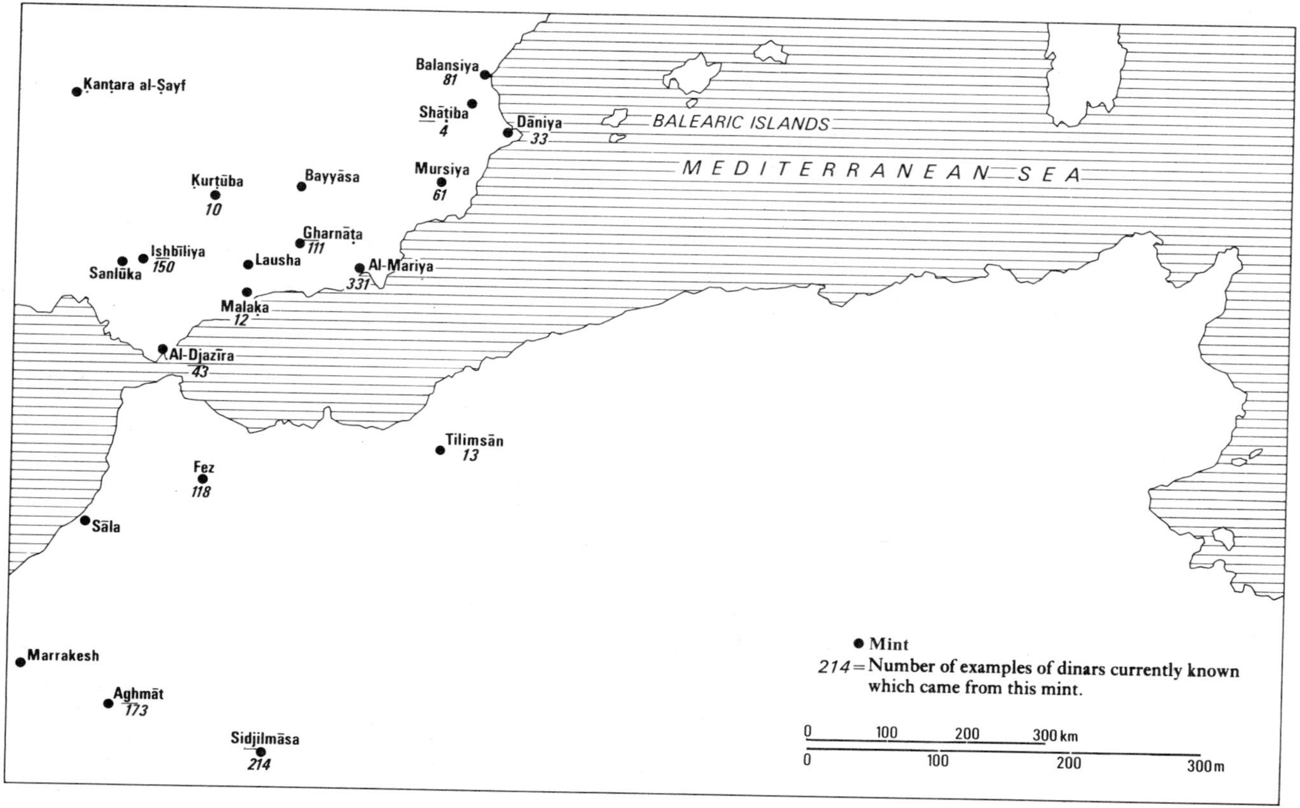

FIG. 14.6 *Almoravid gold coinage: mints*

unless we have to accept that the government was more in control and so could afford to let the mints be more scattered.

All the authors who have studied it conclude that the minting was certainly prolific. The most recent, R. Messier,[184] notes that between 451/1058 and 488/1088 the minting took place in Africa before the conquest of al-Andalus, the earliest dinars being struck at Sidjilmāsa in 448/1056–7. To the series published by this author we must add six dinars found in Mauritania.[185] Overall, mintage was especially prolific after 1100.

Going from the quantitative to the qualitative, still with R. Messier,[186] we see, first, that the standard of fineness was lower than in the Fāṭimid period, the coins containing a certain amount of silver (sometimes over 10 per cent) and copper. There was considerable variation between one mintage and another, but the presence of gold, silver and copper leads Messier to think that this was Sudanese gold, particularly for the minting done at Sidjilmāsa[187] and in the other Maghribī mints, Spanish dinars being in 51 per cent of cases of a different composition.

The abundance and regularity of the mintage, which was virtually unrivalled as far as Fāṭimid Egypt (then certainly deprived of Sudanese gold), made the Almoravid dinars (for the first time in Western Islam) an economically powerful currency even though it no longer attained the prestigious standards of fineness of the Fāṭimid coins.[188] The West had insistently called for 'marabotins';[189] after 1070 the Fāṭimid world itself was keen to have Almoravid dinars.[190]

To finish with these coinage problems it remains to ask ourselves some very difficult questions, to which there are at the moment no definite answers.

Was West African gold treated before being exported to the north? Al-Bakrī speaks of the refining of gold, but links this feature to the export of wire for filigree.[191] As we have seen above, we are inclined to think that *tibr* underwent no refining – which would throw light on R. Messier's analyses – and that it was used as it was in the mints. At the very most it was perhaps melted down in the south to make it easier to transport. At

184. ibid.

185. G. S. Colin, A. G. Babakar, N. Ghali and J. Devisse, 1983. There is also a dinar inscribed in *nashī* (cursive script), published in A. Launois, 1967.

186. R. Messier, 1974.

187. Not without some problems: see A. Huici Miranda, 1959, on a crisis in 1075–6.

188. Egyptian dinars, subject to provisos that we cannot go into here, remained of excellent quality until the end of the eleventh century (A. S. Ehrenkreutz, 1963, p. 259). From then on they lost some of their value, which probably helped to revalue the Almoravid coinages.

189. J. Devisse, 1972.

190. S. D. Goitein, 1967, p. 235: a letter written from Mahdiyya in 1100 mentions great difficulty in obtaining gold, and speaks of the dispatch of 100 dinars struck at Aghmāt in 1088; p. 236: the Jewish bankers of Fusṭāṭ were more at home calculating in Almoravid dinars than in Fāṭimid dinars. See also other interesting accounts in S. D. Goitein, 1973.

191. J. Devisse, 1970, p. 118.

Tegdaoust we found gold wire, drawn out on drawing stones which have also been discovered (Plate 14.3). It was obviously prepared for filigree work[192] which seems to confirm al-Bakrī's statement. If the gold was melted down south of the Sahara, in what form was it finally exported? As small ingots, which were divided up on arrival to be made into coin blanks?[193] Or could these blanks have been cut out before being exported to the north? The idea that ingots, or indeed blanks ready for minting, were exported is all the more appealing because there was no refining problem to speak of, and the gold could be used unrefined and unalloyed without too much concern about its standard of fineness. At Tegdaoust we found five half-ingots of gold, with other gold and silver pieces (Plates 14.4 and 14.5).[194] The five half-ingots, sheared more or less down the middle, had been cast either in a sow channel in the sand or in an ingot mould. One of them has a small copper inclusion. Were these objects intended for goldsmithing locally,[195] or to be divided into blanks for minting?[196] Lastly, in addition to these finds there is the odd case of a gold disc weighing 1.75 gm with an irregular hammered surface.[197]

These questions are still unanswered today. Other finds, laboratory work and future historical thought will no doubt settle them, along with many others.

Trade routes, gold routes and commercial contacts south of the desert

Apart from archaeological evidence, work on Saharan crossings is also assisted by Arabic written sources from the north, particularly from the tenth to the twelfth century. We have already shown how perfunctory Ibn Ḥawḳal's geography of the *Bilād al-Sūdān* still was. We now have to consider the major contributions of al-Bakrī and al-Idrīsī. Let us not choose *a priori* between them, but rather try to understand the concerns and the information that influenced them while they were writing.

192. Unpublished. To be published later. Reference TEG 66 MIV 43 and 44. One of these wires is 15.5 cm long.

193. On minting techniques see P. Grierson, 1975, pp. 139 *et seq.*; indeed, this suggests these questions. G. P. Hennequin, 1972, p. 13, describes the minting operation thus: 'only a given number of coins were cut out from a given weight of metal'.

194. TEG 66 MIV 26-27-28-47 and 48.

195. This treasure includes two rings, an earring and a necklace of gold beads.

196. Various kinds of measurement (in relation to the mitqal, to late tenth-century Fāṭimid dinars and to glass weights found at Tegdaoust) show that these ingots could on average yield between a minimum of 21 dinars and a maximum of 36 dinars. This is of course a purely hypothetical figure. In all, these five half-ingots would have produced between 100 and 150 dinars according to circumstances.

197. The weight does not correspond to any known subdivision of the dinar. Could it be the tray of a balance used in goldsmithing?

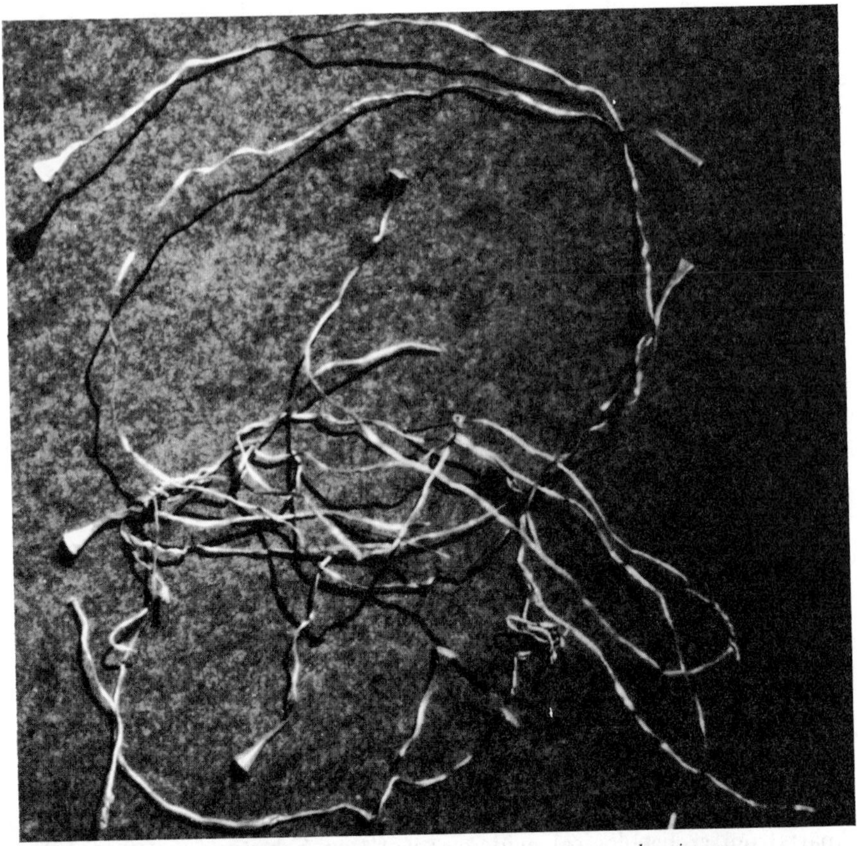

PLATE 14.3 (*above*) *Tegdaoust/Awdāghust: gold wire drawn out on a drawing stone*
PLATE 14.4 (*below*) *Tegdaoust/Awdāghust: half-ingots of gold found on the site*

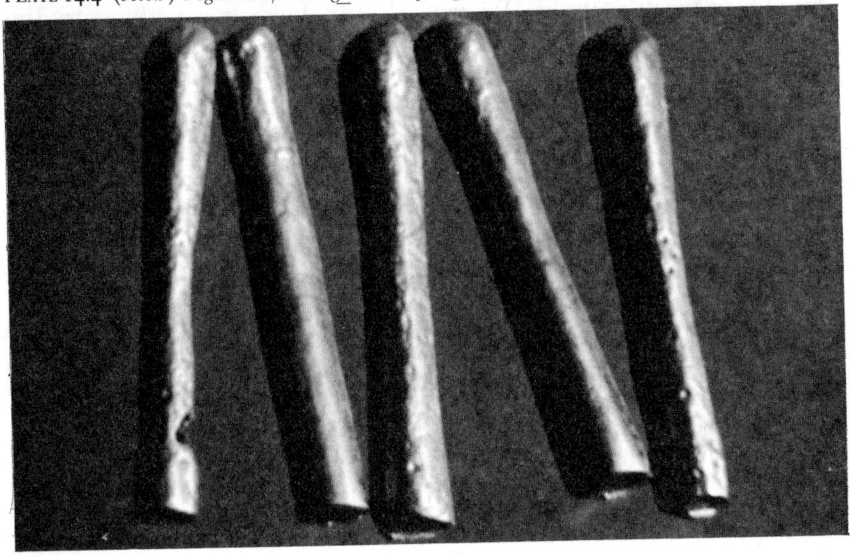

PLATE 14.5 *Tegdaoust/Awdāghust: silver chain (probable date tenth–twelfth century) found during excavation. This object was unfortunately lost in a laboratory*

Al-Bakrī has given a list of his informants, which has a logic of its own.[198] In Fig. 14.7 we have set out seven main routes between the *Bilād al-Sūdān* and the world of the north nearly all derived from different informants. For route No. 1 two sources are quoted: one of al-Bakrī's masters, Aḥmad ibn 'Umar al-'Udhrī,[199] who died at Almeria in 1085, and the writer Muḥammad ibn Yūsuf al-Warrāḳ (904/5–973/4), a native of Spain, who knew Africa from Ifrīḳiya and was associated with Ibāḍite circles. Al-Bakrī admits to borrowing from the latter his first report on Awdāghust.[200] He was also supplied with information on Awdāghust, through al-Warrāḳ, by Abū Bakr Aḥmad ibn Khallūf al-Fāsī and Abū Rustam, the latter being a native of Djabal Nafūsa.[201] Thus it is clear that al-Bakrī's contribution on Awdāghust was very well documented.

In fact, when we compare the information about route No. 1 with what al-Bakrī says about route No. 2, we judge that the big differences are probably due to major discrepancies in his information. For route No. 7 the information about Tīraḳḳā, six days' journey from Rās al-Ma', was supplied by 'Abd al-Malik ibn Nakhkhās al-Gharfa, who also provided the material for the report on Bughrāt, on the Niger near Tīraḳḳā, on the Ghana–Tādmekka route.[202] Someone else, 'Alī 'Abd Allāh al-Makkī,[203] gave the information on Sāma, four days from Ghana. Lastly, Mu'min ibn Yūmar al-Hawwārī gave information about the route that ran from an uncertain point on the Mauritanian coast (where the boats wintered) to Nūl; he also spoke of the stretch from Aghmāt to Nūl.[204]

Al-Bakrī's method of working is clear. He had no means of directly checking the information that he relied on: so he set it out one piece after another, with no way of cross-checking it as it came from his informants.

We ignore here the more easterly routes described by al-Bakrī. One went from Djaddū or Adjadābiya to Kānem[205] via Zawīla (a major hub of the Saharan links) in fifty-four days;[206] al-Bakrī did not regard it as very important, which does not mean that it was not. This route was not 'connected' with the others, not even with the one that went from Ghadāmes to Tripoli via Djabal Nafūsa in ten days[207] which itself was linked to Tādmekka, Gao and Ghana. Another one led in twenty days from Awdāghust to the oases of the Nile via Sīwa, thus joining a Nilotic system that has been fully described.

198. T. Lewicki, 1965b.
199. E. Lévi-Provençal (1960b), p. 157.
200. J. Devisse, 1970, pp. 110 *et seq.*
201. T. Lewicki, 1965b, p. 11. On travelling conditions on this route see above, Chapter 11: peace was probably only established on it by force in 919.
202. T. Lewicki, 1965b, pp. 11–12.
203. ibid., p. 12.
204. ibid.
205. Al-Bakrī, 1913, pp. 26 *et seq.*
206. ibid., pp. 27 *et seq.* At Zawīla, says al-Bakrī, the country of the blacks begins.
207. ibid., pp. 340 *et seq.*

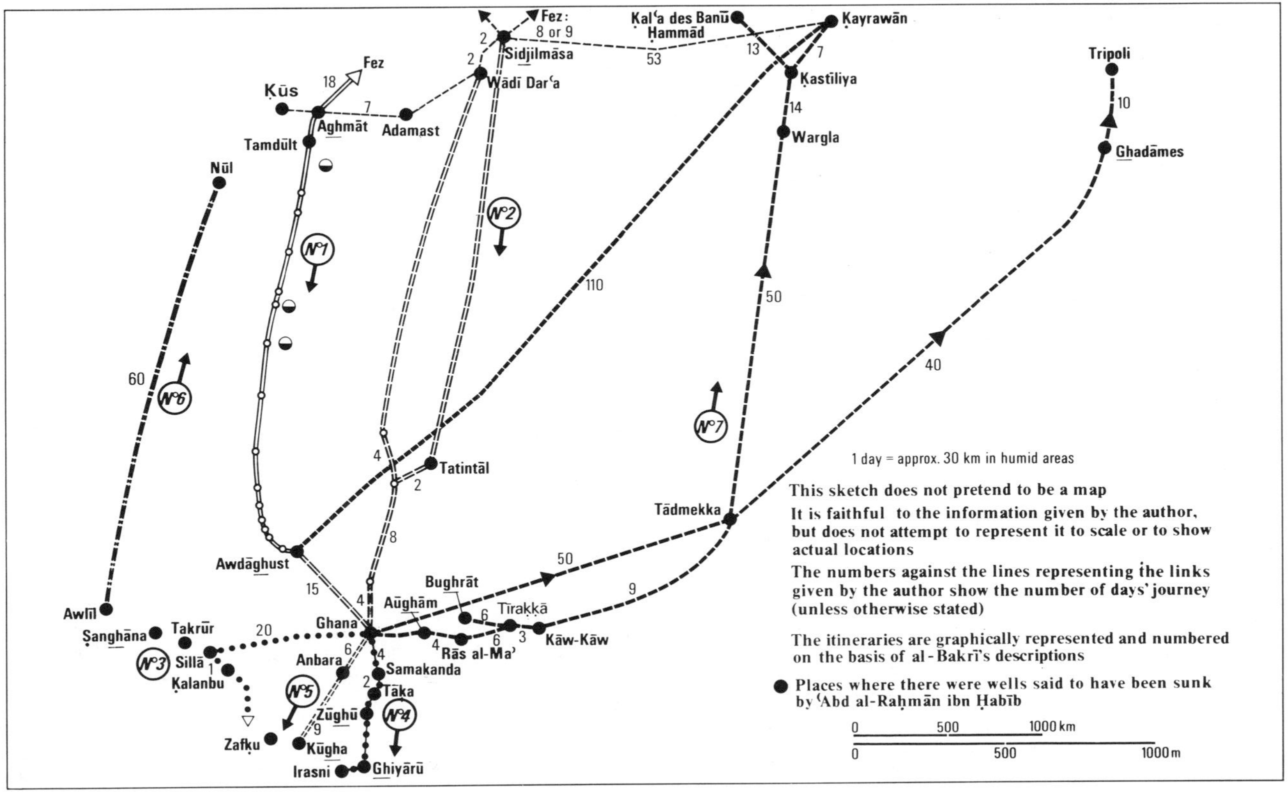
Fez:
8 or 9
Sidjilmāsa
Wādī Darʿa
Kalʿa des Banū Ḥammād
Kayrawān
Ḳastīliya
Wargla
Tripoli
Ghadāmes
Fez
Ḳūs
Aghmāt
Adamast
Tamdūlt
Nūl
Awlīl
Ṣanghāna
Takrūr
Sillā
Ḳalanbu
Zafḳu
Awdāghust
Tatintāl
Tādmekka
Ghana
Aūghām
Bughrāt
Tīraḳḳā
Kāw-Kāw
Rās al-Māʾ
Samakanda
Anbara
Tāka
Zūghū
Kūgha
Irasni
Ghiyārū
110
50
40
60
53
1 day = approx. 30 km in humid areas
This sketch does not pretend to be a map
It is faithful to the information given by the author, but does not attempt to represent it to scale or to show actual locations
The numbers against the lines representing the links given by the author show the number of days' journey (unless otherwise stated)
The itineraries are graphically represented and numbered on the basis of al-Bakrī's descriptions
Places where there were wells said to have been sunk by ʿAbd al-Raḥmān ibn Ḥabīb
0 500 1000 km
0 500 1000 m

FIG. 14.7 *Al-Bakrī's itineraries: western part*

Reverting to the west, we find with the aid of a chart that al-Bakrī's descriptions throw light on each other. Route No. 1 was the 'royal' route, on which details abound, from Tamdūlt to Awdāghust.[208] There were not many links with Awdāghust: it was 15 days journey to Ghana[209] and 110 days to Ḳayrawān,[210] this latter detail being probably modelled on the more realistic estimate of 110 days for the stretch from Gao to Wargla via Tādmekka.[211] In a southward direction Awdāghust seems to have been a *cul de sac*. As for the routes from Sidjilmāsa, on which al-Bakrī was much less accurately informed – routes No. 2 on our chart – which passed further east in quest of salt from Tatintāl[212] in particular, they ended not at Awdāghust but at Ghana.[213] Oddly enough, according to al-Bakrī, Awdāghust was linked neither to the towns on the Senegal River nor to Awlīl: in both cases this seems unlikely, since it had special importance for the former, given that al-Bakrī himself, elsewhere, already names Sillā as Ghana's competitor in the gold trade.[214] As for the stretch from Awlīl to Nūl, its independence is due to that of the informant (route No. 6).

The Ghana system was much more complex and complete. It indicates that links with this town were very important, and that al-Bakrī had plenty of information. But once again the edifice is modelled on the informants. In the south one route led to Ghiyārū. Historians are divided as to the location of the place-names quoted on our route No. 4.[215] The fifth likewise feeds the flames of controversy: some say Kūgha was to the west, others much further east.[216]

The Senegal area is described in route No. 3, but here again localizations and distances are vague. From Ḳalanbu, the last town mentioned, the route led to the 'south'. This was the home of the Zafḳu, in whom T. Lewicki proposes to recognize those whom Yāḳūt later called the Zāfūn and whom

208. ibid., pp. 296 *et seq*. On this route, see the complete geographical interpretation by S. Daveau, 1970, with map. To reach Sidjilmāsa from Awdāghust it was necessary to pass through Tamdūlt; al-Bakrī, 1913, p. 302. S. D. Goitein, 1967, p. 212, stresses that looking at the situation from Cairo, in the eleventh century caravans from West Africa passed through Sidjilmāsa and Ḳayrawān; likewise S. D. Goitein, 1973, pp. 30, 50, 151, gives three eleventh- and twelfth-century texts which show that the route from the west went through Sidjilmāsa.

209. Al-Bakrī, 1913, p. 317: an important point is that he gives this information in a passage which indisputably dates from the eleventh century and was not supplied by al-Wārraḳ.

210. ibid., p. 303.

211. ibid., pp. 338 *et seq*.

212. Only al-Bakrī gives this name.

213. Al-Bakrī, 1913, p. 322.

214. ibid., pp. 324–5.

215. On Samakanda (ibid., p. 334; the people, the Bakam who go naked), see R. Mauny, 1961, p. 126. The country of Gharantal on this itinerary remains unknown (al-Bakrī, 1913, p. 332: a non-Muslim town where Muslims were well received).

216. Al-Bakrī, 1913, pp. 324 *et seq*.; al-Bakrī shows that Kūgha imported cowries, salt and copper.

he localized on the Kolombine, west of present-day Diara, and hence east of the towns mentioned by al-Bakrī.[217] Lewicki even thinks that in the eleventh century this people played an important role in the gold trade to the north.[218] Further 'south' were other 'pagan' peoples. In the case of routes Nos 3, 4 and 5 our knowledge suffers from the almost insurmountable drawback for critical work represented by the heterogeneity of the basic information that al-Bakrī used. Alas, he was neither the first nor the last to do so and in fact it is a miracle that without ever leaving Spain he has left us so much detail to evaluate and criticize. For all that, we must adopt the critical attitude to these sources that their very arrangement makes indispensable.

If we leave Ghana by the bundle of routes No. 7, we repeatedly run into further major difficulties of interpretation: it is noteworthy, for example, that the towns to the north, the east and the south are always said to be four days away from Ghana. What is interesting here is that the piecemeal stretch from Ghana to Gao (seventeen days) is too short, as though the author had been given only a small amount of rather poor information: also noteworthy is the indication 'back to the north' given to the description of the stretches to Wargla and the Djarīd, Ifrīḳiya, Ghadāmes and Tripoli. Here there is no name of a direct informant but the accounts reproduced show that these routes were used[219] at least until the Almoravid domination of the western stretch, and not only from south to north. This eastern network 'from Ghana' forms a coherent whole from its southern terminus to Ḳalʿa of the Banū Ḥammād[220] – hence the information dates from the eleventh century – and to its eastern terminus at Tripoli.[221] There is a good chance that this account represents reliable information for the eleventh century, before the Almoravids. Al-Bakrī mentions a parallel route between Tādmekka and Ghadāmes to look for semi-precious stones; we shall see later that it is highly likely that this route can be completely identified.[222]

Now according to al-Bakrī something was happening at Tādmekka that deserves our attention. The dinars used by the inhabitants, says al-Bakrī, were 'of pure gold'[223] and they had the particular feature of being 'bald' (this is de Slane's literal translation of the Arabic word *ṣulāʿ*). From the way al-Bakrī writes we may reasonably suppose that they were blanks prepared for export to the north that had not yet been imprinted: *ṣulāʿ* in this

217. T. Lewicki, 1971a. Lewicki's arguments are sound.
218. ibid., p. 506.
219. T. Lewicki, 1979, pp. 164–6; J. M. Cuoq, 1975, p. 172.
220. Al-Bakrī, 1913, pp. 105 *et seq.*
221. A wholly consistent delimitation of the area of Ifrīḳiya by Al-Bakrī, 1913, p. 49.
222. It is not surprising that the bundle of data about the links to the north from Gao should fall into a separate account: see al-Bakrī, 1913, pp. 324 *et seq.* Al-Bakrī names the specialist traders at Gao, the Buzurghāniyyūn.
223. Al-Bakrī, 1913, p. 339.

case is presumably the opposite of *manḳush*, which we met earlier. Hence this was not minting but a preparatory stage; the mints were in the north.

Thus without detracting from the value of the texts in question we are inclined to adopt an attitude of discriminating and selective criticism, and to look more closely at the semiological quality of the information – in short to take the view that these sources, like all others, need to be checked against the findings of oral and archaeological investigations. Al-Idrīsī's methods and aims and the information he gives are quite different from his predecessor's.[224] Al-Idrīsī is not content to give a rather empirical description from his 'files' of a set of routes that do not make up a coherent whole. He set out to describe Africa by reference to a rigid framework of climes (*iḳlīm*) and their subdivisions. While he gives the lengths of stretches in days like his predecessor (sometimes taking them from him, sometimes from shared sources), he treats the information quite differently (Fig. 14.8).[225]

As before, the eastern routes can be dealt with very quickly. First, with much exaggeration of the distances, al-Idrīsī studies, in the third section of the first clime, a set of land links from the Niger to the Nile across Kawār. This contains new information that calls for careful critical study. The third section of the second clime is similarly devoted to the description (still with highly overstated distances) of tracks in the central Sahara that emerge in the north via Ghadāmes: this system seems far more independent in relation to the Tādmekka–Wargla route than in al-Bakrī's descriptions. The description of the fourth section of the second clime, devoted to the Nilotic desert and the Nile, seems of little interest. What is striking, therefore, is the attention paid, in the twelfth century, to Niger–Nile and Niger–Chad links and the return to greater independence for the 'Libyan' route that ends up at Ghadāmes and Tripolitania. This would really be something new, if future research confirmed these observations.

Reverting to the first and second sections – and, exceptionally, to the third – of the first, second and third climes, comparisons with al-Bakrī become very interesting. The great meridian route singled out by al-Bakrī has disappeared. In the north, Sidjilmāsa has replaced Tamdūlt;[226] this is perhaps because of the continued obstacle to movement represented by the Barghawāṭa. Going southward, we now avoid Awdāghust and even Ghana. The big novelty is that we come directly to the towns on the Senegal River, despite considerable difficulties due to the crossing of Ḳamnūriyya or the Desert of Nīsar. These towns on the Senegal, where gold is found, are reached in about forty days. From Sillā or Takrūr to Sidjilmāsa took forty days; likewise from Awlīl to Sidjilmāsa; and likewise from the Senegal to Sidjilmāsa via Ḳamnūriyya and Azuḳī. It is true that in one case – a

224. On his methods, see the important study by T. Lewicki, 1966.

225. See Fig. 14.8.

226. The sources certainly confirm the dominance of Sidjilmāsa in the eleventh century. See S. D. Goitein, 1973, pp. 30–151.

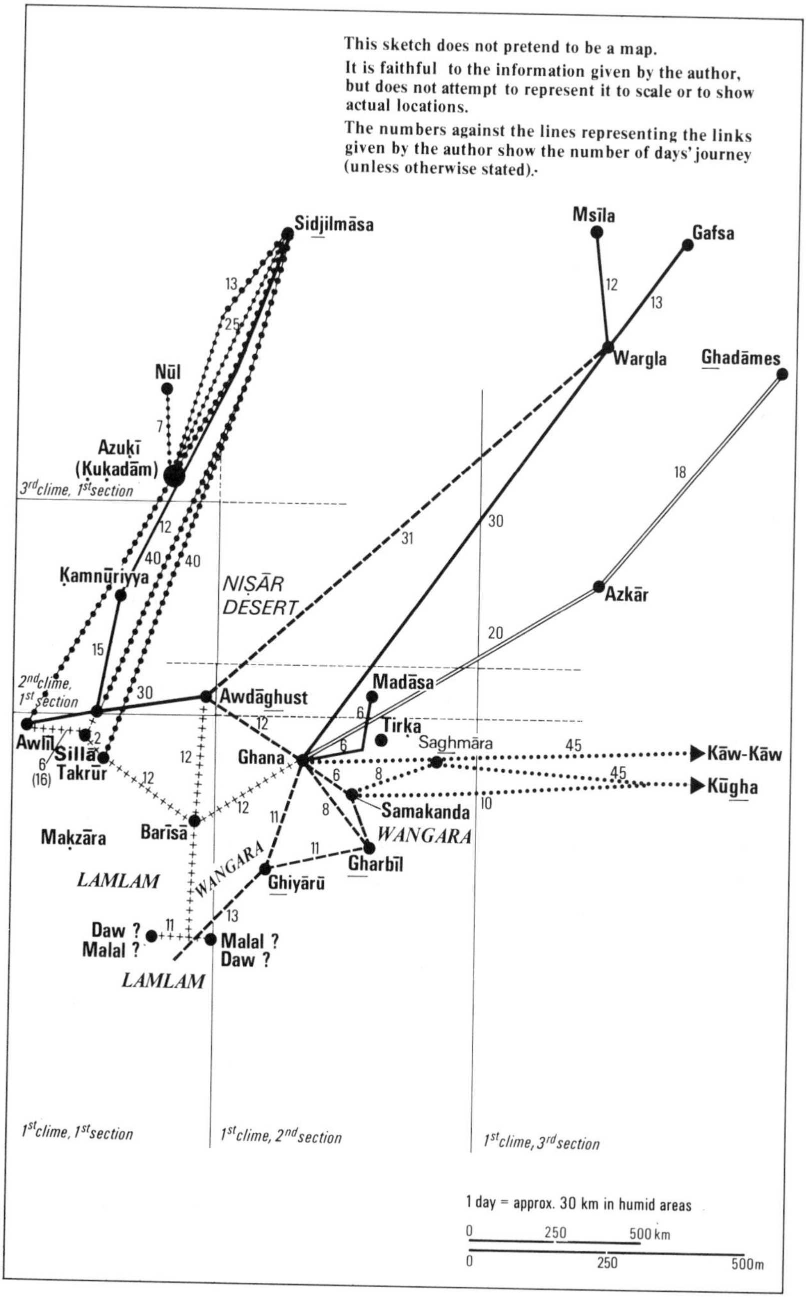
This sketch does not pretend to be a map.
It is faithful to the information given by the author, but does not attempt to represent it to scale or to show actual locations.
The numbers against the lines representing the links given by the author show the number of days' journey (unless otherwise stated).
Sidjilmāsa
Msīla
Gafsa
Wargla
Ghadāmes
Nūl
Azukī
(Kukadām)
3rd clime, 1st section
Kamnūriyya
NISĀR
DESERT
Azkār
2nd clime, 1st section
Awdāghust
Madāsa
Tirka
Saghmāra
Awlīl
Sillā
Takrūr
Ghana
Kāw-Kāw
Kūgha
Samakanda
WANGARA
Makzāra
Barīsā
Gharbīl
LAMLAM
WANGARA
Ghiyārū
Daw ?
Malal ?
Malal ?
Daw ?
LAMLAM
1st clime, 1st section
1st clime, 2nd section
1st clime, 3rd section
1 day = approx. 30 km in humid areas
0 250 500 km
0 250 500m

FIG. 14.8 *Al-Idrīsī's itineraries: western part*

copyist's mistake, or just a mistake – the way via Azuḳī is longer, and that it takes fifty-two days in all from the Senegal to the north: here we are coming closer to Ibn Ḥawḳal's earlier estimates. So from now it is taken for granted that there was a route from Sidjilmāsa to the Senegal River via Azuḳī.

Al-Idrīsī pushes Awdāghust far to the east: one month's journey from Awlīl. Links with it are much less important than a century or two earlier. Though obviously less important economically than the market towns on the Senegal, the town maintained some links which must not be lost sight of. Al-Idrīsī says that Awdāghust was twelve days away from Ghana, and also from Barīsā, which also gave access to trade with the south.

Let us consider for a moment the transliteration of this last name. Barīsā is a reconstruction, but others may be suggested, e.g. Bur. y. sī. It is interesting to note that in Arabic script this other transliteration is not all that different from the Y. r. s. nī found in al-Bakrī. Moreover exactly the same thing applies to Gh. r. n. t. l (al-Bakrī) and Gh. rbīl (al-Idrīsī). The problem may be partly simplified for us insofar as it is legitimate in both cases to equate the places mentioned by both authors, two by two, give or take some nuances of handwriting.

Al-Idrīsī's Barīsā – or Bur. y. sī – like al-Bakrī's Y. r. s. nī – was an important southern location; it was the advance-post for contact with the 'Lamlam' and the Malal. But al-Idrīsī is more precise in his description than his predecessor. Barīsā is also linked, still in twelve days (there must be something odd about this),[227] to the Senegal River system via Takrūr. Barīsā thus becomes a link in both the more northerly systems, via the towns on the Senegal and via Awdāghust and Ghana. Al-Bakrī, by contrast, was less precise about the rôle played by Y. r. s. nī.[228] But also, looking at things from south to north, from Barīsā, Takrūr's domination of the middle Senegal Valley and its hold over the gold trade take on a new aspect, and bring out the changes in equilibrium that had come about over the course of a century in the organization of gold exports.

The Ghana system, which is shifted in its entirety to the second section of the first clime, is both more confused in detail (as though quite contradictory information had come to swell the 'files' of material) and also more realistic as regards distances. But there is inaccuracy in the data for links with the east, to Gao and even to the Niger Bend; from Ghana to the north-east or vice versa, it was thirty days to Wargla (without bothering with the staging post at Tādmekka) and thirty-eight days to Ghadāmes.

227. Arab cartographers are known to have been fond of such constructions. This should arouse critical scepticism or rejection. There are other examples: Ghana–Ghiyārū–Gharbīl are all eleven days apart, and Tīraḳḳā, Samakanda–Ghana all six days apart. Other examples may certainly be found; they have probably been a source of major error.

228. Nevertheless he says (J. M. Cuoq, 1975, p. 103), 'From the country of Y.r.s.nī, *'adjam Sūdān* called Banū Naghmārata get *tibr* and trade in it'.

According to al-Idrīsī, the whole of this second section of the first clime, including the Wanḳāra and the towns of the Niger Bend as far as Tīraḳḳā, was under the domination of Ghana.[229]

We may therefore venture the hypothesis that there were now two major systems competing in the search for gold. One was centred on the towns on the Senegal, and emerged, via Azuḳī,[230] at Sidjilmāsa. It does not need much effort to see in this the direct reflection of Almoravid ascendancy, and even of the policy of the Almoravids, who were allied with Takrūr. The other system, commanding the countries of the Niger, was dominated by Ghana and more closely linked to Wargla than in the past.[231]

Is this an authentic, lasting picture of what had happened since the tenth century or a fleeting glimpse of a brief moment? Have we not here a geography that in the last resort is more ideological than economic, which it would be unwise to trust blindly?[232]

Al-Idrīsī's itineraries, which differ from his predecessor's for the whole of the Sahara area, and quite significantly so, do not constitute the new and decisive material that might have been expected, after two centuries of links, for the areas south of the Senegal and Niger. There are plenty of possible explanations for this, the most probable being that the blacks did not let the merchants from the north travel about much[233] and that conversion to Islam, which was genuine and widespread in the bend of the Senegal and at Gao at the end of the eleventh century, was still hesitant further south. In any case al-Idrīsī should not be relied on any more than one should rely on his predecessors for a detailed account of the life of the blacks south of the rivers.[234] Once again semiology is important and the

229. Al-Idrīsī reports on the opulence of the Muslim town, where wealthy traders live (J. M. Cuoq, 1975, p. 133).

230. It may be thought surprising that Azuḳī is mentioned (rightly, given the importance this town took on after the Almoravid conquest) and that nothing is said about e.g. Tabelbalet, an oasis which at this time probably had facilities for trade with the north (D. Champault, 1969, pp. 23 *et seq.*). It is also true that Azuḳī is described by al-Idrīsī as a prosperous but small town (J. M. Cuoq, 1975, p. 164).

231. Compare this study of the routes with J. O. Hunwick, C. Meillassoux and J.-L. Triaud, 1979.

232. One example, anyway, suggests caution. There is no assessment of the Sidjilmāsa–Ghana stretch, but al-Idrīsī (J. M. Cuoq, 1975, pp. 129, 149) gives a long description of the Madjāba of Nīsar which took fourteen days to cross without finding water: it is a country where the wind blows the sand about. Similarly when describing Azuḳī, al-Idrīsī (J. M. Cuoq, 1975, p. 164) says that it is a stage on the way to Silā, Takrūr or Ghana.

233. The pains taken by al-Idrīsī, as indeed by al-Bakrī before him, to report which are the towns where the merchants from the north were well received, suggests that this information was crucially important.

234. But as we shall see, some new information on the states of the Takrūr, for example, crossed the desert: and some new notes are appearing on towns that were still 'pagan' such as Mallal.

same credence should not be given to repeated information (even if expanded) about the more southerly regions as is given to fresh information about the Sahara crossings.

The siting of trading centres, as we have seen from the start, was closely linked with rainfall; there had to be enough water for the beasts of burden and all the activities of several thousand men. Unfortunately, our knowledge of the development of the environment in the Sahel zone is still very rudimentary. But archaeology raises a whole host of questions (Fig. 14.9). We should like to know all about Sidjilmāsa; unfortunately as things are at present we must be content with written sources, which contribute next to nothing about trans-Saharan trade. The same is true of Aghmāt. We have a little more information about Tamdūlt, thanks to B. Rosenberger.[235] T. Lewicki has given us a highly scientific account of Wargla's links with all parts of West and Central Africa;[236] this shows that we know little about the town's activity before the eleventh century, when it had links with Sidjilmāsa,[237] Tādmekka, Ghana and the gold country.[238] To the north it had trading contacts with the Djarīd and with the Ḳal'a of the Banū Ḥammād; Wargla probably also had caravan links with the Lake Chad area. For the present, we know no more about Ghadāmes than the texts tell us, which is very little.[239] Where trans-Saharan links are concerned, archaeological research in the northern part of Africa has unfortunately yielded as little for the tenth and eleventh centuries as for the preceding two centuries.

Happily, things are better on the other side of the desert. For Azuḳī we now know that the site saw two major occupations: one between the tenth and twelfth centuries and the other between the fifteenth and seventeenth centuries.[240] Work in progress suggests that the Almoravid capital mentioned in the texts is going to yield interesting information.

For Awdāghust the results obtained bring out the fact that in the tenth and eleventh centuries the site was a big town. Industrial activity started there in a non-urban setting as early as the eighth to ninth centuries. In the ninth and tenth centuries, fairly quickly but, as the continuity of the local output of pottery shows, without fundamental cultural change the place began to look like a town, with streets, squares, a mosque, private-enterprise building and the growth of luxury, at any rate in the districts where the merchants from the Maghrib lived. All the excavators have noticed a break in the life of the town in the middle of the eleventh century but it

235. B. Rosenberger, 1970a, p. 79.

236. T. Lewicki, 1976.

237. ibid., p. 16.

238. ibid., pp. 42–3: in the tenth century an Ibāḍite from the Djarīd went to Ghana and from there to Guyāra (identifiable as Ghiyārū); he found the inhabitants of this place going naked, and died in this town (pp. 51–2: discussion about the location of Ghiyārū).

239. Work on this subject is being done by N. Ghali at Université de Paris I.

240. B. Saison, 1981.

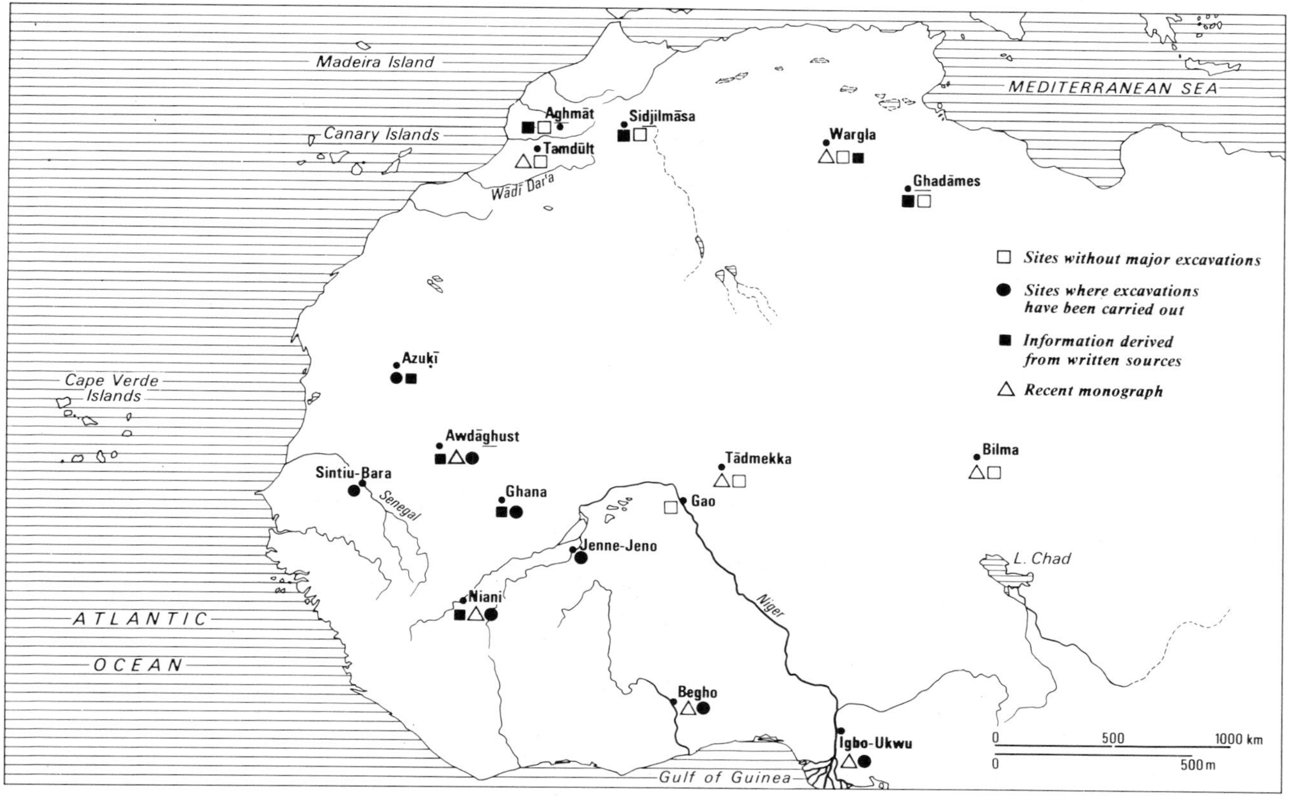

FIG. 14.9 *Sites of trans-Saharan trade, ninth to eleventh centuries*

resumed a different but distinctive way of life after that date.[241] The above datings are confirmed by carbon-14 datings, the glass weights found and the analysis of imported objects. Awdāghust was a town of several thousand inhabitants, very busy in the tenth and eleventh centuries and undoubtedly struck by a disaster in the middle of the latter century. The main reasons for its decline lie outside our chronological framework and present scope.[242]

The excavations at Ghana (Kumbi Saleh) have made it possible there also to measure the long occupancy of the site. Occupations from the eighth to the fifteenth centuries[243] are in layers one above the other to a thickness of more than seven metres and a very important mosque has gradually been uncovered and preserved. The royal capital of which al-Bakrī speaks has not yet been found. Only a very few objects imported from the north have so far been found; but signs of links with Awdāghust are indisputable.

Sintiu-Bara is situated in a historical area of considerable interest,[244] where a great many traces of early urban life have been found.[245] The work done so far does not enable us to connect this site with those mentioned by al-Bakrī and al-Idrīsī. Traces of local metal-working going back to the fifth and sixth centuries have been found there, and also many traces of high-quality pottery.[246] Hence we should bear in mind what al-Idrīsī said about Takrūr and Barīsā, where contacts were made with the merchants from the north: we know what that means from our experience at Tegdaoust, and the discovery of glazed sherds at Sintiu-Bara shows that waiting will not be in vain.[247]

Niani had a more brilliant life in the following period; for the period which concerns us there are no definite traces of links with the trans-Saharan circuits.[248] Nevertheless, the fact that the town certainly existed and probably traded produce with the neighbouring areas makes one wonder about its possible identification with the Mallal of which al-Bakrī speaks.

241. The information is collected together and developed in C. Vanacker, 1979; J. Devisse, D. Robert-Chaleix *et al.*, 1983; J. Polet, forthcoming; D. Robert-Chaleix, forthcoming; B. Saison, forthcoming.

242. See, in particular, J. Devisse, D. Robert-Chaleix *et al.*, 1983.

243. D. Robert, S. Robert and B. Saison, 1976. See also: the annual excavation reports deposited in the Institut Mauritanien de la Recherche Scientifique, and S. Berthier, 1983.

244. See, above, the description of the routes and the map of the sites.

245. B. Chavane, 1980.

246. A. Ravisé and G. Thilmans, 1978, p. 57. Carbon-14 dates: 587 ± 120, 1050 ± 120. G. Thilmans and A. Ravisé, 1980.

247. G. Thilmans, D. Robert and A. Ravisé, 1978.

248. This is not the opinion of W. Filipowiak, 1979, p. 189, who believes that the Arab traders arrived in the tenth century and introduced mud-brick buildings and the cultivation of certain vegetables to Niani. We have some reservations about these interpretations, particularly about the link between mud-brick architecture and the arrival of Arab traders.

Investigations at Jenne-Jeno, based on meticulous stratigraphy and positive datings, are leading to very original findings. Between 400 and 900 a town already existed on this site, near present-day Djenné;[249] and it developed greatly during the following period, from 900 to 1400.[250] Unfortunately up until now the results, which are of crucial importance for regional trade, have had hardly any bearing on trans-Saharan links.

Begho has not yet yielded as much evidence or permitted as many hypotheses. But the mere fact that the earliest traces of activity there go back to the second century of the Christian era shows that it will not be possible much longer to avoid the question of whether goods were not moved about in the savanna area near the forest fringes earlier than has so far been supposed.[251]

Similar speculation stems from the highly controversial results of the fruitful and spectacular research carried out at Igbo-Ukwu.[252] Thurstan Shaw, against the opposition of many colleagues, has wondered whether links did not exist between this area, so close to the Niger Delta, and the north as early as the ninth century.

All recent research radically readjusts the history of technological and commercial exchanges: thanks to it, West Africa is no longer seen as a dependency of the north through the medium of trans-Saharan links. Even when reduced in this way to its proper chronological and quantitative proportions, trans-Saharan trade nevertheless still remains of considerable interest. The changes it introduced in all spheres of activity south and north of the desert will henceforth be able to be gauged more sensibly than before.

The results obtained here and there by archaeology affect economic history and the history of trans-Saharan trade, and it is a great pity that there is still so little information about Gao,[253] Tādmekka,[254] Bilma[255] or even Aïr,[256] to say no more about the towns north of the Sahara. In any case, the historical value of excavation on the sites of towns connected,

249. S. K. McIntosh and R. J. McIntosh, 1980b, p. 190: this was Phase III of the occupation of the site.

250. The fourth and last phase of urban life on this site; ibid; pp. 191–2.

251. M. Posnansky, 1976. In the Dwinfuor district iron-working is attested from the second century.

252. T. Shaw, 1970, 1975; O. Ikimé (ed.), 1980; see Chapters 16 and 18 below.

253. Despite the remarkable research carried out by C. Flight (Birmingham University).

254. T. Lewicki, 1979: little or no information before the tenth century. At that time an Ibāḍite merchant sent sixteen purses each containing 500 dinars, i.e. 8,000 dinars, from Tādmekka to the Djarīd. In Lewicki's view (pp. 165–6) the town was probably in the hands of the Zanāta at that time.

255. The often-quoted article by D. Lange and S. Berthoud, 1977 shows how valuable archaeological research at Kawār would be.

256. S. Bernus and P. Gouletquer, 1974. Whereas for ancient copper metallurgy the results are spectacular.

PLATE 14.6 *Tegdaoust/Awdāghust: oil lamp with reservoir, decorated with pivoting figures; pottery with green glaze. The tip of the spout has been restored*

even indirectly, with trans-Saharan trade seems to have been demonstrated: eveyone will draw from it the lessons of his choice.

Our current image of trans-Saharan trade in the eleventh century is unrealistic and probably over-diagrammatic, given the number of questions, particularly concerning the economy, that still remain unanswered; given also that the first results of archaeological research show that in the realm of the exchange of produce, technologies and even fashions and influences everything is more complex and varied than was thought before.

However written sources and archaeology do enable us to draw up a provisional account of the products that crossed the Sahara. Unfortunately, the information given by the Arabic sources (which reflect the preoccupations of northern exporters) and by archaeology (which takes account of purchases by consumers in the south) do not always, or even often, agree. Al-Bakrī explains that at Awdāghust wheat, dates and raisins were imported at a very high price for a clientele of expatriates from the north;[257] archaeology has so far provided no confirmation of this. Nevertheless, al-Bakrī opens the way for an important piece of research on the trade in dates, which seem to have crossed the Sahara very early, perhaps even with information about their cultivation. No text says anything concerning Awdāghust about other luxury imports for a demanding clientele – those who ate the wheat and the dates – but the excavations reveal a great deal. All the excavation sites[258] show a great increase in the import of semi-luxury objects (glazed oil lamps: see Plate 14.6) or luxury objects

257. J. M. Cuoq, 1975, pp. 83–4. The profit on this trade was certainly very high, even though the consumers and customers were Muslims, like those who sold these rare products.

258. C. Vanacker, 1979, p. 155; B. Saison, 1979; J. Polet, 1980; D. Robert, 1981, p. 209; an increase of 17 per cent in the tenth century; J. Devisse, 1982; 55 per cent of the imports were for the period from the ninth to the eleventh centuries.

PLATE 14.7 *Tegdaoust/Awdāghust: imported glass goblet, probably from Ifrīḳiya or Egypt (?). (Restoration: Mainz Glass Institute, Federal Republic of Germany)*

(cups, vases, glazed perfume-burners and decorated glasses) for this same period: thousands of pieces of evidence of a trade in high-priced goods have been found. For the moment nothing comparable has been found for the same period at the more southerly sites: neither Gao,[259] Sintiu-Bara,[260] Niani[261] or Jenne-Jeno[262] offer finds like the riches of Tegdaoust just described. The same is true for glass, which for the same period was imported to Tegdaoust in very varied forms (phials, vases, cups and goblets, see Plate 14.7)[263] but is very rare on the other sites worked so far. B. Saison has very plausibly argued that even scrap glass was systematically imported, to be melted down locally to make the beads which like other articles of adornment were so much in demand by smart women.[264]

To have a complete picture of this trans-Saharan luxury trade catering

259. R. Mauny, 1952.
260. G. Thilmans, D. Robert and A. Ravisé, 1978.
261. W. Filipowiak, 1979.
262. S. K. McIntosh and R. J. McIntosh, 1980b.
263. C. Vanacker, 1979: finds of complete or reconstructible objects; see chapter by Vanacker in J. Devisse, D. Robert-Chaleix *et al.*, 1983; J. Devisse, 1982: 42 per cent of the glass finds are from the period between the ninth and eleventh centuries.
264. B. Saison, 1979, pp. 659 *et seq.* Many bead moulds were found during the excavations (e.g. Saison, p. 510).

for a North African clientele settled in the Sahel, silver must certainly be added to the wheat, dates, raisins, pottery and glass. It was also worked at Tegdaoust,[265] as were probably the precious and semi-precious stones that circulated beyond Awdāghust. The circulation of precious and semi-precious stones began before 900. It subsequently expanded in step with the needs of a major consumer market, and the provenance of these stones tells us a great deal.

Real agate, which came from Upper Egypt, was rare.[266] Amazonite is more important: Lewicki does not include it in his catalogue of the stones mentioned by the Arab authors[267] but for the centuries that concern us archaeology has yielded many fragments of great interest.[268] The only mines so far identified are a very long way from West Africa: north-east of Tibesti[269] and in the Fezzān.[270] The discovery of large numbers of fragments of this beautiful green mineral in West Africa therefore presupposes some way of moving it all the way from the north-east to the west. Admittedly a very recent study has shown that there are small deposits of amazonite in the Tidjikdja area of Mauritania.[271] Garnet[272] came from the Maghrib; Lewicki shows that some was imported into Egypt during the Fāṭimid period and a beautiful cut garnet has been found at Tegdaoust.[273] As regards the stone that al-Bakrī calls *tasi-n-samt*,[274] Lewicki is correct to reject the translation 'agate' suggested by R. Mauny,[275] but his own translation, 'cornelian' also poses problems. First it must be stressed, to dispose of the legendary imports of Indian cornelian, that there is plenty of corne-

265. B. Saison, 1979: silver jewellery: Plate VI, p. 595; D. Robert, 1980, p. 209: a silver bead, and in the treasure mentioned above, a silver bracelet and three earrings. Be it noted here that according to al-Bakrī, 1913, p. 329, the dogs at the court of Ghana wore gold *and* silver collars with little bells on them made out of the same metals.

266. T. Lewicki, 1967a, pp. 59 *et seq.* Some has been found, without dating or stratigraphy, in the tumuli at Killi and al-Waladji in Mali excavated by Desplagnes (see A. M. D. Lebeuf and V. Paques, 1970, p. 14).

267. T. Lewicki, 1967a.

268. A. M. D. Lebeuf and V. Paques, 1970, p. 14: Killi tumulus, admittedly undated; C. Vanacker, 1979; B. Saison, 1979; J. Polet, 1980, p. 91; D. Robert, 1980, p. 209, mainly for the earliest periods of Awdāghust's existence as a town.

269. P. Huard, 1966, p. 381.

270. T. Monod, 1948, pp. 151 *et seq.*

271. S. Amblard, 1984, p. 216.

272. T. Lewicki, 1967a, pp. 56–7: *bidjādī* in Arabic.

273. TEG 1963, MIV 409. Besides, in the last resort we may wonder whether this is not a different stone. T. Lewicki (1967a: Yaḳūt) reports a kind of zircon, one variety of which is red (a corundum or crystallized alumina) which is very hard and sometimes confused with ruby. Al-Bakrī, says Lewicki, reports a mine where this stone was plentiful, on the Sidjilmāsa–Aghmāt road.

274. J. Devisse, 1970, p. 119, note 2: 'a kind of stone like agate, which is sometimes a mixture of red, yellow and white'.

275. T. Lewicki, 1967a, pp. 53–4.

lian in Africa, in particular in the middle Nile valley;[276] so it is not surprising, leaving aside the distance involved, that we should find traces of it for our period in West Africa.[277] But the definition al-Bakrī gives fits chalcedony much better than cornelian; and many samples of chalcedony for the period in question have been found at Tegdaoust.[278] If we remember that Lewicki's proposed location in the Ahaggar[279] for the source of this mineral mentioned by al-Bakrī certainly corresponds to a chalcedony quarry, this is probably the conclusion. As regards the purpose of these stones, for which there was a great taste in West Africa in the tenth and eleventh centuries,[280] B. Saison was the first, as far as findings at Tegdaoust are concerned, to demonstrate the importance of jewellery combining metals, stones and shells.[281] Lastly, perhaps we should mention the import of cowries, about whose trans-Saharan history we still know so little. They appear at Awdāghust in about the ninth to tenth centuries,[282] and we begin to have traces of trading in them in the north in the eleventh century.[283]

Of course in the case of Awdāghust these imported products were brought in it is worth repeating, for a rich clientele from the north; when it disappeared, after 1100 at the latest, the luxury goods quickly vanished. In this sense Awdāghust seems not to have been (or only very exceptionally so) a redistribution centre for these products imported into the south, but rather a centre for high-value trade between wrought gold,[284] and tanned

276. S. D. Goitein, 1973, p. 283: in 1046 two parcels of cornelian were sent from Alexandria to Tunis.

277. A. M. D. Lebeuf and V. Paques, 1970, p. 14: plentiful at Killi and Waladji, undated; for the period that concerns us here; for Tegdaoust, finds are not unusual: B. Saison, 1979; J. Polet, 1980; D. Robert, 1980; J. Devisse, 1982. At Jenne-Jeno a cornelian bead has been reported; S. K. McIntosh and R. J. McIntosh, 1980b, p. 190, for the period +400–900.

278. C. Vanacker, 1979: fifteen examples; B. Saison, 1979: many examples; J. Polet, 1980 and D. Robert, 1980; J. Devisse, 1982.

279. T. Lewicki, 1967a, p. 54: between In Ouzzal and Timmisao, on a secondary road between Ghadāmes and Tādmekka.

280. J. Devisse, 1970, p. 119, note 1, fully confirmed by archaeological research.

281. B. Saison, 1979, pp. 385 *et seq.*, remarkably cut chalcedony and cornelian beads, cylindrical amazonite jewels; chippings, etc.

282. C. Vanacker, 1979: more likely tenth century; D. Robert, 1980, p. 209: tenth century; J. Devisse, 1981a: more likely ninth century.

283. S. D. Goitein, 1967, p. 154: they were among the goods that usually arrived at ports in Ifrīḳiya; p. 275: some cowries arrived at the port of Tripoli in winter and the consignee complained that these goods sold badly at that time of the year, p. 373: in 1055–6 half a bale of cowries was sold from Ḳayrawān for a sum equivalent to 55 dinars.

284. The texts suggest, and excavation has proved, that Awdāghust certainly took part in oryx-hunting and in the export of hides, perhaps even of the famous Lamṭa shields of which Ibn Ḥawḳal, 1964, p. 91 speaks. See al-Bakrī, 1913, p. 301.

decorated hides, amber from the Atlantic coast,[285] perhaps gum,[286] and the products from the north, of which salt was the only item that could be widely re-exported.

The picture of this trade obviously becomes far more complex as our knowledge gets more detailed. We may now ask a question that research workers will have to bear in mind, namely whether or not there existed in the towns of the Sahel in general a sufficiently rich 'middle class', with tastes more or less like those of the Maghribis, for there to be a demand for the luxury goods in question. At the moment our answer is guarded, and if anything negative for this period; Awdāghust was an exception. Awdāghust was probably also an important centre of copper metallurgy. It imported raw materials, and seems to have made them into quite elaborate alloys and produced luxury goods for local consumption – jewellery and medals[287] – or for re-export. D. Robert thinks that Awdāghust may have been the source of the copper wire used as 'currency' in Ghana.[288]

The results yielded by Awdāghust will certainly be paralleled for all the sites on which similar work is done in the future. This shows how provisional present conclusions on trans-Saharan trade must necessarily be: it was more changeable, more complex and more contradictory than was thought in the past. On the eastern side of the desert, D. Lange and S. Berthoud have shown that the trade of Kawār, which consisted of exports of dates and salt to the south and also alum to the north as far as Wargla, was similarly complex for the same period.[289]

We may therefore wonder whether this trade, under cover of the 'prestige' salt–gold trade, may not have been changeable and drifting, subject to fashion and the balance of power, and less stable than the texts and the fixed nature of the routes suggest: and also whether it really changed life-styles and tastes on both sides of the Sahara.

The time has come to revert to the gold trade itself. Al-Bakrī makes three explicit references to it: one concerns Awdāghust, and the other two form part of the description of two itineraries quite separate from the others (Nos 4 and 5 on Fig. 4.7). The first itinerary went from Ghana to Ghiyārū;[290] first it was four days to Samakanda, then two days to Tāḳa, then one day to an arm of the 'Nile' which the camels forded. From there the route led to the land of Gharntīl,[291] where Muslims did not live, whereas according to al-Bakrī they had settled a little further west at

285. Trade with the coast never stopped, as attested by the large number of shells such as *Anadara senilis* and *cymbium*.

286. Al-Bakrī, 1913, p. 299.

287. C. Vanacker, 1979, pp. 110 *et seq*.; B. Saison, 1979.

288. D. Robert, 1980, pp. 209, 259, 284.

289. D. Lange and S. Berthoud, 1977, pp. 32–5.

290. In Ibn Ḥawḳal this name is spelt Gh.r.yū (or Gh.r.y.wā); in al-Bakrī: Gh.yārū; and in al-Idrīsī: Gh.yāra. Text: J. M.Cuoq, 1975, pp. 101–2.

291. In al-Bakrī this name is spelt Gh.r.n.t.l.; and in al-Idrīsī Gh.rbil or Gh.rbīl.

Yarasnā, where the route ended. The second route, still vaguer,[292] went from Ghana to Kūgha in the south-west, where the best gold mines (*ma'ā-din*) were. What are we to make of the 'gold drives' by Muslim merchants that al-Bakrī's text suggests, which would have taken these merchants far to the south, into almost direct contact with the mining areas? This impetus was apparently much stronger than that described by al-Idrīsī a century later (Fig. 14.10). For the latter the two major gold trade routes were more clearly organized.

The first acted as a link, in towns fairly far to the north such as Takrūr and its dependencies, Barīsā and Sillā, between traders from the north and black merchants who came under Takrūr and travelled around between the towns under its control.[293] Thus there was a system of trade under black control – Takrūr – in an area where a century earlier there had been no such thing, even though al-Bakrī already suggested that Sillā was then trying to compete with Ghana.[294] Barīsā, the southerly point of this system, twelve days[295] from Ghana, Awdāghust and Takrūr, can clearly be located on the Upper Senegal, but outside the gold-mining areas.

If we compare the locations, according to both authors' accounts, of Ghiyārū–Irasna and Ghiyārā–Barīsā, we find that al-Idrīsī's account puts the gold trading centres a long way to the north, and at the same time reduces the area open to prospecting of the Muslim traders who had come to black Africa from the north. There may be many interpretations of such a change. We can now bear in mind that the organization of Takrūr (after 1050, of course) radically altered the geography of gold movements. To fully appreciate the change that had occurred, we must remember that according to al-Idrīsī the route northward from Takrūr led direct to Azukī and Sidjilmāsa.

Al-Idrīsī next decribes a second gold marketing system dominated by Ghana.[296] The most southerly points of this system were Gharbīl and Ghiyārā.[297] The latter, eleven days march from Ghana, lay (on the strength of this information) on an arc running through the Baule, a tributary of the Senegal, and the Inland Niger Delta. Of the two, it would seem reasonable to prefer the Baule, noting, moreover (a further problem), that this would bring Ghiyārā and Barīsā, and consequently the competing systems of Takrūr and Ghana, dangerously close to each other. It should also be noted that Barīsā and Ghiyārā would have been the advance posts of the

292. J. M. Cuoq, 1975, p. 104.

293. ibid., p. 130.

294. ibid., p. 96: '[the king of Sillā] has a vast kingdom, thickly populated: it can almost rival that of Ghana'.

295. Not eleven days, as J. M. Cuoq, 1975, says erroneously in this case, p. 130.

296. ibid., p. 137, 'All the countries we have just mentioned come under the sovereign of Ghana: they supply all his needs and he in turn gives them his protection.'

297. The first of these places al-Bakrī calls Gh-r.n.t.l. and the second Gh.yaru.

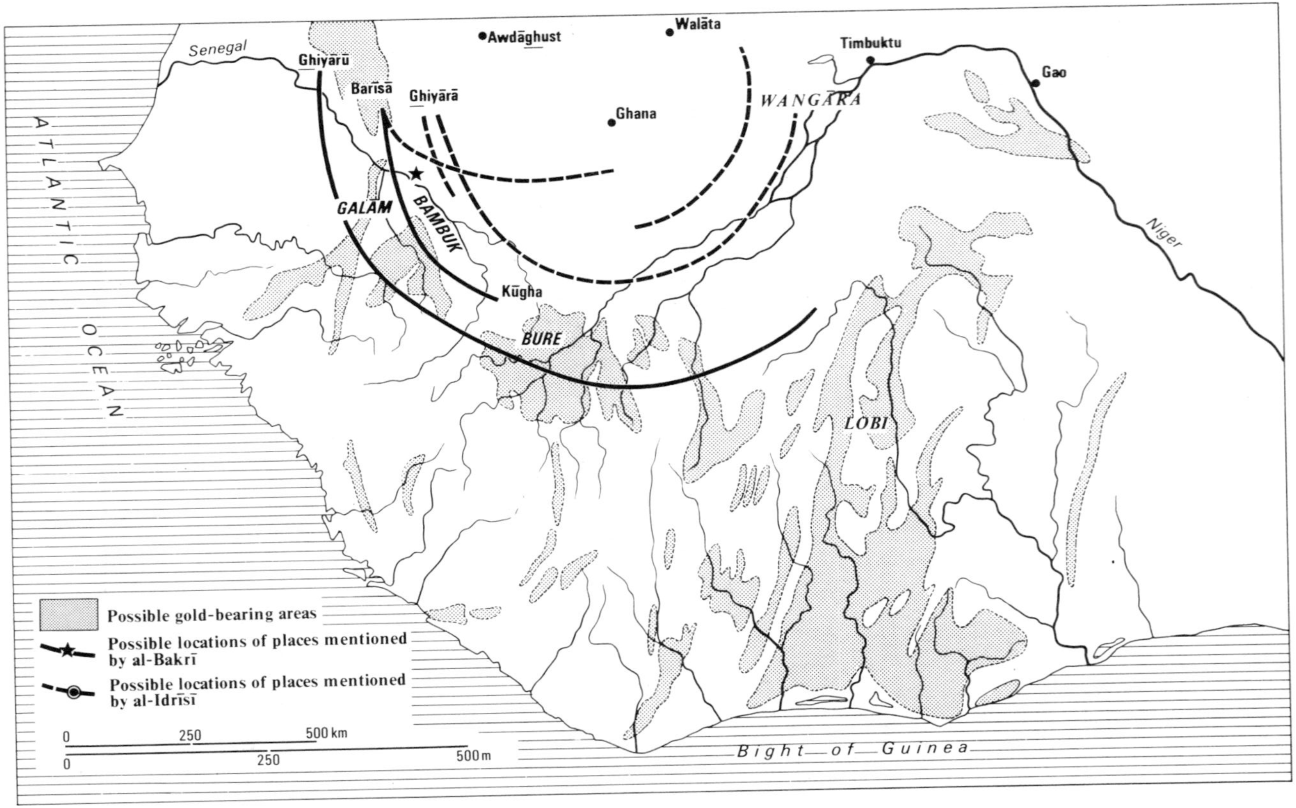

FIG. 14.10 *Gold production areas in West Africa*

two systems in the direction of the mining areas of Galam and Bambuk.[298] Further east the Wangara occupied a vast territory in which gold was plentiful. The very dimensions that al-Idrīsī gives for it (480 km × 240 km), the distance he gives (eight days) between Ghana and Wangara country, his location for Tīraḳḳa, the Wangara town that came under Ghana, and the fact that the Wangara exported their gold to the Maghrib and Wargla – everything suggests that this area corresponds exactly to the Inland Niger Delta between its southernmost point near Bure and the outskirts of Tīraḳḳa. This is a very loose definition of the Inland Delta, but it fits the text well. But once again we are not in the goldmining area.[299]

It should be stressed that much more work than in the past needs to be done on the black merchants mentioned by the sources, beginning with al-Bakrī. Cuoq's translation[300] of the passage in which al-Bakrī speaks of the *'adjam* (non-Arab) traders may be questioned: the main thing is that these traders, called the Banū N.gh.m.ran or Namghmarāna,[301] were once equated by a copyist[302] with the Wangh.m.rāta, and that this gave rise to an important debate: especially since, as all the translators agree, these traders sold gold.[303] The whole question of the Wangara,[304] their location and their economic role will of course one day need to be taken up again. Lastly we must not forget that, although not named, black traders are reported by al-Bakrī and al-Idrīsī at Gharbīl, Ghiyārā and Barīsā, in Takrūr and at Ghana and Gao.

It would be presumptuous to claim to have final solutions for these very difficult questions. At most we need to draw attention again to certain facts. In Ibn Ḥawḳal's time the very vague and remote areas where the blacks lived and found gold were given as one month's journey from Ghana. Later, with al-Bakrī, we see this distance shortened, and with al-Idrīsī we reach a solution that looks reasonable. At the same time the closer we get to this the more we have the impression that the merchants from the north, the informants of the authors we use, did not have direct access to the goldmining areas but had contact with black traders whom we are just begin-

298. It is not without interest that interpreting al-Bakrī's data J. O. Triaud reaches conclusions for Ghiyārū similar to those we put forward here as our interpretation of al-Idrīsī (see J. O. Hunwick, C. Meillassoux and J.-L. Triaud, 1981; see also R. Mauny, 1961, p. 124).

299. In this respect also we feel wholly in agreement with the conclusions of S. K. McIntosh and R. J. McIntosh, 1981.

300. J. M. Cuoq, 1985, p. 102; al-Bakrī, 1913, p. 333.

301. I am indebted for these two readings to Mr Ghali who derived them from the known manuscripts.

302. Bibliothèque Nationale, Paris, Ms 2218, p. 240; information supplied by Mr Ghali.

303. Mr Ghali suggests the following translation: 'the Nunghamarāta [or W.n.gh.m.rāt or W.n.gh.m.rān] who are traders [variant: they are traders] bring the gold to the country and the neighbouring one'.

304. This name appears for the first time with al-Idrīsī. N. Ghali proposes to transliterate it Wan.ḳāra.

ning to get to know. For all that, we need to take account of the hypothesis, suggested by the differences between al-Bakrī's and al-Idrīsī's estimates of distances, that these merchants withdrew northwards between the eleventh and the twelfth century as the reactions of the *Sūdān*, Muslim or not, to the pressure exerted on the Sahel area since the tenth century by the merchants from the north became more organized. Alternatively, the opposite hypothesis may be more accurate: Ibn Ḥawḳal had only an extremely vague knowledge of the land of the blacks on the other side of the Sahel area; al-Bakrī, better informed, still exaggerated the merchants' distances in the south; al-Idrīsī is nearer to the facts, which had not changed since the beginning and marked the firm determination of the black rulers not to allow free access to the gold mines or even a free market for the sale of gold. Much work still remains to be done to discover which of these two hypotheses is nearer to what actually happened.

Cultural effects of the growth of trans-Saharan trade

As regards tastes in food, and their sources, hardly anything changed. The north, with only limited scope to export to the south the knowledge of cultivation of its food plants, wheat and dates, or its fashions in food, exported at high prices to the 'expatriate' merchants settled south of the desert the northern products they wanted. As a transportable commodity dates had a more lasting success than wheat.[305]

The Sahara zone lived without agriculture, except for oasis gardening. According to al-Idrīsī the Sahara got bigger, because the desert advanced, particularly towards the south.[306] In this zone strips of dried camel meat, camel milk and wild grasses[307] made up the staple diet of peoples unacquainted with bread and sparing in their use of water. Snake-meat was an adjunct in the parts where they were common and water was still scarcer, such as the Madjābat of Nīsar[308] and the area north of Gao.[309] The sources say hardly anything about hunting, though it must have been another major source of food.[310]

305. J. M. Cuoq, 1975, p. 131; according to al-Idrīsī, Sidjilmāsa, Tawāt and Wargla were most commonly supposed to be the exporting areas.

306. J. M. Cuoq, 1975, pp. 146 *et seq.*

307. On the place of food-gathering see R. Mauny, 1961, pp. 228 *et seq.*

308. J. M. Cuoq, 1975, pp. 148–9.

309. Al-Idrīsī, J. M. Cuoq, 1975, pp. 151–2. This was the home of the Saghāwa (Zaghāwa?), who used the milk, butter and meat they got from dromedaries, had few vegetables and no wheat and grew a little durra (millet).

310. Al-Bakrī, 1913, p. 321 only mentions hunting in connection with the exportable products it yielded, the hide of the *lamṭ* (oryx) and the fur of the fennec (desert fox). At Jenne-Jeno for the earliest period S. K. McIntosh and R. J. McIntosh have found the remains of crocodiles, tortoises and birds used for food (1980b, p. 188). See R. Mauny, 1961, pp. 257–8.

Awdāghust formed part of this desert or very arid region, but was an exceptional locality because of its water table. In the tenth century, two 'class' diets existed side by side: that of the rich,[311] mainly from the north, who ate wheat, dried and locally grown fruit (figs and grapes) and beef and mutton (which were plentiful and not very expensive), and that of the poorer people, in this case mainly blacks, who used locally grown durra[312] made into a dough or into girdle cakes flavoured with honey imported from the south.[313] Here again archaeology supplements the texts; we have found honeycomb dishes some ten centimetres across which are still used in the south for cooking millet girdle cakes. In the twelfth century, the merchants from the north having left, probably after the Almoravid raid, the town lived mainly, according to al-Idrīsī[314] on dried camel meat, occasionally supplemented by truffles to be found in the area for a few weeks in each year. Insofar as the town survived, it seems to have conformed to the food habits of the surrounding countries.

Westwards across the Senegal and Niger and eastwards in Kawār everything to do with food was completely different. Durra, which was widely grown;[315] rice;[316] fresh, salted[317] or smoked[318] fish; the meat and milk of cattle and more rarely of sheep and goats[319] made up the staple diet. Nothing really changed in three or four centuries except perhaps the

311. We have already had occasion above to draw attention to their love of luxury, which is evident in the quantity and quality of many imported objects and in household luxury. One detail never reported from other archaeological sites in the Sahel may carry final conviction: several kohl sticks for eye make-up were found at Tegdaoust, hewn and carved out of a rot-proof wood.

312. J. M. Cuoq, 1975, p. 149. The durra in question is millet (*Pennisetum*, not sorghum – see R. Mauny, 1961, pp. 238 *et seq.*). Sorghum was rarer; its only archaeological occurrence so far is from Niani (W. Filipowiak, 1979, p. 107) for the eighth and ninth centuries. In the case of Awdāghust a relatively large number of granaries were found during excavations; unfortunately they were always empty for the centuries that concern us here. The profusion of grinding equipment (millstones and grinding mills) for these same periods leaves no doubt about the eating of cereals.

313. On honey, see R. Mauny, 1961, p. 292.

314. J. M. Cuoq, 1975, p. 149.

315. Al-Bakrī, 1913, pp. 324–5.

316. S. K. McIntosh and R. J. McIntosh, 1980b, p. 188; R. M. A. Bedaux *et al.*, 1978.

317. Al-Idrīsī (J. M. Cuoq, 1975, p. 131): fish, which were plentiful, 'are the food of most of the *Sūdān*, who catch them and salt them'.

318. On the possibility that smokehouses existed in the fourth or fifth century see S. K. McIntosh and R. J. McIntosh, 1980b.

319. Oddly, al-Bakrī notes the absence of goats and sheep at Sillā, on the Senegal, whereas cattle were plentiful (al-Bakrī, 1913, pp. 324–5). Between 50 and 400, beef and fish were important in the diet of the people of Jenne-Jeno (S. K. McIntosh and R. J. McIntosh, 1980b, p. 189); sheep and goats only appeared after 900 (p. 191). R. Mauny, 1961, p. 280, already pointed out that the introduction of the long-haired sheep (*Ovis longipes*) into the Sahel seems quite recent.

addition of dates and dried camel meat to the usual foods. In this millet-growing area the nutritional heritage was too long-standing, too well-balanced by practice and too well-adapted to the environment[320] to change. The use of millet beer is also often reported in this third food area;[321] we think we have found traces of it at Tegdaoust, but this will have to be confirmed in the laboratory.

The three food areas were very distinct and hence quite separate and they remained so at least until the twelfth century despite the contacts.[322] Thus it is hardly surprising that none of the very important developments in agricultural techniques[323] that occurred in the north reached the south, where agricultural methods, well adapted to the environment, had remained unaltered for centuries.

Similarly the introduction of certain techniques and objects did not lead to their adoption by the southern cultures. Kilns have been found at Tegdaoust capable of reaching and probably exceeding 1000°C;[324] in morphology they are similar to kilns found at Ṣabra Manṣūriyya, in Tunisia, apparently from the Fāṭimid period, which were connected with glassmaking. They may have been something to do with the making of beads or the smelting of copper alloys: they were no doubt used for oft-repeated attempts to produce coloured glazes on pottery. The kilns did not survive the Almoravid whirlwind. They were not rebuilt after the event; and no similar kilns seem to have been made elsewhere. It was obviously not a question of lack of technical ability, any more than it was so for the production of pottery;[325] these kilns were not something completely and utterly indispensable in the lives of the Sahel people or their neighbours to the south.

The importation of quantities of high-quality oil lamps was followed only by a feeble local imitation.[326] It is uncertain what form of lighting was used in the south.

The arrival of thrown and glazed pottery had an influence that is often apparent on the forms produced locally; though clearly identifiable technical limitations prevented the mere imitation of thrown forms by modelled forms and vice-versa. But these imported objects did not substantially change the output from local potteries, whose techniques, decorations and shapes went back thousands of years. At the most, the con-

320. S. K. McIntosh and R. J. McIntosh, 1980b.

321. For instance al-Idrīsī, in J. M. Cuoq, 1975, p. 132.

322. The insistence of al-Bakrī, still more al-Idrīsī, and much later Ibn Baṭṭūṭa on the features of the *Sūdān*'s food is in itself evidence that the Sahel marked a frontier between types of diet.

323. L. Bolens, 1974.

324. C. Vanacker, 1979, pp. 124 *et seq.*

325. J. Devisse, 1981a.

326. B. Saison, 1979, p. 505.

siderable demand from a people with a high purchasing power over-stimulated output in places where there were colonies of merchants from the north. For the moment, given the tons of pottery fragments found at Tegdaoust, we tend to think that local production did in fact receive such a fillip. This certainly created major problems for the environment: but the continuity of shapes, decorations and techniques demonstrates the cultural stability of the blacks who produced this pottery, even when their customers were Muslims from the north. Apart from the imitation of a few imported shapes and decorations, the pottery-producing area of black Africa remained independent of the one in the north.[327] Nor was it the latter that gave the south its keen taste (responsible nowadays for increasingly surprising finds) for making anthropomorphic (Plate 14.8) and zoomorphic terracotta figurines.[328] In this respect some ancient sites have yielded a fine harvest which gives even more food for thought than the splendid pieces produced in the fourteenth and fifteenth centuries.

The growth of trans-Saharan links, the strong demand for gold and leather in the north, and the more modest demand for northern products (except salt) in the south probably did not bring about great changes in the culture or way of life of the peoples of the north or the south until the twelfth century.

We may think nowadays that these factors were not responsible either for major transfers of basic technology, for example where metals were concerned, either because these transfers took place much earlier or because the south had long since found its own methods of metal production. For copper, which had been worked for at least a thousand years south of the Sahara when the links now in question expanded, we now also know as a result of excavations that manufacturing techniques – *cire perdue* moulds, leaded bronzes[329] and soldering – were developed south of the

327. Much work still remains to be done on the two areas in question. Research workers are often too quick to settle their line of argument in areas in which laboratory techniques give us much help. It remains almost indisputable that the shapes in black Africa are local; that the painted decorations so remarkable at Jenne-Jeno (S. K. McIntosh and R. J. McIntosh, 1980b, pp. 230, 261, 453) are not imitations of objects from the north, and that the tripod and four-legged cups from Niani and the Tellems probably have a common origin on which work needs to be done. Everything or nearly everything remains to be done in this field.

328. Many discoveries at Tegdaoust, to be published in the journals. See already: D. Robert, 1966, and the photograph accompanying this article. See also S. K. McIntosh and R. J. McIntosh, 1980b; Plate IX and p. 189. Recent finds in Niger suggest that there are still surprises in store for us.

329. A. Ravisé and G. Thilmans, 1978. Leaded bronzes are a field for research on their own: indications already exist for Sintiu Bara, Tegdaoust and Igbo-Ukwu, but the direction (if any) in which this technique circulated is at present unknown. Leaded bronzes were also made in Spain and Morocco during the Neolithic period, but no definite diffusionist argument can be deduced from this.

PLATE 14.8 *Tegdaoust/Awdāghust: an unprecedented example of an anthropomorphous statuette (side view) from the pre-Islamic era. The indentations for the hair, eyes and mouth were made with a hollow stalk. The terracotta is coated with an ochre slip*

desert between the sixth and the eighth centuries: although we cannot yet say whether these inventions were indigenous.

In three fields, however, transfers – and not only from north to south – were probably genuinely far-reaching and 'lasting'. The famous article by J. Schacht[330] long ago showed for architecture what T. Lewicki's work revealed for human and economic exchanges: the impact of Ibāḍite models and their crossing of the desert. These are facts which obviously do not apply only to architecture. It would be dangerous, however, to infer the whole from the part, e.g. that the introduction of plans of mosques meant that all building skills were introduced from the north.

But people still often cling to the idea (born of a naive reading of the sources) that architecture as a science was introduced into the Sudan by Mansa Kankū Mūsā after his pilgrimage. This is to confuse the building of certain monuments, mosques and palaces and specifically Muslim town planning, with the art of organizing living space, which is the beginning of

330. J. Schacht, 1954. This study could of course do with revision, but it gave considerable food for thought.

all architecture. Long hidden by pretentious stone architecture,[331] and then by that of cement blocks and corrugated iron, mud architecture is once again becoming the object of attention and serious study.[332] The oldest building at Tegdaoust made considerable use of moulded brick, and walls built of it were to be found on all sides. The art of building with mud[333] and probably with bricks[334] antedates busy trans-Saharan links. This is not surprising given the importance of moulded brick architecture in the culture of Nagada and in ancient and medieval Nubia:[335] it is a safe bet that the African continent very early mastered this way of making use of an adaptable and convenient material.

With Islamization the Muslim merchants probably brought south of the desert their own designs for houses, and in any case the town planning peculiar to the Islamic city. The change is clearly visible at Tegdaoust: streets and enclosed houses very soon appear in place of much simpler lay-outs at the end of the ninth century and in the tenth century. Moreover we may wonder whether some technologies did not cross the Sahara from south to north. When the Almoravid palace at Marrakesh was excavated a wall consisting of two stone-built sections separated by mud rubble was found.[336] At Tegdaoust we have found walls that bear some kinship to this and we may wonder whether the Almoravids did not use a Saharan or Sahelian technique at Marrakesh.[337] The question is only worth raising because another one immediately arises from it, namely that of the painted decorations on the walls. At Tegdaoust for the tenth and eleventh centuries a red-and-white painted decoration, so far unpatterned, was common: it was applied on top of a very thin layer of mud. We may be right to link this with the red-and-white patterned decorations found at Marrakesh and Chichāwa, which date from the Almoravid period, and to wonder about the source of the still famous decorations at Walāta[338] and Ghadāmes.[339]

331. Even on this account alone the received ideas about Kankū Mūsā's role need complete revision. The architecture of Tegdaoust and Kumbi Saleh used stone, and dates from the tenth to eleventh centuries. The pre-fourteenth-century mosques found on these two sites were built of stone.

332. L. Prussin, 1981; an exemplary piece of work in this field: R. McIntosh, 1976.

333. S. K. McIntosh and R. J. McIntosh, 1980b, pp. 189 *et seq.*: between 50 and 900 traces of mud buildings were found. R. M. A. Bedaux *et al.*, 1978: the Tolloy built their granaries out of cylindrical clay bricks. L. Prussin, 1981, thinks that the round house built of cylindrical bricks modelled by techniques similar to those of pottery is the type best suited to African needs.

334. J. Polet, 1980, p. 330. The arrival of bricks cleared the lines and made possible the introduction of corners. On the remarkable brick architecture see L. Prussin, 1981; R. M. A. Bedaux *et al.*, 1978, p. 113.

335. *Dictionnaire archéologique des techniques*, Vol. 1, p. 167.

336. J. Meunié and H. Terrasse, 1952, pp. 10–11. This stone castle, *Ḳasr al-Hadjar*, was built in three months (A. Huici-Miranda, 1959a).

337. From this point of view the Azuḳī excavations are of great importance.

338. G. J. Duchemin, 1950.

339. A. M. Ramadan, 1975, pp. 135, 137.

Discussion has likewise long been underway about the penetration of weaving and cotton south of the Sahara. Let us limit ourselves to that which relates to our period. The nakedness of the people in the Sudan is continually reported by the texts; but this is the result more of the mentality and social background of the editors than of an objective knowledge of the blacks' clothing. Not surprisingly, nakedness and the absence of monotheist religions were to some extent regarded as 'uncivilized'. For the time being archaeology gives no definite answers. Spindle whorls existed at Tegdaoust from the earliest times, but they were only plentiful for periods after the twelfth century.[340] Cotton clothes were probably worn at Tegdaoust in the second half of the eleventh century;[341] cotton plant pollen found at Ogo[342] in Senegal seems to date from about the same period. When describing the area of the towns on the Senegal, al-Bakrī says that at Sillā small cotton loincloths made at Tirinka, where cotton was not plentiful,[343] were used as currency.

If we now put together the information supplied by the texts, the idea is inescapable that in the eleventh and twelfth centuries cotton clothing was still a luxury and a mark of class.[344] According to R. Bedaux, on the other hand, the Niger Bend was already a hub of activity from the eleventh century on.[345] This difficult and important topic is very significant for the history of trans-Saharan links: it may mean, for the period in question here, that imports of fabrics from the north continued on a large scale until the twelfth century: but the question is still very open.[346]

As things are at present, the third topic is still more difficult and tenuous than the previous two. The question is whether the sudden appearance of a demand for gold did not in the tenth century bring about the transfer south of the Sahara of a Muslim system of weighing.[347] The presence at Tegdaoust from the earliest times of scales capable of weighing small quan-

340. An investigation of 155 decorated spindle whorls found at Tegdaoust forms part of J. Devisse, D. Robert-Chaleix *et al.*, 1983; it was conducted by D. Robert-Chaleix.

341. D. Robert, 1980, p. 209.

342. B. Chavane, 1980, p. 139.

343. al-Bakrī, 1913, pp. 325–6.

344. Al-Idrīsī (J. M. Cuoq, p. 129): at Sillā and Takrūr ordinary people wore wool and richer people cotton; at Gao (al-Idrīsī in Cuoq, p. 139) ordinary people dressed in animal skins, traders wore woven clothes and the nobles (?) special clothes (*izār*); at Azuḳī (al-Idrīsī in Cuoq, p. 164) woollen clothes were worn (the clothes of the Gao traders were called *ḳadāwir*). R. M. A. Bedaux and R. Bolland, 1980, reach basic conclusions very different from the foregoing.

345. R. M. A. Bedaux and R. Bolland, 1980, p. 15. It is true that their argument concerns the eleventh to twelfth centuries, and that in two centuries many changes probably took place.

346. At Jenne-Jeno there are no traces of cotton; the spindle whorls found belong to the last stages of development of the site.

347. An essay on this subject by J. Devisse, based on a study by Mme A. Launois, will be found in J. Devisse, D. Robert-Chaleix *et al.*, 1983. Garrard's very efficient work deserves particular attention: see T. F. Garrard, 1975, 1980.

tities.[348] (Plate 14.9), the arrival of glass weights at Tegdaoust, Gao and Kumbi Saleh[349] and probably other forms of weights at other places,[350] lead us to suggest a cautious but fairly positive reply, namely that the basis of a system of weighing probably did follow the demand for gold in the north in the tenth century. But what system was it? Fāṭimid influence is strikingly obvious in the glass weights found at Tegdaoust. Were there not other systems from Spain in the Almoravid world later?[351]

Finally, let us consider what consequences the improvement of trans-Saharan trade had for the states concerned.

In the south either because of conversion to Islam or because of the economic need for a state structure, clearly something took shape (more strongly in Takrūr and Ghana, probably in Gao and perhaps elsewhere) which strengthened the position of the rulers and gave them prestige, power and a new legitimacy.

In the north gold undoubtedly made possible the construction of much stronger state apparatuses than before. The Fāṭimids, the Umayyads and especially the Almoravids derived strength from it which underpinned their independence and influence. Again, the flowering of an exceptionally brilliant and original art may be attributed to the wealth that gold brought to these dynasties, especially the latter and particularly in Morocco. In two centuries the Muslim West acquired an image of considerable importance, even for the internal history of the Muslim world.

The history of trans-Saharan links is one good index among many of the

348. B. Saison, 1979, p. 688.

349. R. Mauny, 1961, p. 415. Initial comments: the weights at Kumbi Saleh were found in the part of the archaeological tell which we know dates probably from the fourteenth to fifteenth centuries, at the earliest from the thirteenth. Hence these are more recent weights than the Tegdaoust ones. The two complete specimens weigh 0.65 gm and 2.43 gm, the three others probably 4.10 gm, 6.54 gm and 7.8 gm. None of them bears any inscription. The weights have now disappeared. For Gao, there are two specimens weighing approximately 5.77 gm and 10.12 gm. These weights are very difficult to classify in any known systems.

350. R. Mauny, 1961, p. 416: Kumbi Saleh, still in the same stratigraphic conditions: weights of 14.85 gm (stone), 14.4 gm (copper), 20.42 gm (iron) and 20.24 gm (iron). For Gao: weights of 14.9 gm (copper) and 9.37 gm (copper), which R. Mauny attributes to the twelfth century. A weight (?) found at Jenne-Jeno (S. K. McIntosh and R. J. McIntosh, 1980b) and weighing about 7 gm poses many problems, and for the moment I would be rather hesitant about its connection with the Muslim system.

351. The diversity of the Muslim systems is well known, both weak systems connected with coins and stronger systems. For example (S. D. Goitein, 1967), the reference system for the Cairo Geniza is as follows: dirham = 3.125 gm; rotl = 450 gm; ūḳiyya = 37.5 gm; and ḳinṭār = 45 kg. The Spanish caliphal system (E. Lévi-Provençal, 1950–3, Vol. 3, pp. 143 *et seq.*): ūḳiyya = 31.48 gm; and rotl = 504 gm, these measures themselves varying according to the goods to be weighed. In Spain the ḳinṭār in the main was 50 kg, and a quarter of it was one arroba, a very important weight; the dirham weight was here 3.148 gm. Thus whenever possible we must reconstruct the system to which the weights found belong, which is what we have tried to do for Tegdaoust on the basis of the weights found.

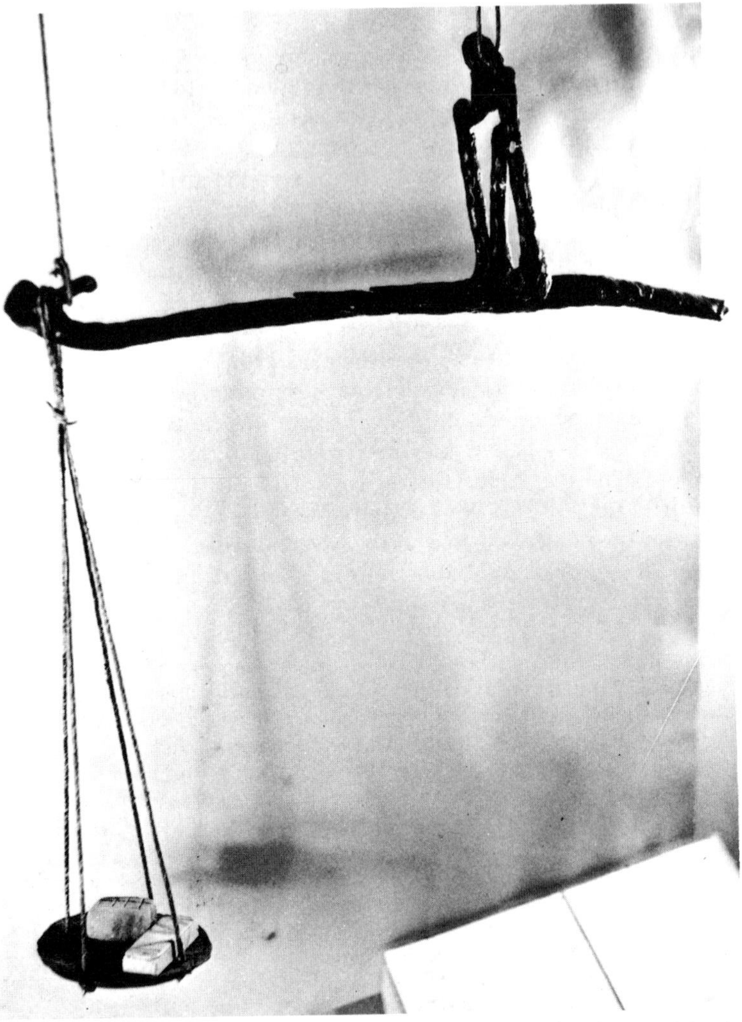

PLATE 14.9 *Tegdaoust/Awdāghust: one of the pairs of scales discovered and restored by the Musée du Fer at Nancy. Hammer-wrought iron, of local manufacture (probable date: eleventh to twelfth centuries).*

continual renewal of research on Africa. Every discovery means rearranging the layout of the picture. Copper in Mauritania and Aïr has in two decades just upset a whole series of long-standing patterns. What will happen when serious attention is given to the scope for exporting Bauchi tin in antiquity, or when serious investigation of the landmarks between the Chad basin and the Nile shows that east–west links have been greatly neglected in favour of north–south links?

So we have tried to open up avenues, to take stock, and to suggest lines of research and topics for consideration rather than to paint a satisfactory 'final' picture of this question. For decades to come the record of this history will have to be regularly taken to bits and put together again in the light of research that is only the threshold of the revelations it is destined to produce. Nothing can better demonstrate the importance of archaeology than this subject; nothing can make people more cautious or more modest about stating the results they have achieved.

15 The Chad region as a crossroads

D. LANGE
in collaboration with
B. W. BARKINDO

The Lake Chad region, which is a savanna zone, has been inhabited by pastoral and agricultural peoples since before the beginning of the Christian era. To the north, where the savanna gradually merges into desert, nomad peoples predominate, though there are also oases with settled communities. To the south, especially along the banks of the rivers that flow into Lake Chad, mainly sedentary cultures are found. The desiccation of the Sahara and the shrinkage of Lake Chad drew peoples from various directions towards the diminishing lake. The coming together of peoples from various no longer viable areas and their attempts to adjust to the changing environment and circumstances form the background of the history of the area.

For a clearer insight into the significance of the historical facts, a precise account of the climatic changes which occurred during the period under review would have been desirable. In fact very little is known about the climate of the Sahel during the first millennium of the Christian era. However, there are several indications that climatic conditions during that period were, on the whole, better than those now prevailing. Particularly noteworthy is the fact that, between the third century and the beginning of the thirteenth century of the Christian era, the waters of Lake Chad flowed almost continuously into the Baḥr al-Ghazāl, which presupposes that the lake level exceeded 286 m.[1] Moreover, J. Maley considers, in the light of various data, that a wet period occurred in the middle of the first millennium, and that the Sahelian region underwent an arid phase in the eleventh century.[2] The area of contact between sedentary and nomadic peoples must therefore have extended further to the north than at present.

Moreover, it cannot be taken for granted that the Lake Chad region was always a crossroads for trade and fruitful interactions. Currently available dates for the spread of iron-working techniques suggest that some populations in the region long remained cut off from the major innovatory trends. The main divide in this regard would seem to be between west and east

1. J. Maley, 1981, pp. 65, 101. Lake Chad's present level is situated at 282 m.
2. ibid., pp. 65, 278.

rather than between north and south. Indeed, it is now known that, to the south of Aïr, at Ekne Wan Aparan, iron-smelting techniques were known as early as -540 ± 90,[3] a date closely concordant with that of -440 ± 140 obtained at Taruga (Nok culture) in central Nigeria.[4] In the region of Termit, between Aïr and Lake Chad, iron-working would seem to have been practised in the seventh century before the Christian era.[5] Elsewhere, iron-working techniques were adopted much later. At Koro Toro, between Lake Chad and Tibesti, the vestiges of a culture based on iron metallurgy have been discovered. Known as *ḥaddād* after the Arabic term for 'blacksmith', this culture flourished only between the fourth and eighth centuries of the Christian era. The painted pottery found on the same sites points to affinities with two major civilizations of the Nile Valley: Meroe and Nubia during its Christian period.[6] Other data are available for the region around the southern shores of Lake Chad. According to relatively unreliable datings, iron was not to be found on the major site of Daima until the fifth or sixth century of the Christian era, and it was later still before iron-smelting techniques were adopted.[7] These few indications concerning the archaeology of iron show that, prior to the foundation of Kānem, the Lake Chad region was remarkable more for its divisions and unequal levels of development than for any unifying factor.

A process of more rapid and spectacular changes appears to have begun around the middle of the first millennium of the Christian era. It was triggered off probably indirectly by the introduction of the camel into the area either from North Africa or – as seems more probable – from the Nile Valley, and its adoption by the Zag͟hāwa and the Tubu. Being far better adapted to the natural conditions prevailing in the Sahara than was the horse, the camel made long desert crossings perfectly feasible, and could transport relatively heavy loads into the bargain. Between the Fezzān and the Lake Chad region, the natural conditions were particularly propitious for crossing the Sahara: a whole series of small oases and natural waterholes and, mid-way, the vast oasis of Kawār, provided an ideal caravan route.

Another opportunity for commerce was with the Nile Valley through Dārfūr and Kordofān. In the absence of any precise archaeological data concerning these routes one can only conjecture; it would seem that in the earlier period trade with the Nile Valley was more important. On the other hand the existence of the ancient kingdom of the Garamantes in the Fezzān was undoubtedly a major factor in the organization of long-distance trade;[8]

3. D. Grébénard, personal communication.
4. B. Fagg, 1969; see also R. Tylecote, 1975.
5. G. Quéchon and J.-P. Roset, 1974, p. 97.
6. F. Treinen-Claustre, 1978, pp. 330–3; see also P. Huard, 1966; Y. Coppens, 1969.
7. G. Connah, 1971, p. 57. Having reassessed previous datings, the same author now proposes +50 as the date of the introduction of iron to Daima (G. Connah, 1981, pp. 146–7).
8. R. C. C. Law, 1967b.

but again the absence of evidence concerning the southern oases of the Fezzān and Kawār, where remains of fortifications of uncertain date are visible to the naked eye, makes any positive conclusion uncertain.[9]

It would seem, however, that as early as the seventh century of the Christian era the central Saharan route was plied by small caravans from the Fezzān, since the celebrated Arab conqueror ʿUḳba b. Nāfiʿ would have found it difficult to penetrate as far as Kawār – which third/ninth century sources assert he did – had the trail not been blazed before him by either Berber or Zag͟hāwa traders.[10] The Kawār oasis[11] was certainly not the final destination of these caravans and the traders had undoubtedly already passed beyond it, to reach the Lake Chad region. In later times the central Saharan route became more important following the establishment of regular trade between the Lake Chad area and the Mediterranean coast which followed the Islamic conquests and the rise of Muslim states in North Africa and later in the Sahara.

In the south, around Lake Chad, a whole series of factors, including not only trade expansion but also the development of better weapons and tools and the evolution of new ways of life to deal with changing circumstances, were to lead to the foundation and expansion of a vast political entity, Kānem-Bornu, whose unifying power and capacity for innovation helped to shape the destiny of the entire region up to the beginning of the colonial era. However, before describing the foundation and early development of that political entity in greater detail, it is proper to give a concise, chronologically balanced account of the principal peoples or, where precise knowledge of them is lacking, of the linguistic groups dwelling between the middle Niger and the Dārfūr mountains.

Peoples and languages of the Chad region

The Arab geographers provide information that throws a revealing light on the early history of Africa. Concerned as they were to recreate as accurate as possible a 'word picture' (*ṣūrat al-arḍ*), these authors gathered geographical data on the Muslim countries and on the lands situated beyond Islam's boundaries. Their information should, however, be treated with caution since most of them had never visited black Africa but gathered their information from traders who were not unbiased and from black African pilgrims many of whom had left home a long time before and may

9. D. Lange and S. Berthoud, 1977; see also H. Ziegert, 1969.

10. Two authors write of the expedition of ʿUḳba b. Nāfiʿ to the Kawār: Ibn ʿAbd al-Ḥakam, 1922, p. 195, and al-Bakrī, 1911, pp. 13–14. The former was writing before 257/871, while the latter wrote his work in 460/1068, albeit basing his account in part on earlier sources. Cf. Chapters 9 and 11 above.

11. The name Kawār is probably of Berber origin, and denotes the 'Blacks' or Negroes. This meaning survived in *ḥasaniyya* (Mauritania) where the term *kūri* (pl. *kowār*) was applied to black Africans whose status was that of freemen.

therefore not have been in a position to know the current situation at home. When describing foreign peoples the Arab geographers often used literary clichés and the names given by them are in many cases generic terms.[12] Thus we invariably encounter references to the *Zandj* in East Africa, the *Ḥabash* in Ethiopia and the *Sūdān* in West Africa, without the defining characteristics of these 'peoples' ever being properly established. In addition to general terms, a few authors also mention ethnonyms passed on by travellers; however, their identification often poses problems. Moreover, the geographical placing of these ethnic entities varies considerably from one author to another. It was not until Ibn Saʿīd produced his *Geography* in the seventh/thirteenth century that highly precise information on the Lake Chad region became available.[13] Only in modern times do we find its equivalent.

Before Ibn Saʿīd, most Arab geographers mention the *Zaghāwa* people when referring to the Central Sudan (an expression used here synonymously with the 'Chad region'). Until the fourth/tenth century, well-informed Arab authors suggest that the Zaghāwa held sway over Kānem; however, al-Idrīsī, writing in the sixth/twelfth century, gives particulars that bring out their purely nomadic nature.[14] Disregarding the lessons to be learned from earlier sources, modern authors have frequently played down the role of the Zaghāwa, either regarding them as a marginal group[15] or, on the contrary, supposing them to be an extremely extensive group, identical to the present-day Tubu.[16] As will be seen below, the Zaghāwa did in fact undergo radical transformations as a result of a dynastic change which occurred in Kānem in the middle of the second half of the fifth/eleventh century. The ethnic balance and the ratio of sedentary to nomadic peoples ceased to be the same after the advent of the new dynasty in Kānem.

The main internal source, the *Dīwān salāṭīn Barnū*, contains an ethnic nomenclature that cannot be checked against that of external sources. For until the end of the seventh/thirteenth century, the chroniclers of the royal court took pains to indicate the names of the ethnic groups from which the successive queen mothers had originated. We know, for example, that in the fourth/tenth and fifth/eleventh centuries the kings of Kānem married women of the Tomaghra, the Kay and the Tubu.[17] Today, the name Tomaghra is applied to a clan dwelling among the Teda, the Kānembu and the Kanuri. The name Kay denotes a Kanuri clan, while Tubu is the generic name used by the Kānembu speakers to refer to the Teda-Daza.

12. Concerning the merits of the Arab sources of this period, see Unesco, *General History of Africa*, Vol. I, ch. 5.
13. D. Lange, 1980.
14. Al-Idrīsī, 1866, pp. 33–4; translation, pp. 39–41.
15. See, for example, Y. Urvoy, 1949, p. 16; A. Smith, 1971, pp. 168–9.
16. M.-J. Tubiana, 1964, p. 18.
17. D. Lange, 1977, pp. 27–32; translation, pp. 67–9.

According to the most likely hypothesis, the traditions recorded in the *Dīwān* refer to the successive matrimonial alliances between the kings of Kānem and the various nomadic groups whose martial prowess the earlier kings found useful in sustaining their power.

Further to the east, between the Zaghāwa and the Nūba, al-Idrīsī situates the Tādjū, whose existence, probably already dating back to the remote past, seems to have been overlooked by earlier authors.[18] According to oral traditions collected by the German traveller Gustav Nachtigal, the Dādjo – probably identical to the Tādjū – gave rise to the first development of Dārfūr as a state structure.[19] The nomadic influence was less perceptible in this region than around Lake Chad. The present distribution of the small Dādjo communities between the Wadai plateau and the Nūba hills, as well as their traditions concerning their origins and their sedentary way of life, indicate rather that they are of Nilotic origin. Nevertheless, in the seventh/thirteenth century, they appear to have been under pressure from the Zaghāwa who, having been excluded from power in Kānem, apparently sought to re-establish a coherent political entity at the southern extremity of the great trans-Saharan route linking the Dārfūr region to Egypt.[20] In fact, the Dādjo surrendered power not to the Zaghāwa but to the Tundjur, resisting assimilation only by withdrawing into areas of refuge. The Zaghāwa, by contrast, were able to preserve their ethnic cohesion, despite the fact that their grazing area had been considerably reduced by the expansion of the Teda-Daza (Tubu). Even today, the Arabs of Chad and the Sudan recognize the specific identity of the Zaghāwa (who call themselves Beri) and the Gorhan (Daza), despite the fact that they survive only in the form of small residual communities, which no longer seem united to anyone but an outside observer.

Taking as his basis a source dating back to the first half of the seventh/thirteenth century, Ibn Saʿīd provides some extremely valuable particulars concerning the Lake Chad region. It is indeed clear from his *Geography* that, in the time of Dūnama Dībalāmi (*c.* 607/1210–646/1248), the Kānem people had not yet driven the ancestors of the Buduma back to the Lake Chad islands, and it is reasonable to suppose that the area inhabited by the Kotoko extended beyond the clay lands (*firki*) of the alluvial plain of the lower Chari. Situating several ethnic groups with great precision, Ibn Saʿīd gives the impression that the Komadugu Yobe valley was still settled by Bede communities (later assimilated by the Kanuri or driven back on to the territory of the Ngizim) and that, on the other side of Lake Chad, the Kurī

18. Al-Idrīsī, 1866, pp. 13, 40; translation, pp. 15, 47.

19. G. Nachtigal, 1879–81, Vol. III, p. 358; for English translation by A. G. B and H. J. Fisher, see G. Nachtigal, 1971–80, Vol. 4, pp. 273–4. See also Unesco, *General History of Africa*, Vol. IV, ch. 16.

20. The route is known by the Arabic expression *ḍarb al-arbaʿīn* ('forty-day route'). It is described by R. S. O'Fahey, 1980, pp. 139–44, who points out its importance for more recent periods.

(today assimilated to the Buduma) still inhabited the *terra firma* to the north of the entrance to the Baḥr al-Ghazāl. South of the lake lived the Kotoko, under a name that appears to belong to Kānembu nomenclature.[21] In all these regions, the Kānembu were therefore already a people of consequence in the seventh/thirteenth century, and it can readily be accepted that in earlier times the area inhabited by Chadic-speaking peoples extended over a large part of Kānem and Bornu. It would, however, be rash to claim that the region's earliest farmers all spoke Chadic languages only, and it would be a mistake to suppose that the sole occupation of all speakers of Saharan languages, including proto-Kanuri languages, was animal husbandry.

South of Lake Chad, in the region of the clay plains of the lower Chari, the Kānembu came into contact with an ancient civilization outstanding for its remarkable figurative art.[22] We know from the archaeological excavations conducted by G. Connah on the Daima site that the inhabitants of the *firki* plains engaged in a mixed economy for an initial period, before the Christian era, when agriculture was practised alongside stock-breeding and fishing. According to the same author, the second period, commencing at the beginning of the Christian era, was marked by the introduction of iron-working techniques. This major innovation had a direct impact upon productivity and upon the process of sedentarization: the intensification of agricultural activities, particularly the practice of flood-retreat cultivation, was to relegate other activities – animal husbandry and fishing – to the background. The emergence during the second period of mud-brick architecture reveals that the inhabitants of Daima had adopted a sedentary way of life quite incompatible with transhumance. During the third period, extending from *c.* +700 to *c.* +1050, the inhabitants of the *firki* plains began to enjoy a life of less austerity: various artefacts deriving from long-distance trade make their appearance for the first time, and the vestiges of a weaving industry are to be found (long before Islam). The production of anthropomorphic and zoomorphic objects appears to have gained new momentum during this period, and, for the first time, Daima potters began to make extremely large earthenware jars, which are today regarded by the inhabitants of the region as the distinctive sign of the 'Sao'. Another major innovation concerned fortifications. In Daima, Connah discovered the remains of a ditch surrounding the dwelling-mound, and it may well be that a defensive wall was erected on other mounds to protect the inhabitants.[23] It would surely not be venturing too far to see the advent of fortifications as the first sign of an external threat that was later to affect the lives of the

21. D. Lange, 1980.

22. J.-P. Lebeuf and A. M. Detourbet, 1950; J.-P. Lebeuf and A. Lebeuf, 1977. The archaeological work of J.-P. Lebeuf is unfortunately characterized by a total lack of concern for chronology.

23. This account of the chronological sequences of the 'Daima culture' closely follows that of G. Connah, 1981, pp. 99–196.

PLATE 15.1 *Bronze objects from excavations at Houlouf (North Cameroon)*

PLATE 15.2 *Primitive anthropomorphous earthenware jar from Houlouf (North Cameroon)*

PLATE 15.3 *Deguesse hill, in the far north of Cameroon*

farmers of the Chari plain to a marked degree. This threat may be fairly readily identified as the expansion of the Kānem peoples.

After many centuries under the political and cultural sway of Kānem-Bornu, the present-day inhabitants of the *firki* plains, the Kokoto, use the term *Sao* or *Soo* to refer to their ancestors. Since the same term recurs in every region in which the Kānem peoples have superseded earlier populations, it is reasonable to suppose that it belonged originally to Kānembu nomenclature, and was used everywhere to denote the indigenous populations which were unable to resist assimilation.[24] In its precise sense, the expression 'Sao civilization' must therefore be applied both to the relatively well-known culture of the ancestors of the Kotoko – corresponding to its established present-day use[25] – and to the earlier cultures of the Komadugu Yobe and the southern part of the Baḥr al-Ghazāl. In architectural terms, however, these three entities seem to have no affinities. Linguistic kinship alone can confer some semblance of unity upon these disparate groups.

Nevertheless, in the case of earlier periods, comparative linguistics provides a number of pointers of considerable interest. It is acknowledged

24. In the Daima region, the Kotoko adopted the Kanuri language only a few generations ago.

25. It is worth noting that Connah, drawing a clear distinction between the cultures of the *firki* plains and those of the Komadugu Yobe, no longer uses the term Sao to refer to a specific archaeologically identified culture.

today that Chadic languages constitute a branch of the great Afro-Asian (or Hamito-Semitic) family. The coherence of the Chadic group is doubtless to be explained by a lengthy evolution of the proto-languages in a geographical environment conducive to linguistic contacts and exchanges. It may be supposed that conditions in various southern regions of the central Sahara became optimal when these received sufficient rainfall during the wet periods. At the beginning of the third millennium before the Christian era, living conditions began to deteriorate rapidly, and it is possible that the proto-Chadic-speaking peoples were already obliged at that time to withdraw into more southerly regions. However, it is not impossible that their withdrawal from Ténéré and the neighbouring regions occurred during a more recent period. As they entered into contact with black African groups they must gradually have lost their Sudano-Mediterranean characteristics. Today, various groups of Chadic-speakers are to be found settled in refuge areas between the Niger and the Wadai Plateau. Of these groups, only the Hausa developed a new dynamism, resulting in a renewed expansion of their language. However, the history of the 'economic take-off' of the Hausa city-states pertains to a later period.[26]

The second major language family of the Chad region is the Nilo-Saharan family. In contrast to Afro-Asian languages, the languages of this family do not extend beyond the black African sphere. The most westerly language of this group is Songhay, which is spoken all along the Niger River, from Jenne to Gaya. Further to the north, however, there are also small groups of farmers (Sudanese) cultivating oases and a few groups of nomadic camel-drivers (of Berber origin) who speak different dialectal forms of Songhay.[27] The second sub-group of the Nilo-Saharan family consists of Saharan languages (Zag͟hāwa, Teda-Daza and Kānembu-Kanuri).[28] Today, all contact between Songhay and Saharan languages has ceased; however, the many lexical forms common to the two language groups suggest that Sudanese herdsmen (and probably also farmers) speaking Nilo-Saharan languages occupied a large part of the region between the great bend of the Niger and the Ennedi mountains. The geographical continuity of this process of settlement must have been broken by the combined effect of the desertification of the Sahara and the advance of the Libyco-Berbers during the last centuries before the Christian era.[29] To

26. See Unesco, *General History of Africa*, Vol. IV, ch. 11.

27. R. Nicolaï, 1979.

28. The linguistic classification followed here is that of J. H. Greenberg, 1963b. Although the inclusion of Songhay in the Nilo-Saharan family has been disputed by P.-F. Lacroix, 1969, R. Nicolaï has shown (in a forthcoming study) that the relationship between the Songhay and Saharan languages is even closer than Greenberg had thought.

29. According to P. Munson, 1980, p. 462, the D͟hār Tichītt region (Mauritania) was invaded by Libyco-Berber warriors in the seventh century before the Christian era. The arrival of the Libyco-Berber in the Aïr by −370 ±40 has been attested (Iwalen site to the south of Mount Grebun: J.-P. Roset, personal communication).

the west, the proto-Songhay-speaking peoples were to initiate the founding of the Kāw-Kāw (Gao), while in the Lake Chad region the proto-Saharan speaking peoples imposed their sway over Kānem. The relatively slight linguistic variation within the Saharan group can be fairly easily explained by the subsequent history of Kānem and, in particular, by the evolution of relations between the central power and the various groups of 'black Saharan nomads'.[30]

The kingdom of Zaghāwa

The first mention of Kānem in written sources is to be found in a text by al-Ya'ḳūbī dated 258/872. This author tells us that in his time Kānem was under the rule of a people called the Zaghāwa.[31] The same people are also mentioned by Ibn Ḳutayba (d. 276/889) on the basis of a report going back to the beginning of the second/eighth century.[32] At the end of the fourth/tenth century, another Arab author, al-Muhallabī, gives a great deal of information about the king of the Zaghāwa from which it is clear that the boundaries of his realm were the same as those of the kingdom of Kānem.[33] Zaghāwa rule over Kānem only came to an end around 468/1075, when a new dynasty, the Sēfuwa, came to power in the same state and drove the Zaghāwa eastward, into a region where they are still to be found today.[34]

But what role exactly did the Zaghāwa play in the founding of Kānem? Al-Ya'ḳūbī states that the various West African peoples he knew of 'took possession of their realms' after a long east–west migration:

> The first of their realms is that of the Zaghāwa. They established themselves at a place called Kānem. Their dwellings are reed huts, and they have no towns. Their king is called Kākura. Among the Zaghāwa there is a clan called Ḥawḍīn: they have a Zaghāwa king.[35]

From the explicit wording of the text it might be deduced that the Zaghāwa were among the earliest inhabitants of Kānem, but without further evidence this is thought to be quite unlikely. The reference to the Ḥawḍīn[36]

30. The expression is used by J. Chapelle, 1957. Concerning the evolution of relations between Kānem and the nomadic groups, more precise information will be found in Unesco, *General History of Africa*, Vol. IV, ch. 10. The following articles containing some more recent interpretations may also usefully be consulted: D. Lange, 1978, 1982a.

31. Al-Ya'ḳūbī, 1983, Vol. 1, pp. 219–20; J. M. Cuoq, 1975, p. 52.

32. Ibn Ḳutayba, 1850, p. 14; J. M. Cuoq, 1975, p. 41.

33. Al-Muhallabī, *apud* Yāḳūt, 1866–73, Vol. 2, p. 932; J. M. Cuoq, 1975, p. 79.

34. D. Lange, 1977, pp. 124–9. On the modern Zaghāwa see M.-J. Tubiana, 1964.

35. Al-Ya'ḳūbī, 1883, Vol. 1, pp. 219–20; J. M. Cuoq, 1975, p. 52.

36. It is possible, as suggested also by other modern writers, that this name refers to the Hausa.

as a particular clan among the Zaghāwa seems to indicate, in fact, that the Zaghāwa were far from being a homogeneous people.

It seems probable that a dominant aristocracy, which produced both the king of Kānem and the king of the Ḥawḍīn gave its name to the whole group of peoples settled in both countries.

Al-Muhallabī, a century later, supplies the important detail that the Zaghāwa (using the term in a broad sense) comprised many peoples. While he does not refer to a dominant aristocracy (the 'true' Zaghāwa) he lays great stress on their king's omnipotence:

> [The Zaghāwa] venerate their king and worship him in place of Allāh the Most High. They imagine that he eats no food. His servants take it to him secretly in his houses: no one knows whence it comes. If any one of his subjects happens to meet the camel carrying the victuals, he is immediately killed on the spot [. . .] As he has absolute power over his subjects, he reduces to slavery whom he wishes [. . .] The religion [of the Zaghāwa] is the worship of their kings: they believe it is they who bring life and death and sickness and health.[37]

The great power of the king of the Zaghāwa, already apparent from al-Ya'ḳūbī's much more concise account, and the very elaborate royal ritual described by al-Muhallabī, must be the result of a considerable number of factors, as has already been mentioned above. It is also unlikely that Kānem was founded as the result of a massive invasion by diverse migrants, as some writers have suggested. The most plausible hypothesis is that a small group of people triggered off state-building development in a region where iron-working techniques had been known since the fourth century of the Christian era (*ḥaddād* culture) and where the possession of horses was not only the mark of very considerable prestige but also a guarantee of superior fighting power. Equipped with weapons made of iron, and having the advantage of contacts, however rudimentary, with the outside world, this group – doubtless the Zaghāwa – gradually brought under its sway the agricultural and pastoral peoples living in the region south-east of Kawār, between Lake Chad and the Baḥr al-Ghazāl[38] the region later to be known as Kānem. The dominant Zaghāwa aristocracy is not likely to have come into being until later, although according to this hypothesis, the Zaghāwa as a whole may not have been ethnically different from the major groups of cultivators and pastoralists over whom they ruled at first. It seems to have been only at a very much later stage, in the time of al-Muhallabī, that diverse ethnic groups were integrated into one and the same state structure.

Al-Idrīsī, in the middle of the sixth/twelfth century, distinguished

37. Al-Muhallabī, *apud* Yāḳūt, 1866–73, Vol. 2, p. 932; J. M. Cuoq, 1975, p. 79.
38. The outfall of Lake Chad, not to be confused with the White Nile tributary of the same name.

between the kingdom of the Zaghāwa and that of Kānem and his evidence has misled many historians about the role of the Zaghāwa in the Lake Chad region. In reality, if al-Idrīsī's reports about the Central Sudan are taken together, if becomes clear that he juxtaposes items of information relating to two different periods in the history of Kānem: the period of Zaghāwa domination and the Sēfuwa period. Instead of putting these items of information into chronological perspective, the author projects them on to the geographical plane.[39] Ibn Sa'īd, writing in the seventh/thirteenth century, puts the Zaghāwa to the east of Kānem, near the Dādjo – where they still live today – and states that the majority of them were at that time under the rule of the king of Kānem.[40] In the light of this body of evidence, we find, in the end, that it is more natural to explain the emergence of the Zaghāwa by the birth and growth of the state of Kānem than to postulate that an earlier ethnic group of Zaghāwa, homogeneous and distinct from the other groups in the region, conquered all the indigenous communities and thereby brought into being the first and largest state to be founded between the Nile and the Niger.

We can go a step further. If it is true that the history of Kānem and that of the Zaghāwa form an inseparable whole up to the fifth/eleventh century, we may deduce that the earliest mention of the Zaghāwa, which we owe to Wahb b. Munabbih, indicates that a state of Kānem was already in existence in his time. Wahb b. Munabbih (d. *c.* 112/730) was one of the famous traditionists of the Yemen in the Umayyad period. His evidence was reported by Ibn Ḳutayba (213/828–276/889). In addition to the Zaghāwa, the text mentions the Nūba, the Zandj, the Fezzān, the Ḥabasha, the Copts and the Berbers.[41] The main point to note is that, according to this early piece of evidence, the Zaghāwa were differentiated both from the Fezzān (the successors of the Garamantes) and from the Berbers. The Zaghāwa were mentioned again at the beginning of the third/ninth century by the great geographer al-Khuwārizmī (d. *c.* 231/840), who shows them on his map both south of the Fezzān and south of the Nubian kingdom of 'Alwa.[42] Half a century later, as we have seen, al-Ya'ḳūbī places the Zaghāwa kingdom in Kānem. Had al-Muhallabī not subsequently described the Zaghāwa kingdom in great detail without mentioning Kānem, we might have been tempted to interpret al-Ya'ḳūbī's reference to Kānem as meaning that the inhabitants of that region had completed an important stage in the general process of becoming settled. All the evidence goes to show that under the concept of Zaghāwa and that of Kānem there lies, in reality, one and the same historial fact: the first mention of the Zaghāwa, dating from the beginning of the second/eighth century, certainly seems to

39. Al-Idrīsī, 1866, pp. 12–15, 33–4; J. M. Cuoq, 1975, pp. 141–51.
40. Ibn Sa'īd, 1970, p. 96; J. M. Cuoq, 1975, p. 211.
41. Ibn Ḳutayba, 1850, pp. 12–13; J. M. Cuoq, 1975, p. 41.
42. Al-Khuwārizmī, 1926, p. 6; J. M. Cuoq, 1975, p. 44.

indicate that the large state at the southern end of the central Saharan route was already in existence then. Moreover, if it is true that in the seventh/thirteenth century the indigenous Kānem traditionists had extensive knowledge of the royal genealogies and that traces of their knowledge are to be found in the *Dīwān* and in information transmitted by al-Maḳrīzī at the beginning of the ninth/fifteenth century, we can even date the beginning of the state of Kānem to slightly before the *hidjra*.[43] The expedition to Kawār undertaken by ʿUḳba b. Nafīʿ in the early days of the Arab conquest shows the importance of north–south exchanges in this region. The control of these exchanges was no doubt in the hands of a Sudanic state beyond the Arabs' range.

Largely on the strength of oral tradition, some authors have taken the view that the *Sao* were the indigenous inhabitants of Kānem, and that from an early date they were under pressure from the nomad peoples further to the north.[44] According to this theory, the *Sao*, being a sedentary people, lived in village communities – or even small fortified towns – and had been organized into chieftaincies since time immemorial. After their subjugation by the Zaghāwa nomads, the latter were believed to have learned from them the forms of political organization which made it possible to establish a large-scale state.

In point of fact, however, none of the assumptions underlying this theory of the foundation of Kānem rest on solid ground. Neither the sharp division between nomads and sedentary peoples, nor the distinction between indigenous and alien peoples, and least of all the postulated existence from an early date of a Sao people (or culture) is a tenable proposition. The Sao appear in written sources for the first time in the middle of the eighth/fourteenth century (*Dīwān*)[45] and they are mentioned by various tenth/sixteenth-century authors: at that time the term 'Sao' was used for a group of peoples established to the east and south-east of Lake Chad and probably speaking Chadic languages. It was only during their long resistance to the expansion of Kānem-Bornu that these peoples developed the forms of political and social organization that gave them their distinctive character. To attribute to the indigenous inhabitants of ancient Kānem the characteristics that were developed in relatively recent times by the indigenous inhabitants of Bornu (situated to the west of Lake Chad) is therefore a gross anachronism.

Moreover, there is no reason to assume that a sharp division existed,

43. D. Lange, 1977, pp. 141–3.

44. Y. Urvoy, 1949, pp. 17–30; J. S. Trimingham, 1962, pp. 105–6, 110–11; J. D. Fage, 1969; R. Cohen, 1962.

45. In connection with the matrimonial alliances of the kings of Kānem, the *Dīwān* records for the sixth/twelfth century the names of some sedentary Kānem clans, but they seem to reappear among the population of present-day Kānem (cf. Unesco, *General History of Africa*, Vol. IV, ch. 10).

particularly as regards ethnic characteristics, between nomads and sedentary peoples, or between indigenous and alien peoples, at the time of ancient Kānem. It would, for instance, be an entirely arbitrary statement to say that the indigenous inhabitants of Kānem, like the Sao, spoke a Chadic language. On the contrary, there may be a certain degree of cultural affinity between the sedentary and nomad groups – such as still exists to this day between the sedentary Kānembu and the nomadic Tubu and Daza (speaking closely related Saharan languages) – and if we accept this, it will be easier to understand how an aristocracy like that of the Zaghāwa (who today also speak a Saharan language) could have come to dominate the rest of the population without the division between two groups of peoples becoming particularly apparent to later foreign observers. Al-Muhallabī's account – the only one to include information about the way of life – suggests peaceful coexistence between cultivators and herdsmen, the power to take coercive action being apparently confined to the king:

> [The kingdom of the Zaghāwa] is under cultivation from one end to the other. Their houses are all reed huts, and likewise the palace of their king . . . As he has absolute power over his subjects, he reduces to slavery whom he wishes. His wealth consists of livestock: sheep, cattle, camels and horses. The principal crops of their country are millet, beans and also wheat. The majority of the King's subjects go naked, wearing nothing but leather loin-cloths. They live by tillage and herding livestock.[46]

The kingdom of the Zaghāwa is not portrayed in this text as an entirely homogeneous whole. On the contrary, the author states at the outset that it comprises 'many nations (*umam*)', which clearly suggests the coexistence of different ethnic groups within a single state structure. At the end of the fourth/tenth century, the kingdom of Zaghāwa evidently expanded considerably, and was no longer confined to the region inhabited by kindred peoples speaking Saharan languages: Kānem proper, lying between Lake Chad and the Baḥr al-Ghazāl, was still the centre of the kingdom, but other peoples on the periphery had been brought under its sway. According to al-Muhallabī, its length was fifteen days' journey and its width the same. In connection with Kāw-Kāw the same author states that the kingdom of the Zaghāwa was larger but the kingdom of Kāw-Kāw more prosperous.[47] It is undeniable that from that time on the largest state in the Central Sudan contributed greatly to the expansion of the Saharan languages and the cultural assimilation of neighbouring peoples. It was only later that the city-states of the Hausa came into being on its western border and the kingdom of Bagirmi was formed to the south-east of Lake Chad, in the

46. Al-Muhallabī, *apud* Yāḳūt, 1866–73, Vol. 2, p. 932. J. M. Cuoq, 1975, p. 79.
47. ibid., Vol. 4, p. 329; J. M. Cuoq, 1975, pp. 77–8.

land inhabited by Sara-Bongo-Bagirmian-speaking peoples, contributing in their turn to the expansion of other Sudanic cultures.[48]

In Kānem, another important development that took place at this time was an increase in the number of sedentary communities, together with the founding of small towns. Al-Ya'ḳūbī, at the end of the third/ninth century, wrote in so many words that the Zaghāwa had no towns.[49] But al-Muhallabī, writing more than a century later, gives the names of two towns, Mānān and Tarāzakī.[50] The town of Mānān is also known to us from the *Dīwān*, and Ibn Sa'īd, in the seventh/thirteenth century, stated that it was the capital of the 'pagan ancestors' of the Sēfuwa.[51] There is evidence to show, however, that in the fifth/eleventh century and the first half of the sixth/twelfth century the kings of Kānem still took their principal wives from two nomad groups, the Tomaghra and the Tubu. It was not until the first half of the thirteenth century, in the reign of Dūnama Dībalāmi (*c.* 607/1210–646/1248), that sedentary elements finally gained the upper hand. This development went hand in hand with the progress of Islamization.

The progress of Islamization

Written sources yield very little material bearing directly on the growth of Islam in Kānem or in the neighbouring regions, and we are reduced to making use of odd scraps of information to build up a very imperfect picture of the process which led first to the conversion of the kings of the old dynasty, and then to the decline of the Zaghāwa and the advent of the Sēfuwa. As regards the beginning of Kānem, it is well established that Islam played no part in the founding of this Sudanic state, nor in the early stages of its development. In Kawār, at the northern extremity of the central Sudan, Islam made a fleeting appearance with the expedition led by 'Uḳbā b. Nafī' shortly after the middle of the first/seventh century, but it probably did not leave a deep impression. It was only in the second/eighth century when the Berbers of the Fezzān and Kawār were converted in large numbers, that Islam began to reach more southerly regions.

48. On the formation of the Hausa city-states, cf. A. Smith, 1970, and Unesco, *General History of Africa*, Vol IV, ch. 11. As regards the origins of Bagirmi, we must probably accept a much earlier date than that suggested by oral tradition. Indeed, the *Dīwān* states that 'Abd Allāh b. Kaday (*c.* 1315–35) waged war against the Lord of Bagirmi (§ 21). Moreover, it would certainly seem that the name *Bakārmī* given by Ibn Sa'īd (mid-seventh/thirteenth century) also refers to Bagirmi (Ibn Sa'īd, 1958, p. 49); J. M. Cuoq, 1975, p. 217.

49. Al-Ya'ḳūbī, 1883, Vol. 1, pp. 219–20; J. M. Cuoq, 1975, p. 52.

50. Al-Muhallabī, *apud* Yāḳūt, 1866–73, Vol. 2, p. 932. In Kawār, al-Muhallabī mentions the towns of Bilma and al-Ḳaṣaba (*ibid.*). Djādo, situated further to the north and at some distance from the great trans-Saharan route, may already have been a staging-post on the Wargla route.

51. Ibn Sa'īd, 1970, p. 95; J. M. Cuoq, 1975, p. 209.

Like many Berber peoples, the inhabitants of the Fezzān initially adopted a heterodox form of Islam, the Ibāḍiyya, thus allying themselves with the Khāridjite faction. The Fezzān, situated at the northen end of the central Saharan caravan route, controlled the bulk of the trade between the Lake Chad area – and *a fortiori* the Kawār oases – and the Muslim world of the Mediterranean. Hence it is quite likely that the earliest form of Islam propagated south of the Sahara by Berber traders was in fact the Ibāḍiyya. Indirect evidence of Ibāḍite influence in Kānem is afforded by an item of bibliographical information concerning Abū ʿUbayda ʿAbd al-Ḥamīd al-Djināwunī, a governor of Djabal Nafūsa, a region where the Ibāḍite sect well survives to this day. It is to the effect that this governor, who lived in the first half of the third/ninth century, knew the language of Kānem in addition to Berber and Arabic.[52] He no doubt learnt the language during a visit to the Central Sudan.

In the Fezzān the situation changed at the beginning of the fourth/tenth century when the new dynasty of the Banū Khaṭṭāb came to power: after that event Arab geographers ceased to mention the heterodox beliefs of the Berbers of the Fezzān, and it is very probable that the political change brought with it a change in the religious trend. This does not necessarily mean that the transition from Ibāḍīyya to Sunna took place with the same speed further south, though Khāridjite resistance eventually petered out there as well.

In fact, nothing very definite can be said on this point, and it is noticeable that al-Yaʿḳūbī – though attesting to the existence of the Ibāḍite sect at Zawīla (the capital of the Fezzān)[53] – is content, in his remarks about the inhabitants of Kawār, to state that they were Muslims:

> Fifteen days journey beyond Zawīla, you come to the town [*madīna*] called Kuwwār inhabited by a Muslim community composed of various peoples. The majority are Berbers. They bring *Sūdān* [slaves].[54]

It is clear from this text that in the second half of the third/ninth century Kawār was inhabited by Berbers; their main occupation seems to have been slave-trading. The other peoples mentioned were probably Sudanic; even at that early date they may have been the Tubu who nowadays live there alongside the Kanuri. Most of the slaves whom the Berber traders of Kawār brought to the Fezzān no doubt came from Kānem, where the king of the Zaghāwa 'reduced to slavery those among his subjects whom he wished'.[55] Al-Yaʿḳūbī himself says that 'the kings of the Sūdān sell the Sūdān [their subjects?] for no reason, and quite apart from any wars'.[56]

52. Al-Shammākhī, *Kitāb al-siyar*, quoted by T. Lewicki, 1964, pp. 309–10; see also T. Lewicki, 1969, p. 97; J. M. Cuoq, 1975, p. 167.
53. Al-Yaʿḳūbī, 1892, p. 345; J. M. Cuoq, 1975, p. 49.
54. ibid.
55. Al-Muhallabī, *apud* Yāḳūt, 1866–73, Vol. 2, p. 932.
56. Al-Yaʿḳūbī, 1892, p. 345.

But this could not be true if we accept the fact that for the purpose of his trade with the outside world, the king of Kānem needed a considerable number of slaves.[57] He must have been capturing most of these from the neighbouring peoples. It was not in his interests that Islam should spread among them, for Islamic law strictly forbids the enslaving of a free Muslim.

At that time, however, the kings of Kānem already seem to have established diplomatic relations with the Muslim states of North Africa. The available sources yield the following information: in 382/992 Ibn Khaṭṭāb, Governor of Zawīla, received a present from one of the countries of the *Bilād al-Sūdān* whose name is not specified,[58] but which, in view of the geographical position of Zawīla, it is reasonable to suppose was Kānem; in the same year, the Zīrīd Sultan of Ifrīḳiya, al-Manṣūr (373/984–386/996), likewise received a gift dispatched by a country of the *Bilād al-Sūdān*, the name of which is not stated.[59] In 442/1031, one of his successors, al-Mu'izz (406/1016–454/1062) received a present of slaves sent by a *malik al-Sūdān*.[60] We cannot be certain that it really was the king of Kānem who initiated these diplomatic missions,[61] but we know that he was at least indirectly in contact with Ifrīḳiya (Tunisia) for according to al-Muhallabī, he wore clothes made of Sousse (Sūs) silk.[62] As regards a later period, Ibn Khaldūn tells us that the kings of Kānem were in touch with the Ḥafṣid dynasty (625/1228–748/1347) from the time of its foundation, and he reports in particular that in 1257 'the king of Kānem and the Lord of Bornu' sent the Ḥafṣid Sultan al-Mustansịr (647/1249–675/1277) a giraffe, which caused a great stir in Tunis.[63] There is nothing surprising about the fact that the king, who was one of the major suppliers of slaves and had some sort of monopoly over their acquisition in his own country, should have courted the goodwill of his principal customers. In the eyes of the Muslim rulers, his economic importance no doubt outweighed any objections to his religious position.

Trade relations with the countries of North Africa and frequent contacts with Muslim merchants could not have gone on for long without enabling Islam to make considerable progress in court circles and certain sections of the population. It would probably be a mistake to visualize the progressive

57. The number of slaves exported northward by Kānem must have been substantial. Zawīla, on the route between Kānem and Tripoli, was according to several sources the biggest slave centre in the Sahara (al-Ya'ḳūbī, 1892, p. 345, al-Iṣṭakhrī, 1870, p. 40; al-Bakrī, 1911, p. 11; J. M. Cuoq, 1975, pp. 49, 65, 81).

58. Ibn 'Idhārī al-Marrākushī, 1948–53, Vol. 1, p. 247; J. M. Cuoq, 1975, pp. 219–20.

59. Ibn 'Idhārī al-Marrākushī, 1948–53, Vol. 1, p. 275.

60. ibid.

61. We have very detailed information about diplomatic relations between Bornu and Tripoli in the seventeenth century: the King of Bornu's envoys brought written messages and presents to the Governors of Tripoli (cf. D. Girard, 1686).

62. Al-Muhallabī, *apud* Yāḳūt, 1866–73, Vol. 2, p. 932.

63. Ibn Khaldūn, 1847–51, Vol. 1, pp. 262, 429; cf. J. M. Cuoq, 1975, p. 351.

Islamization of Kānem as an uninterrupted growth process: it would be strange if the king and the Zaghāwa aristocracy had not tried to curb a movement that threatened to undermine the economic order on which their power was at least partially founded. It is interesting to note in this connection that, according to the *Dīwān*, Arkū b. Būlū (*c.* 414/1023–459/1067), one of the last Zaghāwa kings,[64] established colonies of slaves in several of the Kawār oases and even at Zaylā in the southern Fezzān, a region which today forms part of Libya. This information is of course difficult to check[65] but it is quite understandable that Arkū b. Būlū should have felt impelled by an instinct of self-preservation to extend his sway over the Berber communities of Kawār in order the better to control both their trading activities and their religious proselytizing. The authors of the *Dīwān* do not, of course, state the motives that led to the occupation of Kawār by Kānem, but they abruptly mention the 'mosque' at Sakadam (Seggedine), which may at least be taken as a sign of the importance of the 'religious question'. Moreover, we know that at the same period the king of Ghana was extending his authority over the important trading centre of Awdāghust,[66] and the conjunction of these developments may not be fortuitous.

Arkū's successor was the first Muslim king of Kānem. His name is given in the *Dīwān* in three different forms: Ladsū, Sū (or Sawā) and Ḥū (or Ḥawwā') – the correct form, overlaid by a recent interpolation, no doubt being Ḥū (or Ḥawwā'). The authors of the *Dīwān*, reporting the crucial event in the history of the Chad region, which was the accession to power of a Muslim sovereign in the kingdom of Kānem, were content with an extremely brief note: 'he was invested by the Caliph' (Dīwān, §10). Neither this manner of investiture nor the unorthodox form of the first Muslim king's name admit of the hypothesis of a conversion. On the contrary, it is very likely that after Arkū's death (at Zaylā') the pro-Muslim faction within the old dynasty put forward the strongest candidate it could find having regard to the rules of succession then in force. In the absence of other evidence, we cannot dismiss the possibility that Ḥū (or Ḥawwā') was in reality – as certain pointers suggest – a woman bearing the very Muslim name of Ḥawwā'.[67] He (or she) reigned for only four years, and was succeeded by 'Abd al-Djalīl, whose reign likewise lasted four years. The next

64. It has been established that the *Banū Dūkū* of the *Dīwān* correspond to the *Zaghāwa* mentioned in external sources. See D. Lange, 1977, pp. 113–29.

65. Traces of an early Sudanic presence can easily be recognized in certain archaeological vestiges in the Fezzān: Ganderma, in the vicinity of Trāghen, and Mbīle, to the north of Gatrūn, are fortifications which were undoubtedly erected on the orders of the kings of Kānem (D. Lange and S. Berthoud, 1977, pp. 30–2, 37–8); however, the dates remain uncertain.

66. Al-Bakrī, 1911, p. 180; but see J. Devisse, 1970, pp. 152 ff.

67. If the first Muslim ruler of Kānem was in fact a woman, then the chroniclers' efforts to conceal her real name becomes quite understandable (D. Lange, 1977, pp. 29–30, 67–8).

king, Ḥummay, was the first of a new dynasty, the Sēfuwa.[68] The very short reigns of Ḥū or Ḥawwā', (*c.* 459/1067–478/1071) and 'Abd al-Djalīl (*c.* 478/1071–483/1075) stand in contrast with the long reigns of their predecessors: Ayūma, according to the *Dīwān*, reigned for twenty years (*c.* 376/987–397/1007) Būlū for sixteen years (*c.* 397/1007–414/1023) and Arkū for forty-four years (*c.* 414/1023–459/1067).[69] The shortness of the reigns of the last Zaghāwa rulers may be interpreted as a sign of a serious crisis: after a long period of incubation, when the crucial stage was reached in the growing power of Islam, the Muslims first undermined the stability of the old regime and then brought about a drastic political change.[70]

The advent of the Sēfuwa

By an extraordinary coincidence, the dynastic change that occurred in Kānem around the year 467/1075[71] is not reported clearly in any of the available sources. Consequently there is absolutely no way of establishing for certain the sequence of events that led up to the dynastic change, nor its precise economic and social effects. Since there is a dearth of information about this period despite its great importance, we must make do with what little evidence there is. The first step will be to establish that there really was a change of dynasty at that time, we shall then have to answer the question: 'Who were the Sēfuwa?' We may then be in a position to shed some light on the overall significance of the events that took place.

At the end of the paragraph which the *Dīwān* devotes to 'Abd al-Djalīl, there is a curious passage whose real meaning has escaped most historians:

> That is what we have written about the history of the Banū Dūkū; we shall now proceed to set down the history of the Banū Ḥummay, who professed Islam.[72]

Even since the days of Heinrich Barth[73] this remark has been taken to refer solely to the adoption of Islam – and not to a dynastic change – since the authors of the *Dīwān* indicate in a later passage that the next king,

68. All previous writers, misled by an ambiguous passage in Dīwān (§ 11), have confused the introduction of Islam with the change of dynasty.

69. It seems that more weight should be given to the chronological data supplied by the *Dīwān* than to the report concerning the occupation of Kawār.

70. We cannot completely rule out the possibility that the first two Muslim rulers of Kānem were Ibāḍites.

71. This date is arrived at by adding up the lengths of the reigns given in the *Dīwān* (D. Lange, 1977, pp. 83–94).

72. *Dīwān*, § 11.

73. The German traveller Heinrich Barth visited Bornu – and part of Kānem – in the middle of the thirteenth/nineteenth century, and brought back with him the only two extant copies of the *Dīwān*. We also owe to Barth the first critical history of Kānem-Bornu, which is based on a knowledge both of the country and of the original texts.

Ḥummay, was the son of ʿAbd al-Djalīl. We have seen above, however, that Ḥū (or Ḥawwāʾ) was already a Muslim, as was his (or her) successor, ʿAbd al-Djalīl and this could not have escaped the notice of the chroniclers. Hence the passage just quoted must relate to something other than the introduction of Islam.

It is an eighth/fourteenth century author, Ibn Faḍl Allāh al-ʿUmarī, who establishes the succession of events. Basing his account indirectly on the evidence of Shaykh ʿUthmān al-Kānemī, 'one of their king's close relatives', he writes:

> The first to establish Islam [in Kānem] was al-Hādī al-ʿUthmānī who claimed to be one of the descendants of ʿUthmān b. ʿAffān. After him [Kānem] fell to the Yazaniyyūn of the Banī Dhī Yazan.[74]

The Yazaniyyūn to whom al-ʿUmarī refers are in fact none other that the Sēfuwa, whose name is derived from that of Sayf b. Dhī Yazan. The author says in so many words that the accession to power of the Sēfuwa was preceded by the introduction of Islam.

Much later, at the beginning of the thirteenth/nineteenth century, Muḥammad Bello offers more information about the advent of the Sēfuwa dynasty at a certain stage in the history of Kānem. He refers to a group of Berbers who, having left the Yemen, travelled all the way to Kānem:

> The Berbers found in this country different [ʿ*adjam*] people under the domination of their *Ṭawārik* brothers [called] *Amākīta*. They took their country away from them. During their occupation of the country, their state prospered so much that they dominated the most remote countries of this region.[75]

The first point to note is that the author distinguishes beween two ethnic groups of foreign origin which reigned over Kānem one after the other.[76] This remark in itself leads us to think that the author is referring to the change of dynasty in the fifth/eleventh century. The decisive point is that he makes the second group – and not the first one – come from the Yemen, the homeland of Sayf b. Dhī Yazan, the eponymous ancestor of the Sēfuwa. He must have known that the dynasty that still reigned over Bornu in his days claimed to have come from the Yemen and that it was not they who had founded the state of Kānem, as the *Dīwān* and popular tradition implied, but an earlier group that, according to him, was also of foreign origin.

As to the alleged Berber origins of the successive rulers of Kānem, it

74. Al-ʿUmarī, 1927, pp. 44–5; J. M. Cuoq, 1975, p. 259.

75. M. Bello, 1951, p. 8.

76. In Muḥammad Bello's time the Sēfuwa had left Kānem three and a half centuries earlier to settle in Bornu, west of Lake Chad. Bello, who himself reigned over the 'Caliphate' of Sokoto, west of Bornu, knows this, for he says that the group of Berbers from the Yemen (the Sēfuwa) reached Kānem and not Bornu.

must be borne in mind that Bello's work was written some 800 years after the events under discussion and that in the meantime the role of the Berbers in the Central Sudan had increased enormously, both politically and religiously. The Sēfuwa legend of origin appears to have been primarily the work of Muslim scholars many of whom came to early Kānem from the areas where the Himyarite traditions were still alive. In working out the legend, the clerics were no doubt influenced by the local folk tales and traditions, especially those referring to north–south migrations.[77]

The antiquity of the tradition that tends to conceal the dynastic change by putting the emphasis on the adoption of Islam is attested by Ibn Saʿīd in the thirteenth century. Drawing on sources going back to the reign of Dūnama Dībalāmi (*c.* 607/1210–646/1248) he provides the earliest evidence of the existence in Kānem of a dynasty claiming descent from Sayf b. Dhī Yazan:

> The Sultan of Kānem ... is Muḥammad b. Djīl of the line of Sayf b. Dhī Yazan. The capital of his infidel ancestors, before they were converted to Islam, was Mānān; then one of them, his great-great-great-great-grandfather, became a Muslim under the influence of a jurist, after which Islam spread throughout the land of Kānem.[78]

The great-great-great-great-grandfather of Muḥammad b. Djīl (= Dūnama/Aḥmad b. Salmama/ʿAbd al-Djalīl = Dūnama Dībalāmi) was in fact Ḥummay (*c.* 467/1075–478/1086) and he, as we have seen, was by no means the first Muslim king of Kānem, still less a new convert. The only point in this passage that directly relates to the dynastic change is the change of capital: first Mānān, then Ndjīmī.

Another Arab geographer, al-Bakrī, writing in 460/1067–8 gives us a *terminus a quo* both for the introduction of Islam into Kānem and for the change of dynasty:

> Beyond the Zawīla desert and forty days' journey from that town there lies the land of Kānem, which is very difficult to get to. [The inhabitants of Kānem] are idolatrous Sūdān. It is said that there exists in those parts a clan descended from the Umayyads, who took refuge there when they were persecuted by the Abbāsids. They dress in the fashion of the Arabs and follow their customs.[79]

We do not know for certain to what period this information relates, but it

77. Cf. B. Barkindo, 1985.

78. Ibn Saʿīd, 1970, p. 95; J. M. Cuoq, 1975, p. 211.

79. Al-Bakrī, 1911, p. 11. The fact that this text does not mention Kawār (situated south of Zawīla) could perhaps be used as an argument in support of the report contained in the *Dīwān* (§9) to the effect that Arkū (*c.* 1023–67) had incorporated Kawār into Kānem. But it should be noted that the text does not mention the name of Zaghāwa either. *Co-editor's Note*: N. Levtzion and J. F. P. Hopkins (eds), 1981, p. 64 translate the end of the passage on the descendants of the Umayyads erroneously as 'they still preserve the dress and customs of the Arabs'. The author's translation is more correct.

cannot be later than 460/1067–8.[80] According to the chronology which emerges from the *Dīwān*, that was in fact the very year in which the first Muslim king, who was still a member of the old Zag͟hāwa dynasty, came to power in the kingdom of Kānem. Al-Bakrī, living in far-off Andalusia, could not yet have known of the event even under the most favourable circumstances;[81] and still less could he have known about the change of dynasty, which only happened around 468/1075. So his reference to the 'idolatrous' inhabitants of Kānem squares very well with the information in the *Dīwān*. As for the 'descendents of the Umayyads' who 'dressed *in the fashion of the Arabs*' – and who therefore were not Arabs – they must presumably have been a group of Berbers who had adopted certain Arab customs (at all events, they were not black Africans). This group had perhaps drawn attention to itself by its insubordination to authority and it may quite possibly have been one of the forces that were later to contribute to the success of the pro-Muslim faction within the old dynasty before they brought about the downfall of that dynasty.

Of all the Arab authors, al-Idrīsī (who wrote in 549/1154) should have given us the most accurate account of the changes that took place in Kānem – and the surrounding area – in the second half of the fifth/eleventh century. Writing only three-quarters of a century after the fall of the Zag͟hāwa, he had access to a wealth of information, most of it transmitted to him orally but also some derived from written sources. But in fact al-Idrīsī muddled all his material together, and also threw in some details that were pure inventions. Hence his description of the *Bilād al-Sūdān* must only be used with the greatest caution.

Nevertheless, it emerges from the mass of information provided by al-Idrīsī that in his day 'Kānem' and 'Zag͟hāwa' were two separate entities. All the evidence goes to show that the Zag͟hāwa no longer ruled over Kānem: having lost their ancient privileges, they were apparently living in quite wretched conditions. Most of them seem to have been nomads. Nothing specific is said about the new rulers of Kānem, but some of the author's remarks suggest that the Zag͟hāwa were their subjects. There is the same vagueness about the capital: Mānān and Nd͟jīmi are both mentioned, and Mānān seems to have been the more important town, but it is not clear from the text whether it was the capital of Kānem. No information is given about the religious situation.[82]

It will be deduced from what has gone before that the dynastic change

80. Al-Bakrī bases his account on oral information – some of which dates from a period just preceding the time when he was writing – and also on written sources, the main one as regards the *Bilād al-Sūdan* being a work by Yūsuf al-Warrāk (292/904–5–363/973–4).

81. Al-Bakrī wrote in 460/1067–8. If we add up the lengths of the reigns given in the *Dīwān*, we find that Ḥu (or Ḥawwāʿ) must have come to power in the eighth month of the year 460 AH).

82. Al-Idrīsī, 1866, pp. 12–15, 33–5. A more detailed analysis of this passage will be found in D. Lange, 1977, pp. 124–9.

referred to by Muḥammad Bello and the coming to power of the Yazaniyyūn reported by al-ʿUmarī must have taken place between al-Bakrī's time (460/1067–8) and al-Idrīsī's (549/1154). The dynastic change is then seen to coincide with the expulsion of the Zaghāwa from Kānem. This is as far as we can go on the strength of outside sources, but from analysis of the *Dīwān*, the range of dates for this event which is of crucial importance for the history of the Central Sudan, can be narrowed down to the beginning of Ḥummay's reign (*c.* 467/1075–478/1086) for his predecessor, ʿAbd al-Djalīl, was the last king of the *Banū Dūkū* line and Ḥummay was to be the first of the *Banū Ḥummay* line. The distinction drawn between these two royal houses thus signifies that there was a sharp break in dynastic continuity; it does not coincide with the introduction of Islam.

Who were the new rulers of Kānem? The *Dīwān* provides no answer to this question: while linking Ḥummay genealogically with his predecessor, its authors are silent about his true paternal ancestry.[83] However, the traditions of Kānem and Borno which have been committed to writing in recent times say generally that the new dynasty was descendent from Sayf b. Dhī Yazan.[84]

Several authors have commented on the origin of this new dynasty. Abdullahi Smith suggested that they were a product of the nomad/semi-nomad world, probably Tubu who allied with the other groups through marriage relations in order to come to power. This appears also to be the view of John Lavers.[85] Nur Alkali as well as Bawuro Barkindo believe that they were of local origin but attempted to assume foreign origins in order to gain prestige.[86]

We know that it was during the rule of Ḥummay or of his successors that the Sayfid *niṣba* was introduced. Sayf Ibn Dhī Yazan was a Yemenite hero who, according to legend, helped drive the Ethiopians out of the Yemen in the second half of the sixth century of the Christian era. And it is known that the Berbers of North Africa liked to claim Yemenite descent in order to differentiate themselves from the Adnanite Arabs of the Nadjd and the Ḥidjāz. This attitude was the equivalent in the genealogical field of the adoption of the Khāridjite heterodoxy in religious matters.

It should be noted, however, that Sayf b. Dhī Yazan distinguished himself in battle against an African people. The theme of war between white Muslim Arabs (at a time before the Prophet!) and black Africans who prac-

83. His mother was a Kay [Koyam] – a people of unknown origin – by the name of Takrama, the prefix *ta–* possibly indicating Berber influence. The analysis of the name Ḥummay itself shows the possibility of being derived from the name Muḥammad [loss of the prefix *Mu–* and the ending *–d*, acquisition of a new suffix] as a hypochoristicon, which is still common today among the Tawāriḳ, and other people who were Islamized through Berber influence.

84. Cf. A. Smith, 1971, pp. 165–6.

85. ibid., pp. 166–7; J. E. Lavers, 1980, p. 190.

86. N. Alkali, 1980, pp. 2 ff; B. Barkindo, 1985.

tised a traditional religion (though the Ethiopians were in fact Christians!) came to appeal strongly to the imagination of certain classes of Arabs. In Egypt this theme eventually took the form of a true folk tale or novel which exalts the powers of Sayf b. Dhī Yazan in his innumerable battles with the 'impious blacks'.[87]

Whether those who introduced this strange genealogical concept into the black African environment of the Central Sudan were aware of its racialist overtones remains uncertain. That they were Berbers cannot be doubted; in North Africa the Himyarite legend was still current. H. T. Norris has found out that the Himyarite saga has been ancient and widespread among the Berbers of North Africa and the Sahara.[88] Those who flaunted the name of Sayf b. Dhī Yazan could not have been either Sudanese or Arabs, both of whom had highly respectable genealogies, whereas on the other hand the Berbers were proud of their Himyarite Yemeni origin. The Berber Muslim clerics who elaborated the Sayfid *niṣba* were doubtless attracted also by the similarity in meaning or usage between 'Kānem' meaning South of Teda-Daza, and 'Yemen' often used colloquially to mean south.[89]

All that can be said here is that the Sēfuwa appear to have been of a different genealogy from their Zaghāwa predecessors and that their coming to power was not connected with the introduction of Islam since Ḥummay was not the first Muslim ruler of Kānem. Although there is no concrete evidence to show that the Sēfuwa were not of local origins, there is equally none to say convincingly that they were.

It has been shown that the Islamization of the Central Sudan started with the conversion of the inhabitants of Kawār, who later became the main agents of the expansion of Islam into the kingdom of the Zaghāwa. In Ḥummay's time (467/1075–478/1086) the gradual infiltration of Islam into the various sections of the population had been going on for at least two centuries. The political authorities eventually found that they could not remain indifferent to this process for it was bound to undermine the king's absolute power over his subjects and at the same time help to weaken the position of the Zaghāwa aristocracy. We have seen that the king probably enjoyed a monopoly of the acquisition of slaves and it was clearly in the Berber traders' interests to break the royal monopoly so as to have more direct access to the sources of supply. As for the Zaghāwa artistocracy, it can probably be regarded as the means whereby the king exercised his power over the common people. On the other hand, it was in the interests of the various peoples integrated into the kingdom to embrace Islam as a protection against the king's arbitrary power.

87. R. Paret, 1924, p. 88, has shown that the written form of this tale dates from the beginning of the ninth/fifteenth century. Oral versions certainly existed from a much earlier date.

88. H. T. Norris, 1972, p. 28.

89. Cf. J. E. Lavers, 1980 and B. Barkindo, 1985.

But at the end of the eleventh century, Islam was still restricted to the narrow circles of the royal court and the aristocracy, and it was only much later, at the time of Dūnama Dībalāmi (*c.* 607/1210–646/1248) when it became the instrument of an expansionist policy, that it was able to bridge the gap separating the ruling aristocracy from the ruled peoples and thereby to become a truly popular religion.[90]

Ḥummay came to power in Kānem around the year 468/1075. At the same period, the Berber movement of the Almoravids in the western Sahara was driving southwards to conquer the kingdom of Ghana, where it set up a Muslim dynasty.[91] Further to the east, the Almoravid movement resulted a little later in the establishment of a new Muslim dynasty in the kingdom of Kāw-Kāw (Gao) on the east bank of the Niger.[92] It would not be unreasonable to suppose that the movement led by Ḥummay in the Central Sudan was one of the consequences of the religious ferment that had been stirred up, in a different economic context, among the western Berbers. But unlike the new dynasties of the Western Sudan, the Sēfuwa of Kānem were integrated into an African context, thus ensuring the continuity of the state tradition they had inherited. A century and a half after their seizure of power, the Sēfuwa kings were doing their utmost to eradicate the memory of their real origins and so they linked themselves directly with their Zag͟hāwa predecessors. In the end, the state institutions had proved to be stronger than all particularist tendencies.

90. The theory of a decline of Islam at the beginning of the Sēfuwa period is presented in greater detail in D. Lange, 1978.

91. According to al-Zuhrī, the conquest of Ghana by the Almoravids took place in 469/1076–7 (cf. al-Zuhrī, 1968, pp. 182–3). But cf. Chapter 13 above.

92. J. O. Hunwick, 1980.

16

The Guinea zone: general situation

written in 1977

THURSTAN SHAW

Introduction

I once characterized the thousand years before +1000 in West Africa as 'the silent millennium'.[1] I pointed out how serious for our knowledge of history this silence is, since it must have contained the formative periods essential for the subsequent emergence of those kingdoms and religious centres whose existence we can perceive at the end of the millennium or at the beginning of the next. The time depths of this silent millennium are for the most part too great to be reached by oral traditions;[2] from archaeological evidence more is known about the last few millennia before the Christian era than about the first millennium of the Christian era. This is partly an accident or due to the nature of the sites that have been archaeologically investigated, but in part it may truly represent a change in the way people lived and which has happened hitherto to have brought their remains less prominently to the notice of archaeologists (see below p. 466). In the succeeding centuries, on the other hand, not only do we begin to get historical records but the association of works of art with centralized social and political institutions, which has attracted the attention of both archaeologists and art historians. However, we must try to put together as much of the picture as we can; sometimes this may involve merely recording data we have without being able to interpret it clearly or synthesize it into any more general scheme of things.

The expansion of agriculture

Early developments

The change in the way of life of fundamental importance for our period is from one whose subsistence base was in hunting, gathering and fishing to one in which it depended upon agriculture and stock-raising – or at least depended most upon these activities – because even with fully fledged

1. Cf. Unesco, *General History of Africa*, Vol. I, ch. 24.
2. D. P. Henige, 1974.

farming systems, hunting, gathering and fishing continued to contribute to the food supply, even if not in a major degree. In considering this change as it affected the Guinea zone we should not think of it as a sharp break with the past, as a totally new practice suddenly imported into the area, as happened in many parts of eastern and southern Africa. There are likely to have been many 'stages' through which agriculture and food-production passed; initially the earliest planned seed-sowing of indigenous African cereals south of the Sahara, or in the southern part of what is nowadays the Sahara Desert itself, may simply have been a rather desperate resort of sedentary or semi-sedentary fisherfolk during a period of increasing aridity. Such people would have been accustomed to gaining their livelihood by combining in their diet food drawn from the aquatic resources of their habitat together with grain collected from the wild stands of suitable grasses growing in the neighbourhood. It is probable that with a reduction of fishable areas of water available to them, a greater proportion than before of the food supply would have been derived from this grain. With continuing desiccation the stands of wild grasses would have become thinner and thinner and it would have been necessary to go further afield to harvest them. People always tend to cling to the way of life that they know, and to be able to do this in such a situation, the logical adaptation was to make the wild grass grow more abundantly and nearer the home base, by planting seeds near the dwindling lakes and rivers. It was no discovery that grasses and many other plants grew out of the seeds of the previous year's crop after they have fallen into the ground; folk who gather food from the wild are well aware of this, only before there was no point in *making* it happen, since Nature did it for you! At first this artificial planting was regarded as a temporary expedient, but as time went on more and more reliance had to be placed on it. In this way there was no sudden switch from hunting, gathering and fishing to agriculture, but a progressive change in the proportions of different types of food.[3] Once man had consistently taken a hand in propagating the cereal grasses, genetic changes began to take place in them. This resulted in the process of 'domestication' and in improving them for purposes of human cultivation, harvesting and human consumption.[4]

The exploitation of the oil palm – the most important tree crop of the Guinea zone – offers another example that demonstrates that the change from gathering to agriculture was not a sudden one. There are only small steps between gathering wild nuts fallen from a tree; taking measures to prevent wild animals consuming all the fallen nuts; climbing the tree to obtain the complete cluster of nuts; giving some protection to natural palm seedlings against wild animals, bush-fires or weeds; the assigning of proprietary rights for individuals or families in certain trees or areas of trees;

3. T. Shaw, 1974; J. D. Clark, 1976, pp. 92–3.
4. J. R. Harlan, J. M. J. De Wet and A. B. L. Stemler, 1976b, pp. 6–9.

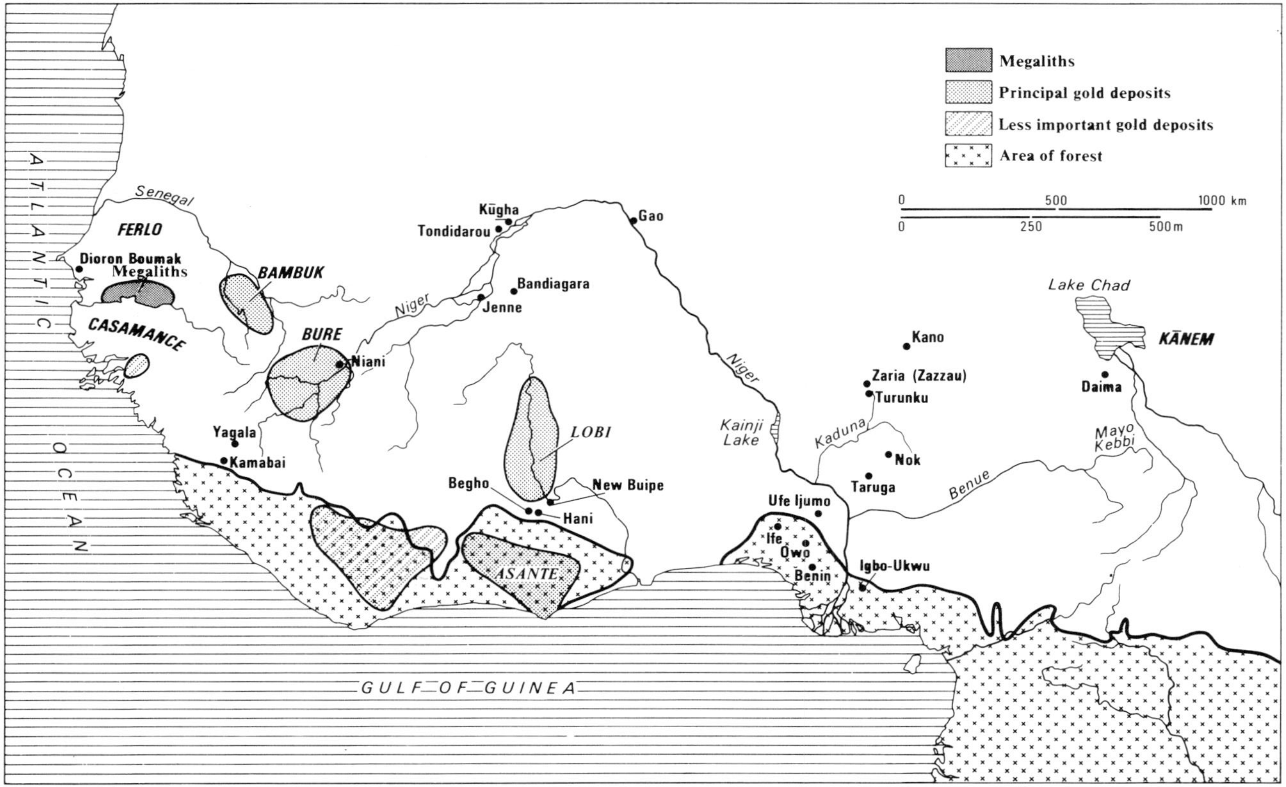

FIG. 16.1 *The Guinea zone: places mentioned in the text*

and finally the intentional planting of palm nuts. Thus the change need not be a sudden one, yet somewhere along the line a change has occurred from gathering the fruits of the wild to planned food production.

Survival of Stone Age hunters

There is no doubt that over most of our area by the beginning of the seventh century, it was food production that provided the basic means of subsistence, rather than hunting and gathering, but there may well have been scattered groups of people, both in the savanna and in the forest, among whom hunting and gathering survived. Perhaps a folk-memory of such groups in the Asante (Ashanti) forests of modern Ghana is enshrined in the stories of the *mmoatia* ('little folk').[5] In the archaeological record now known to us, there are a number of instances where people maintained a Late Stone Age type of technology long after other peoples had adopted metal for their tools and weapons. The people of the earlier millennia of the Late Stone Age were without pottery and ground-stone axes and were undoubtedly hunters, gatherers and fishers; in the later part of the Late Stone Age (sometimes called 'Neolithic') it seems that people were food producers, but just because they had pottery and ground-stone axes we cannot assume this. It may well be, for example, that the people who in the eleventh century left their stone tools behind in the Yagala rock shelter, in Sierra Leone, were predominantly hunters and gatherers.[6]

It is always difficult to obtain direct evidence of agriculture and is largely a matter of chance. The indirect evidence is open to different interpretations: grinding hollows on rock surfaces are almost impossible to date, movable querns and grinding stones can be used for purposes other than food preparation, and wooden objects such as pestles and mortars rarely survive. Nevertheless, a stout and well-carved stick about 1.25 m long and 7.5 cm in diameter was turned up in alluvial deposits worked for tin in central Nigeria. It has been taken to be a pestle or pounding stick, and a sample of wood from it yielded a carbon-14 date in the ninth century.[7]

Crops

The most important cereals in the savanna were bulrush millet (*Pennisetum americanum*), Guinea corn (*Sorghum bicolor*), and two kinds of 'fonio' or 'hungry rice' (*Digitaria exilis* and *D. iburua*). In the Futa Jallon a wild grass (*Brachiaria deflexa*) had been domesticated, and African rice (*Oryza glaberrima*) was dominant in the western part of the Guinea zone. In the

5. R. S. Rattray, 1927, pp. 25–7.
6. J. H. Atherton, 1972; cf. Unesco, *General History of Africa*, Vol. II, ch. 24.
7. B. E. B. Fagg, 1965.

southern savannas and the eastern forests, domesticated African yams formed the staple, especially *Dioscorea cayanensis* and *D. rotundata*. It is possible that the combination of food derived from yams and oil palms, supplemented by proteins from fish, goats, dwarf cattle and bush-meat (including snails) helps to explain the build-up of population in southern Nigeria.[8]

Diseases

By the seventh century also, the incidence of the sickle-cell gene would have built up to levels sufficient to provide the population with considerable protection against malaria; initially the introduction of agricultural methods and ways of life would have increased the incidence of malaria.[9] Mobile hunting bands of about twenty-five people make a much less fertile breeding ground for the establishment of any endemic disease than larger aggregates of settled agricultural populations. In addition, in the case of *falciparum* malaria, the conditions produced by clearing areas in the forest for agriculture favoured the disease. This is because the mosquito *Anopheles gambiae*, the principal vector of *falciparum* malaria, has few suitable natural breeding grounds in the primeval forest, since pools tend not to form on the leaf-covered humus of the forest floor, and where they do are too dark for the habits of *Anopheles gambiae*, which likes to lay its eggs in sunny or well-lit pools. On the other hand open waterholes and domestic rubbish (such as discarded calabashes) of an agricultural village provide ideal breeding grounds for mosquitoes; and the roofs and eaves of thatched huts furnish dark lurking grounds for them during the daytime. We do not know precisely when or how the sickle-cell gene mutation took place. If a child receives it from both parents he will die of sickle-cell anaemia before reaching reproductive age; if he receives it from neither parent he runs a high risk of dying of malaria before reaching maturity; if, however, he receives it from only one parent, he will not die of sickle-cell anaemia and he is provided with a large measure of protection against malaria. Where the incidence of sickle-cell is high in the population, this is always in areas of endemic malaria; it has been able to grow to these high levels in spite of its lethal effect when received from both parents because of the protection it affords against malaria. It has been calculated that it must have taken at least 1500 years to build up to the levels recorded in north-eastern Nigeria; the build-up is probably slower in less humid areas. There tends to be a gradient from south to north in West Africa, with the highest incidence near the coast and a northward diminution.

8. T. Shaw, 1972, p. 159.

9. F. B. Livingstone, 1958; S. L. Wiesenfeld, 1967; D. G. Coursey and J. Alexander, 1968. For skeletal evidence of sickle-cell, see S. P. Bohrer, 1975.

Types of farming and of settlement

We can thus envisage at the beginning of our period a widespread population of village farmers. In some cases (see below) the population density and the ecology of the area was such that permanent settlements were possible, persisting over many generations; in other areas, the food requirements of a community reached a point where it was more economical in terms of labour input for a village to move into an unfarmed area, or one not recently farmed, rather than for farmers to seek land with the necessary fertility further and further away from their village; thus the common long-fallowing system was developed. Where villages remained on one spot for generations and mud houses were rebuilt on the remains of their predecessors every ten to twenty years,[10] the level of the village rose above the surrounding ground and created a mound. Archaeologists have begun to understand how to locate such mounds and a few have been excavated, but it requires much more work than has hitherto been carried out before it will be possible to give a coherent picture of the village farmers who built them, even in a single restricted area. There is a limit to the amount of information that can be obtained by the excavation of a single site.

The other type of village site much more easily escapes notice; it can only be recognized by a surface scatter of potsherds where the ground has been turned over by recent farming; under vegetation it is undetectable, except in some cases by actual vegetation differences. Even where the sites of such villages are spotted, excavation is likely to be less profitable since there is little depth of stratigraphy. This is why we know less about early transient farming villages than we do about sites occupied by the hunters and gatherers of the Late Stone Age, who had a habit of frequently returning to rock shelters and rock overhangs, which can easily be recognized and investigated. Such caves and rock shelters were often utilized temporarily by the later, iron-using agriculturists, for refuges or convenient lodging places during farming activities, but were seldom developed as permanent occupation sites. An exception to this is provided by the Tellem caves of the Bandiagara scarp in present-day Mali, where archaeological and skeletal material from the caves has been intensively studied.[11] The present Dogon people of the area attribute the remains in the caves to the 'Tellem', but say that the caves were unoccupied at the time of their arrival from the west. Carbon-14 dates indicate that the 'Tellem' occupation of the caves only began at the very end of our period and lasted two or three centuries. The 'Tellem' were formerly supposed to have migrated to the east into what is now Burkina Faso and to have been ancestral to the present Kurumba there. However, studies of the physical anthropology of the Kurumba and of the Tellem skeletons indicates that they are genetically different.

10. R. J. McIntosh, 1974.
11. B. T. Bazuin-Sira, 1968; J. Huizinga, 1968; F. Willett, 1971, p. 369.

The diffusion of metallurgy

The making of iron

The farmers used iron, which was widely smelted throughout the Guinea zone by this time. In some parts of the area, the reduction of iron ore had already been practised for a thousand years. Carbon-14 dates for the 'Nok Culture' site of Taruga in present-day Nigeria indicate that iron-ore reduction was being practised there from at least the fourth century before the Christian era.[12] An iron-ore reduction site has been excavated at Hani, in Ghana, and charcoal associated with slag and fragments of tuyères and furnaces provided a carbon-14 date in the second century of the Christian era.[13] Carbon-14 dates in the seventh century are associated with iron-ore reduction furnaces in Nigeria from the foot of the Dala hill in Kano,[14] and in the Kubanni Valley near Zaria;[15] two more recently obtained dates from further excavation among this group of furnaces are from the eighth and tenth centuries, suggesting that this area, near a good source of hard lateritic ore, remained a traditional iron-ore reduction centre over some centuries.[16] South of the River Niger and west of its confluence with the Benue, a group of iron-ore reduction furnaces excavated at Ufe Ijumo has dates in the ninth and twelfth centuries and the level marking the abandonment of the sites yields a fourteenth-century date.[17]

Occupation sites

Apart from actual furnaces for the reduction of iron-ore, a number of occupation sites are now known that offer evidence of the use of iron from the beginning of the Christian era, and many more by the middle of the first millennium. Although the dates are not as early as those of the Taruga iron-smelting furnaces, occupation mounds in the section of the Niger Valley flooded by the Kainji lake and in the nearby Kaduna Valley have in one case produced an initial date of −130,[18] in another dates of +100 and +200,[19] and in another of +200.[20] The earliest occupation dates for the supposed capital of Mali at Niani[21] and for Ife[22] fall in the sixth

12. F. Willett, 1971, p. 369.
13. M. Posnansky and R. McIntosh, 1976, pp. 165–6.
14. F. Willett, 1971, p. 368.
15. M. Posnansky and R. McIntosh, 1976, p. 171.
16. J. E. G. Sutton, 1976, 1977.
17. M. Posnansky and R. McIntosh, 1976, pp. 172, 190.
18. C. Flight, 1973, p. 548.
19. B. M. Fagan, 1969b, p. 153.
20. Author's information, unpublished.
21. W. Filipowiak, S. Jasnosz and R. Wolagiewicz, 1970; D. T. Niane, 1970; F. Willett, 1971, p. 365; see also G. Liesegang, 1975.
22. B. M. Fagan, 1969b, p. 154.

century. So also does the earliest date yet obtained for the use of iron in the area of the Benue–Mayo–Kebbi confluence in Cameroon;[23] at the site of Daima in north-eastern Nigeria south of Lake Chad the estimated date is only a little earlier.[24] It is a little more difficult to interpret the carbon-14 dates published for the neighbouring 'Sao' sites in northern Cameroon and the Republic of Chad.[25] Some of the shell middens of the River Casamance in modern Senegal were accumulating from the beginning of our period as a result of the food-gathering habits of iron-using people; research has suggested that it was the ancestors of the present inhabitants, the Dyula, who were in occupation of the area.[26] In addition to the shellfish exploited, ocean fishing was practised, domestic goats and cattle were kept, and it seems likely that rice had become a staple diet and that its cultivation had made permanent occupation of settlement sites possible. The shell middens of Dioron Boumak in the delta of the Saloum in Senegal seem to have their beginnings towards the end of the eighth century, with an intensification of the exploitation of the shellfish resources from the beginning of the eleventh. The end of this exploitation comes after our period, probably at the time when the Manding were replaced as the coastal population by the Sereer Niominka in the fifteenth century.[27]

Just as it is likely that a hunting and gathering way of life continued in many places for a long time after agriculture first began to be practised, so it is likely that the spread of iron technology was uneven. While our earliest knowledge of it at Taruga dates from several centuries before the Christian era, there are other places in the Guinea area where it was not adopted until a thousand or more years later. During this period there must have been many instances of people with a Late Stone Age technology living not far away from people using iron. As yet we know little about the relationship between such groups practising differing levels of technology – whether there was a peaceful exchange relationship between them, whether there was any kind of confrontation, or whether they occupied different areas and different ecological niches and had little to do with each other. An example of this kind of situation can be seen in northern Sierra Leone, where at Kamabai the uppermost level, with iron tools, slag and pottery, produced carbon-14 dates in the seventh and eighth centuries, whereas at Yagala a Late Stone Age technology apparently persisted into the eleventh century.[28] According to the twelfth-century geographer al-Zuhrī, the people of ancient Ghana raided people who possessed no iron but fought with ebony staves, a poor match for the swords and spears of the people of

23. C. Flight, 1973, p. 550.
24. B. M. Fagan, 1969b, p. 153; G. Connah, 1976.
25. A. Lebeuf and J.-P. Lebeuf, 1970; C. Flight, 1973, pp. 552–3.
26. O. Linares de Sapir, 1971; F. Willett, 1971, p. 361; C. Flight, 1973, p. 545.
27. C. Descamps, G. Thilmans and Y. Thommeret, 1974; C. A. Diop, 1972; M. Posnansky and R. McIntosh, 1976, pp. 184, 193.
28. J. H. Atherton, 1972; F. Willett, 1971, p. 351.

Ghana.[29] We shall not obtain a historically correct picture of the spread of iron-using in West Africa until many more sites of the relevant period distributed in representative localities have been excavated and dated. Before the discovery of the smelting site at Hani dated to the second century of the Christian era (see above p. 467), the earliest known iron in modern Ghana was from the site of New Buipe[30] dated towards the end of the eighth century. It is only recently that archaeological investigation has begun in the highly specialized environment of the Niger Delta. So far no Stone Age site has been discovered there, and the earliest occupation date comes from the end of the ninth century.[31]

In spite of the uneven spread of a knowledge of iron-working, we can take it that by the beginning of our period it was widespread; by the end of the period there must have been very few pockets of Stone Age technology remaining, although it is possible that certain stone tools remained in use.[32] Over most of the area, however, even a folk memory of the use of ground stone axes was lost. When encountered accidentally in the ground, a ceraunic origin was ascribed to them; they were regarded as thunderbolts which descended from the sky with lightning flashes and were held responsible for damage to trees and buildings. As such they came to be revered as vehicles and symbols of divine power and found their way onto the altars of Nyame, Sango and the ancestral *oba*s of Benin. In southern Ivory Coast they developed specialized outsize forms which must surely have had a ritual rather than a functional significance.[33]

Local trade

Undoubtedly one of the most important effects of the spread of iron was an increase in the efficiency of agricultural production. Iron hoes and tools for bush-clearing would have facilitated the creation of those agricultural surpluses that permit a greater division of labour, craft specialization, and ultimately the development of urbanization and support for a royal or priestly court. The process may have been a slow one, and it must not be assumed that it was necessarily 'population pressure' resulting from the agricultural way of life that was the cause, or even one of the causes, of progress towards state formation. On the other hand, there would have grown up local systems of exchange based on specific surpluses and craft specialization. Differences of environment would have fostered the development of such exchange systems, since the products of one environment could be

29. N. Levtzion, 1973, p. 14; N. Levtzion and J. F. P. Hopkins (eds), 1981, p. 98.
30. R. N. York, 1973.
31. M. Posnansky and R. McIntosh, 1976, pp. 170, 189–90.
32. R. S. Rattray, 1923, p. 323; M. D. W. Jeffreys, 1951, p. 1208; D. Williams, 1974, p. 70.
33. B. Holas, 1951.

exchanged for those of another. A riverine area might exchange dried fish for grain grown further away from the river; bush-meat hunted and caught in the savanna might be exchanged for foods only found in the forest. An area smelting iron by exploiting its own rich sources of ore might trade iron products for pottery made in an area better endowed with suitable clay. Gradually such networks would grow, and products of one region would travel, perhaps through several intermediaries, for greater and greater distances. For example, kola nuts, which grow in the forest regions of the south, may have been exchanged for the shea butter produced in the north. This exchange is still important, and may well follow a pattern that is more than a thousand years old. Such local exchange systems may have been important in the development of centralized authority, for once the additional wealth derived from long-distance trade was injected into them, it gave power out of all proportion to what he had previously possessed to the chief who controlled the bartered resources.[34] Undoubtedly this process was one of the most important developments during our period in Guinea, as the tentacles of the more developed trans-Saharan trade began to articulate with the already existing exchange systems. Such expansions of the trading network would not have caused the abandonment of the existing local exchange systems; as has been shown for another region, the development of trade mechanisms tends to be additive rather than sequential.[35]

Just as the development of agricultural systems and of iron-smelting was uneven, so undoubtedly was the development of exchange networks. Where exchange systems were poorly developed, there would be a lack of one of the stimuli towards centralization of authority and state formation, helping to preserve the many stateless societies of West Africa. In the tropical forest culture of South America, the way the lack of homogeneity in the tropical forest (contrary to the picture gained from superficial impressions) led to long-distance trading has been closely studied, together with the way intercommunal warfare failed to disrupt it.[36] Studies of trade in West Africa have tended to concentrate on external trade[37] but the exchange of natural products between the different ecological zones of West Africa is likely to be ancient.

External trade

One of the most interesting pieces of evidence for a concentration of some form of wealth, and, in all probability, a concomitant centralization of social and political authority, is provided by the Senegambian megaliths. An approximately oval region 350 km long from east to west and 175 km

34. R. Horton, 1976, pp. 75, 110–12.
35. T. W. Beale, 1973, p. 143.
36. D. W. Lathrap, 1973.
37. L. Sundstrom, 1974; A. G. Hopkins, 1973.

from north to south (roughly 13°–16° W, 13°–14°30′ N) is remarkable for the number of megalithic monuments within it. Their distribution corresponds closely to the basins of the middle and upper Gambia and Saloum rivers and their tributaries. In this area over 28 000 large dressed stones have been counted.[38] At one site alone (Sine-Saloum) there are some 900 stones arranged in 54 circles. The circles are composed of standing stones, between ten and twenty-four in number, their height above ground varying between half a metre and nearly three metres (see Figs. 16.2; 16.3; 16.4). The commonest shape is cylindrical, others are square or D-shaped in section, others taper towards the top, but all the stones of a particular circle are of the same type. Most stones are flat on top, but some have a hollow or a protruding boss. The internal diameter of the circles varies between four and seven metres. Most circles have a line of similar stones on the eastern side, running north and south. The most remarkable are the rare so-called 'lyre-stones', cut in the shape of a V from a single block of lateritic stone.

Excavation of some of the circles in recent years has demonstrated clearly that they are funerary in character, a number of single and multiple inhumations having been unearthed. Excavation has also provided three carbon-14 dates in the seventh/eighth centuries. Careful examination has shown that there are four types of associated monuments: megalithic circles, stone tumuli (usually having a frontal line of stones to the east like the megalithic circles), stone circles (not marked by megalithic standing stones but by lateritic blocks only just showing above the soil), and earth tumuli.[39]

It is interesting to speculate on what made possible the diversion of so much human effort into the cutting, transporting and erecting of these thousands of stone pillars. Because they are carved out of a surface capping of lateritic stone rich in iron, it has been suggested that the monuments were created by people who gained wealth by smelting iron and supplying it to the surrounding communities. This may have been the case, but if so, the smelting furnaces have not yet been found – any more than the living sites of the megalith builders. This one-sided nature of the archaeological evidence makes it difficult in the present state of knowledge to attempt historical reconstructions. Another suggestion to account for the Senegambian megaliths sees their location as strategically placed to give the occupants of the area control of trade in gold from the goldfields of Bure and Bambuk.[40] If the eighth-century dating is correct, this seems a little early as far west as this for the pull of Arab trade to the north to have been a responsible factor. Although the Arabs conquered the Maghrib early in the eighth century, thereafter their immediate preoccupation was more with the conquest of Visigothic Spain than with the establishment in Morocco

38. V. Martin and C. Becker, 1974a.

39. P. Ozanne, 1966; P. O. Beale, 1966; D. Evans, 1975; G. Thilmans and C. Descamps, 1974, 1975.

40. M. Posnansky, 1973, p. 151.

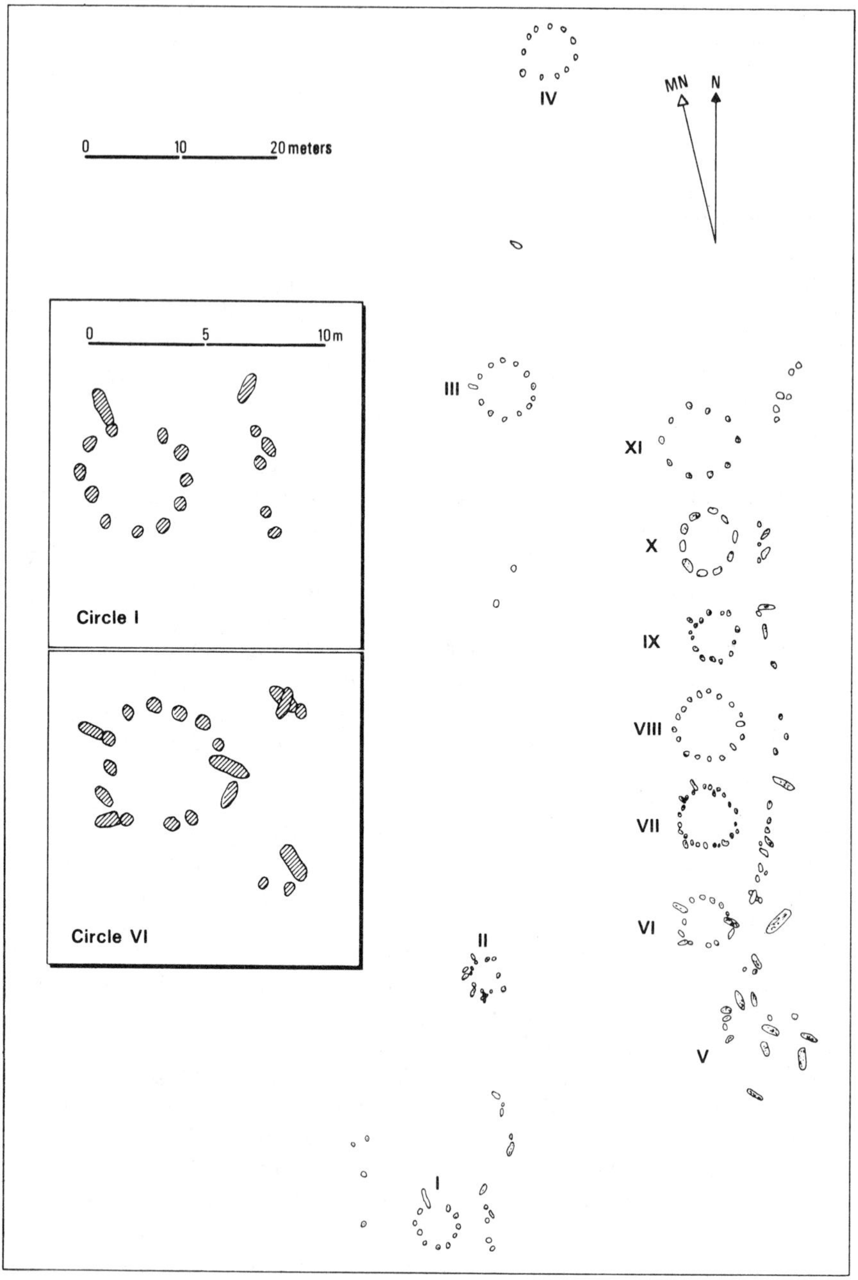

FIG. 16.2 *Plan of the Wassu site*

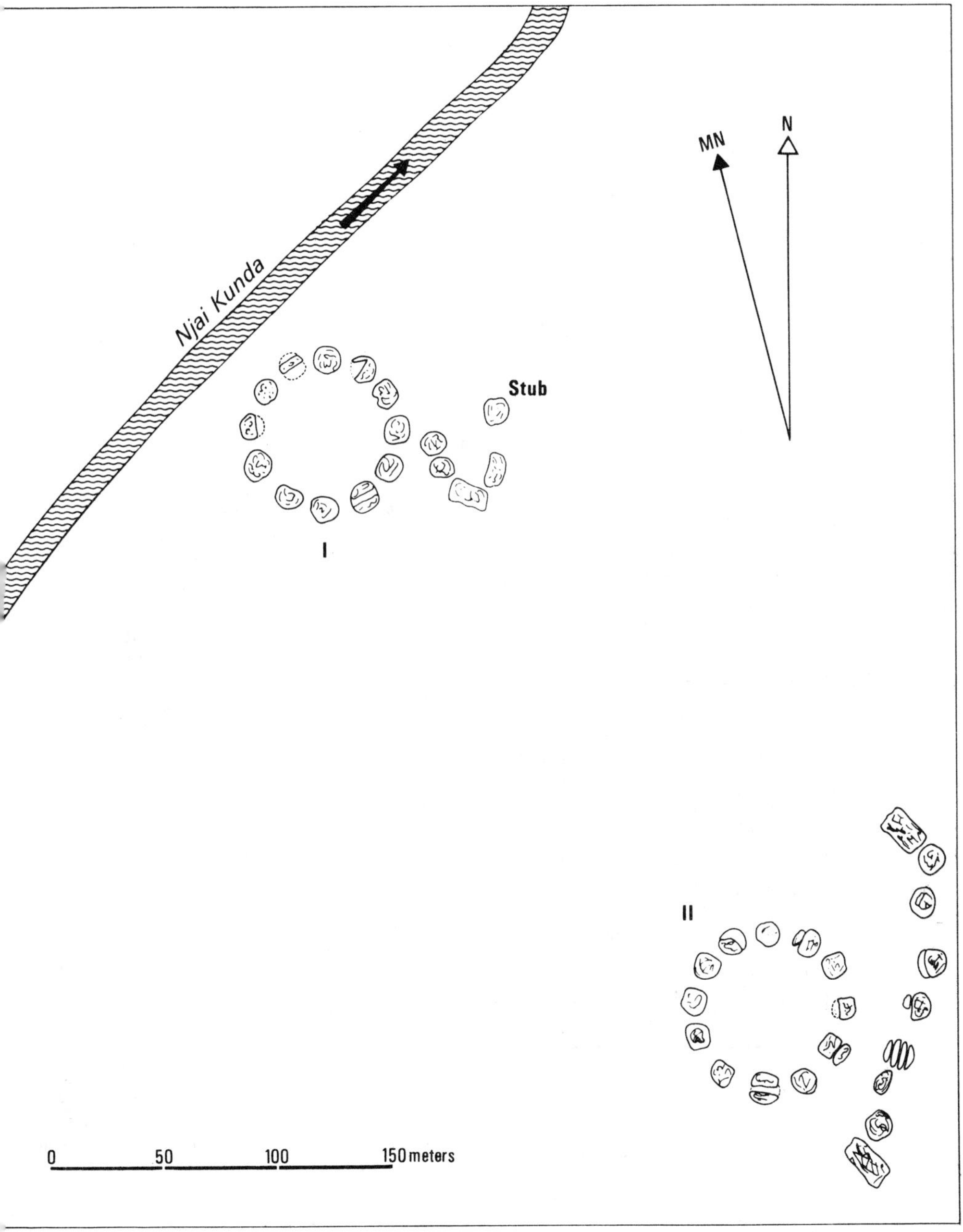

FIG. 16.3 *Two circles at Wassu, with their outlying stones more or less complete in the East*

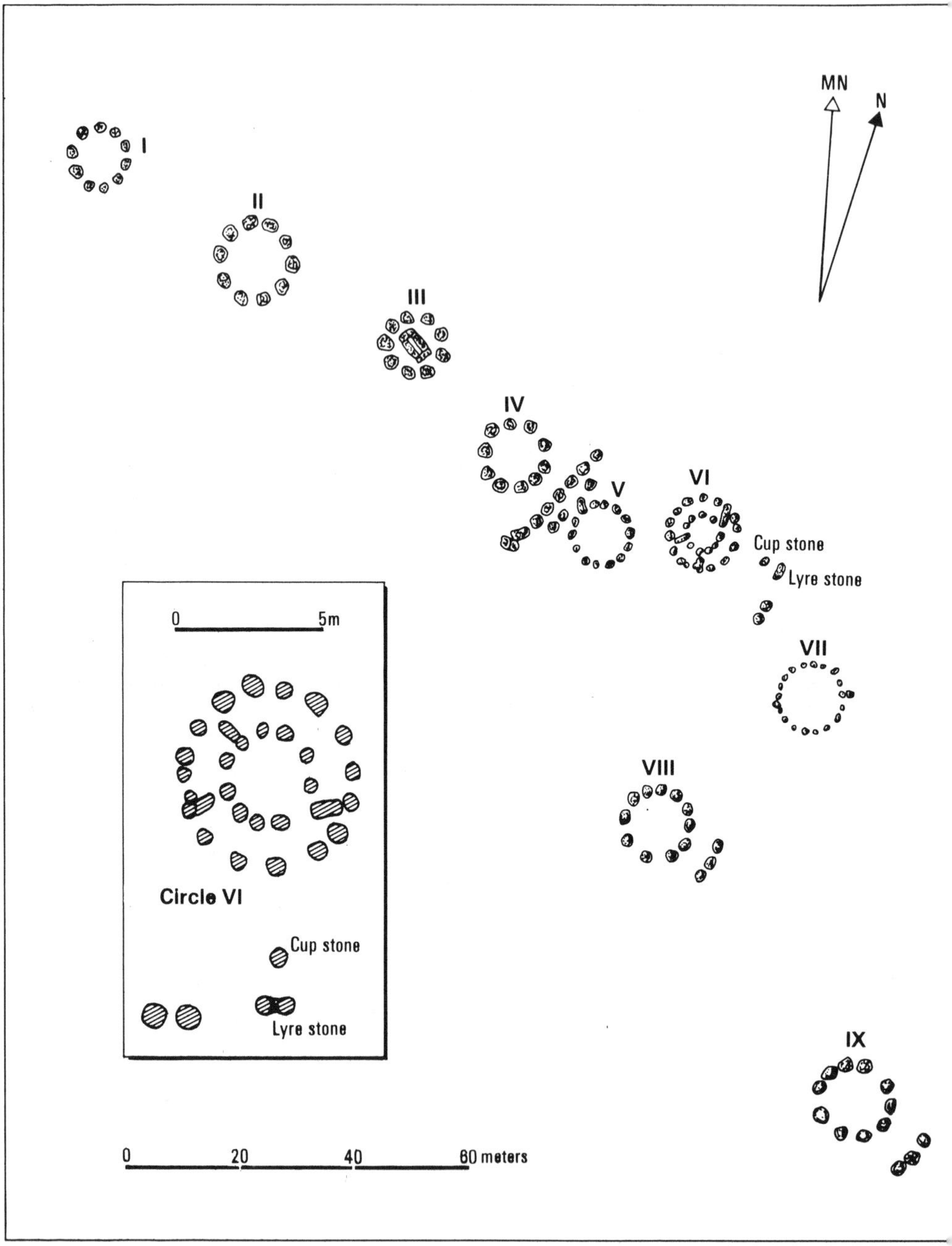

FIG. 16.4 *The lyre stone at Kerbatch*

of settled centres of commerce.[41] If the Senegambian megaliths do in fact predate Arab trade and owe their existence nevertheless to a northward export of gold, perhaps we should envisage the Berber people of the desert as the intermediaries in a trade with Byzantine North Africa. If such a trade existed it would help to explain the comparative rapidity with which the Arabs established commercial relations with the Western Sudan once their occupation of North Africa had become more settled.

To the north of the megalithic area and in the valley of the Senegal is an area of large mounds, some of which have produced pottery comparable with that from the megaliths. Over 4000 have been counted and where excavated contain, like the megaliths, multiple burials. There is a rich profusion of grave goods including gold and carnelian beads, gold and copper ornaments and iron weapons; copper vessels of Moroccan workmanship point to a northward exchange connection. Although there is now an eighth-century carbon-14 date for one of the more southerly mounds, [42] the majority are regarded as belonging to the tenth century.[43] Similarly other mounds with rich finds have been excavated in the upper Niger Valley below Segu; at Kūgha, at the beginning of the great bend of the Niger, one associated with standing stones has been dated to around +1000.[44] In this same middle Niger bend area, the megaliths of Tondidarou, although now plundered and ravaged by modern antiquity collectors and never scientifically excavated, probably date to the same general period and attest to a trade in gold coming down the Niger from the Bure goldfields.[45] It is significant that the development of Kumbi Saleh (ancient Ghana), as the collecting point for gold from this source for the trans-Saharan trade, begins not later than the eighth century. Towards the end of that century Ghana was already famous as 'the land of gold' as far afield as Baghdad, as evidenced by the well-known reference of al-Fazārī.[46] Both Kumbi Saleh and Awdāghust were probably collecting points for gold coming from the Bambuk goldfields, and perhaps it was the greater organization of their trade routes that caused a decline in the social and political importance of communities that had hitherto exploited gold sources further to the west.

There is some indication that before the routes through Taghāza and Sidjilmāsa were developed, the earliest route by which West African gold reached the Arab world was more directly into Egypt, via the Dākhla and Khārja oases.[47] Perhaps we can see a confirmation of this early route in

41. R. Oliver and B. M. Fagan, 1975, p. 157; cf. Chapters 9 and 11 above.
42. M. Posnansky and R. McIntosh, 1976, pp. 184–5.
43. M. Posnansky, 1973, p. 152.
44. R. Mauny, 1961, pp. 109–10.
45. R. Mauny, 1970, pp. 133–6.
46. N. Levtzion, 1973, p. 3; N. Levtzion and J. F. P. Hopkins (eds), 1981, p. 32.
47. N. Levtzion, 1968a, pp. 231–2.

three carbon-14 dates in the sixth, seventh and tenth centuries from the site of Marandet, in Aïr, on the route between Gao and Egypt.[48] Here there are refuse heaps from which some 42 500 crucibles have been excavated, representing the activities of a settlement of artisans. Authorities have disagreed on the metal that was worked,[49] there being rival claims for gold and copper, but the only hard evidence we have as yet is in the form of an analysis of the residues of a crucible, which showed it to be copper and not gold.[50] It is obviously important to learn a lot more about Marandet, to confirm and narrow the dating, and above all to have some idea of the source of the raw materials being used, the destination of the finished products, the identity of the artisans, and the political and commercial control of the organization of the trade. If gold was being used by artisans at Marandet, the raw material would already have travelled a long way from Bambuk and Bure (because it is doubtful whether the Asante goldfields of modern Ghana were yet contributing to this trade) and would be half-way to Egypt. Furthermore, if the crucibles without traces of copper were used for gold, why have none been found in comparable quantities at Kumbi Saleh, Awdāghust, Walāta, Es-Sūḳ and other places known to have been collecting points for gold in the trans-Saharan trade? What was the source of the copper? For a long time research workers have tried to identify the 'Takedda' described by Ibn Baṭṭūṭa in the fourteenth century as a source of copper in the southern Sahara. It was thought that a satisfactory identification had been made with Azelik, 150 km to the north-west of Marandet,[51] where ruins and an abundant scatter of slag and moulds give evidence of Azelik's former importance as a copper-working site. In spite of the earlier claim that the source of copper had been found 13 km east-north-east of Azelik[52] and of more recent work identifying copper deposits in the area,[53] it has been stated that there was insufficient copper ore for exploitation and that it must have been imported copper that was being worked at Azelik, whose carbon-14 dates (twelfth and sixteenth centuries) are later than those for Marandet.[54]

There is plenty of evidence from Arab writers, from al-Bakrī onwards, that copper was an important export into the Guinea zone. It was used as currency in Takedda and Kānem in the fourteenth century.[55] A south-bound caravan that apparently got into difficulties in the Madjābat al-Kubrā in Mauritania early in the twelfth century was carrying 2000 brass

48. H. Lhote, 1972a, 1972b; C. Delibrias, M. T. Guillier and J. Labeyrie, 1974, pp. 44–5; M. Posnansky and R. McIntosh, 1976, p. 183.
49. H. Lhote, 1972a, 1972b; R. Mauny, 1973, pp. 763–4.
50. R. Castro, 1974.
51. R. Mauny, 1961, pp. 140–1, 308–9.
52. J. Lombard and R. Mauny, 1954.
53. S. Bernus and P. Gouletquer, 1976.
54. M. Posnansky and R. McIntosh, 1976, p. 183.
55. N. Levtzion, 1973, p. 120.

rods and jettisoned them.[56] Gold was the prime commodity desired from West Africa by the trans-Saharan merchants, but there were other valuable products to be obtained that yielded high profits, especially ivory and slaves, in areas where no gold was to be obtained, such as the eastern part of the Guinea area. Does the combination of this fact, and the earliness of the copper-working activities at Marandet, taken together with the existence thence of the early trade route direct to Egypt, help to explain the earliness of the carbon-14 dates obtained for the finds at Igbo-Ukwu, far away to the south in the eastern part of the Guinea zone?[57]

The beginnings of centralization

Igbo-Ukwu

Igbo-Ukwu lies some 35 km south-west of Onitsha, the large market town on the east bank of the River Niger, whose political structure has been influenced by Benin. Here, not long before the outbreak of the Second World War, a man digging a water cistern in his compound was surprised to encounter, at no great depth, a number of bronze objects. These later found their way into the Nigerian Museum in Lagos and the Antiquities Department marked the spot down for future excavations, which took place after the war. Three sites adjacent to each other were uncovered. The first was a storehouse or shrine where regalia and ritual objects had been kept and for some reason abandoned intact. The second was the wooden-lined burial chamber of an important personage, and the third was a disposal pit into which ceremonial objects had been cast. The storehouse yielded over seventy large copper and bronze objects and nearly five hundred small items, the burial chamber nineteen large pieces and thirty-two small ones, the disposal pit thirteen large and eighty-seven small items. In the storehouse were over 60 000 beads, and there were over 100 000 in the burial chamber. Highly decorated pottery of a characteristic style occurred at all three sites, with a particular richness in the disposal pit. Such finds were clearly not articles of everyday use by common people, and the treatment accorded the personage in the burial chamber indicates a considerable measure of distinction above others in the community. This distinction may be that accorded to a senior title-holder (*ozo*) of the Igbo title-taking system, perhaps to the *eze nri* himself, the 'priest-king' who until the early years of the present century held powerful ritual and religious sway, though not political power, over large parts of Igboland. The most important part of his function was in connection with the yam crop and the fertility of the land, and was concerned with removing ritual pollutions after taboos had been broken and in settling disputes. In a pre-

56. T. Monod, 1969; C. Flight, 1973, p. 544.
57. T. Shaw, 1970, 1975a, 1977.

(a)

(b)

PLATE 16.1 *Igbo-Ukwu excavation finds:*
16.1(a) (above) miniature bronze pendant head – side view (height: 7.5 cm)
16.1(b) (above, right) bronze pendant representing a decorated ram's head (height: 8.5 cm)
16.1(c) (right) bronze skull of a leopard mounted on a copper rod (length: 24 cm)
16.1(d) (below, right) Bronze pendant ornament in the form of a bird and two eggs, with crotals and beads attached by copper-wire chains (height: 21.5 cm)

(c)

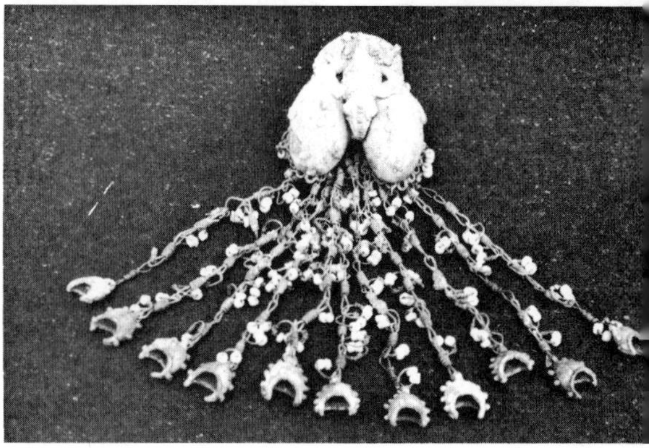

(d)

(e)

(f)

PLATE 16.1 *Igbo-Ukwu excavation finds:*
16.1(e) (above, left) Bronze cylindrical bowl (height 20 cm)
16.1(f) (above, right) Bronze bowl on stand (height: 27.5 cm)
16.1(g) (left) Bronze shell surmounted by an animal (length: 20 cm)
16.1(h) (below, left) Bronze crescent-shaped bowl (length: 14 cm)

(g)

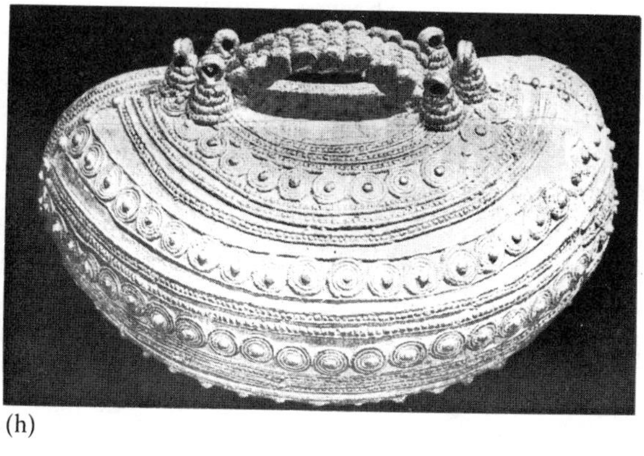
(h)

scientific age, when the causation of such things as fertility and the weather are little understood, it is to be expected that men should have attempted to control such things, vitally affecting their livelihood, in a pre-scientific, religious way. This had happened at the hunter-gatherer stage of existence, but the emphasis had then tended to be upon the plenitude of game and upon successful hunting. When the change to agriculture was effected, the emphasis shifted to the productivity of the land itself and those factors affecting it; it was therefore worthwhile for farming communities to set aside special resources and, often, special persons whose function it was to ensure the fertility of the land. The centralization of social wealth and political power is usually intimately connected with this process and although the manifestations may have been different, it is likely to have been an integral part of the development of other Guinea kingdoms and centralized institutions.

At Igbo-Ukwu there were no recognizable imports other than the metal used for making the bronzes, and the glass beads. Not enough is known about the latter to provide any sure indication of date. The bronzes are in a style utterly unlike those of Benin or Ife and stand in isolation, so that it is difficult to use stylistic features to date them. One is thus thrown back on the carbon-14 dates: wood from a copper-studded stool in the burial chamber fell in the time range from the eighth century to the early eleventh century, and three determinations from charcoal in the disposal pit belonged to the same period; another from the same source, however, fell into the late fourteenth/early fifteenth century; it is similar to the date for the only other excavated bronzes comparable to those from Igbo-Ukwu.[58] The reliability of the earliest carbon-14 dates for Igbo-Ukwu has been disputed[59] but often on erroneous grounds.[60]

Since there is very little copper in Nigeria[61] and no sites of ancient exploitation of this mineral are known, a date in the eleventh century or earlier implies that copper was imported overland from the north, and doubtless there were other imports, such as glass beads, and perishable goods such as salt that have not survived. Eastern Nigeria had no gold to export in exchange, so these luxury goods were probably paid for in ivory and slaves. Some have objected that nowhere else as far south in West Africa do we have evidence for long-distance trade in the period indicated by the carbon-14 dates. This is an argument to be respected, but it must be remembered that the earliest route by which the Arab world obtained gold from the Western Sudan linked ancient Ghana with Egypt via al-Wāhāt, the oases of Kh̲ārja and Dākh̲la (see above p. 475). It was only when this route became too dangerous after the middle of the ninth century that the western route from the Maghrib was developed. There was an 'ivory route'

58. D. D. Hartle, 1967, 1968.
59. B. Lawal, 1973; D. Northrup, 1972.
60. T. Shaw, 1975a.
61. Queried by M. A. Onwuejeogwu, 1974; see T. Shaw, 1975a, p. 513.

in late Roman and Byzantine times from Tripoli to the Lake Chad area along the shortest crossing of the Sahara and it is likely that the Arabs would have also used this route. In the eleventh century al-Bakrī reported that copper was exported southwards from Sūs towards the land of the blacks.[62] The remains of the caravan carrying some two thousand brass rods which came to grief in the Madjābat al-Kubrā were dated to around +1100 (see above p. 476). Thus there is plenty of evidence, not merely for trade in general across the Sahara in the period to which the Igbo-Ukwu finds are assigned by carbon-14 dating, but also for a trade in copper. The only question that remains is whether this trade reached as far south as Igbo-Ukwu. It will only be possible to ascertain this by the excavation of other sites of similar age in the area. A possibility also to be borne in mind and to be checked by future investigation, is that copper could have come from the metalliferous region in the basin of the River Niari, just north of the lower Zaire River.[63]

Perhaps there is some support for the idea that trans-Saharan trade reached well to the south by the eleventh century in two carbon-14 dates obtained from the Nyarko quarter of Begho, in modern Ghana, which became the great collecting point for gold from Asante traded north to Jenne.[64]

Ife

The high point of the Ife culture lies outside our period, since a collation of twenty-five carbon-14 dates from seven different sites excavated there suggest that it is possible to identify the mid-twelfth to the mid-fifteenth centuries as the period *par excellence* of the building of edge-set potsherd pavements, which may themselves be a useful 'marker' of the social, political and economic circumstances that made Ife pre-eminent in its area.[65] If thermoluminescent dating can be trusted, the production of the famous brass heads and other copper-alloy castings belongs to the last century-and-a-half of this three-hundred year period.[66] However, the development of centralized political and religious institutions, with sufficient wealth to patronize outstanding artistic production, does not take place overnight. It is therefore important to take account of the circumstances

62. N. Levtzion, 1968a, pp. 231–2; R. C. C. Law, 1967b; al-Bakrī, 1913, pp. 306–7; N. Levtzion and J. F. P. Hopkins (eds), 1981, p. 69.

63. P. Martin, 1970, p. 143; T. Shaw, 1975a, p. 513.

64. M. Posnansky and R. McIntosh, 1976, p. 166. Investigations since the text of this chapter was written indicate that the 'tell' site of Jenne-Jeno, 3 km south-east of the present city, was occupied from −200 to +1400; the findings throw much light on the origin and development of Jenne. See R. J. McIntosh, 1979; R. J. McIntosh and S. K. McIntosh, 1981; S. K. McIntosh, 1979; S. K. McIntosh and R. J. McIntosh, 1980a, 1980b.

65. T. Shaw, 1978, pp. 157–63.

66. F. Willett and S. J. Fleming, 1976.

that gave rise to these developments, and because this formative stage lies within our period it is proper to give it some consideration. This question of 'the rise' of Ife is related to a wider one, that of the origin of Yoruba urbanism in general, which has puzzled a number of writers.[67]

We can take it that during the first millennium of the Christian era the forest lands of Nigeria became progressively settled by a population practising an agriculture based on yams and oil palms; in the savanna lands immediately to the north of the forest the staples are likely to have been yams, Guinea corn and, in some areas, African rice; in the northern savanna lands yams would have been replaced by bulrush millet. For some thirty generations, bush clearance and agricultural production had been made more efficient by means of metal tools made from locally produced iron. Although fieldwork and excavation have not been sufficiently widespread in Yorubaland to provide archaeological confirmation of this picture, six carbon-14 dates, lying in the sixth to the tenth centuries of the Christian era, from two sites in Ife, are confirmatory evidence of human occupation.[68]

This population is likely to have had three characteristics. First, all settled agricultural populations in pre-scientific times feel that as part of their agricultural practices they have to do something, in the face of the vagaries of the weather and the variability of crop yields, the causes of which are not fully understood, to ensure the fertility of the land and the productiveness of their crops. These things are believed to depend upon the goodwill of supernatural powers. Ordinary folk may not feel confident to handle such potentially dangerous forces, or may be afraid to do so; accordingly they are happy to delegate the task, for a consideration, to specialists who do not have the same hesitancy and who claim to have the necessary expert knowledge. Thus cults and their priests are important in the life of the community.

Secondly, there is commonly a build-up of population. This is not automatic and it is usually slow, but it does take place; there may be setbacks because of famine years and diseases engendered by permanent settlement to which hunters and gatherers are not liable in the same way, but births tend to be more frequent and women to produce and rear more children than among hunters and gatherers. This population increase itself affects agricultural practices and modifies them in the direction of the more efficient exploitation of different ecozones.

Thirdly, this more efficient exploitation of resources is likely to have led to specialization in different ecological areas, with an exchange of products between them (as already described above, pp. 438–9); this would favour the establishment of a recognized system of internal exchange.[69] The complementarity of the resources exploited in the different ecological areas favours occupational specialization and economic interdependence; geo-

67. E.g., W. R. Bascom, 1955; E. Krapf-Askari, 1969.
68. F. Willett, 1971, p. 366.
69. R. McC. Adams, 1966, p. 52.

graphically adjacent segments of the society become symbiotic. Such a situation fosters the institution of redistributive arrangements. That Ife may have occupied a special position in such an exchange network will be suggested later.

Different conditions seem to have prevailed west of the Niger from those in the east, where farmers felt safe enough to live in dispersed homesteads in the middle of their farming land. Whereas defensive earthworks are very rare in Igboland, they are common in Edo and Yoruba country, indicating that, for some reason we can at present only guess at, west of the Niger the needs of defence made the farmers live together in villages within walking distance of their farms. Accordingly the social system which developed among the Yoruba-speaking and Edo-speaking peoples was quite different from that of the Igbo. Because people of different lineages were living close together, the claims of a neighbour began to rival, and then outstrip, those of a kinsman. The demands of kinship tended to threaten the solidarity of the village where its defence needs were concerned, and the disruptive effect of these obligations was damped down by giving certain lineages specified functions in the life of the community, such as providing the chief, the war leader, the historian, the spokesman and the priest. In this way leadership tended to develop into permanent authority. Permanent authority, in its turn, when developed on any large scale, itself requires assistants and an administrative class to help carry out its functions.[70] Or have we put the cart before the horse? Was it the fact that the Yorubas had already developed a hierarchical social system (compared with the segmentary system of the Igbo), with a greater and greater proportion of the fruits of production concentrated at the pinnacle and in the upper layers of the social pyramid, which tended to exacerbate and increase the inter-community rivalry for control of the fruits of production and, perhaps, in the form of land, of the means of production too?

If it is the case that it was the needs of defence that nucleated a scattered agricultural population into villages, what was the nature of the threat? Had the density of population reached the point where there was real competition for the available agricultural land so that one community threatened another? Or did the threat come from outside, as a result of the commercial and military dominance of the trading states to the north, Mali and Songhay? One of our difficulties here is that we do not know enough about the dates at which these various earthworks in Yorubaland were built. It should not be difficult to devise an archaeological research programme to find out. Apart from the fourteenth/fifteenth century inner wall at Benin, the majority of the earthwork systems in the Edo-speaking area appear to have been built as a response to internal imperatives and to be more in the nature of boundaries.[71] Perhaps in fact defensive earthwork

70. R. Horton, 1976.
71. G. Connah, 1975, pp. 98–106; P. J. Darling, 1974, 1976.

building did not begin in Yorubaland until external pressures were felt, as they certainly were after 1100: at its greatest extent the domination of Mali extended down the River Niger to within 100 km of the most northerly Yoruba settlements. We can only guess at how these pressures first exerted themselves, but the most likely demand was for slaves. Slave-raiding southwards from the kingdom of Mali certainly took place, but how early it extended as far east as northern Yorubaland remains uncertain. Slave-raiding was more important in the Central Sudan than in the Western Sudan, because the former produced no gold.[72] As already observed, a system of exchange, in which such things as shea butter from the northern savannas were traded into the forest areas in return for products such as kola, may be older than any long-distance trade. Once this exchange system had been established, and once, as a result of their own contacts, the northern areas found themselves in a position to offer other goods obtained from further afield, these would join the shea butter and other goods and would stimulate the offering in return of additional products from the south.

Given on the one hand the need for cults to ensure the fertility of the land and the success of the crops and for priests to serve them as specialists in supernatural farm management and, on the other hand, the need for the institutionalization of redistributive arrangements, the situation is well on the way to one in which there is the emergence of some form of ceremonial centre.[73] Granted that the priestly function could be performed at the village level, and often still is, nevertheless where there is a build-up towards exchange systems, such specialists may tend more and more to become located at the nodes of such systems. Similarly, the redistributive need could be met by a system of market exchange only, but where there is a priestly functionary mediating supernatural goodwill, to secure the fertility of the land and the welfare of the people, he will expect remuneration for his services, sometimes directly, sometimes in the form of sacrificial offerings to the divine powers, most commonly through a mixture of the two, in which the distinction is blurred. In this situation grew up the ceremonial centre, in which the co-ordinated institutions of temple and palace, of shrines and an *alafin* or *oba*, emerged as the effective redistributive institutions. There is less evidence for the *oni* of Ife having been involved in trade than for the *oba* of Benin: this may be on account of the collapse of Ife's commercial hegemony in the fifteenth/sixteenth century, the disruptions of the Yoruba wars of the nineteenth century, and the lack of continuity in traditions. The *oba* of Benin controlled all trading by individuals outside Benin and alone owned the most valuable articles of trade, slaves, leopard skins, pepper, palm kernels, coral and most ivory. However, one of the Yoruba *ifa oriki*, or divination songs, gives us a hint: it refers to Oduduwa,

72. N. Levtzion, 1973, pp. 174–8.
73. P. Wheatley, 1970, 1971.

the founding hero and first *oni* of Ife, as a trader grown wealthy from the export of locally produced kola nuts who imported horses from the north.[74]

Ife was situated at the centre of a northerly bulge in the forest[75] and was in the heart of a region of ecological diversity. Situated on fertile land in the forest, it was within reach both of the savannas to the north and of the coast to the south, as well as of a major river valley (the Niger) and of a number of lesser riverain environments in the valleys draining south to the Atlantic. Thus we can see how Ife could develop into a ceremonial centre with the *oni* regarded as a sacred figure, supported by tribute and toll on local trade, and in a commanding position by virtue of his pre-eminence in the religious system. Such a centralization of ritual and supernatural authority carried with it a potential for exploitative economic supremacy and for genuine political power. When, therefore, the commercial demands from the north began to make themselves felt, Ife was in a good position to take advantage of them. It is likely that the northern slave-raiders found their task less easy in the forest; they were more easily ambushed, and villages were better able to protect themselves. Therefore, those wanting slaves found it more prudent to buy them from the locally established authorities of these areas than to capture them. The later Atlantic slave-traders found the same thing at the coastal margin of the forest. Commercial slavery became added to domestic bondage and the trade enhanced the wealth and power of the *oni* and his entourage, which itself grew and developed with the system. Where external trade impinged upon African societies not endowed with desirable natural products to export such as gold, but where a process of political centralization had begun, slaves were the most obvious exportable commodity.[76] The most conservative estimate of the number of slaves exported across the Sahara to North Africa in the first half of the nineteenth century is 10 000 a year,[77] and there is plenty of evidence that this trade had been going on for very many centuries. Even if the numbers involved were smaller at the time of Ife's pre-eminence, the trade could well have been the principal source of Ife's wealth. We cannot assume that the many instances in Ife bronzes and terracottas of bound and gagged individuals, of decapitated corpses, and of heads and limbs severed from the body, all represented slaves, but it is likely that this was often so. If slavery was an integral part of the social and commercial system, as well as providing the labour that serviced the court and wealthy traders and officials, it could also have furnished the ritual sacrifices required to preserve the health and prosperity of the king and his free-born subjects. The

74. R. Horton, 1979, p. 101, quoting W. Abimbola, 1975.

75. The possible significance of which was first pointed out in T. Shaw, 1973, subsequently amplified by R. Horton, 1979.

76. J. D. Fage, 1974.

77. A. G. B. Fisher & H. J. Fisher, 1970, p. 60 and Unesco, *General History of Africa*, Volume IV, chs 6 to 10. See also R. A. Austen, 1979.

slaves sold to northern traders were probably paid for in salt, but as the trading relationship became established and this in turn helped to develop the wealth and power of the *oni*, so luxury goods would become added to the imports from the north, and other indigenous products would be offered in exchange. Copper and brass, textiles, beads, bracelets, swords and horses were added to the expensive imports. In the mid-twelfth century al-Idrīsī also mentions spices, perfumes and manufactured iron tools among items exported from southern Morocco to the land of the blacks.[78] How the crafts of brass-casting and glass bead-making became established we cannot tell; perhaps an *oni* demanded of a resident northern merchant that he should import a teacher to instruct his own household slaves; perhaps another merchant decided he could make more profit by establishing a local bead-making industry rather than by importing beads and bangles ready-made. However 'slavery' is defined,[79] seeing it as the essential basis of the economic and social system that gave rise to the art of Ife in no way detracts from that art; the institution of slavery underlay the artistic productions of classical Greece, and we do not think worse of them for that. The copper and brass had to be paid for in some way, since there is virtually no copper in Nigeria and there are many Arab records of its export to West Africa along the costly caravan routes from the north, as already pointed out in connection with Igbo-Ukwu.[80] The other exotic luxuries would also have been expensive but, being mostly perishable, they less obviously demand an explanation of how they were paid for. Perhaps the kola nut trade has a very ancient history[81] and kola and ivory helped to pay the bills;[82] but it is difficult to think of anything other than slaves as the major exportable commodity.[83] The suggestion that trade was important in the formation of the Ife state does not imply that the kingship was dependent on the personnel engaged in this trade.[84] Nevertheless, once external trade injects surplus wealth into the local exchange system, it enormously adds to the power of the chiefs who control its distribution.

There are a number of hints of the influence from the north; the tradition that Obatala, the creator of mankind, was 'white',[85] the technique of brass-casting employed[86] and the location along the Niger of the 'Tsoede' group of bronzes. A majority of these may have originated in Owo[87] and one at least in Ife, but their position along the northern frontier of Yoruba-

78. N. Levtzion, 1973, p. 141.
79. M. Mason, 1973, p. 453.
80. T. Shaw, 1970, pp. 278–9.
81. N. Levtzion, 1973, p. 181.
82. A. Obayemi, 1976, p. 258.
83. A. G. B. Fisher & H. J. Fisher, 1970; T. Lewicki, 1967b, 1971b, p. 657; R. Mauny, 1961, p. 379; A. G. Hopkins, 1973, pp. 78, 83.
84. A. Obayemi, 1976, pp. 258–9.
85. F. Willett, 1970, p. 304.
86. D. Williams, 1974, pp. 179–203.
87. D. Fraser, 1975.

land can be interpreted as indicating the importance of movements coming from this direction.[88]

Other hints of a northerly connection have been claimed in some of the art and architecture of ancient Ife, pointing back ultimately to the late Roman–Byzantine/Arab world of North Africa. This 'influence' has been seen in the employment of the guilloche and rosette patterns;[89] in the impluvium type of house[90] which follows the same plan as the Roman 'atrium' house; and in the stone and potsherd pavements resembling mosaic and tesselated pavements.[91]

These resemblances may be fortuitous, and such things as the guilloche and rosette patterns could easily have arisen independently; similarly the impluvium house and the potsherd pavement could have been locally devised solutions to the problems of architectural design in a climate of hot sunshine and bright light combined with heavy seasonal rainfall. Taken together, these various hints do suggest the likelihood of cultural influence from the north, but it is not a resurrection of the old, discredited 'Hamitic hypothesis', and it is not necessary to invoke wave after wave of large-scale invasions.[92] It may be correct to see these things, along with the traditions of origin, as demonstrating the political imposition of a foreign ruling dynasty, but even this is not necessary,[93] nor do these hints of connections into a world far away from Yorubaland vindicate the idea that the arts of Ife were not really indigenous. Brass-casting and bead-making are likely to have remained a royal prerogative, the latter perhaps connected with the provision of beaded crowns for the sixteen rulers in Yorubaland entitled to wear them by virtue of authority from Ife.[94]

A beginning for the apogee of ancient Ife in the twelfth century would fit in with the likely date of the penetration into Yorubaland of those commercial demands from the northern world of which Ife was able to take advantage. Perhaps the empire of Mali was too far away to provide this stimulus, and we should look rather to the early Hausa states, in the rise of which economic factors played a particularly important role.[95] We know that at a later date Zazzau specialized in slave-raiding southwards, and perhaps the now abandoned urban site of Turunku fulfilled this role at an earlier period; it lies only 300 km from the Niger at Tada. Unfortunately we still know little archaeologically about the early Hausa states, and the site of Turunku has not yet been excavated.

88. T. Shaw, 1973.

89. E. Eyo, 1974, pp. 379–90. Possibly also in the fish-legged figure occurring in Yoruba and Benin art: D. Fraser, 1972.

90. F. Willett, 1967, p. 126; G. Connah, 1969, p. 51.

91. G. Connah, 1969, p. 50.

92. S. O. Biobaku, 1955, pp. 21–3.

93. F. Willett, 1960, p. 232; W. Fagg, 1963, p. 25; D. Fraser, 1972, p. 290.

94. A. Obayemi, 1976, p. 215.

95. R. S. Smith, 1969, pp. 187–8.

17 The Guinean belt: the peoples between Mount Cameroon and the Ivory Coast

B. W. ANDAH *in collaboration with*
J. ANQUANDAH

Viewed from the narrow historiographical standpoint, the seventh to eleventh centuries of the Christian era constitute a silent period in the history of the coast and inland regions of Lower Guinea. For one thing the documentary sources, European or Arab, have little or nothing to offer. They begin to touch on this area only from the thirteenth/fourteenth and sixteenth centuries respectively. Oral tradition on the other hand, more reliable for more recent centuries, become suspect with greater time depth.

Used in conjunction with information from art, archaeological and related anthropological (especially linguistic) sources, it can shed new light on this early period of Lower Guinea history. The art of some Lower Guinea peoples has valuably depicted how people looked and dressed, what their weapons and buildings looked like at different periods, as well as providing us with an independent time scale for the history of such peoples.

In what follows, the above-mentioned sources are examined closely for what they have to tell about the types of terrains that existed in the Lower Guinea region between the seventh and eleventh centuries; who their inhabitants were at the time as distinct linguistic and societal groups; and the manner of their life styles. The forms of relationships that existed between them and outside groups, as well as who these outsiders were, are also investigated.

The ecological setting

The Lower Guinea Coast refers normally to the stretch from Cape Palmas – the border between northern Liberia and Ivory Coast – to Cameroon, and is divided into two natural zones. The western half extending from Cape Palmas to the Benin River is smooth and almost featureless, whereas a zone of submergence stretches from the Benin River to Mount Cameroon (640 km). The featureless stretch is characterized by wide and almost flat coastal plains as well as river outlets often deflected by long-shore drift which moves from south-east to north-west. Between Cape Three Points

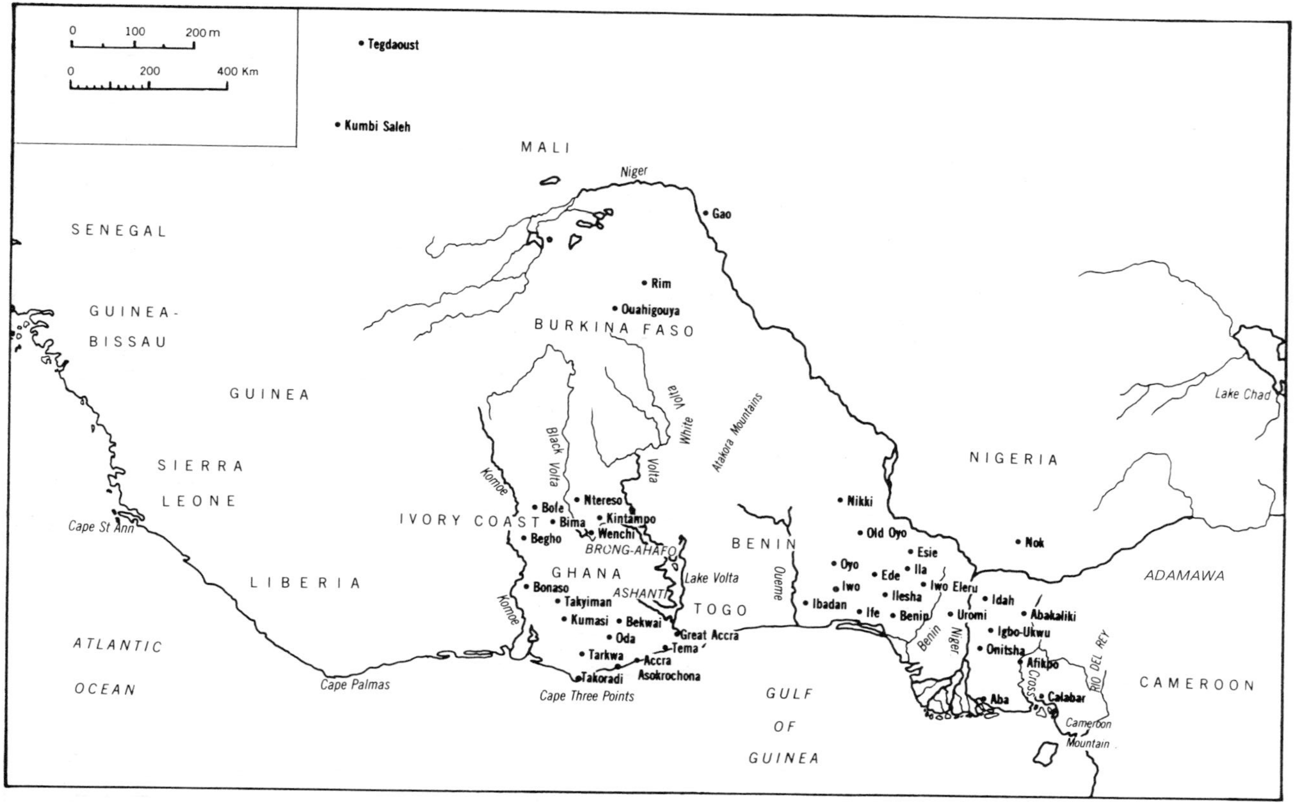

FIG. 17.1 *Towns and sites mentioned in the text*

FIG. 17.2 *Language groups, peoples and kingdoms mentioned in the text*

and the Volta River, low plateaux approach the coast; and dunes are present across estuaries and valley mouths. The zone of submergence, by contrast, comprises the submerging Niger delta which has several openings into the sea; wide, shallow, continually changing bars formed by an eastward coastal drift; and finally estuaries like the Cross River and Rio del Rey which are lined with continuous swamps.

In parts of the coastal zone to the west of the Niger delta, there are some cliffs, and lagoons separated from the ocean by sand ridges. In Ghana and Nigeria outer sand bars of varying width provide effective shelters for the lagoon waterways.

The shore of the mainland north of the lagoons is rocky and cliffed in many places, and modern settlements tend to use the higher sites while the older villages are more frequently at lagoon level.

Behind the coastal strip, there are the southern Asante (Ashanti) plains and upland in Ghana, and the low plateaux in Togo and the Republic of Benin. The Asante uplands have for long been one of the most densely populated parts of West Africa, principally because they are adequately watered, have fertile soils and are marginally situated relative to the northern savanna forest which is restricted to the west of the sandstone escarpment of the Volta basin and the southern end of the Togo mountains. Forest savanna reappears along the coast eastward from Takoradi, changing to true savanna on the Accra plains and extending to the north-east along the dry corridor of the mountains. Mangrove and swamp vegetation occur in the outer edge of the relatively small Volta delta. The open vegetation of the plains is due primarily to the lack of rainfall. Marked differences of soil exist as between the Accra plains and the Volta delta and within the plains themselves.

The Niger delta as a whole is an enormous mass of mixed sediments whereas the Volta has a disproportionately small delta in relation to river length. The Niger delta is large by any standard. East of the Niger there is a broad belt of sedimentary rocks, within which lie the Anambra basin in the north, and the Cross River basin in the south.

The Lower Guinea plains show much greater diversity of climate and vegetation than of landform. The eastern 'dry corridor' crosses the plains from north-east to south-west with mean annual totals of less than 1140 mm extending from the north to the sea and also occurring in the Niger Valley. Immediately to the east of the Atacora Mountains of Togo, annual rainfall averages over 1270 mm along the watershed to Nikki, but totals diminish rapidly northward. To the south-east of the corridor annual totals increase to over 1525 mm. These rainfall totals are reflected in the vegetation pattern. High forest is present in the districts east of Ibadan and south of the watershed, and the greater part of the plains is under open savanna woodland. This open vegetation probably contributed to the development of the relatively large states in this region (e.g. in Yorubaland and the modern Republic of Benin).

Linguistics and early history

Archaeological evidence, especially from surface finds and from shrines (e.g. Ife and Benin in Nigeria), as well as from excavations (e.g. Asokrochona, Kintampo and Ntereso in Ghana; Ugwuelle-Uturu, Iwo Eleru, Afikpo rock shelters in Nigeria) indicate that the Lower Guinea coast and forest now occupied by Kwa-speaking and Benue-Congo-speaking peoples have experienced a long occupation by farmers, and before this by hunters several thousand years ago. Although archaeological and linguistic (glottochronological) evidence suggests a general physical and cultural relationship between the earlier and present inhabitants, such a relationship is yet to be precisely determined. Such delimitation is necessary especially as some of these present inhabitants have myths of origin that tend to show that they have come into their areas of present abode relatively recently.

Linguistic studies suggest that the greater part of the forest belt of West Africa, an area stretching over 1600 km from central Liberia to beyond the Lower Niger in Nigeria is occupied by peoples speaking a series of related languages, with underlying similarities in vocabulary and structure. These are the Kwa and Benue-Congo sub-families of the Niger-Congo language family.

In the central region, the most important (i.e. populous) of these language groupings are Akan (Twi, Fanti, etc.), and Guang dominant in Ghana and Ivory Coast; Gã and Adangbe (Dangme) in southern Ghana; Ewe dominant in Togo and the Republic of Benin and also spoken in south-eastern Ghana. Following Greenberg,[1] the members of the eastern Kwa sub-family in Lower Guinea are Yoruba-Igala; the Nupe group (including Nupe, Gbari, Igbirra and Gade); Edo; the Idoma group (including Idoma, Agatu and Iyala); Igbo; and Ijo. Benue-Congo-speakers are present directly north of and along parts of the Cross River and include the Ibibio, Efik and Ekoi groupings as well as the Tiv.

If underlying similarities in vocabulary and structure characterizing each of these language groups reflect a common proto-language for each, then it means that linguistic evidence points to early cultural continua over the areas they are found in: – Kwa over much of the Guinea forest, Benue-Cross over eastern parts of the Guinea forest and the adjoining savanna – and subsequent diversification from early but unknown dates.

Comparative linguistics suggest that Akan, together with Anyi, Baule, Chakosi, Nzema and Ahanta belongs to a Tano sub-group to which the Guang languages, Abure and Belibe do not belong. Such studies also indicate that the Volta-Comoe languages (Akan group) constitute a true ancestral group to many other Kwa subgroupings; that the Togo remnant languages are distinct from the Ewe and Gã-Adangme groups respectively and that the Akan, Ewe, Guang and Gã-Adangme groups constitute a group less closely related to the Kwa language groups of southern Nigeria.

1. J. H. Greenberg, 1955, 1963a.

The Niger–Benue confluence is generally regarded as a likely centre of origin or dispersal for the eastern Kwa-speaking peoples, while the Benue-Congo speakers are believed to be more recent arrivals in this area from the east. That the divisions between the major Kwa groups must be very old has been inferred from exploratory studies in glottochronology.[2] Although specific time inferences may be considered to be purely speculative, the presence of similarities in important cultural features of the present speakers of these languages, and evidence of having occasionally been influenced similarly does suggest a considerable period of stable divergence of communities in the area.[3] So also is the fact that generally the Kwa languages are very distinctive and divergent from the more widespread linguistic groups that surround them. Indeed they could be survivors of once more widely spread linguistic stocks.

It seems also that there is no clear boundary between some of Greenberg's Kwa (e.g. Igbo) languages and Benue-Cross languages such as Ibibio, Efik and Kele. As noted by Williamson, there are some Benue-Congo languages (like Jukun) without noun-class systems, while some Kwa languages (e.g. Dogama and Edo) have noun-class systems.[4] On the other hand it seems that the Igbo and Efik languages, having been in intimate contact for a long period, could have experienced a certain amount of undetected borrowing, even in basic vocabulary.

Historical geographic evidence furthermore suggests that the already inhabited forest was an obstacle to penetration by later peoples. When such penetration occurred, it was not in the form of mass migrations, but was rather confined to small groups who, even if they exerted great cultural influence, were probably absorbed linguistically and sometimes physically by the local populations.

Apart from principal ethnic groups such as the Akan-Baule of Ghana and the Ivory Coast, the Bini (Edo-speakers), Yoruba, Igbo and Ijo of Nigeria, the Lower Guinea region has also been inhabited by other groups neighbouring the mentioned ones. Many times, the histories of the larger and smaller ethnic groups were inextricably intertwined. Some groups actually intruded into the midst of the others, and there was much cross-cultural influence.

The Gold Coast between 600 and 1100

The period from the seventh to the eleventh century in the Gold Coast (present-day southern and central Ghana) was clearly a formative one, transitional between the prehistoric village complexes antedating the seventh century on the one hand, and the urban, commercial, high-level

2. Cf. R. G. Armstrong, 1962, 1964b.
3. R. G. Armstrong, 1964b, p. 136.
4. K. Williamson, 1971, p. 252.

technology complexes of 1200 and after, on the other. The apparent obscurity of the period 600–1100 is due not to the uneventfulness of the period *per se* (since the earlier prehistoric era −1500–+500 has been heavily documented from several parts of the country), but rather to the relatively small amount of attention given to the period by scholars and the incidence of research.

The prehistoric background

During the first and second millennia before the Christian era various parts of the Gold Coast forest and savanna were settled by village folk who built houses of mud, wood, stone or laterite blocks and practised a subsistence economy combining fishing, hunting, gathering or 'cultivation' of yam, oil palm, fruits, cow pea, hackberry, and *Canarium* fruit and the herding of shorthorn cattle and goats.[5] While the evidence for pastoralism is strong and clear, that for arable or crop farming is rather tenuous, mainly because archaeo-botanical evidence has been hard to find in the tropical soils. Nevertheless, there is such an abundance of technological evidence in the form of polished stone axes and stone hoes for wood-felling, bush-clearing and soil preparation that one cannot but assume that some tubers such as indigenous yam and some grains, such as Guinea corn or millet were cultivated from an early date.

Of the known village sites referred to as the 'Kintampo complex' after the type-site located in the Brong region, 80 per cent have been excavated. The villages so far excavated vary in territorial size from 2000 sq.m (Mumute-Brong), to 115 300 sq.m (Boyase, near Kumasi), and to 21 000 sq.m (Kintampo KI site). Some of the village sites may indeed be comparable to modern villages of Ghana in terms of size and population. The technology and subsistence economies of the prehistoric villages indicate strong adaptations to the environment and specialization among the village folk. There are hints that special areas were reserved for use as potters' workshops, stone-tool knappers' workshops, or grain-milling quarters etc. The Kintampo complex also provides the earliest evidence of ceramic sculpture in the Gold Coast. The populations whose material cultural remains are represented in the Kintampo complex need not have spoken one language in all the regions, as Colin Painter avers, in associating Guan with the Kintampo complex.[6] Indeed, it is possible that any or all of the proto-Akan, proto-Guan and proto-Gã/Dangme languages were in use by the first millennium before the Christian era. From the correlation of linguistic studies on Baule, Agni, Bia and Akan with archaeology, there is emerging the possibility (still yet to be tested) that proto-Akan evolved in the forest and savanna environment straddling the middle and southern

5. C. Flight, 1967, 1976.
6. C. Painter, 1966.

parts of the Ivory Coast and the Gold Coast and that the Kintampo complex, whose sites have now been identified in both countries, may well be the archaeological equivalent of an ecologically adapted proto-Akan speaking populace which knew no territorial boundary such as now exists between the Ivory Coast and Ghana.[7]

The archaeology of the Accra Plains suggests that Late Stone Age hunter-gatherers and fisherfolk who had a shellfish economy and potting technology were already active in the area of Gao lagoon (Tema) between the fourth and second millennia before the Christian era[8] and that they subsequently took to the establishment of village farming settlements such as are attested at the Kintampo complex site of Christian's Village located near the University of Ghana at Legon. At the site of Ladoku, a Late Stone Age flake industry associated with decorated pottery has been found stratified directly below an Iron Age level with Dangme-type Cherekecherete pottery and a bauxite-bead industry dated by carbon-14 to 1325–1475.[9]

While small-scale movement of peoples and trade and cultural contacts are regular features in the evolution of most societies and must be recognized as such, the old idea of mass exodus of people from place to place is, except for rare cases, an unconvincing approach to explaining ethnic and cultural origins. In this respect, the old views of migration origins of the Akan from Egypt or ancient Ghana, and the view of Gã-Dangme origin from what is now the Republic of Benin/Nigeria must, on archaeological and linguistic grounds, be regarded as far fetched.[10]

One of the major landmarks in the cultural evolution of the Gold Coast peoples is the inception and development of iron technology. Its adoption was crucial in the rise of society from a stage of peasant village economy and isolationism to one characterized by high-level technological competence, large-scale agriculture, diverse industries and crafts, complex trade systems and socio-political systems. The earliest evidence for iron technology is from Begho (+105–255) and Abam, Bono Manso (+290–350). Excavations at these sites have produced ruins of furnaces, slag and pottery as well as charcoal usable for dating purposes.

Evidence for the period 600–1100

The period between 600 and 1300 has been described as the 'dark age' in the history of the Gold Coast, in the sense that relatively much less is known of the period than for other periods during the last four millennia. The available evidence, however, leads one to hypothesize that this was essentially a formative period during which a start was made in the laying

7. F. Dolphyne, 1974.
8. J. C. Dombrowski, 1980.
9. J. Anquandah, 1982.
10. Cf. M. E. Kropp-Dakubu, 1976; A. A. Boahen, 1977.

of the infrastructure of society. Because of the relative paucity of evidence for reconstructing the history of this period, one must make allowance for a certain amount of extrapolation of evidence from earlier or later periods and also for the use of circumstantial evidence.

Akanland

The rockshelter site of Amuowi near Bono Manso has a date (+370–510) which is slightly antecedent to the period under discussion. But this date ties in with the date for iron-smelting at Abam, Bono Manso. The Brong of Bono Manso and Takyiman have ethnohistorical traditions which suggest a local origin from the Amuowi sacred hole or rock shelter. Every year, at their *Apoo* festival, the Takyiman Brong recall their traditions of origin in song:

> We came from Amuowi,
> Creator of old;
> We are children of Red Mother Earth
> We came from Amuowi.

The evidence of pottery and dating from the Amuowi excavations suggest that from around the sixth century the Brong of the Bono Manso area were establishing permanent settlements that would lead later to the proto-urban and urban settlement at Bono Manso.[11]

The site of Bonoso has an early date that falls exactly within this period. Excavations conducted there[12] brought to light an iron-smelting industry with slag, iron implements and pottery ornamented with comb impressions. The site is dated by carbon-14 to 660–1085. Oral traditions of the Wenchi Brong assert that their ancestral clans emerged from a hole in the ground at Bonoso near Wenchi after being unearthed by a pig-like quadruped called *wankyie*. The traditions point to Bonoso as the place where the ancestors established their nuclear settlements before moving to their first capital site at Ahwene Koko (Old Wenchi).

A third Brong site belonging to this period is the proto-urban settlement at Begho which oral traditions name after the legendary founder Efua Nyarko. The Nyarko suburb which is dated by carbon-14 to 965–1125,[13] extends over an area of about one square kilometre. The excavations there revealed evidence of iron implements, copper objects, ivory and pottery with slip and painted decorations, akin to ninth-century pottery from New Buipe (Figs. 17.3–17.5). Altogether the data from Nyarko reflects the general tendencies of the period 600-1100, namely, craft and technological specialization with proto-urbanism and possibly the beginnings of the

11. K. Effah-Gyamfi, 1978.
12. J. Boachie-Ansah, 1978.
13. L. B. Crossland, 1976.

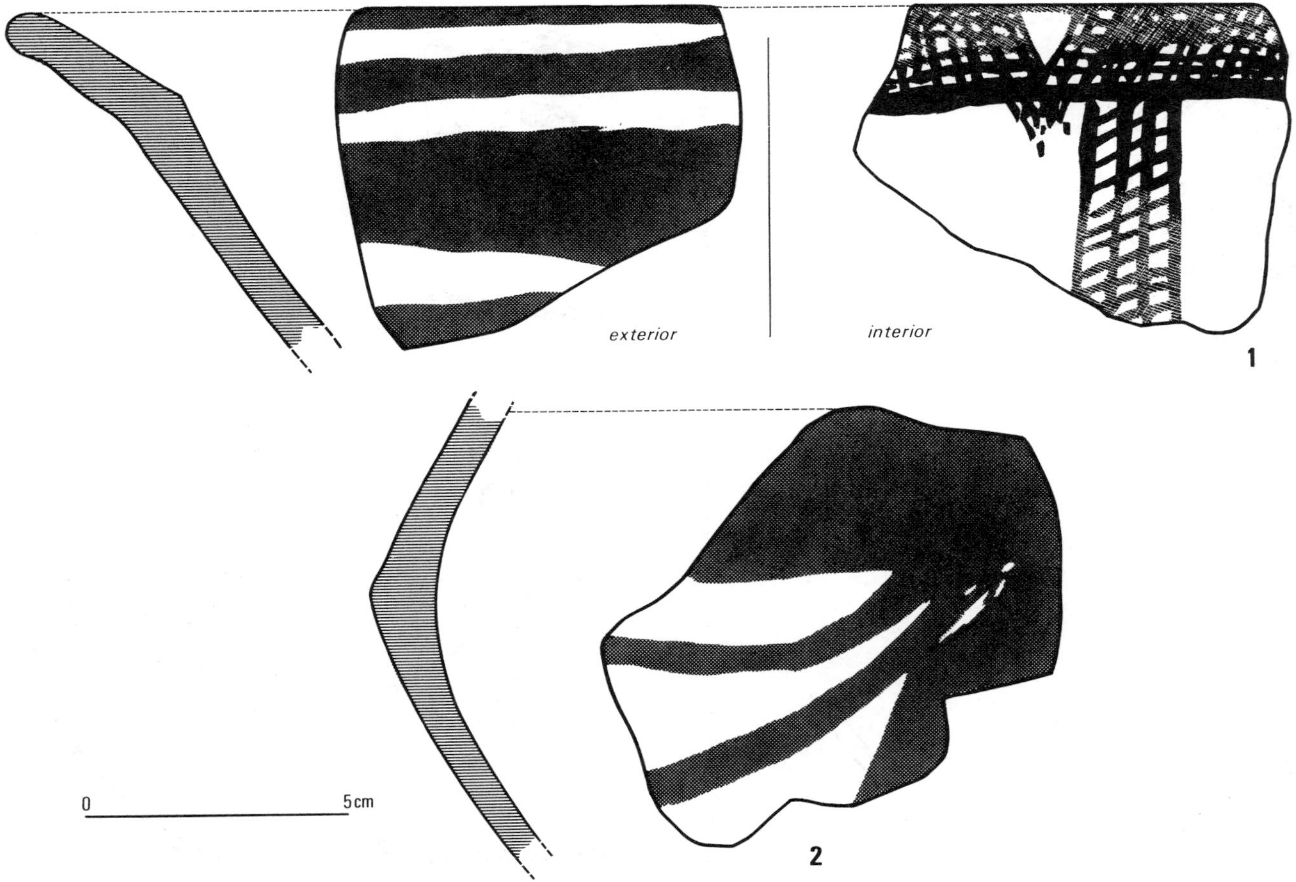

FIG. 17.3 *Tenth- to eleventh-century painted pottery from the Nyarko quarter of the Begho trading metropolis, Republic of Ghana*

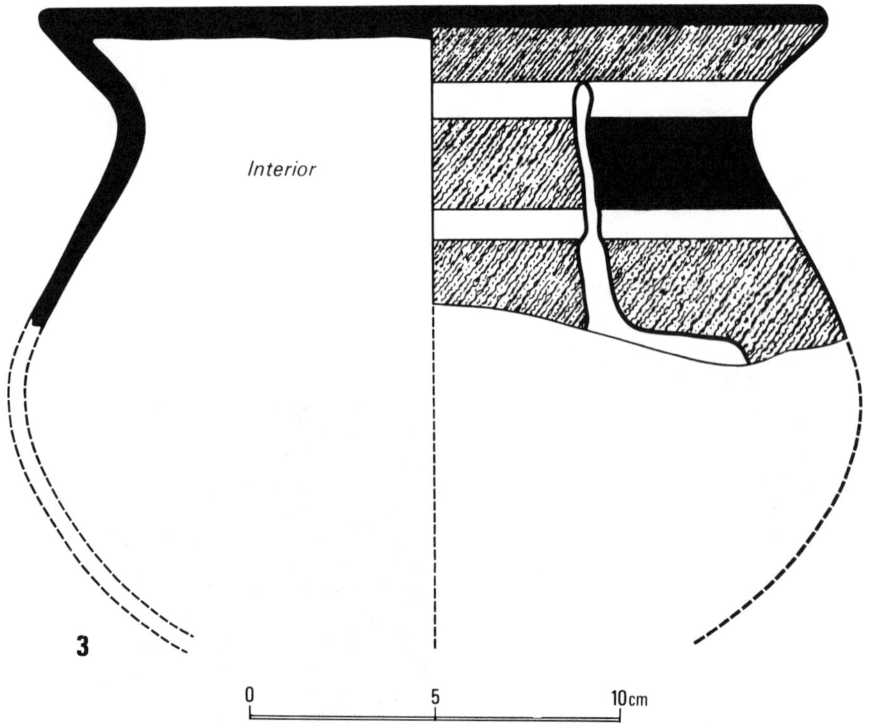

FIG. 17.4 *Seventh- to ninth-century pottery with slip and roulette-impressed decoration from New Buipe, Republic of Ghana*

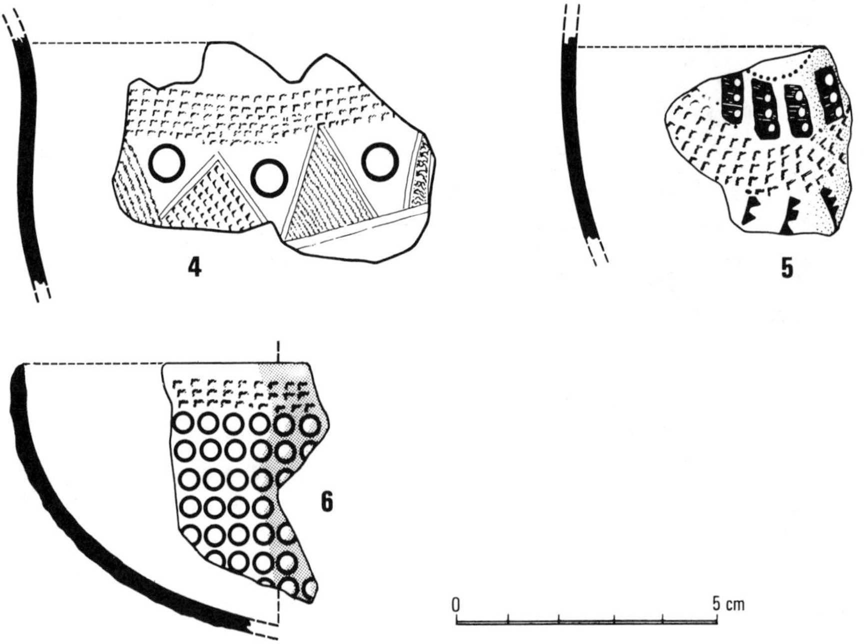

FIG. 17.5 *Seventh- to ninth-century pottery with stamp-impressed decoration from New Buipe, Republic of Ghana (after R. N. York, 1973)*

ivory industry and export trade which was to become important in subsequent centuries. Indeed the ethno-archaeological record points to the Brong region as a pioneering Akan area for the evolution of Iron Age farming, metallurgy, urbanism, state formation and long-distance commerce[14] and the period 600–1100 in Brong, however dimly presented to us by the paucity of evidence, was clearly one of active preparation for the era that was to be the high-water mark of Brong civilization.

The Asante and Wassa areas are well known for their prominent hill-top sites which were the favourite locations of Iron Age settlements of the period between the beginning of the Christian era and 1500. The most notable of these sites are Nkukoa Buoho (near Kumasi), Bekwai, Kwapong, Obuasi Monkey Hill, Nsuta, Tarkwa, Ntirikurom and Odumparara Bepo. The sites appear to have been village settlements with palisades. They are characterized by concentrations of pottery with overhanging lips and profuse ornamentation on bodies and rims. The pottery is sometimes found in association with iron slag, furnace fragments and anachronistic Stone Age carry-overs such as polished stone axes, quartz beads, microliths, grinding stones and occasionally, as at Odumparara, bauxite beads. Although none of the sites has as yet been properly excavated and dated by carbon-14, their characteristic archaic pottery type places them well before the period 1600–1900 when the fashion among potters of Akanland was the complex architectural pot-form with 'smoke-glazing' as ornamentation instead of the earlier picturesque body ornamentation. Oliver Davies[15] described the Asante and Wassa hill-top sites as 'medieval' in date, a term which is manifestly unsatisfactory in the African traditional cultural context. At Nkukoa Buoho near Kumasi, the hill-top complex pottery seems to follow chronologically the Kintampo complex period which suggests that the hill-top profusely decorated pottery of this area belongs to the period 600–1100 or thereabouts. If nothing else does, at least the evidence of iron technology of this complex does point to the foundation-laying character of this period preparatory to the major epoch of urbanization, state formation and long-distance trade evidenced in Adanse, Denkyira and Asante (Figs. 17.6 and 17.7).

The area of Akyem Manso and Akwatia is noted for its production of valuable exportable minerals. Its importance for archaeology, however, lies in its earthen fortifications.[16] These are characterized by high mud embankments constructed as a defensive structure surrounding each village settlement. On the inner side of the embankment was a deep trench or ditch. These earthworks are a common feature at Akwatia, Manso, Oda, Abodum, Kokobin, Domiabra, etc. A number of the fortified sites have been excavated in an attempt to test the two hypotheses advanced to explain their function. The first hypothesis is that they were constructed

14. J. Anquandah, 1982.
15. O. Davies, 1967.
16. ibid.

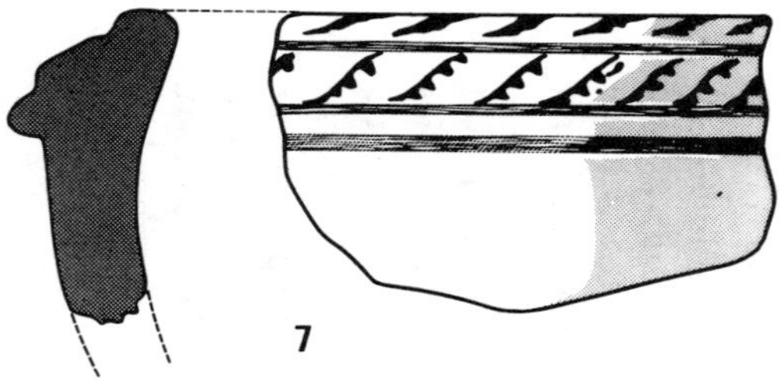

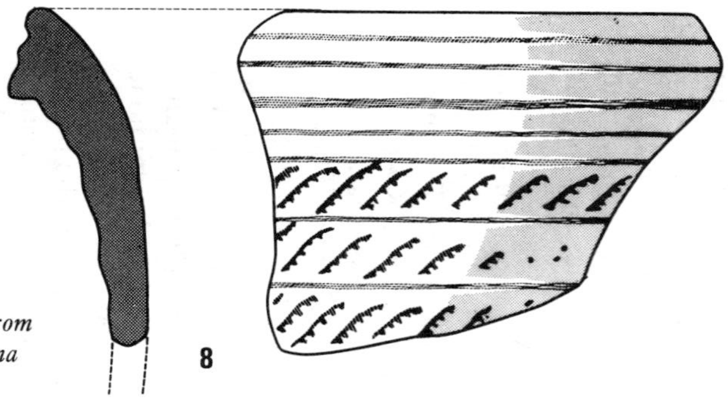

FIG. 17.6 *Pottery with overhanging lip and profuse body ornamentation from period II* (c. *500–1200*) *at Nkukoa Buoho, near Kumasi, Republic of Ghana*

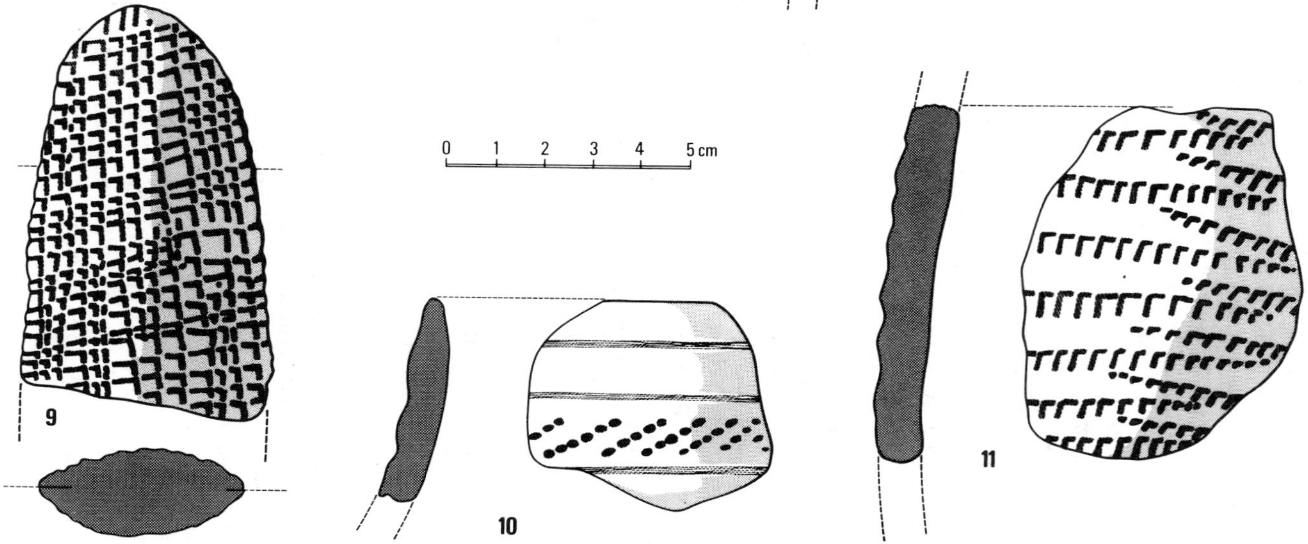

FIG. 17.7 *Kintampo 'neolithic' Complex Culture materials from period I* (c. *−1500 to −500*) *at Nkukoa Buoho, near Kumasi, Republic of Ghana. Left: pot-shaping tool; centre and right: stamped pottery*

for defence. The second is that they were to wall in labour camps built for the exploitation of alluvial gold deposits of the Birim Valley.[17] It appears that the 'defence' school of thought has tended to carry more weight than the 'labour camp' school of thought. The most recent ethno-archaeological studies undertaken at the Akyem Manso earthworks revealed profusely ornamented pottery with overhanging rims (akin to that of the Asante/Wassa hill-top complex), associated with evidence of iron smelting, polished stone axes, beads and grinding stones.[18]

The Guan

Oral traditions state that Kwahuland was among the areas occupied by Guan-speaking people prior to the arrival of Adanse people in the area and that these pre-Akan Guan were called Kodiabe on account of their predilection for a subsistence economy based on oil palm. The traditions name a number of pioneering leaders who led the Guan in establishing settlements in the area, namely, Adamu Yanko, Bransem Diawuo, Odiaboa, Kosa Brempong and Yaw Awere. It is said that around 1200 the Guan settlers who were in occupation of the Afram Plains established their capital at Ganeboafo whence the Atara dynasty ruled the Afram Plains Guan. A commercial centre was set up at Juafo Abotan where brisk commerce was pursued with the Sudanic belt in ivory, kola, cattle, salt and slaves.[19] Archaeology is yet to investigate the substance of these traditions. However, a number of excavations have been undertaken at Bosumpra Cave (the name is thought to be connected with the Guan deity, Bosumpra), and rock shelters at Apreku, Tetewabuo and Akyekyemabuo.[20] The excavations supported by carbon-14 dating indicate that *c.* 1000–1300 the Kwahu scarp was occupied by versatile hunters, fisherfolk, pastoralists and oil palm exploiters who produced 'smoke-glazed' pottery.[21]

Another area where archaeology has been focusing attention on the Guan is Kyerepong Dawu. The indigenous populace of Dawu Akuapem is Guan-speaking, though its language and culture have been considerably overshadowed in recent times by the Akwamu and Akuapem Akan peoples. The area of Dawu and Awukugua is marked by numerous large mounds representing litter deposited by the local people over long periods, which carbon-14 dating fixes at *c.* 1400–1600. Excavations of the mounds have revealed debris including pottery imported from Shai, ivory ornaments, bone combs, copper and iron products, and *akuaba* flat-headed clay sculptures.[22] Although the dating of the middens is a little later than the period

17. P. Ozanne, 1971.
18. D. Kiyaga-Mutindwa, 1976.
19. J. R. Wallis, 1955.
20. F. B. Musonda, 1976.
21. A. B. Smith, 1975; C. T. Shaw, 1944.
22. T. Shaw, 1961.

we are concerned with here, the cultural context associated with the ubiquitous mounds of Akuapem suggests foundation-laying processes which heralded the modern states of the Akuapem Hill-Guan.

The Gã and Dangme

The archaeology and ethnolinguistics of the Accra Plains, examined dispassionately and free from the prejudices of adulterated oral traditions, indicate that the Gã and Dangme peoples have probably been occupying settlements in the Accra Plains for some one to two millennia.[23] Indeed one would go as far as hypothesizing autochthonous Gã and Dangme evolution in the Accra Plains. A number of sites such as Gbegbe, Little Accra, Prampram and Lõlõvõ, though as yet undated, contain ruins of settlements with concentrations of pottery not associated with European imports, thus suggestive of a period before 1400. True, there are settlement sites at Ayawaso, capital of Great Accra, Ladoku and Shai which date to the period 1550–1900, the major period of urbanization, state formation and complex trade systems (Fig. 17.8). On the other hand, Ladoku and Shai were the focus of numerous village settlements belonging to the period 600–1400, among them Cherekecherete, Adwuku, Tetedwa, Pianoyo and Hioweyo. The latest research in Accra Plains Dangmeland indicates that between 1000 and 1300 local Dangme settlers around Prampram, Dawhenya and Shai were evolving a life style of subsistence (pastoralism, fishing, salt-making and terraced agriculture based on Guinea corn cultivation), and a socio-theocratic system that was to lead to the rise of a conurbation or twin-township in 1300–1900 at Shai and Ladoku and a civilization characterised by elaborate herbal science, *Klama* proverbial and philosophical music and a combined theocratic and monarchical system.[24]

Eweland

Research work in Eweland has been confined largely to surface reconnaissance in places like Vume Dugame, Bator, Amedzofe-Avatime, Wusuta and Akpafu. Some of these sites provide quite common evidence of settlements with iron-working. The sites of Akpafu, Wusuta and Kanieme have

23. The question of the origin of the Gã and Dangme is controversial. The view of a migration origin from Dahomey/Nigeria area has been propagated by traditional Elders of Dangmeland including Carl Reindorf, Noa Akunor Aguae Azu, D. A. Puplampu, Nene Lomo II of Ada, Rev. S. S. Odonkor of Krobo and La Nimo Opta III of Doryumu, Shai. This view is supported by scholars like M. E. Kropp-Dakubu, E. O. Apronti, Irene Odotei and Louis Wilson.

24. J. Anquandah, 1982.

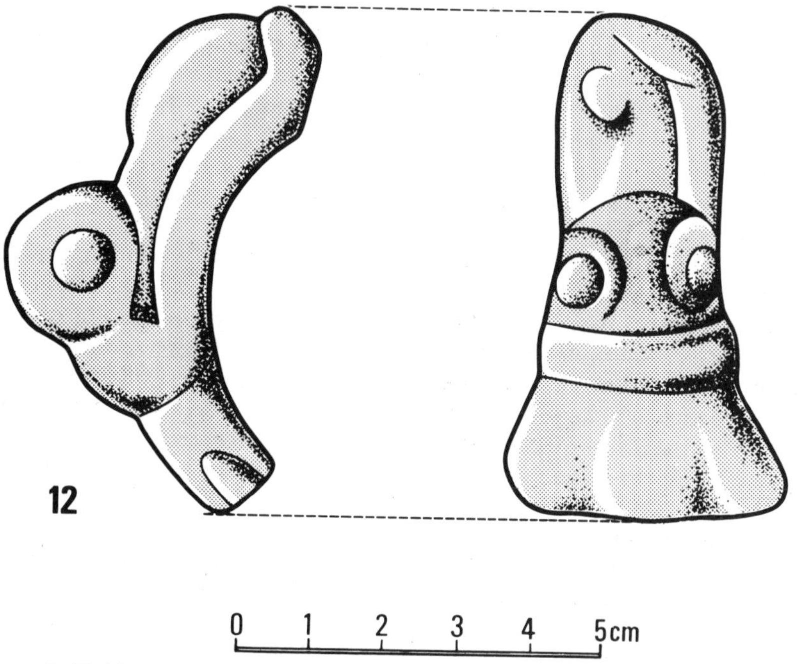

FIG. 17.8 *Shai Dangme potters from Cherekecherete Middle Iron Age site in the Accra Plains (Republic of Ghana) were legatees of seventh- to eleventh-century Iron Age peoples and made pottery decorated with stylized figurines of heads of domestic animals and humans*

traditions of iron-working spread over centuries and the archaeological evidence, though undated, does give support to the traditions. However, there are many sites in the Volta Region which, as indicated above, produce microliths, polished stone axes and stone hoes, suggesting a long continual occupation into modern times. There is really no reason not to associate the present-day Ewe occupants with the Iron Age and Late Stone Age cultural materials distributed widely throughout Ewe country.

Early urban settlement

The available evidence points to the existence of at least two principal types of urban settlements in what is now Ghana prior to European advent; commercial centres like Begho, and state capitals like Bono Manso. Settlements that were mostly trading centres grew up in the Tain–Volta confluence of present-day Ghana. Migrant elements and long-distance trade were important to their growth. Limited archaeological exploration indicated the existence of such settlements in Kitare, Begho, Bicu, Old Bima and Buipe among others.

The evolution of both local and immigrant groups at these sites, and their interrelationships, are yet to be explored in detail through systematic excavation. But present evidence from sites like Jakpawuase seems to suggest that prior to the advent of the Mande this region was reasonably well populated and contained large settlements, as well as clusters of a number of interrelated communities which had previously developed an interwoven network of local trade and exchange probably based on the bartering of food and agricultural produce.

Work at Begho revealed that the culture of this town was predominantly Brong, with evidence for significant outside influences. The quarters of the ancient town are described by Posnansky as consisting of areas of mounds often 'L'-shaped or in the form of hollow squares between one and two metres high and up to twenty metres across. The largest quarter, that of the Brong, consists of several hundred mounds in an area more than a kilometre across. The quarters are one to two kilometres apart, with an exposed outcrop of laterite between them, where the market was said to have been located.[25]

Other important market centres which probably grew up in the same general area at the time of Begho's existence and prospered largely due to the Middle Niger trade in the area include Bima and Bofe. The urban phase of Begho (Bew) was preceded directly by an agricultural-pastoral phase dating as far back as 3500 years ago. The societies involved lived in sizeable settlements and used Kintampo Neolithic-type tools. Evidence, especially pottery, suggests that before the mid-second millennium of the Christian era (especially the eleventh to twelfth centuries) settlements in the Begho vicinity (and pre-urban Begho phase) were mostly those of the indigenous Bono group.

According to Posnansky, Begho also developed as a larger nucleated centre before the advent of long-distance trade, its inhabitants exploiting fertile lands for agriculture, from as far back as the second century of the Christian era. Crops farmed included yams and oil palms with sorghums and millets being added later. In the course of time the town graduated from a Brong (Akan) foundation to incorporate Voltaic-speaking and Mande-speaking people engaged in different occupations.[26]

Begho existed as a trading centre from the eleventh century but did not attain its peak until the fourteenth century. Then it appears to have contained up to five hundred compounds and five thousand people. It comprised five territorially distinct quarters with the largest, that of the Brong, being well over half a kilometre across. Their farmlands stretched much further afield.

Although heterogeneous, the bulk of the population of Begho was probably of local origin (Brong and Pantera). Very little is known of the nature

25. M. Posnansky, 1973, pp. 156–62.
26. M. Posnansky, 1980.

of the society other than what can be inferred from a study of later traditional Akan life. The traditions nevertheless indicate the existence of domestic slaves and an active clan system. The grave goods and the variations in the inhumations indicate a variety of religious attitudes to burials.

Like many other ancient settlements, it is not clear how Bono Manso (16 km north of Takyiman) was founded. Oral information suggests that the site of Bono was founded by a group of people who were once inhabitants of a rock shelter referred to as Amuowi perhaps around the fifth century of the Christian era. According to Effah-Gyamfi the growth and importance of Bono owed much to the integration into one state of various pre-existing chiefdoms in the area around the end of the first millennium.[27] Bono Manso was not the earliest of the large villages and towns in this area; it was simply the first to acquire supremacy over all the settlements in the area through its primary role as the seat of the Bono kings.

Bono had rich deposits of *atwet weboo* (laterite nodules suitable for iron smelting) available to it. Archaeological survey has actually revealed at least five iron-working industrial sites all roughly equidistant from the streams and rivers. One of these sites dates to the fourth century of the Christian era, but some probably belong to the urban phase. Like Amuowi, however, the few pottery remains associated with the site which produced this early date are identical with those found at Bono Manso in the earliest deposits, suggesting the utilization of what became the site of Bono Manso by a society ancestral to the founders of the capital.

Bono Manso was also located at the savanna–forest contact zone where at the regional level savanna items could be exchanged for forest items. At the international level, this was the southernmost point to which pack animals could travel without any health hazards, and therefore the effective area for the exchange of foreign items for those from areas further south. Not only was the area where Bono Manso was located the source of alluvial gold which the Mande traders eagerly sought, it was also the source of kola nuts.

Unlike Begho there is no evidence for the existence of any alien quarter. This means that Bono's population was more ethnically homogeneous than Begho's. Bono's central organization also effectively controlled commercial activities, whereas in Begho commerce seems to have overriden political organization.

Effah-Gyamfi infers from pottery studies that Bono Manso may be an early Akan settlement. According to him the Bono Manso area may have been on the boundary between the early pure Akan cultural group to the south and the early non-Akan and the mixed Akan to the north and north-west respectively.[28] This and linguistic evidence suggest a continuity of many ethnic/cultural groups since the last five hundred years or so.

27. K. Effah-Gyamfi, 1975.
28. ibid.

Yorubaland between 600 and 1100

In Yorubaland, archaeological research has so far been restricted to Ife and Oyo and of these two, only the urban phase of Ife dates back to our period. Archaeological evidence supported by oral traditions indicates that there have been three distinct and major periods in the growth of Ife; these are outlined in some detail by Ozanne.[29]

A traditional Yoruba town apparently comprised several compounds and each compound consisted of houses built around a series of open courtyards of differing sizes and usually containing water pots to catch rain from the roof-tops. There were however important differences between the various towns, reflecting differences in history and ecology. Indeed, if Johnson is right, some of these differences may reflect different kinds of growth. According to him, Ife typifies towns which grew gradually. Such towns started off with one wall only, their surrounding farmland being protected by an *Igbo-Ile*, a dense belt of forest untouched except for certain burials. Later when it became sufficiently important to be threatened by a protracted siege, an outer defensive wall would be built to protect farmlands.[30]

Several historians have suggested that one of the most important agents in the growth of urban and state societies was probably the institution of divine kingship. Wheatley further maintains that divine kingship was introduced through the agency of external contacts rather than by an internally generated redistribution of power in Yoruba society.[31] And even though the precise mode of its diffusion is not known, it is seen as probably providing a powerful impetus towards the development of urban forms. The same scholar, however, admits that Yoruba cities must have been generated rather than imposed, that they were the result of an organic process of internally induced social stratification rather than of the extension of symbolic and organizational patterns already developed elsewhere. Whether or not such an assertion is correct can only be demonstrated by a systematic archaeological study of pertinent towns and village sites in the area. But state systems where the idea of divine kingship played an important role in their development were those of Benin and Nri.

Allison suggests a connection between the stone sculptures of Yorubaland and the classical age of Ife, although these differ stylistically from those of Ife brasses and terracottas. All occur within 100 km of Ife in the central Yoruba forest; with Esie (some 90 km north of Ife) at the edge of the forest region. Several of the sculptures from Esie are found at two villages now in savanna terrain within nine or more sites.[32]

29. P.Ozanne, 1969.
30. S. Johnson, 1921.
31. P. Wheatley, 1970.
32. P. Allison, 1968, pp. 13 ff.

At sacred groves of Ife between the outer and inner walls stand naturalistic figures depicting negroids in a local granite/gneiss. The most outstanding of these are the two figures known as Idena and Ore. A third figure in steatite in a separate grove nearby depicts a kneeling woman. The general treatment of this last figure is described as similar to certain styles of recent Yoruba wood-carving. A variety of other stone objects are grouped around the two granite figures and at other clearings in the Ore grove.

Elsewhere in Ife there are a number of worked standing stones, the most impressive of these being a slim carved granite column known as *Opa Oranmiyan* – the staff of Oranmiyan – Oranmiyan having been one of the children of Oduduwa and the founder of Oyo. It has since been restored (5.5 m high) and ornamented with lines of iron pegs in the form of an elongated trident. In the main marketplace stands the 1.8 m high *Opa Ogun* – staff of Ogun, the god of war and iron – shaped like a cylindrical club.

The Idena and Ore are the only examples of figure sculpture in hard stone at Ife, but at Eshure in the Ekiti country – some 80 km away to the north-east – is a group of carvings with obvious affinities such as the stone figures of Aba Ipetu (eight in all) which are similar in posture, the necklace and arm rings and the arrangements of the cloth, but with more stylized treatment.

In addition to those at Eshure, stone sculptures which show connections with Ife tradition are found at other sites within *c.* 50 km of Ife, like Kuta to the west, Ikirun to the north and Effon to the north-west.

Several terracotta heads of conical form have been found in Ife itself. All of these show some connection with the stone sculpture tradition of Ife. Evidence of a more widespread influence is gradually being revealed, and fragments of the typical Ife potsherd pavements have been found at Benin, to the east and as far away as the Republic of Benin and Togo to the west. Allison suggests though that the origins of the stone sculptures can only be sought in Ife itself.

The largest group of stone sculptures in Yoruba country is at the Igbomina town of Esie, which is still within the forest fringe, though the encroaching front of the savanna is generally only a few miles distant to the north, and has already invaded the forest in many localized patches. The recent history of Esie is connected with Oyo rather than with Ife.

But the stone figures are almost certainly the relics of a former occupation. These representations called *Ere* by Esie people, number more than 800, although one cannot be sure because so many have had their heads and limbs broken off. They all appear to be sculpted in steatite which outcrops at no great distance from the town, and the complete figures are generally about 60 cm high, although they range in size from about 20 cm to nearly 130 cm.

Although today the Igbomina of the savannas claim historic associations with Oyo, the first *Orangun* (head chief) of Ila, a large Igbomina town of the forest, was traditionally one of the seven grandsons of Oduduwa mentioned in the account of the original dispersion from Ife; and in the final confrontation with the Oyo of Ibadan, Ila sided with the Ekiti, Ilesha and the other forest Yoruba.

Tradition associates the objects with previous occupants of the area who were conquered or colonized by Oyo. They were a forest people within the cultural sphere of Ife, whose influence can be detected in several recurrent features of the sculptures.

The naturalistic terracotta and brass sculptures of Ife, which have been dated with some confidence to the eleventh century were certainly created as adornments to the royal ancestor cult of the *Oni* (king) of Ife, so also were the remarkable quartz stools and granite monoliths. The naturalism of the granite/gneiss Idena figure suggests a similar period and inspiration. The fact that the over eight-hundred Esie figures have elaborate headdresses and other ornaments and are mostly seated on stools suggests that they also depict royalty. The style is less realistic than the Ife sculptures and their date may be later.

It is crucial to find out what links if any, chronological and otherwise, exist between the stone sculptures and the terracotta and bronze traditions; and what relationships exist between this stone sculpture tradition and those found in other parts of West Africa. Part of this exercise will require archaeological reconnaissance for pre-Oyo settlements in the Esie and Ijara areas and excavation of these; and a geo-archaeological study of the sources of raw material. Finally ethnographic studies especially of wood and terracotta sculpture will help indicate what technical relationships exist between the stone traditions and others.

In his work on Ife art Willett has noted the many general characteristics which Ife sculptures share with those of Nok,[33] whilst shifting the major emphasis onto naturalistic representation. He also suggests that the naturalistic ears of Ife could have provided a basis for the freely stylized interpretations of Benin. This and other similar evidence is considered by him as indicating connections across time and space and of continuity in artistic tradition in West Africa through more than two millennia.[34] Whether Willett is right or not, the Yoruba appear to constitute a logical point of departure for the study of coastal and inland peoples of Lower Guinea. Remarkable features of their culture were a highly developed urban settlement pattern, a common language with dialectal variations, the peoples' claim to a common history of origin, the worshipping of a common pantheon of gods, again with local variation and emphasis, and finally a very

33. Certain Nok features seem to foreshadow the 'Ife complex' in respect of at least both pottery and figurine traditions. It is even possible that iron tools, and/or knowledge of ironworking were introduced there from Nok while it is not impossible that such knowledge ultimately derived from either Meroe or the north-west, although the evidence presently known does not support such a view.

34. F. Willett, 1967.

PLATE 17.1 *Terracotta head from a figure of an Oni (King), excavated at Ita Yemoo, Ife. Height: 26.3 cm*

PLATE 17.2 *Terracotta head from a figure, possibly of a Queen, excavated at Ita Yemoo, Ife. Height: 23.1 cm*

PLATE 17.3 *Terracotta head found beside the Ifewara Road, Ife. Height: 22.5 cm*

sophisticated art tradition. Furthermore the Yoruba appear to be related to and played an important part in the subsequent founding of some neighbouring kingdoms like those of Benin and Nupe.

The key role of the Yoruba people becomes more clear by looking at the early population movements in southern Nigeria. There was evidently first an early and long-term spread of the Yoruba-Igala group west and southward from an origin point somewhere in the north-eastern part of their current range. Second, Igala traditions relate their early expansion on the east bank of the Niger, with movement eastward against the Idoma and southward against the Igbo-speaking peoples. Third the position of the Itsekiri in the south-western part of the Niger Delta indicates that this Yoruba group expansion may have occurred prior to the expansion of Edo-speakers towards the coast.

An early southward invasion of the Niger Delta by the Ijo-speaking peoples is also inferred.[35] This movement appears to have been followed at a later time first by a southward and east-curving movement of Edo-speaking peoples; second by a general southward Igbo expansion into the uplands west of the Niger, and third by another Igbo push toward the eastern delta coast which was still under way during the development of the slave trade. Eastward expansion by the Igbo against Benue-Congo-speaking peoples north of the Cross River and probably post-dating the slave trade has been documented for very recent times.[36] Such late Igbo expansion is partly associated with rising population pressures on the eastern uplands. These movements may have occurred at the same time as a series of other movements recounted in oral traditions and implied in the intermingling of language groups in the delta. Oral traditions also suggest late expansion of Edo peoples into the central delta, and also of Ijo peoples dispersing from an early centre in the western delta toward the east, where they ultimately came up against the Benue-Congo-speaking Ibibio.

Both Yoruba traditions of origin and archaeological evidence suggest at least that it was in the area of Ife that Yoruba peoples began to show undoubted evidence of having achieved ethnic identity. These and other historical sources indicate that Ife is the earliest so far known ancient Yoruba settlement, ruled by *oni*s who exerted a spiritual power over a wider area for a very long time. In addition Ife settlements served as dispersal points for the subsequent founding of Oyo and five other major Yoruba towns, as well as for the replacement of a former native dynasty at Benin around the fourteenth to fifteenth century. Traditions suggest that Ife was founded as a result of the fact that an invading group with the advantage of iron weapons successfully made their entry into the midst of an indigenous group who were called Igbo.

Whatever the ultimate explanation of the origins or beginnings of Ife, it

35. R. N. Henderson, 1972.
36. G. I. Jones, 1961.

is clear that between the seventh and eleventh century Ife was in the ascendancy culturally as well as politically among the Yoruba and the neighbouring Bini. Some of the bronzes have definitely been dated to the mid eleventh century, and it is possible, although it has not been proved that some of the art in terracotta was of much greater antiquity than the bronzes. More recently archaeology has been supplying some of the missing links to our knowledge of Yoruba history during this crucial period.

Leo Frobenius drew attention to the outstanding historical and archaeological importance of Ife and to the important naturalistic sculpture found there, although his follow-up archaeological work was inadequate by modern standards, and his interpretation of Ife's origin is no longer acceptable.[37] Frobenius worked mostly at Olokun Grove, a site characterized by the working of blue glass *segi* beads. Examples of this bead found at Kumbi Saleh, Tegdaoust and Gao have been shown by X-ray fluorescence analysis to be identical with those found in Ife;[38] this at least suggests some sort of link in the past between Ife and these Sudanic towns. Archaeological evidence supported to a large extent by oral tradition, indicates also that there have been three distinct major periods in the growth of Ife. During the earliest phase dated to −350, Ife was simply a scattered cluster of hamlets, numbering thirteen, according to traditions,[39] located in very well-drained terrain, within the valley of Ife, and occupied by villagers who farmed. The next major phase was the founding of medieval Ife, at which time the communities packed into this area must have had a more elaborate social structure than that of the autonomous hamlets of early Ife.

It is not clear whether this urbanization and the social changes it indicates resulted from independent agreement amongst the communities, or from the imposition of a new order from outside, nor do we really know when exactly these changes were occurring. However, charcoal from medieval layers at Ite Yemoo have been dated to 960, 1060 and 1160. As these may have been relics from an early stage in Ife's development, one has the strong suspicion that at least some of these early but crucial developments of Ife town itself and of its inhabitants occurred somewhere between the seventh and eleventh centuries. Apparently it was also sometime during this period that the road pattern, as retained to this day, to Ede, Old Oyo, and through Ilesha to Benin was first established.

Naturalistic sculpture tradition at Ife also dates back to at least 960 ± 130. Elaborate glass bead work was also present at Ife and Benin. Domestic pottery at Ife appears to be more elaborate than that at Nok especially in the sense that decoration was more varied and included incision (straight lines, zig-zags, stabs and curvilinear designs), burnishing, painting, rouletting (with both carved wood and twisted strings). Cobs or ears of maize and strips of clay were also used or applied for decoration.

37. F. Willett, 1973, p. 117.
38. C. C. Davison, R. D. Giaque and R. D. Clark, 1971.
39. P. Ozanne, 1969, p. 32.

Benin

The excavations by Connah have shown the walls of Benin to be a honeycomb of linear earthworks delimiting territory, and not defensive fortifications.[40] These also suggest that Benin City, like Ife, may originally have been an aggregate of small groups living in proximity to one another in forest clearings. Each of the Benin settlements owed allegiance to the *Oba* but has its own farmlands surrounded by its own bank and ditch. The city was surrounded by a more recent inner wall and an older outer wall. Excavations suggest that the inner wall was not built before the fourteenth century and was most likely erected by the mid-fifteenth century. Sections cut through the wall revealed that it obliterated earlier building sites and cut across an earlier earthwork.[41]

The outer wall on the other hand is attributed by tradition to *Oba* Oguola in the late thirteenth century and archaeological evidence certainly confirms that it is older than the inner wall. Examination of the remains visible on the surface not only indicate that they are earlier than the innermost wall, but also that they could date to anywhere between the eleventh and fifteenth centuries. The extent of these defensive works, especially the inner one, implies the existence at these times of a strong centralized government.

Evidence from art survivals combined with oral tradition also throws some light on this period of Benin history, as for instance can be seen in the useful summary of previous efforts to study Benin art and technology made by Dark.[42] Apparently whether one proceeds from the known to the unknown (with the very stylized type of bronze heads which were still being made after 1897 and which were considered as the most recent), or one starts by accepting the hypothesis that the earliest Benin bronze heads are those which are closest in appearance to the bronze heads of Ife, the resultant ordering has usually turned out to be much the same provided one also accepts certain oral traditions as true markers.

According to Dark's scheme the domestic arts, which included woodcarving, started in the time of Ere, who was the second of the Ogisos, the dynasty before the present one. If, as is suggested by most students of Benin history, the present dynasty, which was founded by Oranmiyan, a prince of Ife, and probably a mythical personage, goes back to +1300,[43] or a bit earlier, and the tradition of there being seventeen Ogisos before that time is accepted,[44] then Ere, the second of them (assuming each king

40. G. Connah, 1975, p. 243.
41. ibid., p. 244.
42. P. J. C. Dark, 1973.
43. R. E. Bradbury, 1959.
44. J. Egharevba, 1960, p. 75.

ruled for an average reign of twenty to twenty-five years), would have begun to rule between 900 and 980.[45]

Dark records that Ere introduced the wooden memorial heads, which are placed on ancestral shrines, and also the royal throne (*ekete*), the rectangular chief's stool (*agba*), the round feather fan (*ezuzu*), the round box (*ekpokin*) made of bark and leather, the swords of authority (*ada* and *eben*), beaded anklets (*eguen*), and collars (*odigba*) and a simple undecorated form of crown. The foundation of the guilds of carvers (*igbesanmwan*) and carpentry (*onwina*) is also credited to Ere's time.[46] The former were recognized as artists working in wood and ivory and the latter as craftsmen, producing undecorated utensils for everyday use, such as wooden plates, bowls, mortars and pestles.[47]

If correct it would mean that the Benin society had reached at the time of Ere the point when the formal organization of artists and craftsmen had become necessary. Further, recognition of an ancestral role in influencing the affairs of the living appears to have been part of Benin beliefs, and was symbolized in the making of the wooden heads, which are used in a memorial context. The practice of making memorial heads, then, could be said to have existed for some 350 or 450 years before brass-casting – which is credited to Oguola's reign – was introduced to Benin and hence before the beginning of the corpus of bronze memorial heads which survive to the present. Although one cannot be certain as to when the sequence of Benin bronze heads began, Dark suggests that this event should be placed sometime around the first quarter of the fourteenth century, that is if 950 is accepted for the beginning of the Ogiso period. If the Ogiso period started earlier then the bronze heads may date earlier (perhaps to the thirteenth century).

In any case, even if the traditional record of the Ogisos presently available is not accurate, it still seems reasonable to assume that the art of carving had been established well before the present dynasty came into existence and that the carvers included in their repertoire the making of wooden heads for ancestor shrines. The stage had thus been long set for the introduction of the manufacture of bronze heads in memory of past kings. Further, though the technology of bronze-working was introduced in

45. Egharevba, the court historian of Benin, assigns the beginning of the Ogiso period to the former date but he would have the present dynasty starting 130 years before the date of 1300 suggested by Dark. If Egharevba calculated in units of twenty or twenty-five years when determining the length of the Ogiso period he would have to place Ere as beginning to reign in 850 or 720. If Egharevba's dates for the reigns of the kings from Ozolua, who was reigning at the time of the Portuguese advent, to Ovonramwen are roughly correct – and most would agree they probably are – then twenty-one kings would have covered a period of 433 years. This means that each reigned on average just over twenty years. The same average is obtained if the first thirty-six kings of the present dynasty are considered as reigning between 1170 and 1914, which is what Egharevba records. Cf. J. Egharevba, 1960, *idem*.

46. P. J. C. Dark, 1973, p. 8.

47. J. Egharevba, 1960.

Benin in Oguola's time, tradition has it that bronze works of art were sent to Benin from Ife before his reign. For how long before, one cannot tell. However, no bronze head in the Benin corpus found in Benin bears the stamp of an Ife artist's head, but there are a few other forms which are said to be strongly Ife in character and which may represent all that survives to this day of the objects sent from Ife to Benin.[48] Dark notes that no comparable piece exists in the Ife record but its lack of existence does not mean that such pieces were not made.[49]

Thus Benin City's emergence apparently resulted basically from a highly successful exploitation of their environment by an iron-using people. Although the origins of Benin City are still difficult to place exactly, they may date from around the beginning of the present millennium. The complex network of linear earthworks and walls that are presently known also suggest that, as at Ife, the city may have come into being through a process of slow fusion of scattered villages having allegiance to a central authority, till Oba Ewuare constructed a true urban unit with a formal defence in the fifteenth century.

Although some traditions claim that the Edo people came to their present abode not too long ago from Egypt, and that here they met people from the Sudan, linguistic evidence suggests that the Edo have occupied their present location for a period of almost four thousand years. For most of this period the village settlement constituted the political unit, in which the fundamental pattern of authority is made up of male age-grade associations. These were autonomous politically, culturally, and economically.

This simple pattern of social organization appears to have been subsequently overlaid by the development of kingship and more complex political units. What led to the development of a new system of political organization in the former village structure is not yet clear. Some authorities have suggested diffusion from the older but nearby Yorubaland, where for many years there was a centralized political unit or kingdom. Others have suggested independent development of relatively large political units in the area. It is also clear that development of large settlements in the Edo region went hand in hand with changes in the level of political organization. Between about the tenth and thirteenth centuries, towns such as Udo, Uromi and Benin are known to have advanced towards urban development.

This initial phase was superseded by a period of 'sorting out' among the early towns which involved some strong political competition. At this

48. F. Willett, 1967, plates 89, 97–9.

49. P. J. C. Dark, 1973, pp. 8–9. Until the Portuguese arrived on the Guinea Coast, the supplies of brass available to the caster must have been very small indeed and this may have made necessary the practice of melting down objects already made in order to obtain materials for casting new ones. While it may therefore be possible that the earliest of the surviving bronze memorial heads were cast after Oguola's time, it would certainly not be right to assign these to a period before Oguola.

period of competition among the chiefdoms (*c.* 1170) and apparently resulting from it, an alien dynasty from Yorubaland was introduced into Benin. This new dynasty apparently began a process by which Benin emerged as the major urban settlement of the area.[50]

The rise of Benin City – its socio-cultural development – can be rightly called the beginnings of Bini civilization. The indices of this civilization included a centralized political organization, an effective defence system, foreign trade, religion and, most important, sophisticated arts and crafts.

Igbo-Ukwu and the Nri 'kingdom'

The earliest corpus of Nigerian bronzes has been unearthed in Igbo country to the east of the Niger. In the course of controlled excavation approximately one-hundred bronzes of distinctive visual aspect were brought to light at Igbo-Ukwu, a small settlement in northern Igboland, in south-eastern Nigeria, and at Ezira 24 km to the east of Igbo-Ukwu.[51]

Among the Igbo-Ukwu and Ezira finds there were bronze objects with parallel marks, various objects described as staff heads, human figurines with anklets and parallel marks, elephant tusks and bronze objects which depict flies, beetles, grasshoppers' (locust?) eggs and heads of animals such as leopards, elephants, rams, monkeys, snails and pythons. There were thousands of pottery fragments, some whole pieces, and a burial chamber in which the occupant was buried in a sitting position in the midst of rich grave-goods which included beads.

Most of the Igbo-Ukwu bronzes are small, except for some vessels about 40 cm in diameter, and human imagery is limited to a few specimens, including a Janus head, a face pendant, an equestrian figure and frontal figures on two 'altar stands'. Igbo-Ukwu's uniqueness extends beyond surface motifs; several object types appear to reflect trends in material culture peculiar to south-eastern Nigeria.

Numerous iconographical elements – floral roundels, crescentic and double spiral patterns, spread-eagled birds – resonate in south-western art. Their presence at Igbo-Ukwu may prefigure these traditions in the south-west, since the site has been dated to the ninth century, making it older than Ife, which had been presumed to mark the inception of Nigeria's great traditions in metal.

Moreover the metallurgical content of the Igbo bronzes is distinctive, recording a consistent leaded bronze composition in contrast to readings characteristic of south-western schools. The entire Igbo-Ukwu find – including clay, glass, iron and copper artefacts – may have constituted the burial goods of an ancient Igbo ruler who exerted control over northern Igbo country and beyond.

50. A. F. C. Ryder, 1969, pp. 7–9.
51. T. Shaw, 1970.

(a)

(b)

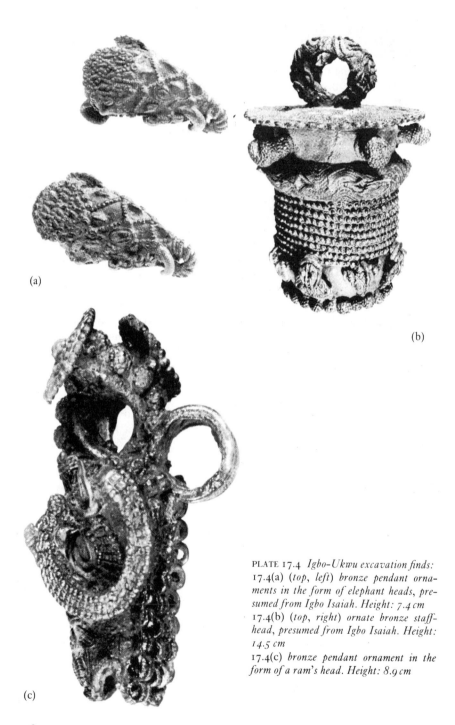

(c)

PLATE 17.4 *Igbo-Ukwu excavation finds:*
17.4(a) (*top, left*) *bronze pendant ornaments in the form of elephant heads, presumed from Igbo Isaiah. Height: 7.4 cm*
17.4(b) (*top, right*) *ornate bronze staff-head, presumed from Igbo Isaiah. Height: 14.5 cm*
17.4(c) *bronze pendant ornament in the form of a ram's head. Height: 8.9 cm*

(d)

(e)

(f)

17.4(d) *Igbo-Ukwu excavation: the bronze roped pot, with bronze altar stand (behind, and to the left) in the store-house of regalia (scale: 1 foot long)*
17.4(e) *(left) globular pot from the store-house of regalia (height: 29 cm)*
17.4(f) *(right) highly decorated pottery vessel from the disposal pit at Igbo-Ukwu (height: 40.6 cm)*

A close study of the archaeological finds in conjunction with the extant cultures by Onwuejeogwu demonstrates some very close parallels between the prehistoric and the extant.[52] Indeed with the help of both lines of evidence, together with fragmentary evidence from Nri oral tradition and the known dispersal of Nri lineages in Igboland, Onwuejeogwu attempted a reconstruction of the socio-political organization of the Nri people from the earliest known times to the eighteenth century. His major conclusion was that the Nri of the Igbo-Ukwu and neighbouring areas had developed a state system sustained and institutionalized by the ritual manipulations of symbols.[53]

All the evidence, archaeological and non-archaeological, suggests the establishment of Nri hegemony and ascendancy in Igboland from as far back as the ninth century and based on the effective manipulation of religious ideologies, doctrines and symbolisms. Spears, clubs, bows and arrows, cutlasses and hoes were transformed into ritual objects, while taboos and abominations were also associated with bloodshed, thereby inhibiting militarism. Colonization and expansion by the Nri kingdom was achieved by sending Nri people to other settlements, the allegiance of such new areas to the *Eze Nri* being obtained through ritual oath. The *Eze Nri*'s will was enforced not through military might but through ritual and mystical sanctions.

Oral tradition specifically ascribes to Nri the origin of local political institutions, in particular the *Ozo* society, a men's title association, and homage is still paid to the town in ritual and title taking ceremonies. Authority was vested in a ruler (*Eze Nri*) and ties with its sphere of influence were maintained by travelling priests who cleansed abominations and conferred rights of leadership. The centralized structure of the Nri polity is unique within Igbo experience and its relationship with its mechanisms such as the *Ozo* lodges is not fully understood. Although nothing survives of the *Eze Nri's* power, title societies continue to be instrumental in local decision-making, despite colonial and national governmental machinery.

Nri influence extended beyond a nuclear northern Igbo region to Igbo settlements on the west bank of the Niger River, and to communities affected by Benin's historic domination of the lower Niger. Onitsha typifies the encounter of Nri-inspired and Bini political styles, the resulting synthesis being a structured ambiguity.[54]

A primary symbol of rank and power, bells were found in burials of important individuals. The finds at Igbo-Ukwu and Ezira exemplify this practice, and it evidently persisted into the early part of this century. The fact that Ezira was a powerful oracle centre that was believed to be the resting place of departed souls underlines the multiple power associations integral to the bronze bell concept.

52. M. A. Onwuejeogwu, 1974.
53. ibid.
54. R. N. Henderson, 1972, p. 297.

A constellation of parallels exists for neighbouring areas in south-eastern Nigeria. To the north, some royal bells were included as grave goods in the burial of Igala kings. In eastern Igbo regions under the hegemony of the Aro, messengers with bell racks signalled the arrival of important personages; chiefs living on the Igbo–Igala frontier employed special bells, and in these areas bells were also ubiquitous elements of shrine furniture.

Inspired by the discoveries at Igbo-Ukwu, recent research based on stylistic analysis and ethnohistorical inquiry suggests that there may indeed exist a south-eastern corpus of bronzes distinguishable from south-western visual concepts. Some of the south-eastern bronze objects housed in museums in Nigeria, the United States, Britain and Europe recall Igbo-Ukwu precedents and conform to categories of material culture valued in traditional Igbo political and religious institutions. The bell is a preponderant element in these bronzes of unknown derivation collected in Nigeria.[55]

There are a few similarities between Igbo-Ukwu, Ife and Benin bronze-casting such as the employment of ram and elephant head motifs, but these may not be significant in art-historical terms. Rather the details of decoration and construction may be more important. For example the ladder-like rows of elongated dots between continuous lines are common to Igbo-Ukwu and the 'Huntsman' style of the Lower Niger bronzes. Significantly, Werner's analyses have also shown that the majority of the Lower Niger figures in the Berlin Museum are, like those of the Igbo-Ukwu, true bronze,[56] whereas the Benin pieces are almost exclusively brass in which the proportion of zinc tended to increase with time.

All these would appear to support William Fagg's assertion that there existed two main style groups in West African metal work, the Ife/Benin/modern Yoruba in central Nigeria, flanked by traditions which employed fine threads of wax or latex in making their models. Until Igbo-Ukwu was dated it was not clear which of these traditions was established first. It would seem now that the Ife/Benin tradition intruded into the area of an older and distinct tradition. Just as has been shown to be true of the later metal-working tradition, it is also very possible that the iron-working tradition at Igbo-Ukwu was distinct from the iron-working tradition of Ife/Benin and Nok.

Igbo-Ukwu excavations clearly indicate that iron-working in south-

55. N. G. Neaher, 1979. The possibility that south-eastern bronzes resulted from a programme of latex modelling deserves serious consideration since documented evidence identifies several groups who utilized tree gums for modelling. The Igbira, the Tiv and the Igala exploited rubbers derived from local varieties of *Ficus*. Bronzes attributed to the first two groups clearly reflect the imprint of a fine medium and it is interesting that the earliest published observer of the Igbo bronzes speculated that a rubber latex was used for modelling. The latex technique centres in areas abundant in rubber-yielding plants and trees, namely the savanna. More than twenty types of such *Ficus* have been identified in Nigeria alone.

56. O. Werner, 1970.

eastern Nigeria is at least as old as the ninth century, and there is every reason to suggest that it was older. Iron-smithing is and was a highly skilled occupation, and often remains exclusive to certain communities and lineages. The most famous of the Igbo smiths in recent times are those from Akwa (east of Onitsha) who apparently first obtained iron (ore) – from the Igbo smelters of Udi – east of Akwa, and only much later received supplies of European iron. Other foci of metallurgical working among the Igbo were the Abiriba – among the Cross River (Eastern) Igbo – iron-smelters as well as iron-smiths and brass-smiths, located near the Okigwe-Arochuku ridge; and the Nkwerre smiths in the southern part of this region.[57]

An excavation in Akwa area yielded fifteen iron gongs and an iron sword similar to those still made by the Akwa smiths as well as a large number of cast bronze bells and other objects which cannot be so readily attributed to Akwa smiths, and which date to $+1495 \pm 95$.[58]

It is not clear what the time/cultural relationship is between Ife and Igbo-Ukwu although Willett thinks it possible that Ife may date much earlier than is presently known, and may even be much nearer Nok than present evidence (tenth to twelfth century) suggests.[59] Indeed, if the Ife beads are the same as the 'akori' beads of the Guinea Coast, as both ethnographic evidence in southern Nigeria and Frobenius suggest,[60] it is then conceivable that the Igbo-Ukwu glass beads were manufactured at Ife. If so it would mean that the Ife culture dates at least as far back as do Igbo-Ukwu finds (ninth century). If some burial goods at Daima in the Chad basin reflect trade contacts between Ife and Daima, then it is quite likely that the cultural parallel may have a time significance. Thus there is a possibility that Ife dates back to at least the sixth century.[61]

The bronzes and beads that have been uncovered reflect the wealth of the economy, and the great artistic skill of the makers of the bronzes, and show the extent to which the area was part of the network of international trade. Shaw has suggested that some of the beads were imported from Venice, but mostly from India via North Africa, and such imports formed part of a major complex of international trade that also involved imports of copper. According to the same author the raw materials for the bronzes namely copper and leaded bronze, were imported from copper mines at Takedda and further afield in the Sahara.[62] While such an international

57. D. Northrup, 1972.
58. D. D. Hartle, 1966, p. 26; 1968, p. 73.
59. F. Willett, 1967.
60. L. Frobenius, 1912, pp. 318–9.
61. G. Connah, 1981, pp. 173 *et seq.* In this regard it seems well worth noting that there is a discontinuity of tradition at Ife in the stone sculpture, glass industry and some architectural features (potsherd pavements) that is largely similar to a cultural discontinuity at Daima (clay figurines and potsherd pavements) dating between the sixth and ninth centuries.
62. T. Shaw, 1975a, p. 513.

trade may well have existed, it is of interest that Onwuejeogwu has indicated that such material was available at Abakaliki and Calabar and may well have come from there.[63] If this was the case, an interesting problem to be resolved would be which of these sources was first exploited by the Igbo-Ukwu craftsmen, the local or the foreign sources, and when?

In the absence of evidence to the contrary, Shaw considers it reasonable to assume that the Igbo-Ukwu bronzes were made by Igbos either in Igbo-Ukwu itself or elsewhere in Igboland. He argues, however, that both raw materials and techniques used were imported from elsewhere. In his view the *cire-perdue* technique of bronze casting is a complicated process which probably spread into West Africa from ancient Egypt and Mesopotamia.[64] If this was the case, adherents of the thesis have yet to demonstrate its validity and the onus lies on them to do this. The argument that the process is very complicated and therefore could not have been discovered independently by the Igbo-Ukwu or any of their West African bronze-casting neighbours (the Sao, south of Lake Chad and gold-casting in Ghana) is not proof.

The material cultures of ancient Igbo-Ukwu, Ife and Benin are often seen as representing high points of Iron Age development in the area. Excavations reveal peoples possessing iron tools and weapons capable of making the forest yield great wealth, utilizing ideas of urbanization and social and religious organization to good effect. Furthermore they were in trading contact with the Arab world and may or may not have obtained knowledge of the art of lost-wax metal casting by this means. Yet despite all these the fact remains that these high points may as much reflect our present ignorance of historical reality since to some extent sheer accident is responsible for our knowledge of them. In other words our high points cannot as yet be studied in the general context of the overall development of Iron Age material culture in southern Nigeria. As rightly noted by Connah, until that can be done we should remember that they may perhaps not be the highest points of attainment and it is very likely that they are not the only points.[65]

Another bronze-casting complex requiring exploration is that of the Cameroon grasslands to the east of Nigeria. Bells are associated traditionally with chieftaincy throughout the region and may have been integral to a system of gift exchange between local rulers. A number of specimens resemble Nigerian types, especially those with segmented banding designs like those of the tulip-shaped bell found along the Cross River corridor; Cameroon bells tend to be larger and much thicker, with distinctive decorative motifs. If any parallel with Nigerian styles exists, it is more likely to consist of provocative affinities with bronzes of the Adamawa region in north-eastern Nigeria along the Cameroon border. In the end, intriguing

63. M. A. Onwuejeogwu, 1974.
64. T. Shaw, 1975a.
65. G. Connah, 1975, p. 248.

visual and thematic correspondences do exist for select Cameroon bronzes, Sao specimens and the Igbo-Ukwu corpus. These deserve fuller scrutiny before a south-eastern Nigerian contribution can be comprehended.[66]

The *Akwanshi*

In the northern part of the Cross River Valley – some 500 km east of Ife – there is evidence of a unique art heritage of hard-stone sculptures. These sculptures known as *Akwanshi* appear to have been the work of ancestors of a restricted group of Ekoid Bantu living in the north, specifically the Nta, Nselle, Nnam, Abanyom and Akagu.

While it is true that where suitable rocks occur in West Africa natural boulders and rocksplinters have often been set up as cult objects, the fact remains that except for half a dozen cases in Yorubaland the sculpturing of hard-stone to represent the human form is confined to a small area of less than a thousand square kilometres on the right bank of the middle Cross River. The area lies in a wide angle formed by the Cross River and one of its confluents, the Ewayon. Here during 1961 and 1962 Allison recorded 295 stones which were shaped with varying degrees of elaboration to represent the human form. Collections of small shaped stones, usually of cylindrical or ellipsoid form, were also found at certain present and former occupation sites in the area.[67]

Allison identified the sculptured stones at twenty-six main sites on land occupied by six formerly independent Ekoi ethnic subgroups and nine other sites at which some sixteen stones were found in ones and twos. The most numerous groups and also the most skilful and original are found on the lands of the Nta (fifty stones) Nselle (ninety stones) and Nnam (ninety-four stones). There are also twenty-two stones at three sites in Abanyom-land and nineteen stones at three sites in Akaguland, but here the workmanship is inferior and the style is derivative. The Nta, Nnam and the best of the Nselle stones are carved in basalt. The Abanyom and Akaju stones are carved from a shelly limestone, some limestone carvings were also found at villages formerly occupied by Nselle. The limestone is probably easier to work but shows a rough finish and weathers badly.

The Nta and Nselle refer to their stones as *Akwanshi* meaning 'the buried dead'; the Nnam and others merely call them *atar*, meaning 'stones', or *ataptal* meaning 'long stones'. Three main styles have so far been distinguished: (1) the Nta style with a cylindrical figure and a definite groove separating the head from the body; (2) the Nnam selected massive boulders and covered them with profuse and well-executed surface decora-

66. N. C. Neaher, 1979.
67. Cf. P. Allison, 1968; 1976.

tion; (3) the Nselle tend towards the Nta style but occasionally produce carvings of individual originality. These styles may also be chronologically significant.

The people of the *Akwanshi* culture (including the Nde) speak distinct but related forms of an Ekoid-Bantu language.[68] In immediate pre-colonial days they were divided into two warring factions who still regard each other with hosility. In recent times the affairs of each community were directed by the elders under whom the young men were organized in age-grade companies. There were also *Ntoon* or priest chiefs whose function in recent times has mainly been religious and ceremonial. The extent of the *Ntoon's* authority varied from a single village to the whole of the subgroup.

Allison tried to reconstruct the genealogy of the *Ntoon* priests for the Nta peoples. Convinced that seniority was a traditional qualification for the selection of the *Ntoon*, Allison contends that each *Ntoon* may not have occupied the post for more than an average of about ten years. Allison believes with justifiable reasons that the *Akwanshi* were memorials of the founders of the dynasty. However, his interpretation of the lifespan of the dynasty as lasting for four to five centuries is based on a rather static functionalist view of the social system of the Ekoi, that is that they were always organized in small rather egalitarian groups. There is an alternative and more reasonable interpretation of the historical data as presently available, namely that the people were organized as a large kingdom not unlike those of Bini and Yorubaland. Indeed the construction of the large and early *Akwanshi* burial memorials predicates such strong, centralized and large-scale socio-political set-ups having sufficient labour forces at their command. If this was so the average rule of the kings would be anything between twenty and thirty years which would mean that the origins of the *Akwanshi* may fall anywhere between the last two or three centuries of the first millennium of the Christian era and the first two to three centuries of the second millennium, that is about the same time as Igbo-Ukwu. The onset of the trans-Atlantic slave trade would appear to have affected this state adversely, leading to social fragmentation and degeneration in the art. The stone sculpture continued in a degenerate form until recent times, mostly today in cylindrical logs of wood.

It is not unlikely that *Nsibidi* writing, which was used by the Ekoi, was one of the achievements of this early civilization in this region. An Nsibidi symbol in the form of a hoop, which represented the former manilla currency and indicated wealth is recognized on certain stones. Such a state must have had a reliable agricultural/technological base, with iron being in use. It also seems reasonable to assume that long-distance trade was a major feature of life connecting such a state to peoples of the north (Tiv, Jukun etc.) west (Igbo-Ukwu, Niger Delta peoples; Bini and Ife) and Bantu-speaking peoples to the east. These are merely intelligent guesses.

68. D. Crabb, 1965.

Quite clearly archaeological work is urgently required in this area, if the substantial gaps in the history of *Akwanshi* state and society are to be filled.

Early trade

This section considers the level of development attained by people in this region especially with respect to the famous sculptures in stone earthenware and in copper alloy, which are generally believed to be medieval, and the towns and rural areas as well as the socio-political systems which sustained the art. If the questions are relatively precise, the answers forthcoming from the various sources available are unfortunately not so. As noted already, most of the Akan, Ewe and Ga-Adangme, and the Yoruba, Edo, Igbo and related groups as presently known were already occupying roughly the same parts of Lower Guinea they live in today in the eleventh to twelfth century and probably much earlier. The Yoruba in particular were by that time already urban dwellers, witness the excavated evidence of towns like Ife, Old Oyo and Ilesha.[69] So also were the Edo as reflected by excavations at Benin. Others like the Igbo-Ukwu in Nigeria and Bono Manso in Ghana had established sophisticated state systems.

These towns were distinguishable from other settlements in terms of their relative size, composition, social organization, structuring and functions. They were more highly nucleated and more populous. In time these towns grew to possess a variety of craft specialists producing goods which were manufactured for more than local consumption, and which came to entail full-time or near full-time participation in the craft. The practice of a variety of technically complex crafts such as metal-working, bead-making and dyeing was soon to be the hallmark of many West African towns. Many of these towns grew to possess strategically located and large-sized markets, placed at frequent intervals in relation to the resources on which they thrived.

Many West African towns in the forest, Sudanic and Sahel belts (e.g. Ife, Benin, Ushongo, Idah, Ugurugu in Nigeria; Notse in Togo) had walls or defensive ditches which provided a tangible demarcation between town and country. Because of the size and more complex social, economic and political system of some towns, inhabitants soon came to have divided or multiple loyalties, whereas the villages were more homogeneous with their single chief, council and shared agrarian experience.

Indeed the attainment of a critical level of technological and subsistence knowledge able to sustain a dense population, and such levels of functional specialization in economic organization as have been described here must have encouraged long-distance trade of various kinds. If this development is viewed archaeologically, what is probably most useful to recognize is not

69. P. Ozanne, 1969.

direct contact trade, or exchange lacking a definite organization, or standardized value of specific materials, but location (i.e. locational analysis), of production, and the character of such locations.

Among many early farming communities in West Africa, polished stone axes (locally known in Ghana as *nyame akume*) were traded over distances of hundreds of kilometres. Greenstone axes from the Bibiani range are found over a large part of southern Ghana. The stone rasps of the Kintampo culture which has produced the earliest evidence of agricultural practices in Ghana around −1500, were made from a dolomitic marl which was evidently traded over substantial distances as it has been found both on the Accra plains and in northern Ghana.[70] At Kumasi, Nunoo excavated a ground-stone axe 'factory' by the banks of the Buruboro and Wiwi streams.[71] The principal evidence here consisted of the roughouts for stone axes and the grooves in the rock outcrop where grinding and polishing of such axes took place; the distribution of these axes has still to be determined. At Rim near Ouahigouya in Burkina Faso, the Late Neolithic/Iron Age levels are associated with axe factory localities, and the site appears to have been a major centre, trading axes to areas lacking the raw material.[72] In any case the substantial distance covered by the dispersal of greenstone axes and rasps, points more to long-distance trade than to a local exchange network.

Also during the Iron Age, there is further evidence of a local trade in pottery in Ghana detected by the recognition of clays in the fabric of pots which are foreign to the areas in which the pots were found. York has indicated that several of the distinctive wares at New Buipe were made from clay sources anything up to 100 km distant from the site. One example is a ware with micaceous paste which has been found at Begho.[73] Priddy has reported even wider distributions, with pots from the Upper Region of Ghana being traded into the Northern Region where little pottery is locally made.[74] The importance of such pottery trade may go beyond indicating culture contacts on a regional basis and demonstrates that very few agricultural societies were entirely self-contained. In this author's view the beginnings of long-distance trade in West Africa are inextricably bound up with the exploitation of the above stone and clay resources as well as metals. In fact it seems reasonable to postulate the existence, from Early Iron Age times, of a complicated and widespread network of long-distance trade radiating from a few central points located in the distinct ecological zones,

70. C. Flight, 1967.
71. R. B. Nunoo, 1969.
72. B. W. Andah, 1973.
73. R. N. York, 1973, pp. 92 and 150–1. Mathewson and Flight showed the distribution of the Kisoto bowl (a small globular bowl, with a slightly beaded rim and made from a distinctive grey fabric) as extending over an area of 90 km around the confluence of the Black and White Voltas. They date this particular ware to the fifteenth to sixteenth centuries.
74. B. Priddy, 1973, p. 3.

and connecting coastal peoples and inland farming peoples on the one hand, as well as people to the south and pastoralists in the north.

Conclusion

The presence of the variety of crafts attested at sites like Igbo-Ukwu suggests the expenditure of a substantial amount of social capital. It also indicates the existence of a sophisticated technology, an accumulation of wealth, the institution of (probably) a ritual leadership and participation in certain trade. According to Shaw the large amount of copper unearthed may have served as currency, and the copper used in the bronzes was necessarily of trans-Saharan origin, while a considerable quantity of the 165 000 beads recovered may have been of Indian manufacture with some perhaps from Venice, although +900 seems too early for postulated contact with Venice.[75] The nearest sources of copper envisaged are in the Azelik area (Takedda) of Aïr in Niger and Nioro in Mali. There is however no way of identifying the exact source of copper used in the Igbo-Ukwu bronzes or of knowing whether their constituents involved long-distance trade from North Africa or whether copper could have come from one of the Sudanic sources. In fact, copper and lead occur at Abakaliki and tin at Afikpo and Calabar.[76] Moreover, Onwuejeogwu claims evidence for ancient mining in these areas.[77] And if he is correct, these more nearby areas would have been much more likely sources of copper. Whatever the source, the quantity of copper items in southern Nigeria before +1300 indicated that trade was on a large scale and had been in existence for probably 500 years prior to that date. Both the excellence of the craftsmanship and the long-distance trade the materials appear to indicate, suggest the existence of a developed agricultural economy probably supplemented by hunting and fishing, and producing a considerable social surplus. Both the Igbo-Ukwu finds and Onwuejeogwu's in-depth study of Nri society have provided much information to support this.

Furthermore, a long-distance trade in luxury goods dependent upon social distinctions could have existed even outside local markets. It could for instance have involved the itinerant trader travelling between royal courts and houses of important peoples as well as attending markets when these were held. In some places as has been shown, regular regional trade developed in special items such as salt, cloth, metal, beads, pottery and stone tools from Late Neolithic/Early Iron Age times. And even such regional trade may not at all times have created entirely new markets, but may rather sometimes have established more regular lines of communication between hitherto existing but periodic local markets. Regional trade in

75. T. Shaw, 1970, Vol. 1, pp. 225–67.
76. M. A. Onwuejeogwu, 1974.
77. ibid.

salt for instance dates back to at least the Late Iron Age (1300–1600) and was both from the Sahara to the Sudan and from the coast to the forest. Several historians have correctly pointed out that the nature of such a trade must have reflected a geographical necessity in south-eastern Nigeria.[78] Large portions of the Niger delta are too swampy and saline to support much agriculture or livestock; on the other hand, the hinterland lacks salt deposits; so both regions find it beneficial to exchange salt and dried fish for agricultural and animal surpluses. According to Jones 'Andoni and Bonny legends suggest a salt boiling industry in the Bonny area before the arrival of the European traders ...'[79] Such trade between the coast and hinterland could conceivably be as old as the very occupation of the coastal regions especially as these peoples probably moved in from the hinterland.

At least one of the regional networks developed to handle exchange of goods between the delta and the hinterland led to the creation of linear marketing networks along the creeks and rivers leading from the delta.[80]

The regional trade in beads has shown more of an east–west than a north–south orientation. One bead type which has never been adequately identified, but which was traded over very long distances round the Gulf of Guinea, was called 'akori'.

Regional trading networks also developed around centres of the textile industry. These had attained considerable sophistication in the 'Igbo-Ukwu cultural era' and persisted to recent times. For instance, in the sixteenth century, Benin people used types of cloth similar in description to that found at Igbo-Ukwu and in the next century they were weaving, importing and exporting large quantities of cloth, some of which may have been of Igbo manufacture, (e.g. the Akwetes of southern Igbo, long famous for their fancy cotton cloth).[81] But the most important of the regional networks in the Igbo hinterland from Igbo-Ukwu times were apparently those including iron and other metals and may have involved itinerant smiths.

78. E. J. Alagoa, 1970, pp. 325–30; D. Northrup, 1972.
79. G. I. Jones, 1963, p. 35.
80. ibid., p. 13; U. Ukwu, 1967, p. 650.
81. D. Forde and G. I. Jones, 1950, p. 43.

18 The peoples of Upper Guinea (between the Ivory Coast and the Casamance)

B. W. ANDAH

Although the view is prevalent among many scholars that there has been an intimate and fundamental connection between Upper Guinea and the Western Sudan at various times in the prehistoric and historic past, no one has clearly identified the nature and course of these relationships through time and for different parts of the Guinea coast. Consequently, as with other similar historical phenomena in African history, this subject of relationship has given rise to hypotheses which often differ either with the type of data relied on, and/or with the manner in which the researcher interprets such data.

It is held by some, for instance, that the peopling of the Upper Guinea coast resulted from the continuous dislocation of population from the interior to the coast. Even within this school of thought opinion differs as to when this drift commenced. McCall, for instance, dates this process back to −5000 when the Sahara began experiencing increasing desiccation, and when in his view the ancestors of the Mande drifted down into the Sahel to introduce agricultural knowledge.[1] A. A. M. Corrêa considers that Western Sudanese states exerted the crucial pressure, and places the beginning of the population drift towards the coast in the third century of the Christian era.[2] At the other end of the spectrum W. Rodney regards the process as having been largely precipitated by political events in the Sudanese states,[3] which do not even date to as far back as the tenth century.

These views, which regard the vast majority of the peoples of Upper Guinea coast as 'refoulés' driven from their original positions inland are no doubt very popular. Yet it is still to be clearly demonstrated how the peoples inhabiting these two vast regions were related physically, linguistically and culturally at various significant points in historic time and who exerted the crucial influence on whom, when and for what reasons.

In this appraisal of the cultural history of the Upper Guinea coast for the period roughly between the seventh and eleventh centuries relevant in-

1. D. F. McCall, 1971.
2. A. A. M. Corrêa, 1943.
3. W. Rodney, 1967.

formation from archaeology, written and oral sources, linguistic and other anthropological data are sifted in an effort to identify the following: the character of the terrain, especially its resource potentials; the human populations of the region; then the languages they spoke, and how they were organized economically, socially and politically. Following from this, an attempt is made to delineate what manner of ties existed between the peoples of the Upper Guinea coast and peoples living to their north at this time. This is done by critically assessing the various hypotheses aimed at accounting particularly for the introduction of iron-working and the establishment of state-organized societies with sophisticated and complex socio-economic systems able to build megalithic monuments.

The ecological setting

Upper Guinea refers here to the western half of the coastlands of West Africa from the Senegal River to Cape Palmas. The stretch from Cape Palmas to the Cameroon is known as Lower Guinea. The coast of Upper Guinea is therefore the southern part of the north-west African coastal region, which stretches from the Strait of Gibraltar to Liberia. Whereas the northern part of this coastal region is characterized by mountains, plateaux and associated troughs, the Upper Guinea stretch contains filled coastal basins and arches. Moderate amounts of rainfall occur in the Senegal and Gambia area, increasing to over 200 cm a year towards Sierra Leone and Liberia. The pattern of rainfall is reflected in the drainage system. In southern Senegal the streams are perennial and the number increases toward the south. Most of these streams are short yet active.

Coastal surface currents (principally Canary) flow southward along the north-western African coast towards Cape Verde to meet the westward-flowing North Equatorial current. Further south the warm Guinea current flows to the east along the Liberian coast.

Geographical units recognizable in this region are Senegambia; the Sierra Leone–Guinea region between the Casamance and Cape Mount (Rodney's Upper Guinea) and the Liberian region between Cape Mount and Cape Palmas.

Inland a major physiographic feature of the Senegambia region is the Senegal Valley. This is flanked on the north and south by low coastal plains and in the north-west by sandstone plateaux with *Hōdh* (Ḥawḍ). In the Sierra Leone–Liberian regions the major landmark is the Guinea Highlands. To the south of this are low coastal plains which stretch uninterrupted to Ghana; while to the north and west there are high plains. Present at the eastern end of the high plains outside of the Upper Guinea region are the Middle Volta basin and the Asante (Ashanti) uplands whereas off the north central part there is the sandstone plateau which occurs immediately south of the Segu and Timbuktu basins.

Most of Senegambia falls within the savanna region which has a

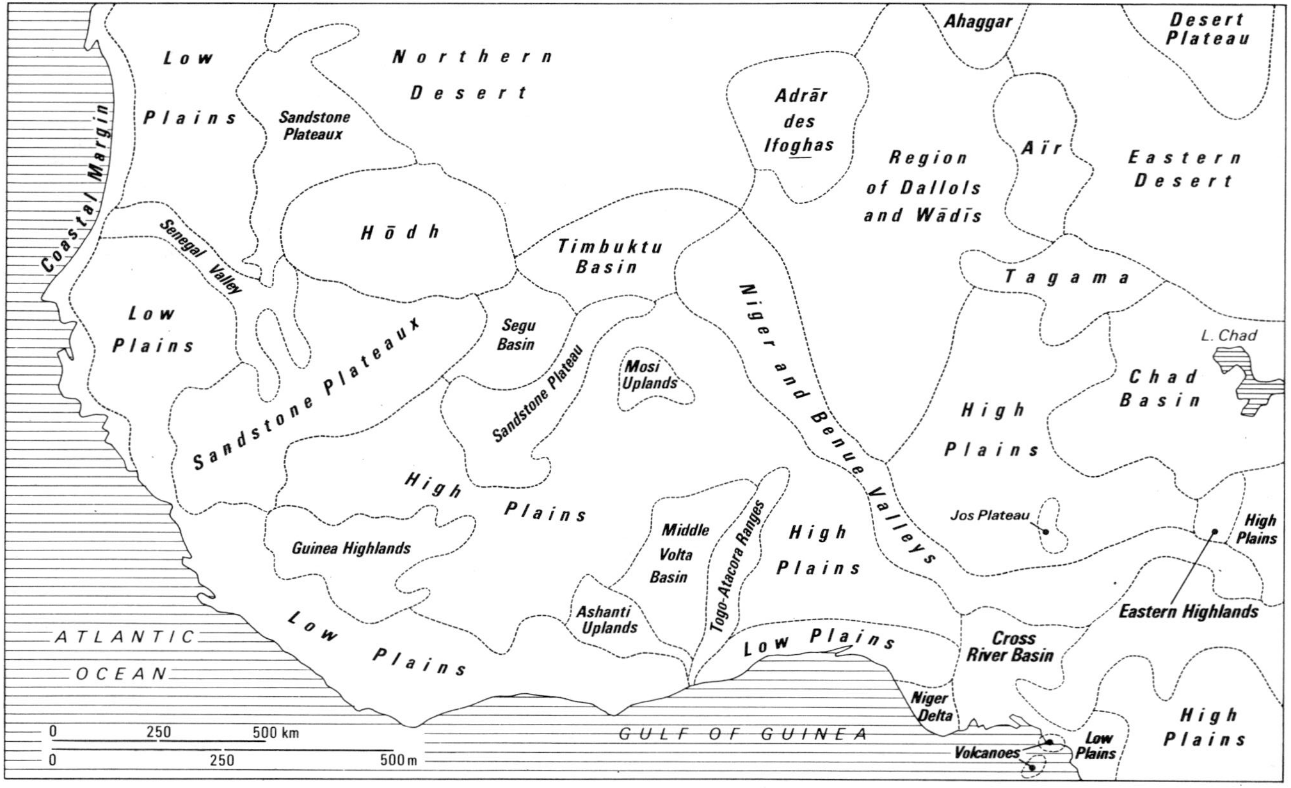

FIG. 18.1 *West Africa: major physical regions*

Sudanian type of climate and vegetation. This covers much of the middle Gambia and the middle Casamance Valley which have highly fertile soils. The southern parts of this zone are high-population density areas. The Lower Casamance region is the wettest and consequently the most densely forested region of Senegambia. Although generally less hot than inland districts it is also humid. This fact notwithstanding, it offers to its heterogeneous peoples, mostly Manden (or Mandenka, Mande, 'Mandingo'), Dyula, Flup, Bainuk and Balante, the most fertile lands as well as the most impressive landscape in the whole of Senegambia.

An uneven line of scarps marks the edge of the sandstone plateaux in the western sector of Upper Guinea. The northern part of Mauritania is true desert while the Senegal Valley with its alluvial deposits is the only major feature that has been attractive to human settlement. Other points settled have been the spring line at the scarp foot and the deep valleys trenched into the scarp edge. The rivers Senegal and Gambia are fed by *wādīs* (marigots) flowing from the sandstone scarps.

The Western Sudan forms the deep hinterland of the Sierra Leone–Guinea zone of the Upper Guinea Coast. Vegetation ranges from forest savanna through true savanna woodland inland to rain-forest in the south, and mangrove swamps in some parts of the coastal fringes.

This zone is further divisible into four natural zones. These are the Guinea (or Coastal) plain characterized by a mountainous region, the uplands and hill country bordering the plain, Futa Jallon and the Upper Niger river basin. Among the distinguishing features of the coastal plain are: an altitude below 150 m, an average annual rainfall of over 250 cm, and a forest or mixed forest savanna-farm vegetation. Its primary crops – palm products, peanuts, rice, kola and others – differed from the main output of adjoining regions which possessed contrasting physical features.

The Futa Jallon (over 1250 m high) represents the south-western continuation of the Manden (Manding) sandstone plateau which occurs between the Hōdh to the north and the Upper Niger basin to the south, and lies almost entirely within the catchment area. Man utilized the valleys of this dissected plateau initially for agricultural settlements and later as routeways for Fulani cattle-rearers and empire-builders.

To the north of the highlands is the Upper Niger basin which is drained by both the Niger and Senegal rivers. Gold is widely dispersed in the pre-Cambrian basement rocks within and these have been long worked by the local people. From Sherbo Island southwards the coast consists mainly of low sandy beaches with river outlets frequently deflected by longshore drift from south-east to north-west.

The Liberian section has a coastline stretching 560 km along the Atlantic Ocean between the Mano and Cavalla rivers. Liberia has a tropical and humid climate; rainfall is heaviest along the coast where it reaches up to 500 cm. Topographically, there are three main zones stretching in an east–west direction parallel to the shoreline:

(1) a coastal or littoral belt between 64 and 80 km wide which is generally low and marked by shallow lagoons, white sand beaches and mangrove marshland;
(2) a very dense rain forest belt rising gently to 330 m above sea level and;
(3) a vast undulating plateau at an elevation of about 660 m. The highest points of the country – the Nimba and Walo Mountains – are located in the north near the Guinea border.

The soil is generally very fertile but subject to leaching. The flora is typical of tropical Africa, with the evergreen forests among the greatest on the continent, containing some 235 different species. Among these are a long list of natural or wild food crops which includes coffee, citrus fruits, cacao, pineapple, avocado, cassava and rice.

The coastal region south of Dakar from southern Senegal, through Guinea, Guinea-Bissau, and the greater part of Sierra Leone is distinguished mainly by drowned muddy estuaries of rivers (e.g. Saloum, Gambia and Casamance) flowing westwards. The main valleys are reasonably well populated, with their broad expanse of alluvium and adequate water for crops like groundnuts and oil palms. But their interfluves suffer increasingly from lateritic crusts towards the interior.

The landscape between the Guinea Highlands and the coastal districts comprises dissected plain – inclined surfaces which slope in a north-north-east – south-south-west direction seaward from the watershed. Freetown is located on a peninsula (with peaks of up to 600 m) which shelters the harbour from south-west winds. Perhaps the geographical features that have exercised the dominant historical influences in the Guinea, Sierra Leone and Liberian regions are the complex of numerous rivers, low plains, marshy land, powerful tides and an extensive continental shelf. There are more than two-dozen principal rivers in the coastal stretch between the Gambia and Cape Mount. These rivers, which flow in a generally westerly or south-westerly direction, constituted, together with their tributaries, important waterways for the inhabitants of this region. None of Liberia's rivers (big and small) are navigable for more than a few kilometres, and they cannot be entered from the sea because of sand bars and perilous rock formations.

The linguistic and ethnic configuration

The peoples of Upper Guinea belong to three main language subgroupings of the Niger-Congo family: Mande, West Atlantic and Kwa (Fig. 18.2).

Mande

By far the most secure and best known of these subgroupings is that of the

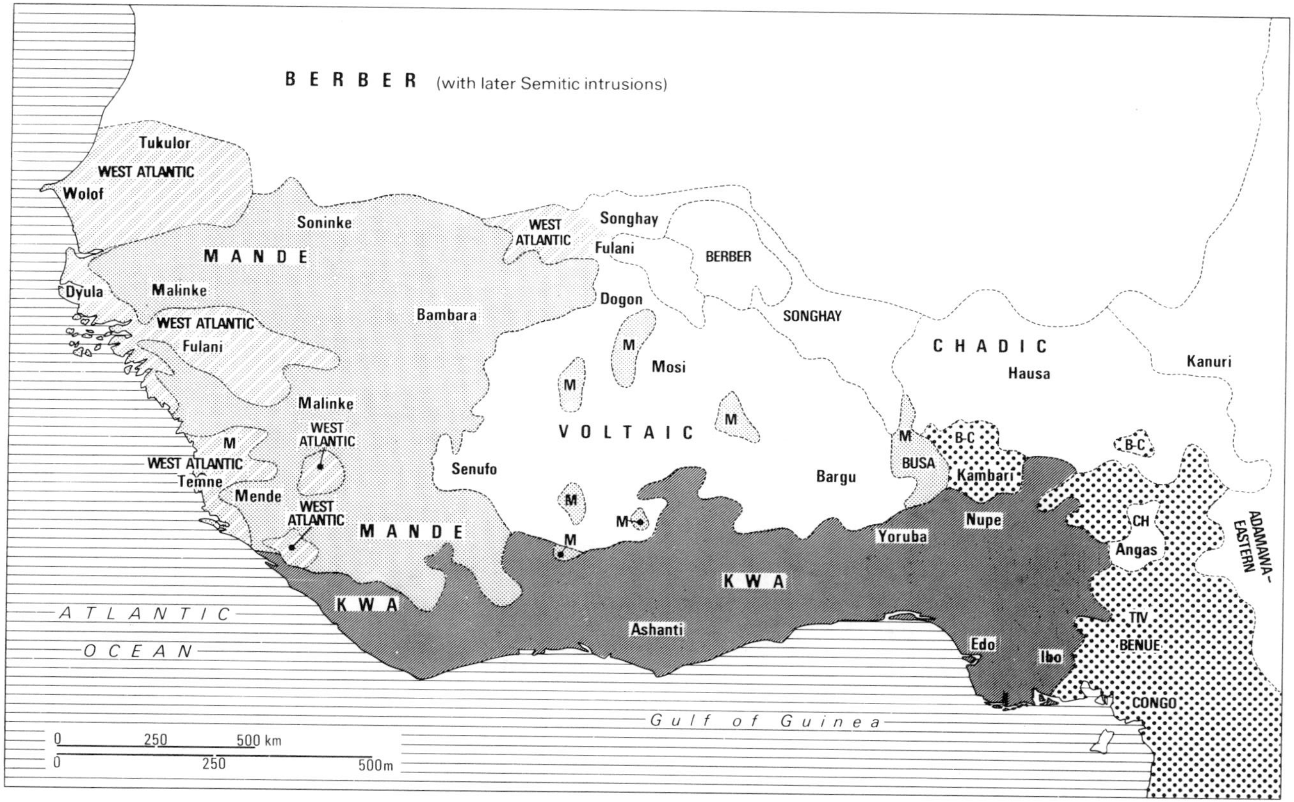

FIG. 18.2 *Language families of West Africa (simplified and with some major individual languages marked)*

Mande, a set of about twenty-five languages which stretches from Busa in Nigeria to The Gambia in the west, and from Soninke in the north to Vai-Kono in the south. Within the Mande subgrouping the position of Bobo-Fing (Sya) in the Burkina Faso remains somewhat enigmatic, while all other Mande languages are generally divided into two groups, the northern or north-western and the southern (or south-eastern).[4] The relative degrees of relationship are clear for many individual languages. The south-west subgroup of the north-western division includes languages such as Mende, Kpelle and Loma, spoken in Sierra Leone, Liberia and Guinea, whereas the northern subgroup of the same division embraces Soninke, Mandenka (Bambara, Malinka, Dyula, etc.), Soso-Yalunke, Vai-Kono, and some others. The southern division was until recently considered to consist of two separate subgroupings, the southern one comprising Mano and a few other smaller languages in Liberia and Ivory Coast, and the eastern one which included a number of small isolated languages (Busa, Bisa, Samo) scattered in Burkina Faso, northern Benin and western Nigeria, but it is now established that both these subgroups are closely related and form therefore only one group.[5]

Mandenka, a subgroup of a subgroup of Mande, has three exceptional features. These are its large numbers of speakers, its extensive geographical spread and its relative cohesion. The Mande-speaking area was the core of the early Western Sudanese states, of which the earliest, the Ghana empire, dates back to over a thousand years. According to oral tradition, Mande expansion into what is now The Gambia took place during the reign of Sundiata in the thirteenth century and the trade settlements to the south date from the fourteenth century, if not before.

The geographical distribution of the Mande-speakers is open to various historical explanations. As the great bulk of the Mande is represented just by the Mandenka it was for a long time held that the original home of all Mande was situated in the Upper Senegal-Niger region in present-day Mali. It was further reasoned that all the other Mande-speakers were offshoots of successive migratory waves from this original centre.[6] This seems to be true of later population movements (known also as the second Mande dispersal) which were directed mostly southwards and westwards.

On the other hand it can be hypothetically presumed that the Mande (or proto-Mande) started their migratory movements from a prehistoric home somewhere in the vicinity of Lake Chad, and after crossing the Niger continued in a general westward or south-westward direction. These migrations must have taken place before those of the Gur (Voltaic)-speaking and Kwa-speaking peoples. Oral traditions of both Bisa (Busanse) and Mosi-Dagomba suggest that the Bisa were in their present locations long before

4. Cf. C. S. Bird, 1970; W. E. Welmers, 1973; R. Long, 1971; M. L. Morse, 1967; A. Prost, 1953, 1981.

5. A. Prost, 1981, pp. 354–5.

6. Cf. J. Vansina, R. Mauny, L. V. Thomas, 1964b, p. 91.

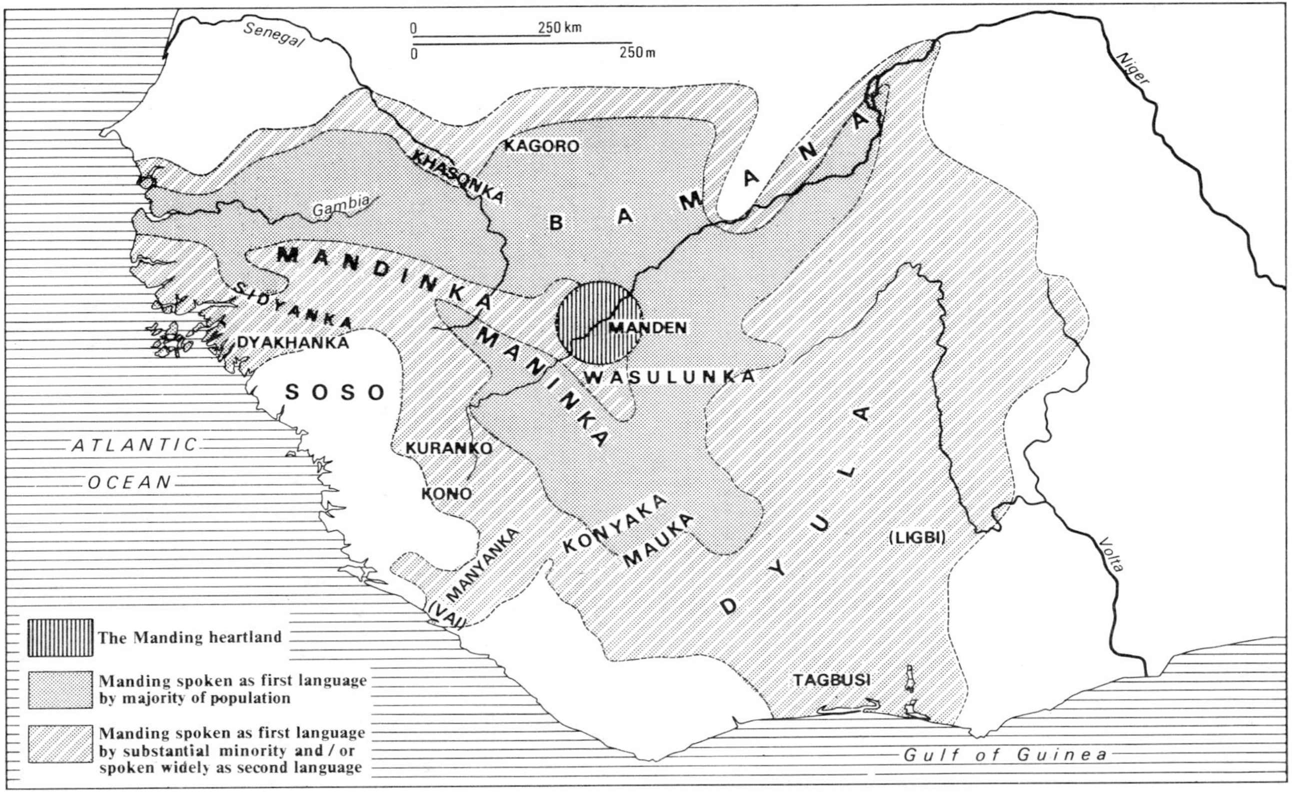

FIG. 18.3 *The 'Manding' peoples and their languages*

the foundation of the Mosi-Dagomba states.[7] The traditions of Busa (in Nigeria) speak of their coming from the east.[8]

All this indicates that the Mande-speaking peoples now living scattered in Burkina Faso, Benin and Nigeria are not the easternmost offshoots of a Mande expansion starting in the west, but rather residues of southern Mande migrations going from east to south-west, as indicated by their close linguistic relationship.[9]

As for the chronological framework, Welmers suggested that the Mande languages represent the earliest break-off from the Niger-Congo family, placing this divergence at *c.* −3300; the split between southern and northern-western Mande would have occurred *c.* −1600.[10] But as these dates are based on glottochronology, the methods of which are coming increasingly under criticism from many linguists, they must be accepted with the utmost caution.

There is no doubt, however, that parts of Liberia and Ivory Coast were during the period covered by this Volume already inhabited by speakers of Mande languages belonging to the southern division. Other Mande peoples – Vai, Kono, Mende, Soso, Kpelle/Guerze, Loma/Toma, etc. – have migrated coastwards in several waves only during the last five or six centuries and their movements are described in the next Volume.[11]

West Atlantic

As against the relative internal homogeneity of the Mande subgrouping, Greenberg's 'West Atlantic' grouping, present also in the savanna zone, is seen by others[12] as *relatively* more disparate, submerging historically significant subgroupings and stages like that of the Mel languages. On the other hand, its classificational break with Kwa appears to be arbitrary, at least in so far as it tends to obscure striking non-contiguous relationships, like the close lexical correspondence between Mel and Akan. However, Dalby's implication that these language groupings of the West Atlantic may not be related at all is open to discussion.

As Welmers quite rightly observes, if West Atlantic represents a very old divergence in Niger-Congo, one would expect some inter-relationship within the branch to be distant, and as such the inclusion of some languages within the group may seem dubious.[13]

7. According to tradition the Dagomba and Mosi states were founded by a son of a Mande hunter and a Voltaic woman, indicating that the Mande were there earlier. Cf. A. Prost, 1945, pp. 50–1; 1981, p. 357; J. Goody, 1964, pp. 211–12.
8. This tradition is linked with the legend of Kisra, cf. P. Mercier, 1970, p. 317.
9. A. Prost, 1981, pp. 357–8.
10. W. E. Welmers, 1958.
11. Cf. Unesco, *General History of Africa*, Vol. IV, ch. 12.
12. E.g., D. Dalby, 1965.
13. W. E. Welmers, 1973, p. 17.

West Atlantic is seen by Sapir to be a group of diverse languages spoken in the coastal area extending from the Senegal–Mauritanian border in the north-west to the Sierra Leone–Liberian border in the south-east.[14] The one exception is Pular (or Fulfude), a language spoken by a savanna people extending from northern Senegal to northern Cameroon and the Chad region. Sapir further noted that in marked contrast to Pular (and to a lesser extent Wolof in Senegal and Temne in Sierra Leone) the majority of the West Atlantic languages are spoken by relatively small and often isolated populations that range in numbers from upwards of 200 000 speakers (e.g. Dyula and Kisi) to as few as several hundred (e.g. Kobiana).[15] Apart from certain common typological features such as noun-class systems and verbal extension suffixes, Sapir finds little that distinguishes the entire group in any obvious way. The diversity of the entire group apparently explains why some scholars (e.g. Dalby) question the relationship of the languages within this group. It does seem however, that Westermann adduced correspondences to link Mel with other West Atlantic languages.[16] Although small in number, these are clear enough to permit the postulation of a unified even if very broad genetic group. Sapir reports that a lexical count based on look-alikes (a pejorative term for putative cognates) clearly and accurately defined the unity of Mel as well as separating out the major sub-groupings and some levels of relationships between these.[17]

Kwa

Greenberg clasifies the Kwa as occupying a belt of about 320 km average width which extends about 2240 km along the West African coast from Monrovia in Liberia in the west, through Ivory Coast, Ghana, Togo and an area between Benin and the eastern Niger delta.[18] While this grouping may well submerge independent language groupings like Nupe and obscure close lexical correspondences between non-contiguous groups like Mel and the Akan languages, Greenberg's middle-range groupings are essentially valid. For instance the four most important of the Kwa languages presently in terms of number of speakers – (1) Akan (Twi, Fanti) dominant in Ghana, (2) Ewe dominant in Togo and the Republic of Benin, and spoken also in south-eastern Ghana; (3) Yoruba dominant in western Nigeria; (4) Igbo dominant in eastern Nigeria – are syllabic, and have musical tones.[19] It is true enough that Greenberg's assignment of languages like Kru and Ijo to Kwa are tentative, yet Ijo for example seems

14. J. D. Sapir, 1971, p. 46.
15. ibid.
16. D. Westermann, 1928.
17. J. D. Sapir, 1971, p. 49.
18. J. H. Greenberg, 1963a.
19. M. H. Stewart, 1971.

to be about as closely related to Yoruba and to Akan as the latter are to each other. Indeed detailed studies, admittedly still in their infancy, indicate that the greater part of the forest belt of West Africa, over a thousand miles from central Liberia to beyond the lower Niger in Nigeria, is occupied by peoples speaking a series of related languages, with underlying similarities in vocabulary and structure. If these reflect a common proto-language, then linguistic evidence points here to an early cultural continuum over much of this forest belt, and subsequent diversification from an early but unknown date. The above-mentioned and several other relationships within Kwa appear to be at least as distant as between some of the easternmost languages assigned to Kwa and languages that clearly belong in Benue-Congo.

Historical-geographic evidence furthermore suggests that the forest was not easily penetrated by later peoples; and when such penetration occurred, it was not in the form of mass migrations. Rather such penetration was confined to small groups, who even if they exerted great cultural influence, were absorbed linguistically by the local populations. It was apparently only in the far west that northerners penetrated in large numbers, establishing warrior chiefdoms like those of the Mende of Sierra Leone, which carried the Mande language family down to the coast.

Hypotheses

For many, the major theme in the historical review of this region is that of an epochal confrontation between two great cultural traditions represented by the precursors of the Mel-speaking peoples of the coast and the expanding Mande-speaking peoples from the highland interior.[20]

It is true that during the period of early European contact, and over the centuries to follow, this region constituted a teeming frontier of immigration, population increase and inter-group competition, as interior peoples moved into the lowland forests of the littoral in search of land and trade. There is also little doubt that the infiltration of Mande-speaking groups from the east was a major contributing factor in this process.

Nevertheless, fundamental problems remain in any efforts to relate these to the broader regional socio-cultural history of the pre-fifteenth century and in particular the late first millennium and the early part of the second millennium. It is not clear for example whether the Mane invasion took place in the fourteenth century as posited by Livingstone, the fifteenth century as suggested by Lamp or the sixteenth century as suggested by Hair.[21] Moreover, related to this are disagreements as to the form it took and its impact on the local people. Whereas for Hair it was a brief war

20. H. Baumann and D. Westermann, 1948; G. P. Murdock, 1959; M. Delafosse, 1931. P. E. H. Hair, 1968a; W. Rodney, 1967.

21. F. B. Livingstone, 1958; F. Lamp, 1979; P. E. H. Hair, 1968a.

resulting in the intruders being assimilated by the local people, for others it was a mass migration with decisive and sometimes disastrous consequences for the indigenous groups.

For instance Rodney and Lamp attribute the destruction of the skills of the Sapes (which include the Bullom, Temne, Limba and Baga and Nalu known today as speakers of Mel languages), who had great reputations as artists and craftsmen, to this intrusion.[22] But the 'Manes' are also regarded as having contributed many new skills such as techniques of iron-working, cotton-weaving and warfare, and gave a great impetus to institutions that were already established like the Poro, Ragbenle and Simo secret societies.

Livingstone, relying on blood studies, especially the parallel distribution of the sickle-cell trait among certain ethnic groups of West Africa with intensive agriculture, suggested that the earliest Mande-speakers to move west (placed by him in the fourteenth century) were primarily hunters and warriors and that subsequent waves of Mande migrants introduced rice cultivation together with iron implements for intensive farming of forest areas by slash-and-burn methods. According to him this process probably began on the fringe forest of the Guinea Highlands and then spread slowly among the peoples of the lowland forest.[23]

Livingstone connected the spread of this trait with the later movements of Mande-speakers from the Western Sudan. According to his thesis the new mode of agriculture introduced into the forest created the environmental conditions favourable to the malaria mosquito and thus enhanced the selective advantage of the sickle-cell gene.

The still prevalent view is that these coastal peoples did not have much cultivation or iron-smelting until Mande-speaking peoples arrived among them, this occurring as recently as the sixteenth century, and that all this resulted in substantial population increase.

A variant of this thesis traces the Mande advent much further back in time and suggests that it constitutes even more of a civilizing force, attributing to the Mande the introduction of agriculture, iron-working, sophisticated socio-political systems, long-distance trade and, with these, more complex economic systems and craft organizations. In this connection, it is variously claimed that the Western Sudanic states, menaced by nomadic Berbers, began to exert pressure which led to population drifts to the coast as early as the third century of the Christian era, that this trend continues today and that there are, as it were, a series of population layers.[24] Spreading outward from the coast are found, first, the remnants of the indigenous peoples. In Sierra Leone, these are the Bullom closely associated with the Kisi and the Krim, the languages of all three being related. Place names seem to indicate that many parts, now occupied by Mende, Kono and Vai, were once Kisi. Along the present Liberian frontier live the

22. W. Rodney, 1967; F. Lamp, 1979.
23. F. B. Livingstone, 1958, p. 553.
24. A. L. Mabogunje, 1971, pp. 7–9.

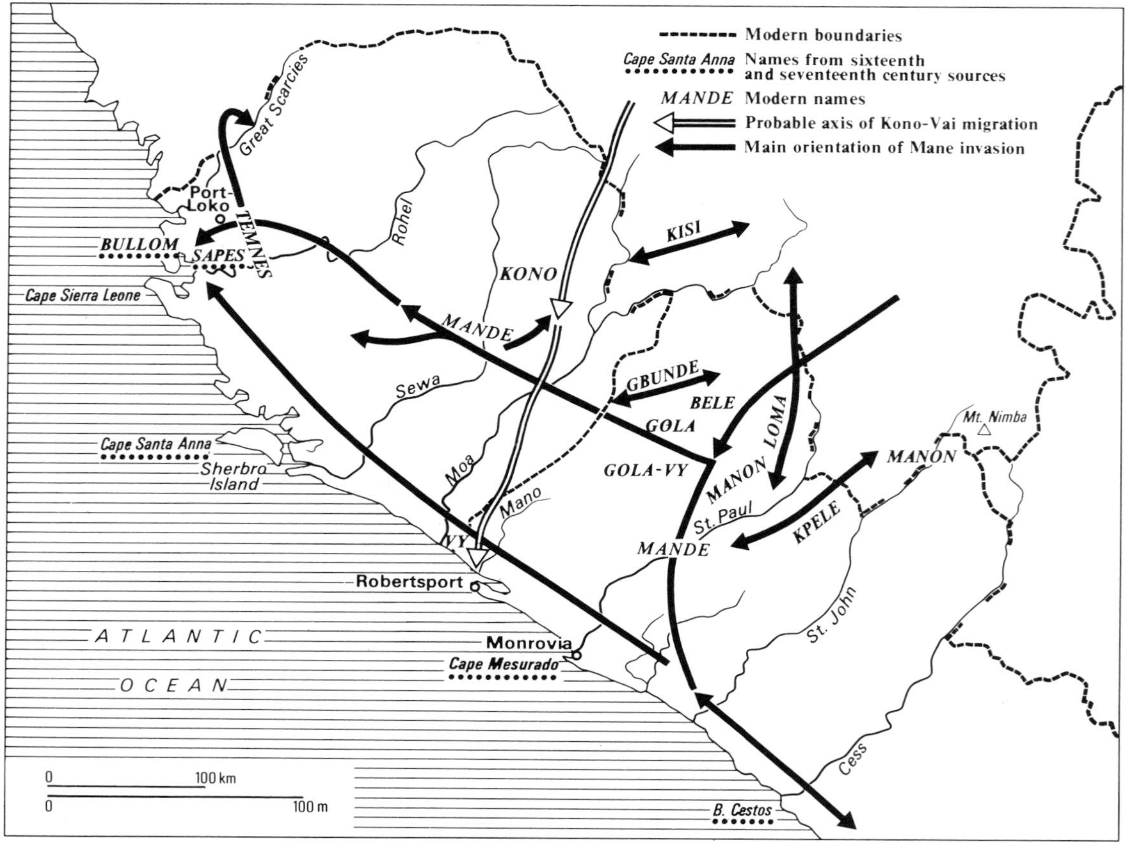

FIG. 18.4 *Population movements in the Upper Guinea Region*

Gola, speaking like the others one of the southern Mel languages, with a system of noun classes similar to that of the Bantu. The Limba, too, have a system of noun classes and are often grouped with the other Mel language speakers in the 'West Atlantic' family.

Somewhat later came the closely related Baga and Temne, speaking a northern Mel language, settling a little inland. These Temne, along with the Nalu, Landuma and Cocoli further north, seem to represent a second, later layer, and have been called the 'Pre-Mandingas'. The Temne, Kisi, Limba, Baga and Landuma were thus all early inhabitants of Futa Jallon. Finally displaced about the thirteenth century by the Mande-speaking Soso, they tended to move west and south to occupy more fertile land towards the coast. The Soso, taking their place, in turn began a move coastwards as they multiplied.

The Sapi and the Landuma remained in the hinterland immediately behind the Nalu and the Baga, but the Temne eventually pushed down to the mouth of the River Sierra Leone, cutting the Bullom in two by the sixteenth century, and becoming one of the most powerful groups of the Sierra Leone coast.

The Baga, Landuma and Temne may have been one people until the Soso drove between them. The former, now occupying Guinea are being gradually absorbed by the Soso. Their counterparts in Sierra Leone, the Temne, have kept their identity and have themselves absorbed members of the coastal Bullom, as well as Loko, Koranko, Fulbe and even Soso further inland.

By focusing attention on aspects of economy, ecology and social structure, Murdock separated the area into two sections: (1) Senegambia represents a solid block of West Atlantic-speakers, distinguished by matrilineality, intensive distribution of Sudanic crops at an early date and a savanna setting, favourable cultural contact and actual intrusion from the Sudan. (2) The zone stretching from coastal Guinea to about the Sassandra River inhabited by a cluster of people referred to as 'the Kru and Peripheral Mande', who are historically and socially closely interrelated with one another, though speaking numerous dialects of the Mande, Kwa (Kru) and West Atlantic (Mel) languages.[25]

D'Azevedo subsequently suggested that a small section (in southern Sierra Leone and north-western Liberia) of this latter area revealed some distinctiveness by its intensive multilingualism, its history of heterogeneous population influx and the existence of inter-tribal confederacies across fluid linguistic boundaries. This sub-area is referred to as 'the Central West Atlantic Region' in order to focus attention on distinctive historical and ethnographic features that seem to set this coastal cluster of ethnic cultures somewhat apart from an area of peoples beyond.[26]

25. G. P. Murdock, 1959.
26. W. L. D'Azevedo, 1962.

An alternative and apparently more reasonable view argues that iron-working and agriculture were firmly established in parts of Upper Guinea before the advent of the 'Mandingo'; the 'Mandingo' advent merely heralded the addition of Sudanic elements to the agricultural system and the socio-political system of the indigenous populations. It is clear from the foregoing that there is still a need to find definitive answers to certain basic questions regarding the cultural history of this region. Some of these concern the times at which peoples came south from the Western Sudan; who they were, from what parts and to what parts they went; the character of these movements and what changes and modifications, if any, occurred as a result. Specifically we would like to know when crops native to Upper Guinea started to be cultivated and when Sudanic elements were introduced, what was their relative importance and how iron-working and long-distance trade became known and with what results.

The process of culture contact was going on in this region for several centuries, long before the famous Mane invasion, and such contact involved the movement of peoples of diverse languages and cultures into a sparsely inhabited coastal forest area and their intermingling. The fact that there is some evidence that most of the ethnolinguistic units that were reported on the coast in the European records between 1440 and 1700 exist today in much the same sequence, though their placement and territorial size may have altered to some degree is noted by adherents of this view as being in its favour. It is also quite rightly pointed out that this does not mean that modern groups, because of similarity of names, languages or placement, are direct genetic or cultural descendants of the ethnic cultures of the past, for this area has undergone vigorous change for centuries.

Senegambia

In the Senegambian region archaeological evidence indicates that the Loudia and Wolof sites in Lower Casamance were occupied from as far back as the first millennium before the Christian era. Up until +200 settlement was sparse and comprised people living in small encampments on low sandy ridges.

Linares de Sapir thinks the people came in from the east since their pottery shares decorative techniques like wavy-line incision 'with Neolithic pottery of wide distribution from Cape Verde to Southern Algeria and even beyond to Central Africa'.[27] These coastal dwellers subsequently adapted to coastal life, which fact is testified to by the presence of mollusc remains. De Sapir conjectures that the people had commenced to cultivate wet rice at this time (i.e. between −200 and +200).[28] Such new and radi-

27. O. Linares de Sapir, 1971; cf. also Unesco, *General History of Africa*, Vol. II, ch. 24.
28. According to A. Portères, 1950, Senegambia was a secondary centre of *Oryza glaberrima* (West African rice) propagation.

cal adaptation was introduced by new settlers, possibly ancestors of the Dyula, who came from the south and displaced the previous few occupants, who were relatively few in number.

During the third major phase of occupation sheep and/or goat domesticates were kept; cattle continued to be present while fish was a most common element in the diet.

In the fourth and final phase identified, two new animal domesticates, pig and dog, appear. Pottery is generally similar to that of the preceding period although the small lidded bowl was no longer being made by the inhabitants then, as is true now also of the Dyula. De Sapir interprets the archaeological evidence, especially pottery, as indicating that the Dyula came to occupy all of the alluvial valleys between the Casamance River delta and the Sondrougou River in the course of the three latter phases.

Apart from Casamance, the mouth of the Senegal River near St Louis and the Sine-Saloum delta (Joal, Gandoul and Bandiala) were similarly inhabited from about as early if not earlier. De Sapir notes that even though some middens found in these other estuaries may be 'terminal Neolithic', most date from the Early Iron Age, while some were occupied when the Europeans arrived. One such complex of shell-midden settlement at Dionevar contains well over forty burials. Recent excavations revealed Iron Age materials (hoe blade, beads and bracelets, and pottery).[29] There are general ceramic parallels between the Casamance and Saint-Louis areas. In both Casamance and Cape Verde, decorative techniques assigned to the Neolithic also continue into the Early Iron Age. Both areas also share vague similarities in the shapes of vessels (spheroids and ovoids of various sizes and middle-sized jars with flared necks).

Linguistic evidence does not appear to support the idea that the Dyula group came from the east. Rather it places the centre of ancient Dyula dispersion to the south, in the coastal section of Guinea-Bissau, where the Mandyak and the Balante, both linguistically related to the Dyula are found. Like the Dyula these people are also wet-rice cultivators and employ the unique hand spade, the *kayando*. Archaeologically it is also questionable since the practice of shellfish gathering, the shell-tempered pottery and the presence of fish remains during the second major phase of occupation, indicate a coastal rather than an inland eastern origin.

About +300, the Dyula were exploiting the rich fauna of mangrove channels and marigots, and were probably also practising agriculture, perhaps an advanced stage of rice cultivation. Many recognizable features of Dyula culture were already present from the second distinctive occupation period onwards. Groups lived on sandy ridges in or near alluvial valleys, just as they do today, discarding their rubbish in particular places. Middens formed contain pottery fragments and other refuse which com-

29. C. Descamps, G. Thilmans, Y. Thommeret, 1974; G. Thilmans and C. Descamps, forthcoming.

pare with present Dyula material culture. It is not known whether or not the Dyula buried pots with their dead, since no graves were found in or near these sites.

Over the past eighty or so years several great complexes of stone circles (megaliths) have been discovered in the Senegambian region, to the north of the River Gambia, in an area of more than 30 000 sq km, stretching from Fara-fenni, some 360 km from the river mouth, to as far east as Tamba-counda in the Senegal (see Figs 16.2–16.4). The stones were usually quarried from the low laterite hills which dot this savanna region. The earliest-known ones consist of standing stones and lines of lateritic blocks between eight and twenty-four in number and up to 4 m high. One group at Dialloumbere, perhaps the largest concentration yet known, consists of at least fifty-four circles, each circle up to 8 m across. But the size of the interior of the circle varies according to the size and number of stones; and circles are usually in twos and threes. Some of the interiors of the circles are flat, while some are hollowed, but more often they are slightly raised. The stones in any particular circle are all of the same size – usually anywhere from 1–2 m tall. In shape the stones are generally rounded pillars. Most circles have a pair of stones oriented due east from them, and occasionally there are huge stones cut in the shape of a letter Y.[30]

Archaeological work has shown that these monuments are burial grounds. It seems that these circles of stones were originally much higher and covered with sand and laterite and that the rows of adjoining circles were the cemeteries of dynasties of kings or priests, while the smaller groups are those of local chiefs or priests. There is also the suggestion that the eastward orientation of the Y-shaped stone and pairs of outliers may reflect sun worship.

Pottery from these megaliths appears to parallel material found in the tumuli of the Rao and Sine, and Sahelian regions of Senegal.[31] Although previously dated to the fourteenth century,[32] excavations by Dakar University in the Sine-Salum area indicate dates around + 1000.[33]

So far, more than 4000 mounds have been discovered, some as high as 5 m and up to 40 m across. Those excavated reveal multiple burials; at Dioron Boumak there were forty-one.[34] The profusion of grave goods includes gold and carnelian beads, iron weapons, ornaments of gold and copper and, in one grave, a gold pectoral. It is possible to date the emergence of metals – ornaments and other burial objects – in this region to a period from the fourth to the sixth century of the Christian era. The carnelian beads, however, come from sites that date to before the eleventh century and point to a circulation of this material, probably from the Nile Valley.

30. G. Thilmans, C. Descamps and B. Khayat, 1980.
31. M. Posnansky, 1973.
32. J. Joire, 1955.
33. G. Thilmans and C. Descamps, 1974; 1975.
34. ibid.

Other mounds with similar rich finds have been excavated in the upper Niger Valley, mainly below Segu. At Kūgha one mound associated with standing stones has been dated to around +1000.[35] This affluence was almost certainly due to the control of the mineral resources and to the agricultural potential of the Inland Delta of the Niger.

It is clear from the above that there were important contacts and connections between the Western Sudan and Senegambia during this period of megalith builders. The Arab geographer al-Bakrī described an eleventh-century burial of a king of Ghana which is similar in some respects to the Senegambian burials.[36] To some modern historians such evidence and earlier dating estimates of burials indicate derivation (not precluding movement of the Soninke) from the seat of the state of Ghana in the Western Sudan. The weight of evidence available suggests that the megaliths and related socio-cultural achievements were the work of the ancestors of people living in the area today, mainly 'Mandingo', Wolof and Fulbe. As far as is known only the Dyula were known to have lived there at the time of the circle building. However, the fact that pottery found in some complexes (e.g. Wassu) differs considerably from that found in others (e.g. Fara-fenni) may indicate that many ethnic groups – but with identical cultures – conducted these burials. Moreover the variety of styles in the stone-carving argues for a development over a long period.

Guinea–Sierra Leone–Liberia

In Sierra Leone, man appears to have had easy access to caves and rock-shelters located in the wooded savanna regions, especially in the highland zone in the north-east. He occupied caves and shelters like Kamabai, Yagala, Kabala, Kakoya, Yengema and Bunumbu from early times, sometimes well before the Late Stone Age. Excavations at Kamabai and Yagala (rock shelters less than 320 km north of Cape Mount) by Atherton, and at Yengema by Coon revealed iron-using phases in their later levels, dating from as early as the seventh or eighth century; stone tools continued in use until at least the fourteenth century.[37] Important food items for peoples here from Neolithic times must have included oil palm, locust beans, wild yams, game, fish, honey and small fruits. Huge smelting sites are present in north-eastern Sierra Leone in Koranko country; unfortunately there are no dates.

The most recent two levels (3 and 4) of Kamabai were dated to between the sixth and ninth centuries and the sixth and tenth centuries. Pottery from these levels, especially those with chevron triangular impressions were markedly different from pottery recovered from smaller sites around

35. R. Mauny, 1961, pp. 109–10.
36. Al-Bakrī, 1913, p. 176.
37. J. H. Atherton, 1972; C. Coon, 1968.

Koidu[38] and north-eastern Bo.[39] The 'Iron Age' level was succeeded, at least in north-eastern Bo, by a tradition called 'Sefadu-Tankoro' by Hill, characterized by iron-working (slag and tuyère fragments). At one site a partially vitrified crucible and a mould, apparently used for lost-wax casting of brass, were found. Iron artefacts were retrieved together with chipped-stone tools from one such site in what Hill thinks may be a ritual deposit accumulated over a very short period of time. A few non-ceramic sites and stray finds of stone tools are also interpreted as suggesting that industries analogous or even homologous to the Lower and Middle Yengeman of Yengema cave were widespread in the Eastern and Southern provinces.[40]

The fact cannot be gainsaid that there were contacts between the forest and savanna peoples of this part of the Upper Guinea region, from very early times. Trade was particularly important as a means of contact and interaction. Silk, cotton, and a little gold were traded for oysters round the northern rivers (i.e. Scarcies, Mellacourie, etc). However, contrary to what some think, there is evidence for the flourishing of civilizations in the forest areas from early times. Among this are the steatite ancestor figures in Sierra Leone and Liberia, known as *nomoli* and *pomdo*,[41] and the megaliths already alluded to above, but also from Guinea through Sierra Leone to Liberia. Some scholars have suggested that both traditions were approximately contemporaneous with the introduction of iron, implying that iron and these traditions were introduced into the forest areas.[42]

Some of the contemporary pottery features (e.g. the globular pottery with constricted neck and flared rim, made today in the north of Sierra Leone) appear to continue traditions begun in the Neolithic era and resembling those from Futa Jallon in Guinea. Whether pottery and iron-working were introduced into the forest region or not, the region between Senegal and the Ivory Coast manifested features of complex state organization long before recorded history. And these manifestations were in character largely independent of the civilization of the Middle Niger region.

Liberian rain-forest 'early Iron Age' pottery appears to share similarities with the Iron Age of Zimbabwe in the earlier half of the first millennium of the Christian era.[43] This complex included channelled, stamped and corded ware in jar and carinated bowl forms, pole and daub huts and slightly raised platforms, slag from iron-smelting, fertility worship symbols of women and cattle clay figurines, ostrich-shell beads and copper and bronze objects. The last three groups of artefacts have not so far been

38. P. Ozanne, 1966, p. 15.
39. M. H. Hill, 1970.
40. ibid.
41. J. H. Atherton and M. Kalous, 1970.
42. A. P. Kup, 1975.
43. K. G. Orr, 1971–2, p. 77.

found in Liberian complexes. Liberian pottery also shows striking similarities with Early Iron Age pottery from other parts of West Africa. For example the stamped ware found in Mali, Senegal and Ghana sites show specific similarities in rocker and dentate stamps as well as other design elements on comparable vessel forms and ware types.

The Liberian pottery finds fall into distinguishable groups which appear to have validity in cultural analysis. In regard to the ethnographic materials the 'Mandingo'-Lomo-Kpelle-Mano wares are sufficiently alike to form a genetically related sub-tradition. This is in effect a continuum of traits with the most varied and complex in the 'Mandingo' ware and the simplest in the Mano wares. In regard to designs and vessel forms the 'Mandingo' are the most varied and complex and the Mano the least so. Actually, the Lomo-Kpelle-Mano potteries are considerably less complex. According to Orr this agrees with the culturally more sophisticated position of the 'Mandingo' of the nuclear Mande and the others, the so-called peripheral Mande.[44] The Bofota, Samquelle I and Gbanshay ceramics appear to be most closely related to the peripheral Mande pottery family and according to Orr are *undoubtedly* earlier although he has no seriation in the styles to indicate how much earlier.

The known examples of *pomtan* and *nomoli*, the names usually applied to a variety of stone sculptures, number in thousands and have been found over an area stretching from Sherbro Island to the Kisi country of Guinea, some 350 km to the north; and from western Liberia westwards to the Temne country, a distance of about 220 km. Occurrence of the carvings appears to be more or less continuous throughout the area, although there are wide stylistic differences between the *pomtan* (sing., *pomda*) of Kisi and the *nomoli* found in Sierra Leone. The terrain has a high-forest vegetation and is populated by agricultural peoples who cultivate rice as their main crop, but belong to two different language groups. The Kisi people to the north, and the Bullom-Sherbro on the coast speak languages of the same group, but which differ basically from the language of the Mande and Kono who occupy the country which divides them. Besides being numerous and widely distributed, the *nomoli* and *pomtan* are small enough to be readily portable and became early available for study in European collections.

Although the tendency has been to discount the Mande as having been the makers of these stone figures, since they are thought to have arrived late, Atherton and Kalous hold a contrary view. They are convinced that the Mende are made up of an earlier aboriginal population group and a more recent 'Mandingo' element. In their view the aboriginal group known as 'Sapes' to early visitors (and excluding related coastal peoples such as the Sherbro) were responsible for making the *nomoli*. Their supporting evidence includes representation by the *nomoli* of such physical features as

44. ibid.

large heads wearing the characteristic long drooping moustache of the northern Mande.[45].

As against this view Person inferred – from studies of local tradition, place names and early European chronicles – that the area in which the *nomoli* occur was once entirely occupied by peoples of the West Atlantic language group.[46] However all relevant evidence indicates that his placement of the time when the Mande moved south to their present point as four centuries ago is much too recent. It seems for instance that in the more remote forested highlands of the Niger watershed, the Kisi, although a people of very mixed ethnic origins, preserved not only their language, but much of their cultural traditions, including that of stone-carving, which continues in a less sophisticated form to the present. Recent archaeological evidence from Sierra Leone which indicates that a metal-using culture with a distinctive pottery tradition was widespread in this region from the sixth to the seventh century also points to some relationship between this iron culture and the *nomoli* tradition.

On the basis of stylistic similarities, Atherton and Kalous have claimed that the first *nomoli* must have been made in imitation of clay figurines of the Western Sudan. According to them the tradition of making *nomoli* must have been introduced from the Western Sudan at the same time as the first appearance of some rather distinctive pottery (as well as iron) at Kamabai, namely sometime in the sixth or seventh century.[47] While it is quite possible that the stone sculptures were being made during the Early Iron Age, these scholars adduce no evidence to show that the knowledge of stone-carving was brought in from the Western Sudan to the north. Indeed they prefer to ignore the fact that wooden sculptures very similar to the stone objects (and not clay ones) are present in this region, and that the knowledge for the stone sculptures may have been acquired through first working in wood. The suggestion of outside introduction also does not take into account the fact, among others, that this tradition is uniquely a stone not a clay one and the sculptures represent a wide variety of styles. In any case if the tradition was presaged by working in clay it seems very odd that no clay figurines (terracottas) have been found in association even though clay was being used by the local people for making pots.

Allison points out that a majority of the sculptures were of talc or steatite, with smaller numbers in chlorite schist and amphibolite, and a few in hard rocks such as granite, dolerite and sandstone.[48] Given the large number of sculptures, it would seem reasonable to expect that they were usually made either by or as near as possible to rich sources of raw material. Its great abundance, its very wide distribution, the fact that stone and wood rather than clay were used, and the variety of styles, all point to a

45. J. H. Atherton and M. Kalous, 1970, p. 307.
46. Y. Person, 1972.
47. J. H. Atherton and M. Kalous, 1970, p. 312.
48. P. Allison, 1968, p. 37.

home-grown, rather than an imported tradition, which blossomed in these diverse forms in response mainly to local cultural and ecological pressures and differences. If indeed the first *nomoli* were made in imitation of clay figurines of the Western Sudan as Atherton and Kalous claim, it is very strange that the forest-dwellers never attempted to fashion such clay objects – since such an exercise would by all accounts have been easier as well as possible – as clay was available and being used for making pots. It is also equally strange that these folks, so good at imitating others, not only learnt so fast but quickly translated this new lesson into several local idioms and materials, yet were not able to discover the potentials of these heavily abundant raw materials on their own, but had to wait to see the one or two odd clay figurines, before Pandora's box could be unlocked for them. Not only is it more logical in the face of presently available evidence to accept that the *nomoli* were largely the independent achievement of people who had been living in the terrain for a very long time, but it is necessary to examine seriously the possibility that this art/scientific tradition was exported northwards from the southern source. Indeed it may well not be an accident that a stone-sculpturing tradition is found in various other parts of the Guinea region, such as at Esie in Yorubaland, and in the *Akwanshi* culture among the Ekoi of the Cross River region.

Nor does dating evidence support the idea that knowledge of *nomoli*-making came from the Sudanic area through the indirect route of terracotta art. In the course of archaeological work in Jenne-Jeno in the Inland Niger Delta a terracotta statuette was recovered from a secure archaeological context dated sometime between 1000 and 1300.[49] If this date heralds the beginnings of this art tradition in this region it means that it is much later than the beginnings of the *nomoli* stone-working tradition of Sierra Leone which has been dated by association to the sixth to seventh century.

The great majority of sculptures of all types represent the male human figure although the genitals are seldom portrayed. The typical *nomoli* is usually between about 15 cm and 20 cm high and the *pomdo* between about 7.5 cm and 15 cm, although a few specimens over 30 cm high have been collected in all parts of the area. The *pomtan* are typically cylindrical in form and consist basically of a cylinder surrounded by a featureless globular head which has inevitably led to their being described as phalli.

From this simplified formal expression, the carvings develop to a fully realized representation of the human figure. As in the case of the much larger *Akwanshi* of the Cross River, the head is given human features and engraved, or low-relief arms are added to the body.[50] A few bulbous stylizations of the female form also occur. Finally, well-sculptured human figures of both sexes are found, though the males are more numerous. These show considerable elaboration in the form of headgear or dressed

49. R. J. McIntosh and S. K. McIntosh, 1979, pp. 51–3.
50. Cf. Chapter 17 above.

hair, beads and ornamental body-scars. The male figures are often beaded and some have curved noses and bared teeth and carry a staff or weapon in their hands. Still retaining the typical cylindrical form of the *pomtan* are a few groups in which a large central figure is surrounded by a number of smaller ones. These more elaborate figures and groups occur rarely in the collections made in the Kisi country of Guinea and probably derive mainly from the southern Kisi of Sierra Leone and from the Kono country which borders both Kisi and Mande.

The popular belief throughout the area is that the carvings are of divine origin, although the Kisi elders agree that the *pomtan* were made by their forefathers at some very remote period, and are always the manifestation of some particular ancestor. Among the Mande on the other hand, the *nomoli* are significantly connected with the old landowners, and not with their own ancestors. When found, they are set up on a shrine in the farmland where it is believed that their presence will ensure a good rice crop.

Indeed linguistic evidence seems to suggest that as from about 2500 years ago the southern Sierra Leone, northern Liberia region and part of adjacent Guinea were occupied by Mel-speakers, who were probably expanding at the expense of Kwa-speakers. At about the same time, Mande languages were spreading from a hearth in the Mali-Guinea border area and differentiating. One branch of Mande ancestral to Kono-Vai, Koranko, Malinke and others spread north, eventually expanding widely in the Sudan. Later on, the Kono-Vai branch spread south-westwards separating Kisi and Gola from the other Mel language. Subsequently and quite recently another Mande group, already internally distinct, expanded north-westwards, splitting Kisi from Gola if they were not already physically separated and cutting across the Kono-Vai salient. This northwestward thrust of Mande (known as Mande Loko) was subsequently divided by the eastward expansion of Temne-speaking people north of the area.[51] Hill has raised the possibility that the appearance of the Sefadu Tankoro archaeological tradition is associated with the south-westward expansion of Kono-Vai.[52] But this suggestion leaves an important question unanswered: why one linguistic expansion – Kono-Vai – is visible while another precisely similar one – Mande-Loko – is not.

There is little evidence of a direct connection between the movement of the Vai of north-western Liberia (who speak a northern Mande language) towards the coast and that of the Ligbi towards eastern Ivory Coast, despite linguistic similarities. More probably the Vai entered present-day Sierra Leone in company with the Kono. Traditions that the Kono were 'left behind' sound misleading: it is more likely that the Kono, Vai and speakers of the now extinct 'Dama' language formed a continuous band from eastern Sierra Leone to the sea, cutting off the Gola and Kisi from

51. P. E. H. Hair, 1968a; 1968b.
52. M. H. Hill, 1972, pp. 1–2.

other Mel-speakers. Later (perhaps before the mid-seventeenth century) this band must have been split by the westward movement of south-western Mande-speakers.

The 'migration' of the Vai need not have involved a mass exodus or conquest. What was probably involved was the gradual creation of trade corridors, with a few northern Mande-speakers resident on the coast and a large number carrying salt, dried fish and other wares from the coast towards the head of the Niger. Although the corridors were eventually to some extent disrupted, the Vai language survived near the coast, because of its importance in trade and because links with the Manden were never entirely severed.

Convinced also that both salt and fish must have been prominent in long-distance trade long before European trade began, Hill came to the conclusion that (1) the extension of Manden speakers into the forest zone and ultimately to the coast was tied to the establishment of trade routes; (2) that these trade routes, in turn, were linked (reciprocally?) to the increase of population in the area affected; (3) that increasing population provided the basis for the development of more complex political systems, appropriate to a people essentially dependent on foreign trade and probably modelled on those of the Western Sudan; (4) that prestige of the Manden language of traders and/or rulers contributed to the replacement of a probable Mel antecedent tongue or tongues by ancestral Kono/Dama/Vai.[53]

According to recent research the northern Mande-speaking groups did not arrive suddenly in the forest regions, but came gradually and in small groups; there is also growing awareness that this must have happened much earlier than was originally thought. The role of long-distance trade in stimulating major socio-political development as well as the influence that may have been exercised in this respect by the main purveyors of the trade, i.e. the Vai, seems to be significant. It is now recognized as a real possibility that the Vai came into Liberia many centuries before the 1455 date suggested by Person.[54]

Linguistic evidence offers some interesting indications on these questions: Jones reports that Kono and Vai have apparently borrowed some words from south-western Mande languages (for instance their terms for 'fish', 'fowl', 'canoe', 'camwood', 'cotton' and 'iron'), some of which they share with Mel and south-western Mande languages but not with Manden (e.g. 'short', 'smallpox') and at least one which they seem to share only with Kisi (i.e. 'elephant'). These borrowings may be culturally significant; if so it means that the development of Kono-Vai civilization was a very gradual process receiving cross-fertilization from various directions and at various times.[55]

In this regard, Person's picture of the movement which put the Vai and

53. ibid.
54. Y. Person, 1971.
55. A. Jones, 1981.

Kono in place as simply a quick incursion dated to the fifteenth or sixteenth century is not fully convincing; historical processes which last decades or centuries can hardly be explained in terms of a single battle or the action of one leader. Equally, new trade routes are mostly created by a gradual evolution, not a sudden military conquest.

What we are concerned with rather is the movement of parties for political or economic reasons which dragged on over the centuries. The result was the modification of populations through intermarriage, the transformation of social structures and the expansion or regression of languages. Many of the events Person describes, including the arrival of the Vai, probably took place centuries earlier and at a much slower pace.

According to Jones, the number of Vai-speakers was increased by intermarriage with the indigenous population; not just Mel-speakers but also the Die who, according to the nineteenth-century sources, used to occupy a larger area on the coast. Thus the Vai ceased to be regarded as complete strangers.[56] Traditions which talk of migrations, conquests and territorial spread make more sense if we think in terms of trade paths (sometimes extended and safeguarded, perhaps, by military actions). In addition to a small core of Vai on the coast, there was probably a large number of people speaking Vai or a related language and moving up and down the corridors which connected the Mandenka country with the coast. Perhaps settlements were formed as 'nodes' along these corridors; but it is unlikely that such settlements controlled large pieces of territory.

With respect to fields of research which might yield further clues about Vai origins, Jones aptly notes that if additional written sources from the sixteenth and seventeenth centuries are discovered, they are unlikely to tell us much that is new on this subject. He thinks that oral traditions could be of some help, regarding for example traditions of eastern Sierra Leone and north-western Liberia. The Kamara factor is singled out as deserving further investigation; and in general it is correctly noted that it would be helpful to know how widespread the use of Manden names by non-Manden-speaking people is in particular areas. Linked with this is the need for socio-anthropological research, which might indicate to what extent the Vai have retained Manden characteristics in the social and cultural spheres.

Hardly any archaeological research has yet been conducted in the Vai

56. ibid., p. 162. Jones also points out that it has never been satisfactorily explained just why Northern Mande languages are so often used for trade, though it may have something to do with their grammatical simplicity. But the point that needs stressing is that Vai was adopted as a trade language and that this has important historical implications. Jones observes that the adoption of Vai as a trade language seems to imply that there existed a market for the goods in which Vai-speakers dealt. Possibly non-Vai were willing to accept Vai as a *lingua franca* because they somehow saw it as representing a 'superior' civilization. Perhaps Vai did not carry as strong ethnic connotations as some languages. It is even conceivable that the spread of Vai was assisted by the spread of disease introduced by Vai-speakers, as has been suggested with regard to Bantu expansion. But there is as yet hardly any evidence for testing such an idea.

area. If Hill's evidence for the influx of distinctive pottery and a new settlement pattern north of the Vai area is confirmed,[57] this may well have implications for theories about the emergence of the Vai, although it would be dangerous to draw borders simply on the basis of pottery style. The sites of some coastal settlements are indicated on early seventeenth-century maps, and these would be worth investigating, if only to find out roughly how large they were. More work needs to be done on the *nomoli*; and it is crucial to have information on the early use of iron in this area.

A major contribution, however, must come from linguists. During the last fifteen years much progress has been made in classifying the languages of this area into 'groups' or 'branches'. It is to be hoped that some attention will now be paid to bridging the gaps between these groups and discovering what individual languages in different groups have in common. Until this is done it will never be possible to express for example how 'different' Vai is from Mande or from Krim. Loan-words are a particularly important field for further research. A comparison of dialects within the Mande, Vai, Krim and Gola languages would also be revealing. Finally a linguistic explanation could perhaps be offered for the apparent discrepancy between the present distribution of Mel-speakers and of river names beginning with *Ma*.

It appears then that there was contact from very early on between the Sudanic and Guinea-forest peoples leading to some drift southward and eastward of Sudanic peoples like the Soninke and Mande into parts of the lowland forest regions. It is very doubtful, however, that these came in such superior numbers as to replace indigenous peoples. Indeed, more often than not the indigenous peoples were not simple Kwa hunter-gatherers or fishers as has often been postulated. Nor is it true that both indigenous folks and the immigrants usually remained culturally stagnant or even retrogressed due to isolation and unfavourable ecology, as Murdock has suggested.[58] The historical facts rather reveal a continuous dynamic interaction of groups inhabiting the region, resulting in distinctive regional modifications.

Some relationship existed between ethnic stock, language affiliation and cultural type, but it was not necessarily as close, or as regular as has been posited by some. Widely spaced coastal peoples such as the Wolof, Sereer, Dyula, Nalu, Temne, Kisi and Gola, speaking languages of the West Atlantic subfamily may represent remnants of ancient inhabitants of the region, but these did not constitute an 'ancient primitive' forest culture of an original Negro stock that presumably inhabited all of western Africa in prehistoric times. Nor were the Kwa-speaking peoples of south-eastern Liberia and the western Ivory Coast the most primitive of these groups. Indeed the bulk of archaeological and related evidence available so far

57. M. H. Hill, 1972, pp. 1–2.
58. G. P. Murdock, 1959, pp. 70–1, 259–60.

shows conclusively that intensive agriculture, large centralized monarchies, occupational guilds and hereditary classes, military organizations, and trade and market systems were features of life among many of these peoples well before the earliest Sudanic intrusions and influences were experienced, and certainly between the seventh and eleventh centuries.

Both archaeological and ethnological evidence also appears to lend support to the thesis of a dynamic interaction between various peoples coming in contact at various times rather than to the view that important features such as iron-working, and state life were achieved through cultural imposition from the Sudan. These lines of evidence indicate that rice has been a more important and intensively cultivated crop along the West Atlantic coast than either cotton, millet or sorghum, to which proponents of the primacy of the Sudanic region seem to attach undue importance, and which may have been introduced by northern immigrants or through contact with the north.

Southern Liberia and the western Ivory Coast appear to be the locus of a sharp division of these agricultural traditions. The Bandama River, which separates the Baule and the Kru peoples, is also the northern boundary of intensive yam cultivation. Where yams appear in agriculture north of this boundary, it is reported that their harvest is not associated with the elaborate ritual that is found among the Agni and other Kwa-speaking peoples further to the south.

Whereas north of the Saint Paul River and eastward along the fringes of the forest area, rice continues as a basic crop in intensive agriculture for all the peoples of the Central West Atlantic region, important Sudanic cultigens such as millet, cotton and sorghum have scarcely intruded further west than the Guinea–Liberian border, or further south than to the Temne, Mande, Koranko, and Kono of Sierra Leone. In the northwestern province of Liberia, these crops are not planted by the De, Gola, and western Kpelle, except where 'Mandingo' peoples have settled in relatively recent times or where this influence is known to have obtained over long periods in the past. The latter condition did exist in a narrow corridor along the Saint Paul River as far west as the present town of Boporo, and also among those sections of the Kisi, Loma, and Gio peoples whose territories reach well into the highland plains of Guinea.

Conclusion

The current state of knowledge on the history of the Upper Guinea region in the period covered by this Volume may be considered as unsatisfactory. What we have presented here is no more than a provisional attempt to collect and discuss the available results of archaeological and linguistic research so far done in the region. But there are still more gaps than hard facts in our knowledge and we are dealing mostly with hypotheses that need further corroboration. This situation calls for a more systematic research strategy based on collaboration of specialists in various fields. No less important, however, is a new and unbiased approach enabling us to see the history of the Upper Guinea peoples in a perspective which will present them not merely as subjects of outside influence, be it from the north, or later from the south, but as active participants in the historical process.

19

The Horn of Africa

T. T. MEKOURIA

A map of seventh-century Ethiopia would not have a definite outline. On it would be marked the small number of towns and regions mentioned by Cosmas Indicopleustes in his *Christian Topography*, written in about the middle of the sixth century. This gives first-hand information about regions bordering on the Nile, the Red Sea and the Indian Ocean. It tells us, for example, that 'from Axum . . . to the lands of incense called Berbera which, lying on the ocean coast, are to be found not close to but far from Sasou, the furthest region of Ethiopia, it is a journey of some forty days'.[1]

Cosmas also wrote about merchants in their hundreds who travelled all over these regions, trading cattle, salt and iron and also, no doubt, the products of Byzantine craftsmanship, in exhange for 'gold nuggets'. There was also trade in spices, incense and cassia. The Axumite king exercised control over a large part of this trade 'through the agency of the governor of Agaw', states the writer from Alexandria, who was himself a merchant. The two big cities of the time were Axum and its port Adulis. We have no reason to think that the general situation was fundamentally different in the seventh century. Having reached its zenith in the preceding century, the kingdom of Axum had no doubt lost none of its power, although there is no direct information on this period. To be sure, the dangers facing it were to increase, and the decline was soon to set in. Still, at the beginning of the eighth century, a caliph of the Umayyad dynasty had the four kings of the world drawn on the walls of his palace in Ḳuṣayr ʿAmra, in Jordan. These were the sovereigns of Visigothic Spain, Byzantium, Persia and Axum. This testifies to their importance, even if the caliph in question claimed to have conquered them.[2]

The decline of the kingdom of Axum

The first historical reference to the kingdom of Axum was made at the beginning of the second century of the Christian era, or perhaps at the end of

1. Cosmas Indicopleustes, 1968, pp. 361–2.
2. U. Monneret de Villard, 1948, pp. 175–80; P. K. Hitti, 1956, p. 271.

the first century, in the *Periplus of the Erythraean Sea.* It enjoyed a period of exceptional prestige during the reign of Ezana in the fourth century. His wealth was derived from cattle-breeding, agriculture and, above all, from trading, especially in ivory. The kingdom maintained trade relations with the Mediterranean world and several places around the Indian Ocean through its port of Adulis and the Red Sea. This trade contributed greatly to the economic development of the country and, through the various activities that resulted from it, led to the growth of towns. As F. Anfray observes, these were essentially market towns.[3] He suggests considering as such several ancient sites whose buried remains are to be found throughout the high plateau of Tigre and Eritrea, such as Axum, Henzat, Haghero-Deragoueh, Degoum, Etch-Maré, Tokonda, Aratou and others still. These towns, which archaeologists are gradually bringing to light, were vast and crowded urban centres with tightly packed dwellings.

As early as the third century, the necessities of trade encouraged the creation of coinage, and these coins have given us the name of some twenty kings for the whole of the Axumite period, most of whom, from Endybis to Hataza, would otherwise have remained unknown.

The inscriptions inform us of events of historic importance such as the destruction of Meroe and the armed interventions in South Arabia during the reign of King Ezana – called Abraha, which means 'Illumina', in the traditional text – whose titles carved on the monuments indicate that he was 'King of Axum, Himyar, Kasu, Saba, Ḥabas̱hat, Raydan and Salhin, Tsiamo and Bēḏja.'[4]

From this period, Christianity became the dominant religion. The work of evangelization, begun by Bishop Frumentius – the Abba Salama, Kessate Berhan of Ethiopia tradition – was carried on in the fifth century by monks from the Byzantine empire.

Trade did not slacken in the sixth century. Quite the reverse was true and there are many sites dating from this period, especially on the edge of the Eritrean plateau. A large quantity of pottery has been found at Matara and includes many amphorae imported from the Mediterranean. This is something borne out by Cosmas Indicopleustes who describes the activities of the port of Adulis, 'the town of the Ethiopians . . . where we merchants from Alexandria and Ela trade'. He states that there were countless elephants in Ethiopia. 'They are elephants with large tusks. From Ethiopia, these tusks are sent by boat to India, Persia, the country of the Himyarites and Romania [i.e. the Roman Empire (Byzantium)]'.

During his stay in Adulis, Cosmas noted the preparation being made for the expedition that Caleb was to undertake in South Arabia which, for many years, was to remain under Ethiopian control.[5] The end of the cen-

3. Cf. Unesco, *General History of Africa*, Vol. II, p. 369.
4. E. Littman, 1913, pp. 4–35.
5. Cosmas Indicopleustes, 1968, pp. 368–70.

tury witnessed the collapse of Himyarite culture. The Sassanids of Persia took control of the Arabian Peninsula and clashed with Byzantines for control of the Red Sea trade.[6] This deprived Axum of some of its outlets.

The situation also changed in the north-west of the kingdom, which the local text calls 'Soba-Noba'. Alodia, Muḳurra and Nobadia formed Christianized states with which it can be assumed that Axum still had links.

The beginning of the seventh century marked a turning point for the kingdom of Axum. A page in the history of Axumite power was turned. Another age was to begin, that of its decline, for which documentary evidence is rarer, although this does not mean that it is non-existent. The Axumite towns continued for an as yet undetermined period. This we know from archaeology. The coins found on the sites at Axum, Matara and Adulis tell us the names of the kings who reigned during the seventh century and certainly part of the eighth: Ella-Gabaz, Anaeb, Armah, Yathlia, Za Ya-Abiyo, La Madhen, Wazena, Ghersem and Hataza. Their heads on the coins are surrounded by inscriptions in Ge'ez, still the liturgical language today. The reverse sides of the coins bear the Christian cross.

Ella-Gabaz and Armah are mentioned in Byzantine and Arab chronicles. According to al-Ṭabarī, Ella-Gabaz was the grandfather of Armah. Coins from the reign of Armah are numerous at the archaeological sites (Plate 19.1). He is shown sitting on a ceremonial seat.[7]

In about 615, during the reign of King Armah, or more probably that of his father, Ella-Tsaham, a significant event took place. Some followers of Muḥammad whose lives were threatened found refuge at the court of Axum where they were favourably received. As the Prophet had told him, 'if you are in Abyssinia, you will find a king under whom no one is persecuted. It is a land of justice where God will grant you relief from your troubles'. When the chiefs of Mecca, enemies of the Prophet, asked that the fugitives should be handed back to them, the king refused to satisfy their demands, considering that the religion of his guests was not without resemblance to the Christian faith which he practised. In addition, the law of hospitality had to be observed.[8]

The seventh century marked the birth and growth of Islam. Arab unity was to be shaped around Muḥammad. Islam gradually spread along the edge of the Red Sea. The favourable attitude of the first Muslims towards the Axumite kingdom lasted only a relatively short time. There were increasing clashes. The Axumites made incursions on to the Arab coast, provoking retaliatory action from the Muslims. In the eighth century, the Muslims occupied the Dahlak Islands which were part of the empire of Axum. Tombs have been discovered there with epitaphs carved in Kufic script. One of these is the epitaph of Mubārak, the founder of the dynasty,

6. Cf. N. V. Pigulevskaya, 1969.
7. C. Conti Rossini, 1928, Vol. 1, pp. 205–10.
8. ibid., p. 262; cf. also Chapter 26 below.

FIG. 19.1 *The Horn of Africa*

PLATE 19.1 *Coinage of King Armah, seventh century of the Christian era*

which established its domination over the archipelago in the eleventh century.[9]

Archaeological evidence gives ground for thinking that Adulis, the Axumite port, was destroyed in about the eighth century, and that the trading activities which until then had been under the control of the Axumite king were brought to a complete halt. As regards the events taking place in the interior of the country, however, history remains silent, or almost so. It merely records a weakening of the royal power which,

9. The inscription indicates that he died on 11 Dhu l-ḥidjdja 486/3 December 1093. Cf. B. Malmusi, 1895; G. Oman, 1974 a and b; S. Tedeschi, 1969.

strangely, was to show renewed vigour for a while, if one considers the accounts of two Arab historians.

In the third/ninth century, al-Yaʿḳūbī talks about a Christian sovereign governing a vast country whose capital is Kaʿbar or Kuʿbar.[10] In the fourth/tenth century, al-Masʿūdī improved on the description given by his predecessor: 'The capital of Abyssinia is called Kuʿbar. It is a large city and the seat of the Kingdom of Nadjāshī. The country has many towns and extensive territories reaching as far as the sea of Abyssinia. It encompasses the coastal plain facing the Yemen where one finds many cities such as Zaylāʿ, Dahlak and Nasiʿ, in which the Muslim subjects of the Abyssinians live'.[11] The exact location of Kuʿbar, the royal capital, is still a mystery.[12]

The Bēdja

One of the factors that contributed to the waning of the kingdom of Axum from the seventh century onwards and its disappearance in the eighth, was without doubt the invasion of the northern regions of Ethiopia by the Bēdja whose 'force of expansion', as the historian C. Conti Rossini calls it, was at the time considerable. One of the most powerful of the Bēdja groups, the Zanāfidj, invaded the Eritrean plateau through the Barḳa Valley.

During preceding periods, the Bēdja people had organized themselves into several 'kingdoms', occupying a vast area from Axum to Upper Egypt. These Bēdja formed a single ethnic group with the Blemmyes mentioned by authors writing in Latin. The Blemmyes were well known from the third century onwards, and the first mention of the Bēdja (or Bega) also appears in an inscription from the same century made by an Axumite king and copied in the sixth century by Cosmas.

Their warlike spirit was particularly evident during the reign of Ezana in the fourth century, and several inscriptions from this reign in Ge'ez, imitation South Arabian and Greek, read like bulletins from the campaign against these unruly peoples. In addition, one of the titles the Axumite sovereign gives himself is king of the Bēdja.

This occupation of the north of Ethiopia by the Bēdja – hence the present name of Begemder, Bēdja country – no doubt resulted from the fact that the power of Axum had weakened somewhat, but the pressure that the Bēdja were to exercise from then on was to hasten the decline of Axumite power.

10. Al-Yaʿḳūbī, 1883, p. 219.

11. Al-Masʿūdī, 1861–77, Vol. 3, p. 34.

12. C. Conti Rossini, 1928, Vol. 1, p. 51 identified Kuʿbar with Axum, seeing the Arabic name as a graphic corruption. However, it is probable that at that time Axum no longer existed as a capital.

From the third/ninth to the fifth/eleventh centuries, the only sources concerning the Bēdja are Arab authors, first among them being al-Ya'ḳubī (d. 897), and, second, Ibn Ḥawḳal and al-Uswānī. These authors provide a great deal of information on the ethnic situation in the north of Ethiopia and between the Nile and the Red Sea. Because of the difficulties of Arabic script, which allows a large number of different readings, most of the ethnonyms and toponyms still remain a mystery. In spite of the efforts of several scholars, only a limited number of these names have been identified.[13]

Starting from the area near the Nile, al-Ya'ḳūbī lists and gives the position of five Bēdja 'kingdoms', going from the Nile towards the sea, and then southwards. The first kingdom, the nearest to the Muslim country of Aswān, was Naḳis which was inhabited by several small peoples whose names are listed but have not yet been deciphered. These peoples lived near the second kingdom, Baḳlīn or Taflīn, in the Eritrean Sahel, the Rora plateau and the middle valley of the River Barakat. To the east of the Baḳlīn lived the Bāzīn whose descendants are probably the present-day Kunama who are called Bazen by their neighbours. The kingdom of the Djarin stretched from Bāḍī' (Massawa) as far as the country of the Baḳlīn towards the Barakat. The last group consisted of the Ḳata'a, whose territory extended from Bāḍī' to Faykun or Fankun. These Ḳata'a were Christians and found themselves under the influence of the Nadjāshī. Arab merchants traded with these people and gradually brought about their conversion to Islam.[14]

It is surprising to find that the Arab accounts make no mention of the Tigre who lived in this area of Eritrea at this time. It is quite possible, however, that the people called the Zanāfidj, mentioned by al-Ya'ḳūbī and Ibn Sulaym al-Uswānī in their lists of the Bēdja groups, were in reality the Tigré, as has been shown by A. Zaborski.[15]

In Eritrea and northern Tigré, there are still traditions recalling these ancient peoples under the legendary names of Rom and Balaw (and sometimes Belew Kelew, mostly in the Chimezana). Place names also record their existence, especially that of the Belew who five or six centuries ago extended their supremacy as far as the coastal area. The Beni 'Amer, who today lead a nomadic existence in northern Eritrea and Sudan, are the descendants of the former Bēdja.[16]

Under the pressure of these warlike Bēdja groups, Axum's kings and leading citizens left Axum for more southerly areas which were free from the perils of the invaders. In addition, life in the former area of Axumite rule was becoming uncertain.

13. Cf. J. H. Kramers, 1954; A. Zaborski, 1965, 1970, 1971.

14. Al-Ya'ḳūbī, 1883, pp. 217–19.

15. A. Zaborski, 1971, pp. 118 *et seq.* The al-Zanāfidj called their God *akzabhir*, a Semitic word, whereas the Bēdja spoke a Cushitic language.

16. C. Conti Rossini, 1928, ch. 12; E. Cerulli, 1971, pp. 42–53.

As has been said, at the start of the seventh century the political situation around the Red Sea changed almost completely. The Byzantine empire, itself threatened by Persian conquests, shrank back. The Persians were more and more in evidence and established bases on the African coast. Although archaeologists have not yet paid much attention to them, there are remains to be found in various places where the memory of the Furs is preserved. Ethiopia was the ally of Byzantium whose power was being weakened. Little by little, the Arabs pushed the Byzantines back. In Egypt they won complete victories. In Ethiopia the successors of Armah were isolated. The country was then enveloped by a kind of darkness lit only by faint historical glimmers. No inscription has been discovered for this period of the seventh and eighth centuries except one rather clumsily carved inscription on the base of a throne in Axum. It is in Ge'ez and seems to be of a later period. It mentions a certain *Ḥaḍānī* Dan'el (a pretender to the throne?) who rebelled against his sovereign and forbade the king access to his city. This inscription contains little information on the events of the period other than that a person of high standing rebelled, which can mean that traditional power had weakened somewhat.[17]

On the threshold of the second millennium

During the second half of the tenth century something serious happened which affected the life of the country. This event is related by two Arab sources, the *History of the Patriarchs of Alexandria* and the account given by the well-known geographer, Ibn Ḥawḳal.

The *History of the Patriarchs* mentions a certain queen of the Banū al-Hamwiya, from the south, who sacked the Axumite area and destroyed its churches. She drove out the king, who appealed to the Coptic patriarch, Cosmas, through the Nubian king Djirdjīs/George, asking him to send a metropolitan.[18] As we know, the See of Axum had been held since the fourth century by a Coptic ecclesiastic from Alexandria. In the fifth century, Ethiopia embraced the Monophysite doctrine, adopting the Egyptian liturgy.[19]

About the same time, Ibn Ḥawḳal wrote concerning the events taking place in Ethiopia:

> Regarding the land of the Abyssinians, it has been governed for many years now by a woman. She killed the king of the Abyssinians who was known by the title of *Ḥaḍānī*. She has hitherto ruled in complete independence over her own country and the areas surrounding the land of the *Ḥaḍānī* in the south of Abyssinia. It is an immense

17. Cf. Y. M. Kobishchanov, 1962.
18. J. Perruchon, 1894, pp. 359–62.
19. Cf. Unesco, *General History of Africa*, Vol. II, ch. 16.

> country, without definite borders, which deserts and lonely places render difficult of access.

In another place, Ibn Ḥawḳal, who wrote his book in about 367/977, states that this queen had come to power thirty years before.[20]

Driven from power, the unfortunate king took refuge in remote Shoa, feeling his overthrow to be the result of divine rage provoked by the dismissal of a bishop, as is shown in a passage of the letter that he sent to the Nubian king Djirdjīs II, at the time when Abba Philotheos (Filatewos, 979–1003) was patriarch of Alexandria. The king wrote among other things:

> ... by dismissing the duly elected Abba Petros [Peter] and accepting Minas the usurper, the kings who preceded us transgressed the law ... Because of this, God became angry with us ... Our enemies rose against us and led many of us into captivity. They put the country to the torch and destroyed our churches ... we have become wanderers ... The heavens no longer send rain and the earth no longer gives us its fruits ... We are now like abandoned sheep, without a shepherd.[21]

After the probable intervention of the Nubian king, Djirdjīs, the patriarch appointed a certain Abba Daniel as bishop of Axum. Before he could take up his duties, however, the king who in about 970 to 980 was still fighting the implacable queen, died.[22]

The documents are contradictory in what they say about this queen. Some say that she was the queen of the Falashas (Ethiopian Jews) and a daughter of chief Gideon. Others state that she was the granddaughter of king Wedem-Asfere, and others still claim that she was the daughter known as Mesobe-Work of the last Axumite king, Delnaad.[23]

The Ethiopian Church still remembers this queen whom it calls Goudite (the monster) or Esato (the fiery one), without however telling us what her real name was. Likewise, the name of the royal writer of the letter is, unfortunately, not made known to us, although it could well have been Delnaad, the last Axumite king.

Conti Rossini suggested that the word *Al-Hamwiya* in the title of the queen be read as *Al-Damūta*, which might indicate the region of Damot – to the south and south-east of the Blue Nile – as her land of origin.[24] These events could then be interpreted as a reaction by the small peoples in

20. Ibn Ḥawḳal, 1964, Vol. 1, pp. 56 and 16.

21. Cf. T.-T. Mekouria, 1959, pp. 334–6. Synaxarion for the feast of 12 Hadar/20 November.

22. According to E. Cerulli, 1971, pp. 258–69, the sending of the letter by the Ethiopian king to the Nubian king Djirdjīs seems to have taken place before 978.

23. Mesobe-Work means 'gilded basket' – a basket that is richly worked, round, with a base, made of compressed straw, on which are put flat loaves of bread (*ingera*), which comprise the national dish.

24. C. Conti Rossini, 1928, Vol. 1, p. 286.

the interior of Ethiopia against the expansion by the Axumite Christian kings into the south of the country.

Ethiopian histories for this dark period contain royal genealogies. Most of these are found in the *Chronicle of the Reign of Emperor Menelik*, written at the start of the twentieth century by a church dignitary, Neboure-Id Guèbrè Sellassié:

> . . . Kaleb . . . was a good king. He begat Gabra Meskal, under whose reign Yared composed the *Degoua*.[25] It was he who founded Debre-Damo, the domain of our father Abuna Aregawi. Gabra Meskal begat Kostentinos who begat Wesen-Segued, who begat Fere-Senay, who begat Aderaz, who begat Akale-Wedem, who begat Guerma-Asfere, who begat Zergaz, who begat Degna Mikael . . . who begat Bahr-Ikla, who begat Gum, who begat Asguamgum, who begat Letem, who begat Telatem, who begat Ode-Gosh, who begat Aizour. This last king reigned for only half a day and died. And if anyone asks about the manner of his dying, it was on this wise. The day on which he began to reign, he said: 'Do not stop my people from coming to me. Let them come, let them look at my face, let them greet me'! Thus he was besieged by so many people that, trampled underfoot, he died . . . Aizour begat Dedem who begat Wedem-Asfere who reigned until he was seven score and ten years old, and begat Armah who begat Denaguej, who begat Delnaad.[26]

This table of royal successions starting from the sixth century is obviously apocryphal. It was composed at a later date, but might still contain a few grains of truth.[27]

Other traditions relate that the last king, Delnaad, could have taken refuge in a country in the south. In about the ninth century, he supposedly founded the Saint Stephen (Stifanos) monastery at Lake Hayk, near which he is also said to have built his residence. A no doubt legendary account but one which might have stemmed from important events, has it that his daughter married a prince from Bugena, the region near the Lasta in which a new dynasty was to take root in the twelfth century.[28]

This people from the Lasta, who were to play a role in the history of Ethiopia, belonged to the Agaw, who for centuries had been living in the south-west of the country. In his *Christian Topography*, Cosmas Indicopleustes mentions a governor of the Agaw in the sixth century.[29]

It is possible that the flight of the last Axumite king and the legend of his daughter, Mesobe-Work, who married Mera Tekle Haymanot, the first

25. Antiphon for all the feast days of the year.
26. Guèbrè Sellassié, 1930, pp. 16–20.
27. C. Conti Rossini, 1909.
28. According to one tradition, this new dynasty is said to have been established in the tenth or eleventh century.
29. Cosmas Indicopleustes, 1968, pp. 360–1.

king of the new Zague dynasty, according to the traditional genealogy is a romanticized version of an episode that really occurred. Be that as it may, after the glories of the Axumite period, this new dynasty supplanted the old and legitimate dynasty of the Ezanian family and established itself in the centre of Ethiopia.

After so much destruction, the new dynasty set up its own political system once it had settled in the central provinces, yet it retained many of Axum's traditions and cultural traits. This new reign reached its zenith in the twelfth and thirteenth centuries, as witnessed by the great kings of the Zague dynasty of whom the most famous is Lalibela.

Literature

Ethiopian literature is biblical and Christian in origin. From the outset, ecclesiastical circles gave it its essential stamp. From the fourth century, the Ge'ez language predominated at court as well as in church. The translations which occupy a large place in this literature are written in this language.

The first books were translations of the Bible, done in the monasteries established from the end of the fifth century onwards. Translation continued during the succeeding centuries, principally from Greek. The New Testament was translated from the version approved by the Patriarch of Antioch by Syrian Monophysite ecclesiastics who in the fifth and sixth centuries took refuge in Ethiopia, where they did much to spread Christianity.

With regard to the Old Testament, apart from the canonical books recognized by the Council of Trent, the Ethiopians translated several biblical books considered by other churches to be apocryphal. These include the *Book of Enoch*, the *Book of Jubilees*, the *Ascension of Isaiah*, the *Shepherd* by Hermas and the *Apocalypse* of Esdras. It is noteworthy that these apocryphal books have come down to us in full in the Ge'ez language alone, while only fragments survive in other languages. In those dark ages Ethiopia thus made one of its major contributions to Christian literature.

The list of translations also includes theological treatises among which was the *Qerillos*, according to a compilation made by Saint Cyril of Alexandria. Another work that greatly contributed to the development of the religious spirit of the Ethiopian clergy was the translation of *The Rule of Pachomius*, Saint Pachomius being the founder of eastern monasticism. The same period also saw the translation from Greek of the *Physiologos*, a collection of semi-legendary accounts of animals, plants and minerals with moral conclusions.

These texts were all apparently translated before the seventh century. However, there is reason to believe that some versions of them were recopied during the period under study, because during this time – from the seventh to the eleventh century – Christianity continued to extend its influence primarily, if not exclusively, through monasticism, which is per-

PLATE 19.2 *Gospel book of Abba-Guerima showing the figure of St Mark (eleventh century)*

haps the most important phenomenon in the history of that obscure period.[30]

The fact that no original works have come down to us from that period does not in itself mean that those centuries were totally lacking in original intellectual activity. On the contrary, it seems to have been at this time that the foundations were laid for the flowering of literature in the fourteenth century. Of this flowering, E. Cerulli has rightly observed: 'The artistic maturity of these writings in no way represents a literature in its infancy: and the standard of writing presupposes a discipline which cannot be rapidly acquired without a long tradition'.[31]

Architecture

According to several traditions, the first monasteries in the north of the country were established in the fifth and sixth centuries. The violent sackings that took place in this area over the centuries led to the complete destruction of most of the buildings. None the less, substantial remains can still be found in some areas.[32]

30. I. Guidi, 1932, pp. 11–21.
31. E. Cerulli, 1956, p. 35.
32. C. Conti Rossini, 1928, pp. 219–25.

The 'Nine Saints' (Teseatu Kidusan) who are traditionally said to have come from the Byzantine world, are seen as being the originators of monastic life proper. They settled in remote parts of the Axum region. One of their oldest foundations is to be found east of Adwa on a high rocky platform in the Tigré Mountains. It is called Debre-Damo.

A church, recently restored, was established there in very remote times. It is one of the very small number of churches that were preserved from destruction. Specialists date them to about the tenth century, but tradition holds that the first church was built in the sixth century at Debre-Damo, on the initiative of king Gebra-Masqal, son of Kaleb, at the spot chosen by Abba Za-Mikael Aragawi, one of the Nine Saints.

The church that one sees today is rectangular in shape and measures 20 m × 9.70 m. The method of construction remains faithful to Axumite architectural tradition in which stone and wood are used together. The doors and windows have the same frames as one sees, for example, on the giant stelae of Axum, with the projecting butt-ends of beams as well as the alternately projecting and recessed parts that are one of the features of Axumite architecture. The church has a single storey with galleries above the naves. It also has a most important decorative feature consisting of a wooden panelled ceiling decorated with different designs representing animals and geometric patterns of oriental inspiration and dating back to the end of the first millennium. Various objects discovered at Debre-Damo are evidence of the antiquity of this building.[33]

Although this church was the first to show what the buildings put up around the tenth century were like, it is not now the only example of the architecture of this period. Excavations undertaken in the 1970s have brought to light other churches in northern Ethiopia which various pieces of archaeological evidence link to that distant age of the Axumite decline and the advent of a new period when the seat of government moved south, monastic life developed, and a new culture came into being. The churches in question, which we will mention here as evidence of this particular aspect of history, are those of Zarema, Agowo and Berakit.[34]

The church in the village of Zarema, east of Atsbi on the eastern Tigré plateau is shaped like a cross. This church is dedicated to St George (Kedus Ghiorghis) and is probably a latter-day survival of the square-shaped, colonnaded buildings of the Axumite period. The carvings on the wooden ceilings, above the aisles, are of exceptional interest both because of the composition and because of the technique. Attention should be drawn here to the rare preservation in this church of beautiful wooden capitals finely carved with crosses and palmettes. According to C. Lepage, 'this carving derives directly from the decorative Mediterranean art of the seventh and eighth centuries, especially that of Coptic Egypt. It bears no

33. D. Matthews and A. Mordini, 1959, pp. 1–59.

34. In writing these paragraphs on architectural remains, I have drawn substantially on the studies by C. Lepage.

PLATE 19.3 *Interior of the Church of Tcherqos (St Cyriacus) at Agowo, ninth to tenth centuries of the Christian era.*

trace of Islamic decorative art'. While still a matter of doubt, the original date of the church of Zarema-Ghiorghis seems, in the opinion of the author whose work is being used as a reference here, to go 'very far back'. 'The ninth or tenth century would be well within the realms of possibility'.[35]

The church of Agowo, like that of Zarema, is to be found in the Atsbi area. It is a small basilica of stone and wood built against a cliff, under a rocky overhang. As in Axumite buildings, the walls show the butt-ends of beams, and the ceiling of the central nave has wooden panels which are not,

35. C. Lepage, 1973.

however, decorated as they are at Debre-Damo. The rooms on the eastern side also have ceilings with slanted beams and small wooden panels constructed in an original way. The framework of the openings in the walls is typical of Axumite architecture. This church bears the name of Tcherqos (Cyriac). Its oldest parts probably date back to the eleventh century, but it was restored at a later date (Plate 19.3).

Rock churches

The churches of Debre-Damo, Zarema-Ghiorghis and Agowo-Tcherqos, which we dealt with above, are churches that have been built in the conventional way. A large number of churches carved out of the living rock are to be found in northern Ethiopia where the roots of Christianity go very deep. They are of considerable interest in more ways than one. They originated in the period under review; they have close links with Axumite architecture; and some of them are remarkably well executed.[36]

A large group of churches are to be found in the Guerealta area, to the north of Mekele. Other churches are to be found all over the neighbouring districts of Tembien, Amba Senayt and Atsbi. These churches reproduce, in the rock, the interior of a normally built church with pillars, capitals and a framework. A total of about one hundred and twenty rock churches have been listed in these areas. Among the oldest are the hypogea of Degum-Sellassie in Guerealta, which have been dated to as far back as the tenth century. Certain archaeological considerations could lead to their being attributed a date about two centuries earlier. These three hypogea are very skilfully cut into the rock and are parallel to each other. There is a deep crypt with a staircase leading into it, as in the large Axumite tombs at Axum, Matara and elsewhere. Nearby, also cut into the rock, is a baptismal font that is strikingly similar to the one discovered by F. Anfray at the Matara site and dated to the sixth or seventh century.[37] These rock hypogea are thought to have been used for burials. It is interesting to note that the ruins of a building of the Axumite period lie nearby.

Some twenty kilometres from the Degum-Sellassie site is the church of Maryam of Berakit, which is situated about a hundred kilometres south-east of Axum to the north-west of Guerealta. It is a remarkable example of Ethiopian rock art. It has been hewn out of a rocky eminence in the middle of the valley. C. Lepage, who has written a detailed study on it, says that it is the 'rock equivalent of a kind of very distinctively Axumite basilica'. He also observes that its shape can be compared with the constructed church at Debre-Damo.[38]

There is no doubt that the first thing that strikes one on seeing a church

36. Cf. G. Gerster, 1968, 1970, 1974.
37. F. Anfray, 1974.
38. C. Lepage, 1972.

of this kind is its relationship with Axumite architecture. To start with, they are geographically close, there are extant Axumite remains, and then in the architectural order there are several features that are shared with Axumite tradition, such as the smallness of the proportions, the characteristic basilica plan of the small churches of the sixth and seventh centuries at Enda-Tcherqos near Axum, at Matara, Tokonda and Kohayto, the flat ceilings, the pillars and the capitals. These features lead us to attribute to a church like the one at Berakit a date close to the Axumite period.

Ornamentation

In several old buildings, including those dealt with in this chapter, carving is to be found, chiefly on the ceilings, capitals and arches.

In the church of Debre-Damo, carved decorations are still to be seen on the panels of the wooden ceilings of the porch. They mostly represent animals such as lions, antelopes, zebu cattle, snakes, camels, elephants, buffaloes, goats, donkeys, giraffes, leopards, as well as imaginary animals, plant motifs and geometrical shapes. The capitals also display this liking for decoration. The cross is often the central motif, surrounded by interlaced designs and palmettes. The artists of remote antiquity knew all the different types of ornamentation used in Mediterranean countries, especially Coptic Egypt. In the churches of Zarema, Debre-Damo and Agowo, there are friezes in a square frame, identical to the framework of the windows, carved into the rock as a decoration. The church of Zarema-Ghiorghis is among the most decorated of the ancient buildings in northern Ethiopia.

There are no wall paintings in these churches at the present time. One may wonder whether such paintings decorated their walls in ancient times, as is the case with the later churches like Beta-Maryam in Lalibela for example, but the walls of the oldest known churches today bear no trace of them. The small size of the walls seems to have left very little space for painted decoration. Still it is possible that such decorations did exist at one time. We have the eyewitness account, recorded by al-Ṭabarī, of a woman in Muḥammad's entourage who went to Axum in the seventh century and who, on her return to Medina, remembered with admiration the 'marvellous paintings on the walls' of the cathedral. However, no painting, not even a trace, has survived from these ancient times.

With regard to the manuscripts, we know that several ancient books were translated from Greek and Syriac from the fifth or sixth century onward, but it is difficult to know whether these manuscripts were decorated with paintings as none of them seems to have withstood the destructive action of time and, sometimes, of men, with the exception of two beautiful gospel-books preserved in the old monastery of Abba-Guerima, near Adwa in Tigré. The paintings decorating some pages of these manuscripts bear a degree of resemblance to the Byzantine art of Syria. A study has been made of them by J. Leroy, who dates them to the eleventh century (Plate 19.2). There is no doubt that these ancient manuscripts carried on a tradition of which real evidence may perhaps one day be discovered in a church lost in the mountains of northern Ethiopia.[39]

39. J. Leroy, 1968; D. Matthews and A. Mordini, 1959; D. R. Buxton, 1971.

20 Ethiopia's relations with the Muslim world

E. CERULLI

The relations which since earliest times have linked the populations of the two shores of the Red Sea, Arabs and Ethiopians, began to change with the rise of Islam, as from then on they were expressed as relations between Christians and Muslims.

The traditions collected in the biographies of the Prophet Muḥammad record various episodes involving early contacts of nascent Islam with Ethiopia:

(1) The letter of Muḥammad to the *negus* (Arabic *nadjāshī*) inviting him to join the new religion, starting with the Qoranic passage (4:169) which invites 'the People of the Book' (*ahl al-Kitāb*) to reconsider the person of Jesus in the light of Islamic teachings.[1]

(2) The mission to Ethiopia of ʿAmr ibn al-ʿĀṣ, the future Muslim conqueror of Egypt, who was sent, when still a 'pagan', by the Meccan oligarchy to the *negus* to oppose the progress of Islam, but instead was converted to the Islamic religion.

(3) The emigration to Ethiopia of Djaʿfar ibn Abī Ṭālib, cousin of Muḥammad and brother of the future Caliph ʿAlī ibn Abī Ṭālib, who went to the court of the *negus* with other Muslims in order to escape the hostilities of the Ḳurayshites. According to some traditions he succeeded in converting the *negus*; the latter, in his turn, to avoid the hostility of his Christian subjects, resorted to the stratagem of concealing in his breast the text of the passage of the Qoran mentioned above and thus pretended to swear in a way conformable to the Christian faith.

This action of Djaʿfar perhaps later inspired the claims of various princes and leaders of Ethiopia and Somalia to be descended from members of Abī Ṭālib's family, as we shall see later on.

(4) Another group of traditions of early Islam concerns Bilāl, the faithful slave of Ethiopian origin. Bilāl became a freed slave of Abū Bakr (the future first Caliph), and was, according to the legend, the second male convert to Islam, the first being Abū

1. V. Vacca, 1923–5.

> Bakr himself. In fact, the first person converted to Islam was a woman: Khadīdja, the wife of the Prophet Muḥammad. A trusty follower of the Prophet, Bilāl, was appointed by him *mu'adhdhin* with the task of calling the faithful to prayer in the mosque; and he remained in this office until the Caliphate of ʿUmar, when he went with the Muslim army to Syria, where he died and was buried.

Many other traditions generally refer to the Ethiopian Bilāl and the Prophet's predilection for him and people of the same origin, like the saying 'Who brings an Ethiopian man or an Ethiopian woman into his house, brings the blessing of God there'.

This affection for the Ethiopians also gave rise to some opuscula of Arabic literature.[2] There is the work of Ibn al-Djawzī (d. 596/1200) with the pompous title 'The Lightening of the darkness on the merits of the Blacks and Ethiopians' (*Tanwīr al- ghabash fī faḍl al-Sūdān wa l-Ḥabash*). The Egyptian polyhistor al-Suyūṭī (d. 911/1505) wrote a special treatise entitled 'The Raising of the status of the Ethiopians' (*Rafʿ sha'n al-Ḥubshān*), which he later summarized in his other work 'Flowers of the thrones on the history of the Ethiopians' (*Azhār al-ʿurūsh fī akhbār al-Ḥubūsh*). Another work of this kind is 'The Coloured brocade on the good qualities of the Ethiopians' (*Al-Ṭirāz al-mankūsh fī maḥāsin al-Ḥubūsh*)[3] written in 991/1583 by Muḥammad ibn ʿAbd al-Bāḳī al-Bukhārī al-Makkī.

It became fashionable to insert in these works one or more chapters on Ethiopian words which are supposed to occur in the Revelation, i.e. in the Qoran and also in the *ḥadīth*s, i.e. traditional accounts of the Prophet's deeds and sayings. Some of the words listed as such are not Ethiopian but of an origin that remained unknown to Arabic authors. But many others are clearly of Ethiopian (*Geʿez*) origin; at the beginning of the seventh century they were in common usage in Arabia.[4] In some cases a genuine Arab word was given a specific religious meaning under the influence of the cognate Ethiopian. The linguistic observations of Arabic authors are of interest also for the linguistic history of Ethiopian languages, because the saying 'The *sīn* of Bilāl is *shīn* with God' gives the *terminus ante quem* for the transition from *sh* to *s* in the pronunciation of Ethiopian, since it is already reported by Ibn Saʿd, who wrote in 230/844–5.[5]

2. B. Lewis, 1971, p. 37.
3. German translation by M. Weisweiler, 1924.
4. Cf. A. Jeffery, 1938. In the Qoran we find the following Ethiopian words: *mishkat*, from Eth. *maskot*, window; *kiflain*, dual of Eth. *kefl*, portion, part; *burhān*, an evident proof, Eth. light, illumination; *tābūt*, Eth. Ark of Covenant, chest; *hawāriyyūn*, Eth. disciples, apostles; *maṣhaf*, Eth. a copy, book; *māʾida*, table, Lord's table; *malak*, angel, etc. Ethiopian too is the word *sana*, attributed to Bilāl (Eth. *sannay*, beautiful), and also *minbar*, pulpit, Eth. *manbar*.
5. Ibn Saʿd, 1905–28, Vol. 3, pp. 165–70.

The Muslim settlement on the Dahlak Islands

Relations between the nascent Muslim state and Ethiopia did not have a friendly character. Already during Muḥammad's life an Ethiopian fleet attacked the Arabian port of S̲h̲uʿayba and some years later the Caliph ʿUmar was forced to send four ships and two hundred men against 'the Ethiopians who committed many evil deeds to Muslims in Arabia',[6] but this expedition against the Axumites seems to have achieved little.

Throughout the seventh century the Red Sea remained firmly in Ethiopian hands and only gradually did the Muslims gain the upper hand. In 702 the Ethiopians attacked Ḥid̲j̲āz for the last time and their fleet occupied D̲j̲idda for a while, thus creating panic in Mecca. Whether these attacks were undertaken by regular Axumite forces or by Ethiopian pirates remains obscure. In any case as a retaliation for the last attack the Arabs occupied and destroyed Adulis[7] and established themselves on the Dahlak Islands in the Gulf of Masāwa, opposite Adulis. These islands afforded the possibility of controlling the sea traffic of Ethiopia, because Adulis was a stopping place on the route to the Indies, and this traffic was one of the main resources of the Axum state, together with the caravan route to the Nile Valley which also made Adulis the outlet for goods coming from Nubia. From the second half of the eighth century on, no more Ethiopian naval raids are mentioned and the same is true about Ethiopian seafaring in general. It seems that the Arabs had destroyed the Ethiopian navy which appears again on the scene only in the fourteenth century. During these centuries the Muslims exercised full control of the seaborne trade of the Red Sea, thus increasing the isolation of Ethiopia.

The occupation of Dahlak took place early in the Umayyad period and the islands were also used as a place of political exile. We have evidence of this already during the reign of Caliph Sulaymān (96/715–99/717) when the Arab poet al-Aḥwaṣ was exiled to the Dahlak Islands for some of his satirical verses.[8]

Subsequently, under the Abbasids, the islands served as a base for ensuring a safe sea voyage for the pilgrims to the Holy Places, at a time when the Red Sea was infested by pirates.

At the beginning of the fourth/tenth century an independent Muslim principality was established on the Dahlak Islands. This state played a highly important role in the economic history of Ethiopia as well as in the spread of Islam in this region.[9] It took over the ancient trade of Adulis and maintained brisk trade relations with Christian Ethiopia.[10]

6. Al-Ṭabarī, 1879–1901, Vol. 1, p. 1889.
7. R. Paribeni, 1908.
8. Cf. K. Petráček, 1960. It is noteworthy that in modern times, too, the Nokra Island was used as a penal station for politicians regarded as undesirable by the Italian Fascist government.
9. Cf. Chapter 3 above.
10. Al-Yaʿḳūbī, 1883, p. 219.

Evidence of the mercantile activity of the Dahlak sultanate exists in an Arabo-Jewish document of the Fāṭimid epoch, found in the Cairo Geniza. The document states that a merchant originating from Tripolitania (he is called al-Lebdī, i.e. native of Leptis Magna) on his passage from Egypt to India stopped at Dahlak for business purposes sometime before the year 490/1097.

We have a rich documentation on the duration of the Sultanate on the Dahlak Islands and also on the degree of Islamic culture of its inhabitants in more than two hundred Arabic inscriptions found on the main island, Dahlak Kabīr, which are now in various museums (Modena, Treviso, Bar-le-Duc, Cairo and Asmara).

The oldest of these inscriptions is dated 298/911 and the most recent bears the date of 946/1539. They are written in a grammatically correct Arabic and, with many quotations from the Qoran, follow the formulae in use at that time in neighbouring Islamic countries.[11] These inscriptions also allow us to reconstruct partially the genealogy and succession of the sultans of Dahlak, mainly from the fifth/eleventh century on.[12]

Alongside these documents indicating the continuous presence of the Arabs, the tradition which is widespread along the African coast from the Gulf of Masāwa to that of Djibuti must not be neglected. This tradition attributes to the 'Furs' (Persians) the construction of monuments, in general large cisterns for the collection of water, the remains of which can still be seen in Dahlak Kabīr and in Adal. This may be evidence of the presence of Persian traders or commercial agencies on the African coast, or it may document the fact that the sovereigns of both coasts of the Red Sea employed Persian engineers for these constructions, given the renown acquired by the Persians in the Muslim world for their water storage and distribution works. Three Dahlak inscriptions mention personages who died on these islands and whose *nisba* (indicative of the place of origin) was al-Ḳaysī, derived from the name of the Arab 'tribe' of Ḳays, which succeeded Sīrāf, the famous trade emporium, in the hegemony of the Arab/Persian Gulf traffic in the fourth/tenth century.[13]

The Muslim states of southern Ethiopia

The African coast of the Red Sea thus kept its old function in the traffic to the Indies, although within the new economic system of the Islamic world. But of course the Muslim merchants very soon pushed forward from the coast into the neighbouring regions of Ethiopia in search of merchandise for their commerce. In the north we thus have documentation of a Muslim

11. On these inscriptions see B. Malmusi, 1895; G. Oman, 1974b (with a full up-to-date bibliography).

12. Cf. R. Basset, 1893; G. Wiet, 1953; S. Tedeschi, 1969.

13. G. Puglisi, 1969; 1953.

trading centre even in the territory of the kingdom of Axum, namely, in Endertā, at the edge of the Tigrai near the River Mareb. The presence of these Muslims is documented by a group of Arabic inscriptions which are dated from 391/987 to 549/1154, dates which, as can be seen, correspond to the period of greatness of the sultanate of the Dahlak Islands, with which this trading centre must have been connected.[14]

But while in the north the Christian state of Axum prevented a greater extension of Islam, its development in the south of Ethiopia was very different. Here, too, it set out from the sea along the natural route which leads from the Gulf of Djibuti through the depression of the valley of the River Ḥawāsh to the richest regions of the south and west of the Ethiopian plateau. Once again, therefore, the spread of Islam follows the trade routes; indeed, even today *naggadie*, which in Amharic means 'merchant', typically means 'Muslim' in the language of the Oromo (Galla) of southern Ethiopia.[15]

Various southern Ethiopian populations, from the coast of the Red Sea and the Gulf of Aden up to the Blue Nile, were thus converted to Islam. And in this way various Muslim sultanates were formed; what had been local state organizations probably being transformed into Islamic states. In these sultanates a hereditary aristocracy was dominant which was, or pretended to be, of Arab origin, while the mass of the population were Ethiopian and probably belonged to the Cushite family of the Sidamas. During the historical period in which the documents enable us to follow these sultanates, although they were often at war with each other they were under the hegemony of one of them which imposed its authority on the others; and on the other hand they had relations, generally not very friendly, with the state of Christian Ethiopia which, as we shall see, was to come ever closer to them in its movement of expansion.

The first of these sultanates was that of Dāmūt which, as the great Arab historian Ibn Khaldūn records, exercised its hegemonic sway as far as Ifāt (i.e. as far as the region between the present Shoa and the lowland plain of Dancalia). It is difficult to locate this sultanate precisely, because today 'Dāmūt' is a region north of the Blue Nile and south of Godjam, but in East Africa other cases have already been noted where populations forced to move have taken the name of the old country with them into the new territories and given it to their new home. In any case Dāmūt must have been a territory in the south-west of Ethiopia in the sector nearest to the Blue Nile.

Ibn Khaldūn relates how Dāmūt was attacked and conquered by the Negus of Christian Ethiopia and how a race called Walasmaʿ lived in it, which then emigrated further east and settled in Ifāt where it formed another sultanate.[16]

14. C. Pansera, 1945; M. Schneider, 1967, 1969.
15. Cf. Chapter 3 above.
16. Ibn Khaldūn, 1925–56, Vol. 2, p. 108.

We are better documented on the sultanate of Shoa which was in its turn to exercise sway over Muslim southern Ethiopia. The sultanate comprised at least the eastern zone of present Shoa. It was governed by a dynasty of sultans who declared themselves to be Makhzūmī, because they said they were descended from the famous Banū Makhzūm, a Meccan *ḳabīla* to which Khālid ibn al-Walīd, the first Muslim conqueror of Syria, belonged. The names of the sultans preserved in the document mentioned above prove the use of an Ethiopian language of the Semitic family, although it is different from those known hitherto. But the hypothesis should also be considered that the *Chronological Repertory* preserves only the official 'reign names', while the sultans could have had a Muslim personal name, as was still the case recently with the Muslim populations of the Ethiopian West (the Sultan of Genina, known in 1928 by the Oromo (Galla) name of Abba Djifar meaning 'Lord of the dappled steed', had his Muslim name of Muḥammad ibn Dā'ūd).

The Makhzūmī dynasty, according to the document mentioned above, ruled over Shoa at least from the year 283/896–7 and its sovereigns succeeded each other for four centuries until 684/1285, when the last Sultan and his family were deposed and murdered by the Sultan of Ifāt.[17] Among the names of the Makhzūmī sultans preserved to us it is worth noting some that appear characteristic: Girāmgaz'i (i.e. 'terrific lord') who reigned from 660/1262 to 662/1263, when he abdicated in favour of his brother Dil-gāmis. The name of this successor Dil-gāmis can be interpreted as 'victorious buffalo' or 'buffalo in Victory', according to a type of regal name that is attested in Christian Ethiopia also.[18] Thus the name of Sultan Ḥarb-ar'ad means 'terror of the spears' and this too is a type of regal name common in Christian Ethiopia. It suffices to mention Negus Sayfa Ar'ad, 'terror of the swords'. Ḥarb-ar'ad was reigning in Muslim Shoa in 502/1108.

It should also be pointed out that, according to the document already referred to, it appears that women had a certain importance in political power in the sultanate of Shoa, which corresponds rather to the Ethiopian tradition than to the official situation of the other Muslim countries. Thus the *Chronological Repertory* of Shoa begins by recording the dating from a queen; then the marriages of two sultans are recorded. And the second of these marriages, that of Sultan Dil-mārrah with the daughter of the Sultan of Ifāt in 669/1271 is an attempt at a marriage alliance, when Ifāt was becoming more threatening in its attitude to Shoa.

The history of Shoa as it emerges from the *Chronological Repertory* consists of a series of internal struggles between the various leaders, and externally a series of raids and wars against the neighbouring Muslim states, especially against Ifāt. But it is also recorded in this document that in 677/1278 Sultan Dil-mārrah, defeated and deposed by his internal enemies,

17. Cf. E. Cerulli, 1941.
18. Dil-gāmis reigned from 1263 to 1269.

took refuge with the Negus of Christian Ethiopia. This is an important piece of historical evidence proving that the consolidation of Christian Ethiopia under the rule of the first Solomonids began to exert an influence on the weakening of the Sultanate of Shoa caused by its fratricidal struggles. Moreover, it should be noted, in this connection, that the *Chronological Repertory* also lists among the dates of the Shoan sultans the date of the death of Negus Yekuno Amlāk, the first Solomonid sovereign of Christian Ethiopia. Similarly and for opposite reasons this document lists the date of the fall of the Abbasid caliphate at the hands of the Mongols in 656/1258.

The sultanate of Shoa finally lost its independence as a result of the action of the neighbouring Sultanate of Ifāt. At the end of the civil strife which had troubled Muslim Shoa from 675/1276 to 678/1280 the Sultanate of Ifāt intervened directly in the weakened Shoan state, and on 26 April 1280 (19 Dhū l-ḥidjdja 678) occupied the centre of Shoa and put an end to that sultanate.

Since the commercial route through the Nile Valley had been definitely closed to Christian Ethiopia and the sea route to the Indies had been reduced to a minimum, because of the consolidated and extended Muslim expansion, what had been the Christian kingdom of Axum was compelled to seek its expansion southwards, that is towards the centre of the Ethiopian plateau. Accordingly there was first a transfer of the capital from Axum to the central region of Lasta and then, after the Solomonid dynasty had become established on the throne, its further transfer to the frontier of Shoa which was then Muslim. Moreover the monastery of St Stephen on Lake Ḥayq was recognized as the Christian religious centre, before it too was transferred to Absbo (Babra Barkān) right in Shoan conquered territory. These events naturally caused Christian Ethiopia to exert strong pressure on the Muslim states of southern Ethiopia, which were thus directly threatened; and while, as we shall see, the individual sultans set about their defence, there also arose independent movements of reaction headed by Muslim religious leaders. The first of which we have knowledge was the one led by the *shaykh* Muḥammad Abū ʿAbdallāh in 693/1298–9, during the reign of Negus Wedem Raʿad in Christian Ethiopia. This is recorded by the Egyptian chronicler al-Mufaḍḍal, although with the addition of popular legendary details. The Negus succeeded by a skilful political manoeuvre in separating the *shaykh* Muḥammad from some of his followers; in the end he offered the Muslim agitator and those who had remained loyal to him a settlement in territory controlled by Christian Ethiopia, and in this way the movement of Muḥammad Abū ʿAbdallāh failed.[19]

Meanwhile in the Muslim areas of southern Ethiopia, as we have seen, the hegemony of Muslim Shoa was succeeded by the hegemony of Ifāt.

19. Cf. al-Mufaḍḍal, 1919–20.

The Sultanate of Ifāt

The Sultanate of Ifāt, which thus succeeded that of Shoa in the hegemony over the Islam of southern Ethiopia, was ruled by a dynasty which had the name (of local origin) of Walasmaʿ. They came firstly into Ifāt as refugees from the ancient Muslim state of Dāmūt, as Ibn Khaldūn testifies. However, the Walasmaʿ dynasty also boasted a distant Arab origin and, according to the oral tradition preserved to our times, considered its progenitor to be ʿAḳīl ibn Abī Ṭālib, brother of Caliph ʿAlī and of Djaʿfar ibn Abī Ṭālib who, as we have seen, had been one of the first Muslims to take refuge in Ethiopia. According to the apologetic writing, the *History of the Walasmaʿ*, on the contrary, the founder of the dynasty ʿUmar ibn Dunyā-ḥawz[20] was descended from al-Ḥasan, one of the two sons of Caliph ʿAlī.

The first part of the *History of the Walasmaʿ* seems however to be legendary; for example, the duration of 120 years for the life of ʿUmar Walasmaʿ, who reigned for 80 of them; and the tradition regarding the holy Sultan Djamāl al-dīn ibn Baziyū who had the genii at his command, one of whom brought him a letter from the Nile in an hour and another brought him water from the River Ḥawāsh (these may be assimilations of the ideas of Ethiopian 'paganism' on the minor divinities living in running waters).

The first date mentioned in the *History of the Walasmaʿ* is that of 778/1376–7; but the synchronisms with the Ethiopian Chronicles and with the Arab historians permit earlier datings. For example, Sultan Ṣabr al-dīn fought for a long time against Negus 'Amda Ṣeyon (who reigned from 1314 to 1344). Therefore, however that may be, since the legendary tradition reckons a total of ninety-six years for the duration of the reigns from Sultan Ṣabr al-dīn to ʿUmar Walasmaʿ, if as a vague assumption we adhered to this date, we should have to put the foundation of the Walasmaʿ dynasty of Ifāt at the end of the twelfth century, with all the necessary reserves and doubts due to the imperfection of the documentation we have quoted.

Ṣabr al-dīn, made war on Christian Ethiopia and he is represented, also in the Ethiopian Chronicles, as the most important of the Muslim sovereigns of the South: he is in fact designated as 'King of the Infidels' (Negusa ʿelwan). This confirms the position of hegemony which Ifāt meanwhile held in the first half of the fourteenth century of the Christian era after the fall of the Sultanate of Shoa.[21] But two more useful items of historical in-

20. For this name it might be possible to think of a Semitic-Ethiopian word which would correspond to the Ethiopian (Geʿez): *ḥawz* and interpret the name: Dunyā-ḥawz as Mundi suavitas (almost 'deliciae generis humani'!). It would then be a relic of ancient Ethiopian tradition in the names of the Walasmaʿ princes. In any case the name Walasmaʿ is not Arabic, but I have not been able to reconstitute it with Ethiopian words, at least to date. It is perhaps composed of the ancient Semitic 'WA' which means 'of', 'related to' and 'ALʿASMĀʾ' which means 'the gills'.

21. Cf. J. Perruchon, 1889.

formation are furnished by the Ethiopian Chronicle on the war of Sultan Ṣabr al-dīn. The first is the first documentation of the use of *ḳāt* by Ethiopian Muslims. The *ḳāt* (this is the Arabic word; in Amharic it is *chāt*) is a shrub (*Catha edulis*), whose leaves have a slight stimulating effect. The use of *ḳāt* ('which keeps the family awake at night', as a popular song says) is the characteristic feature of the Muslims in Ethiopia. Here we see it already so much used that Ṣabr al-dīn in his warlike boasting proclaims that he will take possession of the capital of Christian Ethiopia and 'will plant *ḳāt* there, because the Muslims like this plant very much'.

A second important point for Ethiopian history in the Chronicle cited is a reference by the chronicler to the fact that after the victory of the negus over the Muslims, when the Christian sovereign wished to take advantage of his success in order to advance into the Muslim country and establish his armed forces there, he came up against the opposition of his soldiers. Having obtained the victory and the booty, they wanted to return home and enjoy the fruits of it, and did not understand the need for a permanent occupation of the enemy country. This psychological fact is interesting because we shall find a similar happening two centuries later (in the sixteenth century) this time with the Muslim soldiers of the *Imām* Aḥmed ibn Ibrāhīm, who likewise showed their repugnance for a permanent conquest of the territory of the defeated peoples. Thus, according to the Ethiopian chronicler, the soldiers say to the Christian sovereign: 'O Negus, you have fought and have saved us from the hands of the infidel; and now by your counsel let us go back to our villages'. And the Negus replies: 'Animals return to their pasture'. No differently two centuries later will the Arab chronicler represent the Muslim soldiers, who after the victory say to their leader Aḥmed ibn Ibrāhīm: 'O Imām of the Muslims, you see what has happened. Many of our soldiers have been slain. Many of us are covered with wounds. We have only scanty provisions. Lead the army to our country. There they will reorganize us and we will reorganize our ranks'. But in the end in both cases the soldiers accept the order of their leader, although only after showing their discontent.[22]

The advance southwards of the new Solomonid dynasty of Christian Ethiopia and the expansion in Shoa of Muslim Ifāt were bound to lead to a struggle between the two states. The first encounter of which we have record is in the chronicle of Negus ʿAmda Ṣeyon I, when the Ethiopian sovereign states that, at the beginning of his reign, he had defeated Sultan Ḥaḳḳ al-dīn of Ifāt and slain the Muslim prince Darāder, brother of Ḥaḳḳ al-dīn.[23] It should be pointed out here that the Arabic *History of the Walasmaʿ* makes no mention of Ḥaḳḳ al-dīn or of this war but since the Muslim chronicler attributes the beginning of the struggles of the Christians to Sultan Ḥaḳḳ al-dīn II, who reigned from 1376 to 1386 (many

22. W. G. Conzelman, 1895.
23. G. W. B. Huntingford, 1965.

decades after Ḥaḳḳ al-dīn I), it may be a mistake on the part of the chronicler or of his source.

But the first war between Ethiopia and Ifāt that is amply documented for us is the one waged during the reign of Negus ʿAmda Ṣeyon I (1314–44) and of Sultan Ṣabr al-dīn I in 1332.[24] Ṣabr al-dīn attacks the troops of the Negus who have entered Shoa, but is defeated after a fierce struggle and is forced to make an act of submission. The Negus appoints prince Djamāl al-dīn, brother of Ṣabr al-dīn, to be Sultan of Ifāt, but because of the spurious origin of his power he fails to acquire authority; and shortly after he is ousted by a vast movement of Muslim reaction stirred up by a religious agitator, the Ḳāḍī Ṣāleḥ. The latter manages to form a league of Muslim princes, among whom the Sultan of Adal (to the east of Ifāt) distinguishes himself, this time in the first place. However, the Negus manages to win once again, and this time his victory is the start of a new era among the petty Muslim states of the south, because from now on the hegemony passes from Ifāt to the Sultanate of Adal, although the power remains with the prince of the Walasmaʿ dynasty. So we may say that in two centuries (the thirteenth and fourteenth) the political centre of Ethiopian Islam was shifted three times, and always in a west–east direction towards the edge of the plateau: from Dāmūt to Shoa, from Shoa to Ifāt, and from Ifāt to Adal.

The victory won by Negus ʿAmda Ṣeyon over the Muslims impelled his successors to undertake a series of military operations in the south. Thus Negus Dāwit I (1382–1411) defeated and killed in battle Sultan Ḥaḳḳ al-dīn II in 776/1376–7; and his successor, Negus Yesḥaq, defeated Sultan Saʿad al-dīn, the successor of Ḥaḳḳ al-dīn II, and pushed on towards the sea as far as Zāylaʿ. Of the victories of Negus Yesḥaq there survives a long victory song sung by his soldiers, which is valuable for us because it preserves the names of the various Muslim countries which that Negus, in his war against Saʿad al-dīn, had conquered and laid waste. The poetic document thus completes and specifies the list of the Muslim countries which about a century before had joined the Islamic league formed as a result of the preaching of the Ḳāḍī Ṣāleḥ, as we have seen, against Negus ʿAmda Ṣeyon. On the Muslim side, Sultan Saʿad al-dīn, who fell in battle against the Christians in 1415, became the eponymous hero of the Muslim resistance against the invading Neguses and from that time the Muslim south that had remained independent took the name of 'land of Saʿad al-dīn' (*barr Sa'ad al-dīn*).

But the Sultanate of Adal, now at the head of Ethiopian Islam, recovered after a few decades; and there followed a strong and complex attempt to invade Shoa, now not only Christian but also the seat of the Neguses. The Muslim army was led by Sultan Shihāb al-dīn Aḥmed Badlāy (who in the Ethiopian Chronicles is called: Arwē Badlāy, 'the wild beast Badlāy'). After

24. Cf. J. Perruchon, 1889–90.

some initial successes Badlāy was defeated by Negus Zareʿa Yāʿqob in a great battle at Egubbā on 29 December 1445, and the Sultan fell in the fighting. The Negus pursued the Muslim army as far as the River Ḥawāsh and gained a booty which seemed really wonderful to the Christian Ethiopians. This was because the commercial relations which the Sultanate of Adal had with the potentates of the Arabian Peninsula enabled the Muslims to obtain luxury articles which the Christian Ethiopians, still blocked in their relations with the outside world, could not yet procure. Thus a Christian document, for example, records:

> And the robes [of the Sultan] and the robes of his chief men were adorned with silver and shone on every side. And the dagger that he [the Sultan] had at his side was richly ornamented with gold and precious stones; and his amulet was adorned with drops of gold; and the lettering of the amulet had been made with gold paint. And his umbrella was from the country of Syria of a workmanship that caused those who looked at it to marvel, and on it were painted winged serpents.

After the battle of Egubbā the Sultans of Adal, where the dynasty of the Walasmaʿ, formerly sultans of Ifāt, had continued, established their capital at Dakar at the edge of the eastern lowland plain. But a few years later Negus Eskender took the offensive, entered Adal, and conquered and destroyed Dakar. However, on its way back to its territory in Shoa, the Christian army was surprised in 1475 by that of the Sultan of Adal, Shams al-dīn ibn Muḥammad, and Negus Eskender was defeated and died in the battle. But the Muslims did not follow up this victory, because Adal was paralysed and impoverished by the struggles of the various emirs for the supremacy of the country.

Then the capital was transferred again eastward to Aussa down in the lowland until finally Sultan Abū Bakr ibn Muḥammad ibn Aẓhar al-dīn transferred the capital from Adal to Harar in 926/1520. He thus founded the dynasty of the Emirs of Harar, which for three centuries held power in the Muslim state which from that time on was called the emirate of Harar. This was because Muḥammad ibn Abū Bakr ibn Aẓhar al-dīn, who had shifted the capital to the south for reasons of safety, held supreme power in name only, since he maintained on the throne the princes of the Walasmaʿ dynasty for whom he kept the title of Sultan. In this way he avoided charges of illegitimacy and secured for his effective power the nominal one of the old dynasty. His successors did the same, until the Walasmaʿ dynasty became extinct in obscure circumstances.

The new Sultanate of Harar was also soon torn by civil strife; and this lasted until a strong personality arose, namely, the future *Imām* Aḥmed ibn Ibrāhīm who gained the ascendancy and concentrated all power in his hands.

21 The East African coast and the Comoro Islands

F. T. MASAO and H. W. MUTORO

This chapter attempts to re-evaluate the history of the east African coast and the Comoro Islands, hereafter conveniently referred to as the East African coast and its environs, between the seventh and eleventh centuries of the Christian era. It aims to correct the false picture that has been painted by historians and/or archaeologists of the colonial school of thought, who relied on external sources, incomplete data or mere rumours to present a synthesis which in most cases has been a history of foreign traders and colonizers who are credited with the civilization of the coast. The role of outsiders in the early history of the East African coast cannot be denied but it is one thing to be part of a process of change and completely another to claim responsibility for the process. Recent research findings based on new scientific methods and techniques in archaeology, history, ethnography, etc., which continue to come to light[1] have not only broadened our data base but are also slowly but surely making it very clear that the history of the East African coast and its environs is the history of autochthonous African populations and their interaction with the environment.

The geographical background

The East African coast and its environs in this context refers to that stretch of land lying approximately between longitude 38°E and 50°E and latitude 11°N and 25°S , and stretching between the coasts of Somalia in the north and Mozambique in the south. It is an area which is under the influence of the monsoon winds system, a factor which in one way or another has influenced the historical development of the coast communities. Most of the area, except northern Kenya and Somalia, has good rainfall and fertile soils which can support agricultural activities. This region can conveniently be divided into three major eco-geographical zones: the Islands (e.g. Lamu,

1. The authors have in mind, for example, the works of J. de V. Allen, 1982; M. Horton, 1981; H. W. Mutoro, 1979, 1982b.

Pate, Manda, Aldabra, the Comoros, etc.), the Peninsula and the hinterland. These zones are characterized by remains of settlements whose cultural uniqueness makes it very probable that they are the products of an autochthonous African population. Although abandoned today, the remains of these settlements still physically stand above the general surface as ruins and can be detected on aerial photographs and on topographic maps. For those that were not permanent, their presence has been shown in the archaeological record either by post holes or by high mounds that are surrounded by a vegetation cover which is either rich and tall or very poor and stunted.

Although the ecozones in which these settlements were located are today characterized by a poor vegetation cover and a small animal population, there is sufficient evidence from fossil pollen and bone remains to show that this was not the case during the formative years when these areas were being settled. The estuarine systems on which island settlements, like Lamu, Manda, Pate, Shanga, etc., are situated were for instance flanked by dense mangrove forests, which not only provided security and shelter to the inhabitants of these settlements but also a source of income (i.e. from sales of mangrove poles); today they are almost completely dilapidated. Also what is left of the Peninsula along the coastal mainland, on which settlements like Gedi, Mwana, Ntwapa, etc., were situated is a low thorn-bush belt which builds up into moist wooded grassland patches that are no doubt derived from former dense forests or woodlands which today are exemplified by *Kaya* forests in the hinterland. The hinterland ecozone, which is characterized by the *Kaya* settlements, is perhaps the only living example of what the ecosystem was like during the early settlement period of the region under review. Beyond the *Kaya* forest ridge, vegetation consists of a poor savanna which degenerates into the Tary desert vegetation that today supports *Waata* hunter-gatherers and *Kwavi* pastoralists.

It is in these ecological zones that East African coastal settlements and the civilization associated with them emerged and were in time to integrate the whole region with the wider world beyond. These settlements – *Midzi* or *Miji* (towns) – covered as much as fifty hectares at the height of their power and splendour.[2] In time, however, they slowly but steadily declined and were subsequently abandoned to nature by their owners. Their ruins and monuments today litter the entire region under review and a closer look at their distribution and geographical location coupled with recent archaeological findings leaves no doubt that the occupants of these settlements were in constant mutual societal interaction and with their neighbours further afield. A reconstruction of the history of these societies therefore demands a frame of reference that is regional, multidisciplinary and symbiotic in perspective.

2. Kaya Mudzi Mwiru covered an area of 32 ha, Kaya Singwaya 20 ha, and Kaya Bomu 24 ha.

The problems

The majority of works dealing with the pre-colonial history of the East African coast have however, failed us in this respect. This failure is due mainly to two factors: the traditional methodology on which the research was based, and the colonialist approach of those who undertook it. The methodology is traditional because it did not explicitly specify what research problems the archaeologist was out to solve and how he was going to solve them. The aim apparently was to cover as many areas as possible just because such areas had not been investigated before. It is thus not surprising to find that as a result of the apparent hurry involved, a number of settlements were either superficially investigated or were ignored altogether.

On many occasions only one or two holes were dug on a settlement of considerable dimensions, as is attested by site reports or published works. In such cases, the data recovered from such a hole was then used to describe the behaviour patterns of the settlement as a whole. This approach is improper because human behaviour is patterned, and data from one or two excavated holes cannot be representative of all the behaviour patterns of a settlement as a whole. The colonialist attitude in the historiography is reflected in the perception as well as interpretation of the data recovered. Firstly, coastal culture was perceived in terms of trait lists which represented ideas, beliefs, mental templates or norms of people that made them. This means that the interpretation that followed, particularly with regard to variability and change in the culture, was given in terms of diffusion from some superior cultural centres in the Middle East and beyond, rather than as resulting from the people's adaptation to their changing environment. This traditional explanation of the settlement history of the East African coast and its environs is to be found in works of many scholars, as will be seen presently.

According to F. B. Pearce the settlements in this region were founded by Persians and Arabs as is evidenced by what he called the Shīrāz and Arab style of architecture.[3] W. H. Ingrams went further to suggest that if the founders of these settlements were Persians, then they were of a Shī'ā faith of Islam.[4] L. W. Hollingsworth even went a step further arguing that, in addition to these immigrants being Shīrāz and therefore Persian in origin, they also introduced stone buildings as well as ideas of manufacturing lime and cement, and the arts of wood-carving and cotton-weaving.[5] Similar sentiments were expressed by James Kirkman who, after visiting several of these settlements, concluded that the 'historical monuments of East Africa belong not to the Africans but to the Arabs and Arabized Persians mixed in

3. F. B. Pearce, 1920, p. 399.
4. W. H. Ingrams, 1931, pp. 133, 153.
5. L. W. Hollingsworth, 1974, pp. 39–40.

blood with Africans, but in culture utterly apart from the Africans who surrounded them.'[6] The difference between Pearce and Kirkman is that while the former sees the Shīrāzī or Persian architecture as preceding the Arab style, the latter sees it the other way round. Neville Chittick is no exception to these views.[7] He not only sees these immigrants from Shīrāz (Sīrāf) – who he claims founded settlements in this region – as consisting mostly of men, but also argues that even the economy on which these settlements were based was alien: 'Though the origins of these civilizations were in those lands on which they economically depended, it was always seawards that the cities of the coast faced, looking out over the great maritime region constituted by the Indian Ocean and its Coasts'.[8]

Protagonists of foreign origins of settlements in this region under review have used epigraphy, documentary evidence as well as place names to support their thesis but their evidence has been found to be inadequate and unconvincing. For instance, while it is true that two epigraphic remains of the thirteenth century found in Mogadishu bear Persian names, these are too few to form a basis for any solid conclusions. In addition to this, settlements in this region were already flourishing by this time.

Names resembling those in Arabia or Persia, e.g. al-Ḳaḥṭānī, al-Ḥaḍramī, etc., have also been cited as evidence for Arabo-Persian origins of the East African coastal settlements. Such names have been reported from Mogadishu and Tongoni in northern Tanzania.[9] It should be noted here that the thirteen names or inscriptions recovered from Mogadishu were subjected to a thorough scrutiny and only two of them mention people of demonstrably Persian origin.[10] Although the single tile from Tongoni reported by Burton is still at large, it is very unlikely that such a tile was Persian in origin. Even if it were, it alone does not provide us with enough evidence to show that Tongoni was a Persian settlement. Finally, documentary evidence has also been cited to support the theory that the settlements of the East African coast and its environs had Persian origins. In the long list compiled by B. G. Martin, for instance, it has been found that none of these is convincing and none shows the existence of these settlements before +1750.[11]

In an attempt to fix a date for the foundation by aliens of these coastal cities, imported pottery was taken and used as the best evidence for dating. Toward this end, we are told, Manda was founded in the third/ninth century, Takwa in the tenth/sixteenth–eleventh/seventeenth century, and Kilwa in the fourth/tenth to fifth/eleventh or sixth/twelfth century.[12] In

6. J. Kirkman, 1954, p. 22.
7. H. N. Chittick, in all his works.
8. H. N. Chittick, 1974, Vol. 1, p. 245.
9. Cf. E. Cerulli, 1957, Vol. 1, pp. 2–10; B. G. Martin, 1974, p. 368.
10. J. de V. Allen, 1982, p. 10. Some later inscriptions indicate Arab origin.
11. B. G. Martin, 1974, pp. 368 ff.
12. J. Kirkman, 1954, pp. 174–82; H. N. Chittick, 1974, Vol. 1, pp. 235–7.

this connection, carbon-14 dates (which are scientifically derived and are as such more objective) were ignored because the dates obtained were regarded as too early. The local ceramics, which can either be cross-dated with the well-known ones in the neighbourhood or can be dated by thermoluminescence, were treated in isolation, as if to imply that they were not the product of these settlements and even if they were, their dates would contradict conclusions that had already been reached, i.e. that prior to the arrival of foreigners from Shīrāz, etc., no settlements existed in this region. Had this been the case, one would expect to find a number of sites in the region with an assemblage that is dominantly different and foreign to the area, particularly when compared with the stratigraphy. But this type of evidence has not come to light yet. Excavations at Takwa, for instance, yielded well over five million potsherds of locally made ceramics compared to five hundred potsherds of imported ceramics.[13] Excavations at other sites like Manda, Kaya Singwaya, Kaya Mudzi Mwiru, Gedi, Kilwa, Shanga, Mudzi Mwiru and Fungo, to name a few, have also revealed an enormous preponderance of locally made ceramic materials over imported materials.[14] Against this background one wonders how a settlement can belong to foreigners when, first, there is no evidence and, secondly, its material cultural remains are predominantly those of an indigenous population.

Another methodological shortcoming that needs to be tested is the way in which these sites have been dated to fit with the coming of these Arabs and Persians. All coastal towns have in this respect been dated on the basis of imported pottery. Often this was done on the basis of a single potsherd recovered from a single test pit. Consistent archaeological excavations in these settlements have continued to unearth potsherds belonging to even earlier time periods than the ones quoted above. This is exemplified by the site of Takwa which on the basis of imported pottery was dated to the tenth or eleventh/sixteenth or seventeenth centuries.

This site has also provided Chinese celadons and Islamic monochromes of the fifth/eleventh to seventh/thirteenth century.[15] The questions to ask are: What criteria were used in determining the dating? Why were the fifth/eleventh to seventh/thirteenth century potsherds not considered? Should we ignore the carbon-14 dates just because they do not fit into the expected scheme of diffusion?

On this note we wish to point out that the imported pottery dates for East African coastal settlements, suggested by earlier researchers, were based on incomplete data. Our own comparison of all the dates provided by imported pottery vis-à-vis those provided by carbon-14 (e.g. Stratum 3

13. H. W. Mutoro, 1979, pp. 68–110.

14. J. Kirkman, 1954; H. N. Chittick, 1967; M. Horton, 1981; H. W. Mutoro, 1982a, 1982b.

15. H. W. Mutoro, 1979, pp. 111–21.

data of 1195 ± 135 for Takwa) leads to the conclusion that all the imported pottery dates for the coast must be treated with greater caution than has previously been done. We wish to stress that imported pottery like other imported luxury exchange items such as drinking glasses, beads, wine cups, cloth, etc., may tell us a lot about the life style and economy of the society as well as the degree of interaction with its neighbours. We have to consider them when working out the site's chronology but this must not be done to the exclusion of other more objective and scientific methods of dating like carbon-14. The dates established on the basis of imported pottery must not be seen as marking the time when the settlements were founded, as has been often maintained.

Secondly, in any field research, one needs to clarify the sampling procedure being used in the selection of the data that is to be analysed or dated. A single potsherd from one or two test pits on a settlement cannot be considered to be representative of all the potsherds on the site. We also have to take note of the fact that human settlement systems are often capable of growing from very humble beginnings to complex dimensions. On attaining this stage, such settlements generally span greater ecological ranges, thus becoming more complex and more widespread. To understand the process of cultural evolution and change within these settlements, we have first of all to note the behaviour patterns of the extinct societies and to see that a wide section of the settlement is sampled and excavated to get the representative data that can help us in our analysis and explanation. While it is true that we cannot excavate the whole settlement, it is necessary that the procedure we are using to determine which areas of the settlement to be excavated is made explicit. All points on the settlement should at least be given an equal chance of being selected for excavation.

Another aspect of colonial prejudice is reflected in the types of settlements that were selected for investigation. It goes without saying that virtually all past efforts were concentrated on and confined to stone-built settlements, e.g., Manda, Kilwa, Takwa, Mwana, Gedi, etc., which, as we have already stated, were attritued to and seen as belonging to the aliens. Those settlements that were not built in stone were ignored not just because they were uninteresting but also because they were not 'architectural' in the fullest sense of the word. The point being emphasized here is that settlements are cultural systems and as such are neither univariate phenomena nor can their functioning be understood in terms of a single variable, i.e., the spatial-temporal transmission of ideas from higher culture centres to lower centres. They rather should be seen in a multivariate spectrum of events whose operation can only be understood in terms of many causally relevant variables which either function interdependently or in varying combinations. It is up to us researchers, therefore, to isolate these causative variables in an effort to establish the relations that existed between them. To achieve such a goal we certainly have to go beyond the traditional paradigm that glorifies the racial superiority of the colonizing

PLATE 21.1 *Excavations on the Manda site*

people by employing a new paradigm that can solve the problems in an objectively conceived frame of reference.

In the absence of any adequate and convincing data to support the view that settlements on the East African coast were founded by aliens, it thus becomes probable that the original progenitors of the coastal culture were the indigenous African populations. The evidence for their presence and possible involvement in the establishment of these settlements is attested by the archaeological as well as documentary evidence to which we now turn.

The sources

Archaeology

Although archaeological work in this region is still in its infancy, already considerable evidence has come to light to show that the region was at different time periods populated by the so-called Early, Middle and Later Stone Age societies. These were subsequently succeeded by the Early and Later Iron Age populations. Evidence for Early, Middle and Later Stone Age settlements in this region has been found at several sites.[16] Mtongwe, just off the road to Kwale in southern Kenya, is one of those sites that is

16. G. Omi, 1982; H. N. Chittick, 1963.

being properly excavated by a Japanese research team from Nagoya University. Located on Changamwe terrace, the settlement measures 800 m by 300 m and comprises thirty localities.[17] A detailed discussion of the artefactual remains and the behaviour patterns of the populations that produced them is not only well known but also falls outside the scope of this chapter. It will, however, suffice to say that a large assemblage of cultural remains was recovered all attesting to the existence, in this region, not only of human activities, but also of human settlements going back beyond the frequently quoted ninth century of the Christian era.

Evidence for Early and Later Iron Age settlement in the region is also abundant. First and foremost is the site of Kwale located on the Kinango road some 6 km from present-day Kwale town. This site was excavated in the mid-1960s by Robert Soper and a wide variety of items of pottery, iron slag, implements, etc. were retrieved, attesting to the existence here of an Iron Age population by the first quarter of the first millenium of the Christian era.[18] Related, contemporary cultural material remains have also been reported from excavations as well as surface sites in a number of areas in central and coastal Tanzania and Kenya. Such areas include the Usambara Mountains, the South Pare Hills, the Mijikenda *Kaya* settlements (e.g. *Kaya* Mudzi Mwiru, *Kaya* Fungo, *Kaya* Singway, etc)., to name but a few.

At Gedi for instance, a special kind of sixth/twelfth-century ornamented ware has been excavated from a stratum below the city foundations. This particular ware has been described as ribbed ornamented ware and compared with sherds of ribbed black ware found in upper levels at Great Zimbabwe. The ornamentation and style are undisputedly African, but the sherds have been ascribed on the basis of negative evidence to Oromo (Galla) rather than Bantu or Swahili.[19] Both at Unguja Ukuu and Manda, sites dating to the third/ninth century have been found. However, it is reported by Chittick that the blue-glazed Islamic ware is by far the commonest import but unfortunately no statistics are given to enable comparison with the local ware.[20]

At Nzwani in the Comoro Islands, a range of sherds datable probably to $+430 \pm 70$ have been found, showing that the islands were settled before the coming of the Arabs, probably by Afro-Indonesians, though whether these were from Madagascar or from a South-East African coastal settlement is unclear. However as has rightly been pointed out by Shepherd, since Comorians are Bantu-speaking, the later hypothesis is the more likely.[21] In addition, Wa-Ngazija (the islander) tradition is one of arrival from the mainland.

17. G. Omi, 1982.
18. R. Soper, 1967, p. 1.
19. J. Kirkman, 1954, p. 73.
20. H. N. Chittick, 1975, p. 37.
21. G. Shepherd, G. 1982, p. 7.

In Kilwa, both periods 1a and 1b (ninth to twelfth century) which predate the Shīrāzī dynasty, are marked by homogeneous cultural material including slag as evidence of iron smelting and evidence of the manufacture of beads, pottery and fish debris.[22] Chittick, however, on the basis of the pottery – which to him displays 'a considerable degree of technical skill' – is of the opinion that the settlement of Kilwa was not autochthonous. This bias cannot be entertained too seriously because not only do the chronicles leave no doubt that Kilwa's population at this time was local, but similar red-finished ware occurs at other coastal sites such as Unguja Ukuu and Manda.[23] The fact that no such pottery has been reported from the hinterland does not mean that this innovative technique could not have developed independently in the coastal towns. Besides, the hinterland has yet to be thoroughly investigated and until this is done it would be presumptuous to think that pottery is restricted to the coast.

The two diagnostic local wares of this period are bag-shaped cooking pots with incised decoration on rim or shoulder and red burnished ware. Shallow bowls with inturned rims also occur. Imported wares were sgraffito and white tin-glazed Persian sherds.[24] It is of interest to note that there is some resemblance between the incised decoration on the necks of pots of Type I and pottery from the Usambara Mountains designated as Group C which, though undated, is obviously later than the Early Iron Age wares.[25] Other archaeological finds from this period include knives, arrowheads, fish hooks, hollow tubes, iron points and nails and carnelian beads. As at Manda, glass beads do not occur before the fourth/tenth century.[26]

At Unguja Ukuu on Zanzibar Island, the earliest local pottery is dated to around the fourth/tenth century, or equivalent to Manda period 1a.[27] Although Gedi is said to have been founded in the sixth/twelfth century and is therefore outside the chronological confines of this chapter, it is of interest to note that the quantity of sherds of local earthenware greatly exceeded the imported sherds, although a greater portion were body sherds and therefore of no diagnostic importance. In short, the local ware was unglazed and sparingly incised, indented, applied or rarely colour ornamented. Linear incised ornamentation is locally regarded as characteristic of the Swahili, Wasanya and Oromo, fingernail indented ornamentation as of Wanyika origin and applied ornamentation as typical of the Oromo peoples' pottery.[28] The African element, i.e. the ribbed ornamented ware and the hemispherical bowls from the earliest levels, is undisputed, and as

22. H. N. Chittick, 1974, Vol. 1, p. 235.
23. ibid., p. 237.
24. ibid., Vol. 2, p. 319.
25. ibid., Vol. 1, p. 237.
26. ibid., Vol. 2, pp. 482–3.
27. H. N. Chittick, 1975, p. 37.
28. J. Kirkman, 1954, p. 71.

has been seen earlier, this type of pottery is of at least a tenth-century date and resembles pottery from the Central Africa sites of Great Zimbabwe and Mapungubwe.

The scarcity of ribbed ornamented ware after the foundation of the city indicates that there must have been local people there before the arrival of the Arabs and the supplanting of the local earthenware technique by the foreign technique. Consequently, imported wares including blue and green glazed earthenwares (Islamic), 'yellow and black' glazed earthenware and celadon and blue and white celadon (China) became more abundant than local earthenware after the foundation of the city.[29] The finger-nail ornamented cooking pots may be of historical importance as evidence of the migration of peoples. These cooking pots, which are still made today by the Giriama, were found at Gedi. This particular ornamentation is now regarded as characteristic of the Wanyika[30] as opposed to the incised decoration practised by the Swahili.[31]

Archaeological evidence throughout the east coast leaves no doubt that in all cases there were local inhabitants with their own civilizations before the coming of the Arabs. Available evidence supports the contention that at least for the central and southern parts of the coast, the inhabitants were Bantu.

Written sources

The above archaeological evidence for the autochthonous origins of the settlements in this region during the period under review is further corroborated by written sources. The majority of these were produced by Arab authors, but there are also some fragmentary accounts in Chinese; however, the interpretation of the few place-names they mention and thus their localization is rather uncertain. It was merely the preponderance of the Arabic written materials that constituted one of the chief reasons why the East African coast has been for such a long time considered to be an Arabo-Persian colony, or a cultural appendix of the larger Islamic world in which the local people played only an insignificant role. But a careful reading of the most important Arabic works and their unbiased interpretation will show a quite different picture to that painted by the former school of historiography.

The Arabs called the inhabitants of eastern Africa south of the Juba River, al-Zand̲j (or al-Zind̲j), a term whose etymology continues to be obscure.[32] There is no doubt that the Arabs and other Muslims understood

29. J. Kirkman, 1954, p. 94.
30. The Wanyika is a general term used to refer to the Mijikenda group of people.
31. J. Kirkman, 1954, p. 75.
32. On the oldest history of the name Zand̲j, cf. L. M. Devic, 1883, pp. 15–35; E. Cerulli, 1957, Vol. 1, pp. 233–7.

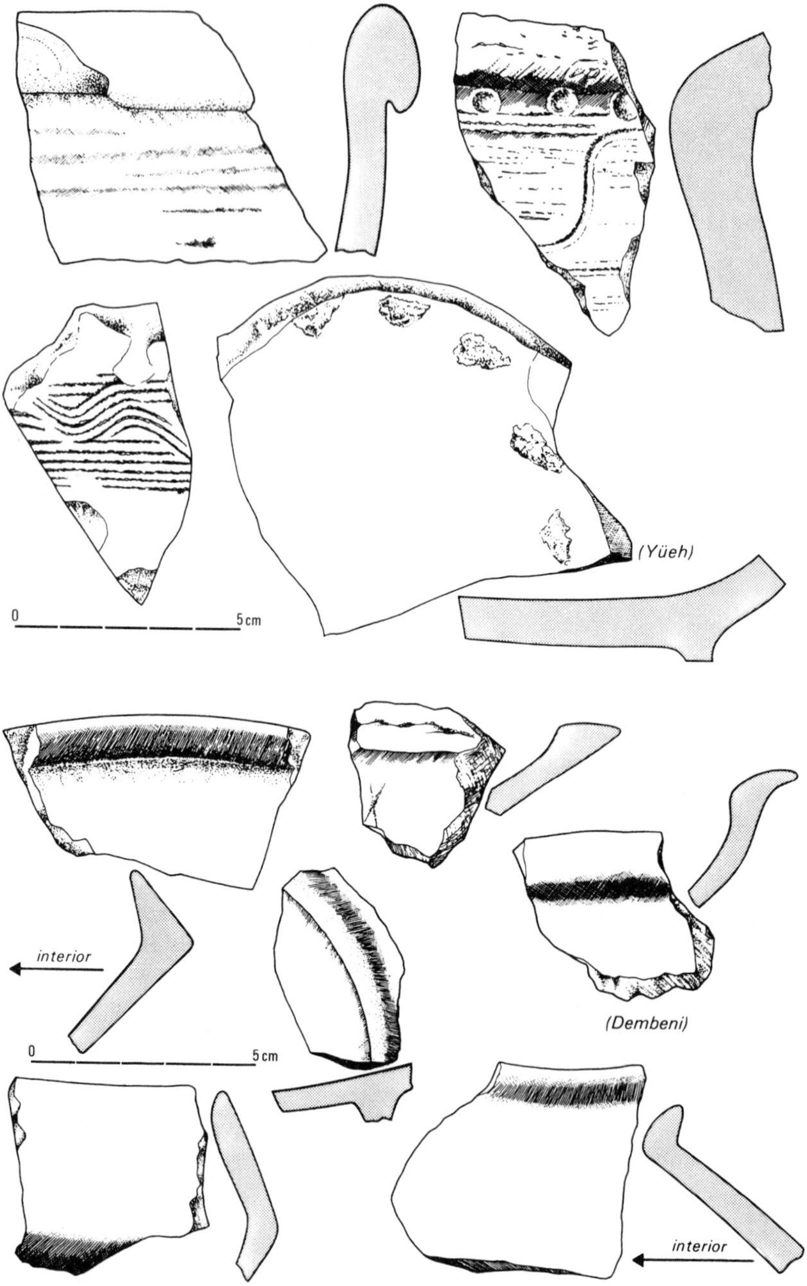

FIG. 21.1 *Pottery excavated at Mro Deoua, Comoro Islands: top, Middle Eastern and Yüeh pottery; bottom Dembeni red pottery*

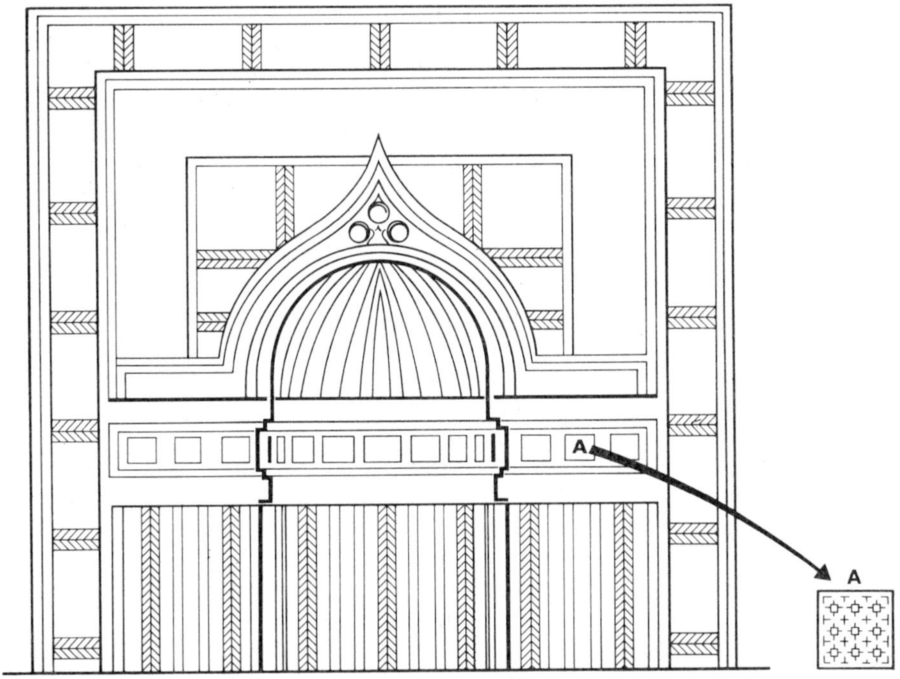

FIG. 21.2 *Old Shīrāzī mosque of Domoni Anjouan, Comoro Islands (eleventh century)*

NOTE TO FIGS 21.1 AND 21.2

Since this chapter by F. T. Masao and H. W. Mutoro was written, important archaeological excavations have been carried out in the Comoro Archipelago, in particular by H. T. Wright, 1984; C. Allibert, A. Argan and J. Argan, 1983; and C. Chanudet and P. Vérin, 1983).

It is now clear that the archipelago was already occupied in the ninth century. The people of the four islands made a red and black pottery, known as 'Dembeni', which resembles the pottery found by N. Chittick in the lower levels of the same period at Kilwa and Manda. Another tradition of local pottery called Majikavo used an *Arca* shell-pattern decoration and shows some resemblance to the discoveries made at sites in the north of Madagascar.

The first inhabitants of the Comoros traded with the outside world, particularly with the towns of Sīrāf and Sohar, through which oriental Yüeh pottery, Middle Eastern (opaque tin-glazed) pottery and also glassware and other luxury objects arrived.

The Comorians of the Dembeni culture knew how to work metal, fished and grew rice.

In the eleventh century, significant cultural changes took place. Stone buildings made their appearance. One of the oldest mosques is undoubtedly the one at Domoni, which has frequently been rebuilt.

A new kind of Middle Eastern pottery – the sgraffito – appears at this stage and the Majikavo pottery takes on a simpler form of decoration and is called Hanyundro. Steatite cooking pots imported from Madagascar appear to be common at this time. Weights used in spinning are evidence of the making of clothes.

this term to mean the negroid and Bantu-speaking peoples living on the coast and in the interior of East Africa. Some Zandj words quoted by Arab authors point quite distinctly to their Bantu origins: the geographer Ibn al-Faḳīh (writing *c.* 280/902–3) was the first to mention that the name of God in the Zandj language is *l-makludjulu*;[33] a similar word is furnished also by al-Mas'ūdī (d. 345/956) in the form *malkandjulu*, and by Muṭahhar al-Maḳdīsī (*fl.* 355/966) as *malakui* and *djalui*.[34] All these forms are derived from the Bantu *mkulu* (great person) and the reduplication – *mkulunkulu* – indicates someone very great. The nearest to this ancient form is the Zulu *unkulunkulu*. The Bantu character of the Zandj is further supported by such words as *waflīmī*, meaning kings or chiefs, corresponding exactly to the Bantu/Kiswahili *mfalme* (pl. *wafalme*),[35] or *inbīla* (rhinoceros) from Bantu *mpela* (Kiswahili *pera* or *pea*), and *makwandju* (the tree, *Tamarindus indica*) from Kiswahili *mkwanju*, both these words being cited by the famous scientist al-Bīrūnī (d. 442/1050–1).[36]

Nowhere in Arabic sources from this period – and among these are the copious reports by Ibn al-Faḳīh, Buzurg ibn Shahriyār, al-Mas'ūdī, al-Bīrūnī and, a bit later, al-Idrīsī – do we find any mention of large settlements or colonies of expatriates from Muslim countries. The coast is described as inhabited and, what is more important, ruled by the local Zandj population. Especially in the account of al-Mas'ūdī, who visited the coast for the last time in 304/916–17, there is a stress on the non-Muslim character of the Zandj state. The famous tale of Buzurg ibn Shahriyār about the kidnapping of the Zandj king by Arab slavers offers further evidence of the independent development of the coastal Bantu peoples.[37] Even from the comparatively late al-Idrīsī (d. 560/1165) who incorporated into his work information from earlier sources, we gain the impression that political power in all coastal settlements had been in the hands of indigenous Africans.

On the other hand all Arabic sources speak about a constantly expanding trade between the East African coast and the lands surrounding the Indian Ocean, and about regular visits of Arab, Persian and Indian merchants. This intercourse was nothing new, as in the preceding period the Graeco-Roman authors had already described the commercial links between this region and other parts of the Indian Ocean area.[38] The importance of the international trade for the history of the East African coast and its economic and cultural impact on the African peoples there will be discussed presently.

33. Ibn al-Faḳīh, 1885, p. 78.
34. Al-Mas'ūdī, 1861–77, Vol. 3, p. 30; Muṭahhar al-Maḳdīsī, 1899–1919, Vol. 1, p. 63.
35. Al-Mas'ūdī, 1861–77, Vol. 3, pp. 6 and 29.
36. Al-Bīrūnī, 1887, p. 100; al-Bīrūnī, 1941, p. 126.
37. Buzurg ibn Shahriyār, 1883–6, pp. 50–60; G. S. P. Freeman-Grenville, 1962b, pp. 9–13. Cf. also P. Quennell, 1928, pp. 44–52.
38. Cf. Unesco, *General History of Africa*, Vol. II, ch. 22.

The fallacy of the former school of historiography consisted in the mixing up of commercial relations with permanent settlement by the visitors and/or their political supremacy. Since the colonizing process in modern times proceeded along the line of trade–political supremacy–cultural change, it was erroneously concluded that the same must have happened in earlier times along the East African coast although there was not a trace of evidence to support such a view.

As for the permanent presence of Arabo-Persian elements in large numbers in the coastal settlements and their alleged founding of them, there is for this period only one indication and even this one is highly ambiguous. Al-Masʿūdī tells us that the island of Ḳanbalū (Pemba) is inhabited by a Muslim people, although their language is the Zandj one, and he adds that the Muslims conquered the island, making the local people prisoners. In another place the same source mentions that Ḳanbalū has a mixed population of Muslims and non-Muslim Zandj, the king being from among the Muslims.[39] Nowhere does the author maintain that these Muslims were Arabs or Persians; their Zandj language points rather to a group of Islamized Bantu-speakers. In any case the island was inhabited by the Zandj prior to the Muslim conquest.

Oral traditions

The third main source for the history of the East African coast is the oral tradition preserved in the local chronicles of Pate, Lamu, Kilwa and some other cities, the majority of these chronicles were written down either in Kiswahili or in Arabic only in the nineteenth century. An earlier version of the *Kilwa Chronicle* is contained in the sixteenth-century *Decadas da Asia* of João de Barros, being thus much closer in time to the earlier period. In many of these traditions an attempt is made to forge links between the ruling dynasty or class and some of the famous persons and/or cities of Middle Eastern history. This is a common trend in traditions of nearly all African Islamized societies and the result is the unnecessary prolonging of the authentic traditions into past centuries and their embroidering with great names of early Islamic ages.

While oral tradition can be useful in researching the history of a preliterate people, this source has not been fully utilized by historians because of their reliance on written sources. Although most oral tradition would have low reliability due to the antiquity of the period covered here, it is nevertheless a source for Mombasa's three groups (*Taifa tatu*) – Wa-Changamwe, Wa-Kilindini and Wa-Tangana – whose tradition claims that they were the original inhabitants until their sovereignty was overthrown by the Shīrāzī rulers in the second half of the thirteenth century.[40]

39. Al-Masʿūdī, 1861–77, Vol. 1, p. 205, Vol. 3, p. 31.
40. J. S. Trimingham, 1964, p. 14.

Until now, most historians have used these sources only to produce histories of diffusion and migrations of peoples and ideas to the African coast, the resultant synthesis being that the history and civilization of the coast is alien. It is thus necessary to review the history in a new approach which will identify the local components in the genesis of East African coast civilization and show that it is basically autochthonous and adapted to the region. This does not deny occasional foreign inputs for we are not dealing with a closed culture.

The coastal peoples

The Arab geographers divided the eastern African coast into three parts: the land of the Barbar (*bilād al-Barbar*) in the north, the land of the Zandj (*bilād al-Zandj*) between the Webi Shebele River and some point on the coast opposite to Zanzibar, and the Sofala country (*arḍ* or *bilād Sufāla*) to the south. Whether the mysterious country of *Wāḳ-Wāḳ* is to be placed even farther southwards on the African continent or whether it meant Madagascar, is difficult to decide owing to the confused accounts.

The land of the Barbar covered approximately the coast of present-day Somalia, both the northern part facing the Gulf of Aden, where the town of Berbera still exists, and the part to the south of Cape Guardafui. There is little doubt that the name Barbar has been applied by the Arabs to the Somali and other Cushitic-speaking peoples of the Horn of Africa. These people were sometimes referred to as 'black Berbers' to distinguish them from the North African Berbers. The term Berber had been already employed by the *Periplus of the Erythraean Sea*, Ptolemy and Cosmas Indicopleustes in the same sense.[41] Although some scholars argue that the boundaries between the Barbar country and the land of the Zandj lay on the Juba River,[42] there is enough evidence to show that the Bantu population lived as far north as the Webi Shebele. Bantu-speaking groups, like the Shidla, Shabeli, Dube and Elay still exist along the lower Webi Shebele, and the group known as the Gosha lives to the north of the Juba. At Brava the people still speak Chimbalazi, one of the northern dialects of Kiswahili. Nevertheless it seems that some Somali elements had already penetrated in the fourth/tenth or fifth/eleventh century to the coastal region between Mogadishu and Brava; in the mid-sixth/twelfth century al-Idrīsī already located fifty villages of the Hawiya – a Somali group – along the bank of an unnamed river, probably the Webi Shebele.[43] The same author mentions also Merka as one of the last towns in the land of the Barbar.

The land of the Zandj seems to have attracted more attention than all the other parts of the coast, mainly because of the brisk trade of the Zandj with

41. Unesco, *General History of Africa*, Vol. II, ch. 22.
42. V. V. Matveyev, 1960.
43. E. Cerulli, 1957, Vol. 1, pp. 41–5.

the countries around the Indian Ocean. The descriptions furnished by Arab authors leave no doubt that the coastal people were of Negro stock even if al-Iṣṭakhrī (*fl.* 340/951) mentions that in the cooler parts of East Africa lived 'white Zandj'.[44] Whether his informants (he himself never visited Africa) had in mind some Cushitic-speaking peoples inhabiting the hilly regions in the interior who differed from their Negro neighbours by their colour, remains unsolved.

The authors before the sixth/twelfth century do not mention any coastal place by its name, only the settlements on the offshore islands. Apart from Ḳanbalū (most probably Pemba Island), visited by al-Mas'ūdī, only one other name is mentioned by an early author; al-Djāḥiẓ (d. 255/869) divides the Zandj into two branches, the *Ḳanbalū*, and the *Lundjūya*, which is clearly a corruption from the Bantu word for Zanzibar, Ungudja.[45] The same author also relates a highly interesting account, found nowhere else, about a sea expedition led by a prince of Oman which – probably at the end of the seventh century – reached the land of the Zandj and was there destroyed by local peoples.

Al-Idrīsī is the first among the authors writing in Arabic to furnish the names of several coastal settlements of the land of the Zandj and Sofala. After al-Nadjā, the last town of the Barbars, he speaks about Badhūna and Ḳarḳūna as the two settlements bordering with the Zandj. From his text it is not entirely clear whether these two were inhabited by the Zandj or by Barbars, but he states that the Badhūna people are under the rule of the Zandj king. Then follow – going from north to south – Malindi, Manbasa (Mombasa) where the king of the Zandj resides, and al-Banās (or al-Bayās) the last place of the Zandj, touching already the Sofala country. The identification of al-Banās is not yet established definitively but it seems that it is to be located somewhere between Tanga and Sadani.[46]

To the south of the land of Zandj began the Sofala country, called by the Arabs *Sufāla al-Zandj* (Sufala of the Zandj) to distinguish it from Indian Sofala, near Bombay.[47] Because the African Sofala was famous for its gold, it was also known as *Sufāla al-dhahab* (Golden Sofala) or *Sufāla al-tibr* (Sofala of gold sand). Although some later authors mention the town of Sofala, the earlier geographers rather understood under this name (whose meaning is either 'low-lying land' or 'shoal water') a whole stretch of the coast between Pangani and southern Mozambique. According to their accounts the Sofala peoples were akin to the Zandj and were in commercial

44. al-Iṣṭakhrī, 1870, p. 36.

45. Cf. al-Djāḥiẓ, 1903, p. 36; it could be read also as *Landjūya*, the la- being an archaic Bantu prefix.

46. Al-Idrīsī, 1970, p. 59, gives the distance between Mombasa and al-Banās as one day and a half on the sea. Taking into account the average speed of Arabic sailing vessels at this period as being 3 knots (cf. G. F. Hourani, 1951, pp. 110–11), this will correspond to *c.* 108 nautical miles (200 kms).

47. The Indian Sofala corresponded to the ancient port of Surparaka.

intercourse with traders coming from Arab countries and India. The general tone of al-Bīrūnī's narrative gives the impression that Sofala was a well-known and frequently visited country, not an exotic and faraway land. It represented the terminal of voyages, as no ship ventured to sail further owing to sea dangers. Highly interesting is al-Bīrūnī's remark that beyond Sofala the Indian Sea joins the Western (Atlantic) Ocean.[48]

Settlements must have been scattered all along the coast and although the *Periplus* mentions only Rhapta and Menouthias, it is reasonable to expect that there were several small villages built of mud and wattle which later on developed into prominent metropolises such as Mogadishu, Gedi, Manda, Kilwa, and Ḳanbalū.

By the third/ninth century most of the towns on the East African coast were inhabited by the Swahili. The degree of affluence differed from one town to another depending on social organization and economic activities. Very few would have been built of stone in the initial stages, but as the settlements prospered, more and more stone architecture would result. Kilwa and Mafia as shown by archaeological excavations were characterized by mud-and-wattle houses, a fishing economy, local pottery and iron products, and limited local trade.[49]

Social organization

The *Periplus* mentions savage people remarkable for their stature, and organized under separate chiefs for each place.[50] As the reference does not indicate anything about the language, these people could have been as well Bantu-speakers as speakers of any other language group.

The coastal settlements were always self-governing and generally independent, their links with each other following varying patterns of alliance and hostility. Now and again, Kilwa, Pate and Mombasa attained a precarious hegemony when powerful enough to exact tribute.[51]

Islamic influence was nowhere responsible for the type of government which developed. It arose out of the nature of the situation. Maritime city-states had long existed on the Ethiopian coast and the maritime economic basis of settlement which came into existence on the East African coast required a wide outlook and centralized power capable of exacting taxes and tribute.

In the Benadir states authority seems to have been originally exercised by a council of lineage heads as in Mogadishu, Brava and Siyu throughout their independent history; one of these heads came to be recognized as a *primus inter pares*. But most coastal towns acquired chiefs, often an immi-

48. Al-Bīrūnī, 1934, p. 122; al-Bīrūnī, 1933, p. 711.
49. H. N. Chittick, 1974, Vol. 1, p. 36.
50. J. W. T. Allen, 1949, p. 53.
51. J. S. Trimingham, 1964, p. 11.

grant Arab or Persian accepted voluntarily as in Pate, presumably because he was outside the sphere of clan rivalries.[52]

The mixture of indigenous people and immigrants resulted in an ethnically mixed and economically specialized society. This led to the characteristic pattern of socio-economic differentiation and social stratification, with individual groups living together in their own ward and quarter (*mtaa*) of the town and different groups in wards ranked hierarchically against one another.[53] The early Arabic writers, Al-Djāḥiẓ and al-Mas'ūdī indicate that the settlements were ruled by local kings who were apparently elected and had their own armies.

T. Spear has rightly pointed out that a Swahili history which emphasizes Arab roots and Arab culture is based only on that layer which developed in the nineteenth century. It is necessary to go beyond this to uncover deeper layers, such as the ones relating to the Sanye and Batawi in Pate, which have been almost but not quite obliterated by subsequent developments in the societies and traditions. We must seek to uncover the meanings these have for Swahili historians if we are to be able to use them to construct our own histories.[54]

The Kiswahili language

The coastal settlements or small towns, it must be assumed, brought together different people, the majority of whom were of Bantu stock, a condition which must have favoured the development of Kiswahili.

The term Swahili is derived from the Arabic *sāḥil* (pl. *sawāḥil*)–'coast', and was employed first for the region stretching from Mogadishu to Lamu. The Kiswahili language (literally, 'the language of the coast') developed, of course, only later with the introduction of many Arab and Persian loanwords, that accompanied the progressive Islamization of the coastal people. It would be therefore more proper to speak – at least before the sixth/twelfth century – about proto-Kiswahili as the Bantu language that formed the basis on which later Kiswahili developed. Many authorities argue that Kiswahili was first concentrated in the area north of the Tana Delta and along the Somali coast and then spread from there southward.[55]

Al-Mas'ūdī's quotation of some Zandj words[56] leaves no doubt about the Bantu character of their language. It is therefore likely that some form of proto-Kiswahili was spoken on the coast; in no case was it a pidgin language since the same author mentioned the rich eloquence of the people and the existence of accomplished orators among them.

52. ibid., p. 14.
53. T. Spear, 1982, p. 6.
54. ibid., p. 19.
55. J. de V. Allen, 1981, p. 323; T. Spear, 1982, p. 16; 1978, p. 25.
56. Cf. p. 598 above.

It has been reported that between 800 and 1300 about nineteen settlements were situated north of the Tana, but that there were others such as Mombasa, Malindi, Zanzibar, Pemba, Kilwa and Ḳanbalū in the south.[57] These towns nurtured the development of Kiswahili while subsequent migration from the core area spread the language.

Linguistic evidence gathered by Derek Nurse has pointed more clearly to a Kiswahili synthesis along the northern coast. Further studies have left no doubt that Kiswahili is a Bantu language closely related to the Pokomo and Mijikenda languages previously spoken along the Somali and northern Kenyan coast. Kiswahili seems to have developed in this area as people speaking the language that was ancestral to Mijikenda, Pokomo and Kiswahili became divided, their language consequently diverging into separate dialects and eventually separate languages.[58]

As the society of coastal townspeople who were the speakers of Kiswahili became more complex and as commerce became important, interaction with Arab traders increased. As a result, a number of Arabic words and the Arabic script were adopted into Kiswahili. Subsequently, the language spread down the coast as it was carried by traders from Somalia and northern Kenya around the ninth century. As the traders expanded their activity down the coast, they established new settlements and interacted with the societies in which they settled. This gradually facilitated the adoption of Islam as the religion of the rulers.[59]

This view is contrary to the thesis propounded by some historians who view the Kiswahili-speaking peoples of the East African coast as members of an Arab diaspora which due to trade spread all over the coast during the last two thousand years. They argue that the Swahili culture has very strong Arab elements, that the language uses Arabic script, that the stone buildings and mosques are constructed in the Arabic manner and that the religion of Islam which is predominant along the coast and the genteel social behaviour of the Swahili are all Arab, especially when contrasted with the African cultures of the interior.

This perspective is essentially diffusionist as it assumes that cultural innovation and historical development in East Africa could only come from outside. It is also racist to assume that race and culture are so inextricably linked that a separate 'race' of immigrants had to carry these new ideas. These historians failed to investigate the possible African roots of the Swahili culture as reflected in the language, in religious beliefs and values and in the economy or social structure.[60]

Recent studies of Swahili culture and society reveal that African components are far more prominent than is allowed for by the diffusionists' arguments:

57. J. de V. Allen, 1981, p. 323.
58. T. Spear, 1982, p. 16.
59. ibid., pp. 17–18; T. Spear, 1978, p. 25.
60. T. Spear, 1982, p. 2.

(1) The Kiswahili grammatical structure as well as the greater part of the vocabulary are closely related to the Mijikenda and Pokomo languages, while its literature reflects the African oral code.

(2) The material culture of the Swahili has no analogues in Arabia or Persia. The Swahili stone architecture has no detailed parallels to justify the conclusion that it originated in the Near East, Arabia or Persia. Instead it developed locally out of the mud and wattle architecture prominent along the coast as a result of increasing economic wealth and socio-economic differentiation.[61] The coastal architecture which has been so much used as a proof that the coastal urban centres were founded by Arabs uses no materials which are not locally obtainable. Coral and coralline limestone which dominated the buildings were locally quarried. The mortar and plaster were also made from the available coral and gypsum.

(3) Even the Islam of the coast bears strong traces of historical traditional African religions in the prominence in it of beliefs in spirits and spirit possession, ancestor worship, witchcraft and divination which can be found in local traditions of Islam, co-existing with the more orthodox legal tradition.[62]

Islam

It would seem that the role of Muslims and their very number has been exaggerated by many historians, a bias perhaps inherent in the fact that most of the pre-tenth/sixteenth century written sources are Arabic. Although Islam had reached the northern part of the East African coast by the second/eighth century and the southern part well before the fifth/eleventh century, it was not until the eighth/fourteenth century that a distinctive Islamic coast civilization which can be called Shīrāzī differentiated itself.[63]

For a long time Islam was professed only by the immigrants from Arabia or Persia who were settled in the coastal towns. It seems that these expatriate merchants had not developed any large-scale proselytizing activity, so that the number of native Muslims remained rather restricted. Gradually some people in the immediate entourage of the immigrants as well as those Africans who were interested in commercial intercourse with the foreigners accepted Islam as their religion. The evidence of al-Mas'ūdī already quoted[64] points to the island of Ḳanbalū as inhabited by Muslims speaking the Zandj language, and it is generally accepted that Islam was implanted on the East African islands before it spread to the mainland.

61. ibid., P. S. Garlake, 1966, p. 113.
62. T. Spear, 1982, p. 2.
63. J. S. Trimingham, 1964, p. 11.
64. Cf. p. 598 above.

The overall picture of the expansion of Islam is rather blurred but it seems that until the sixth/twelfth century or even later, Islam was not a factor which would play a major part in shaping and influencing the societies of the coast to any noteworthy extent. The majority of local people were still adhering to their traditional beliefs, as witnessed by many Arabic authors.

The spread of Islam is connected closely with the problem of the Shīrāzī. The oral tradition and the Swahili written chronicles of late origin maintain that some merchants from the Persian Gulf, especially from Sīrāf, the port for the famous city of Shīrāz (in the Persian province of Fārs) came to East Africa during the ninth and tenth centuries. This is supported by ceramics from Manda and Unguja Ukuu.[65] Some of the imported ware is known to have been produced in Iraq, a part of which had been conquered in 290/902–3 by the Ḳarmatians, an extreme Shī'ite sect whose centre of power was located in al-Aḥsā region of Arabia, bordering the Persian Gulf. Although there is no direct evidence, it seems that the Ḳarmatians participated in the trade with East Africa. Various accounts from Kilwa indicate a probable Ḳarmatian colonization of the northern portion of the coast (the Benadir coast) in the tenth century. Archaeological evidence seems to support the traditional dating associated with the Seven Brothers story, which is a part of the 'number seven' legend supposedly connected with the Ḳarmatians and designates the period between 274/887 and 312/924 as that in which the colonization of the coast occurred.[66] The tradition claims connection between the Ḳarmatian state of al-Aḥsā and the founding of the states of Mogadishu, Brava, Marka, and possibly those of the Lamu archipelago and Zanzibar, too. It also claims that Kilwa was founded in the same period (tenth century) as the Benadir towns. However, this hypothesis cannot be entertained too seriously because Kilwa did not emerge as a primary power until the emergence of what Chittick[67] has postulated as a dynasty of South Arabian origin at the end of the thirteenth century. The Benadir coastal towns date from at least two hundred years earlier than the towns of Kilwa, Sofala and those on the Comoro Islands.[68]

The importance of the Shīrāzī as a socio-political force is questionable because the Shīrāzī immigrant traders who settled on the coast came as individuals and not as families. Naturally they were captured by a Bantu language while at the same time retaining their distinction from Africans. The language (Kiswahili), as already pointed out, developed on the Benadir coast and the system of inter-settlement communication ensured a general uniformity in all the settlements, though each developed its own

65. But the same ware could have reached the East African coast not only through Sīrāf merchants but through others working out of other major commercial centres, cf. R. C. Pouwels, 1974, p. 67.

66. ibid., pp. 68–9.

67. H. N. Chittick, 1970, p. 274.

68. R. C. Pouwels, 1974, pp. 70–1; J. S. Trimingham, 1964, pp. 3–4.

dialect. The result of the interaction was a Bantu-Islamic civilization moulded by Arabo-Persian elements but preserving Bantu features.

The Shīrāzī have been credited with the introduction of a highly developed stone architecture, the use of lime and cement, many fruits, carpentry, cotton-weaving, and various sciences including the use of the Persian solar calendar. However, it is now contended that the Shīrāzī as such did not introduce all these, but rather that their development was accelerated by the prosperity brought by the trade. Undeniably some fruit trees must have been introduced by the Arabo-Persians, but the arts of stonemasonry and carpentry were known along the coast before the coming of the Shīrāzī.

Oral tradition relating to the Persian influence on the Benadir coast is supported by the fact that the mosque of Arbaʿ Rukun in Mogadishu contains an inscription dated 667/1268–9 in the name of a Khusraw ibn Muḥammad al-Shīrāzī;[69] an earlier tomb inscription from 614/1217 bears the name of a person whose *nisba* al-Nīsābūrī al-Khurasānī points also to a Persian origin.[70] However, there is little evidence of much direct Persian activity to the south of the Somali coast. Nevertheless, there are indications that from the twelfth century on, groups of merchants – the majority of whom were descendants of intermarriage between Arabo-Persians and local populations on the Benadir coast – started to migrate south and carried the Arabo-Islamic culture to the islands of Zanzibar, Pemba, Kilwa and Mafia. These, together with the Ozi, Malindi and Mombasa town states, remained Shīrāzī, although increasingly Bantuized, until after the Portuguese conquest.[71]

Architecture

Stone buildings among coastal settlements seem to have first been concentrated in the area north of the Tana Delta, an area which has been referred to as Swahilini. However, before the third/ninth century, the majority of the buildings in many of the settlements were, as already pointed out, mud and wattle houses. The roofs were of thatch, as are those found today, either of the fronds of the *mwaa* palm or of the *makuti* (bound leaves of the coconut tree). Even in subsequent periods such houses were still built, as they still are in present-day coastal towns. Short lengths of stone-built walls have been found but it is not certain whether they were part of larger structures.[72]

As far as the origin of the coastal stone architecture is concerned, many historians have attributed it to Persia and Arabia. However, this diffusionist view is eschewed here in favour of more acceptable explanations. It has

69. E. Cerulli, 1957, Vol. 1, p. 9; local pronounciation of the name is Khisarwa.
70. ibid., pp. 2–3.
71. Cf. J. S. Trimingham, 1964, pp. 10–11.
72. H. N. Chittick, 1974, Vol. 1, p. 235.

already been pointed out that in no one region in the Near East are there sufficiently numerous or detailed parallels to enable clear conclusions on Persian or Arabic origin to be made. All the raw materials (coralline, limestone, coral, mortar, plaster) have always been found locally in plenty and there is nothing to prevent an innovative architectural element developing locally. However, some influence from traders and other immigrants cannot be ruled out.[73]

Economic activities

Agriculture

In economic terms, the coastal society was an urban–rural continuum with many earning their living from agriculture.[74] No doubt there were also pastoralists, especially in the north, on the Benadir coast. As Chinese sources of as early as the ninth century tell us, the inhabitants of the Barbar coast lived on meat and milk and on blood which they drew from cattle. The practice of drinking fresh blood drawn from cattle is practised even today by the Maasai.

The majority of Swahili, especially those living in the smaller and medium-sized settlements, but some of those in the larger ones too, were primarily agriculturalists. The custom of townsmen going into the country for three or four months every year to cultivate crops, as reported by M. Ylvisaker, was probably much more widespread throughout the Swahili world in earlier centuries.[75]

In Arabic sources we do find fragmentary accounts about crops and cultures. The chief crops seem to have been sorghum (*d̲h̲urra*) as well as yams whose local name *al-kilārī* is attested by al-Mas'ūdī. Another edible plant cultivated by the Zand̲j̲ was *al-rāsan*, identified as *Coleus*.[76] The diet of the coastal people was supplemented by bananas, coconuts, rice, tamarind and in some places even by grapes; sugar-cane is also mentioned. Whether honey was a product of apiculture or of wild-bee honey gathering remains unclear.

The Chinese traveller-writer Tuan Ch'eng Shin (d. 863) noted that the five grains were not eaten in Barbara while Wang Ta-yüan remarked that yams replaced grain in Zanzibar; Fei Hsin seems to have thought it strange that the inhabitants of Brava should have grown onions and garlic instead of gourds.[77]

Archaeological investigations in Kilwa have shown that the only grain to

73. J. M. Gray, 1951, p. 5; P. S. Garlake, 1966, p. 113.
74. J. de V. Allen, 1981, p. 330.
75. ibid., p. 329.
76. Al-Mas'ūdī, 1861–77, Vol. 3, p. 30.
77. P. A. Wheatley, 1975, p. 93.

have been grown was sorghum, as evidenced by carbonized seeds. No implements for grinding grain have been found from earlier times but in later periods rotary querns were also used as they are now, but such would have vanished from the archaeological record.[78]

Fishing and seafaring

The coastal communities obviously engaged in a fair amount of maritime activities (fishing, canoe-building, sailing). Many Arabic authors insist on the Zandj being fisheaters and add that for this purpose they sharpen their teeth. All along the coast the people were active in fishing but some places are mentioned where this was the main occupation, as for example in Malindi, where the inhabitants exported their catch. It seems that the people on the more southern parts of the coast were to a high degree dependent on sea food, not only fish but turtles and molluscs as well. On some islands the Zandj gathered shells for making ornaments but not for food. In Sofala they dived for pearls.

Although boatbuilding and navigation are inseparable from fishing, Arabic authors are silent about this side of the Zandj way of life. Only Buzurg ibn Shahriyār mentions numerous boats (*zawārīḳ*) that surrounded Arab ships near the Sofala coast. The same author wrote that among the ship captains on the Indian ocean were some Zandj; this indicates that the eastern Bantu were acquainted not only with coastal navigation but also with that of the high seas as well.[79] The use of the boat known as *dau la mtepe*[80] in the first century of the Christian era on the Benadir coast and on what is now the Tanzania coast is clearly referred to in the *Periplus*.[81] In addition to the *mtepe* there was also another type of boat known as *ngalawa*. The latter is a rather narrow dugout boat which by itself would be unstable and dangerous in open sea. However, the lack of stability is overcome by an outrigger balancing device.[82] Besides East Africa, this feature is also found in Indonesia, western New Guinea and Madagascar. Both the single and the double outrigger are found in the Comoros, otherwise only the double outrigger occurs in East Africa in rather sporadic distribution, being most common in Zanzibar and central coastal Tanzania.

The origin of the *ngalawa* is disputable. However, on linguistic and structural details, the *ngalawa* seems to have been developed on the East

78. H. N. Chittick, 1974, Vol. 1, p. 236.

79. Buzurg ibn Shahriyār, 1883–6, p. 54; on the other hand al-Idrīsī, 1970, pp. 60–1, categorically denies the existence of Zandj ships capable of long distance sea voyages.

80. *Mtepe* (a sewn boat) is distributed all over the coast but it is commoner in the central and southern parts of the East African coast.

81. J. T. Miller, 1969, p. 168.

82. A. H. J. Prins, 1959, p. 205.

African coast, probably in the Comoros in post-Portuguese times and thereafter spread to other East African areas.[83]

The sewn boat *mtepe* and the smaller variant *dau la mtepe* are however much older. They have been plying along the coast for a long time and are now both extinct except for a few specimens in museums. Their origin is also debatable. Linguistically, it would appear as if the *mtepe* is indigenous to East Africa, but structural details would suggest an Indian prototype, the *mtepe* being a Perso-Arabization of this prototype.[84] Graffiti on the walls of a house in the Gedi ruins depicts what is unmistakably a *mtepe* and has been provisionally dated to the fifteenth or sixteenth century. Other engravings occur at Kilwa, Songo Mnara and Ungwana which date from between the thirteenth and eighteenth centuries.[85] Perhaps these depictions are meant to underscore the role of shipping and therefore of trade on which the prosperity of the settlements so much depended. Both *mtepe* and *dau la mtepe* are represented in the engravings. Other engravings occur at Farkwa and Fort Jesus.[86]

Animal husbandry

While there are no doubts about the existence, since ancient times, of animal husbandry to the north of the Juba River, the situation obtaining to the south is unclear. On one hand, al-Mas'ūdī reports that cattle were employed by the Zandj as riding oxen (with saddles and reins) in war – the *mfalīmī* having 300 000 cavalry – and Buzurg mentions sheep and other domestic animals.[87] Al-Idrīsī on the other hand categorically insists on the absence of any beasts of burden or cattle among the people on the eastern coast, and other Arabic authors, too, are totally silent about animal husbandry.[88] As is well known, the coastal parts of East Africa are at present infested by tsetse and thus quite unsuited for cattle-keeping; but it is not impossible that in earlier times some stretches were tsetse free, thus making animal husbandry practicable.[89]

Hunting

Although hunting must have formed a part of the basic economy, there is

83. ibid., pp. 205–10.
84. ibid., pp. 210–13.
85. ibid., p. 211; P. S. Garlake, 1964, p. 197.
86. P. S. Garlake, 1966, pp. 197, 206; J. Hornell, 1942.
87. Al-Mas'ūdī, 1861–77, Vol. 3, pp. 6–7; Buzurg ibn Shahriyār, 1883–6, p. 151.
88. Al-Idrīsī, 1970, p. 60.
89. H. N. Chittick, 1977, p. 188, erroneously maintains that al-Mas'ūdī's cattle-keeping (and cattle-riding) people were of Ethiopian (Cushitic) stock. The whole context, however, of all fragments dealing with cattle points unmistakably to the black Zandj in the southern part of the coast.

rather scanty direct evidence about it. Arab authors were fascinated chiefly by elephant hunting, and even gave some details about its techniques, especially those that used poison, either for poisoning the water from which these animals drank (al-Masʿūdī) or to tip the points of weapons (al-Bīrūnī). Other hunted animals were leopards (*al-numūr*), lions, 'wolves' (apparently jackals) and monkeys. Most of the game was hunted for export purposes (ivory, skins) and although we do not find any mention of hunting for food, it seems more than likely that the meat of animals killed (elephants) would have been consumed.

Mining

Among minerals it was gold that attracted the main attention of the Arab authors, and Sofala was considered to be one of the most famous gold lands of the known world. Although al-Idrīsī wrote about the coastal towns of Djāsṭa and Daghūṭa (not yet identified but surely somewhere on the Mozambique coast) as the places where gold was found, it is evident from all other written sources that the main gold mines were located in the interior of the Sofala country and that the coastal settlements served only as export ports. Al-Bīrūnī mentions that gold in Sofala was found in the form of grains; the same kind has been discovered in the Great Zimbabwe archaeological complex.

Gold did not serve as a universal means of exchange among the eastern coast inhabitants but they were well aware of its value as a currency and an export commodity. On the other hand iron and copper were more valued by the local people and al-Masʿūdī wrote that they used iron for ornaments instead of gold and silver.

The main evidence for iron-mining is offered by al-Idrīsī who pointed out that the main centres of iron production were Malindi and Mombasa in the north and Djanṭāma and Dandāma in the south.[90] Iron became one of the major export commodities of these places, forming the main source of revenue. Although there is no reason to doubt al-Idrīsī's veracity, his account poses some problems. No large smelting ovens have yet been found in the vicinity of Mombasa and Malindi;[91] moreover all Arab authors are silent about iron-working or production of iron tools and weapons, activities which would have been natural for a region allegedly rich in iron. This does not mean, of course, that these activities did not exist on the coast but it seems that they were on a rather localized and small scale. Al-Idrīsī alluded to this when he noted that although the population of the Zandj country is numerous, they have few weapons.[92] Further archaeological research is needed to elucidate this important problem.

90. Al-Idrīsī, 1970, pp. 59–60, 68–9.

91. It is, of course, possible that al-Idrīsī's Malindi refers rather to the region of Manda where slag from iron smelting has been discovered archaeologically.

92. Al-Idrīsī, 1970, p. 61.

Commercial activities

The East African coast is one of the few regions in sub-Saharan Africa that entered early into continuous trade relations with the outside world.[93] The emergence, from the seventh century on, of a powerful Islamic empire in the Middle East contributed vastly to the growth of trade in the Indian Ocean including the East African coast. The establishment of an increasingly expanding market in Islamic countries during the period under discussion offered new possibilities for the coastal settlements to develop an export trade. Not only was the volume of trade increased but to the traditional commodities new ones were added, thus contributing to the diversification and specialization of various coastal towns. It was trade too that favoured the differential development of towns which depended on relative success as trading centres. The tempo of migrations and trade seems to have increased in the ninth and tenth centuries and it was during this time that coastal trading centres such as Mogadishu, Marka, Brava, Mombasa, Manda and Unguja Ukuu were founded and expanded. Towns rose and fell individually according to the vagaries of trade, one generation building elegantly in stone while the next reverted to mud and wattle. But during the period under consideration perhaps the only prominent towns were Manda in the Lamu archipelago and Ḳanbalū. The others seem to have attained their prominence only after the eleventh century.[94]

The commerce and trade of the coastal towns may be looked at from three different angles: trade with foreigners, trade within the coastal settlements and trade with the interior.

Trade with foreigners

The items of trade which attracted Arabs, Persians, Indians and Indonesians to the coastal towns were many and varied, but the most important were ivory, tortoiseshell, ambergris, incense, spices, slaves, gold and iron. Although there is no evidence of direct contact, some African products were known and in demand in China during the Tang period (618–906). The East African coast was known as a prolific source of ambergris which was introduced to China by the end of this dynasty.[95] By the seventh century, sweet oil of storax, tortoiseshell from Barbara, 'dragon's blood' (resins of *Dracaena schizantha*, and *D. cinnabari*) and aloes (plant juice) were among the exports to China.[96] The ninth-century Chinese records also mention that the inhabitants of Barbara were in the habit of selling

93. Cf. Unesco, *General History of Africa*, Vol. II, ch. 22.
94. T. Spear, 1982, p. 5; G. Shepherd, 1982, pp. 7–10.
95. P. A. Wheatley, 1975, p. 105; J. Kirkman, 1954, p. 95.
96. P. A. Wheatley, 1975, p. 105.

their womenfolk to foreign traders. Later Chao Ju-kua told how savages with lacquer-black bodies from Kumr Zangi (Zanzibar) were enticed by food and then captured.[97] According to al-Idrīsī, the Arabs of Oman also enticed children by offering dates and then abducted them into slavery.[98] The well-known story told by Buzurg ibn S̲h̲ahriyār about the kidnapping of the king of the Zand̲j̲ offers an insight into another manner of obtaining slaves.[99]

The slave trade poses a problem of interpretation. For the period between the seventh and twelfth centuries there is practically no direct evidence in written sources about slave trading along the East African coast. The above-mentioned incidents show that slaves were procured by capturing or abducting local peoples rather than by purchasing them. Now, this method is hardly effective in the long run and can be employed only occcasionally, thus producing a restricted number of slaves; its regular or prolonged use is out of question as it leads to the hostility of the coastal people and affects adversely the development of normal commercial intercourse.

On the other hand the mass employment of the so-called Zand̲j̲ slaves in irrigation works in lower Iraq – those who, in the ninth century led the famous slave revolt – seems to indicate that there must have been a continuous flow of enslaved peoples from East Africa to Islamic countries.[100]

A solution to this apparent contradiction is offered by the possibility that although the black slaves in southern Iraq were of different origins – from Ethiopia, from the Horn or from other parts of Africa, with a proportion of East Africans – they were for some reason collectively known as the 'Zand̲j̲'. This does not mean that no slave trade at all existed on the East African coast; it surely did but its volume could not have been very great since otherwise it would have not escaped the notice of Arab authors. Although they brought very detailed accounts of all export and import commodities, slaves do not figure among these.

From the early days the East African ports were known for their exports, most of them being the time-honoured natural products: ivory, which was sent as far as China, ambergris, leopard skins and tortoiseshell. The export of gold from the southern parts began in fourth/tenth century, whereas in the sixth/twelfth century al-Idrīsī considered iron to be the main commodity exported by many coastal towns. The Benadir coast was famous for its exports of incense, perfumes and aromatic oils, such as balsam and myrrh.

As far as imports are concerned, the main items recorded by the Arab and Chinese sources are ceramics (Islamic and Chinese), cloth, beads and glass. By the beginning of the twelfth century, South Asian immigrants who had arrived in northern Madagascar and the Comoro Islands some

97. ibid.
98. Al-Idrīsī, 1970, p. 61.
99. Buzurg ibn S̲h̲ahriyār, 1883–6, pp. 51–60.
100. Cf. Chapter 26 below.

centuries earlier, were exporting soapstone vessels to Kilwa, Manda and further afield.[101]

At Kilwa, excavations of the predynastic period (probably at the end of the sixth/twelfth century) have shown that among the imported objects (Islamic pottery and glass beads) the proportion of glass to foreign pottery was greater than in the subsequent period. In addition to glass beads, cornelian beads from Cambay in India were found. As for imported pottery to East Africa, the earliest is the Islamic sgraffito, a ware with a mottled glaze applied over a slight slip. It is a characteristic Islamic ware known from third/ninth-century Samarra (in Iraq) to the early tenth/sixteenth century. In East Africa, sgraffito is probably most characteristic for the seventh/thirteenth century.[102] However, sgraffito was also the least common type found. The largest imports, especially in the case of Gedi, were blue and green glazed earthenware, and yellow and black, celadon and blue, and white porcelain from China.[103] In the fifth/eleventh century, Duyvendak records that Chinese exports consisted largely of gold, silver, copper, cash, silk and porcelain. Chinese coins have been found all over the coast and they continued to reach East Africa until the seventh/thirteenth century.[104]

Trade within the coastal settlements

The larger towns tended to be oriented more towards international maritime trade than the smaller ones, which depended largely on agriculture and fishery. But at the same time there must have been frequent interaction between one settlement and another regardless of their size. Although we have no record of much of the inter-coastal trade during the period under review, it is known from published reports that Kilwa was trading with other important cities such as Manda.[105]

At Manda, recent excavations have shown that at levels datable to the ninth to tenth centuries, there is a lack of glass beads just as there is at Kilwa. Neither Manda nor Kilwa seem to have had any significant trade with the interior. Consequently, glass beads of an early date are extremely rare in the interior.[106]

Trade with the interior

The question of early contacts between the coastal settlements and the

101. G. Shepherd, 1982, p. 15.
102. P. S. Garlake, 1966, p. 53.
103. J. Kirkman, 1954, p. 94; 1966, pp. 18–19.
104. G. S. P. Freeman-Grenville, 1959, p. 253.
105. H. N. Chittick, 1974, Vol. 1, p. 236.
106. ibid., Vol. 2, p. 483.

interior still remains a crucial problem. It is inconceivable that there was no intercourse at all, but no evidence – in this case only archaeology is called for to find it – of any importance has been as yet produced. The only region where there was a significant trade with the interior seems to have been the Sofala coast; the gold that was exported from this country came mainly from what is now Zimbabwe. But it would be premature to conclude that the coastal people ventured, in this early period, far into the interior.

There was probably no long-distance trade in the usual sense of the word; what we can imagine at most is that goods which came from a long distance were bartered from one people to another, not carried by caravans as in the nineteenth century. The coastal towns must have relied for agricultural products on their immediate hinterland neighbours. In exchange for these, as well as for ivory and skins, the peasants received dried fish or shell beads. It is also likely that the hinterland peoples came with their products to the towns or to periodic markets just behind the coast. These contacts left no durable traces; the local pottery of the coast is unrelated to that of the interior.

Conclusion

During the period under discussion the East African coast witnessed the beginnings of various historical processes that came to full fruition only after the twelfth century. But it was probably during this period that the foundation of an African culture was laid, upon which was later built the rich Swahili culture. The political and social development of the coastal Bantu-speaking peoples started to be influenced by the rise of international trade on the Indian Ocean. At first the impact was felt mostly in the economic field as some of the coastal settlements oriented themselves more to foreign trade; gradually politics, culture and religion were permeated by the norms brought by immigrants from Islamic countries. The first region to come under these external influences was that to the north of the Juba River; from there, in later centuries, new waves of migrants carried the elements of the mixed culture to the south. At the same time all immigrants – never very numerous – underwent a process of Bantuization. The most outstanding result of this process of interchange and intermarriage has been the Swahili language and culture, in which features of African and Oriental origin were welded together.

22 The East African interior

C. EHRET

The seventh to the eleventh centuries of the Christian era appear on the whole to have been a period of consolidation of previous trends in the East African interior. The notable ethnic and economic transformations of the earliest Iron Age lay several centuries in the past, at the turn of the eras and during the two or three centuries thereafter when Bantu communities spread into widely scattered areas and iron technology began widely to be practised. The next era of equivalent transformation would not be for centuries still to come. that is not at all to say that the period of the seventh to eleventh centuries was without interest. New ethnic expansions took place, changing the linguistic map and creating new challenges to be dealt with by established communities. and sometimes the accumulation of small changes grew into something new and significantly different from just the sum of its parts.

Population movements

The two most widely encountered groupings of peoples at the beginning of the seventh century were the southern Cushites and the Bantu. Nilotic and Khoisan-speaking peoples were significant, though less numerous actors in the events of the mid-first millennium.

The Cushites

The first Southern Cushites had settled in northern Kenya during the third millennium before the Christian era, and some of their linguistic descendants had spread still farther south, as far as central northern Tanzania by the late second millennium. Peoples speaking the early Southern Cushitic languages can be identified as the makers of the various archaeological cultures which belong to the Savanna Pastoral Neolithic tradition of East Africa.[1] As the archaeological name suggests, from the beginning of

1. S. H. Ambrose, 1982.

their settlement the Southern Cushites kept cattle and small livestock as well, apparently, as donkeys. What is not yet adequately recognized in the archaeology but clearly indicated in the linguistic record is that many of the Southern Cushites were grain cultivators,[2] some of them from fairly early times using both irrigation and animal manure to increase their yields.

The Southern Cushites of the early first millennium of the Christian era were a varied lot. Along the Tana River and in parts of the near interior of the Kenya coast lived the Dahaloans. Those along the Tana were apparently cultivators like the Bantu-speaking Pakomo and Elwana who were later to absorb and replace them in the present millennium.[3] At least one hunter-gatherer community in the modern Witu area had taken up the Dahalo language as its own, ceasing to speak its formerly Khoisan language but bringing a number of Khoisan words containing click sounds into its new language.[4]

In the deeper interior the Rift Southern Cushites predominated. One such society, remembered in oral tradition by the name Mbisha, lived in the Taita Hills.[5] Around Mount Kilimanjaro and southward onto the Maasai steppe can be placed the Old Asa-speaking communities, while in parts of central Tanzania lived the closely related Old Kw'adza and Iringa Southern Cushites (see Fig. 22.1). The latter three societies spoke what were probably still at that time little more than dialects of a single diverse language. Both the Old Asa and Old Kw'adza societies apparently co-existed, like the later food-producers of those regions, with hunter-gatherer bands, some of whom took up the languages of the dominant farmers and herders.[6] West of the Rift Valley in Tanzania lay the lands of the aptly named West Rift peoples, at one time probably extending through all the areas south of the Mau forest of Kenya and as far west as the south-western Lake Victoria region, but by +600 probably centred on the Serengeti and Ngorongoro regions. Many of the Rift Southern Cushites of the seventh century may have been pre-eminently pastoral in economy. Still, it seems probable that others, especially around Kilimanjaro, the Taita Hills, and the edges of the Rift Valley, lent primary attention to their crops.

The other significant Southern Cushitic communities of the era spoke Mbuguan languages. Two sets of communities can be discerned in the linguistic record. One, the Kirinyaga Cushites, apparently preceded the Bantu settlers of Mount Kenya; they are probably the people remembered as the Gumba in the modern-day traditions of the region, and they prob-

2. C. Ehret, 1980a.

3. The evidence includes cultivation terms apparently borrowed from Dahalo into Pokomo.

4. C. Ehret, 1974a, pp. 10–11, 67.

5. C. Ehret and D. Nurse, 1981a, 1981b.

6. C. Ehret, 1974a, p. 15.

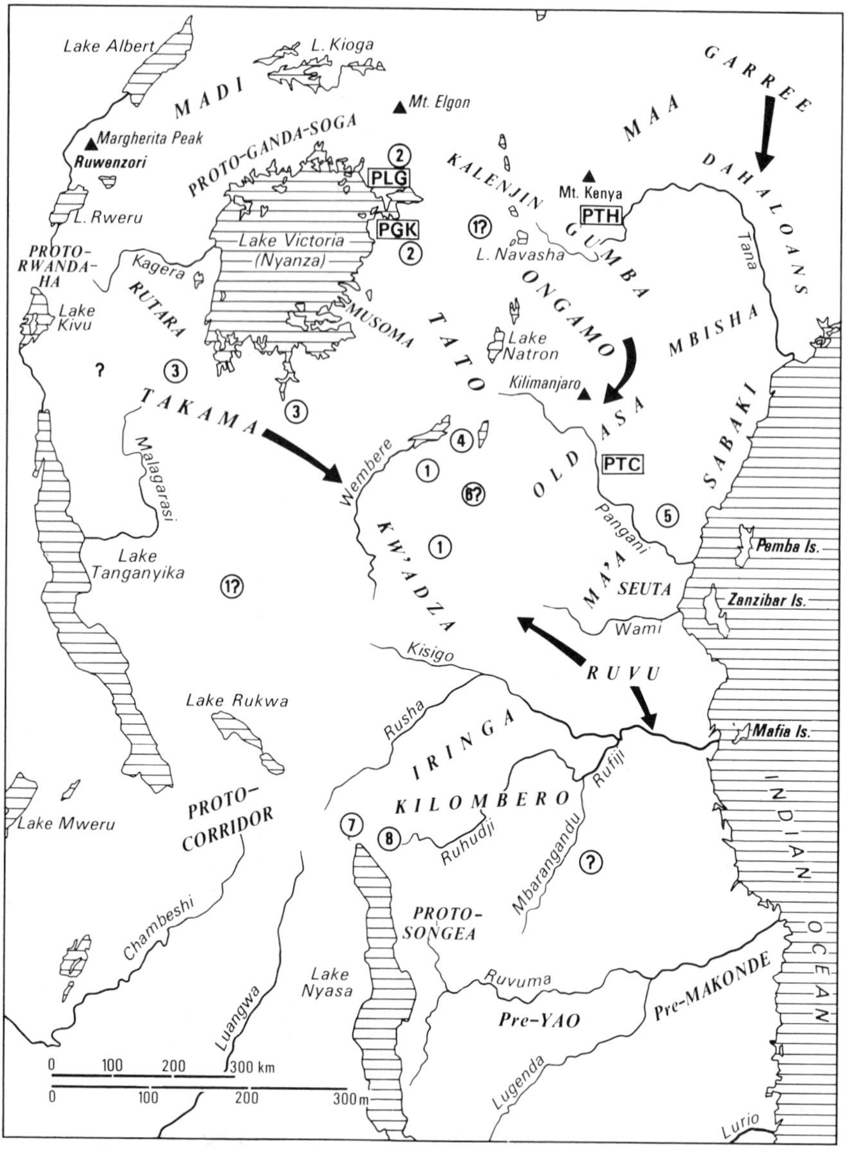

FIG. 22.1 *Major eastern African societies from about the seventh to the ninth century*

IRINGA	Ethnic groups
➡	Probable directions of ethnic expansions during or following the period of the seventh to ninth centuries
1	Khoisan hunter-gatherers
2	Plateau Southern Cushites
3	Nyanza Southern Cushites
4	Proto-West Rift Southern Cushites
5	Pre-Asu
6	Pre-Rango
7	Pre-Nyakyusa
8	Proto-Njombe
PGK	Proto-Gusii-Kuria (Mara)
PLG	Proto-Luyia-Gusii
PTC	Proto-Taita-Chaga
PTH	Pre-Thagicu

Note: Despite the close similarity in self-names, the Ma'a are a Southern Cushitic people quite distinct from the Maa, who spoke an Eastern Nilotic language.

ably included hunter-gatherers as well as farmers among their numbers.[7] The second Mbuguan group, the Old Ma'a, were apparently centred by this time in north-eastern Tanzania, probably to the east of the Old Asa and south of the Pangani River, in parts of the upper Wami watershed where the ecological conditions allowed extensive cattle-raising. The oral traditions of the present-day Ma'a remember their movement into this region from the direction of Kenya, at a time preceding the seventeenth century.[8] Apparently the Ma'a have attached an authentic, but very ancient tradition at the beginning of the more circumstantial accounts of their recent history, for the linguistic evidence concurs with tradition but places the movement from the north *much* earlier than the seventeenth century.[9]

The Khoisan

The Southern Cushitic expansions of the last three millennia before the Christian era had wholly incorporated many Khoisan communities. Other such societies had continued to coexist as hunter-gatherers living alongside food-producing Cushites, but had taken up the language of those dominant neighbours. As we have already seen, most of the Southern Cushite speech communities seem to have included this kind of associated but economically distinct people during the later first millennium. But around the fringes of the Southern Cushitic areas of central Tanzania, at least two Khoisan groups have been able to maintain their languages down to the present. The Hadza survived as a unit by Lake Eyasi, in lands marginal to farming and inimical by reason of tsetse fly to cattle. But even they probably had been significantly influenced in material culture by nearby West Rift people by the seventh century of the Christian era, obtaining pottery of a Savanna Pastoral Neolithic style, for instance, from Southern Cushites.[10] The other community, the Sandawe, survived by adopting agriculture and so gaining the economic basis for successfully competing with other food-producers. The sources of their knowledge were apparently Old Kw'adza-speakers living in or near Kondoa and the modern Sandawe areas.[11] Unfortunately the era of the Sandawe shift to agricultural pursuits cannot yet be decided. It is unlikely to be as late as the eighteenth century as some observers have thought.[12] The beginning of the

7. ibid., pp. 27–8; additional evidence allows attribution now of the language to the Mbuguan branch of Southern Cushitic.
8. S. Feierman, 1974, pp. 74–5.
9. C. Ehret, 1974a, p. 13.
10. S. H. Ambrose, 1982.
11. This relation is abundantly evident in Sandawe food-producing vocabulary, which has many old Kw'adza loanwords; separate publication of this evidence has not yet been made, however. See also Unesco, *General History of Africa*, Vol. IV, ch. 19.
12. E.g. J. L. Newman, 1970.

Sandawe shift to food production could have begun as early as the period of the seventh to eleventh centuries since the Old Kw'adza were probably already in place by then. But it could also date to the centuries between 1100 and 1700.

The Central Sudanic speakers

Far to the west, in the Great Lakes region, Central Sudanic-speaking communities seem to have held the same kind of historical position as the Southern Cushites had in central and eastern East Africa. Herders of cattle and small livestock, cultivators of sorghum and finger millet, and avid fishers, the Central Sudanians first rose to prominence in the areas near the Nile River in far southern Sudan and far northern Uganda, probably in about the third millennium before the Christian era. Sometime later, a new front of Central Sudanic settlement opened up to the south in the Lake Victoria basin. The evidence of this expansion, little investigated so far, takes two forms. Pollen studies, which reveal changes in vegetation attributable to agricultural activities in the basin, place the inception of the agricultural era at no later than about three thousand years ago in areas to the west and just north of Lake Victoria.[13] In archaeology the probable reflection of this cultural and economic expansion of Central Sudanians is Kansyore pottery.

Like their contemporaries, the southern Cushites to the east of the Great Lakes region, the Central Sudanic farmers and herders of the last three millennia before the Christian era entered into close relations with neighbouring food-collecting communities. A notable reflection of such relations can be seen in the wide adoption of Kansyore pottery by hunter-gatherers, for instance along the west and to the south of Lake Victoria.[14] As part-time fisherfolk the Central Sudanians would have competed directly for one of the principal food resources of their predecessors in the basin and so may have assimilated the hunter-gatherers to their ways and absorbed them into their societies more rapidly and thoroughly than did the Southern Cushites.

The Nilotes

East of Lake Victoria the initial challenge to the predominant position of the first farmers came from the Southern Nilotes, who began to move southward out of the Uganda–Sudan border regions sometime around the middle of the first millennium before the Christian era and are to be identi-

13. E.g. R. L. Kendall, 1969; M. E. S. Morrison, 1968; M. E. S. Morrison and A. C. Hamilton, 1974. For historical interpretation of these data, see D. Schoenbrun, 1984, note 47.

14. S. H. Ambrose, 1982, p. 133.

fied as the makers of the Elmenteita archaeological tradition.[15] The Southern Nilotes took up residence in the higher areas along and to the west of the central Rift Valley in Kenya, incorporating a considerable body of Southern Cushites into their society and apparently entering into close economic relations with hunter-gatherer communities of the forested fringes of the Rift Valley and with the more purely pastoral Southern Cushitic people who continued to occupy the valley floor.[16] From the hunters they would have obtained products such as honey, beeswax and skins, while with herders of the Rift Valley they would probably have exchanged grain for livestock. By the seventh century of the Christian era, two distinct descendant societies of the early Southern Nilotes had emerged, the pre-Kalenjin north of the Mau, and the Tato, from whom the modern Dadoga derive, to the south of that range. The Tato were centred at first, it would seem, in the Loita highlands and spread at some later period, but before 1100, south-eastward from there into the Old Asa country of the Maasai steppe.[17]

Bantu expansion

But the more serious challenge to the earlier ways of agricultural life was posed by the Early Iron Age Bantu expansion into East Africa. It was a challenge that was not always immediately evident, for the Bantu immigrants were initially rather selective in their areas of settlement.

The first appearance of the new agricultural communities on the East African scene was at the far west of the Great Lakes region. Speaking a number of different dialects of a language known to modern scholars as proto-Eastern Bantu, they appear to have established themselves in parts of the western, central and southern Lakes region earlier than the middle of the last millennium before the Christian era.[18] By this point in time two major kinds of economic change were underway in the north-western part of East Africa. One was the spread of iron-working with its attendant effects on the technology of tool-making: the age of stone tools was thus beginning to draw to an end rather earlier there than elsewhere in eastern Africa. The second, of probably greater long-range importance, was the emergence of a more complex agriculture, principally among the communities speaking the proto-Eastern Bantu language. Coming with a livelihood based on yam cultivation, they had begun to adopt in addition the crops of the farming societies who had preceded them in the eastern side of the continent, gaining thereby a new potential flexibility in adapting to the great variety of East African environments.[19] By the close of the era a few

15. ibid., pp. 139–44.
16. C. Ehret, 1971, pp. 39, 114.
17. ibid., pp. 55–7; C. Ehret, 1980b.
18. C. Ehret, 1973. See also J. Vansina, 1984, for recent bibliography and views.
19. C. Ehret, 1974b.

Eastern Bantu communities, under the influence of their Central Sudanian neighbours and, to the south of Lake Victoria, of Southern Cushites as well, had also begun to take an increasing interest in cattle-raising. Moreover, the population of people speaking Eastern Bantu dialects apparently grew considerably during the last several centuries before the Christian era, by absorbing many of the erstwhile Sudanians[20] and probably by natural increase as well. At the turn of the era the Eastern Bantu of the Lakes region and adjoining parts of eastern Zaire had grown into a sufficiently large population to support a vast new scattering out of Bantu emigrants to new and distant regions of settlement all across eastern and south-eastern Africa.

In East Africa some of the new settlers went far to the east, to the coastal areas of southern Kenya and to parts of the mountainous areas of north-eastern Tanzania, in particular to the Pare and Ngulu ranges. These were the makers of Kwale pottery. A slightly later offshoot of this settlement had arrived at Mount Kenya by the fifth century of the Christian era. That latter group of settlers probably brought the dialect of Eastern Bantu which was ancestral to the Thagicu languages, spoken across the eastern highlands of Kenya today. Archaeological continuity between Kwale ware, Gatung'ang'a pottery of the twelfth century on Mount Kenya, and more recent wares, though not yet fully demonstrable, seems a plausible hypothesis[21] and fits the linguistic indications as well. The people of the Pare Mountains settlement can be suggested to have spoken the closely related dialect from which the later Chaga, Dawida and Saghala languages derive.[22] Although Kwale ware is known from sites on nearby Kilimanjaro, it was most probably traded to there from the early Bantu inhabitants in Pare, from which pottery has long been imported because of the paucity of suitable clay on Kilimanjaro.

A second early movement of early Eastern Bantu into coastal East Africa was that of the north-east-coastal people, probably by or before the middle of the first millennium of the Christian era. The inception of this settlement has yet to be archaeologically identified. By the seventh century an array of north-east-coastal communities stretched probably from north of the mouth of the Tana River to the hinterland of modern Dar es Salaam in Tanzania and were to coalesce into four societies: the Sabaki in Kenya, the Seuta to their south, the Ruvu in the regions inland from the central Tanzania coast, and the pre-Asu perhaps already in the South Pare Mountains.[23] In a number of areas, especially north of the Pangani River, this

20. C. Ehret, 1973.
21. R. Soper, 1982, pp. 236–7.
22. C. Ehret and D. Nurse, 1981b.
23. See the arguments in Unesco, *General History of Africa*, Vol. IV, ch. 19. Sabaki and Ruvu are geographical names given by scholars to peoples whose self-names have been lost to history; other such names used in this chapter include Takama, Njombe, Kirinyaga, Iringa, and the like.

expansion can be suggested to have incorporated the previously established Kwale people of the coastal hinterland.[24]

Several Early Iron Age Bantu settlements ended up in far southern East Africa. The Kilombero people had settled in or around the valley of that name, while people ancestral in language to others of the modern peoples of southern Tanzania settled farther south, in the Songea highlands and south of the Ruvuma. Still other areas of settlement arose at the northern end of Lake Malawi among them those of the peoples from whose dialects the Nyakyusa, Corridor (Fipa, Nyamwanga, Nyiha, Mambwe), and Mjombe (Hehe, Bena, Kinga) languages variously stem. These last three areas of settlement are known so far only through the testimony of linguistics.[25]

The final notable early Eastern Bantu settlements which need mention were along the western shore of Lake Victoria, especially north of the Wami Gulf, and in western parts of north-central Tanzania. The Wami Gulf settlers, makers of a variety of Urewe pottery, were the probable base out of which the Luyia-Gisu societies of later times were to emerge. The second-mentioned settlement, by makers of Lelesu pottery, may have been ephemeral. Alternatively, Lelesu ware may have been made by the community from which derive the Irangi, who live today in the Kondoa area of central Tanzania.

Other Eastern Bantu societies took shape, of course, among those communities that continued to reside in the Great Lakes region. The proto-Lacustrine people, both from linguistic argument and from the combined indications of oral tradition and archaeology as to population continuities,[26] are best placed as inhabitants of the Bukoba area at the turn of the eras. The proto-Takama people may have lived to the south of the proto-Lacustrine society, while still other communities, incorporated into expanding Lacustrine societies at various later times, had found a place for themselves in Rwanda and Burundi and other areas on the western side of the region.

Hence, by the seventh century Eastern Bantu farming communities could be found in a scattered and very uneven distribution – widely through the central and southern Great Lakes region; probably continuously through the immediate hinterland of the central and northern Tanzanian and the Kenyan coasts; in the Pare mountains; in a patch on the slopes of Mount Kenya; along the western side of Lake Victoria; in several adjoining clumps in central southern Tanzania; and possibly in one area in north-central Tanzania. The common factor in this distribution was the

24. The evidence for this conclusion consists of early loanwords from a Thagicu – or Taita-Chaga-related language, which are found in Sabaki languages and are not clearly attributable to contacts of the last few centuries. A few such loans may also occur rarely in some southern Somali languages.

25. D. Nurse, 1982. See also Unesco, *General History of Africa*, Vol. IV, ch. 19.

26. P. R. Schmidt, 1978.

usual correlation of Bantu settlement with areas of more than 900–1000mm of rain a year, occasionally somewhat lower in highland areas where lower evaporation rates made up the difference. Eastern Bantu settlement in the Early Iron Age seems, in other words, to have gone to areas most like those from which it came: wooded or forested lands with sufficient rainfall for the yam-based planting agriculture that had propelled the earliest Bantu movements out of West Africa.[27] To be sure, all the East African Bantu of this era had African grain crops, but the pattern of settlement suggests that yam cultivation remained very important.

What made the wetter areas doubly attractive is that they must frequently have been areas little or not at all utilized by the established Southern Cushitic and Nilotic food-producers, places where the dangers of direct competition for land could be avoided. Along the East African coast many areas would have been tsetse-infested and thus unattractive to the cattle-herding Cushites and Nilotes. In southern Tanzania, Bantu settlement went into areas often similarly unsuited to livestock-raising and, in any case, not yet reached by Southern Cushitic expansion,[28] while in the Pare Mountains and on Mount Kenya we can imagine that Bantu immigrants moved into forested zones above the plains and forest fringes already exploited by neighbouring Cushites. In many of these areas hunter-gatherer bands must have operated but, as food-collectors, were at a distinct disadvantage in the competition for resources with incoming food-producers. Except in the colder highland forests, hunter-gatherers were probably assimilated into the intrusive Bantu communities before very many centuries had passed.

The one notable exception to the pattern of Bantu settlement was the movement of the Lelesu-ware makers into quite dry parts of central Tanzania. If this community survived as a separate society into later eras, it would have to have made rapid and major subsistence adaptations not required of other Bantu settlements, shifting wholly to grain cultivation in its farming and perhaps greatly expanding the proportion of food obtained through hunting. The evidence for connecting the Lelesu people to any later Bantu-speaking society is as yet lacking, so this intriguing possible history cannot presently be followed up.

Several areas of the interior of East Africa remained unsettled by food-producing communities in the seventh century. The most notable such region covered a large part of western Tanzania. A second large area lay in the heart of south-western Tanzania. Presumably Khoisan hunter-gatherer bands continued to pursue an independent food-collecting existence in these areas and continued to do so often into much later eras. But the necessary archaeological study to demonstrate this proposition remains to be done.

27. C. Ehret, 1982a.
28. G. Waite and C. Ehret, forthcoming.

A few Eastern Cushitic societies were also prominent, principally located in what is today northern Kenya. On the north side of Mount Kenya lived people speaking an early form of Yaaku. The Yaakuan Eastern Cushites had spread into the region as early, possibly, as the first or second millennium before the Christian era. Apparently mainly pastoralists, though with knowledge of grain cultivation, they had incorporated the Mbuguan Southern Cushites who preceded them in north-central Kenya,[29] and their language was also taken up by at least one previously Khoisan-speaking hunter-gatherer community of the north slopes of Mount Kenya.[30]

In the Lake Turkana basin other Eastern Cushites resided, the offspring of societies, related to the modern Danenech and Arbore of the north end of the lake, which had spread widely across the basin in the last millennium before the Christian era. Present-day scholars have given the name Baz to these otherwise unnamed groups,[31] makers probably of the archaeo-astronomic monuments of the Lake Turkana region.[32]

Early Somali and Rendille

Further east, the vast lowland running from the Tana River to the Shebelle basin in Somalia was already the home for several centuries of the early Somali and Rendille peoples.[33] There are indications that their expansion into these regions, beginning probably around the turn of the era, proceeded at the expense not only of fairly numerous hunter-gatherers of uncertain language affiliations, but of Dahaloan herding communities.[34] But by the seventh century of the Christian era the regions of the Juba and Shebelle rivers had become largely if not entirely Somali-speaking.[35]

The north-eastern regions of the East African interior stood off economically from the rest. Containing the driest areas of East Africa, they had become by the seventh century the centre of emergence of a new form of pastoralism in which camels, better adapted to such climes, often replaced cattle as the chief subsistence animals. What went along with the most specialized versions of camel-herding was a new social development, of a nomadic pattern of life, unknown then or later in any more southerly part of East Africa. The extent to which this shift in livelihood and residence patterns had proceeded by the seventh century is unclear. The linguistic

29. C. Ehret, 1974a, p. 33; but linguistic affiliations of the particular Southern Cushites are not identified there.

30. ibid., pp. 33, 88.

31. B. Heine, F. Rottland and R. Vossen, 1979.

32. S. H. Ambrose, 1982. These people are perhaps early Nilotes.

33. B. Heine, 1978.

34. Preliminary indications of research project into Somali history presently being undertaken by M. N. Cali and C. Ehret.

35. M. N. Cali, 1980.

evidence suggests that it was rather far advanced among the pre-Rendille, who lived in the driest areas, and among some of the Somali-speakers.[36] On the other hand, many of the Somali communities lived in somewhat better-watered areas where cattle could have held their own with camels, and the Somali speech area even in those centuries included the sedentary agricultural societies along the Juba and Shebelle for whom cattle would have been much more useful animals.[37] We can expect that the Baz people of the Turkana basin also kept camels, though perhaps not so prominently as peoples living eastward from the lake.

The supposed Indonesian element

One last ethnic element, not directly present in the interior, nevertheless had a major economic impact in the longer run, and that was the Indonesian element. Arriving at the coast via the Indian Ocean sea lanes sometime around the third to the sixth centuries of the Christian era, the pre-Malgache found a more permanent place for themselves elsewhere, through their subsequent settlement of Madagascar. But they may have brought with them part of the South-east Asian crop complex, eminently suited to several of the local climates of East Africa. The most important of the new crops was the banana, which in time proved especially adaptable to warmer highland climes. Other crops, all of which like the banana needed substantial rainfall (or else irrigation), included Asian yams, taro and sugar-cane. Rice was presumably introduced also by the pre-Malgache but, unlike the other crops, did not apparently spread much beyond the coastal belt until the nineteenth century.[38]

Ethnic processes

The persistence in the seventh to eleventh centuries of trends already established in the first six centuries of the Christian era can be depicted from a variety of standpoints.

From the geographical point of view, the various Bantu-speaking societies remained mostly within the relatively restricted ecological bounds of their Early Iron Age settlement areas, although they must have continued to expand their numbers within those zones and to extend their effective use of the potentialities of those spheres, probably clearing more forest, for instance, in the highland zones and spreading to the limits of the suitable environments outside the highlands. The linguistic evidence also indicates growth by a continuing process of assimilation of non-Bantu-speaking groups in a number of areas. In north-eastern Tanzania, for example, a

36. B. Heine, 1981.
37. M. N. Cali, 1980.
38. C. Ehret, forthcoming.

considerable component of Old Ma'a-speakers was apparently incorporated into proto-Seuta society as part of the expansion of Seuta territories in the Ngulu Mountains and Uzigula.[39]

Differences and distinctions among Bantu societies continued to grow, too. All the Bantu of East Africa at the beginning of the Christian era spoke dialects of a single Eastern Bantu language. In the seventh century the mutual intelligibility of the various Bantu dialects must have widely been coming to an end, and by the eleventh century the process of differentiation had proceeded to such an extent that a goodly number of separate languages could be distinguished – the North-east-Coastal language, itself consisting of four distinct dialects or dialect groups: Seuta, Sabaki, Ruva and Asu; Lacustrine of the central Great Lakes region, with at least three dialects so distinct already as to be close to separate languages; the Takama language, again with several dialects spoken by communities living somewhere to the south of Lake Victoria; the proto-Gusii-Kuria language along the south-eastern side of the lake; proto-Luyia-Gisu of the north-eastern shores; Thagicu, probably the language of the makers of Gatung'ang'a ware of Mount Kenya; proto-Taita-Chaga, spoken by the fashioners of Maore ware in North Pare, Kilimanjaro and the Taita Hills, with three dialects, two of them spoken in the Taita area; and the several languages of far southern Tanzania.[40] The Sabaki and Ruvu divisions of North-east-Coastal Bantu were themselves already diverging into groups of dialects before the eleventh century. The original Sabaki society had broken up into proto-Swahili, proto-Pokomo, proto-Mijikenda, and Elwana societies, while the spread of some Ruvu-speakers inland toward present-day Ukagulu had led to the emergence of separate East and West Ruvu peoples.

The split-up of the Taita-Chaga into three societies can also be laid to population movement in these centuries. The proto-Taita-Chaga people are believed to have been among the early makers of Maore pottery, which appears in the North Pare Mountains in the latter part of the first millennium of the Christian era.[41] The first split of the Taita-Chaga group involved a movement of a small set of people into the Taita Hills at some point late in the millennium; their dialect of Taita-Chaga developed into the present Saghala language. A subsequent period of movement from North Pare to Taita brought a second Taita-Chaga dialect, the ancestor of modern Dawida, into the region. Both sets of Bantu immigrants entered into a long period of cultural interchange with the Mbisha, the Rift Cushitic people already resident in and around the hills.[42] The remaining Taita-Chaga inhabitants of North Pare developed directly into the proto-Chaga of the beginning of the present millennium, the descendants of whom

39. C. Ehret, 1974a, p. 13.
40. See also Unesco, *General History of Africa*, Vol. IV, ch. 19.
41. C. Ehret and D. Nurse, 1981b.
42. ibid.

would become the focal point of social and economic reorganization of the Kilimanjaro region in later centuries.[43]

Significant movements of Bantu-speaking people appear to have taken place in the Great Lakes region also in the second half of the first millennium of the Christian era and brought about a considerable expansion of the territories inhabited by Lacustrine societies. The original Lacustrine society probably took shape among the Early Iron Age Bantu settlers in the then heavily forested areas along the western and south-western shore of Lake Victoria. They were presumably the makers of the kind of Urewe pottery known from Bukoba and prominently associated there with impressive early iron-working sites. Their ethnic neighbourhood at the turn of the era had included Southern Cushites, probably the Rift peoples who had spread as far as the southern side of Lake Victoria, and Central Sudanians, from whose language the Lacustrine word for 'cow', among others, came. Some outward movement of Lacustrine people had already taken place by the first centuries of the Christian era, implanting the Lacustrine dialects from which the Rwanda-Ha and Konjo languages would in time evolve in areas to the west, near the great Western Rift Valley that marks the divide between the Congo and Victoria basins. A second period of outward movement, which linguistic evidence places a bit before the middle of the first millennium, spread people of Lacustrine background to the north of Lake Victoria. The causes of these outward movements may be connected to over-use of the environment, through growth of population and so of agricultural demands on the soils and perhaps most importantly through over-clearing of forest to make charcoal for iron-smelting, an early specialization of the region amply attested in the archaeology.[44] It is with this second period of expansion that the divergence of the remaining Great Lakes society into separate Rutara and Ganda-Soga sets of communities began, apparently by movement away of considerable numbers of people who spread north around the north-western and northern side of the lake, incorporating pre-existing Central Sudanic communities and in the process developing into the distant forebears of the present-day Ganda and Soga populations. The Rutara society evolved among those who stayed on, probably in reduced numbers, in the areas in and about the Bukoba region.[45]

A final period of outward movement from the areas along the west of Lake Victoria began probably toward the very end of the period covered in this volume. It involved the expansion of Rutara language and culture north-westward into the regions that would one day become Nkore, Mpororo, and Bunyoro. That movement of ideas and practices is likely to have marked the inception of the era of the 'Bachwezi', a period only dimly and fabulously remembered in the later oral traditions, but one in which

43. See Unesco, *General History of Africa*, Vol. IV, ch. 19.
44. D. Schoenbrun, 1984; M. C. van Grunderbeck *et al.*, 1983a, 1983b.
45. ibid.

the key political ideas and economic structures of the later kingdoms first began to be put into effect.

The grasslands and high plains of the central interior of East Africa continued throughout the period to be predominantly inhabited by speakers of Nilotic and Cushitic languages, but apparently with the territories of Southern Nilotes increasing and those of Southern Cushites greatly declining. The Dadoga took shape probably during those centuries, as a society of especially but not entirely, pastoral economy in the areas extending from the west side of the Rift Valley of far southern Kenya to the northern and central Maasai plains of Tanzania.[46] They expanded, it appears, at the expense of peoples closely related in language to the Old Asa and Old Kw'adza.[47] In central Maasailand they coexisted with specialized hunter-gatherer communities who were to maintain the East Rift language called Asa (not to be confused with the Bantu language Asu) down to recent decades.[48] Other Tato Southern Nilotes inhabited the fine grazing lands immediately south of the Mau forest. One Bantu society, ancestral to the Sonjo, appears to have found a niche for itself in the midst of the Tato speech area, since the modern Sonjo language contains loanwords attributable to early Dagoga contacts. Presumably they persisted as a separate factor in the history of the region by pursuing irrigation agriculture along the Rift escarpment like their more recent descendants.[49]

The proto-Kalenjin society came into being among the Southern Nilotes who lived north of the Mau. The evolution of the society in the centuries before 1000 involved a long-term incorporation of Southern Cushitic peoples.[50] A notable Bantu element was also incorporated, principally, it would appear, through the practice of Kalenjin men marrying wives from a society speaking an early version of the Luyia-Gisu language.[51] From the end of the first millennium the Kalenjin began to expand over considerable new territory, from Mount Elgon in the north-west as far as the southern Nyandarua range and the Rift Valley areas of central and southern Kenya. One notable development of this era of expansion was the adoption of Kalenjin speech by the remaining hunter-gatherer bands of the forested areas adjoining the Rift and also within the Mau forests. Other Kalenjin expansions carried westward into the modern-day Luyia-speaking land south of Mount Elgon where both Bantu and Southern Cushitic communities had apparently previously been established.[52]

Another region of significant ethnic realignment in the period before

46. C. Ehret, 1971, pp. 55–7.
47. A large set of East Rift loanwords occurs in Dadog. East Rift is the sub-group of Southern Cushitic to which Asa and Kw'adza belong.
48. C. Ehret, 1974a, pp. 14–15.
49. C. Ehret, 1971, p. 55.
50. ibid., p. 48.
51. C. Ehret, 1976, p. 13.
52. C. Ehret, 1971, pp. 50–1.

1100 can be discerned, and that was northern Uganda. To the west of the region the Madi, a Central Sudanic people, expanded across the areas on the east and north-east of Lake Edward, becoming a not insignificant element among the peoples of western Uganda who were absorbed into the expanding Northern Rutara society during the first half of the second millennium.[53] Other Madi were to remain the major people of central northern Uganda down to the era of Luo expansion at mid-millennium.[54]

On the eastern side of northern Uganda the major society in the seventh century was that of the Western Kuliak, who occupied the lands from mounts Moroto and Napak in the south to the modern Sudan border on the north. By 1000 or thereabouts Western Kuliak unity had broken down in the face of the intrusion of the Ateker, an Eastern Sudanic-speaking people, into the heart of the region. The frequency of Western Kuliak loanwords in Ateker vocabulary indicates that this expansion was accomplished by a very extensive incorporation of erstwhile Kuliak people into the early Ateker society.[55] How far this process had proceeded by the eleventh and twelfth centuries is unclear. The remaining Kuliak were probably at that time, however, still a numerically significant element of the population and not yet entirely restricted to mountainous redoubts as they are today.

The Ateker settlers whose arrival in eastern Uganda set off the process of ethnic shift there apparently came out of the block of Eastern Nilotic peoples living in those centuries in the far southern Sudan, just northward of the present-day Uganda boundary. In the early first millennium of the Christian era this population was composed of the cultural and linguistic forebears of the Bari and Lotuko clusters of peoples, who still reside in some of those areas today, and of the proto-Maa-Ongamo as well as the Ateker. At the same period the ancestors of the Didinga-Murle peoples lived apparently to the immediate north-east of the Eastern Nilotes, also on the plains of the far southern Sudan. They had an early influence on the Ateker before the Ateker expansion southward into eastern Uganda,[56] but did not directly intrude into events in northern Uganda till later eras, after 1100. Another set of peoples of importance in much later eras of East African history, the Luo, resided just north of the Eastern Nilotes in the seventh to eleventh centuries, but to the west apparently of the pre-Didinga-Murle, in parts of the Sudd regions near and to the east of the Nile River in the southern Sudan.

The most notable departure from these trends of gradual ethnic shift and progressive expansion of communities was the appearance of a wholly new ethnic element on the central East African scene, the Maa-Ongamo. (The Maa, who include the modern Maasai, are not to be confused with

53. This is suggested by the presence of Madi loanwords in the northern Rutara dialects.
54. See Unesco, *General History of Africa*, Vol. IV, ch. 20.
55. C. Ehret, 1982b, p. 25.
56. G. J. Dimmendaal, 1982.

the *Ma'a*, a Southern Cushitic people discussed above!). From an origin point near the Lotuko area of far southern Sudan, the proto-Maa-Ongamo society spread south toward the Baringo and Laikipia regions, north and north-west of Mount Kenya, by about the eighth century of the Christian era. Their initial southward expansion appears to have incorporated many of the Baz, the Lowland Eastern Cushites who previously inhabited the Turkana basin.[57] South of Baringo and in Laikipia the formerly dominant communities were probably Southern Nilotic and Southern Cushitic in language.[58] A significant Southern Nilotic impact is apparent on proto-Maa-Ongamo culture, notably in the Maa-Ongamo adoption of circumcision and the long, oval Southern Nilotic style of shield.[59] Once in the Mount Kenya region, the proto-Maa-Ongamo then split in relatively short order into two societies. The Maa proper came to dominate the Baringo basin and Laikipia and continued to be strongly influenced by their Kalenjin neighbours on the south and west.[60] The Old Ongamo spread south, through the Rift and perhaps the gap between Mount Kenya and the Nyandarua range, to concentrate in the plains of the Kilimanjaro and Pare Mountain region,[61] where they influenced the livestock-raising side of life among the Taita-Chaga peoples who lived there in the late first millennium. In the early part of the present millennium the Ongamo began to be absorbed in significant numbers into the proto-Chaga society.

Economic activities

In the economy, too, the patterns of activity established in the early centuries of the first millennium of the Christian era still greatly constrained the directions of change in the period of the seventh to eleventh centuries.

One notable effect was the strong correlation which continued to obtain between ethnicity and the type of food production practised. Southern Nilotes had immigrated into western Kenya a thousand years before as mostly pastoral people with some cultivation of grains. From the kinds of locations the Tato and Kalenjin peoples favoured and from the kinds of word-borrowing between them and their neighbours,[62] it appears that in general their subsistence strategies had not yet greatly changed even as late as 1000. The spread of the Maa-Ongamo, who were Eastern Nilotes, into

57. C. Ehret, 1974a, pp. 40–1; B. Heine, F. Rottland and R. Vossen, 1979.

58. C. Ehret, 1971, pp. 52–4, places this settlement further south than now seems probable. The Southern Cushitic loanword set in Maa has not yet been given the careful study it deserves, and its extinct source language is therefore of uncertain placement in the Southern Cushitic group.

59. C. Ehret, 1971, p. 53.

60. C. Ehret, 1971, pp. 74–5, 166–71, conflates evidence of these contacts with evidence of a later contact situation, for which see Unesco, *General History of Africa*, Vol. IV, ch. 19.

61. C. Ehret, 1974a, pp. 40–1; R. Vossen, 1978.

62. C. Ehret, 1971, pp. 144–62.

central parts of East Africa only reinforced the tendency for Nilotic speech to be associated with cattle-raising and the cultivation of grains as staples. With such an economy the Nilotes understandably came into direct conflict for land with the more pastoral of the Southern Cushites, and successful Southern Nilotic expansion often meant the incorporation of formerly dominant Cushite communities. For the same reason, the Maa-Ongamo spread in its turn incorporated Southern Nilotes.

Bantu-speaking societies remained largely the practitioners of a different type of farming, planting agriculture, so called because its major crops are not reproduced from seed but from parts of the cultigen itself which are planted in the earth. The Bantu societies also knew of and sowed a variety of seed crops, including sorghum and, in highland areas, finger millet, and often kept cattle.[63] But until very late in the first millennium, African varieties of yam, the ancient staple of West African planting agriculture, probably continued to be a pre-eminent food source nearly everywhere among the Bantu of interior East Africa. The early successful crops of the South-east Asian complex were also planted cultigens needful of considerable rainfall. Including Asian yams, taro, and bananas among others, the crops must have been taken up with particular ease by Bantu-speaking societies, by reason both of their climatic situations and their prior acquaintance with planting agriculture. The addition of the crops could only have added to the success of the Bantu economies and helped put off significant change in agricultural strategies.

There were some exceptions to these broad tendencies. The Sonjo have been mentioned as a Bantu community that used extensive irrigation and manuring to cultivate a variety of crops on otherwise marginal land. The pattern they followed was one of probable Southern Cushitic inspiration, and their adoption of that pattern of life may well date back before 1100. On the escarpment of the Kerio Valley of central Kenya several small communities, by 1100 speaking the particular varieties of early Kalenjin that have developed into the present-day Marakwet dialects, may similarly have been irrigating as well as manuring their lands and living primarily by intensive cultivation rather than by livestock-raising. And in parts of Tanzania in the period 600–1100 could be found Bantu societies that must have placed a proportionately much greater reliance on grains and other seed crops than on yams. One of these was the West Ruvu community, which by splitting off to the west late in the period moved into higher and drier lands, probably in the Kagulu area of east-central Tanzania, suited to cattle-raising as well as grain crops. A possibly older Bantu adaptation to drier conditions was that of the proto-Takama, from whose language Kimbu, Nyamwezi-Sukuma, Rimi (Nyaturu), and Iramba derive. Their earliest settlement areas may have been near or to the west or north-west of the Wembere River of west-central Tanzania. In that case yams would

63. C. Ehret, 1974b.

have been a successful crop only in areas of wet soils, such as along the Wembere itself, and the development of greater reliance on grain crops would therefore have been essential to the early Takama expansions – a development already beginning, it appears, by the eleventh century.[64]

In one case the unfolding of previous trends in subsistence led to the emergence of a truly new approach, highland planting agriculture, which combined existing crops and practices into the most productive system yet devised in East Africa. The new staple was the banana. Knowledge of the banana had clearly diffused well inland by the later second half of the first millennium of the Christian era, apparently via the Pare region as far as Mount Kenya, for the same root word for the plant turns up in Taita-Chaga and in Thagicu and was borrowed from the proto-Thagicu language by the proto-Maa-Ongamo of the Mount Kenya region, by or before the tenth century.[65] But it was in the Pare Mountains that the transition to a mature form of the highland planting agriculture apparently took place, close to the turn of the millennium. The Dawida, who had split from the proto-Chaga and left North Pare to settle the Taita Hills around perhaps the tenth or eleventh century, continued into recent times to give priority to the yam. In contrast, the proto-Chaga of the same centuries developed a very complex system of terms for bananas and banana cultivation, attesting to the contemporaneous supplanting of the yam by the banana as their primary item of diet. What made highland planting agriculture of north-eastern Tanzania so especially productive was the systematic use of irrigation and animal manure. Procedures of cultivation of Southern Cushitic source were applied to a crop of South-east Asian origin by peoples of an already planting-agricultural tradition. It can hardly be a coincidence that the spreading out of the Chaga speech community all around the east and south sides of Kilimanjaro can be placed in the immediately succeeding centuries.

Knowledge of bananas did not enter the East African interior only from the Kenya or northern Tanzania coast, however, and in fact that direction would have to be considered a relatively minor source. The linguistic evidence also depicts a separate spread of bananas into the Great Lakes region directly from the south, ultimately from Malawi and the Zambezi basin, as part and parcel of a much wider spread of the new crop from the lower Zambezi region, through the Congo basin, and all across West Africa. It is this wider spread of the banana that has been given recognition so far in the studies of the botanists.[66] The southerly introduction of the plant, via the wetter far western fringes of East Africa, probably brought knowledge of the crop to the Great Lakes Bantu and to peoples of Mount Elgon well

64. See also Unesco, *General History of Africa*, Vol. IV, ch. 19.

65. Proto-Chaga-Dawida *maruu, Proto-Thagicu *marigo, and proto-Maa-Ongamo *mariko.

66. Note especially N. W. Simmonds, 1962; also J. Barrau, 1962. (Note by co-editor: J. Barrau now has a somewhat different opinion).

before 1000. Similar developments of something approaching the highland planting agriculture of north-eastern Tanzania eventually emerged in several regions where bananas could be fruitfully cultivated, among them the Mount Elgon region, from whence it probably spread later to Busoga and Buganda,[67] the Bukoba area, and the region far to the south, at the north end of Lake Malawi. But the innovation of intensive banana cultivation seems in each such case a solution independently arrived at, encouraged by similar needs to expand food production capacities in comparable environmental conditions, and arising, except possibly in the instance of Mount Elgon, later in time than the Chaga case, usually in the eras since 1100.

The trend toward the supplanting of stone tool technology by iron-working continued throughout the period of the seventh to eleventh centuries. Metals seem to have entered the interior of East Africa from two directions at the turn of the era, from the west or north-west via the Great Lakes region and from the east coast. The Bantu communities of settlement of the beginning of the first millennium of the Christian era apparently frequently included iron-workers among them, and knowledge of iron-making seems also to have diffused around the north of Mount Elgon as far as the Southern Nilotic peoples west of the Rift Valley, perhaps almost as early.[68] In northern Tanzania, some of the Southern Cushites appear to have known of iron as early as the period of Bantu settlement.[69] Their acquaintance with metals is likely to have come from the Indian Ocean seaboard where traders from the Near East were bartering iron by no later than the first or second century.[70] But iron-working was slow to establish itself in the central interior. In many areas it may have long remained a rare commodity, used in ornamentation but too valuable to waste on tools. Only in the period of the eighth to tenth centuries did the Elmenteitan tool tradition, presumed to be the work of central Kenyans of Southern Nilotic speech, finally collapse and disappear, at a time when new iron-using immigrants, the Maa-Ongamo, were making their presence felt. Among West Rift people of northern Tanzania, iron-working may possibly be similarly late in fully supplanting stone tool technology. But by 1100 stone tools must have been relative rarities almost everywhere in the East African interior, except possibly in drier portions of the Ruaha basin of south-eastern Tanzania and in parts of western Tanzania where hunter-gatherers may have remained in possession for some centuries longer.

For most times and places between 600 and 1100 trade was an enterprise irregularly engaged in and serving to fill special limited needs, such as for food in a famine year, or to dispose of occasional surpluses, as of ostrich

67. See also Unesco, *General History of Africa*, Vol. IV, ch. 19.

68. C. Ehret, 1971, p. 44, suggests this dating.

69. This is indicated by the fact that some key words for iron and iron-working in Taita-Chaga, Sonjo, and Thagicu are Southern Cushitic loanwords; see C. Ehret, unpublished (b).

70. The *Periplus of the Erythraean Sea* describes this trade.

eggshells collected by hunter-gatherers and used by many peoples for making beads. Certain recurring patterns of exchange existed: for instance, the export of obsidian from producing areas in central Kenya, where it was still being used for Elmenteitan stone blades as late as the eighth or ninth centuries, and the trading of cowry shells inland from the east coast.[71] But such exchanges passed progressively from community to neighbouring community without significant long-distance carriage of goods and without regular markets or merchants.

Only one occupational specialization, blacksmithing, existed in the seventh century. It would not have been an occupation universally found in interior East African societies, and many communities would have traded for their iron and so might only distantly have been acquainted with smelting or even forging until later centuries.

An additional specialized occupation may have arisen in about the eighth and ninth centuries when ethnic pottery distinctions partially broke down in the central Kenyan areas inhabited by Southern Nilotes and the intruding Maa-Ongamo communities. Thereafter a single kind of pottery, Lanet ware, began to be used by a number of Nilotic-speaking groups.[72] It seems probable that it was at this point in time that potting began to be, as it has remained, a specialized occupation followed principally by hunter-gatherers of the Rift and Mau. The resulting increase in hunter-gatherer dependence on exchange relations with Nilotes may help to explain why the subsequent proto-Kalenjin expansion after 1000 was accompanied by a general adoption of Kalenjin speech by food collectors all around the Rift.

As noted previously, a trade in pottery also probably existed between North Pare and Kilimanjaro, the sellers being Bantu communities and the buyers most probably the Old Asa who lived about Kilimanjaro in those eras. Potting in Pare and among the Rift Valley hunters would have been, however, a part-time occupation of people who for the most part were engaged in supplying their own household needs. The existence of specialization did not thus lead immediately to the appearance of institutionalized and regular markets, but it may have led to the establishment in several areas of central East Africa of particular locations where people habitually went to seek out needed goods. Between Kilimanjaro and the North Pare region, which was a major area of manufacture of both iron and pots,[73] the process may have gone even further, toward the setting up of actual regular markets by the early second millennium.[74]

Social organization

A universal characteristic of the societies of the East African interior from

71. S. H. Ambrose, 1982. C. Ehret, 1971, p. 98.
72. S. H. Ambrose, 1982.
73. Cf. I. N. Kimambo, 1969, ch. 4 and elsewhere.
74. L. J. Wood and C. Ehret, 1978.

the seventh to the eleventh centuries was the smallness of scale of both residential and political units, despite a notable variety in the principles of social organization followed by different peoples. The commercial conditions that were conducive on the coast to the development of towns were lacking in the interior; the economic base capable of supporting large polities apparently was also missing.

The most common residential unit of the northern interior was a neighbourhood of dispersed homesteads. It was an old pattern going back to the eras of early Southern Cushitic settlement and also characteristic of the Southern Nilotic settlers of the last millennium before the Christian era. The Bantu immigrants at the turn of the era had come out of a background where village life had been the rule, but the spread of Bantu speech did not necessarily lead to the establishment of villages. Where Bantu settlement had encountered and absorbed significant Cushitic or Nilotic communities, the older pattern of habitation tended to persevere, as for instance in the Kenya highlands and parts of northern Tanzania. Farther south, however, villages were the common residential theme among Bantu-speakers.

Southern Cushitic societies seem usually to have been composed of autonomous clans, each with a recognized clan headman. Among early Bantu settlers a similar pattern, of a clan headed by a hereditary clan chief, can be reconstructed as typical.[75] But it seems probable that Bantu clan chiefship was an actively political position, with responsibilities in most areas of community life, whereas the Cushitic clan headman may principally have been concerned with presiding over the allotment of land, a commodity easily supplied in those days of much lesser population densities. The frequent dropping out of use of the old root word for chief (**-kumu*)[76] in Bantu languages of the East African interior suggests that the chiefly role must often have been greatly modified over the course of cultural assimilation between Bantu and non-Bantu even though an Eastern Bantu language might become the language of the new society. The dating of this kind of development is generally unclear, but some instances of it probably fit in the period between 600 and 1100. The Thagicu clan head (Gikuyu *muramati*), for example, looks rather more like a variation of the Southern Cushitic pattern than a derivation from the Bantu prototype.[77] Since the institution goes back to the period before 1100 among the Thagicu, it may well be an element of continuity deriving from the Gumba side of the Thagicu background and reflecting the social interactions between Southern Cushites and Bantu-speakers on Mount Kenya in those centuries.

In two cases there arose among the Eastern Bantu communities a new kind of chiefly position in which the chief was not tied to a single clan but ruled over a territory inhabited by people of different clan affiliations. The

75. J. Vansina, 1971, p. 263, thinks the kin tie was looser than that postulated here.
76. It becomes *-fumu* and refers to 'diviners' rather than to 'chiefs'; see below.
77. G. Muriuki, 1974, p. 75.

earliest example of such a development, among the Great Lakes people, probably took place before the times this chapter is directly concerned with. Already in the proto-Great Lakes language, spoken no later than the very start of our era, the original Bantu root word for 'chief' had come to apply instead to the doctor-diviner (the so-called 'witch-doctor'), and a different word was applied to the political head of the society. A plausible explanation is that a new stratum of chiefship had emerged in the proto-Great Lakes society and that the older petty chiefs had been relegated for the most part to religious-cum-medical roles, a pattern of political change not unknown in the later history of the Great Lakes region.[78] The economic basis for a larger-scale chiefship existed at and before the turn of the era in the form of control over primary access to the newly important material, iron. It was in just those areas along the west of Lake Victoria, where the proto-Great Lakes people are believed to have resided, that a particularly highly developed iron-smelting industry had arisen in the second half of the last millennium before the Christian era.[79] In the multi-ethnic contact situation in which the proto-Great Lakes people lived, the new class of chiefs could have further enhanced their positions by acting as adjudicators between kin groups of different ethnicity and hence becoming the foci for the integration of peoples of Central Sudanic, Southern Cushitic and Great Lakes background into one society.[80] The possession of such an institution may go far to explain the continuing success of Great Lakes expansion at several points in the first millennium.

It is possible, however, that by the time of the Rutara expansion early in the second millennium a new basis for chiefly (and even kingly) power, capable potentially of supporting a considerably larger-scale political unit, was taking hold in the western Great Lakes region. That basis was chiefly or royal power over the access to and redistribution of surpluses in cattle.[81] The first emergence of really large polities based on such a political economy apparently lies in the succeeding eras after 1100.[82]

The second development of territorial chiefship in the period before the twelfth century took place on a very small scale among the proto-Chaga of the start of the second millennium of the Christian era, apparently coincident with the emergence of the mature highland planting agriculture. The characteristic social development of this era in North Pare and parts of Kilimanjaro, strongly apparent from the linguistic sources, was the incorporation of sizeable groups of Old Asa and Old Ongamo into the proto-

78. I. Berger, 1981, sees something of this nature as occurring in the rise of the Lakes region states of recent centuries.

79. P. R. Schmidt, 1978, p. 278 and elsewhere.

80. As A. Southall, 1954 has shown to be the case in the more recent example of the Alur of the northwestern Lakes region.

81. This hypothesis was suggested already by C. Ehret *et al.*, in an unpublished paper of 1972 and independently proposed on different evidence by I. Berger, 1981.

82. See Unesco, *General History of Africa*, Vol. IV, ch. 20.

Chaga society. It can be suggested that the highland planting system gave a decisive productive advantage to the earliest Chaga and so set off Chaga expansion, and that chiefship took on its new form because the chiefly role provided an integrative focus for the assimilation of people of different ethnic and hence different kin affiliations. The new sort of chiefdom thus produced must have been significantly larger in population than the typical clan unit of the previous times, but still quite tiny in comparison with East African kingdoms of recent centuries and probably smaller than the typical lacustrine chiefdom of the same era.

The largest scale of potential social and political co-operation was probably not reached, however, by the societies of the East African interior which had hereditary leaders during those centuries, but rather by Southern Nilotes and Maa-Ongamo peoples. The age-set institutions of these communities, different in their particular structures but alike in their social effects, drew together all the young men from all the neighbourhoods of homesteads over a wide area. The limits of recruitment into a particular named age set tended to be defined by the limits of the society. By belonging to a common age set, men from distant areas gained a basis for co-operating in raiding other peoples when young and for keeping peace with one another in their maturity. Possession of such institutions probably helps to explain why Nilotic language and Nilotic ethnic identity tended to supplant Southern Cushitic over the long run. When conflict arose, or when other troubles such as famine struck, the Nilotes had, at least potentially, a wider group of people from whom support might be sought.

In this connection the disappearance of age organization among many of the Bantu of eastern Africa, and of circumcision also, becomes an interesting problem. In the interior regions the Early Iron Age settlers, as linguistic reconstruction clearly shows, circumcised their boys and formed them into age sets,[83] although these were probably locally recruited and lacked the formality of structure and range of social roles possessed by the comparable institutions among the Nilotic-speakers. Yet the several Bantu societies of the first millennium in southern Tanzania – which often preserved older features of culture lost farther north, such as matrilineal descent and clan chiefship – nevertheless dropped circumcision and age grouping at undetermined but probably quite early times in their histories. Circumcision tended rather to be preserved only where there were neighbouring Southern Cushitic and Southern Nilotic societies, who also had this practice; and age institutions tended to persist among Bantu-speakers in northern areas of the interior where reinforcement by Nilotic example can be detected.

83. Proto-Eastern Bantu had the roots *-al- (*-aluk-, *-alik-, *-alam-) and *-tiin- (retained in Chaga, Seuta, and known also in Mongo of Zaire) for 'to circumcise'; the old Bantu root *-kula for age set has lasted down to today only in Gusii-Kuria and Luyia-Gisu in East Africa, but is also known from some north-western Bantu languages (it was wrongly explained by C. Ehret, 1976, p. 19, n. 33).

In some cases this kind of influence could be quite strong and had its most significant impact during the period from the seventh to the eleventh centuries. One set of examples are the generation-set systems of the Thagicu peoples of Mount Kenya, for which a partially Southern Nilotic inspiration, dating at the latest to proto-Thagicu times, must be presumed.[84] A second notable case is that of the Chaga, whose age-set ideas show a major Maa-Ongamo contribution, probably specifically from the Old Ongamo during the proto-Chaga period at the turn of the millennium.[85] In Chaga society the control of the transformed age institutions passed into the hand of the new kind of local, non-clan chief, who used it for defence and as a source of labour, whereas on Mount Kenya generation sets became the focus of political activity and the basis for wider area co-operation in a group of societies lacking hereditary political roles. What can be suggested is that age sets served no compelling need in more southerly areas where only sparse hunter-gatherer populations greeted Bantu settlement. Farther north, however, the age-grouping practices of neighbouring food producers reinforced or led to modification of the ideas of Bantu-speakers; and, in particular, the adoption of Nilotic models sometimes provided effective new means of incorporating non-Bantu into Bantu societies and of coping with the pressures, in the later first and very early second millennia, of new Nilotic expansions.

Religious systems

Most peoples of the period of the seventh to eleventh centuries followed one or the other of two major religious systems.

Across much of the Kenya interior and south through central Tanzania there prevailed the belief in a single Divinity, usually identified metaphorically with the sky. The existence of evil was understood in this religion to derive usually from divine retribution or judgment.[86] Ancestor spirits were not significant objects of religious concern. Versions of the religion among Cushitic-speaking peoples sometimes added a belief in lesser spirits capable of harm, and some of the rift Southern Cushites had developed a different celestial metaphor, linking Divinity to the sun rather than to the sky in general. This latter variety of the religion had been adopted some centuries before the turn of the era by the Southern Nilotic ancestors of the Tato and the Kalenjin.

84. C. Ehret, 1971, p. 43.

85. The age set system closely resembles that of the Maa, but cannot specifically be derived from the Maasai; hence we are left with the earlier Maa-Ongamo contact, that between Old Ongamo and early Chaga, as an alternative source of the influence; or else the Chaga system retains the older Bantu system modified by Ongamo example.

86. For a detailed description of one variety of this religion, see E. E. Evans-Pritchard, 1956.

In much of the southern half of the East African interior and through much of the Great Lakes region, a different religion prevailed. Brought in by Bantu settlers at the start of the Early Iron Age, this set of beliefs recognized the existence of a creator God, but its primary religious observances were directed toward the ancestors. Evil was attributed most often to human malice and envy: to the work of persons called, in European translations of the African names for them, 'witches' or 'sorcerers'. In the Lakes region there eventually arose an additional stratum of spirit belief. Spirits of higher status and farther-reaching influence than one's ancestors are now widely turned to by supplicants in that region. This level of religious practice may go back to proto-Lacustrine times at the turn of the era,[87] but it seems probable that it began to take on pre-eminent importance only during the second millennium, as the religious counterpart of, and often reaction to, the growth of political scale in later eras.

In the central East African interior where both religions were practised, the trend of the past two thousand years has been toward blending the elements of the two philosophies. A couple of significant manifestations of this trend belong to the period from the seventh to the eleventh centuries. In western Kenya the idea of the ancestors as an important focus of religious observance diffused, presumably from the pre-Luyia-Gisu, eastward to the pre-Kalenjin during that era, and the concept of witchcraft had apparently become part of the Kalenjin explanation of evil by the end of the first millennium also.[88] In North Pare and adjoining areas of Kilimanjaro, the God-sun metaphor took hold in proto-Chaga religious thought at around the beginning of the second millennium.[89] The proto-Chaga incorporation of Old Asa people apparently added Southern Cushitic concepts of Divinity onto a still active concern for the ancestors, derived from the Bantu portion of the Chaga heritage, just as the contemporaneous assimilation of Old Ongamo people brought about a major modification of age organization in the society. But elsewhere the era does not seem to have been marked by great change in values or beliefs.

Conclusion

If in the East African interior, then, the half a millennium between 600 and 1100 was not an era of sweeping change, still it was a period marked by varied kinds of lesser change in different parts of the wider region. Varia-

87. I. Berger, 1981; P. R. Schmidt, 1978.

88. Cf. C. Ehret, 1971, p. 157. A systematic distinguishing of 'witchcraft' from other, more benign uses of medicine had developed in proto-Kalenjin vocabulary but cannot be reconstructed for the earlier proto-Southern Nilotic stage.

89. The use of the older Bantu word for 'sun' to name God is found throughout Chaga, whereas both Dawida and Saghala retain the older Eastern Bantu root word for God, *Mulungu. Hence the shift of metaphor arose only in proto-Chaga after the latest split, that of Dawida, had occurred.

tion in domestic economy continued largely to follow the ethnic and geographical distributions laid down in the first few centuries of our era; planting agriculture with some grain cultivation tended to be pursued by Bantu-speakers in better-watered and well-wooded lands, while different combinations of grain cultivation with livestock-raising were engaged in by Nilotes and Cushites in the drier northern and central zones. Hunter-gatherers of Khoisan language may still have had parts of western and south-eastern Tanzania almost entirely to themselves. But at the same time considerable transfer of non-material and even material culture between societies is evident; the beginning of economic specialization takes hold in some areas; and in a number of instances notable new amalgamations of peoples arose. The most striking instance, the melting of Nilotes, Southern Cushites, and Bantu into the proto-Chaga, created a truly new society that incorporated basic ideas and practices from each of the three cultural backgrounds. Chaga became the language of the new society, probably because it was the pre-Chaga-speakers who had pioneered the highland planting agriculture on which the Chaga economy rested.

A characteristic of the period was the marked insulation of the East African interior from the currents of change so prominent in the Indian Ocean. A few crops of Indonesian source, such as the banana, had begun spreading inland in the period preceding the seventh century, but no further significant additions to culture and livelihood seem to have come from that direction between the seventh and eleventh centuries. The highland planting agriculture that arose at about the tenth or eleventh century, surely in response to local conditions, indeed used the banana as its staple; but the agriculture itself was built up of ideas and practices of a much more ancient African provenance and owed nothing to contemporary Indian Ocean influences.

At the coast a major growth in commercial activities took place during approximately the ninth and tenth centuries. The direct East African participants in the expanding trade relations of the western Indian Ocean, we have every reason to presume, were the proto-Swahili, whom we can visualize as inhabitants of seaside settlements, most probably located along the northern Kenya and far southern Somali coasts. Merchants of the time extended their activities far south along the coast itself, as far apparently as the Limpopo River region, where already by the eleventh and twelfth centuries a kingdom, centred on the site of Mapungubwe, had begun to profit from the trade in Zimbabwe gold.[90] But commerce appears not at all to have penetrated the East African interior. A few shells reached far inland, passing by way of small-scale local exchanges from community to community; but apparently the East African hinterland offered nothing of interest to Indian Ocean commerce which was not also available within a few kilometres of the shore. Interior peoples on the whole were able to

90. T. N. Huffman, personal communication, July 1981.

supply their own perceived material needs throughout the period and for centuries still to come.

One other major development, of considerable long-range importance but less overtly visible in the East African interior, may have been underway during the second half of the first millennium. The more intensive exploitation of the land that is implied in the farming practices of most Bantu societies of that period suggests, namely, that Bantu-speaking areas had already begun to be areas of build-up of population. In the second millennium those areas increasingly became population reservoirs out of which many of the more significant population movements and most of the major currents of change were to flow.

23 Central Africa to the north of the Zambezi

D. W. PHILLIPSON

The start of the Iron Age

By the beginning of the period with which this chapter is primarily concerned, almost all the region under consideration was occupied by Early Iron Age peoples, many of whom may have been speakers of Bantu languages. In many areas, remnants of technologically distinct earlier populations continued to live alongside the Early Iron Age folk, from whom they may also have been differentiated linguistically.[1] The earlier phases of the Iron Age in this region have been described in an earlier volume of this History.[2] Here, it may be recalled that archaeologists now have reasonable confidence in grouping the Early Iron Age industries south of the equatorial forest into a single Industrial Complex. Archaeologists differ in their classification of the Early Iron Age industries: here it will be convenient to summarize the hierarchy of terms preferred by the present writer. The cultural entity as a whole is referred to as the *Early Iron Age Industrial Complex*; it is subdivided into an *eastern stream* and a *western stream*. On the basis of the typology of the various pottery wares, several geographically restricted *groups* are recognized within each stream (see Fig. 23.1). Each group is named, following the accepted practice of Africanist archaeologists, after the site at which its associated pottery was first recognized and described. The Early Iron Age within the territory of individual groups may, in certain cases, be further subdivided – this time chronologically – into sequential *phases*. It is necessary to reiterate that two streams may provisionally be recognized in the archaeological record of this complex, and that a certain correspondence may be observed between the expansion processes and the relative chronology of these streams on the one hand, and the linguistically reconstructed course of the spread of the Bantu languages on the other.[3] Both streams appear to be derived, at least in part, from the Urewe settlements of the interlacustrine

1. For a consideration of the processes of interaction between the two groups see S. F. Miller, 1969; also D. W. Phillipson, 1977a, ch. 10.
2. Cf. Unesco, *General History of Africa*, Vol. II, chs 21, 23, 25, 27 and 29.
3. D. W. Phillipson, 1976b, 1977a, ch. 8.

region during the closing centuries of the last millennium before the Christian era. The eastern stream's expansion may be shown to have begun around the second century of the Christian era with the inception of the Kwale-ware tradition in the coastal regions of Kenya and Tanzania: however, its main southward extension was not achieved until the fourth century, when Early Iron Age culture was brought to most parts of eastern sub-equatorial Africa as far to the south as the Transvaal and southern Mozambique. It was at this stage that Early Iron Age settlement of the eastern stream took place in the more easterly parts of the region which forms the subject of this chapter, i.e. in Malawi and in those parts of Zambia which lie to the east of the Luangwa River. A later expansion of the eastern stream, from a centre south of the Zambezi in what is now The Republic of Zimbabwe, took place in about the sixth century but affected only a very small part of our present region, the Victoria Falls area in the extreme south of Zambia.

The Early Iron Age of Natal and much of the southern Transvaal is best attributed, in the present writer's view, to the western stream. Indeed, it is to the western stream that the Early Iron Age of most of the region here discussed belongs. The archaeology of the western stream is for the most part far less well known than that of its counterpart further to the east. It has been suggested that the western stream arose, around the beginning of the Christian era, in the country south of the lower Congo, through the fusion or interaction of two distinct Bantu-speaking populations. One of these appears to have penetrated through the equatorial forests directly southward from the original centre of Bantu speech in what is now Cameroon. It is probably represented in the archaeological record by the so-called 'Leopoldian neolithic' of Lower Zaire, which has recently been reinvestigated by Pierre de Maret.[4] The second Bantu-speaking element appears, like the later eastern stream, to have been an offshoot of the Urewe settlements of the interlacustrine region. It may be demonstrated archaeologically by Urewe-type pottery once reported to have been found near Tshikapa in southern Kasai (unfortunately in a poorly documented and undated context),[5] as well as by the general Urewe affinities of the western-stream pottery tradition as a whole. Most probably it was by means of this southwards and westwards expansion around the forest fringes that domestic cattle and sheep, as well as cereal agriculture and, perhaps, knowledge of metallurgical techniques, were brought to the south-western savanna. These developments may have given rise to a southward expansion of Iron Age culture from Kongo country, through Angola into northern Namibia, accompanied by Bantu languages ancestral to such modern tongues as Moundu and Herero which Bernd Heine[6] has classified as the

4. P. de Maret, 1975.

5. J. Nenquin, 1959. It has, however, recently been shown that there is considerable doubt as to where this material was actually found.

6. B. Heine, 1973; B. Heine, H. Hoff and R. Vossen, 1977.

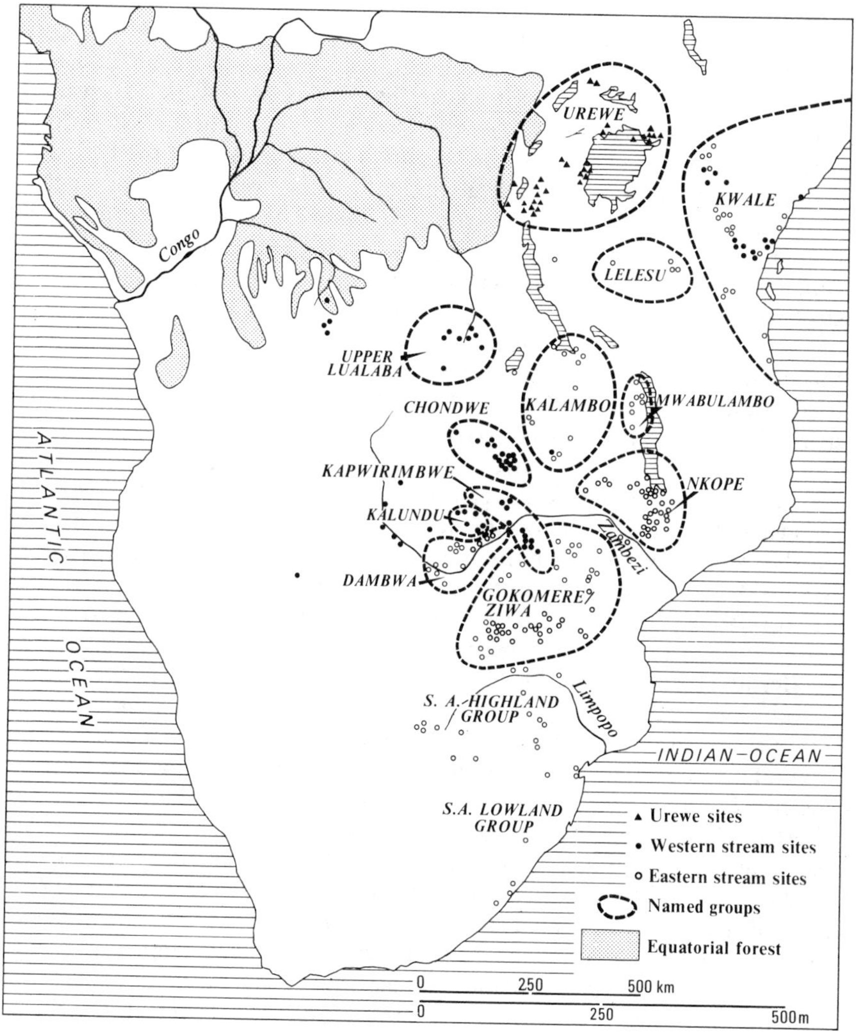

FIG. 23.1 *Archaeological cultures in eastern and southern Africa*

West Highland group. The only dated archaeological site that may be attributed to an early phase of this expansion is at Benfica, on the Atlantic coast near Luanda, where pottery showing strong affinity to that of the Early Iron Age of other western-stream areas occurs in a second century of the Christian context.[7] Moreover, certain elements of Early Iron Age culture, i.e. knowledge of pottery manufacture and the herding of sheep and cattle, appear to have been transmitted to the Khoisan-speakers of southern Namibia and the western Cape – far beyond the southernmost limit of Bantu penetration – by about the second or third century of the Christian era. Since it is hard to envisage a source for these innovations other than the western stream of the Early Iron Age, their date may be interpreted as providing a *terminus ante quem* for the latter's expansion into southern Angola.[8] Further details concerning the early expansion of the western stream are not yet available: such archaeological data as we have are attributed to the second half of the first millennium of the Christian era, and for the most part come from the eastern part of the western stream area – Shaba and western Zambia – where its advent appears to have been delayed until about the fifth or sixth century.

The outline presented above is not contradicted by such conclusions of comparative Bantu linguists as can be used to form the basis of a historical reconstruction of Bantu language development. Indeed, it has been argued by the present writer that the western stream's original dispersal from Kongo country to the south of the lower reaches of the Congo River may be correlated with a secondary centre of Bantu language dispersal which has been placed in just this area as a result of recent linguistic studies both by Bernd Heine and by David Dalby.[9] Their contention is that Bantu speech spread directly southwards from its Cameroonian homeland by either a coastal or a river route to the area that is now Lower Zaire. This would have been a movement quite independent from the one that brought another Bantu language along the northern fringes of the forest to the interlacustrine region. Those Bantu languages that have been spoken in recent times to the south of the equatorial forest all appear to be derived, directly or indirectly, from a centre of dispersal near Lower Zaire. The first stage of dispersal from this centre appears to have given rise to languages ancestral to those that Heine has named the Western Highland group, spoken today through highland Angola and southwards into northern Namibia. Further stages involved basically eastward dispersal, as will be described below.

To amplify this general outline it is necessary to present a summary of the archaeological evidence from these regions that appears to belong to this period of expansion by Bantu-speakers. It will be convenient to com-

7. J. R. dos Santos and C. M. N. Everdosa, 1970.

8. This argument is developed in D. W. Phillipson, 1977a, chs 6 and 10.

9. B. Heine, 1973; B. Heine, H. Hoff and R. Vossen, 1977; for alternative views, as well as a fuller statement of those held by the present writer, see L. Bouquiaux (ed.), 1980.

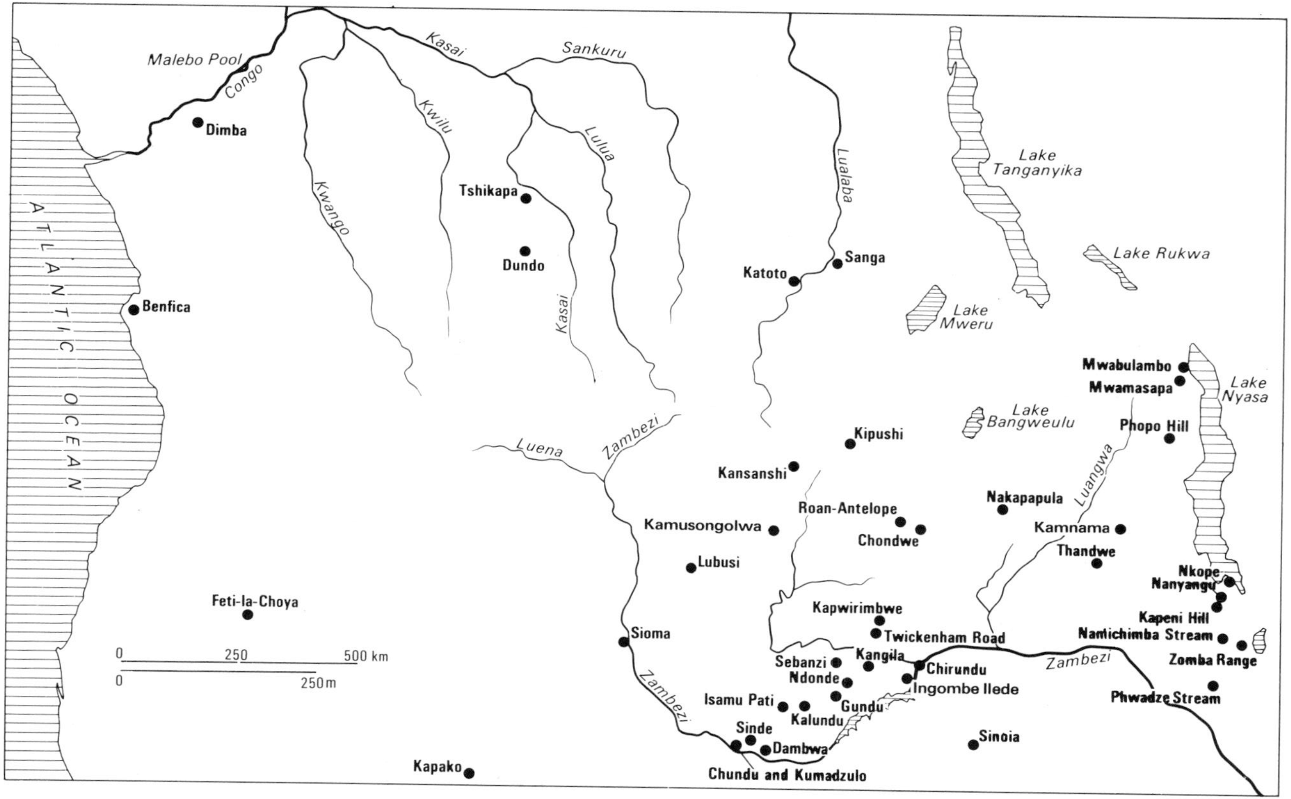

FIG. 23.2 *Archaeological sites in central Africa*

mence this overview in Lower Zaire and Angola and then to proceed eastwards.

The western stream of the Early Iron Age

Chronologically the earliest of the relevant prehistoric industries is that from Lower Zaire which has conventionally been known as the 'Leopoldian neolithic'. It is characterized by necked pottery vessels with elaborate grooved decoration which is reminscent of that seen on some Early Iron Age ceramics from other regions. No metal artefacts are associated with this pottery; instead there are abundant ground stone 'axes'. Several sites of this industry have recently been investigated by Pierre de Maret who has obtained carbon-14 dates that indicate an age in the last four centuries before the Christian era.[10] Material attributed to this industry is known from the Kinshasa area on the southern side of the Malebo (Stanley) Pool, and from there westwards to near the Atlantic seaboard, occurring mainly in the caves and rock-shelters of the province of Lower Zaire, although a few open-air occurrences have also been reported. Significantly, no trace of this industry has yet been discerned in the more open savanna country of northern Angola. This observation, coupled both with the apparently sudden appearance of ground stone artefacts in this one restricted part of a region where they are otherwise extremely rare, and also with the occurrence of comparable industries to the north of the forest, in West Africa and on the island of Fernando Poo,[11] lends support to the hypothesis that the 'Leopoldian neolithic' was introduced to the Lower Zaire region from an essentially northerly direction.

In other occurrences in Lower Zaire, for which absolute age determinations are not yet available, but which may be assumed to post-date the 'neolithic' material noted above, more varied pottery has been recovered which shows rather stronger similarities to that known in Early Iron Age contexts further to the east. In particular, affinities with the Urewe ware of the interlacustrine region seem to be much closer in this material, notably that from Dimba cave near Mbanza Ngungu, than they are in the 'Leopoldian neolithic'.[12] Further to the south, as noted above, pottery from Benfica also shows strong Early Iron Age affinities: it is dated to about the second century of the Christian era, and this would be a plausible date for the Lower Zaire material also.

Our knowledge of the Early Iron Age in regions of Angola further inland, and in the neighbouring Kasai Province of Zaire, is even more scanty. Near Tshikapa, close to Kasai's southern border, it has been claimed that mining operations in the Lupembe valley yielded four nearly complete pot-

10. P. de Maret, 1975.
11. A. Martin del Molino, 1965.
12. G. Mortelmans, 1962.

tery vessels that would not be out of place typologically in an assemblage of Urewe ware from the interlacustrine region.[13] It is unfortunate that the circumstances of this discovery are poorly recorded, and that there is no basis for estimating the absolute age of the context in which the pottery was preserved. Not far to the south, across the Angola border, two small collections of pottery from the Dundo area are dated to the last quarter of the first millennium of the Christian era.[14] The sherds differ markedly from the (presumably earlier) Tshikapa specimens, but nevertheless show several Early Iron Age typological features alongside characteristics that have continued into the modern pottery of northern Angola. Broadly contemporary sites are known, albeit poorly, from southern Angola and northern Namibia. By the seventh or eighth century, a substantial Iron Age settlement had been established at Feti la Choya, near the confluence of the Kunene and Kunyongauna rivers, but information about the associated artefacts that has been published is insufficiently detailed to enable us to evaluate its affinities. In the extreme north of Namibia, at Kapako close to the western end of the Caprivi Strip,[15] a site with traces of iron-working has yielded pottery that its excavator sees as related to other wares of the Early Iron Age's western stream, notably that from Kapwirimbwe which will be discussed below. No trace of Early Iron Age settlement has yet been reported from more southerly parts of Namibia, but it must be emphasized that appropriate research has for the most part not so far been undertaken.

Our most detailed knowledge of the archaeology of the western stream of the Early Iron Age comes from the Upemba depression in the valley of the upper Lualaba in Shaba.[16] The earliest Iron Age settlement so far discovered in this region is at Kamilamba, dated to about the sixth or seventh century of our era. The pottery shows strong affinities with material of the same age from western Zambia. In about the tenth century, or shortly before, began the use of an extensive series of cemeteries which has been investigated on several occasions during the last twenty years, the best known being that at Sanga on Lake Kisale. The Sanga cemetery appears to have remained in use until about the seventeenth or eighteenth century, but throughout this period the typology of the associated pottery seems to the present writer to have been rooted in an Early Iron Age tradition.

The dead were buried in an extended or slightly flexed position, accompanied by abundant grave goods. The most frequent items were pottery vessels, those prior to *c.* 1300 of our era being of the style known as Kisalian, followed by those attributed to the Kabambian tradition. Metal objects were also abundant, including elaborate copper ornaments such as

13. J. Nenquin, 1959. It is doubtful whether this material was really found at Tshikapa.
14. J. D. Clark, 1968, pp. 189–205.
15. B. Sandelowsky, 1973.
16. J. Nenquin, 1963; J. Hiernaux, E. de Longrée and J. de Buyst, 1971; J. Hiernaux, E. Maquet and J. de Buyst, 1973; P. de Maret, 1977.

PLATE 23.1 *Early Kisalian tomb (eighth to tenth centuries), Kamilamba site. Of particular interest are the ceremonial hatchet and the anvil against the skull.*

chains, bangles and twisted belts and necklets. Iron is represented by hoes and axes rather than by weapons: there are also a number of small flange-welded bells. Copper cross-shaped ingots of various sizes were common in Kabambian graves but rare in Kisalian ones: there is evidence that these probably served as some form of currency.

Some 140 km further upstream along the Lualaba is the site of Katoto, where there is a further cemetery in many ways comparable with those of the Upemba depression. The pottery, although typologically distinct, like-

PLATE 23.2 *Tomb from the classical Kisalian period (tenth to fourteenth centuries), Sanga site*

wise belongs to an Early Iron Age tradition, although it has stronger affinities than does the Kasalian both with Urewe ware and with ceramics from western Zambia. It is probable that Katoto will prove to be of earlier date than the Sanga cemetery.

It is unfortunate that no domestic living sites have yet been discovered that may be attributed to the population responsible for the upper Lualaba cemeteries. The latter sites do, however, attest to the material wealth and technological sophistication that had been attained in this area by the beginning of the present millennium. A relatively high population density had evidently developed by this time, and there can be little doubt that a major factor contributing to this was the presence of the rich mineral deposits of the Copperbelt at no great distance to the south. As will be shown below, this mining area attracted trading contacts over an enormous area among the Early Iron Age folk, even though mining remained on a relatively small scale. This sequence is of particular importance and interest since, as de Maret points out, it occurs in an area where 'oral traditions have placed the origin of Luba kingship to which many kingdoms of the central savanna trace their origin'.

Archaeological research on the Copperbelt itself has taken place only in Zambian territory. Numerous Early Iron Age settlement sites have been located, and these are attributed to the Chondwe group, named after a site some 45 km south of Ndola.[17] Chondwe group villages were generally situated beside rivers and streams: one, at Roan Antelope near Luanshya, was also adjacent to a prehistoric copper working. Copper bangles have been found at Chondwe at a level dated to between the sixth and the eighth centuries of the Christian era; impressions of similar objects used to decorate pottery strongly suggest that the use of copper most probably goes back to

17. E. A. C. Mills and N. T. Filmer, 1972; D. W. Phillipson, 1972.

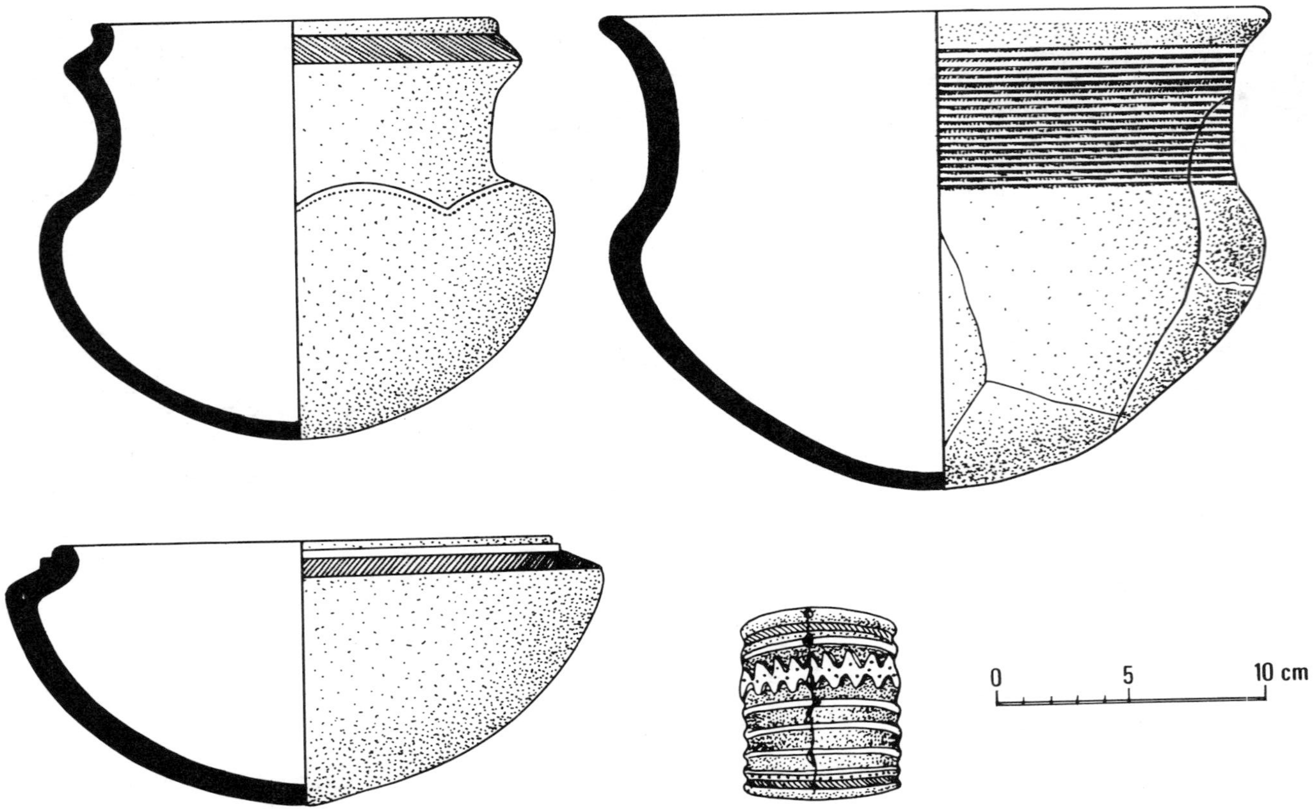

FIG. 23.3 *Pottery and an ivory bangle from Sanga (after Nenquin, 1963; Hiernaux, de Longrée and de Buyst, 1971)*

the first Early Iron Age settlement of the area, about the beginning of the sixth century.

Particular interest attaches to the presence at several sites, including Roan Antelope, of scattered Early Iron Age potsherds of types that are characteristic of the tradition of distant regions – the middle Zambezi valley and southern Malawi for example – rather than of the local Chondwe group pottery tradition. These occurrences are probably best interpreted as evidence for inter-group contact. Most probably this contact took the form of men (see p. 656 below) travelling from afar to the copper-producing area in order to obtain metal. Since there is reason to believe that potting was the work of men, during the Early Iron Age in this part of Africa, it is likely that the 'foreign' pottery referred to above was made by these visitors: there is thus no need to suppose either that whole families travelled to the mines in search of metal or that such fragile objects as pots were themselves traded over large distances.

To the west of the main Copperbelt, on the Zambezi/Congo watershed near Solwezi, the prehistoric mining area at Kansanshi has recently been investigated by Michael Bisson.[18] Here, the earliest Iron Age occupation, of about the fifth century, is associated with evidence for copper-working. The pottery is distinct from that of the Chondwe group (although both types are attributed to the western streams of the Early Iron Age) and shares features with wares found on widely dispersed sites in the Kalahari Sand country of western Zambia. Here, the most informative sites are those at Sioma on the upper Zambezi not far to the south of the Barotze floodplain, and at Lubusi in Kaoma District.[19] Early Iron Age settlement, associated with the working of iron and (to judge from bangle impressions on the pottery) copper, is attested from the sixth century if not the end of the fifth. Only along the Zambezi valley does the coverage of research enable the distribution of these sites to be plotted with any degree of comprehensiveness. Recent research by N. Katanekwe suggests that settlement by the western stream of the Early Iron Age did not penetrate far downstream of Sioma.

The only other areas of Zambia to be subject to western stream settlement are the Lusaka and Southern Province plateaux, where the Early Iron Age sites are attributed to the Kapwirimbwe and Kalundu groups respectively.[20] The pottery of the first of these, as at the eponymous village site near Lusaka where the brief period of occupation is dated to about the fifth century, shows many affinities to that of the Chondwe group on the Copperbelt. At Kapwirimbwe, the presence of semi-permanent structures is indicated by post-holes, but plans of individual buildings could not be distinguished. Large quantities of debris from collapsed *daga* (puddled mud) structures appear to be the remains of iron-smelting furnaces: the

18. M. S. Bisson, 1975; and reports forthcoming.
19. J. O. Vogel, 1973a; D. W. Phillipson, 1971.
20. D. W. Phillipson, 1968, 1970b; B. M. Fagan, 1967.

working of iron seems to have been conducted on a large scale within or immediately adjacent to the village, but copper was unknown. The inhabitants of Kapwirimbwe herded domestic cattle, bones of which were recovered during the excavations.

The later phases of the Kapwirimbwe group are best known from a site at Twickenham Road in suburban Lusaka. At some time between the ninth and the early twelfth centuries, fine elaborately decorated pottery was in use that clearly belongs to a development of the same tradition as was represented at Kapwirimbwe. Domestic goats were kept, and wild animals hunted. As at Kapwirimbwe, iron was worked on a substantial scale, but it was only in the final phase of the Early Iron Age at Twickenham Road that copper made its appearance. It is interesting to note that pottery more closely resembling that of the Chondwe group appears in the Lusaka sequence at the same time. At both Kapwirimbwe and Twickenham Road were recovered perforated pottery colanders which, it is suggested, may have been used for the preparation of salt.

The former extent of the Kapwirimbwe group is not easy to ascertain, but closely related pottery has been recorded from as far to the west as Mumbwa Cave and from the Chirundu region of the Zambezi valley. The Early Iron Age 'Sinoia tradition' of ceramics of the Lomagundi and Urungwe Districts of Zimbabwe is so similar to that from Kapwirimbwe and Twickenham Road that it also is probably best subsumed into the same group.[21] These sites are quite distinct from their contemporaries in other parts of Zimbabwe and are of interest as the only representatives of the western stream of the Early Iron Age yet to have been identified south of the Zambezi.

On the Southern Province or Batoka plateau south of the Kafue, the first Kalundu group settlements may have been established before the end of the fourth century. Some sites were occupied on a repeated or prolonged basis resulting in the accumulation of deep stratified archaeological deposits. The pottery and other items of material culture have much in common with those of the Kapwirimbwe group. At Kalundu Mound, near Kalowo, domestic animals (cattle and sheep/goats) accounted for less than two-fifths of the bones recovered, indicating that hunting still played an important part in the economy. With the Kalundu group we conclude this survey of the Central African manifestations of the Early Iron Age's western stream.

The eastern stream of the Early Iron Age

In Malawi and eastern Zambia, the Early Iron Age industries, although clearly belonging to the same Industrial Complex as those described above from more westerly regions, are nevertheless markedly distinct. They are

21. P. S. Garlake, 1970; T. N. Huffman, 1971.

attributed to an eastern stream and appear to be derived reasonably directly from the Urewe group settlements of the interlacustrine region.

Studies of pottery typology enable two variants to be recognized in the Early Iron Age of Malawi. These are the Mwabulambo group in the north, named after a site on the Lufilya River, and – in the south – the Nkope group which takes its name from a locality on the western shore of Lake Malawi, north of Mangochi.[22] Despite the large number of Early Iron Age sites that have now been located in Malawi, the nature and location of the geographical boundary between these two groups is not well known. The distribution of Nkope ware extends westwards across the watershed into the greater part of south-eastern Zambia lying to the east of the Luangwa River, while its spread into adjacent parts of Mozambique is attested by material collected by Carl Wiese in 1907 and now housed in the Museum für Völkerkunde, Berlin.[23] The carbon-14 dates for Malawi Early Iron Age sites indicate that their florescence began early in the fourth century of the Christian era; and it has been shown statistically that the Mwabulambo group may have been established at a slightly earlier date than its more southerly counterpart.[24]

Only small-scale test excavations have been undertaken on the Early Iron Age sites so far investigated in Malawi; and the information that is available from them is correspondingly scant. Traces of substantial houses, built of mud applied over a wooden framework (pole and *daga*), were preserved at Phopo Hill near Lake Kazuni. Iron, in the form of slag and finished artefacts, has been recovered from several sites, notably Nanyangu in the Ncheu District and Zomba Range. Copper, on the other hand, has not been recovered. Shell beads occurred in association with Nkope ware in a storage pit at Phwadze Stream in the Chikwawa District that is dated to the fifth or sixth century of the Christian era. The only coastal object from an Early Iron Age context in Malawi is a broken cowry shell from a late Nkope site on the Namichimba Stream, Mwanya. Bones that have been identified from these sites are all of wild species.[25]

In the Chipata District of south-eastern Zambia, a relatively sparse Early Iron Age presence seems to have been established around the beginning of the fourth century, although an indigenous stone-tool-using population also appears to have survived well into the present millennium. The only Early Iron Age village site that has so far been investigated in this area is at Kamnama on the Malawi border north of Chipata. The settlement covered an area of some five hectares, but its occupation was apparently brief, being dated between the third and the fifth centuries.[26]

The eastern stream settlements south of the Zambezi being outside the

22. P. A. Cole-King, 1973.
23. D. W. Phillipson, 1976a, p. 17.
24. D. W. Phillipson, 1975.
25. K. R. Robinson, 1970, 1973, 1976.
26. D. W. Phillipson, 1976a, pp. 38–45.

geographical range of this chapter, it is necessary now to turn our attention to the Early Iron Age in the Victoria Falls region of southern Zambia. This has been termed the Dambwa group after a site lying on the outskirts of the town of Livingstone.[27] The distribution of the Dambwa group extends along the Zambezi valley from the vicinity of Chirundu upstream almost as far as Sioma, and also southwards at least into the Wankie area of modern Zimbabwe. It is bordered on the north by regions where the Early Iron Age industries, as described above, are attributed to the western stream. There can be little doubt that the Dambwa group owes its origin to a north-westward expansion of eastern stream Early Iron Age folk from the Zimbabwean plateau. The carbon-14 dates indicate that the main florescence of the Dambwa group in the Victoria Falls region did not begin until the sixth century of the Christian era. This was significantly later than the inception of western stream settlement in the areas only a short distance to the north.

The best-known sites of the Dambwa group are Kumadzulo, occupied between the fifth and seventh centuries, and the slightly later settlement of Dambwa. Four successive phases have been recognized on the basis of the pottery typology, but all belong to a single developing ceramic tradition that has been named the Shongwe tradition.[28]

Sites of the Dambwa group have yielded bones of domestic cattle and small stock, in addition to those of wild animals. Traces of buildings at Kumadzulo are interpreted as the remains of remarkably small rectangular pole-and-*daga* houses. Contact with the east coast trade had begun by the seventh century, as is indicated by a fragment of imported glass recovered from the ruins of one of the houses at Kumadzulo, and by some cowry shells from the nearby Chundu Farm site. Glass beads, however, do not occur in Early Iron Age contexts in this area. Locally made iron tools include hoes, axes, knives, spear-points and arrowheads. A copper bar and bangles have also been recovered, indicating trade with copper-producing areas such as the Hook of the Kafue or the Wankie region of Zimbabwe.

Excavations at Chundu Farm have thrown much light on the local Early Iron Age burial customs. These may be compared with those that prevailed during somewhat later times in the upper Lualaba cemeteries described above. The dead were buried tightly contracted in individual pit-like graves, while similar pits were dug nearby for the deposition of grave goods. These usually comprised pairs of pottery vessels forming a covered container for a funerary cache of such objects as iron hoes, axes, iron or copper bangles, cowry shells or shell beads. One of these caches also contained two seeds that have been tentatively identified as those of squash and a bean. The Chundu Farm site is dated to about the eighth century of the Christian era.[29]

27. S. G. H. Daniels and D. W. Phillipson, 1969; J. O. Vogel, 1971.
28. J. O. Vogel, 1972a.
29. J. O. Vogel, 1972b, 1973b.

The Early Iron Age/Later Iron Age transition

In many parts of Bantu-speaking Africa, the Later Iron Age societies have been less intensively studied by archaeologists than have their Early Iron Age predecessors. Consequently, at least for the period with which we are here concerned, before that at which oral tradition becomes a significant historical source, the centuries after about the beginning of the eleventh century of the Christian era represent a virtual lacuna in our knowledge of central African history. Despite the lack of abundant data, however, a picture is beginning to emerge of a sharp break in the local pottery traditions of most areas early in the eleventh century of the Christian era.[30] One of the few areas where some degree of continuity over this period may be demonstrated is in southern Zambia; and this is a convenient place at which to commence the following survey.

The relevant archaeological material here is that attributed to the Kalomo industry; and there are convincing reasons for regarding the Kalomo pottery tradition as having developed from a late phase of the Dambwa group sequence of the Victoria Falls region.[31] Thence, around the end of the ninth century of the Christian era, its practitioners appear to have begun to expand to the north and north-west on to the Batoka plateau where their characteristic pottery rapidly displaced that of the Early Iron Age Kalundu group. This transition was first noted at the Kalundu site near Kalomo where it is, however, obscured by the disturbed stratigraphy; it is also exposed further to the north at Gundu and Ndonde in the Choma District.[32] However, the best picture of the Kalomo industry as a whole is obtained at Isamu Pati, west of Kalomo, a site where there was no previous Early Iron Age occupation.[33]

Some Kalomo industry villages seem to have consisted of rings of unsubstantial circular houses set around open areas that may have served as cattle kraals. These villages were continuously or repeatedly occupied over several centuries.

Iron-working seems to have been practised by the inhabitants of these Kalomo industry sites on a smaller scale than by their Early Iron Age predecessors. Although axes and hoes have been found, they are extremely rare: knives, razors and points for spears and arrows being the tools most frequently encountered. Copper was used mainly for bangles. A steady decrease in the importance of hunting is indicated by the way in which bones of wild animals are now outnumbered by those of domestic species. There is evidence for the cultivation of sorghum, but one has the impression that here – as in other areas of eastern and southern Africa – the economy of the

30. J. E. G. Sutton, 1972; D. W. Phillipson, 1975.
31. J. O. Vogel, 1975.
32. Unpublished excavations by B. M. Fagan; D. W. Phillipson, 1970a.
33. B. M. Fagan, 1967.

opening centuries of the Later Iron Age was heavily dependent upon the herding of domestic animals, principally cattle. The presence of glass beads, cowry shells and conus shells shows that contact with the east coast trade was now stronger than it had been in earlier times.

In about the second half of the eleventh century of the Christian era the Kalomo industry on the Batoka plateau was abruptly replaced by a southward spread of a further distinct industry, known as Kangila, which seems to have originated in or near the lower Kafue valley. The Kangila industry also spread to the Victoria Falls region, where its interface with the Kalomo industry is dated at Sinde about a hundred years later than the corresponding event on the plateau: this time-lag may be regarded as a function of the slow southwards dispersal of the Kangila industry.[34]

Our archaeological evidence for the early development of the Kangila industry is difficult to interpret, being based on excavations at only two sites: Sebanzi near Monze and Ingombe Ilede not far from the Zambezi/Kafue confluence. At the latter site the occupation probably began in the seventh or eighth centuries; the corresponding event at Sebanzi was probably later. At both sites the stratigraphy and chronology are unclear, but the pottery may be confidently regarded as ancestral to that found at Kangila on the plateau near Mazabuka. The Kangila village itself was occupied briefly in about the fifteenth century of the Christian era, and thus represents a late phase of the industry to which it has given its name. Apart from the pottery, its inhabitants' material culture and economy appear to have been very similar to those of the Kalomo industry.[35]

Outside the Southern Province, the most widespread Later Iron Age pottery type recognized in Zambia is that attributed to the Luangwa tradition. Its distribution covers the whole of Zambia to the north and east of a line extending from the lower Kafue to Lubumbushi, and extends also into the neighbouring parts of Zaire, Malawi, Mozambique and Zimbabwe. The Luangwa tradition thus occurs in areas where the Early Iron Age had belonged to the Kalambo, Nkope, Chondwe and Kapwirimbwe groups, representing both the eastern and the western streams. It first appears in the archaeological record during the eleventh century of the Christian era, and makes a sudden and complete break with the preceding Early Iron Age traditions. The nature and date of this interface are best illustrated at Twickenham Road and at Chondwe, while confirmatory evidence comes from rock-shelter sites in the north and east, as at Nakapapula and Thandwe. Throughout its area of distribution, the Luangwa pottery tradition has been continued into recent times by such peoples as the Bemba, Chewa, Nsenga and northern Lunda.[36]

34. J. O. Vogel, 1973c. Vogel refers to the Kangila tradition as 'Early Tonga', but the present writer prefers to avoid attributing tribal names to prehistoric material.

35. B. M. Fagan and D. W. Phillipson, 1965; B. M. Fagan, 1969b; D. W. Phillipson and B. M. Fagan, 1969.

36. D. W. Phillipson, 1974.

There is a very pronounced contrast between the pottery of the Luangwa tradition and that of its Early Iron Age predecessors, and no suggestion of a gradual development from one to the other. However, the Early Iron Age ware that is typologically closest to the Luangwa tradition is that of the Chondwe group. It has been suggested that the ancestor of the Luangwa tradition may prove to have been more closely related to the Chondwe group pottery than to that of any other of the Early Iron Age groups that are at present known.[37] The most likely explanation of these archaeological observations is that the inception of the Luangwa tradition was occasioned by a relatively large-scale movement of people, in which whole families took part, from an area located to the north or north-west of the Zambia/Shaba Copperbelt. If Luangwa tradition pottery was then (as it invariably is today) the work of women, the suddenness of its appearance may be explained by postulating that Early Iron Age ceramics were made by men.[38]

A similar picture is now emerging in Malawi, Nkope ware being replaced around the beginning of the eleventh century of the Christian era by that named after Kapeni Hill in the Ncheu District. At about the same time, Mwamasapa ware (which takes its name from a site near Karonga) took over from Mwabulambo ware as the characteristic pottery type in the northern part of the country. Both these Malawi Later Iron Age wares appear to be related in some way to those of the Luangwa tradition. As in Zambia, little is yet known concerning the archaeology of these first Later Iron Age communities. Pole-and-*daga* houses are indicated at some sites, as also are less permanent beehive-shaped structures. Iron and occasional copper objects were in use throughout this period. Imported glass beads, initially rare, became progressively more frequent. Seeds of sorghum have been recovered in association with Mwamasapa pottery, while cattle bones occur on several Later Iron Age sites, widely distributed through Malawi.[39] We shall return in a later section of this chapter to a consideration of these Later Iron Age communities in Malawi and the eastern half of Zambia; meanwhile we must briefly describe the remarkably contrasting situation that prevailed at this time in the regions further to the west.

To the west of the area occupied by industries of the Luangwa tradition there is apparent a much greater degree of continuity from the ceramic industries of the Early Iron Age into those of the present millennium. For example, in the Mongu, Kabompo, Zambezi, Mwinilunga and Kaoma Districts of western Zambia the modern pottery tradition, which has been named the Lungwebungu tradition, shows many features in common with that of the local Early Iron Age, as exemplified at the Lubusi site described above.[40] Recent research suggests that this continuity may not have been

37. D. W. Phillipson, 1972.
38. D. W. Phillipson, 1974.
39. P. A. Cole-King, 1973; K. R. Robinson, 1966c, 1970.
40. D. W. Phillipson, 1974.

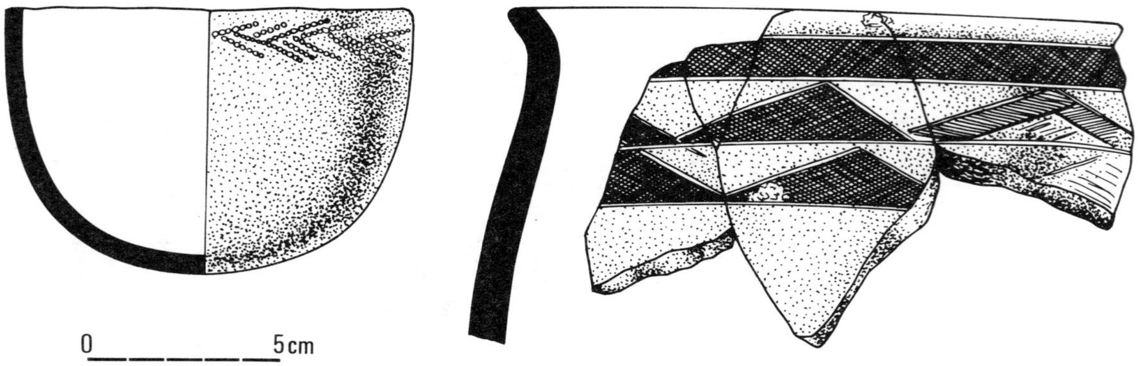

FIG. 23.4 *Luangwa tradition pottery from Makwe rock-shelter, eastern Zambia (after Phillipson, 1976)*

so direct as was previously thought,[41] nevertheless there is no evidence here for a pronounced break in the archaeological record early in the present millennium, such as heralded the advent of the Later Iron Age further to the east. Between the areas of the Lungwebungu and Luangwa pottery traditions, in the country now occupied by the Kaonde, yet another pottery style is attested at sites such as Kamusongolwa and Kansanshi, dated between the eleventh and the thirteenth centuries.[42]

Thus the overall picture of central Africa during the eleventh century of the Christian era that emerges is one of a marked east–west dichotomy. In the east the Early Iron Age industries were abruptly terminated and replaced; in the west their counterparts continued with relatively little modification. The upper Lualaba cemeteries of Sanga and Katoto, described above, are further evidence for this continuity in the western half of our area: typologically they belong with the Early Iron Age Industrial Complex, yet chronologically they bridge the gap and extend into the period occupied elsewhere by the Later Iron Age industries – a period to which, indeed, these cemeteries' main period of use belongs. It is now necessary to turn away from purely archaeological arguments in order to consider the meaning and significance of these observations in historical terms.

The first point to be emphasized is the much greater degree of Early Iron Age/Later Iron Age continuity in the western half of central Africa in contrast to the situation in the east. Interestingly, this east–west division does not coincide with the 'tribal' subdivisions of the region, as this is reflected in the extant oral tradition. For example, peoples who traditionally trace their origins to the Lunda and Luba empires are found in both the eastern and the western areas. Furthermore, there are today 'tribes' bearing the name of Lunda which make, in one case, Luangwa pottery (Kazembe's Lunda of the Luapula valley) and, in the other, that of the Early Iron Age-derived Lungwebungu tradition (the western Lunda of north-western Zambia).[43] It is thus clear that the inception of the Later Iron Age and the traditionally recalled emergence of its constituent societies were essentially disparate processes. This is confirmed by the chronological implications of the most recent interpretation of the oral traditions. These would place the political developments that gave rise to the Luba empire as early as the fourteenth or even the thirteenth century, a date still significantly more recent than that attested by archaeology for the start of the Later Iron Age.[44]

It is when we compare the archaeological data with that of linguistics that it is possible tentatively to propose a meaningful correlation. Attention was drawn above to the Western Highland group of the Bantu languages, which Heine and Dalby derive from a dispersal centre near the lower

41. R. M. Derricourt and R. J. Papstein, 1976.
42. M. S. Bisson, 1975.
43. D. W. Phillipson, 1974, 1977b.
44. J. C. Miller, 1976; D. Birmingham, 1977.

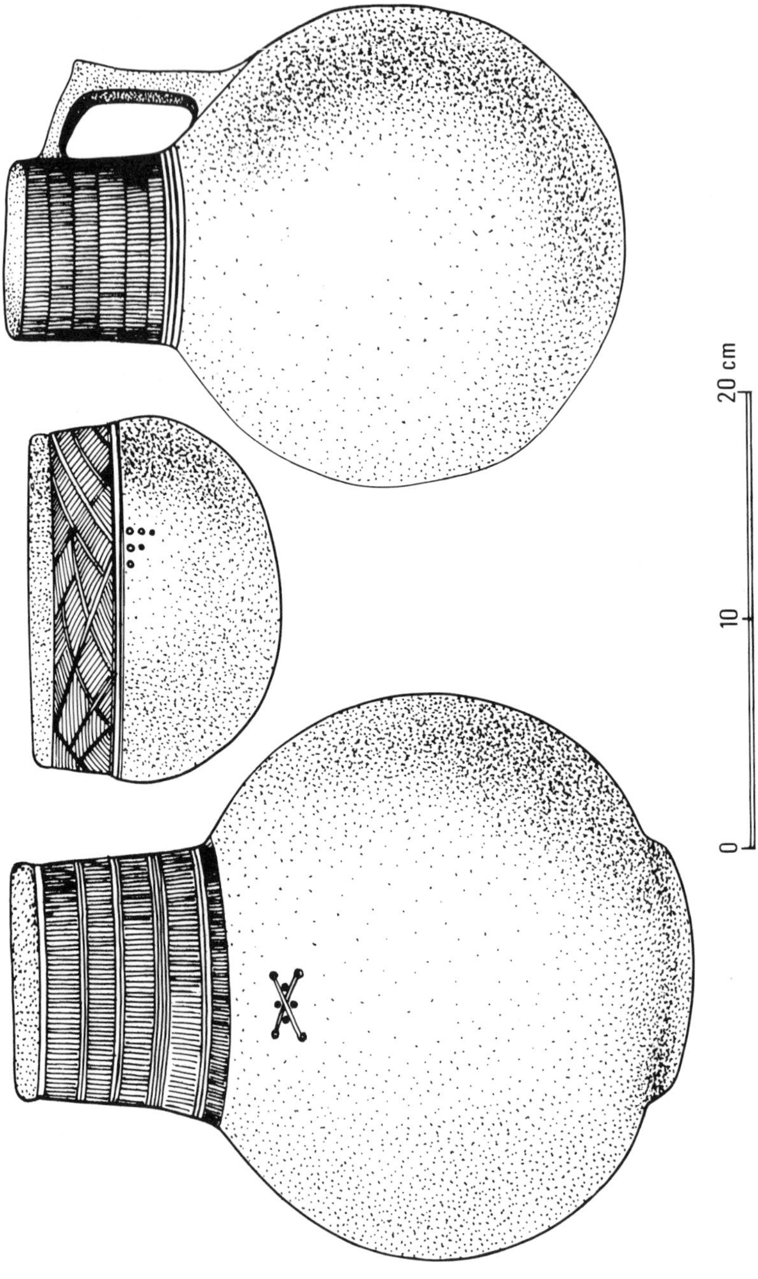

FIG. 23.5 *Modern Lungwebungu tradition pottery (after Phillipson, 1974)*

Congo. Subsequent to the establishment of these Western Highland languages they themselves gave rise to a tertiary dispersal centre in the Shaba area. It is to this centre that most linguists would now trace the last major diaspora of the Bantu languages, that which led to the introduction, throughout the eastern half of Bantu Africa, of the closely interrelated languages which Heine has called the Eastern Highland group.[45] The present writer has shown elsewhere that there are grounds for linking the inception of the Later Iron Age industries in the eastern regions with the spread of the people who spoke these Eastern Highland languages.[46] The continuation of the older and more diverse western languages compares with the greater degree of Early Iron Age/Later Iron Age continuity in the west. The geographical distribution of the Eastern Highland languages coincides with the area where a sharp break in the archaeological sequence took place at the start of the Later Iron Age. Likewise, the westerly origin of the Eastern Highland languages is in accord with that of several Later Iron Age industries, notably the Luangwa tradition.

This is the picture of central Africa from the seventh to the eleventh centuries of the Christian era that archaeology and linguistics combine to present. Throughout the region, Early Iron Age peoples, probably Bantu-speakers, were in occupation by the beginning of this period, although in many areas stone-tool-using hunter/gathering peoples continued to survive, often in a client relationship with their farming neighbours. These Early Iron Age communities are known almost exclusively from archaeology: they may be divided into two streams – eastern and western – of distinct but related origin. They were evidently peasant farming societies, probably lacking any large-scale systems of centralized political authority. Towards the close of the first millennium we can, however, detect a marked increase in wealth, trade activity and population density in the upper Lualaba area.[47] It was from this general region that, in about the eleventh century, began the process of population expansion that resulted in the introduction of Later Iron Age culture to much of eastern central Africa. Thus were established the populations from which the more developed Later Iron Age societies subsequently emerged.

45. B. Heine, H. Hoff and R. Vossen 1977; D. Dalby, 1975, 1976.
46. D. W. Phillipson, 1976c; 1977a, ch. 8.
47. Cf. M. S. Bisson, 1975.

24 Southern Africa to the south of the Zambezi

T. N. HUFFMAN

The most important development in the Iron Age prehistory of southern Africa occurred one thousand years ago in the Shashi/Limpopo basin. It was here that Bantu-speakers evolved the Zimbabwe Culture. To explain the history and importance of this development, I first consider ethnic movements identified by ceramic style and culture systems recognized in settlement layout. I then turn to the impact of external trade on local politics and the consequent evolution of the Zimbabwe Culture at Mapungubwe.

Ethnic movements and culture systems: 700–1000

Archaeologists in southern Africa use ceramic style to trace the movements of Iron Age people because stylistic units demarcate the distribution of ethnic entities in space and time. This is so because (1) ceramic style, as part of patterned behaviour, is created and transmitted through groups of people, (2) the transmission of a style must be partially accomplished through verbal communication, and, (3) as long as the identity of the manufacturers and users of style are the same, the distribution of that style must also represent the distribution of a group of people speaking the same language. This set of premises does not mean, however, that another stylistic group could not have spoken the same language.

On the basis of these premises, the languages spoken by Iron Age people in central and southern Africa can be confidently identified from the ceramic evidence as members of the Bantu family. Since the earliest Iron Age ceramics in this region belong to a single stylistic complex[1] and since one of these styles can be traced directly to the ceramics of modern-day Shona-speakers,[2] a Bantu language must have been the principal tongue of all the Early Iron Age groups. For the reasons given above, this one ceramic continuum is sufficient to establish the link between Iron Age entities and Bantu languages.

1. T. N. Huffman, 1982; T. M. Maggs, 1980a, 1980b; D. W. Phillipson, 1977a.
2. T. N. Huffman, 1978.

At the beginning of the eighth century of the Christian era, several ethnic groups of Bantu-speakers lived in southern Africa (see Fig. 24.1). One group, named after the present-day town of Sinoia, had only recently moved across the Zambezi,[3] but the ancestors of the others had been in the general area since the beginning of the Iron Age.[4] The area with which we are most concerned – modern-day south-western Matabeleland, east-central Botswana and the far northern Transvaal – was occupied largely by Zhizo people. The ceramic sequence shows that they inhabited this area for another 250 years before newcomers known as Leopard's Kopje moved into south-western Zimbabwe. This later ethnic movement is demonstrated by a major stylistic discontinuity between Zhizo and tenth-century Leopard's Kopje ceramics.[5] Zhizo ceramics include jars with bands of stamp impressions and incisions on the lower rim and a textured line on the shoulder, while Leopard's Kopje jars are decorated with incised triangles, loops and meanders on the neck. This ceramic disjunction occurs at the same time as a threefold increase in late Zhizo settlements called Toutswe in Botswana.[6] Evidently, many Zhizo people chose to leave the area rather than be incorporated in the new Leopard's Kopje group.

Some archaeologists believe that the spread of Leopard's Kopje at the beginning of the eleventh century of the Christian era was part of a single expansion of Bantu-speakers from central Africa across the subcontinent.[7] Leopard's Kopje ceramics, however, are not closely related to contemporaneous styles in Zambia or Malawi or to the new style that appeared at sites related to Blackburn on the Natal coast in the tenth century.[8] Instead, Leopard's Kopje forms the third phase of a stylistic continuum that includes eighth- to ninth-century Klingbeil ceramics[9] and fifth- to seventh-century pottery in the central Transvaal.[10] Furthermore, the tenth-century replacement of Zhizo in south-western Zimbabwe by Leopard's Kopje and then the eleventh-century replacement of Maxton people in northern Zimbabwe by a group related to Leopard's Kopje known as Gumanye (formerly Zimbabwe Period II and Lower Zimbabwe) shows that these Leopard's Kopje people moved north across the Limpopo River, not south across the Zambezi.[11] Moreover, groups related to Leopard's Kopje who did not move north, such as Eiland, continued in some areas

3. P. S. Garlake, 1970; T. N. Huffman, 1979; D. W. Phillipson, 1977a; K. R. Robinson, 1966b.

4. T. M. Evers, 1980; E. O. M. Hanisch, 1980, 1981; T. N. Huffman, 1974b; T. M. Maggs and M. A. Michael, 1976; D. W. Phillipson, 1977a; K. R. Robinson, 1966a.

5. T. N. Huffman, 1974b.

6. J. R. Denbow, 1982, 1983.

7. D. W. Phillipson, 1977a.

8. O. Davies, 1971; T. M. Maggs, 1980a; T. Robey, 1980.

9. T. M. Evers, 1980.

10. T. M. Evers, 1982; R. R. Inskeep and T. M. Maggs, 1975.

11. T. N. Huffman, 1978.

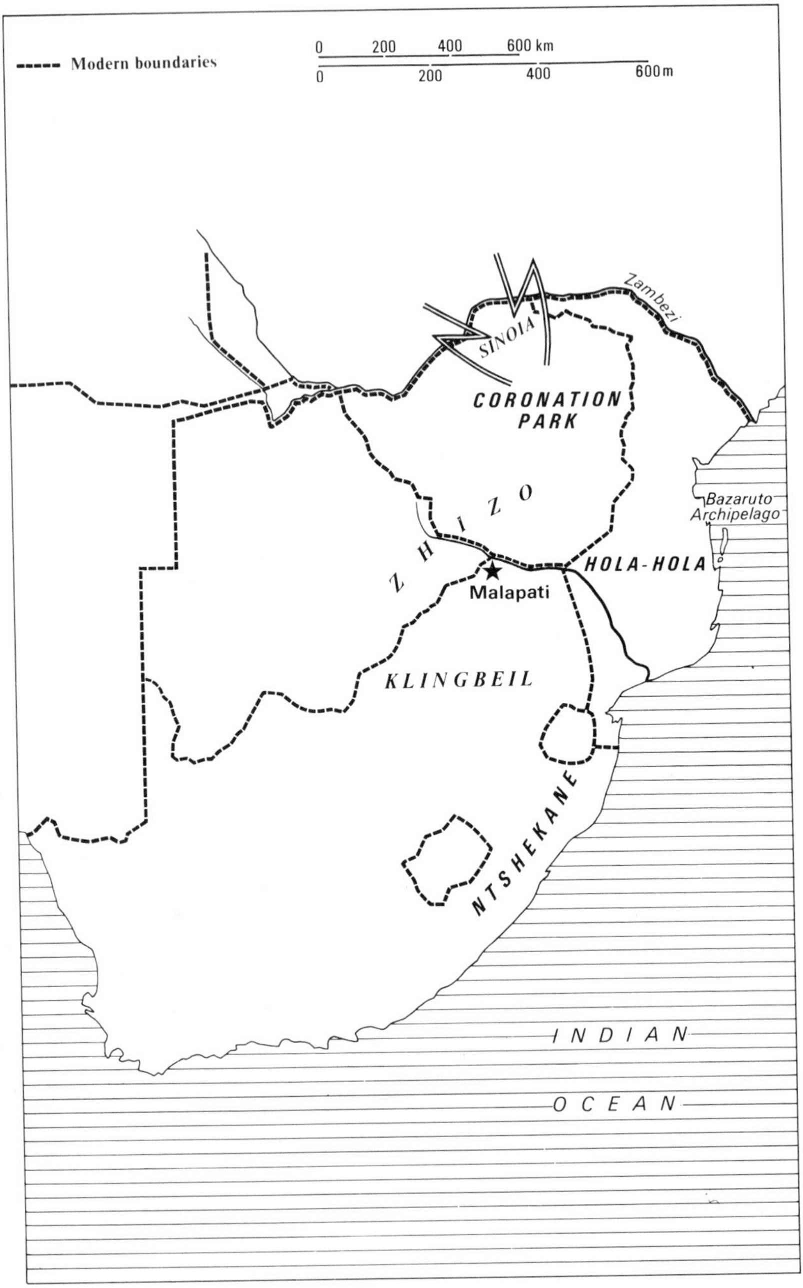

FIG. 24.1 *Some of the ethnic groups defined by ceramic style in southern Africa between 700 and 900: names in capital letters are mentioned in the text; the star marks the Zhizo site of Schroda*

until the fourteenth century.[12] Population replacements thus occurred at various times in southern Africa, and they originated from places other than central Africa (see Fig. 24.2).

Leopard's Kopje and Gumanye are part of the ceramic continuum mentioned earlier that links Bantu language with Iron Age peoples. Leopard's Kopje and Gumanye, therefore, were the ancestors of many present-day Shona-speakers.

Ceramic units such as Leopard's Kopje, however, only identify groups of people. To understand how these people lived, we must turn to economic and other data. The location and type of Iron Age sites, as well as the associated artefacts, show that these people were mixed farmers. For example, most early Iron Age settlements were located in broken country where the resources needed by mixed farmers – water, wood, cultivable soils and pasture – occurred in close proximity. In contrast, pastoralists preferred open grasslands like the Kalahari, while hunter-gatherers once occupied almost every kind of terrain. Iron Age settlements, furthermore, were relatively permanent compared with the transient camps of herders and hunter-gatherers. The remains of pole-and-*daga* (a mud and dung mixture) structures are common, and the amount of refuse indicates that even the smallest homesteads were usually occupied for several years. The features and artefacts in these semi-permanent settlements include storage pits, raised storage bins, grindstones and iron hoes, all of which indicate a technology adapted to grain cultivation. The ceramics in these settlements typically occur in a wide range of shapes and sizes, and this range also attests cultivation, since most hunter-gatherers did not use pottery at all and the pottery of pastoralists was usually limited to a few small portable shapes. Cultivators, on the other hand, need several shapes and sizes to prepare and to serve foods made from grain, such as porridge and beer. Some of the actual crops have also been recovered from Iron Age sites in this region: for instance, carbonized sorghum has been found in Zhizo,[13] Toutswe[14] and Leopard's Kopje sites[15]; while *Eleusine* (finger millet) and *Pennisetum* (bullrush millet) have also been recovered from Leopard's Kopje sites;[16] and various legumes are known from Sinoia,[17] and Leopard's Kopje sites.[18] These seeds complement the other data and together form the evidence for a cultivation component in Iron Age economy.

A herding component is also well attested in the archaelogical record for

12. J. R. Denbow, 1981.
13. E. O. M. Hanisch, 1980, 1981.
14. J. R. Denbow, 1983.
15. T. N. Huffman, 1974b; A. Meyer, 1980.
16. E. O. M. Hanisch, 1980; T. N. Huffman, 1974b.
17. T. N. Huffman, 1979.
18. T. N. Huffman, 1974b.

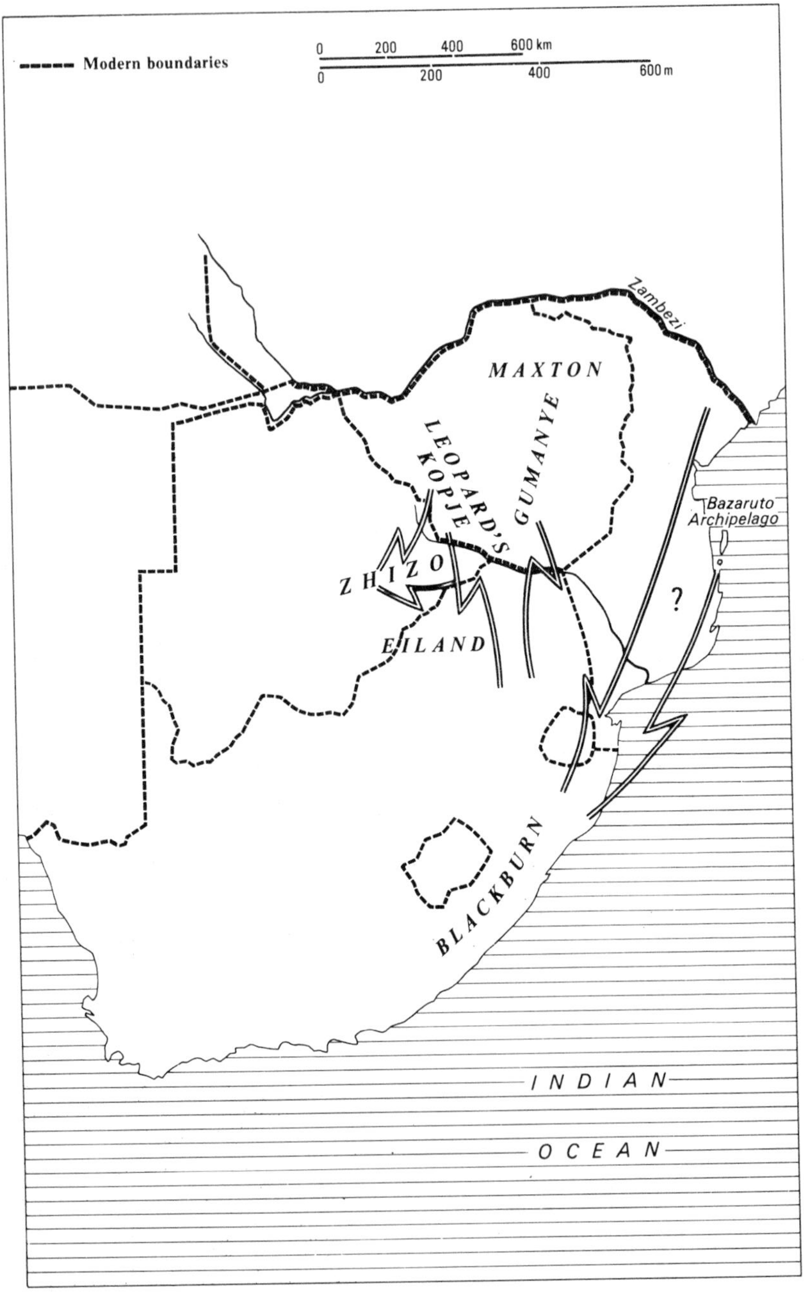

FIG. 24.2 *Ethnic groups and movements in southern Africa between 950 and 1000*

the seventh to eleventh centuries, for bones of domestic caprines (sheep and goat) and cattle have been found in virtually every known Iron Age group at this time.[19] Until recently, though, it was commonly thought that the Leopard's Kopje people were the first in southern Africa to begin cattle-keeping on a large scale. This in turn was part of a belief that two distinct economies existed during the Iron Age: an Early Iron Age one that centred on cultivation and a Later Iron Age economy based on cattle.[20] Recent research, however, invalidates this economic distinction.

An extensive reconnaissance along the eastern fringe of the Kalahari in Botswana[21] discovered that both eighth- to ninth-century Zhizo and tenth- to eleventh-century Toutswe sites are characterized by thick deposits of cattle dung, so thick that the deposits sometimes became vitrified through internal combustion.[22] These Zhizo herds, therefore, were as large as those of the later Leopard's Kopje people. Although comparable data are not available for Zimbabwe, Zhizo people along the edge of the Kalahari apparently kept more cattle than their Zhizo relatives to the east. Whatever the case, this research shows that economic variation between Iron Age communities was more likely due to conscious decisions about exploiting environmental and political opportunities, than to fixed historical or cultural traditions.

Indeed, other recent research also highlights the common culture of most Early and Late Iron Age societies in southern Africa and shows that nearly all Iron Age people shared the same attitudes to cattle, regardless of whether they kept large herds. To evaluate the importance of cattle in Iron Age society, I now analyse settlement organization.

It is possible to use the organization of space to determine the culture system of Iron Age groups because the use of space is a cultural variable: every society divides its spatial environment into distinct locations where a limited range of culturally related activities are permitted. Fortunately for Iron Age research, anthropologists have recently determined the spatial code and underlying culture system of the Southern Bantu.[23]

This Bantu Cattle Culture is characterized by a cluster of interrelated values concerning the political role of men, the benevolence of ancestor spirits and the mediating function of cattle. Domestic cattle within this system belong to the domain of men: they are the principal form of wealth, the main avenue to wives and children, and the basis of success, status and power. These ideas generate a specific spatial pattern in which a men's

19. Cf. the works of J. R. Denbow, T. M. Evers, E. O. M. Hanisch, T. N. Huffman, J. H. N. Loubser, T. M. Maggs, M. P. J. Moore, T. Robey, K. R. Robinson, E. A. Voigt and R. Welbourne. Listed in the Bibliography.

20. R. Oliver, 1982; R. Oliver and B. M. Fagan (eds), 1975; D. W. Phillipson, 1977a.

21. J. R. Denbow, 1982, 1983.

22. J. S. Butterworth, 1979; J. R. Denbow, 1979.

23. A. Kuper, 1982a.

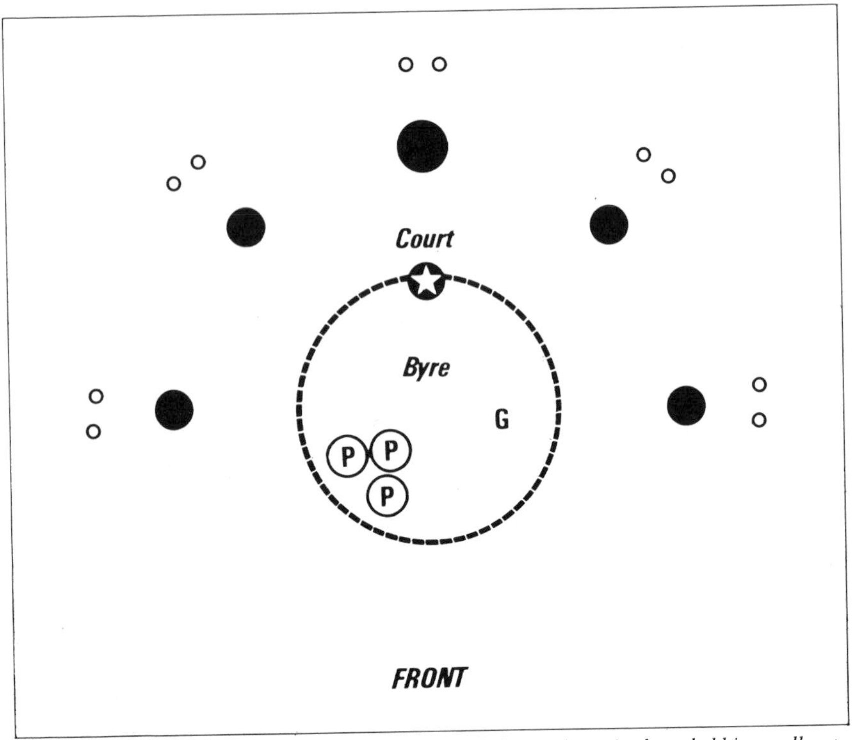

FIG. 24.3 *Spatial organization of the Bantu Cattle Culture: the senior household is usually upslope and behind the men's court and cattle byre, which contains grain storage pits (P) and graves (G). The small circles represent raised grain bins at the back of the individual households*

court is placed in the centre of the settlement in or near the cattle byre of the headman. The headman and other important people are buried in this kraal, and communal storage pits (or special grain bins) are also dug here as a protection against famine. The huts of a man's wives are placed around this central zone according to a system of status expressed through some alternating use of left and right positions. In settlements with independent households this status system determines the location of households around the headman, and in individual houses one side is reserved for men and the other for women in accordance with the same principle. Attitudes to profane and sacred activities, on the other hand, determine what is found in front and back positions. The front of the household and settlement is allocated to public and profane activities, while the back is reserved for private and sacred activities: for example, ancestral objects are kept at the back of a hut, privately (as opposed to communally) owned grain bins are placed behind the huts of their owners, and a sacred rainmaking area is located at the back of a settlement behind the quarters of the headman. Because this sacred/profane dimension is arranged more-or-less at right angles to that concerned primarily with status, the most important person is at the back of the settlement in the most protected position. If the front of the settlement faces downslope, then status and ritual importance are also expressed through height (see Fig. 24.3).

Despite considerable variability, this general pattern applies to many different ethnic groups in southern Africa, but it is not found among the matrilineal Bantu in central Africa, who own few if any cattle, nor among the cattle-owning non-Bantu-speakers in East Africa. The pattern instead appears to be restricted to patrilineal Bantu who exchange cattle for wives.[24] If this correlation is correct, the presence of this pattern in the archaeological record is conclusive evidence for a distinctive Bantu system of values concerning politics and cattle.

Although this entire spatial pattern cannot be physically uncovered in a prehistoric context, it is possible to find specific constellations of features that are exclusive to the Bantu Cattle Culture. Central cattle byres containing pits and human burials in particular appear to be sufficient. Using this kind of evidence, the Bantu Cattle Culture can be traced from historic times directly back to the seventh century in southern Africa. For example diagnostic features of the spatial pattern characterize eighteenth-century stone-walled settlements attributed to Northern Transvaal Ndebele,[25] eighteenth- to sixteenth-century stone-walled settlements associated with Sotho-Tswana speakers,[26] sixteenth- to fourteenth-century Moloko (the archaeological name for the Sotho-Tswana ceramic complex) settlements without stone walls,[27] fourteenth- to twelfth-century Woolandale sites,[28] twelfth- to tenth-century Leopard's Kopje,[29] Eiland[30] and Toutswe sites,[31] and tenth- to seventh-century Zhizo settlements, including those with apparently small herds.[32] Indeed, these diagnostic features show that Zhizo people during the Early Iron Age had the same basic attitudes toward cattle as historic Nguni.

Archaeologists previously underestimated the importance of cattle to Zhizo society because most excavations were designed to retrieve ceramic samples, not economic data. As a consequence, archaeologists seldom recognized dung deposits or realized the significance of activity areas to the interpretation of economic data. Research projects specifically designed to investigate lifeways show that herding and farming were complementary

24. ibid.
25. J. H. N. Loubser, 1981.
26. D. P. Collett, 1979, 1982; T. M. Evers, 1981, 1984; S. L. Hall, 1981; T. M. Maggs, 1976; R. J. Mason, 1968, 1969, 1974; M. O. V. Taylor, 1979, 1984.
27. B. N. S. Fordyce, 1984; E. O. M. Hanisch, 1979; R. J. Mason, 1974.
28. T. N. Huffman, 1984; K. R. Robinson, 1966a.
29. G. A. Gardner, 1963; E. O. M. Hanisch, 1980; T. N. Huffman, 1974b.
30. J. R. Denbow, 1981; J. H. N. Loubser, 1981; M. P. J. Moore, 1981.
31. J. R. Denbow, 1982, 1983.
32. ibid., E. O. M. Hanisch, 1980, 1981; T. N. Huffman, 1974b, 1984.

aspects of one system: separate Early and Late Iron Age types of economy did not exist.

Now that the cultural background to Zhizo and Leopard's Kopje communities has been established, our understanding of the Bantu Cattle Culture can be used to interpret the important events and changes that occurred in the Shashi/Limpopo area. I first concentrate on the largest settlements.

The size of a settlement in the Bantu Cattle Culture is a direct result of political power: the larger the settlement, the more important the leader. The largest and politically most important Zhizo settlement so far discovered anywhere is Schroda, just south-east of the modern border between Zimbabwe, Botswana and South Africa.[33] The largest known Leopard's Kopje settlement is K2,[34] located about six kilometres south-west of the earlier Zhizo capital.

At one time K2 was thought to be a Khoisan rather than a Bantu settlement.[35] This interpretation was greatly influenced by skeletal analyses that identified human burials from K2 as Boskop-Bush with no Negroid traits.[36] More recent analyses, however, show that the K2 people came from an essentially Negroid breeding population,[37] as did other Leopard's Kopje, Eiland and Zhizo communities, including Schroda.[38] This radically different interpretation of Iron Age communities is the result of better comparative collections and better methods of analysis. Earlier analyses concentrated univarially on a few traits thought to be significant, whereas recent studies attempt to characterize the total morphological pattern of an individual through multivariate procedures. The skeletal evidence now complements that from ceramic style and settlement organization and shows that K2 and Schroda people, like most other prehistoric Southern Bantu, were Negroes.

The K2 and Schroda people were probably attracted to the Shashi/Limpopo area because of its natural resources. Given sufficient rainfall, this is a good environment for mixed agriculturalists: the broken sandstone ridges provide cultivable soils and mixed woodland; the warm temperature and relatively low rainfall generate sweet savanna grasses; and the Shashi and Limpopo rivers ensure a more-or-less permanent water supply. In addition, the Mopani woodland between the two rivers is prime elephant country, and ivory would have been easily available: even today this area is rich in elephant. Furthermore, the rivers that drain the western gold reefs of Zimbabwe flow into the Shashi and Limpopo near their confluence; and so it would have been possible to pan for alluvial gold in the vicinity of

33. E. O. M. Hanisch, 1980, 1981.
34. J. F. Eloff and A. Meyer, 1981; G. A. Gardner, 1963; A. Meyer, 1980.
35. G. A. Gardner, 1963.
36. A. Galloway, 1937, 1959.
37. G. P. Rightmire, 1970.
38. E. O. M. Hanisch, 1980; T. N. Huffman, 1974; J. H. N. Loubser, 1981.

Schroda and K2.[39] I now show how external trade led to the evolution of the Zimbabwe Culture. I later show how this trade hypothesis is superior to other interpretations that emphasize the roles of religion and cattle.

Trade and politics: 1000–75

Archaeological evidence for contact between coastal merchants and Iron Age people in the Shashi/Limpopo area is clear. In fact, ninth-century Schroda is the earliest site in southern Africa to yield a substantial number of glass beads and ivory objects, and K2 has produced more ivory and glass beads than all other contemporaneous settlements combined.[40] What is more, archaeologists in Mozambique have recently located eighth- to twelfth-century coastal trading stations that probably supplied the glass beads first to Schroda and then K2.

Reconnaissance of the coastal plain around Vilanculos Bay and the Bazaruto Archipelago (the bay and peninsula in Fig. 24.1 next to 'Hola-Hola') discovered sites with Persian pottery and Islamic glass.[41] Preliminary excavations at one of these sites, Chibuene,[42] uncovered an eighth- to ninth-century deposit that contained glazed and unglazed wares like those from the early periods of Kilwa and Manda further up the east coast. This Early Iron Age deposit also yielded several hundred wound and drawn, yellow, green and blue glass beads like those from Schroda and K2. Indeed, some tubular blue beads in the collection are the same type as the earliest glass beads found anywhere in Zimbabwe. The Vilanculos area thus appears to have had the earliest coastal trading stations in south-eastern Africa, and the Shashi/Limpopo area appears to have been one of the first in the interior of southern Africa to be integrated in the Indian Ocean commercial network.

The recently discovered coastal stations together with Schroda and K2 were elements in the network described by al-Masʿūdī in the tenth century:

> The sailors of Oman . . . go on the sea of the Zandj as far as the island of Kanbalu and the Sofala of the Demdemah, which is on the extremity of the country of the Zandj and the low countries thereabout. The merchants of Siraf are also in the habit of sailing on this sea . . . The sea of the Zandj reaches down to the country of Sofala and of the Wāḳ-Wāḳ which produces gold in abundance and other marvels . . . Although constantly employed in hunting elephants and gathering ivory, the Zandj make no use of ivory for their own domestic purposes. They

39. T. G. Trevor and E. T. Mellor, 1908; M. Watkeys, Department of Geology, Witwatersrand University, personal communication.
40. E. A. Voigt, 1983.
41. P. J. J. Sinclair, 1981.
42. P. J. J. Sinclair, 1982.

> wear iron instead of gold and silver ... [Tusks] ... go generally to Oman, and from there are sent on to China and India.[43]

We know now from other sources that glass beads, cloth and sometimes glazed ceramics were brought back to southern Africa from China and India in exchange for the gold and ivory. Significantly, these imported commodities were different from the traditional wealth in cattle in at least one way.

In traditional Zhizo and Leopard's Kopje economies cattle had to be constantly circulated to maintain the system. Wealthy men would have loaned their cattle to poor people, and rich and poor alike would have exchanged cattle for wives. Traditional wealth, therefore, could not be hoarded without destroying the system. In contrast to cattle, the distribution of gold, ivory, glass beads and cloth could be completely controlled without undermining the economy because these commodities were storable. Besides these storage qualities, the trade goods were imported in huge quantities. As a consequence, hereditary leaders could become exceedingly wealthy. Wealth and political power were linked in the traditional system because, among other reasons, the more marriages and loans a chief could make, the more alliance and allegiances he established. According to later Portuguese documents, some of the trade goods were used for bride wealth and so once these commodities were translated into traditional economic values, the trade wealth also furthered political power.

When the Leopard's Kopje people moved into the Shashi/Limpopo area, they probably took the ivory trade away from Schroda before the trade wealth could have much impact on Zhizo society. A dramatic increase in the political power of the leaders at K2, however, is reflected in the midden associated with the chief's court. The court midden in the Bantu Cattle Culture characteristically comprises broken beer pots, the ash from the council fire, the remains of cattle slaughtered as fines or tribute, and the remains of wild animals shared among men or given as tribute to the chief. This debris is thrown into the central byre or kept next to the court, rather than mixed with other refuse elsewhere. Therefore, the magnitude of a court midden results directly from the intensity and duration of men's activity that takes place there. Originally K2 was organized like Schroda: small homesteads with their cattle byres flanked the central court of the chief. By 1020, however, the court midden at K2 became so large that it engulfed the nearby byre. At about the same time the cattle were moved out of the central area (Fig. 24.4). This removal of the central byre was the first alteration in the spatial organization of the Bantu Cattle Culture, and it was a direct consequence of increased political activity and associated changes in the relative economic value of cattle.

By 1075 the court midden had grown to a height of nearly six metres above the old byre, and the raised valley in which K2 was situated was

43. Quoted in B. Davidson, 1964, pp. 115–16.

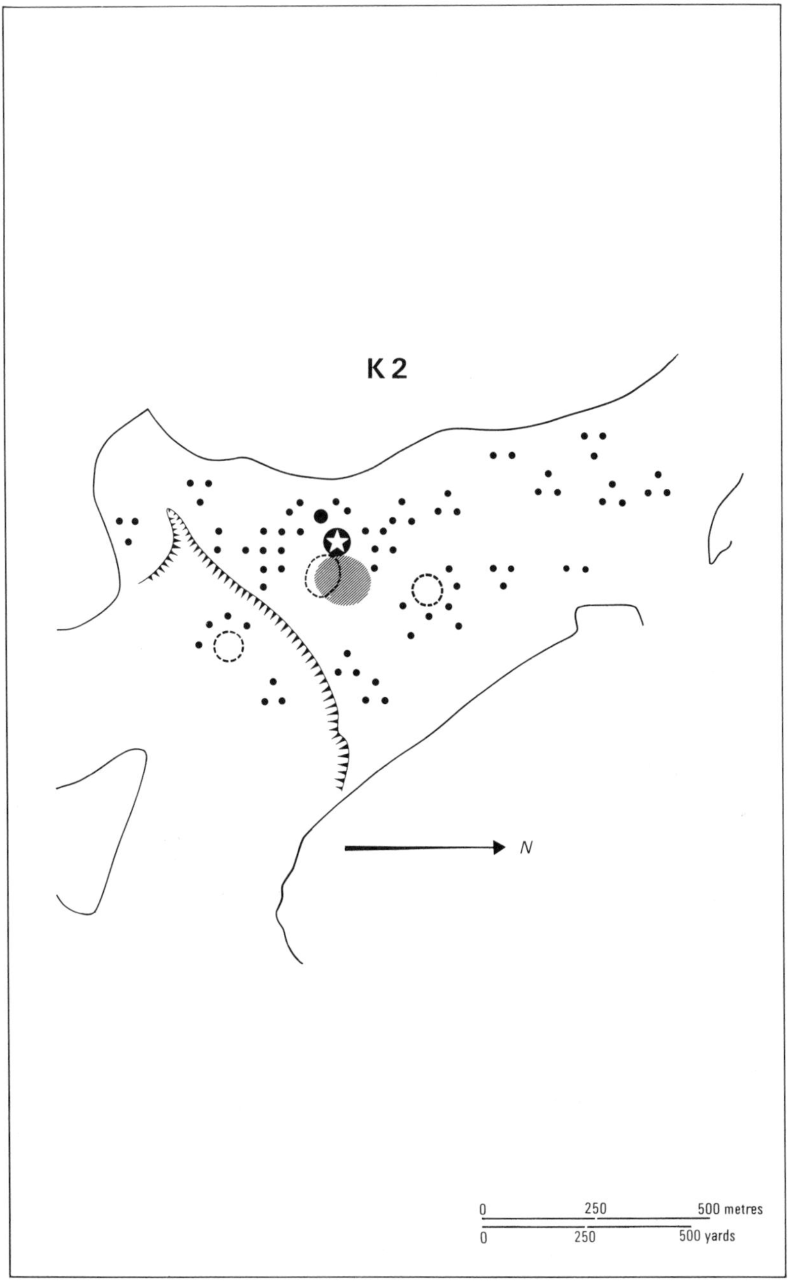

FIG. 24.4 *Stylized reconstruction of K2 at* c. *1050: the star marks the men's court; the large midden (hatched area) below the court covers an earlier cattle byre (dotted circle)*

completely occupied. Recent excavations and carbon-14 dates[44] show that the abrupt abandonment of K2 at this time coincided with an instantaneous increase of K2 people around Mapungubwe Hill, less than a kilometre away. Since two or three times more living space was available at Mapungubwe, it is reasonable to presume that the capital was shifted there in order to accommodate a growing population. A natural amphitheatre at the bottom of Mapungubwe Hill probably sheltered the new court because this is the only sizeable area inside the town centre free of residential debris (Fig. 24.5). The absence of cattle dung anywhere in the vicinity indicates that a byre was not erected with the court; and so, the previous alteration in the spatial pattern at K2 was perpetuated at Mapungubwe. Subsequent spatial transformations show that the origins of the Zimbabwe Culture lay here rather than at Great Zimbabwe itself.

Mapungubwe, the first Zimbabwe capital: 1075–1220

The spatial organization of the Zimbabwe Culture differs in several ways from the Bantu Cattle pattern: the king lived inside a stone enclosure on a hill above the court, not at the base of the hill; elite were buried in hills rather than in the byre; royal wives lived in their own area rather than with the king; and important men maintained prestigious residences on the outskirts of the capitals.[45] I now show that these and other features occurred for the first time at Mapungubwe.

When the capital was relocated at Mapungubwe, some people moved onto the hill above the court (Fig. 24.5). It is reasonable to presume that these people included the chief and his household, since they would have lived upslope and behind the court at K2. This shift from upslope to uphill is the first time in the prehistory of southern Africa that leaders were so physically separated from their followers, and it is the first indication of an institutionalized class structure.

Shortly after the move from K2 to Mapungubwe, the K2 ceramic style began to change. Some might argue that this change signalled the appearance of a new people, but the ceramic differences are not stylistically or numerically abrupt: instead, the surface finish was refined, the earlier K2 designs merely became more complex, and the new types only gradually replaced the others. Rather than an ethnic replacement, these changes may have been due to the emergence of full-time ceramic specialists, who were a consequence of the burgeoning population and developing class structure. Further research is necessary, however, to clarify the impact of social change on ceramic style.

Other artefacts indicate continued contact with coastal traders. Spindle-

44. J. F. Eloff and A. Meyer, 1981; M. Hall and J. C. Vogel, 1980; A. Meyer, 1980.
45. T. N. Huffman, 1981, 1982.

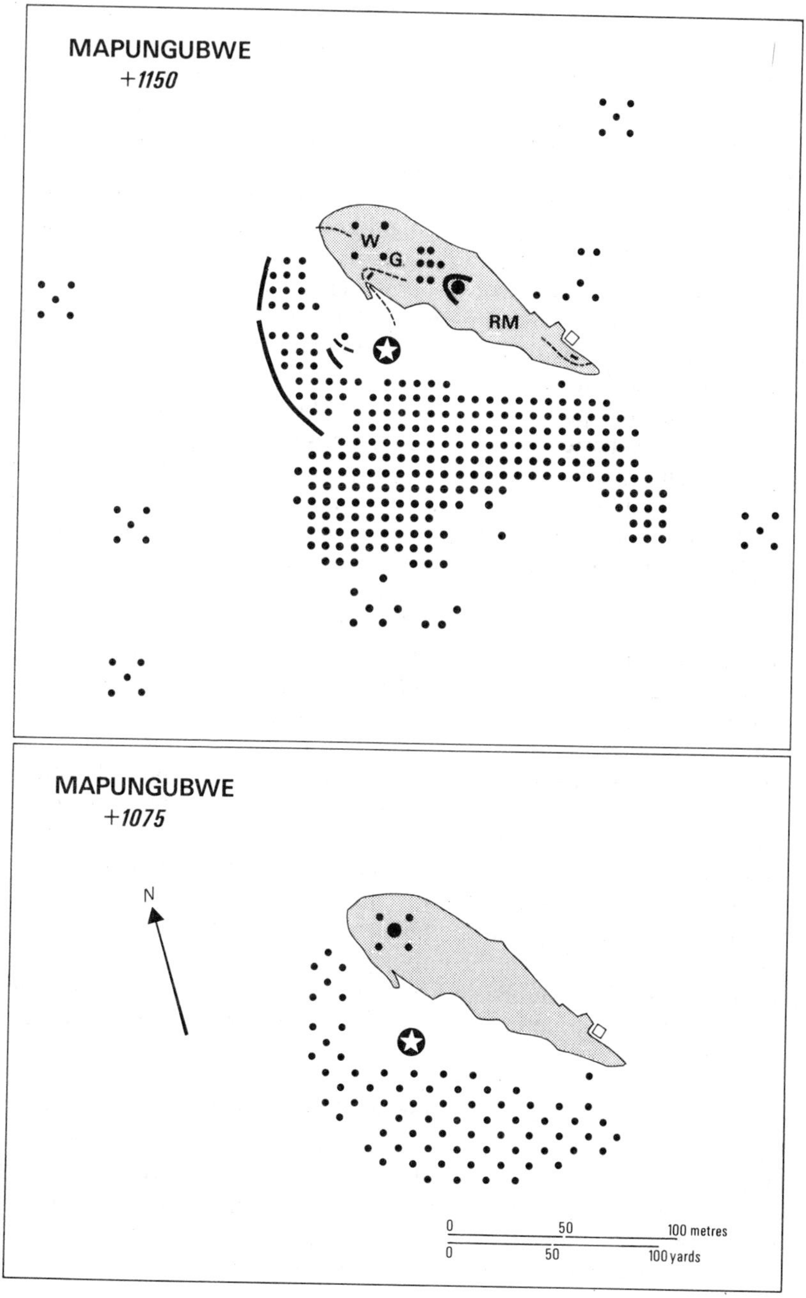

FIG. 24.5 *Stylized reconstruction of Mapungubwe at 1075 and 1150: the star marks the men's court; W = wives' area; G = grave area; RM = rain-making area*

whorls appear at about 1100 at Mapungubwe.[46] These flat circular discs with central perforations were used as weights for spinning cotton thread.[47] Since cotton-weaving was a well-established craft in Swahili towns by this time, the spindle-whorls at Mapungubwe, the earliest known in the interior, mark the introduction of weaving by coastal traders and perhaps the start of another craft speciality.

At the beginning of the trade, gold was probably more a means to wealth than wealth itself, but by about 1150 gold objects had been locally manufactured. Unique items such as a rhinoceros and a 'sceptre' made from thin sheets of gold tacked onto wooden cores were found in elite burials on the royal hill.[48] This is the first time in the Iron Age of southern Africa that gold was used as a status symbol; and so it is the earliest evidence that gold had acquired a local intrinsic value.

By this time the spatial organization of Mapungubwe had been transformed into a new pattern in which stone walls demarcated important areas (Fig. 24.5). One stone-walled residence was sited next to the court at the base of the hill. This residence was most likely occupied by the principal councillor, the man in the Zimbabwe Culture who organized court cases and appointments with the king. The main staircase led from this area through a narrow cleft to the hilltop: paired sockets in the sandstone probably held wooden steps, and a short length of coursed walling marked the top of the passage. More sockets at the top may have supported a palisade fence which surrounded the hill and funnelled traffic to the right of the graveyard. On this right-hand side several huts had been erected in front of a large arc of stone walling that enclosed a special hut complex. Rare Chinese celadon from this complex, together with the stone wall, indicate that the king lived here. Stone boards for a men's game in the foremost hut complex suggest that male retainers lived in this area, such as the soldiers, praisers and musicians described in later Portuguese documents for other Zimbabwe kings. The opposite side of the graveyard is reached by an inconspicuous passageway on the north-west end of the hill. The huts on this other side have yielded the only grindstones from the hilltop; and so they were probably occupied by royal wives. Therefore, the new pattern included a formal distinction between the wives' residence and that of the king and his retainers.

Other features were continuities from the older Bantu Cattle pattern. For example, since the ritual rain pots behind the homestead of the chief in the older pattern were inextricably linked to the chief's homestead, they were probably moved to the top of the hill when the royal family moved from K2. The corresponding area on Mapungubwe Hill is devoid of normal residential debris, yet it is reached by a special stone-walled pathway at the eastern end of the hill. It is likely, then, that this was a national rain-

46. A. Meyer, 1980.
47. P. Davison and P. Harries, 1980.
48. L. Fouché, 1937.

making centre behind the king's apartment, as the Eastern Enclosure was at Great Zimbabwe. Consequently, the eastern pathway up the hill demarcates the back of the town, and the long wall on the opposite side marks the front, as at Great Zimbabwe.

The distribution of occupational debris shows that the bulk of the population resided within this western wall, but a few families lived on high spots outside the urban centre (Fig. 24.5). In the Bantu Cattle pattern men who are competitors for chieftainship, such as brothers, uncles and important affines, usually live outside the protective circle formed by the chief's immediate supporters.[49] Because the same kind of competition would have existed at Mapungubwe, it is likely that the prestigious residences around the edge of the town were inhabited by such important men.

These important residences are similar to elite hilltop settlements some distance away from Mapungubwe: for example, Little Muck, 13 km away; Mmangwa, 40 km to the west;[50] Mapela Hill, 85 km north-west;[51] and Macena Hill, 96 km north-east. They are invariably near low-lying Mapungubwe-phase villages which were still organized around central cattle byres, for example at Mtetengwe.[52] These different kinds of settlements provide the best archaeological evidence for a three-tiered political hierarchy: the low-lying sites were probably inhabited by commoners; the small hilltop sites were probably occupied by district leaders; and the capital at Mapungubwe would have been the supreme authority. The elite residences on the outskirts of the capital, then, were probably the town houses of these district leaders. Thus, the class structure of Mapungubwe society is evident in the regional distribution of settlements as well as in the spatial organization of the capital.

The sequence of changes from K2 to Mapungubwe and the similarities between Mapungubwe and Great Zimbabwe demonstrate that the Zimbabwe Culture evolved out of the Bantu Cattle Culture in the Shashi/Limpopo area. Mapungubwe, consequently, should be considered as the first Zimbabwe capital.

This sequence also clarifies the roles of religion and cattle in the evolution of the Zimbabwe Culture. Some historians believe that the Mbire moved south across the Zambezi and developed the Zimbabwe kingdom through the power of their religion before the gold trade was established with the coast.[53] The archaeological evidence is clear, however, that the important ethnic movement was from the south and that the elaborate ritual that surrounded Zimbabwe kings accompanied the external trade and growth of political power rather than preceding it. Therefore, new religious forces could not have caused the rise of the Zimbabwe Culture.

49. I. Schapera, 1970.
50. M. J. Tamplin, 1977, p. 38.
51. P. S. Garlake, 1968.
52. K. R. Robinson, 1968.
53. D. P. Abraham, 1962, 1966; P. S. Garlake, 1973.

Other Africanists believe that the Zimbabwe Culture arose through the ownership of cattle herds and the consequent development of grazing strategy for these large areas. As herds naturally increased, it is argued, concepts of private property developed around cattle. Since the best grazing strategy for these large herds was a transhumance cycle, according to this hypothesis, control of distant pasturages became essential, and this forced the development of a centralized political authority.[54] The first objection to this interpretation is that cattle herds did not dramatically increase immediately before the development of the Zimbabwe Culture, for the thick dung deposits and spatial organization of the seventh-century Zhizo settlements show that cattle-oriented societies existed at least four hundred years before Mapungubwe was established. My second objection concerns the postulated transhumance cycle. The numerous commoner sites with substantial dung deposits in the Mapungubwe region negate the possibility of any regular, large-scale movement of cattle and people to distant pasturages, for the physical remains show that these settlements were just as permanent as Early Iron Age communities.

More important than these substantive errors, however, is the confusion between political centralization and cultural change. Various cattle-based societies within southern Africa have been highly centralized, such as the Bamangwato, Matabele, Zulu and Swazi, and yet these societies still had the same cultural values as the rest of the Southern Bantu, and, accordingly, their settlements were still organized according to the same principles that underlay K2 and Schroda. It follows then that private wealth in cattle may have been a necessary precursor to the evolution of Zimbabwe, but it was not a sufficient cause.

Thus, neither the cattle nor the religious hypothesis explains the present data. The complete trade hypothesis, on the other hand, accounts for the long period of cattle-keeping before the rise of Mapungubwe, the enlarged court midden at K2, the move from K2 to Mapungubwe, the subsequent spatial alterations at Mapungubwe, and the continuity of the Bantu Cattle Culture in other parts of southern Africa. As this chapter has shown, the transformations at K2 and Mapungubwe that lead to the Zimbabwe Culture were the result of increased political power made possible by the ivory and gold trade.

54. P. S. Garlake, 1978.

25 Madagascar

B. DOMENICHINI-
RAMIARAMANANA

The history of Madagascar before +1000, sometimes even before +1500, is often seen as an area of uncertainty in which numerous and contradictory hypotheses have been put forward for decades without ever being able to secure general agreement.[1] The written sources brought to light in the Island at best go back to the twelfth century, and the growth of archaeology has been too recent[2] – and its means too limited – for it to provide us with reliable statistical and chronological results,[3] which would place historical reconstructions on wholly reliable bases. Making use of non-Malagasy sources, since the old works of G. Ferrand, has been virtually limited to works in the Arabic language; in any case, use of these sources involves knowledge of many languages with which specialists on Madagascar are not normally familiar, and mastery of knowledge that is usually far beyond the capacities of the small teams currently in existence. It no doubt takes a fair amount of boldness to write a history of Madagascar from the inside between the seventh and eleventh centuries of the Christian era.

It was tempting to begin using the oral sources in all the forms in which they can be found today in Madagascar, and this is what we have done in this chapter. These sources have survived in a variety of circumstances. Sometimes, especially in the south-east, they have been attached to documents written in Arabic-Malagasy script (*volan'Onjatsy* or *sorabe*);[4] sometimes they have been absorbed, in the form of traces that are difficult to interpret, in sources that have been much reworked;[5] sometimes they are

1. See Unesco, *General History of Africa*, Vol. II, ch. 28, and the bibliography. See also E. Ralaimihoatra, 1971b, 1974.
2. J. P. Domenichini, 1981b.
3. For an interesting survey of the question, see D. Rasamuel, 1985, 1986.
4. On which much important work is being done today in Madagascar itself, under the guidance of Professor Ludwig Munthe.
5. This is the case, for example, with a source recently located in Lower Manan-jara by B. Domenichini-Ramiaramanana, among the Ravoaomena Andria-manavanana, a tiny minority group that claims to be the descendants of the local dynasty that existed before that of the Zafi(n–d)Raminia, whose arrival in the north-east of the Island has been dated to the late eleventh century. The traditions of these latter, constructed over almost a millennium of virtually continuous domination, largely obliterated those of earlier groups.

texts of a highly formal nature, used in rituals that are still performed;[6] sometimes, finally, they are scattered sources, where the context is not very clear, that are being collected more and more throughout the country.

Nevertheless, we think it important to show how research in progress in the Island, untrammelled by the problematic of colonialism, and of any quest for legitimacy based on racism or, even worse, evolutionism, and making proper use of both oral sources and the rich contributions of multi-disciplinary approaches, has begun to open up new perspectives.[7] We shall not enter here into the still very lively discussion between the – increasingly rare – supporters of a short chronology [8] and the supporters of a long chronology,[9] nor into highly ideological debates on the forms and stages of the peopling of the Island; we shall not try and say who the *Vazimba* were, about whom so much remains to be discovered, nor shall we deal with the tales of settlement by 'Arabs', which were for a long time taken literally as accounts of the origin of a good many Malagasy groups. All these are matters that require serious examination and study before debates about them are resumed. We want here, rather, to open up discussion on other matters, using other sources of information.[10]

The problem of understanding oral sources

An enormous effort is under way in Madagascar to collect and study all possible sources in this area. Like everywhere else, they demand a precise methodology; in the case of Madagascar, linguistics plays a very important role in opening up the historical information that these sources contain.

A manuscript recently edited and transcribed by Ludwig Munthe[11] has drawn attention especially to a whole corpus of very scattered information about a 'giant' named *Darafify*[12] which requires close critical atten-

6. We shall give some examples of this.

7. B. Domenichini-Ramiaramanana and J. P. Domenichini, 1979 and 1983.

8. See J. Poirier, 1965; P. Ottino, 1974a and P. Vérin, 1974.

9. Perrier de la Bathie (quoted by H. Deschamps, 1972, p. 35) proposed a range of from five centuries to four millennia *since* the destruction of the forest in the central Highlands, which were probably the last region of the Island to be inhabited.

10. B. Domenichini and J. P. Domenichini, 1984. The first version of this text (1983) which developed various points in the article quoted in note 7, was the object of a series of discussions not only with experts on Madagascar but also with experts on East Africa and the western Indian Ocean and experts on South-east Asia and Austronesia.

11. L. Munthe, 1982. The published manuscript is that of a *sorabe*. It bears the scientific reference A6 and is kept in Oslo.

12. The systematic collection of sources relating to *Darafify* and other 'giants' is only just beginning. It reveals the wealth of memory, orally transmitted, throughout the east and south.

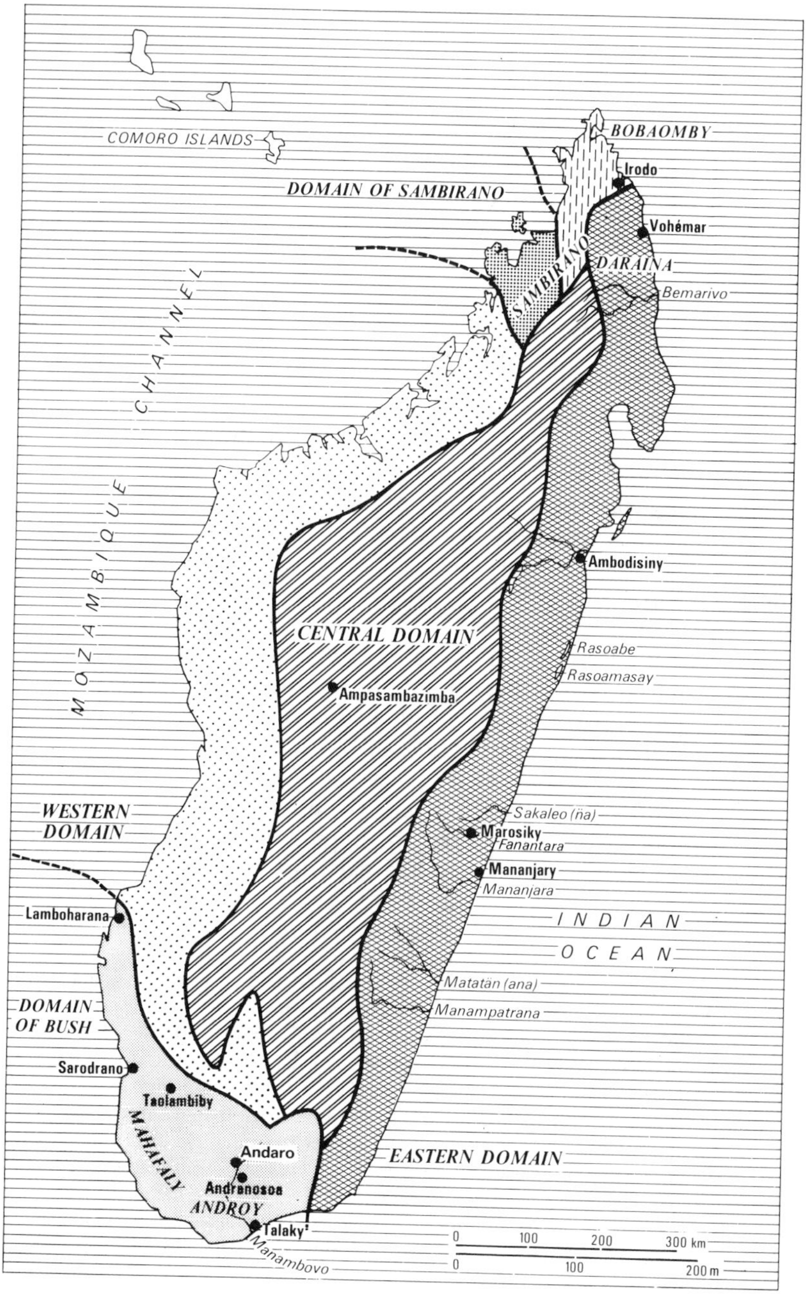
COMORO ISLANDS
BOBAOMBY
Irodo
DOMAIN OF SAMBIRANO
Vohémar
SAMBIRANO
DARAINA
Bemarivo
MOZAMBIQUE CHANNEL
CENTRAL DOMAIN
Ambodisiny
Rasoabe
Rasoamasay
Ampasambazimba
WESTERN DOMAIN
Sakaleo (ña)
Marosiky
Fanantara
Mananjary
Mananjara
INDIAN OCEAN
Lamboharana
Matatàn (ana)
Manampatrana
DOMAIN OF BUSH
Sarodrano
Taolambiby
MAHAFALY
Andaro
Andranosoa
ANDROY
EASTERN DOMAIN
Talaky
Manambovo
0 100 200 300 km
0 100 200 m

FIG. 25.1 *Madagascar and the Comoros*

tion.[13] The first thing was to know whether the names provided by this cycle, for the 'giants' in question, had any historical validity or not. The profound homogeneity of the Malagasy language, which derives from the unity of its underlying Austronesian foundation[14] and does not, as has been claimed, date from the Merina expansion in the eighteenth and nineteenth centuries, makes it possible not only to identify borrowings from other languages rather easily and locate them chronologically in the cultural history of the country, but also to work at least momentarily and in the same way on any tradition transmitted in Malagasy.

We had, thanks to the Oslo A6 manuscript, a document in Malagasy which appeared, in addition, to be the most complete and coherent version of the story of Darafify and his intervention in a particular region. Analysis of it enabled us not only to uncover some of the political and social circumstances under which it was transmitted, but also to conclude that the *katibo* in the south-east had taken good care to respect its formal character, even if they had no hesitation about removing from it anything that might undermine the reputation as first 'civilizers' of the region usually attributed to their ancestors who had 'come from Arabia'. It was thus possible, as a first step, to proceed to the study of names. Each of these was, in accordance with Malagasy usage, formed according to precise rules, which are perfectly 'decodable'.

The first clear information provided by the names of the 'giants' in question was that these names are made up of a masterly mixture of words of Austronesian, Sanskrit or Persian origin, but they all relate to the trade in aromatics, spices, perfumes and medicinal herbs.[15] The form adopted by these various elements made possible the acceptance of the whole range of such terms as neologisms which had arisen in the Island during a period (prior to Islam) of contacts between Madagascar and the regions considered and put forward to suggest the hypothesis according to which the regions of Madagascar concerned had participated in trade in the Indian Ocean prior to the seventh century.

Darafify, *Darofipy*, *Darafely Fatrapaitañ(ana)* are formed from simple

13. For the corpus as it stands, we were dealing with documents which had not only been torn from their context but also transformed – even deformed – by transcriptions and translations made by men whose acquaintance with oral cultures in general and/or Malagasy cultures in particular were quite obviously inadequate or even non-existent. And it might seem *a priori* that treatment by the archaeology of language (B. Domenichini-Ramiaramanana, 1983 and 1985) might, in these circumstances, not provide all the guarantees that it can in the case of traditions that are formulated in the mother tongue of the group concerned and methodically collected in the normal context in which they are displayed. The archaeology of language is a philological approach in the broadest sense of the term and in semantic analysis has recourse to both etymology and dialectical comparisons and the symbolic code of the culture, which is manifested even in the traditional techniques of conscious or unconscious manipulation of linguistic data.

14. B. Domenichini-Ramiaramanana, 1976.

15. ibid.

words which, except *dara*, are still used in Malagasy and we need to look at how they are used. *Fi(m)py–fify* relate to food, cosmetic and pharmaceutical products; among these was no doubt what Etienne de Flacourt identified in the seventeenth century as being the *Costus* of Madagascar.[16] If we refer to ethnoscience, this first category of products included, first, animal products coming mainly from the operculum of the *Murex* genus of shellfish and especially of the *Murex trunculus*, which are still used in powder form in the south-west. A second group in this category are vegetable products derived essentially from certain *Myristicacaeae* (the bark and gum of *Haematodendron* or *Mauloutchia sp.*,[17] but probably also from the root of a herbaceous plant.[18] Also in this category of *fi(m)py–fify* were the various varieties of wild pepper (*Piper borbonese* DC), presently known as 'pink pepper' (*Piper pachyphyllum* Baker and *Piper pyriofolium* Vahl) inherent in the term *Darafely*.[19] At the beginning of the nineteenth century, Barthélémy Hugon[20] identified them as being the 'true cubeb of the Arabs', who were first great consumers of it and later re-exported it.

Finally there was benjamin (*fatra* or *Styrax benzoin* Dryander) remembered in the name of the giant Fatrapaitañ(ana), but which seems not then to have been the main export product of the Matatañ(na), since it appears through this name that the measure (*fatra*) of benjamin (*fatra*) was a gift made to the purchaser when a sale was concluded (*paitanana*). And in the field that concerns us here, this main product must have been *fimpy*, which botanists have recognized as being abundant in the south-east. As for benjamin itself, which as a fixative for more volatile essences is mainly used to increase the value of these – whence no doubt its status in the trade of the Matatañ(na). Miller[21] suggested identifying it with the *cancanum* mentioned by classical authors, which the *Periplus of the Erythraean Sea* included among the imports of Arabia from Malao (in present-day Somalia). And *cancanum*, according to Miller, reached this port along the 'Cinnamon Route' that he situated as passing by way of Madagascar and East Africa, 'in the time of the Roman Empire (−29/+641)'.

There are yet other products that appear in the sources of the 'Darafify Cycle', but their names were not used, as the preceding ones were, to make up the names of giants. To give them their proper names, the *(ha)ramy* (*Canarium madagascariense*, *C. boivini* and *C. multiflorum* Engler) are known today as 'Madagascar incense' or 'white African incense'; as regards

16. E. de Falcourt, 1661, p. 131.
17. P. Boiteau, 1976, p. 71.
18. ibid., p. 69. See: name of *fifinatsy* or *Bulbostylis firingalavensis* Cherm.
19. The peppers are designated in Malagasy by the old names of *Voamperifery* and *Tsimperifery*, derived from borrowings from Sanskrit in the Asiatic period of the history of the language. They are also designated by the more recent name of *Darafilofilo*, a word used only in the north.
20. E. Heckel, 1903, p. 120.
21. J. I. Miller, 1969, p. 39.

cinnamons referred to in the placename *Ambodisiny*, a probable calque of the former *Andarasiny*, they still retain some traces of their ancient importance today: among some groups, in the solemn planting of a cinnamon root at the birth of a first son in a family.[22]

Linguistics shows then that there is a link, which may yet become conscious, between the names of 'legendary' figures who incarnate a very abstract ancient history and the plants and precious products of Madagascar, especially in the eastern part of the Island.

For the historian, the next stage is much more difficult. On the one hand, we need to know whether the very indirect allusions that he has collected have any real historical content, and whether it might be possible to situate them in even a relative chronology; and whether this chronology in turn fits into a reliable chronology of trade in the Indian Ocean. These points will be looked at below. On the other hand – and this relates more to the internal history of the Island – we need to elicit, still within a likely chronology, the history of the power relationships among groups for ancient periods in the life of the peoples of the Island: this is certainly research of a most challenging kind but also research that is the least spectacular to report in a book such as the present one; therefore, in this *General History*, we shall omit it entirely, since the results already known and in the process of being published are available elsewhere. But we should perhaps mention some general features that are useful to the historian.

First of all, the names which have just been mentioned are, historically, difficult to use. Each of them constitutes a collective symbol and not the individual name of a 'historic hero'; when one speaks of 'the Darafify', 'the Darofipy' and others, one is simply talking of a number of episodes in the history of the Island, which probably pre-date the eleventh century. But it also describes *a given group at a given time in its history*, for example when it attempted to corner the production and export of certain products; at other times, or on other occasions, the same group was perhaps known by other names.

Treating peoples as 'giants', like treating them as 'dwarfs' are also codes,

22. Today, in the Island, cinnamons include both introduced *Cinnamona* and endemic *Cinnamosma*, which include one of the famous 'conquerors of every problem' (*mandravasarotra*, *Cinnamosma fragrans* Baillon) so often prescribed by both empiricists and diviners. When they are not called *kanely*kanelina* (<French *cannelle*), from names spread during colonization with the development of the exploitation of *Cinnamomum zeylanicum* Breyn, cinnamons, in everyday language, are usually described by names of Austronesian origin, *hazomanitra* 'perfumed wood' and *hazomamy* 'sweet wood', except in the north. There, despite the extreme openness of the language to borrowings from French, people continue to call them nostalgically *darasiny* (<Persian *dār čīnī* 'cinnamon', literally, 'wood/tree from China' or 'gate of China') as in Persian and languages that have borrowed this word from it, either directly or through Arabic. And it is thus, as it were, indirectly, under this latter name, that they are mentioned in the Darafify cycle through the toponym of Ambodisiny, 'At the foot/feet of the cinnamon(s)/Near the cinnamons'.

PLATE 25.1 *Cinnamon-tree:* Cinnamomum zeylanicum

the key to which we need to discover, with no thought of using these facts as actual historical realities. Just as treating people as 'dwarfs' was used by Malagasy tradition in the case of the Vazimba, to confirm their political consignment to oblivion in various parts of the island, so treating people as 'giants' was no doubt used, in the case of the Darafify – and thus too of their opponents – in order to immortalize groups which were so prestigious that many local traditions endeavoured to preserve the memory of them.

The rewriting of traditions, their contradictions and the opposing legitimacies that they attempted to secure are inextricably mixed up. It is probably impossible, without lengthy surveys in which anthropology and linguistics would have a major role to play, to conclude too rapidly, straightaway, on the basis of the few undeniably historical features that can certainly be found in the 'Darafify cycle' and which relate to the internal history of the Island, that a part of the history of the Island can already be written based on them. They constitute irreplaceable elements of potential. But who were these 'Darafify', who came from the north-east, and who are said, at a time that is difficult to specify, to have sought to escape from what the oral sources stress was their traditional condition as cattle-rearers? They are said then to have become involved, through tact, or by force, depending on places and cases, in a trade (how regular? on what scale?) which may have carried (using Austronesian (?) or Persian (?) middlemen) products in demand in the world to the north of Madagascar. It should be noted that the regions of the Island involved in these obscure events were situated in the eastern coastal part and the south.

The geographical area within which the powerful group of the Darafify – tempted to acquire a monopoly of this trade – intervened is already broadly delimited by the places where the traditions forming the cycle were collected. It is more narrowly defined not only by the places where the facts and events recorded occurred, but also by the places where the human achievements attributed to them are still to be found, almost all of which are connected with the working of chlorite-schist (quarries and manufactured goods). It then comes out quite clearly that this area, although it had an extension into the Mahafale in the south-west (given as the last region reached by a migration that had chosen to cut across country, leaving the east coast somewhere south of the Manampatrana[23]) stretched essentially from the extreme north of the Island to the basin of the Matataña(na). It embraced, in short, except for the extreme south, the whole eastern seaboard of the Island, which is moreover particularly rich in these aromatics, spices, perfumes and medicinal herbs, and the conditions under which they were exploited (production and commercialization) also emerge quite clearly from the deciphering of proper names, particularly all those recorded in the text of the Oslo A6 manuscript. Surveys already conducted

23. On the importance of the Maropaika gate for moving from east to west and vice versa, see E. Ralaimihoatra, 1966, p. 54.

along the lower Mananjara have shown the scale of the ideological reworking suffered by the tradition of the Ravoaimena Andriamanavanana, when the Zafi(n–d) Raminia arrived.

The part of the history of the lower Mananjara after the arrival of the Zafi(n–d) Raminia is probably to be dated after the end of the eleventh century. Nevertheless, knowledge of it seems to be fundamental for anyone seeking to understand the later evolution of political and social organization in various regions of the Island; it is equally vital for anyone wanting to have a better understanding of the context within which the export trade developed, whose ups and downs probably profoundly marked the earlier period.

By revealing both the community of origins between the old princes of the Darafify and Zafi(n–d) Raminia and the impact of their solidarity on the history of Madagascar, this history forces us to turn to the pre-Malagasy history of the Zafi(n–d) Raminia. This history, over which much ink has already been spilled, is certainly still very little known. However, from relatively reliable data it can already be agreed that, while delimiting the area of the activities of these great Austronesian traders, which included most of the Indian Ocean covered by sea routes, the successive migrations of the Zafi(n–d) Raminia, from Sumatra to the shores of the Red Sea, and from there to India (Mangalore), and then to Madagascar, might equally reflect the general movement of sea-borne trade among the Austronesians which, at least partly, embraced Malagasy external trade from the seventh to the eleventh century. But before attempting to go so far, it is no doubt desirable to complete our survey of life in Madagascar, through the contributions of disciplines whose main sources owe but little to the linguistic sciences.

Ethno-botany or archaeology: is it likely that the products mentioned were exported?

The present-day vegetation of Madagascar is generally considered to be the direct or indirect result of human activity. The disappearance, about the beginning of the present millennium, of some animals (large lemurs, large 'ostriches' or *Aepyornis*, large land tortoises, giant crocodiles, dwarf hippopotamuses, etc.) that lived in this original environment, and whose cemeteries are to be found often around old water points, seems at least to indicate that there had already been a considerable change in the forest cover, even if it may also be supposed that there was also a period of relatively lower rainfall in order to explain the drying up of some regions. And it may moreover be noted that in some sites dating from our period (Lamboharana, +730 ± 80; Taolambiby, +900 ± 150; and Ambasambazimba, +915 ± 50), traces of human industries (teeth pierced for ornamentation, pottery, etc.) are found associated with the remains of these sub-fossil animals; doubt as to whether they are exactly contemporaneous arises from our ignorance as to their respective situations in the stratigraphy.[24]

Whether it is a matter of the flora or the fauna, the action of men in other times was not only negative, as there is a tendency too often to portray it. In the area of the flora, the wealth of endemic species (86 per cent) and the rarity of particular types (less than 8 per cent) that are the typical features of the Malagasy flora, testify both to the length of time that Madagascar has been an island and to the fact that the island was once attached to a large continent, the present-day remnants of which are covered with a similar primitive flora. It is a situation that suggests that the immigrants to Madagascar, wherever they came from, found there plants identical to or closely resembling those in their own country or countries of origin, many of which were plants that were already traded or could be traded in due course. It is enough, to be convinced on this point, to examine, for example, the list of plants made by Flacourt,[25] who naturally paid particular attention to commerical plants, and to compare it with the lists drawn up for imports from Egypt, the Roman Empire and Persia.

Two questions are thus posed: were these plants and products of animal origin, the memory of which has been retained in the oral sources, especially in the east of the Island, collected and sold in ancient times? That is what we are now going to analyse. Were they integrated into a trading area that included, before Islam and in its early days, all or part of the Indian Ocean? That is what we shall look at below. According to the census made by Perrier de la Bathie,[26] 48 per cent of non-endemic Malagasy plants were imported by man. More remarkable still, and something that could not be explained by biogeography – which would normally expect to find more non-endemic plants in the west, separated from East Africa simply by the Mozambique Channel, than in the east, separated from any other continent by the vastness of the Indian Ocean – 57.14 per cent of these plants are found in the windward region – and, exceptionally, in the Sambirano (north-west) – whereas there are only 14.28 per cent found in the leeward region, the remaining 28.75 per cent being common to both regions. Perrier de la Bathie felt that the introduction of these plants occurred indirectly through the activity of man, after the break-up of the continent to which Madagascar initially belonged. He used this to demonstrate in passing the antiquity of the human presence in the Island.[27] The planting of valuable species and the acclimatization of new plants was no doubt undertaken before the destruction of the forest by silviculturists or at least by true wandering land-clearers, who were generally careful about restoring the soil and the vegetable formations. Archaeological research is

24. J. P. Domenichini, 1981a, p. 70.
25. E. de Flacourt, 1661, pp. 111–46.
26. H. Perrier de la Bathie, 1936.
27. ibid., pp. 143–4. For a recent survey see C. Chanudet, 1979.

less developed than research in biogeography or palaeontology, and it has so far brought to light only one site pre-dating our period (Saradrano, a fishermen's site in the south-west, $+490 \pm 90$),[28] but it has on the other hand revealed some that do date to our period. And, as with vegetation formations, these sites have as it were confirmed in advance some of the facts recently established by the decoding of oral tradition which, in turn, should make it possible to propose a better-based interpretation of the results of surveys and excavations.

In the northern region that tradition gives as the place of origin of the Darafify, between Bobaomby and Daraina, at the bottom of a bay protected from the swell of the open sea by Nosy Valasola ('The island residence of the envoy' or 'The island reliquary'[29]), Nosy Fiherenana ('The island of return'), Nosy Komankory ('The island of pigs') and Nosy Ankomba ('The island of lemurs'), is to be found Irodo, from the name of a present-day village and on the river that empties into this bay. Since there has been no pollen analysis, there is nothing yet to confirm or refute the exploitation there of the *dara* and other commerical plants remembered here in the name Daraina ('From which *dara* were made'/'Where the *dara* are plentiful'). But Battistini has pointed out that the coastal plain, where shells of the eggs of the *Aepyornis* (*vorompatra* 'bird of the deforested zones') have been found, 'is almost wholly covered by a *satrana* savanna, which is certainly a degraded formation',[30] and the region situated south of Ampasimena bears the name of Ankaibe, describing a zone that was put to fire by land-clearers and herdsmen.

The three coastal sites that have been the object of surveys have revealed a population with the same culture characterized, according to Vérin, by 'the styles of its pottery (pots, jars, legged bowls), the use of chlorite-schist (pots, bowls) and the consumption of *Pyrazus palustris*'. Archaeologists estimate that this site, which was in use at least until the middle of the fifteenth century, was already occupied in the ninth and perhaps even in the seventh century.[31] In those early times, fishermen knew how to work iron and glass and were in contact with an Arab-Persian trading area.[32] Among the shells (*Pyrazus palustris*, *Ostrea mytoloides*, *Turbo*, etc.), no doubt mainly destined for consumption and craftwork (spoons carved from *Turbo*), are found, but in small quantities, *Murex* which provided *fimpy*, a

28. R. Battistini and P. Vérin, 1971, and, particularly for the dating, R. Battistini, 1976.

29. Thinking of the frequent use of islands as cattle pens in the north, one is tempted to translate *Nosy Valasolo* as 'the island that is a substitute for an enclosure', but that would normally be *Nosy Solovala*, since *solo* is only found as a substantive.

30. R. Battistini and P. Vérin, 1967, p. xix(a).

31. Carbon-14 datings: Kigoshi: GAK 380: 1200 ± 140 BP; GAK 692: 1090 ± 90 BP; GAK 350b: 980 ± 100 BP; giving a maximum range of from $+610$ to $+1070$.

32. R. Battistini and P. Vérin, 1967, p. xix(a). P. Vérin, 1975, repeats the 1967 text but replaces 'seventh to ninth century' by 'ninth to eleventh century' without further explanation.

perfume still sought today by Muslim 'Indians' in Madagascar and whose name is to be found, as we have seen, in the name of Darafify.

Other sites dating at least partly from our period are to be found in the far south of the Island, in present-day Antandroy country, which it was until recently thought was only peopled in the eighteenth to nineteenth centuries, since no European source ever mentioned the obvious signs of its early occupation, despite the fact that its population was relatively dense and seems to have lasted until the sixteenth century. These are essentially two groups both situated on the banks of the Manambovo ('The river with traps/water holes'), that of the site of Talaky[33] ('The well seen'), astride the mouth, and that of the site of Andranosoa[34] ('At the good water'), partly occupied by the imposing Manda(n–d)–Refilahatra (46 ha) ('Citadel of the Great One who brings rank/order'), at the confluence of the Manambovo with the River Andranosoa. To these two groups can be added upriver that of the site of Andaro[35] ('With barks/skins/leathers' or 'feet of daro'), composed of Mahirane (25 ha) ('The clear-sighted/intelligent/clever ones'), and Ambonifanane (6 ha) ('Above the hydra/snake/grave', 'With the ruling hydra/snake/grave'), a group that has not been given an absolute date, but which clearly belongs to the same culture as (inter)fluvial sites and stone forts such as Manda(n–d)–Refilahatra-Andranosoa, and goes back to a period when, in inhabited places, the various species of sub-fossil fauna could still be found.

Like the written sources, the oral sources, including the Darafify cycle, are silent about these sites, whose populations, such as the ones who occupied Andranosoa, were part of a territorial organization with ritual ceremonies in which various clusters took part (cf. the nature of the zebu remains found in the rubbish heap at Andranosoa),[36] but have disappeared without leaving any trace in the region, whose present-day inhabitants know nothing whatsoever about their distant predecessors. The carbon-14 datings are interesting:[37] they indicate a period from +940 to +1310 as the extreme limits, with a greater likelihood for the eleventh century. It remains to be explained what riches that could have been exported by Talaky were exploited by the populations settled in the hinterland. There is nothing in observations made so far that can convey an accurate picture.

Even though the south was perhaps already at this time affected by the beginnings of drought, it certainly had different climatic conditions in the tenth and eleventh centuries, which probably meant that the Manambovo was a river whose flow was greater and did not yet have the enormous seasonal variations that it has today. Its upper reaches then crossed a wooded region that made possible an economic life that rested in part on

33. R. Battistini, P. Vérin and R. Rason, 1963.
34. C. Radimilahy, 1980, 1981.
35. C. Radimilahy, 1980.
36. D. Rasamuel, 1983.
37. GIF 4571: 920 ± 90 BP: GIF 4570: 730 ± 90 BP; for Talaky: 840 ± 80 BP.

metal-working, a heavy consumer of fuel. This metal-working involved copper and iron, and ores of these metals have been found, but also, unlike for the copper ore around Bemarivo in the north, so have traces of ancient exploitation. However, copper, which was to enjoy great fortune in later periods, seems at first to have led there only to craft jewellery production notably of the *vangovango* bracelets with a broken ring that have been found as far away as Irodo and that are still called, even when they are made of silver, by the name *haba*. Once again, the linguistic associations are interesting. The Cham *haban* and the čuru *saban* both mean copper in the continental Austronesian domain;[38] *saba* in both Malagasy and in Comorian is still the usual word for copper today.[39]

Iron was exploited in significant quantities. Here, the metal does not seem to have been worked on the spot, since the usual practice of re-use, attested to by ethnography, is not enough to explain the striking contrast between the abundance of traces of exploitation of the ore (ashes, charcoal, slag) and the virtual absence of iron objects, the sites of the period having yielded only one bracelet (Andranosoa), a harpoon and fish-hooks (Talaky). To this might be added – in a country where the existence of stone tools has not yet been attested – marks of axes and knives on bones (Andaro, Andranosoa). No doubt the smelted products were largely exported through Talaky, whose development, if not its foundation, thus appears to be linked to its role as an outlet to the sea of export products from the interior, which moreover were apparently not limited to smelted products.

The toponym Andaro[40] and the discovery made there of numerous remains of the bones of young animals suggests that young animals were consumed there in large quantities. This no doubt had less to do with the gastronomic tastes of the inhabitants than with the need to slaughter the animals before their skin (*daro*) was too spoiled by brambles and thorns. Sheep skins may have been a second export product. And it may well be that the large surplus of meat that was thus obtained was salted and smoked, using techniques of preservation known to have existed at the time. This preserved meat could naturally have been a third export product. But, if the maritime traffic was heavy, this meat probably served mostly to supply the boats. Nor is it impossible that some of it was destined for local consumption. It is already quite certain that these inhabitants of the interior in the south who, following the traditional Malagasy way of doing things,[41] used a very refined cuisine based on boiling and sophisti-

38. G. Ferrand, 1909.

39. M. Ahmed Chamanga and N. J. Guenier, 1979, but note that *saba* in Malagasy can sometimes mean silver. In Kiswahili *shaba* means copper.

40. The toponym may refer to the exportable plants mentioned above in the discussion of the oral sources.

41. B. Domenichini-Ramiaramanana, 1977, 1981.

cated methods of preparing meat (art of carving, etc.),[42] were at least not deficient in animal proteins.

In addition to sheep, they also reared – but in smaller numbers, it would seem – oxen and goats, the consumption of which is attested by the leftovers from meals, which also show the consumption of products of hunting (bones of birds, hedgehogs, and other small rodents) and fishing (fish bones, crab claws, shells of sea urchins, freshwater and seawater shellfish). As for their food plants, which are not mentioned in the historical tradition and for which there is no archaeological evidence, no doubt they at least included those among the earliest plants domesticated on the Island that were present in the region, yams and taros or similar plants, which could also be gathered in the forest, as they still are today. And to them may be added, in addition to the calabash gourd with its many uses which is widely found there, the providential Madagascar periwinkle (*Catharanthus roseus* Linn.), which Malagasy sailors knew traditionally and probably diffused among other sailors at a very early date.[43] This is certainly not, strictly speaking, an edible plant, but the appetite-reducing properties of its leaves relieve hunger pangs, and earned it the name of *tonga* (literally: 'which enables (one) to arrive') in the south. Indeed, it is not necessary to penetrate into the hinterland to procure it, for it is rather a coastal species, even managing to survive in salty areas. Thus it may be supposed that the boats that must have called in at Talaky could take it on board as canoes of today do.

The tiny part of Talaky that has been explored, on the east bank, has only revealed one fisherman's dwelling (in addition to the harpoon and the fishing hooks, and weights for fishing lines or nets); its everyday objects are rather simple utilitarian pieces and cannot bear comparison with those from sites in the interior (varied and quite richly decorated pottery, various pieces of jewellery, etc.). But, as at the site at Irodo, spoons carved from *Turbo* shells have been found, and, as at the sites at Andaro and Andranosoa, the local pottery bears traces of graphitizing with no apparent utilitarian purpose that has, it seems, been found outside Madagascar (on ancient as well as contemporary pottery) only on certain pieces of pottery from East Africa (Lelesu tradition) and southern Africa (Gokomere-Ziwa-Zhizo tradition) and on those in the Sa-huynh-Kalanay tradition (especially in ancient Champa), in the Austronesian area.[44] And the presence on the sites along the upper reaches of the Manambovo of chlorite-schist weights and pottery imitating stone models, sea products and overseas products

42. D. Rasamuel, 1983.

43. P. Boiteau, 1977.

44. See particularly, for eastern Africa, R. Soper, 1971; for southern Africa, Unesco, *General History of Africa*, Vol. II, ch. 27; for continental south-east Asia, W. G. Solheim, 1965; and for an overview of the data, B. Domenichini-Ramiaramanana and J.-P. Domenichini, 1983, pp. 12–15. The technique of graphitizing luxury products is also found in the Great Lakes region, but after 1450.

(sgraffito from Arabia and other imported pottery not yet precisely dated, ivory pendants from Africa or Asia), is final proof that Talaky, which must have been the transit point for all of it, was not a site of fishermen of the Sarodrano type. Moreover, without yet even mentioning the sites on the west bank, the group of sites on the plateau overlooking the dune sites where the survey was conducted is already too far from the sea for men who were simply engaging in subsistence fishing, and the fact that it covers such a large area would itself suggest other types of activities, e.g., large-scale fishing whose produce must have been in part preserved and sold like the mutton. But all this still requires confirmation.

This inadequacy of the data, which is already perceptible at the level of a single site, is much more so when one thinks of the size of the country. But further research, systematically directed towards the study of river mouth sites and, upstream, of economically strategic zones on the sides of the basins, would no doubt make it possible soon to proceed to a reconstruction of the economic and social life of the whole of Madagascar at this key period in its ecological and political history. For, the data from archaeology, in their present state, combined with the data from ethnography and tradition, already suggest the existence of a remarkable cultural and material unity which comes through both in conceptions that are still alive in present-day Malagasy civilization and in the features of the material culture dated from this period. Some of these – notably the imported pottery – prove clearly that some Malagasy groups were part of a network of relations that reached out into areas that the study of traditions had not previously brought out: the countries on the continent bordering the South China Sea, on the one hand, and the countries bordering the Mozambique Channel on the other. And this must naturally lead to extending to these 'new' areas the search for data that might throw light on the history of Madagascar.

Madagascar in the international context

From the elaborate data of tradition to the more direct data provided by archaeology, the area of Madagascar has thus already provided, for our period, various indications of relations with a wide area overseas, some points in which are barely mentioned, while others are stressed. But given the present gaps in this documentation, nothing can be deduced from it immediately either as to the true nature of the relations between the Island and each of these points, or as to their intensity. The indications provided by the study of the oral sources and by archaeology make it possible to abandon, finally – we would like to hope – the hypothesis of a short chronology, which placed the peopling of Madagascar at the end of the first millennium,[45] thus, by the same token disproving research that based its

45. Cf. J. Poirier, 1965; P. Ottino, 1974a and P. Vérin, 1974.

arguments on it.[46] There is no longer any doubt that man was present in Madagascar, at least in the regions on which recent surveys have thrown new light, long before +1000. If we include the study of non-Malagasy sources, which must of course be handled extremely carefully, since Madagascar is never mentioned by a name that is unambiguous, the period from the seventh to the eleventh century, despite what is still obscure about it, can no longer be accepted, in Malagasy history, as the time when peopling began. The time has even come to abandon once and for all so far as concerns Malagasy history, all debates arising from the inadequacy of knowledge about the world of Austronesia. The Island appears indeed to have been situated, without canvassing all the evidence that we have, in a broad oceanic context.

The history of navigation in the Indian Ocean remains to be written; for the present, there are only partial studies and it is difficult to build a wholly reliable synthesis out of these. The maritime expansion of the Arab-Muslim world from the eleventh century onwards at least has probably overshadowed, in the plethora of sources and studies, the part played by other peoples and other regions in the earliest navigations. Perhaps more attention needs to be paid than has been so far to the degree of perfection reached – by the first century of the Christian era – in the sailing techniques of those whom the Chinese in the first millennium embraced under the name *Kun-lun*, among whom the Austronesians were probably a majority or in any event very numerous. But it seems that what was being referred to were mainly seafaring peoples of continental and insular South-east Asia.[47] These Austronesians were the first to be recognized as being the builders of the great sewn boats intended for sailing the high seas, which the Chinese authors from the third to the ninth century described by the name of *kun-lun bo*, describing them as ships with woven sails averaging 50 m in length and capable of transporting between 500 and 1000 people and a cargo of between 250 and 1000 tons.[48] Rafts and canoes with an outrigger or outriggers may perhaps have continued to transport some Austronesian immigrants at the end of the first millennium to Madagascar – poverty and courage, like the taste for adventure, are timeless. However, it is no longer possible, for periods after the third century – and perhaps even before this time[49] – to tie the date of the peopling of the Island to the

46. Cf. for example, J. Bernard, 1983.

47. The best-known to the Chinese were certainly the founders of the future Indianized Austronesian kingdom of Champa. This kingdom was born of a victory by the Kun-lun over the Chinese province of Je-Nan in +137; later, it frequently demonstrated its unruliness and spirit of conquest, including against China, of which it had become theoretically a tributary.

48. P. Y. Manguin, 1979.

49. Just as Chinese missionary monks voyaged, until the mid-eighth century (see G. Ferrand, 1919 (March–April), pp. 245–6) on the boats of the Kun-lun, so the Chinese envoys to the southern seas from the time of the emperor Wu (−140/−86) were already travelling on the trading ships of the 'Barbarians'.

sailing capacities of those 'frail skiffs', that some supporters of the short chronology – overlooking both Donque's warning[50] and the quick journey to the east coast of Madagascar by way of Ceylon, the Maldives and the Chagos demonstrated by Paul Adam[51] – still see happening necessarily at the end of a slow advance extending over several centuries punctuated by more or less long-lived settlements along the shores of the Indian Ocean. Such settlements did perhaps exist; but, from very early on, their creation, rather than an ineluctable need flowing from the state of technical knowledge, could have derived from the outcome of the choice and strategy of the users of an oceanic space whose routes had been recognized for many years, and whose economic and political geography was known. Thus, we feel today that for the Austronesians in antiquity, the peopling of Madagascar, if not necessarily its discovery, was probably already part of a process where the place left to chance had ceased to be dominant.

If it is agreed that the Austronesians were the first to sail towards Madagascar (whose peopling, language and culture bear their imprint – on this point no doubt has emerged during recent research), there is good reason, given the evidence looked at above, to examine closely the hypothesis that the Island was integrated into an inter-regional trade system which provided a demand for a number of valuable products.[52] Timber, caulking gum, aromatics and spices were, from a very early date, supplied by gathering techniques in the Island; these included cinnamon which seems to have been one of the most profitable products in such trade, whose exploitation by protected gathering techniques was a speciality of ancient Champa.[53]

There is no denying that this hypothesis clashes with many received ideas and that it contains features that are still very fragile alongside ones that are firmly established. It rests first on the likely participation of Austronesians in the transport of persons and goods in the western Indian Ocean at the beginning of the first millennium. Various pieces of evidence suggest the possible presence of the 'vessels of black men'[54] – *kun-lun-bo* – close to Africa; the reference by the *Periplus of the Erythraean Sea* to sewn boats with woven sails on the northern coast of Azania;[55] the tall 'man-

50. See G. Donque, 1965, p. 58, giving 'the proof that geographical determinism does not exist'.

51. P. Adam, 1979.

52. B. Domenichini-Ramiaramanana and J.-P. Domenichini, 1983, 1984.

53. Personal communication from G. Condominas based on the documentation assembled by Louis Condominas on 'Les Moïs de Haut Son-Tran'.

54. See the expression *kolandio phonta* which, in the *Periplus*, 'describes the boats sailing between India and south-east Asia (Chryse)' (P.-Y. Manguin, 1979). In this expression, which some authors have already connected with *kun-lun-bo*, the first element is to be related to *Kuladan* or *Koladya* which, according to Xu Yun-qiao, basing himself notably on an article by Chen Ching-ho, devoted to the founding ancestors of the kingdom of Lin-yi (the ancient name of Champa), means 'land of black men' and is to be related to the migrations of the Kun-lun.

55. These might however derive from Egyptian boats.

eating Ethiopians' of its southern coast mentioned by Ptolemy;[56] the sewn boats with a single rudder that probably belonged to the Chams,[57] present in the Red Sea in the sixth century.[58] The list of facts reported by Miller can be added to the fact that the cultivation of banana trees from South-east Asia in East Africa is very old, that coconut oil was exported through Rhapta in the time of the *Periplus*, that war elephants ridden by Seres[59] were present in the 'Ethiopian' army before the third century,[60] that sea-faring Cham traders participated in the Zandj slave trade[61] both to Asia and to the Middle East[62] and that an acute awareness of the unity and weight of the black world was attributed to the Zandj by al-Djāḥiẓ.[63] All

56. See H. N. Chittick, 1968b, p. 103. The *Book of the Marvels of India* in the tenth century, still spoke of the 'man-eating Zandj' in the land of Sofala (see A. Miquel, 1975, p. 172). But cannibalism, according to Pierre Alexandre, concerns only a minority of African groups and is to be found rather in Central Africa.

57. P.-Y. Manguin, 1979, says 'to the continentals', but the same author (1972, p. 44) specifies that the Vietnamese 'have never been a seafaring people'.

58. See H. N. Chittick, 1979b.

59. Although this name normally describes the Chinese, and J. H. Needham, 1970, pp. 140–1, following Pelliot and including rather improperly south and south-east China, does not rule out that the possibility that in antiquity there might have been 'Chinese' ocean voyaging as far as the port of Adulis, these Seres were not Chinese. In fact, these Seres, from whom the emperor received domestic or trained elephants, on the same terms as tribute from the Barbarians in the south as silk, aromatics, spices, etc. did not have war elephants; and those of the Chams, who may moreover be suspected to be behind these Seres and who were using these 'tanks' as much as the Indians, were still sowing terror in the Chinese army until the middle of the fifth century (see G. Maspéro, 1928, p. 72).

60. See Héliodore [Heliodorus], 1960, Vol. 3, pp. 59–61. On this trade in elephants, see Unesco, *General History of Africa*, Vol. II, p. 185.

61. G. Maspéro, 1928, p. 34, translating the *Ling W(a)i Tai Ta* (*Ling Dai Da* in Pinyin), Vol. 2, p. 11, says that 'Most Chams carry on the business of slave traders; their junks transport men instead of goods'. The slaves whom the Chams traded, raiding for them or purchasing them at very high prices or in exchange for 'scent wood' – see the *Tchou Fan Tche* (*Zhu Fan Zhi*) by Tchao Jou-Koua (Chau Ju-kua) quoted on the same page of Maspéro – came partly from the eastern Austronesian islands (Moluccas, etc.); but the same Ling Wai Dai Da, published in 1178 by Zhou Qu-fei, asserted that some came from Kun-lun Zengqi, or 'Zandj land of the Kun-lun', 'in the south-western sea'.

62. Many of these Zandj slaves whose presence in China is known from 724 (tribute offered to the court by the Nousantarian rulers of Srīvijāya), were destined for the Arabs who, according to Zhou Qu-fei, paid a high price for them and used them particularly as porters (see translation in G. Ferrand, 1919 (March–April), p. 253).

63. *Livre de la Supériorité des Noirs sur les Blancs* (Book of the Superiority of Blacks over Whites), an unpublished translation kindly made available by Jean Devisse. The black world mentioned in this work ranges from the Zandj of Africa to the 'Chinese' of south-east China, by way of the Austronesians of Zābadj who appear in it as Nousantarians (see on this A. Miquel, 1975, p. 78, who, taking al-Zābadj as a doublet of Djāvaga, also sees in it the whole of the Sumatra-Java nexus or Sumatra alone). But Zābadj, which corresponded to the Suvarnadvipa in Sanskrit (see al-Bīrūnī, quoted by G. Coedès, 1964, p. 264), which sometimes describes parts of the continent (see Coedès, 1964, p. 160) is perhaps connected with the *ZaBai* of Ptolemy, in whom some writers have thought they recognized Champa (see G. Maspéro, 1928, p. 2).

these are so many factors among others that testify to the antiquity and durability of contacts.

The second series of factors whose qualitative and quantitative importance will need to be assessed in the years to come relates to the part played by Madagascar in this possible movement of Austronesian boats westward. In a work which has been much criticized, Miller puts the integration of the Island into this trade at a very early date.[64] It seems to us, given the evidence found in the oral sources and archaeology, that Madagascar was not only, as Miller believed, a screen serving to maintain commercial secrecy about the land of cinnamon and cassia, misleadingly placed in the Horn of Africa. The east coast of Madagascar was, moreover, a country rich in a number of the main products in the international trade of Antiquity and the high Middle Ages – including notably the eaglewood[65] that Miller identified with the *tarum* arriving by the 'Cinnamon Route' – and had in addition the advantage not only of being away from the zones crisscrossed by rival fleets, but also close to the principal outlets, and particularly to the African ports contributing to supplying Egypt, and through it the Mediterraneann world.[66] The east coast of Madagascar, no doubt, supplied its products during the period covered here. The absence on the coast of Africa of certain plants, of great cultural importance, such as *Calophyllum inophyllum*,[67] even inclines us to believe that Madagascar, where this plant is present, was visited earlier by the Austronesians than was East Africa. They brought both new immigrants and goods not available in Madagascar, either for local consumption or for external trade.

All that we have said above concerns, of course, the period preceding that dealt with in this volume. Since we believe that at this remote time Madagascar was already participating heavily in the Indian Ocean trade, obviously the next step is to attempt to follow the stages in this participation between the seventh and eleventh centuries. And we do so without

64. J. I. Miller, 1969, who puts (p. 171) the peopling of Madagascar in the second millennium before the Christian era, is certainly not alone in looking to such an early date; the earliest dates are suggested by physical anthropologists, from A. Rakoto-Ratsimananga, 1939, who puts it *c.* −550, to R. Fourquet *et al.* at the Institut Pasteur, 1974, who put forward the hypothesis of a 'pre-Dravidian proto-Australoid origin'. See also note 9. In his book, J. I. Miller does not study the period covered by this volume.

65. See E. de Flacourt, 1661, p. 131.

66. See for example, J. Leclant, 1976, p. 270, who mentions cinnamon among the products arriving from East Africa that Egypt re-exported to the Mediterranean during the 25th dynasty (−664−−525).

67. *Calophyllum inophyllum* Linn. is found all round the Indian-Pacific basin except in Africa. This gap led Perrier de la Bathie to place its ocean migration in very early times (see Y. Cabanis *et al.*, 1969–70, p. 280). But the tree, which also provides timber for boats and caulking gum, was among the plants systematically cultivated by Indianized groups for the requirements of religious ritual and royal ceremonial (see A. G. Haudricourt and L. Hédin, 1953, p. 541). On the important place it occupies in Malagasy culture, see B. Domenichini-Ramiaramanana, 1983, pp. 483–6.

concealing, from ourselves or from the reader, the fact that this chronological framework rests on a preliminary postulate: our certainty, based on surveys conducted in Madagascar, that the Island was actively involved in the oceanic trade by the beginning of the first millennium.

The first difficulties that traders from Madagascar met with seem to have been related to the ineffectiveness of the alliance between Axum and Byzantium against Sassanid Persia. The Sassanids, thanks to the conquest of South Arabia (570) which they remained in control of until the conversion of the last governor to Islam in 628,[68] succeeded no doubt in partially taking over the legacy of the South Arabians in the sea trade in the Indian Ocean, including the Red Sea. Then conquered – and soon converted – Persia was to some extent integrated to the expansionist policy of the Arab-Islamic world, whose conquest of Egypt (641–2) completed the seizure of control of the trade routes in the west by the Arabs and Persians.

Whether active or passive, the initial adaptation of the Island to this situation manifestly consisted in entering into relations with Persian-speaking importers, which is what explains how their influence is perceptible through the data yielded by the soil of Madagascar. Some of them were, moreover, probably present on the African coast. But the at least partial change in partners and the interruption of overland routes, which lay behind not only the decline in the incense trade but also no doubt that in other products coming up against competition with those of the Arab-Persian world, also perhaps impeded the trade in cinnamon, which was already in competition with Ceylon which had been backed by the Sassanids since the fourth century. And when, taking advantage of the troubles at the end of the seventh and beginning of the eighth century in South Arabia, it seems,[69] the people of al-Ḳumr (Comoros and Madagascar) embarked on the conquest of Aden in their outrigger boats, it should perhaps be seen as a partially successful attempt to restore the situation. For these conquerers, some of whom had settled down in Yemen, and had made Aden into their home port from where they would set out each season, 'sail[ing] together in a single monsoon', had succeeded in establishing a direct sailing route between their country of origin and south Arabia, a voyage that the Arabs and Persians in the thirteenth century, according to the testimony of Ibn al-Mudj̲āwir, were still taking three monsoons to complete. Thus, in spite of everything, they were able to compete with their rivals, since the Arab and Persian seafarers, who seem not to have known of the Comoros and Madagascar until the tenth century – and only had a clear idea of them by the twelfth century – continued to receive Malagasy products on the East African coast, which they would coast along.

Major upheavals affected the life of the western Indian Ocean in the

68. See J. I. Miller, 1969, p. 220.

69. We follow O. C. Dahl, 1951, and H. Deschamps, 1972, in their understanding of 'Empire of the Pharaohs' as 'Roman rule in Egypt'.

ninth century. At present, it is difficult to be clear about the detailed situation of trade during this century. In this and the immediately following centuries, as far as the Arabic sources lead one to suppose, the voyages of the 'Malagasy' seafarers probably usually ended at Aden. Their long familiarity with Muslim countries led to the conversion of some Malagasy to Islam, and it may even be wondered whether some voyages from al-Ḳumr to Aden and the entrance to the Persian Gulf did not in the end become part of the organization of Arab-Persian trade. One fact in any case seems virtually certain, and that is that it was Malagasy seafarers converted to Islam who initiated the sailors of Oman and Sīrāf into the direct sailing route to the north of the Island, where the earliest settlements can still be found at Onjatsy,[70] and also to the island of Ḳanbalū, which al-Mas'ūdī said was 'inhabited by a mixed population of Muslims and idolatrous Zandj' and which it can still not be ruled out may have been situated somewhere in al-Ḳumr, where it would have to be looked for in the north-west.[71] But wherever exactly Ḳanbalū was situated, this clearly implies that it was at the latest by the beginning of the tenth century that the rivalry with the Arabs and Persians was no longer experienced so intensely by all Malagasy. And since that was happening at a time when, taking advantage of the situation created by the massacre of Muslims in Canton (878) and the growth of the power of Śrīvijāya, the world of the Kun-lun, through control of the straits, had just gained a real advantage over rival navies (Arab-Persian and Indian, on the one hand, Chinese on the other), things were not going to stay like that.

This control of the straits, perhaps reaching as far as the Sunda Strait, succeeded in making the Malacca peninsula, in the kingdom of Śrīvijāya, the terminus for all ships going to or coming from China. For China had become one of the largest markets of the time, and much of the trade of all the countries in the south-west of the Indian Ocean cut off from the Mediterranean had turned towards it. Madagascar, of which at least the eastern part continued to be part of the Kun-lun orbit, participated of course in this trade. In the episode of the attack of Ḳanbalū (945), it is sometimes accepted that the attackers called Wāḳ-Wāḳ by the Arabic sources came from Madagascar.[72] The explanation for this raid given by Ibn Lākīs in *The Marvels of India* is accepted as satisfactory: the expedition was looking for Zandj to take into slavery and products suitable for their country and for China (ivory, tortoise-shell, leopard skins and ambergris). In fact, while

70. The Onjatsy, whose history is obscure and who, in times of tension, were rejected as 'non-Arabs' and described as 'people from the sands of Mecca', may however have arrived in the north before the Zafi(n–d)–Raminia. The most convincing etymology at present remains the one that links this name to that of the Azd given by sailors from Oman.

71. A. Miquel, 1975, pp. 171–2 only rùles out the possibility of placing Ḳanbalū in Madagascar – but we say rather al-Ḳumr by including in it the Comoro archipelago – because he could see no economic benefit in such a voyage.

72. ibid., p. 173. Against this interpretation: R. Mauny, 1965, pp. 7–16.

there is no need to question these admitted motives, the interest of which lies in bringing out the fact that there did exist in the Island a market supplied by trade with the continent, from which came ivory and panther skins – as well as, probably, Zandj captives – such an expedition would be much less well explained in the context of the development of Malagasy trade with China than in that of a rivalry between the Muslim world and the Kun-lun world that Ibn Lākis called Wāḳ-Wāḳ.[73]

However, although piracy and raiding were common throughout this period, and although Malagasy history in more recent periods also provides glaring examples of it, the expedition including a 'thousand vessels' that had come from the south to attack Ḳanbalū was not only led by Malagasy from the east coast. It also included Wāḳ-Wāḳ from the Far East, whose expeditions in these regions in the far south, for which there is evidence elsewhere,[74] could not have been motivated by the quest for products which they could leave to their allies in Madagascar to take care of and which were plentiful in their own regions and were the objects of their centuries-old trade with China. Everything indicates to us that what was important for these Kun-lun or Wāḳ-Wāḳ was to oppose the Muslim advance southward, which was supported by the Islamized Malagasy, and to protect access to the mines of gold and other metals. Perhaps it can be accepted that the iron in southern Madagascar, which was so well protected by those who were exploiting it, might in itself constitute a resource that it was worth fighting to keep a monopoly of.[75]

Expeditions such as that of 945 seem to have slowed down the advance of the Muslim navy for a long time. But the homogeneity of the Kun-lun world had already been affected by the proselytism of Islam. It may be that it was at this time that migrations such as that of the Zafi(n–d) Raminia left the shores of the Red Sea. At the same time, the Island began to develop its relations with East Africa – which may well have been different but which was also Islamized – probably exporting there chlorite-schist objects that it produced, as the imports of Kilwa from the tenth century onwards would tend to suggest.[76]

This new assessment of the economic and naval relations between Madagascar and the Kun-lun world, on the one hand, and between the Island and the Arab-Persian world, on the other, raises new questions that relate, this time, to the internal life of the Island. The concordant observations, six centuries apart, of the *Hudūd al-ʿĀlām* and admiral Sīdī ʿAli

73. For a detailed examination of what follows, see B. Domenichini-Ramiaramanana and J.-P. Domenichini, 1983 and 1984.

74. See A. Miquel, 1975, p. 173.

75. A tribute offered in 974 by the Chams included 'forty pounds of iron' (see G. Maspéro, 1928, p. 121).

76. See P. Vérin, 1975, p. 937, who is in agreement with the opinion expressed time and again by J. Devisse in discussing H. N. Chittick's hypothesis. This latter envisages only an importation coming from South Arabia.

Čelebi seem to show that the old political and social structures in the south firmly resisted new influences. This should lead experts on Madagascar to take up again an examination of the question of 'Arab' influence which has been used too systematically to explain various features of ancient Malagasy culture. But such an examination relates rather to a study of periods after the eleventh century. The sole fact that should retain our attention is that the major alteration in perspective that we are called upon to make in this field should be the fruit of a synthesis of all the sources currently available to write the history of the period from the seventh to the eleventh century. In this exercise there is much to think about, when one realizes not only the many gaps that still exist in the evidence for this period, but also the extent of our ignorance of the previous period.

Just as the excessive influence hitherto attributed to Arab influence is today called into question, so too can one foresee that many points in the history of Madagascar in the Indian Ocean between the seventh and eleventh century, such as it comes through in our three aspects, will be the object of later revisions. There is then a great temptation to say – and this will be our conclusion – that the essential point, in the immediate future, lies perhaps less in recognition of an important turning-point in the past of the Island and in the facts that appear to be historically established or are virtually so, than in the fact of having 'experimentally' established the equal importance, rarely recognized, of the various categories of sources, and the need to exploit all of them equally systematically.

26 The African diaspora in Asia

Y. TALIB
based on a contribution by F. SAMIR

Although the presence of Africans outside their home continent has been attested since Antiquity, it was only during the period under review that their role in the various fields of human activities in the Muslim countries in the Middle East, in the Indian subcontinent, the Malay Archipelago and the Far East became increasingly important. Our sources on these activities are unfortunately still scanty and widely dispersed in many works and documents, written in various, mostly oriental, languages. Moreover, no systematic scholarly study has ever been done on the African diaspora in Asia.[1] This chapter is therefore a preliminary attempt to bring together available data on early relations between Africa and Arabia, as well as on the political, social, economic and cultural aspects of the African presence in the aforementioned areas.

Early contacts between Africa and Arabia: The pre-Islamic period

Commercial relations between South-western Arabia and the East African littoral as depicted by the unknown author of the *Periplus of the Erythraean Sea*[2] which probably dates to the late first or early second century of the Christian era, went back several centuries before. It appeared that the wealthy and powerful kingdom of ʿAwsān[3] in the Yemen owed its status as a great trading centre to its extensive commercial links with East Africa. Its prosperity and power suffered an irrevocable decline when it passed under the suzerainty of Qataban in the latter half of the fifth century before the Christian era.

1. Since this chapter was drafted, I. Van Sertima (ed.), 1985 – a work on the African presence in Asia in Antiquity – has been published.
2. See G. W. B. Huntingford, 1980.
3. For full details see H. von Wissmann and Maria Höfner, 1952, pp. 287–93.

The paucity of data makes it difficult to ascertain the first establishment of these trade contacts as well as how far down the East African seaboard they extended during the pre-Roman period. A. M. H. Sheriff[4] has convincingly suggested the second century of the Christian era as a likely date. During the Roman period they appear to have exercised a virtual monopoly of the entire coastal trade of East Africa.

The economic unification and growing opulence of the Roman empire gave an added impetus to South Arabian mercantile activity. The growing need for exotic products such as ivory on the domestic market inevitably absorbed the East African 'region ... into the international system of trade centred on the Mediterranean through the south-west Arabian state of Himyar'.[5] This was accompanied by 'political domination' and 'social penetration' bringing about the rise of various seagoing and trading peoples of mixed parentage and acting out the role of vassals and local agents of the then prevailing international system of trade.[6]

The official conversion of Axum to Monophysite Christianity[7] in the early part of the fourth century of the Christian era was an historical event of great significance. A vital link was forged with the foremost Christian power of the time, the Byzantine empire. Consequently, the Axumites emerged as the promoters of Byzantine foreign policy, especially in its commercial and religious aspects. This deeply involved Ethiopia in South Arabian affairs, the most important manifestation of which was the Ethiopian invasion of the south-western corner of the Arabian peninsula in 525.[8]

It has been presumed by early Arabian[9] and Christian[10] authors that this invasion of the Yemen was chiefly occasioned by the general persecution of Yemenite Christians leading to the wholesale massacre of the important Monophysite Christian community of Nadjrān[11] by the king of

4. Cf. Unesco, *General History of Africa*, Vol. II, ch. 22.

5. ibid., p. 561.

6. 'From here after two courses off the mainland lies the last mart of Azania called Raphta, which has its name from the afore-mentioned sewn boats, where there is a great deal of ivory and tortoise shell. The natives of this country have large bodies and piratical habits, and each place likewise has its own chief. The Mopharitic chief rules it according to an agreement by which it falls under the kingdom which has become first in Arabia. Under the king the people of Mauza hold it by payment of tribute, and send ships with captains and agents who are mostly Arabs and are familiar through residence and intermarriage with the nature of the places and their language.' See G. W. B. Huntingford, 1980, p. 30.

7. Cf. Unesco, *General History of Africa*, Vol. II, ch. 16.

8. This date is based on the inscription found at Ḥusn al-Ghurāb – the fortress and look-out guarding the ancient port and trading city of Ḳana' on the southern coast of Arabia. For details see K. Mlaker, 1927.

9. Ibn Isḥāḳ, 1955, pp. 14–33.

10. A. Moberg, 1924; F. M. E. Pereira, 1899.

11. On events in South Arabia during the sixth century see the following; D. S. Attema, 1949; J. Ryckmans, 1956; S. Smith, 1954; N. V. Pigulevskaya, 1960, 1961.

the Himyarites, Dhū Nuwās,[12] a convert to the Jewish faith and also the leader of the pro-Persian party in the country. To avenge his coreligionists, and upon the instigation of the Byzantines, the Axumite king, Ella Aṣbeḥa launched a punitive expeditionary force across the Straits of Bāb al-Mandab. Dhū Nuwās was overthrown and a native Christian by the name of Sumayfaʿ Ashwaʿ was installed as ruler.[13]

However, the real motive for the invasion as credited in South Arabian inscriptions and the account given by Procopius[14] was economic in nature. The demand for luxuries in the Byzantine world was enormous. The trade in these rare and precious commodities, especially silk, was virtually in the hands of the Persians, who not only kept prices at a very high level but exacted payment for them in Roman gold. If this pattern of trade relations was to have continued it would have resulted in a great drain on the wealth of Rome to the profit of its rival Persia.

Consequently, one of the most important elements of Byzantine foreign policy under Justinian (*reg.* 527–65) was a circumvention of the Persian monopoly of the trade by the establishment of a southern sea route to the farther East through Ethiopian intermediaries and an attempt to prevent it from falling into the hands of the Persians or pro-Persian elements in South Arabia. This policy was doomed from the start.

In 535 Sumayfaʿ was deposed by the local population and replaced with one Abraha,[15] the former slave of a Roman merchant of Aduḷis.[16] For most of his reign, Abraha – to the disappointment of Justinian – adopted a neutral stance in the long-drawn-out struggle between the rival powers of the day. It was only at the close of his rule that he tilted the balance in the Byzantines' favour by marching northwards at the head of an expeditionary force against the Ḥidjāz in 570.[17] It was an ill-fated attempt. His army

12. He is known to Arab tradition by this epithet – 'Lord of the Curls'. In other sources he is referred to as 'Dunaan' (A. Moberg, 1924, p. xlii). In the *Book of the Himyarites*, he is given the name of 'Masrūḳ', an appellation that is also found in two other sources. See D. S. Attema, 1949, p. 7, note 32. He is referred to in Christian sources variously as 'Dimnus', 'Damian', 'Dimianos', 'Damnus' and in Abyssinian texts as 'Phinʿhas'. Djawād ʿAlī, 1952–6, Vol. 3, p. 190. His real name upon his conversion to Judaism is Yūsuf Ashʿar. S. Smith, 1954, p. 456.

13. Procopius, 1954, p. 189. He is referred to here as 'Esimiphaeus'.

14. K. Mlaker, 1927, p. 60. Procopius, 1954, pp. 193–4.

15. A. F. L. Beeston, 1960, states that the details of Abraha's life given by Muslim historians are largely stories of folklore origin which had been attached arbitrarily to the name of a famous personage. For more precise information one has to refer to the account given by Procopius, 1954, pp. 191–4 and fragmentary South Arabian epigraphic sources. A critical examination of the extant sources on the career of Abraha or Abramos is given in S. Smith, 1954, pp. 431–41.

16. Procopius, 1954, p. 191.

17. Classical Muslim sources attribute the motive of the expedition to Abraha's jealousy of the Meccan sanctuary and a futile attempt to substitute his Church at Ṣanʿā as the place of pilgrimage for the whole of Arabia. A. F. L. Beeston, 1960, p. 103. See equally P. K. Hitti, 1970, p. 64.

was put to rout and decimated by epidemics.[18] This year, called the 'Year of the Elephant'[19] in classical Arabic sources was claimed to have been the year in which the Prophet of Islam – Muḥammad – was born.[20] It was also the year in which Ethiopian domination in the Yemen was put to an end by the Sassanids under the command of Wahrīz.[21]

The pre-Islamic and early Islamic periods

Blacks in pre-Islamic Arabia

The geographical proximity of Arabia to Africa and the centuries-long links across the Red Sea led to an early presence of many Africans on the Arabian Peninsula. These Africans of both sexes, of various origin, but mostly from Ethiopia, Somalia, Nubia and the east coast, came thither in various capacities, but mostly as slaves. On the other hand, a great number of Ethiopian warriors, who came with the invading army, must have remained in South Arabia and elsewhere, in due course being absorbed by the predominantly Arab population. Arabic literary sources have preserved scattered accounts of various kinds about people of African origin living in Arabia before the advent of Islam.

Several poets of the pre-Islamic era (Djāhiliya) were known collectively as the 'Aghribat al-ʿArab' (The Crows of the Arabs) because of the swarthy complexions they inherited from their mothers. The most famous among them were ʿAntara b. Shaddād,[22] Khufāf ibn Nadba[23] and Sulayk b. al-Sulaka.[24] The latter belonged to the saʿālik,[25] celebrated wandering bands of 'robber-knights' famed for their chivalry and honour despite their predatory activities. However, the most illustrious of the 'Crows' was ʿAntara of the *ḳabīla* of ʿAbs born of an Abyssinian bond-maid named Zabība.

He flourished during the Dāḥis-Ghabrā[26] conflicts between his paternal

18. Ibn Isḥāḳ, 1955, pp. 26–7.

19. Al-Ṭabarī, 1329 AH, Vol. 30, p. 195. C. Conti Rossini, 1921 has contested this account of the march of the Abyssinians against the Ḥidjaz accompanied by their elephants.

20. M. Rodinson, 1971, p. 38 is of the view that this is improbable. The most commonly accepted year is 571.

21. A. Christensen, 1944.

22. For detailed studies on ʿAntara see the following: A. Thorbecke, 1867; H. Derenbourg, 1905, pp. 3–9; al-Iṣfahānī, 1868–9, Vol. 8, pp. 237–46.

23. He was descended from an Arab father of the Banū Sulaym and a black slave mother named Nadba. He accompanied the Apostle of Islam in his triumphal entry into Mecca bearing the standard of his 'tribe'; see Ibn Ḳutayba, 1850, p. 126; al-Iṣfahānī, 1868–9, Vol. 20, pp. 2–9.

24. al-Iṣfahānī, Vol. 18, pp. 133–9. Thābit ibn Djābir or more popularly known as Taʿabbata Sharran of the tribe of Fahm and of an African mother was ranked among them.

25. A detailed account is given in Y. Khalīf, 1959.

26. 'These fights were due to a dispute involving a race between two horses, Dāḥis and Ghabrā, on which occasion the tribe of ʿAbs accused the tribe of Dhubyān of having had recourse to stratagems to assure the victory of their horse'. I. Goldziher, 1966, p. 14.

tribe and that of Abū Dhubyān and distinguished himself by his valour and strength, thereby gaining glory for his kinsmen. Eventually, he was freed and became an honoured member of his tribe. His verses on his numerous battles, vicissitudes and love for ʿAbla are considered the finest creations of the 'Djāhiliya' poetry, assuring him an honoured rank amongst the Muʿallaḳāt poets.[27] As his fame spread far and wide, his exploits became in the later Islamic times the theme of an extremely popular cycle of romance entitled 'Sīrat ʿAntar' (The Story of ʿAntara).[28] He emerged as the national hero of the Arabs.

In the merchant city of Mecca the defence and protection of its caravan routes was entrusted to a troop of mercenaries, known as the *Aḥābīsh*, a term held to be connected with the Arab name for Ethiopians, *al-Ḥabash*. Although it seems that the Ethiopians formed the core of this troop, it consisted also of other African slaves and Arabic nomads from the Tihāma (the coastal plain along the Red Sea shore) and Yemen.[29] Their leading role as the main military force in the retinue and escort of the patrician families of the city is well attested in many Arabic sources, where the military skill, discipline and prowess of these African 'soldiers of fortune' are repeatedly stressed.

The great reliance on mercenaries resulted mainly from the fact that the Ḳurayshites, to whom the Meccan inhabitants belonged, were few in numbers and were thus unable to muster any considerable army from their own ranks to defend their city and to protect their far-reaching commercial interests. Many of the *Aḥābīsh* later took an active part in the military expeditions against the nascent Muslim state of Medina and fought at the battles of Badr and Uḥud.[30]

Blacks in Muḥammad's entourage

Tradition asserts that among the first converts to Islam in Mecca were many slaves, some of them of African origin.[31] In the tenets of the new religion preached by Muḥammad these socially handicapped people had found the possibility of attaining human dignity and self-respect, and the opportunity to join a new community where a man was judged primarily by his religious fervour and his pious acts, and not merely by his social or

27. 'The term, which literally means "suspended" has not yet been satisfactorily explained. A story of later concoction asserts that they were the winning poems at poetic tournaments held at the fair of ʿUkāẓ, transcribed in gold and hung up in the Kaʾba at Mecca'. H. A. R. Gibb, 1963, p. 22; J. Berque, 1979.

28. Cf. G. Rouger, 1923; B. Heller, 1931.

29. Cf. Lammens, 1916; W. M. Watt, 1953, pp. 154–7; M. Hamidullah, 1956, pp. 434–7.

30. One of these Aḥābīsh, Waḥshī b. Ḥarb, an Ethiopian slave, slew the Prophet's uncle Hamza in the battle of Uḥud.

31. 'I heard ʿAmmār (b. Yāsir) say: I saw the Apostle of God while there was none with him but five slaves, two women and Abū Bakr', in al-Bukhārī, 1978, Vol. 5, pp. 24–5.

racial origins. Thus in the early difficult years of the Prophet's activities there had already emerged a number of converts who were black or had black ancestors who played considerable roles in the life of the nascent Islamic politico-religious community.

One such early convert was ʿAmmār ibn Yāsir, whose mother Sumayya was a former slave of the Ḳurayshite clan of Banū Makhzūm; he participated in the first migrations to Ethiopia and later returned to Medina, taking part in all the campaigns of the Prophet. The Caliph ʿUmar (3/634–23/643) appointed him as governor of Kūfa, one of the most important posts in the new administration of the early Islamic state. Being later a zealous adherent of the ʿAlī's cause, he fell during the first civil war in the battle of Ṣiffīn (37/617). He belonged also to the transmitters of the *ḥadīth*s (accounts of Muḥammad's deeds and sayings).[32]

The most celebrated of the Prophet's early circle of black companions was Bilāl b. Rabāḥ, an Ethiopian slave whose mother Ḥamāmah and brother Khālid were also slaves in Mecca. He is described in early Muslim accounts as 'tall, thin, hollow-cheeked and having a stentorian voice'. Before Caliph Abū Bakr bought and freed him, he was persecuted and tortured by his owner because of his religious convictions. He became the first *mu'adhdhin* (one who calls to prayer) in Islam and took part in all the early Islamic campaigns including those in Syria, where he died of plague in Damascus (20 or 21/640–41).[33] His services to Islam as well as those of the other black *mawālī*s can be summed up in the words of one modern biographer of the Prophet as 'having filled the modest but indispensable role of ordinary believers. Their tireless devotion, total selflessness and absolute lack of mental doubts and soul-searchings, coupled with the invaluable service they rendered in practical matters, made them examples to be held up to caviling opponents'.[34]

One other early black convert to Islam who made valuable contributions in the military field was al-Miḳdād b. ʿAmr al-Aswad. He was one of the earliest of the companions and assisted the Prophet in all his battles. Being the only Muslim who fought on horseback during the battle of Badr, he was thus given the title Fāris al-Islam (the knight of Islam).[35]

Slaves who embraced Islam were manumitted and thereby became *mawālī* (clients) of the Prophet and other prominent Muslims. Early Islamic writings allude to several of them, namely al-Ra'ay al-Aswad al-Ḥabashi,[36] Mihdja' who fell in the battle of Badr,[37] Abū Laḳīt of Nubian origin, who was employed by ʿUmar b. al-Khattāb as an official in the

32. Ibn Ḳutayba, 1850, pp. 131–2; Ibn Hishām, 1936, Vol. 1, p. 279; Ibn Saʿd, 1904–40, Vol. 8(1), pp. 165–76.

33. Ibn Ḳutayba, 1850, p. 88; Ibn Saʿd, 1904–40, Vol. 3(1), pp. 165–70.

34. M. Rodinson, 1971, p. 130.

35. Ibn Ḳutayba, 1850, p. 134.

36. Ibn Saʿd, 1904–40, Vol. 3(1), p. 33.

37. Ibn Ḳutayba, 1850, p. 78.

dīwān (state chancellery),[38] Rabāḥ,[39] one of the Prophet's bearers, Abū Muwayhibah,[40] a transmitter of several *ḥadīths*,[41] and Ṣāliḥ b. Shuḳrān who was a close associate of Caliph ʿUmar.

In the midst of the early Muslim community were to be found several black female emancipated slaves. Umm Ayman Baraka[42] who nursed the Prophet in his childhood and was a respected member of his household. Fudda,[43] the maid in the employ of the Prophet's daughter, and Naba'a,[44] a slave girl of Muḥammad's uncle Abū Ṭālib, who was credited with having transmitted a *ḥadīth* on Muḥammad's nocturnal journey (*isrā'*) to Jerusalem.

Muslim links with Ethiopia

Five years after the proclamation of Islam (615), a number of Muslims sought refuge in neighbouring Ethiopia in order to escape the persecutions of the Ḳurayshites in Mecca.[45] The warm reception extended to them by the negus (nadjāshī in Arabic accounts)[46] and his court ushered in a period of cordial relations between the two religious communities. This was echoed in early Islamic traditions.

According to one account, the negus, referred to as Nadjāshī al-Aṣḥama b. Abdjar, declared his belief in the Prophet's mission.[47] Mention is also made of the nadjāshī sending his son with a deputation of some sixty Ethiopians to the Prophet Muḥammad.[48] Their boat foundered when they were in the middle of the sea and they all perished. It is also reported that the Prophet grieved on learning of the nadjāshī's death and offered special prayers for his soul.[49]

Their sojourn in Ethiopia greatly impressed these early Muslim migrants and influenced the future development of their new faith. Muslim biographical sources (*tabaḳāt*) enumerate not a few Ethiopian converts to

38. Ibn Ḥadjar al-ʿAsḳalānī, 1970, Vol. 7, p. 352.
39. Ibn Ḳutayba, 1850, p. 72; Ibn Ḥadjar al-ʿAsḳalānī, 1970, Vol. 2, p. 452.
40. Ibn Ḳutayba, 1850, p. 73.
41. ibid., p. 72.
42. ibid., pp. 70–1.
43. Ibn Ḥadjar al-ʿAsḳalānī, 1970, Vol. 8, p. 75.
44. ibid.
45. The first migration (*hidjra*) comprised eleven men and four women, the prominent members were ʿUthmān and his wife Rukaya, daughter of the Prophet (Ibn Saʿd, 1904–40, Vol. 1, p. 136). This was followed several years later by a larger group of migrants – eighty-three men and some women (Ibn Hishām, 1936, Vol. 1, p. 353.
46. Ibn Hishām, 1936, Vol. 1, p. 353.
47. ibid., pp. 35, 359. Hartmann interprets his Abyssinian name as Ella Ṣaḥam, see M. Hartmann, 1895, pp. 299–300.
48. Ibn Hishām, 1936, Vol. 1, p. 366. Ibn Ḥadjar al-ʿAsḳalānī, 1970, Vol. 1, p. 300.
49. See al-Wāḥidī, 1315 AH, pp. 103–4.

Islam who migrated to Medina and ranked amongst the Prophet's companions. They were referred to as the 'Ethiopian monks' (*ruhbān al-ḥabasha*).[50] Four of them had Abraha as their name. One of them was said to have been the grandson of Abraha, the invader of Mecca,[51] yet another was the female slave of Umm Ḥabība[52] (one of the Prophet's spouses) during her Ethiopian exile. Another account placed the son and nephew of the nadjāshī by the Prophet's side at Medina.[53] It is interesting to note that many of the children of these Muslim migrants were Ethiopian born.

These traditions considerably shaped Muslim attitudes towards Ethiopia, whence such eulogies as Ibn al-Djawzī's (d. 1208) 'Tanwīr al-ghabash fī faḍl al-sūdān wa'l-ḥabash' (The lightening of the darkness on the merits of blacks and Ethiopians), Al-Suyūṭī's (d. 1505) 'Raf'sha'n al-ḥubshān' (The raising of the status of the Ethiopians) and that by Muḥammad b. 'Abd al-Bāḳī al-Bukhārī (sixteenth century) – 'Al-tirāz al-manḳūsh fī maḥāsin al-ḥubūsh' (The coloured brocade on the good qualities of the Ethiopians).[54]

The status of Africans in Muslim society

The Qoranic view

The Qoran – the ultimate Islamic text – would naturally form the basis of any discussion on Muslim attitudes on race and colour. Yet surprisingly, as observed by Bernard Lewis,[55] only two passages in the Qoran have a direct bearing on the subject. The first of these is to be found in Sūra 30, verse 22, which reads 'Among God's signs are the creation of the heavens and of the earth and the diversity of your languages and of your colours'. This forms part of a larger section enumerating the signs and wonders of God. The diversity of 'languages and colours' is cited as only another sign of the omnipotence and versatility of the Creator.

The other passage, Sūra 49, verse 13, is more definite: 'O people! We have created you from a male and a female and we have made you into confederacies and tribes so that you may come to know one another. The noblest of you in the eyes of God is the most pious, for God is omniscient and well-informed.'

Consequently, one finds no instances of racial or colour prejudice in the Qoran, nor even awareness of it. The aforementioned passages do, however, indicate a 'consciousness of difference' with the second quotation

50. Ibn Ḥadjar al-'Asḳalānī, 1970, Vol. 1, p. 22.
51. ibid., Vol. 7, p. 476.
52. ibid., Vol. 1, p. 21; Vol. 2, p. 417.
53. ibid., Vol. 4, p. 575.
54. Quoted in B. Lewis, 1971, p. 37, note 45; cf. now G. Ducatez and J. Ducatez, 1980.
55. B. Lewis, 1971, pp. 6–7.

putting the stress on piety rather than birth. It is obvious that the question of race never became an issue in the Qoran.[56]

Various designations of blacks in Arabic

In Arabic medieval sources the inhabitants of tropical Africa are usually divided into four great categories: the Sūdān, the Ḥabasha, the Zandj and the Nūba.

The term *as-sūdān* (plural of *al-aswad*, 'black') is the most general, being applied to all people of black colour without pointing to the place of origin. Sometimes even the Indians, the Chinese and other people of Asia were included in this category. In a narrower sense the Sūdān became gradually to mean the black Africans living to the south of the Maghrib, i.e. the inhabitants of the *Bilād al-sūdān* ('the Land of the Blacks') par excellence.

As for the *Ḥabasha* (the Ethiopians), their geographical proximity as well as their association with Muḥammad's early history made them the best-known group of Africans. Some authors, however, employed this term in a larger sense, counting among the Ḥabasha even people living as far as the Niger or on the frontiers of Egypt.[57]

The *Zandj* (or *Zindj*) refer mostly to the Bantu-speaking peoples from the East African coast, who since pre-Islamic times had been brought as slaves to Arabia, Persia and Mesopotamia.[58] Their high numbers in these countries soon gave the name the general meaning of 'black' and of 'slave'.

The *Nūba* (Nubians) became known to the Arabs after the conquest of Egypt; it is, however, very likely that the name covered also all Africans originating in the countries to the south of Nubia proper, i.e. the Nilotic-speaking and Eastern Sudanic-speaking groups, who came to the lands of the Caliphate via Nubia.[59]

The provenance of slaves

The Arab Muslims were not the originators of the trade in black African

56. The condemnation of racial prejudice and discrimination with an insistance on the primacy of piety over 'noble or purely Arab birth' is specifically indicated in a number of *ḥadīths*. See al-Bukhāri, 1978, p. 79, where the Prophet gave the command of an expedition to Usāmah b. Zayd despite the objection of some people on account of his swarthy complexion, inherited from his mother, Umm Ayman.

57. This extension of the Ḥabasha westwards and northwards is perhaps an echo from the Graeco-Roman authors who also mentioned the Ethiopians far in the west. Cf. J. Desanges, 1962, p. 16.

58. The derivation and meaning of *Zandj* is still unsolved. Usually it is derived from Egyptian *Zink*, the people of Punt. For other explanations cf. P. Pelliot, 1959, pp. 598–603. See also chapter 21 above.

59. Cf. Y. F. Hasan, 1967, pp. 42–6. The Arabic sources do not tell us much about the areas from which these slaves were obtained.

PLATE 26.1 *The Battle of the Clans, from Khamsa of Nizāmī, a manuscript dated 866/1461, Baghdad*

slaves. The enslavement of Nubians and other Africans can be traced back to Pharaonic times. This is attested by the numerous representations of slaves in Egyptian art.[60] Black slaves were equally to be found in the Hellenistic and Roman worlds.[61] According to Maurice Lombard,[62] the black slave traffic conducted by the Muslims was of the utmost commercial importance:

> no slaves were to be had inside the Muslim world, because once the phase of conquest was over, there was no room for anyone within the frontiers except Muslims or protected subjects (*dhimmī*) such as Jews, Christians or Zoroastrians, none of whom could be reduced to slavery but for rare exceptions, like the occasion when the Copts of the Delta revolted and were led away into slavery. Slaves had to be sought elsewhere in countries near and far and obtained either by raids or by purchase from weaker, less tightly knit societies incapable of defending themselves.

One of the major areas where slaves might be procured were those parts of Africa inhabited by the blacks, i.e. the eastern littoral, Nubia, Ethiopia, and the Central and Western Sudan.[63]

The slave trade from the eastern coast started long before the coming of Islam.[64] In the eighth and ninth centuries the demand for slave labour increased, linked with agricultural development in lower Iraq and with the expansion of international trade in the Indian Ocean. The Bantu-speaking peoples – more and more known under the name of the Zandj – were procured either by capture in raids or bought in exchange for shoddy goods from the petty kings of the hinterland. They were then shipped from the counting-houses on the coast to the island of Socotra and the emporium of Aden, assembly points from which they reached their final Egyptian and Mesopotamian destinations via the Red Sea and the Persian Gulf respectively. It was in Iraq that the greatest concentration of black slaves was to be found; this eventually led to the outbreak of the Zandj revolt one of the bloodiest and most destructive revolts in Islamic history.[65]

Another major source of supply of servile labour to the Muslim world was Nubia. According to Yūsuf Faḍl Ḥassan, 'it was primarily for commercial reasons that the Arabs penetrated into Al-Muḳurra' and ʿAlwa in the early centuries of Islam. Arab merchants brought grain, beads and combs, and took back ivory, ostrich feathers, cattle and slaves. It is prob-

60. See J. Vercoutter, 1976.

61. F. M. Snowden, 1970, passim.

62. M. Lombard, 1971b.

63. Since there is no study on the slave trade in Western Africa one cannot be certain about its volume or even of its factual existence.

64. A. Popovic, 1976, pp. 53 ff (on the name Zandj), pp. 62 ff (the earliest mention of their presence and their revolts).

65. See M. Lombard, 1971b, p. 153.

able that the last item constituted the main activity of the Arab merchants'.[66] Some slaves were acquired as annual tribute paid by Nubia (*baḳt*) to the rulers of Muslim Egypt.[67] The majority of slaves thus procured were destined for the Egyptian market, largely for military use.[68]

The Ethiopians were imported along the valleys of the Blue Nile and the Nile or passed through the transit ports of 'Aydhāb and Zāyla' on the African coast of the Red Sea into Egypt or Arabia. The Somalis from the Berbera area were shipped via Zāyla' to Aden and the great distribution centre of Zabīd, thereby supplying the slave markets of the Ḥidjāz, Syria and Iraq.[69]

The final source of supply was the Western Sudan. Slaves from the region of the Sahel (Ghana, Gao, Kānem and Zaghāwa) were either conveyed to the major urban centres of the Maghrib and Muslim Spain via Nūl Lamṭa and Sidjilmāsa or through the central Saharan region to Wargla and Djarīd and then onward to Ifrīḳiya, Fezzān, Tripolitania and Cyrenaica en route for Egypt and other regions of the Muslim East.[70] This was greatly facilitated by the presence of colonies of Muslim traders[71] in several sub-Saharan countries, especially Ghana and Gao. These merchants traded with the local princes and acted as bridgeheads for the trans-Saharan traffic in gold, salt and slaves. Other non-Islamized groups, the Zaghāwa for example, were also in contact with the Islamized Berbers of the Hoggar or of inner Cyrenaica who were the forwarding agents for this lucrative overland trade.[72]

The slave market (*Sūḳ al-raḳīḳ*)

Not all the details concerning the organization of the slave trade in the Muslim world of this period are known to us. Nevertheless, we are acquainted with some of its salient features.

Slave markets, referred to in some countries as 'places of display' (*mā'riḍ*), were found in every important town throughout the Muslim empire. Some of these in the ninth century were situated at the opening of major international commercial routes and thereby played the role of distributing centres. The markets of Bukhārā, Samarkand, Nīshāpūr, Rayy,

66. Y. F. Hassan, 1967, p. 42.
67. On the *baḳt* see Chapters 7 and 8 above.
68. The demand for 'Nubian' slaves was not limited to Egypt even though it remained the principal mart. One finds that in 977 Ibn Ziyād, ruler of a dynasty with its centre at Zabīd in the Yemen received from the ruler of the island of Dahlak amongst other items a 'tribute of one thousand heads of slaves whereof five hundred were Abyssinian and Nubian female slaves'. See al-Ḥakamī, 1892, p. 6.
69. M. Lombard, 1971b, p. 200.
70. ibid., p. 201.
71. See A. Mez, 1922, p. 444, for the commercial role of these Muslim colonies.
72. Cf. Ibn Ḥawḳal, 1938, p. 61, and 1964, p. 153.

Balkh, and Marw served as terminal stations for the columns of Slav or Turkish slaves. Zabīd, Aden in the Yemen and Baṣra in Lower Mesopotamia were centres through which black slaves were forwarded. Yet other markets were situated in the middle of heavily populated areas where there was a maximum utilization of slave labour. These were Baghdad, Cairo, Cordova and Mecca. Al-Ya'ḳūbī (third/ninth century) described one of the most famous of these slave marts – Samarra – as 'consisting of a vast quadrangle intersected with internal alleys. The houses contained lower and upper rooms and stalls for slaves'.[73]

The buying and selling of slaves became an intricate affair. Slaves had to be carefully examined by midwives and at times by doctors before they were put up for display to prospective buyers. Details on the merits and de-merits of slaves as well as the best kind of work they were suited for were grouped in the form of manuals. One such slave buyer's vademecum was that by the Christian physician of the fifth/eleventh century – Ibn Buṭlān – entitled 'Risāla fī shirā al-rāḳīḳ wataḳlīb al-'abīd'.[74] Ibn Buṭlān collected and popularized, at least among slave-buyers, a great many prejudices borrowed mostly from Greek and Latin literature, partly medical. The literature, particularly under the influence of the physiognomists of the fifth and following centuries attempted to link physical appearance due to environmental conditions with character traits. In Ibn Buṭlān's discussion of the relative merits of coloured slave girls we find many curious observations such as the one about the Zandj women:

> Their defaults are innumerable; the darker, the uglier; they are not up to much ... Dancing and beating the rhythm are engrained in their nature. And since their manner of speech is unintelligible, they are given to blowing [musical instruments] and dancing. It is said: were the Zandj to fall from heaven, he would beat the rhythm in falling.[75]

Repeating many physiognomists' stereotypes, Ibn Buṭlān wrote that 'fat lips are the sign of stupidity',[76] or that 'dark black eyes signalize cowardice, and if they are goat-like, it is a sign of ignorance'.[77]

Al-Mas'ūdī, a century before Ibn Buṭlān, reproduced the famous passage of Galen attributing ten not very favourable properties to blacks, in particular, the last one being 'an excessive petulance'. And he adds that Galen interpreted the predominance of this property to an imperfect organization of the brain which in turn results in feeble intelligence.[78]

This text, with some variants, is to be found in many other authors; it helped to spread a pernicious idea – which has as yet not entirely dis-

73. Al-Ya'ḳūbī, 1892, p. 259; A. Mez, 1922, p. 156.

74. Ed. by 'Abd al-Salām Hārūn in *Nawādir al-Makhṭuṭāt*, 4, 6, Cairo, 1373/1954. For a comprehensive study of this guide see F. Sanagustin, 1980. See also H. Müller, 1980.

75. F. Sanagustin, 1980, p. 233.

76. ibid., p. 227.

77. ibid., p. 226.

78. Al-Mas'ūdī, 1962, p. 69.

appeared – about the lightheartedness of the blacks, due to the environment and the influence of sun. These judgements are, however, based on the differences caused by climate and environment.[79] This theory of climates had a long life among the authors writing in Arabic and later also among Europeans as well.[80]

Slave markets were under strict state control in order to protect the buyers from unethical business practices. Transactions were not exclusively held in public. Slaves were also procured through the services of agents (*dallāl*) on payment of a commission. However, most of these slave merchants known as importers (*djallāb*) or cattle dealers (*nakhkhās*) inspired contempt for their occupation or envy for their wealth.[81]

Prices of slaves were determined according to their place of origin, sex, age, physical condition and abilities. As a rule, whites were dearer than blacks. Allusions to the varying prices of slaves are to be found in classical Arabic accounts. About the middle of the second/eighth century, 200 dirhams was the average price of a slave. In Oman a good black slave could be bought for between 25 and 30 dinars. A winsome girl fetched 150 dinars, *c.* 300/912. The Abyssinian Abu' l-Misk Kāfūr, who later became regent of Egypt (334/945–356/966), was reported to have been purchased in 312/924 for the paltry sum of 18 dinars, even though he was a eunuch. The vizier al-Ṣāḥib b. ʿAbbād purchased a Nubian slave for 400 dinars, a price regarded as being too high, for a pretty swarthy Nubian female could be had for only 200 dinars.[82] However, slaves endowed with exceptional talents fetched astronomical prices. Trained dancing girls had price tags of between 1000 and 2000 dinars. Singers in Baghdad in 918 were almost all of servile origins. A female singer was sold in an aristocratic circle in 912 for 13 000 dinars.[83]

Islam and slavery in the Indian Ocean

Islam, given the political and social context of its birth in Arabia, could not

79. Equally negative characteristics were attributed to northern peoples (Turks, Slavs, etc.) who lived also under 'abnormal' – from the point of view of inhabitants of the mild zone – conditions.

80. See for example M. Bergé, 1972, pp. 165–76.

81. F. Sanagustin, 1980, pp. 168–9.

82. A. Mez, 1922, pp. 153–4. An anecdote on the estimation of the value of the celebrated black poet Nusayb by apprisers on the orders of the Umayyad Caliph ʿAbd al-Azīz ibn Marwan provides us with valuable indications as to the range of prices prevailing then. A black slave was worth 100 dinars and if he was a good shepherd it rose to 200 dinars. One who shaped arrows and fledged them was worth 300 dinars and an excellent archer, 400 dinars. A reciter of poems fetched the sum of 500 dinars. A gifted poet was priced at 1000 dinars. See Ibn Khallikān, 1843–71, Vol. 3, p. 626, note 13. For a comprehensive study on prices, see the valuable study by E. Ashtor, 1969.

83. A. Mez, 1922, p. 154. See equally S. D. Goitein, 1963; S. Rasheed, 1973; C. Pellat, 1963.

suppress slavery as an institution nor preach for its abolition as a doctrine. It strived, however, to moderate the system and to reduce the severity of its moral and legal aspects. In doing so, Islam accepted a modified form of slavery having as its basis a certain respect for human beings; the vanquished in war were no longer killed off, but made prisoners. This was in marked contrast with previous practices and constituted progress.

Slavery of any form shocks us today. This was not so for preceding generations living as they did in a completely different period and milieu, where even the notion of liberty was almost absent. The supremacy of the concept of the group within a lineage context went unchallenged, making a non-gregarious existence well-nigh impossible. Many an isolated individual found social existence only as a 'client' of dependent status. Moral judgements on the institution of slavery during the period under review must be passed with caution.[84]

The Qoran (4:36) enjoins believers to treat their slaves with kindness (*iḥsān*) and makes the emancipation of a slave a worthy act and work of charity (2:177; 90:13).[85]

'Tradition delights in asserting that the slave's lot was among the latest preoccupations of the Prophet. It has quite a large store of sayings and anecdotes, attributed to the Prophet or to his Companions, enjoining real kindness towards this inferior social class.'[86]

Slaves were to be treated as brothers. They should not be addressed in contemptuous terms. Slave and master should sit at the same table, and be provided with the same garments. The master should not let a slave do onerous tasks and if he committed an offence the punishment meted out should not be harsh or excessive. Manumission is recommended as a happy solution and a way for the master to make amends for the excessive chastisement of his slave. In return, it was the slave's duty to show unswerving loyalty.[87] It can be noted from the foregoing that the Muslim religious ethic follows closely 'the line of Qoranic teaching, it even lays perceptible emphasis upon the humanitarian tendencies of the latter on the question of slavery'.[88]

The conquest and development of major trade gave rise in Muslim lands to an ever-increasing importance of servile labour, until it became a social phenomenon of the first order. Muslim jurists of the great Sunni schools were consequently inclined to study this question. Areas of concern were the provenance of slaves, their status in a new social setting, the composite quality of a slave both as a thing and a person, and lastly his manumission.

R. Brunschwig has observed that despite the strictness professed by cer-

84. F. Sanagustin, 1980, pp. 17–18.
85. R. Brunschwig, 1960; R. Roberts, 1908 pp. 41–7.
86. R. Brunschwig, 1960, p. 25.
87. On *ḥadīth*s pertaining to slaves, see al-Tahawī, 1950–1, pp. 368, 377 and 378. Ibn Ḥadjar, al-Asḳalānī, 1970, Vol. 4, p. 320. Al-Ghazālī, 1861, Vol. 2, p. 199.
88. R. Brunschwig, 1960, p. 25.

tain doctors of law, the *fikh* has never evolved an adequately clear system of sanctions to suppress the kidnapping or sale of persons, Muslim or non-Muslim. Still less does one see any positive denunciation of the practice of castrating young slaves, although it was condemned in principle[89]

Unlike the ancient laws of Babylon, which recognized several causes of slavery,[90] Muslim law acknowledges only two sources of legitimate slavery; birth in servitude and capture in war.[91] In the first case, a slave is identified as one who is born of slave parents. The child assumes at birth his mother's status, free or slave. This is equally applied to children born of a free woman, even if the father is a slave. However, a major exception is made of a child born of a free man and a female slave in his employ who is regarded as free born. If this was not so, the child would have become his master's slave. This was of wide occurrence.[92]

However, birth in bondage could not constitute a never-ending source of supply of servile labour on account of the free status of children born under the system of legal concubinage as well as the high incidence of manumissions, which tended further to diminish their numbers. The persistence of the institution of slavery in the Islamic world therefore had to depend on 'the constantly renewed contribution of peripheral or external elements, either directly captured in war or imported commercially under the fiction of Holy War, from foreign territory (*dār al-ḥarb*)'.[93]

From the juridico-religious view-point, the slave is seen as possessing 'a kind of composite quality, partaking of the nature both of thing and of person. Considered as a thing, he is subject to the right of ownership ... exercised by a man or woman and [is] the object of all the legal operations proceeding from this position: sale, gift, hire, inheritance and so on.'[94]

Reducing a slave to the level of a 'mere commodity', Islamic canon law inevitably places him on the same footing as that of a beast of burden (*dawābb*).[95] This was given frequent expression in the theoretical treatises on public law of the period, especially regarding the role of the *muḥtasib* in ensuring the proper treatment meted out by masters to their animals and slaves.[96]

Regarded as a person, the slave in principle had certain rights and responsibilities but these were evidently not comparable to those of a free man. However, a singular feature of slavery as practised in the Muslim

89. ibid., p. 26. The practice of castration is against the teachings of Islam. See Qoran, 4: 18. On eunuchs, see C. Orhanlu, 1978.

90. These were (1) birth in servitude; (2) selling oneself into slavery in cases of insolvency; (3) the sale of minors; (4) abduction of minors; and (5) prisoners of war. For details, see I. Mendelsohn, 1949, pp. 1–23.

91. R. Brunschwig, 1960, p. 26.

92. ibid.

93. ibid.

94. ibid.

95. See al-Māwardī, 1922, p. 257.

96. R. Brunschwig, 1960, p. 26.

world was that the slave, despite his quasi-subservience to his master, was still allowed to administer property, transact business and save money. In some cases, he might enrich himself and rise to high office. Nevertheless, the equivocal status of a slave, at once the owner of property and the possession of his master, was a constant source of difficulty.

A Muslim slave is permitted to marry with his master's consent. He may have a family of his own, but not the right of custody of his children. Equally authorized are unions of slaves with one another, and of a slave with a free woman other than his mistress, or that of a female slave with a free man. However, the wedlock of any free man or woman with their own slaves is prohibited. The Malikī school of law confers upon the slave the right to have a maximum of four wives just like his free coreligionists. The other schools of law entitle him only to a maximum of two wives. He equally retains the husband's usual right of repudiation (*ṭalaḳ*).[97]

It was, however, the system of legal concubinage which had greater social significance, on account of its widespread application and impact on the social life of the period. 'Both pre-Islamic Arab custom and the Koran recognized the right of the master to take his female slaves as concubines, and a slave woman who had borne a child to her master was called *umm al-walad*'.[98] The freedom and legitimacy of children born of such cohabitations depended entirely on the acknowledgement of their father, the master. This appeared to have been regularly given.

Moreover, the master disposes of the right of chastisement (*ta'dhīb*) of his slave. If the latter suffered maltreatment to the point of sustaining severe bodily injuries it is recommended that he be sold or enfranchised.[99]

Finally, the slave could not in theory ascend to positions of authority (*wilāyāt*), whether public or private. However, there was greater flexibility in the actual implementation of this ruling. It was quite customary for men in high positions to employ slaves in subordinate functions and delegate some of their authority to them and in the case of slaves of a caliph or a prince they could become as a matter of fact far more powerful than free men.[100]

The slave has the same religious duties (*'ibādāt*) as that of any other Muslim. Nevertheless, his servile condition acquits him from observing scrupulously certain religious obligations that entail liberty of movement, such as the Friday prayer, the pilgrimage and the *djihād*. He is also not considered competent to hold religious office.[101]

The state of bondage though perpetual in principle was, however, subject to being modified and terminated under exceptional conditions. This

97. ibid., p. 27.

98. J. Schacht, 1950, p. 264. Qoran, 4:3,24; 23:6,50; 70:30.

99. R. Brunschwig, 1960, p. 27. On the position of the slave under Islamic penal law, see ibid., p. 29.

100. F. Sanagustin, 1980, p. 23.

101. R. Brunschwig, 1960, p. 27.

was effected in various ways. First, there was enfranchisement (*'itḳ*) regarded as a work of piety and conferred unilaterally by the master. It was irrevocable.[102] Secondly, the promise of freedom of a master to his slave, to take effect on his death. This post-mortem grant is known as *tadbīr* and the beneficiary a *mudabbar*.[103] Thirdly, the competence given to master and slave to enter into a contractual enfranchisement (*kitāba*). This meets with Qoranic approval (24:33). Under this contract, the master offered his slave the chance of buying back his liberty by using his own savings in instalments. The finalization of payment entitled him to the full legal rights of a free-born man.[104] Finally, there was the legal provision already alluded to conferring liberty and legitimacy on children born of a slave woman (a concubine) and her master.

On emancipation, the slave though having the full civic rights of a freed man still remained, as did his male descendants, attached in perpetuity to his former master, now his 'patron' and his family by a 'bond of clientship' – *walā*. Both 'patron' and 'client' are referred to as *mawlā* and in the plural form as *mawālī*.[105]

Employment and social conditions

As aptly pointed out by Mez, despite the lack of instances of racial or colour prejudice in the Islamic body of values and despite the provision of legal guarantees and the favours of fortune, one must not be led to paint too rosy a picture of the social status of the black Muslim slave in the first centuries of Islam.[106] In daily life and in the realities of social relationships prejudice – though not shown exclusively towards Africans – was widespread.

This marked aversion toward blackness and later on to dark-complexioned peoples characterized the views of a number of Muslim geographers, *adab* writers and poets as well as those of the common man as expressed in the popular lore of the period. An early interpretation of the inferior status of the black was based on the biblical story of how Ḥām, one of the sons of Noah, was damned black for his 'sin'. The curse of blackness, and with it slavery, passed on to all black peoples who descended from Ḥām. This explanation, particularly popular among professional tellers of legends and stories (*ḳuṣṣaṣ*) but even among serious scholars like al-Ya'ḳūbī (third/ninth century), was not generally accepted. Al-Hamdānī explicitly refuted this tradition – which according to him originated with the Jews –

102. ibid., p. 30.
103. J. Schacht, 1950, p. 265, note 8; also R. Brunschwig, 1960, p. 30.
104. See J. Schacht, 1950, pp. 111–12.
105. R. Brunschwig, 1960.
106. A. Mez, 1922, pp. 161–2. For a detailed study of the status of black slaves in medieval Muslim society see G. Rotter, 1967.

on the ground of a Qoranic verse (6:164) 'Each soul will earn only on its own account and none will be laden with another burden'. And he concludes, again with reference to the environmental factors: 'Black, white or brown skin of man has no other cause than the climate as we have mentioned it in this book'.[107]

Ibn Khaldūn, too, rejects the hereditary curse:

> 'The genealogists who do not know anything about the nature of things, have imagined that the Blacks are sons of Ḥām, son of Noah, and that the colour of their skin is the result of Noah's curse, which has caused the blackness of Ḥām and the slavery inflicted by God on his descendants. If the Thora says that Noah has cursed his son Ḥām, it does not speak about the colour of the latter. The curse only made Ḥām's sons slaves of his brothers' descendants. To link the skin colour of Blacks with Ḥām means an ignorance of the true nature of heat and cold, and of their influence on climate and on created beings'.[108]

Black slaves were employed for various purposes in medieval Muslim society; mainly as menial servants, concubines and eunuchs in harems, craftsmen, business assistants, members of forced collective labour forces in state enterprises and as soldiers. Their contribution in building the economic, political and social base of medieval Islamic states was considerable.

At the bottom of the social ladder were to be found the 'Zandj' consisting mainly of East African slaves. In the extensive salt flats of Lower Mesopotamia, these slaves toiled in gangs of 500 to 5000, at the task of digging away the nitrous top soil (*sebākh*) and laying bare the fertile ground beneath for cultivation, possibly of sugar, as well as to obtain the saltpetre that occurred in the upper stratum and pile it up in stacks. Their labour was supervised by agents and overseers. Life in the salt flats and marshes and the conditions under which these labourers (*kassāḥīn*) worked and lived were indeed dreadful. The great Muslim annalist al-Ṭabarī indicated that these miserable souls were underfed and often fell victim to recurrent malarial epidemics and other diseases. These, coupled with the harsh treatment they received at the hands of their taskmasters engendered smouldering resentment and led to frequent revolts.[109]

The use of collective forced labour in large-scale projects was not only confined to the area of the Shaṭṭ al-ʿArab in lower Iraq, but also occurred

107. Al-Hamdānī, 1954, Vol. 1, pp. 29–31; see B. Lewis, 1971, pp. 29–38; Ibn Ḳutayba, 1850, pp. 13–14; al-Masʿūdi, 1861–77, Vol. 1, pp. 75–80; G. Vajda, 1971.

108. Ibn Khaldūn, 1967–9, Vol. 1, pp. 167–8.

109. 'They were fed only on a "few handfuls" of flour, semolina, and dates', quoted in B. Lewis, 1971, p. 66. Our information on these work sites of the Zandj is scanty and essentially based on the accounts given in al-Ṭabarī, 1879–1901, Vol. 3, pp. 1747–50.

in the province of al-Baḥrayn.[110] In the eleventh century a force of 30 000 blacks was obliged to do rough work under the Karmathians.[111] Zandj slaves, according to Ibn al-Mudjāwir, were also purchased for work in the stone quarries of Aden.[112]

However, the nature of employment of the vast majority of slaves was essentially domestic and military, with far more tolerable working and living conditions. In many modest and well-to-do households, domestic chores were taken care of by one or more slaves including manumitted ones.[113] They were the cooks, chambermaids, wet nurses, doorkeepers, water-carriers and the like. Attractive female slaves, as concubines, gratified the sexual pleasures of their masters. In the harems of the wealthy, talented female slaves were afforded the possibilities of becoming singers, musicians, dancers and poets, and thereby beguiling the leisure moments of their lords.

The mating of Arab males with black women goes back to pre-Islamic times, the women generally being Nubians and Sudanese. However, Ethiopian girls were highly esteemed. Such relationships took the form of concubinage rather than marriage.[114] In the Umayyad and Abbasid periods, it was a common practice at every social level.[115] A number of Arabic poets became enamoured of their swarthy bondmaids. Amongst them was to be found ʿAshā Sulaym, who cohabited with a pitch-dark bondmaid, Danānīr by name.[116] The celebrated bard al-Farazdaḳ (d. 114/732) took Umm Makkiya – 'the negress' – for wife.[117] They became inseparable. The blind Abbasid poet, Bashār ibn Burd (d. 167/783) extolled the virtues of his dark-complexioned life companion.[118] Abū Shīs, yet another poet of the period (d. 196/811), likened the raven-black complexion of his mate to that of 'sweet-smelling musk'.[119]

A famous text from the third/ninth century – al-Djāḥiẓ's defence of the blacks against their detractors[120] – shows clearly how much the blacks

110. The province of al-Baḥrayn comprised the coast (and its hinterland) between present-day Kuwait and Ḳatar.

111. B. Lewis, 1971, p. 66.

112. Ibn al-Mudjāwir, 1957, Vol. 1, p. 126.

113. See C. Pellat, 1953, p. 234.

114. B. Lewis, 1971, p. 93.

115. As expressed by the poet al-Riyāshī in the following verse (al-Mubarrad, 1864, Vol. 1, p. 302):

> Sons of concubine have become,
> So numerous amongst us;
> Lead me, O God, to a land,
> Where I shall see no bastards.

116. al-Djāḥiẓ, 1964, Vol. 1, p. 214.

117. ibid.

118. al-Iṣfahānī, 1868–9, Vol. 8, p. 46.

119. Amin Aḥmad, 1969b, Vol. 1, p. 86.

120. Al-Djāḥiẓ, 1903.

and whites were used to living together, at various social levels, particularly in Baṣra. The same author offers, moreover, many examples of the consideration in which the people from Africa and the Indian Ocean were held, at least until the time when the Zandj revolt caused many changes in attitudes.[121]

The system of concubinage, favoured by Muslim institutions, resulted in the mingling of races and constituted an important element in the rural and urban populations. Although there was a continuous flow of people of African origin to Muslim countries, the facility of their being easily assimilated into the extant social framework has left a different mark on the population structure in this region as compared with other areas with a numerous African diaspora. One of the most striking results of this assimilation process is the non-existence of large homogeneous racial groups with their own separate history and culture such as are sometimes to be found in the Americas.

In the upper layers of medieval Muslim society concubinage with slave-girls of African origin was nothing exceptional. A number of princes and caliphs, especially of the Abbasid dynasty, had slave mothers, some of whom were black Africans. The literature of this period informs us that the mothers of Prince Ibrāhīm b. al-Mahdī and of the Caliph al-Muḳtafī (d. 555/1160) were a 'negress' and a Nubian, respectively.[122] A Sudanese slave-girl, the concubine of al-Ẓāhir, gave birth to the future Fāṭimid Caliph al-Mustanṣir. She was a remarkable woman and ruled over Egypt after al-Ẓāhir's death and during her son's minority.[123] This period of Fāṭimid history is of particular importance. Al-Zāhir's mother favoured largely the black warriors whose influence on Egyptian policy correspondingly increased. This provoked a hostile reaction from the Turks, the second group of expatriate warriors, and from this time on skirmishes between the blacks and the Turks became very frequent. The least fortunate of the female black slaves in Muslim society were those forced into prostitution despite Qoranic prohibition.

Male black slaves who were eunuchs filled the palaces of the great of the land, especially as guardians of the harems.[124] Some of them managed to rise to high office and played key roles in state affairs in the medieval period. This can be illustrated by several examples. The black eunuch Kāfūr al-Ikhshīdī (356/966) rose to become regent of Egypt,[125] Mufliḥ – 'the black' – the favourite of Caliph al-Rāḍī (d. 329/940) was responsible

121. Al-Djāḥiẓ's book *Kitāb fakhr al-Sūdān 'ala' l-Bīḍān* will be shortly edited and translated into French by A. Miquel, G. Ducatez, J. Ducatez and J. Devisse.

122. Ibn Khallikān, 1843–71, Vol. 1, pp. 16–20.

123. M. Lombard, 1971b, p. 150.

124. During the reign of the Abbasid Caliph al-Muktadir (295/908–320/932), the palace eunuchs numbered 11 000, comprising 7000 blacks and 4000 whites. For details, see Al-Sābi', 1964.

125. Ibn Khallikān, 1843–71, Vol. 2, pp. 524–8. Cf. chapter 7 above.

for the formulation of state policies.[126] The chamberlain of the Buwayhid prince ʿAḍud al-Dawlah (d. 372/982) was shakr (sugar), a black eunuch. He was the only one who succeeded in securing the confidence of his suspicious and tyrannical master, an honour coveted by all.

Outside the house or the palace, many black slaves served as shop assistants or transacted business themselves with a considerable measure of independence. Al-Djāḥiẓ alludes to a negress, Khulayda by name, who hired dwelling houses to pilgrims in Mecca.[127] Others tilled their masters' fields or served as watchmen of their masters' orchards. One reads of a black slave being paid three loaves a day for keeping watch and ward.[128] Al-Shāfiʿī, the founder of one of the four Islamic schools of law (d. 204/819), owned several slaves, of whom one was a Nubian employed as a baker.[129] Al-Balādhurī mentions a quarter of Kūfa named after the black cupper ʿAntara. Yet others were hired out with two-thirds of their earnings going to their masters. ʿAmr b. Wabara[130] (second/eighth century), profited from such a practice. The poet Abū l-ʿAtāhiya (d. 211/826), a potter by profession, had several black slaves as his assistants.[131]

The military role of slaves was one of the salient features of Islamic civilization and had considerable repercussions on the foreign and domestic policies of many Muslim states.[132] Bernard Lewis notes that 'Black soldiers appear occasionally in early Abbasid times and after the slave rebellion in Iraq, in which blacks displayed terrifying military prowess, they were recruited in large numbers'.[133] It is related that under the Abbasid Caliph al-Amīn (d. 198/813) a special corps of Ethiopian bodyguards with the designation 'Crows' was formed.[134] In the fierce struggle for power during the reign of al-Muḳtadir (d. 320/932), 7000 blacks fought on the side of the caliphal party.[135] Aḥmad ibn Ṭūlūn (d. 884), governor of Egypt and later its virtual ruler, mustered a large army of black slaves, especially Nubians. It is related that upon his death he left, among other possessions, 24 000 white *mamlūk*s and 45 000 blacks. These were organized in separate corps and accommodated in separate quarters at the military cantonments.[136]

According to Arabic chronicles of the period, black regiments referred to as *ʿabīd al-shirāʿ* (slaves obtained through purchase) became an important part of the Fāṭimid military forces. Their role became all the more promi-

126. Miskawaih, 1914, Vol. 1, p. 104.
127. Al-Djāḥiẓ, 1964, Vol. 2, p. 130.
128. Al-Ibshīhī, 1851/2, Vol. 1, p. 140.
129. Al-Shāfiʿī, 1903, Vol. 4, p. 48.
130. Al-Ṭabarī, 1879–1901, Vol. 6, p. 153.
131. al-Iṣfahānī, 1868–9, Vol. 3, p. 129.
132. For a detailed study, see D. Pipes, 1980.
133. B. Lewis, 1971, p. 69.
134. Al-Sābiʾ, 1958, p. 16.
135. ibid., p. 8.
136. B. Lewis, 1971, p. 69; M. Lombard, 1971b, p. 195.

nent during the reign of al-Mustanṣir (1035–94) on account of the unflinching support they received from the Caliph's mother, a Sudanese slave-woman of stout character. At the height of their influence, they numbered 50 000.[137]

The revolts of the Zandj

The Zandj rose in arms against the Caliphate on several occasions.[138] The first insurrection (70/689–90) was in Baṣra during the reign of Khālid b. 'Abd Allāh. It was of minor importance, consisting as it did of small bands of slaves given to plundering and acts of vandalism in the Euphrates area. It was easily quelled by the caliphal forces, with some of its prominent members being put to the sword.[139]

A second rebellion in 75/694 was of greater significance. It was better organized and ably led by the chief of the Zandj, Riyāḥ, who was otherwise widely known as the 'Lion of the Zandj' (*Shīr Zandj*). He sowed terror throughout the region of the Euphrates and at al-Ubulla. Judging from the series of battles these insurgents waged against governmental forces, their numbers must have been large. This rebellion could only be suppressed with the reinforcement of the caliphal army by Baṣran volunteers.[140]

In 132/749–50, during the reign of Caliph Abū l-'Abbas al-Ṣaffāḥ a regular force of 4000 soldiers was launched against the rebels at Mosul in northern Mesopotamia, resulting in a massacre that was said to have cost the lives of more than 10 000 inhabitants – men, women and children.[141]

Another Zandj uprising followed the abortive Alid revolt against the forces of the Abbasid Caliph al-Manṣūr in Medina (145/765). Members of the defeated party incited their black slaves and *mawāli* (clients) to attack the garrison of Abbasid troops in the city. This led to chaos. The governor was deposed and the black rebels seized military depots. Fearing a worsening situation, the patrons calmed their slaves and the authority of the Abbasids was once again restored. However, harsh punishments were meted out to the Zandj ring leaders.[142]

The Zandj revolt of 255/869 was undoubtedly the greatest protest movement by black African slaves in medieval Islam. It lasted more than fourteen years and passed through two distinctive periods (255/869–266/879

137. Ibn Muyassar, 1919, pp. 16–17.

138. The first detailed study of the Zandj revolt was T. H. Nöldeke, 1892. This was followed by several other studies both in Arabic and European languages. A good detailed account in Arabic is that by F. al-Sāmir, 1971. However, the most complete study of the revolt to date is that of A. Popovic, 1976.

139. See A. Popovic, 1976, pp. 62–3; F. al-Sāmir, 1971, p. 19; al-Balādhurī, 1883, Vol. II, p. 305.

140. Ibn al-Athīr, 1855–6, Vol. 4, pp. 188, 314–15.

141. ibid., Vol. 5, pp. 340–1.

142. Al-Ṭabarī, 1879–1901, Vol. 3, p. 286.

and 266/879–270/883). The first period was one of expansion and great success for the insurgents. The second phase consisted of a prolonged struggle against superior forces and the eventual collapse of the Zandj state. The war theatre was the region of lower Mesopotamia and Southern Persia.[143]

The leader of this revolt was an Arab, ʿAlī b. Muḥammad and widely referred to as 'Ṣāḥib al-Zandj' (Master of the Zandj).[144] After a series of abortive endeavours at sedition in a number of cities and provinces of the region 'including Baṣra where he narrowly escaped capture and imprisonment, he went to the saltpetre area'.[145] On the 26th Ramaḍān 255/7 September 869 he aroused the Zandj serfs to rebellion.[146]

In the beginning, in order to legitimize and seek support for his cause, he claimed Alid ancestry. He did not, however, adhere to Shīʿīte doctrine but instead to that of the Khāridjites, whose egalitarian principles allowed even an Ethiopian to be caliph.[147]

The revolt began as a class conflict between the exploited Zandj slaves and their masters. It rapidly turned, however, into an open and violent war against the Caliphate. It was, therefore, a political and social struggle rather than a racial one.[148] The dearth of sources provides us with only meagre accounts of the movement's size, composition, organization and the like, and even these are often unreliable and must be approached with caution. A further difficulty resides in the fact that contemporary and later historians largely confined their attention to the military campaigns and were openly hostile to the insurgents, depicting them as 'enemies of God' living in a state of irreligion and lawlessness.[149]

As correctly observed by Nöldeke, 'the number of 300 000 fighting men claimed for the negro leader was greatly exaggerated. The Zandj may very well have outnumbered their assailants, whose strength was given at 50 000, at least at the beginning of the struggle; but the latter were, on the whole, certainly much better equipped, fed and continually reinforced by newly arriving troops'.[150]

The black slaves involved in the revolt were scattered over a wide area in lower Mesopotamia and southern Persia in large bands of 500–5000 labourers.[151] The Zandj contingents of ʿAlī b. Muḥammad consisted of the following main groups:

The Zandj Non-Arabophone slaves from the coast of East Africa, who

143. A. Popovic, 1976, p. 83.
144. For details on ʿAlī b. Muḥammad, see *ibid.*, pp. 71–81.
145. B. Lewis, 1950, p. 104; F. al-Sāmir, 1971, pp. 102–3.
146. A. Popovic, 1976, p. 79.
147. T. H. Nöldeke, 1892, p. 151; F. al-Sāmir, 1971, p. 82.
148. See F. al-Sāmir, 1971, p. 59; L. Massignon, 1929.
149. A. Popovic, 1976, p. 157.
150. T. H. Nöldeke, 1892, pp. 167–8; Ibn al-Athīr, 1885–6, Vol. 11, p. 41.
151. Al-Ṭabarī, 1879–1901, Vol. 3, pp. 1747–50.

were imported into the region from an undetermined period. Al-Djāḥiẓ distinguished four sub-groupings; Ḳunbula, Landjāwiyya, Naml and Kilāb.[152] These were able to communicate with their leader only through an interpreter.

The Ḳarmātiyya These were an ill-defined group of African slaves, in all probability hailing from the Sudan. They were Arabophone. They had no links with the Ḳarāmita movement.[153]

The Nūba These were not only Nubians but also included Nilotic peoples as well. They were also Arabic-speaking.[154]

The Furātiyya Slaves dwelling on the banks of the lower Euphrates, south of the city of Wāsiṭ. They were clearly distinguished from the Zandj and spoke Arabic.[155]

The Shūridjīyya These were the labourers (*kassāḥīn*) employed on the salt flats of lower Mesopotamia. Their designation is a derivation of the Persian word *shōra*, meaning nitrous earth.[156] Under this grouping are also to be found some free men and manumitted slaves as well as the hired hands employed on the date and sugar plantations.[157]

Finally, there were the *Beduins* inhabiting the marshy districts south of Wāsiṭ. The ranks of the insurgents were swelled by the desertion of black soldiers from the caliphal armies.

It is not our intention to give here a detailed account of the various military campaigns of the Zandj revolt, but only a summary of the principal events.

In 256/870, the Zandj army conquered the flourishing port of al-Ubulla and destroyed it.[158] The fall of al-Ubulla terrified into submission the inhabitants of the Persian port of ʿAbbadān[159] on the eastern bank of the Shaṭṭ al-ʿArab. This paved the way for the invasion in the same year of the adjoining province of Khūzistān. The Zandj made themselves masters of Djubbā and the capital al-Ahwāz.[160] The following year (257/871) witnessed the occupation and sacking of the principal port of Iraq, Baṣra. This was the most spectacular of the Zandj victories and a great blow to the Abbasid Caliphate. The terrible fate of Baṣra remained alive in the minds of succeeding generations.[161] The Zandj forces then successfully ad-

152. C. Pellat, 1953, p. 41; Al-Ṭabarī, 1879–1901, Vol. 3, pp. 1756–7.
153. Al-Ṭabarī, 1879–1901, Vol. 3, p. 1749.
154. ibid., p. 1745.
155. ibid., p. 1757.
156. See L. Massignon, 1929.
157. Al-Ṭabarī, 1879–1901, Vol. 3, p. 1753.
158. Ibn al-Athīr, 1885–6, Vol. 7, p. 94.
159. Al-Ṭabarī, 1879–1901, Vol. 3, p. 1837.
160. Ibn al-Wardī, 1868, Vol. 1, p. 234.
161. Al-Ṭabarī, 1879–1901, Vol. 3, pp. 1847–57; Masʿūdī, 1861–77, Vol. 4, pp. 207–8. The tragic fate of Baṣra has been immortalised by Ibn al-Rūmī (283?/896?). See Ibn al-Rūmī, 1924, pp. 419–27.

vanced northward, capturing and sacking along the way the cities of Wāsiṭ (264/877–8), Nu'mānīya (265/878) and Djardjarāyā, 110 km below Baghdad. This was the culminating point of their northward expansion.[162]

Between 267/881 and 270/883, the Abbasid crown prince al-Muwaffaḳ undertook the offensive and pushed the invading forces southward and finally imposed a complete economic blockade on their capital, al-Mukhtāra.[163] After a siege of three years the city succumbed to assault on the 2 Ṣafar 270/11 August 883. The leader of the revolt and many of his commanders were slain.[164]

There is no doubt that the economic, political and social consequences of this long revolt profoundly affected the whole Islamic world. At the same time it made Muslims more averse to Africa and Africans in general. The import of Zandj slaves seems subsequently to have been restricted or put under control. Another consequence was the widespread diffusion of the unfavourable image of the black in Islamic countries, from Noah's curse to the themes propagated by Ibn Buṭlān.

The cultural Role of Africans in the Islamic world

The contribution of Africans in the cultural sphere as poets, authors, musicians and experts in the Islamic sciences of Qoranic exegesis, transmission of traditions and canon law was an important one.[165]

On the testimony of classical Arabic authors, Africans were endowed with eloquence. During the Umayyad and Abbasid Caliphates there were a number of distinguished black poets. An anthology of poems by one, 'Irār b. 'Amr, son of a black slave-girl, is preserved for posterity in the *Kitāb al-Aghānī* and *Ḥamāsa*.[166] He flourished during the reign of 'Abd al-Malik (d. 86/705) and was in the service of the governor of the province of Iraq, al-Hadjdjādj (d. 95/714). Another black poet of unique talent and eloquence during this period was al-Hayḳatān.[167] However, the most celebrated and eminent of these poets was Abū Miḥdjān (d. 108/726–7). He was born in the Ḥidjāz of Ethiopian parents and in his youth worked as a camel-driver. Being ambitious, he addressed a series of panegyrics to the Umayyad Prince 'Azīz b. Marwān, making such an impression that he was purchased from his owner by Marwān for a thousand dinars and manu-

162. Ibn al-Djawzī, 1938–40, Vol. 5, pp. 45–50.

163. The capital of the Zandj, according to Nöldeke, 'covered a large area and included extensive fields and palm groves. It lay somewhat below Baṣra, abutted on the west bank of the Tigris and was intersected by the canal Nahr Abī' l-khāṣīb', T. H. Nöldeke, 1892, p. 156.

164. F. al-Sāmir, 1971, pp. 151–2; A. Popovic, 1976, pp. 152–5; T. H. Nöldeke, 1892, p. 174.

165. See A. Badāwī, 1976; S. S. Haas, 1942.

166. al-Iṣfahānī, 1868–9, Vol. 10, pp. 65–6; al-Tammām, 1828–47.

167. al-Djāḥiẓ, 1964, Vol. 1, p. 182.

mitted.[168] In the early years of the Abbasid dynasty a black Kūfan poet – Abū Dulāma (d. 161/*c.* 778) – was famed for his wit, amusing adventures, acquaintance with general literature and talent for poetry. Caliph al-Manṣūr found pleasure in the verses and drollery of this gifted, bibulous, frivolous black court poet and jester.[169]

The first really great representative of Arabic artistic prose was ʿAmr Baḥr al-Djāḥiẓ (The goggle-eyed) of Baṣra (d. 255/868–9) where he lived to the age of 96.[170] His grandfather was a black camel-driver, named Fazāra – a *mawlā* of ʿAmr ibn Ḳila'.[171] Though deformed in person, as implied in his sobriquet, al-Djāḥiẓ was amply compensated with an incisive mind and a sagacious spirit.[172] His learning was encyclopaedic and he was a versatile author of numerous works on almost every branch of knowledge. One of his finest productions was the *Kitāb al-ḥayawān* (The Book of Animals).[173] He was equally famed as a freethinker and composed a discourse on the fundamentals of religion. An offshoot of the Mu'tazilite sect was called 'al-Djāḥiẓīya' after him.[174]

The Africans excelled also in the musical arts and several black virtuosi dominated the musical scene during the first two centuries of the Islamic era, especially in the Ḥidjāz where 'in the palaces and houses of the nobility and the wealthy, music and musicians came in for special indulgence'.[175] The first and greatest musician of the period was the black Abū ʿUthmān Sa'id ibn Misdjaḥ (d. *c.* 715). His desire to learn exotic musical techniques brought him to Persia and Syria. Upon his return to Ḥidjāz he introduced Byzantine and Persian melodies in the singing of Arabic songs. Ibn Misdjaḥ reached the height of his musical attainments during the reign of the Umayyad Caliph ʿAbd al-Malik (684–705) and he was acclaimed as one of the four great singers of the epoch.[176]

Another celebrated black musician was Abū ʿAbbād Ma'bad ibn Wahb (d. 126/743). He was a mulatto from Medina and flourished during the reigns of three Umayyad caliphs, being hailed as the Prince of the Medinese singers. Among his pupils was also Sallāma al-Ḳass, the mulatto female singer and favourite of Caliph Yazīd b. ʿAbd al-Malik. Many other black musicians and singers attained glory during the Abbasid Caliphate.

Arabic biographical sources (*ṭabaḳāt*) mention a number of African traditionists and scholars of religion. One of the most eminent was the

168. Cf. U. Rizzitano, 1938, pp. 316–18; D. Sallūm, 1967.
169. Ibn Khallikān, 1843–71, Vol. 1, pp. 534–9; al-Iṣfahānī, 1868–9, Vol. 1, p. 199; Vol. 10, p. 245; M. Cheneb, 1922.
170. I. Goldziher, 1966, p. 81.
171. See C. Pellat, 1953, pp. 51–4.
172. ibid., pp. 56–8.
173. Cairo edition of 1323–5/1905–7 in two volumes.
174. Ibn Khallikān, 1843–71, Vol. 2, p. 405.
175. H. G. Farmer, 1929, p. 43.
176. ibid., pp. 77–78.

black *mawlā*, Abū 'Abd Allāh Sa'īd ibn D̲j̲ubayr ibn Hishām (d. *c.* 94/712), an authority on the rites of the Pilgrimage, Qoranic exegesis, laws of divorce and questions of ritual.[177] Another, Abū 'Atā b. Rabāḥ (d. 115/733–4) was described as 'black in colour, blind in one eye, flat-nosed, one-armed, lame of a leg and woolly haired'.[178] His authority as a traditionist was widely acknowledged and the 'office of *muftī* at Mecca devolved to him'. Yet he was unostentatious and led the life of a devout ascetic.[179] The first to distinguish himself in the fields of *ḥadīth* and *fiḳh* in Islamic Egypt was Yazīd b. Abī Ḥabīb (d. 128/745), the son of a Nubian prisoner of war.[180] Al-D̲j̲āḥiẓ spoke highly of the black *mawlā* – Faradj al-Ḥadjām of Baṣra, whose role as a traditionist was beyond reproach.[181] A celebrated ascetic and great *ṣūfī* doctor was the black eunuch Abū' l-Ḥasan al-Bag̲h̲dādī, generally known by the name of K̲h̲ayr al-Nassādj (d. 322/934). He worked as a silk weaver, before he was manumitted by his master. He was equally reputed as an *'adl* (irreproachable witness).[182]

Africans in India, South-east Asia and China

Evidence of the presence of Africans in India during this period is scanty. As observed by J. Burton-Page 'there is little information concerning the numbers, status and functions of the Habs̲h̲īs in the earliest Muslim period'.[183] It is probable that a thorough and systematic examination of the Indian National Archives as well as the rich body of vernacular literatures of southern and western India would provide us with much valuable data. At present we are in a better position regarding our information on the presence of black African slaves in Indonesia and China, owing to the availability of brief historical notices and paleographical and icono-graphical materials.

Black African slaves were known in the Malay Archipelago as far back as the early part of the eighth century of the Christian era and were generally referred to as the Zandj.[184] Chinese links with this area also brought black slaves to China. In the Chronicle of the T'ang Dynasty of China, under the

177. Ibn Ḳutayba, 1850, p. 227.
178. ibid.
179. ibid., p. 203.
180. I. Goldziher, 1971, Vol. 2, p. 77.
181. al-D̲j̲āḥiẓ, 1964, Vol. 1, p. 182.
182. Ibn al-D̲j̲awzī, 1938–40, Vol. 6, p. 304.
183. J. Burton-Page, 1971, p. 14.
184. 'It is with the value of 'negro' and often of 'negro slave' that the word Zängi passed to Indonesia, Central Asia and the Far East. A Javanese inscription of 860 mentions the J̌ĕṅgī, while other spellings J̌aṅgi and J̌eṅi occur in inscriptions dated 1135, 1140 and 1294. J̌aṅgi or J̌ĕṅgī is still the name of the negroes in Malay, it is Joṅgī in Batak.' P. Pelliot, 1959, p. 598. For the same word in Chinese sources, see ibid., pp. 599–601. The designation 'Ḥabs̲h̲i' for blacks or African slaves is of later application. For an example given in the Malay legal digests of the eighteenth century, see R. J. Maxwell, 1932, p. 254.

events of 724 is recorded the reception of an embassy sent by the Ruler of the kingdom of Śrīvijāya centred at Palembang in Sumatra. A Zandj girl was offered along with other exotic items as tribute.[185] This was not an isolated event, as between 813 and 818 another Indonesian kingdom, that of the Javanese nation of Kalinga despatched three missions to the court of the T'ang Emperor, Hsien Tsung. Among the rarities presented as tribute were several Zandj boys and girls.[186] It is also recorded in the Chronicle of the Sung Dynasty that in 976 an Arab merchant brought to the Imperial Court 'a black K'un Lun slave with deep-set eyes and black body'.[187]

These 'black youths and maidens' were hardly passing 'curiosities for the cultivated courts of the eighth and ninth centuries' but in reality represented only part of the large group of African slaves imported into the region by Arab merchants. Chou Ch'u-fei, a Chinese official, in his work *Ling-wai Tai-ta* compiled at Kwee Lin in 1178, showed an awareness of this traffic in African slaves. 'Writing of an undetermined sector of the East African coast, which he calls *K'un-lun Ts'eng-chi*', he noted that 'savages with lacquer-black bodies and frizzy hair were enticed by offers of food and then captured'.[188] Thousands of these negroes, he further remarked, were sold as 'foreign slaves'.[189] It appears that a proportion of this human merchandise was shipped by Arab traders to China via the Malay Archipelago. Canton was the principal port of entry and distributing centre.[190]

There is also evidence of the role played by African slaves in the social and economic fields. In another passage, 'the *P'ing-chou K'o-tan* adds that these "devil slaves" were employed on shipboard to caulk leaky seams below the water-line from the outside as they were expert swimmers who do not close their eyes under water'.[191] They also appear to have been reasonably common as household servants of the wealthy classes in the main urban areas.[192] G. Ferrand, drawing on Chinese classical sources,

185. G. Ferrand, 1922, pp. 7–8; P. Pelliot, 1959, p. 599, mentions two *sěng-ch'i* (Zandj) girls.

186. P. Pelliot, 1959, p. 599.

187. Chou Ju-kua, 1911, p. 32.

188. P. Wheatley, 1961, p. 54.

189. ibid.

190. This has been attested by the Chinese scholar of the Sung Period, Chu Yu, who in his work entitled *P'ing-chou k'ōtan* (1119) wrote: 'In Kuang-chou (Canton) most of the wealthy people keep devil-slaves (*kuei-nu*), who are very strong and can lift [weights of] several hundred catties. Their language and tastes are unintelligible [to the Chinese]. Their nature is simple and they do not abscond. They are also called 'wild men' (*yeh-jen*). Their colour is as black as [Chinese] ink, their lips are red, their teeth white and their hair curly and yellow [*sic*]. There are both males and females among them . . . They live on the islands beyond the sea.' Quoted in P. Wheatley, 1961, pp. 54–5. See equally Chang Hsing-Lang, 1930.

191. Cited in P. Wheatley, 1961, p. 55. Also in Chou Ju-kua, 1911, pp. 31–2.

192. Chou Ju-kua, 1911, p. 32. 'Many families [in China] buy black people to make gatekeepers of; they are called *kui-nu* or "devil-slaves" or *hei siau ssi* (black slaves or servants)'.

speaks of their role as musicians in the Sumatran kingdom of Śrīvijāya (San-fo-ts'i).[193]

The worldwide presence of Africans was not initially brought about by the forced mass exodus to the Americas. It has been observed that already from the seventh to the eleventh century, large numbers of Africans were to be found in many parts of Asia, occupying various social positions and making important contributions in the economic, political and cultural fields. It is regrettable that this image of the impact of Africa on Asia, though of major historical importance, is still a fragmentary one and is based on non-African sources. For a complete and balanced account, there is an urgent need to study how Africans saw themselves in relation to others in their lands of exile.

193. G. Ferrand, 1922, p. 16. 'Les esclaves provenant du K'ouen-louen font de la musique pour les gens du pays, en sautant sur le sol et en chantant'.

27

Relations between the different regions of Africa

A. BATHILY *with the collaboration of* C. MEILLASSOUX

The period from the seventh to the eleventh century of the Christian era showed a remarkable growth of relations between the various regions of Africa. The fact that this growth coincided with Muslim expansion led certain authors, such as Raymond Mauny, to say that it was the Arab conquest and Islamization that brought tropical Africa out of its isolation and linked it up with the rest of the world again.[1] Yet, despite considerable gaps in the sources – partly made good by the growing number of archaeological discoveries in recent years – present data bear out the words of Catherine Coquery-Vidrovitch that 'one of the characteristics of African societies is never to have lived in isolation. The continent of Africa has known two major phenomena: population mobility and the volume of long-distance trade.'[2] The work of E. W. Bovill,[3] C. A. Diop[4] and T. Obenga[5] among others, has shown the vitality of the relations between the regions north and south of the Sahara since Antiquity.[6] Moreover, it has been appositely demonstrated how the socio-economic context in which Islam came into being was strongly influenced by the development of trade between Ethiopia, the Mediterranean and the Indian Ocean.[7] These comments having been made, it must nevertheless be recognized that the integration of some parts of Africa into the Arab empire set up in the seventh century[8] gave new momentum to inter-African relations. Arab and Muslim influence produced a chain reaction right across the continent, and became the decisive feature in the development of the Maghrib, Egypt and the Saharan peoples from the eighth century onwards.[9] Elsewhere it acted as an external factor whose importance varied according to the geographical posi-

1. R. Mauny, 1970, p. 138.
2. C. Coquery-Vidrovitch, 1974, p. 349.
3. E. W. Bovill, 1935, 1958.
4. C. A. Diop, 1955, 1967.
5. T. Obenga, 1973; cf. also R. C. C. Law, 1967b.
6. Cf. Unesco, Vol. II, *General History of Africa*, Chs 20 and 22.
7. E. R. Wolf, 1951; see also M. Rodinson, 1968.
8. On the Muslim expansion, see R. Mantran, 1969 and Chapters 2 and 3 above.
9. Cf. Chapters 7 to 12 above.

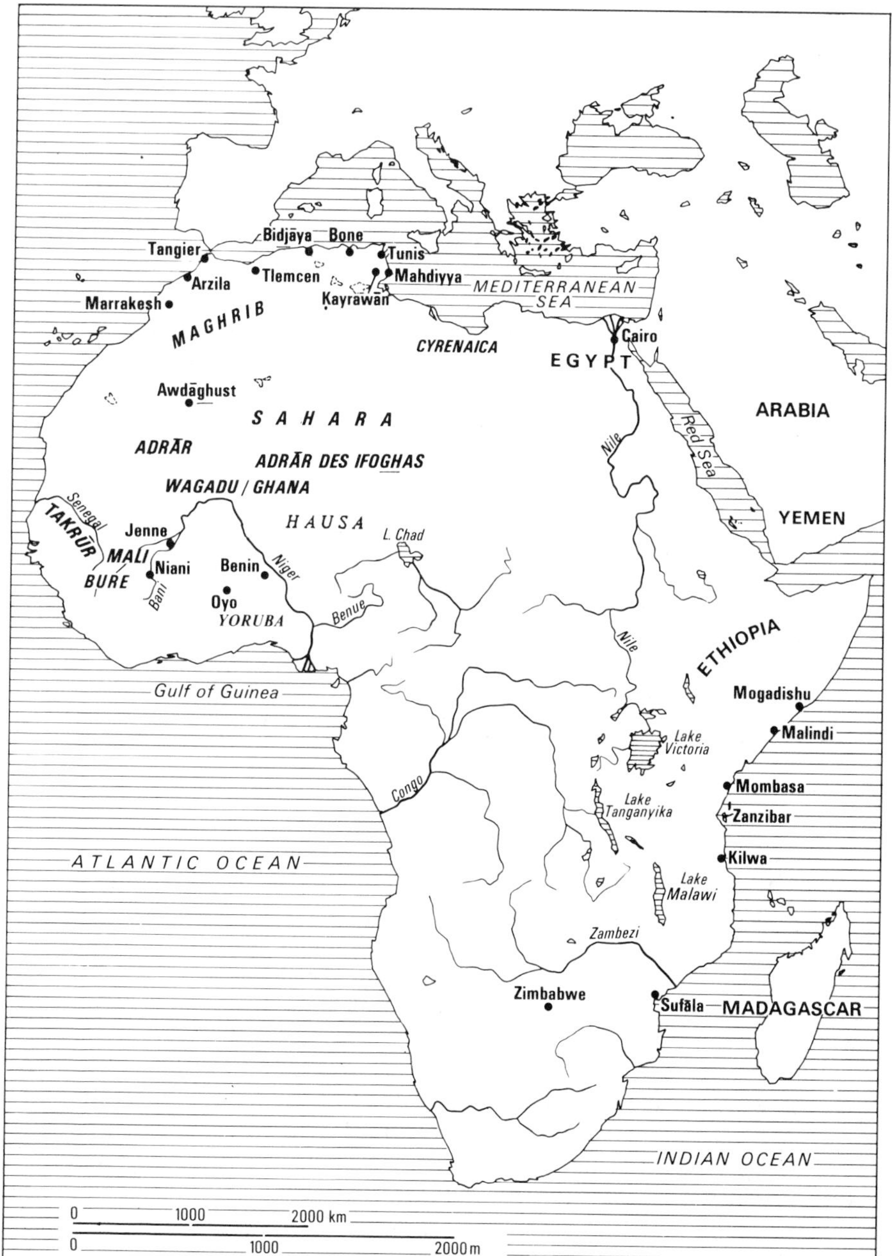

FIG. 27.1 *Relations between the different parts of Africa from the seventh to the eleventh century*

tion of the various regions in relation to the routes of penetration taken by the Muslims.[10]

The growth of inter-regional trade

The itineraries left by Arab geographers are evidence of the development of trade between the various parts of the continent from the eighth century onwards. The Arab conquest did not only bring about a profound change in the political geography of the Mediterranean world, which was dominated between the seventh and eleventh centuries by the Muslim empire; in particular it also gave 'international' trade unusual dynamism even after the disintegration of that empire. In spite of the constant turbulence that characterized the superstructure of the empire (revolts, schisms, etc.), the Muslim world remained the mainspring of world trade until the thirteenth century. Maurice Lombard's classic article has brought out the fundamental role of African gold in the establishment of Muslim power.[11] Until the European expansion of the fifteenth century, the fates of Africa and the Arab world were closely linked.[12]

Inter-African trade during the period under consideration was characterized by three fundamental features: progress in means of communication; expansion of the commercial network; and an increase in the volume of trade. Although to the best of our knowledge, no systematic work exists on the African economy of this period, the few clues furnished by Arabic written sources and archaeology amply bear out the above point of view.

Progress in means of communication

By strengthening permanent links between North Africa and western Asia, the Arab conquest created favourable conditions for the large-scale use of camels. According to some authors the camel, a most opportune animal for desert regions, was introduced into Africa about the first century of the Christian era; according to others, on the other hand, certain species of camels which were extinct during the historical period were found on the continent at the end of the Neolithic period.[13]

But wherever the camel came from, researchers on the whole agree in recording the widespread use of this beast of burden in trans-Saharan trade from the Islamic period onwards. Thus in Morocco cross-breeding of the two-humped camel of central Asia with the Arabian camel or one-humped dromedary, together with the techniques of selection, produced two types

10. See for example Chapters 19 to 21 above.

11. M. Lombard, 1947; cf. also M. Malowist, 1966 and R. A. Messier, 1974. In recent years the Lombard thesis has been severely criticized by C. Cahen, 1977, pp. 323–57; 1981.

12. E. F. Gautier, 1935.

13. Cf. the discussion in Unesco, *General History of Africa*, Vol. II, ch. 20.

PLATE 27.1 *From one encampment to the next: transhumance of shepherds in the Sahel region of Mali (near Gumbu du Sahel)*

of camel. One, slow of gait, but capable of carrying heavy loads, was used for trade; the other, faster and lighter, was used for warfare and for carrying messages (*mehari*).[14] The western Sahara was also famous for the breeding of camels. According to al-Bakrī the king of the Ṣanhādja possessed over 100 000 thoroughbred camels for his army.[15] The number of camels making up the various caravans that plied between the Sudan, the Maghrib and Egypt all the year round ran into thousands.

One of the positive aspects of Muslim expansion is that it gave considerable impetus to navigation. At the behest of the Aghlabids and Fāṭimids powerful fleets were built up which enabled Muslim merchants to maintain the flow of trade between East Africa and the countries of the Indian Ocean, Red Sea and Mediterranean. Large harbours with dockyards for shipbuilding were constructed in the Maghrib, such as Tunis (eighth century), Bidjāya (Bougie) and Mahdiyya (915), Algiers (946), Oran (902) and Arzila (tenth century). In Egypt the old port of Alexandria was revived. It was between the eighth and eleventh centuries that the typical large Mediterranean trading vessel, with a raised hull and two lateen-rigged masts, was evolved under the aegis of the Muslim navy; technically, it was a cross between the merchant ship of the ancient Mediterranean and the ship designs of the Indian Ocean.[16] Well before the introduction of the compass and other navigational instruments the Muslim seamen were able to ply the seas over great distances by employing a method known as the 'sidereal rose';[17] the compass and astronomical tables were to make these voyages safer.

14. N. Pacha, 1976, p. 49; cf. also Chapter 14 above.
15. J. M. Cuoq, 1975, p. 2; N. Levtzion and J. F. P. Hopkins (eds), 1981, p. 69.
16. M. Lombard, 1971a, p. 67; A. R. Lewis, 1951.
17. V. A. Teixeira da Mota, 1963; see also G. Tibbets (ed.), 1971.

Expansion of the commercial network

Between the seventh and the eleventh centuries trade between the various regions of the continent was booming. The growth of cities was the most obvious sign of this development of commercial activity. In about 757 an old nomad camel drivers' fair in the Tafilālet became a town, Sidjilmāsa, which until the eleventh century served as the main staging-post for trans-Saharan trade between the Western Sudan and the western Maghrib.[18] Ḳayrawān, later to replace the old city of Carthage, was founded. In the mid-eighth century Tāhert came into being in the central Maghrib.[19] In about 800 the Idrīsids made Fez into a flourishing city. Under the Fāṭimids Cairo was the pivot between the Muslim East, the Muslim West and Africa south of the Sahara. In the western Sahara, Awdāghust, political capital of the Ṣanhādja Berbers, became the market place linking black Africa with Barbary,[20] after the manner of Zawīla[21] in the central Sahara. Routes that were much used or little used according to the favourability or otherwise of the political situation linked these markets to others south of the Sahara. Thus, Ghana/Kumbi Saleh, capital of the empire of Ghana/Wagadu, Sillā and Yaresi on the Senegal River and Kāw-Kāw on the Niger connected the Muslim world with the savanna lands and those of the West African forest. On the East African coast, Muslim merchants founded trading centres such as Mogadishu, Barāwa (Brava), Malindi, Mombasa, Kilwa and Sofala on the mainland and on the islands of Pate, Ḳanbalū (Pemba), Kizimkaẓi (Zanzibar).[22] In the eleventh century these centres became great cosmopolitan markets specializing in the transit of goods from East Africa (Zimbabwe), eastern and southern Asia and the Muslim world.

Thus the new growth of towns that took place from the seventh century onwards as a result of the development of trade led to the expansion of the trade network and then speeded up the integration of the various regional and local economies.

Increase in the volume of trade

The growth of the volume of trade was the direct result of the keen demand created by urban development, population growth in certain regions (e.g. the Maghrib and Bantu regions) and the expansion of foreign markets

18. Ibn Ḥawḳal in J. M. Cuoq, 1975, p. 71; N. Levtzion and J. F. P. Hopkins (eds), 1981, p. 45; al-Bakrī in J. M. Cuoq, 1975, p. 95; N. Levtzion and J. F. P. Hopkins (eds), 1981, pp. 64–6.

19. Ibn al-Saghīr in J. M. Cuoq, 1975, pp. 55–6; N. Levtzion and J. F. P. Hopkins (eds), 1981, pp. 121–2; T. Lewicki, 1962.

20. Al-Muhallabī in J. M. Cuoq, 1975, p. 76; N. Levtzion and J. F. P. Hopkins (eds), 1981, p. 168; al-Bakrī in J. M. Cuoq, 1975, pp. 81–2.

21. Al-Bakrī in J. M. Cuoq, 1975, pp. 81–2.

22. See Chapter 21 above.

(India, China and the Arab empire). Products intensively traded during this period fall into four main categories: raw materials; subsistence products; luxury items for domestic use; and luxury goods. Depending on circumstances and places, a single item may have occupied different positions in this range.

Raw materials

The most important raw materials were iron, flax, cotton, gum and indigo. Iron manufactured in the empire of Ghana, probably in the area between the Faleme and Senegal rivers, was exported to other parts of Senegambia and the Niger. We know for certain that East and Southern Africa supplied India with iron. The Nilotic countries no doubt participated in this trade with India and even with the Muslim world. In the Maghrib the deposits at Ceuta and Oran and in the area between Salé and Marrakesh were still being worked in the eleventh century.[23]

Trade in flax, cotton, gum and indigo is connected with the development of the textile industry. The growing of flax has been reported in the Maghrib, and of cotton in several areas (Senegal River, Ethiopia, the Maghrib, etc.). Gum, which was used in the finishing of fabrics, came either from the gum-tree forests of the western Sahara or from Kordofān. Indigo, which is perhaps of Asian (Indian) origin, was grown from the eleventh century in the Maghrib, which must have supplied it to the Western Sudan.

Subsistence products

The distribution of subsistence products ranked first in volume in inter-African trade. Wheat from the Maghrib was exported by caravan via Si<u>dj</u>ilmāsa to the western Sahara and the Sudan. Despite its large domestic market, Egypt could still export cereal surpluses by caravan to Libya and Nubia and by boat to Cyrenaica. According to al-Bakrī, the wheat harvest in the Bē<u>dj</u>a region in Ifrīḳiya was always to be relied on; and in good years the city supplied 1000 camel-loads a day to several cities including Ḳayrawān and Tunis.[24]

Millet, sorghum, rice and shea-butter from the Western Sudan and olive oil from the Maghrib were exported in all directions. Dried smoked fish prepared on the coast and in countries on rivers was sent to the interior. The salt trade was the main branch of the subsistence trade. Rock salt from the Sahara (Ta<u>gh</u>āzā) and sea salt competed with each other in the interior; but they could never satisfy the keen demand, as is witnessed by the very

23. N. Pacha, 1976, p. 60; B. Rosenberger, 1970a.
24. Al-Bakrī, 1913, p. 120.

high value of this commodity, which according to Ibn Ḥawḳal could reach 200–300 dinars a camel load.[25]

Luxury items for domestic use

Luxury items for domestic use consisted predominantly of slaves and camels. As on all continents at that time, slavery in Africa was a socially legitimate practice. Arabic sources stress the importance of the trade in black slaves by Muslim merchants, but in fact this trade worked both ways. In the royal courts of the Sudan there were Berber and Arab slaves, and no doubt slaves of European origin.[26] It is reasonable to suppose that economic growth and its corollaries (urban development and the splendour of court life) brought about a keen demand for manpower in black Africa and in the Muslim East and West. Hence the intensification of the slave trade implied by the Arabic chronicles of the period.

Nevertheless, to put forward estimates of the number of slaves exported by black Africa to the Muslim world, as R. Mauny and T. Lewicki have done, is extremely hazardous. Mauny believes that the number of black slaves exported was somewhere around 20 000 a year or two million per century during the Middle Ages[27] whilst according to Lewicki 12–16 million black slaves passed through Cairo in the sixteenth century alone.[28] Such estimates are obviously exaggerated. There are at least three reasons to explain why this trade fell short of the figures put forward:

The low level of development of the Muslim economy of the period, which could not absorb such a quantity of slaves. Except for the Zandj (black slaves) from lower Iraq[29] no large body of blacks historically linked to the trans-Saharan slave trade existed anywhere in the Arab world.

The high cost of slaves, because of the risks inherent in the desert crossing, which would not have permitted such a massive exodus.[30] In this connection, it is significant that in the Arabic iconography of the period, the slave merchant was often depicted as a man with a hole in his purse.

Until the Crusades the Muslim world drew its slaves from two main sources: Eastern and Central Europe (Slavs) and Turkestan. The Sudan only came third. But it must be added that black slaves were appreciated above all as domestic workers – eunuchs, concubines, wet nurses, cooks, etc.[31] The descendants of these concubines and wet nurses were integrated

25. J. M. Cuoq, 1975, p. 75; N. Levtzion and J. F. P. Hopkins (eds), 1981, p. 49.

26. Although this practice appears in fourteenth-century sources (Ibn Baṭṭūṭa in J. M. Cuoq, 1975, pp. 316, 390) it probably went on in the previous centuries.

27. R. Mauny, 1961.

28. T. Lewicki, 1967b.

29. Cf. Chapter 26 above.

30. For prices on Iraqi markets see E. Ashtor, 1969, pp. 88 ff, 361 ff.

31. Thus according to al-Bakrī an excellent black cook was worth 100 *mithḵāls* and more at Awdāghust; see J. M. Cuoq, 1975, p. 84.

into Muslim society as full citizens, as illustrated by the cases of Isā ibn Yazīd, the supposed chief of a group of emigrants who founded Sidjilmāsa[32] and Abū Yazīd, born at Gao of a black mother and a Berber father, who became a famous preacher and led the Fāṭimids to within an ace of their downfall (late tenth century).[33]

Owing to the development of trade between black Africa and the Muslim world, Arab horses multiplied in the savanna lands where the absence of trypanosomiasis made their survival possible. The trade in Arab horses (barbs), which was monopolized by the Sudanic states, led to the gradual disappearance of the smaller, local pony-like race whose presence was still mentioned in the eleventh century by al-Bakrī.[34]. Numidia and Nubia gradually came to specialize in the breeding of Barbary horses, which they then exported to the Western and Central Sudan.

Luxury goods

Luxury goods consisted predominantly of textiles, precious metals, pearls and ivory. The geographical literature of the period lays particular stress on the flowering of textile crafts in the Maghrib and Egypt. Silk goods from Gabès and woollen goods from Ḳayrawān were prized on all markets. Awdāghust exported red and blue dyed garments.[35] The town of Taranka on the middle Senegal was famous for its fine cotton loincloths or *shaḳḳiyyāt*, which merchants sent to the north and to the neighbouring countries.[36] Following the work of Charles Monteil, some historians see in the progress of the textile crafts and the fabric trade a consequence of the expansion of Islam. In fact the social changes (urban development, enrichment of the ruling classes through foreign trade, and population growth) seem to have been the root causes that dictated the development of increasingly extensive textile crafts in all areas. Clearly, the new conditions meant that people could no longer rely for their clothing on makeshift expedients like animal skins or textiles made from the bark of certain trees, as they had in earlier periods when the population was more scattered, society less highly organized and certain moral values consequently not yet current.

As regards precious metals, gold of course held first place. During the period that concerns us several producing areas existed that supplied the rest of the continent and foreign markets to an unequal extent. In decreasing order of importance these areas were: Bambuk/Galam and Bure in West Africa; Southern Africa; and Nubia.

32. Al-Bakrī, 1968, p. 43.
33. On Abū Yazīd, see R. Le Tourneau, 1954, and Chapter 12 above.
34. J. M. Cuoq, 1975, p. 102; N. Levtzion and J. F. P. Hopkins (eds), 1981, p. 89. The problem of horses in the Sudan is discussed by H. J. Fisher, 1972, 1973a.
35. Al-Bakrī, 1913, p. 159.
36. C. Monteil, 1926.

Copper was used as a raw material in the manufacture of art objects and other luxury items. Cut up into rings it served as currency in some localities (e.g. Sillā on the Senegal River).[37] In any case it was extensively traded between the producing areas (Katanga, Aïr, western Sahara), the Yoruba countries and northern Africa, where the growth of the arts led to keen demand.[38]

The southern Maghrib and the Central Sudan were famous for their pearls and precious stones (agate, amazonite, etc.). Thus the Bēdja country between the Nile and the Red Sea contained deposits of precious stones and emeralds that were worked by the Muslims.[39]

The dissemination of techniques

Trade, and the population mobility that went with it, were instrumental in bringing about the dissemination of techniques. But in this respect, our sources are even more meagre. The Arab geographers which we use as a source were more interested in the mechanism of the distribution of goods than in their production. Archaeological data are still too contradictory to allow us to advance positive opinions about the development of techniques during the period under consideration. The present state of our knowledge suggests that five branches of activity made progress and spread on the continent. These were mining and metallurgy; agriculture; crafts; trading techniques; and techniques of war.

Mining and metallurgy

Mining and metallurgy were booming in all areas. According to S. Gsell, the mining industry's most active period in the Maghrib was not Antiquity but the Middle Ages.[40] In the Muslim West, attempts were made to improve the technique for treating ores. In Muslim Spain a new process was used for separating gangue from azurite (a copper ore). It consisted of soaking the ore in oil and then throwing it into a rapidly flowing stream; the particles of metal, buoyed up by the oil, were carried away by the current, while the earthy matter dropped to the bottom. It seems highly probable that this method was in use in the Maghrib.[41] The debate on the spread of iron in Africa continues, but L. M. Diop's thesis,[42] which argues for the indigenous origin of iron-working, seems preferable to the hypotheses of

37. Al-Bakrī in J. M. Cuoq, 1975, p. 97; N. Levtzion and J. F. P. Hopkins (eds), 1981, p. 78.
38. Cf. Chapter 16 above.
39. Al-Ya'ḳūbī in J. M. Cuoq, 1975, p. 50; al-Mas'ūdī, 1861–77, Vol. 3, pp. 43–50.
40. S. Gsell, 1913–28, Vol. 8, p. 16.
41. N. Pacha, 1976, p. 60.
42. L. M. Diop, 1968.

dissemination from outside supported by several historians; in any case it is now established that many African peoples went from the Stone Age to the Iron Age during the first millennium of the Christian era. This seems to be true of the Bantu[43] and the peoples living on the Atlantic coast west of the empire of Ghana.[44] Be that as it may, the social processes going on on the continent as a whole most probably led to the intensification and perhaps to the improvement of the techniques for the manufacture of metals.

Agriculture

In the sphere of agriculture, the period is distinguished by the spread of farming techniques and new plants. Thus in the Maghrib and the Saharan oasis a new system of irrigation involving the use of *foggāra* or stone conduits was adopted, and this made it possible to extend the cultivation of new crops such as rice, cotton and sugar cane.[45]

The Gangara farming area (Assaba, in Mauritania), consisting of walled fields and terracettes whose ruins are still visible, no doubt dates from the Almoravid period.[46] In East Africa, rice-growing in flooded fields seems to have been introduced by Asian immigrants.

Under the impetus of inter-regional trade, plants or new species were spread outside their area of origin. Thus some varieties of rice of Asian origin reached as far as the Egyptian oases and southern Morocco. Sorghum, a plant from Africa south of the Sahara, began to be grown in Upper Egypt, Cyrenaica, the Algerian Tell and even in Syria and southern Europe. The species of wheat known in the oral traditions of the Soninke of Wagadu as *darma yille* (Adrār millet) spread southwards into the Sahel.

The cultivation of olive trees made considerable progress in the Maghrib, to the point of completely changing the countryside of the region. The date palm, a native of Mesopotamia and the Persian Gulf, was found in Egypt in the Pharaonic period; but the planting of it was intensified between the seventh and eleventh centuries. Southern Tunisia and the western Sahara were the main centres of the date palm. The Muslim and Jewish commercial communities introduced to the Sudanic towns (Ghana and Kānem) vegetables such as melons and cucumbers which were grown in gardens. The growing of bananas and coconuts was linked with the growth of the Indian Ocean trade.

Crafts

The process of dissemination of craft techniques is far less well known.

43. G. W. B. Huntingford, 1963; G. Mathew, 1963; P. L. Shinnie (ed.), 1971; see also Chapters 6 and 23 above.

44. J. M. Cuoq, 1975, p. 120; N. Levtzion and J. F. P. Hopkins (eds) 1981, p. 98.

45. N. Pacha, 1976, p. 46.

46. C. Toupet, 1966, p. 19.

Two facts deserve mention. According to Al-Bakrī, Sfax, famous for its sheets, was indebted to Alexandria for the methods of pressing used by the people of that city.[47]

The manufacture of paper from flax, and then from cotton on the Chinese model brought about a veritable revolution from the end of the tenth century onwards. While the parchment and papyrus used until then for the transmission of texts could not provide the conditions for a democratization of knowledge, cheap paper made by the new process gave a general impetus to intellectual activity.[48]

The development of trading techniques

The development of trade and the growth in the volume of goods that resulted from it led to the adoption of increasingly sophisticated methods of payment. The most striking feature of this development was the progressive monetization of the regional economies. While the Maghribian monetary system was linked to that of the Muslim world (which was based on the gold dinar), a wide range of currencies existed in other parts of the continent: various kinds of shells, including cowries (*Cypraea moneta*) from the Maldive Islands, copper rings, bars of salt and pieces of fabric were used concurrently for trading purposes.

In the Muslim world in particular, trading techniques developed remarkably. Merchants in that region already used drafts, bills of exchange (*suftādja*) and promises to pay (*shakk* or cheque). Thus Ibn Ḥawḳal, writing towards the end of the tenth century, said that he had seen a cheque in Awdāghust made out in favour of one of the people of Sidjilmāsa and drawn against a certain tradesman of Awdāghust for the sum of 4000 dinars.[49] At that time tradesmen engaged in trans-Saharan enterprises set up a highly efficient network organized either on a family basis or on the basis of joint stock companies, with correspondents in all the important places. They did business with countries outside the sphere of Muslim influence with the help of intermediaries (interpreters) recruited in the entrepôt centres such as Ghana/Kumbi Saleh, as Yāḳūt so appositely pointed out.[50] The 'silent trade' mentioned by a number of chroniclers after Herodotus[51] seems, as Paulo Farias has shown, to be one of the myths that die hard.[52]

47. Al-Bakrī, 1913, pp. 46–7.
48. Cf. on this question Chapter 1 above.
49. J. M. Cuoq, 1975, p. 71, but see N. Levtzion, 1968a; on trade and currency in the Muslim world, cf. M. Lombard, 1971a, Chapters 5 to 8.
50. J. M. Cuoq, 1975, p. 183; N. Levtzion and J. F. P. Hopkins (eds), 1981, p. 172.
51. Herodotus, 1872, Book IV, p. 237.
52. P. F. de Moraes Farias, 1974.

Techniques of war

In the countries of the Sudanic savanna the increase in imports of Arab horses and the growth of iron metallurgy on the one hand, and the internal development of the societies of the region on the other, led to a profound change in military tactics. Cavalry rather than infantry began to play a predominant rôle in battles. Weapon technology also changed. The bow and arrow, the 'democratic weapon' characteristic of egalitarian societies[53] which could be made by every individual, was progressively replaced by iron weapons whose manufacture presupposed a more highly developed social context. The manufacture of shields also made definite progress during this period. Thus the shields known as *lamṭa* manufactured by a Saharan *ḳabīla* of the same name, enjoyed a great reputation as far as the Maghrib.[54] All in all, thanks to speedier methods of locomotion (horses and camels) and the improvement of weapons, war was henceforth to play the prime rôle in the process of social evolution within African social groupings.

The expansion of Islam and its social significance

From the point of view of the movement of ideas, the period from the seventh to the eleventh century was characterized by the spread of Islam at the expense not only of Christianity and Judaism but also of polytheism. At the end of the seventh century only a minority consisting of the Arab conquerors professed Islam in the Maghrib and Egypt, but by the end of the eleventh century the whole of the Maghrib, Egypt and the western Sahara and large groups of peoples in West, Central and East Africa had gone over to Islam. This extraordinary rise of Islam has been attributed to various causes. According to Mauny, the successes of Islam in West Africa were due to conversion by force and the simplicity of its doctrine, which was 'easy for a black to accept'.[55]

These explanations are superficial. While the domination of Rome, Byzantium and more recently colonialism, which made themselves tools of Christianity, were accompanied by violence, the expansion of Islam via tropical Africa took the form of an increasingly massive influx of merchants. Moreover, the supposed simplicity of Islam as compared to Christianity is more a value judgement based on prejudice than on objective analysis of the two religions.

Let us sum up by saying that Islam owed its expansion to the new economic and social conditions directly or indirectly created by the commercial

53. J. Goody, 1971, p. 43.
54. Al-Ya'ḳūbī in J. M. Cuoq, 1975, p. 49; Ibn al-Faḳīh in J. M. Cuoq, 1975, p. 54.
55. R. Mauny, 1961, p. 520.

and political expansion of the Arab empire, in correlation with the internal development processes of African societies.[56]

Basic features of the development of African societies from the seventh to the eleventh century

Three essential features characterized the social changes of this period: major population movements; acceleration of the process of social differentiation, as a result of the division of labour; development of the class struggle, as manifested in revolts and civil wars in several states.

Population movements

Population movements markedly changed the human geography of the continent. Whatever the outcome of debates about the Bantu migrations, the movement of this people across Central, East and Southern Africa continued during the period that concerns us.[57] The political strife that marked the beginning of the Arab conquest, and in particular the development of trans-Saharan trade, led to several Berber groups being driven into the Sahara. It was perhaps the pressure of these newcomers that caused the exodus of certain black peoples such as the proto-Wolof and the Serer from Tāgant (Mauritania) to the south-west (western Senegal). The Soninke Dyula (tradesmen) of Ghana, who were middlemen in the trans-Saharan trade, founded a series of commercial centres on the Niger and its tributaries, the most prosperous of which were to be Dia and Jenne.[58] The population of the East African coast and Madagascar was swollen by the arrival of successive waves of migrants from Arabia, India, western Asia and Indonesia.[59]

Social differentiation

The acceleration of the process of social differentiation was the result of a more sophisticated division of labour, which in turn was the consequence of the development of trade. The major feature in this sphere was the emergence in the Maghrib and the Sudan of a class of professional middlemen trading between the different regions. These traders managed to transcend their racial differences (Berbers, Arabs, Jews and blacks) and constitute a genuine class, conscious of where its own interests lay. Traders held a dominant economic position in the societies, and even aspired to

56. See Chapters 3 and 4 above.
57. B. A. Ogot (ed.), 1974; see also Chapters 5 and 6 above.
58. On the founding of Jenne, see C. Monteil, 1903. But the recent research by S. K. McIntosh and R. J. McIntosh has proven the much earlier origin of this town.
59. B. A. Ogot, 1974; Chapters 4, 5 and 21–25 above.

take over political power, or at least to use the states as mere police devices for ensuring the security of business transactions.

As regards the military aristocracy, which held political power, foreign trade enabled it to acquire additional means of domination (arms and horses in the case of the Sudanic states, gold in the case of the Muslim states) that tended to strengthen its sway over the ordinary people. Thus in most of these states an increasingly sharp demarcation separated those who benefited from trade (aristocracy and traders) from the common people (peasants and small urban craftsmen). The general consequence of the development of trade was that it broke up social structures founded on kinship and the ethnic group to produce a new social order based on ownership of the means of production (land in the Maghribian states) and trade. The formation of Zimbabwe in the eleventh century and the establishment of the Kongo kingdom (finally completed in the fourteenth century) and the Hausa states was probably to some extent influenced by the changes taking place on the East African coast and in Egypt and the Sahara as a result of the trade boom in the Indian Ocean, the Red Sea and the Mediterranean. A recent version of the legend of Sundiata, the famous Mande emperor of the thirteenth century, suggests that the slaving expeditions of the Malinke princes in league with the Soninke traders acted as a stimulus to the emergence of the empire of Mali.[60] But, unlike many authors, we believe that trade was not the motive force behind the setting up of these states.[61] It merely accelerated the process on the basis of the internal dynamic of these societies, which had reached a level of maturity that allowed them to react favourably to external stresses. In particular making a surplus as a result of improved productivity was the basis on which trade with foreign communities was built up. Thus the social phenomena of this period were the outcome of the dialectic of the production and distribution of goods. Be that as it may, the expansion of Islam during this period was the result of interaction between the economic shifts and the social changes that agitated most regions of Africa, in particular the Maghrib, Egypt, the Sahara, East Africa and the Central and Western Sudan. Islam and its universalist doctrine amounted to more than the old polytheism overlaid by the ethnic variants of Christianity and Judaism, which were no longer valid for the expression of conflicts of interest between the various social groups. Thus the K͟hāridjite movement, Abū Yazīd's revolt and other messianic movements that disturbed the Maghribian states during the period that concerns us, represented in social terms the rejection of the established order, and above all a determination to put an end to social injustice.[62] The violence with which the Almoravid movement first attacked Awdāg͟hust, a city of Muslim traders, was due not so much to the

60. W. Kamisokho, 1975.

61. Cf. Centre d'Etudes et de Recherche Marxiste, 1974, in particular J. Suret-Canale, 1974.

62. C. A. Julien, 1952, p. 63.

fact that the latter had accepted the sway of non-Muslim Ghana[63] as to concern on the part of the Berber masses of the western Sahara to appeal to truth, to rectify injustices and abolish unfair taxation.[64]

In the states of the Western and Central Sudan (Ghana, Gao and Kānem), the dominant economic position occupied by the Muslims was what enabled them gradually to gain an ascendancy over society as a whole. In Ghana the emperor chose his interpreters and most of his ministers from among the Muslims. In Gao no one could reign without being converted to Islam.[65] Again, the conversion of one of the kings of Mali in the eleventh century under the influence of a Muslim whose prayers supposedly ended the drought[66] is an indication of the growing ideological influence of the followers of Islam in Sudanic societies. The proselytism of the king of Takrūr, Wār Diabi[67] is another indication of Islam's power of attraction. The economic role and the social prestige of the Muslims were thus the decisive reasons for the success of their religion.

The development of the class struggle

The development of the class struggle, and of social conflicts in general, took place with an intensity that varied according to local peculiarities and the degree of domination and exploitation that operated within each social group. For the Maghrib, C. A. Julien, A. Laroui and to a lesser extent G. Marçais have analysed the revolts and schismatic movements of the period as episodes in the class struggle.[68]

In the Sudanic states the picture is less clear. But the fall of the empire of Ghana/Wagadu at the end of the eleventh century was probably the final consequence of a process of internal decay. According to our hypothesis this decay was due to the conflicts between two groups within the ruling class of Ghana: one Islamized and allied with the traders, and the other loyal to the traditional religion and rural society. Internal dissensions were then aggravated with the sharpening of the contradictions between the people as a whole and the ruling class.[69] Whatever the merits of this hypothesis, it has nevertheless been established that inter-African trade exerted contradictory influences on social groups on the continent. In some cases it favoured political integration (the Almoravid and Fāṭimid empires, and later Mali and Songhay); in others it led on the contrary to the disintegration of state structures inherited from earlier periods (Ghana and the Christian empire of Ethiopia).

63. Al-Bakrī in J. M. Cuoq, 1975, p. 92.
64. ibid., p. 86. Cf. Chapter 13 above.
65. Al-Bakrī in J. M. Cuoq, 1975, p. 109. Cf. Chapter 3 above.
66. ibid., pp. 102–3.
67. ibid., p. 96.
68. C. A. Julien, 1952, p. 28; A. Laroui, 1970, pp. 91–2; G. Marçais, 1946, pp. 34–44.
69. See A. Bathily, 1975, pp. 34–44.

Conclusion

The period from the seventh to the eleventh century marked a peculiar stage in the history of the continent of Africa. The present state of our knowledge does not allow us to grasp every aspect of this development, but it may confidently be asserted that the expansion of the Arab empire was one of its main features. The above study of trade relations and the dissemination of techniques and ideas suggests two basic comments by way of description of the historical movement of African societies during this period.

First, the African economy as a whole remained a self-sufficient one within which productivity standards followed consumption standards. Goods were traded on the basis not of their exchange value as such but of their use value. Economic links between the various regions were based on complementarity between the goods they respectively produced; and these were more subject then than now to natural conditions because of the low level of productivity. But comparison of the various social groups shows that they were unevenly developed. This uneven development is illustrated by the fact that some societies had reached a very advanced process of social differentiation, with a very elaborate economic structure tending towards the establishment of a market economy (the Maghrib and the Sudan), whilst other communities were still at the stage of food-gathering or hunting in hordes. Hence the difficulty the historian has in defining a mode of production specific to Africa taken as a whole.[70]

Secondly the analysis of specific social groups outlined in this chapter leads to one major observation. From the seventh to the eleventh century, thanks to advances in the economic integration of its regional economies, Africa was able to satisfy most of its needs both of essentials and of luxury items. In the context of the world economy of the period, formed of the Mediterranean and Indian Ocean systems, Africa held a predominant position, especially through its gold exports.

70. See the discussion of this subject in Centre d'Etudes et de Recherche Marxiste, 1974, in particular J. Suret-Canale, 1974; C. Coquery-Vidrovitch, 1976.

28

Africa from the seventh to the eleventh century: five formative centuries

J. DEVISSE and J. VANSINA

Introduction

Historical research over the last thirty years has taught us, especially for Africa, that there are no uniform models and no automatic periodizations that can be safely applied, especially for the period we are dealing with here. There are even good grounds for questioning the broad limits – the seventh and eleventh centuries of the Christian era – chosen for this volume. The earlier date does indeed have some real meaning for the northern part of the continent, where Islam appeared, at least after the middle of the century; and it does for other regions too, quite unrelated to Islam, where, in so far as we know at present, the sixth and seventh centuries saw the emergence of new features that were to develop over the following centuries: this is particularly true for central and southern Africa; it is doubtless wise to recall that this same date – the seventh century, or the first century AH – used to be considered as very significant for West Africa; this is no longer so and research has 'won' about a millennium: in West Africa, the origins of the great changes examined in this volume lie in the first or even the second millennium before the Christian era.[1] It is the same for the eleventh century. While it is very significant for West Africa, where it marks the establishment of Mālikite Sunnism and a clear alteration in the relations of force between Muslims and non-Muslims, it probably does not have the same importance in other regions of the continent. However, the impression remains that after 1100 a new world was coming into being in some parts of the continent, for example with the flourishing of the Yoruba cities and the cities on the coast of East Africa, and the birth of the empire of Mali. The following centuries saw the growth of kingdoms in Central Africa, new kingdoms in West Africa and the expansion of pastoralists such as the Khoi, the Fulani and the Baḳḳāra.

There have been many attempts to find a few general traits to character-

1. The most significant recent works are: S. K. McIntosh and R. J. McIntosh, 1980b; J. Devisse, 1982.

ize the overall evolution of the continent during these five centuries; but none really stands up to examination, whether one thinks of the continent as a whole or of any particular part of it. Neither the Muslim expansion, so characteristic north of the equator, nor what has been called the 'second Iron Age' – to which we shall have to return later – constitute indisputable *general* points of reference.

These simple observations should inspire us to be wary: research is making rapid progress and each of its discoveries calls into question the whole gamut of our previous certainties: there can be no doubt that this situation will become even more marked in the coming years. This indicates how hypothetical, how fragile in several cases, and certainly how provisional, are the conclusions that can be drawn today from the analysis of these five centuries. But it is still right that they should be set out for researchers and readers to reflect on. And first of all it deserves repeating that, over these five centuries and for the first time so clearly, it is possible to trace, with all the methodological caution and all the regional nuances necessary, a series of comparable developments throughout the continent.

During these centuries, the geographical distribution of the main socio-cultural landscapes of Africa became stabilized and took shape. They saw the maturation of economies, socio-political formations and collective representations that were to underlie later historical movements. During these centuries slow germination was underway that explains the flowering that was to follow.

The first striking general characteristic, some of whose origins lie well before the seventh century in some regions, is the organization of areas of sedentarization where agricultural production became dominant. The development of technologies constitutes a second major feature; this development involved a better exploitation of resources, the division of labour and the spread of exchange. The complexity of political regimes becomes decipherable to the historian, while at the same time the collective representations, religions, ideologies and the whole range of means of cultural expression that were to ensure their reproduction and transmission to later generations took shape.

The sedentary organization of space

Sedentarization is not in itself a mark of progress; it does not, as is too often said, stand in opposition to the freedom of the semi-nomadic or nomadic pastoralists or to the unsettled life of hunter-gatherers. Everywhere, it resulted, quite clearly, from a new relationship with the environment, made necessary both by climatic changes, almost always unfavourable, and by the demographic growth and increasing complexity of societies seeking to organize the lands on which they lived. It is highly likely that sedentarization increases demographic growth and promotes the division of labour; it makes agricultural progress all the more necessary. Such growth, which corresponds to an increase in the amount of labour necessary for the production of food, forms the best survival strategy invented by human groups, in Africa as in other continents, but not everywhere does it find the conditions essential for it. The study of these changes, in this period, is only just beginning; it is far from having provided clear results for the whole continent. Everywhere, however, where surveys have been carried out – they are above all the province of archaeology – they reveal the importance of quantitative research into food-use patterns and the significance – in terms of quantity, nature and quality – of variations observed in traces of evidence of diet.

Central and Southern Africa

The Bantu expansion really came to an end in about the sixth century.[2] The subcontinent was thenceforward occupied by farmers where the climatic conditions allowed. Appropriate food production complexes were established. In the forests of Central Africa, a farming technique based on a field cleared each year was developed. Yams, plantains and vegetables were grown there; food-growing was only one element in a complex in which trapping and gathering remained very important. South of the forest, in the tsetse-fly-infested savannas,[3] the agricultural system was built around two fields a year; one cleared in the gallery forest and another in the savanna. Cereals were dominant and the complex was completed by hunting rather than trapping, while gathering was only a supplementary activity. In eastern and south-eastern Africa, as well as in the southern part of Central Africa, food production was based on stock-raising and an agriculture based on the growing of cereals cultivated in the savanna, the main crops being millets, sorghum or finger millet, depending on local variations in humidity. Hunting, trapping, gathering and small-scale fishing activities were less important than in Central Africa. As in many other regions, stock-raising predominated in the drier regions: this was the case in Botswana, northern Uganda and southern Sudan, as well as in neighbouring areas of Kenya. However, this was not always a matter of the perpetuation of old methods of stock-raising. Spectacular advances were under way, after 800, in the raising of cattle. By 600, wholly pastoral ways of life, using cattle, only existed in the Horn of Africa, in the Sahel, on the edge of the Sahara (especially in Mauritania?) and probably in an area stretching from southern Sudan east of the White Nile as far as central Tanzania. But, from the ninth century a new variant of the south-eastern African economic complex developed in Botswana.[4] Cattle-raising came to dominate in it. It

2. J. Vansina, 1984; D. W. Phillipson, 1977a; T. N. Huffman, 1982, pp. 133–8 and see Chapter 6 above.

3. The tsetse fly needs to be studied in detail from a historical perspective. See J. Ford, 1971.

4. J. R. Denbow, 1979, 1984.

took several centuries to perfect a pastoral system that would enable the Khoi-Khoi to occupy all the sites favourable to stock-raising in Namibia and Cape Province. They were to do so in the following period.

Eastern Africa

In eastern Africa in the widest sense, the historical movement of pastoralist expansion was probably linked to the diffusion of breeds of humped cattle – zebu and Sanga – better adapted to the dry heat than other breeds. These breeds, long known in Egypt and Axum, were to be found in Christian Nubia. But, so far as we know at present, they are to be found only after 1200 in the White Nile region and in the Horn of Africa. One author[5] links the expansion of Nilotic pastoralists to the acquisition of this type of cattle after 1200 and also sees it as the stimulus behind the expansion of the Maasai in East Africa and the Arabic-speaking Bakkāra in the Nilotic Sudan, also after 1200. But the Sanga breed, which is found as far as South Africa where it gave birth to another breed, is older than the zebu breed.[6] It may have spread during the centuries we are looking at and it may even have had something to do with the Khoi expansion. The whole question requires further study. It is of great importance, since in addition to the cases mentioned, this breed may have played a role in the establishment of pastoralists in the Great Lakes region, which occurred during the period under review,[7] and above all it may have led to a more intensive use of all the arid lands of East Africa. South-western Africa, too dry for agriculture, did not undergo very profound changes, even though the raising of ovines was practised there by the beginning of the Christian era.

Western Africa

Western Africa underwent an evolution that was at once comparable and different. In the forest zones and the rich savannas, phenomena comparable to those we have just looked at occurred. Population growth was probably already being accompanied by a dangerous destruction of the forest

5. N. David, 1982a, pp. 86–7; 1982b, pp. 54–5.

6. On this breed see H. Epstein, 1971. Thorax vertebrae of the Sanga breed were found at Tsodilo in the north-western corner of the present-day Kalahari, dated *c.* + 1000; cf. J. R. Denbow, 1980, pp. 475–6. Some figurines representing a humped ox, probably a Sanga, date from the Klamomo (Zambia) site *c.* 1000. It has also been claimed that the zebu was present in Madagascar well before the year 1000. See plate Z1, Fig. 1, in B. Fagan and J. Nenquin (eds), 1966. See also J. O. Vogel, 1975, p. 91, Fig. 93 and compare it with other figures on the same page; B. Fagan, 1967, pp. 65–70, illustration 67. For the Androy (Madagascar), see C. Radimilahy, 1981, p. 63.

7. If we identify their arrival with the change in ceramic style, their arrival could be dated to the eighth century. See F. Van Noten, 1983, p. 62; M. C. Van Grunderbeck, E. Roche and H. Doutrelepont, 1983a, p. 44, 1983b.

(a)

(b)

(c)

(d)

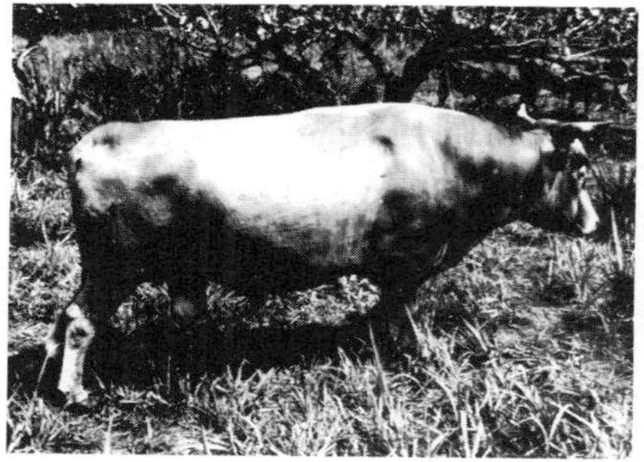

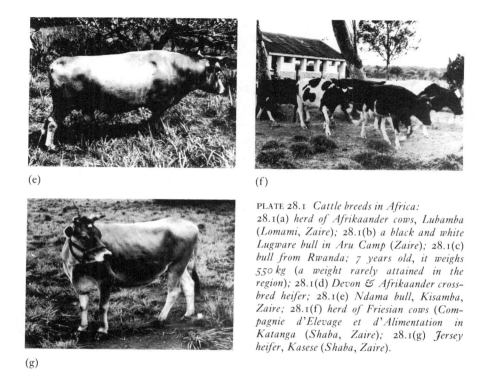

(e)

(f)

(g)

PLATE 28.1 *Cattle breeds in Africa:*
28.1(a) *herd of Afrikaander cows, Lubamba (Lomami, Zaire);* 28.1(b) *a black and white Lugware bull in Aru Camp (Zaire);* 28.1(c) *bull from Rwanda; 7 years old, it weighs 550 kg (a weight rarely attained in the region);* 28.1(d) *Devon & Afrikaander crossbred heifer;* 28.1(e) *Ndama bull, Kisamba, Zaire;* 28.1(f) *herd of Friesian cows (Compagnie d'Elevage et d'Alimentation in Katanga (Shaba, Zaire);* 28.1(g) *Jersey heifer, Kasese (Shaba, Zaire).*

cover. The meagre indications that we have for Sierra Leone and Liberia lead one to suppose that farmers were the first occupants of the region; in the forests of Benin (Nigeria) the advance of the farmers into the forest is particularly well documented.[8]

In the drier parts of the savanna and in the Sahelian zone, the climate had been changing for several centuries; the effects of this deterioration were felt, locally, during the period dealt with in Volume II of the *General History of Africa* and also during the one with which we have just dealt. While we do not yet know precisely how these changes occurred, there is more or less general agreement that there was a gradual shift from the north-east towards the south-west or south of peoples who were becoming sedentarized and were domesticating plants. In areas where there did not exist water reserves formed by river basins, which had themselves also been in the process of organization for several millennia,[9] they followed the rains and the minima necessary for a true agriculture. The complexity of the forms of settlement in the flood plains of the Senegal and of the Inland Niger Delta are gradually becoming clear; for numerous reasons, not all of which are economic or climatic, these two areas of land surrounded by rivers became areas of high human density and greater economic complexity before the Christian era.[10] The progressive desiccation of the regions between the north banks of the two rivers and the Sahara, which was accompanied by the digging of deeper wells,[11] the withdrawal of farmers and their replacement by pastoralists and, later, by cameleers seems to have gone hand in hand with increasing density on the still quite well-watered lands to the south of the two rivers.

We are now more or less in a position to sketch the outlines of a few typical zones. The Sahel was an area of stock-raising, in which the population subsisted on milk, supplemented by the picking of grain-yielding grasses, and with hunting to complete the diet; cultivation there was only possible where the underground water-table permitted the drawing of water and irrigation. Fishing, which existed in the Neolithic period,[12] had disappeared everywhere and this major change had deprived the inhabitants of their most constant and abundant basic food sources: these were now to be found only in the river valleys; perhaps it was the 'taste for fish' that led, in the Sahelian zone, to the buying of dried or smoked fish from the south but as yet there is no archaeological evidence to confirm it. Hunting itself

8. P. J. Darling, 1979.

9. J. Devisse, 1985b.

10. *Atlas National du Sénégal*, 1977, plate 18 and commentary.

11. In the twelfth century, al-Idrīsī (J. M. Cuoq, 1975, pp. 147 and 152) states – it is said too rarely – that north of the Senegal bend ... 'there are tracks where the markers are no longer known and the track is disappearing because there are so few travellers. *The water is going deeper and deeper in the ground ...*' (our emphasis); archaeology has confirmed this statement.

12. V. Roux, 1980.

probably did not provide sufficient resources for growing populations.[13] Importation became essential when various economic imperatives obliged the peoples to live in an insufficiently productive environment.[14]

The valleys were areas of complex organization, in strips parallel to the rivers, where land was probably bitterly fought over as the number of inhabitants, the division of labour and the organization of authority developed. The waters were the province of an old and well-established settlement of fishermen;[15] in the seventh century they were certainly already practising the drying – perhaps even the smoking – and export of fish.[16] The waters supplied many other foodstuffs; turtles, shellfish, hippopotamus and crocodile meat.[17] Then came the long, narrow and complementary strips of low-water crops and crops that were more difficult to grow as one moved away from the river; these had already been areas of sedentarization *par excellence* for centuries when our period opened.[18] When one follows the process of settlement of farmers on the least dry lands, one finds that it was very destructive of the environment as a result of large-scale ground-clearing.[19]

A few kilometres away from the privileged area of the river basins – especially of the vast Inland Niger Delta – there is evidence of already highly elaborate forms of agricultural organization, sparing of water and skilful in making use of all the plants useful to life. While not all aspects of this skilled agriculture were yet in place before the seventh century – we still lack archaeological surveys – it seems highly likely that many of these refined technologies for exploiting the soil, the carriers of 'ethnic groups' later to be well known, such as the Sereer, were becoming organized between the seventh and ninth century.

The lands situated to the north of the rivers were progressively transformed into pasture areas as they were gradually abandoned by farmers for lack of rain. The spread of the Fulani, from present-day Senegal, began, most probably in these areas, in the eleventh century, perhaps earlier; perhaps it too was linked to the acquisition of zebu cattle.

The Sahara

During the previous two or three millennia, the Sahara and its northern and southern fringes had gradually been abandoned by its inhabitants as

13. A. Holl, 1983.
14. Al-Bakrī, 1913, p. 158 gives information on these imports.
15. G. Thilmans and A. Ravisé, 1983; J. Gallais, 1984; S. K. McIntosh and R. J. McIntosh, 1980b.
16. S. K. McIntosh and R. J. McIntosh, 1980b, for Jenne-Jeno.
17. Al-Bakrī, 1913, p. 173 gives a good description of hippopotamus hunting by the people living on the banks of the Senegal.
18. Cultivation of rice – *Oryza glaberrima* – is attested by the excavations at Jenne-Jeno. It remains to be determined whether this was irrigated rice or dry rice.
19. B. Chavane, 1985.

depleting resources failed to provide them with adequate food. The introduction of the camel into these areas, from the third century of the Christian era on, constituted a revolution in food supply as well as in transport.[20]

The geographical space of the vastness of the Sahara and the surrounding areas was totally reorganized. The oases were no longer the sole inhabited areas. They became staging points in systems of transhumance that made use of all the routes that had an abundance of wells. The adoption of the camel made possible heavy transport over great distances, a factor that must be taken into account in any discussion of the rise of trans-Saharan relations, a phenomenon that became large-scale towards the end of the Byzantine period.

In the space of a few centuries groups of camel-breeders and those controlling the routes took control of the desert. The peoples of the Sahara, who were overwhelmingly Berber-speaking, played a new sort of active role, following several centuries of torpor and the migration of a section of them towards the edges of the desert. This recovery by the masters of the desert, coinciding with the increased demand for gold by the Muslim states to the north, was to give the Sahara, in the tenth and eleventh centuries, an historical importance that it had not known for a long time. This throws light, among other things, on the 'adventure of the Almoravids'.

Northern Africa

In northern Africa it is more difficult to discern the evolution of production zones, probably in part because of the lasting consequences of ancient colonial urban settlement. The relationship between the countryside and these towns, with its rejections and revolts, is generally better known than the organization of the producing communities themselves. At most, for example, one can glimpse, through the sources, that the Barg͟hawāṭa in Morocco managed a coherent economy, based on wheat and in a position to export, at the time when the Arab sources mention it (tenth to eleventh centuries); that Sūs was producing sugar cane (but since when and in what circumstances?) in the ninth century; that Ifrīḳiya – by the time we have descriptions of it in the ninth century – was an enormous production zone, heavily oriented towards export of its products by sea. But the archaeological excavations remain to be carried out that would enable us to build up pictures comparable to those we now have for other parts of the continent.

In the various stretches of the Nile Valley, long since organized, there is nothing strikingly comparable to note. Here, in Egypt at least, the food problem was no longer simply one of production but one of urban overconsumption, and our period saw the emergence of profound crises of wheat supply, a sign of the beginning of a new economic era; feeding an agglomeration like Cairo, which had several hundred thousand inhabitants

20. R. W. Bulliet, 1975, pp. 111–40.

in the eleventh century, posed problems out of all proportion to those facing the producing and consuming communities of black Africa.[21] These crises were so serious that they called into question the policy of the rulers – whoever they were – governing the country and necessitated heavy imports. Feeding the inhabitants of Egypt was a state matter involving, on a country-wide level, the need to adopt a production, financial and import policy; and it therefore falls almost wholly outside the analysis we are attempting for the rest of Africa.

The description left by the Fāṭimid envoy to the ruler of Dūnḳūla (Dongola),[22] al-Uswānī, after his journey to Nubia (*c.* 976), shows clearly that we are here dealing with an area that straddles regions differing greatly from one another. The north of Nubia, north of the second cataract, at Baṭn al-Ḥadjar, participated in the Egyptian economy, even though it was firmly controlled by the Christian ruler in Dūnḳūla. South of the second cataract was a new economic world.[23] Villages were numerous and productive, the traveller tells us.[24] Gradually, as he moved beyond the last cataracts, to the south, and reached the farthest kingdom, ʿAlwa, he entered a zone where there were no palm trees or vines, but white sorghum appeared 'which looks like rice and from which they make their bread (?) and their beer'.[25] Meat was plentiful because of the large number of herds. Here we are among the societies of black Africa, and the author, moreover, indicates that, despite his curiosity and his mission, he had been able to obtain almost none of the information he was seeking.[26]

In the present state of research, we are unable to say whether comparable developments occurred in Ethiopia or Madagascar, nor whether they were earlier – as in the case of Ethiopia – or later.

The movement of African societies

The general movement of African societies, from the seventh to the eleventh century, while contradictory in its forms depending on place and time, was, broadly speaking, directed towards consolidating earlier situations, and adjusting and perfecting food production complexes to meet growing needs. There was certainly, during these centuries, a natural population increase. Even though this was very slow and though we know

21. On the famines, see for example, T. Bianquis, 1980, and Chapter 7 above.

22. We here adopt the Arab form of this name, often given in the form Dongola. It is an important site, about which archaeology has recently taught us a great deal.

23. Al-Uswānī (G. Troupeau, 1954, p. 282): 'One no longer sees either dinar or dirham ... The currencies circulate below the cataract to trade with the Muslims, but above it, the inhabitants do not practise either buying or selling' (*sic*).

24. G. Troupeau, 1954, p. 283: he saw palm trees, vines, gardens and meadows with camels in them.

25. ibid., p. 188.

26. On this period, see W. Y. Adams, 1977; on Alwa and the recent excavations, see D. A. Welsby, 1983.

little about it, we cannot ignore it. It was accompanied, in many regions, by a growing deterioration in relations with the environment. The two phenomena combined, probably, to give rise to slow population movements, which were not migrations but which research is gradually bringing to light. This is the case with the reverse movement from the Transvaal towards Zimbabwe, beginning apparently in the eighth or ninth century, which seems to be linked to the effects of overpopulation; it is the case too in the Inland Niger Delta, with the occupation, in the tenth and eleventh centuries, of previously unexploited mounds above the flood plain.[27] A much more refined study of climatological variations would add greatly to our understanding of these questions; even moderate and short-lasting changes probably precipitated phenomena of relative overpopulation or, on the contrary, created temporarily more favourable conditions.[28] In recent years there have been inconclusive attempts to explain the migration of the Banū Hilāl and the Banū Sulaym by environmental considerations.[29]

The new production dynamics led of course to social changes. To some extent it may be said that the main processes of the integration of groups into coherent societies go back to this period. It was assuredly a time of 'ethnogenesis', of the absorption of old groups into larger ones and of relative linguistic integration, at least locally; and all this was far from being undramatic and struggle-free.

In the forest of Central Africa, the specialization of hunter-gatherer persisted and the hunters retained their pygmy physical type. But they lived in close symbiosis with the farmers, adopted their languages and were socially and culturally absorbed to become a 'caste' in large groupings. In most regions, the autochthonous peoples were wholly absorbed by the end of the eleventh century, as in Zimbabwe and in Zambia.[30] Absorption proceeded more slowly in eastern Angola and the neighbouring areas of Zambia where a Late Stone Age still existed in the fifteenth century. In these regions, the hunter-gatherers slowly retreated, particularly as the growing population densities affected the distribution of game. They remained intact in southern Angola on lands where the Bantu-speaking farmers did not penetrate.

In West Africa, already complex communities settled on the forest fringes and in forest zones. Their spatial arrangements brought together hunters, gatherers and agriculturalists in more complex societies in which there developed internal networks of fictive kinship and external ones of spatial alliances intended to ensure the survival of the group through a regional balance of forces. In riverain areas, things were even more complex: production provided surpluses that made trade possible over medium dis-

27. R. M. A. Bedaux, T. S. Constandse-Westermann, L. Hacquebord, A. G. Lange and J. D. van der Waals, 1978.

28. The climatic explanation is often used, between the eighth and eleventh century, for the central plateau in Zimbabwe. See Chapter 24 above.

29. Bibliography in J. Devisse, 1972, pp. 67–9.

30. R. Gerharz, 1983, p. 26; D. Phillipson, 1977, pp. 247–52.

tances,[31] and the division of labour became more pronounced between specialized producers, even if the old complementarities between hunters, gatherers, fishermen and agriculturalists were maintained. The nature of authority was now more complex.

In such more sedentary groups, settled on the land, in environments better exploited until population pressure condemned the groups to various forms of segmentation, the African societies developed new technologies, and not only for food production. At this time, securing better living accommodation quite clearly became a goal: the archaeology of the mud habitat has not yet provided much of the information that it can tell us. But already, at least for West Africa, there are B. Chavane's comments;[32] and those of W. Filipowiak,[33] who thinks – wrongly in our opinion – that whitewash was only used in Niani after it had been introduced by the Muslims, but who also says that local mud was used to build mud walls over a wooden framework as early as the sixth century; the research of S. and R. J. McIntosh which is conclusive on the presence of the art of mud-building at Jenne-Jeno before any contact with the north;[34] R. Bedaux's findings on the Bandiagara region;[35] and L. Prussin's conclusions on savanna building technology.[36] This leaves out of consideration the discovery of structures built of sun-dried bricks, at Tegdaoust,[37] and Kumbi Saleh,[38] since these were contemporaneous with contacts with Islam, even though the archaeologists who excavated them are certain that they did not involve imported techniques. In this area, as in so many others, everything still remains to be done to make the soil of Africa yield up all the information that we need. It is enough to recall that the process of 'Nubian vaulting', known in the Egyptian Old Empire,[39] made a spectacular

31. S. K. McIntosh and R. J. McIntosh, 1980b. In the period before the Christian era. And also R. Håland, 1980. See also, on Ife, Chapter 16 above.

32. Through soil analysis B. Chavane, 1985, has shown that the human group whose homes he excavated, to be dated certainly to the ninth and tenth centuries and which is on the left bank of the Senegal, not far from the river, were building houses using clay walls. See also, on the use of clay at Tondidaru, in the seventh century, P. Fontes *et al.*, 1980 and R. Håland, 1980.

33. W. Filipowiak, 1979.

34. S. K. McIntosh and R. J. McIntosh, 1980. See also R. J. McIntosh, 1974.

35. R. M. A. Bedaux, 1972.

36. L. Prussin, 1981.

37. J. Devisse, D. Robert-Chaleix *et al.*, 1983, pp. 85–93.

38. S. Berthier, 1983.

39. The very special technique of building using 'Nubian' vaults is clearly set out in G. Jéquier, 1924, pp. 303–6. For the Christian period, there are examples in U. Monneret de Villard, 1935–57. The attention of architects has recently been drawn back to them by the works of Hassan Fathy: see H. Fathy, 1981, pp. 60–1. Recent excavations in the Oases – at Balāṭ – by the Institut Français d'Archéologie Orientale du Caire have uncovered vast vaults of this type dating from the end of the Old and the Middle Empire. The method was used again successfully in the eleventh and twelfth centuries for roofing Nubian churches with sun-dried bricks; see E. Dinkler (ed), 1970.

reappearance in the tenth and eleventh centuries for the roofing of many churches in the Christian kingdoms of Nubia to appreciate that the study of African architecture still remains largely a closed book, but that it is possible and that is has great historical importance.[40] Of course, research on the ways in which living spaces that are homes are conceived leads directly to the history of techniques and also the history of societies.

Techniques and why they should be studied

The history of African technologies remains to be written. So here we have to raise more problems than we can solve. Some technologies, such as pottery, basketry, tanning, woodworking, stone-working and perhaps salt extraction, were already centuries-old before 600. None of them was unchanging, before or after 600: a technique such as the making of hunting nets, certainly very old, obviously evolved and it would be useful to study this evolution, between Egypt, West Africa and Central Africa for example, in terms of the animals hunted, the hunting techniques used and the types of societies and food. All anthropological studies, in any case, show that there is a relationship between the methods of weaving nets, their size and the size of the meshes, and how they are kept and used, on the one hand, and socio-economic structures on the other; but we know only of a few points that stand out in a centuries-long evolution, not the continuities. In the same way, we do not know anything about the evolution of techniques for extracting salt, nor even how the quantities produced and consumed changed over time. We can be quite certain that the latter varied as a function both of population pressure and types of food.[41]

One of the most pressing needs in African history and archaeology is the careful and detailed study of technical changes, and of the circumstances that precipitated or encouraged them. Pottery, metals and weaving can act as examples, as yet very incomplete, of what studies of these matters can contribute to the history of the continent.

Pottery

Pottery is 9000 years old in some parts of Africa, such as in Aïr in modern Niger.[42] Its use was linked to more and more pronounced forms of sedentarization but not always to the appearance of agriculture. It has become customary, especially in eastern and southern Africa, to designate certain types of pottery by the name of the principal site where they were discovered. When dated by the excavators in satisfactory conditions these

40. J. Devisse, 1981b.
41. See J. Bernard, 1982.
42. M. Cornevin, 1982; J.-P. Roset, 1983.

PLATE 28.2 *House built of clay brickwork: a vaulted chamber.*

have then been used as indicators of chronological sequences. In this way, a link has often been made between the appearance of types of pottery and the appearance of successive iron ages – a notion to which we shall return – and, too often, to the migration of peoples bearing with them, in one package, iron, agriculture and pottery.[43] Today, the trend is in the opposite direction. Laboratory studies complement formal observation and classification.[44] The production of pottery, qualitatively and quantitatively, has become a demographic and economic indicator – giving information about trade and the area in which objects circulate[45] – as well as a cultural indicator. The series of revelations made by archaeology in recent years is an indicator of what a more profound archaeology of African pottery has in store for us: the discovery of the anthropomorphic terracottas of Ife, Owo, following those of Nok,[46] the equally striking ones around the upper Niger,[47] those just beginning to be uncovered in Niger,[48] the rare but interesting artefacts that excavations in Mauritania have brought to light,[49] and the evidence of rooms and courtyards paved with fragments of potsherds[50] – these constitute the most spectacular elements in a corpus that is rapidly being enriched. Pottery has been treated as a vehicle of changes in techniques, in detail (how the clay is prepared, fired, waterproofed), and as an indicator of variations in taste, but also as an indicator of objects available for ornament in the everyday life of the producers, as a good indicator of – an altogether relative – wealth, as an essential part of the furniture whose position in habitats provides solid information to researchers, and has thus become an object vital for our knowledge of the African past, especially for the period we are studying in this volume. For, from this period on, the sequences are almost certain down to the present day. At any event, we have learned to treat this 'merchandise' quite differently from the way it used to be treated, which was quite unsystematic.

Leopard's Kopje pottery, named after its type-site in Zimbabwe, is one element in the creation of a much more complex society leading to the formation of a state about or before 900.[51] Conversely, the appearance of Kisalian pottery at Sanga in southern Zaire in the eighth century was not

43. Good information in D. W. Phillipson, 1977a. On the misuse of systematization about pottery and the expansion of the Bantu-speakers, see P. de Maret, 1980.

44. J. Devisse, 1981a; D. Robert, 1980.

45. A. Louhichi, 1984, has provided proof, through laboratory study, that pottery was transported across the Sahara, from present-day Tunisia or Algeria to the Sahel. See also J. Devisse, D. Robert-Chaleix *et al.*, 1983.

46. E. Eyo and F. Willett, 1980, 1982.

47. B. de Grunne, 1980.

48. B. Gado, 1980, pp. 77–82.

49. J. Devisse, D. Robert-Chaleix *et al.*, 1983, p. 188; D. Robert, 1980.

50. On these pavements, see F. Willett, 1967, 1971 and G. Connah, 1981. Other examples have come to light more recently in Burkina Faso and Benin.

51. See Chapter 24 above.

PLATE 28.3 *Terracotta statuettes were produced within the territory of the present-day Republic of Niger between the sixth and tenth centuries. An example of discoveries made in 1983 and hitherto unpublished.*

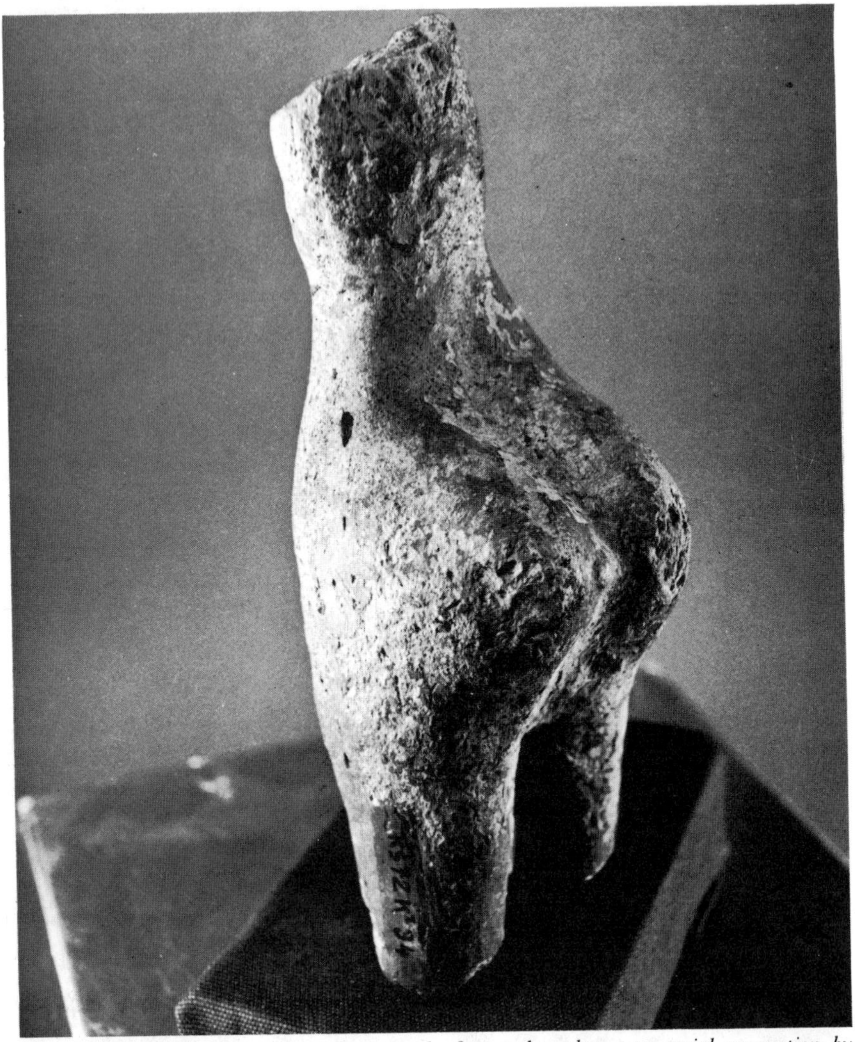

PLATE 28.4 *Female torso in terracotta made from ochre clay. 1972 trial excavation by J. Devisse at Kumbi Saleh.*

accompanied by any such phenomenon.[52] It is more likely to mark the appearance of a community of fishermen-agriculturalists of a new type. The new pottery in Rwanda in the same or the following century might be the sign of a quite minor change although it marks the abandonment of the concentration of iron-smelting furnaces. But it could also signal a more profound transformation flowing from the integration of specialized pastoralists into society.

52. F. Van Noten, 1982.

PLATE 28.5 *Potsherd pavement: the corner of a courtyard, excavated at Ita Yemoo, Ife. Scale is in feet.*

Metals

A few decades ago, there was much writing on the production of metals in Africa. The debates were all the more lively because they rested on a very slender information base.[53]

African gold has long been surrounded by myths and by a sort of historical magic. Today we know a little more about it, and we are at last moving from the imaginary to more quantified assessments.[54] Present-day Zimbabwe came into prominence at this time, the last of the old producing regions, after Nubia and West Africa. In this latter zone, alluvial gold was certainly exploited, as it was in Nubia, before 600: the demand might have been local; it could also have come for the north of the continent; at any event, it is more likely that it was so in the Byzantine period.[55] The quantities were small, and it is unlikely that it was extracted by digging mines. With the establishment of the Muslim states, one of the first users of the gold being surely the Aghlabids, demand grew and throughout the period looked at here, exports of gold were larger. It is extremely difficult to assert that a mining technology involving the systematic digging of mines had been developed before the tenth century, even in the case of Nubia. It is likely that the more and more widespread discovery of areas of active panning was enough, for a long time, to meet the demand: it is today certain that gold from the forest zones of West Africa was, by *c.* 1100, already being exported, it, too, going northwards. The evidence of written sources makes it certain that mines were being dug in the fourteenth century;[56] archaeology has also provided proof of it on the Zimbabwe Plateau.[57] Given then that the real growth of demand, in quantity, dates from the tenth and eleventh centuries and that no one has yet shown that the quantities transported were increased between the tenth and fourteenth century, it is not at all unreasonable to think that the digging of mines was already occurring in the tenth century. It is no doubt possible too that the persistence, over a very long period, of stories about gold being found in the roots of plants reflects a certain degree of reality, if one thinks of gold-panning, and also reflects the desire never to say too much about the true conditions and the exact regions in which African gold was produced. Metal-smelting

53. For iron, for example, a survey of these debates can be made: N. Van der Merwe, 1980, argues (pp. 500–1) for a history of 'pyrotechnology'. See also the review by J. E. G. Sutton, 1984, pp. 222–3, remarking that already in the first centuries of the Christian era the furnaces in Buhaya were different from those in Rwanda; this technical variability is also found in the Great Lakes region. See also P. L. Shinnie, 1971; N. Van de Merwe, 1980, and J. Devisse, 1985a.

54. Information on this is to be found in several chapters in this volume.

55. See T. F. Garrard, 1982, basing himself on numismatics and metrology.

56. Al-ʿUmarī, 1927, p. 81: 'The sultan [Mansa Mūsā] . . . told me that there were pagan peoples in his empire . . . whom he used to extract gold in the mines. He also told me that the gold mines consisted of holes dug to the depth of a man's height or almost'.

57. R. Summers, 1969.

PLATE 28.6 *Gold filigreed jewelry found at Tegdaoust, Mauritania (Denise Robert excavations)*

was known in the regions where it was exploited;[58] it remains difficult and would perhaps be incautious to say that techniques of gold-working did not exist in the producing regions; it is likely that filigree-work, so widespread in Andalusia and North Africa as early as the tenth century, reached the south from these regions: filigreed gold ornaments dating from the eleventh or twelfth century have been found at Tegdaoust. And filigree was used for objects in copper alloys at Igbo-Ukwu in Nigeria.[59]

South of the Sahara copper often rivalled gold as the favoured metal and the raw material for luxury articles and had done so for a very long time.[60] In this field too, there have been many surprises in recent years and research has made enormous advances. Areas where the raw material was produced and the metal was smelted were, in the seventh century – and in many cases much earlier – more numerous than was formerly thought. Mauritania, Niger – Aïr again – the Copperbelt (Zaire and Zambia), the Transvaal (Phalaborwa), were producing and exporting it throughout the centuries dealt with in this volume.[61] Trade in this metal, attested to by the Arabic sources of the tenth to twelfth centuries and by a number of archaeological discoveries, certainly brought copper and copper alloys from the north to the area south of the Sahara but the picture that we have of this trade today is much more complex than it was formerly; what was yesterday accepted as dogma can no longer be accepted: that products and techniques came exclusively from the north. In Central Africa, copper became a standard currency from 900 on and although copper ornaments and bangles have not yet been found in the Transvaal, the Phalaborwa

58. For Tegdaoust, see Chapter 14 above.

59. T. Shaw, 1970.

60. E. Herbert, 1984.

61. Important recent surveys: N. Echard (ed.), 1983. The recent work of D. Grebenart will also be looked forward to with great interest. See also for the Upemba, in Zaire, P. de Maret, 1981.

mine was producing the metal, and was no doubt not the only one to be doing so.

The extraction techniques seem to have been limited to the digging of pits and horizontal galleries; systems of deep galleries were rare, for this metal as for gold; essentially, no doubt, this was because of the rise of underground water levels during the rainy seasons. Knowledge of how to cast copper existed in Mauritania and in Aïr long before the Christian era, and in the fifth to sixth centuries in the Copperbelt. Lost-wax moulds dating from the eighth to ninth centuries have been found in the excavations at Tegdaoust (Mauritania)[62] and processes well adapted to the various types of metal have been recognized at Igbo-Ukwu, where euphorbia latex replaced wax.[63] Today, all that we know enables us to say that the metallurgy of copper and its alloys was perfectly mastered, in tropical Africa in the sixth, seventh and eighth centuries. Hammering, cold spinning and casting using the lost-wax process were used, each with the appropriate metal and zinc – and lead-based bronzes and brass – the tin probably came from modern central Nigeria – provided a known and knowledgably used range of different metals for the production of different objects; even welding was effected according to the known qualities of various metals. It should be noted in passing that some coppers and alloys in West Africa contain a lot of arsenic, which probably provides an important clue to the source of objects found during excavations.[64]

Contrary to all formerly received ideas, the existence of an ancient and well-mastered copper metallurgy must today be accepted; it does not mean totally excluding highly diverse types of relations with Mediterranean or Asian metallurgies and, no doubt, many revisions will yet have to be made in our mental maps, as laboratory research, in particular, makes us better informed.

It is no different with iron. In the past a chronology of two successive iron ages was drawn up that, it was hoped, would be usable for the whole of the black world, the 'second age' appearing precisely during the centuries we are looking at here. An attempt was made to show that significant differences marked the passage from the first age to the second, notably an increase in quantities produced, an improvement and diversification of qualities, and the appearance of new modes of settlement producing characteristic pottery types. More recent research, once again, has destroyed this 'model'.[65] It is probably dangerous to continue to speak of two clearly distinct sequences, especially for the continent as a whole and, once again,

62. D. Robert, 1980 (to be published, see D. Robert-Chaleix, forthcoming).

63. Which leads one to suppose a prior adaptation in the Sahelian zone, which is rich in euphorbia.

64. C. Vanacker, 1983a.

65. Major recent works indicative of the reasons for calling into question this approach are P. de Maret, 1979, pp. 233–5; M. C. Van Grunderbeck, E. Roche and H. Doutrelepont, 1983b; earlier: P. Schmidt, 1978.

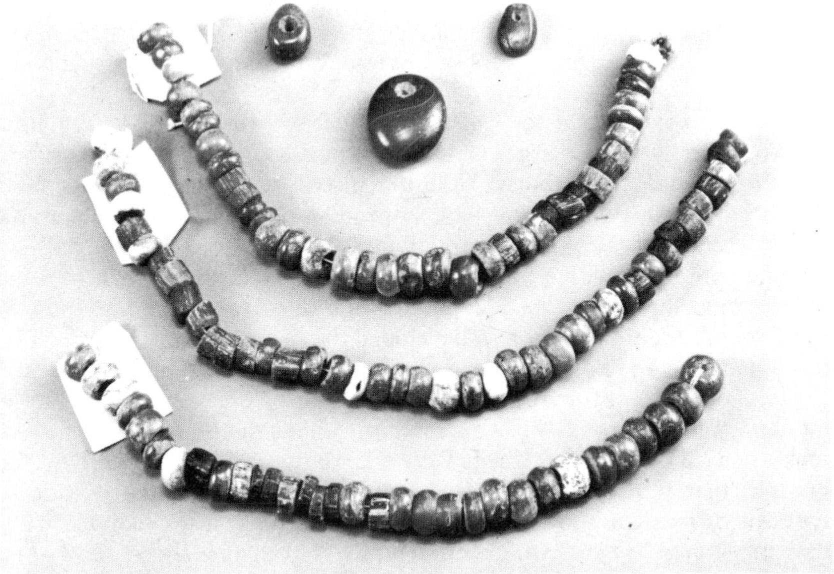

(a)

PLATE 28.7(a) (*top*) *Carnelian pendants and strings of carnelian and glass beads, from the burial chamber at Igbo-Ukwu, beads from Igbo Richard*

PLATE 28.7(b) (*below*) *Strings of coloured glass beads from the store-house regalia at Igbo-Ukwu*

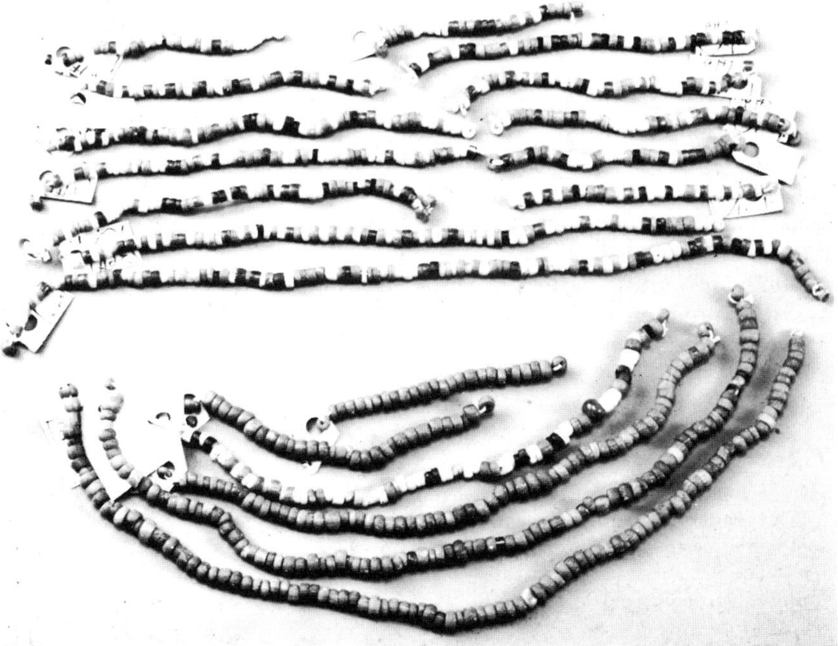

(b)

there is a need for more subtle analyses and to accept the heterogeneity of the phenomena and the diversity of significant dates depending on the region.[66]

The technological history of iron in Africa still remains very little known, despite detailed studies of certain metallurgical sites in West and East Africa and at Phalaborwa.[67] Different types of iron might have been produced, but we do not know how far production was controlled, nor how the different processes, from extraction to the final product, evolved, beginning with the building of furnaces. Plans changed, the manner of using them changed, the fuels changed, the raw product was worked in different ways and all the tools used also developed. Even the concentration or dispersion of the industry is little known. We know that in Rwanda and Burundi one type of furnace was abandoned during our period and that the industry was dispersed. But we know little about the type of furnace that took its place or what the effects were on production or the quality of the product that followed the dispersion. The cartographic distribution of types of furnace and equipment (bellows, hammers, mauls, anvils, wire-drawing stones, etc.), as well as fuels and ways of using them, shows that there was major technological activity in the past.[68] All this information remains episodic and poorly correlated and is thus unable to throw the light it should on the technological evolution that one can guess at but which is very inadequately known. We know that iron was present, in numerous regions, from the seventh century onwards and that it supplied the raw materials for implements – axes, working hoes – weapons – cutlasses, spears, arrowheads, harpoon tips, knives – various utensils – scissors, needles – and also for ornaments – necklaces, bracelets, rings. We also know that, on the other hand, there was hoarding: proof of this is provided by the presence of mauls, often in the form of an anvil, sometimes found in context, but which have unfortunately not yet been dated. Ethnographical data at least make it possible to pose a certain number of problems: what was the iron used for? what was its real importance? How was it related to copper and other objects of value or jewels or exchange materials region by region and period by period? A history of iron metallurgy and the use of its products is certainly destined in part to overturn many received interpretations.

Textiles

There has been weaving in Egypt and Nubia for millennia. After the be-

66. Seminar on iron metallurgy by the direct reduction process. University of Paris-I, EHESS, Paris, 1983. Proceedings to appear in 1985. There were major African contributions to this meeting. See also J. Devisse, 1985a.

67. The Phalaborwa site is situated in the Transvaal, south-east of Mapungubwe and north of Lydenburg.

68. See for example W. Cline, 1937 or L. Frobenius and R. von Wilm, 1921–31, for example, plan of bellows, Heft 1, Blatt 4.

ginning of the Christian era, Coptic techniques reached heights never later surpassed. But cotton as a raw material was recent. The plant had probably been imported to Meroe.[69] No one disputes the importance and influence of Egyptian weaving, particularly between the seventh and eleventh century.[70] The debates, which are once again very lively, relate to the development of weaving, especially using cotton, south of the Sahara.[71] The sources and archaeology provide key elements. Cotton was present in the villages in the Senegal floodplain, by the tenth century;[72] and cloths made from narrow woven strips dated to the tenth to eleventh centuries have been found in the Tellem caves.[73] It is important to point out that cotton and cotton-weaving were widespread in Ethiopia and, as early as *c.* 900, in southern Mozambique and at Mapungubwe.[74] Cotton was already being cultivated and woven in tropical Africa in the ninth to tenth centuries. Weaving required two key elements: the spindle whorls for spinning, and looms. Archaeological discoveries, in both areas, are still few and far between and remain difficult to interpret. Positively identified spindle whorls[75] are abundant for the thirteenth to fourteenth centuries; in the present state of our knowledge they are rarer for earlier periods. As far as looms are concerned, they are different in Mozambique – but knowledge is limited – as compared with West Africa; in the latter case, they can be reconstituted through articles found in excavations. The narrow loom with two heddles was used, as it still is today. This allows long strips some 30 cm wide to be woven and was perhaps introduced before 1000, possibly from the Nile Valley.[76] In subsequent centuries weaving and the sale of cloth were to become economically very important and generated secondary activities such as indigo growing. It is thus important to discover the origins of this activity which not only supplied new articles of clothing, but was also very rapidly to provide indications of social distinction and objects to be exchanged and hoarded.

Here a major place must be given to the making of mats and carpets, which supplied a large export trade towards the Orient from present-day Tunisia from the ninth century, but of whose techniques we know very little.

In sub-Saharan Africa, not only cotton was woven.[77] The raffia palm

69. W. Y. Adams, 1977, pp. 331, 371 (loom).
70. M. Lombard, 1978, pp. 151–74.
71. R. Boser-Sarivaxévanis, 1972, 1975.
72. B. Chavane, 1980.
73. R. M. A. Bedaux and R. Bolland, 1980.
74. P. K. Davison and P. Harries, 1980 (spindle whorls at Mapungubwe, tenth and eleventh centuries).
75. There are no obvious formal differences between some old spindle whorls and objects intended for quite different uses.
76. M. Johnson, 1977.
77. J. Picton and J. Mack, 1979.

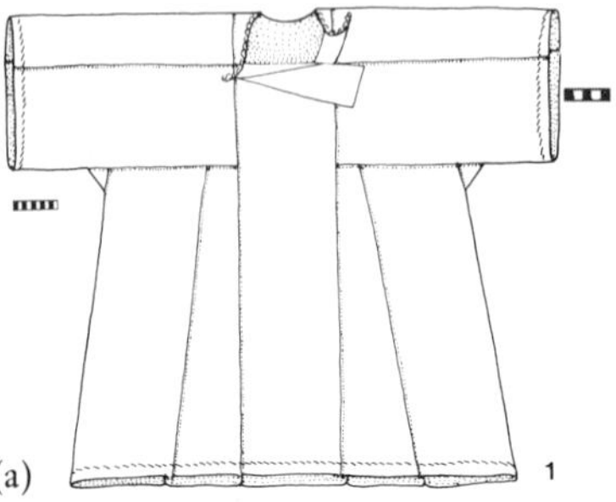
(a)

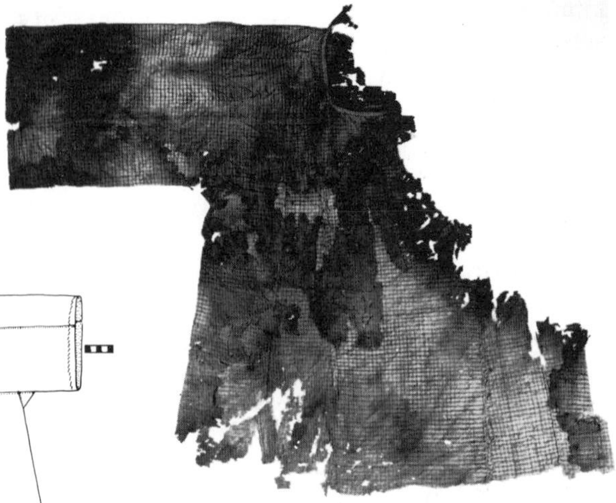
(b)

PLATE 28.8(a) (*above, left*) *Reconstruction of the trapezoidal tunic, from grotto Z (twelfth-thirteenth centuries of the Christian era)*
PLATE 28.8(b) (*above, right*) *Trapezoidal cotton tunic, from grotto C (eleventh-twelfth centuries of the Christian era)*
PLATE 28.8(c) (*below*) *Tellem skull with cotton head covering, from grotto C (eleventh-twelfth centuries of the Christian era.*

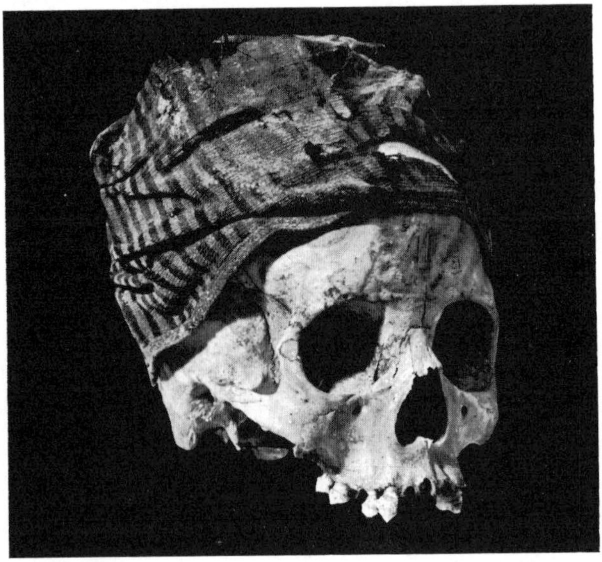
(c)

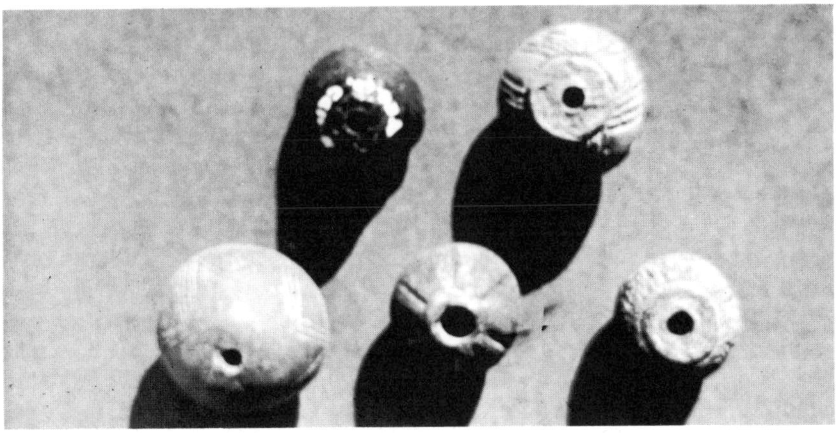

PLATE 28.9 *Spindle whorls found at Tegdaoust*

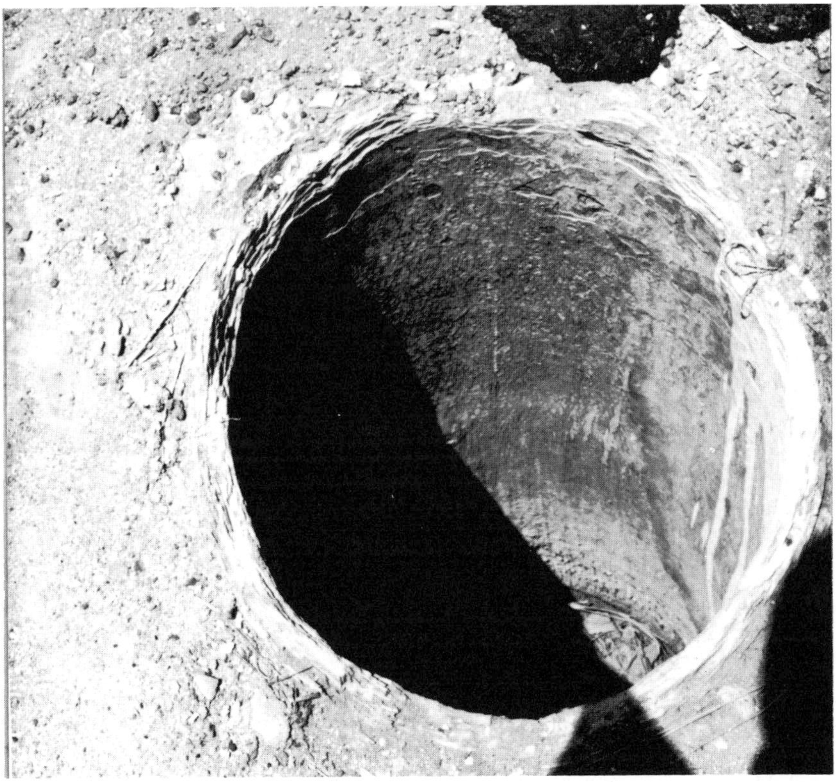

PLATE 28.10 *Indigo dye-pit in north of the Ivory Coast*

produces a fibre that can be woven.[78] Where this palm tree grows, in West and Central Africa, the fibre is woven on quite a broad vertical or horizontal loom, with one main heddle. We do not know how old this practice is. It is not impossible that this loom is older than the West African loom, but it may be of more recent invention.[79] One of the Nok figurines appears to be wearing a cloth over its shoulder; but it is not altogether certain that it is indeed a cloth.

Raffia fabric was particularly important in Central Africa, where the technique of decorating it was highly developed before the sixteenth century and where raffia squares were used as money. In the forest zone, although this is not really weaving in the strict sense of the term, the production of bark cloth treated by hammering was highly developed. In the open savanna, leather remained the main clothing material. These facts run counter to the argument that the practice of weaving cotton spread as a result of the Muslim impact, as a consequence of the desire to combat nakedness. This line of reasoning begins to carry little conviction as soon as one realizes that other forms of clothing were known.

Demonstrating the importance of a history of technology, and the fact that this history is virtually unknown, must suffice for the present. This is one of the key gaps in African history. Excavations combined with ethnographic studies will help to fill it.

Salt

Among all the commodities whose production most likely increased in quantity during our period,[80] salt represents a particularly interesting one. The techniques of producing and consuming it cut across all the aspects we have touched on above; we shall be dealing with commercialization later. Salt was obtained from the Sahelian, Ethiopian and East African salt mines in the form of rock salt bars; there is an abundant literature on this point.[81] It was also obtained from evaporating sea or lagoon water,[82] by collecting deposits, as in the lower valley of the Sine Saloum in Senegal, and through highly sophisticated techniques using the ashes of xerophilous plants to extract the salt from them by leaching.[83] In addition, where rock salt or sea salt were not available, people had succeeded in cultivating plants producing it, in marshy areas in particular. However, the superiority of sea salt or Sahara salt was such that it was exported over great distances; in some

78. H. Loir, 1935.

79. It would perhaps be interesting to compare the study of it with the one now under way of the silk-weaving loom found in Madagascar.

80. B. M. Fagan, and J. E. Yellen, 1968; J. E. G. Sutton and A. D. Roberts, 1968; J. Devisse, 1972; D. W. Phillipson, 1977.

81. See for example D. W. Phillipson, 1977a, pp. 110 and 150.

82. For an evocative anthropological study see J. Rivallain, 1980.

83. L. Ndoricimpa *et al.*, 1981; E. Torday and T. A. Joyce, 1910.

PLATE 28.11 *Salt production – Walata: a caravan from the sebkhra of Idjil (Mauritania), carrying loads of bar-salt*

regions, notably Ethiopia, at certain periods, salt was used as currency. Salt was a greater source of income for coastal dwellers than fresh or dried fish and shellfish; they exchanged it for all sorts of products that they needed. It is difficult to conceive of the settlement of peoples in the salty areas of the Niger delta – and this probably happened in the period we are looking at – without the supply of foodstuffs and implements from the interior, but thanks to salt this supply posed no problems.[84] In the same way, the inhabitants of the Sahara secured the cereals they needed by exchanging them in the Sahel for salt from their mines. The example of salt thus takes us from technological considerations to the unequal distribution of resources and the trade that resulted from it.

The various forms of trade

Local exchanges, over larger or smaller areas, had certainly been going on for a very long time, in essential products such as salt or metals and also in jewelry and ornaments, which were sometimes transported over great distances.

Certain zones, where technological development was intense, became

84. Dates from the ninth century onwards: M. Posnansky and R. McIntosh, 1976, p. 170; O. Ikime (ed.), 1980, pp. 68–72.

areas of high production of raw materials and elaboration of finished products, and within them developed staging points in the transport of these products along the networks that were progressively being organized. In recent years, archaeology has fully revealed the existence of such networks south of the Senegal and Niger rivers, on which all the other sources were silent;[85] this throws a much clearer light on the genesis of such political entities as Takrūr, Ghana or Gao. During the five centuries we are looking at, trade developed spectacularly, and its high point was the trans-Saharan trade. Before the beginning of the period some internal Sahelian trade existed as no doubt did links with the Nile Valley and North Africa, especially along a link between Lake Chad, Kawār and the Fezzān. The indicators we possess (metrology, numismatics, finds in West Africa) make it possible to hypothesize that it was the adoption of transport by camel that made long-distance trade across the desert a paying proposition. But it still remains true that from *c.* 800 this trade underwent a dramatic increase. The classical Saharan system with exports of gold and foodstuffs going north in exchange for the import of salt from the desert and manufactured products from the north became established in our period.[86] This trade extended a very long way south. In the ninth century, it probably delivered thousands of beads to Igbo-Ukwu and this site was also linked to the sea to the south.[87] And by *c.* 1100, the trade had reached the edges of the forest in the area that later came to be called the Gold Coast (present-day Ghana). North as well as south of the desert, the expansion of trans-Saharan trade had major consequences. First among these was the development of state institutions, from Morocco to Egypt, between the eighth and the eleventh centuries; the picture was the same to the south, between the Atlantic and Lake Chad, during the same centuries. Then, of course, the trade led to the development of trading groups that were more or less well organized and more or less dependent on the political authorities.

The role of Ethiopia in international trade collapsed with the major changes in the great Indian Ocean traffic between the sixth and eighth centuries: Adulis lost its role and Axum went into decline. The coast of East Africa, conversely, assumed much more importance, even if at present we are much better informed about the stages of this transformation after the twelfth century than before.

In the eighth century, traces of imports have been found from the coasts of Somalia to those of southern Mozambique.[88] Here too gold played a major role, especially in the south. Here too, international trade took place in the framework of a vigorous regional trade. Gold, ivory, wood and slaves

85. S. K. McIntosh and R. J. McIntosh, 1980b; J. Devisse, 1982.

86. See Chapters 11, 12, 13, 14, 15 and 27 above.

87. T. Shaw, 1970.

88. Chapters 22 and 26 above, and P. J. J. Sinclair, 1982. The presence of the Zandj in China and India soon after 700 indicates the spread of this trade, even at a date earlier than that of towns so far found.

were exported as well as a few luxury products, while imports included luxury products, such as beads and cloth. Already it was an unequal exchange, but an unequal exchange that gave an impetus to the development of internal communications: at least an attempt has been made to prove this for the Limpopo region[89] where this trade speeded up or strengthened the construction of large political entities.

Overall economic growth and commercial expansion were not, however, comparable in all societies on the continent. During these centuries, North Africa belonged to the centre of a 'world' economy. Technologies developed there through diffusion from one end of the Muslim world to the other and with them particular production systems; for example, the planting of sugar cane or date palms.[90] The cultural creation of a Muslim and Arab world facilitated and intensified contacts, no doubt even more than attempts at political unification. Egypt, Tunisia, and the leading Muslim cities in Morocco became great manufacturing centres which exported, notably to West Africa. East Africa was linked in an even more complex way to the economy of the Muslim world, as well as to the Asian economies of China, India,[91] and Indonesia.

On the other hand, there remained regions that were hardly affected by international trade or not at all. Southern and Central Africa provide the most extreme examples, although in Central Africa a regional commercial zone centred on the Copperbelt developed that was in indirect contact with the Indian Ocean before 1100. It was based on the exchange of products from different environments and from salt mines. To judge from later periods, salt and iron, fish and raffia cloth, palm oil and *mbafu* oil, and red dyewood were exchanged, and the general movement was above all from north to south, crossing the ecological zones. Still in Central Africa, the River Zaire and some of its affluents were no doubt already in use as a cheap means of communication, although no evidence of this has yet been found before the period following the one we are concerned with.

The interior of eastern Africa remains a problem. No trace of imports has been found there and it has been concluded from this that there were no links between these regions and the neighbouring coast.[92] It is difficult to believe that this was so. Perhaps these imports were limited to salt and cloth, the products exported being, in addition to ivory, other luxury objects such as the large rock crystals the Fāṭimids were so fond of.[93]

89. See Chapter 24 above.

90. A. M. Watson, 1983, provides the most recent but perhaps exaggerated survey.

91. Al-Idrīsī, in the twelfth century, notes that iron was exported from the coast of present-day Kenya to India. See Chapters 1 and 21 above.

92. Although there is still the problem of the similarities observed between pottery from the interior and locally produced coastal pottery (see for example H. N. Chittick, 1974, on Kilwa).

93. Which came perhaps from the Laikipia plateau where they are common (personal communication from J. de Vere Allen).

Whatever the case, relations with international trade were at best indirect. In addition, this sector did not form a single regional trading zone. A few small production centres (mainly of salt) can be detected, no doubt serving rather small areas. Further north, in Ethiopia, regional trade doubtless survived and probably spread with the extension of monastic foundations and the transfer of the centre of the kingdom to Lasta. Southern Ethiopia, especially Shoa, saw its links with the outside world develop and the settlement of Muslim traders exporting through the coast of the Horn. The Christian kingdoms of the Nile also remained isolated from intercontinental trade. Two very different economies coexisted there. One, subsistence farming, involved the vast majority of the population; it was not necessarily stagnant, as we have seen above. The other had a dual driving force. One part consisted of complex trade arrangements with the Muslims, who supplied the Nubian court and the privileged groups with Mediterranean products – cloths, wines, grains – in exchange for slaves.[94] The quest for the latter necessitated a second sector consisting of commercial relations with the Chad basin area, and with areas of the continent to the south of Nubia: the circulation of Nubian pottery in Dārfūr and Koro Toro north-east of Lake Chad has begun to provide evidence that these relations did indeed exist. It is striking that these are not mentioned at all by al-Uswānī, in the account mentioned above,[95] although this Fāṭimid envoy speaks of the relations between Dūnḳūla and the Red Sea from the great bend made by the Nile: 'Hippopotamuses abound in this country and roads lead from there towards Sawākin, Bāḍi, Dahlak and the islands of the Red Sea'.[96]

This sketch of commercial activity shows that a good half of the continent was already involved in large-scale trade and that in most of the other parts regional networks were coming into being. Complete absence of a network, even a regional one, was rare, but was probably the case in a few pockets: Namibia and the Cape region, the forests of Liberia and the neighbouring regions perhaps, and the interior of East Africa and part of the savanna lands between Cameroon and the White Nile. But it is possible that this impression is merely a product of our own lack of information.

But the fact remains that there were major innovations in the overall situation of the continent compared with the previous period. The integration of the Sahara, of West Africa, of the eastern coast and of the interior of part of Zimbabwe and the Transvaal into an intercontinental trading network was new, as was the development of regional trade networks. This commercial dynamism was a first fruit of sedentarization and the adjustment of production systems that we have described. Despite all the gaps, we now know enough to assert that this period represents a starting-point from which the economies and trade were to develop with even more intensity, volume and complexity between 1100 and 1500. The regional

94. On this aspect of trade, see L. Török, 1978.
95. G. Troupeau, 1954. See above.
96. ibid., p. 285.

networks would develop and coalesce but always in a subordinate position in relation to the areas of international trade. And by *c.* 1500 hardly any part of the continent would remain outside a regional trading area. Thus in our period communications over large areas of the continent were forged, linking the human settlements with one another, carrying ideas and social customs along with the goods traded.

Societies and power

The social history of the continent also still remains to be written for the period that concerns us. We know virtually nothing of the real life of the times, the arrangements regarding kinship and living and working together. Even the history of the institutions that structured these relationships such as the family, the extended family (often called the lineage),[97] the household, marriage, and work groups remains unknown. These structures have left few traces in the written or archaeological sources. Moreover, although they are fundamental, they have low visibility, because of their very permanence. The appearance given is one that demonstrates stable features linked to human nature. Yet this is simply not so, although many researchers have allowed themselves to be taken in by it, as if clans, lineages and marriages had always functioned in the same way.

The consequences of the division of labour are more visible, even if the vocabulary here also tends to be misleading and to involve us in schematism. It is quite certain that the division of labour progressed spectacularly between the seventh and the eleventh centuries, and that societies were becoming stratified. Analysis and classification of the phenomena is as yet in its infancy. It is easier, in some parts of the continent, to show that wide divergences of economic and social statuses – classes – appeared in this period than to understand, other than by the application of abstract theories, how relations between these classes actually functioned. In northern Africa, in Nubia, in Ethiopia, we see aristocrats whose landed property, however acquired, was the basis of their power. In North Africa, this aristocracy surrounded itself with numerous clients – *mawālī*; it sometimes protected non-Muslim groups, and owned slaves, servants, workers or warriors; it had sufficient power to be able sometimes to oblige the official power-holders to treat with it. It may well have been more or less the same in Nubia or Ethiopia. Further south, things are less clear; researchers are still engaged in lively debates on the existence of clearly distinct classes at this time; and in even more lively ones on the existence of closed castes, comparable to those occasionally found in Africa in more recent periods. Al-Mas'ūdī's oft-cited allusion to those who exhort the crowd and the

97. The term lineage is more an ideological term than a concept describing social realities. See A. Kuper, 1982b, pp. 71–95.

princes to live according to the examples given by the ancestors and the kings of former times,[98] should not lead us to think that these are 'bards' nor that they were members of a 'caste'. The equally frequent reference to 'bards' in Sundiata's suite, in the thirteenth century, is only proof of their existence at a time when the traditions that speak of them had been fixed or reworked; as to the dates of these fixings or reworkings, here too the debate is far from closed.

The most recent research, at least for West Africa, tends rather to suggest that castes were of recent rather than ancient appearance.[99] Much more work is therefore probably needed, with clear testing of all possible research hypotheses, before prematurely freezing a description of societies in the midst of change and at different stages in this change in different places.

To return a moment to what was probably happening between the seventh and eleventh century in Central Africa, things were rather different from what they were in the north and west of the continent. In equatorial Africa, some division of labour, partly regulated by the growing symbiosis between agriculturalists and hunter-gatherers, appeared. The forest people in some cases attached themselves to groups of hunters (especially pygmies) by supplying them with food (especially plantains) and iron implements, and later also with equipment such as heavy hunting nets in exchange for game and honey. This symbiosis necessitated significant surpluses of foodstuffs; it could not have developed before plantains became a basic crop, nor before the period when the density of agriculturalists had increased to the point where it disturbed the hunters. For this reason, we feel that these systems developed during the period studied in this volume. It must be noted that this arrangement was quite different from the regular commercial relations between agriculturalists in the forest and professional fishermen who supplied them with fish, pottery and vegetable salt in exchange for vegetable foodstuffs. These older relations had been formed from the time these regions were occupied. They were based on relations of equality, which is not true for the symbiotic relations.

Naturally, and above all when archaeology enables us to take the exact measure of it, the place where the ongoing social changes will be seen best is in the towns. They are clearly to be seen at Tegdaoust;[100] and also by examining the Sanga tombs, where inequality is clearly visible and increasing with time. The history of the process of urbanization is also undergoing radical revision.[101] It was long thought that it was linked exclusively with Muslim influence; it is a fact that Muslims were great founders of towns wherever they lived, both at this time and in more recent ones. But it is

98. Al-Masʿūdī, 1965, p. 330.
99. See the interesting views in A. R. Ba, 1984.
100. J. Devisse, D. Robert-Chaleix *et al.*, 1983.
101. J. Devisse, 1983, for example.

today becoming clearer and clearer that urban agglomerations existed before Islam: this has been spectacularly shown for Jenne-Jeno,[102] and in the south-east of the continent as well;[103] these examples are more conclusive than those involving towns where the settlement of Muslims played an obvious role, such as was the case with Kumbi Saleh,[104] Tegdaoust,[105] and Niani.[106] It is of the greatest importance for the future of this research on urbanization that the fruitful work done at Ife,[107] Igbo-Ukwu,[108] Benin,[109] Begho and Kong,[110] should be pursued and developed. Similarly, research on Nyarko, on the edge of gold-bearing areas of the forests of modern Ghana, which was already a town as early as the eleventh century, should be pursued.[111] No doubt other proto-urban or urban centres founded during this period will be discovered. One thinks of Kano, Zaria, and Turunku and the oldest towns along the lower Shari River.

This urbanization of western Africa calls into question a whole series of received ideas, particularly the one that the phenomenon of towns was a more or less late implantation by traders from North Africa. Contrary to the impression left by the vast majority of ethnographic works or those by social anthropologists until very recently, West Africa was not a collection of villages brought together in ethnic groups with distinct and rural cultures and languages living cheek by jowl without influencing one another. As soon as towns appeared, they became cultural centres that influenced vast areas around them. Complex cultural and social spaces were formed before the eleventh century, which is what explains the diffusion of languages such as the Mande languages, Yoruba and Hausa. For a long time, the scale of these societies, their internal dynamics, and their evolution were thus misunderstood.

New questions along the same lines can now be raised concerning the trading posts along the east coast and in Madagascar, their African and Malagasy foundations and the place of Muslim traders in their develop-

102. S. K. McIntosh and R. J. McIntosh, 1980b.

103. See Chapter 24 above.

104. S. Berthier, 1983.

105. J. Devisse, D. Robert-Chaleix *et al.*, 1983, p. 169.

106. M. Filipowiak, 1979.

107. F. Willett, 1967 and 1971. Generally speaking, the development of the Yoruba settlements – towns and villages – merits the continuation of studies already embarked on. See the useful and little-known work by J. O. Igué, 1970–80. The author relies heavily on the well-known work by A. L. Mabogunje, 1962.

108. T. Shaw, 1970. More recently, see Chapter 16 above, and E. Eyo and F. Willett, 1980, 1982.

109. G. Connah, 1972.

110. Research carried out by the Institut d'Art, d'Archéologie et d'Histoire of the University of Abidjan under the direction of Mr Victor T. Diabaté.

111. J. Anquandah, 1982, p. 97. Generally speaking, urbanization in Ghana also deserves study; for how long had the town of Ladoku, near Accra, and already flourishing in the sixteenth century, been in existence (J. Anquandah, 1982, p. 70)?

ment.[112] Already it is being asked whether in eastern Africa – but how far northwards and southwards? – Swahili culture, with which the development of towns seems to coincide, was not, from its very beginnings, an urban civilization; the debate is far from closed.[113] The trading posts situated in present-day Mozambique[114] maintained contacts with the Limpopo Valley and indirectly made a contribution to the creation of a first proto-urban centre at Mapungubwe, an administrative centre and the first stage in a development that would culminate in the creation of Zimbabwe in the thirteenth century.

Equal attention should be paid, in the north of the continent, to the creation, in this period, of important towns on which sometimes very limited research has yet been done. While the evolution of Fez, Ḳayrawān, Marrakesh, and Rabat, for example, is well known, there has been very little work done on Sidjilmāsa or Tāhert – creations of the seventh century – on Sadrāta and the whole of the Mzāb, on Ghadāmes, or on the Egyptian and Nubian cities of the middle Nile Valley.[115] This formative period was thus also one during which a new urbanization was restructuring space. This phenomenon, all in all, affected only half the continent; but it still remains true that it was characteristic of the whole of Africa.

The Muslim conquest of the northern part of the continent, after a short period of theoretical unity under the authority of the eastern caliphs, led to a political break-up of vital importance for the future. New states came into being in Egypt and present-day Tunisia, and also around important cities such as Fez, Tāhert, and Sidjilmāsa. They became more and more firmly established in the ninth and tenth centuries. In particular they nearly always used West African gold to ensure the quality of their currency. The territorial bases of this state organization were strengthened, first in Ifrīḳiya, then in Egypt under the Fāṭimids.[116] The most disturbed periods of the eleventh century did not call into question a fact that was gradually becoming established: the territorial basis of the Muslim dynastic rulers, especially in Tunisia and in Egypt and then in the eleventh century in Almoravid Morocco, had become a more or less stable, more or less permanent reality. Muslim states, with their functions and their machinery, were established in this period, even though the dynasties changed, even though

112. See Chapters 13, 14, 15, 21 and 25 above. The expansion of the trading posts as far south as the Sabi dates from the eighth century (P. J. J. Sinclair, 1982).

113. T. H. Wilson, 1982.

114. See Chapter 22 above. See also 'Trabalhos de Arqueologia ...', 1980; P. J. J. Sinclair, 1982.

115. On Ḳūs, a caravan centre in upper Egypt, see J. C. Garcin, 1976. On the importance of funerary steles as a document for demographic, economic and cultural history see M. al-Ṭawāb 'Abd ar-Raḥmān, 1977. On the towns of Nubia, in particular, the importance of the Polish excavations at Faras and Dongola, see Chapter 8 above. On the recent excavations at Sūba, the capital of the southernmost Nubian kingdom, see D. A. Welsby, 1983.

116. See Chapters 7, 10 and 12 above.

incidents of varying seriousness such as Abū Yazīd's revolt,[117] or the 'Hilalian invasion'[118] or Christian attacks from Sicily, from time to time disturbed, sometimes profoundly, the chances of state territorial control and dynastic continuity.

In West Africa, the organization of states probably began before 600, but becomes apparent during the period studied here. Gao, Ghana and Kānem are today apparently well known, although much work remains to be done on the genesis of the state in all three cases. But there are many other areas, where less research has so far been done, and for which the existence of state authorities is no longer in doubt during the period involved. This was certainly the case with Takrūr, on whose origins a recent thesis throws new light.[119] Our inadequate information has led us, apart from these certainties, to believe that African authorities were no more than 'chiefdoms' without any great territorial consistency: but is it legitimate to look at the case of Ife in this way? Again, are we to believe that the power of Sumaoro Kante, in the Soso that rivalled Ghana and the Mande *Mansaya* until its defeat by Sundiata in the thirteenth century, was not yet a state? Research still has much to teach us in this field too. And what was happening among the Hausa or the Yoruba?

The presence of fortifications to the west of the lower Niger, in the lands that were to become the kingdom of Benin, indicates not simply a concentration of power that was territorial in character but also a bitter struggle to enlarge the territorial base of the various states in the process of being formed. This contrasts with the situation to the east of the lower Niger where the absence of fortifications might indicate either a territorial unity headed by Igbo-Ukwu, or the presence of a totally different form of land occupation and political structures; how, politically, should the discovery of a splendid tomb at Igbo-Ukwu be interpreted?

In north-east Africa, the period saw the apogee of the Christian kingdoms formed in the sixth century, particularly in the three sections of Nubia, where the economic and cultural success was still evident in the eleventh century.[120] Ethiopia was in a worse situation, but the monarchy re-established itself, after the collapse of Axum, at Lasta, in the eleventh

117. On this subject, a new study, just being completed by an Algerian researcher, Mrs Nachida Rafaï, using a new translation of the Arabic sources, will bring out the bitterness of the struggle between Abū Yazīd and the Fāṭimids.

118. The debate remains open on the economic, social and political consequences of this 'invasion'. A recent translation of the key text by al-Idrīsī (Hadj Sadok, 1983) provides new food for thought.

119. A. R. Ba, 1984.

120. One has only to refer to the monuments found by the excavators at Dongola for example, particularly churches and a royal palace, to appreciate that, in a rather poor country, the Nubian state possessed important assets and played an international role. On Alwa and the recent excavations, see D. A. Welsby, 1983; these excavations confirm the economic and cultural dynamism of Nubia in the eleventh century.

century. At the same time, a series of Muslim principalities was formed in the east and south, reaching the Ethiopian lakes.

The organization of a dominant authority in each town seems to have been the rule along the eastern coast. In present-day Zimbabwe, a state was formed in the tenth century, with its capital at Mapungubwe, and Great Zimbabwe appeared in the thirteenth century. In Central Africa or the interior of East Africa, large-scale territorial developments have not yet been observed. All that one can say is that at Sanga the data suggest a slow evolution towards a 'chiefdom', an evolution that only became clearly established towards the end of the tenth century.[121]

Outside these developments, we have no direct evidence on the subject of other types of political organization. It can be argued that in eastern and south-eastern Africa, the spatial organization of habitations suggests collective rule carried on by leaders of large groups and based on a kinship ideology. But this line of argument has been questioned very recently.[122] It is argued that it relies too heavily on analogies derived from the ethnographic literature of the last two centuries. But it still remains the case that in the present state of our knowledge, what can be observed is the perpetuation of the power of rulers no doubt established before the seventh century. In such cases there was no dynastic pre-eminence, no hierarchies, no marked difference in standards of living. The fact that we are here dealing with agglomerated sites suggests the likelihood of a collective government. The data also probably indicate that the territory thus controlled was very small, corresponding perhaps to a village. Altogether comparable examples can be studied in the forest zones of West Africa.

Collective representations: religions, ideologies, arts

A large part of the African continent was divided between two monotheisms. Islam was continually expanding between the seventh and eleventh century.[123] Christianity disappeared from the whole of northern Africa[124] where it had been established in the Roman period and continued to exist solidly only in Nubia and Ethiopia; a large Christian minority survived in Egypt. Both monotheisms had built a universalizing civilization with which they endeavoured to replace the pre-existing cultures, to a greater or lesser degree, depending on place and time. Christianity was far from being able to overcome the internal divisions that were, to a large degree, the product of its intimate union with the post-Roman authorities. Neither the Copts nor the Nubians nor the Ethiopians were linked to

121. P. de Maret, 1977–8.
122. Critique by M. Hall, 1984.
123. See Chapters 3, 4 and 10 above.
124. Its last cultural manifestations and its last traces date from the eleventh century. See Chapter 3 above.

Rome, or even to Byzantium. However brilliant these African Christianities may have been, and they were particularly rich in monasteries, they lived on without much contact with the worlds outside, at least so far as concerns the Mediterranean. A study is needed, particularly for the period discussed here, of their relations with the Christians of Asia, also separated from Rome and Byzantium, in particular with the Nestorians, whose ecclesiastical organization extended as far as China; too few questions have been asked in this area.

The influence of Islam, a religion and a culture that spread right across the known world from Asia to the Atlantic and, for long, separated the blacks in Africa from the peoples to the north of the Mediterranean, grew stronger and stronger, as it achieved greater unity. In the tenth century this unity was strongly threatened by the temporary triumph of Fāṭimid Shī'ism throughout Muslim Africa. In the eleventh century the advance of Sunnism, based, in Africa, on Mālikite law, began. It was a way of life that gradually came to dominate, made up of legal and social observances and respect for the fundamental rules of Islam. Gradually, Muslim norms were to triumph, in profoundly Islamized areas, over older cultural ways. Broadly speaking, it can be estimated that this had happened throughout the north of the continent by the end of the eleventh century.[125] Advances were made in the Sahel and along the East African coast; but in these last two cases the real cultural triumph of Islam was to come only in the following period. And it is probable that in future we shall have to pay greater attention to the compromises that power-holders were forced into when they converted to Islam, in the Sahel and elsewhere, faced as they were with societies whose functioning ancestral religious norms were incompatible with certain of the demands of Islam.[126] It is this that explains both the slowness of progress in some areas, the prolonged urban character of the process of Islamization and the outraged violence of pious jurists against 'slack' rulers, a violence whose effects were felt over several centuries, especially after the fourteenth century. An early example of this violence is perhaps to be sought in the Islamization by the Almoravids of some areas of West Africa at the end of the eleventh century.

For historians, it would be much more important to know what African religion was at the time. We can only interpret the few snippets of information we have with the help of information relating to much more recent periods. There is much talk of 'rain-makers', of 'charms', of 'ancestor

125. Cf. Chapters 2 and 4 above. Beneath the appearance of unity interesting survivals of syncretic cults, of Christianity, Judaism and Khāridjism did persist. This is not the place to discuss them.

126. An example of compromise of which al-'Umari speaks as late as the fourteenth century: Mansa Mūsā of Mali revealed, in Cairo, that there existed within his empire 'pagan populations *whom he did not oblige to pay the tax on infidels*, but whom he employed to extract gold from the mines'. Cf. also Chapter 3 above.

worship', of 'idols' – the word comes from monotheistic sources – of 'sorcery'. This sort of approach simply hides our ignorance; it stresses the reassuring continuities and eliminates any evolution; it remains dangerously vague. Here we are in the presence of another great lacuna in research on ancient Africa, a lacuna that it will be possible to fill only partially and only then by developing new methodologies.

The notion that cultures have of the authorities to whom they entrust the leadership of societies is, of course, linked both to the dominant ideologies and to economic structures. We have seen above the probable diversity of concrete forms of authority. The monotheisms placed all authority in the light of the service of God and of a delegation of authority made by Him: even if the *imām* of Tāhert did not resemble the imāmal power of the Fāṭimids, even if the latter saw themselves as closer to God and the caliphs of the Prophet than the Aghlabid *amīr*s or Idrīsid princes; whatever the case, these dynasties ruled in the name of God and Qoran. The situation was exactly the same, in terms of the relationship with God, with the Nubian kings and the Neguses of Ethiopia, although as yet we know little for this period of the theoretical analysis of this relationship to God.[127]

The situation was different in parts of Africa that had remained faithful to its religion and the socio-economic structures that it gave rise to. The development of large states led to the appearance of an interesting and novel conception of power, often improperly called 'divine kingship'. For more than a century, scholars have noted that the ideologies of kingship were very similar from one end of Africa south of the Sahara to the other. The holder of power was 'sacred', that is respected in so far as he fulfilled the conditions of the human contract that bound him to his group; and also feared, as he – and he alone – was obliged to transgress the ordinary rules of social life; the example most often cited of these transgressions is incest. This individual had a positive effect on the environment and fertility, on rain and water, on food, on social harmony, on the life of the community. By tacit consent, he possessed supernatural powers inherent in his function or obtained through an accumulation of charms. The queen-mother or the king's sisters or even his wife played a major ritual role. Some points of etiquette and symbols associated with kingship were very similar everywhere. The king must have no physical defect. His feet must not touch the bare earth. He must not see blood or corpses; he remained invisible to the people and hid his face; he only communicated with others through intermediaries. He ate alone and no one must see him drink. G. P. Murdock even went so far as to say that all the African kingdoms resembled one another like peas in a pod.[128] If he should fail seriously in one of his obligations especially as regulator of the harvests, in the integrity of his

127. Although it is perfectly easy to analyse in the case of Roman Christianity. See for example J. Devisse, 1985b.

128. G. P. Murdock, 1959, p. 37.

body or by exceeding his power, the individual in question was more or less summarily physically eliminated.[129] Here, no doubt, lies the greatest concrete difference in the exercise of power in comparison with the Mediterranean worlds.

Similarities between African political powers used to be explained in terms of a shared, single pharaonic origin. This view is less universally accepted today and there is greater stress on the antiquity, local origin and roots in local rites and beliefs of some of the typical features of these political powers: their relations with the land, the source of food, with hunting, with rain, for example. It is also likely that these powers borrowed from one another their most attractive and impressive features: a degree of uniformity perhaps emerged from these borrowings. One example will suffice: that of single or double flange-welded clapperless iron bells. This type of emblem developed in West Africa but is to be found *c.* 1200 in Shaba, at Katoto, in the case of the single bell, while the double bell appears in Zimbabwe in the fifteenth century. The single bell was associated with political and above all military authority, the double bell with kingship proper. There was thus diffusion from Nigeria to Zimbabwe (and to the kingdom of Kongo) before 1500 and from Nigeria to Shaba before 1200, again, probably during the centuries with which we are dealing here.[130] Here is a tangible sign of the diffusion of an element of the divine kingship complex, through channels that are as yet unknown.

An ideology of royalty was certainly also associated with the creation of a kingdom at Mapungubwe. We believe that here the connection between the king and rain was crucial. The king was the supreme rain-maker controlling the rainfall. This was obviously a crucial attribute in a country where rainfall was variable and all crops depended on it. But we know virtually nothing of the other components of this ideology. That of Zimbabwe was to derive from it and when we have information about it – but five centuries later – a good proportion of the elements found in West Africa are also present there.

Thus the factors that favoured the appearance of one or other characteristic feature of this 'divine' kingship were very changeable in time and space. Here again, one must be careful to avoid being overly systematic. Forms of etiquette, rituals, beliefs and symbols varied from century to century and from place to place. Even in the nineteenth century, they were not identical from one kingdom to another and the list of 'divine kingship

129. One example: al-Mas'ūdī, 1965, p. 330: 'As soon as the king [of the Zandj] exercised his power tyrannically and strayed from the rules of equity, they put him to death and excluded his posterity from the succession'. The putting to death of a king for a physical defect or after a given number of years of reign has been the subject of an enormous literature. But despite the presence of these rules as ideological norms in many kingdoms, no case of it has yet been proved.

130. J. Vansina, 1969.

traits' is a composite list. It is rare to find all its features together in a single kingdom. Murdock's similarity is thus in part fictive.

The complexity of the aspects of power appears almost physically in the period under review. In the regions where trade became essential, power could not be indifferent to the way in which it was controlled; nor could it be to the mastery of gold, copper or iron for example. Thus aspects of power that did not exist in a society of hunter-gatherers or in a simple farming group made their appearance.

The rulers of Ghana were assuredly supposed, like others, to be physically strong: the deception reported by al-Bakrī to hide the blindness of one of them is sufficient proof of that;[131] but it was still the commercial power of these kings that most caught the attention of Arab writers.

Thus, the history of political power seems, in the final analysis, in Africa as elsewhere, to be much more linked to economic and social changes than to ideology: ideology created, as the need arose, the justifications and rituals necessary for the stability and legitimacy of the rulers. What happened then when two legitimacies confronted each other? For example, the legitimacy of the king subject to Allāh and the legitimacy – in the same individual – of the master of iron casting, associated in an ancient alliance with the magician-founders. Merely to ask the question is to answer it. African political powers faced, before the seventh century as after the eleventh and in the centuries in between, contradictions, tensions, choices and evolutions as in any other region of the globe. What is probably today most striking and most disconcerting for historians in this field is the extreme flexibility of the ideological adaptations that reduced contradictions and conflicts, at least so long as the demands of Christianity or Islam did not supervene.

Religion and ideologies treat of the cultural substance. The arts are the expression of this substance. At this level, a distinction is made between two groups of different traditions: the tradition of the *oikoumene*[132] and the tradition of the arts of regional tradition. For the latter, we possess direct knowledge only of the visual remains.

The Muslim world subordinates art to the life of the Islamic community. Collective monuments, even if they are built at the instance of the political authorities are, primarily, those where this community meets to pray and perform acts of faith. The mosque is at the centre of Muslim architecture. There do of course exist styles, recognizable at first glance, due to the prevailing order, the fashion of the times or the functions given to this or that part of the building; certainly too, each dynasty endeavoured to put its stamp on its mosques. Neither the Tulunids in Fusṭāṭ, nor the Aghlabids in Ḳayrawān, nor the Fāṭimids in Mahdiyya or Cairo nor the Almoravids in Morocco or Spain nor the Almohads were exceptions to this

131. Al-Bakrī, 1913, pp. 174–5.
132. See Ch. 8, note 94 above.

rule. But, over and above differences of detail, the mosque proclaimed the unity of the Muslim *umma*.

In all other areas, the discreet luxury of an aristocracy of government, war or trade might develop. This class was never ostentatious, but developed, in these centuries, a taste for luxury that shows clearly in the production of cloths, sculpted ivories and wood, ceramics, mosaics or sometimes murals. In this field as in that of architecture, borrowings moved, following fashion, from one continent to another. And the taste for luxury is so obvious that the 'expatriates' who settled south of the Sahara to trade carried it with them in its most beautiful forms and products.[133]

Before the end of the eleventh century, the Muslim world produced luxury goods, fine objects that sold very well: already, for example, at Fusṭāṭ at the end of the tenth century, Chinese celadons, hitherto imported at great expense were being copied.

The arts of Nubia and Ethiopia, more self-contained, yet still borrowing from the Mediterranean basin, have been mentioned in this volume. The place taken by murals in Christian art is in sharp contrast to Muslim practice. The slight influence of the one on the other – of Muslim art on Christian art and vice-versa – is worth stressing. It is negative proof that styles did not spread automatically but followed religious and political lines of force. In this sense, visual art was still an expression of the dominant ideology and world view.

It was long thought and written that nothing remained of the visual arts of Africa south of the Sahara, since wood, the preferred material of artistic expression, did not stand the ravages of time! Moreover, if these arts did exist, they could have been no more than what was disparagingly called 'tribal'. The journey across the world of the magnificent exhibition of *Treasures of Ancient Nigeria*[134] has put such notions where they belong and led, along with other recent discoveries and exhibitions, to the question being reopened. Nok has impressed many people over many years:[135] this figurative ceramic art, whose products, in so many varied styles, were spread over almost a millennium beginning in the seventh century before the Christian era, revealed at one stroke the historical depth of the African artistic past. There was then a tendency to move on directly to the production of Ife, in the twelfth century, Ife being seen as the consequence of Nok. The error lay in believing that not much existed for the period between these two manifestations and that ceramic art was limited to Nigeria. Today, it has become clear that Nok was not a closed entity, that figurative ceramic art was also found beyond it and that during our period a plastic art developed that has been found from Tegdaoust to Jenne-Jeno,

133. See the remarkable recent work by a Tunisian researcher on this: A. Louhichi, 1984.

134. E. Eyo and F. Willett, 1980, 1982.

135. See Unesco, *General History of Africa*, Vol. II, Ch. 24.

in Niger,[136] south of Lake Chad[137] and no doubt elsewhere, notably too at Igbo-Ukwu. There are great stylistic differences. In the present state of research, one may speak of a regional Upper Niger tradition that expressed itself not only in ceramics but in small metal objects and, *c.* 1100, at Bandiagara, also in wood. It is likely that many other objects in wood were carved at this time but have perished. The preservation of wooden neck-rests and a few statuettes at Bandiagara is due to conditions of conservation that were exceptional, but which may be found elsewhere.

Throughout West Africa a figurative expression existed that used baked clay to conserve its products; this production and these techniques were spread over centuries and go back well before the seventh century. Study of them needs now to be co-ordinated and rationalized. But we must also mention in passing the very fine artistic quality of ceramic vases found at Sintiu-Bara, in Senegal, dated to the sixth century, which it seems very likely can be considered as cultural indicators over a much wider geographical area.[138] What did this artistic output correspond to? What did it represent as an aesthetic need, as an ideological projection? Who ordered it? All so many questions that remain, for the present, unanswered.

In Central Africa two wooden items, the one a helmet mask representing an animal, the other a head on a post dating from the end of the first millennium have survived. They at least show that the practice of carving existed in Angola. Rock drawings are abundant in Angola, and even more so in Central Africa: they have unfortunately been neither carefully collated, nor studied nor, *a fortiori*, dated.[139] In East Africa, a few figurines of cattle dating from this period come from the White Nile and human figurines from Uganda. In Southern Africa, the period of ceramic masks in the Transvaal came to an end *c.* 800. There is perhaps a link with some gold-covered objects found at Mapungubwe. These objects were certainly the precursors of the stone sculpture that developed later in Zimbabwe. But Mapungubwe was only one case among many in the region. Elsewhere, there were, in our period, clay figurines of cattle and of other domestic animals and of human females in sites of the Leopard's Kopje tradition. They are also found in older sites in Zimbabwe (Gokomere). In central Zambia (Kalomo), similar figurines of the period studied here show strong stylistic differences to those in Zimbabwe. It should not be forgotten, finally, that the very rich rock art in Zimbabwe died out in the eleventh century, while less complex rock-art styles continued to exist in Namibia and Southern Africa, no doubt the work of the San.

Enough has been said to show that a plastic art existed everywhere south of the *oikoumene*, but that so far only traces of it have been discovered. The

136. B. Gado, 1980. Other discoveries have been made more recently by the same author.

137. G. Connah, 1981, pp. 136 *et seq.*

138. G. Thilmans and A. Ravisé, 1983, pp. 48 et seq. See also Chapter 13 above.

139. On Angolan rock drawings, cf. C. Ervedosa, 1980, with a full bibliography.

spread of stylistic provinces is not yet clear. And we have only vague ideas about the role played by these works and their purpose. Even in the cases where objects have been found, as in Southern Africa, there has not been enough research. One day, however, it can be anticipated that some gaps will be filled and that we will be able to reconstruct a history of art for the arts of regional tradition as has been done for the art of the *oikoumene*. Contrary to what is so often said and repeated, it is not at all certain that these ancient African arts were as strongly dominated by religious needs and ideas as they were in the *oikoumene*, unless of course, any and every ideology and value system is called religion.

Conclusion

Five centuries of growing stability, of societies putting down roots, of development in the widest sense of the word. Five centuries marked both by the more coherent exploitation of various environments and the appearance of Islam, which, in the long run, altered the old balances. Five centuries of unequal development, from which some regions of the continent emerge fully from the documentary shadow and enable us to reconstruct, through patient work and methodological inventiveness, the technical, social, cultural and political changes under way. Five centuries during which too some regions remain very inadequately known, which means that we have not done enough work. Central Africa, certainly, was at this time involved in a process of intense socio-political organization: one senses it almost everywhere, but too often the evidence is still lacking.

When one measures the distance research has travelled, especially for these five centuries, over the last twenty years, a journey of which this volume bears the imprint, one cannot but consider this period as one of those on which very serious efforts should be concentrated, in all fields of research, to fill out the knowledge, so intriguing but so incomplete, that we already have of it.

An observer living in 600 could not, even in the broadest outline, have foreseen what Africa would be in 1100. But an observer living in 1100 could have predicted in broad outline what the human situation in the continent would be in 1500 and on the cultural level even in 1900. And that is the significance of the five formative centuries that have been presented in this volume.

Members of the International Scientific Committee for the Drafting of a General History of Africa

The dates cited below refer to dates of membership.

Professor J. F. A. Ajayi
(Nigeria), from 1971
Editor Volume VI

Professor F. A. Albuquerque Mourao
(Brazil), from 1975

Professor A. A. Boahen
(Ghana), from 1971
Editor Volume VII

H. E. Boubou Hama
(Niger), 1971–8 (resigned)

H. E. M. Bull
(Zambia), from 1971

Professor D. Chanaiwa
(Zimbabwe), from 1975

Professor P. D. Curtin
(USA), from 1975

Professor J. Devisse
(France), from 1971

Professor M. Difuila
(Angola), from 1978

Professor H. Djait
(Tunisia), from 1975

The late Professor Cheikh Anta Diop
(Senegal), 1971–86; deceased 1986

Professor J. D. Fage
(UK), 1971–81 (resigned)

H. E. M. El Fasi
(Morocco), from 1971
Editor Volume III

Professor J. L. Franco
(Cuba), from 1971

The late Mr M. H. I. Galaal
(Somalia), 1971–81; deceased 1981

Professor Dr V. L. Grottanelli
(Italy), from 1971

Professor E. Haberland
(Federal Republic of Germany), from 1971

Dr Aklilu Habte
(Ethiopia), from 1971

H. E. A. Hampate Ba
(Mali), 1971–8 (resigned)

Dr I. S. El-Hareir
(Libya), from 1978

Dr I. Hrbek
(Czechoslovakia), from 1971
Assistant Editor Volume III

Dr A. Jones
(Liberia), from 1971

The late Abbé Alexis Kagame
(Rwanda), 1971–81; deceased 1981

Professor I. N. Kimambo
(Tanzania), from 1971

Professor J. Ki-Zerbo
(Upper Volta), from 1971
Editor Volume I

Mr D. Laya
(Niger), from 1979

Dr A. Letnev
(USSR), from 1971

Dr G. Mokhtar
(Egypt), from 1971
Editor Volume II

Professor P. Mutibwa
(Uganda), from 1975

Professor D. T. Niane
(Senegal), from 1971
Editor Volume IV

Professor L. D. Ngcongco
(Botswana), from 1971

Professor T. Obenga
(People's Republic of the Congo),
from 1975

Professor B. A. Ogot
(Kenya), from 1971
Editor Volume V

Professor C. Ravoajanahary
(Madagascar), from 1971

The late Professor W. Rodney
(Guyana), 1979–80; deceased 1980

The late Professor M. Shibeika
(Sudan), 1971–80; deceased 1980

Professor Y. A. Talib
(Singapore), from 1975

The late Professor A. Teixeira da Mota
(Portugal), 1978–82; deceased 1982

Mgr T. Tshibangu
(Zaïre), from 1971

Professor J. Vansina
(Belgium), from 1971

The late Rt Hon. Dr E. Williams
(Trinidad and Tobago), 1976–8;
resigned 1978; deceased 1980

Professor A. A. Mazrui
(Kenya)
Editor Volume VIII, not a
member of the Committee

Professor C. Wondji
(Ivory Coast)
Assistant Editor Volume VIII, not
a member of the Committee

Secretariat of the International Scientific Committee
M. Glélé, Director, Division of Studies
and Dissemination of Cultures,
1, rue Miollis, 75015 Paris

Biographies of authors

CHAPTER 1 — I. Hrbek (Czechoslovakia); specialist in Arabic, African and Islamic history as well as in the Arabic sources of the history of Africa; author of many works and articles in these fields; researcher at the Oriental Institute, Prague, and scientific consultant to the Czechoslovak Academy of Sciences.

CHAPTER 2 — M. El Fasi (Morocco); author of a number of works (in Arabic and French) dealing with linguistic history and literary criticism; former Vice-Chancellor of the Ḳarāwiyyīn University in Fez.

CHAPTER 3 — I. Hrbek/M. El Fasi.

CHAPTER 4 — Z. Dramani-Issifou (Benin); specialist in relations between Black Africa and the Maghrib; author of numerous papers and an important work on the subject.

CHAPTER 5 — F. de Medeiros (Benin); specialist in African historiography; author of works on the relations between Black African world and the other peoples.

CHAPTER 6 — S. Lwango-Lunyiigo (Uganda); specialist in early African history, particularly the African Iron Age; author of numerous works on the subject.

J. Vansina (Belgium); specialist in African history; author of numerous works and articles on pre-colonial history of Africa; Professor of History, the University of Wisconsin, Madison (U.S.A.).

CHAPTER 7 — T. Bianquis (France); specialist in tenth- and eleventh-century history of Arab Orient; author of a work entitled *Histoire de Damas et de la Syrie sous la domination fatimide*; former director of the Institut français d'études arabes, Damascus; at present lecturer in Islamic history and civilization at the University Lumière-Lyon II.

CHAPTER 8 — S. Jakobielski (Poland); specialist in Christian archaeology; has published works on Coptic script; lecturer in Archaeology of Nubia, Catholic Academy of Theology, Warsaw; member of Polish Centre of Mediterranean Archaeology in Cairo.

CHAPTER 9 — H. Mones (Egypt); specialist in general history of Islam; has published works on this subject; Professor of History, Faculty of Arts, University of Cairo; member of the Arabic language Academy, Cairo.

CHAPTER 10 — M. Talbi (Tunisia); Islamologist; has published many works and articles on the various aspects of Islamic religion and culture; former teacher at the Faculty of Arts, Tunis.

CHAPTER 11 — T. Lewicki (Poland), specialist in the history of the Maghrib and in the history of Sudan in the Middle Ages; author of numerous works on the subject; Professor at Jagellonne University, Krakow.

CHAPTER 12 — I. Hrbek.

CHAPTER 13 — J. Devisse (France); specialist in the history of North-West Africa from the fourth to the sixteenth century; archaeologist; has published many articles and works on the history of Africa; Professor of African History at the University of Paris I, Panthéon-Sorbonne.

I. Hrbek.

CHAPTER 14 J. Devisse.

CHAPTER 15 D. Lange (Federal Republic of Germany); specialist in the pre-colonial history of the central Sudan; has published various works on this period; former teacher at the University of Niamey.

B. Barkindo (Nigeria); specialist in pre-colonial and early colonial inter-state relations in the Chad basin; author of numerous works on the subject; lecturer in History, Bayero University, Kano.

CHAPTER 16 Thurstan Shaw (U.K.); author of numerous works on the prehistory of West Africa; Professor of Archaeology; Vice-President of the Pan-African Congress on Prehistory; President of the Prehistoric Society.

CHAPTER 17 B. W. Andah (Nigeria); specialist in African history, archaeology and anthropology; author of numerous works on the subject; Professor of Archaeology and Anthropology at the University of Ibadan.

J. R. Anquandah (Ghana); specialist in history and archaeology of Africa from the early Metal Age to c. 1700; has published numerous works on the subject; lecturer in Archaeology, University of Ghana, Legon.

CHAPTER 18 B. W. Andah.

CHAPTER 19 Tekle-Tsadik Mekouria (Ethiopia); historian, writer; specialist in the political, economic and social history of Ethiopia from its origins to the 20th century; retired.

CHAPTER 20 E. Cerulli (Italy); ethnologist; author of works on the subject.

CHAPTER 21 F. T. Masao (Tanzania); archaeologist; specialist in the Later Stone Age and Prehistory rock art; author of numerous works on the subject; Director, the National Museums of Tanzania.

H. W. Mutoro (Kenya); specialist in African archaeology; author of numerous works on the subject.

CHAPTER 22 C. Ehret (U.S.A.); linguist and historian of East Africa; has published many works and articles on the pre-colonial and colonial history of East Africa; teaches at the University of California, Los Angeles.

CHAPTER 23 D. W. Phillipson (U.K.); museum curator and archaeologist; specialist in the prehistory of sub-Saharan Africa with emphasis on the eastern and southern regions; author of numerous works on these topics and editor of the *African Archaeology Review*; lecturer at the University of Cambridge.

CHAPTER 24 T. N. Huffman (U.S.A.); specialist in social and cultural anthropological archaeology and the prehistory of sub-Saharan Africa; author of works on the subject.

CHAPTER 25 (Mme) B. Domenichini-Ramiaramanana (Madagascar); specialist in Malagasy language and literature; author of numerous works on the civilization of Madagascar; Vice-President of the section of Language, Literature and

Arts at the Malagasy Academy; teaches oral literature and cultural history at the University of Madagascar; Senior Researcher in the sciences of the language at the Centre national de la recherche scientifique (CNRS), Paris.

CHAPTER 26 Y. A. Talib (Singapore); specialist in Islam, the Malay world and the Middle East, particularly South-West Arabia; author of works on the subject; Associate Professor; Head, Department of Malay Studies, National University of Singapore.

F. El-Samir (Iraq); specialist in Islamic history; author of numerous works on the subject.

CHAPTER 27 A. Bathily (Senegal); specialist in the history of Western Sudan from the eighth to the nineteenth centuries; has published numerous works on the subject.

C. Meillassoux (France); specialist in economic and social history of West Africa; author of many works on the subject; Senior Researcher at the CNRS, Paris.

CHAPTER 28 J. Devisse/J. Vansina.

Bibliography

The publishers wish to point out that while every effort has been made to ensure that the details in this Bibliography are correct, some errors may occur as a result of the complexity and the international nature of the work.

Abbreviations and list of periodicals

AA *American Anthropologist*, Washington, DC
AARSC *Annales de l'Académie Royale des Sciences Coloniales*, Brussels
AAW *Abhandlungen der Königlich Preussischen Akademie der Wissenschaften*, Berlin
AB *Africana Bulletin*, Warsaw: Warsaw University
Actes Coll. Bamako I *Actes du 1er Colloque International de Bamako, organisé par la Fondation SCOA pour la Recherche Scientifique en Afrique noire.* (Projet Boucle du Niger), Bamako, 27 January–1 February 1975. Paris: Fondation SCOA, 1976
Actes Coll. Bamako II *Actes du 2è Colloque International de Bamako, organisé par la Fondation SCOA pour la Recherche Scientifique en Afrique noire* (Projet Boucle du Niger), Bamako, 16–22 February 1976. Paris: Fondation SCOA, 1977
Actes 1er Coll. Intern. Archéol. Afr. *Actes du Premier Colloque International d'Archéologie Afrique.* (Fort-Lamy, 11–16 Décembre 1966), Fort-Lamy: Inst. National Tchadien pour les Sciences Humaines, 1969
Actes Coll. Intern. Biolog. Pop. Sahar. *Actes du Colloque International de Biologie des Populations Sahariennes*, Algiers, 1969
Actes VIe Congr. PPEQ *Actes du Sixième Congrès Pan-Africain de Préhistoire et des études du Quaternaire*, Dakar: Cambéry, 1967
AE *Annales d'Ethiopie*, Paris
AEH *African Economic History*, Madison, Wisconsin
AES *Afrikanskiy etnograficheskiy sbornik*, Moscow-Leningrad
AF *Altorientalische Forschungen, Schriften zur Geschichte und Kultur des Alten Orients*, Akademie der Wissenschaften der DDR, Berlin
AFLSHD *Annales de la Faculté des Lettres et Sciences Humaines*, Université de Dakar
Africa (IAI) *Africa*, International African Institute, London
Africa (INAA) *Africa*, Institut National d'Archéologie et de l'Art, Tunis
African Arts *African Arts*, African Studies Center, University of California, Los Angeles
AHES *Annales d'Histoire Economique et Sociale*, Paris
AHS *African Historical Studies* (became *IJAHS* in 1972), Boston University, African Studies Center
AI *Annales Islamologiques* (earlier *Mélanges*), Cairo: Institut Français d'Archéologie Orientale du Caire
AIEOA *Annales de l'Institut d'Etudes Orientales de l'Université d'Alger*, Alger: Faculté des Lettres
AIMRS *Annales de l'Institut mauritanien de Recherche Scientifique*, Nouakchott
AION *Annali dell' Istituto Orientale di Napoli*, Naples
AJ *Africana Journal*, New York
AJPA *American Journal of Physical Anthropology*
AKM *Abhandlungen für die Kunde des Morgenlandes*, Deutsche Morgenlandische Gesellschaft, Leipzig
AL *Annali Lateranensi*, Vatican
ALR *African Language Review* (now) *African Languages*, London: International African Institute
ALS *African Language Studies*, London: School of Oriental and African Studies
AM *Africana Marburgensia*, Marburg
AMRAC *Annales du Musée Royal d'Afrique Centrale*, Sciences Humaines. Tervuren, Belgium
AN *African Notes*, Ibadan: University of Ibadan, Institute of African Studies
ANM *Annals of the Natal Museum*, Durban
Annales ESC *Annales–Economies, Sociétiés, Civilisations*, Paris
Ann. Rev. Anthropol. *Annual Review of Anthropology*
ANYAS *Annals of the New York Academy of Sciences*, New York
AQ *Africa Quarterly*, New Delhi

Arabica *Arabica: Revue des études*, Leiden: Brill
Ar. Anz. *Archäeologischer Anzeiger*, Berlin (West)
ARB *Africana Research Bulletin*, Freetown: Institute of African Studies
Archaeology *Archaeology*, Boston: Archaeology Institute of America
Archaeometry *Archaeometry*, Oxford: Research Laboratory of Archaeology and the History of Arts
Archeologia *Archeologia*, London
Archéologia *Archéologia*, Paris
AROR *Archiv Orientalní, Oriental Archives*, Prague
Ars Orientalis *Ars Orientalis: the Arts of Islam and the East*, Washington, DC: Smithsonian Institution
AS *African Studies* (continues as *Bantu Studies*), Johannesburg
ASAG *Archives Suisses d'Anthropologie générale*, Geneva
ASR *African Studies Review*, Camden, New Jersey
Atti IV Congr. Int. Studi Etiop. *Atti de IV Congresso Internazionale di studi etiopici, Roma 10–15 Aprile 1972*, Roma: Accad. Naz. dei Lincei
AuÜ *Afrika und Übersee*, Hamburg
AUA *Annales de l'Université d'Abidjan*, Abidjan
AUM *Annales de l'Université de Madagascar*, Tananarive.
Azania *Azania: Journal of the British Institute of History and Archaeology in Eastern Africa*, London
BA *Baessler Archiv*, Berlin, Museum für Völkerkunde
BAB *Bulletin Antieke Beschaving. Annual Papers on Classical Antiquity*, Leiden
BASEQA *Bulletin de l'Association sénégalaise pour l'étude du Quarternaire africain*, Dakar-Fann
BASP *Bulletin of the American Society of Papyrologists*
BCCSP *Bolletino del Centro Camuno di Studi Preistorici*
BCEHS *Bulletin du Comité d'Etudes Historiques et Scientifiques de l'Afrique occidentale française*, Dakar
BEO *Bulletin d'Etudes Orientales*, Damascus: Institut Français de Damas
BGA *Berliner geographische Abhandlungen*, Berlin: Freie Universität
BIE *Bulletin de l'Institut d'Egypte*, Cairo
BIFAN *Bulletin de l'Institut Français (later Fondamental) de l'Afrique Noire*, Dakar
BMAPM *Bulletin du Musée d'Anthropologie Préhistorique de Monaco*
BMNV *Bulletin du Musée National de Varsovie*, Warsaw
BNR *Botswana Notes and Records*, Gaborone
BS *Bantu Studies*, Johannesburg
BSA Copte *Bulletin de la Société d'Archéologie Copte*, Cairo
BSARSC *Bulletin des Séances de l'Académie Royale des Sciences Coloniales*, Brussels
BSGAO *Bulletin de la Société de Géographie et Archéologie d'Oran*, Oran
BSOAS *Bulletin of the School of Oriental and African Studies*, London
BSPF *Bulletin de la Société Préhistorique Française*, Paris
BUPAH *Boston University Papers in African History*, Boston: Boston University, African Studies Center
Byzantion *Byzantion*, Brussels
Cahiers du CRA *Cahiers du Centre de Recherches Africaines*, Paris
CAMAP *Travaux du Centre d'Archéologie Méditerranéenne de l'Académie Polonaise des Sciences*, Warsaw
CCM *Cahiers de Civilisation Médiévale*
CEA *Cahiers d'Etudes Africaines*, Paris: Mouton
CHM *Cahiers d'Histoire Mondiale*, Paris: Librairie des Méridiens
CORSTOM *Cahiers de l'Office de la Recherche Scientifique et Technique d'Outre-Mer*, Paris
C-RAI *Compte-Rendu des Séances de l'Académie des Inscriptions et Belles-Lettres*, Paris
CSSH *Comparative Studies in Society and History*, Cambridge
CT *Cahiers de Tunisie: Revue des Sciences Humaines*, Tunis: Faculté de Lettres
CUP *Cambridge University Press*
EHA *Etudes d'Histoire Africaines*, Kinshasa
EP *Etnografia Polska*, Wroclaw
EUP *Edinburgh University Press*
FO *Folia Orientalia*, Krakow
GNQ *Ghana Notes and Queries*, Legon
GSSJ *Ghana Social Science Journal*, Legon
HA *History in Africa: A Journal of Method*, Waltham, Massachusetts
Hespéris *Hespéris*, Rabat: Institut des Hautes Etudes Marocaines
L'Homme *L'Homme, Cahiers d'Ethnologie, de Géographie et de Linguistique*, Paris

HT *Hespéris-Tamuda*, Rabat: Université Mohammed V, Faculté de Lettres et des Sciences Humaines
HUP Harvard University Press
IAI Institute of African Studies, London
IC *Islamic Culture*, Hyderabad
IFAN Institut fondemental de l'Afrique noire
IJAHS *International Journal of African Historical Studies*, Boston
IJAL *International Journal of American Linguistics*, Chicago: Linguistic Society of America
IRSH Institut de Recherches Humaines, Niamey
Islam *Der Islam: Zeitschrift für Geschichte und Kultur des islamischen Orients*, Berlin
JA *Journal asiatique*, Paris
JAH *Journal of African History*, Cambridge: Cambridge University Press
JAL *Journal of African Languages*, London
J. Afr. Soc. *Journal of the African Society*, London
JARCE *Journal of the American Research Center in Egypt*, Boston, Massachusetts
JAS *Journal of African Studies*, Los Angeles
JEA *Journal of Egyptian Archaeology*, London
JES *Journal of Ethiopian Studies*, Addis Ababa
JESHO *Journal of Economic and Social History of the Orient*, Leiden
JHSN *Journal of the Historical Society of Nigeria*, Ibadan
JRAS *Journal of the Royal Asiatic Society of Great Britain and Ireland*, London
JSA *Journal de la Société des Africanistes*, Paris
JSAIMM *Journal of the South African Institute of Mining and Metallurgy*, Johannesburg
KHR *Kenya Historical Review*, The Journal of the Historical Association of Kenya, Nairobi
KS *Kano Studies*, Kano, Nigeria
KSINA *Kratkiye Soobcheniya Instituta Narodow Azii Akademii Nauk SSSR*, Moscow-Leningrad
KUP Khartoum University Press
Kush *Kush*, Journal of the Sudan Antiquities Service, Khartoum
Likundoli *Likundoli*, Sér. B, Archives et Documents, Lubumbashi
LNR *Lagos Notes and Records*, Lagos
LSJ *Liberian Studies Journal*, Newark, Delaware
MAIB-L *Mémoires de l'Académie des Inscriptions et de Belles-Lettres*, Paris
Man *Man*, London
MBT *Madjallat al-buḥūth al-ta'rīkhīyya*, Tripoli
MHAOM *Mélanges d'Histoire et d'Archéologie de l'Occident Musulman*, Algiers, 1957, 2 vols
MLI *Mare-Luso-Indicum*
MSOS *Mitteilungen des Seminars für Orientalische Sprachen an der Friedrich-Wilhelm Universität zu Berlin*
NA *Notes Africaines*: Bulletin d'Information de l'IFAN, Dakar
NAA *Narodui Azii i Afriki*, Moskva
Nyame Akuma *Nyame Akuma*, Calgary: University of Calgary, Department of Archaeology
NC *Nubia Christiana*, Warsaw, Academy of Catholic Theology
NCAA *Nouvelles du Centre d'Art et d'Archéologie*, Antananarivo, Université de Madagascar
NUP Northwestern University Press
Odu, *Odu*, Ife
OH *Orientalia Hispanica*, Leiden: Brill
Omaly sy Anio *Omaly sy Anio*, Antananarivo
OUP Oxford University Press
PA *Présence Africaine*, Paris-Dakar
Paideuma *Paideuma. Mitteilungen zur Kulturkunde*, Frankfurt
PBA *Proceedings of the British Academy*, London
Proc. KNAW *Proceedings-Koniglijke Nederlansche Akademie van Wetenschapen*, Amsterdam
Proc. Preh. Soc. *Proceedings of the Prehistoric Society*, Cambridge
PS *Palestinskiy Sbornik*, Moscow-Leningrad
PUF Presses Univeritaires de France
PUP Princeton University Press
RA *Revue Africaine.* Journal des travaux de la Société Historique algérienne, Alger
RAC *Rivista di Archeologia Cristiana*, Pontificia Commissione di archeologia sacra, Rome
RAI Royal Anthropological Institute, London
Radiocarbon *Radiocarbon, Annual Supplement to the American Journal of Sciences*, New York
REI *Revue des Etudes Islamiques*

RFHOM *Revue française d'Histoire d'Outre-mer*, Paris
RHES *Revue d'Histoire Economique et Sociale*, Paris
RHM *Revue d'Histoire Maghrébine*, Tunis
RHPR *Revue d'Histoire de la Philosophie religieuse*, Strasbourg
RIE *Revista del Instituto Egipcio*, Madrid
RMAOF *Revue militaire de l'A.O.F*
RMN *Rocznik Muzeum Narodowego w Warszawie*, *Annuaire du Musée National de Varsovie*, Warsaw
RO *Rocznik Orientalistyczny: Polish Archives of Oriental Research*, Warszaw
ROMM *Revue de l'Occident Musulman et de la Méditerranée*, Aix-en-Provence
RPAR *Rendiconti della Pontificia Accademia Romana di Archeologia*, Rome
RPC *Recherche, Pédagogie et Culture*, Paris: AUDECAM
RS *Revue Sémitique*, Paris
RSE *Rassegna di studi etiopici*, Rome
RT *Revue tunisienne*
SAAB *South African Archeological Bulletin*, Cape Town
SAJS *South African Journal of Science*, Johannesburg
Sankofa *Sankofa: The Legon Journal of Archaeology and Historical Studies*, Legon
SE *Sovietskaya Etnografiya*, Moscow
SFHOM Société française d'histoire d'Outre-Mer, Paris
SI *Studia Islamica*, Paris
SJE *The Scandinavian Joint Expedition to Sudanese Nubia Publications*, Uppsala, Lund, Odense, Helsinki
SLLR *Sierra Leone Language Review*, Freetown
SNR *Sudan Notes and Records*, Khartoum
Sources Orales et Histoire *Sources Orales et Histoire*, Valbonne, CEDRASEMI
STB *Sudan Texts Bulletin*, Coleraine, New University of Ulster
SUGIA *Sprache und Geschichte in Afrika*, Cologne, Institut für Afrikanistik der Universität zu Köln
SWJA *South-Western Journal of Anthropology* (now *Journal of Anthropological Research*), Albuquerque, New Mexico
Taloha *Taloha*, Tananarive
Tarikh *Tarikh*, Historical Society of Nigeria
THSG *Transactions of the Historical Society of Ghana*, Legon
TIRS *Travaux de l'Institut de Recherches Sahariennes*, Alger
TJH *Transafrican Journal of History*, Nairobi: East African Literature Bureau
TNR *Tanganyika Notes and Records* (now *Tanzania Notes and Records*), Dar es Salaam
UJ *Uganda Journal*, Kampala
UWP University of Wisconsin Press
WA World Archaeology, Henley-on-Thames, England
WAAN *West African Archaeological Newsletter*, Ibadan
WAJA *West African Journal of Archaeology*, Ibadan
WZHU-S *Wissenschaftliche Zeitschrift der Humboldt Universität Ges. Sprachwissenschaft*, Berlin DDR
WZKM *Wiener Zeitschrift für die Kunde des Morgenlandes*, Vienna
YUP Yale University Press
ZÄS *Zeitschrift für Ägyptische Sprache und Altertumskunde*, Leipzig
ZDMG *Zeitschrift der Deutschen Morgenländischen Gesellschaft*, Leipzig

Bibliography

al-ʿAbbādī, A. M. (1960) 'Dirāsa hawla Kitāb al-Ḥulal al-Mawshīyya ...', *Tiṭwān*, 5, 1960, pp. 139–58.
al-ʿAbbādī, A. M. and al-Kattānī, M. I. (1964) *Al-Maghrib al-ʿarabī fi l-ʿaṣr al-wāsiṭ* (Dar al-Bayḍā).
Abdalla, A. M. (ed.) (1964) *Studies in Ancient Languages of the Sudan* (Papers presented at the Second International Conference on Language and Literature in the Sudan, 7–12 December 1970, Khartoum: KUP).
ʿAbd ar-Raḥmān, M. ʿAbd al-Ṭawāb (1977) *Stèles islamiques de la nécropole d'Assouan. I* (Cairo: IFAO).
ʿAbd al-Wahhāb, Ḥ. Ḥ. (1965–72) *Al-Warakāt* (3 vols, Tunis).
Abimbola, W. (1975) *Sixteen Great Poems of Ife* (Niamey).
Abir, M. (1970) 'Southern Ethiopia' in R. Gray and D. Birmingham (eds), pp. 119–38.

Abitbol, M. (1979) *Tombouctou et les Arma. De la conquête marocaine du Soudan nigérien en 1591 à l'hégémonie de l'empire peul du Macina en 1833* (Paris: Maisonneuve-Larose).
Abitbol, M. (1981) 'Juifs maghrébins et commerce trans-saharien du VIIIe au XVe siècle' in *(Le) sol, la parole et l'écrit*, Vol. 2, pp. 561–77.
Abraham, D. P. (1962) 'The early political history of the kingdom of Mwene Mutapa (850–1589)' in *Historians in Tropical Africa* (Salisbury: University College of Rhodesia and Nyasaland), pp. 61–91.
Abraham, D. P. (1966) 'The roles of "Chaminuka" and the Mhondoro-cults in Shona political history' in E. Stokes and R. Brown (eds), pp. 28–46.
al-Abshīhī, A. (1872) *Kitāb al-Mustaṭraf fi kull fann al-mustaẓraf* (Cairo).
Abū l-'Arab Tamīn (1920) *Kitāb Tabaḳāt 'Ulamā Ifrīḳiyya*, ed. by M. Ben Cheneb (Algiers: Publ. de la Fac. des Lettres).
Abu 'l-Fidā (1840) *Géographie d'Aboulféda*, Arabic text ed. by M. Reinaud et M. G. de Slane (Paris: Imprimerie Royale).
Abu 'l-Fidā (1848–83), *Géographie d'Aboulféda* trans. by M. Reinaud et S. Guyard (3 vols, Paris: Imprimerie Royale).
Abu Ṣāliḥ (1969) *The Churches and Monasteries of Egypt and some Neighbouring Countries*, tr. by B. T. Evetts and A. J. Butler (Oxford: Clarendon Press, reprint).
Abu Tammām (1828–47) *Ḥamāsa*, ed. by G. Freytag (2 vols, Bonn).
Abun-Nasr, J. M. (1971) *A History of the Maghrib* (Cambridge: CUP).
Adam, P. (1979) 'Le peuplement de Madagascar et le problème des grandes migrations maritimes' in M. Mollat (ed.), pp. 349–56.
Adams, R. McC. (1966) *The Evolution of Urban Society* (London: Weidenfeld & Nicolson).
Adams, W. Y. (1962a) 'Pottery kiln excavations', *Kush*, **10**, pp. 62–75.
Adams, W. Y. (1962b) 'An introductory classification of Christian Nubian pottery', *Kush*, **10**, pp. 245–88.
Adams, W. Y. (1964) 'Sudan Antiquities Service excavations at Meinarti, 1962–3', *Kush*, **12**, pp. 227–47.
Adams, W. Y. (1965a) 'Sudan Antiquities Service excavations at Meinarti 1963–4', *Kush*, **13**, pp. 148–76.
Adams, W. Y. (1965b) 'Architectural evolution of the Nubian church 500–1400 AD', *JARCE*, **4**, pp. 87–139.
Adams, W. Y. (1966) 'The Nubian Campaign – a retrospect' in *Mélanges offerts à K. Michałowski* (Warsaw: PWN), pp. 13–20.
Adams, W. Y. (1967–8) 'Progress Report on Nubian pottery, 1. The native wares', *Kush*, **15**, pp. 1–50.
Adams, W. Y. (1970) 'The evolution of Christian Nubian pottery' in E. Dinkler (ed.), pp. 111–128.
Adams, W. Y. (1977) *Nubia – Corridor to Africa* (London: Allen Lane).
Adams, W. Y. (1978) 'Varia Ceramica', *Etudes Nubiennes*, 1978, pp. 1–23.
Adams, W. Y. (1982) 'Qasr Ibrim, an archaeological conspectus' in J. M. Plumley (ed.), 1982a, pp. 25–38.
Afigbo, A. E. (1973) 'Trade and trade routes in nineteenth century Nsukka' *JHSN*, **7**, 1, pp. 77–90.
Ahmed Chamanga, M. and Gueunier, N.-J. (1979) *Le dictionnaire comorien–français et français–comorien du R. P. Sacleux* (Paris: SELAF).
Aḥmad, K. (1976) *Islam, Its Meaning and Message* (London: Islamic Council for Europe).
Ajayi, J. F. A. and Crowder, M. (eds) (1971, 1976, 1985) *History of West Africa*, Vol. 1 (London: Longman, 1st edn 1971, 2nd edn 1976, 3rd edn 1985).
Alagoa, E. J. (1970) 'Long-distance trade and states in the Niger Delta', *JAH*, **11**, 3, pp. 319–29.
Alexandre, P. (1981) *Les Africains. Initiation à une longue histoire et à des vieilles civilisations, de l'aube de l'humanité au début de la colonisation* (Paris: Editions Lidis).
Al-Hajj, M. A. (1968) 'A seventeenth-century chronicle on the origins and missionary activities of the Wangarawa', *KS*, 1, 4, pp. 7–42.
'Alī, Djawād (1952–6) *Ta'rikh al-'Arab ḳabla 'l-Islām* (8 vols, Baghdād).
Alkali, N. (1980) 'Kanem-Borno under the Safawa' (unpublished PhD thesis, Ahmadu Bello University).
Allen, J. de V. (1981) 'Swahili culture and the nature of East coast settlement', *IJAHS*, **14**, pp. 306–34.
Allen, J. de V. (1982) 'The "Shirazi" problem in East African coastal history', *Paideuma*, **28**, pp. 9–27.
Allen, J. W. T. (1949) 'Rhapta', *TNR*, **27**, pp. 52–9.
Allibert, C., Argan, A. and Argan, J. (1983) 'Le site de Bagameyo (Mayotte)', *Etudes Océan Indien*, **2**, pp. 5–10.
Allison, P. (1968) *African Stone Sculpture* (London: Lund Humphries).
Allison, P. (1976) 'Stone sculpture of the Cross River Nigeria', *BCCSP*, **13–14**, pp. 139–52.

Amari, M. (1933–9) *Storia dei Musulmani di Sicilia* (2nd edn, 3 vols, Catania: Prampolini).
Amblard, S. (1984) *Tichitt-Walata (R.I. de Mauritanie). Civilisation et industrie lithiques* (Paris: ADPF).
Amilhat, P. (1937a) 'Les Almoravides au Sahara', *RMAOF*, **9**, 34, pp. 1–39.
Amilhat, P. (1937b) 'Petite chronique des Id ou Aïch, héritiers guerriers des Almoravides sahariens', *REI*, **1**, pp. 41–130.
Ambrose, S. H. (1982) 'Archaeology and linguistic reconstructions of history in East Africa' in C. Ehret and M. Posnansky, (eds), pp. 104–57.
Amīn, Aḥmad (1969a) *Fadjr al-Islām* (Beirut, 10th edn).
Amīn, Aḥmad (1969b) *Ḍuḥa al-Islām* (3 vols, Beirut, 10th edn).
Andah, B. W. (1973) 'Archaeological reconnaissance of Upper Volta' (unpublished PhD thesis, University of California, Berkeley).
Anderson, R. (1981) 'Texts from Qasr Ibrim', *STB*, **3**, pp. 2–4.
Anfray, F. (1974) 'Deux villes axoumites: Adoulis et Matara'. *Atti IV Congr. Intern. Studi Etiop.*, pp. 725–65.
Anquandah, J. (1976) 'The rise of civilisation in the West African Sudan. An archaeological and historical perspective', *Sankofa*, **2**, pp. 23–32.
Anquandah, J. (1982) *Rediscovering Ghana's Past.* (London: Longman).
Arkell, A. J. (1951–2) 'The History of Darfur: 1200–1700 A.D.', *SNR*, **32**, pp. 37–70, 207–38; **33**, pp. 129–55, 244–75.
Arkell, A. J. (1961) *A History of the Sudan from the Earliest Times to 1820* (London: Athlone Press, 2nd revised edn).
Armstrong, R. G. (1960) 'The development of kingdoms in Negro Africa', *JHSN*, **2**, 1, pp. 27–39.
Armstrong, R. G. (1962) 'Glottochronology and African linguistics' *JAH*, 3, 2, pp. 283–90.
Armstrong, R. G. (1964a) *The Study of West African Languages* (Ibadan: Ibadan UP).
Armstrong, R. G. (1964b) 'The use of linguistic and ethnographic data in the study of Idoma and Yoruba history' in J. Vansina *et al.* (eds), pp. 127–44.
Arnold, T. W. (1913) *The Preaching of Islam. A History of the Propagation of the Muslim Faith* (2nd edn, London: Constable).
Ashtor, E. (1969) *Histoire des prix et des salaires dans l'Orient médiéval.* (Paris: SEVPEN).
Ashtor, E. (1976) *A Social and Economic History of the Near East in the Middle Ages* (London: Collins).
Assimi, K. (1984) 'Les Yarsé. Fonction commerciale, religieuse et légitimité culturelle dans le pays moaga (Evolution historique) (Thèse de doctorat de 3ème cycle, Université de Paris).
Atherton, J. H. (1972) 'Excavations at Kamabai and Yagala rock shelters', *WAJA*, **2**, pp. 39–74.
Atherton, J. H. and Kalous, M. (1970) 'Nomoli', *JAH*, **11**, 3, pp. 303–17.
Atlas National du Sénégal (1977) (Dakar).
Austen, R. A. (1979) 'The trans-saharan slave trade: a tentative census' in H. Gemery, and J. Hogendorn (eds), pp. 23–76.
Azaïs, R. P. and Chambord, R. (1931) *Cinq années de recherches archéologiques en Ethiopie, province du Harar et Ethiopie méridionale* (Paris).
d'Azevedo, W. L. (1962) 'Some historical problems in the delineation of a central West Atlantic region', *ANYAS*, **96**, art. 2.
Asín-Palacios, M. (1914) *Abenmasarra y su escuela; orígenes de la filosofía hispano-musulmana* (Madrid: Imprenta Ibérica).
Attema, D. S. (1949) *Het Oudste Christendom in Zuid-Arabië* (Amsterdam: Noord-Hollandsche).

Ba, A. R. (1984) 'Le Takrūr des origines à la conquête par le Mali, VIe–XIIIe siècle' (Thèse de doctorat de 3ème cycle, Université de Paris VII–Jussieu).
Badawi, A. (1976) *Al-Sūd wa'l-haḍārah al-'Arabiyah* (Cairo).
al-Bakrī (1911) *Description de l'Afrique septentrionale.* (Arabic text ed. by Baron Mac Guckin de Slane (2nd edn, Algiers: Adolphe Jourdan).
al-Bakrī (1913) *Description de l'Afrique septentrionale par el-Bekri*, tr. by Baron Mac Guckin de Slane (revised and corrected edn of 1859 1st edn, Paris: Geuthner).
al-Balādhurī (1866) *Liber expugnationis regionum* ... [*Kitāb Futūḥ al-Buldān*], ed. by M. J. de Goeje (Leiden: Brill).
al-Balādhurī, Aḥmad b. Yaḥyā (1883) [*Anṣāb al-Ashrāf*]. *Anonyme arabische Chronik. Bd. XI, vermutlich das Buch der Verwandschaft und Geschichte der Adligen* ed. by W. Ahlwardt (Greifswald).
al-Balādhūrī (1957) *Futūḥ al-Buldān* ed. by Ṣalāḥ al-Munadjdjid (Cairo).
Balog, P. (1981) 'Fāṭimid glass jetons: token currency or coin weights?', *JESHO*, **24**, pp. 91–109.
Balogun, S. A. (1980) 'History of Islam up to 1800' in O. Ikime (ed.), pp. 210–23.

Barcelo, M. (1975) 'El hiato en las acunaciones de oro en al-Andalus, 127–317/744–5–929', *Moneda y Credito*, **132**, pp. 33–71.

Barcelo, M. (1979) 'On coins in al-Andalus during the Umayyad Emirate (138–300)', *Quaderni ticinesi di numismatica e antichità classiche*, Lugano, pp. 313–23.

Barkindo, B. (1985) 'The early states of the Central Sudan: Kanem, Borno and some of their neighbours to *c.* 1500 A.D.' in J. F. A. Ajayi and M. Crowder (eds) (1985), pp. 225–54.

Barns, J. (1974) 'A Text of the Benedicite in Greek and Old Nubian from Kasr el-Wizz', *JEA*, **60**, pp. 206–11.

Barrau, J. (1962) 'Les plantes alimentaires de L'Océanie, origines, distribution et usages', *Annales du Musée colonial de Marseille*, **7**, pp. 3–9.

Barreteau, D. (ed.) (1978) *Inventaire des études linguistiques sur les pays d'Afrique Noire d'expression française* (Paris: SELAF).

Barros, João de (1552) *Decadas da Asia* (4 vols, Lisbon, 2nd edn, 1778).

Barth, H. (1857–8) *Reisen und Entdeckungen in Nord und Central Africa in den Jahren 1849 bis 1855* (5 vols, Gotha: J. Perthes).

Barth, H. (1857–9) *Travels and Discoveries in North and Central Africa* (3 vols, New York: Harper).

Barth, H. (1860–1) *Voyages et découvertes dans l'Afrique septentrionale et centrale pendant les années 1849 à 1855* (4 vols, Paris-Brusells: A. Bohné).

Bascom, W. R. (1955) 'Urbanization among the Yoruba', *American Journal of Sociology*, **60**, pp. 446–53.

Basset, H. (1920) *Essai sur la littérature des Berbères* (Algiers: Carbonel).

Basset, H. (1952) *Les langues berbères* (London: OUP).

Basset, R. (1893) 'Les inscriptions arabes de l'Ile de Dahlak', *JA*, 9th series, **1**, pp. 77–111.

Bastin, Y., Coupez, A., and de Halleux, B. (1981) 'Statistique lexicale et grammaticale pour la classification historique des langues bantoues', *BSARSC* (forthcoming).

Bates, M. L. (1981) 'The function of Fāṭimid and Ayyūbid glass weights', *JESHO*, **24**, pp. 63–92.

Bathily, A. (1975) 'A discussion of the traditions of Wagadu with some reference to ancient Gh̲āna', *BIFAN* (B), **37**, **1**, pp. 1–94.

Bathily, I. D. (1969) 'Notices socio-historiques sur l'ancien royaume soninké du Gadiaga, présentées, annotées et publiées par Abdoulaye Bathily', *BIFAN* (B), **31**, pp. 31–105.

Batrān, A. A. (1973) 'A contribution to the biography of Shaikh Muhammad ... al-Mag̲h̲ili', *JAH*, **14**, 3, pp. 381–94.

Battistini, R. (1976) 'Les modifications du milieu naturel depuis 2000 ans et la disparition de la faune fossile à Madagascar', *BASEQA*, **47**, pp. 63–76.

Battistini, R. and Vérin, P. (1967) 'Irodo et la tradition vohémarienne', *Taloha*, **2**, pp. xvii–xxxii.

Battistini, R. and Vérin, P. (1971) 'Témoignages archéologiques sur la côte vezo de l'embouchure de l'Onilahy à la Baie des Assassins', *Taloha*, **4**, pp. 19–27.

Battistini, R., Vérin, P. and Rason, R. (1963) 'Le site archéologique de Talaky, cadre géologique et géographique, premiers travaux de fouilles', *AUM* (Série Lettres et Sciences Humaines), **1**, pp. 112–53.

Baumann, H. and Westermann, D. (1948) *Les peuples et les civilisations de l'Afrique* (Paris: Payot).

Bazuin-Sira, B. T. (1968) 'Cultural remains from the Tellem caves near Pégué (Falaise de Bandiagara), Mali, West Africa', *WAAN*, **10**, pp. 14–15.

Beale, P. O. (1966) *The Anglo-Gambian Stone Circles Expedition 1964/65* (Bathurst: Government Printer).

Beale, P. O. (1968) 'The stone circles of the Gambia and the Senegal', *Tarikh*, **2**, **2**, pp. 1–11.

Beale, T. W. (1973) 'Early trade in highland Iran: a view from a source area', *WA*, **5**, **2**, pp. 133–48.

Becker, C. H. (1902–3) *Beiträge zur Geschichte Ägyptens unter dem Islam* (2 vols, Strassburg: Trübner).

Becker, C. H. (1910) 'Zur Geschichte des östlichen Sudan', *Der Islam*, **1**, **2**, pp. 153–77.

Bedaux, R. M. A. (1972) 'Tellem, reconnaissance archéologique d'une culture de l'Ouest africain au Moyen Âge – Recherches architectoniques', *JSA*, **42**, pp. 103–85.

Bedaux, R. M. A. (1974) 'Tellem, reconnaissance archéologique d'une culture de l'Ouest africain au Moyen âge: les appuie-nuques', *JSA*, **44**, pp. 7–42.

Bedaux, R. M. A. and Bolland, R. (1980) 'Tellem, reconnaissance archéologique d'une culture de l'Ouest africain au Moyen âge: les textiles', *JSA*, 50, pp. 9–24.

Bedaux, R. M. A., Constandse-Westermann, T. S., Hacquebord, L., Lange, A. G. and Van der Waals, J. D. (1978) 'Recherches archéologiques dans le Delta intérieur du Niger', *Palaeohistoria*, **20**, pp. 91–220.

Beeston, A. F. L. (1960) ''Abraha' in H. A. R. Gibb *et al.* (eds), pp. 102–3.

Békri, C. (1957) 'Le Kharijisme berbère: quelques aspects du royaume rustumide', *AIEOA*, **15**, pp. 55–108.

Bel, A. (1903) *Les Benuou Ghânya, derniers représentants de l'empire Almoravide et leur lutte contre l'empire Almohade* (Paris: Leroux).

Bello, M. (1951) *Infaku'l maisuri*, ed. by C. E. J. Whitting (London: Luzac).

Ben Achour (1985) 'L'onomastique arabe au sud du Sahara: ses transformations' (Thèse de doctorat de 3ème cycle, Université de Paris I).

Ben Romdhane, K. (1978) 'Les monnaies almohades, apsects idéologiques et économiques' (2 vols, thèse de doctorat de 3ème cycle, Université de Paris, VII).

Berchem, M. van (1952) 'Deux campagnes de fouilles à Sedrata en Algérie', *C-RAI*, pp. 242–6.

Berchem, M. van (1954) 'Sedrata. Un chapitre nouveau de l'histoire de l'art musulman. Campagnes de 1951 et 1952', *Ars Orientalis*, **1**, pp. 157–72.

Bercher, H., Courteaux, A., and Mouton, J. (1979) 'Une abbaye latine dans la société musulmane: Monreale au XIIe siècle', *Annales, ESC*, **34**, 3, pp. 525–47.

Bergé, M. (1972) 'Mérites respectifs des nations selon le Kitāb al-Intā 'wa-l-Mu'anasa d'Abu Ḥayyān al-Tamḥīdī (+414 H/1023)', *Arabica*, pp. 165–76.

Berger, I. (1981) *Religion and Resistance in East African Kingdoms in the Precolonial Period* (Tervuren: Musée Royale de l'Afrique Centrale).

Bergman, I. (1975) *Late Nubian Textiles* (Uppsala: SJE, 8).

Bernard, A. (1932) *Le Maroc*. (8th edn, Paris: Alcan).

Bernard, J. (ed.) (1982) 'Le sel dans l'histoire', *Cahiers du CRA*, **2**.

Bernard, J. (1983) *Le sang et l'histoire* (Paris: Buchet-Chastel).

Bernus, S. and Gouletquer, P. (1974) *Approche archéologique de la région d'Azelik et de Tegidda N-Tesamt (Agadez)* (Niamey: CNRS).

Bernus, S. and Gouletquer, P. (1976) 'Du cuivre au sel: recherches ethno-archéologiques sur la région d'Azelik (campagnes 1973–75)', *JSA*, **46**, 1–2, pp. 7–68.

Berque, J. (1979) *Les dix grands odes arabes de L'Anté-Islam. Les* Mu'allaqât *presentées et traduites de l'arabe* (Paris: Sindbad).

Berthier, P. (1962) 'En marge des sucreries marocaines: la maison de la plaine et la maison des oliviers à Chichaoua', *HT*, **3**, pp. 75–7.

Berthier, S. (1976) 'Une maison du quartier de la mosquée à Koumbi Saleh' (2 vols, Mémoire de maîtrise, Université de Lyon II).

Berthier, S. (1983) 'Etude archéologique d'un secteur d'habitat à Koumbi-Saleh' (2 vols, thèse de 3ème cycle, Université de Lyon II).

Beshir, I. B. (1975) 'New light on Nubian–Fatimid relations', *Arabica*, **22**, pp. 15–24.

Bianquis, T. (1980) 'Une crise frumentaire dans l'Egypte fatimide', *JESHO*, **23**, pp. 87–101.

Biobaku, S. O. (1955) *The Origin of the Yorubas* (Lagos: Government Printer, Lugard Lectures).

Biobaku, S. O. (ed.) (1973) *Sources of Yoruba History* (Oxford: Clarendon Press).

Bird, C. S. (1970) 'The development of Mandekan (Manding): a study of the role of extra-linguistic factors in linguistic change' in D. Dalby (ed.), pp. 146–59.

Birmingham, D. (1977) 'Central Africa from Cameroun to the Zambezi' in R. Oliver (ed.), pp. 519–66.

al-Bīrūnī (1887) *Alberuni's India* . . ., Arabic text ed. by E. C. Sachau (London: Trübner).

al-Bīrūnī (1888) *Alberuni's India* . . ., English text ed. by E. C. Sachau (2 vols, London: Trübner).

al-Bīrūnī (1933) in Y. Kamal (ed.) *Monumenta Cartographica Africae et Aegypti*, Vol. 3 (Leiden: Brill).

al-Bīrūnī (1934) *The Book of Instruction in the Elements of the Art of Astrology by al-Bīrūnī*, tr. by R. Wright (London: Luzac).

Bisson, M. S. (1975) 'Copper currency in central Africa: the archeological evidence', *WA*, **6**, pp. 276–92.

Bivar, A. D. and Shinnie, P. L. (1970) 'Old Kanuri capitals' in J. D. Fage and R. A. Oliver (eds), pp. 289–302.

Blachère, R. (1966) *Le Coran* (Paris: PUF).

Blachère, R., Chouémi, M., Denizeau, C. (1967–) *Dictionnaire arabe–français–anglais* (Paris: Maisonneuve & Larose).

Blanck, J.-P. (1968) 'Schema d'évolution géomorphologique de la Vallée du Niger entre Tombouctou et Labhérange (République du Mali)', *BASEQA*, **19–20**, pp. 17–26.

Blau, O. (1852) 'Chronik der Sulṭâne von Bornu', *ZDMG*, **6**, pp. 305–30.

Bleek, W. H. I. (1862–9) *A Comparative Grammar of South African Languages* (2 vols, Cape Town: Juta/London: Trübner).

Bloch, M. (1977) 'Disconnection between power and rank as a process: an outline of the development of kingdoms in Central Madagascar', *AES*, **17**, pp. 107–48.

Boachie-Ansah, J. (1978) 'Archaeological contribution to Wenchi history' (unpublished MA thesis, University of Ghana, Legon).
Boahen, A. A. (1977) 'Ghana before the Europeans' *GSSJ*, 1.
Bohrer, S. P. (1975) 'Radiological examination of the human bones' in G. Connah, pp. 214–17.
Boiteau, P. (1974–9) 'Dictionnaire des noms malgaches de végétaux', *Fitoterapia* (Milano) 1974, **2**, p. 39; 1979, **4**, p. 192.
Boiteau, P. (1977) 'Les proto-Malgaches et la domestication des plantes', *Bull. de l'Académie Malgache*, **55**, 1–2, 1979, pp. 21–6.
Bolens, L. (1974) *Les méthodes culturales au Moyen Age d'après les traités d'agronomie andalous: traditions et techniques* (Geneva: Editions Médecine et Hygiène).
Bomba, V. (1977) 'Traditions about Ndiadiawe Ndiaye, first Buurba Djolof. Early Djolof, the southern Almoravids and neighbouring peoples', *BIFAN*, (B), **39**, 1, pp. 1–35.
Bomba, V. (1979) 'Genealogies of the Waalo matrilineages of Dioss Logre and Tediegue. Versions of Amadou Wade and Yoro Dyao', *BIFAN* (B), **41**, 2, pp. 221–47.
Bonnassié, P. (1975) *La Catalogne du milieu du Xe à la fin du XIe siècle. Croissance et mutations d'une société* (2 vols, Toulouse: Université de Toulouse-le-Mirail).
Boser-Sarivaxévanis, R. (1972) *Les tissus de l'Afrique occidentale.* (Basel: Basler Beiträge zur Ethnologie).
Boser-Sarivaxévanis, R. (1975) *Recherches sur l'histoire des textiles traditionnels tissés et teints de l'Afrique occidentale* (Basel: Basler Beiträge zur Ethnologie).
Boulnois, J. (1943) 'La Migration des Sao du Tchad', *BIFAN* (B), **5**, pp. 80–121.
Boulnois, J. and Hama, B. (1954) *L'empire de Gao* (Paris: Miasonneuve).
Bouquiaux, L. and L. Hyman (eds) (1980) *L'expansion bantoue* (Paris: SELAF).
Bovill, E. W. (1933) *Caravans of the Old Sahara* (London: OUP).
Bovill, E. W. (1958) *The Golden Trade of the Moors* (London: OUP).
Bradbury, R. E. (1959) 'Chronological problems in the study of Benin History', *JHSN*, 1, 4, pp. 263–86.
Brett, M. (1969) 'Ifrīqiya as a market for Saharan trade from the tenth to the twelfth century, A.D.', *JAH*, **10**, 3, pp. 347–64.
Brett, M. (1972) 'Problems in the interpretation of the history of the Maghrib in the light of some recent publications', *JAH*, **13**, 3, pp. 489–506.
Brett, M. (1975) 'The military interest of the Battle of Haydarān' in V. J. Parry, and M. E. Yapp (eds), pp. 78–88.
Brothwell, D. R. (1963) 'Evidence of early population change in central and southern Africa: doubts and problems', *Man*, **63**, pp. 101–4.
Browne, G. M. (1979–81) 'Notes on Old Nubian', I–III, *BASP*, **16**, 1979, pp. 249–56; IV–V, *BASP*, **17**, 1980, pp. 37–43; VI–VII, *BASP*, **17**, 1980, pp. 129–41; VIII–X, *BASP*, **18**, 1981, pp. 55–67.
Browne, G. M. (1982a) 'The Old Nubian verbal system', *BASP*, **19**, pp. 9–38.
Browne, G. M. (1982b) *Griffith's Old Nubian Lectionary* (Rome-Barcelona: Papyrologica Castroctaviana, 8).
Browne, G. M. (1983) *Chrysostomus Nubianus. An Old Nubian Version of Ps.- Chrysostom 'In Venerabilem Crucem Sermo'* (Rome-Barcelona: Papyrologica Castroctaviana, **9**).
Brunschwig, R. (1942–47) 'Ibn ʿAbd al-Hakam et la conquête de l'Afrique du Nord par les Arabes. Etude critique', *AIEOA*, **6**, pp. 108–55.
Brunschwig, R. (1947) *La Berbérie orientale sous les Hafsides. Des origines à la fin du XVe siècle* (2 vols, Paris: Maisonneuve).
Brunschwig, R. (1957) 'Fiqh fatimide et histoire d'Ifrīqīyya', *MHAOM*, **2**, pp. 13–20.
Brunschwig, R. (1960) ''Abd' in H. A. R. Gibb *et al.* (eds) (1960) pp. 24–40.
Brunschwig, R. (1967) 'Conceptions monétaires chez les juristes musulmans', *Arabica*, **14**, pp. 113–43.
Brunschwig, R. (1974) 'L'Islam enseigné par Ḥāmid b. Ṣiddīq de Harar (XVIIIe siècle)', *Atti IV Congr. Int. Studi Etiop*, **1**, pp. 445–54.
Bryan, M. A. (1959) *The Bantu Languages of Africa* (London: IAI).
Budge, E. A. W. (1909) *Texts relating to Saint Mena of Egypt and Canons of Nicaea in a Nubian Dialect* (London: OUP).
al-Bukhārī (1978) *Kital al-jāmīʿ al-ṣahiḥ* (tr. and notes by Muḥammad Asad (New Delhi).
Bulliet, R. W. (1975) *The Camel and the Wheel* (Cambridge, Mass.: HUP).
Burke III, E. (1975) 'Towards a history of the Maghrib', *Middle Eastern Studies*, **2**, 3, p. 306.
Burton-Page, J. (1971) 'Habshī' in B. Lewis *et al.* (eds), pp. 14–16.
Butterworth, J. S. (1979) 'Chemical analysis of archaeological deposits from Thatswane Hills, Botswana', *SAJS*, **75**, 9, pp. 408–9.

Buxton, D. R. (1971) 'The rock-hewn and other medieval churches of Tigré Province, Ethiopia', *Archaeologia* (London), **103**, pp. 33–100.
Buzurg Ibn Shahriyār (1883–6) *Kitāb 'Adjā'ib al Hind*; 1883 edn. ed. by P. A. van der Lith (Vol. 1) and 1886 French transl. by M. Devic (Vol. 2), *Livre des merveilles d'Inde* (Leiden: Brill).

Cabanis, Y., Chabonis, L. and Chabonis, F. (1969–70) *Végétaux et groupements végétaux de Madagascar et des Mascareignes* (Tananarive: BDPA).
Cahen, C. (1961) 'La changeante portée sociale de quelques doctrines sociales' in *L'Elaboration de l'Islam*, pp. 5–22.
Cahen, C. (1965) 'Quelques problèmes concernant l'expansion économique musulmane au haut moyen âge', *Settimani di Studio del Centro Italiano di studi sull'alto medioevo*, **12**, pp. 391–432.
Cahen, C. (1968) 'Quelques mots sur les Hilaliens et la nomadisme', *JESHO*, **11**, pp. 130–3.
Cahen, C. (1970) 'Le commerce musulman dans l'Océan Indien au Moyen âge' in *Sociétés et Compagnies de commerce en Orient et dans l'Océan Indien.* (Paris: SEVPEN), pp. 180–93.
Cahen, C. (1972) 'L'administration financière de l'armée fatimide d'après al-Makhzumi', *JESHO*, **15**, 1–2, pp. 305–27.
Cahen, C. (1977) *Les peuples musulmans dans l'histoire médiévale* (Damascus: Institut Français de Damas).
Cahen, C. (1979) 'L'or du Soudan avant les Almoravides, mythe ou réalité?', *RFHOM*, **66**, pp. 169–75.
Cahen, C. (1980) 'Commercial relations between the Near East and the Western Europe from the VIIth to the XIth century' in K. I. Semaan (ed.) pp. 1–25.
Cahen, C. (1981) 'L'or du Soudan avant les Almoravides: mythe ou réalité?' in (*Le*) *Sol, la Parole et l'Ecrit*, Vol. 2, pp. 539–45.
Cahen, C. (1983) *Orient et Occident au temps des croisades* (Paris: Augier).
Cali, M. N. (1980) 'Outline of early Somali history from a linguistic perspective' (Paper delivered at International Conference of Somali Studies, Muqdishu, July 1980).
Calvocoressi, D. and David, N. (1979) 'A new survey of radiocarbon and thermoluminescence dates for West Africa', *JAH*, **20**, 1, pp. 1–29.
Camps, G. (1969) 'Haratin-Ethiopiens, réflexions sur les origines des négroïdes sahariens' in *Actes, Coll. Intern. Biolog. Pop. Sahar.*, pp. 11–20.
Camps, G. (1970) 'Recherches sur les origines des cultivateurs noirs du Sahara', *ROMM*, **7**, pp. 35–45.
Camps, G. (1979) 'Les relations du monde méditerranéen et du monde subsaharien durant la préhistoire et la protohistoire' in *Recherches Sahariennes*, **1**, pp. 9–18.
Camps, G. (1980) *Berbères, aux marges de l'histoire* (Paris: Hespérides).
Canard, M. (1942–7) 'L'impérialisme des Fāṭimides et leur propagande', *AIEOA*, **6**, pp. 162–99.
Canard, M. (ed.) (1958) *Vie de l'ustadh Jaudhar* (Algiers: Publications de l'Institut d'Etudes Orientales de la Faculté des Lettres d'Alger).
Canard, M. (1965) 'Fāṭimids' in B. Lewis *et al.* (eds), pp. 850–62.
Cancellieri, J. A. (1982) *Economie génoise et or du Soudan aux XIIe et XIIIe siècles* (Rome: Ecole française de Rome, ronéo).
Carbou, H. (1912) *La région du Tchad et du Ouadaï* (2 vols, Paris: Leroux).
Castiglione, L., Hajnóczi, G., Kákosy, L. and Török, L. (1974–5) *Abdallah Nirqi 1964, The Hungarian Excavations in Egyptian Nubia* (Budapest: Acta Archaeologica Academiae Scientiarum Hungaricae, **26**–**27**).
Castro, R. (1974) 'Examen de creusets de Marandet (Niger)', *BIFAN* (B), **36**, 4, pp. 667–75.
Caudel, M. (1900) *L'Afrique du Nord. Les Byzantins, les Berbères, les Arabes, avant les invasions* (Paris: Leroux).
Cenival, P. de and Monod, T. (1938) *Description de la côte d'Afrique de Ceuta au Sénégal par Valentin Fernandes* (Paris: Larose).
Centre d'Etudes et de Recherche Marxiste (1974) *Sur le 'mode de production asiatique'* (2nd edn, Paris: Editions Sociales).
Cerulli, E. (1936) *Studi Etiopici* (Rome: Istituto per l'Oriente).
Cerulli, E. (1941) 'Il sultanato dello Scioa nel secolo XIII secondo un nuovo documento storico', *RSE*, **1**, pp. 5–42.
Cerulli, E. (1956) *Storia della letteratura etiopica* (Milan: Nuova Accademia Editrice).
Cerulli, E. (1957–64) *Somalia. Scritti vari editi ed inediti* (3 vols, Rome: Amministrazione Fiducitaria Italiana di Somalia).
Cerulli, E. (1971) *L'Islam di ieri e di oggi.* (Rome: Istituto per l'Oriente).
Chamla, M.-C. (1968) *Les populations anciennes du Sahara et des régions limitrophes. Etudes des restes osseux humains néolithiques et protohistoriques* (Paris: Arts et Métiers graphiques).

Champault, F. D. (1969) *Une oasis du Sahara nord-occidental: Tabelbala.* (Paris: CNRS).
Chang Hsing-Lang (1930) 'The importation of Negro slaves to China under the T'ang Dynasty' *Bulletin of the Catholic University of Peking*, 7, pp. 37–59.
Chanudet, C. (1979) 'Problèmes actuels de biogéographie malgache', *Ambario* (Antananarivo), 1, 4, pp. 373–8.
Chanudet, C. and Vérin, P. (1983) 'Une reconnaissance archéologique de Mohéli, *Etude Océan Indien*, 2, pp. 11–58.
Chapelle, J. (1957) *Nomades noirs du Sahara* (Paris: Plon).
Chapelle, J. (1980) *Le peuple tchadien, ses racines et sa vie quotidienne.* (Paris: L'Harmattan and ACCT).
Chapelle, J. (1982) *Nomades noirs du Sahara: les Toubous* (Paris: L'Harmattan).
Charnay, J.-P. (1980) 'Expansion de l'Islam en Afrique Occidentale', *Arabica*, 28, pp. 140–53.
Chavane, B. (1980) 'Recherches archéologiques sur la moyenne vallée du Sénégal' (Thèse de 3ᵉ cycle, Université d'Aix-Marseille, 2 vols).
Chavane, B. (1985) *Villages anciens du Takrūr. Recherches archéologiques dans la vallée moyenne du Sénégal* (Paris: Karthala).
Cheneb, M. (1922) *Abu Dulama, poète-bouffon de la cour des premiers califes abbasides* (Algiers).
Chittick, H. N. (1959) 'Notes on Kilwa', *TNR*, 53, pp. 179–203.
Chittick, H. N. (1963) 'Kilwa and the Arab settlement of the East African coast', *JAH*, 4, 2, pp. 179–90.
Chittick, H. N. (1965) 'The "Shirazi" colonization of East Africa', *JAH*, 6, 3, pp. 275–94.
Chittick, H. N. (1966) 'Unguja Ukuu: the earliest imported pottery, and an Abbasid dinar', *Azania*, 1, pp. 161–3.
Chittick, H. N. (1967) 'Discoveries in the Lamu archipelago', *Azania*, 2, pp. 46–67.
Chittick, H. N. (1968a) 'Two traditions about the early history of Kilwa', *Azania*, 3, pp. 197–200.
Chittick, H. N. (1968b) 'The coast before the arrival of the Portuguese' in B. A. Ogot and J. A. Kieran (eds), pp. 98–114.
Chittick, H. N. (1969) 'A new look at the history of Pate', *JAH*, 10, 3, pp. 375–91.
Chittick, N. H. (1969) 'An archaeological reconnaissance of the southern Somali coast', *Azania*, 4, pp. 115–30.
Chittick, H. N. (1974) *Kilwa: An Islamic Trading City on the East African Coast* (2 vols, Nairobi: British Institute in Eastern Africa).
Chittick, H. N. (1975) 'The peopling of the East African coast' in H. N. Chittick and R. I. Rotberg (eds), pp. 16–43.
Chittick, H. N. (1977) 'The East Coast, Madagascar and the Indian Ocean' in R. Oliver (ed.), pp. 183–231.
Chittick, H. N. (1979a) 'The Arabic sources relating to the Muslim expansion in the western Indian Ocean' in *Mouvements de Populations dans l'Océan Indien* (Paris: Champion), pp. 27–31.
Chittick, H. N. (1979b) 'Sewn boats in the Western Indian Ocean and a Survival in Somalia' in *ICIOS*, 3, *History of the Commercial Exchange and Maritime Transport* (Perth).
Chittick, H. N. (1980) 'L'Afrique de l'Est et l'Orient: les ports et le commerce avant l'arrivée des Portugais' in Unesco (1980), pp. 15–26.
Chittick, H. N. and Rotberg, R. I. (eds) (1975) *East Africa and the Orient* (New York: Africana Publishing).
Chou Ju-Kua (1911) *Chou Ju-Kua. His Work on the Chinese and Arab Trade in the Twelfth and Thirteenth Centuries, entitled Chu-fan-chi* (tr. by F. Hirth and W. W. Rockhill, St Petersburg: Imperial Academy of Sciences).
Christensen, A. (1944) *L'Iran sous les Sassanides* (Paris-Copenhagen: Geuthner).
Christophe, L.-A. (1977) *Campagne internationale de l'Unesco pour la sauvegarde des sites et monuments de Nubie. Bibliographie* (Paris: Unesco).
Churakov, M. (1960) 'Maghrib nakanune kharidjitskogo vosstaniya' [The Maghrib at the dawn of the Kharidjite revolt], *Palestinskiy Sbornik*, 5, 68, pp. 66–84.
Churakov, M. (1962) 'Kharidjitskiye vosstaniya v Magribe' [The Kharidjite revolts in the Maghrib], *Palestinskiy Sbornik*, 7, 70, pp. 101–29.
Churakov, M. V. (1966) 'Borba Kharidjitov Sidjilmasūi' [The struggle of the Kharidjites of Sidjilmāsa] in *Arabskie strany: Istoriya, Ekonomika* (Moscow: Nauka).
Cipolla, C. (1961) 'Appunti per una nuova storia della moneta nell'alto medioevo', *Settimani di Studio del Centro Italiano di studi sull'alto medioevo*, 8, pp. 619–25.
Cissoko, S. M. (1975) *Tombouctou et l'empire songhay.* (Dakar-Abidjan: Nouvelles Editions Africaines).

Clark, J.D. (1968) *Further Palaeo-anthropological Studies in Northern Lunda.* (Lisbon: Publicacoēs cult. Co. Diam. Angola, 78).
Clark, J.D. (1970) *The Prehistory of Africa* (London: Thames & Hudson).
Clark, J.D. (1976) 'Prehistoric populations and pressures favoring plant domestication' in Harlan, J. R. *et al.* (eds) pp. 67–105.
Clarke, S. (1912) *Christian Antiquities in the Nile Valley: A Contribution towards the Study of the Ancient Churches* (Oxford: Clarendon Press).
Cline, W. (1937) *Mining and Metallurgy in Negro Africa* (Menasha: The American Anthropologist).
Coedès, G. (1964) *Les Etats hindouisés d'Indochine et d'Indonésie* (Paris: de Boccard).
Cohen, R. (1962) 'The Just-so So? A spurious tribal grouping in Western Sudanic history', *Man*, **62**, pp. 153–4.
Cohen, R. (1966) 'The Bornu king lists', *BUPAH*, **2**, pp. 39–84.
Cole-King, P. A. (1973) *Kukumba mbiri mu Malaŵi: a summary of archaeological research to March, 1973* (Zomba: Government Press).
Colin, G. S., Babakar, A. O., Ghali, N. and Devisse, J. (1983) 'Un ensemble épigraphique almoravide: découverte fortuite dans la région de Tikjikja: chaton de bague découvert à Tegdaoust' in J. Devisse, D. Robert-Chaleix *et al.* (eds) pp. 427–44.
Collett, D. P. (1979) 'The archaeology of the stone walled settlements in eastern Transvaal, South Africa' (unpublished MSc thesis, University of the Witwatersrand).
Collett, D. P. (1982) 'Excavations of stone-walled ruin types in the Badfontein Valley, eastern Transvaal, South Africa', *SAAB*, **37**, 135, pp. 34–43.
Colloque de Nouakchott (1976) *Colloque de Nouakchott sur les problèmes de la desertification au sud du Sahara* (17–19 December 1973) (Dakar: NEA).
Colloque de Saint-Denis (1972) *Colloque de Saint-Denis (Réunion) sur les mouvements de populations dans l'Océan Indien.*
Condé, A. (1974) *Les sociétés traditionelles mandingues* (Niamey: CRDTO).
Condominas, G. (1965) *L'exotique est quotidien* (Paris: Plon).
Connah, G. (1968) 'Radiocarbon dates for Benin city and further dates for Daima, N. E. Nigeria', *JHSN*, **4**, pp. 313–20.
Connah, G. (1969) 'Ife' in T. Shaw (eds), pp. 47–53.
Connah, G. (1971) 'Recent contributions to Bornu chronology', *WAJA*, **1**, pp. 55–60.
Connah, G. (1972) 'Archaeology in Benin' *JAH*, **13**, 1, pp. 25–39.
Connah, G. (1975) *The Archaeology of Benin* (Oxford: Clarendon Press).
Connah, G. (1976) 'The Daima sequence and the prehistoric chronology of the Lake Chad region of Nigeria', *JAH*, **17**, 3, pp. 321–52.
Connah, G. (1981) *Three Thousand Years in Africa. Man and his Environment in the Lake Chad Region of Nigeria* (Cambridge: CUP).
Conrad, D. C. and Fisher, H. J. (1982) 'The conquest that never was: I. The external Arabic sources', *HA*, **9**, pp. 21–59.
Conrad, D. C. and Fisher, H. J. (1983) 'The conquest that never was: II. The local oral sources', *HA*, **10**, pp. 53–78.
Conti Rossini, C. (1909) 'Les listes des rois d'Aksum', *JA*, **14**, pp. 263–320.
Conti Rossini, C. (1921) 'Expeditions et possessions des Habašat en Arabie', *JA*, July/September, pp. 5–36.
Conti Rossini, C. (1928) *Storia d'Etiopia* (Bergamo: Istituto Italiano d'Arti Grafiche).
Conzelman, W. E. (1895) *Chronique de Galâwdêwos, roi d'Ethiopie* (Paris: Bouillon).
Coon, C. (1968) *Yengema Cave Report* (Philadelphia: University of Pennsylvania, University Museum Monographs).
Coppens, Y. (1969) 'Les cultures protohistoriques et historiques du Djourab' in *Actes Ier Coll. Intern. Archéol. Afr.*, pp. 129–46.
Coquery-Vidrovitch, C. (1969) 'Recherches sur un mode de production africain', *La Pensée*, **144**, pp. 61–78.
Coquery-Vidrovitch, C. (1974) 'Recherches sur un mode de production africain' in Centre d'Etudes et de Recherche Marxiste, pp. 345–67.
Corippus (1970) *Flavii Cresconii Corippi Iohannidos, seu De bellis Libycis, libri VIII*, ed. by J. Diggle and F. R. D. Goodyear (Cambridge: CUP).
Cornevin, M. (1982) 'Les Néolithiques du Sahara australe et l'histoire générale de l'Afrique', *BSPF*, **79**, pp. 439–50.
Cornevin, R. (1960) *Histoire des peuples de l'Afrique Noire* (Paris: Berger-Levrault).
Corrêa, A. A. M. (1943) *Raças do império* (Oporto: Portucalense Editora).
Corso, R. (1949) 'Il velo dei Tuàregh' *Annali, Istituto Orientale di Napoli*, **3**, pp. 151–66.

Cosmas Indicopleustes (1968) *Topographie chrétienne*. (Paris: Le Cerf).
Coulon, C. (1983) *Les musulmans et le pouvoir en Afrique noire* (Paris: Karthala).
Couper, A., Evrard, J. B. and Vansina, J. (1975) 'Classification d'un échantillon de langues bantoues d'après la lexicostatistique', *Africana Linguistica*, **6**, pp. 131–58.
Coursey, D. G. and Alexander, J. (1968) 'African agricultural patterns and the sickle cell', *Science*, **160**, pp. 1474–5.
Courtois, C. (1957) 'Remarques sur le commerce maritime en Afrique au XIe siècle', *MHAOM*, **2**, pp. 51–9.
Crabb, D. (1965) *Ekoid Bantu Languages of Ogoja* (London: OUP).
Crossland, L. B. (1976) 'Excavations at Nyarko and Dwinfuor sites of Begho–1975', *Sankofa*, **2**, pp. 86–7.
Crowfoot, J. W. (1927) 'Christian Nubia', *JEA*, **13**, pp. 141–50.
Cuoq, J. M. (1975) *Recueil des sources arabes concernant l'Afrique occidentale du VIIIe au XVIe siècle (Bilād al-Sūdān)* (Paris: CNRS).
Curtin, P. D. (1971) 'Pre-colonial trading networks and traders: the Diakhanké, in C. Meillassoux (ed.), pp. 228–39.
Curtin, P. D. (1975) *Economic Change in Precolonial Africa. Senegambia in the Era of the Slave Trade* (Madison: UWP).

al-Dabbāgh (1901) *Ma 'ālim al-Īmān* (4 Vols, Tunis).
Dachraoui, F. (1961) 'Contribution à l'histoire des Fatimides en Ifriqiyya', in *Arabica*, **8**, **2**, pp. 141–66.
Dachraoui, F. (1964) 'Le commencement de la prédication Ismailienne en Ifrīqīyya', *SI*, **20**, pp. 92–109.
Dachraoui, F. (1981) *Le Califat fatimide du Maghreb. Histoire politique et institutions* (Tunis: STD).
Daghfūs, R. (1981) 'Al-'awamīl al-iḳtiṣādiyya li-hidjra Banī Hilāl wa-Banī Sulaym min Miṣr ilā Ifrīḳīya' [The economic factors of the B. Hilāl and B. Sulaym emigration from Egypt to Ifrīḳīya], *Awrāq* (Madrid), **4**, pp. 147–63.
Dahl, O. C. (1951) *Malgache et Manjaan. Une comparaison linguistique* (Oslo: Egede-Instituttet).
Dalby, D. (1965) 'The Mel languages: a reclassification of the Southwest Atlantic', *ALS*, **6**, pp. 1–7.
Dalby, D. (ed.) (1970) *Language and History in Africa* (London: Cass).
Dalby, D. (1975) 'The prehistorical implications of Guthrie's *Comparative Bantu*. Part I: problems of internal relationship', *JAH*, **16**, 4, pp. 481–50.
Dalby, D. (1976) 'The prehistorical implications of Guthrie's *Comparative Bantu*. Part II: Interpretation of cultural vocabulary', *JAH*, **17**, 1, pp. 1–27.
Daniels, C. M. (1968) 'Garamantian Excavations: Zinchecra, 1965–1967', *Libya Antiqua*, **5**, pp. 113–94.
Daniels, S. G. H. and Phillipson, D.W. (1969) 'The Early Iron Age site at Dambwa near Livingstone' in B. M. Fagan, D. W. Phillipson and S. G. H. Daniels (eds), Vol. 2, pp. 1–54.
Dark, P. J. C. (1973) *An Introduction to Benin Art and Technology* (Oxford: Clarendon Press).
Darling, P. J. (1974) 'The earthworks of Benin', *Nigerian Field*, **39**, 3, pp. 128–37.
Darling, P. J. (1976) 'Notes on the earthworks of the Benin empire', *WAJA*, **6**, pp. 143–9.
Darling, P. J. (1979) 'Fieldwork surveys in the Benin and Ishan kingdoms', *Nyame Akuma*, **15**, pp. 35–9.
Datoo, B. A. (1970) 'Rhapta: the location and importance of East Africa's first port', *Azania*, **5**, pp. 65–76.
Daveau, S. (1970) 'Itineraire de Tamadalt à Awdaghust selon al-Bakri' in D. Robert, S. Robert and J. Devisse (eds), pp. 33–8.
Daveau, S. and Toupet, C. (1963) 'Anciens terroirs Gangara', *BIFAN* (B), **25**, pp. 193–214.
David N. (1982a) 'Prehistory and historical linguistics in Central Africa: points of contact' in C. Ehret, and M. Posnansky (eds), pp. 78–95.
David, N. (1982b) 'The BIEA Southern Sudan Expedition of 1979: interpretation of the archaeological data' in J. Mack and P. Robertshaw, pp. 49–57.
Davidson, B. (1964) *The African Past* (London: Longmans).
Davies, O. (1967) *West Africa before the Europeans* (London: Methuen).
Davies, O. (1971) 'Excavations of Blackburn', *SAAB*, **26**, 103–4, pp. 165–78.
Davison, C. C., Giaque, R. D. and Clark, J. D. (1971) 'Two chemical groups of dichroic glass beads from West Africa', *Man*, (ns) **6**, 4, pp. 645–59.
Davison, P. and Harries, P. (1980) 'Cotton weaving in south-east Africa: its history and technology', *Textile History*, **11**, pp. 176–92.
De Heinzelin, J. (1962) 'Ishango', *Scientific American*, June, pp. 105–18.

Delafosse, M. (1912) *Haut-Sénégal-Niger (Soudan français)* (3 vols, Paris: Larose).
Delafosse, M. (1924) 'Les relations du Maroc avec le Soudan à travers les âges', *Hespéris*, **9**, pp. 153–74.
Delafosse, M. (1924) 'Le Ghana et le Mali et l'emplacement de leurs capitales', *BCEHS*, **8**, pp. 479–542.
Delafosse, M. (1931) *The Negroes in African History and Culture* (Washington, DC: Associated Publishers).
Delibrias, G., Guillier, M. T. and Labeyrie, J. (1974) 'Gif natural radiocarbon measurements, VIII', *Radiocarbon*, **16**, 1, pp. 15–94.
Denbow, J. R. (1979) 'Iron Age research in eastern Botswana', *Nyame Akuma*, **14**, pp. 7–9.
Denbow, J. R. (1979) '*Cenchrus ciliaris*: an ecological indicator of Iron Age middens using aerial photography in eastern Botswana', *SAJS*, **75**, 9, pp. 405–8.
Denbow, J. R. (1980) 'Early Iron Age remains from Tsodilo Hills', *SAJS*, **76**, pp. 474–5.
Denbow, J. R. (1981) 'Broadhurst – a 14th century AD expression of the Early Iron Age in south-eastern Botswana', *SAAB*, **36**, 134, pp. 66–74.
Denbow, J. R. (1982) 'The Toutswe traditions: a study in socio-economic change in Botswana Society', in *Settlement in Botswana* (London: Heinemann), pp. 73–86.
Denbow, J. R. (1983) 'Iron Age economics: herding, wealth and politics along the fringes of the Kalahari Desert during the Early Iron Age' (unpublished PhD thesis, Indiana University).
Denbow, J. R. (1984) 'Prehistoric herders and foragers of the Kalahari: the Evidence for 1500 years of 'interaction' in C. Schrire (ed.), pp. 175–93.
Derenbourg, H. (1905) 'Le poète antéislamique Antar' in Derenbourg, *Opuscules d'un Arabisant* (Paris: Charles Carrington), pp. 3–9.
Derricourt, R. M. and Papstein, R. J. (1976) 'Lukolwe and the Mbwela of northwestern Zambia', *Azania*, **11**, pp. 169–76.
Desanges, J. (1962) *Catalogues des tribus africaines de l'antiquité classique à l'Ouest du Nil* (Dakar: University of Dakar, Section d'Histoire).
Desanges, J. (1976) 'L'Iconographie du noir dans l'Afrique du nord antique' in J. Vercoutter, J. Leclant, F. Snowden (eds).
Descamps, C., Thilmans, G. and Thommeret, Y. (1974) 'Données sur l'édification de l'amas coquillier de Dioron Boumak', *BASEQA*, **41**, pp. 67–83.
Deschamps, H. (1960), *Histoire de Madagascar* (Paris: Berger Levrault).
Deschamps, H. (1968) *Le Sénégal et la Gambie* (Paris: PUF).
Deschamps, H. (ed.) (1970–1) *Histoire générale de l'Afrique noire* (2 vols, Paris: PUF).
Deschamps, H. (1972) *Histoire de Madagascar* (Paris: Berger Levrault).
Despois, J. (1965) 'Fazzān' in B. Lewis, C. Pellat and J. Schacht (eds), pp. 875–7.
Deverdun, G. (1959–66) *Marrakech des origines à 1912* (2 vols, Rabat: Ed. Techniques nord-africaines).
Devic, L. M. (1983) *Le Pays des Zendjs ou la côte orientale d'Afrique au Moyen âge* (Paris: Hachette).
Devisse, J. (1970) 'La question d'Audagust', in D. Robert, S. Robert and J. Devisse (eds), pp. 109–56.
Devisse, J. (1972) 'Routes de commerce et échanges en Afrique occidentale en relation avec la Méditerranée. Un essai sur le commerce africain médiéval du XIe au XVIe siècle', *RHES*, **50**, 1, pp. 42–73, **50**, 3, pp. 357–397.
Devisse, J. (1974) 'Une enquête à développer: le problème de la propriété des mines en Afrique de l'Ouest du VIIIe au XVIe siècle' in *Miscellanea Charles Verlinden* (*Bulletin de l'Institut Historique Belge de Rome*, **44**), pp. 201–19.
Devisse, J. (1979a) *L'image du Noir dans l'Art Occidentale, Vol. 2, part 1, Des premiers siècles chretiens aux 'Grandes Decouvertes'. De la menace demoniaque à L'incarnation de la sainteté* (Fribourg: Office du Livre).
Devisse, J. (1979b) 'L'arrière plan africain des relations internationales au Xe siècle' in *Occident et Orient au Xe siècle, Actes du IXe Congrès de la Société des historiens médievistes* (*Dijon: 2/4 June 1978*) (Paris: Société les Belles Lettres), pp. 145–65.
Devisse, J. (1981a) 'Pour une histoire globale de la céramique africaine' in (*Le*) *sol, la parole et l'ecrit*, pp. 179–203.
Devisse, J. (1981b) 'L'Afrique noire' in 'Le grand Atlas de L'architecture mondiale', *Encyclopedia Universalis* (Paris), pp. 72–83.
Devisse, J. (1982) 'L'apport de l'archéologie à l'histoire de l'Afrique occidentale entre le Ve et le XIIe siècle', C-RAI, pp. 156–77.
Devisse, J. (1983) 'Histoire et tradition urbaine du Sahel' in *Lectures de la ville africaine contemporaine* (Actes du 7e Séminaire consacré aux transformations de l'architecture dans le monde islamique, Dakar, 1983). pp. 1–10.

Devisse, J. (1985a) 'Les Africains et l'eau, la longue durée' in *Actes du Colloque de l'Université de Paris I sur la Politique de l'eau en Afrique* (1983).

Devisse, J. (1985b) 'Fer et espace dans l'histoire de l'Afrique', *Annales ESC* (forthcoming).

Devisse, J., Robert-Chaleix, D. *et al.* (1983) *Tegdaoust III. Recherches sur Awdaghust* (Paris: ADPF).

Diallo, T. (1972) 'Origine et migrations des Peul avant le XIX siècle', *AFLSHD*, **2**, pp. 121–93.

Dictionnaire archéologique des techniques (1963) (2 vols, Paris: Edition de l'Accueil).

Didillon, H., Didillon, J.-M., Donnadieu, C. and Donnadieu, P. (1977), *Habiter le désert, les maisons mozabites. Recherches sur un type d'architecture traditionnelle pré-saharienne* (Brussels).

Diehl, C. (1896) *L'Afrique byzantine* (Paris: Leroux).

Dimmendaal, G. J. (1982) 'Contacts between Eastern Nilotic and Surma groups in linguistic evidence' in J. Mack and P. Robertshaw (eds), pp. 101–10.

Dinkler, E. (ed.) (1970) *Kunst und Geschichte Nubiens in Christlicher Zeit, Ergebnisse und Probleme auf Grund der jüngsten Ausgrabungen.* (Recklinghausen: Verlag Aurel Bongers).

Dinkler, E. (1975) 'Beobachtungen zur Ikonographie des Kreuzes in der nubischen Kunst' in K. Michalowski (ed.), pp. 20–30.

Diop, C. A. (1955) *National nègre et culture* (Paris: Editions Africaines).

Diop, C. A. (1960) *L'Afrique noire précoloniale* (Paris: Présence Africaine).

Diop, C. A. (1967) *Antériorité des civilisations nègres: Mythe ou vérité historique?* (Paris: Présence Africaine).

Diop, C. A. (1972) 'Datations par la méthode du radiocarbone, série III', *BIFAN*, (B), **34**, 4, pp. 687–701.

Diop, C. A. (1981) *Civilisation ou barbarie* (Paris: Présence Africaine).

Diop, L. M. (1968) 'Métallurgie traditionelle et âge du fer en Afrique', *BIFAN* (B), **30**, 1, pp. 10–38.

al-Djaddawī, M. (1963) *Al-Raḳīḳ fi 'l-ta'rīkh wa-fī 'l-Islām*, Vol. 1 (Alexandria).

al-Djāḥiẓ Abū 'Uthmān 'Amr (1903) *Tria opuscula*, ed. by G. van Vloten (Leiden: Brill).

al-Djāḥiẓ Abū 'Uthmān 'Amr (1964) *Rasā'il al-Djāḥiẓ: Risāla Fakhr al-Sūdān 'alā' l-Bīḍān* (ed. by 'A Hārūn, 2 vols, Cairo).

Djaït, H. (1973) 'L'Afrique arabe au VIIIe siècle (84–184/705–800)', *Annales ESC*, **28**, 3.

Djait, H., Talbi, M., Dachraoui, F., Bouib, A. and M'Rabet, M. A. (n.d.) *Histoire de la Tunisie: le Moyen âge* (Tunis: Société Tunisienne de Diffusion).

al-Djanhānī, H. (1968) *Al-Ḳayrawān 'abra 'uṣūr izdihār al-ḥaḍārat al-islāmiyya fi l-Maghrib al-'Arabī* (Tunis).

Dobrzeniecki, T. (1973–5) 'Maiestas Domini', I, *RMN*; **17**, 1973; II, *RMN*, **18**, 1974, pp. 216–308; III, *RMN*, **19**, 1975, pp. 5–263.

Dobrzeniecki, T. (1974) 'Maiestas Crucis in the mural paintings of the Faras Cathedral. Some iconographical notes', *BMNV*, **15**, pp. 6–20.

Dobrzeniecki, T. (1980) 'Nubijska Maiestas Domini z katedry w Faras w Muzeum Narodowym w Warszawie' [Nubian Maiestas Domini of the Cathedral of Faras in the Warsaw National Museum], *RMN*, **24**, pp. 261–341.

Doke, C. M. (1938) 'The Earliest records of Bantu', *Bantu Studies*, **12**, pp. 135–44.

Dolphyne, F. (1974) 'The languages of the Ghana–Ivory Coast border', *Actes du Colloque interuniversitaire Ghana–Côte d'Ivoire* (Abidjan: Université Nationale).

Dombrowski, J. C. (1980) 'Early settlers in Ghana' (Legon: University of Ghana, Inter-Faculty Lecture).

Domenichini, J.-P. (1978), 'Antehiroka et Vazimba. Contribution à l'histoire de la société du XVIIIe au XIXe siècle', *Bull. Ac. Malg.*, **56**, 1–2, (1982), pp. 11–21.

Domenichini, J.-P. (1981a) 'La plus belle énigme du monde, ou l'historiographie coloniale en question', *Omaly sy Anio*, **13**–14, pp. 57–76 and 84–5.

Domenichini, J.-P. (1981b) 'Problématiques passées et présentes de l'archéologie à Madagascar', *RPC*, **55**, pp. 10–15.

Domenichini-Ramiaramanana, B. (1976) *Le Malgache, Essai de description sommaire* (Paris: SELAF).

Domenichini-Ramiaramanana, B. (1977) 'Malagasy cooking' in J. Kuper (ed.), pp. 111–15.

Domenichini-Ramiaramanana, B. (1978) 'Qu'est-ce qu'un hainteny?' in R. Etiemble (ed.) *Colloque sur la traduction poétique* (Paris: Gallimard) pp. 103–6.

Domenichini-Ramiaramanana, B. (1981) 'La Cuisine malgache' in J. Kuper (ed.), pp. 120–5.

Domenichini-Ramiaramanana, B. (1983) *Du Ohabolana au hainteny. Langue, littérature et politique à Madagascar* (Paris: Karthala/CRA).

Domenichini-Ramiaramanana, B. (1984) 'De la légende à l'histoire: le cycle de Darafify ou le

commerce des aromates, épices, parfums et simples', *Communication à l'Académie Malgache*, séance de section du 28 Juin 1984.
Domenichini-Ramiaramanana, B. (1985) 'Madagascar dans l'Océan Indien du Haut Moyen âge d'après les traditions de la côte orientale', *Sources Orales et Histoire*, **1**, (forthcoming) (Valbonne: CEDRASEMI).
Domenichini-Ramiaramanana, B. and Domenichini, J.-P. (1979) 'La tradition malgache, une source pour l'histoire de l'Océan Indien', *Taloha*, **8**, pp. 57–81.
Domenichini-Ramiaramanana, B. and Domenichini, J.-P. (1983) 'Madagascar dans l'Océan Indien avant le XIIIe siècle', *NCAA*, **1**, pp. 5–19.
Domenichini-Ramiaramanana, B. and Domenichini, J.-P. (1984) *Les premiers temps de l'histoire malgache. Nouvelle définition d'un champ de recherche* (Antananarivo: forthcoming).
Donadoni, S. (ed.) (1967) *Temit 1964. Missione Archeologica in Egitto dell'Università di Roma* (Rome: Università degli Studi).
Donadoni, S. (1969) 'Mētēr Basileōs' [King's Mother] *Studi Classici e Orientali* (Pisa), **18**, pp. 123–5.
Donadoni, S. (1970) 'Les fouilles à l'église de Sonqi Tino' in E. Dinkler (ed.), pp. 209–18.
Donadoni, S. and Curto, S. (1968) 'Le pitture murali della chiesa di Sonki nel Sudan' in *La Nubia Cristiana*, Quaderno No 2 de Museo Egizio di Torino (Turin: Fratelli Fozzo-Salvati), pp. 1–13.
Donadoni, S. and Vantini, G. (1967–8), 'Gli scavi nel diff di Sonqi Tino, Nubia Sudanese', in: *RPAR*, **40**, pp. 247–73.
Donque, G. (1965) 'Le contexte océanique des anciennes migrations: vents et courants dans l'Océan Indien', *Taloha*, **1**, pp. 43–59.
Donzel, E. van, Lewis, B., Pellat, C. (eds), *Encyclopaedia of Islam*, Vol. 4 (2nd edn, Leiden: Brill).
Doresse, J. (1971) *Histoire sommaire de la Corne orientale de l'Afrique* (Paris: Geuthner).
Dos-Santos, J. and Everdosa, C. M. N. (1970) 'A Estacão arqueologica de Benfica, Luanda', *Revista da Fac. de Ciencias da Universidade de Luanda*, **5**, pp. 33–51.
Douglas, M. (1981) *De la souillure. Essai sur les notions de pollution et de tabou* (Paris: Maspéro).
Dozy, R. (1874) *Geschichte der Mauren in Spanien bis zur Eroberung Andalusiens durch die Almoraviden (711–1110)* (2 vols, Leipzig: Grunow).
Dozy, R. (1932) *Histoire des Musulmans d'Espagne jusqu'à la conquête de l'Andalousie per les Almoravides (711*–1110) (2nd edn, Leiden: Brill).
Dramani-Issifou, Z. (1981) 'Routes de commerce et mise en place des populations du nord du Bénin actuel' in *(Le) sol, la parole et l'écrit*. Vol. 2, pp. 655–72.
Dramani-Issifou, Z. (1982) *L'Afrique noire dans les relations internationales au XVI siècle. Analyse de la crise entre le Maroc et le Sonrhaï* (Paris: Karthala–CRA).
Dramani-Issifou, Z. (1983a) 'Islam et société dans l'empire sonrhaï: sur quelques aspects des relations entre Gao et Tombouctou aux XVe–XVIe siècles d'après les Ta'rikhs soudanais', *L'Information historique*, **45**, pp. 244–52.
Dramani-Issifou, Z. (1983b) 'Les nouvelles interprétations des relations entre le Maghreb et l'Afrique soudanaise au XVIe siècle' in *Actes du Second Colloque euro-africain sur 'Le Passé du Sahara et les zones limitrophes des Garamantes au Moyen âge'*. Paris, 15–16 Décembre 1983.
Dramani-Issifou, Z. (1984) 'Quand les voyageurs arabes découvraient le pays des noirs', *Balafon-Mémoire de l'Afrique*, **62**, pp. 20–7.
Du Bourguet, P. (1970) 'La peinture murale compte: quelques problèmes devant la peinture murale nubienne' in E. Dinkler (ed.), pp. 303–12.
Ducatez, G. and Ducatez, J. (1980) 'Formation des dénominations de couleur et de luminosité en arabe classique et pré-classique: essai de périodisation selon une approche linguistique et anthropologique', *Peuples méditerranéens*, **10**, pp. 139–92.
Duchemin, G. J. (1950) 'A propos des décorations murales des habitations de Oualata (Mauritanie)', *BIFAN* (B), **12**, pp. 1095–110.
Duyvendak, J. J. L. (1949) *China's Discovery of Africa* (London: Probsthain).

Echallier, J. L. (1970) 'Forteresse et villages désertés du Toūat Goūrara (Sahara algérien)' (Thèse de 3ème cycle, Paris, Ecole Pratique des Hautes Etudes).
Echard, N. (ed.) (1983) *Métallurgies africaines. Nouvelles contributions* (Paris: Société des Africanistes).
Effah-Gyamfi, K. (1975) *Traditional History of the Bono State. An Archaeological Approach* (Legon: Institute of African Studies).
Effah-Gyamfi, K. (1978) 'Bono Manso, an archaeological investigation into early Akan urbanism' (unpublished PhD thesis, University of Ghana, Legon).
Egharevba, J. (1960) *A Short History of Benin* (3rd edn, Ibadan: Ibadan University Press).
Ehrenkreutz, A. S. (1959) 'Studies in the monetary history of the Near East in the Middle Ages', *JESHO*, **2**, pp. 128–61.

Ehrenkreutz, A. S. (1963) 'Studies in the monetary history of the Near East in the Middle Ages, II: the standard of fineness of western and eastern dinars before the Crusades', *JESHO*, **6**, pp. 243–77.

Ehrenkreutz, A. S. (1977) 'Numismatico-statistical reflections on the annual gold coinage production of the Ṭūlūnid Mint in Egypt', *JESHO*, **20**, pp. 267–81.

Ehret, C. (1971) *Southern Nilotic History: Linguistic Approaches to the Study of the Past* (Evanston: NUP).

Ehret, C. (1972) 'Bantu origins and history: critique and interpretation', *TJH*, **2**, pp. 1–9.

Ehret, C. (1973) 'Patterns of Bantu and Central Sudanic settlement in central and southern Africa (1000 BC–500 AD)', *TJH*, **3**, pp. 1–71.

Ehret, C. (1974a) *Ethiopians and East Africa: The Problems of Contacts* (Nairobi: East African Publishing House).

Ehret, C. (1974b) 'Agricultural history in central and southern Africa, (ca 1000 BC to AD 500)', *TJH*, **4**, 1–25.

Ehret, C. (1974c) 'Some trends in precolonial religious thought in Kenya and Tanzania' (Paper delivered at Conference on the Historical Study of African Religions, Limuru, Kenya, June 1974).

Ehret, C. (1976) 'Aspects of social and economic change in Western Kenya, AD 500–1800' in B. A. Ogot (ed.), pp. 1–20.

Ehret, C. (1980a) *The Historical Reconstruction of Southern Cushitic Phonology and Vocabulary* (Berlin: Reimer).

Ehret, C. (1980b) 'The Nilotic languages of Tanzania' in E. C. Polomé and C. P. Hill (eds), pp. 68–78.

Ehret, C. (1982a) 'Linguistic inferences about early Bantu history' in C. Ehret and M. Posnansky (eds), pp. 57–65.

Ehret, C. (1982b) 'Population movement and culture contact in the southern Sudan, *c.* 3000 BC to AD 1000: a preliminary linguistic overview' in J. Mack and P. Robertshaw (eds), pp. 19–48.

Ehret, C. (forthcoming), 'East African words and things: aspects of nineteenth century agricultural change in East Africa' in B. A. Ogot (ed.).

Ehret, C. (unpublished a) 'The invention of highland planting agriculture in northeastern Tanzania: social repercussions of an economic transformation'.

Ehret, C. (unpublished b) 'Technological change in central and southern Africa, ca. 1000 BC to AD 500'.

Ehret, C. and Nurse, D. (1981a) 'The Taita Cushites', *SUGIA*, 3, pp. 125–68.

Ehret, C. and Nurse, D. (1981b) 'History in the Taita Hills: a provisional synthesis', *KHR*, 7–8.

Ehret, C. and Posnansky, M. (eds) (1982) *The Archaeological and Linguistic Reconstruction of African History* (Berkeley, Los Angeles and London: University of California Press).

L'Elaboration de l'Islam (1961) Colloque de Strasbourg, 12–14 Juin 1959 (Paris: PUF).

Eloff, J. F. and Meyer, A. (1981) 'The Greefswald sites' in E. A. Voigt (ed.), pp. 7–22.

Epstein, H. (1971) *The Origins of the Domestic Animals in Africa* (2 vols, New York: Africana Publishing).

Ervedosa, C. (1980) *Arqueologia Angolana* (Luanda: Ministério da Educaçao Nacional).

Etudes Nubiennes (1978) Colloque de Chantilly, 2–6 Juillet 1975 (Cairo: IFAO-Bibliothèque d'Etude, Vol. 77).

Etudes d'orientalisme dediées à la mémoire de E. Lévi-Provençal (1962) (Paris: Maisonneuve & Larose).

Eustache, D. (1970–1) *Etudes sur la monnaie antique et l'histoire monétaire du Maroc, I: Corpus des dirhams idrisites et contemporains. Collection de la Banque du Maroc et autres collections mondiales publiques et privées* (Rabat: Banque du Maroc).

Evans, D. (1975) 'Stonehenges of West Africa', *Country Life*, 16 January, pp. 134–5.

Evans-Pritchard, E. E. (1956) *Nuer Religion* (Oxford: Clarendon Press).

Evers, T. M. (1980) 'Klingbeil Early Iron Age sites, Lydenburg, eastern Transvaal, South Africa', *SAAB*, 35, 131, pp. 46–57.

Evers, T. M. (1981) 'The Iron Age in the eastern Transvaal' in E. A. Voigt (ed.), pp. 65–109.

Evers, T. M. (1982) 'Excavations at the Lydenburg Heads site, eastern Transvaal, South Africa', *SAAB*, 37, 135, pp. 16–33.

Evers, T. M. (1984) 'Sotho-Tswana and Moloko settlement patterns and the Bantu cattle pattern', in M. J. Hall *et al.* (eds), pp. 236–47.

Ewert, C. (1971) *Islamische Funde in Balaguer und die Aljaferia in Zaragoza* (Berlin: De Gruyter).

Eyo, E. (1974) 'Recent excavations at Ife and Owo, and their implications for Ife, Owo and Benin studies (unpublished PhD thesis, University of Ibadan).

E. Eyo and F. Willett (1980, 1982) *Treasures of Ancient Nigeria* (New York: Knopf [1980], London: Royal Academy of Arts in association with Collins [1982].

Fagan, B. M. (1967) *Iron Age Cultures in Zambia, I: Kalomo and Kangila.* (London: Chatto & Windus).

Fagan, B. M. (1969a) 'Excavations at Ingombe Ilede, 1960–1962' in B. M. Fagan, D. W. Phillipson and S. G. H. Daniels (eds), pp. 55–161.

Fagan, B. M. (1969b) 'Radiocarbon dates for sub-Saharan Africa, VI', *JAH*, **10**, 1, pp. 149–69.

Fagan, B. M. and Nenquin, J. (eds) (1966) *Inventaria Archeologica Africana* (Tervuren: Musée Royale de l'Afrique Centrale).

Fagan, B. M. and Phillipson, D. W. (1965) 'Sebanzi, the Iron Age sequence of Lochinvar and the Tonga', *J. Roy. Anthropol. Inst.*, **45**, pp. 253–94.

Fagan, B. M., Phillipson, D. W. and Daniels, S. G. H. (eds) (1967–9), *Iron Age Cultures in Zambia* (2 vols, London: Chatto & Windus).

Fagan, B. and Yellen, J. E. (1968) 'Ivuna: ancient salt working in southern Tanzania', *Azania*, **3**, pp. 1–44.

Fage, J. D. (1964) 'Some thoughts on state-formation in the Western Sudan before the seventeenth century', *BUPAH*, **1**, pp. 17–34.

Fage, J. D. (1969) *A History of West Africa* (4th edn, Cambridge: CUP).

Fage, J. D. (1974) *States and Subjects in Sub-Saharan African History* (Johannesburg: Witwatersrand University Press, Raymond Dart Lecture).

Fage, J. D. (ed.) (1978) *The Cambridge History of Africa, Vol. 2: c. 500* BC–AD *1050* (Cambridge: CUP).

Fage, J. D. (1980) 'Slaves and society in western Africa c. 1445–1700', *JAH*, **21**, 3, pp. 289–310.

Fage, J. D. and Oliver, R. A. (1970) *Papers in African Prehistory* (Cambridge: CUP).

Fagg, B. E. B. (1965) 'Carbon dates from Nigeria', *Man*, **54**, pp. 22–3.

Fagg, B. (1969) 'Recent work in West Africa: new light on the Nok Culture', *WA*, **1**, 1, pp. 41–50.

Fagg, W. (1963) *Nigerian Images* (London: Lund Humphries).

Fall, Y. (1982) 'Silla: problématique d'un site de la vallée du Fleuve du Sénégal', *ASAG*, **46**, pp. 199–216.

Farias, P. F. de Moraes (1966) 'A reforma de Ibn Yāsīn', *Afro-Asia* (Salvador de Bahia), **2**–3, pp. 37–58.

Farias, P. F. de Moraes (1967) 'The Almoravids: some questions concerning the character of the movement during its periods of closest contact with the Western Sudan', *BIFAN* (B), **24**, 3–4, pp. 794–878.

Farias, P. F. de Moraes (1974) 'Silent trade: myth and historical evidence', *HA*, **1**, pp. 9–24.

Farmer, H. G. (1929) *A History of Arabian Music to the XIIth century* (London: Luzac).

Fathy, H. (1981) *Des architectures de terre ou l'avenir d'un tradition millénaire* (Paris: Centre Georges Pompidou).

Fazlur, R. (1966) *Islam* (London: Weidenfeld & Nicolson).

Feierman, S. (1974) *The Shambaa Kingdom* (Madison: UWP).

Ferrand, G. (1891–1902) *Les Musulmans à Madagascar et aux Iles Comores* (3 vols, Paris: Leroux).

Ferrand, G. (1909) *Essai de phonétique comparée du malais et des dialectes malgaches* (Paris: Geuthner).

Ferrand, G. (1919) 'Les K'ouen-louen et les anciennes navigations interocéaniques dans les mers du Sud', *JA*, 11th series, **13**, pp. 239–333, 431–92; **14**, pp. 5–68, 201–41.

Ferrand, G. (1922) 'L'empire Sumatranais de Çrīvijaya', *JA*, 11th series, **20**, pp. 1–104.

Ferrand, G. (1929) 'Waḳwāḳ' in M. T. Houtsma *et al.* (eds), pp. 1105–9.

Filesi, T. (1962) *Le relazioni della Cina con l'Africa nel Medio-Evo* (Milan: Giuffrè).

Filesi, T. (1970) *China and Africa in the Middle Ages* (London: Cass).

Filipowiak, W. (1979) *Etudes archéologiques sur la capitale médiévale du Mali* (Szczecin: Muzeum Narodowe).

Filipowiak, W., Jasnosz, S., Wolagiewicz, R. (1970) 'Les recherches archéologiques polono-guinéennes à Niani en 1968', *Materialy Zachodnio-pormorskie*, **14**, pp. 575–648.

Fisher, A. G. B. and Fisher, H. J. (1970) *Slavery and Muslim Society in Africa* (London: Hurst).

Fisher, H. J. (1972) '"He swalloweth the ground with fierceness and rage": the horse in the Central Sudan. I. Its introduction', *JAH*, **13**, 3, pp. 367–88.

Fisher, H. J. (1973a) '"He swalloweth the ground with fierceness and rage": the horse in the Central Sudan. II. Its use', *JAH*, **14**, 3, pp. 355–79.

Fisher, H. J. (1973b) 'Conversion reconsidered: some historical aspects of religious conversion in Black Africa', *Africa*, **43**, pp. 27–40.

Fisher, H. J. (1977) 'The eastern Maghrib and the central Sudan' in R. Oliver (ed.) (1977), pp. 232–330.

Flacourt, E. de, (1661) *Histoire de la Grande Ile Madagascar ... avec une relation de ce qui s'est passé ès* *années 1655, 1656 et 1667* (Paris: Pierre Bienfait. Edition prepared by A. Grandidier, G. Grandidier and H. Froidevaux, 1913).

Fleischhacker, H. von (1969) 'Zur Rassen-und Bevölkerungsgeschichte Nordafrikas unter besonderer Berücksichtigung der Aethiopiden, der Libyer und der Garamanten', *Paideuma*, **15**, pp. 12–53.

Flight, C. (1967) 'The prehistoric sequence in the Kintampo area of Ghana', *Actes VIe Congr. PPEQ*, pp. 68–9.

Flight, C. (1973) 'A survey of recent results in the radiocarbon chronology of northern and western Africa', *JAH*, **14**, 4, pp. 531–54.

Flight, C. (1975) 'Gao, 1972: first interim report: a preliminary investigation of the Cemetery at Sané', *WAJA*, **5**, pp. 81–90.

Flight, C. (1976) 'The Kintampo culture and its place in the economic prehistory of West Africa' in J. Harlan *et al.* (eds), pp. 211–21.

Flight, C. (1978) 'Gao, 1974: second interim report: excavation in the Cemetery at Sané', *WAJA*, **7**.

Flury, S. (1922) 'The Kufic inscriptions of Kisimkazi Mosque, Zanzibar, 500 A.H. (A.D. 1107)', *JRAS*, April, pp. 257–64.

Forand, P. (1971) 'Early Muslim relations with Nubia', *Islam*, **48**, pp. 111–21.

Ford, J. (1971) *The Role of the Trypanosomiases in African Ecology: A Study of the Tsetse Fly Problem* (Oxford: Clarendon Press).

Forde, D. and Jones, G. I. (1950) *The Ibo and Ibibio-speaking Peoples of South-Eastern Nigeria* (London: IAI).

Fordyce, B. N. S. (1984) 'The prehistory of Nylsvley' in B. Walker (ed.).

Foucauld, C. E. de (1940) *Dictionnaire abrégé touareg–français de noms propres* (*dialecte de l'Ahaggar*) (Paris: Larose).

Fouché, L. (ed.) (1937) *Mapungubwe: Ancient Bantu Civilization on the Limpopo* (Cambridge: CUP).

Fournel, H. (1875–81) *Les Berbères; étude sur la conquête de l'Afrique par les Arabes* (2 vols, Paris: Imprimerie nationale).

Fourquet, R., Sarthou, J.-L., Roux, J. and Acri, K. (1974) 'Hémoglobine S et origines du peuplement de Madagascar. Nouvelle hypothèse sur son introduction en Afrique', *Arch. Inst. Pasteur de Madagascar*, **43**, pp. 185–220.

Fraser, D. (1972) 'The fish-legged figure in Benin and Yoruba art' in D. Fraser and H. M. Cole (eds), pp. 261–94.

Fraser, D. (1975) 'The Tsoede bronzes and Owo Yoruba art', *African Arts*, **8**, 3, pp. 30–5.

Fraser, D. and Cole, H. M. (1972) *African Art and Leadership* (Madison: UWP).

Freeman-Grenville, G. S. P. (1959) 'Some problems of East African coinage from early times to 1890', *TNR*, **53**, pp. 250–60.

Freeman-Grenville, G. S. P. (1960) 'East African coin finds and their historical significance', *JAH*, **1**, 1, pp. 31–43.

Freeman-Grenville, G. S. P. (1962a) *The Medieval History of the Coast of Tanganyika* (London: OUP).

Freeman-Grenville, G. S. P. (1962b) *The East African Coast. Select Documents from the first to the earlier nineteenth century* (Oxford: Clarendon Press).

Frend, W. H. C. (1972a) 'Coptic, Greek and Nubian at Qasr Ibrim', *Byzantinoslavica*, **33**, pp. 224–9.

Frend, W. H. C. (1972b) *The Rise of the Monophysite Movement: Chapters in the History of the Church in the Fifth and Sixth Centuries* (Cambridge: CUP).

Frend, W. H. C. (1979) 'The cult of military saints in Christian Nubia' in C. Andresen and G. Klein (eds) *Theologia Crucis – Signum Crucis. Festschrift für E. Dinkler zum 70. Geburstag* (Tübingen: J. C. B. Mohr), pp. 155–63.

Frobenius, L. (1913) *The Voice of Africa* (2 vols, London: Hutchinson).

Frobenius, L. and Wilm, R. von (1921–31) *Atlas Africanus* (Munich: Beck).

Gado, B. (1980) *Le Zarmatarey. Contribution à l'histoire des populations d'entre Niger et Dallol Mawri* (Niamey: Institut de Recherche en Sciences Humaines).

Gado, B. (1981) 'La recherche archéologique et historique au Niger' *Recherche, Pédagogie et Culture*, **55**, pp. 33–40.

Gallais, J. (1984) *Hommes du Sahel, espace, temps et pouvoirs* (Paris: Flammarion).

Galloway, A. (1937) 'The skeletal remains of Mapungubwe' in L. Fouché (ed.), pp. 127–74.

Galloway, A. (1959) *The Skeletal Remains of Bambandyanalo* (Johannesburg: University of the Witwatersrand Press).

Gao Jinyuan (1984) 'China and Africa: the development of relations over many centuries', *African Affairs*, **83**, 331, pp. 241–50.

Garcin, J.-C. (1976) *Un centre musulman de la Haute-Egypte médiévale: Qūṣ* (Cairo: IFAO).
Gardner, G. A. (1963) *Mapungubwe*, Vol. 2 (Pretoria: J. L. van Schaik).
Garlake, P. S. (1966) *The Early Islamic Architecture of the African Coast* (London and Nairobi: British Institute in Eastern Africa).
Garlake, P. S. (1968) 'Test excavations at Mapela Hill, near the Shashi River, Rhodesia', *Arnoldia (Rhod.)*, 3, 34, pp. 1–29.
Garlake, P. S. (1970) 'Iron Age site in the Urungwe district of Rhodesia', *SAAB*, **25**, 97, pp. 25–44.
Garlake, P. S. (1973) *Great Zimbabwe* (London: Thames & Hudson).
Garlake, P. S. (1978) 'Pastoralism and Zimbabwe', *JAH*, **19**, 4, pp. 479–94.
Garrard, T. F. (1975) 'Pottery and stone goldweights from Ghana', *Sankofa*, **1**, pp. 60–8.
Garrard, T. F. (1982) 'Myths and metrology. The early trans-Saharan gold trade', *JAH*, **23**, 4, pp. 443–61.
Gartkiewicz, P. M. (1973) 'Stary Kościół w Dongoli na tle sakralnej architektury wczesnośredniowiecznej Nubii' [The Old Church in Dongola against the background of sacral architecture in Early Medieval Nubia], *Kwartalnik Architektury i Urbanistyki* (Warsaw), **18**, pp. 207–39.
Gartkiewicz, P. M. (1975) 'The central plan in Nubian church architecture' in K. Michałowski (ed.), pp. 49–64.
Gartkiewicz, P. M. (1980) 'New outline of the history of Nubian church architecture', *BAB*, **55**, pp. 137–44.
Gartkiewicz, P. M. (1982a) 'An introduction to the history of Nubian church Architecture', *NC*, **1**, pp. 43–105.
Gartkiewicz, P. M. (1982b) 'Remarks on the cathedral at Qasr Ibrim' in J. M. Plumley (ed.) (1982a), pp. 87–94.
Gartkiewicz, P. M. (1983) 'Some remarks on the building-history of the Cathedral in Faras', *Nubian Letters*, (The Hague: Society for Nubian Studies), **1**, pp. 21–39.
Gast, M. (1972) 'Témoignages nouveaux sur Tin Hinan, ancêtre légendaire des Touareg Ahaggar', *ROMM*, **9**, (Mélanges Le Tourneau), pp. 395–400.
Gaudio, A. (1978) *Le dossier de la Mauritanie* (Paris: Nouvelles Editions Latines).
Gautier, E. F. (1927) *L'Islamisation de l'Afrique du Nord. Les siècles obscurs du Maghreb* (Paris: Payot).
Gautier, E. F. (1935) 'L'or du Soudan dans l'histoire', *AHES*, **7**, pp. 113–23.
Gautier, E. F. (1937) *Le passé de l'Afrique du Nord. Les siècles obscurs* (Paris: Payot).
Gemery, H. A. and Hogendorn, J. S. (eds) (1979) *The Uncommon Market: Essays in the Economic History of the Atlantic Slave Trade* (New York: Academic Press).
Gerharz, R. (1983) 'Rock paintings and ruins: pictures from the history of Zimbabwe' in K. H. Striedter (ed.), *Rock Paintings from Zimbabwe* (Wiesbaden: Steiner).
Gerster, G. (1968) *Kirchen im Fels; Entdeckungen in Äthiopien* (Stuttgart: Kohlkammer).
Gerster, G. (1970) *Churches in Rock; Early Christian Art in Ethiopia* (London: Phaidon).
Gerster, G. (1974) *Äthiopien: das Dach Afrikas* (Zürich: Atlantis).
al-Ghazālī (1861) *Iḥyā' 'ulūm al-dīn* (Būlāḳ).
Gibb, H. A. R. (1963) *Arabic Literature: An Introduction* (2nd edn, Oxford: Clarendon Press).
Gibb, H. A. R., Kramers, J. H., Lévi-Provençal, E. and Schacht, J. (eds) (1960) *Encyclopaedia of Islam*, Vol. 1 (2nd edn, Leiden/London: Brill/Luzac).
Girard, D. (1686) *Discours historique de l'état de Borno* (Paris: Bibliothèque Nationale, Fonds Français, 12.220 [appendice]).
Godlewski, W. (1978) 'Some problems connected with Nubian baptisteries', *Etudes Nubiennes*, 1978, pp. 107–17.
Godlewski, W. (1979) *Faras VI. Les baptistères nubiens* (Warsaw: PWN).
Godlewski, W. (1981) 'Throne hall at Old Dongola (the Sudan)', *AB*, **30**, pp. 39–51.
Godlewski, W. (1982a) 'The mosque-building in Old Dongola' in P. van Moorsel (ed.), pp. 21–8.
Godlewski, W. (1982b) 'Some comments on the wall painting of Christ from Old Dongola' in J. M. Plumley (ed.) (1982a), pp. 95–9.
Goitein, S. D. (1962) 'La Tunisie du XIe siècle à la lumière des documents de la *Geniza* du Caire' in *Etudes d'orientalisme dédiées à la mémoire de E. Lévi-Provençal*, Vol. 2, pp. 559–79.
Goitein, S. D. (1963) 'Slaves and slave-girls in the Cairo Geniza Records', *Arabica*, **9**, pp. 1–20.
Goitein, S. D. (1966) *Studies in Islamic History and Institutions* (Leiden: Brill).
Goitein, S. D. (1967) *A Mediterranean Society. Vol. I: Economic Foundations.* (Berkeley and Los Angeles: University of California Press).
Goitein, S. D. (1973) *Letters of Medieval Jewish Traders* (Princeton: PUP).
Goldziher, I. (1925) *Vorlesungen über den Islam.* (2nd edn, Heidelberg: Carl Winter).
Goldziher, I. (1966) *A Short History of Classical Arabic Literature* (Hildesheim: Georg Olms).
Goldziher, I. (1971) *Muslim Studies* (2 vols, London: Allen & Unwin).

Gołgowski, T. (1968) 'Problems of the iconography of the Holy Virgin murals from Faras', *Etudes et Travaux*, 2 (CAMAP, 6), pp. 293–312.
Gołgowski, T. (1969) 'Scènes de la Passion et de la Résurrection sur une peinture de Faras', *Etudes et Travaux*, 3 (CAMAP, 8), pp. 207–29.
Golvin, L. (1957) *Le Magrib central à l'époque des Zirides* (Paris).
Goody, J. (1964) 'The Mande and the Akan hinterland' in J. Vansina, *et al.* (eds), pp. 193–218.
Goody, J. (1971) *Technology, Tradition and the State in Africa* (London: OUP).
Grabar, O. (1957) *The coinage of the Tulunids* (New York: American Numismatic Society, Numismatic Notes and Monographs, **139**).
Gray, J. M. (1951) 'A History of Kilwa, Part 1', *TNR*, **31**, pp. 1–24.
Gray, J. M. (1954) 'The Wadebuli and the Wadiba', *TNR*, **36**, pp. 22–42.
Gray, J. M. (1962) *History of Zanzibar from the Middle Ages to 1856* (London: OUP).
Gray, R. (ed.) (1975) *The Cambridge History of Africa, Vol. 4, c. 1600 to c. 1790* (Cambridge: CUP).
Gray, R. and Birmingham, D. (eds) (1970) *Pre-colonial African Trade. Essays on Trade in Central and Eastern Africa before 1900* (London: OUP).
Grebenart, D. (1983) 'Les débuts de la métallurgie en Afrique occidentale' (2 vols, Thèse de Doctorat d'Etat, Université d'Aix-en-Provence).
Greenberg, J. H. (1955) *Studies in African Linguistic Classification* (New Haven: Compass Publishing).
Greenberg, J. H. (1963a) 'The languages of Africa', *IJAL*, **29**, 1, pp. 1–177.
Greenberg, J. H. (1963b) *Languages of Africa* (Bloomington: University of Indiana Press).
Greenberg, J. H. (1966) *The Languages of Africa* (The Hague: Mouton).
Greenberg, J. H. (1972) 'Linguistic evidence regarding Bantu origins', *JAH*, **12**, 2, pp. 189–216.
Grierson, P. (1961) Contribution to 'La discussione sul tema: gli scambi internazionali e la moneta', *Settimani di Studio de Centro Italiano di studi sull'alto medioevo*, 8, pp. 683–721.
Grierson, P. (1975) *Monnaies et monnayage: introduction à la numismatique* (Paris: Aubier).
Griffith, F. L. (1913) 'The Nubian texts of the Christian period', *AAW*, Phil. Hist. Classe, 8.
Griffith, F. L. (1928) 'Christian documents from Nubia', *PBA*, **14**, pp. 117–46.
Grottanelli, V. L. (1955) *Pescatori dell' Oceano Indiano* (Roma: Cremonse).
Grottanelli, V. L. (1975) 'The peopling of the Horn of Africa' in H. N. Chittick and R. I. Rotberg (eds), pp. 44–75.
Grunderbeck, M. C. van, Roche, E. and Doutrelepont, H. (1983a), *Le premier âge du Fer au Rwanda et au Burundi. Archéologie et environnement* (Butare: INRS, Publ. **23**).
Grunderbeck, M. C. van, Roche, E. and Doutrelepont, H. (1983b) 'La métallurgie ancienne au Rwanda et au Burundi', *Journée de Paléométallurgie*, pp. 1–15.
Grunne, B. de (1980) *Terres cuites anciennes de l'ouest africain* (Louvain La Neuve: Institut Supérieur d'Archéologie et d'Histoire de l'Art).
Gsell, S. (1913–28) *L'Histoire ancienne de l'Afrique du Nord* (8 vols, Paris: Hachette).
Gsell, S., Marçais, G. and Yver, G. (1935) *L'Algérie* (Paris: Boivin).
Guèbrè Sellassié (1930) *Chronique du règne de Ménélik II.* (Tr. and annotated by M. de Coppet) (Paris: Maisonneuve).
Guidi, I. (1932) *Storia della litteratura etiopica* (Roma: Istituto per Oriente).
Guthrie, M. (1948) *The Classification of the Bantu Languages* (London: OUP).
Guthrie, M. (1962) 'Some developments in the prehistory of the Bantu languages', *JAH*, **3**, 2, pp. 273–82.
Guthrie, M. (1967–71) *Comparative Bantu* (4 vols. Farnborough: Gregg).

Haas, S. S. (1942) 'The contribution of slaves to and their influence upon the culture of early Islam' (unpublished PhD dissertation, Princeton University).
Hadj-Sadok, M. (1983) *Al-Idrīsī: le Magrib au XIIe siècle après J.C.* (*VIe siècle de l'Hégire*) (Paris: Publisud).
Hägg, T. (1982) 'Some remarks on the use of Greek in Nubia' in J. M. Plumley (ed.) (1982a), pp. 103–7.
Hair, P. E. H. (1968a) 'Ethnolinguistic continuity on the Guinea Coast', *JAH*, 8, 2, pp. 247–68.
Hair, P. E. H. (1968b) 'An ethnolinguistic inventory of the Lower Guinea Coast before 1700 (part I)', *ALR*, 7, pp. 47–73.
Hair, P. E. H. (1974) 'Barbot, Dapper, Davity: a critique of sources on Sierra Leone and Cape Mount', *HA*, 1, pp. 25–54.
al-Hakamī (1892) *Yaman, its Early Medieval History . . .*, ed. and tr. by H. C. Kay (London: Arnold).
Håland, R. (1980) 'Man's role in changing habitat of Mema during the old kingdom of Ghana', *Norwegian Archeological Review*, **13**, 1, pp. 31–46.

Hall, D. G. (1964) *A History of South-East Asia* (2nd edn, London: Macmillan).
Hall, M. (1984) 'The myth of the Zulu homestead: archaeology and ethnography', *Africa* (IAI), **54**, pp. 65–79.
Hall, M. and Vogel, J. C. (1980) 'Some recent radiocarbon dates from southern Africa', *JAH*, **21**, 4, pp. 431–55.
Hall, M. J., Avery, G., Avery, D. M., Wilson, M. L. and Humphreys, A. J. B. (eds) (1984) *Frontiers: Southern African Archaeology Today* (Oxford: BAR, Cambridge Monographs in African Archaeology, **10**).
Hall, S. L. (1981) 'Iron Age sequence and settlement in the Rooiberg, Thabazimbi area' (MA Thesis, University of the Witwatersrand).
Hallam, W. K. R. (1966) 'The Bayajida legend in Hausa folklore', *JAH*, **7**, 1, pp. 47–60.
Hamani, D. (1985) 'L'Ayar (Aïr) nigérien du XVe au XIXe siècle' (Thèse de doctorat d'Etat, Université de Paris I).
al-Hamdānī (1954) *Al-Iklīl*, ed. by O. Löfgren (Uppsala: Almqvist & Wiksells).
al-Hamdānī (1958) *On the Genealogy of Fatimid Caliphs* (Cairo: American University at Cairo, School of Oriental Studies, Occasional Paper, **1**).
Hamidullah, M. (1956) 'Les "Aḥābīsh" de La Mecque' in *Studi orientalistici in onore di Giorgio Levi della Vida* (Rome: Pubblicazioni dell'Istituto per l'Oriente), pp. 434–47.
Hanisch, E. O. M. (1979) 'Excavation at Icon, northern Transvaal' in *S. Afr. Archaeol. Soc., Goodwin Series*, **3**, pp. 72–9.
Hanisch, E. O. M. (1980) 'An archaeological interpretation of certain Iron Age sites in the Limpopo/Shashi Valley' (unpublished MA thesis, University of Pretoria).
Hanisch, E. O. M. (1981) 'Schroda: a Zhizo site in the northern Transvaal' in E. A. Voigt (ed.), pp. 37–53.
Harlan, J. R., De Wet, J. M. J. and Stemler, A. B. L. (eds) (1976a) *Origins of African Plant Domestication* (The Hague and Paris: Mouton).
Harlan, J. R., De Wet, J. M. J. and Stemler, A. B. L. (1976b) 'Plant domestication and indigenous African agriculture' in Harlan, J. R. *et al.* (eds) (1976a), pp. 3–19.
Harris, J. E. (1971) *The African Presence in Asia* (Evanston: NUP).
Hartle, D. D. (1966) 'Bronze objects from the Ifeka gardens site Ezira', *WAAN*, **4**.
Hartle, D. D. (1967) 'Archaeology in eastern Nigeria', *Nigeria Magazine*, **93**, pp. 134–43.
Hartle, D. D. (1968) 'Radiocarbon dates', *WAAN*, **9**, p. 73.
Hartmann, M. (1895) 'Der Naǧāšī Aṣhama und sein Sohn Armā", *ZDMG*, **49**, 1895, pp. 299–300.
Hasan, Y. F. (1966) 'The penetration of Islam in the eastern Sudan' in I. M. Lewis (ed.), pp. 144–59.
Hasan, Y. F. (1967) *The Arabs and the Sudan* (Edinburgh: EUP).
Hasan, Y. F. (ed.) (1971) *Sudan in Africa: Studies presented to the First International Conference sponsored by the Sudan Research Unit, 7–12 February 1968* (Khartoum: KUP).
Hasan, Y. F. (1973) *The Arabs and the Sudan* (3rd edn, Khartoum: KUP).
Haudricourt, A. G. and Hedin, L. (1943) *L'Homme et les plantes cultivées.* (Paris: Gallimard).
Havighurst, A. F. (1958) *The Pirenne Thesis: Analysis, Criticism and Revision* (Boston: Heath).
Heckel, E. (1903) *Les plantes médicinales et toxiques de Madagascar.* (Marseille-Paris: Institut Colonial-Challamel).
Heine, B. (1973) 'Zur genetischen Gliederung der Bantu-Sprachen', *AU*, **56**, pp. 164–85.
Heine, B. (1978) 'The Sam languages: a history of Rendille, Boni and Somali', *Afroasiatic Linguistics*, **6**, pp. 23–115.
Heine, B. (1981) 'Some cultural evidence on the early Sam-speaking people of eastern Africa', *SUGIA*, **3**, pp. 169–200.
Heine, B., Hoff, H. and Vossen, R. (1977) 'Neuere Ergebnisse zur Territorial-geschichte der Bantu' in W. J. Möhlig, F. Rottland and B. Heine (eds), pp. 57–70.
Heine, B., Rottland, F., Vossen, R. (1979) 'Proto-Baz: some aspects of early Nilotic-Cushitic contacts', *SUGIA*, **1**, pp. 75–91.
Héliodore (1960) *Les Ethiopiens* (*Théagène et Charidée*) (3 vols, Paris: Les Belles Lettres).
Heller, B. (1931) *Die Bedeutung des arabischen 'Antarromans für die vergleichende Litteraturkunde* (Leipzig: Eichblatt).
Henderson, R. N. (1972) *The King in Every Man: Evolutionary Trends in Onitsha Ibo Society.* (New Haven: YUP).
Henige, D. P. (1974) *The Chronology of Oral Tradition: Quest for a Chimera* (Oxford: Clarendon Press).
Hennequin, G. P. (1972) 'Problèmes théoriques et pratiques de la monnaie antique et médiévale', *AI*, **10**, pp. 1–55.

Hennequin, G. P. (1974) 'Points de vue sur l'histoire monétaire de l'Egypte musulmane au Moyen âge', *AI*, **12**, pp. 1–36.
Herbert, E. (1984) *Red Gold of Africa: Copper in Precolonial History and Culture* (Madison: UWP).
Herodotus (1872) *Histoires* (Paris: Ed. Muller).
Hiernaux, J. (1968) 'Bantu expansion: the evidence from physical anthropology confronted with linguistic and archaeological evidence', *JAH*, **9**, 4, pp. 505–15.
Hiernaux, J., De Longrée, E. and De Buyst, J. (1971) *Fouilles archéologiques dans la vallée du Haut-Lualaba, I, Sanga (1958)* (Tervuren: Musée Royale de l'Afrique Centrale).
Hiernaux, J., Maquet, E. and De Buyst, J. (1973) 'Le cimetière protohistorique de Katoto, vallée du Lualaba, Congo-Kinshasa', *Actes du VI Congrès Panafricain de Préhistoire*, pp. 148–58.
Hill, M. H. (1970) 'Towards a culture sequence for Sierra Leone', *Africana Res. Bull.* (Freetown) **1**, 2.
Hill, M. H. (1972) 'Speculations on linguistic and cultural history in Sierra Leone' (Paper presented at the Conference on Manding Studies, SOAS London, 1972).
Hinkel, F. (1977–) *The Archaeological Map of the Sudan*, Fasc. I–X (Berlin: Akademie-Verlag, Fasc. II and III have appeared, others forthcoming).
Hinkel, F. (1978) *Auszug aus Nubien* (Berlin: Akademie-Verlag).
Hintze, F. (1971–7) 'Beobachtungen zur altnubischen Grammatik, I–II' *Berliner Beiträge zur Ägyptologie und Sudanarchäologie: WZHUS*, **20**, 3, 1971, pp. 287–93; III, *AF*, **2**, 1975, pp. 11–24; IV in K. Michałowski (ed.), 1975, pp. 65–9; V, *AF*, **5**, 1977, pp. 37–43.
Hirschberg, H. Z. (1963) 'The Problems of the Judaized Berbers', *JAH*, **4**, 3, pp. 313–39.
Hirschberg, H. Z. (J. W.), (1974) *A History of Jews in North Africa, Volume I: From Antiquity to the Sixteenth Century* (Leiden: Brill).
Hiskett, M. (1984) *The Development of Islam in West Africa* (London: Longman).
Hitti, P. K. (1956) *History of the Arabs* (6th edn, London: Macmillan).
Hitti, P. K. (1970) *History of the Arabs* (10th edn, London: Macmillan).
Hodge, C. T. (ed.) (1971) *Papers on the Manding* (Bloomington: Indiana University Publications, African Series, 3).
Hodgkin, T. (1975) *Nigerian Perspectives. An Historical Anthology* (2nd edn, London: OUP).
Hoenerbach, W. (ed.) (1967) *Der Orient in der Forschung, Festschrift für Otto Spies* (Wiesbaden: Harrassowitz).
Hofmann, I. (1967) *Die Kulturen des Niltals von Aswan bis Sennar, vom Mesolithikum bis zum Ende der Christlichen Epoche* (Hamburg: Hamburgischer Museum für Völkerkunde).
Holas, B. (1951) 'Deux haches polies de grande taille de la Basse Côte d'Ivoire', *BIFAN*, **13**, 4, pp. 1174–80.
Holl, A. (1983) 'Essai sur l'économie néolithique du Dhar Tichitt (Mauritanie)' (Thèse de 3ème cycle: Université de Paris I).
Hollingsworth, L. W. (1974) *A Short History of the East Coast of Africa* (3rd edn, London: Macmillan).
Hopkins, A. G. (1973) *An Economic History of West Africa* (London: Longman).
Hornell, J. (1934) 'Indonesian influence on East African culture', *JRAI*, **64**, pp. 305–33.
Hornell, J. (1942) 'The sea-going *mtepe* and *dáu* of the Lamu Archipelago', *TNR*, **14**, pp. 27–37.
Horton, M. (1981) 'Excavations at Shanga' (preliminary report).
Horton, R. (1976) 'Stateless societies in the history of West Africa' in J. F. A. Ajayi and M. Crowder (eds) (1976), pp. 72–113.
Horton, R. (1979) 'Ancient Ife: a reassessment', *JHSN*, **9**, 4, pp. 69–150.
Hourani, G. F. (1951) *Arab Seafaring in the Indian Ocean in Ancient and Early Medieval Times* (Princeton: PUP).
Houtsma, M. T., Wensinck, A. J., Arnold, T. W. and Lévi-Provençal, E. (eds) (1929) Encyclopaedia of Islam (1st edn, Leyden and London: Brill and Luzac).
Hrbek, I. (1953) 'Die Slawen im Dienste der Fatimiden', *AROR*, **21**, 4, pp. 543–81.
Huard, P. (1966) 'Introduction et diffusion du fer au Tchad', *JAH*, **7**, 3, pp. 377–404.
Huffman, T. N. (1970) 'The Early Iron Age and the spread of the "Bantu"', *SAAB*, **25**, pp. 3–21.
Huffman, T. N. (1971) 'A guide to the Iron Age of Mashonaland', *Occas. Papers Nat. Museum Rhodesia*, **4**, 1, pp. 20–44.
Huffman, T. N. (1974a) 'The linguistic affinities of the Iron Age in Rhodesia', *Arnoldia* (Rhod.), **7**.
Huffman, T. N. (1974b) *The Leopard's Kopje Tradition* (Salisbury: National Museums and Monuments of Rhodesia, Museum Memoir, **6**).
Huffman, T. N. (1978) 'The origins of Leopard's Kopje: an 11th century defaquane', *Arnoldia* (Rhod.), 8, 23, pp. 1–23.
Huffman, T. N. (1979) 'Test excavations at Naba and Lanlory, northern Mashonaland', *S. Afr. Archaeol. Soc., Goodwin Series*, **3**, pp. 14–46.

Huffman, T. N. (1981) 'Snakes and birds: expressive space at Great Zimbabwe', *AS*, **40**, 2, pp. 131–50.
Huffman, T. N. (1982) 'Archaeology and ethnohistory of the African Iron Age', *Ann. Rev. Anthropol.*, **11**, pp. 133–50.
Huffman, T. N. (1984) 'Leopard's Kopje and the nature of the Iron Age in Bantu Africa', *Zimbabweana*, **1**, 1.
Hugot, H. J. (1962) *Mission Berliet Ténéré-Tchad (1960), Documents scientifiques* (Paris: Arts et Métiers graphiques).
Hugot, H. J. (1966) 'Mission à l'Ile de Tidra', *BIFAN* (B), **28**, pp. 555–64; 1019–23.
Hugot, H. J. *et al.* (1973) *Tichitt I. Rapport scientifique* (ronéo).
Hugot, H. J. (1974) *Le Sahara avant le désert* (Paris: Editions des Hespérides).
Hugot, H. J. (1979) 'Le Néolithique saharien' (Thèse de Doctorat ès Lettres, Université de Paris X–Nanterre).
Huici-Miranda, A. (1959a) 'La Salida de los Almoravides del desierto y el reinado de Yusuf b. Tāšfīn: adaraciones y rectificaciones', *Héspéris*, **47**, pp. 155–82.
Huici-Miranda, A. (1959b) ''Alī b. Yūsuf y sus empresas en El-Andalus', *Tamuda*, **7**, pp. 77–122.
Huici-Miranda, A. (1960) 'El Rawḍ al-quirṭās y los Almorávides', *HT*, **1**, pp. 513–41.
Huici-Miranda, A. (1961) 'Un fragmento inedito de Ibn 'Idhārī sobre los Almorávides', *HT*, **2**, pp. 43–111.
Huici-Miranda, A. (1962) 'Contribución al estudio de la dinastia almorávide: el gobierno de Tašfīn Ben 'Alī Ben Yūsuf en el-Andalus' in *Etudes d'orientalisme dédiées à la mémoire de E. Lévi-Provençal*, Vol. 2, pp. 605–21.
Huici-Miranda, A. (1962) 'Los Banu Hud de Zaragoza, Alfonso I el Batallador y los Almoravides' in *Estudios de Edad Media de la Corona de Aragon*, (Zaragoza), **7**, pp. 7–38.
Huici-Miranda, A. (1963) 'Nuevas aportaciones de "Al-Bayān al-Mughrib" sobre los Almorávides', *Al-Andalus*, **28**, pp. 313–30.
Huizinga, J. (1968) 'New physical and anthropological evidence bearing on the relationship between Dogon, Kurumba and the extinct West African Tellem populations', *Proc. KNAW*, (C), **71**, 1, pp. 16–30.
Al-Ḥulal al-Mawshīyya (1936) (ed. by I. Allouche, Rabat: IHEM).
Al-Ḥulal al-Mawshīyya (1952) in A. Huici-Miranda, *Colección de crónacas arabes de la Reconquista. Tomo I. Al-Hulal al-Mawshīyya* (Tetuan: Editori Marroquí).
Huntingford, G. W. B. (1965) *The Glorious Victories of Amda Seyon, King of Ethiopia* (Oxford: Clarendon Press).
Huntingford, G. W. B. (1963) 'The peopling of the interior of Africa by its modern inhabitants' in R. Oliver and G. Mathew (eds), pp. 58–93.
Huntingford, G. W. B. (tr. and ed.) (1980) *The Periplus of the Erythraean Sea* (London: Hakluyt Society).
Hunwick, J. O. (1980) 'Gao and the Almoravids: a hypothesis' in B. K. Swartz and R. F. Dumett (eds), pp. 413–30.
Hunwick, J. O., Meillassoux, C. and Triaud J.-L. (1981) 'La géographie du Soudan d'après al-Bakrī. Trois lectures' in *(Le) Sol, la Parole et l'Ecrit*, Vol. 1, pp. 401–28.

Ibn 'Abd al-Ḥakam (1922) *The History of the Conquest of Egypt, North Africa and Spain, known as the Futūḥ Miṣr of Ibn 'Abd al-Ḥakam*, ed. by C. C. Torrey (New Haven: YUP).
Ibn 'Abd al-Ḥakam (1947) *Conquête de l'Afrique du Nord et de l'Espagne*, ed. and tr. by A. Gateau (Algiers: Bibliothèque Arabe Française, II).
Ibn 'Abd Rabbihi (1876) *Al-'Iḳd al-farīd* (3 vols, Cairo).
Ibn 'Abdūn (1955) 'Risāla fi l-ḳaḍā' wa-l-ḥisba' in E. Lévi-Provençal (ed.) *Trois traités hispaniques de ḥisba* (Cairo: Institut français d'archéologie du Caire).
Ibn Abī Dīnār (1869–70) *Kitāb al-mu'nis fī akhbār Ifrīkīyya wa-Tūnis* (Tunis).
Ibn Abī Zar' (1843–6) [*Rawḍ al-Kirṭās*] *Annales regum Mauritaniae a condito Idrisarum imperio ad annum fugae 726* . . ., ed. by C. J. Tornberg (2 vols, Uppsala: Litteris Academicis).
Ibn Abī Zar' (1936) *Rawḍ al-Kirṭās*, ed. by M. al-Hāshimī al-Filālī (2 vols, Rabat).
Ibn al-Abbār (1963) *Al-Hulla al-Siyarā* (2 vols, Ed. H. Mu'nis, Cairo).
Ibn al-Athīr, 'Alī b. Muḥammad (1885–6) *Al-Kāmil fī 'l-Ta'rikh* (12 vols, Cairo).
Ibn al-Djawzī, Abū 'l-Faradj (1938–40) *Kitāb al-Muntaẓam* (10 vols, Hyderabad).
Ibn al-Faḳīh (1885) *Compendium libri Kitāb al-boldān*, ed. by M. J. de Goeje (Leiden: Brill).
Ibn al-Mudjāwir (1957) *Ta'rīkh al-Mustabṣir*, ed. by O. Löfgren (Leiden: Brill).
Ibn al-Rūmī (1924) *Dīwān*, ed. by K. Kaylānī (Cairo).

Ibn al-Saghīr (1975) 'Chronique d'Ibn Saghir sur les imams Rostemides de Tahert', CT, **23**, 91–2, pp. 315–68.
Ibn al-Wardī (1868) *Tatimmat al-Mukhtaṣar fi akhbār al-bashār* (Cairo).
Ibn Baṭṭūṭa (1969) *Voyages d'Ibn Battûta*, ed. and tr. by C. Defrémery et B. R. Sanguinetti (reprint of 1st edn 1854–8, with notes by V. Monteil, Paris: Anthropos).
Ibn Ḥadjar al-'Askalānī (1970) *Al-Iṣāba fī tamyīz al-Ṣaḥāba* (8 vols, ed. by A. M. al-Bajjāwī, Cairo).
Ibn Ḥammād (1927) *Histoire des rois 'obaidides, les califes fatimides*, ed. and tr. by M. Vonderheyden (Algiers: Carbonal).
Ibn Ḥawkal (1938) *Opus Geographicum*, ed. by J. H. Kramers (Leiden: Brill).
Ibn Ḥawkal (1964) *Configuration de la terre* (*kitāb Surat al-Arḍ*), tr. by J. H. Kramers and G. Wiet (2 vols, Paris: Maisonneuve & Larose).
Ibn Hazm (1962) *Djamharat Ansāb al-'Arab*, ed. by 'Abd al-Salām Hārūn (Cairo).
Ibn Hishām (1936) *Al-Sīra al-Nabawiyya* (4 vols, Cairo).
Ibn 'Idhārī al-Marrākushī (1848–51) *Histoire de l'Afrique et de l'Espagne intitulée al-Bayano 'l Mogrib* (2 vols, ed. by R. Dozy, Leiden: Brill).
Ibn 'Idhārī al-Marrākushī (1948–51) *Histoire de l'Afrique du Nord et de l'Espagne musulmane, intitulée Kitab al-bayān al-mughrib, et fragments de la chronique de 'Arib* (4 vols, new edn of 1848–51 edn by R. Dozy from new ms, by G. S. Colin and E. Lévi-Provençal, Beirut: Da Assakafa).
Ibn 'Idhārī al-Marrākushī (1967) *Al-Bayān al-mughrib fī Akhbār al-Andalus wa-l-Maghrib* (4 vols; Beirut: Ed. Iḥsān 'Abbās).
Ibn Isḥāḳ (1955) *The Life of Muhammad: A Translation of Iṣhāq's Sīrat Rasūl Allāh*, tr. by A. Guillaume (Lahore: OUP).
Ibn Khaldūn (1847–51) *Histoire des Berbères et des dynasties musulmanes de l'Afrique septentrionale* tr. by Baron de Slane (2 vols, Algiers: Imprimerie du gouvernement).
Ibn Khaldūn (1867) *Kitāb al-'Ibār* (7 vols, Cairo).
Ibn Khaldūn (1925–56) *Histoire des Berbères et des dynasties musulmanes de l'Afrique septentrionale*, tr. Baron de Slane (1st edn, 1852–6), new edition ed. by P. Casanova (4 vols, Paris: Geuthner).
Ibn Khaldūn (1956–9) *Kitab al-'Ibar* (4 vols, reprinted 1961, Beirut).
Ibn Khaldūn (1967–9) *Al-Muqaddima. Discours sur l'histoire universelle.* Trad. par V. Monteil (3 vols, Beirut: Com. Libanaise pour la traduction des chefs-d'oeuvre).
Ibn Khallikān (1843–71) *Ibn Khallikan's Biographical Dictionary*, tr. by Baron de Slane (4 vols, Paris: Oriental Translation Fund of Great Britain and Ireland).
Ibn Ḳutayba (1850) *Ibn Coteibas Hanbuch der Geschichte* [Kitāb al-ma'ārif], ed. by F. Wüstenfeld (Göttingen: Vandenhoeck und Ruprecht).
Ibn Miskawayh (1920–1) *The Experiences of the Nations* in *The Eclipse of the Abbasid Caliphate; Original Chronicles of the Fourth Islamic Century*, ed. by H. F. Amedroz and D. S. Margoliouth (6 vols, Oxford: Blackwell).
Ibn Muyassar (1919) *Annales d'Egypte* (*Akhbār Miṣr*) (ed. by H. Massé, Cairo: PIFAO).
Ibn Sa'd (1904–40) [*Kitāb al-tabaḳāt al-kubrā*] *Biographien Muhammeds, seiner Gefährten und der späteren Träger des Islams bis zum J. 230 der Flucht* (9 vols, ed. by E. Sachau *et al.*, Leiden: Brill).
Ibn Sa'īd (1970) *Kitāb al-Djughrāfiyya* ed. by al-'Arabī (Beirut).
Idris, H. R. (1955) 'Deux maîtres de l'école juridique kairouanaise sous les Zīrīdes (XIe siècle): Abū Bakr b. 'Abd al-Raḥmān et Abū 'Imrān al-Fāsī', *AIEOA*, **13**, pp. 30–60.
Idris, H. R. (1962) *La Berberie orientale sous les Zirides: 10e–12e siècle* (2 vols, Paris: Maisonneuve).
Idris, H. R. (1968a) 'De la réalité de la catastrophe hilalienne', *Annales ESC*, **13**, **2**, pp. 390–6.
Idris, H. R. (1968b) 'L'invasion hilalienne et ses conséquences', *CCM*, **11**, pp. 353–71.
Idris, H. R. (1971) 'L'Occident musulman (Ifriqiya et al-Andalus) à l'avènement des Abbāsides d'après le chroniqueur zīrīde al-Raqīq', *REI*, **39**, **2**, pp. 109–91.
Idris, H. R. (1972) 'L'Ecole malikite de Mahdiya: l'Imām al-Mazārī' in *Etudes d'orientalisme dédiées à la mémoire de E. Lévi-Provençal*, Vol. 1, pp. 153–64.
al-Idrīsī (1866) *Description de l'Afrique et de l'Espagne* (Arabic text and translation by R. Dozy and M. J. de Goeje, Leyden: Brill).
al-Idrīsī (1970) *Opus geographicum*, ed. by A. Bombaci *et al.* (Naples–Rome).
Igué, O. J. (1970–80) *Contribution à l'étude de la civilisation Yoruba.* (Cotonou: Université Nationale du Bénin).
Ikime, O. (ed.) (1980) *Groundwork of Nigerian History* (Ibadan: Heinemann).
Ingrams, W. H. (1931) *Zanzibar, its History and its People* (London: Witherby).
Inskeep, R. R. and Maggs, T. M. (1975) 'Unique art objects in the Iron Age of the Transvaal', *SAAB*, **30**, 119–20, pp. 114–38.
al-Isfahānī, Abu 'l-Faradj (1868–9) *Kitāb al-Aghānī* (Būlāḳ).

Al-Iṣṭakhrī (1870) *Kitab masalik al-mamalik. Viae Regnorum* (ed. by M. J. de Goeje, Leiden: Brill).
Ivanow, W. (1942) *Ismaili Tradition Concerning the Rise of the Fatimids.* (London: OUP, Islamic Research Association Series, **10**).
Ivanow, W. (1952) *Brief Survey of the Evolution of Ismailism* (Leiden: Brill).

Jacques-Meunier, D. (1961) *Cités anciennes de Mauritanie* (Paris: Klincksieck).
Jakobielski, S. (1966a) 'La liste des évèques de Pakhoras', *Etudes et Travaux*, 1 (*CAMAP*, 3), pp. 151–70.
Jakobielski, S. (1966b) 'Two Coptic foundation stones from Faras' in *Mélanges offerts à Kazimierz Michalowski* (Warsaw: PWN), pp. 101–9.
Jakobielski, S. (1970) 'Polish excavations at Old Dongola, 1969' in E. Dinkler (ed.), pp. 171–80.
Jakobielski, S. (1972) *Faras III: A History of the Bishopric of Pachoras on the basis of Coptic Inscriptions* (Warsaw: PWN).
Jakobielski, S. (1975) 'Polish Excavations at Old Dongola, 1970–1972' in K. Michałowski (ed.), pp. 70–5.
Jakobielski, S. (1978) 'Polish Excavations at Old Dongola, 1973–1974 seasons', *Etudes Nubiennes*, pp. 129–40.
Jakobielski, S. (1981) 'Nubian Christian architecture', *ZÄS*, **108**, pp. 33–48.
Jakobielski, S. (1982a) 'Polish Excavations at Old Dongola 1976 and 1978' in J. M. Plumley (ed.) (1982a), pp. 116–26.
Jakobielski, S. (1982b) 'Portraits of the bishops of Faras' in J. M. Plumley (ed.) (1982a), pp. 127–42.
Jakobielski, S. (1982c) 'A brief account of the churches at Old Dongola' in P. van Moorsel (ed.), pp. 51–6.
Jakobielski, S. (1982d) 'Remarques sur la chronologie des peintures murales de Faras aux VIIIe et IXe siècles, *NC*, **1**, pp. 142–72.
Jakobielski, S. and Krzyzaniak, L. (1967–8) 'Polish excavations at Old Dongola, third season, December 1966–February 1967', *Kush*, **15**, pp. 143–64.
Jakobielski, S. and Ostrasz, A. (1967–8) 'Polish excavations at Old Dongola, second season, December 1965–February 1966', *Kush*, **15**, pp. 125–42.
Jean de Nikiou (1883) *Chronique de Jean, Evêque de Nikiou*, ed. and tr. by H. Zotenberg (Paris: Bibliothèque Nationale).
Jeffery, A. (1938) *The Foreign Vocabulary of the Qur'ān* (Baroda: Oriental Institute).
Jeffreys, M. D. W. (1951) 'Neolithic stone implements (Bamenda, British Cameroons)', *BIFAN*, **13**, 4, pp. 1203–17.
Jéquier, G. (1924) *Manuel d'archéologie égyptienne* (Paris: Picard).
Johnson, M. (1977) 'Cloth strips and archaeology', *WAJA*, **7**, pp. 169–78.
Johnson, S. (1921) *The History of the Yorubas from the Earliest Times to the Beginning of the British Protectorate* (London: Routledge).
Johnston, H. H. (1919–22) *A Comparative Study of the Bantu and Semi-Bantu Languages* (2 vols, Oxford: Clarendon Press).
Joire, J. (1955) 'Découvertes archéologiques dans la région de Rao (Bas-Sénégal)', *BIFAN* (B), **17**, 3–4, pp. 249–333.
Jones, A. (1981) 'Who were the Vai?', *JAH*, **22**, 2, pp. 159–78.
Jones, G. I. (1961) 'Ecology and social structure among the north-eastern Ibo', *Africa*, **31**, pp. 117–34.
Jones, G. I. (1963) *The Trading States of the Oil Rivers* (London: OUP).
Julien, C.-A. (1952) *Histoire de l'Afrique du Nord: Tunisie–Algérie–Maroc. De la conquête arabe à 1830* (Paris: Payot).
Julien, C.-A. (1970) *History of North Africa: Tunisa–Algeria–Morocco. From the Arab conquest to 1830* (London: Routledge & Kegan Paul).

Kagabo, J. (1982) 'Les "Swahili" du Rwanda. Etude sur la formation d'une minorité islamisée' (Thèse de 3ème cycle, Paris: EHISS).
Kamal, Y. (1926–38) *Monumenta Cartographica Africae et Aegypti* (13 vols, Cairo/Leiden: Brill).
Kamisokho, W. (1975) 'L'empire du Mali' in *Premier Colloque International de Bamako, 27 janvier–1 février 1975* (Fondation SCOA pour la Recherche scientifique en Afrique noire).
Keenan, J. H. (1977) 'The Tuareg veil', *Middle Eastern Studies*, **13**, pp. 3–13.
Kendall, R. L. (1969) 'An ecological history of the Lake Victoria basin', *Ecological Monographs*, **39**, pp. 121–76.
Kent, R. K. (1970) *Early Kingdoms in Madagascar, 1500–1700.* (New York: Holt, Rinehart & Winston).

Keswani, D. K. (1980) 'Influences culturelles et commerciales indiennes dans l'océan Indien, de l'Afrique et Madagascar à l'Asie du Sud-Est' in Unesco (1980), pp. 37–50.

Khalīf, Y. (1959) *Al-Shu'arā' al-ṣa 'ālīk fī'l 'aṣal-djāhili* (Cairo).

Khalis, S. (1966) *La vie littéraire à Seville au XIe siècle* (Paris: SNEA).

Khayar, I. H. (1976) *Le refus de l'école. Contribution à l'étude des problèmes de l'éducation chez les musulmans de Ouaddaï (Tchad)* (Paris: Maisonneuve).

al-Khuwārizmī (1926) *Das Kitāb Ṣūrat al-Arḍ des Abū Ǧa'far Muḥammad ibn Mūsā al-Huwārizmī* ed. by Hans von Mžik (Leipzig: Harrassowitz).

Ki-Zerbo, J. (1978) *Histoire de l'Afrique noire* (Paris: Hatier).

Kiethega, J.-B. (1983) *L'or de la Volta Noire: exploitation traditionnelle, histoire et archéologie* (Paris: Karthala).

Kimambo, I. N. (1969) *A Political History of the Pare of Tanzania* (Nairobi: East African Publishing House).

Kirkman, J. S. (1954) *The Arab City of Gedi: Excavations at the Great Mosque, Architecture and Finds* (London: OUP).

Kirkman, J. S. (1966) *Ungwana on the Tana* (The Hague: Mouton).

Kirwan, L. P. (1935) 'Notes on the topography of the Christian Nubian kingdoms', *JEA*, **21**, pp. 57–62.

Kirwan, L. P. (1982) 'Some thoughts on the conversion of Nubia to Christianity' in J. M. Plumley (ed.) (1982a), pp. 142–5.

Kitāb al-Istibṣār (1852) *Description de l'Afrique par un géographe arabe anonyme du VIe siècle de l'hégire* (Arabic text edited by M. Alfred Kramer, Vienna).

Kiyaga-Mulindwa, D. (1976) 'The earthworks of the Birim valley, southern Ghana' (unpublished PhD dissertation, Johns Hopkins University).

Kobishchanov, Y. M. (1962) 'Skazaniye o pokhode hadani Dan'ela' *NAA*, **6**.

Kołodziejczyk, K. (1982) 'Some remarks on the Christian ceramics from Faras' *NC*, **1**, pp. 173–89.

Konaré-Ba, A. (1977) *Sonni 'Ali Ber* (Niamey: IRSH, Etudes nigériennes, **40**).

Kramers, J. H. (1954) 'L'Erythrée au Xe siècle' in *Analecta Orientalia*, (Leiden: Brill), Vol. 1, pp. 159–72.

Krapf-Askari, E. (1969) *Yoruba Towns and Cities* (Oxford: Clarendon Press).

Krause, M. (1970) 'Zur Kirchen und Theologiegeschichte Nubiens' in E. Dinkler (ed.), pp. 71–86; the same reprinted as 'Neue Quellen und Probleme zur Kirchengeschichte Nubiens' in F. Altheim and R. Stiehl, *Christentum am Roten Meer*, Vol. 1 (Berlin–New York: W. de Gruyter), pp. 510–15.

Krause, M. (1978) 'Bischof Johannes III von Faras und seine beiden Nachfolger. Noch einmal zum Probleme eines Konfessionswechsels in Faras' *Etudes Nubiennes*, pp. 153–64.

Kronenberg, A. and Kronenberg, W. (1965) 'Parallel cousin marriage in medieval and modern Nubia', *Kush*, **13**, pp. 241–60.

Kropp-Dakubu, M. E. (1972) 'Linguistic prehistory and historical reconstruction: the Ga-Adangme migrations', *THSG*, **13**, 1, pp. 87–111.

Kubbel, L. E. (1963) 'Iz istoriii drevnego Mali', *AES*, **5**, pp. 1–118.

Kubińska, J. (1974) *Faras IV: Inscriptions grecques chrétiennes* (Warsaw: FWN).

Kubińska, J. (1976) 'L'Ange Litakskuel en Nubie', *Le Muséon*, **89**, pp. 451–5.

Kup, A. P. (1975) *Sierra Leone: A Concise History* (Newton Abbot: David & Charles).

Kuper, A. (1982a) *Wives for Cattle: Bridewealth and Marriage in Southern Africa* (London: Routledge & Kegan Paul).

Kuper, A. (1982b) 'Lineage theory: a critical retrospect' *Annual Review of Anthropology*, **11**, pp. 71–95.

Kuper, J. (ed.) (1977) *The Athropologist's Cookbook* (London: RAI).

Kuper, J. (ed.) (1981) *La Cuisine des ethnologues* (Paris: Berger-Levrault).

Kuper, R. (ed.) (1978) *Sahara: 10.000 Jahre zwischen Weide und Wüste.* (Köln: Museen der Stadt Köln).

Lacam, J. (1965) *Les Sarrasins dans le Haut Moyen âge français* (Paris: Maisonneuve & Larose).

La Chapelle, F. de (1930) 'Esquisse d'une histoire du Sahara occidental', *Hespéris*, **11**, pp. 35–95.

Lacoste, Y. (1966) *Ibn Khaldoun. Naissance de l'histoire, passé du Tiers-Monde* (Paris: Maspéro).

Lacroix, P.-F. (1969) 'L'Ensemble songhay-djerma: problèmes et thèmes de travail', *AUA*, Série H, pp. 87–99.

Laforgue, P. (1940) 'Notes sur Aoudaghost, ancienne capitale des Berbères Lemtouna', *BIFAN*, **2**, pp. 217–36.

Lagardère, V. (1976) 'Les Almoravides jusqu'au règne de Yūsuf b. Tāshfīn (430/1039–500/1106)' (Thèse de doctorat de 3ème cycle, Université de Bordeaux, III).

Lagardère, V. (1978) 'Le gouvernement des villes et la suprématie des Banū Turğūt au Maroc et en Andalus', *ROMM*, **25**, pp. 49–65.
Lagardère, V. (1979) 'Esquisse de l'organisation des Mūrabiṭūn à l'epoque de Yūsuf b. Tašfīn (430–1039/500–1106)', *ROMM*, **27**, pp. 99–114.
Lagardère, V. (1981) 'L'unification du malékisme oriental et occidental à Alexandrie: Abū Bakr aṭ-Ṭurṭūšī', *ROMM*, **31**, pp. 47–62.
Lagardère, V. (1983) 'La Tariqa et la révolte des Murīdūn en 539/1144 en Andalus', *ROMM*, **35**, pp. 157–70.
Lambert, N. (1971) 'Les industries sur cuivre dans l'Ouest saharien', *WAJA*, **1**, pp. 9–21.
Lammens, H. (1916) 'Les "Aḥābīš" et l'organisation militaire de La Mecque au siècle de l'Hégire, *JA*, 8, pp. 425–82.
Lamp, F. (1979) *African Art of the West Atlantic Coast. Transition in Form and Content* (New York: L. Kahen Gallery).
Lange, D. (1977) *Le Dīwān des sultans du [Kānem-]Bornū: chronologie et histoire d'un royaume africain (de la fin du Xe siècle jusqu'à 1808)* (Wiesbaden: Steiner).
Lange, D. (1978) 'Progrès de l'Islam et changement politique au Kānem du XIe au XIIIe siècle: un essai d'interprétation', *JAH*, **19**, 4, pp. 495–513.
Lange, D. (1979a) 'Un texte de Maqrīzī sur les "races des Sūdān"', *AI*, **15**, pp. 187–209.
Lange, D. (1979b) 'Les lieux de sépulture des rois sēfuwa (Kānem-Bornū): textes écrits et traditions orales', *Paideuma*, **25**, pp. 145–57.
Lange, D. (1980) 'La région du lac Tchad d'après la Géographie d'Ibn Sa'īd. Texte et cartes', *AI*, **16**, pp. 149–81.
Lange, D. (1982a), 'L'éviction des Séfuwa du Kānem et l'origine des Bulāla', *JAH*, **23**, 3, pp. 315–31.
Lange, D. (1982b) 'L'Alun du Kawār: une exportation africaine en Europe', *Cahiers du CRA*, **2**.
Lange, D. and Berthoud, S. (1977) 'Al-Qaṣaba et d'autres villes de la route centrale du Sahara', *Paideuma*, **23**, pp. 19–40.
Largeau, V. (1879) *Le Pays de Rirha, Ouargla. Voyage à Rhadamès* (Paris: Hachette).
Laroui, A. (1970) *L'histoire du Maghreb: un essai de synthèse* (Paris: Maspéro).
Laroui, A. (1977) *The History of the Maghrib: An Interpretative Essay* (Princeton: PUP).
Lathrap, D. W. (1973) 'The antiquity and importance of long distance trade relationships in the moist tropics of pre-Columbian South America', *WA*, **5**, 2, pp. 170–86.
Launois, A. (1964) 'Influence des docteurs malékites sur le monnayage ziride de type sunnite et sur celui des Almoravides', *Arabica*, **11**, pp. 127–50.
Launois, A. (1967) 'Sur un dinar almoravide en *nashī*', *Arabica*, **14**, pp. 60–75.
Lavers, J. E. (1974) 'Islam in the Bornu Caliphate: a survey', *Odu*, **5**, pp. 27–53.
Lavers, J. E. (1980) 'Kanem and Borno to 1808' in O. Ikime (ed.), pp. 187–209.
Law, R. C. C. (1967a) 'Contacts between the Mediterranean civilisations and West Africa in pre-Islamic times', *LNR*, **1**, 1, pp. 52–62.
Law, R. C. C. (1967b) 'The Garamantes and trans-Saharan enterprise in classical times', *JAH*, 8, 2, pp. 181–200.
Lawal, B. (1973) 'Dating problems at Igbo-Ukwu', *JAH*, **14**, 1, pp. 1–8.
Lebeuf, A. and Lebeuf, J.-P. (1970) 'Datations au C14 de sites Sao (Cameroun et Tchad)', *NA*, **128**, pp. 105–6.
Lebeuf, A. M. D. and Paques, V. (1970) *Archéologie malienne* (Paris: Catalogues du Musée de l'Homme, série C, Afrique Noire, 1).
Lebeuf, J.-P. (1962) *Archéologie tchadienne: les Sao du Cameroun et du Tchad* (Paris: Hermann).
Lebeuf, J.-P. (1981) 'Travaux archéologiques dans les basses vallées du Chari et du Logone (1963–1980)', *C-RAI*, pp. 636–56.
Lebeuf, J.-P. and Detourbet, A. M. (1950) *La civilisation du Tchad* (Paris: Payot).
Lebeuf, J.-P. and Lebeuf, A. (1977) *Les Arts des Sao: Cameroun, Tchad, Nigeria* (Paris: Chêne).
Lebeuf, J.-P., Lebeuf, A. M. D., Treinen-Claustre, F. and Courtin, J. (1980) *Le gisement sao de Magda-Fouilles 1960–68 (Tchad)* (Paris: Société d'ethnographie).
Leclant, J. (1958–74) 'Fouilles et travaux en Egypte et au Soudan' *Orientalia*, **27**–43.
Leclant, J. (1975–83) 'Fouilles et travaux en Egypte et au Soudan', *Orientalia*, **44**–52.
Leclant, J. (1976) 'L'Egypte, terre d'Afrique dans le monde gréco-romain' in J. Vercoutter *et al.* (eds), Vol. 1, pp. 269–85.
Leclant, J. and Huard, P. (1980) *La culture des chasseurs du Nil et du Sahara* (Algiers: SNED, Mémoires du CRAPE, **29**, 1 and 2).
Leclant, J. and Leroy, J. (1968) 'Nubien' in *Propyläen Kunstgeschichte (Byzanz und Christlichen Osten)*, 3 (Berlin), pp. 361–6.

Leo Africanus [Jean Léon l'Africain] (1956) *Description de l'Afrique*, tr. A. Epaulard, with notes by A. Epaulard, T. Monod, H. Lhote and R. Mauny (2 vols, Paris: Maisonneuve).

Lepage, C. (1972) 'L'église rupestre de Berakit', *AE*, 9, pp. 147–92.

Lepage, C. (1973) 'L'église de Zaréma (Ethiopie)', *C-RAI*, pp. 416–54.

Leroy, J. (1968) 'Un nouvel évangéliaire éthiopien illustré du Monastère d'Abba Garima' in *Synthronon. Art et Archéologie de la fin de l'Antiquité et du Moyen âge* (Paris: Klincksieck), pp. 75–87.

Le Rouvreur, A. (1962) *Saháliens et Sahariens du Tchad* (Paris: Berger-Levrault).

Lespinay, C. de (1981) 'Le chameau et l'histoire de l'Afrique pré-islamique. Approche critique des sources' (Mémoire de maîtrise, Université de Paris I).

Lessard, J.-M. (1969) 'Sijilmassa: la ville et ses relations commerciales au XIe siècle d'après al-Bakrī', *HT*, **10**, pp. 5–37.

Le Tourneau, R. (1949), *Fès avant le protectorat* (Casablanca: SMLE).

Le Tourneau, R. (1954) 'La révolte d'Abu Yazid au Xe siècle', *CT*, **2**, pp. 103–25.

Le Tourneau, R. (1958) 'Barghawāṭa' in B. Lewis *et al.* (eds), pp. 1043–5.

Lévi-Provençal, E. (1928) *Documents inédits d'histoire almohade* (Paris: Geuthner).

Lévi-Provençal, E. (1938) 'La Fondation de Fès', *AIEOA*, **4**.

Lévi-Provençal, E. (1948) 'Réflexion sur l'empire almoravide au début du XIIe siècle' in Lévi-Provençal, *Islam d'Occident; études d'histoire médiévale* (Paris: Maisonneuve), pp. 240–56.

Lévi-Provençal, E. (1950–3) *Histoire de l'Espagne musulmane* (3 vols, Paris-Leiden: Brill).

Lévi-Provençal, E. (1954a) 'Un nouveau récit de la conquête de l'Afrique du Nord par les Arabes', *Arabica*, **1**.

Lévi-Provençal, E. (1954b) 'Un nuevo documento sobre la conquista de Norte de Africa por los árabes', *Revista de Instituto Egipcio de Estudios Islamicos en Madrid*, **2**, 1–2, pp. 169, 193–239.

Lévi-Provençal, E. (1955) 'Le titre souverain des Almoravides et sa légitimation par le califat abbaside', *Arabica*, **2**, pp. 266–88.

Lévi-Provençal, E. (1957) 'La fondation de Marrakech (462/1070)', *MHAOM*, **2**, pp. 117–20.

Lévi-Provençal, E. (1960a) ''Abd al-Raḥman b. Ḥabīb b. Ḥabīb b. Abi 'Ubayda' in H. A. R. Gibb *et al.* (eds), p. 86.

Lévi-Provençal, E. (1960b) 'Abu 'Ubayd al-Bakrī' in H. A. R. Gibb *et al.* (eds), pp. 155–7.

Lévi-Provençal, E., Garcia-Gomez, E. and Oliver Asín, J. (1950) 'Novedades sobre la batalla llamada de al-Zallāqa', *Al-Andalus*, **15**, pp. 111–55.

Levtzion, N. (1968a) 'Ibn Ḥawqal, the cheque and Awdaghost', *JAH*, **9**, 2, pp. 223–33.

Levtzion, N. (1968b) *Muslims and Chiefs in West Africa. A Study of Islam in the Middle Volta Basin in the Pre-colonial Period* (Oxford: Clarendon Press).

Levtzion, N. (1973) *Ancient Ghana and Mali* (London: Methuen).

Levtzion, N. (1978) 'The Sahara and the Sudan from the Arab conquest of the Maghrib to the rise of the Almoravids' in J. D. Fage (ed.), pp. 637–84.

Levtzion, N. (1979) ''Abd Allāh b. Yāsīn and the Amoravids' in J. R. Willis (ed.), pp. 78–112.

Levtzion, N. (1981) 'Ancient Ghana: a reassessment of some Arabic sources', in *(Le)Sol, la Parole et l'Ecrit*, Vol. 1, pp. 429–37.

Levtzion, N. and Hopkins, J. F. P. (eds) (1981) *Corpus of Early Arabic Sources for West African History* (Cambridge: CUP).

Levy, R. (1957) *The Social Structure of Islam* (Cambridge: CUP).

Lewicki, T. (1939) 'Sur l'oasis de Ṣbrū (Ḍbr, Shbrū) des géographes arabes', *RA*, **378**, pp. 45–64.

Lewicki, T. (1951–2) 'Une langue romane oubliée de l'Afrique du Nord. Observations d'un arabisant', *RO*, **17**, pp. 415–80.

Lewicki, T. (1955) *Etudes ibāḍites nord-africaines. Partie I* (Warszawa: PWN).

Lewicki, T. (1957) 'La répartition géographique des groupements ibāḍites dans l'Afrique du Nord au Moyen âge', *RO*, **21**, pp. 301–43.

Lewicki, T. (1959) 'A propos d'une liste de tribus berbères d'Ibn Ḥawḳal', *FO*, **1**, pp. 128–35.

Lewicki, T. (1960) 'Quelques extraits inédits relatifs aux voyages des commerçants et des missionnaires ibāḍites nord-africains occidental au Moyen âge', *FO*, **2**, pp. 1–27.

Lewicki, T. (1962) 'L'état nord-africain de Tāhert et ses relations avec le Soudan occidental à la fin du VIIIe et au IXe siècle', *CEA*, **4**, 8, pp. 513–35.

Lewicki, T. (1964) 'Traits d'histoire du commerce saharien: marchands et missionnaires ibādites au Soudan occidental et central au cours des VIIIe–IXe siècles', *Ethnografia Polska*, **8**, pp. 291–311.

Lewicki, T. (1965a) 'Animal husbandry among medieval agricultural people of Western and Middle Sudan (according to Arab sources)', *Acta Ethnographica Academiae Scientiarum Hungaricae*, **14**, 1–2, pp. 165–78.

Lewicki, T. (1965b) 'L'Afrique noire dans le Kitāb al-Masālik wa'l-Mamālik d'Abū 'Ubayd al-Bakrī (XIe siècle)', *AB*, **2**, pp. 9–14.

Lewicki, T. (1965c) 'A propos du nom de l'oasis de Koufra chez les géographes arabes du XIe et du XIIIe siècle', *JAH*, **6**, 3, pp. 295–306.
Lewicki, T. (1965d) 'Prophètes, devins et magiciens chez les Berbères médiévaux', *FO*, **7**, pp. 3–27.
Lewicki, T. (1966) 'A propos de la génèse de *Nuzhat al-Mūstāq fi-Istirāq al-āfāq* d'al-Idrisi', *Studi Maghrebini*, **1**, pp. 41–55.
Lewicki, T. (1967a) 'Les ecrivains arabes du Moyen âge au sujet des mines de pierres précieuses et de pierres fines en territoire africain et de leur exploitation', *AB*, **7**, pp. 49–67.
Lewicki, T. (1967b) 'Arab trade in negro slaves up to the end of the XVIth century', *AB*, **6**, pp. 109–11.
Lewicki, T. (1969) *Arabic External Sources for the History of Africa to the South of Sahara* (Wroclaw-Warszawa-Kraków).
Lewicki, T. (1970) 'Les origines de l'islam dans les tribus berbères du Sahara occidental: Mūsā ibn Nuṣayr et 'Ubayd Allāh ibn al-Ḥabhāb', *SI*, **32**, pp. 203–14.
Lewicki, T. (1971a) 'Un état soudanais médiéval inconnu: le royaume de Zāfūn(u)', *CEA*, **11**, 44, pp. 501–25.
Lewicki, T. (1971b) 'Al-Ibāḍiyya' in B. Lewis *et al.* (eds), pp. 648–60.
Lewicki, T. (1973) 'Le monde berbère vu par les écrivains arabes du Moyen âge' in *Actes du Premier Congrès d'Etudes des cultures méditerranéennes d'influence arabo-berbère* (*Algiers: SNED*), pp. 31–42.
Lewicki, T. (1974) *West African Food in the Middle Ages according to Arabic Sources* (Cambridge: CUP).
Lewicki, T. (1976) *Etudes maghrébines et soudanaises* (Warsaw: Editions Scientifiques de Pologne).
Lewicki, T. (1977) 'L'exploitation et le commerce de l'or en Afrique de l'Est et du Sud-Est au Moyen âge d'après les sources arabes', *FO*, **18**, pp. 167–86.
Lewicki, T. (1978) 'L'Origine nord-africaine des Bafour' in *Actes du Deuxième Congrès International des Cultures de la Méditerranée Occidentale*, **2** (Algiers: SNED), pp. 145–53.
Lewicki, T. (1981) 'Les origines et l'islamisation de la ville de Tādmakka d'après les sources arabes' in (*Le*) *sol, la parole et l'écrit*, Vol. 1, pp. 439–44.
Lewis, A. R. (1951) *Naval Power and Trade in the Mediterranean A.D. 500–1100* (Princeton: PUP).
Lewis, B. (1940) *The Origins of Isma'ilism* (Cambridge: CUP).
Lewis, B. (1950) *The Arabs in History* (London: Hutchinson).
Lewis, B. (1971) *Race and Color in Islam* (New York: Harper & Row).
Lewis, B. (1982) *Race et couleur en pays d'Islam* (Paris: Payot).
Lewis, B., Pellat, C. and Schacht, J. (eds) (1958, 1965) *The Encyclopedia of Islam*, new edn, Vol. 1 (1958); Vol. 2 (1965) (Leiden/London: Brill/Luzac).
Lewis, B., Ménage, V. L., Pellat, C. and Schacht, J. (eds) (1971) *The Encyclopedia of Islam*, new edn, Vol. 3 (Leiden/London: Brill/Luzac).
Lewis, I. M. (ed.) (1966) *Islam in Tropical Africa* (London: OUP).
Lewis, I. M. (1974) 'Islamic frontiers in Africa and Asia: Africa south of the Sahara' in J. Schacht and C. E. Bosworth (eds) (1974), pp. 105–15.
Lhote, H. (1955) *Les Touaregs du Hoggar* (Paris: Payot).
Lhote, H. (1955–6) 'Contribution à l'histoire des Touaregs soudanais', *BIFAN*, **17**, pp. 334–70; **18**, pp. 391–407.
Lhote, H. (1972a) 'Recherches sur Takedda, ville décrite par le voyageur arabe Ibn Battouta, et située en Aïr', *BIFAN*, (B), **34**, 3, pp. 429–70.
Lhote, H. (1972b) 'Une étonnante découverte archéologique au Niger', *Archéologia*, **5**, pp. 63–7.
Liesegang, G. (1975) 'Mounds and graves near Famanougou, Mali', *Nyame Akuma*, **7**, pp. 27–8.
Linares de Sapir, O. (1971) 'Shell middens of Lower Casamance and problems of Diola protohistory', *WAJA*, **1**, pp. 23–54.
Lister, F. C. (1967) *Ceramic Studies of the Historic Periods in Ancient Nubia* (Salt Lake City: University of Utah, Anthropological Paper, **8**, Nubian series, **2**).
Littman, E. (1913) *Deutsche Aksum-Expedition, Vol. 4, Sabaische, Griechische und Abbessinische Inschriften* (Berlin: Reimer).
Livingstone, F. B. (1958) 'Anthropological implications of sickle cell gene distribution in West Africa', *AA*, **60**, 3, pp. 533–62.
Lockhart, L. (1960) 'Al-Ahwāz' in H. A. R. Gibb *et al.* (eds) p. 305.
Loir, H. (1935) *Le tissage du raphia au Congo belge* (Tervuren: Musée du Congo Belge).
Lombard, J. and Mauny, R. (1954) 'Azelik et la question de Takedda', *NA*, **10**, 64, pp. 99–101.
Lombard, M. (1947) 'Les bases monétaires d'une suprématie économique: l'or musulman du VIIe au XIe siècle', *Annales ESC*, **2**, pp. 143–60.
Lombard, M. (1971a) *Monnaie et Histoire d'Alexandre à Mahomet* (Paris: Mouton).
Lombard, M. (1971b) *L'Islam dans sa première grandeur* (*VIIIe–XIe siècle*) (Paris: Flammarion).

Lombard, M. (1978) *Les Textiles dans le monde musulman du VIIIe au XIIe siècle.* (Paris and The Hague: Mouton).
Long, R. (1971) 'A comparative study of the Northern Mande languages' (unpublished PhD dissertation, Indiana University).
Loubser, J. H. N. (1981) 'Ndebele archaeology of the Pietersburg area' (unpublished MA thesis, University of the Witwatersrand).
Louhichi, A. (1984) 'La céramique musulmane d'origine médiévale importée à Tegdaoust. Etude archéologique; étude de laboratoire' (Thèse de 3ème cycle, Université de Paris I).
Lucas, A. J. (1931) 'Considération sur l'ethnique maure et en particulier sur une race ancienne: les Bafour', *JSA*, **1**, pp. 151–94.
Lucchesi-Falli, E. (1982) 'Some parallels to the figure of St. Mercurius at Faras' in J. M. Plumley (ed.) (1982a), pp. 162–9.
Łukaszewicz, A. (1978) 'Quelques remarques sur un saint anachorète de Faras', *Etudes et Travaux*, **10**, (*CAMAP*, 20) pp. 355–62.
Łukaszewicz, A. (1982) 'En marge d'une image de l'anachorète Aaron dans la cathédrale de Faras', *NC*, **1**, pp. 192–213.
Lwanga-Lunyiigo, S. (1976) 'The Bantu problem reconsidered', *Current Anthropology*, **17**, 2, pp. 282–6.

Mabogunje, A. L. (1962) *Yoruba Towns* (Ibadan: Ibadan University Press).
Mabogunje, A. L. (1971) 'The Land and Peoples of West Africa' in J. F. A. Ajayi and M. Crowder (eds), (1971) Vol. 1, pp. 1–32.
McCall, D. F. (1971) 'The cultural map and time profile of the Mande speaking peoples' in C. T. Hodge (ed.).
MacGaffey, W. (1966) 'Concepts of race in the historiography of north-east Africa', *JAH*, **7**, 1, pp. 1–17.
McIntosh, R. J. (1974) 'Archaeology and mud wall decay in a West African village', *WA*, **6**, 2, pp. 154–71.
McIntosh, R. (1976) 'Finding lost walls on archaeological sites. The Hani model', *Sankofa*, **2**, pp. 45–53.
McIntosh, R. J. (1979) 'The development of urbanism in West Africa: the example of Jenne, Mali' (unpublished PhD thesis, Cambridge University).
McIntosh, R. J. and McIntosh, S. K. (1979) 'Terra cotta statuettes from Mali', *African Arts*, **12**, 2, pp. 51–3, 91.
McIntosh, R. J. and McIntosh S. K. (1981) 'The Inland Niger Delta before the empire of Mali: evidence from Jenne-Jeno', *JAH*, **22**, 1, pp. 1–22.
McIntosh, S. K. (1979) 'Archaeological exploration in *terra incognita*: excavation at Jenne-Jeno (Mali)' (unpublished PhD dissertation, University of California, Santa Barbara).
McIntosh, S. K. (1981) 'A reconsideration of Wangara/Palolus, Island of Gold', *JAH*, **22**, 1, pp. 145–58.
McIntosh, S. K. and McIntosh R. J. (1980a) 'Jenne-Jeno: an ancient African city', *Archaeology*, **33**, 1, pp. 8–14.
McIntosh, S. K. and McIntosh, R. J. (1980b) *Prehistoric Investigations in the Region of Jenne (Mali)* (2 vols, Oxford: BAR, Cambridge Monographs in African Archaeology, **2**).
McIntosh, S. K. and McIntosh, R. J. (1981) 'West African prehistory', *American Scientist*, **69**, 6, pp. 602–13.
Mack, J. and Robertshaw, P. (eds) (1982) *Culture History in the Southern Sudan, Archeology, Linguistics, Ethnohistory.* (Nairobi: British Institute in Eastern Africa).
Madelung, W. (1961) 'Das Imamat in der frühen ismailitischen Lehre', *Der Islam*, **37**, pp. 43–135.
Mādjid, ʿAbd al-Munʿim (1968) *Ẓuhūr k͟hilāfāt at-Fāṭimiyyīn wa suḳūṭuhā.* (Cairo).
Maggs, T. M. (1976) *Iron Age Communities of the Southern Highveld* (Pietermaritzburg: Natal Museum, Occ. Publ. Natal Museum, **2**).
Maggs, T. M. (1980a) 'The Iron Age sequence south of the Vaal and Pongola rivers: some historical implications' *JAH*, **21**, 1, pp. 1–15.
Maggs, T. M. (1980b) 'Mzonjani and the beginning of the Iron Age in Natal', *ANM*, **24**, 1, pp. 71–96.
Maggs, T. M. and Michael, M. A. (1976) 'Ntshekane: an Early Iron Age site in the Tugela Basin, Natal', *ANM*, **22**, 3, pp. 705–40.
Mahjoubi, A. (1966) 'Nouveau témoignage épigraphique sur la communauté chrétienne de Kairouan au XIe siècle' *Africa* (INAA), **1**, pp. 85–104.
al-Maḳḳarī (1840–3) *The History of the Mohammedan Dynasties in Spain*, tr. by P. de Gayangos (2 vols, London: W. H. Allen).

al-Maḳḳarī (1855–1861) *Analectes sur l'histoire et la littérature des Arches d'Espagne* (2 vols, ed. by R. Dozy, G. Duget, L. Krehl et W. Wright, Leiden: Brill).
al-Maḳḳarī (1969) *Kitāb Nafḥ al Ṭīb* (2 vols, Ed. Iḥsān 'Abbās, Beyrūt).
Maley, J. (1981) *Etudes palynologiques dans le bassin du Tchad et paléoclimatologie de l'Afrique nord-tropicale de 30.000 ans à l'époque actuelle.* (Paris: ORSTOM).
al-Mālikī (1951) *Riyāḍ al-Nufūs*, Vol. 1 (ed. H. Mu'nis: Kahira).
Malmusi, B. (1895) *Lapidi della necropoli musulmana di Dahlak* (Modena: Società tipografica).
Malowist, M. (1966) 'Le commerce d'or et d'esclaves au Soudan occidental' *AB*, **4**, pp. 49–72.
Mamour, P. H. (1934) *Polemics on the Origin of the Fatimi Caliphs* (London: Luzac).
Manguin, P.-Y. (1972) *Les Portugais sur les côtes du Viet nam et du Campa. Etude sur les routes maritimes et les relations commerciales d'après les sources portugaises.* (*XVIe–XVIIIe siècles*) (Paris: EFEO).
Manguin, P.-Y. (1979) 'The South-East Asian trading ship. An historical approach' in ICIOS, **5**. *The History of Commercial Exchange and Maritime History* (Perth).
Mantran, R. (1969) *L'expansion musulmane VIIe–XIe siècle* (Paris: PUF).
Marçais, G. (1946) *La Berbérie musulmane et l'Orient au Moyen-Age* (Paris: Aubier).
Marçais, G. (1953) 'Sîdî Ukba, Abû l-Muhâdjir et Kusaila', *CT*, **1**, pp. 11–17.
Marçais, W. (1938) 'Comment l'Afrique du Nord a été arabisée', *AIEOA*, **4**, pp. 1–22.
Maret, P. de (1975) 'A carbon-14 date from Zaire', *Antiquity*, **49**, pp. 133–7.
Maret, P. de (1977) 'Sanga: new excavations, more data and more related problems', *JAH*, **18**, 3, pp. 321–37.
Maret, P. de (1977–8) 'Chronologie de l'âge du fer dans la dépression de l'Upembe en République du Zaire' (3 vols, Brussels: unpublished Thèse de Doctorat).
Maret, P. de (1979) 'Luba roots: the first complete Iron Age sequence in Zaire' *Current Anthropology*, **20**, pp. 233–5.
Maret, P. de (1980) 'Les trop fameux pots à fossette . . . du Kasai' *Africa Tervuren*, **26**, pp. 4–12.
Maret, P. de (1981) 'L'évolution monétaire du Shaba central entre le VIIe et le XVIIIe siècle', *AEH*, **10**, pp. 117–49.
Maret, P. de and Nsuka, F. (1977) 'History of Bantu metallurgy: some linguistic aspects', *HA*, **4**, pp. 43–66.
Marquart, J. (1913) *Die Benin-Sammlung des Reichsmuseums für Völkerkunde in Leiden* (Leiden: Brill).
Martens, M. (1972) 'Observations sur la composition du visage dans les peintures de Fara, VIIIe–IX siècles', *Etudes et Travaux*, **6** (*CAMAP*, 13), pp. 207–50.
Martens, M. (1973) 'Observations sur la composition du visage dans les peintures de Faras, IXe–XIIe siècles', *Etudes et Travaux*, **8** (*CAMAP*, 14), pp. 163–226.
Martens-Czarnecka, M. (1982a) *Faras VII. Les éléments décoratifs sur les peintures de la cathédrale de Faras* (Warsaw: PWN).
Martens-Czarnecka, M. (1982b) 'Remarques sur les motifs décoratifs des peintures de la cathédrale de Faras' in J. M. Plumley (ed.) (1982a), pp. 170–8.
Martens-Czarnecka, M. (1982c) 'General results of using decorative ornaments and motifs on Faras murals as a criterion for their dating' *NC*, **1**, pp. 214–22.
Martens-Czarnecka, M. (1982d) 'Influences extérieures dans l'art nubien', *AB*, **31**, pp. 59–73.
Martin, B. G. (1969) 'Kanem Bornu and the Fazzān: notes on the political history of a trade route.' *JAH*, 10, 1, pp. 15–27.
Martin, B. G. (1974) 'Arab migrations to East Africa in medieval times', *IJAHS*, 7, 3, pp. 367–90.
Martin, P. (1970) 'The trade of Loango in the seventeenth and eighteenth centuries' in R. Gray and D. Birmingham (eds), pp. 138–61.
Martin, V. and Becker, C. (1974a) *Répertoire des sites protohistoriques du Sénégal et de la Gambie* (Kaolack).
Martin, V. and Becker, C. (1974b) 'Vestiges protohistoriques et occupation humaine au Sénégal', *Annales de Démographie historique*, pp. 403–29.
Martin del Molino, A. L. (1965) *Secuencia cultural en el néolitico de Fernando Po* (Madrid: Trabajos de Prehistoria del Seminario de Historia Primitiva del Hombre de la Universidad de Madrid y del Instituto Español de Prehistoria del Consejo Superior de Investigaciones Cientificas, **17**).
Mason, M. (1973) 'Captive and client labour and the economy of the Bida emirate, 1857–1901', *JAH*, **14**, 3, pp. 453–71.
Mason, R. J. (1968) 'Transvaal and Natal Iron Age settlements revealed by aerial photography and excavation', *AS*, **27**, 4, pp. 1–14.
Mason, R. J. (1969) *Prehistory of the Transvaal: A Record of Human Activity* (Johannesburg: Witwatersrand University Press).

Mason, R. J. (1974) 'Background to the Transvaal Iron Age – new discoveries at Olifantspoort and Broederstroom', *JSAIMM*, 74, 6, pp. 211–16.
Maspéro, G. (1928) *Le royaume de Champa* (Paris-Brussels: G. Van Oest).
Massé, H. (1966) *L'Islam* (Paris: A. Colin, 9th edn.).
Massignon, L. (1929) 'Zandj' in M. T. Houtsma *et al.* (eds), p. 1213.
al-Mas'ūdī (1861–77) *Les Prairies d'or*, ed. and tr. by C. Barbier de Meynard et P. de Courteille (9 vols, Paris: Imprimerie Impériale).
al-Mas'ūdī (1962–5) *Les Prairies d'or*, tr. by C. Pellat (Paris).
al-Mas'ūdī (1964) *Murū' al-Dhahab wa ma'ādin al Djawhar*, ed. by M. Abdulhamid (4 vols, Cairo).
Mathew, G. (1963) 'The East African coast until the coming of the Portuguese' in R. Oliver and G. Mathew (eds), pp. 94–128.
Matthews, D. and Mordini, A. (1959) 'The monastery of Debra Damo, Ethiopia', *Archaeologia*, **97**, pp. 1–58.
Matveyev, V. V. (1960) *Northern Boundaries of the Eastern Bantu (Zinj) in the Tenth Century, According to Arab Sources* (Moscow: Oriental Institute).
Mauny, R. (1951) 'Etat actuel de la question de Ghana' *BIFAN*, **13**, pp. 463–75.
Mauny, R. (1955a) 'Notes d'histoire et d'archéologie sur Azougui, Chinguetti et Ouadane', *BIFAN* (B), **17**, pp. 142–62.
Mauny, R. (1955b) 'Disques énigmatiques de poterie', *NA*, **68**, p. 17.
Mauny, R. (1961) *Tableau géographique de l'Ouest Africain au Moyen Age d'après les sources écrites, la tradition, l'archéologie* (Dakar: IFAN).
Mauny, R. (1965) 'The Wakwak and the Indonesian invasion in East Africa in 945 AD', *Studia* (Lisbon), pp. 7–16.
Mauny, R. (1970) *Les siècles obscurs de l'Afrique noire: histoire et archéologie* (Paris: Fayard).
Mauny, R. (1973) 'Notes bibliographiques', *BIFAN*, (B), **35**, 3, pp. 759–66.
Mauny, R. (1978) 'Trans-Saharan contacts and the Iron Age in West Africa' in J. D. Fage (ed.), pp. 272–341.
al-Māwardī (1922) *Al-aḥkām al-sulṭāniyya* (Cairo).
Maxwell, R. J. (1932) 'The law relating to slavery among the Malays', *Journal of the Malayan Branch of the Royal Asiatic Society*, **10**, 1, p. 254.
Medeiros, F. de (1973) 'Recherches sur l'image des noirs dans l'occident médiéval, 13–15e siècles' (Thèse de doctorat, Université de Paris).
Meeussen, A. E. (1969) *Bantu Lexical Reconstructions* (Tervuren, stenciled).
Meier, F. (1981) 'Almoraviden und Marabute', *Die Welt des Islams* (ns), **21**, pp. 80–163.
Meillassoux, C. (ed.) (1971) *The Development of Indigenous Trade and Markets in West Africa* (London: OUP for IAI).
Meillassoux, C. (ed.) (1975) *L'esclavage en Afrique précoloniale* (Paris: Maspéro).
Meinardus, O. (1967) 'The Christian kingdoms of Nubia', *Nubia, Cahiers d'Histoire Égyptienne*, **10**, pp. 133–64.
Meinhof, C. (1899) *Grundriss einer Lautlehre der Bantusprachen* (Leipzig: Brockhaus).
Meinhof, C. (1906) *Grundzüge einer vergleichenden der Grammatik der Bantusprachen* (Berlin: Reimer).
Mekouria, T. T. (1959) *History of Ethiopia: Axum-Zagwé* (in Amharic, Addis Ababa).
Mendelsohn, I. (1949) *Slavery in the Ancient Near East* (New York: OUP).
Mercier, E. (1888–91) *Histoire de l'Afrique septentrionale (Berbérie) depuis les temps les plus reculés, jusqu'à la conquête française* (3 vols, Paris: Leroux).
Mercier, P. (1970) 'Guinée centrale et orientale' in H. Deschamps (ed.), Vol. 1.
Merwe, N. J. Van Der (1980) 'The advent of iron in Africa' in T. A. Wertime and J. D. Muhly (eds), pp. 463–506.
Messier, R. A. K. (1974) 'The Almoravids: West African gold and the gold currency of the Mediterranean world', *JESHO*, **17**, 1, pp. 31–47.
Messier, R. A. (1980) 'Quantitative analysis of Almoravid dinars', *JESHO*, **23**, pp. 102–18.
Metcalf, D. M. (1972) 'Analyses of the metal contents of medieval coins, methods of chemical and metallurgical investigation of ancient coinage', *Royal Numismatic Society Special Publication*, **8**, pp. 383–434.
Metzger, B. M. (1968) 'The Christianization of Nubia and the Old Nubian versions of the New Testament' in *Historical and Literary Studies: Pagan, Jewish and Christian* (Grand Rapids, Michigan), pp. 111–22.
Meunié, J. and Allain, C. (1956) 'La forteresse almoravide de Zagora', *Hesperis*, **53**, pp. 305–23.
Meunié, J. and Terrasse, H. (1952) *Recherches archéologiques à Marrakech* (Paris: Arts et Métiers graphiques).

Meyer, A. (1980) ''n Interpretasie van die Greefswald potwerk' (unpublished MA thesis, University of Pretoria).
Mez, A. (1922) *Die Renaissance des Islams* (Heidelberg: C. Winter).
Michałowski, K. (1962) *Faras, Vol. 1, Fouilles Polonaises 1961* (Warsaw: PWN).
Michałowski, K. (1964a) 'Polish Excavations at Faras, 1962–63', *Kush*, **12**, pp. 195–207.
Michałowski, K. (1964b) 'Die wichtigsten Entwicklungsetappen der Wandmalerei in Faras' in K. Wessel (ed.), pp. 79–94.
Michałowski, K. (1965a) 'La Nubie chrétienne', *AB*, **3**, pp. 9–25.
Michałowski, K. (1965b) 'Polish excavations at Faras, fourth season, 1963–64', *Kush*, **13**, pp. 177–89.
Michałowski, K. (1965c) *Faras, Vol. 2, Fouilles Polonaises 1961–1962* (Warsaw: PWN).
Michałowski, K. (1966a) 'Polish excavations at Old Dongola: first season, November–December 1964', *Kush*, **14**, pp. 289–99.
Michałowski, K. (1966b) *Faras, centre artistique de la Nubie chrétienne* (Leiden: Instituut vor het Nabije Oosten).
Michałowski, K. (1967) *Faras, die Kathedrale aus dem Wüstensand* (Einsiedeln, Zurich, Cologne: Benzinger Verlag).
Michałowski, K. (1970) 'Open problems of Nubian art and culture in the light of the discoveries at Faras' in E. Dinkler (ed.) (1970), pp. 11–20.
Michałowski, K. (1974) *Faras, Wall Paintings in the Collection of the National Museum in Warsaw* (Warsaw: Wydawnictwo Artystyczno–Graficzne).
Michałowski, K. (ed.) (1975) *Nubia – récentes recherches. Actes du Colloque Nubiologique International au Musée National de Varsovie, 19–22 juin 1972* (Warsaw: National Museum).
Michałowski, K. (1979) 'Faras, seventeen years after the discovery', in F. Hintze (ed.) *Africa in Antiquity – the Arts of Ancient Nubia and the Sudan, Proceedings of the Symposium held in conjunction with the Exhibition, Brooklyn, September 29–October 1, 1978, Meroitica*, 5 (Berlin: Humboldt-Universität), pp. 31–9.
Migne, J.-P. (ed.) (1844–64) *Patrologiæ cursus completus, series Latina* (Paris).
Mileham, G. (1910) *Churches in Lower Nubia* (Philadelphia: University Museum).
Miller, J. C. (1976) *Kings and Kinsmen: Early Mbundu States in Angola* (London: OUP).
Miller, J. I. (1969) *The Spice Trade of the Roman Empire (29 BC to AD 641)* (Oxford: Clarendon Press).
Miller, S. F. (1969) 'Contacts between the Later Stone Age and the Early Iron Age in Southern Central Africa', *Azania*, **4**, pp. 81–90.
Millet, N. B. (1964) 'Gebel Adda. Preliminary Report, 1963–64', *JARCE*, **3**, pp. 5–14.
Millet, N. B. (1967) 'Gebel Adda. Preliminary Report, 1965–1966', *JARCE*, **6**, pp. 53–63.
Mills, E. A. C. and Filmer, N. T. (1972) 'Chondwe Iron Age site, Ndola, Zambia', *Azania*, **7**, pp. 129–47.
Miquel, A. (1975) *La géographie humaine du monde musulman jusqu'au milieu du XIe siècle* (Paris: Mouton).
Miquel, A. (1977) *L'Islam et sa civilisation, VIIe–XXe siècles* (Paris: A. Colin).
Miskawaih (1914) *Tadjārib al-umam* (Cairo).
Mlaker, K. (1927) 'Die Inschrift von Ḥuṣn Ghurāb', *WZKM*, **34**, pp. 54–75.
Moberg, A. (1924) *The Book of the Himyarites. Fragments of a Hitherto Unknown Syriac Book* (Lund: Gleerup).
Modat, C. (1919) 'Les populations primitives de l'Adrar mauritanien', *BCEHS*, **4**, pp. 372–91.
Möhlig, W. J., Rottland, F. and Heine, B. (eds) (1977) *Zur Sprachgeschichte und Ethnohistorie in Afrika* (Berlin: Reimer).
Mollat, M. (1971) 'Les relations de l'Afrique de l'Est avec l'Asie: essai de position de quelques problèmes historiques', *CHM*, **13**, 2, pp. 291–316.
Mollat, M. (ed.) (1979) *Mouvements de populations dans l'Océan Indien* (Paris: Champion).
Monès, H. (1947) *Fatḥ al 'Arab li l-Maghrib* (Cairo).
Monès, H. (1962) 'Le malikisme et l'échec des Fatimides en Ifrikiya' in *Etudes d'orientalisme dédiées à la mémoire de E. Lévi-Provençal*, Vol. 1, pp. 197–220.
Monneret de Villard, U. (1927) *Il Monastero di San Simeone presso Aswan* (Milan: S. Giuseppe).
Monneret de Villard, U. (1935–57) *La Nubia mediévale* (4 vols, Cairo: Service des Antiquités de l'Egypte).
Monneret de Villard, U. (1938) *Storia della Nubia cristiana* (Rome: Orientalia Christiana Analecta, 118).
Monneret de Villard, U. (1948) 'Aksum e i quattro re del mondo', *AL*, **12**, pp. 175–80.
Monod, T. (1948) *Mission scientifique au Fezzan, 1944–45, 2è partie: Reconnaissance au Dohone* (Algiers: Institut de Recherches Sahariennes de l'Université d'Alger).

Monod, T. (1958) *Majābat al-Koubra. Contribution à l'étude de l'Empty Quarter ouest-Saharien* (Dakar: IFAN).
Monod, T. (1969) 'Le "Maden Ijâfen"; une épave caravanière ancienne dans la Majâbat al-Koubrâ', *Actes 1er Coll. Intern. Archéol. Afr.*, pp. 286–320.
Monod, T. (1973a) *Les déserts* (Paris: Horizons de France).
Monod, T. (1973b) 'Les monnaies nord-africaines anciennes de Corvo (Açores)', *BIFAN* (B), **35**, pp. 231–5.
Monteil, C. (1903) *Soudan français. Monographie de Djenné, cercle et ville* (Tulle: Mazeirie).
Monteil, C. (1926) 'Le coton chez les noirs', *BCEHS*, 9, pp. 585–684.
Monteil, C. (1929) 'Les empires du Mali', *BCEHS*, **12**, pp. 291–443.
Monteil, C. (1953) 'La légende de Ouagadou et l'origine des Sarakolé' in *Mélanges ethnologiques* (Dakar: IFAN) pp. 359–408.
Monteil, C. (1977) *Les Bambara du Ségou et du Kaarta. (Etude historique, ethnographique et littéraire d'une peuplade du Soudan français)* (Paris: Maisonneuve & Larose).
Monteil, V. (1968) 'Al-Bakri (Cordoue, 1068); routier de l'Afrique blanche et noire du Nord-Ouest' *BIFAN* (B), **30**, pp. 39–116.
Monteil, V. (1980) *L'Islam noir. Une religion à la conquête de l'Afrique* (3rd edn, Paris: Editions du Seuil).
Moore, M. P. J. (1981) 'The Iron Age of the Makapan Valley area, central Transvaal' (unpublished MA thesis, University of the Witwatersrand).
Moorsel, P. van (1966) 'Une théophanie nubienne', *RAC*, **42**, pp. 297–316.
Moorsel, P. van (1970a) 'Die Wandmalereien der zentrale Kirche von Abdallah Nirqi' in E. Dinkler (ed.), pp. 103–111.
Moorsel, P. van (1970b) 'Die stillende Gottesmutter und die Monophysiten' in E. Dinkler (ed.), pp. 281–90.
Moorsel, P. van (1972) 'Die Nubier and das glorreiche Kreuz', *BAB*, **47**, pp. 125–34.
Moorsel, P. van (1975) 'Bilder ohne Worte. Problems in Christian Nubian iconography' in K. Michałowski (ed.), pp. 126–9.
Moorsel, P. van (ed.) (1982) *New Discoveries in Nubia. Proceedings of the Colloquium on Nubian Studies, the Hague, 1979.* (Leiden: Instituut voor het Nabije Oosten – Egyptologische Uitgaven, 2).
Moorsel, P. van, Jacquet, J. and Schneider, H. D. (1975) *The Central Church of Abdallah Nirqi* (Leiden: Brill).
Moreau, J.-L. (1982) *Africains musulmans. Des communautés en mouvement* (Paris: PA, Abidjan: INADES édition).
Morrison, M. E. S. (1968) 'Vegetation and climate in the uplands of south-west Uganda during the later Pleistocene period. I. Muchoya Swamp, Kigizi district', *Journal of Ecology*, **156**, pp. 363–84.
Morrison, M. E. S. and Hamilton, A. C. (1974) 'Forest clearance and other vegetational changes in the Rukiga Highlands during the past 8000 years', *Journal of Ecology*, **62**, 1, pp. 1–31.
Morse, M. L. (1967) 'The question of Samogo' *JAL*, **6**, pp. 61–80.
Mortelmans, G. (1962) 'Archéologie des Grottes Dimba et Ngovo', *Actes du IV congrès Panafricain de Préhistoire*, pp. 407–25.
al-Mubarrad (1864–92) in W. Wright (ed.) *Kāmil* (2 vols, Leipzig).
Mubitana, K. (ed.) (1977) *The Sculpture of Zambia* (Lusaka).
al-Mufaḍḍal (1918–21) *The Mufaḍḍalīyāt: An Anthology of Ancient Arabian Odes*, ed. by C. J. Lyall (Oxford: Clarendon Press).
al-Muḳaddasī (1877) *Aḥsān al-taḳāsim. Descriptio imperii moslemici* (ed. by M. J. de Goeje, Leyden: Brill, 2nd edn, 1906).
Müller, C. D. G. (1975) 'Die nubische Literatur, Bestand und Eigenart' in K. Michałowski (ed.), pp. 93–100.
Müller, C. D. G. (1978) 'Die nubische Literatur, Bestand und Eigenart', *Etudes et Travaux*, **10**, (*CAMAP*, 20) pp. 375–7.
Müller, H. (1980) *Die Kunst des Sklavenkaufs nach arabischem, persischem and türkischen Ratgebern von 10. bis zum 18. Jhdt* (Freiburg: Klaus Schwarz).
Munson, P. (1968) 'Recent archeological research in the Dhar Tichitt region of South-Central Mauritania', *WAAN*, **10**, pp. 6–13.
Munson, P. (1970) 'Corrections and additional comments concerning the Tichitt Tradition', *WAAN*, **12**, pp. 47–8.
Munson, P.J. (1971) 'The Tichitt tradition: a late prehistoric occupation of the southern Sahara' (unpublished PhD dissertation, University of Illinois).
Munson, P. (1980) 'Archaeology and the prehistoric origins of the Ghana empire', *JAH*, **21**, 4, pp. 457–66.

Munthe, L. (1982) *La tradition arabico-malgache vue à travers le manuscrit A-6 d'Oslo et d'autres manuscrits disponibles* (Antananarivo: TPFLM).

Murdock, G. P. (1959) *Africa, Its Peoples and Their Culture History* (New York: McGraw-Hill).

Muriuki, G. (1974) *A History of the Kikuyu, 1500–1900* (Nairobi: OUP).

Musca, G. (1964) *L'Emirato di Bari: 847–871* (Bari: Dedalo).

Musonda, F. B. (1976) 'The archaeology of the Late Stone Age along the Voltaian scarp' (unpublished MA thesis, University of Ghana, Legon).

Muṭahhar al-Maḳdīsī (1890–1919) *Le livre de la création et de l'histoire*, ed. and tr. by C. Huart (6 vols, Paris: Publications de l'ELOV).

Mutoro, H. W. (1979) 'A contribution to the study of cultural and economic dynamics of the historical settlements on East African coast, with particular reference to the ruins of Takwa, North Coast' (unpublished MA thesis, University of Nairobi).

Mutoro, H. W. (1982a) 'New light on the archeology of East African coast', *KHR*, **9**, 1–2.

Mutoro, H. W. (1982b) 'A survey of the Kaya settlement system on hinterland Kenya coast' (Report to the Ministry of Culture and Social Services, Government of Kenya).

Nachtigal, G. (1879–89) *Saharâ und Sûdân* (3 vols, Berlin–Leipzig: Weidmann).

Nachtigal, G. (1971–80) *Sahara and Sudan*, Vols 1, 2 and 4, Engl. tr by A. G. B. Fisher and H. J. Fisher (London: C. Hurst).

al-Naqar, U. (1969) 'Takrūr: the history of a name', *JAH*, **10**, 3, pp. 365–74.

al-Nawawī (1951) *En-Nanawi: Les Quarante Hadiths*, tr. by G. H. Bousquet (Algiers: La Maison des Livres).

Ndoricimpa, L. et al. (1981) 'Technologie et économie du sel végétal au Burundi' in *La Civilisation ancienne des peuples des Grands Lacs: colloque de Bujumbura* (Paris: Karthala), pp. 408–16.

Neaher, N. C. (1979) 'Nigerian bronze bells', *African Arts*, **12**, 3, pp. 42–7.

Needham, J. H. (1974) *La tradition scientifique chinoise* (Paris: Hermann).

Nenquin, J. (1959) 'Dimple based pots from Kasai, Belgian Congo', *Man*, **59**, art. 242.

Nenquin, J. (1963) *Excavations at Sanga 1957* (Tervuren: Musée Royale de l'Afrique centrale).

Newman, J. L. (1970) *The Ecological Basis for Subsistence Change among the Sandawe of Tanzania* (Washington, DC: National Academy of Sciences).

Niane, D. T. (1970) 'Notes sur les fouilles de Niani, ancienne capitale du Mali', *WAAN*, **12**, pp. 43–6.

Nicholson, R. A. (1907) *A Literary History of the Arabs* (Cambridge: CUP).

Nicholson, S. E. (1976) 'A climate chronology for Africa: synthesis of geological, historical and meteorological information and data' (unpublished PhD dissertation, University of Wisconsin, Madison).

Nicholson, S. E. (1979) 'The methodology of historical climate reconstruction and its application to Africa', *JAH*, **20**, 1, pp. 31–50.

Nicolaï, R. (1979) 'Les dialectes du songhay. Contribution à l'étude des changements linguistiques' (Thèse d'Etat, Université de Nice).

Nicolaisen, J. (1963) 'Niewolnictwo wśród pasterskich plemion Tuaregów', *Problemy afrykanistyki pod redakcja S. Strelcyna*, pp. 65–70.

Nicolas, G. (1978) 'L'enracinement ethnique de l'Islam au sud du Sahara' *CEA*, **16**, 71, pp. 347–77.

Nöldeke, T. H. (1892) 'Ein Sklavenkrieg im Orient' in Nöldeke, *Orientalische Skizzen* (Berlin: von Gebrüder Paetel), pp. 153–84.

Norris, H. T. (1971) 'New evidence on the life of ʿAbdallāh b. Yāsin and the origins of the Almoravid movement', *JAH*, **12**, 2, pp. 255–68.

Norris, H. T. (1972) *Saharan Myth and Saga* (Oxford: Clarendon Press).

Northrup, D. (1972) 'The growth of trade among the Igbo before 1800', *JAH*, **13**, 2, pp. 217–36.

Noten, F. van (1982) *The Archeology of Central Africa*, with contribution by D. Cohen, P. de Maret, J. Moeyersons and E. Roche (Graz).

Noten, F. van (1983) *Histoire archéologique du Rwanda* (Tervuren: Musée Royal de l'Afrique centrale).

Noth, A. (1967) 'Das ribāt der Almoraviden' in W. Hoenerbach (ed.), pp. 503–10.

Nunoo, R. B. (1969) 'Buruburo factory' *Actes 1er Coll. Intern. Archéol. Afr.* pp. 321–3.

Nurse, D. (1974) 'A linguistic sketch of the north-east Bantu languages with particular reference to Chaga history' (unpublished PhD thesis, University of Dar es Salaam).

Nurse, D. (1982) 'Bantu expansion into East Africa: linguistic evidence' in C. Ehret and M. Posnansky (eds), pp. 199–222.

Nurse, D. and Phillipson, D. W. (1974) *The North-eastern Bantu Languages of Tanzania and Kenya: A Classification* (Dar es Salaam: Dar es Salaam University Press).

Obayemi, A. (1976) 'The Yoruba and Edo-speaking peoples and their neighbours before 1600' in J. F. A. Ajayi and M. Crowder (eds) (1976), pp. 196–266.
Obenga, T. (1971) *L'Afrique dans l'antiquité. Egypte pharaonique, Afrique noire* (Paris: Présence Africaine).
L'Occidente e l'Islam nell'Alto Medievo (1965) (2 vols, Spoleto: Centro Italiano di Studi sull'Alto Medievo).
O'Fahey, R. S. (1980) *State and Society in Darfur* (London: C. Hurst).
Ogot, B. A. (ed.) (1974) *Zamani: A Survey of East African History* (2nd edn, Nairobi: East African Publishing House).
Ogot, B. A. (ed.) (1976) *Kenya before 1900* (Nairobi: East African Publishing House).
Ogot, B. A. (ed.) (forthcoming) *Kenya in the Nineteenth Century.*
Ogot, B. A. and Kieran, J. A. (eds) (1968) *Zamani: A Survey of East African History* (Nairobi: East African Publishing House).
Olagüe, I. (1974) *La révolución islámica en occidente* (Barcelona: Fundación Juan March).
Olderogge, D. A. (1960) *Zapadnuiy Sudan v XV–XIX vv. Ocherki po istorii i istorii kulturyi* (Moscow and Leningrad: IAN).
Oliver, R. (1966) 'The problem of the Bantu expansion', *JAH*, **7**, 3, pp. 361–76.
Oliver, R. (ed.) (1967) *The Middle Age of African History* (London: OUP).
Oliver, R. (ed.) (1977) *The Cambridge History of Africa, Vol. 3: c. 1050–c. 1600* (Cambridge: CUP).
Oliver, R. (1979) 'Cameroon – The Bantu cradleland', *SUGIA*, **1**, pp. 7–20.
Oliver, R. (1982) 'The Nilotic contribution to Bantu Africa', *JAH*, **23**, 4, pp. 433–42.
Oliver, R. and Fagan, B. M. (eds) (1975) *Africa in the Iron Age: c. 500 BC to AD 1400* (Cambridge: CUP).
Oliver, R. and Fage, J. D. (1962) *A Short History of Africa* (Harmondsworth: Penguin).
Oliver, R. and Mathew, G. (eds) (1963) *History of East Africa*, Vol. 1 (Oxford: Clarendon Press).
Oman, G. (1974a) 'La necropoli islamica di Dahlak Kebir. Il materialo epigraphico', *Akten d. VII. Kongresses fur Arabistik und Islamwissenschaft (Göttingen 1974)* (Göttingen: Vandenhock Z. Ruprecht), pp. 273–81.
Oman, G. (1974b) 'The Islamic necropolis of Dahlak Kebir in the Red Sea: report on a preliminary survey carried out in April 1972', *East and West*, **24**, 3–4, pp. 249–95.
Omi, G. (1982) *Mtongwe. The Preliminary Report* (Nagoya-Tokyo).
Onwuejeogwu, M. (1974) 'The political organization of Nri, south-eastern Nigeria' (unpublished MPhil. thesis, University of London).
Orhanlu, C. (1978) '*Khaṣī*' in E. van Donzel *et al.* (eds), pp. 1087–93.
Orr, K. G. (1971–2) 'An introduction to the archaeology of Liberia', *LSJ*, **4**, pp. 55–80.
Osman, A. (1982a) 'Medieval Nubia: retrospects and introspects' in P. Van Moorsel (ed.), pp. 69–90.
Osman, A. (1982b) 'The post-medieval kingdom of Kokka: a means for a better understanding of the administration of the medieval kingdom of Dongola' in J. M. Plumley (ed.), 1982a, pp. 185–97.
Ottino, P. (1974a) *Madagascar, les Comores et le Sud-Ouest de l'Océan Indien* (Tananarive: Université de Madagascar, Centre d'Anthropologie culturelle et sociale).
Ottino, P. (1974b) 'Le Moyen-Age de l'Océan Indien et le peuplement de Madagascar' in *Annuaire des Pays de l'Océan Indien* (Aix-en-Provence: CERSOI), pp. 197–221.
Ottino, P. (1983) 'Les Andriambahoaka malgaches et l'héritage indonésien', in F. Raison (ed.), pp. 71–96.
Ould el-Bah, A. (1982) *Les Almoravides à travers les sources orales en Mauritanie* (Mémoire-Université de Paris I).
Ozanne, P. (1966) 'The Anglo-Gambian Stone Circles Expedition', *WAAN*, **4**, pp. 8–18.
Ozanne, P. (1969) 'A new archaeological survey of Ife', *Odu*, (ns), **1**, pp. 28–45.
Ozanne, P. (1971) 'Ghana' in P. L. Shinnie (ed.), pp. 36–55.

Pacha, N. (1976) *Le commerce au Maghreb du XIe*–XIVe siècle (Tunis: Faculté des Lettres de Tunis).
Pacheco Pereira, D. (1956) *Esmeraldo de Situ Orbis. Côte occidentale d'Afrique, du Sud marocain au Gabon*, tr. by R. Mauny (Bissau).
Painter, C. (1966) 'The Guang and West African historical reconstruction', *GNQ*, **9**, pp. 58–65.
Palmer, H. R. (1908) 'The Kano Chronicle' *JRAI*, **38**, pp. 58–98.
Palmer, H. R. (1928) *Sudanese Memoirs: being mainly translations of a number of Arabic manuscripts relating to the Central and Western Sudan* (3 vols, Lagos: Govt Printer. Reprinted, 1967, London: Cass, in one volume).
Palmer, H. R. (1928–9) 'The Central Sahara and the Sudan in the XIIth century', *J. Afr. Soc.*, **28**, pp. 368–78.
Palmer, H. R. (1936) *The Bornu, Sahara and Sudan* (London: Murray).

Pansera, C. (1945) 'Quatro stele musulmane presso Uogher Hariba nell' Enderta', *Studi etiopici raccolti da C. Conti Rossini* (Rome: Istituto per l'Oriente), pp. 3–6.
Paret, R. (1924) *Sīrat Saif Ibn Dhī Yazan, ein arabischer Volksroman* (Hannover: Lafaire).
Paribeni, R. (1908) 'Richerche nel luogo dell'Antica Adulis', *Antichita Publicati per Curia della Accademia Nazionale dei Lincei*, **18**, pp. 438–572.
Parry, V. J. and Yapp, M. E. (eds) (1975) *War, Technology and Society in the Middle East* (London: OUP).
Pearce, F. B. (1920) *Zanzibar, the Island Metropolis of Eastern Africa* (London: T. F. Unwin).
Pellat, C. (1953) *Le milieu Baṣrien et la formation de Gāhiz* (Paris: Adrien-Maisonneuve).
Pellat, C. (1963) 'Les esclaves-chanteuses de Gāhiz', *Arabica*, **10**, pp. 121–47.
Pelliot, P. (1959) 'Çanghibar' in Pelliot, *Notes on Marco Polo*, Vol. 1, (Paris: Imprimerie nationale), pp. 598–603.
Pereira, F. M. E. (1899) *Historia dos martyres de Nagran, versâo ethiopica* (Lisbon: Imprensa nacional).
Pérès, H. (1953) *La poésie andalouse en arabe classique du XIe siècle* (Paris: Maisonneuve).
Perrier de la Bathie, H. (1926) *Biogéographie des plantes de Madagascar* (Paris: Ed. Géographiques, Maritimes et Coloniales).
Perruchon, J. (1889) 'Histoire des guerres d'Amda Sion, Roi d'Ethiopie' *JA*, 8th series, **14**, pp. 271–363, 381–493.
Perruchon, J. (1893) *Les chroniques de Zar'a Yâ'eqôb et Ba'eda Mâryâm, rois d'Ethiopie de 1434 à 1478* (Paris: Bouillon).
Perruchon, J. (1894) 'Notes pour l'histoire d'Ethiopie' *RS*, **2**, pp. 78–93.
Person, Y. (1968–75) *Samori, une révolution Dyula* (3 vols, Dakar: IFAN).
Person, Y. (1971) 'Ethnic movements and acculturation in Upper Guinea since the fifteenth century', *AHS*, **4**, 3, pp. 669–89.
Person, Y. (1972) 'Les Mandingues dans l'histoire' (Paper presented at the Conference on Manding Studies, SOAS, London, 1972).
Person, Y. (1981) 'Nyaani Mansa Manudu et la fin de l'empire du Mali' in (*Le*) *sol, la parole et l'écrit*, Vol. 2, pp. 613–54.
Petitmaire, N. (1978) 'Die atlantische Sahara, der Mensch Zwischen Wüste und Ozean', in R. Kuper (ed.).
Petráček, K. (1960) 'Al-Aḥwaẓ' in H. A. R. Gibb *et al.* (eds), p. 305.
Phillipson, D. W. (1968) 'The Early Iron Age site of Kapwirimbwe, Lusaka', *Azania*, **3**, pp. 87–105.
Phillipson, D. W. (1970a) 'Notes on the later prehistoric radiocarbon chronology of eastern and southern Africa', *JAH*, **11**, 1, pp. 1–15.
Phillipson, D. W. (1970b) 'Excavations at Twickenham Road, Lusaka', *Azania*, **5**, pp. 77–108.
Phillipson, D. W. (1971) 'An Early Iron Age site on the Lubusi River, Kaoma District, Zambia', *Zambia Museums Journal*, **2**, pp. 51–7.
Phillipson, D. W. (1972) 'Early Iron Age sites on the Zambian copper belt', *Azania*, **7**, pp. 93–128.
Phillipson, D. W. (1974) 'Iron Age history and archaeology in Zambia', *JAH*, **15**, 1, pp. 1–25.
Phillipson, D. W. (1975) 'The chronology of the Iron Age in Bantu Africa', *JAH*, **16**, 3, pp. 321–42.
Phillipson, D. W. (1976a) *The Prehistory of Eastern Zambia* (Nairobi: British Institute in Eastern Africa).
Phillipson, D. W. (1976b) 'The Early Iron Age in eastern and southern Africa: a critical reappraisal', *Azania*, **11**, pp. 1–23.
Phillipson, D. W. (1976c) 'Archaeology and Bantu linguistics', *WA*, **8**, pp. 65–82.
Phillipson, D. W. (1977a) *The Later Prehistory of Eastern and Southern Africa* (London: Heinemann).
Phillipson, D. W. (1977b) 'Zambian Sculpture on historical evidence' in K. Mubitana (ed.), pp. 85–8.
Phillipson, D. W. and Fagan, B. M. (1969) 'The dates of the Ingombe Ilede burials', *JAH*, **10**, 2, pp. 199–204.
Picton, J. and Mack, J. (1979) *African Textiles. Looms, Weaving and Design* (London: British Museum Publications).
Pigulevskaya, N. V. (1960, 1961) 'Les rapports sociaux à Nedjran au début du VIe siècle de l'ère chrétienne', *JESHO*, **3**, pp. 113–30; **4**, pp. 1–14.
Pigulevskaya, N. V. (1969) *Byzanz auf den Wegen nach Indien* (Berlin: DAW).
Pipes, D. (1980) *Slaves, Soldiers and Islam: The Genesis of a Military System* (New Haven: YUP).
Pirenne, H. (1937) *Mahomet et Charlemagne* (4th edn, Paris: Alcan).
Plumley, J. M. (1970) 'Some examples of Christian Nubian art from the excavations at Qasr Ibrim' in E. Dinkler (ed.), pp. 129–40.
Plumley, J. M. (1971a) 'Pre-Christian Nubia (23 BC–535 AD): evidence from Qasr Ibrim', *Etudes et Travaux*, 5 (*CAMAP*, 11), pp. 7–24.
Plumley, J. M. (1971b) 'The stele of Marianos, Bishop of Faras', *BMNV*, 11, pp. 77–84.

Plumley, J. M. (1975a) 'The Christian period in Qasr Ibrim, some notes on the MSS finds' in K. Michałowski (ed.), pp. 101–7.
Plumley, J. M. (1975b) *The Scrolls of Bishop Timotheos* (London: Egypt Exploration Society).
Plumley, J. M. (1978) 'New light on the Kingdom of Dotswo', *Etudes Nubiennes*, pp. 231–41.
Plumley, J. M. (ed.), (1982a) *Nubian Studies. Proceedings of the Symposium for Nubian Studies, Selwyn College, Cambridge* (Warminster: Aris & Phillips).
Plumley, J. M. (1982b) 'The Christian period in Nubia as represented on the site of Qasr Ibrim' in P. van Moorsel (ed.), pp. 99–110.
Plumley, J. M. (1982c) 'New evidence on Christian Nubia in the light of recent excavations', *NC*, 1, pp. 15–24.
Plumley, J. M. (1983) 'Qasr Ibrim and the Islam', *Etudes et Travaux*, 12 (*CAMAP*, 24), pp. 157–70.
Plumley, J. M. and Adams, W. Y. (1974) 'Qasr Ibrim 1972', *JEA*, **60**, pp. 212–38.
Plumley, J. M., Adams, W. Y. and Crowfoot, E. (1977) 'Qasr Ibrim 1976', *JEA*, **63**, pp. 29–47.
Poirier, J. (1965) 'Données écologiques et démographiques de la mise en place des Proto-Malgaches', *Taloha*, 1, pp. 61–82.
Polet, J. (1980) 'Fouille d'un quartier de Tegdaoust. Urbanisation, architecture, utilisation de l'espace construit' (Thèse de 3e cycle, Université de Paris, I).
Polet, J. (forthcoming) *Tegdaoust IV. Recherches sur Aoudaghost. Fouille d'un quartier: urbanisation, architecture, utilisation de l'espace construit* (Paris).
Polomé, B. C. and Hill, C. P. (eds) (1980) *Language in Tanzania* (London: IAI).
Pomerantseva, N. (1982) 'The iconography of the Christian paintings of Nubia', in J. M. Plumley (ed.) (1982a), pp. 198–205.
Poncet, C. (1954) 'L'évolution des genres de vie en Tunisie', *CT*, **2**, pp. 315–23.
Poncet, J. (1967) 'Le mythe de la "catastrophe" hilalienne', *Annales ESC* **9–10**, pp. 1099–120.
Popovic, A. (1976) *La révolte des esclaves en Iraq au IIIe/IXe siècle* (Paris: Geuthner).
Portères, A. (1950) 'Vieilles agricultures africaines avant le XVI ème siècle. Berceaux d'agriculture et centres de variation', *L'Agronomie Tropicale*, **5**, 9–10, pp. 489–507.
Posnansky, M. (1964) 'Bantu genesis', *UJ*, **25**, 1, pp. 86–92.
Posnansky, M. (1971) 'Ghana and the origins of West African trade', *AQ*, **11**, 2, pp. 111–25.
Posnansky, M. (1973) 'Aspects of early West African trade', *WA*, **5**, 2, pp. 149–62.
Posnansky, M. (1976) 'New radiocarbon dates from Ghana', *Sankofa*, **2**, pp. 60–3.
Posnansky, M. (1977) 'Brass casting and its antecedents in West Africa', *JAH*, **18**, 2, pp. 287–300.
Posnansky, M. (1980) 'Some reflections of a temporary nature on towns in general and on Begho, Ghana, in particular' in *African Studies Fall Colloquium on Indigenous African Towns*, University of California, Los Angeles.
Posnansky, M. and McIntosh, R. (1976) 'New radiocarbon dates for northern and western Africa', *JAH*, 17, 2, pp. 161–95.
Pouwels, R. C. (1974) 'Tenth-century settlement on the East African coast: the case of Qarmatian/Isma'ili connections', *Azania*, **9**, pp. 65–74.
Priddy, B. (1973) 'Pottery traditions in Ghana, their significance for the archaeologist' (cyclostyled seminar paper, Department of Archaeology, University of Ghana, Legon).
Procopius (1954) *History of the Wars, Books I and II* (ed. and tr. by H. B. Dewing, London).
Prost, A. (1945) 'Notes sur les Boussané', *BIFAN*, 7, pp. 47–53.
Prost, A. (1953) *Les langues Mandé-Sud du groupe mana-busa* (Dakar: IFAN).
Prost, A. (1981) 'Les Mandé-sud en Afrique occidentale', in *(Le) sol, la parole, et l'écrit*, Vol. 1, pp. 353–9.
Prussin, L. (1981) 'Building technologies in the West African savannah', in *(Le) sol, la parole et l'écrit*, Vol. 1, pp. 227–45.
Puglisi, G. (1953) 'Le citerne di Dahlak Chebir e di Adal nell'archipelago delle Dahlak' *Bolletino di Istituto di Studi Etiopici (Asmara)* 1, pp. 53–70.
Puglisi, G. (1969) 'Alcuni vestigi dell'isola di Dahlak Chebir e la leggenda dei Furs' in *Proc. 3rd Intern. congress of Ethiopian Studies* (Addis Abeba), pp. 35–47.
Puygaudeau, O. du (1966) 'Une carte des chars à boeufs révèle les rapports trois fois millénaires entre le Maghreb et le Soudan', *Archéologia*, **3**, pp. 37 *et seq.*

Quéchon, G. and Roset, J.-P. (1974) Prospection archéologique du massif de Termit (Niger), *Cahiers de l'ORSTOM sér. scien. hum.* **11**, 1, 1974, pp. 85–104.
Quennell, P. (1928) *The Book of the Marvels of India* (London: Routledge).

al-Rabī' ibn Ḥabīb (n.d.) *Musnad.*

Radimilahy, C. (1980) *Archéologie de l'Androy. Contribution à l'étude des phases de peuplements* (Antananarivo, Centre d'Art et d'Archeologie).
Radimilahy, C. (1981) 'Archéologie de l'Androy', *RPC*, **55**, pp. 62–5.
Raison, F. (ed.) (1983) *Les souverains de Madagascar. L'Histoire royale et ses résurgences contemporaines* (Paris: Karthala).
Rakoto-Rastimamanga, A. (1939) 'Tâche pigmentaire et origine des Malgaches' (Thèse de sciences, Université de Paris).
Ralaimihoatra, E. (1948) 'Vazimba et Hova à Madagascar', *Revue de Madagascar*, pp. 35–48.
Ralaimihoatra, E. (1966) *Histoire du Madagascar* (Tananarive: Société Malgache d'Edition).
Ralaimihoatra, E. (1971a) 'Le contexte et la signification du terme Vazimba dans l'histoire de Madagascar', *Bull. Acad. Malg.*, **47**, pp. 183–4.
Ralaimihoatra, E. (1971b) 'Elements de connaissance des proto-Malgaches', *Bull. Acad. Malg.*, **49**, 1, pp. 29–33.
Ralaimihoatra, E. (1974) *Etapes successives du peuplement de Madagascar: relations avec l'Asie du Sud-Est, l'Océan Indien et l'Afrique* (Tananarive, roneo).
Ramadan, A. M. (1975) *Réflexions sur l'architecture islamique en Libye* (Tripoli).
Rasamuel, D. (1983) 'Alimentation et techniques anciennes dans le Sud malgache à travers une fosse à ordures du XIe siècle', *Etudes Océan Indien/Tsiokantimo* (Paris/Tuléar), **5**, pp. 81–110.
Rasamuel, D. (1985) 'Culture matérielle ancienne à Madagascar: contribution des pays riverains de l'Océan Indien dans le mouvement des idées dans l'Océan Indien occidental' in *Actes de la Table Ronde de Saint-Denis [25–28 juin 1982]* (Saint-Denis, La Réunion), pp. 113–25.
Rasamuel, D. (1986) *Fanongoavana, site ancien des Hautes Terres* (Paris: CRA-Karthala).
Rasheed, S. (1973) 'Slave girls under the early Abbasids' (unpublished PhD thesis, University of St Andrews).
Rassart, M. (1972) 'Visages de Faras, caractéristiques et évolution stylistique', *Etudes et Travaux*, **6** (CAMAP, 13), pp. 251–75.
Rassart, M. (1978) 'Quelques considérations sur les rapports thématiques et stylistiques entre l'Egypte Copte et la Nubie chrétienne' in A. Destrée (ed.), *Mélanges Armand Abel* (Leiden: Brill), Vol. 3, pp. 200–20.
Rattray, R. S. (1923) *Ashanti* (Oxford: Clarendon Press).
Rattray, R. S. (1927) *Religion and Art in Ashanti* (Oxford: Clarendon Press).
Ravelojoana (1937) *Fireketana ny fiteny sy ny zavatra malagasy* (Dictionnaire encyclopédique malgache) (Tananarive: Fiainana).
Ravereau, A. (1981) *Le M'zab, une leçon d'architecture* (Paris: Sindbad).
Ravisé, A. and Thilmans, G. (1978) 'A propos d'une clochette trouvée à Sintiou-Bara (Fleuve Sénégal)', *NA*, **159**, pp. 57–9.
Ravoajanahary, C. (1980) 'Le peuplement de Madagascar: tentative d'approche', in Unesco, 1980, pp. 91–102.
Reinaud, J. (1836) *Invasion des Sarrazins en France* (Paris).
Renaudot, E. (1713) *Historia Patriarcharum Alexandrinorum Jacobitorum* (Paris).
Rey, G. de (1972) *Les Invasions des Sarrasins en Provence pendant les VIIIe, IXe et Xe siècles* (2nd edn, Paris).
Reygasse, M. (1940) 'Fouilles de monuments funéraires de type 'chouett' à Abalessa (Hoggar)', BSGAO, **61**, fasc. 214.
Reygasse, M. (1950) *Monuments funéraires préislamiques de l'Afrique du Nord* (Paris: Arts et Métiers graphiques).
Richards, D. S. (ed.) (1970) *Islam and the Trade of Asia* (Oxford: Cassirer).
Rightmire, G. P. (1970) 'Iron Age skulls from southern Africa re-assessed by multiple discriminant analysis', *AJPA*, **33**, 3, pp. 147–68.
(La) rime et la raison (1984) (Catalogue de l'exposition de la Collection de Ménil, Grand Palais, Paris, 1984).
Rivallain, J. (1980) 'Le sel dans les villages côtiers et lagunaires du Bas-Dahomey: sa fabrication, sa place dans le circuit du sel africain', *AUA* (série 1: Histoire), 8, pp. 81–127.
Rizzitano, U. (1938) 'La poesia de Abū Miḥdjān, N. b. R. e necessita di uno studio piu completo sui poeti minori de secolo Ummayyade', *Actes XXe Congr. Int. Or.*, pp. 316–18.
Robert, D. (1966) 'Statuette anthropomorphe du site de Tegdaoust (Mauritanie orientale)', *NA*, **112**, pp. 142–3.
Robert, D. (1970) 'Les fouilles de Tegdaoust', *JAH*, 11, 4, pp. 471–94.
Robert, D. (1980) 'Une "concession médiévale" à Tegdaoust: implantation évolutive d'une unité d'habitation' (2 vols, thèse de 3e cycle, Université de Paris, I).

Robert, D., Robert, S. and Devisse, J. (eds) (1970) *Tegdaoust I. Recherches sur Aoudaghost* (Paris: Arts et Métiers Graphiques).
Robert, D., Robert, S. and Saison, B. (1976) 'Recherches archéologiques: Tegdaoust-Koumbi Saleh', *AIMRS*, **2**, pp. 53–84.
Robert, S. (1976) 'Archéologie des sites urbains des Hodh et problèmes de la désertification au Moyen âge' in *Colloque de Nouakchott*, pp. 46–55.
Robert-Chaleix, D. (forthcoming) *Tegdaoust V. Recherches sur Aoudaghost. Une concession médiévale, implantation et evolution d'une unité d'habitation* (Paris).
Robert-Chaleix, D. and Sognane, M. (1983) 'Une industrie métallurgique ancienne sur la rive mauritanienne du fleuve Sénégal' in N. Echard (ed.), pp. 45–62.
Roberts, R. (1908) *Das Familien, Sklaven und Erbrecht in Koran* (Leipzig).
Robey, T. (1980) 'Mpambanyoni: a Late Iron Age site on the Natal south coast', *ANM*, **24**, 1, pp. 147–64.
Robineau, C. (1967) 'L'Islam aux Comores, une étude d'histoire culturelle de l'Ile d'Anjouan' in P. Vérin (ed.), pp. 39–56.
Robinson, K. R. (1958) 'Four Rhodesian Iron Age sites: a brief account of stratigraphy and finds', *Occ. Pap. Natn. Mus. Sth. Rhod.*, **3A**, **22**, pp. 77–119.
Robinson, K. R. (1966a) 'The Leopard's Kopje Culture, its position in the Iron Age of Southern Rhodesia', *SAAB*, **21**, 81, pp. 5–51.
Robinson, K. R. (1966b) 'The Sinoia Caves, Lomagundi District, Rhodesia', *Proc. Trans. Rhod. Sci. Ass.* **51**, pp. 131–55.
Robinson, K. R. (1966c) 'A preliminary report on the recent archeology of Ngonde, northern Malawi', *JAH*, **7**, 2, pp. 169–88.
Robinson, K. R. (1968) 'An examination of five Iron Age structures in the Umguza Valley, 14 miles north of Bulawayo, Rhodesia', *Arnoldia (Rhod.)* 3, 35, pp. 1–21.
Robinson, K. R. (1970) *The Iron Age in the Southern Lake Area of Malawi* (Zomba).
Robinson, K. R. (1973) *The Iron Age of the Upper and Lower Shire, Malawi* (Zomba).
Robinson, K. R. (1976) 'A note on the spread of Early Iron Age ceramics in Malawi', *SAAB*, **31**, pp. 166–75.
Rodinson, M. (1969) *Mahomet* (Paris: Seuil).
Rodinson, M. (1971) *Mohammad* (London: Allen Lane).
Rodney, W. (1967) 'A reconsideration of the Mane invasions of Sierra Leone', *JAH*, **8**, 2, pp. 219–46.
Rodziewicz, M. (1972) 'Die Keramikfunde der deutschen Nubienunternehmungen 1968–69', *Ar. Anz.*, **4**, pp. 643–713.
Rosenberger, B. (1970a) 'Les vieilles exploitations minières et les anciens centres métallurgiques du Maroc', *Revue de géographie du Maroc*, **17–18**, pp. 71–102.
Rosenberger, B. (1970b) 'Tamdult, cité minière et caravanière pré-saharienne, IXe–XIVe siècles', *HT*, **11**, pp. 103–39.
Roset, J.-P. (1983) 'Nouvelles données sur le problème de la néolithisation du Sahara méridionale: Air et Ténéré au Niger', *Cahiers de l'ORSTOM* (série Géologie) **13**, 2, pp. 119–42.
Rosso, J.-C. and Petitmaire, N. (1978) 'Amas coquilliers du littoral atlantique saharien', *BMAPM*, **22**, pp. 79–118.
Rostkowska, B. (1972) 'Iconographie des personnages historiques sur les peintures de Faras', in *Etudes et Travaux*, **6**, (*CAMAP*, 13) pp. 195–205.
Rostkowska, B. (1981) 'Classical traditions in Christian art of the Nile Valley', in M. Mulett and R. Scott (eds), *Byzantium and the Classical Tradition – The University of Birmingham thirteenth Spring Symposium of Byzantine Studies*, 1979 (Birmingham: University of Birmingham), pp. 149–54.
Rostkowska, B. (1982a) 'Nobadian painting: present state of investigations', *NC*, **1**, pp. 283–304.
Rostkowska, B. (1982b) 'The title and office of the king's mother in Christian Nubia', *AB*, **31**, pp. 75–8.
Rotter, G. (1967) *Die Stellung des Negers in der islamisch-arabischen Gesellschaft bis zum XVI. Jhdt* (Bonn).
Rouger, G. (1923) *Le roman d'Antar d'après les anciens textes arabes* (Paris: L'Edition d'art).
Roux, V. (1980) 'Oscillation climatique et néolithisation: la pêche', *Cahiers du CRA* (Série Histoire) **1**, pp. 3–38.
Rozenstroch, M. (1984) 'Liongo Fumo. Légende et signification politique' (Thèse de doctorat de 3ème cycle, Université de Paris VII).
Ryder, A. F. C. (1969) *Benin and the Europeans 1485*–1897 (London: Longmans).
Ryckmans, J. (1956) *La persécution des chrétiens himyarites au VIe siècle* (Istanbul: Nederlands Historisch-Archaeologisch Instituut in het Nabije Oosten).

al-Sābi', Abū' l'Ḥasan (1958) *Al-wuzara'* (Cairo).
al-Sābi', Hilāl (1964) *Rusūm dār al-khilāfa* (ed. M. 'Awwād, Baghdad).
as-Sa'dī, A. see Ta'rīkh al-Sūdān.
Sahlins, M. (1972) *Stone Age Economics* (London: Tavistock).
Saison, B. (1979) 'Fouille d'un quartier artisanal de Tegdaoust' (2 vols, Thèse de Doctorate de 3e cycle, Université de Paris, I).
Saison, B. (1981) 'Azugi, archéologie et histoire en Adrar Mauritanien', *Rercherche, Pédagogie et Culture*, 55, pp. 66–74.
Saison, B. (forthcoming) *Tegdaoust VI. Recherches sur Aoudaghost. Fouille d'un quartier artisanal* (Paris).
al-Salāwī (1954) *Al-Istiḳṣā li-Akhbār al-Maghrib al-Aḳṣā'* (2nd edn, Al-Dār al-Baydā Casablanca).
Saliège, J. F., Person, A., Barry, I. and Fontes, P. (1980) 'Premières datations de tumulus pré-islamiques au Mali: site mégalithique de Tondidarou', *Comptes rendus de l'Académie des Sciences*, 291 (D), 12, pp. 981–4.
Sallūm, D. (1967) *Shi'r Nuṣaib b. Rabāḥ* (Baghdad).
al-Samīr, F. (1971) *Thawrat al-Zandj* (2nd edn, Beirut).
Sanagustin, F. (1980) 'Un aide-mémoire à l'usage de l'acheteur d'esclaves' (unpublished thèse de doctorat, University of Paris, III).
Sandelowsky, B. (1973) 'Kapako, an Early Iron Age site on the Okavango River, South West Africa', *SAJS*, 69, p. 325.
Sanders, E. R. (1969) 'The Hamitic hypothesis, its origin and functions in time-perspective', *JAH*, 10, 4, pp. 521–32.
Sanneh, L. O. (1976) 'The origins of clericalism in West African Islam', *JAH*, 17, 1, pp. 49–72.
Sanneh, L. O. (1979) *The Jakhanke. The History of an Islamic Clerical People of the Senegambia* (London: IAI).
Santarem, M. F. de B. (1842) *Notice sur André Alvarez d'Almada et sa description de la Guinée* (Paris: Bertrand).
Sapir, J. D. (1971) 'West Atlantic: an inventory of the languages, their noun class systems and consonant alteration' in T. Sebeok (ed.), pp. 45–112.
Sauvaget, J. (1949) 'Les epitaphes royales de Gao', *Al-Andalus*, 14, pp. 123–41.
Säve-Söderbergh, T. (1970) 'Christian Nubia. The excavations carried out by the Scandinavian Joint Expedition to Sudanese Nubia' in E. Dinkler (ed.) (1970), pp. 219–40.
Scanlon, G. (1970) 'Excavations at Ḳasr el-Wizz. A preliminary report I', *JEA*, 56, pp. 29–57.
Scanlon, G. (1972) 'Excavations at Ḳasr el-Wizz. A preliminary report II', *JEA*, 58, pp. 7–42.
Schacht, J. (1950) *The Origins of Muhammadan Jurisprudence* (Oxford: Clarendon Press).
Schacht, J. (1954) 'Sur la diffusion des formes d'architecture religieuse musulmane à travers le Sahara', *TIRS*, 11, pp. 11–27.
Schacht, J. and Bosworth, C. E. (eds.) (1974) *The Legacy of Islam* (2nd edn, Oxford: Clarendon Press).
Schapera, I. (1970) *Tribal Innovators: Tswana Chiefs and Social Change 1795–1940* (London: Athlone Press).
Schmidt, P. (1975) 'A new look at interpretations of the Early Iron Age in East Africa', *HA*, 2, pp. 127–36.
Schmidt, P. R. (1978) *Historical Archeology: A Structural Approach to an African Culture* (Westport, Conn.: Greenwood Press).
Schmidt, P. (1981) *The Origin of Iron Smelting in Africa: A Complex Technology in Tanzania* (Providence, RI, Brown University, Research Papers in Archeology, no 1).
Schneider, M. (1967) 'Stèles funéraires arabes de Quiha', *AE*, 7, pp. 107–22.
Schneider, M. (1969) 'Stèles funéraires de la région de Harar et Dahlak (Ethiopie), *REI*, 37, 2, pp. 339–43.
Schoenbrun, D. (1984) 'Forests of words: early agricultural history in lacustrine East Africa, ca. 1000 BC to ca. AD 1000' (Seminar paper, University of California, Los Angeles, March 1984).
Schrire, C. (ed.) (1984) *Past and Present in Hunter Gatherer Studies* (New York: Academic Press).
Sebeok, T. (ed.) (1971) *Current Trends in Linguistics*, Vol. 7 (Bloomington: Indiana University Press).
Seligman, C. G. (1930) *Races of Africa* (London: Butterworth).
Seligman, C. G. (1935) *Les Races de l'Afrique* (Paris: Payot).
Semaan, K. I. (ed.) (1980) *Islam and the Medieval West* (Albany: State University of New York Press).
Semonin, P. (1964) 'The Almoravid movement in the Western Sudan', *THSG*, 7, pp. 42–59.
Sergew, H. S. (1972) *Ancient and Medieval Ethiopian History to 1270* (Addis-Ababa: United Printers).
van Sertima, I. (ed.) (1985) *African Presence in Early Asia* (New Brunswick: Transaction Books).

Severus ibn al-Mukaffa' (1904) *Historia Patriarcharum Alexandronorum.* [CSCO, Script. Arab., ser. III, vol. IX] (ed. by C. F. Seybold, Beyrouth: Univ. St-Joseph).
Seydou, C. (1977) *Bibliographie générale du monde Peul* (Niamey: IRSH, Etudes nigériennes, **43**).
al-Shafi'ī (1903) *Kitāb al-'amm* (Cairo).
Shaw, C. T. (1944) 'Report on excavations carried out in the cave known as "Bosumpra" at Abetifi, Kwahu, Gold Coast Colony', *Proc. Prehist. Soc.*, **10**, pp. 1–67.
Shaw, T. (1960) 'Excavations at Igbo-Ukwu, Eastern Nigeria: an interim report', *Man*, **60**, pp. 161–4.
Shaw, T. (1961) *Excavation at Dawn* (Edinburgh: Nelson).
Shaw, T. (ed.) (1969a) *Lectures on Nigerian Prehistory and Archaeology* (Ibadan: Ibadan University Press).
Shaw, T. (1969b) 'The Late Stone Age in the Nigerian forest' in *Actes Ier Coll. Intern. Archéol. Afr.*, pp. 364–75.
Shaw, T. (1970) *Igbo-Ukwu: An Account of Archeological Discoveries in Eastern Nigeria* (2 vols, London: Faber).
Shaw, T. (1972) 'Early agriculture in Africa', *JHSN*, **6**, 2, pp. 143–91.
Shaw, T. (1973) 'A note on trade and the Tsoede bronzes', *WAJA*, 3, **pp. 233–8**.
Shaw, T. (1974) 'Hunters, gatherers and first farmers in West Africa' (Paper prepared for Conference on Hunters, Gatherers and First Farmers outside Europe held at Leicester University).
Shaw, T. (1975a) 'Those Igbo-Ukwu radiocarbon dates: facts, fictions and probabilities', *JAH*, **16**, 4, pp. 503–17.
Shaw, T. (ed.) (1975b) *Discovering Nigeria's Past* (London: OUP).
Shaw, T. (1977) *Unearthing Igbo-Ukwu* (Ibadan: OUP).
Shaw, T. (1978) *Nigeria. Its Archaeology and Early History* (London: Thames & Hudson).
Shepherd, G. (1982) 'The earliest Swahilis: a perspective on the importance of the Comoro Islands in the south-west Indian Ocean before the rise of Kilwa' (Paper presented to the Conference on Swahili Language and Society, London, SOAS, April 1982).
Shinnie, P. L. (1954) *Medieval Nubia* (Khartoum: Sudan Antiquities Services, Museum Pamphlet, **2**).
Shinnie, P. L. (1961) *Excavations at Soba* (Khartoum: Sudan Antiquities Services, Occasional Paper, **3**).
Shinnie, P. L. (1965) 'New light on medieval Nubia', *JAH*, **6**, 3, pp. 263–73.
Shinnie, P. L. (1971) 'The culture of medieval Nubia and its impact on Africa' in Y. F. Hasan (ed.), pp. 124–8.
Shinnie, P. L. (ed.) (1971) *The African Iron Age* (Oxford: Clarendon Press).
Shinnie, P. L. (1974) 'Multilingualism in medieval Nubia' in A. M. Abdalla (ed.), pp. 41–7.
Shinnie, P. L. (1975) 'Excavations at Debeira West' in K. Michałowski (ed.), pp. 116–20.
Shinnie, P. L. (1978a) 'Christian Nubia' in J. D. Fage (ed.), pp. 556–88.
Shinnie, P. L. (1978b) 'Trade in medieval Nubia', in *Etudes Nubiennes*, pp. 253–64.
Shinnie, P. L. and Chittick, H. N. (1961) *Ghazali – A monastery in the Northern Sudan* (Khartoum: Sudan Antiquities Service, Occasional Paper, **5**).
Shinnie, P. L. and Shinnie, M. (1978) *Debeira West. A Medieval Nubian Town* (Warminster: Aris & Phillips).
Simmonds, N. W. (1962) *The Evolution of the Bananas* (London: Longmans).
Simon, H. (1946) 'Le Judaïsme berbère dans l'Afrique ancienne', *RHPR*, **26**, pp. 1–31.
Sinclair, P. J. J. (1981) 'An archaeological outline of two social formations of the Later Iron Age in Zimbabwe and Mozambique' in *10th Proc. Cong. Union Int. Scient. Prehist. Protohist.* (Mexico, D. F., Sections VII–IX), pp. 64–5.
Sinclair, P. J. J. (1982) 'Chibuene – an early trading site in southern Mozambique', *Paideuma*, **28**, pp. 150–64.
Smith, A. (1970) 'Some considerations relating to the formation of states in Hausaland', *JHSN*, **5**, 3, pp. 329–46.
Smith, A. (1971) 'The early states of the Central Sudan' in J. F. A. Ajayi and M. Crowder (eds) (1971), pp. 158–201.
Smith, A. (1972) 'The legend of the Sefuwa' (unpublished seminar paper, Ahmadu Bello University).
Smith, A. B. (1975) 'Radiocarbon dates from Bosompra Cave, Abetifi, Ghana' *Proc. Prehist. Soc.*, **41**, pp. 179–82.
Smith, R. S. (1969) *Kingdoms of the Yoruba* (London: Methuen).
Smith, S. (1954) 'Events in Arabia in the 6th century AD', *BSOAS*, **16**, pp. 425–68.
Snowden, F. M. (1970) *Blacks in Antiquity – Ethiopians in the Graeco-Roman Experience* (Cambridge, Mass.: Harvard University Press).
(Le) sol, la parole et l'écrit. Mélanges en hommage à Raymond Mauny (1981) (2 vols, Paris: SFHOM).

Solheim, W. G. (1965) 'Indonesian culture and Malagasy origins', *Taloha*, **1**, pp. 33–42.
Soper, R. C. (1967) 'Kwale: an early Iron Age site in south-eastern Kenya', *Azania*, **2**, pp. 1–17.
Soper, R. C. (1971) 'A general review of the Early Iron Age in the southern half of Africa', *Azania*, **6**, pp. 5–37.
Soper, R. C. (1982) 'Bantu expansion into eastern Africa: archaeological evidence' in C. Ehret and M. Posnansky (eds), pp. 223–44.
Southall, A. (1954) 'Alur tradition and its historical significance', *UJ*, **18**, pp. 137–65.
Spear, T. (1978) *The Kaya Complex. A History of the Mijikenda Peoples of the Kenya Coast* (Nairobi: Kenya Literature Bureau).
Spear, T. (1982) 'The Shirazi in Swahili traditions, culture and history' (Paper presented to the Conference on Swahili Language and Society, London, SOAS, April 1982).
Stenning, D. J. (1959) *Savannah Nomads: A Study of the Woodaabe Pastoral Fulani of Western Bornu Province, Northern Region, Nigeria* (London: OUP).
Stepniewska, B. (1971) 'Portée sociale de l'Islam au Soudan occidentale aux 14e–16e siècles', *AB*, **14**, pp. 35–8.
Stern, S. M. (1950) 'An Embassy of the Byzantine Emperor to the Fāṭimid Caliph al-Mu'izz', *Byzantion*, 20, pp. 239–58.
Stern, S. M. (1961) 'Ismā'īls and Qarmatians', in *L'Elaboration de l'Islam*, pp. 99–108.
Stevenson, R. (1956) 'A survey of the phonetics and grammatical structure of the Nuba Mountain languages', *AU*, **40**, pp. 73–84, 93–115.
Stevenson, R. (1971) 'The significance of the Sudan in linguistic research, past, present and future' in Y. F. Hasan (ed.), pp. 11–25.
Stewart, M. H. (1979) 'The role of the Manding in the hinterland trade of the Western Sudan: a linguistic and cultural analysis', *BIFAN* (B), **41**, 2, pp. 280–302.
Stigand, C. H. (1913) *The Land of Zinj* (London: Constable).
Stillman, N. (1972) 'Un témoignage contemporain de l'histoire de la Tunisie Zirid', *HT*, **13**, pp. 37–59.
Stokes, E. and Brown, R. (eds) (1966) *The Zambezian Past* (Manchester: Manchester University Press).
Stricker, B. H. (1940) 'A study in medieval Nubian', *BSOAS*, **10**, pp. 439–54.
Strong, S. A. (1895) 'History of Kilwa', *JRAS*, **20**, pp. 385–430.
Strothmann, R. (1928) 'Berber und Ibâditen', *Der Islam*, **17**, pp. 258–79.
Summers, R. (1969) *Ancient Mining in Rhodesia and Adjacent Areas* (Salisbury: National Museum of Rhodesia).
Sundstrom, L. (1974) *The Exchange Economy of Pre-colonial Tropical Africa*. (London: Hurst).
Suret-Canale, J. (1974) 'Les sociétés traditionnelles en Afrique tropicale et le concept de mode de production asiatique' in *Centre d'Etudes et de Recherche Marxiste*, pp. 101–33.
Sutton, J. E. G. (1972) 'New radiocarbon dates for eastern and southern Africa', *JAH*, **13**, 1, pp. 1–24.
Sutton, J. E. G. (1976) 'Iron-working around Zaria', *Zaria Archaeology Paper*, **8** (Centre for Nigerian Cultural Studies, Ahmadu Bello University).
Sutton, J. E. G. (1977) 'Radiocarbon dates for the Samaru West ironworks', *Zaria Archaeology Paper*, 8 (Addendum).
Sutton, J. E. G. (1979) 'Towards a less orthodox history of Hausaland', *JAH*, **20**, 2, pp. 179–201.
Sutton, J. E. G. (1984) 'Archaeology in Rwanda and Burundi' (Book Review), *JAH*, **25**, 2, pp. 222–3.
Sutton, J. E. G. and Roberts, A. D. (1968) 'Uvinza and its salt industry', *Azania*, **3**, pp. 45–86.
Swartz, B. K. and Dumett, R. E. (eds) (1980) *West African Cultural Dynamics* (The Hague: Mouton).
al-Suyūṭī (1969) *Ta'rīkh al-khulafā'* (Cairo).

al-Ṭabarī, M. b. Dj. (1879–1901) *Annales: Ta'rīkh al-rusūl wa'l-mulūk*. (15 Vols. ed. J. M. de Goeje *et al.* Leiden: J. Brill).
al-Ṭabarī (1329 AH) *Tafsīr al-Ḳurān* (Būlāḳ).
al-Ṭabarī (1962–7) *Ta'rīkh al-rusūl wa-l-mulūk*, ed. by M. Abū 'l-Faḍl Ibrāhīm (Cairo).
al-Tahawī, Abū Dja'far (1950–1) *Mukhtaṣar al-Tahawī* (Cairo: 1370 AH).
Talbi, M. (1962) 'Kairouan et le mālikisme espagnol', *Etudes d'Orientalisme dédiées à la mémoire de Lévi-Provençal* (Paris: Maisonneuve & Larose).
Talbi, M. (1966) *L'Emirat Aghlabide, 184–296 (800–909). Histoire politique*. (Paris: Maisonneuve).
Talbi, M. (1971) 'Un Nouveau fragment de l'histoire de l'Occident musulman (62–196/682–812). L'épopée d'Al-Kahina', *RT*, **19**, pp. 19–52.
Talbi, M. (1973) 'Hérésie, acculturation et nationalisme des Berbères barġawāṭa' in *Actes du Premier Congrès d'Etudes des Cultures méditerranéennes d'influence arabo-berbère* (Alger: SNED), pp. 217–33.

Talbi, M. (forthcoming) *Etudes d'histoire Ifriqiyenne.*
Tamplin, M. J. (1977) *Preliminary Report on an Archaeological Survey in the Republic of Botswana* (Peterborough: Trent University).
Tamrat, T. (1972) *Church and State in Ethiopia, 1270–1527* (Oxford: Clarendon Press).
Tandia, B. (1982–3) 'Sites d'habitats anciens sur la rive mauritanienne du fleuve Sénégal. Premières prospections' (Mémoire de fin d'Etudes, Ecole Normale Superieure de Nouakchott).
Ta'rīkh al-Fattāsh (1913–14), ed. and tr. by O. Houdas and M. Delafosse (Paris: Leroux).
Ta'rīkh al-Sūdān (1900) *Tarikh es-Soudan, par Abderrahmane ben Abdallah ben Imram ben Amir Es-Sadi*, tr. by O. Houdas (Paris: Leroux).
Tauxier, L. (1937) *Moeurs et histoire des Peuls* (Paris: Payot).
Taylor, M. O. V. (1979) 'Late Iron Age settlements on the northern edge of the Vredefort Dome' (unpublished MA thesis, University of the Witwatersrand).
Taylor, M. O. V. (1984) 'Southern Transvaal stone walled sites – a spatial consideration' in M. J. Hall *et al.* (eds), pp. 248–51.
Tedeschi, S. (1969) 'Note storiche sulle isole Dahlak' in *Proc. of the 3rd Intern. Conf. of Ethiopian Studies* (Addis Ababa) pp. 49–74.
Teixeira da Mota, V. A. (1963) 'Méthodes de navigation et cartographie nautique dans l'Océan Indien avant le XVIe siècle', *Studia* (Lisbon), 11, pp. 45–9.
Terrasse, H. (1949–50) *Histoire du Maroc* (2 vols, Casablanca: Atlantides).
Terrasse, H. (1951) 'Consequences d'une invasion berbère: le rôle des Amoravides dans l'histoire de l'Occident' in *Mélanges d'histoire du moyen âge dediées à la mémoire de Louis Halphen* (Paris: PUF), pp. 673–81.
Terrasse, H., Meunié, J. and Deverdun, G. (1957) *Nouvelles recherches archéologiques à Marrakech* (Paris).
Thelwall, R. (1978) 'Lexicostatical relations between Nubian, Daju and Dinka' in *Etudes Nubiennes*, pp. 265–86.
Thelwall, R. (1982) 'Linguistic aspects of greater Nubian history' in P. van Moorsel (ed.), p. 121.
Thilmans, G. (1979) 'Les disques perforés en céramique des sites proto-historiques du Fleuve Sénégal', *NA*, **162**, pp. 59–61.
Thilmans, G. and Descamps, C. (1974) 'Le site mégalithique de Tiékène-Boussoura (Sénégal). Fouilles de 1973–4', *BIFAN*, (B), **36**, 3, pp. 447–96.
Thilmans, G. and Descamps, C. (1975) 'Le site mégalithique de Tiékène-Boussoura (Sénégal). Fouilles de 1974–5', *BIFAN* (B), **37**, 2, pp. 259–306.
Thilmans, G. and Descamps, C. (forthcoming) *Protohistoire du Sénégal*, Vol. 3.
Thilmans, G., Descamps, C. and Khayat, B. (1980) *Protohistoire du Sénégal. Recherches archéologiques. Vol. I. Les sites mégalithiques* (Dakar: IFAN).
Thilmans, G. and Ravisé, A. (1983) *Protohistoire du Sénégal. Vol. II. Sintiou-Bara et les sites du Fleuve* (Dakar: IFAN).
Thilmans, G., Robert, D. and Ravisé, A. (1978) 'Découverte d'un fragment de poterie émaillée à Sintiou Bara (fleuve Sénégal)', *NA*, **159**, pp. 59–61.
Thomassey, P. and Mauny, R. (1951) 'Campagne de fouilles à Koumbi Saleh', *BIFAN*, **13**, pp. 436–62.
Thomassey, P. and Mauny, R. (1956) 'Campagne de fouilles de 1950 à Koumbi Saleh (Ghana?)', *BIFAN*, **17**, pp. 117–40.
Thompson, L. A. and Ferguson, J. (eds) (1969) *Africa in Classical Antiquity* (Ibadan: Ibadan University Press).
Thorbecke, A. (1867) *Antarah, ein vorislamischer Dichter* (Leipzig).
Tibbets, G. R. (ed.) (1971) *Arab Navigation in the Indian Ocean Before the Coming of the Portuguese* (London: Luzac).
Tibbets, G. R. (1979) *A Study of the Arabic Texts Containing Material on South-East Asia* (Leiden: Brill).
Torday, E. and Joyce, T. A. (1910) *Notes ethnographiques sur les peuples communément appelés Bakuba, ainsi que sur les peuplades apparentées. Les Bushongo* (Tervuren: Musée du Congo Belge).
Török, L. (1975) 'Man in the Vessel, an intepretation of a Nubian fresco representation' in K. Michałowski (ed.), pp. 121–5.
Török, L. (1978) 'Money, economy and administration in Christian Nubia', *Etudes Nubiennes*, 1978, pp. 287–311.
Toupet, C. (1966) *Description du milieu physique de Massif de l'Assaba (Mauritanie)* (Dakar: IFAN).
Toupet, C. (1976) 'L'evolution du climat de la Mauritanie du Moyen âge jusqu'à nos jours' in *Colloque de Nouakchott*, pp. 56–63.

Toupet, C. (1977) *La sédentarisation des nomades en Mauritanie centrale sahélienne* (Paris: Librairie Honoré Champion).
'Trabalhos de arqueologia e antropologia' (1980) in *Arqueologia e conhecimento do passado*, **1** (Maputo: Eduardo Mondlane University).
Treinen-Claustre, F. (1978) 'Eisenzeitliche Funde aus dem Nord-Tschad' in R. Kuper (ed.), pp. 330–3.
Trevor, T. G. and Mellor, E. T. (1908) 'Report on a reconnaissance of the north-western Zoutpansberg District' in *Special Publication Transvaal Mines Department* (Pretoria: Government Printer).
Triaud, J.-L. (1968) 'Quelques remarques sur l'islamisation du Mali des origines à 1300', *BIFAN* (B), **30**, 4, pp. 1329–51.
Trigger, B. G. (1965) *History and Settlement in Lower Nubia* (New Haven: Yale University Publications in Anthropology, **69**).
Trigger, B. G. (1967) *The Late Nubian Settlement at Arminna West* (New Haven-Philadelphia: Publications of the Pennyslvania-Yale Expedition to Egypt, **2**).
Trigger, B. G. (1970) 'The cultural ecology of Christian Nubia' in E. Dinkler (ed.), pp. 347–87.
Trimingham, J. S. (1949) *Islam in the Sudan* (London: OUP).
Trimingham, J. S. (1952) *Islam in Ethiopia* (London: OUP).
Trimingham, J. S. (1959) *Islam in West Africa* (London: OUP).
Trimingham, J. S. (1962) *A History of Islam in West Africa* (London: OUP).
Trimingham, J. S. (1964) *Islam in East Africa* (London: OUP).
Tritton, A. S. (1958) 'Theology and philosophy of the Isma'ilis', *JRAS*, pp. 178–88.
Troupeau, G. (1954) 'La description de la Nubie d'al-Uswānī (IVe/Xe siècle)', *Arabica*, **1**, pp. 276–88.
Tubiana, M.-J. (1964) *Survivances préislamiques en pays Zaghawa* (Paris: Institut d'Ethnologie).
Turay, A. K. (1978) 'Language contact: Mende and Temne – a case study', *Africana Marburgensia*, **11**, 1, pp. 55–73.
Tylecote, R. (1975) 'Iron smelting at Taruga, Nigeria', *Journ. Hist. Metall. Soc.* Soc., **9**, pp. 49–56.

Ukwu, U. (1967) 'The development of trade and marketing in Igboland', *JHSN*, **3**, pp. 647–62.
al-'Umarī ibn Faḍl Allāh (1927) *Masālik al abṣār fī mamālik al-amṣār: l'Afrique moins l'Egypte*, tr. by Gaudefroy-Demombynes (Paris: Geuthner).
Unesco (1980) *Relations historiques à travers l'Océan Indien* (Paris: Unesco, Histoire générale de l'Afrique, Etudes et Documents, **3**).
Urvoy, Y. (1936) *Histoire des populations du Soudan central* (*colonie du Niger*) (Paris: Larose).
Urvoy, Y. (1941) 'Chronologie du Bornou', *JSA*, **11**, pp. 21–32.
Urvoy, Y. (1949) *Histoire de l'Empire du Bornou* (Paris: Larose).

Vacca, V. (1923–5) 'Le ambascerie di Maometto ai Sovrani secondo Ibn Ishāq ed. al-Wāqidī', *RSO*, **10**, pp. 87–109.
Vajda, G. (1971) 'Ḥām' in B. Lewis *et al.* (eds), pp. 104–5.
Vallvé, J. (1967) 'Sobre algunas problemas de la invasion musulmana', *Anuario de Estudios Medievales*, **4**, pp. 261–367.
Vanacker, C. (1973) 'Géographie économique de l'Afrique du Nord, selon les auteurs arabes du IXe au milieu du XIIe siècle', *Annales ESC*, **28**, 3, pp. 659–80.
Vanacker, C. (1979) *Tegdaoust II. Recherches sur Aoudaghost. Fouille d'un quartier artisanal* (Nouakchott: Institut Mauritanien de la Recherche Scientifique).
Vanacker, C. (1983a) 'Cuivre et métallurgie du cuivre à Tegdaoust' in N. Echard (ed.), pp. 89–108.
Vansina, J. (1969) 'The bells of kings', *JAH*, **10**, 2, pp. 187–97.
Vansina, J. (1971) 'Inner Africa' in *Horizon History of Africa* (New York: American Heritage Publishing Company) pp. 261–73.
Vansina, J. (1979–80) 'Bantu in the crystal ball', *HA*, **6**, pp. 287–333; **7**, pp. 293–325.
Vansina, J. (1984) 'Western Bantu expansion', *JAH*, **25**, 2, pp. 129–44.
Vansina, J., Mauny, R. and Thomas, L. V. (eds) (1964a) *The Historian in Tropical Africa* (London: OUP).
Vansina, J., Mauny, R. and Thomas, L. V. (1964b) 'Introductory summary' in Vansina, J. *et al.* (eds), pp. 59–103.
Vantini, G. (1970a) *The Excavations at Faras: A Contribution to the History of Christian Nubia* (Bologna: Nigrizia).
Vantini, G. (1970b) 'Le Roi Kirki de Nubie à Baghdad: un ou deux voyages?' in E. Dinkler (ed.), pp. 41–8.
Vantini, G. (1975) *Oriental Sources Concerning Nubia* (Heidelberg and Warsaw: Heidelberger Akad. d. Wiss. and Polish Acad. of Sciences).

Vantini, G. (1981a) *Christianity in the Sudan* (Bologna: EMI).
Vantini, G. (1981b) 'Les fresques de Faras et l'histoire', *BSA Copte*, **23**, pp. 183–97.
Vercoutter, J. (1970) 'Les trouvailles chrétiennes françaises à Aksha, Mirgissa et Sai' in E. Dinkler (ed.), pp. 155–6.
Vercoutter, J. (1976) 'The iconography of the black in ancient Egypt from the beginnings to the twenty-fifth dynasty' in J. Vercoutter, F. M. Snowden and J. Desanges, *The Image of the Black in Western Art* (Lausanne), pp. 33–78.
Vercoutter, J., Leclant, J., Snowden, F. M. and Desanges, J. (1976) *L'Image du Noire dans l'Art occidental*, Vol. 1 (Fribourg: Office du Livre).
Vérin, P. (ed.) (1967) *Arabes et islamisés à Madagascar et dans l'Océan Indien* (Tananarive: Revue de Madagascar).
Vérin, P. (1974), 'Archeology in Madagascar (1971–1973)', *The Far Eastern Prehistory Association Newsletter*, **3**, pp. 37–40.
Vérin, P. (1975) *Les Echelles anciennes du commerce sur les côtes nord de Madagascar* (Lille: Université de Lille).
Vérin, P. (1980) 'Les apports culturels et la contribution africaine au peuplement de Madagascar' in Unesco 1980, pp. 103–24.
Vilá, J. B. (1956) *Los Almorávides* (Tetuán).
Viré, M. M. (1958) 'Notes sur trois épitaphes royales de Gao', *BIFAN* (B), **20**, pp. 368–76.
Viré, M. M. (1959) 'Stèles funéraires musulmanes soudano-sahéliennes', *BIFAN* (B), **21**, pp. 459–500.
Vogel, J. O. (1971) *Kumadzulo* (Lusaka).
Vogel, J. O. (1972a) 'The Shongwe tradition', *Zambia Museums Journal*, **3**, pp. 27–34.
Vogel, J. O. (1972b) 'On Early Iron Age funerary practice in southern Zambia', *Current Anthropology*, **13**, pp. 583–6.
Vogel, J. O. (1973a) 'The Early Iron Age sites at Sioma mission western Zambia', *Zambia Museums Journal*, **4**, pp. 153–69.
Vogel, J. O. (1973b) 'Some Early Iron Age sites in southern and western Zambia', *Azania*, **8**, pp. 25–54.
Vogel, J. O. (1973c) 'The Mosiatunya sequence', *Zambia Museums Journal*, **4**, pp. 105–52.
Vogel, J. O. (1975) *Simbusenga. The Archeology of the Intermediate Period of the Southern Zambia Iron Age* (Lusaka: Zambia Museum Papers, **4**).
Voigt, E. A. (1980) 'Reconstructing Iron Age economies of the northern Transvaal: a preliminary report', *SAAB*, **35**, 131, pp. 39–45.
Voigt, E. A. (ed.) (1981a) *Guide to Archaeological Sites in the Northern and Eastern Transvaal* (Pretoria: Transvaal Museum).
Voigt, E. A. (1981b) 'The Faunal remains from Schroda' in E. A. Voigt (ed.), pp. 55–62.
Voigt, E. A. (1983) *Mapungubwe: An Archaeozoological Interpretation of an Iron Age Community* (Pretoria: Transvaal Museum, Transvaal Museum Monograph, **1**).
Vossen, R. (1978) 'Notes on the territorial history of the Maa-speaking peoples', *KHR*, **6**.

al-Wāḥidī (1315 AH) *Ashāb al-nuzūl* (Cairo).
Wai-Ogosu, B. (1974) 'Pleistocene man in Africa with special reference to West Africa', *JHSN*, **7**, 2 pp. 357–68.
Waite, G. and Ehret, C. (forthcoming) 'Linguistic perspectives on the early history of southern Tanzania', *TNR*.
Walker, B. (ed.) (1984) *The Structure and Function of a South African Savanna Ecosystem*.
Wallis, J. R. (1955) 'The Kwahus and their connection with the Afram plains', *THSG*, 1, 3, pp. 10–26.
Wang Gungwu (1980) 'Les Chinois et les pays situés de l'autre côté de l'Océan Indien' in *Unesco* (1980) pp. 69–75.
Wansbrough, J. (1968) 'The decolonization of North African history', *JAH*, **9**, 4 pp. 643–50.
Wansleben, J. M. (1677) *Histoire de l'eglise d'Alexandrie* (Paris).
Watson, A. M. (1983) *Agricultural Innovations in the Early Islamic World. The Diffusion of Crops and Farming techniques, 700–1100* (Cambridge: CUP).
Watt, W. M. (1953) *Muhammad at Mecca* (Oxford: Clarendon Press).
Weeks, K. R. (1967) *The Classic Christian Townsite at Arminna West* (New Haven-Philadelphia: Publications of the Pennsylvania-Yale Expedition to Egypt, **3**).
Weisweiler, M. (1924) *Buntes Prachtgewand über die guten Eigenschaften der Abessinier* (Hannover: Lafaire).
Weitzmann, K. (1970) 'Some remarks on the source of the fresco paintings of the cathedral of Faras' in E. Dinkler (ed.) (1970), pp. 325–46.

Welbourne, R. (1975) 'Tautswe Iron Age site: its yield of bones', *BNR*, **7**, pp. 1–16.
Welmers, W. E. (1958) 'The Mande languages' in *Georgetown Univ. Monograph Series on Languages and Linguistics*, **11**, pp. 9–24.
Welmers, W. E. (1971) 'Niger Congo Mande' in T. Sebeok (ed.), pp. 113–40.
Welmers, W. E. (1973) *African Language Structures* (Berkeley: University of California Press).
Welsby, D. A. (1983) 'Recent work at Soba East in Central Sudan', *Azania*, **18**, pp. 165–80.
Wenig, S. (1978) *Africa in Antiquity: The Arts of Ancient Nubia and the Sudan* (2 vols, New York: Brooklyn Museum).
Wensinck, A. J. *et al.* (1933–69) *Concordance et indices de la tradition musulmane* (7 vols, Leiden: Brill).
Werner, O. (1970) 'Metallurgische Untersuchungen der Benin Bronzen des Museums für Völkerkunde Berlin', *Baessler-Archiv*, **18**, pp. 71–153.
Wertime, T. A. and Muhly, J. D. (1980) *The Coming of the Age of Iron* (New Haven: YUP).
Wessel, K. (ed.) *Christentum am Nil* (Recklinghausen: Vertag Aurel Bongers).
Westermann, D. (1928) 'Die westatlantische Gruppe der Sudansprachen', *MSOS*, **31**, 3, pp. 63–86.
Wheatley, P. (1961) 'Geographical notes on some commodities involved in the Sung maritime trade', *Journal of the Malayan Branch of the Royal Asiatic Society*, **32**, 2, p. 54.
Wheatley, P. (1970) 'The significance of traditional Yoruba urbanism', *CSSH*, **12**, 4, pp. 393–423.
Wheatley, P. (1971) *The Pivot of the Four Quarters* (Edinburgh: EUP).
Wheatley, P. (1975) 'Analecta Sino-Africana Recensa' in H. N. Chittick and R. I. Rotberg (eds), pp. 76–114.
Whitehouse, D. (1970) 'Siraf a medieval port on the Persian Gulf', *WA*, **2**, pp. 141–58.
Wiesenfeld, S. L. (1967) 'Sickle-cell trait in human biological and cultural evolution', *Science*, **157**, pp. 1134–40.
Wiet, G. (1932) *L'Egypte byzantine et musulmane*, Vol. 2 of *Précis de l'Histoire de l'Egypte* (Cairo).
Wiet, G. (1937) *L'Egypte arabe* (Paris: Société de l'histoire nationale).
Wiet, G. (1953) 'Roitelets de Dahlak', *BIE*, **34**, pp. 89–95.
Wiet, G. (1966) *Introduction à la littérature arabe* (Paris: Unesco-Maisonneuve).
Willett, F. (1960) 'Ife and its archaeology', *JAH*, **1**, 2, pp. 231–48.
Willett, F. (1967) *Ife in the History of West African Sculpture* (London: Thames & Hudson).
Willett, F. (1970) 'Ife and its archaeology' in J. D. Fage and R. A. Oliver (eds), pp. 303–26.
Willett, F. (1971) 'A survey of recent results in the radiocarbon chronology of western and northern Africa', *JAH*, **12**, 3, pp. 339–70.
Willett, F. (1973) 'Archaeology' in S. O. Biobaku (ed.), pp. 111–39.
Willett, F. and Fleming, S. J. (1976) 'A catalogue of important Nigerian copper-alloy castings dated by thermoluminescence', *Archaeometry*, **18**, 2, pp. 135–46.
Williams, D. (1969) 'African iron and the Classical World' in L. A. Thompson and F. Ferguson (eds), pp. 62–80.
Williams, D. (1974) *Icon and Image* (London: Allen Lane).
Williamson, K. L. A. (1971) 'The Benue-Congo languages and Ijo' in T. Sebeok (ed.), pp. 245–306.
Willis, J. R. (1979) 'Reflections on the diffusion of Islam in West Africa', in J. R. Willis (ed.), pp. 1–15.
Willis, J. R. (ed.) (1979) *Studies in West African History*. Vol. 1, *The Cultivators of Islam* (London: Frank Cass).
Wilson, T. H. (1982) 'Spatial analysis and settlement patterns on the East African coast', *Paideuma*, 28, pp. 201–20.
Wissman, H. von and Höfner, M. (1952) *Beiträge zur historischen Geographie der vorislamischen Südarabien* (Wiesbaden: Steiner).
Wolf, E. R. (1951) 'The social organisation of Mecca and the origins of Islam', *SWJA*, vol. 7, pp. 329–56.
Wood, L. J. and Ehret, C. (1978) 'The origins and diffusion of the market institution in East Africa', *Journal of African Studies*, **5**, pp. 1–17.
Wright, H. T. (1984) 'Early seafarers of the Comoro Islands: the Dembeni Phase of the IXth–Xth centuries AD', *Azania*, **19**, pp. 13–59.
Wrigley, C. C. (1960) 'Speculations on the economic prehistory of Africa', *JAH*, **1**, 2, pp. 189–204.
Wüstenfeld, F. (1881) *Geschichte der Fatimiden-chalifen. Nach arabischen Quellen* (Göttingen: Dieterich).

al-Ya'ḳūbī (1870–94) *Kitāb al-buldān*, ed. by M. J. de Goeje (Leiden: Brill).
al-Ya'ḳūbī (1883) *Ibn Wadhih qui dicitur al-Ja'qūbī Historiae* (*Kitāb al-ta'rīkh*) (2 vols, ed. M. T. Houtsma, Leiden: Brill).
al-Ya'ḳūbī (1892) *Kitāb al-Buldān* (ed. by M. J. de Goeje, Leiden: Brill).
al-Ya'ḳūbī (1937) *Les pays*, tr. by G. Wiet (Cairo: Institut Française d'Archéologie Orientale).

al-Ya'ḳūbī (1962) *Description du Maghreb en 276/889, Extrait du Kitāb al-Buldān*, Arabic text by H. Pérès, tr. by G. Wiet (Algiers: Institut d'Etudes Orientale).
Yāḳūt (1866–73) *Jacut's Geographisches Wörterbuch* [*Mu'jam al-buldān*] (6 vols, ed. by F. Wüstenfeld, Leipzig: Brockhaus).
Yāḳūt (1907) *Mu'djam al-buldān* (10 vols, Cairo: 1325 AH).
York, R. N. (1973) 'Excavations at New Buipe', *WAJA*, **3**, pp. 1–189.

Zaborski, A. (1965) 'Notes on the medieval history of the Beja tribes', *FO*, **7**, pp. 289–307.
Zaborski, A. (1970) 'Some Eritrean place-names in Arabic medieval sources', *FO*, **12**, pp. 327–37.
Zaborski, A. (1971) 'Beja and Tigrē in 9th–10th century period', *RO*, **35**, 1, pp. 117–30.
Zaghlūl, S. (1965) *Ta'rīkh al-Maghrib al-'Arabī* (Cairo).
Zaydān, J. (n.d.) *Al-'Arab ḳabla 'l-Islām* (Cairo: Dār al-Hilāl).
Zaydān, J. (1902) *Ta'rīkh al-Tamaddun al-Islāmī* (5 vols, Cairo).
Ziegert, H. (1969) 'Überblick zur jüngeren Besiedlungsgeschichte des Fezzan', *BGA*, 8, pp. 49–58.
al-Zuhrī (1968) *Kitāb al-Dju'rāfiyya. Mappemonde du Calife al-Ma'mun réproduite par Fazārī (IIIe/IXe s.), rééditée et commentée par Zuhrī (VIe/XIIe s.).* Arabic text by Muḥammad Hadj-Sadok, *BEO*, **21**, pp. 1–312.
Zyhlarz, E. (1928a) *Grundzüge der nubischen Grammatik im christlichen Frühmittelalter* (*Altnubisch*), *AKM*, 18, 1.
Zyhlarz, E. (1928b) 'Zur Stellung des Darfur-nubischen', *WZKM*, **35**, pp. 84–123, 188–212.
Zyhlarz, E. (1932) 'Neue Sprachdenkmäler des Altnubischen' in S. R. K. Glanville (ed.) *Studies presented to F. Ll. Griffith* (London: OUP, pp. 187–97).

Index